TEST CRICKET LISTS

TEST CRICKET LISTS

The Ultimate Guide to International Test Cricket

Graham Dawson & Charlie Wat

Foreword by Richie Benaud

The Five Mile Press

The Five Mile Press

The Five Mile Press Pty Ltd
950 Stud Road, Rowville
Victoria 3178 Australia
Website: www.fivemile.com.au
Email: publishing@fivemile.com.au

First edition published 1982
Second edition published 1992
Third edition published 1996
Fourth edition published 1998
This edition published 2006

Formatting: Charlie Wat
Peter Bourne, SBR Productions Olinda Victoria

Photo section images: 1: Copyright © The Age, Melbourne, Australia; 2: AFP Photo/Dean Treml; 3: AP Photo/NZPA, Ross Setford; 4: Copyright © The Age, Melbourne, Australia; 5: AP Photo/Anjum Naveed; 6: Copyright © The Age, Melbourne, Australia; 7: Copyright © The Age, Melbourne, Australia; 8: AP Photo/Adil Bradlow; 9: Copyright © The Age, Melbourne, Australia; 10: AFP Photo/Rob Elliott; 11: Copyright © The Age, Melbourne, Australia; 12: Copyright © The Age, Melbourne, Australia; 13: EPA/Jon Hrusa; 14: Copyright © The Age, Melbourne, Australia; 15: AFP Photo/Philip Brown; 16: Copyright © The Age, Melbourne, Australia.

Printed in China

National Library of Australia Cataloguing-in-Publication data

Test cricket lists: the ultimate guide to international test cricket.
5th ed.

ISBN 10: 1 74178 249 X
ISBN 13: 978 1 74178 249 3

1. Cricket - Records. 2. Cricket - Statistics. 3. Test matches (Cricket). I. Wat, Charlie. II. Dawson, Graham.

796.35865

About the Authors

GRAHAM DAWSON

Graham Dawson has been one of Australia's leading radio and television sporting commentators for more than 30 years.

He has broadcast or reported on 93 Test matches and more than 200 One Day Internationals. He was a member of the commentary teams that broadcast the Centenary Test match in 1977, as well as the 1975 and 1992 World Cup finals at Lord's and the Melbourne Cricket Ground respectively.

As well as his cricket broadcasting commitments, Graham has been a radio or television commentator at five summer Olympics and six Commonwealth Games.

He has broadcast more than 1,290 Australian Football League matches – which is a record number for any commentator.

In 1999, Graham was inducted into the Australian Media Hall of Fame at the MCG.

He was a useful park cricketer, before broadcasting commitments relegated his playing to the infrequent social match; although he *was* captain of his school First XI when the former England fast bowler, Frank Tyson, was coach.

CHARLIE WAT

Charlie Wat began his career as a statistician in 1962 when he was a Melbourne schoolboy. Inspired by *Wisden Cricketers' Almanack*, he started keeping his own Test records.

He has contributed to *The Australian Cricketer* and *The Sunday Observer*. He has also provided the statistics for Brian Crowley's *A History of Australian Batting 1850–1986* and *A History of Australian Bowling and Wicket-keeping 1850–1986*, as well as providing the scorecards and statistics for Jack Pollard's *The Complete Illustrated History of Australian Cricket* (1995). He was also a contributor to *The Cricketer Quarterly: Facts and Figures*, and is a current contributor to *Wisden Cricketers' Almanack.*

In 1992, Charlie provided the stats for the second edition of *Test Cricket Lists* and also came on board the next year for The Five Mile Press' *Australian First Class Cricket.*

His greatest regret is that he was overseas when Gary Sobers scored 254 for a World XI against Australia at the MCG in January 1972. However, this is tempered to a certain degree by the fact that he was able to watch the world's best players in the 1970 'Test' series between England and the Rest of the World.

Foreword

Cricket lives in a whiz-bang world of computers, mobile telephones, un-wired or wireless connections and, theoretically, smaller and smaller briefcases into which fit the modern-day versions of books of statistics. It is true that the amount of cricket played in this twenty-first century requires that statistics be kept up to date almost by the day, an imposing task able to be achieved only by computers.

It is also true that nothing for me replaces the written word. One tiny book I always carry with me is only 100 pages long and is written by Professor William Strunk Jr and the American essayist E B White, and it is simply called *The Elements of Style*. This is a legacy of my father having been a schoolteacher with a love of the English language and a hope that his two sons would derive a similar love and appreciation, whether it be in the reading of books, writing them, or keeping up with the latest news and records of cricket.

For almost 25 years I have been a devotee of the written word produced by Graham Dawson, first of all in 1982, with the statistical assistance of Ross Dundas and, for the past 14 years, of Charlie Wat, one of the more dedicated keepers of the faith of cricket records. *Test Cricket Lists* sits in my office at Coogee and is one of those books which can be read and re-read; there is always something jumping out of the page at you as a reminder that the ageing memory can be fallible.

The style of this new edition of *Test Cricket Lists* will not have altered greatly; after all a cricket match has in essence remained unchanged since the first game between Australia and England in 1876–77, even though the Laws may well have varied in many ways. Whether or not those changes brought in by Imperial and International Boards or Councils have been for the good of the game could be argued for many hours without reaching any agreement. In my experience, few have really worked and eventually commonsense has prevailed.

In this book, the section 'Famous Test Matches' will lead the way and it is fitting that at the top will be the 2005 Ashes series in England and, to me, this is the greatest in which I have ever been concerned. Until that magnificent summer I had three views about outstanding matches: that the greatest series in which I took part was the Tied Test series of 1960–61, from the purely selfish personal point of view the best match was Old Trafford 1961 and the finest series, 1981 when Ian Botham at Headingley began his season of mayhem against Australia.

All that changed with Edgbaston, Old Trafford and then Trent Bridge in 2005, plus Kevin Pietersen's century at The Oval, and the twists and turns and extraordinary excitement of the final four matches made it a series never to be forgotten. Everything is set for another tremendous battle in Australia in 2006–07, and this book will be invaluable now and in years to come for all cricket lovers. Oddities of the game, statistics and stories on every page make it a book to be treasured.

Richie Benaud
September 2006

To Bill
Whose courage and fighting spirit
has been an inspiration

Contents

Acknowledgements

It has been a great pleasure to have been involved in another edition of *Test Cricket Lists*.

Since the previous publication, the highest individual innings scored has been broken twice. India's Kumble became only the second bowler to take all ten wickets in an innings, while Sri Lanka's Sangakkara and Jayawardene established a new record partnership for all wickets, against South Africa. These and many more magnificent contests appear in the expanded 'Famous Test Matches' section of this edition.

Once again, statistician Charlie Wat has been superb. His attention to detail and presentation of the statistics are matched only by great knowledge, understanding and love of the game, all of which has proved to be a constant source of strength.

In compiling this volume, I am again indebted to the works of some far more knowledgeable students of the game than me. In particular, I acknowledge my debt to the *Wisden Book of Test Cricket*, compiled and edited by Bill Findall; and the *Wisden Cricketers' Almanack,* edited by Matthew Engel.

I would like to thank my good friend the 'goal umpire', David Mitchell, for allowing me access to his extensive collection of the *Wisden Cricketers' Almanack,* and my beautiful daughter Shona for her typing and proofreading skills.

I would also like to thank Richie Benaud for the wonderful words he has written in the introduction to this book. Richie was a childhood hero when he was captain of Australia and it has been an honour and privilege to have been able to work with him on several Test matches.

To David Horgan, Janet Rowe, Lorelei Waite and Peter Bourne from The Five Mile Press, thank you for your continued support, encouragement and patience.

In order to meet the publication deadlines, figures and statistics are current up to and including the fourth Test between England and Pakistan in August 2006.

Graham Dawson

Graham Dawson
September 2006

A Guide to the Symbols

General

* signifies not out or unbroken partnership as appropriate
# signifies retired hurt

Scorecards

* indicates the captain of the team
† indicates the wicket-keeper

All other symbols are explained in whichever section they appear.

Key to duplicate named players

Two players named Anwar Hossain represented Bangladesh in Tests:

Anwar Hossain[1]	Mohammad Anwar Hossain — b Lalbagh, 10 December 1983 (RHB, WK) 1 Test in 2002-03.
Anwar Hossain[2]	Mohammad Anwar Hossain — b Munshiganj, 31 December 1981 (RHB, RFM) 4 Tests 2003-04 to 2005.

Two players named Ijaz Ahmed have represented Pakistan in Tests:

Ijaz Ahmed[1]	Ijaz Ahmed — b Sialkot, 20 September 1968, (RHB, LM) 60 Tests 1986-87 to 2000-01.
Ijaz Ahmed[2]	Ijaz Ahmed — b Lyallpur (now Faisalabad), 2 February 1969, (RHB, OB) 2 Tests in 1995-96.

Two players named Enamul Haque represented Bangladesh in Tests:

Enamul Haque[1]	Enamul Haque — b Comilla, Chittagong, 27 February 1966 (LHB, SLA) 10 Tests 2000-01 to 2002-03.
Enamul Haque[2]	Enamul Haque — b Sylhet, Chittagong, 5 December 1986 (RHB, SLA) 10 Tests 2003-04 to 2005-06.

Two players named Manjural Islam represented Bangladesh in Tests:

Manjural Islam[1]	Mohammad Manjural Islam — b Khulna, 7 November 1979 (LHB, LFM) 17 Tests 2000-01 to 2003-04.
Manjural Islam[2]	Qazi Manjural Islam Rana — b Khulna, 4 May 1984 (LHB, SLA) 6 Tests 2003-04 to 2004-05.

Two players named Shakeel Ahmed represented Pakistan in Tests:

Shakeel Ahmed[1]	Shakeel Ahmed — b Daska, 12 November 1971 (RHB, WK) 3 Tests 1992-93 to 1994-95.
Shakeel Ahmed[2]	Shakeel Ahmed — b Kuwait City, Kuwait, (LHB, SLA) 1 Test in 1998-99.

In August 2005 Yousuf Youhana changed his name to Mohammad Yousuf. For consistency I have not updated his change of name in these records.

Ground Names

'Bombay' became known as 'Mumbai' in November 1995 and 'Madras' became known as 'Chennai' in June 1996. The new names have been used for matches played at these grounds since the changes.

Spelling

Players' names have been spelt as they appear in the cricketing records of their own country.

Part 1

Famous Test Matches

Since the first official Test match in 1876, cricket has produced many unforgettable games and memorable moments. Opening with The Ashes 2005 series and the historic England v Pakistan match in August 2006, this section then goes back in time to explore some of the most famous Test matches in cricket history.

THE ASHES 2005

ENGLAND v AUSTRALIA 1st TEST

Lord's, London
21, 22, 23, 24 July 2005
Australia won by 239 runs

Australia 190 (S.J. Harmison 5 for 43) and 384 (M.J. Clarke 91, S.M. Katich 67, D.R. Martyn 65); England 155 (K.P. Pietersen 57, G.D. McGrath 5 for 53) and 180 (K.P. Pietersen 64 not out)

I had arrived in England ten days before the first Test and could not believe how the upcoming Test series, with the prospect of regaining the Ashes, had gripped the country. Everywhere I travelled people wanted to talk cricket. It was just about the only topic of conversation on everyone's lips.

Ponting called correctly and took first use of a typical Lord's pitch. In the forty-first over Australia had been dismissed for a disappointing 190. England's four-pronged pace attack had bowled with great fire and hostility, particularly Harmison, who claimed his sixth bag of 5 wickets in an innings. Langer who went in first, top scored with 40. There was a lack of respect and discipline in Australia's batting while the innings exposed the Australians to the reverse swing that would continue to haunt them throughout the series.

A magnificent spell from McGrath (he captured 5 for 16 from 10 overs straight after tea) turned the game in Australia's favour. Trescothick, who fell first ball after the interval, became McGrath's 500th Test wicket. Only Pietersen, on debut, with 57 offered any resistance and it took a splendid outfield catch by Martyn, running full speed around the mid wicket boundary, to end his innings.

Pietersen then became the villain of the home team's fans when he dropped Clarke, 21, at short cover, with Australia 3 for 139. Taking full advantage of this good fortune Clarke and Martyn put on a match winning partnership of 155 for the fourth wicket. Katich, 67, was able to conjure up a further 95 runs with numbers 10 and 11 (Gillespie and McGrath) to give Australia a lead of 419.

Strauss and Trescothick started confidently in pursuit of the victory target. However, Lee and Warne soon had the visitors in the driver's seat. Again it was Pietersen who offered the strongest resistance as he reached his second half century of the match. Fittingly it was McGrath who wrapped up England's second innings on the fourth afternoon. Four second innings wickets gave him nine for the match.

The confidence with which England started the campaign was in tatters. Would the team be able to turn it around?

ENGLAND v AUSTRALIA 2nd TEST

Edgbaston, Birmingham
4, 5, 6, 7 August 2005
England won by 2 runs

England 407 (M.E. Trescothick 90, K.P. Pietersen 71, A. Flintoff 68) and 182 (A. Flintoff 73, S.K. Warne 6 for 46); Australia 308 (J.L. Langer 82, R. T. Ponting 61) and 279

The considerable psychological advantage Australia had gained as a result of its resounding win at Lord's was handed back before a ball was bowled in anger at Edgbaston.

McGrath rolled an ankle in the warm-up and wasn't able to take his place in the starting line-up, but even without his premier fast bowler Ponting still sent England in after calling correctly. It was a poor decision to rival that of his predecessor at Calcutta in 2001.

England plundered Australia's pedestrian attack and scored at better than five runs per over throughout the opening day to reach 407. This was England's highest first day total since World War II. Pietersen and Flintoff were particularly savage on Australia's bowlers and brought up their century partnership at a run a ball in just over an hour.

Australia's response should have been ever so much better. Hayden went first ball, falling for the three card trick, driving Hoggard straight to short cover. Ponting, who was in imperious form, top edged Giles to short fine leg while the laconic Martyn ran himself out in the last over before lunch. This time the tail didn't support Gilchrist who was left stranded on 49.

Outstanding bowling by Warne and Lee reduced England to 9 for 131, a lead of 230. Not enough on a slow unresponsive pitch. Flintoff, with the support of S.Jones, added 51 priceless runs for the last wicket. Flintoff's total of nine sixes for the match was a record for an Ashes Test. Warne was at his teasing and tormenting best in taking 6 for 46 from 23 overs.

When Harmison bowled Clarke at the end of the third day Australia still required 107 runs with only Lee and Kasprowicz to support Warne. Flintoff's constant aggressive bowling forced Warne onto his stumps at 220. Kasprowicz bravely supported Lee as the visitors got to within three of victory. S.Jones had missed a difficult chance at third man with 15 required before Harmison's short pitched delivery had Kasprowicz gloving a leg side catch to the keeper, G. Jones.

England had won a classic contest by two runs, Flintoff came of age as a world class all rounder and the fight for the Ashes was on in earnest.

ENGLAND v AUSTRALIA 2005 (First Test)

Lord's, St John's Wood Road, London, 21, 22, 23, 24 July. Australia won by 239 runs.

AUSTRALIA

J.L.Langer	c Harmison b Flintoff	40	(1)	run out	6
M.L.Hayden	b Hoggard	12	(2)	b Flintoff	34
R.T.Ponting*	c Strauss b Harmison	9	(3)	c sub (J.C.Hildreth) b Hoggard	42
D.R.Martyn	c G.O.Jones b S.P.Jones	2	(4)	lbw b Harmison	65
M.J.Clarke	lbw b S.P.Jones	11	(5)	b Hoggard	91
S.M.Katich	c G.O.Jones b Harmison	27	(6)	c S.P.Jones b Harmison	67
A.C.Gilchrist†	c G.O.Jones b Flintoff	26	(7)	b Flintoff	10
S.K.Warne	b Harmison	28	(8)	c Giles b Harmison	2
B.Lee	c G.O.Jones b Harmison	3	(9)	run out	8
J.N.Gillespie	lbw b Harmison	1	(10)	b S.P.Jones	13
G.D.McGrath	not out	10	(11)	not out	20
Extras	(B 5, LB 4, NB 11, W 1)	21	(B 10, LB 8, NB 8)		26
	Total	190			384

ENGLAND

M.E.Trescothick	c Langer b McGrath	4	(1)	c Hayden b Warne	44
A.J.Strauss	c Warne b McGrath	2	(2)	c & b Lee	37
M.P.Vaughan*	b McGrath	3	(3)	b Lee	4
I.R.Bell	b McGrath	6	(4)	lbw b Warne	8
K.P.Pietersen	c Martyn b Warne	57	(5)	not out	64
A.Flintoff	b McGrath	0	(6)	c Gilchrist b Warne	3
G.O.Jones†	c Gilchrist b Lee	30	(7)	c Gillespie b McGrath	6
A.F.Giles	c Gilchrist b Lee	11	(8)	c Hayden b McGrath	0
MJ.Hoggard	c Hayden b Warne	0	(9)	lbw b McGrath	0
S.J.Harmison	c Martyn b Lee	11	(10)	lbw b Warne	0
S.P.Jones	not out	20	(11)	c Warne b McGrath	0
Extras	(B 1, LB 5, NB 5)	11	(B 6, LB 5, NB 3)		14
Total		155			180

ENGLAND	O	M	R	W		O	M	R	W
Harmison	11.2	0	43	5	Harmison	27.4	6	54	3
Hoggard	8	0	40	1	Hoggard	16	1	56	2
Flintoff	11	2	50	2	Flintoff	27	4	123	2
S.P.Jones	10	0	48	2	S.P.Jones	18	1	69	1
					Giles	11	1	56	0
					Bell	1	0	8	0

AUSTRALIA	O	M	R	W		O	M	R	W
McGrath	18	5	53	5	McGrath	17.1	2	29	4
Lee	15.1	5	47	3	Lee	15	3	58	2
Gillespie	8	1	30	0	Gillespie	6	0	18	0
Warne	7	2	19	2	Warne	20	2	64	4

FALL OF WICKETS

	A	E	A	E
1st	35	10	18	80
2nd	55	11	54	96
3rd	66	8	100	104
4th	66	19	255	112
5th	87	21	255	119
6th	126	79	274	158
7th	175	92	279	158
8th	178	101	289	164
9th	178	122	341	167
10th	190	155	384	180

Umpires: Aleem Dar and R.E.Koertzen

ENGLAND v AUSTRALIA 2005 (Second Test)

Edgbaston, Birmingham, 4, 5, 6, 7 August. England won by 2 runs.

ENGLAND

M.E.Trescothick	c Gilchrist b Kasprowicz	90	(1)	c Gilchrist b Lee	21
A.J.Strauss	b Warne	48	(2)	b Warne	6
M.P.Vaughan*	c Lee b Gillespie	24	(4)	b Lee	1
I.R.Bell	c Gilchrist b Kasprowicz	6	(5)	c Gilchrist b Warne	21
K.P.Pietersen	c Katich b Lee	71	(6)	c Gilchrist b Warne	20
A.Flintoff	c Gilchrist b Gillespie	68	(7)	b Warne	73
G.O.Jones†	c Gilchrist b Kasprowicz	1	(8)	c Ponting b Lee	9
A.F.Giles	lbw b Warne	23	(9)	c Hayden b Warne	8
M.J.Hoggard	lbw b Warne	16	(3)	c Hayden b Lee	1
S.J.Harmison	b Warne	17	(10)	c Ponting b Warne	0
S.P.Jones	not out	19	(11)	not out	12
Extras	(LB 9, NB 14, W 1)	24		(LB 1, NB 9)	10
Total		407			182

AUSTRALIA

J.L.Langer	lbw b S.P.Jones	82	(1)	b Flintoff	28
M.L.Hayden	c Strauss b Hoggard	0	(2)	c Trescothick b S.P.Jones	31
R.T.Ponting*	c Vaughan b Giles	61	(3)	c G.O.Jones b Flintoff	0
D.R.Martyn	run out (Vaughan)	20	(4)	c Bell b Hoggard	28
M.J.Clarke	c G.O.Jones b Giles	40	(5)	b Harmison	30
S.M.Katich	c G.O.Jones b Flintoff	4	(6)	c Trescothick b Giles	16
A.C.Gilchrist†	not out	49	(7)	c Flintoff b Giles	1
S.K.Warne	b Giles	8	(9)	hit wicket b Flintoff	42
B.Lee	c Flintoff b S.P.Jones	6	(10)	not out	43
J.N.Gillespie	lbw b Flintoff	7	(8)	lbw b Flintoff	0
M.S.Kasprowicz	lbw b Flintoff	0	(11)	c G.O.Jones b Harmison	20
Extras	(B 13, LB 7, NB 10, W 1)	31		(B 13, LB 8, NB 18, W 1)	40
Total		308			279

AUSTRALIA	O	M	R	W		O	M	R	W
Lee	17	1	111	1	Lee	18	1	82	4
Gillespie	22	3	91	2	Gillespie	8	0	24	0
Kasprowicz	15	3	80	3	Kasprowicz	3	0	29	0
Warne	25.2	4	116	4	Warne	23.1	7	46	6

ENGLAND	O	M	R	W		O	M	R	W
Harmison	11	1	48	0	Harmison	17.3	3	62	2
Hoggard	8	0	41	1	Hoggard	5	0	26	1
S.P.Jones	16	2	69	2	Giles	15	3	68	2
Flintoff	15	1	52	3	Flintoff	22	3	79	4
Giles	26	2	78	3	S.P.Jones	5	1	23	1

FALL OF WICKETS

	E	A	E	A
Wkt	1st	1st	2nd	2nd
1st	112	0	25	47
2nd	164	88	27	48
3rd	170	118	29	82
4th	187	194	31	107
5th	290	208	72	134
6th	293	262	75	136
7th	342	273	101	137
8th	348	282	131	175
9th	375	308	131	220
10th	407	308	182	279

Umpires: B.F.Bowden and R.E.Koertzen

ENGLAND v AUSTRALIA 3rd TEST

Old Trafford, Manchester
11, 12, 13, 14, 15 August 2005
Match Drawn

England 444 (M.P. Vaughan 166, M.E. Trescothick 63, I.R. Bell 59) and 6 for 280 Dec. (A.J. Strauss 106, I.R. Bell 65. G.D. McGrath 5 for 115); Australia 302 (S.K. Warne 90, S.P. Jones 6 for 53) and 9 for 371 (R.T. Ponting 156)

Australia selected McGrath to play in the Test only a week after severely damaging his ankle in the warm-up at Edgbaston while England's confidence continued to grow after Vaughan won the toss. The Old Trafford curator compared the pitch to concrete.

Again England scored over 400 in the first innings although not quite at the same rate as in the previous match. This time the captain was the mainstay of his team's innings although he was dropped by Gilchrist on 41 and at the same score was bowled by a McGrath no-ball. The gamble taken on McGrath back-fired as his figures of 0 for 86 were his worst in Test cricket.

Australia's top order again performed poorly. Most got set but not one went on to get the big score required. Warne and Gillespie were together at the end of the second day with the visitors 7 for 214 and in danger of following-on.

The famous Manchester rain came to Australia's rescue on the third day when only 14 overs play was possible. The eighth wicket partnership flourished, yielding 86 runs and in a match in which the leg spinning wizard was to become the first man to claim 600 Test wickets, it would have been appropriate for him to score his maiden Test century. He fell 10 runs short.

With the follow-on avoided England pushed ahead looking to make a suitable declaration. Strauss reached his first century against Australia while Bell, who had looked out of his depth earlier in the series, scored his second half century of the match. This was the only innings of the series in which Warne went wicketless. When Vaughan made the declaration Australia required a record score of 423 to win, or to bat for 108 overs to save the game.

Ponting, who went in early on the final day, played a superb innings that ended with him ninth man out with just four overs of the match remaining. McGrath had to survive with Lee against Harmison and Flintoff. This was achieved to the great relief of the visitors who were able to thank the famous Manchester weather Gods for reducing the third day so drastically.

After three absorbing matches England had a realistic chance of regaining the Ashes for the first time in nineteen years.

ENGLAND v AUSTRALIA 4th TEST

Trent Bridge, Nottingham
25, 26, 27, 28 August 2005
England won by 3 wickets

England 477 (A. Flintoff 102, G.O. Jones 85, M.E. Trescothick 65, M.P. Vaughan 58) and 7 for 129; Australia 218 (S.P. Jones 5 for 44) and 387 (J.L. Langer 61, S.M. Katich 59, M.J. Clarke 56)

For the second time in the series Australia could not include its leading fast bowler because of injury. This time McGrath missed because of an elbow complaint. The out-of-form Gillespie was omitted with Kasprowicz and debutant, Tait, coming into the line-up.

It was not until Flintoff and G. Jones came together early on the second day that England gained the ascendancy. They added 177 for the sixth wicket at nearly five runs per over. McGrath's steadiness was sorely missed.

Once again, Australia's top order batting was lamentable. This time it was Hoggard who did the early damage before S. Jones removed the lower order to claim his second five wicket haul in successive matches. Vaughan decided to enforce the follow-on, the first time for Australia since September 1988 in Karachi.

Unfortunately for England S. Jones limped off after only four overs at the start of Australia's second innings. The visitors did bat with more determination but not one batsman could get the big score required to set England a competitive target. There were three half centuries and two scores in the forties. Australia's cause was not helped by the senseless run out of the captain by Martyn. Pointing had reached 48 and was playing in a similar vein to his match saving innings at Old Trafford.

Warne weaved some more magic and with Lee's support, had England a jittery 4 for 57 and then 7 for 116 after G. Jones had spooned the wily leg spinner to mid-off. Hoggard joined Giles with 13 still required by England to take the led in the series. The Australian's needed to take 3 for 11 to retain the Ashes. Thoughts of Headingley, 1981, came flooding back but obviously not to Giles and Hoggard who carried England across the line. The home team now was in reach of its dream of regaining the Ashes.

ENGLAND v AUSTRALIA 2005 (Third Test)

Old Trafford, Stretford, Manchester, 11, 12, 13, 14, 15 August. Match Drawn.

ENGLAND

M.E.Trescothick	c Gilchrist b Warne	63	(1)	b McGrath	41
A.J.Strauss	b Lee	6	(2)	c Martyn b McGrath	106
M.P.Vaughan*	c McGrath b Katich	166	(3)	c sub (B.J.Hodge) b Lee	14
I.R.Bell	c Gilchrist b Lee	59	(4)	c Katich b McGrath	65
K.P.Pietersen	c sub (B.J.Hodge) b Lee	21	(5)	lbw b McGrath	0
M.J.Hoggard	b Lee	4			
A.Flintoff	c Langer b Warne	46	(6)	b McGrath	4
G.O.Jones†	b Gillespie	42	(7)	not out	27
A.F.Giles	c Hayden b Warne	0	(8)	not out	0
S.J.Harmison	not out	10			
S.P.Jones	b Warne	0			
Extras	(B 4, LB 5, NB 15, W 3)	27		(B 5, LB 3, NB 14, W 1)	23
Total		444		6 wickets declared	280

AUSTRALIA

J.L.Langer	c Bell b Giles	31	(1)	c G.O.Jones b Hoggard	14
M.L.Hayden	lbw b Giles	34	(2)	b Flintoff	36
R.T.Ponting*	c Bell b S.P.Jones	7	(3)	c G.O.Jones b Harmison	156
D.R.Martyn	b Giles	20	(4)	lbw b Harmison	19
S.M.Katich	b Flintoff	17	(5)	c Giles b Flintoff	12
A.C.Gilchrist†	c G.O.Jones b S.P.Jones	30	(6)	c Bell b Flintoff	4
S.K.Warne	c Giles b S.P.Jones	90	(9)	c G.O.Jones b Flintoff	34
M.J.Clarke	c Flintoff b S.P.Jones	7	(7)	b S.P.Jones	39
J.N.Gillespie	lbw b S.P.Jones	26	(8)	lbw b Hoggard	0
B.Lee	c Trescothick b S.P.Jones	1	(10)	not out	18
G.D.McGrath	not out	1	(11)	not out	5
Extras	(B 8, LB 7, NB 15, W 8)	38		(B 5, LB 8, NB 19, W 2)	34
Total		302		9 wickets	371

AUSTRALIA	O	M	R	W		O	M	R	W
McGrath	25	6	86	0	McGrath	20.5	1	115	5
Lee	27	6	100	4	Lee	12	0	60	1
Gillespie	19	2	114	1	Warne	25	3	74	0
Warne	33.2	5	99	4	Gillespie	4	0	23	0
Katich	9	1	36	1					

ENGLAND	O	M	R	W		O	M	R	W
Harmison	10	0	47	0	Harmison	22	4	67	2
Hoggard	6	2	22	0	Hoggard	13	0	49	2
Flintoff	20	1	65	1	Giles	26	4	93	0
S.P.Jones	17.5	6	53	6	Vaughan	5	0	21	0
Giles	31	4	100	3	Flintoff	25	6	71	4
					S.P.Jones	17	3	57	1

FALL OF WICKETS

	E	A	E	A
Wkt	1st	1st	2nd	2nd
1st	26	58	64	25
2nd	163	73	97	96
3rd	290	86	224	129
4th	333	119	225	165
5th	341	133	248	182
6th	346	186	264	263
7th	433	201	-	264
8th	434	287	-	340
9th	438	293	-	354
10th	444	302	-	-

Umpires: B.F.Bowden and S.A.Bucknor

ENGLAND v AUSTRALIA 2005 (Fourth Test)

Trent Bridge Ground, Nottingham, 25, 26, 27, 28 August. England won by 3 wickets.

ENGLAND

M.E.Trescothick	b Tait	65	(1)	c Ponting b Warne	27
A.J.Strauss	c Hayden b Warne	35	(2)	c Clarke b Warne	23
M.P.Vaughan*	c Gilchrist b Ponting	58	(3)	c Hayden b Warne	0
I.R.Bell	c Gilchrist b Tait	3	(4)	c Kasprowicz b Lee	3
K.P.Pietersen	c Gilchrist b Lee	45	(5)	c Gilchrist b Lee	23
A.Flintoff	lbw b Tait	102	(6)	b Lee	26
G.O.Jones†	c & b Kasprowicz	85	(7)	c Kasprowicz b Warne	3
A.F.Giles	lbw b Warne	15	(8)	not out	7
M.J.Hoggard	c Gilchrist b Warne	10	(9)	not out	8
S.J.Harmison	st Gilchrist b Warne	2			
S.P.Jones	not out	15			
Extras	(B 1, LB 15, NB 25, W 1)	42		(LB 4, NB 5)	9
Total		477		7 wickets	129

AUSTRALIA

J.L.Langer	c Bell b Hoggard	27	(1)	c Bell b Giles	61
M.L.Hayden	lbw b Hoggard	7	(2)	c Giles b Flintoff	26
R.T.Ponting*	lbw b S.P.Jones	1	(3)	run out (sub G.J.Pratt)	48
D.R.Martyn	lbw b Hoggard	1	(4)	c G.O.Jones b Flintoff	13
M.J.Clarke	lbw b Harmison	36	(5)	c G.O.Jones b Hoggard	56
S.M.Katich	c Strauss b S.P.Jones	45	(6)	lbw b Harmison	59
A.C.Gilchrist†	c Strauss b Flintoff	27	(7)	lbw b Hoggard	11
S.K.Warne	c Bell b S.P.Jones	0	(8)	st G.O.Jones b Giles	45
B.Lee	c Bell b S.P.Jones	47	(9)	not out	26
M.S.Kasprowicz	b S.P.Jones	5	(10)	c G.O.Jones b Harmison	19
S.W.Tait	not out	3	(11)	b Harmison	4
Extras	(LB 2, NB 16, W 1)	19		(B 1, LB 4, NB 14)	19
Total		218			387

AUSTRALIA	O	M	R	W		O	M	R	W
Lee	32	2	131	1	Lee	12	0	51	3
Kasprowicz	32	3	122	1	Kasprowicz	2	0	19	0
Tait	24	4	97	3	Warne	13.5	2	31	4
Warne	29.1	4	102	4	Tait	4	0	24	0
Ponting	6	2	9	1					

ENGLAND	O	M	R	W		O	M	R	W
Harmison	9	1	48	1	Hoggard	27	7	72	2
Hoggard	15	3	70	3	S.P.Jones	4	0	15	0
S.P.Jones	14.1	4	44	5	Flintoff	29	4	83	2
Flintoff	11	1	54	1	Harmison	30	5	93	3
					Giles	28	3	107	2
					Bell	6	2	12	0

FALL OF WICKETS

	E	A	A	E
Wkt	1st	1st	2nd	2nd
1st	105	20	50	32
2nd	137	21	129	36
3rd	146	22	155	57
4th	213	58	161	57
5th	241	99	261	103
6th	418	157	277	611
7th	450	157	314	116
8th	450	163	342	-
9th	454	175	373	-
10th	477	218	387	-

Umpires: Aleem Dar and S.A.Bucknor

ENGLAND v AUSTRALIA 2005 (Fifth Test)

Kennington Oval, London, 8, 9, 10, 11, 12 September. Match Drawn.

ENGLAND

Batsman	1st innings	Runs		2nd innings	Runs
M.E.Trescothick	c Hayden b Warne	43	(1)	lbw b Warne	33
A.J.Strauss	c Katich b Warne	129	(2)	c Katich b Warne	1
M.P.Vaughan*	c Clarke b Warne	11	(3)	c Gilchrist b McGrath	45
I.R.Bell	lbw b Warne	0	(4)	c Warne b McGrath	0
K.P.Pietersen	b Warne	14	(5)	b McGrath	158
A.Flintoff	c Warne b McGrath	72	(6)	c & b Warne	8
P.D.Collingwood	lbw b Tait	7	(7)	c Ponting b Warne	10
G.O.Jones†	b Lee	25	(8)	b Tait	1
A.F.Giles	lbw b Warne	32	(9)	b Warne	59
M.J.Hoggard	c Martyn b McGrath	2	(10)	not out	4
S.J.Harmison	not out	20	(11)	c Hayden b Warne	0
Extras	(B 4, LB 6, NB 7, W 1)	18		(B 4, NB 5, W 7)	16
Total		373			335

AUSTRALIA

Batsman	1st innings	Runs		2nd innings	Runs
J.L.Langer	b Harmison	105	(1)	not out	0
M.L.Hayden	lbw b Flintoff	138	(2)	not out	0
R.T.Ponting*	c Strauss b Flintoff	35			
D.R.Martyn	c Collingwood b Flintoff	10			
M.J.Clarke	lbw b Hoggard	25			
S.M.Katich	lbw b Flintoff	1			
A.C.Gilchrist†	lbw b Hoggard	23			
S.K.Warne	c Vaughan b Flintoff	0			
B.Lee	c Giles b Hoggard	6			
G.D.McGrath	c Strauss b Hoggard	0			
S.W.Tait	not out	1			
Extras	(B 4, LB 8, NB 9, W 2)	23		(LB 4)	4
Total		367		0 wickets	4

AUSTRALIA	O	M	R	W		O	M	R	W
McGrath	27	5	72	2	McGrath	26	3	85	3
Lee	23	3	94	1	Lee	20	4	88	0
Tait	15	1	61	1	Warne	38.3	3	124	6
Warne	37.3	5	122	6	Clarke	2	0	6	0
Katich	3	0	14	0	Tait	5	0	28	1

ENGLAND	O	M	R	W		O	M	R	W
Harmison	22	2	87	1	Harmison	0.4	0	0	0
Hoggard	24.1	2	97	4					
Flintoff	34	10	78	5					
Giles	23	1	76	0					
Collingwood	4	0	17	0					

FALL OF WICKETS

Wkt	E 1st	A 1st	E 2nd	A 2nd
1st	82	185	2	-
2nd	102	264	67	-
3rd	104	281	67	-
4th	131	323	109	-
5th	274	329	126	-
6th	289	356	186	-
7th	297	359	199	-
8th	325	363	308	-
9th	345	363	335	-
10th	373	367	335	-

Umpires: B.F.Bowden and R.E.Koertzen

ENGLAND v AUSTRALIA 5th TEST

Kennington Oval, London
8, 9, 10, 11, 12 September 2005
Match Drawn

England 373 (A.J. Strauss 129, A. Flintoff 72, S.K. Warne 6 for 122) and 335 (K.P. Pietersen 158, A.F. Giles 59, S.K. Warne 6 for 124); Australia 367 (M.L. Hayden 138, J.L. Langer 105, A. Flintoff 5 for 78) and 0 for 4.

The climax of one of the most engrossing series ever staged didn't disappoint the millions of supporters of the great game.

England was not able to select S. Jones because of the injury he suffered at Trent Bridge but instead of going with the same team balance opted for the safety first selection and played Collingwood and not Anderson. McGrath returned for Australia although there were still some concerns about his fitness.

Vaughan won the toss for the third time in a row and had no hesitation in batting first. The mercurial Warne ripped out the top order before Strauss and Flintoff added 143 for the fifth wicket. Strauss scored a second century in his first Ashes series. Warne captured six wickets in an innings for the second time in the series. He was to make it three times in England's second innings.

Nearly 130 overs play was lost during the second, third and fourth days, many by the choice of Australia's batsmen because of poor light. This was a surprising decision as the visitors had to win the match to retain the Ashes. The out-of-form Hayden laboured to a century at a rate of a run every two and a half balls. It was the first time he had passed fifty in the series. For the fourth time in a row England gained the first innings lead even though Australia had an opening stand of 185.

When the final day started England's lead was 40 with 9 wickets in hand. Australia needed an early breakthrough. McGrath and Warne obliged, England going to lunch at 5 for 127. An Australian victory was now a distinct possibility. Pietersen then launched one of the great counter attacks of all time. His innings of 158 was scored at almost a run a ball with an Ashes record seven sixes. He received outstanding support from Giles, 59 and their eighth wicket stand of 109 ensured the Ashes would return to England. Pietersen was missed by Gilchrist early in his innings and then by Warne at slip when on 15. This was a more straightforward chance. Who knows what may have happened if that catch had been held.

The England players and supporters celebrated long and hard at regaining the Ashes. Fittingly Flintoff and Warne were the players of the series with Flintoff the inaugural winner of the Compton–Miller Medal.

RECENT HIGHLIGHTS

ENGLAND v PAKISTAN 2006

Kennington Oval, London
17, 18, 19, 20 August
Match awarded to England

England 173 and 4 for 298 (K.P. Pietersen 96, A.N. Cook 83, A.J. Strauss 54); Pakistan 504 (Yousuf Youhana 128, Mohmmad Hafeez 95, Imran Farhat 91, Faisal Iqbal 58 not out)

This was the first time in more than 1,800 Test matches that a team had forfeited a match by refusing to take the field.

Pakistan had been in a strong position to win the Test, as they had dominated proceedings for most of the four days' play.

The following explains how the drama unfolded at 'The Oval' on that historic Sunday.

2.34 pm Umpires Doctrove, West Indies, and Hair, Australia, examine the ball after Umar Gul's 14th over.

Ball is changed.

England awarded five penalty runs.

3.45 pm Bad light stops play; tea taken early.

4.43 pm Umpires and England batsmen return to the field for resumption of play. Pakistan team does not reappear.

4.54 pm Umpires remove bails, ending play.

5.24 pm Pakistan team returns to the field.

5.34 pm Pakistan team returns to the dressing rooms.

6.05 pm Fourth umpire advises teams there will be no further play.

6.30 pm Match referee, Procter, in discussion with umpires.

10.10 pm England Cricket Board, Chief Executive Officer, David Collier, announces that the match is over. England declared the winner of the Test as Pakistan is deemed to have forfeited the match.

ENGLAND v PAKISTAN 2006 (Fourth Test)

Kennington Oval, London, August 17, 18, 19, 20, 21, 2006. Match awarded to England.

ENGLAND

M.E.Trescothick	c Mohammad Hafeez b Umar Gul	6	(1)	c Kamran Akmal b Mohammad Asif	4
A.J.Strauss*	c Kamran Akmal b Mohammad Asif	38	(2)	lbw b Danish Kaneria	54
A.N.Cook	lbw b Shahid Nazir	40	(3)	lbw b Umar Gul	83
K.P.Pietersen	c Kamran Akmal b Mohammad Asif	0	(4)	c Kamran Akmal b Shahid Nazir	96
P.D.Collingwood	lbw b Mohammad Asif	5	(5)	not out	26
I.R.Bell	c Faisal Iqbal b Danish Kaneria	9	(6)	not out	9
C.M.W.Read†	b Umar Gul	33			
S.I.Mahmood	b Umar Gul	15			
M.J.Hoggard	c Kamran Akmal b Mohammad Asif	3			
S.J.Harmison	not out	8			
M.S.Panesar	b Umar Gul	0			
Extras	(B 4, LB 5, NB 7)	16		(B 8, LB 3, NB 10, PEN 5)	26
Total		**173**		**4 wickets**	**298**

PAKISTAN

Mohammad Hafeez	c Strauss b Hoggard	95
Imran Farhat	c Trescothick b Hoggard	91
Younis Khan	c Read b Mahmood	9
Yousuf Youhana	c Read b Hoggard	128
Inzamamul Haq*	c Strauss b Harmison	31
Faisal Iqbal	not out	58
Kamran Akmal†	c Collingwood b Harmison	15
Shahid Nazir	c Hoggard b Mahmood	17
Umar Gul	lbw b Panesar	13
Danish Kaneria	c Trescothick b Harmison	15
Mohammad Asif	c Cook b Harmison	0
Extras	(B 4, LB 9, NB 8, W 110	32
Total		**504**

AUSTRALIA	O	M	R	W		O	M	R	W
Mohammad Asif	19	6	56	4	Mohammad Asif	17	1	79	1
Umar Gul	15.2	3	46	4	Umar Gul	14	1	70	1
Shahid Nazir	11	1	44	1	Mohammad Hafeez	4	1	13	0
Danish Kaneria	8	1	18	1	Danish Kaneria	29	6	94	1
					Shahid Nazir	8	1	26	1

PAKISTAN	O	M	R	W	O	M	R	W
Hoggard	34	2	124	3				
Harmison	30.5	6	125	4				
Mahmood	27	3	101	2				
Panesar	30	6	103	1				
Collingwood	6	0	29	0				
Pietersen	2	0	9	0				

FALL OF WICKETS

	E	P	E	P
Wkt	1st	1st	2nd	2nd
1st	36	70	8	-
2nd	54	148	115	-
3rd	54	325	218	-
4th	64	379	277	-
5th	91	381	-	-
6th	112	398	-	-
7th	158	444	-	-
8th	163	475	-	-
9th	173	504	-	-
10th	173	504	-	-

Umpires: B.R.Doctrove and D.B.Hair

OTHER FAMOUS TEST MATCHES

AUSTRALIA v ENGLAND 1876-77

Melbourne Cricket Ground, Melbourne
15, 16, 17, 19 March 1877
Australia won by 45 runs

Australia 245 (C. Bannerman 165 retired hurt) and 104 (A. Shaw 5 for 38); England 196 (H. Jupp 63, W.E. Midwinter 5 for 78) and 108 (T. Kendall 7 for 55)

This is regarded as the first official Test match. England was represented by professional players who had been touring Australia during the 1876-77 season, but it would have been a stronger team had it included the leading amateur cricketers of the day.

Australia won the toss and batted first. Charles Bannerman dominated the innings and, after receiving the first ball in Test cricket, went on to score the first Test century. He eventually retired hurt after making 165 in an Australian total of 245. Surrey opener Harry Jupp top-scored in England's first innings with a patient knock of 63.

Shaw and Ulyett combined to bowl Australia out for 104, but the target of 154 proved too much for the England batsmen. The Victorian Kendall captured seven wickets for 55 runs as England was dismissed for 108; Australia won by 45 runs.

A collection at the ground for the injured Bannerman raised £165. (See scorecard on page 25.)

ENGLAND v AUSTRALIA 1880

Kennington Oval, London
6, 7, 8 September 1880
England won by 5 wickets

England 420 (W.G. Grace 152, A.P. Lucas 55, Lord Harris 52) and 5 for 57; Australia 149 (F. Morley 5 for 56) and 327 (W.L. Murdoch 153 not out)

This was the first Test match to be played on English soil, and the Australian team was weakened by the absence of its greatest bowler of the time, Spofforth.

The England team, led by Lord Harris, included for the first time three brothers, E.M., W.G. and G.F. Grace. E.M. Grace opened the England innings with W.G. Grace, whose 152 was the first Test century scored by an Englishman. The third and youngest brother, B.F. Grace, made the first 'pair' of ducks in Test cricket, but his outfield catch to dismiss the Australian Bonnor was also long remembered. The batsmen were on their way back for the third run when he held the catch.

He died less than a month later after catching a severe cold in a club game. The cold developed into congestion of the lungs, and he was dead within three days.

ENGLAND v AUSTRALIA 1882

The Ashes match
Kennington Oval, London
28, 29 August 1882
Australia won by 7 runs

Australia 63 (R.G. Barlow 5 for 19) and 122 (H.H. Massie 55); England 101 (F.R. Spofforth 7 for 46) and 77 (F.R. Spofforth 7 for 44)

This most remarkable and exciting match will be remembered for as long as cricket history exists. The Ashes match was Australia's first Test victory in England. The win was set up by Spofforth's magnificent bowling, and his figures of 14 for 90 enhanced his reputation as the finest bowler in the world.

Australia was bundled out for 63 after winning the toss. England's reply was not much better, and the team was dismissed for 101. Australia's second innings was an improvement on the first, and Massie led the way with 55 in an opening stand of 66 with Bannerman, but the rest struggled. By mid-afternoon on the second day, Australia had been dismissed for 122, with a lead of just 84 runs. England looked comfortable in the second innings when W.G. Grace and Ulyett took the score to 51 after the early loss of Hornby and Barlow, but inspired bowling by 'the Demon' (Spofforth) and Boyle, supported by magnificent fielding, carried Australia to a thrilling victory. See page 27 for the complete scoreboard.

The day after the match, the *Sporting Times* carried an 'In Memoriam' announcement as follows:

IN AFFECTIONATE REMEMBERANCE
OF
ENGLISH CRICKET
which died at Kennington Oval on 29th August 1882.
Deeply lamented by a large circle
of sorrowing friends and
acquaintances.
R.I.P.
N.B. — The body will be cremated and
the ashes taken to Australia.

AUSTRALIA v ENGLAND 1884-85

Sydney Cricket Ground, Sydney
20, 21, 23, 24 February 1885
Australia won by 6 runs

Australia 181 (T.W. Garrett 51 not out, W. Flowers 5 for 46) and 165 (W. Bates 5 for 24); England 133 (T.P. Horan 6 for 40) and 207 (W. Fellows 56, J.M. Reid 56, F.R. Spofforth 6 for 90)

Australia crawled to 0 for 40 at lunch before a violent storm hit the ground. When play finally resumed on the damp

AUSTRALIA v ENGLAND 1876-77 (First Test)

Melbourne Cricket Ground, 15, 16, 17, 19 March. Australia won by 45 runs

AUSTRALIA

C. Bannerman	retired hurt	165		b Ulyett	4
N.Thompson	b Hill	1		c Emmett b Shaw	7
T.P.Horan	c Hill b Shaw	12		c Selby b Hill	20
D.W. Gregory*	run out	1	(9)	b Shaw	3
B.B.Cooper	b Southerton	15		b Shaw	3
W.E.Midwinter	c Ulyett b Southerton	5		c Southerton b Ulyett	17
E.J. Gregory	c Greenwood b Lillywhite	0		c Emmett b Ulyett	11
J.M.Blackham†	b Southerton	17		lbw b Shaw	6
T.W.Garrett	not out	18	(4)	c Emmett b Shaw	0
T.K.Kendall	c Southerton b Shaw	3		not out	17
J.Hodges	b Shaw	0		b Lillywhite	8
Extras	(B 4, LB 2, W 2)	8		(B 5, LB 3)	8
Total		**245**			**104**

ENGLAND

H.Jupp	lbw b Garrett	63	(3)	lbw b Midwinter	4
J.Selby†	c Cooper b Hodges	7	(5)	c Horan b Hodges	38
H.R.J.Charlwood	c Blackham b Midwinter	36	(4)	b Kendall	13
G.Ulyett	lbw b Thompson	10	(6)	b Kendall	24
A.Greenwood	c E.J. Gregory b Midwinter	1	(2)	c Midwinter b Kendall	5
T.Armitage	c Blackham b Midwinter	9	(8)	c Blackham b Kendall	3
A.Shaw	b Midwinter	10		st Blackham b Kendall	2
T.Emmett	b Midwinter	8	(9)	b Kendall	9
A.Hill	not out	35	(1)	c Thompson b Kendall	0
J.Lillywhite*	c and b Kendall	10		b Hodges	4
J.Southerton	c Cooper b Garrett	6		not out	1
Extras	(LB 1)	1		(B 4, LB 1)	5
Total		**196**			**108**

ENGLAND	O	M	R	W		O	M	R	W
Shaw	55.3	34	51	3	Shaw	34	16	38	5
Hill	23	10	42	1	Ulyett	19	7	39	3
Ulyett	25	12	36	0	Hill	14	6	18	1
Southerton	37	17	61	3	Lillywhite	1	0	1	1
Armitage	3	0	15	0					
Lillywhite	14	5	19	1					
Emmett	12	7	13	0					
AUSTRALIA	O	M	R	W		O	M	R	W
Hodges	9	0	27	1	Kendall	33.1	12	55	7
Garrett	18.1	10	22	2	Midwinter	19	7	23	1
Kendall	38	16	54	1	D.W.Gregory	5	1	9	0
Midwinter	54	23	78	5	Garrett	2	0	9	0
Thompson	17	10	14	1	Hodges	7	5	7	2

FALL OF WICKETS

	A	E	A	E
Wkt	1st	1st	2nd	2nd
1st	2	23	7	0
2nd	40	79	27	7
3rd	41	98	31	20
4th	118	109	31	22
5th	142	121	35	62
6th	143	135	58	68
7th	197	145	71	92
8th	243	145	75	93
9th	245	168	75	100
10th	245	196	104	108

Umpires: C.A.Reid and R.B.Terry

pitch Australia collapsed, finishing the day at 8 for 97. When Spofforth went at 101 Australia was in real trouble. But fortunately Garrett, 51, and Evans, 33, added 80 runs for the last wicket in a match-winning partnership. Barnes — the leading wicket-taker on the tour — refused to bowl after a disagreement with his captain, Shrewsbury.

The England innings finished quickly as Horan and Spofforth bundled out the visitors for 133, Flowers top-scoring with 24. Australia then built on its first-innings lead of 48 before Bates struck. England's target was now 214. At 5 for 61 and then 6 for 92 the game appeared lost. It was Flowers and Reid who combined for a 102-run partnership that turned the game the visitors' way, before Australia's great bowlers, Spofforth and Trumble, wrapped up the England tail. 'The Demon' Spofforth captured ten wickets in a match for the third time.

AUSTRALIA v ENGLAND 1886-87

Sydney Cricket Ground, Sydney
28, 29, 31 January 1887
England won by 13 runs
England 45 (C.T.B. Turner 6 for 15) and 184 (J.J. Ferris 5 for 76); Australia 119 and 97 (W. Barnes 6 for 28)

After being sent into bat, England was bundled out for its lowest score against Australia (45). Turner and Ferris, both on debut, bowled unchanged in England's innings. Australia gained a first-innings lead of 74 after being dismissed for 119. Moses and Jones top-scored with 31. England's lead was only 29 with just three wickets in hand. On the final day, England's Briggs compiled the top score for the game, 33, to set Australia 111 runs for victory. Moses, 24, and Jones, 18, again batted well, but it was Barnes and Lohmann who triumphed and bowled England to a great win.

ENGLAND v AUSTRALIA 1890

Kennington Oval, London
11, 12 August 1890
England won by 2 wickets
Australia 92 (F. Martin 6 for 50) and 102 (F. Martin 6 for 52); England 100 and 8 for 95 (J.J. Ferris 5 for 49)

Played on a slow wicket soaked by heavy rain, this was a match dominated by the ball. In his only Test against Australia, the Kent bowler Martin spearheaded England's victory with match figures of 12 for 102.

In a nerve-tingling finish with England needing one run to tie and two to win, Sharpe joined MacGregor at the wicket. The Australian bowler Ferris continually beat Sharpe, but wasn't able to claim the wicket Australia desperately needed. At last, Sharpe put bat to ball; he and his partner MacGregor ran for a suicidal single, but Barrett's return was too high for Ferris to reach. England won the match on the overthrow.

AUSTRALIA v ENGLAND 1894-95

Sydney Cricket Ground, Sydney
14, 15, 17, 18, 19, 20 December 1894
England won by 10 runs
Australia 586 (S.E. Gregory 201, G. Giffen 161, F.A. Iredale 81, J. Blackham 74, T. Richardson 5 for 181) and 166 (J. Darling 53, R. Peel 6 for 67); England 325 (A. Ward 75, J. Briggs 57) and 437 (A. Ward 117, J.T. Brown 53)

This high-scoring match featured many highlights and records: the aggregate of 1514 runs was a new mark, Australia's score of 586 remained an Australian record for 30 years, the ninth-wicket partnership of 154 by Gregory and Blackham still remains Australia's best and, for the first time, a team won after following-on. Giffen produced an outstanding all-round performance for Australia: 161 and 41 with the bat, and 8 for 238 from 118 overs with the ball. But luck went against the Australians. First, Blackham sustained a severe thumb injury and couldn't keep wicket in England's second innings. Then after five days' play, with Australia needing just 64 runs with eight wickets in hand to win, the heavens opened and the rain tumbled down. The next day followed with blazing sunshine, and Australia was caught on a classic 'sticky' wicket. Briggs and Peel took full advantage of the conditions to bowl England to a memorable victory. The details of this absorbing Test are set out on page 29.

ENGLAND v AUSTRALIA 1896

Old Trafford, Manchester
16, 17, 18 July 1896
Australia won by 3 wickets
Australia 412 (F.A. Iredale 108, G. Giffen 80, G.H.S. Trott 53, T. Richardson 7 for 168) and 7 for 125. (T. Richardson 6 for 76); England 231 (A.A. Lilley 65 not out, K.S. Ranjitsinhji 62) and 305 (K.S. Ranjitsinhji 154 not out)

In this classic match, the two outstanding performers were on the defeated England team. Richardson returned match figures of 13 for 239 from 110 overs, and Ranjitsinhji, playing in his first Test, scored 62 and a masterly 154 not out. Australia's victory was set up by the top-order batsmen. Iredale, 108, Giffen, 80, and Trott, 53, led the way to the Australian first-innings total of 412. In England's first innings, Lilley and the 'Prince" (Ranjitsinhji) both compiled half-centuries, but it was not enough to avoid the follow-on. In their second innings, Ranjitsinhji played one of the great Test innings. He scored 154 not out in his three hours and ten minutes at the crease, but the team was all out for 305. What should have been a formality for Australia almost turned into a nightmare. Richardson bowled superbly. He had Australia on the brink at 7 for 100 before Trumble and Kelly were able to scramble for the last 25 runs needed to record Australia's first Test win in England for eight years.

ENGLAND v AUSTRALIA 1882 (Only Test)

Kennington Oval, London, 28, 29 August. Australia won by 7 runs

AUSTRALIA

A.C.Bannerman	c Grace b Peate	9		c Studd b Barnes	13
H.H.Massie	b Ulyett	1		b Steel	55
W.L.Murdoch*	b Peate	13	(4)	run out	29
G.J.Bonnor	b Barlow	1	(3)	b Ulyett	2
T.P.Horan	b Barlow	3		c Grace b Peate	2
G.Giffen	b Peate	2		c Grace b Peate	0
J.M.Blackham†	c Grace b Barlow	17		c Lyttelton b Peate	7
T.W.Garrett	c Read b Peate	10	(10)	not out	2
H.F.Boyle	b Barlow	2	(11)	b Steel	0
S.P.Jones	c Barnes b Barlow	0	(8)	run out	6
F.R.Spofforth	not out	4	(9)	b Peate	0
Extras	(B 1)	1		(B 6)	6
Total		**63**			**122**

ENGLAND

R.G.Barlow	c Bannerman b Spofforth	11	(3)	b Spofforth	0
W.G.Grace	b Spofforth	4	(1)	c Bannerman b Boyle	32
G.Ulyett	st Blackham b Spofforth	26	(4)	c Blackham b Spofforth	11
A.P.Lucas	c Blackham b Boyle	9	(5)	b Spofforth	5
Hon.A.Lyttelton†	c Blackham b Spofforth	2	(6)	b Spofforth	12
C.T.Studd	b Spofforth	0	(10)	not out	0
J.M.Read	not out	19	(8)	b Spofforth	0
W.Barnes	b Boyle	5	(9)	c Murdoch b Boyle	2
A.G.Steel	b Garrett	14	(7)	c and b Spofforth	0
A.N.Hornby*	b Spofforth	2	(2)	b Spofforth	9
E.Peate	c Boyle b Spofforth	0		b Boyle	2
Extras	(B 6, LB 2, NB 1)	9		(B 3, LB 1)	4
Total		**101**			**77**

ENGLAND	O	M	R	W		O	M	R	W
Peate	38	24	31	4	Peate	21	9	40	4
Ulyett	9	5	11	1	Ulyett	6	2	10	1
Barlow	31	22	19	5	Barlow	13	5	27	0
Steel	2	1	1	0	Steel	7	0	15	2
					Barnes	12	5	15	1
					Studd	4	1	9	0

AUSTRALIA	O	M	R	W		O	M	R	W
Spofforth	36.3	18	46	7	Spofforth	28	15	44	7
Garrett	16	7	22	1	Garrett	7	2	10	0
Boyle	19	7	24	2	Boyle	20	11	19	3

FALL OF WICKETS				
	A	E	A	E
Wkt	1st	1st	2nd	2nd
1st	6	13	66	15
2nd	21	18	70	15
3rd	22	57	70	51
4th	26	59	79	53
5th	30	60	79	66
6th	30	63	99	70
7th	48	70	114	70
8th	53	96	117	75
9th	59	101	122	75
10th	63	101	122	77

Umpires: L.Greenwood and R.Thoms

ENGLAND v AUSTRALIA 1902

Old Trafford, Manchester
24, 25, 26 July 1902
Australia won by 3 runs

Australia 299 (V.T. Trumper 104, C. Hill 65, R.A. Duff 54, J. Darling 51, W.H. Lockwood 6 for 48); and 86 (W.H. Lockwood 5 for 28); England 262 (Hon. F.S. Jackson 128, L.C. Braund 65) and 120 (H. Trumble 6 for 53)

Australia went into this vital Test one up with two matches to play, and England had made four changes to the team that had lost the previous Test at Sheffield. Significantly, Jessop and Hirst were left out of the team, and F.W. Tate, a bowler with no batting ability, was included for his first Test. Trumper played a magnificent innings for Australia and posted his century before lunch. With Hill, 65, Duff, 54, and Darling, 51, making useful contributions, Australia posted 299, a somewhat disappointing total after the opening stand of 135. England's reply was dominated by Jackson, 128, and Braund, 65, who scored 193 out of 262. With a lead of 37, Australia collapsed in its second innings and was dismissed for a paltry 86. Only Darling, 37, and Gregory, 24, reached double figures. Tate dropped Darling early in his innings. If the catch had been taken, Australia would have struggled to reach 50.

With light rain falling, England needed 124 to square the series. After a steady start, the wickets began to tumble — 15 runs were needed with two wickets to fall when Rhodes joined Lilley. But shortly afterwards Lilley fell to a magnificent outfield catch by Hill.

With eight runs required, Tate was the last man, and the rain was coming down in torrents. After a delay of 45 minutes, play resumed. Rhodes calmly played three balls from Trumble, then Tate faced Saunders. The first ball was snicked for four; Tate survived the next two and was then clean-bowled by the fourth ball of the over.

Australia had snatched victory by three runs. Both Lockwood and Trumble bowled superbly. Lockwood claimed eleven wickets and Trumble claimed ten.

ENGLAND v AUSTRALIA 1902

Kennington Oval, London
11, 12, 13 August 1902
England won by 1 wicket

Australia 324 (H. Trumble 64 not out, M.A. Noble 52, G.H. Hirst 5 for 77) and 121 (W.H. Lockwood 5 for 45); England 183 (H. Trumble 8 for 65) and 9 wickets for 263 (G.L. Jessop 104, G.H. Hirst 58 not out)

The classic contest is always referred to as 'Jessop's match' for it was Jessop (known as 'the Croucher') who eventually won the game for England.

Darling called correctly, and Australia took advantage of the good weather and pitch to compile 324. Trumble's 64 not out proved his all-round ability.

England made a modest reply, scoring 183 with Trumble claiming 8 for 65.

Australia's second innings started disastrously with Trumper being run out for 2. After this early setback, the Australia batsmen struggled and only Hill, 34, and Armstrong, 21, were able to score more than 20. Australia was all out for 121, for a lead of 262.

England collapsed and was at one point 5 for 48. The match looked to be over. Then 'the Croucher' joined Jackson, and the pair turned the game around for the home team. In 75 minutes Jessop smashed 104 runs with 17 boundaries and a five. But 15 runs were still required when the last man, Rhodes, joined Hirst.

Legend has it that Hirst said to Rhodes, 'We'll get them in singles.' However, although these men of Yorkshire did manage to score the runs needed to record a famous victory, they did not do it in singles.

AUSTRALIA v ENGLAND 1903-04

Sydney Cricket Ground, Sydney
11, 12, 14, 15, 16, 17 December 1903
England won by 5 wickets

Australia 285 (M.A. Noble 133) and 485 (V.T. Trumper 185 not out, R.A. Duff 84, C. Hill 51, W. Rhodes 5 for 94); England 577 (R.E. Foster 287, L.C. Braund 102, J.T. Tyldesley 53) and 5 for 194 (T.W. Hayward 91, G.H. Hirst 60 not out)

Under the leadership of Pelham Warner, this touring party was the first to come to Australia under the MCC's banner. Previous tours to Australia had been privately sponsored, and team selection had been undertaken by individuals.

Noble was Australia's new captain, and he started well by winning the toss and making the top score, 133, in a respectable total of 285. England struggled at first, but Foster and Braund turned the tide. After two days' play, the visitors trailed by 42 runs with six wickets in hand. On the third day, Foster's innings blossomed. He struck 38 boundaries in a new Test record score of 287. England's total of 577 was a new innings high for Test cricket.

Foster shared century partnerships with Braund, 192, Relf, 115, and Rhodes, 130. The Foster-Rhodes last-wicket partnership still stands as an English record.

A superb, unbeaten century from Trumper, with valuable contributions from Duff and Hill, carried Australia's second innings to 485. Rhodes was once more the pick of England's bowlers. He finished with 5 for 94 from a marathon spell of 40 overs.

England's target was 194 runs. The team was in trouble at 4 for 82, then Hirst was missed by Laver after just one run had been added. After the let-off, the Yorkshireman assisted Hayward to wipe off the deficit. Hirst and Hayward saw England home by five wickets with Hayward, 91, being dismissed near the end of the match.

AUSTRALIA v ENGLAND 1894-95 (First Test)

Sydney Cricket Ground, 14, 15, 17, 18, 19, 20 December. England won by 10 runs

AUSTRALIA

J.J.Lyons	b Richardson	1		b Richardson	25
G.H.S.Trott	b Richardson	12		c Gay b Peel	8
G.Giffen	c Ford b Brockwell	161		lbw b Briggs	41
J.Darling	b Richardson	0		c Brockwell b Peel	53
F.A.Iredale	c Stoddart b Ford	81	(6)	c and b Briggs	5
S.E.Gregory	c Peel b Stoddart	201	(5)	c Gay b Peel	16
J.C.Reedman	c Ford b Peel	17		st Gay b Peel	4
C.E.McLeod	b Richardson	15		not out	2
C.T.B.Turner	c Gay b Peel	1		c Briggs b Peel	2
J.M.Blackham*†	b Richardson	74	(11)	c and b Peel	2
E.Jones	not out	11	(10)	c MacLaren b Briggs	1
Extras	(B 8, LB 3, W 1)	12		(B 2, LB 1, NB 4)	7
Total		**586**			**166**

ENGLAND

A.C.MacLaren	c Reedman b Turner	4	b Giffen	20
A.Ward	c Iredale b Turner	75	b Giffen	117
A.E.Stoddart*	c Jones b Giffen	12	c Giffen b Turner	36
J.T.Brown	run out	22	c Jones b Giffen	53
W.Brockwell	c Blackham b Jones	49	b Jones	37
R.Peel	c Gregory b Giffen	4	b Giffen	17
F.G.J.Ford	st Blackham b Giffen	30	c and b McLeod	48
J.Briggs	b Griffen	57	b McLeod	42
W.H.Lockwood	c Giffen b Trott	18	b Trott	29
L.H.Gay†	c Gregory b Reedman	33	b Trott	4
T.Richardson	not out	0	not out	12
Extras	(B 17, LB 3, W 1)	21	(B 14, LB 8)	22
Total		**325**		**437**

ENGLAND	O	M	R	W		O	M	R	W
Richardson	55.3	13	181	5	Richardson	11	3	27	1
Peel	53	14	140	2	Peel	30	9	67	6
Briggs	25	4	96	0	Lockwood	16	3	40	0
Brockwell	22	7	78	1	Briggs	11	2	25	3
Ford	11	2	47	1					
Stoddart	3	0	31	1					
Lockwood	3	2	1	0					

AUSTRALIA	O	M	R	W		O	M	R	W
Jones	19	7	44	1	Jones	19	0	57	1
Turner	44	16	89	2	Turner	35	14	78	1
Giffen	43	17	75	4	Giffen	75	25	164	4
Trott	15	4	59	1	Trott	12.4	2	22	2
McLeod	14	2	25	0	McLeod	30	7	67	2
Reedman	3.3	1	12	1	Reedman	6	1	12	0
Lyons	2	2	0	0	Lyons	2	0	12	0
					Iredale	2	1	3	0

FALL OF WICKETS

	A	E	E	A
Wkt	1st	1st	2nd	2nd
1st	10	14	44	26
2nd	21	43	115	45
3rd	21	78	217	130
4th	192	149	245	135
5th	331	155	290	147
6th	379	211	296	158
7th	400	211	385	159
8th	409	252	398	161
9th	563	325	420	162
10th	586	325	437	166

Umpires: C.Bannerman and J.Phillips

SOUTH AFRICA v ENGLAND 1905-06

Old Wanderers, Johannesburg
2, 3, 4 January 1906
South Africa won by one wicket
England 184 and 190 (P.F. Warner 51); South Africa 91 (W.S. Lees 5 for 34) and 9 wickets for 287 (A.W. Nourse 93 not out, G.C. White 81)

In this low-scoring match, England gained a first innings lead of 93. Faulkner bowled superbly to capture 4 for 26 and restrict England's second innings to 190. Crawford batted well in both innings, scoring 44 and 43.

When Nourse joined White, the home team was struggling at 6 for 105 and England appeared likely to win. Nourse played with remarkable maturity as he and White carried the score to 226. After White's departure, Vogler and Schwarz fell at 230 and 239 respectively. The last man in was South Africa's captain Sherwell; when he arrived at the crease, 45 runs were still required for victory. Amid great excitement Nourse and Sherwell hit the runs needed to win. It was South Africa's first Test victory.

AUSTRALIA v ENGLAND 1907-08

Melbourne Cricket Ground, Melbourne
1, 2, 3, 4, 6, 7 January 1908
England won by 1 wicket
Australia 266 (M.A. Noble 61, J.N. Crawford 5 for 79) and 397 (W.W. Armstrong 77, M.A. Noble 64, V.T. Trumper 63, C.G. Macartney 54, H. Carter 53, S.F. Barnes 5 for 72); England 382 (K.L. Hutchings 126, J.B. Hobbs 83, A. Cotter 5 for 142) and 9 wickets for 282 (F.L. Fane 50)

The first Test in Sydney was close, but this one was even closer.

Australia's 266 was a modest effort after an 84-run opening stand by Trumper and Macartney. The skipper, Noble, top-scored with 61.

This match saw the test debut of Hobbs. He made 83 and paved the way for Hutchings to smash 126 with 25 fours and a six. England finished with 382 for a lead of 116.

Five batsmen scored half-centuries as Australia compiled a second innings total of 397, despite the untiring effort of Barnes who captured 5 for 72 from 27.4 overs.

England needed to score 282 to win the match and level the series. After the fifth day, it was 4 for 159 and anyone's game. When Rhodes was run out, it was 8 for 209 with 73 runs still required. Barnes and Humphries added 34, but 39 were still needed when the last pair was at the crease.

Finally, with one run needed, the batsmen went for a suicidal single. But Hazlitt's throw was wild and England scored a thrilling victory.

AUSTRALIA v SOUTH AFRICA 1912

Old Trafford, Manchester
27, 28 May 1912
Australia won by an innings and 88 runs
Australia 448 (W. Bardsley 121, C. Kelleway 114, S.J. Pegler 6 for 105); South Africa 265 (G.A. Faulkner 122 not out, W.J. Whitty 5 for 55) and 95 (C. Kelleway 5 for 33)

This was the first match in the triangular tournament of 1912. The Australians started confidently as Kelleway and Bardsley scored freely, compiling a 202-run partnership for the third wicket. Low-order batsmen Matthews and Whitty hit lustily in a last-wicket stand of 63.

Faulkner played a lone hand for South Africa. Dropped at 36, he carried his bat for 122. Whitty had broken the back of the batting with a fiery spell before Matthews ended the innings with the first of his two hat-tricks for the day. Beaumont was bowled, and both Pegler and Ward were trapped lbw.

Forced to follow-on, South Africa's second innings was a dismal effort. At 5 for 70 Matthews bowled Taylor and then caught and bowled both Schwarz and Ward, capturing his second hat-trick. Ward bagged a 'king pair', being the third victim of both hat-tricks.

SOUTH AFRICA v ENGLAND 1922-23

Newlands, Cape Town
1, 2, 3, 4 January 1923
England won by 1 wicket
South Africa 113 and 242 (R.H. Catterall 76, H.W. Taylor 68, G.G. Macaulay 5 for 64); England 183 (J.M. Blanckenberg 5 for 61) and 9 for 173 (A.E. Hall 7 for 63)

England gained the ascendancy on the first day, dismissing South Africa for 113 and being 4 for 128 in reply. Fender was the best of England's bowlers and finished with 4 for 29. Carr, 42 and Russell, 39, batted well for the visitors.

However, though the first day went well for the visitors, the second day saw a complete turnaround in fortunes. South African bowlers Blanckenberg and Hall demolished the middle and lower-order England batsmen and the English lead was restricted to just 70 runs.

After Hearne went out at two for his second duck in the match, Catterall and Taylor dominated the batting and, at the close of the day's play, they had taken the South African's second-innings score to 134.

Macaulay and Kennedy bowled England back into the match on the third day. South Africa's lead was 172. Inspired by Hall's fine bowling, the home team struck back and England finished the day at 6 for 86.

Then England captain, Mann, and Jupp added 68 for the

seventh wicket to give the visitors a glimmer of hope. When the last man, Macaulay, joined Kennedy, five runs were still needed for victory. Kennedy hit a four before a single by Macaulay finished the match.

As well as the exciting finish, this match was a memorable game for a number of reasons. Macaulay took the wicket of Hearne with his very first ball in Test cricket, and he also made the winning run; Hall, the other debutante in the match, took 11 for 112 and almost bowled South Africa to victory.

ENGLAND v AUSTRALIA 1928-29

Exhibition Ground, Brisbane
30 November, 1, 3, 4, 5 December 1928
England won by 675 runs

England 521 (E.H. Hendren 169, H. Larwood 70, A.P.F. Chapman 50) and 8 for 342 dec. (C.P. Mead 73, D.R. Jardine 65 not out, C.V. Grimmett 6 for 131); Australia 122 (H. Larwood 6 for 32) and 66

This was Brisbane's first Test match and one of only two to be played at the Exhibition Ground. The 675-run winning margin is the largest Test match victory, by runs, ever recorded.

Under Chapman, who had regained the Ashes at Kennington Oval in 1926, England had one of its strongest teams. But many of the Australian stalwarts including Collins, Bardsley, Macartney, Andrews, Taylor and Mailey, had retired after the last tour of England.

Hendren, playing perhaps his finest innings against Australia, scored a masterly 169 as England reached 521. Towards the end of the innings, Gregory injured his knee attempting to take a return catch and was told by the doctor that he would never play again.

It was in this match that Bradman made his debut, although he failed, scoring only 18 and 1. He was subsequently left out of the team for the second test.

Larwood crashed through Australia's batting. He captured 6 for 32, and, with Tate claiming 3 for 50, the home team was bundled out for 122.

With Kelleway indisposed with food poisioning and Gregory out of the match, Chapman decided to bat again. He eventually made the first declaration in a Test in Australia at 8 for 342.

Australia's target: just 742 runs! On a difficult pitch, the effort put up by the home team was abysmal: all out for 66 in just 25.3 overs. Woodfull carried his bat in making 30.

Larwood had an outstanding match: he scored 70 and 37 and took 6 for 32 and 2 for 30. And, to round it off, he took four catches in Australia's second innings.

WEST INDIES v ENGLAND 1929-30

Sabina Park, Kingston, Jamaica
3, 4, 5, 7, 8, 9, 10, 11, (no play) 12, (no play) April 1930
Match Drawn

England 849 (A. Sandham 325, L.E.G. Ames 149, G. Gunn 85, E.H. Hendren 61, R.E.S. Wyatt 58, J. O'Connor 51, O.C. Scott 5 for 266) and 9 for 272 dec. (E.H. Hendren 55, A. Sandham 50); West Indies 286 (R.K. Nunes 66) and 5 for 408 (G.A. Headley 223, R.K. Nunes 92)

This was the final test of the first series played between these teams in the Caribbean. England had won at Port-of-Spain by 167 runs, and then the West Indies won at Georgetown by 289. With the series level, it was decided to play the test in Kingston to a finish. Sandham, who batted for more than ten hours, posted the first triple century in Test cricket. His innings was the backbone of the massive England total of 849. The West Indies trailed by 563, but the England captain, the Hon. F.S.G. Calthorpe, did not enforce the follow-on. Sandham scored 50 in the second innings to give him a match aggregate of 375.

The West Indies was set 836 to win and posted a highly respectable 5 for 408 before rain and a waiting ship ended the match. The 20 year-old George Headley made his debut in the series, scoring 703 runs with four centuries at an average of 87.

ENGLAND v AUSTRALIA 1930

Lord's Cricket Ground, London
27, 28, 30 June, 1 July 1930
Australia won by 7 wickets

England 425 (K.S. Duleepsinhji 173, M.W. Tate 54) and 375 (A.P.F. Chapman 121, G.O.B. Allen 57, C.V. Grimmett 6 for 167); Australia 6 wickets for 729 dec. (D.G. Bradman 254, W.M. Woodfull 155, A.F. Kippax 83, W.H. Ponsford 81) and 3 for 72

This was the match in which Bradman played the innings he considered to be (technically) the best in his life.

Australia had gone to Lord's one down, but determined to square the series. Duleepsinhji contributed a century, 173, in his first Test against Australia in England's total of 425.

Woodfull and Ponsford gave Australia a flying start and posted 162 for the first wicket. With Bradman's arrival, the scoring rate increased. At stumps, 'the Don' was 155 not out, with Australia 2 for 404 — 829 runs had been scored in two days' play. On the third day, Bradman and Kippax continued on to post a 192-run partnership. Woodfull declared at tea with a new record score for Australia of 729 (since broken). Bradman's chanceless 254 had taken just five and a half hours to compile.

Grimmett struck early in England's second innings, dismissing Hobbs and Woolley and when he removed

Hammond just after play resumed on the final day, Australia knew victory was a distinct possibility. Chapman scored a fine century, but it wasn't enough to save the match. Australia's target was 72, and they had plenty of time to polish off the runs. The Bradman era had dawned!

AUSTRALIA v ENGLAND 1932-33

Sydney Cricket Ground, Sydney
2, 3, 5, 6, 7, December 1932
England won by 10 wickets

Australia 360 (S.J. McCabe 187 not out, H. Larwood 5 for 96) and 164 (H. Larwood 5 for 28); England 524 (H. Sutcliffe 194, W.R. Hammond 112, Nawab of Pataudi, Sr. 102) and 0 for 1

This was the first test of the infamous Bodyline series, but unfortunately illness prevented 'the Don' from taking part in the game.

McCabe played one of the truly great Test innings. He hit 25 boundaries in his four-hour stay at the crease and scored 51 of a 55-run last-wicket partnership in just 33 minutes. In a sign of what was to come throughout the series, Larwood and Voce did the damage for England with five and four wickets respectively.

The Nawab of Pataudi, snr, playing for England, became the third Indian prince after 'Ranji' and 'Duleep' to score a century in his first Test against Australia. Sutcliffe and Hammond were the other century-makers as England gained a lead of 164. Then Larwood, bowling with great pace, ripped the heart out of the Australian batting. Only Fingleton, 40, and McCabe, 32, offered any resistance, and England wrapped up the match.

AUSTRALIA v ENGLAND 1932-33

Melbourne Cricket Ground, Melbourne
30, 31 December 1932, 2, 3, January 1933
Australia won by 111 runs

Australia 228 (J.H.W. Fingleton 83) and 191 (D.G. Bradman 103 not out); England 169 (H Sutcliffe 52, W.J. O'Reilly 5 for 63) and 139 (W.J. O'Reilly 5 for 66)

The great Don Bradman returned to the Australian line-up after missing the first Test in Sydney. Woodfull elected to bat first and was quickly back in the pavilion. When O'Brien went shortly afterwards 'the Don' strode out to join Fingleton. On his first ball he attempted to hook Bowes but only succeeded in edging it onto his stumps.

Fingleton was the mainstay of Australia's innings, top-scoring with a patient 83, and England could not match the home side's modest total of 228. Wall and O'Reilly were the chief destroyers for Australia.

The third day crowd of 70 000 was a record and the patrons did not go home disappointed as their hero Bradman scored a superb 103 not out in a total of 191.

England's target was 251 runs. When the fourth day began this had been reduced to 208 with all wickets in hand. Once again it was O'Reilly, this time with the assistance of Ironmonger, who proved to be damaging on the responsive pitch. O'Reilly's match-winning ten-wicket haul was the first of three he was to claim in Test cricket.

AUSTRALIA v ENGLAND 1932-33

Adelaide Oval, Adelaide
13, 14, 16, 17, 18, 19 January 1933
England won by 338 runs

England 341 (M. Leyland 83, R.E.S. Wyatt 78, E. Paynter 77, T.W. Wall 5 for 72) and 412 (W.R. Hammond 85, L.E.G. Ames 69, D.R. Jardine 56); Australia 222 (W.H. Ponsford 85) and 193 (W.M. Woodfull 73 not out, D.G. Bradman 66)

This must have been one of the most unpleasant Test matches ever played. The 'Bodyline' controversy had reached its ugliest; in fact, ill-feeling was so great that Jardine had to persuade local officials to close the ground while the England team had its final practice session the day before the match.

Jardine elected to bat first, but his team was soon in desperate trouble with the score at 4 for 30. Leyland, 83, and Wyatt, 78, added 156 for the fifth wicket before Verity helped Paynter carry the total beyond 300.

The crowd became hostile early in Australia's innings when Woodfull was struck a painful blow above the heart by a Larwood thunderbolt. Later in the innings, Oldfield went down after misjudging a Larwood delivery. This incident stirred the crowd to fever pitch, and they began to count the England team 'out' — 'one, two, three, four, five, six, seven, eight, nine, ten, out!'. Australia was dismissed for 222 with Ponsford, 85, top-scoring. England produced an even team performance in its second innings. With six batsmen reaching 40, the total climbed to 412. Australia's target was 532, which proved far too difficult a task. Only Bradman, 66, and Woodfull, who carried his bat for 73, offered any resistance.

It was during this match that the Australian captain, Woodfull, made his famous utterance to the MCC tour management, Sir Pelham Warner and Lionel Palairet: 'There are two teams out there and one of them is trying to play cricket.'

AUSTRALIA v ENGLAND 1932-33

Woolloongabba, Brisbane
10, 11, 13, 14, 15, 16 February 1933
England won by 6 wickets

Australia 340 (V.Y. Richardson 83, D.G. Bradman 76, W.M. Woodfull 67) and 175; England 356 (H. Sutcliffe 86, E. Paynter 83) and 4 for 162 (M. Leyland 86)

England regained the Ashes with their third win of the Bodyline series on the day that Archie Jackson died.

Woodfull took Richardson in with him first and they posted Australia's best opening partnership of the series. Bradman built on the solid foundation and, along with Woodfull, carried the total to 200. However, the middle and lower order failed to capitalise on the home team's promising start.

In reply, England really struggled after a painstaking opening partnership between Jardine and Sutcliffe had realised 114. Paynter was the English hero. Suffering from acute tonsillitis he left a nursing home sick-bed to play a match-winning innings of 83. He added 92 with Verity for the ninth wicket, to gain a 16-run lead for the visitors.

Australia's top order failed in the second innings. A mix-up between debutants Darling and Bromley saw Darling run out, and the innings quickly folded. Leyland played one of his finest knocks to take England within sight of victory before the first-innings hero Paynter won the match by hitting McCabe for six.

ENGLAND v AUSTRALIA 1934

Lord's, London
22, 23, 25 June 1934
England won by an innings and 38 runs

England 440 (L.E.G. Ames 120, M. Leyland 109, C.F. Walters 82); Australia 284 (W.A. Brown 105, H. Verity 7 for 61) and 118 (H. Verity 8 for 43)

This Test became know as 'Verity's Match'. Batting first, England compiled 440, with Leyland and the wicketkeeper, Ames, both scoring centuries. Walters, who was relieved of the captaincy after the first Test, returned to form with 82. By the close of play on the second day (Saturday) Australia had reached 2 for 192, but rain over the weekend drenched the pitch. The England left-arm spinner Verity was able to exploit the conditions perfectly when play resumed.

Australia lost its last 8 wickets for 81, with Verity claiming 6 for 37. Forced to follow-on, the visitors were demolished by this Yorkshireman. Australia was all-out for 118 – Verity taking 8 for 43. On the final day, he took 14 wickets for 80 runs and so equalled Rhodes' earlier record of 15 wickets in Anglo-Australian Tests.

This was England's first win against Australia at Lord's since 1896, and they have not won against Australia at the home of cricket since.

ENGLAND v AUSTRALIA 1934

Kennington Oval, London
18, 20, 21, 22 August 1934
Australia won by 562 runs

Australia 701 (W.H. Ponsford 266, D.G. Bradman 244) and 327 (D.G. Bradman 77, S.J. McCabe 70, W.E. Bowes 5 for 55, E.W. Clark 5 for 98); England 321 (M. Leyland 110, C.F. Walters 64) and 145 (C.V. Grimmet 5 for 64)

This was the final Test of the summer and with the series tied at one apiece, there was no restriction on the number of days' play to get a result. England recalled Woolley at the age of 47 to make the last Test appearance by a pre-1914 Test player, but this move backfired. Woolley scored 4 and 0 and while deputising for the injured Ames in Australia's second innings, conceded a record number of byes (37) for a Test innings.

After Brown had fallen cheaply, Ponsford and Bradman combined to create one of the greatest partnerships in the game's history. Australia's champion batsmen added 451 for the second wicket in five and a quarter hours. Bradman's classic knock included one six and 32 fours; while Ponsford hit a five and 27 boundaries in his highest ever Test innings.

After an opening stand of 104 between the English batsmen Walters and Sutcliffe, only Leyland provided resistance against the Australians. In a superb knock he added 110 of 185 runs to the score. Despite leading by 380, Woodfull did not enforce the follow-on. England, left to make 708 for victory, were bundled out for just 145 with Grimmet doing most of the damage. For the second time in four years, Australia regained the Ashes on the captain's birthday.

ENGLAND v AUSTRALIA 1938

Kennington Oval, London
20, 22, 23, 24 August 1938
England won by an innings and 579 runs

England 7 for 903 dec. (L. Hutton 364, M. Leyland 187, J. Hardstaff Jnr 169 not out, W.R. Hammond 59, A. Wood 53); Australia 201 (W.A. Brown 69, W.E. Bowes 5 for 49) and 123.

This will always be remembered as 'Hutton's match'. On a belter of a pitch, he and Leyland added 318 on the first day after Edrich had become O'Reilly's 100th wicket against England. The second-wicket partnership was broken with the run-out of Leyland, but not before 382 had been added to the score.

By stumps on the second day, England had reached 5 for 634 with Hutton 300 no out.

Australia's fielding was outstanding as the team attempted to defend Bradman's record Test score for Anglo-Australian tests. Hutton eventually was dismissed for 364, the highest Test innings at the time. He played the then longest innings in first-class cricket, batting for more than 13 hours.

Hammond finally declared at 7 for 903, which was the highest total in Test cricket until 1997-98. With both Bradman (who injured an ankle bowling) and Fingleton unable to bat, Australia's reply was a moderate 201. Brown, who opened, was last man out for 69. The second innings was even worse – all out for 123 – and England had inflicted the heaviest defeat in Test history. The margin was an innings and 579 runs.

SOUTH AFRICA v ENGLAND 1938-39

Kingsmead, Durban
3, 4, 6, 7, 8, 9, 10, 11, 13, 14 March 1939
Match drawn

South Africa 530 (P.G.V Van der Bijl 125, A.D. Nourse 103, A. Melville 78, R.E. Grieveson 75, E.L. Dalton 57, R.T.D. Perks 5 for 100) and 481 (A. Melville 103, P.G.V. Van der Bijl 97, B. Mitchell 89, K.G. Viljoen 74); England 316 (L.E.G Ames 84, E. Paynter 62) and 5 for 654 (W.J. Edrich 219, W.R. Hamond 140, P.A. Gibb 120, E. Paynter 75, L. Hutton 55)

This was the famous 'timeless' Test. There was play on nine out of ten possible days, and the game only ended because the ship that was to take the England team home could wait no longer. After the tenth day, England was just 40 runs away from achieving an amazing victory.

Details of the close-of-play scores on each day were as follows:

Day 1: South Africa 2 for 229
Day 2: South Africa 6 for 423
Day 3: South Africa all out 530
England 1 for 35 (rain stopped play)
Day 4: England 7 for 268 (bad light stopped play)
Day 5: England all out 316
South Africa 3 for 193
Day 6: South Africa all out 481
England 0 for 0 (bad light stopped play)
Day 7: England 1 for 253 (bad light)
Day 8: Rain
Day 9: England 3 for 496
Day 10: England 5 for 654
(interruptions because of rain)

NEW ZEALAND v AUSTRALIA 1945-46

Basin Reserve, Wellington
29, 30 March 1946
Australia won by an innings and 103 runs

New Zealand 42 (W.J. O'Reilly 5 for 14) and 54; Australia 8 for 199 dec. (W.A. Brown 67, S.G. Barnes 54, J. Cowie 6 for 40)

This was the first Test to be played between the countries and the first for Lindwall, Miller and Tallon — who were to become three of Australia's finest Test players. New Zealand batted first on a rain-affected pitch. The Kiwis lost their last eight wickets for just five runs as O'Reilly, playing his final Test, captured five wickets in an innings for the eleventh time.

The match ended on the second afternoon after eight and a half hours of play. New Zealand's aggregate of 96 was their lowest score in all Tests, and the match aggregate of 295 was the third lowest of any completed Test. Australia and New Zealand would not meet again in a Test until 1973-74.

ENGLAND v AUSTRALIA 1948

Headingley, Leeds
22, 23, 24, 26, 27 July 1948
Australia won by 7 wickets

England 496 (C. Washbrook 143, W.J. Edrich 111, L. Hutton 81, A.V. Bedser 79) and 8 for 365 dec. (D.C.S. Compton 66, C. Washbrook 65, L. Hutton 57, W.J. Edrich 54); Australia 458 (R.N. Harvey 112, S.J.E Loxton 93, R.R. Lidwall 77, K.R. Miller 58) and 3 for 404 (A.R. Morris 182, D.G. Bradman 173 not out)

This was a memorable match with many highlights. England batted better than at any other stage in the series, and was content to have scored 496. But it should have been more, for at one stage on the second day they were 2 for 423. Australia started poorly and lost Morris, Hassett and Bradman cheaply (3 for 68). Then Harvey, in his first Test against England, joined Miller, and they proceeded to hit themselves out of trouble. After Miller departed, Loxton took over and he smashed five sixes and eight fours in an innings of 93. The 19-year-old Harvey reached his century; then Lindwall added 77 and Australia trailed by only 38 runs. England again batted soundly in the second innings and, by the end of the fourth day, was 8 for 362 (a lead of 400). Yardley batted on for five minutes the following morning, so he could use the heavy roller in the hope that it would further break up the pitch.

Australia only needed to draw the match to retain the Ashes, but when Bradman joined Morris they went for victory. They got there with less than fifteen minutes remaining. Bradman fed the strike to Harvey to allow him to hit the winning runs.

It was the Don's last innings at Leeds. In four Tests at the ground he scored 963 runs at an average of 192.6.

SOUTH AFRICA v ENGLAND 1948-49

Kingsmead, Durban
16, 17, 18, 20 December 1948
England won by 2 wickets

South Africa 161 and 219 (W.W. Wade 63); England 253 (L. Hutton 83, D.C.S. Compton 72, N.B.F. Mann 6 for 59) and 8 for 128 (C.N. McCarthy 6 for 43)

This match was played on the same pitch as the 'timeless' Test ten years before. However, this time the pitch played at varying heights and with the ball swinging late in the humid atmosphere, conditions were not easy for batting. Bedser and Gladwin utilised the conditions beautifully and with the support of some magnificent fielding, the South Africans were dismissed for a disappointing 161.

England's batsmen, apart from Hutton and Compton, struggled against the South African spinners Mann and A.M.B. Rowan. The pitch started turning appreciably on the second day and they were able to take advantage of the conditions. Two and a quarter hours were left for play when South Africa's second innings ended – England's target for victory was 128 runs.

England's final innings was played in drizzling rain and poor light but both teams were determined to play on. McCarthy, in his first Test, claimed 6 for 33 in a devastating spell that gave South Africa a winning chance.

Compton and Jenkins added 45 for the seventh wicket to stem the tide for England.

Bedser and Gladwin were at the crease with Tuckett to bowl the last over.

Eight runs were from the eight-ball over. With three balls left, any one of four results (a win, loss, draw or tie) was possible. Bedser levelled the scores with a single from the sixth delivery, then Gladwin missed the seventh, and after a mid-pitch conference, the batsmen decided to run whatever happened on the final ball. Gladwin swung at the last ball, missed, but then ran the leg bye that gave England the most narrow and exciting of victories.

SOUTH AFRICA v AUSTRALIA 1949-50

Kingsmead, Durban
20, 21, 23, 24 January 1950
Australia won by 5 wickets

South Africa 311 (E.A.B. Rowan 143, A.D. Nourse 66) and 99 (I.W. Johnson 5 for 34); Australia 75 (H.J. Tayfield 7 for 23) and 5 for 101 (R.N. Harvey 151 not out, S.J.E. Loxton 54)

This was a truly remarkable victory by Australia after South Africa gained a first-innings lead of 236 runs. Rowan's patient knock of 143 was the backbone of the Springboks' innings which carried on well into the second day. It is contended that Hassett, the Australian captain, in conjunction with his bowlers, Miller and Johnson, did not attempt to take South African wickets on the second day. The South African innings eventually finished on 311. By stumps, Australia was dismissed for a paltry 75, with ten wickets falling for 44. Tayfield, the off-spinner, claimed 7 for 23. Nourse, South Africa's skipper, had the weekend to decide whether he should enforce the follow-on. With rain threatening, he decided to bat again. South Africa's collapse was worse than Australia's, with the last eight wickets falling for just 14 runs. South Africa was dismissed for 99 — and Australia needed 336 to win.

On a wearing, turning pitch, Harvey proceeded to play possibly his finest Test innings, He finished on 151 not out and was involved in match-winning partnerships with Loxton (135 for the fifth wicket), and McCool (106 unbroken for the sixth).

Australia got home by five wickets to be 3-0 up in the series.

AUSTRALIA v ENGLAND 1950-51

Woolloongabba, Brisbane
1, 2 (no play), 4, 5 December 1950
Australia won by 70 runs

Australia 228 (R.N. Harvey 74) and 7 for 32 dec.; England 7 for 68 dec. (W.A. Johnston 5 for 35) and 122 (L. Hutton 62 not out)

Hassett won the toss for Australia and decided to take advantage of the near-perfect batting conditions.

England did remarkably well to bowl out the home team on the first day for 228. Only Harvey, 74, and Lindwall, with a patient 41, took advantage of the conditions. Bedser and Bailey were the pick of the English bowlers.

A typical Brisbane thunderstorm washed out play on Saturday and rain delayed the start until half an hour before lunch on Monday. What followed was one of the most amazing day's play in Test cricket history — 20 wickets fell for just 102 runs!

Brown declared England's innings while still 160 runs behind in the hope that his bowlers would also be able to take advantage of the conditions. They were — and Australia was soon 3 for 0. Hassett declared the innings at 7 for 32 for an overall lead of 192 runs. Bedser and Bailey were the only two bowlers used in the innings, both finishing with seven wickets for the match.

With a target of 193, England's innings started disastrously with Lindwall bowling Simpson first ball. Brown shuffled his order with his finest batsmen, Hutton and Compton, coming in at eight and nine respectively. Hassett's bold declaration was vindicated as England crashed to 6 for 30 at stumps.

On the fourth day, Hutton played one of the great Test innings. He made 62 not out while 92 runs were added on the treacherous pitch. Unorthodox spinner Iverson claimed four wickets in his first Test to seal the Australia victory.

AUSTRALIA v WEST INDIES 1951-52

Melbourne Cricket Ground, Melbourne
31 December 1951, 1, 2, 3 January 1952
Australia won by 1 wicket

West Indies 272 (F.M.M. Worrell 108, K.R. Miller 5 for 60) and 203 (J.B. Stollmeyer 54, G.E. Gomez 52); Australia 216 (R.N. Harvey 83, J. Trim 5 for 34) and 9 for 260 (A.L. Hassett 102, A.L. Valentine 5 for 88)

The injured Worrell scored a superb century in the first innings to carry the West Indies to 272, but Miller captured 5 for 60 to spearhead Australia's attack. The visitors, however, gained a first-innings lead of 56 after a disappointing reply from Australia. Only Harvey, 83, mastered the attack of which Trim, with 5 for 34, was the star.

Despite half-centuries by Stollmeyer and Gomez, the West Indies could only manage 203 in the second innings for a lead of 259. The captain, Hassett, scored a superb 102, but, despite his efforts, Australia looked beaten when the ninth wicket fell at 222. With 38 runs needed, Johnston joined Ring at the crease. As they crept closer to the target, confusion became evident in the West Indies team: Ring and Johnston took 13 off a Valentine over, and seven off the next by Ramadhin. Then Ramadhin limped off and nearly everyone was trying to set the field.

Johnston deflected Worrell to fine leg for the single that won an unlikely victory. Later, Johnston was reported to have said: 'I was never worried. I knew we couldn't make the runs.'

INDIA v ENGLAND 1951-52

Chepauk (Chidambaram Stadium), Madras
6, 8, 9, 10 February 1952
India won by an innings and 8 runs

England 266 (J.D.B. Robertson 77, R.T. Spooner 66, M.H. Mankad 8 for 55) and 183 (J.D.B. Robertson 56); India 9 for 457 dec. (P.R. Umrigar 130 not out, Pankaj Roy 111, D.G. Phadkar 61)

This was India's first Test victory after almost 20 years and 24 previous matches. Carr, deputising for the ill Howard, won the toss and made first use of the excellent batting conditions.

Robertson, Spooner and Graveney gave England a sound start until Mankad produced his match-winning spell — his figures of 38.5-15-55-8 are the best by an Indian bowler in all Tests against England — and wicketkeeper Sen assisted with four stumpings.

The death of King George VI was announced during the first day's play and arrangements were changed to make the following day the rest day. India batted far more positively than in the previous matches of the series. Umrigar, who had originally been left out of the team, led the way with an unbeaten 130 — his maiden Test century. (Umrigar gained his reprieve when Adhikari sustained a wrist injury just before the game.) Pankaj Roy scored his second century of the series and this got the home team's innings away to a flying start.

Trailing by 191 runs and with the pitch deteriorating, England struggled in the second innings. Robertson top-scored again but the consistent Watkins was the only other batsman to offer any real resistance to the Indian spinners, Mankad and Ghulam Ahmed.

Both bowlers collected four wickets, giving Mankad a total of twelve for the match. The Indian players and officials were jubilant at the victory after such a long wait for success.

ENGLAND v AUSTRALIA 1953

Lord's, London
25, 26, 27, 29, 30 June 1953
Match Drawn

Australia 346 (A.L. Hassett 104, A.K. Davidson 76, R.N. Harvey 59, A.V. Bedser 5 for 105) and 368 (K.R. Miller 109, A.R. Morris 89, R.R. Lindwall 50); England 372 (L. Hutton 145, T.W. Graveney 78, D.C.S. Compton 57, R.R. Lindwall 5 for 66) and 7 for 282 (W. Watson 109, T.E. Bailey 71)

England recalled its chairman of selectors, F.R. Brown, at the age of 42 to play his first Test for two years. After the Australians won the toss, Hassett went in first with Morris. They posted an opening stand of 65 before Morris was brilliantly stumped by Evans off Bedser.

Harvey joined the captain Hassett and they proceeded to add 125 for the second wicket. But Wardle then picked up three wickets in ten deliveries to rip the heart out of the Australian middle order. Davidson held the tail together with an aggressive 76 scored out of 117 runs made while he was at the crease.

Hutton and Graveney launched England's innings with an impressive range of stroke play that had been missing from Test cricket for some years. Hutton, playing one of his finest knocks in a five and a quarter hour stay at the crease, passed 2000 runs in Tests against Australia.

Like the Australian innings, the England middle and lower order collapsed, the last eight wickets falling for just 93 runs.

Trailing by 26 runs, Australia's second innings followed a similar patten to the first, although this time it was Morris and Miller who added 165 for the second wicket. Lindwall's half-century in 45 minutes gave the tail some sting and Australia a lead of 342.

England had an hour to bat on the fourth day and in that time lost Hutton, Kenyon and Graveney for 20 runs. Watson was dropped in the last over of the day.

When Compton fell early on the final morning an Australian victory looked assured. Bailey joined Watson at 12.42 pm and this pair stayed together until 5.50 pm, 40 minutes before stumps.

Their partnership was worth 163 runs and it saved the English team from defeat, with the Australian spinners failing to capitalise on the favourable conditions.

ENGLAND v AUSTRALIA 1953

Kennington Oval, London
15, 17, 18, 19 August 1953
England won by 8 wickets
Australia 275 (R.R. Lindwall 62, A.L. Hassett 53) and 162 (G.A.R. Lock 5 for 45); England 306 (L. Hutton 82, T.E. Bailey 64) and 2 for 132 (W.J. Edrich 55 not out)

In this match, England regained the Ashes which had been in Australia's possession for 19 years. The first four Tests in this damp summer had been drawn. The final match began with Hassett giving Australia a solid start after calling correctly for the fifth time in the series. A shower of rain during the luncheon break freshened up the wicket, and the England bowler Trueman (playing his only Test of the summer) took full advantage of the lively strip. Australia slumped from 2 for 107 to 5 for 118. Only aggressive late-order batting by Lindwall gave Australia's innings respectability. Hutton, 82, played a fine captain's knock for England. Bailey and Bedser added 44 for the last wicket, and England gained a first-innings lead of 31.

After Hassett's dismissal, Morris and Hole (promoted to No.3) carried Australia's second innings score to 59. Then followed a sensational fifteen minutes in which the Ashes were lost: Hole was given lbw to Laker then Lock's first ball to Harvey bowled him. Miller was caught at short let off Laker for a duck, and Morris was trapped in front from the first ball of Lock's next over. Four wickets had fallen for just two runs.

Archer scored 49 with some strong hitting before Australia was all out for 162.

England, needing just 132 to regain the Ashes, acquired the runs with little difficulty. Compton made the winning hit off Morris. This was the signal for thousands of delighted fans to stream on to the ground to acknowledge their heroes.

WEST INDIES v ENGLAND 1953-54

Bourda, Georgetown, British Guiana
24, 25, 26, 27 February, 1,2, March 1954
England won by 9 wickets
England 435 (L. Hutton 169, D.C.S. Compton 64, S. Ramadhin 6 for 113) and 1 for 75; West Indies 251 (E.D. Weekes 94, C.A. McWatt 54) and 256 (J.K. Holt 64)

There was controversy before the match when the England captain, Hutton, objected to the appointed umpires standing in the Test. Inter-island jealousies meant that two other Georgetown umpires had to be used. Hutton won the toss but the advantage seemed lost with the early dismissal of Watson and May. Hutton then proceeded to play one of his best Test innings. His knock of 169 was the foundation of the sizeable England total and the innings lasted until early on the third day. Then in the thirty-five minutes before lunch Statham, bowling with great hostility, removed Worrell, Stollmeyer and Walcott. Rain washed out play for the rest of the day.

The batting collapse continued the next morning until seven wickets were down for 139. Of these runs, Weeks had made a memorable 94. McWatt and Holt set about restoring the West Indies' innings. Holt, batting with a runner because of a pulled leg muscle, went in at number nine rather than opening as usual. Ninety-nine had been added by this pair before McWatt was run out by May. Sections of the crowd disagreed with Umpire Menzies' decision and started hurling bottles and wooden packing-cases on to the field. It was an ugly scene with several players lucky to escape injury. The British Guiana Cricket Association officials suggested to Hutton that he takes his players from the field, but Hutton wanted to remain on the ground to press home his team's advantage.

England enforced the follow-on and although several of the West Indian batsmen got a reasonable start, no-one played the big innings that was required to save the game.

In England's final innings, Watson completed the visitors' victory by hitting a six.

ENGLAND v PAKISTAN 1954

Kennington Oval, London
12, 13 (no play), 14, 16, 17 August 1954
Pakistan won by 24 runs
Pakistan 133 and 164 (J.H. Wardle 7 for 56); England 130 (D.C.S Compton 53, Fazal Mahmood 6 for 53) and 143 (P.B.H. May 53, Fazal Mahmood 6 for 46)

England rested Bailey and Bedser from the game and included Loader and Tyson to boost their Test match experience. This pair had been selected for the MCC tour to Australia later in the year, but Bailey's omission left England with a long 'tail'.

Rain prevented play starting until 2.30 pm and Pakistan, after winning the toss, soon found themselves in trouble. The debutants, Loader and Tyson, had the visitors reeling at 7 for 51. Kardar led the fightback with a patient 36 before 56 was added for the last two wickets.

Further rain washed out play on the second day. When play resumed, conditions were difficult for batting with the ball rising awkwardly from a good length. Fazal Mahmood and Mahmood Hussain exploited the conditions superbly with Fazal bowling 30 overs unchanged throughout the innings.

With the pitch drying out in Pakistan's second innings, the English spinners came into their own. It was Wardle who looked likely to spin the home side to victory as the visitors slimped to 8 for 82. But once again the tail wagged — Wazir Mohammad and Zulfiqar Ahmed posting 58 for the ninth wicket.

England needed 168 for victory and looked likely to score the runs on the fourth afternoon. Simpson and May added 51 in forty minutes for the second wicket; but the aggressive approach and the absence of Bailey's steadiness from the middle order saw the wickets tumble. When the final day began, England required 43 for victory with four wickets in hand. Fazal captured six wickets for the second time in the match to bowl Pakistan to a memorable win. It was their first victory over England and the first time a visiting country had won a Test match on their first tour of England.

AUSTRALIA v ENGLAND 1954-55

Sydney Cricket Ground, Sydney
17, 18, 20, 21, 22 December 1954
England won by 38 runs
England 154 and 296 (P.B.H. May 104, M.C. Cowdrey 54); Australia 228 and 184 (R.N. Harvey 92 not out, F.H. Tyson 6 for 85)

Morris, captaining Australia in the absence of the injured Johnson, invited England to bat first. The decision was vindicated with the visitors bowled out for a modest total of 154. The Australian pace quartet of Lindwall, Archer, Davidson and Johnston shared the wickets with two, three, two and three respectively. Wardle, coming in at number nine, top scored with an invaluable 35.

Australia's reply was disappointing. They gained a lead of only 74 runs despite the fact that six batsmen got a start — Archer led the way with a hard-hitting 49. England's speedsters did the damage. Bailey and Tyson captured four wickets each while Statham picked up the other two.

England then looked to be in real trouble with Hutton, Bailey and Graveney out and only 55 runs on the board. However, May and Cowdrey gave the visitors some hope with a partnership of 116.

May went on to compile his first century against Australia in just under five hours. Again the England tail wagged, and this time Appleyard and Statham put on 46 for the last wicket. Tyson had been knocked out when he turned his back on a Lindwall bouncer and was struck on the back of the head.

Australia required 223 for victory and Tyson bowled with great pace and hostility despite his painful blow. He was superbly supported by Statham who operated into a strong wind. Only Harvey offered any resistance to the pace of the English pair. He played one of his finest innings to remain 92 not out and almost single-handedly pulled off an Australian victory. However, Tyson's six wickets gave him ten for the match, spearheading England to victory.

AUSTRALIA v ENGLAND 1954-55

Melbourne Cricket Ground, Melbourne
31 December 1954, 1, 3, 4, 5, January 1955
England won by 128 runs
England 191 (M.C. Cowdrey 102) and 279 (P.B.H. May 91, W.A. Johnston 5 for 25); Australia 231 (J.B. Statham 5 for 60) and 111 (F.H. Tyson 7 for 27)

More than 300 000 people attended this New Year Test. It has been remembered as the 'watering of the wicket' match. The respected Melbourne Age cricket writer Percy Beames saw the MCG curator watering the pitch on the Sunday rest day. Fortunately, this watering helped England more than Australia.

Cowdrey rescued England with one of his great innings. After the magnificent bowling of Miller had England reeling at 4 for 41, Cowdrey's century carried the visitors to 191. Australia's reply was not much better, but the tail wagged sufficiently to give the home team a 40-run lead. The pitch was at its best the Monday following the Sunday watering. Johnston bowled superbly for Australia, but England's 279 (including 91 from May) set Australia a target of 240.

With Morris and Favell out, Australia was 2 for 72 at the end of the fourth day, needing only a further 165 to win. When Harvey fell to a brilliant leg-side catch by Evans off Tyson, England's danger-man was gone. Australia crashed, losing eight wickets for 36 in only 80 minutes on the final morning. A 'typhoon' had wrecked Australia: Tyson returned 7 for 27 as England went 2-1 up in the series.

ENGLAND v AUSTRALIA 1956

Old Trafford, Manchester
26, 27, 28, 30, 31, July 1956
England won by an innings and 170 runs
England 459 (Rev. D.S. Sheppard 113, P.E. Richardson 104, M.C. Cowdrey 80); Australia 84 (J.C. Laker 9 for 37) and 205 (C.C. McDonald 89, J.C. Laker 10 for 53)

This was 'Laker's Match' on a dust bowl of an Old Trafford pitch. Groundsman Bert Stack as good as admitted he was instructed to prepare the wicket to suit the England spinners, Laker and Lock. (See scoreboard on page 40.)

There were no problems for Richardson and Cowdrey. They compiled 174 for the first wicket and, with Sheppard scoring a century, England posted a daunting 459. McDonald and Burke started Australia's innings steadily, scoring 48 for the first wicket. But after McDonald's dismissal, the rest capitulated, and Australia was all out for 84. After tea on the second day, Laker had taken seven wickets for eight runs from 22 balls. Laker's first nine overs had yielded 0 for 21; his next 7.4 returned 9 for 16.

Australia followed-on, 375 runs behind. McDonald was soon to retire hurt and out came Harvey who was dismissed first ball, a full toss from Laker to Cowdrey. (The great left-hander had made a pair on the same day!) Rain permitted only 49 minutes of play on the third day (Saturday) when Burke was dismissed. On Monday, there was more rain, and only 19 overs of play were possible, but McDonald and Craig survived on the soft, rain-affected pitch. On the final day, they continued until lunch to give the visitors some hope of survival.

Sunshine ended Australia's hopes. Laker utilised the sticky wicket to spin a web over the batsmen. Craig went just after lunch after almost four and a half hours of defiant defence. Mackay, Miller and Archer followed in quick succession. When McDonald went for 89 after more than five and a half resolute hours at the crease, it was all but over. Maddocks was trapped in front to give Laker 'all ten'. All hell erupted, the result and retention of the Ashes forgotten in the thrill of Laker's historic achievement. His figures were 16.4-4-37-9 and 51.2-23-53-10.

SOUTH AFRICA v ENGLAND 1956-57

New Wanderers, Johannesburg
15, 16, 18, 19, 20 February 1957
South Africa won by 17 runs

South Africa 340 (R.A. McLean 93, T.L. Goddard 67, J.H.B. Waite 61) and 142; England 251 (P.B.H. May 61) and 214 (D.J. Insole 68, M.C. Cowdrey 55, H.J. Tayfield 9 for 113)

South Africa won the toss for the first time in the series and decided to adopt a more positive approach to its batting. Goddard and Waite set up the innings with a 112-run partnership for the second wicket. McLean, who top-scored with a hard-hitting 93, was dropped at slip on 3. South Africa's total of 340 was their highest score of the series in a rubber dominated by the bowlers of both sides.

England were making reasonable progress at 2 for 131, with May and Insole having added 71 for the third wicket, when Insole was run out in unusual circumstances. Tayfield unsuccessfully appealed for lbw. The ball flew to Goddard at slip, but Insole thought the ball had gone through the slips and started for a run. Goddard ran in and easily removed the bails. Compton, with the support of the tail-enders, took England's total to 251.

South Africa's 89-run lead proved decisive, although a lion-hearted effort by the England attack restricted the Springboks' second innings to 142. Goddard completed a fine double, top-scoring with 49.

The visitors needed 232 for victory. They lost Bailey late on the fourth afternoon and started the final day requiring 213 to win. Tayfield bowled unchanged for four hours and fifty minutes sending down 35 eight-ball overs. He was to bowl South Africa to its first win at home on a turf pitch. Tayfield was the first South African bowler to take nine wickets in an innings and 13 in a match. Loader, the last wicket to fall, was caught by Tayfield's brother Arthur who was substituting for Funston.

WEST INDIES v PAKISTAN 1957-58

Kensington Oval, Bridgetown, Barbados
17, 18, 20, 21, 22, 23 January 1958
Match Drawn

West Indies 9 for 579 dec. (E.C. Weekes 197, C.C. Hunte 142, O.G. Smith 78, G.S. Sobers 52) and 0 for 28; Pakistan 106 and 8 for 657 dec (Hanif Mohammad 337, Imtiaz Ahmed 91, Saeed Ahmed 65)

This was the first Test to be played between the two countries and it was a match of many records. Nasim-ul-Ghani, aged 16 years and 248 days, became the youngest Test player ever. On the first day of the game, Hunte scored a brilliant century on debut to set up a sizeable West Indies total. Weekes then proceeded to blast the Pakistani attack all over the ground.

Pakistan followed-on 473 runs behind after a miserable display with the bat realised only 106. Hanif then proceeded to play the longest innings in Test history – he batted for 16 hours and 53 minutes, hitting 24 boundaries in a great knock of 337. He shared in century partnerships with Imtiaz Ahmed (152), Alimuddin (112), Saeed Ahmed (154) and his brother Wazir (121).

Hanif was finally dismissed after tea on the final (sixth) day, having started his innings mid-afternoon on the third day. Although the match resulted in a draw, Pakistan's 8 for 657 will be remembered as the highest total after following-on in all Tests.

WEST INDIES v PAKISTAN 1957-58

Sabina Park, Kingston, Jamaica
26, 27, 28 February, 1, 3, 4, March 1958
West Indies won by an innings and 174 runs

Pakistan 328 (Imtiaz Ahmed 122, W.Mathias 77, Saeed Ahmed 52, E.S. Atkinson 5 for 42) and 228 (Wazir Mohammad 106, A.H. Kardar 57); West Indies 3 for 790 dec. (G.S. Sobers 365 not out, C.C. Hunte 260, C.L. Walcott 88 not out)

This crushing win by the West Indies was dominated by Sobers' great innings. The 21-year-old left-hander broke the Test record individual score of 364, set by Hutton for England against Australia at Kennington Oval in 1938.

Sobers batted for just over ten hours, which was three hours less than Hutton. He received grand support from Hunte — their partnership was worth 446 and was only broken by the run-out of Hunte for 260. They became only the fourth pair to bat through a whole day's play and it was also Sobers' first century in Test cricket.

ENGLAND v AUSTRALIA 1956 (Fourth Test)

Old Trafford, Manchester, 26, 27, 28, 30, 31 July. England won by an innings and 170 runs

ENGLAND

P.E.Richardson	c Maddocks b Benaud	104
M.C.Cowdrey	c Maddocks b Lindwall	80
Rev.D.S.Sheppard	b Archer	113
P.B.H.May*	c Archer b Benaud	43
T.E.Bailey	b Johnson	20
C.Washbrook	lbw b Johnson	6
A.S.M.Oakman	c Archer b Johnson	10
T.G.Evans†	st Maddocks b Johnson	47
J.C.Laker	run out	3
G.A.R.Lock	not out	25
J.B.Stratham	c Maddocks b Lindwall	0
Extras	(B 2, LB 5, W 1)	8
Total		**459**

AUSTRALIA

C.C.McDonald	c Lock b Laker	32		c Oakman b Laker	89
J.W.Burke	c Cowdrey b Lock	22		c Lock b Laker	33
R.N.Harvey	b Laker	0		c Cowdrey Laker	0
I.D.Craig	lbw b Laker	8		lbw b Laker	38
K.R.Miller	c Oakman b Laker	6	(6)	b Laker	0
K.D.Mackay	c Oakman b Laker	0	(5)	c Oakman b Laker	0
R.G.Archer	st Evans b Laker	6		c Oakman b Laker	0
R.Benaud	c Statham b Laker	0		b Laker	18
R.R.Lindwall	not out	6		c Lock b Laker	8
L.V.Maddocks†	b Laker	4	(11)	lbw b Laker	2
I.W.Johnson*	b Laker	0	(10)	not out	1
Extras		-		(B 12, LB 4)	16
Total		**84**			**205**

AUSTRALIA	O	M	R	W		O	M	R	W
Lindwall	21.3	6	63	2					
Miller	21	6	41	0					
Archer	22	6	73	1					
Johnson	47	10	151	4					
Benaud	47	17	123	2					
ENGLAND	O	M	R	W		O	M	R	W
Statham	6	3	6	0	Statham	16	10	15	0
Bailey	4	3	4	0	Bailey	20	8	31	0
Laker	16.4	4	37	9	Laker	51.2	23	53	10
Lock	14	3	37	1	Lock	55	30	69	0
					Oakman	8	3	21	0

FALL OF WICKETS

	E	A	A
1st	174	48	28
2nd	195	48	55
3rd	288	62	114
4th	321	62	124
5th	327	62	130
6th	339	73	130
7th	401	73	181
8th	417	78	198
9th	458	84	203
10th	459	84	205

Umpires: D.E.Davies and F.S.Lee

AUSTRALIA v WEST INDIES 1960-61 (First Test)

Wolloongabba, Brisbane, 9, 10, 12, 13,14 December. Match Tied

WEST INDIES

C.C.Hunte	c Benaud b Davidson	24	c Simpson b Mackay	39
C.W.Smith	c Grout b Davidson	7	c O'Neill b Davidson	6
R.B.Kanhai	c Grout b Davidson	15	c Grout b Davidson	54
G.S.Sobers	c Kline b Meckiff	132	b Davidson	14
F.M.M.Worrell*	c Grout b Davidson	65	c Grout b Davidson	65
J.S.Solomon	hit wkt b Simpson	65	lbw b Simpson	47
P.D.Lashley	c Grout b Kline	19	b Davidson	0
F.C.M.Alexander†	c Davidson b Kline	60	b Benaud	5
S.Ramadhin	c Harvey b Davidson	12	c Harvey b Simpson	6
W.W.Hall	st Grout b Kline	50	b Davidson	18
A.L.Valentine	not out	0	not out	7
Extras	(LB 3, W 1)	4	(B 14, LB 7, W 2)	23
Total		**453**		**284**

AUSTRALIA

C.C.McDonald	c Hunte b Sobers	57	b Worrell	16
R.B.Simpson	b Ramadhin	92	c sub (L.R.Gibbs) b Hall	0
R.N.Harvey	b Valentine	15	c Sobers b Hall	5
N.C.O'Neill	c Valentine b Hall	181	c Alexander b Hall	26
L.E.Favell	run out	45	c Solomon b Hall	7
K.D.Mackay	b Sobers	35	b Ramadhin	28
A.K.Davidson	c Alexander b Hall	44	run out	80
R.Benaud*	lbw b Hall	10	c Alexander b Hall	52
A.T.W.Grout†	lbw b Hall	4	run out	2
I.Meckiff	run out	4	run out	2
L.F.Kline	not out	3	not out	0
Extras	(B 2, LB 8, NB 4, W 1)	15	(B2, LB 9, NB 3)	14
Total		**505**		**232**

AUSTRALIA	O	M	R	W		O	M	R	W
Davidson	30	2	135	5	Davidson	24.6	4	87	6
Meckiff	18	0	129	1	Meckiff	4	1	19	0
Mackay	3	0	15	0	Benaud	31	6	69	1
Benaud	24	3	93	0	Mackay	21	7	52	1
Simpson	8	0	25	1	Kline	4	0	14	0
Kline	17.6	6	52	3	Simpson	7	2	18	2
					O'Neill	1	0	2	0

WEST INDIES	O	M	R	W		O	M	R	W
Hall	29.3	1	140	4	Hall	17.7	3	63	5
Worrell	30	0	93	0	Worrell	16	3	41	1
Sobers	32	0	115	2	Sobers	8	0	30	0
Valentine	24	6	82	1	Valentine	10	4	27	0
Ramadhin	15	1	60	1	Ramadhin	17	3	57	1

FALL OF WICKETS

	W	A	W	A
Wkt	1st	1st	2nd	2nd
1st	23	84	13	1
2nd	42	138	88	7
3rd	65	194	114	49
4th	239	278	127	49
5th	243	381	210	57
6th	283	469	210	92
7th	347	484	241	226
8th	366	489	250	228
9th	452	496	253	232
10th	453	505	284	232

Umpires: C.J.Egar and C.Hoy

Pakistan was limited to two fit bowlers after the first five balls with Nasim-ul-Ghani (fractured thumb) and Mahmood Hussain (pulled thigh muscle) unable to bowl. The captain Kardar went into the match with a broken finger on his left hand yet he bowled 37 overs of left-arm spinners.

Because of these injuries, Pakistan batted two men short in the second innings and despite a determined rearguard action by Wazir Mohammad and Kardar, the match finished early on the final day with victory going to the West Indies.

AUSTRALIA v WEST INDIES 1960-61

Woolloongabba, Brisbane
9, 10, 12, 13, 14 December 1960
Match Tied

West Indies 453 (G.S. Sobers 132, F.M.M. Worrell 65, J.S. Solomon 65, F.C.M. Alexander 60, W.W. Hall 50, A.K. Davidson 5 for 135) and 284 (F.M.M. Worrell 65, R.B. Kanhai 54, A.K. Davidson 6 for 87); Australia 505 (N.C. O'Neill 181, R.B. Simpson 92, C.C. McDonald 57) and 232 (A.K. Davidson 80, R. Benaud 52, W.W. Hall 5 for 63)

This Test will live forever in cricket history. It was the first tie in almost 500 matches, and was truly one of the great games highlighted by many outstanding individual efforts.

Sobers, 132 with 21 fours, played one of the greatest innings ever, according to the Australian Captain, Benaud. The grace of Worrell (who scored 65 in each innings), the 181 runs scored by O'Neill, the fast bowling of Hall and the magnificent all-round performance of Davidson (who scored 44 and 80 and captured 5 for 135 and 6 for 87) also contributed to the memorable impact of this match. So to the final day: Hall and Valentine added 25 valuable runs to the West Indies' tally, leaving Australia 233 to win in just over five hours. Midway through the afternoon session, all looked lost as Simpson, Harvey, McDonald, O'Neill, Favell and Mackay were back in the pavilion with only 92 on the board. But Davidson and Benaud staged a tremendous fightback, adding 134 for the seventh wicket before Solomon threw Davidson out.

Grout joined his captain with seven runs needed to win. He took a single and faced the last over which was to be bowled by Hall (at this time they were still bowling eight-ball overs). The first ball took Grout on the thigh for one leg-bye so now five were needed. The next delivery was a bouncer; Benaud swung, got a faint edge, and was caught behind by Alexander.

Meckiff was the new batsman. He played his first ball defensively, then Grout called him for a bye from the next. Four were now needed to win from four balls, with two wickets in hand. Grout skied the next ball towards square leg; Kanhai was waiting to take the catch, but Hall charged towards the ball, causing his team-mates to scatter. The big fast bowler, however, muffed the chance, and the batsmen ran a single.

Three balls to go, three runs to win. Meckiff swung the next ball towards the mid-wicket boundary, and the game looked over as the batsmen turned to complete the third run. But Conrad Hunte returned fast and flat to Alexander beside the bails, with Grout just short of his crease.

The scores were tied as the last man, Kline, joined Meckiff with two balls left. He pushed the first ball to square leg, and Meckiff called for the single. Jo Solomon gathered, and from 20 metres and with one stump at which to aim, ran Meckiff out — a thrilling finish to a magnificent game of cricket and the first tie in Test match history. See the final scoreboard on page 41.

AUSTRALIA v WEST INDIES 1960-61

Adelaide Oval, Adelaide
27, 28, 30, 31 January, 1 February 1961
Match drawn

West Indies 393 (R.B. Kanhai 117, F.M.M. Worrell 71, F.C.M. Alexander 63 not out, R.Benaud 5 for 96) and 6 for 432 dec. (R.B. Kanhai 115, F.C.M. Alexander 87 not out, C.C. Hunte 79, F.M.M. Worrell 53); Australia 366 (R.B. Simpson 85, R. Benaud 77, C.C. McDonald 71, L.R. Gibbs 5 for 97) and 9 for 273 (N.C. O'Neill 65, K.D. Mackay 62 not out)

This match produced an even longer period of suspense than did the tied Test in Brisbane. Kanhai produced his best batting of the series, ripping a century off Australia's attack in each innings. The West Indian wicketkeeper Alexander added great depth to his team's batting, scoring 63 not out and 87 not out from the lower order.

Worrell was again among the run-scorers with 71 and 53. Australia sorely missed the injured Davidson on a belter of an Adelaide pitch.

The highlight of Australia's first innings was the hat-trick taken by Gibbs. The victims were Mackay, Grout and Misson. It was the first hat-trick in Australia — West Indies Tests, and the first to be taken in Australia for 57 years.

Worrell's declaration left Australia 460 to score in about six and a half hours. When McDonald, Favell and Simpson fell before stumps on the fourth day, things were serious.

O'Neill, 65, Burge, 49, and Grout, 42, batted well. But the match seemed over just after tea when Australia was 9 for 207 with 110 minutes still to play. The last man, Kline (who had been dismissed repeatedly in the nets), walked out to join Mackay. The pair remained calm in the crisis as Worrell continually changed his bowlers. The new ball was seen off and the spinners kept out. Mackay faced the last over from Hall and was so determined to save the game that he took several deliveries on the body. His courage was rewarded! The last pair saved the day for Australia.

AUSTRALIA v WEST INDIES 1960-61

Melbourne Cricket Ground, Melbourne
10, 11, 13, 14, 15 February 1961
Australia won by 2 wickets

West Indies 292 (G.S. Sobers 64) and 321 (F.C.M. Alexander 73, C.C. Hunte 52, A.K. Davidson 5 for 84); Australia 356 (C.C. McDonald 91, R.B. Simpson 75, P.J.P. Burge 68, G.S. Sobers 5 for 120) and 8 for 258 (R.B. Simpson 92, P.J.P. Burge 53)

This was the deciding match of one of the most exciting series ever played. Both teams agreed to play a sixth day, if required, to obtain a result. Benaud surprised most people when he invited the West Indian visitors to bat. However, it was not the spearhead Davidson who did the damage but Misson and the spinners who claimed most of the wickets. Six of the West Indies batsmen reached 30 but no-one was able to play the commanding innings required to lay the foundation for a sizeable total.

Before a world-record MCG crowd of 90,800 on the second day, Simpson and McDonald posted the highest opening partnership of the series (146) to place the home team in a sound position. The middle order, apart from Burge, failed to capitalise on the excellent start and at the end of the innings Australia's lead was just 64 runs.

Once again the West Indies' batsmen made a reasonable start but only Alexander and Hunte reached 50. Simpson dismissed the dangerous Sobers — caught at the wicket for the second time in the match — while tragically for the visitors, Solomon was run out again after being well set.

Simpson started the chase for victory at breakneck speed. Eighteen runs came from the first over and 24 from the first ten balls he received. The innings ebbed and flowed until Grout, with Australia 7 for 254, late-cut Valentine. The off-bail fell to the ground and wicketkeeper Alexander pointed to the bail, while the batsmen ran two. Umpire Egar conferred with square leg umpire Hoy and they decided that Grout was not out. Ironically, Grout was then dismissed without further addition to the score.

Mackay and Martin ran a bye to win a thrilling Test and thousands from the final-day crowd of 41,186 swarmed on to the ground to celebrate the climax of a memorable series. The teams were given a ticker-tape parade through the streets of Melbourne two days later.

ENGLAND v AUSTRALIA 1961

Old Trafford, Manchester
27, 28, 29, 31 July, 1 August 1961
Australia won by 54 runs

Australia 190 (W.M. Lawry 74, J.B. Statham 5 for 53) and 432 (W.M. Lawry 102, A.K. Davidson 77 not out, N.C. O'Neill 67, R.B. Simpson 51); England 367 (P.B.H. May 95, K.F. Barrington 78, G.Pullar 63) and 201 (E.R. Dexter 76, R.Benaud 6 for 70)

It was one Test apiece when the English and Australian teams arrived in Manchester for the fourth match of the series. The pitch was the complete opposite to the dust bowl of 1956. Once again, Australia's innings was held together by Lawry, who scored 74 in a disappointing total of just 190. Statham exploited the conditions and bowled superbly, returning five wickets for 53 from 21 overs.

England reached 6 for 358 before Simpson crashed through the English lower order, capturing 4 for 2 off just 26 balls. Simpson was bowling because Benaud was still struggling with the shoulder injury which caused him to miss the second Test at Lord's.

The Ashes were at stake, and Australia's batsmen put their heads down. Lawry scored his second century of the series, and with O'Neill, 67, and Simpson, 51, gave Australia a lead of 154 runs with four wickets in hand at the start of the final day's play.

Mackay, Benaud and Grout fell for the addition of three runs when the No. 11 batsman, McKenzie, joined Davidson. The pair produced one of the finest last-wicket partnerships seen, so that when Flavell bowled the 19-year-old McKenzie, 98 runs had been added. The home team was left with 256 to score at 67 per hour. After a steady start by Pullar and Subba Row that realised 40, 'Lord Ted' Dexter accepted the challenge. He hammered the Australian attack to score 75 in 84 minutes, before Benaud switched to bowl around the wicket. The change worked! Dexter was caught behind, with England 2 for 150, and England crashed to 9 for 193 with Australia's captain producing a match-winning spell at the crease. Benaud's return — injured shoulder and all — was 6 for 70 from 32 overs. When Davidson captured the last wicket Australia had won by 54 runs and, more importantly, they had retained the Ashes.

ENGLAND v WEST INDIES 1963

Lord's, London
20, 21, 22, 24, 25 June 1963
Drawn

West Indies 301 (R.B. Kanhai 73, J.S. Solomon 56, F.S. Trueman 6 for 100) and 229 (B.F. Butcher 133, F.S. Trueman 5 for 52); England 297 (K.F. Barrington 80, E.R. Dexter 70, F.J. Titmus 52 not out, C.C. Griffith 5 for 91) and 9 for 228 (D.B. Close 70, K.F. Barrington 60)

This Test did much for cricket in England. Fortunes fluctuated over five days before the game ended in a thrilling draw.

The West Indies opened proceedings with 301. 'Fiery Fred' (F.S. Trueman) took 6 for 100 before Shackleton, with three wickets from four balls, finished off the innings. Dexter savaged the attack for 70 and, with Barrington's 80, England's deficit was only four runs. The West Indies started the second innings poorly: 2 for 15 became 5 for 104 before Butcher rescued the side with a superb 133. There was another late-order collapse when five wickets fell for 15 runs on the fourth morning, leaving England 234 runs to win and almost two days' play to make them.

England slumped to 3 for 31, and lost Cowdrey with a broken arm. At the close of play on the fourth day, England needed 118 with 6 wickets in hand. The pre-lunch session on the final day was washed out, and England had 200 minutes to score the 118 required. At tea, the score had advance to 5 for 171, with 63 needed in 85 minutes. Close continued to score freely and seemed likely to take England to victory. When the 200 was posted, 34 runs were needed in 45 minutes, with five wickets still in hand. Then the drama started – Hall had Titmus and Trueman out in one over, and then Griffith dismissed Close. Now fifteen runs were needed in twenty minutes, with two wickets in hand, including the injured Cowdrey. Allen and Shackleton reduced the margin to six runs from three balls, then Shackleton was run out! Cowdrey came out with his broken left arm in plaster (fortunately for England, he went to the non-striker's end). Allen blocked the last two balls for the game to end in a nail-biting draw.

ENGLAND v AUSTRALIA 1964

Headingley, Leeds
2, 3, 4, 6 July 1964
Australia won by 7 wickets

England 268 (J.M. Parks 68, E.R. Dexter 66, N.J.N. Hawke 5 for 75) and 229 (K.F. Barrington 85); Australia 389 (P.J.P Burge 160, W.M. Lawry 78) and 3 for 111 (I.R. Redpath 58 not out)

Australia did well to bowl England out on the first day. Hawke and McKenzie were in fine form as they restricted the home team to 268. Dexter and Parks played many handsome strokes but neither were able to get through the sixties.

Burge joined Lawry with Australia in a comfortable position at 2 for 124. Lawry was run out five runs later and the middle order collapsed, leaving the visitors 7 for 178 and struggling against the English spinners, Titmus and Gifford. Burge was 38 not out when Dexter decided to take the new ball with Australia 7 for 187.

Forty-two runs came from the first seven overs bowled by Trueman and Flavell. Burge and Hawke added 105 for the eighth wicket, in better than even time. Burge reached his century just before stumps.

The following morning, Grout assisted Burge in compiling an 89-run partnership for the ninth wicket. The last three wickets had realised 221 runs and Burge had played one of the great innings in Anglo-Australian Tests, batting for five and a quarter hours and hitting 24 boundaries.

Apart from Barrington, England's batsmen struggled against the Australian attack which was supported by superb fielding. Australia was never troubled to make the 109 required for victory.

The win in this match was the only result in the series and enabled Australia to retain the Ashes. It will always be remembered as 'Burge's Match'.

SOUTH AFRICA v AUSTRALIA 1966-67

New Wanderers, Johannesburg
23, 24, 26, 27, 28 December 1966
South Africa won by 233 runs

South Africa 199 (J.D. Lindsay 69, G.D. McKenzie 5 for 46) and 620 (J.D. Lindsay 182, R.G. Pollock 90, P.L. Van der Merwe 76, H.R. Lance 70, A. Bacher 63, E.J. Barlow 50); Australia 325 (W.M. Lawry 98, R.B. Simpson 65) and 261 (T.R. Veivers 55, T.L. Goddard 6 for 53)

This was Australia's first defeat in a Test match on South African soil. Although the ground had been saturated by days of rain, Van der Merwe batted first after winning the toss. It certainly looked like he had made a grave mistake when the score stood at 5 for 41. Lindsay and Lance added some respectability with a stand of 110, but 199 looked anything but a winning total. Simpson and Lawry posted 118 before the captain was dismissed for 65. Australia passed South Africa's total with the loss of just one wicket but then Australia collapsed losing 9 for 121, resulting in a lead of 126.

Lindsay made a match-winning century and R.G. Pollock also produced a classic innings of 90. The Australians put down some vital chances, the most crucial when Lindsay was 10 and Van der Merwe 2. This pair shared a record seventh-wicket partnership of 221. South Africa's score proved to be way beyond the visitors, with Goddard returning career-best figures of 6 for 53 to bowl his team to a historic victory.

INDIA v WEST INDIES 1966-67

Eden Gardens, Calcutta
31 December 1966, 1 (no play), 3, 4, 5 January 19676
West Indies won by an innings and 45 runs
West Indies 390 (R.B. Kanhai 90, G.S. Sobers 70, S.M. Nurse 56); India 167 (L.R. Gibbs 5 for 51) and 178 runs.

This match will be remembered not for the cricket but for the riot that caused the second day's play to be abandoned. The authorities had sold more tickets than there were seats so the disappointed Indian spectators invaded the ground, clashed with police and set fire to several of the stands. The players, naturally concerned for their own safety, were reluctant to continue the match. It came close to being abandoned until assurances were received from important government officials that there would be no further trouble.

The game was played on an under-prepared pitch so the toss virtually decided the outcome. After both openers were run out, cautious batting placed the visitors in a match-winning position. With the ball spinning viciously and coming off the pitch at an uneven height, Sobers and Gibbs triumphed, leading the West Indies to a comprehensive victory.

WEST INDIES v ENGLAND 1967-68

Queen's Park Oval, Port-of-Spain, Trinidad
14, 15, 16, 18, 19 March 1968
England won by 78 wickets
West Indies 7 for 526 dec. (R.B. Kanhai 153, S.M. Nurse 136, G.S. Camacho 87) and 2 for 92 dec.; England 414 (M.C. Cowdrey 148, A.P.E. Knott 69 not out, G. Boycott 62, B.F. Butcher 5 for 34) and 3 for 215 (G. Boycott 80 not out, M.C. Cowdrey 71)

This was the fourth match of the series and the only one in which a result was obtained. England had had the better of the first three matches but this time the West Indies dominated proceedings until the final day.

An aggressive start by Camacho laid the foundation for Nurse and Kanhai to plunder the bowling. This pair added 273 for the third wicket to leave the home side in a seemingly impregnable position.

Cowdrey played a superb captain's knock to lead the fightback until the part-time spinner Butcher ran through the lower middle order to record career-best figures of 5 for 34. With a lead of 112 and the success of the leg spinners, Rodriguez and Butcher, Sobers gambled and declared the West Indies' second innings at 2 for 92 — leaving England to reach 215 in two and three quarter hours. Again it was Cowdrey and Boycott who led the way for the visiting team. They paced the innings perfectly after Edrich, 29, had laid the foundation for an improbable victory. Boycott was there when the match was won with three minutes and eight balls remaining. The West Indian captain Sobers was severely criticised in the Caribbean for the generosity of his declaration.

ENGLAND v AUSTRALIA 1968

Kennington Oval, London
22, 23, 24, 26, 27, August 1968
England won by 226 runs
England 494 (J.H. Edrich 164, B.L. D'Oliveira 158, T.W. Graveney 63) and 181; Australia 324 (W.M. Lawry 135, I.R. Redpath 67) and 125 (R.J. Inverarity 56, D.L. Underwood 7 for 50)

England was to win this memorable match with just five minutes of the match remaining.

Rain sent the players from the field one minute before lunch on the last day with Australia in real trouble at 5 for 86. Then a freak storm flooded the ground during the interval and looked likely to prevent the English victory. However, the ground staff mopped up — assisted by volunteers from the crowd — to enable play to resume at 4.45 pm with just 75 minutes of the match remaining. Rain had played havoc with earlier matches in the rubber and again looked likely to deprive England of a win. No-one will ever forget the sight of hundreds of people mopping up pools of water on Kennington Oval!

Inverarity and Jarman continued to defend stoutly on the deadened pitch. Cowdrey tried his front-line bowlers — Snow, Brown, Illingworth and Underwood — then introduced D'Oliveira who bowled Jarman with the last ball of his second over. Cowdrey immediately recalled Underwood to the attack and the left-armer found the pitch more to his liking as it dried out in the afternoon sun. He removed Mallett and McKenzie in his first over, Gleeson survived until twelve minutes to six, and Inverarity — who had batted for over four hours since the start of the innings — was the last man out at five to six. England thoroughly deserved the victory to square the series.

Of the four centuries scored in the series, three were made in this match — Edrich and D'Oliveira for England, and Lawry for Australia.

AUSTRALIA v WEST INDIES 1968-69

Adelaide Oval, Adelaide
24, 25, 27, 28, 29 January 1969
Match Drawn
West Indies 276 (G.S. Sobers 110, B.F. Butcher 52) and 616 (B.F. Butcher 118, M.C. Carew 90, R.B. Kanhai 80, D.A.J. Holford 80, G.S. Sobers 52, A.N. Connolly 5 for 122); Australia 533 (K.D. Walters 110, I.M. Chappell 76, W.M. Lawry 62, K.R. Stackpole 62, G.D. McKenzie 59, A.P. Sheahan 51) and 9 for 339 (I.M. Chappell 96, W.M. Lawry 89, K.R. Stackpole 50, K.D. Walters 50)

Despite the fact that the match ended in a draw it was a dramatic and exciting finish. The West Indies batted poorly on the first day after winning the toss, with most of the visitors' batsmen throwing their wickets away on the easy-paced pitch. Sober's 110 came in just over two hours but apart from Butcher, the skipper lacked support. It was also a surprise to many of the pundits that Sobers continued to bat down the order at number six or seven.

Australia replied aggressively with Redpath's 45 the lowest score from the top six. The West Indies' attack was undermanned, as Hall had been left out of the line-up for the first time in many years. The home team had a lead of 257 and it looked only a matter of time before another comfortable victory was achieved.

However, the West Indies batsmen clicked and played with a determination that had been missing since the first Test of the series. Carew and Kanhai launched an assault on 'mystery' spinner Gleeson and hit him out of the attack. Shortly before tea on the fourth day, the visitors' lead was 235 with two wickets in hand. Hendriks joined Holford in a ninth-wicket stand of 122 which carried West Indies past 600 and to relative safety.

Australia's target on the last day was 360 in five and three-quarter hours. Positive batting by Lawry, Stackpole, Chappell and Walters, who were scoring at more than four runs per over, had the home team 3 for 298 with the last 15 overs to be bowled. Along the way there was some drama when Redpath, the non-striker, was run out by the bowler, Griffith, without a warning for backing-up before the ball had been bowled.

The final 15 overs produced a nerve-tingling finish. Chappell went lbw to Griffith and then Walters, Freeman and Jarman were run out by a mixture of good fielding and poor calling by Sheahan. When McKenzie swept Gibbs to square leg and Gleeson was lbw to Griffith, Sheahan and Connolly had 26 balls to face. Sobers took the new ball against Connolly but he was able to survive, leaving Australia 21 runs and West Indies one wicket, short of victory.

AUSTRALIA v ENGLAND 1970-71

Sydney Cricket Ground, Sydney
12, 13, 14, 16, 17 February 1971
England won by 62 runs

England 184 and 302 (B.W. Luckhurst 59, J.H. Edrich 57); Australia 264 (G.S. Chappell 65, I.R. Redpath 59) and 160 (K.R. Stackpole 67)

This was the seventh and final Test with Australia needing to win to level the series and retain the Ashes. Ian Chappell replaced Lawry as captain but the former skipper's batting would be sorely missed.

Chappell invited England to bat in his first Test as captain. The gamble paid off with the visitors dismissed for a modest 184. Interestingly, it was the spinners Jenner and O'Keeffe who did the damage claiming three wickets apiece.

Australia struggled in reply and at 4 for 66 looked likely to trail on the first innings. However, stubborn resistance from Redpath, Greg Chappell and Walters, 42, carried Australia to a lead of 80. There was some high drama late on the second day when Jenner ducked into a short-pitched ball from Snow, who was then warned by umpire Rowan for the persistent use of bouncers, which in turn led to a protest from the England captain, Illingworth. The crowd demonstrated against Snow and Illingworth, Snow being assaulted by a spectator who had lent over the boundary fence. Illingworth led his side from the field and only returned after being warned by the umpires that his team could forfeit the game.

A timely opening partnership of 94 by Edrich and Luckhurst restored the balance England's way and with useful contributions from the rest of the top order, Australia was set 223 to win.

After dismissing Eastwood in the first over of the home team's second innings, England's spearhead Snow, broke his hand on the boundary fence when going for a catch. It mattered not as Illingworth and Underwood mesmerised Australia's batsmen with their wily spin. Only Stackpole and Greg Chappell offered any resistance as the home team surrendered meekly.

England had reclaimed the Ashes for the first time since 1958-59.

WEST INDIES v INDIA 1970-71

Queen's Park Oval, Port-of-Spain, Trinidad
6, 7, 9, 10 March 1971
India won by 7 wickets

West Indies 214 (C.A. Davis 71 not out) and 261 (R.C. Fredericks 80, C.A. Davis 74 not out, S. Venkataraghavan 5 for 95); India 352 (D.N. Sardesai 112, S.M. Gavaskar 65, E.D. Solkar 55, J.M. Noreiga 9 for 95) and 3 for 125 (S.M. Gavaskar 67 not out)

This was a memorable match on many counts. It was India's first victory against West Indies and it saw the debut of India's greatest batsman, Gavaskar, who had the honour of hitting the winning run.

The West Indies batted first on a sub-standard pitch and could not have had a worse start, losing Fredericks from the first ball of the match. The home team slumped to 4 for 62 before Sobers joined Davis and attempted to hit his way out of trouble. At the end of the innings the bowlers, Holder and Shillingford, added some valuable runs with Davis. However, 214 was a disappointing total.

Gavaskar and Mankad gave India a sound start, although

they did have their share of good fortune. Sardesai provided the big score from the middle order that was to guarantee a sizeable first innings lead for the visitors. At the same time, the 34-year-old off-spinner Noreiga, playing in only his second Test, became the first bowler to take nine wickets in an innings for West Indies.

After trailing by 138 the home team adopted a positive approach to wipe off the deficit. By stumps on the third day they had gone twelve runs ahead with only one wicket lost. An unfortunate accident before the start of the fourth day turned the wheel India's way. Davis, who was 33 not out, was struck over the eye while practising and had to go to hospital for stitches. He returned to find four wickets had fallen for only 19 runs. Davis carried his bat again but this time the wily Indian spinners were too crafty for the West Indies tail.

The visitors had more than eight hours in which to score the 124 needed for victory. With Gavaskar in full cry they wasted no time and completed the historic victory on the fourth day.

ENGLAND v PAKISTAN 1971

Headingley, Leeds
8, 9, 10, 12, 13 July 1971
England won by 25 runs
England 316 (G. Boycott 112, B.L. D'Oliveira 74) and 264 (B.L. D'Oliveira 72, D.L. Amiss 56); Pakistan 350 (Zaheer Abbas 72, Wasim Bari 63, Mushtaq Mohammad 57) and 205 (Sadiq Mohammad 91)

England won the deciding Test on the final day in a match that could have gone either way.

Illingworth won the toss but the home team got away to a poor start with Luckhurst and Edrich out cheaply. Boycott's third century in successive innings was the backbone of England's effort. He put on 135 in an enterprising stand with D'Oliveira, with Illingworth, Hutton and Lever all adding valuable runs in the lower order.

When Pakistan reached 2 for 198 shortly before stumps on the second day, with Zaheer Abbas and Mushtaq Mohammad in full flight, the visitors looked likely to gain a commanding lead. Lever and Hutton broke through with the new ball to tip the scales England's way. The third day's play was the slowest in England's Test history, seven wickets falling for just 159 runs. Wasim Bari laboured for more than four hours to record his highest Test score and build a Pakistani lead of 34.

Despite Luckhurst 'bagging a pair' and Boycott failing, the home team gave themselves a chance with some resolute batting from Edrich, Amiss, D'Oliveira and Illingworth. Salim Altaf crashed through the tail taking 4 for 9, the last five England wickets falling for 16.

Aftab Gul and Sadiq Mohammad had wiped 25 runs off the target of 231 by stumps on the fourth day. The final day started disastrously for Pakistan with Aftab Gul out third ball and Zaheer Abbas caught from the next. Sadiq Mohammad looked the likely match-winner as he defended resolutely against the good balls and smashed the loose deliveries to the boundary. With Asif Iqbal, Sadiq took the score to 160 before Gifford had Asif Iqbal stumped. D'Oliveira swung the game England's way by removing Sadiq and Intikhab Alam for three runs. Lever ended the match taking three wickets in four balls. Wasim Bari equalled the Test record by holding eight catches in the match.

ENGLAND v INDIA 1971

Kennington Oval, London
19, 20 (no play), 21, 23, 24 August 1971
India won by 4 wickets
England 355 (A.P.E. Knott 90, J.A. Jameson 82, R.A. Hutton 81) and 101 (B.S. Chandrasekhar 6 for 38); India 284 (F.M. Engineer 59, D.N. Sardesai 54, R. Illingworth 5 for 70) and 6 for 174

This was India's first Test win in England and the victory brought to an end England's record run of 26 Tests without defeat.

After winning the toss the home team scored 355 on the first day at nearly three and a half runs per over. Jameson smashed an aggressive 82 at the top of the order before Knott and Hutton established a record seventh-wicket partnership of 103 in just over an hour, Knott's 90 coming from only 117 deliveries.

Rain prevented play on the second day and when it started fifteen minutes late on the third India got away to a poor start, Gavaskar and Mankad falling cheaply. In a welcome return to form, Sardesai and skipper Wadekar, 48, put on 93 for the third wicket to restore the balance. Illingworth did his best to upset India's plans by removing Wadekar, Sardesai and Viswanath in 23 balls without conceding a run. Then Solkar, 44, and Engineer hit back with an attractive 97-run stand for the sixth wicket. Abid Ali, 26, and Venkataraghavan, 24, took India to within 71 runs of the home team.

It was expected that England would set the visitors a sizeable target on the final day. However, Wadekar attacked with his spinners and in just 45.1 overs the home team was bundled out for 101. Chandrasekhar produced a match-winning spell of 6 for 38 to give him eight wickets for the match.

Illingworth was not going to give up the match without a great fight. He bowled superbly, but without luck, conceding only 40 runs from 36 overs, and operated in tandem with Underwood. Again Wadekar and Sardesai held the top order together as the visitors crawled ever so carefully to victory, Engineer's experience proving invaluable as the final 40 runs were scored.

The win was greeted with unbridled joy by millions of supporters across India.

WEST INDIES v NEW ZEALAND 1971-72

Sabina Park, Kingston, Jamaica
16, 17, 18, 19, 21 February 1972
Match Drawn

West Indies 4 for 508 dec. (L.G. Rowe 214, R.C. Fredericks 163) and 3 for 218 dec. (L.G. Rowe 100 not out); New Zealand 386 (G.M. Turner 223 not out, K.J. Wadsworth 78) and 6 for 236 (M.G. Burgess 101)

This was New Zealand's first Test match in the Caribbean and it was an amazing game of cricket.

Sobers won the toss and Fredericks and Rowe proceeded to put the game out of New Zealand's reach on the first day. Their partnership realised 269 before Fredericks was finally dismissed for 163. In his first Test innings, the local hero Rowe made 214.

When the visitors had slumped to 5 for 108 shortly before lunch on the third day they looked headed for an overwhelming defeat. Wadsworth, whose previous highest score had been 21, joined Turner in a match-saving partnership of 220. Wadsworth, who had played the support role to perfection, was finally dismissed for 78. Turner, New Zealand's premier batsman, carried his bat for the second time. His innings of 223 was the highest score by any batsman carrying his bat in Tests.

The West Indies declaration was delayed until Rowe had reached his second hundred of the match. Perhaps Sobers waited too long, as New Zealand required 341 in 310 minutes for victory. When Holford dismissed Dowling and Turner shortly after lunch the home team had a glimmer of hope. However, a fighting century by Burgess enabled New Zealand to save the game.

Rowe became the first player to score hundreds in both innings of his first Test and was the third, after Walters and Gavaskar to score a century and a double-century in the same match. His aggregate of 314 was a record for any debutant.

ENGLAND v AUSTRALIA 1972

Lord's, London
22, 23, 24, 26 June 1972
Australia won by 8 wickets

England 272 (A.W. Greig 54, R.A.L. Massie 8 for 84) and 116 (R.A.L. Massie 8 for 53); Australia 308 (G.S. Chappell 131, I.M. Chappell 56, R.W. Marsh 50, J.A. Snow 5 for 57) and 2 for 81 (K.R. Stackpole 57 not out)

Australia won what has become known as 'Massie's match' on the fourth afternoon to maintain its fine record at the 'home of cricket'.

England batted first on a hard fast pitch that was ideal for pace bowling while for the first three days the atmosphere was heavy and suited to swing. Boycott, Luckhurst and Edrich fell cheaply before the middle order dug in to retrieve the situation.

The next six batsmen all got set but only Greig reached fifty. Knott, 43, Snow, 37, Smith, 34, D'Oliveira, 32, and Illingworth, 30, failed to capitalise on their start. Lillee bowled with great pace and hostility to capture two early wickets but it was his Western Australian team-mate, Massie, who did the damage. In his first Test, the fast-medium swing bowler captured 8 for 84 from 32.5 overs. Only Trott, for Australia against England in 1894/95, and Valentine, for West Indies against England in 1950, had previously taken eight wickets in an innings on debut.

Francis and Stackpole fell cheaply before the Chappell brothers combined in a 75-run partnership for the third wicket. Ian, the more aggressive, fell to a suspect outfield catch by Smith for an attractive 56. When Walters was dismissed for 1 the visitors were again in trouble at 4 for 84. Greg then received valuable support from another Western Australian debutant, Edwards. This pair added 106 for the fifth wicket before Edwards fell to another splendid outfield catch by Smith. Greg Chappell, who brought up his century shortly before stumps on the second day, was finally dismissed for a magnificent 131. Hard hitting by Marsh and Colley gave the visitors a slender lead of 36. Snow bowled superbly finishing with 5 for 57 from 32 overs.

The capacity Saturday crowd did not know what was in store as England started its second innings. A short ball from Lillee struck Boycott on the body before dropping onto the off-bail. Luckhurst was next to go, caught Marsh bowled Lillee for four. Under cloudy skies the England batsmen had no answer to the superb swing bowling of Massie. The last pair of Gifford and Price put on 35 which was the best stand of the innings. Massie's second innings figures 8 for 53 from 27.2 overs were even better than his first. His match return of 16 for 137 was a record on debut until Hirwani of India captured 16 for 136 against the West Indies in 1987/88.

With only 81 required for victory, Australia wrapped up the match on the fourth afternoon by eight wickets.

The match-winner, Massie, had made one of the greatest debuts in the game's long history.

AUSTRALIA v PAKISTAN 1972-73

Sydney Cricket Ground, Sydney
6, 7, 8, 10, 11 January 1973
Australia won by 52 runs

Australia 334 (I.R. Redpath 79, R. Edwards 69) and 184; Pakistan 360 (Mushtaq Mohammad 121, Asif Iqbal 65, Nasim-ul-Ghani 64, G.S. Chappell 5 for 61) and 106 (M.H.N. Walker 6 for 15)

Pakistan won the toss and sent Australia in to bat on a green and responsive pitch. However, the pace trio of Asif Masood, Salim Altaf and Sarfraz Nawaz failed to take advantage of the favourable conditions. Redpath's patient innings of 79 was the cornerstone of Australia's total of 334. Sarfraz with 4 for 53 was the best of the visitors' bowlers.

Mushtaq Mohammad and Asif Iqbal, who came together with the score at 131, added 139 for the fifth wicket. The home team's premier bowler, Lillee, sent down only ten overs before a back problem caused him to leave the field. Greg Chappell exploited the conditions with his lively medium-pace deliveries to return 5 for 61.

With Pakistan leading by 26 the game was wide open. In the final session of the third day, Salim Altaf and Sarfraz Nawaz bowled the visitors to the edge of victory. Walker's dismissal early on the fourth morning left Australia 75 runs in front with just two wickets in hand. Massie joined the debutant Watkins in a match-winning 83-run partnership for the ninth wicket. It wasn't a swashbuckling affair as the pair occupied the crease for two and a half hours. Both Salim and Sarfraz claimed four wickets apiece, giving Sarfraz eight for the match and Salim seven.

The target for Pakistan was 159 with more than a day to play. Lillee bowled Nasim-ul-Ghani, 5, with the score on seven then Edwards took one of the great catches at cover point to remove Sadiq for 6. Zaheer Abbas, 26, and Majid Khan, 11, resumed on the final morning with only 111 required. However, the batsmen were overwhelmed by the occasion and the superb bowling of Lillee and Walker. Lillee reduced his pace because of the back problem while Walker, in only his second Test, captured 6 for 15 from 16 overs to win the match.

INDIA v ENGLAND 1972-73

Eden Gardens, Calcutta
30, 31 December 1972, 1, 3, 4 January 1973
India won by 28 runs

India 210 (F.M. Engineer 75) and 155 (A.S. Durani 53, A.W. Greig 5 for 24); England 173 (B.S. Chandrasekhar 5 for 65) and 163 (A.W. Greig 67, B.S. Bedi 5 for 63)

Almost 70,000 spectators packed the famous Eden Gardens stadium each day of the match, which fluctuated throughout every session.

India batted first after winning the toss. Tight English bowling supported by splendid fielding restricted the home team to 5 for 148 on the first day. Skipper Wadekar held the top order together with a patient 44 before he was tragically run out. Wicketkeeper Engineer played with his customary bravado. Coming in at number seven he scored 75 out of 110 runs while he was at the crease.

England struggled in reply. The Indian spinners Bedi, Chandrasekhar and Prasanna were able to weave their spell over the visitors' batsmen. Greig, 29, Knott, 35, and Old, 33 not out, bolstered the middle order but they fell 36 runs short on the first innings.

Hostile bowling by debutant Old put India on the back foot at the start of their second innings. Durani (batting with a runner) and Viswanath put on 71 for the third wicket in what proved to be a match-winning partnership. Greig, bowling a mixture of medium-pace cutters and fast off-spinners, captured 5 for 24 from 19.5 overs to give England some hope of victory.

Greig followed up his superb spell with the ball with a fine knock. He joined Denness with the visitors in desperate trouble at 4 for 17, but by stumps it was 4 for 105. The final day started with England needing a further 86 for victory with six wickets in hand. However, when Chandrasekhar removed Greig, Knott and Denness the balance had returned to India. Cottam was the batsman out in the first over after lunch as India scored a thoroughly-deserved win in a stirring low-scoring contest.

WEST INDIES v AUSTRALIA 1972-3

Queen's Park Oval, Port-of-Spain, Trinidad
23, 24, 25, 27, 28 March 1973
Australia won by 44 runs

Australia 332 (K.D. Walters 112, I.R. Redpath 66, G.S. Chappell 56) and 281 (I.M. Chappell 97, L.R. Gibbs 5 for 102); West Indies 280 (R.B. Kanhai 56, A.I. Kallicharran 53) and 289 (A.I. Kallicharran 91, R.C. Fredericks 76)

Australia pulled off a fighting victory on a turning pitch in Trinidad. Walters played one of his great Test innings. He scored 100 between lunch and tea on the first day (Later, in December 1974 in Perth he was to score 100 between tea and stumps against England.)

The West Indies replied with 280 to trail by 52 runs in the first innings. They were disadvantaged by the fact that their number three batsman, Rowe, tore the ligaments in his right ankle on the first day and was therefore unable to bat in either innings of the match.

Ian Chappell's gutsy 97 was the foundation of Australia's second effort with the bat. He was seventh out at 231, and then some strange bowling by Gibbs allowed the last three wickets to add 50 (including 33 for the last wicket between Walker and Hammond).

The home team's target was 334. At lunch on the final day, an improbable victory seemed likely when Kallicharran and Foster were together with the score at 4 for 268. The tireless Walker snared 'Kalli' on the first ball after lunch and then O'Keeffe removed Foster. The rout continued with O'Keeffe picking up one of his best returns in the Test arena taking 4 for 57 from 24.1 overs.

NEW ZEALAND v ENGLAND 1974-75

Eden Park, Auckland
20, 21, 22, 23, 25 February 1975
England won by an innings and 83 runs

England 6 for 593 dec. (K.W.R. Fletcher 216, M.H. Denness 181, J.H. Edrich 64, A.W. Greig 51); New Zealand 326 (J.M. Parker 121, J.F.M. Morrison 58, K.J. Wadsworth 58, A.W. Greig 5 for 98) and 184 (J.F.M. Morrison 58, G.P. Howarth 51 not out, A.W. Greig 5 for 51)

The match ended amid great drama when the New Zealand number eleven, Chatfield, deflected a bouncer from Lever into his temple and collapsed with a hairline fracture of the skull. Chatfield's heart stopped beating for several seconds and only heart massage and mouth-to-mouth resuscitation by Bernard Thomas, the England physiotherapist, saved his life. Lever, who was visibly distressed by the incident, was reassured by Chatfield that the accident was his fault.

The dramatic finish to the match diverted attention from the excellent cricket that had been played on the first four days of the game. England had made a shaky start before Denness added 117 for the third wicket with Edrich and 266 for the fourth with Fletcher, who batted for seven hours to record his highest Test score of 216.

Despite a splendid century from Parker and half-centuries from Morrison and Wadsworth, New Zealand followed on 267 runs behind. By the fourth day the pitch had bare patches and the ball turned with uneven bounce, bringing Greig and Underwood into their own. During the match Greig took his 100th wicket, becoming the fourth English all-rounder to score 2000 runs and take 100 wickets. Underwood became the fourth English bowler to take 200 wickets when he dismissed Congdon in New Zealand's second innings.

While Chatfield will always remember his first Test with mixed emotions, he recovered to play a further 42 times for his country and take 123 wickets.

ENGLAND v AUSTRALIA 1975

Headingley, Leeds
14, 15, 16, 18, 19 (no play) August 1975
Match Drawn

England 288 (D.S. Steele 73, J.H. Edrich 62, A.W. Greig 51, G.J. Gilmour 6 for 85) and 291 (D.S. Steele 92); Australia 135 (P.H. Edmonds 5 for 28) and 3 for 220 (R.B. McCosker 95 not out, I.M. Chappell 62)

This game at Headingley was the third Test of a four-match series. Australia, holding the Ashes, was leading 1-0.

England collapsed from 5 for 268 to be all out for 288. Gilmour was the wrecker, capturing a career-best 6 for 85 from 31 overs. Australia was bundled out for 135 in reply. Edmonds, on debut, was the destroyer with 5 for 28 from 20 overs.

Steele with 92 (after 73 in the first innings) and Greig, 49 (after his 51 in the first 'dig'), carried the home team to 291. The lead was 444 runs as Australia chased an improbable victory. By the end of the fourth day, they were in with a chance at 3 for 220.

When the ground staff arrived the next morning, they discovered to their horror that the pitch had been vandalised. Not only had the wicket been dug up but oil had also been poured onto it. Play was impossible and so the game was abandoned. Ironically, it started raining at about midday so little play would have been possible on the final day anyway.

WEST INDIES v INDIA 1975-76

Queens Park Oval, Port-of-Spain, Trinidad
7, 8, 10, 11, 12 April 1976
India won by 6 wickets

West Indies 359 (I.V.A Richards 177, C.H. Lloyd 68, B.S. Chandrasekhar 6 for 120) and 6 for 271 dec. (A.I. Kallicharran 103 not out); India 228 (M.A. Holding 6 for 65) and 4 for 406 (G.R. Viswanath 112, S.M. Gavaskar 102, M. Amarnath 85)

In this match, India scored over 400 in the fourth innings to win. The only previous occasion had been at Headingley in 1948 (see page 21). Richards, with 177, mastered the Indian spinners, and made nearly half the West Indies first-innings total of 359. The youthful Holding ripped through the visitors, who were bowled out for 228, leaving a deficit of 131. The home team built on the first-innings lead and, after Kallicharran reached his century, Lloyd declared. India needed 403 in a day and a half. (Australia's target at Leeds had been 404.)

Gavaskar, at his best, smashed 86 with twelve fours before stumps were drawn at 1 for 134. India needed 269 runs in six hours. After Gavaskar's early departure, Viswanath took over and, with Amarnath as the sheet anchor, they progressed steadily towards an extraordinary victory. The West Indian spinners bowled poorly and without the skill of their opposite numbers. Even though 'Vishy' and Amarnath were run out, Patel took over and India was home with seven overs to spare.

AUSTRALIA v ENGLAND 1976-77

The Centenary Test
Melbourne Cricket Ground, Melbourne
12, 13, 14, 16, 17 March 1977
Australia won by 45 runs

Australia 138 and 9 for 419 dec. (R.W. Marsh 110 not out, I.C. Davis 68, K.D. Walters 66, D.W. Hookes 56); England 95 (D.K. Lillee 6 for 26) and 417 (D.W. Randall 174, D.L. Amiss 64, D.K. Lillee 5 for 139)

The Centenary of Test cricket was celebrated with a special match at Melbourne 100 years after that first match in March 1877. Australia, sent in on a lively pitch, was bundled out for just 138. The huge Sunday crowd roared as Lillee and Walker crashed through England's batting. England was all out for 95 as a result of the onslaught. Lillee took 6 for 26 and Walker 4 for 54.

The MCC officials were concerned; the match seemed certain to be over by the fourth day of play. However, the Queen and Duke of Edinburgh were not due to attend until the afternoon of the fifth day.

The pitch was now favouring the batsmen. Although the homeside was in trouble at 3 for 53 in the second innings, they were able to turn that situation around. Marsh reached his first Test century against England, and the 21-year-old Hookes, on debut, hit Greig for five successive fours. The gutsy McCosker (who had his jaw fractured in the first innings) batted at number ten and scored 25 in an invaluable partnership of 54 with Marsh. Chappell declared Australia's innings with his team leading by 462.

Randall and Amiss gave England a glimmer of hope with a third-wicket stand of 166. O'Keeffe had both Randall and Greig caught at short leg by Cosier, then Lillee trapped Knott in front.

The result was an Australian victory by 45 runs — the same margin by which they had won the first match 100 years earlier. See page 52 for final scoreboard.

NEW ZEALAND v ENGLAND 1977-78

Basin Reserve, Wellington
10, 11, 12, 14, 15 February 1978
New Zealand won by 72 runs

New Zealand 228 (J.G. Wright 55, C.M. Old 6 for 54) and 123 (R.G.D. Willis 5 for 32); England 215 (G. Boycott 77) and 64 (R.J. Hadlee 6 for 26)

This was the 48th match in 48 years between the two countries. Wright, playing his first Test, laid the foundation for New Zealand's innings. His 55 was scored in almost six hours and, with Congdon, 44, the home team reached a modest 228. Old bowled into the howling gale and finished with 6 for 54 from 30 overs. If Wright was laborious, then Boycott was, too. His 77 took almost seven and a half hours to compile. England lost its last six wickets for 32 runs to trail by 13 runs on the first innings. New Zealand's second-innings collapse was just as dramatic. The home team went from 1 for 82 to be all out for 123, with the last nine wickets falling for 41 runs. Willis was the destroyer, taking 5 for 32. England's target was 137, but by the end of the fourth day the innings was in tatters: eight wickets had fallen for 53 runs. Rain delayed the inevitable on the final morning for 40 minutes. It then took the Kiwis 49 minutes to claim the last two wickets, both falling to Richard Hadlee, who finished with 6 for 26. England was all out for 64.

New Zealand defeated England for the first time amid chaotic scenes at the Basin Reserve.

WEST INDIES v AUSTRALIA 1977-78

Bourda, Georgetown, Guyana
31 March, 1, 2, 4, 5 April 1978
Australia won by three wickets

West Indies 205 (A.E. Greenidge 56, S. Shivnarine 53) and 439 (H.A. Gomes 101, A.B. Williams 100, S. Shivnarine 63, D.R. Parry 51); Australia 286 (R.B. Simpson 67, S.J. Rixon 54, G.M. Wood 50) and 7 for 362 (G.M. Wood 126, C.S. Serjeant 124)

A pre-match dispute between the West Indies Board and their captain, Lloyd, over team selection resulted in all the players contracted to World Series Cricket withdrawing from the team. As a result of this action, Kallicharran was named captain and the team comprised six new caps. It was hardly the perfect preparation for an important Test match for the West Indies.

Hostile bowling by Thomson and Clark restricted the inexperienced line-up to 205 with two of the debutants, A.E. Greenidge and Shivnarine scoring half-centuries. Australia lost Darling and Ogilvie before the close and by lunch on the second day were 6 for 146. Simpson, Rixon and Yardley retrieved the situation for the visitors with some splendid batting which saw Australia gain a lead of 81. Two of the new caps, Phillip with four and Clarke three, were amongst the wickets and they both bowled with good pace and hostility. Another of the debutants, Williams, turned the game for the West Indies with a cavalier knock. He raced to his century from just 118 deliveries and then departed next ball. Williams received excellent support from nightwatchman Parry in a third-wicket partnership of 77. Gomes, who took over from Williams, was less aggressive but equally effective. Gomes reached his century in three hours and 25 minutes with eleven boundaries and, like Williams, was dismissed next ball after completing his hundred. Shivnarine again played a vital role with the bat, putting on 70 with Gomes for the seventh wicket and 62 with Holder for the ninth. Australia had two days in which to score 359 for victory.

After forty minutes on the fourth day it looked like a certain West Indies win. Darling, Ogilvie and Simpson had been dismissed by Clarke with only 22 runs on the board. However, Wood and Serjeant played with great determination in a stand of 251 to give the visitors some hope of pulling off a memorable victory. When the century-makers and Cosier fell in the final session it was again anyone's match.

Australia started the fifth day needing a further 69 with four wickets in hand. Wicketkeeper Rixon with 39 not out, Laughlin 24, and Yardley 15 not out, saw the visitors home.

The total of 7 for 362 was at the time the third-highest fourth innings score to win a Test.

AUSTRALIA v ENGLAND 1976-77 (Centenary Test)

Melbourne Cricket Ground, 12, 13, 14, 16, 17 March. Australia won by 45 runs

AUSTRALIA

Batsman	1st innings	Runs		2nd innings	Runs
I.C.Davis	lbw b Lever	5		c Knott b Greig	68
R.B.McCosker	b Willis	4	(10)	c Greig b Old	25
G.J.Cosier	c Fletcher b Lever	10	(4)	c Knott b Lever	4
G.S.Chappell*	b Underwood	40	(3)	b Old	2
D.W.Hookes	c Greig b Old	17	(6)	c Fletcher b Underwood	56
K.D.Walters	c Greig b Willis	4	(5)	c Knott b Greig	66
R.W.Marsh†	c Knott b Old	28		not out	110
G.J.Gilmour	c Greig b Old	4		c Knott b Greig	16
K.J.O'Keeffe	c Brearley b Underwood	0	(2)	c Willis b Old	14
D.K.Lillee	not out	10	(9)	c Amiss b Old	25
M.H.N.Walker	b Underwood	2		not out	8
Extras	(B 4, LB 2, NB 8)	14		(LB 10, NB 15)	25
Total		**138**		**(9wkts dec.)**	**419**

ENGLAND

Batsman	1st innings	Runs		2nd innings	Runs
R.A.Woolmer	c Chappell b Lillee	9		lbw b Walker	12
J.M.Brearley	c Hookes b Lillee	12		lbw b Lillee	43
D.L.Underwood	c Chappell b Walker	7	(10)	b Lillee	7
D.W.Randall	c Marsh b Lillee	4	(3)	c Cosier b O'Keeffe	174
D.L.Amiss	c O'Keeffe b Walker	4	(4)	b Chappell	64
K.W.R.Fletcher	c Marsh b Walker	4	(5)	c Marsh b Lillee	1
A.W.Greig*	b Walker	18	(6)	c Cosier b O'Keeffe	41
A.P.E.Knott†	lbw b Lillee	15	(7)	lbw b Lillee	42
C.M.Old	c Marsh b Lillee	3	(8)	c Chappell b Lillee	2
J.K.Lever	c Marsh b Lillee	11	(9)	not out	4
R.G.D.Willis	not out	1		not out	5
Extras	(B 2, LB 2, NB 2, W 1)	7		(B 8, LB 4, NB 7, W 3)	22
Total		**95**			**417**

ENGLAND	O	M	R	W		O	M	R	W
Lever	12	1	36	2	Lever	21	1	95	2
Willis	8	0	33	2	Willis	22	0	91	0
Old	12	4	39	3	Old	27.6	2	104	4
Underwood	11.6	2	16	3	Greig	14	3	66	2
					Underwood	12	2	38	1
AUSTRALIA	O	M	R	W		O	M	R	W
Lillee	13.3	2	26	6	Lillee	34.4	7	139	5
Walker	15	3	54	4	Walker	22	4	83	1
O'Keeffe	1	0	4	0	Gilmour	4	0	29	0
Gilmour	5	3	4	0	Chappel	16	7	29	1
					O'Keeffe	33	6	108	3
					Walters	3	2	7	0

FALL OF WICKETS

	A	E	A	E
Wkt	1st	1st	2nd	2nd
1st	11	19	33	28
2nd	13	30	40	113
3rd	23	34	53	279
4th	45	40	132	290
5th	51	40	187	346
6th	102	61	244	369
7th	114	65	277	380
8th	117	78	353	385
9th	136	86	407	410
10th	138	95	-	417

Umpires: T.F.Brooks and M.G.O'Connell

WEST INDIES v AUSTRALIA 1977-78

Sabina Park, Kingston, Jamaica
28, 29, 30 April, 2, 3, May 1978
Match Drawn

Australia 343 (P.M. Toohey 122, G.N. Yallop 57) and 3 for 305 dec. (P.M. Toohey 97, G.M. Wood 90); West Indies 280 (H.A. Gomes 115, S. Shivnarine 53, T.J. Laughlin 5 for 101) and 9 for 258 (A.I. Kallicharran 126)

Australia was denied an almost certain victory when spectators rioted and invaded the ground after Holder had been given out caught behind by Umpire Malcolm. Thirty-eight balls of the mandatory final 20 overs remained when the incident occurred. Officials of both teams had decided to extend the match into a sixth day but had not consulted nor informed the umpires of this decision. One of them, Gosein, was adamant there was no provision in the laws or playing conditions for the match to be extended so he refused to continue, as did the third umpire, John Gayle. Although Malcolm was prepared to stand, no other official of first-class status was available so the match was abandoned as a draw.

The visitors had held sway from the start with Toohey's maiden century making up the cornerstone of Australia's total of 343. Left-arm spinner Jumadeen polished off the tail, taking the last four wickets in 28 balls. Gomes' splendid hundred held the West Indies innings together after they had slumped to be 5 for 63. He shared stands of 96 with Shivnarine, 46 with Phillip, and 57 with Holder.

Aggressive batting by Australia in its second innings gave the visitors the opportunity to declare late on the fourth day, leaving the home team 369 for victory with Toohey and Wood both just missing out on well-deserved centuries.

Skipper Kallicharran held the West Indies innings together with a determined century but it was problematical that Parry and Jumadeen would have been able to survive against the Australian spinners, Yardley and Higgs, on a turning pitch.

AUSTRALIA v PAKISTAN 1978-79

Melbourne Cricket Ground, Melbourne
10, 11, 12, 14, 15 March 1979
Pakistan won by 71 runs

Pakistan 196 and 9 for 353 dec. (Majid Khan 108, Zaheer Abbas 59); Australia 168 and 310 (A.R. Border 105, K.J. Hughes 84, A.M.J. Hilditch 62, Sarfraz Nawaz 9 for 86)

This Test was the first of a two-match series and came at the end of an Australian season in which six Tests had been played in an Ashes series and Pakistan had completed a successful tour of New Zealand.

Yallop sent Pakistan in after winning the toss. Hogg responded with a fiery opening spell which reduced the visitors to 4 for 40. The situation became even worse after Javed Miandad and Wasim Raja had been removed, with Pakistan in real trouble at 6 for 99. Mushtaq Mohammad played a gritty captain's knock, top-scoring with 36. He received valuable support from Imran Khan, 33, and Sarfraz Nawaz, 35, which carried Pakistan to a modest 196. Hogg was the pick of the bowlers finishing with 4 for 49.

Australia's reply was poor. Openers Wood and Hilditch collided while running which forced Wood to retire hurt. Apart from new cap Whatmore, who top-scored with a patient 43, the home team struggled. Imran bowled superbly taking 4 for 26 from 18 overs. There was a stir when Hogg was run out after leaving the crease before the ball was 'dead'. Mushtaq asked umpire Harvey to reverse his decision, but the request was denied. Umpire Harvey, standing in his first Test, was the elder brother of Neil, the celebrated Australian left-hand batsman.

Pakistan consolidated its position with some aggressive batting. Majid Khan led the way with his seventh century, his 108 featuring sixteen majestic boundaries. The declaration was made mid-afternoon on the fourth day with Australia set 382 for victory.

With Wood inconvenienced, Whatmore opened and put on 49 with Hilditch who fell just before stumps for 62. Australia started the final day needing 265 to win with eight wickets in hand. Within half an hour, Yallop was foolishly run out. Border and Hughes, with a mixture of splendid batting and good fortune, carried Australia to 3 for 305 by half past four. Seventy-seven runs were needed with seven wickets in hand. Sarfraz Nawaz then produced one of the greatest spells in Test history. In 65 balls the home team was dismissed for 310. Sarfraz had taken 7 for 1 from 33 deliveries to finish with 9 for 86 and the other dismissal had been a run-out. Pakistan had pulled off a great victory, as a result of the inspired bowling by Sarfraz.

NEW ZEALAND v WEST INDIES 1979-80

Carisbrook, Dunedin
8, 9, 10, 12, 13 February 1980
New Zealand won by 1 wicket

West Indies 140 (D.L. Haynes 55, R.J. Hadlee 5 for 34) and 212 (D.L. Haynes 105, R.J. Hadlee 6 for 68); New Zealand 249 (B.A. Edgar 65, R.J. Hadlee 51) and 9 for 104

After Lloyd called correctly, Hadlee tore the heart out of the visitors' innings. They were 3 for 4 after Hadlee had bowled 13 deliveries. Haynes with 55 played a lone hand, as the West Indies were bowled out for 140.

Against hostile fast bowling, Edgar and Howarth played with great courage and determination for New Zealand, with Edgar taking almost five hours to score 65. After a middle order collapse, Hadlee and Cairns added 64 in 34 minutes for the eighth wicket. Cairns hit Parry for 3 sixes in one over, and Hadlee's 51 runs included nine fours.

New Zealand's lead was a valuable 109 runs. Again it was Haynes who held the visitors' innings together. He scored 105 out of 212, and added 88 for the fifth wicket with King and 63 for the sixth with Murray to save the side.

New Zealand needed 104 to win. By lunch on the final day they had reached 2 for 33. Under intense pressure from the pace battery (Holding, Croft and Garner), they crashed to be 7 for 54 and appeared to be beaten.

Again Hadlee and Cairns came to the rescue. They added 19 for the eighth wicket before Cairns and Troup put on 27 for the ninth. At tea it was 8 for 95. With one run added, Holding hit Cairns' off-stump without dislodging the bail. Cairns went when the score reached 100. Boock, the No.11 batsman, joined Troup. He survived the last five balls of Holding's over. Garner continued the attack. The first ball produced a bye. On the second ball, Boock survived an appeal for lbw. He defended the next two before pushing the fifth ball behind point for two runs. With scores level, the batsmen scampered a leg bye to produce a thrilling New Zealand victory.

Hadlee's eleven wickets included a Test record – eight lbw decisions (of the total twelve lbw decisions made in the match).

AUSTRALIA v INDIA 1980-81

Melbourne Cricket Ground, Melbourne
7, 8, 9, 10, 11 February 1981
India won by 59 runs

India 237 (G.R. Viswanath 114) and 324 (C.P.S. Chauhan 85, S.M. Gavaskar 70); Australia 419 (A.R. Border 124, K.D. Walters 78, G.S. Chappell 76) and 83 (Kapil Dev 5 for 28)

This was a sensational match – not only because of Australia's amazing second-innings collapse on the final day, but because India had come near to forfeiting the match on the previous day when the captain, Gavaskar, disagreed with an lbw decision and wanted to call off the game.

Chappell sent India in on an MCG pitch that had been criticised all summer. The decision was vindicated when India slumped to 6 for 115. They were kept in the match by Viswanath, who went in at 2 for 22, and was ninth man out making 114. In reply, Australia struggled early before Chappell and Border added 108 for the fourth wicket. Border reached his century on the third morning, and then Walters and Marsh held the lower order together.

Australia had a significant lead of 182, although resolute batting by Gavaskar and Chauhan had reduced this to 74 at the end of the third day. Then, 35 minutes before lunch, the 'Gavaskar incident' occurred. Gavaskar was given out, but he indicated that he had hit the ball on to his pad. As he walked past his partner, Chauhan, he urged him to leave the field with him. Fortunately, the Indian team manager, Wing Commander Durrani, intervened and ordered Chauhan to continue his innings.

When Chauhan was dismissed shortly after, Lillee became Australia's leading Test wicket-taker. Vengsarkar, Viswanath and Patil helped rebuild India's innings, but a late-order collapse let Australia needing only 143 to win.

India's attack was seriously depleted. Kapil Dev had pulled a thigh muscle and didn't bowl on the fourth evening. Yadav suffered a fractured toe batting in the first innings when he was struck by a Pascoe yorker, and Doshi had a fractured instep and was greatly distressed. Nevertheless Australia was reeling at 3 for 24 at the end of the day, with Dyson, Wood, and Chappell all back in the pavilion. The injured Kapil Dev joined the fray on the final morning and, despite the disability, bowled unchanged to capture five of the last seven wickets to fall. India managed an unlikely victory by 59 runs.

ENGLAND v AUSTRALIA 1981

Headingley, Leeds
16, 17, 18, 20, 21 July 1981
England won by 18 runs

Australia 9 for 401 dec. (J. Dyson 102, K.J. Hughes 89, G.N. Yallop 58, I.T. Botham 6 for 95) and 111 (R.G.D. Willis 8 for 43); England 174 (I.T. Botham 50) and 356 (I.T. Botham 149 not out, G.R. Dilley 56, T.M. Alderman 6 for 135)

For this third Test of the series, Brearley replaced Botham as England's captain. Hughes won the toss for the third time in succession for Australia, and batted first. Dyson's solid century and the skipper's 89 steered Australia to the relative safety of 401 before the declaration.

Australia's pace bowlers, Lillee, Alderman and Lawson, bundled England out for 174. The deposed Botham, who had taken six wickets in Australia's innings, top-scored with 50.

England followed on, 227 runs behind, but the second innings proceeded along similar lines to the first. Taylor became Alderman's fourth victim for the innings, and England's score was 7 for 135.

Botham proceeded to play one of the great Test hands and, with admirable support from the tail, at least avoided the innings defeat and gave his team a glimmer of hope. With Dilley, 56, he added 117 for the eighth wicket in 80 minutes; with Old, 29, it was 67 for the ninth; and with Willis, 2, it was 37 for the last. Botham finished with 149 not out and posted his century from 87 balls. (Jessop had smashed 104 in 75 minutes at Kennington Oval in 1902 — see page 15.)

Australia had almost the entire final day to score 130 to win. With the score at 1 for 56, Willis changed ends to bowl with the wind. He proceeded to take eight of the last nine wickets to fall and, in a career-best performance, returned 8 for 43 from 15.1 overs as England snatched a dramatic 18-run victory.

This was only the second time that a team following-on had won a Test match. The previous occasion was in Sydney in December 1894 (see page 26).

Early in England's second innings, odds of 500 to 1 for an England victory were posted in the betting tents at Headingley.

ENGLAND v AUSTRALIA 1981

Edgbaston, Birmingham
30, 31 July, 1, 2 August 1981
England won by 29 runs
England 189 (T.M. Alderman 5 for 42) and 219 (R.J. Bright 5 for 68); Australia 258 and 121 (I.T. Botham 5 for 11)

Less than two weeks after England's unbelievable win at Headingley, they did it again at Edgbaston. The ball dominated to the extent that no batsman scored 50. This had not happened since January 1935 when the West Indies played England on a rain-affected pitch at Bridgetown.

Despite some concern about the wicket, Brearley chose to bat after winning the toss. The skipper top-scored with a patient 48; the next best was Botham who made 26. For the third time in the series, Alderman claimed five wickets in an innings. By stumps on the first day England had struck back with Old removing Dyson and Border.

Tight bowling and alert fielding by the home team restricted Australia's lead to 69 runs. Hughes top-scored with 47, debutant Kent made 46 and Yallop, 30. Emburey bowled his off-spinners with great control, finishing with 4 for 43 from 26 overs.

When Bright, bowling his left-arm orthodox into the bowler's footmarks, had dismissed Gower, Boycott, Gooch and Willey, and Lillee had Botham caught behind, England's lead was just 46 with only four wickets in hand. Gatting, who top-scored with 39, kept the game alive with valuable support from the bowlers. Emburey remained 37 not out while Old made 23.

Australia's target was 151, 21 more than was required at Headingley. Old struck before stumps on the third day, trapping Wood in front. The visitors required 142 with two days to play.

Willis gave England some hope by removing Dyson and Hughes within forty minutes on the fourth morning. Yallop, who made 30 for the second time in the match, and Border carefully took the score to 87. Australia still looked likely winners as Border, with Kent's assistance, moved the total to 105.

With just 46 needed, Emburey dismissed Australia's sheet-anchor and with Border gone the brittleness of the visitors' batting was exposed. Botham, who had been reluctant to bowl, destroyed the lower order taking 5 for 1 in 28 balls to end the match.

On only the second Sunday during which there had been Test cricket played in England, the home team had scored a remarkable victory to the delight of the capacity crowd.

AUSTRALIA v PAKISTAN 1981-82

W.A.C.A. Ground, Perth
13, 14, 15, 16, 17 November 1981
Australia won by 286 runs
Australia 180 and 424 (K.J. Hughes 106, B.M. Laird 85); Pakistan 62 (D.K. Lillee 5 for 18) and 256 (Javed Miandad 79, B. Yardley 6 for 84)

This was another incident-filled match. On the previous occasion these teams played in Perth, in March 1979, Sikander Bakht had been run out by the bowler while he was backing up and Hilditch was given out 'handled the ball'.

There were to be no such controversial dismissals in this game but Pakistan was bowled out in just 21.2 overs for its lowest Test score of 62. Alderman, who had taken 42 wickets in his first series in England earlier in the year, captured the wicket of Riswan-uz-Zaman with his first ball in a Test on home soil. Lillee became the third bowler, after S.F. Barnes and Grimmett, to take five wickets in an innings 20 times.

The low point of the match came on the fourth afternoon when there was an ugly confrontation between the Pakistan captain, Javed Miandad, and Australia's premier fast bowler. Lillee, who claimed that he had been provoked by abuse from Javed, deliberately impeded and then aimed a kick at the visiting captain. It was left to Umpire Crafter to separate the combatants as Javed aimed to hit Lillee with his bat.

Despite a disappointing first innings total of 180, Australia comprehensively outplayed the visitors, highlights being a controlled century from Hughes and six second innings wickets to the off-spinner Yardley.

AUSTRALIA v WEST INDIES 1981-82

Melbourne Cricket Ground, Melbourne
26, 27, 28, 29, 30 December 1981
Australia won by 58 runs
Australia 198 (K.J. Hughes 100 not out, M.A. Holding 5 for 45) and 222 (A.R. Border 66, B.M. Laird 64, M.A. Holding 6 for 62); West Indies 201 (H.A. Gomes 55, D.K. Lillee 7 for 83) and 161

Australia won a memorable Test that ended the West Indies' sequence of 15 matches without defeat.

Chappell somewhat surprisingly decided to bat on a damp pitch and when Holding removed Laird and the skipper with successive balls in the fifth over, it looked as if the Australian captain had made a mistake. The situation got progressively worse as 2 for 4 became 3 for 8, then 4 for 26 and 5 for 59. Hughes proceeded to play one of the great innings. With a mixture of resolute defence and scorching strokes he remained 100 not out in a total of 198. When the number eleven Alderman joined him, Hughes was on 71. Their 43-run partnership was the second best of the innings. Holding was easily the pick of the four-pronged pace battery and thoroughly deserved his five-wicket haul.

The West Indies were left with 35 minutes to bat on the first day, and this produced some more dramatic cricket. Alderman had Bacchus caught at fourth slip then Lillee had Haynes caught by Border at second slip and the visitors were 2 for 5. Nightwatchman Croft was trapped in front by Lillee and it was 3 for 6. The big crowd roared like it was a football match when Lillee bowled Richards with the last ball of the day's play, leaving West Indies 4 for 10.

Lillee started the second day needing two wickets to break Gibb's world record of 309. Dujon, on debut as a specialist batsman, was the first, caught at deep backward square after an impressive innings of 41. Gomes was next, caught at slip by Chappell. West Indies finished with a lead of three runs. On an improving pitch, Australia's openers Wood and Laird produced the best partnership of the match, Wood contributing 46 in a stand of 82. Border then held the innings together with another pugnacious knock. He top-scored with 66 after Laird had made 64. The only other batsman to reach double figures was Yardley with 13. Holding was once again magnificent taking 6 for 62. His match figures of 11 for 107 still remain the best for a West Indies bowler against Australia. Wicketkeeper David Murray took nine catches for the match to establish another West Indian record.

The target for victory was 220 but when Alderman removed Bacchus and Richards in the second over Australia held the whip hand. Dujon played another fine knock but he lacked support. Yardley with 4 for 38 and Lillee 3 for 44 were the pick of Australia's bowlers, the record-breaking fast bowler claiming 10 for 127 for the match.

AUSTRALIA v ENGLAND 1982-83

Melbourne Cricket Ground, Melbourne
26, 27, 28, 29, 30 December 1982
England won by three runs

England 284 (C.J. Tavaré 89, A.J. Lamb 83) and 294 (G.Fowler 65); Australia 287 (K.J. Hughes 66, D.W. Hookes 53, R.W. Marsh 53) and 288 (D.W. Hookes 68, A.R. Border 62 not out, N.G. Cowans 6 for 77)

This was one of the great Test matches. In terms of runs, the only closer Tests were a tie between Australia and the West Indies in Brisbane, 1960-61 (page 29); a tie between India and Australia in Madras, 1986-87 (page 45); the West Indies' one run win over Australia in Adelaide, 1992-93 (page 49); and England's victory by two runs against Australia at Edgbaston in 2005 (page 74).

Chappell sent England in on a slightly damp pitch. The visitors were soon struggling at 3 for 56 before Tavaré and Lamb added 161 for the fourth wicket in sparkling fashion. England's tail failed to wag, and the innings ended at 284.

On the second day, Australia was bowled out for 287. After Cowans dismissed Dyson and Chappell with successive deliveries, Hughes grafted a patient 66 to hold the Australian innings together. Both Hookes and Marsh, with a mixture of aggression and good fortune, scored half-centuries.

The pattern continued on the third day with England being dismissed for 294. This time, it was the lower order that held the innings together. Botham scored his 46 at a run a ball before Pringle and Taylor realised 61 in an eighth-wicket partnership.

Australia's target was 292. An occasional ball was keeping low on the relaid pitch, but the outfield was unusually fast (the result of a prolonged drought that had restricted the watering of the ground).

Fortunes fluctuated throughout Australia's innings. Early on, England was on top. Chappell fell cheaply, again to Cowans, and when Dyson was brilliantly caught by Tavaré at slip it was 3 for 71. Australia regained the initiative when Hughes and Hookes posted a century partnership for the fourth wicket.

Then the inspired spell from Cowans tipped the scales England's way. He captured 4 for 19 in seven overs to have the home team in desperate trouble at 9 for 218. Thomson joined Border with 74 runs still required. By stumps, the last pair had taken the score to 255 — they were half-way there. On the final morning 18 000 spectators turned up for the climax to what had been the most enthralling Test since the tie at the Gabba 22 years earlier.

Willis kept the field back for Border to enable him to take singles. The pugnacious left-hander had been out of touch, and the lack of pressure helped play him back to form. The new ball had been taken early on the final morning with the score at 259, but still the last pair defied the England team. Botham started the eighteenth over of the day with four runs needed for an Australian victory. Thomson fended at the first ball, edging it to Tavaré at second slip. The straightforward catch bounced out, but within reach of Miller at first slip. He completed the catch, and England won the titanic struggle by three runs. With that final wicket, Botham became only the second English Test player (Rhodes being the other) to score 1000 runs and take 100 wickets against Australia.

PAKISTAN v INDIA 1982-83

Niaz Stadium, Hyderabad
14, 15, 16, 18, 19 January 1983
Pakistan won by an innings and 119 runs

Pakistan 3 for 581 dec. (Javed Miandad 280 not out, Mudassar Nazar 231); India 189 (B.S. Sandhu 71, M. Amarnath 61, Imran Khan 6 for 35) and 273 (M. Amarnath 64, S.M. Gavaskar 60, D.B. Vengsarkar 58 not out)

The feature of this match was the third-wicket partnership between Mudassar Nazar and Javed Miandad. Their stand realised 451 runs which equalled the then world Test record for any wicket (Legendary Australia batsmen Ponsford and Bradman had added 451 for the second wicket at Kennington Oval in 1934). Mudassar and Miandad both made their highest Test score.

Pakistan outclassed India for the third successive match to record its most emphatic series victory over its subcontinental neighbour.

In this game, Viswanath played his eighty-fifth consecutive Test to equal the then record of Sobers. In the series, Pakistan's captain, Imran Khan, was outstanding. He captured 40 wickets.

ENGLAND v NEW ZEALAND 1983

Headingley, Leeds
28, 29, 30 July, 1 August 1983
New Zealand won by 5 wickets

England 225 (C.J. Tavaré 69, A.J. Lamb 58, B.L. Cairns 7 for 74) and 252 (D.I. Gower 112 not out, E.J. Chatfield 5 for 95); New Zealand 377 (J.G. Wright 93, B.A. Edgar 84, R.J. Hadlee 75) and 5 for 103 (R.G.D. Willis 5 for 35)

After a long run of seventeen defeats and eleven draws, this was New Zealand's first Test victory in England.

Howarth sent the home team in on a seamer's pitch. It was a successful opening day for the visitors, and England was bowled out for 225. Just before tea, only two wickets had fallen when Martin Crowe took a brilliant diving catch at square leg to remove Lamb. Cairns, with 7 for 74, became the first New Zealand bowler to capture seven wickets in a Test innings against England.

Edgar was forced to retire hurt early on the second day, but his opening partner, Wright, became New Zealand's sheet anchor. On his way to scoring 93 in almost five hours, he was involved in two tragic run-outs – both Howarth and Jeff Crowe were victims of his indecision. Later, Edgar returned and with the hard-hitting Hadlee, carried New Zealand's first-innings total to 377.

England's second effort was only a slight improvement on the first. But Gower, in scoring his first century at home in four years, held the innings together.

New Zealand required 101 to win, but with Willis in full flight, Kiwi hearts were fluttering as Coney walked to the crease with the score at 4 for 61. Jeff Crowe went at 83, then Hadlee joined Coney, and they proceeded to wipe off the deficit with more than a day to spare.

ENGLAND v WEST INDIES 1984

Lord's Cricket Ground, London
28, 29, 30 June, 2, 3 July 1984
West Indies won by 9 wickets

England 286 (G.Fowler 106, B.C Broad 55, M.D. Marshall 6 for 85) and 9 for 300 dec. (A.J. Lamb 110, I.T. Botham 81); West Indies 245 (I.V.A. Richards 72, I.T. Botham 8 for 103) and 1 for 344 (C.G. Greenidge 214 not out, H.A. Gomes 92 not out)

England controlled the match for four of the five days, only to be convincingly defeated at the end. Fowler and Broad, on debut, scored a rare century opening stand against the West Indies pace battery. Fowler applied himself for over six hours to post his second Test century. The last six English wickets fell for only 43 as Marshall cleaned up the tail to finish with 6 for 70.

Botham knocked over the top order to have the West Indies in trouble at 3 for 35. Richards and Lloyd dug in until Botham trapped Richards in front for 72.

Umpire Barry Meyer later admitted that he had considered recalling Richards, fearing he may have made a mistake. Botham was magnificent and finished with 8 for 103 as England gained a first innings lead of 41 runs.

This advantage was quickly lost as the home team slumped to 3 for 36. Lamb, with support from Gatting and Botham, turned the innings around. The irrepressible Botham hammered 81, while Lamb finished with 110.

When Gower declared early on the final morning the West Indies required 342 to win in five and a half hours.

Greenidge proceeded to play a superb innings. He made the England attack look pedestrian as he plundered 29 boundaries in compiling a brilliant double-century. Greenidge and Gomes added an unbroken 287 for the second wicket to bring the West Indies home with almost twelve overs to spare.

For the first time, a 'Man of the Match' award was shared — Botham joined Greenidge for the honour.

Finally, of the 30 dismissals in the match, twelve were lbw, thereby equalling the record set at Dunedin in 1979-80.

WEST INDIES v ENGLAND 1985-86

Recreation Ground, St John's, Antigua
11, 12, 13, 15, 16 April 1986
West Indies won by 240 runs

West Indies 474 (D.L. Haynes 131, M.D. Marshall 76, M.A. Holding 73, R.A. Harper 60) and 2 for 246 dec. (I.V.A. Richards 110 not out, D.L. Haynes 70); England 310 (D.I. Gower 90, W.N. Slack 52, G.A. Gooch 51) and 170 (G.A. Gooch 51)

This was the final Test of a five-match series, and was historic on two counts.

Firstly, the West Indies emulated Australia's achievement in winning all five home Tests on more than one occasion – they had previously defeated India 5-0 in the 1961-62 series. Secondly, and more significantly, Richards, in scoring 110 not out in the West Indies second innings, recorded the fastest Test century ever produced in terms of balls faced – he faced 56 to reach three figures, and 58 in all. The previous best had been J.M. Gregory's 67 against South Africa at Johannesburg in 1921-22.

Richards' innings was played without blemish while England was trying to make run-scoring as difficult as possible. For the most part there were six men on the boundary and sometimes as many as nine. His innings occupied 83 minutes, and he scored 110 of the 146 runs made in that time.

The details were as follows:

..36126141 (24 off 10)
.211.412.1 (36 off 20)
112.211.. (45 off 30)
.1.1624441 (68 off 40)
12..664612 (96 off 50)
..21.461 (110 off 58)

INDIA v AUSTRALIA 1986-87

Chepauk (Chidambaram Stadium), Madras
18, 19, 20, 21, 22 September 1986
Match Tied

Australia 7 for 574 dec. (D.M. Jones 210, D.C. Boon 122, A.R. Border 106) and 5 for 170 dec.; India 397 (Kapil Dev 119, R.J. Shastri 62, K.R. Srikkanth 53, M. Azharuddin 50, G.R.J. Matthews 5 for 103) and 347 (S.M. Gavaskar 90, M. Amarnath 51, G.R.J. Matthews 5 for 146, R.J. Bright 5 for 94)

This match resulted in the second tie in Test history. (Australia was also involved in the first tie — against the West Indies — in 1960-61. See page 42.) At the finish, it was Australia who managed to avoid defeat, even though they had dominated proceedings for the first four days' play. Australia declared both its innings, and lost only twelve wickets in the match.

Australia's first innings continued until early on the third day. Jones' double-century was the cornerstone of the visitors' highest Test score in India, and Boon and Border were the other century makers. However, the Indian skipper, Kapil Dev, made sure that Australia batted again by blasting a century off 109 balls with 21 fours.

The off-spinner Matthews picked up five wickets in an innings for the first time. From the 49 overs remaining on the fourth day, Australia scored 170. This allowed Border to declare on the final morning, setting India 348 to win from a minimum of 87 overs.

After a steady start, Gavaskar and Amarnath picked up the batting tempo and, when they went to tea at 2 for 190, India had a realistic chance of winning the match. The target for the final session was 158 runs from 30 overs. At the start of the final 20 overs, 118 runs were needed with seven wickets in hand.

Gavaskar, 90, went out at 251; when Kapil Dev was out two runs later, Australia again had a chance. Shastri, Pandit and Chetan Sharma turned the game India's way until only 18 runs were needed from 30 balls. The situation changed again when Sharma and More were dismissed in an over by Bright. Yadav, who had hit Matthews for six, was ninth out at 344, bowled by Bright.

With just eight balls remaining, Maninder Singh joined Shastri and defended two balls from Bright, giving Shastri the strike for the last over from Matthews. The first ball was blocked. He went for a big hit off the second ball and mistimed the stroke. But after a misfield he was able to take two runs.

The third ball was pushed to mid-wicket for a single and the scores were tied. Maninder defended the fourth, but from the fifth delivery he was trapped lbw. The match ended in a thrilling tie before 30 000 excited fans. Matthews picked up his second five-wicket haul, and the left-armer Bright gained the other five. All ten wickets in India's second innings had fallen to spin. See page 59 for the final scoreboard.

INDIA v PAKISTAN 1986-87

Chinnaswamy Stadium, Bangalore
13, 14, 15, 17 March 1987
Pakistan won by 16 runs

Pakistan 116 (Maninder Singh 7 for 27) and 249; India 145 (D.B. Vengsarkar 50, Iqbal Qasim 5 for 48, Tauseef Ahmed 5 for 54) and 204 (S.M. Gavaskar 96)

INDIA v AUSTRALIA 1986-87 (First Test)

Chidambaram Stadium, Chepauk, Madras, 18, 19, 20, 21, 22 September. A tie

AUSTRALIA

D.C.Boon	c Kapil Dev b Sharma	122	(2)	lbw b Maninder Singh	49
G.R.Marsh	c Kapil Dev b Yadav	22	(1)	b Shastri	11
D.M.Jones	b Yadav	210		c Azharuddin b Maninder Singh	24
R.J.Bright	c Shastri b Yadav	30			
A.R.Border*	c Gavaskar b Shastri	106	(4)	b Maninder Singh	27
G.M.Ritchie	run out	13	(5)	c Pandit b Shastri	28
G.R.J.Matthews	c Pandit b Yadav	44	(6)	not out	27
S.R.Waugh	not out	12	(7)	not out	2
T.J.Zoehrer†					
C.J.McDermott					
B.A.Reid					
Extras	(B 1, LB 7, NB 6, W 1)	15		(LB 1, NB 1)	2
Total	**(7 wkts dec.)**	**574**		**(5 wkts dec.)**	**170**

INDIA

S.M.Gavaskar	c and b Matthews	8		c Jones b Bright	90
K. Srikkanth	c Ritchie b Matthews	53		c Waugh b Matthews	39
M.Amarnath	run out	1		c Boon b Matthews	51
M.Azharuddin	c and b Bright	50		c Ritchie b Bright	42
R.J.Shastri	c Zoehrer b Matthews	62	(7)	not out	48
C.S.Pandit	c Waugh b Matthews	35	(5)	b Matthews	39
Kapil Dev*	c Border b Matthews	119	(6)	C Bright b Matthews	1
K.S.More†	c Zoehrer b Waugh	4	(9)	lbw b Bright	0
C.Sharma	c Zoehrer b Reid	30	(8)	c McDermott b Bright	23
N.S.Yadav	c Border b Bright	19		b Bright	8
Maninder Singh	not out	0		lbw b Matthews	0
Extras	(B 1, LB 9, NB 6)	16		(B 1, LB 3, NB 2)	6
Total		**397**			**347**

INDIA	O	M	R	W		O	M	R	W
Kapil Dev	18	5	52	0	Sharma	6	0	19	0
Sharma	16	1	70	1	Kapil Dev	1	0	5	0
Maninder Singh	39	8	135	0	Shastri	14	2	50	2
Yadav	49.5	9	142	4	M. Signh	19	2	60	3
Shastri	47	8	161	1	Yadav	9	0	35	0
Srikkanth	1	0	6	0					

AUSTRALIA	O	M	R	W		O	M	R	W
McDermott	14	2	59	0	McDermott	5	0	27	0
Reid	18	4	93	1	Reid	10	2	48	0
Matthews	28.2	3	103	5	Matthews	39.5	7	146	5
Bright	23	3	88	2	Bright	25	3	94	5
Waugh	11	2	44	1	Border	3	0	12	0
					Waugh	4	1	16	0

FALL OF WICKETS

	A	I	A	I
Wkt	1st	1st	2nd	2nd
1st	48	62	31	55
2nd	206	65	81	158
3rd	282	65	94	204
4th	460	142	125	251
5th	481	206	165	253
6th	544	220	-	291
7th	573	245	-	331
8th	-	330	-	334
9th	-	334	-	344
10th	-	397	-	347

Umpires: D.N.Dotiwalla and V.Vikramraju

This was the fifth and final match in a series in which the first four games had been drawn. The Test was played on a pitch that encouraged the spinners, although both teams thought the conditions would be helpful to the seamers.

Imran batted first after winning the toss. It wasn't long before the visitors were in deep trouble. Maninder Singh produced career-best figures of 7 for 27 as he spun Pakistan out for their lowest score against India of 116.

Vengsarkar played resolutely in scoring 50, placing the home team in a position to establish a sizeable first-innings lead. But Tauseef and Iqbal captured the last six wickets for 19 runs. India's lead was deteriorating rapidly.

Imran shuffled his batting order in the second innings and sent Miandad in first with Rameez. It was a titanic struggle with first one team, then the other, gaining the ascendancy until Yousuf and Tauseef added 51 for the ninth wicket. Pakistan's lead was 220.

Gavaskar played a great innings on a pitch that enabled the off-spinner to bowl bouncers. Unfortunately, India's master batsman didn't get enough support, with only Vengsarkar, Azharuddin and Binny reaching double figures. The Test victory gave Pakistan its first series win in India, and only its third victory in any Test series outside Pakistan.

AUSTRALIA v NEW ZEALAND 1987-88

Melbourne Cricket Ground, Melbourne
26, 27, 28, 29, 30 December 1987
Match Drawn

New Zealand 317 (J.G. Wright 99, M.D. Crowe 82, C.J. McDermott 5 for 97) and 286 (M.D. Crowe 79, A.I.C. Dodemaide 6 for 58); Australia 357 (P.R. Sleep 90, S.R. Waugh 55, A.I.C. Dodemaide 50, R.J. Hadlee 5 for 109) and 9 for 230 (D.C. Boon 54, R.J. Hadlee 5 for 67)

This final Test of the three-match series was a classic contest that developed into a nail-biting finish. New Zealand was put in to bat and had reached 1 for 119 when Jones deflected McDermott; Australia's wicketkeeper, Dyer, rolled over, then held the ball aloft claiming the catch. The umpires conferred, and the decision was given against the batsman. The television replays, however, showed the ball leaving the 'keeper's gloves and rolling on the ground. With that controversy behind them, the visitors went on to score 317.

Wright became the third New Zealand batsman to be dismissed for 99 in a Test innings.

Australia's middle and lower order staged a grand recovery to give the home team a 40-run first innings lead. Sleep, 90, Waugh, 55, and Dodemaide, 50 on debut, led the fightback after Australia had slumped to 5 for 121. Martin Crowe again played beautifully in New Zealand's second innings and struck twelve majestic boundaries in an innings of 79.

The all-rounder Dodemaide followed his first innings half-century with 6 for 58 from 28.3 overs in the second – and in doing so made a fine start to his Test career.

With the New Zealand second innings ending on the third ball of the final day, Australia required 247 for victory from a minimum of 92 overs. At 4 for 176, the target was only 71 from 28 overs when Hadlee was recalled to the attack. He bowled superbly until the end of the match, and almost single-handedly pulled off an unexpected victory for the visitors.

McDermott and Whitney, the last pair, had to survive for 4.5 overs to save the match and give Australia the Trans-Tasman Trophy for the first time. Hadlee had taken ten wickets in a Test match for a record eighth time, and had joined Botham on 373 wickets.

INDIA v WEST INDIES 1987-88

Chepauk (Chidambaram Stadium), Madras
11, 12, 14, 15 January 1988
India won by 255 runs

India 382 (Kapil Dev 109, Arun Lal 69) and 8 for 217 dec. (W.V. Raman 83); West Indies 184 (I.V.A. Richards 68, N.D. Hirwani 8 for 61) and 160 (A.L. Logie 67, N.D. Hirwani 8 for 75)

In this match India recorded the most convincing of all its victories over the West Indies. The player mainly responsible was a new cap, the 19-year-old leg spinner Hirwani. He captured eight wickets in each innings, which equalled the performance of Australia's Massie at Lord's in 1972. Coincidentally, Hirwani returned match figures of 16 for 136 — Massie's were an almost identical 16 for 137.

Shastri was captaining India for the first time. He won the toss and batted first on what was an under-prepared pitch. The home team was struggling at 6 for 156 but then the former captain, Kapil Dev, joined another new cap, Ajay Sharma, at the crease. This pair added 113 runs for the sixth wicket, and Kapil Dev's contribution was a match-winning 109 runs from 119 balls. Given the difficult batting conditions, 382 was a most respectable score.

The West Indies struggled from the start of its innings, and certainly missed the experienced opener Greenidge. Richardson batted for two hours to make 36, while Richards produced some amazing strokes in compiling 68. The follow-on was avoided on the third morning as Hirwani, on debut, finished with 8 for 61 from 18.3 overs.

With time on its side, India steadily increased its lead. Raman, yet another new cap, showed considerable maturity in making 83. Walsh was again the pick of the West Indies bowlers, toiling manfully to finish with 4 for 55.

The West Indies required 416 to win, or more realistically, to bat for one and a half days to save the game. Their batsmen played as if it was a limited overs match, and the Test was over on the fourth day.

This time, Hirwani finished with 8 for 75 from 15.2 overs, and India's wicketkeeper, More, excelled in the difficult conditions. He stumped six batsmen in the match, five of them in the second innings and in doing so made two Test records.

ENGLAND v AUSTRALIA 1989

Old Trafford, Manchester
27, 28, 29, 31 July, 1 August 1989
Australia won by 9 wickets

England 260 (R.A. Smith 143, G.F. Lawson 6 for 72) and 264 (R.C. Russell 128 not out, J.E. Emburey 64, T.M. Alderman 5 for 66); Australia 447 (S.R. Waugh 92, M.A. Taylor 85, A.R. Border 80, D.M. Jones 69) and 1 for 81

This was the fourth Test of a six-match series. Australia had won the first two Tests and the third was drawn. Gower decided to bat first after winning the toss. This time Lawson made the early breakthrough and England was soon in trouble at 3 for 57. Smith played superbly to score his maiden Test century, but only Gower and Foster offered any support. Foster contributed 39 in an eighth-wicket partnership of 74.

Taylor and Marsh put on 135 for the first wicket as Australia set about building a sizeable first-innings advantage. When the innings ended early on the morning of the fourth day, the visitors' lead had reached 187.

Just after lunch, the match was all but over. England had crashed, losing 6 for 59, with Lawson and Alderman claiming three wickets apiece. Rain delayed the inevitable – after all, the match was being played in Manchester!

On the final day, Russell and Emburey batted through the first session. Emburey finally went for 64 after adding 142 with Russell for the seventh wicket. The gritty wicket-keeper became the fourth England player to score his maiden first-class century in a Test match. Alderman, who was surprisingly 'wicketless' in the first innings, picked up five in the second, while Lawson claimed three to finish with nine for the match.

The target of 78 presented no problems for Australia and, when Boon hit Cook to the boundary, there was great rejoicing in the visitors' camp. The Ashes had been regained in England for the first time since 1934.

ENGLAND v INDIA 1990

Lord's, London
26, 27, 28, 30, 31 July 1990
England won by 247 runs

England 4 for 653 dec. (G.A. Gooch 333, A.J. Lamb 139, R.A. Smith 100 not out) and 4 for 272 dec. (G.A. Gooch 123, M.A. Atherton 72): India 451 (M. Azharuddin 121, R.J. Shastri 100, Kapil Dev 77 not out, D.B. Vengsarkar 52, A.R.C. Fraser 5 for 104) and 224

This high-scoring Test was a match of many records. The aggregate number of runs, 1603, was two more than the previous record for Lord's (established in 1930 when England played Australia).

Azharuddin sent England in to bat. Late on the second day, Gooch was able to declare at 4 for 653. The skipper was dropped behind by More on 36, and then went on to record the highest Test score at Lord's. Gooch's 333 included 3 sixes and 43 fours; it was the third-highest Test score made by an English cricketer and the sixth-highest overall. Lamb and Smith also compiled centuries while the partnership of 308 by Gooch and Lamb was the best for any wicket for England against India.

The visitors replied in a positive manner: Azharuddin scored his century off just 88 balls; Shastri, in a new role as opener, also reached three figures. It was 9 for 430 when the last man, Hirwani, joined Kapil Dev, and India needed 24 runs to avoid the follow-on. Hirwani survived one ball from Fraser; then Hemmings bowled to Kapil Dev. The champion all-rounder blocked the first two balls before launching an unbelievable assault on the hapless off-spinner. Four successive deliveries were smashed down the pitch for six. Fraser dismissed Hirwani with the next ball.

Gooch continued on from his first-innings massacre of the Indian attack. His 123 came off only 113 balls, and included 4 sixes and 13 fours. His match aggregate of 456 was 76 more than the previous record held by Greg Chappell. India was left with seven hours to bat to save the match, or score 472 to win. On a wearing pitch, the task was always going to prove too difficult, and it was Gooch who ended the game by throwing out Sharma. England won handsomely by 247 runs.

NEW ZEALAND v SRI LANKA 1990-91

Basin Reserve, Wellington
31 January, 1, 2, 3, 4, February 1991
Match Drawn

New Zealand 174 and 4 for 671 (M.D. Crowe 299, A.H. Jones 186, J.G. Wright 88); Sri Lanka 497 (P.A. de Silva 267, A.P. Gurusinha 70, A. Ranatunga 55, D.K. Morrison 5 for 153)

This match will be remembered forever as the Test in which a new world Test record partnership for any wicket was established. Sri Lanka dominated the first half of the match and had played itself into a winning position before New Zealand produced a superb fightback to save the game. Ratnayake and Labrooy, with four wickets apiece, combined on the opening day to bowl the home team out for 174. Aravinda de Silva then hammered the New Zealand bowlers to all parts of the ground as he posted his country's highest Test score. His 267 contained 40 fours, and was scored from 376 balls. Sri Lanka declared on the third day with a lead of 323. New Zealand had the task of batting for 15 hours to save the game. Wright and Franklin posted 134 for the opening stand, but then both batsmen were out within 14 runs. This set the stage for the highest partnership in Test history. The New Zealand captain, Martin Crowe, joined Jones and in just over nine hours together added 467, surpassing the previous best of 451. (Ponsford and Bradman scored 451 for the second wicket against England in 1934, and Mudassar Nazar and Javed Miandad made their partnership of 451 against India in 1982-83).

Jones was out for 186, and Crowe was dismissed in the final over of the match for 299.

WEST INDIES v SOUTH AFRICA 1991-92

Kensington Oval, Bridgetown, Barbados
18, 19, 20, 22, 23 April 1992
West Indies won by 52 runs

West Indies 262 (K.L.T. Arthurton 59, D.L. Haynes 58) and 283 (J.C. Adams 79 not out, B.C. Lara 64); South Africa 345 (A.C. Hudson 163, K.C. Wessels 59) and 148 (K.C. Wessels 74, P.N. Kirsten 52, C.E.L. Ambrose 6 for 34)

It was an historic occasion when Wessels led his teammates out at the Kensington Oval in Barbados. It was South Africa's first Test for 22 years and its first ever clash against the West Indies. The West Indies Board selected Bridgetown as the venue for the only Test match; the home team had not lost there since 1935 when England won by four wickets.

Wessels followed the usual procedure at Kensington Oval and sent the West Indies in to bat. Haynes and Simmons added 99 before lunch, but then both openers fell in the space of nine balls from Snell. Richardson and Arthurton put on 82 for the fourth wicket before the middle and lower order collapsed. The last six wickets fell for only 22 runs.

South Africa gained a first-innings lead of 83. Opener Hudson scored 163 on debut to become the first South African cricketer to score a century in his first Test match. It was his country's 173rd Test. Only Wessels, 59, and Kuiper, 34, offered any worthwhile contributions apart from the century-maker. Adams was the most successful bowler with 4 for 43. By stumps on the third day, South Africa had a firm grip on the match. The West Indies' lead was only 101 with just three wickets in hand. Donald and Snell had ripped the heart out of the home team's batting, taking three wickets apiece. After the rest day, however, the tail wagged and 99 runs were added on the fourth day, including 62 for the last wicket by Adams and Patterson. Adams, on debut, completed a fine double. He held the middle and lower order together with 79 not out.

South Africa's target was 201. By the end of the fourth day's play, they were just 79 runs away from victory with eight wickets in hand. Wessels had played magnificently and was 74 at the close (he and Kirsten had added 95 for the third wicket, after the openers Hudson and Rushmere had gone cheaply). On the final day, the visitors were routed by sustained hostile fast bowling from Ambrose and Walsh. Both bowlers claimed four wickets apiece as South Africa lost 8 for 26. Only Wessels and Kirsten reached double figures. 'Extras' was third top score on 11, Pringle was next best with 4. The West Indies won a memorable match by 52 runs.

AUSTRALIA v WEST INDIES 1992-93

Adelaide Oval, Adelaide
23, 24, 25, 26 January 1993
West Indies won by 1 run

West Indies 252 (B.C. Lara 52, M.G. Hughes 5 for 64) and 146 (R.B. Richardson 72, T.B.A. May 5 for 9); Australia 213 (C.E.L. Ambrose 6 for 74) and 184 (J.L. Langer 54)

This was one of the greatest Test matches ever played and the closest of all Tests decided on a run basis. (See scoreboard on page 63).

Haynes, 45, and Simmons, 46, got the West Indies off to a flying start with an opening stand of 84 but the visitors failed to capitalise on this foundation. On a pitch that offered more assistance to the bowlers than normal, only Lara and Murray — apart from the openers — played an innings of consequence. The lion-hearted Hughes was rewarded for his persistence with another five-wicket haul for the Australians.

Australia had a taste of what was in store for them when Taylor fell on the first evening and the debutant Langer had his helmet split by some fierce bowling from the West Indies. Australia's woes continued on the rain-shortened second day when Boon was forced to retire hurt after being struck on the arm.

Ambrose was at the peak of his form and bowled the visitors to a 39-run first innings lead.

The third day of this fluctuating match saw 17 wickets fall for 259 runs. A hostile spell of fast-bowling from McDermott reduced the visitors to 4 for 65 before Richardson and Hooper addd 59 for the fifth wicket. However, careless batting then saw the West Indies lose their last six wickets for only 22 runs. May, playing his first Test for almost four years, captured 5 for 5 from 32 deliveries.

AUSTRALIA v WEST INDIES 1992-93 (Fourth Test)

Adelaide Oval, 23, 24, 25, 26 January. West Indies won by 1 run

WEST INDIES

D.L.Haynes	st Healy b May	45		c Healy b McDermott	11
P.V.Simmons	c Hughes b S.R.Waugh	46		b McDermott	10
R.B.Richardson*	lbw b Hughes	2		c Healy b Warne	72
B.C.Lara	c Healy b McDermott	52		c S.R.Waugh b Hughes	7
K.L.T.Arthurton	c S.R.Waugh b May	0		c Healy b McDermott	0
C.L.Hooper	c Healy b Hughes	2		c Hughes b May	25
J.R.Murray†	not out	49		c M.E.Waugh b May	0
I.R.Bishop	c M.E.Waugh b Hughes	13		c M.E.Waugh b May	6
C.E.L.Ambrose	c Healy b Hughes	0		st Healy b May	1
K.C.G.Benjamin	b M.E.Waugh	15		c Warne b May	0
C.A.Walsh	lbw b Hughes	5		not out	0
Extras	(LB 11, NB 12)	23		(LB 2, NB 12)	14
Total		**252**			**146**

AUSTRALIA

M.A.Taylor	c Hooper b Bishop	1	(2)	Murray b Benjamin	7
D.C.Boon	not out	39	(1)	lbw b Ambrose	0
J.L.Langer	c Murray b Benjamin	20		c Murray b Bishop	54
M.E.Waugh	c Simmons b Ambrose	0		c Hooper b Walsh	26
S.R.Waugh	c Murray b Ambrose	42		c Arthurton b Ambrose	4
A.R.Border*	c Hooper b Ambrose	19		c Haynes b Ambrose	1
I.A.Healy†	c Hooper b Ambrose	0		b Walsh	0
M.G.Hughes	c Murray b Hooper	43		lbw b Ambrose	1
S.K.Warne	lbw b Hooper	0		lbw b Bishop	9
T.B.A.May	c Murray b Ambrose	6		not out	42
C.J.McDermott	b Ambrose	14		c Murray b Walsh	18
Extras	(B7, LB 3, NB 19)	29		(B1, LB8 NB 13)	22
Total		**213**			**184**

AUSTRALIA	O	M	R	W		O	M	R	W
McDermott	16	1	85	1	McDermott	11	0	66	3
Hughes	21.3	3	64	5	Hughes	13	1	43	1
S.R.Waugh	13	4	37	1	S.R.Waugh	5	1	8	0
May	14	1	41	2	May	6.5	3	9	5
Warne	2	0	11	0	Warne	6	2	18	1
M.E.Waugh	1	0	3	1					
WEST INDIES	O	M	R	W		O	M	R	W
Ambrose	28.2	6	74	6	Ambrose	26	5	46	4
Bishop	18	3	48	1	Bishop	17	3	41	2
Benjamin	6	0	22	1	Benjamin	12	2	32	1
Walsh	10	3	34	0	Walsh	19	4	44	3
Hooper	13	4	25	2	Hooper	5	1	12	0

FALL OF WICKETS

	W	A	W	A
Wkt	1st	1st	2nd	2nd
1st	84	1	14	5
2nd	99	16	49	16
3rd	129	46	63	54
4th	130	108	65	64
5th	134	108	124	72
6th	189	112	137	73
7th	206	181	145	74
8th	206	181	146	102
9th	247	197	146	144
10th	252	213	146	184

Umpires: D.B.Hair and L.J.King

Australia had two days in which to score 186 and thus regain the Frank Worrell Trophy. The openers went cheaply but Langer and M. Waugh carefully carried the score beyond fifty. Waugh went out for 26 with the total on 54. Shortly after lunch Ambrose removed S. Waugh, Border and Hughes with Walsh chipping in to dismiss Healy — Australia had lost 4 for 10 and the team was now reeling at 7 for 74.

Langer's determined resistance continued and 28 more runs were added before Warne fell to Bishop. May — on his 31st birthday and with a fractured finger — valiantly continued the struggle.

It was Bishop who finally removed the doughty Langer — his great effort of four and a quarter hours at the crease had yielded the home team's only half-century of the match.

McDermott, at number eleven, supported May bravely. They carried Australia to within two runs of victory before a lifting delivery from Walsh brushed McDermott's glove and Umpire Hair upheld the West Indies appeal. So it was the visitors who were celebrating on Australia Day, winning a thrilling match by the narrowest of possible margins.

AUSTRALIA v SOUTH AFRICA 1993-94

Sydney Cricket Ground, Sydney
2, 3, 4, 5, 6 January 1994
South Africa won by 5 runs

South Africa 169 (G. Kirsten 67, S.K. Warne 7 for 56) and 239 (J.N. Rhodes 76 not out, S.K. Warne 5 for 72); Australia 292 (M.J. Slater 92, D.R. Martyn 59) and 111 (P.S. de Villiers 6 for 43)

South Africa scored a thrilling victory after Australia had held control for most of the match.

The visitors were bowled out on a suspect pitch for a disappointing 169. Hudson fell cheaply before G. Kirsten and Cronje added 90 for the second wicket. Warne ripped through the middle and lower order — in one spell he claimed 5 for 5 in 22 balls — while his figures of 7 for 56 were the best for Australia against South Africa at home. Apart from Kirsten and Cronje, only de Villiers reached double figures.

Slater, playing with unusual caution, guied Australia to a 123-run lead. The other major contributions came from Martyn and the captain Border. The Australian supporters may have been concerned that the lead wasn't greater as the team had to bat last in the match and the Australians had a poor record when chasing a target. South Africa's opening bowlers, Donald and de Villiers, stuck to their task and claimed four wickets apiece.

When the fifth wicket of the South African second innings had fallen for 110, the match looked lost for the Springboks. However, Rhodes played superbly and with the assistance of Richardson and Donald, South Africa gained a lead of 116. Rhodes and Richardson put on 72 for the sixth wicket while 36 was added for the last by Rhodes and Donald.

The brilliant Warne once again mesmerised the South African batsmen as he claimed his first ten-wicket haul in Test cricket. Australia needed 117 to win its first Test against South Africa for 27 years. Shortly before stumps on the penultimate day, the home team was cruising at 1 for 51. Then de Villiers removed Taylor, Boon and nightwatchman May to set the stage for an exciting finish to what had been a truly absorbing match.

With free admission, an estimated crowd of 12 000 turned up on the final morning. When Donald bowled Border in the very first over of the day the game had swung South Africa's way. Then Donald struck again, removing M. Waugh with a fast yorker, and when the acting captain Cronje threw down the stumps to run out Warne, the Australian team was on the ropes at 8 for 75.

McDermott made some telling blows and while he and Martyn were together the Australians still had some hope. After 35 had been added for the ninth wicket, Martyn holed out to cover. McGrath was dismissed in the next over and South Africa had pulled off a stunning victory. The Australian score of 111 was the same as that recorded in 'Botham's match' at Headingley in 1981.

WEST INDIES v ENGLAND 1993-94

Queen's Park Oval, Port-of-Spain, Trinidad
25, 26, 27, 29, 30 March 1994
West Indies won by 147 runs

West Indies 254 (R.B. Richarson 63) and 269 (S. Chanderpaul 50, A.R. Caddick 6 for 65); England 328 (G.P. Thorpe 86, C.E.L. Ambrose 5 for 60) and 46 (C.E.L. Ambrose 6 for 24)

The West Indies pulled off an amazing victory after England had held the upper hand for the first three days of the match.

Richardson elected to bat on a somewhat suspect pitch. He was the sheet anchor of the team's struggle for runs on the opening day, taking more than four hours to score 63. From the relative safety of 1 for 158, the middle order capitulated against the accuracy of Fraser and Lewis with the last nine wickets falling for 94 runs.

England gained a first innings lead of 76 after some resolute batting by Thorpe, Atherton and Hick and some spirited hitting by Salisbury at the end. Ambrose collected yet another five-wicket haul in an innings and was largely responsible for restricting England's lead.

When Richardson, Lara and Haynes had been dismissed

with the deficit still 25, the visitors were in the box seat. Arthurton and Adams added 80 carefully compiled runs for the fourth wicket. But both fell shortly before stumps to once again leave the advantage with England. Chanderpaul, who was dropped twice, with the support of the 'keeper Murray and the bowlers, put on 126 valuable runs on the fourth day to give the West Indies a handy lead of 193.

Because of rain interruptions, 15 overs remained to complete they day's pay. Atherton fell lbw to the first ball of the innings, Ramprakash ran himself out off the fifth and Smith was bowled by the second ball of Ambrose's second over. Worse was to follow; Hick went at 21, and Stewart, the only batsman to reach double figures, was bowled at 26. Walsh at last got into the act and had Salisbury caught at slip. Ambrose then removed Thorpe and Russell to leave England in tatters at 8 for 40.

Walsh claimed the last two wickets early the next morning but not before six runs had been scored. England's lowest Test innings of 45 was narrowly avoided – but at least the team of 1887 won that match in Sydney! Ambrose and Walsh had bowled through the innings, Ambrose taking his third ten-wicket haul in Test cricket.

WEST INDIES v ENGLAND 1993-94

Recreation Ground, St John's, Antigua
16, 17, 18, 20, 21 April 1994
Match Drawn

West Indies 5 for 593 dec. (B.C. Lara 375, S. Chanderpaul 75 not out, J.C. Adams 59) and 0 for 43; England 593 (R.A. Smith 175, M.A. Atherton 135, C.C. Lewis 75 not out, R.C. Russell 62).

This match earned a significant place in cricket history with an innings of 375 by Lara. This beat the previous highest individual score in Test cricket by ten runs. Lara broke the record on the third morning of the match from the 530th ball he faced. Fittingly, Sir Garfield Sobers, who had held the record, came onto the ground to congratulate the new record-holder after he had pulled a short ball from Lewis to the boundary.

Lara's innings was compiled on a flat, lifeless pitch that gave absolutely no assistance to the bowlers, however, the outfield was remarkably slow.

England equalled West Indies total of 593 after centuries from Smith and Atherton. Their partnership of 303 was a new third wicket record for England against West Indies.

Although the game, for the most part, was a total stalemate it will always be remembered for the glittering memories provided by Lara's new record individual score.

PAKISTAN v AUSTRALIA 1994-95

National Stadium, Karachi
28, 29, 30 September, 1, 2 October 1994
Pakistan won by 1 wicket

Australia 337 (M.G. Bevan 82, S.R. Waugh 73, I.A. Healy 57) and 232 (D.C. Boon 114 not out, M.E. Waugh 61, Wasim Akram 5 for 63); Pakistan 256 (Saeed Anwar 85) and 9 for 315 (Saeed Anwar 77, Inzamamul Haq 58 not out, S.K. Warne 5 for 89)

This was the seventh Test to be decided by a margin of one wicket. It was the first Test Australia had played since the retirement of former captain Allan Border, who had appeared in 153 successive matches. Mark Taylor, the new captain, did win the toss but unfortunately he became the first player to mark his first Test as captain by 'bagging a pair'.

Australia took the honours on the opening day compiling 7 for 325. Bevan, on debut, scored a stylish 82. He added 121 in better than even time with S. Waugh, whose 73 included 13 boundaries. Keeper Healy contributed yet another useful half-century.

The last three wickets fell for just twelve runs on the second morning. Pakistan started brightly with Saeed Anwar and Aamir Sohail posting 90 for the first wicket in even time. A middle-order collapse left the home side struggling at 7 for 209 at stumps on the second day. A breezy 39 from Wasim Akram carried the Pakistan total to 256.

Despite Taylor going cheaply again, the visitors built on the 81-run lead, with Boon and M. Waugh pushing the score to 2 for 171 shortly before the close of the day's play. Pakistan then struck back with Waqar Younis removing M. Waugh for 61 and Wasim Akram dismissing both Bevan and S. Waugh first ball. The determined Tasmanian Boon posted his nineteenth Test century, which was his first against Pakistan, but the Australian tail failed to wag.

The home team's target was 314 with almost two full days' play remaining. Saeed Anwar again batted positively giving his side a good start for the second time in the match. However, when Saleem Malik fell for 43 just before stumps the game was evenly balanced with the home team at 3 for 155.

The spinner Warne ripped out the Pakistan middle order on the final morning to set up what looked a certain Australian victory. When the last man in for the home side, Mushtaq, joined Inzamamul Haq, 56 runs were still needed. Some brave batting brought the scores closer until just three were required.

Warne bowled to Inzamamul Haq who went down the pitch to a ball pitched outside the leg stump. It missed the bat, flicked the pad and sped away for four leg byes. Pakistan had won a thrilling match to retain its unbeaten record in Karachi. (See final scoreboard on page 66.)

PAKISTAN v AUSTRALIA 1994-95 (First Test)

National Stadium, Karachi, 28, 29, 30 September, 1, 2 October. Pakistan won by 1 wicket

AUSTRALIA

M.J.Slater	lbw b Wasim Akram	36	lbw b Mushtaq Ahmed	23
M.A.Taylor*	c and b Wasim Akram	0	c Rashid Latif b Waqar Younis	0
D.C.Boon	b Mushtaq Ahmed	19	not out	114
M.E.Waugh	c Zahid Fazal b Mushtaq Ahmed	20	b Waqar Younis	61
M.G.Bevan	c Aamer Sohail b Mushtaq Ahmed	82	b Wasim Akram	0
S.R.Waugh	b Waqar Younis	73	lbw b Wasim Akram	0
I.A.Healy†	c Rashid Latif b Waqar Younis	57	c Rashid Latif b Wasim Akram	9
S.K.Warne	c Rashid Latif b Aamer Sohail	22	lbw b Waqar Younis	0
J.Angel	b Wasim Akram	5	c Rashid Latif b Wasim Akram	8
T.B.A.May	not out	1	b Wasim Akram	1
G.D.McGrath	b Waqar Younis	0	b Waqar Younis	1
Extras	(B 2, LB 12, NB 8)	22	(B 6, LB 4, NB 5)	15
Total		**337**		**232**

PAKISTAN

Saeed Anwar	c M.E.Waugh b May	85		c and b Angel	77
Aamer Sohail	c Bevan b Warne	36		run out	34
Zahid Fazal	c Boon b May	27		c Boon b Warne	3
Saleem Malik*	lbw b Angel	26		c Taylor b Angel	43
Basit Ali	c Bevan b McGrath	0	(6)	lbw b Warne	12
Inzamamul Haq	c Taylor b Warne	9	(8)	not out	58
Rashid Latif†	c Taylor b Warne	2	(9)	lbw S.R.Waugh	35
Wasim Akram	c Healy b Angel	39	(7)	c and b Warne	4
Akram Raza	b McGarth	13	(5)	lbw b Warne	2
Waqar Younis	c Healy b Angel	6		c Healy b Warne	7
Mushtaq Ahmed	not out	2		not out	20
Extras	(LB 7, NB 4)	11		(B 4, LB 13, NB 3)	20
Total		**256**		**(9 wkts)**	**315**

PAKISTAN	O	M	R	W		O	M	R	W
Wasim Akram	25	4	75	3	Wasim Akram	22	3	64	5
Waqar Younis	19.2	2	75	3	Waqar Younis	18	2	69	4
Mushtaq Ahmed	24	2	97	3	Mushtaq Ahmed	21	3	51	1
Akram Raza	14	1	50	0	Akram Raza	10	1	19	0
Aamer Sohail	5	0	19	1	Aamer Sohail	7	0	19	0
Saleem Malik	1	0	7	0					

AUSTRALIA	O	M	R	W		O	M	R	W
McGrath	25	6	70	2	McGrath	6	2	18	0
Angel	13.1	0	54	3	Angel	28	8	92	2
May	20	5	55	2	S.R.Waugh	15	3	28	1
Warne	27	10	61	3	Warne	36.1	12	89	5
S.R.Waugh	2	0	9	0	May	18	4	67	0
					M.E.Waugh	3	1	4	0

FALL OF WICKETS

	A	P	A	P
Wkt	1st	1st	2nd	2nd
1st	12	90	1	45
2nd	41	153	49	64
3rd	75	154	171	148
4th	95	157	174	157
5th	216	175	174	174
6th	281	181	213	179
7th	325	200	218	184
8th	335	234	227	236
9th	335	253	229	258
10th	337	256	232	-

Umpires: H.D.Bird and Khizer Hayat

SOUTH AFRICA v PAKISTAN 1994-95

Wanderers, Johannesburg
19, 20, 21, 22, 23 January 1995
South Africa won by 324 runs
South Africa 460 (B.M. McMillan 113, J.N. Rhodes 72, P.S. de Villiers 66 not out) and 7 for 259 dec. (D.J. Cullinan 69 not out); Pakistan 230 (Saleem Malik 99, P.S. de Villiers 6 for 81) and 165 (Inzamamul Haq 95)

This was the first Test to be played between the two countries and resulted in South Africa's biggest ever home victory.

Positive batting on the first day saw South Africa score at almost four runs an over. McMillan completed his maiden Test century from 146 balls while he and Rhodes added 157 for the sixth wicket. On the second morning, de Villiers and Donald realised 71 for the last wicket in just 35 minutes.

Pakistan's reply was a disappointing 230 with only skipper Salim Malik taking the attack to the home team. He struck 16 boundaries before falling one short of a third hundred in successive Tests.

Cronje did not enforce the follow-on as he was concerned about the deteriorating state of the pitch. He declared South Africa's second innings at lunch on the fourth day leaving Pakistan five sessions to score 490.

Donald and de Villiers soon had the visitors 3 for 5 with the match as good as over. This time, only Inzamamul Haq played an innings of any substance. His 95 was like an oasis in the desert. Man-of-the-match de Villiers became the first South African to take ten wickets and score 50 in a Test match.

This game was also notable because it was played amidst alleged rumours of match-fixing by certain members of the Pakistan team.

SOUTH AFRICA v NEW ZEALAND 1994-95

Wanderers, Johannesburg
25, 26, 27, 28, 29 November 1994
New Zealand won by 137 runs
New Zealand 411 (S.A. Thomson 84, M.D. Crowe 83, K.R. Rutherford 68) and 194 (C.R. Matthews 5 for 42); South Africa 279 (D.J. Richardson 93, D.J. Cullinan 58) and 189 (W.J. Cronje 62, M.N. Hart 5 for 77)

New Zealand surprised the confident South Africans with the ease of their win. M. Crowe and Rutherford batted with calm assurance through most of the first day to leave the visitors soundly placed. However, when three quick wickets fell on the second morning the home team was back in the match. Thomson, who top-scored in the innings, held the lower order together before Doull, 31 not out, and De Groen, 26, added 57 for the last wicket.

South Africa was soon in trouble and were 3 for 38 within an hour. Wicketkeeper Richardson, batting with a guard on his broken right thumb, led the recovery that saw the home team avoid the follow-on. He scored 93 out of the 132 runs added in the three hours that he was at the crease.

De Villiers then produced a superb spell of bowling to remove Murray, Young, Crowe and Rutherford while Matthews picked up Fleming to have the Kiwis reeling at 5 for 34. However, Parore, 49, Hart, 34, Thomson, 29, and Nash, 20, dug in to carry New Zealand to 194, leaving South Africa with 327 to score on a wearing pitch.

They started the final day needing 198 to win with eight wickets in hand. The match was all over before lunch, the last seven wickets falling for 39 runs. Doull captured 4 for 33 to support Hart, the left-arm orthodox spinner, who exploited the bowlers' foot-marks for a career best 5 for 77.

AUSTRALIA v ENGLAND 1994-95

Melbourne Cricket Ground, Melbourne
24, 26, 27, 28, 29 December 1994
Australia won by 295 runs
Australia 279 (S.R. Waugh 94 not out, M.E. Waugh 71) and 7 for 320 dec. (D.C. Boon 131); England 212 (G.P. Thorpe 51, S.K. Warne 6 for 64) and 92 (C.J. McDermott 5 for 42)

Atherton invited Australia to bat on a damp pitch that offered the England bowlers considerable encouragement. However, they failed to take full advantage of the conditions, with the Waugh twins providing the backbone of the home team's total of 279. S.R. Waugh was left unconquered on 94. He held the lower order together, as he had done so often in the past.

Luck was against the visitors as Stewart had his right index finger broken by the first ball after lunch on the second day. Resolute batting by Atherton and Thorpe then carried England to 1 for 119, and a position of comparative safety, before Warne struck with his lethal leg-spinners. When Gooch hit a return catch to McDermott from the first ball of the third day's play, the visitors' hopes had all but disappeared.

Australia built on its lead of 67 runs, and with Boon occupying the crease for more than six hours to compile his first Test century at the Melbourne Cricket Ground, Taylor was able to declare, leaving England with 388 needed for victory.

After Fleming removed Gooch and Hick with only ten runs on the board, the visitors were in desperate trouble. McDermott crashed through the middle-order before Warne removed De Freitas, Gough and Malcolm with successive deliveries. De Freitas was lbw, Gough caught behind and Malcolm was snapped up by Boon at short-leg. It was the first hat-trick in Ashes Tests since Trumble at Melbourne in 1903-04.

Australia's trump cards, McDermott with eight wickets and Warne with nine, had bowled the home team to a comprehensive victory.

AUSTRALIA v ENGLAND 1994-95

Adelaide Oval, Adelaide
26, 27, 28, 29, 30 January 1995
England won by 106 runs

England 353 (M.W. Gatting 117, M.A. Atherton 80) and 328 (P.A.J. De Freitas 88, G.P. Thorpe 83, J.P. Crawley 71, M.E. Waugh 5 for 40); Australia 419 (G.S. Blewett 102 not out, M.A. Taylor 90, I.A. Healy 74, M.J. Slater 67) and 156 (I.A. Healy 51 not out)

An under-manned England team surprised with its first Test win in Australia for eight years.

Gatting's painstaking knock was the basis of the visitors' innings. He was at the crease for nearly seven hours scoring 117, including 77 minutes in the 90s and 31 minutes on 99.

The home team gained a first innings lead of 66 by adopting a far more positive approach. The local hero, Blewett, became the 16th Australian to score a hundred on debut, he and Healy adding 164 runs for the sixth wicket. Taylor and Slater had scored another big opening partnership before a slump left Australia 5 for 232. A further collapse saw the home team lose its last five wickets for just 23 runs.

Encouraged by the bowler's efforts to wrap up the tail, Thorpe led the England counter-attack with an aggressive 83. However, wickets continued to fall and when Lewis was bowled by Fleming, the visitors were 6 for 181. Crawley and De Freitas carried the total to 220 by stumps on the fourth day but with a lead of only 154, England's prospects of saving the game looked remote. De Freitas turned the match with his bold innings. He scored 88 from just 95 balls in a two-hour stay at the crease.

Australia had 67 overs to score 263 and took unnecessary risks in chasing the victory target. On a superb pitch, saving the game should not have presented the home team with any problems at all. Malcolm and Lewis bowled with tremendous hostility to reduce Australia to 8 for 83 before Healy and Fleming survived for nearly two hours. But it was in vain, as the last wicket fell with 35 balls remaining.

ZIMBABWE v PAKISTAN 1994-95

Harare Sports Club, Harare
15, 16, 18, 19 February 1995
Pakistan won by 99 runs

Pakistan 231 (Inzamamul Haq 101) and 250 (Inzamamul Haq 83, Ijaz Ahmed 55); Zimbabwe 243 and 139 (Aamir Nazir 5 for 46)

Pakistan joined England (against Australia in 1888) and South Africa (against New Zealand in 1995) as one of very few teams to come from behind and win a three-Test series. They were the first to do so away from home.

Fortunes fluctuated constantly in this low-scoring match. Streak bowled with pace and hostility to have the visitors 4 for 83 before Ijaz Ahmed, 41, and Inzamamul Haq retrieved the situation with a stand of 76. Aamir Nazir, 0 not out, was there while 27 runs were added for the last wicket which enabled Inzamam to score his fourth century.

Zimbabwe's reply was disappointing. The home team gained a twelve-run lead, but it should have been more as six batsmen passed 20. A. Flower top-scored with 37, while Aaqib Javed, with 4 for 64, was the pick of the visitors' bowlers.

Once again, Inzamamul Haq and Ijaz Ahmed held the Pakistan batting together with a stand of 116 for the fourth wicket before the last six fell for 20. Streak, who needed cortisone injections to overcome a side strain, picked up another four-wicket haul. Zimbabwe had nearly two days to score 239 for their first series win. However, the Pakistan pace trio bowled with sustained hostility to rout the home team. Aamer Nazir took five wickets in an innings for the first time, in only his fifth Test.

WEST INDIES v AUSTRALIA 1994-95

Kensington Oval, Bridgetown, Barbados
31 March, 1, 2 April 1995
Australia won by ten wickets

West Indies 195 (B.C. Lara 65, C.L. Hooper 60) and 189 (G.D. McGrath 5 for 68); Australia 346 (I.A. Healy 74 not out, S.R. Waugh 65, M.A. Taylor 55) and 0 for 39

Richardson returned to lead his country in Test cricket after an illness had kept him out of the game. Australia had lost both its opening bowlers, McDermott and Fleming, to injury before a ball was bowled in the series.

Reiffel and Julian reduced the West Indies to 3 for 6 before Lara and Hooper proceeded to smash the visitors' attack. A breathtaking opening session saw the home team 3 for 116 at lunch. Hooper and then Adams fell shortly after the break before S. Waugh claimed a juggling catch in the gully to dismiss Lara. Television replays confirmed that the ball hit the ground. This dismissal may have been pivotal in deciding the Test, as the lower order offered little resistance. Julian was Australia's surprise packet, picking up four top-order wickets.

The visitors had the opportunity to put the match out of the West Indies' reach but until Healy and Julian added 60 for the seventh wicket, the innings had stuttered along. The top six batsmen all reached double figures with only Taylor and S. Waugh posting half-centuries.

The West Indies' second effort with the bat was even more disappointing than the first. Adams, 39 not out, and Richardson, 36, were the only batsmen to show any resistance. McGrath seized the opportunity to spearhead Australia's attack with his first five-wicket haul in Tests.

It was the first time for thirty years that West Indies had lost in three days and it was only their third defeat at Bridgetown.

WEST INDIES v AUSTRALIA 1994-95

Sabina Park, Kingston, Jamaica
29, 30 April, 1, 2 May 1995
Australia won by an innings and 53 runs

West Indies 265 (R.B. Richardson 100, B.C. Lara 65) and 213 (W.K.M. Benjamin 51); Australia 531 (S.R. Waugh 200, M.E. Waugh 126, G.S. Blewett 69)

Richardson won his fourth consecutive toss and took first use of the magnificent batting pitch. Williams fell without a run on the board before the skipper and Lara posted a century in only 20 overs. Lara's dismissal at 103, caught behind off Warne, turned the game Australia's way. Richardson was eighth out with the score at 251, after posting his first hundred of the series. The West Indies' total of 265 was their best effort in four Tests, but it was well short of what should have been scored under the conditions.

When S. Waugh joined his twin brother at the crease, Australia was 3 for 73 and the game was in the balance. Shortly before stumps, M. Waugh departed but the pair had put on 231 from 57 overs in a match-winning partnership. It was the eighth Test century for both, Mark's coming from 146 balls and Steve's from 183. The longer the partnership continued the more dispirited West Indies became. With splendid support from Blewett and Reiffel, S. Waugh reached his maiden double-century before being last man out after a stay of nearly ten hours at the crease.

With their spirit broken and facing a deficit of 266, the home team was soon in more trouble as Reiffel removed Richardson, Williams and Lara with only 46 runs on the board. Warne dismissed the last four batsmen to inflict a shattering defeat on the West Indies.

Australia regained the Sir Frank Worrell Trophy, last held in 1975-76. The West Indies had lost a series for the first time since New Zealand in 1979-80 and they had been beaten in the Caribbean for the first time since I. Chappell's team in 1972-73.

It was a truly significant Australian victory.

ENGLAND v WEST INDIES 1995

Lord's, London
22, 23, 24, 25, 26 June 1995
England won by 72 runs

England 283 (R.A. Smith 61, G.P. Thorpe 52) and 336 (R.A. Smith 90, G.A. Hick 67); West Indies 324 (K.L.T. Arthurton 75, J.C. Adams 54, A.R.C. Fraser 5 for 66) and 223 (S.L. Campbell 93, B.C. Lara 54, D.G. Cork 7 for 43)

After being soundly defeated in the first Test of the series, England played with great character to win a match that could have gone either way.

Atherton chose to bat on a pitch that provided some movement and bounce for the West Indies' pace-bowling quartet. England's innings was held together by a partnership of 111 for the fourth wicket by Thorpe and Hick, and 50 for the eighth by Cork and Martin. The home team's total of 283 left the game wide open.

The visitors' reply followed a similar path to England's innings and there is no doubt the West Indies missed a golden opportunity to wrest the initiative. Four of the recognised batsmen reached forty but no-one went on to play the big innings that was required. The lion-hearted Fraser was at his miserly best, taking 5 for 66 from 33 overs.

Trailing by 41 on the first innings, England was in real trouble with both openers back in the pavilion and a lead of only ten runs. Their position became worse when Thorpe was struck in the head and forced to retire. However, resolute batting by Smith for 90, Hick for 67 and Thorpe for 42 on his return, gave the home team a glimmer of hope.

Needing only 296 to win this see-sawing Test, the West Indies started the final day at 1 for 68 with their leading batsman Lara, on 38, the key to victory. When Gough had the talented batsman caught behind, he opened the door for England. It was Cork, playing in his first Test, who proved to be the match-winner. His figures of 7 for 43 were the best on debut for an England bowler in Test history, as the home team pulled off a memorable win.

SOUTH AFRICA v ENGLAND 1995-96

New Wanderers, Johannesburg
30 November, 1, 2, 3, 4 December 1995
Match Drawn

South Africa 332 (G. Kirsten 110, D.J. Cullinan 69, D.G. Cork 5 for 84) and 9 for 346 dec. (B.M. McMillan 100 not out, D.J. Cullinan 61, J.N. Rhodes 57); England 200 (R.A. Smith 52) and 5 for 351 (M.A. Atherton 185 not out)

Atherton played one of the great innings to save the match for his team after a South African victory looked certain on the fourth day.

England's attack bowled poorly and failed to take advantage of the favourable conditions after Atherton had sent the home team in to bat. Positive batting and aggressive running by Kirsten placed the momentum with South Africa. The left-handed opener was rewarded with his maiden century. Apart from Cullinan's 69, there were useful contributions from Cronje, 35, McMillan, 35, and Pollock, 33, that lifted the home team to a respectable 332.

The visitors were bundled out for a disappointing total of 200 on the second day. Only Smith, 52, Stewart, 45, and Thorpe, 34, offered any resistance to the South African bowlers. With a lead of 122, the home team pushed on for victory, Cullinan again producing a dazzling array of strokes. Inexplicably the South African batsmen came off for bad light with 7.3 overs remaining on the third day with the lead at 428. Somewhat surprisingly the innings continued for another 92 minutes to allow McMillan to complete his second Test century.

England was left with five sessions to survive. After Stewart, Ramprakash, Thorpe and Hick had fallen on the fourth day, the visitors' prospects of saving the game looked remote. Atherton had a life on 99 when he forced Donald into the hands of Kirsten at short-leg and the ball popped straight out again. Wicketkeeper Russell joined his skipper with over four and a half hours to play. Russell had already broken the world record for dismissals in a Test by taking eleven catches. He had a life on five when Pringle dropped a return catch. Russell batted for 277 minutes while Atherton played the fourth-longest innings for England. His 643 minutes was bettered by only Hutton (797) against Australia at Kennington Oval in 1938, Barrington (683) against Australia at Old Trafford in 1964 and Radly (648) against New Zealand at Auckland in 1977-78. It was a great captain's knock.

AUSTRALIA v SRI LANKA 1995-96

Melbourne Cricket Ground, Melbourne
26, 27, 28, 29, 30 December, 1995
Australia won by 10 wickets

AUSTRALIA 6 for 500 dec. (S.R. Waugh 131 not out, D.C. Boon 110, R.T. Ponting 71, M.J. Slater 62) and 0 for 41; Sri Lanka 233 (A. Ranatunga 51, R.S. Kaluwitharana 50, G.D. McGrath 5 for 40) and 307 (A.P. Gurusinha 143)

This match will always be remembered for the no-balling of Sri Lanka's champion spin bowler Muralidaran by umpire Hair for throwing. It was the first time Muralidaran had been called for an illegal action. It came in his 22nd Test and completely stunned the M.C.G. Boxing Day crowd of more than 55,000.

After being called seven times in three overs Muralidaran switched ends and bowled until tea on the second day. When umpire Hair advised the Sri Lankans he was ready to call him from square leg.

The drama of the no-balling of a bowler, who at a time later in his career, became the leading wicket taker in Test cricket completely over shadowed anything else associated with the match.

Ranatunga's gamble in sending Australia in on a benign pitch backfired. Boon scored his 21st century in what was to be his penultimate Test while S. Waugh completed a stylish 131 not out. Ponting in his second Test innings reached fifty again, a sign of things to come.

McGrath's pace and hostility was too much for the visitors, and they were forced to follow-on. Only Gurusinha offered any real resistance before the Australians took an unbeatable two nil lead in the series.

PAKISTAN v ZIMBABWE 1996-97

Sheikhupura Cricket Stadium, Sheikhupura
17, 18, 19, 20, 21 October 1996
Match Drawn

Zimbabwe 375 (G.W. Flower 110, P.A. Strang 106 not out, Shahid Nazir 5 for 54) and 7 for 241 (D.L. Houghton 65); Pakistan 553 (Wasim Akram 257 not out, Saqlain Mushtaq 79, Saleem Malik 52, P.A. Strang 5 for 212)

This was the first match played at Test cricket's newest ground. The ground was given a remarkable baptism. On a grassless pitch the Pakistan captain, Wasim Akram, played a record-breaking innings while the Zimbabwean leg spinner P.A. Strang produced an outstanding all-round performance.

Strang joined G.W. Flower with Zimbabwe in desperate trouble at 6 for 142. Their partnership realised 131 before the Strang brothers put on 87 for the ninth wicket. Paul Strang posted his maiden first class century in just under five hours.

ZIMBABWE v ENGLAND 1996-97 (First Test)

Queens Sports Club, Bulawayo, December 18, 19, 20, 21, 22, 1996. Match Drawn

ZIMBABWE

G.W.Flower	c Hussain b Silverwood	43		lbw b Gough	0
S.V.Carlisle	c Crawley b Gough	0		c Atherton b Mullally	4
A.D.R.Campbell*	c Silverwood b Croft	84		b Croft	29
D.L.Houghton	c Stewart b Croft	34		c Croft b Tufnell	37
A.Flower†	c Stewart b Tufnell	112		c Crawley b Tufnell	14
A.C.Waller	c Crawley b Croft	15		c Knight b Gough	50
G.J.Whittall	c Atherton b Silverwood	7	(8)	c Croft b Tufnell	56
P.A.Strang	c Tufnell b Silverwood	38	(9)	c Crawley b Croft	19
H.H.Streak	b Mullally	19	(10)	not out	8
B.C.Strang	not out	4	(7)	c Mullally b Tufnell	3
H.K.Olonga	c Knight b Tufnel	0		c Stewart b Silverwood	0
Extras	LB 4, NB 13, W 3	20		B 4, LB 6, NB 2, W 2	14
Total	**376**				**234**

ENGLAND

N.V.Knight	lbw b Olonga	56		run out (B.C.Strang/A.Flower)	96
M.A.Atherton*	lbw b P.A.Strang	16		b Ologna	4
A.J.Stewart†	lbw b P.A.Strang	48		c Campbell b P.A.Strang	73
N.Hussain	c B.C.Strang b Streak	113		c Carlisle b P.A.Strang	0
G.P.Thorpe	c Campbell b P.A.Strang	13	(6)	c Campbell b Streak	2
J.P.Crawley	c A.Flower b P.A.Strang	112	(5)	c Carlisle b Whittall	7
R.D.B.Croft	lbw b Olonga	7			
D.Gough	c G.W.Flower b Olonga	2	(7)	not out	3
C.E.W.Silverwood	c Houghton b P.A.Strang	0			
A.D.Mullally	c Waller b Streak	4			
P.C.R.Tufnell	not out	2			
Extras	B 4, LB 4, NB 24, W 1	33		B 2, LB 13, Nb 1, W 3	19
Total		**406**		**6 wickets**	**204**

ENGLAND	O	M	R	W		O	M	R	W
Mullally	23	4	69	1	Gough	12	2	44	2
Gough	26	4	87	1	Mullally	18	5	49	1
Silverwood	18	5	63	3	Croft	33	9	62	2
Croft	44	15	77	3	Silverwood	7	3	8	1
Tufnell	26.5	4	76	2	Tufnell	31	12	61	4

ZIMBABWE	O	M	R	W		O	M	R	W
Streak	36	8	86	2	Streak	11	0	64	1
B.C.Strang	17	5	54	0	Olonga	2	0	16	1
P.A.Strang	58.4	14	123	5	P.A.Strang	14	0	63	2
Olonga	23	2	90	3	G.W.Flower	8	0	36	0
Whittall	10	2	25	0	Whittall	2	0	10	1
G.W.Flower	7	3	20	0					

FALL OF WICKETS

Wkt	Z	E	Z	E
1st	3	48	6	17
2nd	129	92	6	154
3rd	135	160	57	156
4th	205	180	82	178
5th	235	328	103	182
6th	252	340	111	204
7th	331	344	178	-
8th	372	353	209	-
9th	376	378	233	-
10th	376	406	234	-

Umpires: R.S. Dunne and I.D.Robinson

The home team found themselves in a similar predicament when Saqlain Mushtaq joined his skipper with Pakistan at 7 for 237. They proceeded to post a new world record of 313 for the eighth wicket in a Test match, easily passing the 246 set by Ames and Allen for England against New Zealand in 1931. Wasim Akram's 257 not out was the highest Test score returned by a number eight batsman, exceeding Imitaz Ahmed's 209 for Pakistan against New Zealand in 1955-56. Akram smashed twelve sixes in his innings, breaking the previous best in Tests (Hammond's 10 against New Zealand in 1932-33).

P.A. Strang finished with 5 for 212 from 69 overs to become the 18th player to score a century and take five wickets in an innings in the same Test. He also had the dubious honour of becoming the 13th bowler in Test history to concede 200 runs in an innings.

PAKISTAN v NEW ZEALAND 1996-97

Gaddafi Stadium, Lahore
21, 22, 23, 24 November 1996
New Zealand won by 44 runs

New Zealand 155 and 311 (C.L. Cairns 93, S.P. Fleming 92 not out, Mushtaq Ahmed 6 for 84); Pakistan 191 (Moin Khan 59, S.B. Doull 5 for 46) and 231 (Mohammad Wasim 109 not out)

This was only New Zealand's second win in Pakistan and it came after a break of 27 years. However, the home team was without its dynamic skipper, Wasim Akram, who withdrew on the morning of the match with a shoulder injury.

Despite having the advantage of winning the toss, New Zealand was bundled out for a modest 155, Waqar Younis and Mushtaq Ahmed claiming four wickets each.

The visitors struck back, Doull ripping the heart out of the Pakistan top order to have the home team reeling at 5 for 37. However, resolute batting by the bottom half of the order gave Pakistan a lead of 36 runs.

New Zealand slumped to 5 for 101 on the third morning before Cairns joined Fleming. Cairns, in the manner of his father before him, carved 93 from 89 balls in a 141-run partnership. Doull then assisted Fleming to add 49 for the last wicket, which left Pakistan with a target of 276 for victory.

Again the home team's top order failed, with 6 for 60 being the tale of woe. Debutant Mohammad Wasim restored some respectability with an elegant century. But only Moin Khan provided any worthwhile support as the veteran off-spinner, Patel, wrapped up the innings claiming 4 for 36.

ZIMBABWE v ENGLAND 1996-97

Queens Sports Club, Bulawayo
18, 19, 20, 21, 22 December 1996
Match Drawn

Zimbabwe 376 (A. Flower 112, A.D.R. Campbell 84) and 234 (G.J. Whittall 56, A.C. Waller 50); England 406 (N. Hussain 113, J.P. Crawley 112, N.V. Knight 56, P.A. Strang 5 for 123) and 6 for 204 (N.V. Knight 96, A.J. Stewart 73)

After 1345 Test matches in 119 years, this was the first ever game that was drawn with the scores level. It was also the first Test played between the two countries, the home team having the added incentive of knowing the Test and County Cricket Board had opposed their application for Test status in 1992.

New skipper Campbell and A. Flower, who had recently relinquished the position, were the backbone of Zimbabwe's competitive first innings total. Flower posted his third Test century in a stay of just over six hours, while Campbell had scored 50 for the ninth time without reaching three figures.

Centuries by Hussain and Crawley gave the visitors a 30-run lead. Their fifth-wicket partnership realised 148 runs, however the England batsmen should have adopted a more positive approach to gain the ascendancy. But when the home team lost five wickets for 107 with one day to play, the visitors still looked likely winners.

Positive batting, which produced half-centuries to Waller and Whittall, left England with 205 needed for victory in 37 overs. After Atherton's early departure, Knight and Stewart took up the challenge. Eighty-seven runs were needed with 15 overs remaining. However, this was not a one-day game so there was no 30-yard circle or fielding restrictions.

Fifty-nine runs from ten overs became 33 from five but Stewart, Hussain, Crawley and Thorpe had been dismissed in the chase for victory. Finally, 13 was required from the last over with Streak bowling to Knight. All nine fieldsmen were on the boundary. The first ball was down leg-side, and splendid running by Gough scored two from the second. Knight lifted England's hopes with a six over square leg, leaving five runs needed from three balls. The fourth delivery was well wide of the off-stump but not called by Umpire Robinson. Two more runs came from the fifth ball of the over. Streak then fired in the perfect yorker which Knight played into the covers. Flower removed the bails after a fine throw from B. Strang, before the batsmen had crossed for the winning run. (See final score on page 71.)

NEW ZEALAND v ENGLAND 1996-97

Eden Park, Auckland
24, 25, 26, 27, 28 January 1997
Match Drawn

New Zealand 390 (S.P. Fleming 129, B.A. Pocock 70, C.L. Cairns 67) and 9 for 248 (N.P. Astle 102 not out); England 521 (A.J. Stewart 173, G.P. Thorpe 119, M.A. Atherton 83, D.G. Cork 59)

New Zealand found an unlikely batting hero in their number eleven, Morrison, who survived for 165 minutes to hold England out. The same batsman has a record of 24 Test ducks!

Atherton sent the Kiwis in but his pace bowlers wasted the conditions with their inaccuracy. Fleming's maiden century and aggressive batting by Cairns carried New Zealand to a respectable total of 390.

England replied with 521. Stewart's 173, the highest score by an English wicketkeeper, which beat the previous best of 149 by Ames at Kingston in 1930. Thorpe produced another solid if unspectacular century, while Atherton returned to form with an elegant 83.

By lunch on the final day, England had the game as good as won, with New Zealand 8 for 105 and only Doull and Morrison to support Astle. Doull made 26, hitting lustily to avoid the innings defeat before Morrison and Astle produced their superb rear-guard effort.

NEW ZEALAND v ENGLAND 1996-97

Lancaster Park, Christchurch
14, 15, 16, 17, 18 February 1997
England won by 4 wickets

New Zealand 346 (S.P. Fleming 62, A.C. Parore 59, C.L. Cairns 57, R.D.B. Croft 5 for 95) and 186 (C.L. Cairns 52); England 228 (M.A. Atherton 94 not out) and 6 for 307 (M.A. Atherton 118)

This was a remarkable victory for England as only once before, at Melbourne in January 1929, had they scored more than 300 in the fourth innings to win a Test.

With Germon injured, Fleming became New Zealand's youngest skipper. He lost the toss and then proceeded to top-score with 62 in an innings of 346 that took almost nine hours to complete. It was an innings of missed opportunities as six batsmen passed 20.

England's reply was disappointing, falling 118 runs short of the home team's total. Atherton played a lone hand for the visitors, carrying his bat for 94 in a patient knock that took almost six hours to compile. Allott marked his return to Test cricket with four wickets, including three of the first five to fall.

New Zealand failed to drive home its advantage and by lunch on the fourth day had been dismissed for 186. This left the visitors with ample time to reach the target of 305.

Once again, the sheet anchor of England's innings was skipper Atherton who was at the crease for 399 minutes making 118. Until his dismissal, he had been on the field for the first 26 and a half hours of the match. Hussain and Thorpe fell in quick succession, leaving England 6 for 231 and still 74 runs short of the victory target. However, there was to be no further success for New Zealand as Crawley and Cork steered the visitors to victory. The match was won with just 12.2 overs remaining. The 18-year-old Vettori bowled with maturity beyond his years to claim 4 for 97 from 57 overs.

SOUTH AFRICA v AUSTRALIA 1996-97

Wanderers, Johannesburg
28 February, 1, 2, 3, 4 March 1997
Australia won by an innings and 196 runs

South Africa 302 (W.J. Cronje 76, D.J. Richardson 72 not out) and 130; Australia 8 for 628 dec. (G.S. Blewett 214, S.R. Waugh 160, M.T.G. Elliott at 85)

This was the first match in a three Test series that was billed as the world championship decider.

The South Africans were in trouble early as McGrath exploited the conditions superbly to remove Hudson, Kallis and Kirsten in his first ten-over spell. Only the skipper Cronje made a worthwhile contribution in the top order. Late on the first day, wicketkeeper Richardson hit lustily to add respectability to the home team's score. Australia's reply was dominated by a record fifth-wicket partnership of 385 by S. Waugh and Blewett. (Waugh was playing with his twin brother for the 44th time, breaking the record of Ian and Greg Chappell). During the partnership, Waugh and Blewett became the ninth pair to bat through a day's play, and it was the twelfth time in Test history that a full day's play had failed to produce a wicket. The partnership was the best ever against South Africa while Blewett's 214 was the highest score by an Australian in South Africa.

On a wearing pitch, Australian spinners Warne and Bevan bowled the visitors to a commanding victory before lunch on the final day, Bevan ending the match with four wickets for two runs from twelve deliveries.

SOUTH AFRICA v AUSTRALIA 1996-97

St. George's Park, Port Elizabeth
14, 15, 16, 17 March 1997
Australia won by 2 wickets

South Africa 209 (B.M. McMillan 55, J.N. Gillespie 5 for 54) and 168; Australia 108 and 8 for 271 (M.E. Waugh 116)

Taylor sent Australia in on a pitch that the Australian captain labelled 'under-prepared'. Hostile fast bowling by both McGrath and Gillespie had the home team reeling at 4 for 22 within the first hour's play. The experienced pair of McMillan and Richardson added 85 runs for the eighth wicket to restore some credibility to the innings.

Australia's batsmen failed to come to terms with the difficult conditions and were dismissed for 108, their second lowest total in South Africa. Elliott top-scored with a painstaking 23, and only four Australian batsmen reached double figures. South Africa suffered a telling blow when their opening bowler Pollock was forced from the field with a hamstring injury.

When the home team reached 0 for 83 by stumps on the second day, Australia looked a beaten side. However, the match was turned upside-down by a mixture of high-quality bowling and poor batting on the third morning. Apart from the openers, Bacher with 49 and Kirsten 43, only Cronje and Pollock (batting with a runner) reached double figures. Gillespie and Bevan claimed three wickets apiece to spearhead Australia's fight-back.

The target of 270 was a testing one on a difficult pitch. Taylor went cheaply and when Hayden was run out in a mix-up with Elliott, the visitors were in trouble at 2 for 30. M. Waugh, playing in his 100th Test innings, then carried Australia to within twelve runs of victory. Waugh's 116 was one of the finest centuries in Test history and certainly his most valuable in an illustrious career. With his dismissal and those of Bevan and Warne, Australia still required five runs with two wickets in hand.

Healy ended the match triumphantly swinging Cronje over backward square leg for six.

WEST INDIES v INDIA 1996-97

Kensington Oval, Bridgetown, Barbados
27, 29, 30, 31 March 1997
West Indies won by 38 runs

West Indies 298 (S. Chanderpaul 137 not out, B.K.V. Prasad 5 for 82) and 140 (A. Kuruvilla 5 for 68); India 319 (S.R. Tendulkar 92, R.S. Dravid 78) and 81

Brian Lara captained the West Indies for the first time in the absence of the injured Walsh. Tendulkar sent the home team in on a pitch that was going to favour the pace bowlers for the duration of the match. After 13 half-centuries in 18 Tests, Chanderpaul finally reached the three figures, with his 137 not out forming the backbone of the West Indies innings.

Tendulkar and Dravid produced the best batting of the match in their 170-run partnership for the third wicket. The West Indies fast bowlers delivered 30 no-balls in India's innings and perhaps it should have been more, with video replay suggesting that Bishop overstepped the line when he had Tendulkar caught in the gully. To its credit the home team fought back to claim the last six wickets for 66 and restrict the visitors' lead to just 21 runs.

India's pace trio of Prasad, Kuruvilla and Ganesh, bowling a fuller length than their West Indian counterparts, had the home team in desperate trouble at 9 for 107 when Dillon joined Ambrose. Their 33-run partnership was the highest of the innings and left the visitors needing 120 for victory.

On a pitch that was becoming increasingly difficult, this was never going to be an easy target. Sustained hostile bowling by Ambrose, Bishop and Rose dismissed India for 81 (their lowest score in the West Indies) and the home team had snatched yet another victory from 'the jaws of defeat'.

SRI LANKA v INDIA 1997-98

Premadasa Stadium, Colombo
2, 3, 4, 5, 6 August 1997
Match Drawn

India 8 for 537 dec. (S.R. Tendulkar 143, M. Azharuddin 126, N.S. Sidhu 111, R.S. Dravid 69); Sri Lanka 6 for 952 dec. (S.T. Jayasuriya 340, R.S. Mahanama 225, P.A. de Silva 126, A. Ranatunga 86, D.P.M. Jayawardene 66

Two of cricket's most imposing records were broken on a docile pitch in Colombo.

Sri Lanka's total of 6 for 952 easily surpassed England's 7 for 903 declared at Kennington Oval in 1938. Jayasuriya and Mahanama added 576 for the second wicket. They cruised past the previous highest Test partnership of 467 set by Crowe and Jones of New Zealand against Sri Lanka at Wellington in 1990-91. Jayasuriya's score of 340 was the fourth highest in Test history. The three higher scores were Lara's 375, Sobers' 365 not out and Hutton's 364.

Jayasuriya started the final day requiring 50 runs to break the record. Local officials let the public in free with the prospect of a new record score but many in the crowd of more than thirty thousand were still finding their vantage point when Jayasuriya was dismissed, caught at silly point by Ganguly off Chauhan. Kulkarni became the twelfth bowler to take a wicket with his first ball in Test cricket when he had Atapattu caught behind by Mongia.

The Sri Lankan run feast had come after India had plundered the home team's attack, scoring 537 at better than three runs per over. Centuries were scored by Sidhu, Tendulkar and Azharuddin who put on 221 for the fourth wicket. India's captain, Tendulkar, claimed that his team had only lost wickets because they took chances trying to score runs. (See final score on page 75.)

SRI LANKA v INDIA 1997-98 (First Test)

R.Premadasa (Khettarama) Stadium, Colombo, August 2, 3, 4, 5, 6, 1997 — Match Drawn

INDIA

N.R.Mongia†	c Jayawardene b Pushpakumara	7
N.S.Sidhu	c Kaluwitharana b Vaas	111
R.S.Dravid	c and b Jayasurija	69
S.R.Tendulkar*	c Jayawardene b Muralidaran	143
M.Azharuddin	c and b Muralidaran	126
S.C.Ganguly	c Mahanama b Jayasuriya	0
A.R.Kumble	not out	27
R.K.Chauhan	c Vaas b Jayasuriya	23
A.Kuruvilla	c Atapattu b Pushpakumara	9
N.M.Kulkarni		
B.K.Venkatesh Prasad		
Extras	B 10, NB 12	22
Total	**8 wickets declared**	**537**

SRI LANKA

S.T. Jayasuriya	c Ganguly b Chauhan	340
M.S.Atapattu	c Mongia b Kulkarni	26
R.S.Mahanama	lbw b Kumble	225
P.A.de Silva	c Venkatesh Prasad b Ganguly	126
A.Ranatunga*	run out (sub Jadeja/Mongia)	86
D.R.M.Jayawardene	c Kulkarni b Ganguly	66
R.S.Kaluwitharana†	not out	14
W.P.U.J.C.Vaas	not out	11
K.R.Pushpakumara		
M.Muralidaran		
K.J.Silva		
Extras	B 27, LB 10, NB 14, W 7	58
Total	**6 wickets declared**	**952**

SRI LANKA	O	M	R	W	O	M	R	W
Vaas	23	5	80	1				
Pushpakumara	19.3	2	97	2				
Jayawardene	2	0	6	0				
Muralidaran	65	9	174	2				
Silva	39	3	122	0				
Jayasuriya	18	3	45	3				
Atapattu	1	0	3	0				
INDIA	O	M	R	W	O	M	R	W
Venkatesh Prasad	24	1	88	0				
Kuruvilla	14	2	74	0				
Chauhan	78	8	276	1				
Kumble	72	7	223	1				
Kulkarni	70	12	195	1				
Ganguly	9	0	53	2				
Tendulkar	2	1	2	0				
Dravid	2	0	4	0				

FALL OF WICKETS

Wkt	I	SL	I	SL
1st	36	39	-	-
2nd	183	615	-	-
3rd	230	615	-	-
4th	451	790	-	-
5th	451	921	-	-
6th	479	924	-	-
7th	516	-	-	-
8th	537	-	-	-
9th	-	-	-	-
10th	-	-	-	-

Umpires: K.T.Francis and S.R.Randell

AUSTRALIA v SOUTH AFRICA 1997-98

Sydney Cricket Ground, Sydney
2, 3, 4, 5 January 1998
Australia won by an innings and 21 runs
South Africa 287 (W.J. Cronje 88, H.H. Gibbs 54, S.K. Warne 5 for 75) and 113 (S.K. Warne 6 for 34); Australia 421 (M.E. Waugh 100, S.R. Waugh 85, R.T. Ponting 62)

Australia's champion leg-spinner, Warne, captured his 300th Test wicket on the way to another match-winning performance. It was exactly six years to the day since he had captured his first victim at the highest level.

South Africa batted first on the best Sydney pitch for many years. The visitors' lack of initiative on the opening day went a long way to deciding the result. Only 197 runs were scored from 97 overs for the loss of five wickets. Cronje was uncharacteristically restrained with a patient 88. Gibbs, with a maiden half-century, added 97 for the fourth wicket with his captain. Warne, wicketless on the first day, returned to top form on the second morning taking the last five wickets for 29 as South Africa slumped from 5 for 228 to be all out for 287.

On such a good pitch the home team set about gaining a sizeable lead. With Taylor, Elliott and Blewett out and only 103 on the board, the visitors had a chance to fight their way back into the match. However, the Waugh twins produced another memorable partnership despite some of the most hostile bowling seen in Sydney for years. With the second new ball, Donald was at his fiery best but was not able to make the vital breakthrough. Ponting and Healy, who finished 46 not out, gave Australia a 134-run advantage.

After McGrath and Reiffel had picked up an early wicket, Warne was at his brilliant best as he reduced South Africa to 7 for 55. A storm delayed play for three hours, but the hardy souls who stayed at the ground were not disappointed as Warne bowled Kallis for wicket number 300 to produce scenes of great jubilation. Reiffel dismissed Symcox and Donald to end the match at nine minutes past seven in the gloomy weather with the SCG lights blazing.

WEST INDIES v ENGLAND 1997-98

Sabina Park, Kingston
29 January 1998
Match Abandoned
England 3 for 17

The first Test of the series was abandoned after just 56 minutes and 10.1 overs. It was the first Test to have been called off because of a dangerous pitch. Umpire Venkataraghavan had contacted match referee Jarman as early as the third over expressing his concern about the state of the pitch.

Physiotherapist Wayne Morton had been called upon to treat England's batsmen six times in less than an hour's play. Opener Stewart called his captain Atherton on to the field at the drinks break and after consultation with West Indies' captain Lara and Jarman, the umpires suspended play and later decided to abandon the match.

It was deemed that the results of the 10.1 overs play would count in the players' career statistics.

AUSTRALIA v SOUTH AFRICA 1997-98

Adelaide Oval, Adelaide
30, 31 January, 1, 2, 3 February 1998
Match Drawn
South Africa 517 (B.M. McMillan 87 not out, G. Kirsten 77, W.J. Cronje 73, A.M. Bacher 64, P.L. Symcox 54) and 6 for 193 dec. (G. Kirsten 108 not out); Australia 350 (M.A. Taylor 169 not out, M.E. Waugh 63, S.M. Pollock 7 for 87) and 7 for 227 (M.E. Waugh 115 not out)

South Africa, who needed to win the match to square the series, was unable to select its pace-bowling spearhead Donald while Australia was without its three leading fast bowlers, McGrath, Gillespie and Reiffel.

Cronje won the toss again and batted on a typical Adelaide 'belter'. Against the inexperienced new-ball attack of Kasprowicz and Bichel, Bacher and Kirsten added 140 for the first wicket. Cronje, playing with more purpose than in Sydney then scored 73 in just under three hours. With the visitors at 7 for 305, the home team had fought back well before McMillan, in a return to form, realised 214 for the last three wickets with Pollock, who scored 40 from 67 deliveries; Klusener, 38 off 59; and Symcox, 54 from just 42 balls.

Australia's reply was built around the captain's gutsy innings. Taylor had not played in the one-day series so was fresher than most of his teammates. In extremely hot conditions, he batted for over eight hours to become the ninth Australian to carry his bat.

In a game of many individual highlights, Pollock's 7 for 87 from 41 overs in the searing heat was an outstanding performance. Pollock's magnificent bowling had given South Africa a realistic chance of winning the match and levelling the series.

Kirsten played another splendid innings to compile his sixth century and allow Cronje to declare at 6 for 193, leaving Australia 361 to win from 109 overs. This was never going to be an attainable target and was even less likely after both Taylor and Elliott were out with only 17 on the board.

M. Waugh was then to play one of his most responsible knocks for his country. Even though he was dropped four times, his patient century was to save the side. There was a moment of high drama in the seventh over of the final hour. Waugh was hit on the elbow by Pollock, the ball carrying to Symcox in the gully, who appealed for the catch. As Waugh turned, he lost control of his arm and his bat broke the wicket. An appeal for hit-wicket followed. Third umpire Davis was consulted and correctly ruled in the batsman's favour as the bails were not dislodged in the act of facing the ball or in taking a run.

It was a tense end to a wonderful match.

WEST INDIES v ENGLAND 1997-98

Queen's Park Oval, Port of Spain, Trinidad
5, 6, 7, 8, 9 February 1998
West Indies won by 3 wickets

England 214 (N. Hussain 61 not out, A.J. Stewart 50) and 258 (A.J. Stewart 73, C.E.L. Ambrose 5 for 52); West Indies 191 (B.C. Lara 55, A.R.C. Fraser 8 for 53) and 7 for 282 (C.L. Hooper 94 not out, D. Williams 65, S.C. Williams 62)

This Test was added to the England tour itinerary after the match in Kingston had been abandoned on the first day.

The game was played on a mediocre pitch which produced slow uneven bounce and where patience was a real virtue. Atherton won the toss and decided to bat first. Stewart played stylishly for his half-century, but only Hussain batted with the resolve required in the difficult conditions, Fraser staying with him for 90 minutes on the second morning while 42 runs were added for the ninth wicket.

Fraser then dominated proceedings with the ball as he returned career-best figures of 8 for 53. New skipper Lara top-scored for the home team with 55 but only Chanderpaul, 34, and Ambrose, 31, offered any real support. With a lead of 23, England had an opportunity to press home the advantage and received an added bonus when Lara used Benjamin and McLean to open the bowling and not the experienced Ambrose and Walsh. Stewart was again the pick of England's batsmen, but this time he received more support so that by the end of the third day the visitors were 4 for 219, leading by 242.

On the fourth morning, Ambrose produced one of his great spells taking 5 for 16 from 7.5 overs as the last six wickets fell for 30 runs. West Indies required 282 to record an amazing victory. S. Williams, 62, held the top order together with one of his most responsible knocks but when half the team was out for 121 it was England who looked likely to win.

The little wicketkeeper D. Williams joined the enigmatic Hooper and they added 57 before stumps, so 101 was still required when the final day started. Fraser dropped a return catch from Williams from the first ball of the day and from that moment the home team looked more likely to succeed. Williams was dismissed after a 129-run partnership but by then only 29 was required for victory. Ambrose fell cheaply but Hooper found a capable partner in Benjamin and they carried the West Indies to a memorable win. In a match in which there were many outstanding individual performances, Hooper was a worthy man-of-the-match.

WEST INDIES v ENGLAND 1997-98

Queen's Park Oval, Port of Spain, Trinidad
13, 14, 15, 16, 17 February 1998
England won by 3 wickets

West Indies 159 (A.R.C. Fraser 5 for 40, A.R. Caddick 5 for 67) and 210 (J.C. Adams 53); England 145 (C.E.L. Ambrose 5 for 25) and 7 for 225 (A.J. Stewart 83)

Because of the farce in Jamaica when the Test was abandoned after just 56 minutes of play, back-to-back matches were played in Trinidad. A different pitch was used for this match than for the game the West Indies had won three days earlier.

Atherton invited the West Indies to bat but the decision looked likely to back-fire with the home team at 1 for 72 just after lunch and Lara in dominant form. Accurate bowling from Caddick and Fraser supported by excellent catching turned the match, reducing the West Indies from 1 for 93 to be all out for a modest 159. Nine wickets had fallen for 66 in 40 overs.

England's reply was no better despite reasonable contributions from Stewart, 44, Thorpe, 32, Butcher, 28, and Russell, 20 not out. No other batsman reached double figures as Ambrose, revelling in the conditions, claimed another five-wicket haul.

The West Indies, after leading by 14 runs, had increased their advantage to 85 with eight wickets in hand at the end of the second day. Lara, who was on 30, again loomed as England's danger man. When Fraser trapped him in front for 47 the visitors had regained the initiative. Chanderpaul and Adams, with a 56-run partnership for the sixth wicket, went some way to restoring the West Indies' supremacy. However, when three wickets fell for just one run, England was again in the driver's seat. Adams then managed to eke out 51 valuable runs with McLean and Walsh. Fraser and Headley both picked up four wickets, Fraser finishing with nine for the match.

The visitors had more than two days to score the 225 required for victory. Atherton and Stewart had polished off 52 from the target by the end of the third day. Unseasonal rain frustrated both teams on the fourth day as England laboured towards victory. Atherton and Stewart had scored more than half the runs required with their 129-run opening stand.

The final day started with the visitors still needing to score 38 with six wickets in hand. Rain delayed play for 45 minutes and then Thorpe, Russell and Caddick fell in quick succession before Butcher and Headley took England to a nail-biting victory.

ENGLAND v SRI LANKA 1998

Kennington Oval, London
27, 28, 29, 30, 31 August 1998
Sri Lanka won by 10 wickets

England 445 (J.P. Crawley 156 not out, G.A. Hick 107, M.R. Ramprakash 53, M. Muralidaran 7 for 155) and 181 (M. Muralidaran 9 for 65); Sri Lanka 591 (S.T. Jayasuriya 213, P.A. de Silva 152, A. Ranatunga 51).

This was a one off Test that came at the end of a gruelling home season for England.

Ranatunga surprisingly sent England in and commented later that he wanted to give his trump card, off-spinner Muralidaran, a rest between innings.

By compiling a respectable 445 England had appeared to have played themselves into a position of relative safety. Hick's 107 was a painstaking affair while Crawley's 156 not out was a little more attractive. Perhaps they were both thinking more about selection for the upcoming Ashes Tour. Muralidaran sent down 59 overs to claim 7 for 155.

Sri Lanka seized the iniative on the third day when they scored 367 for the loss of just two wickets. Jayasuriya and de Silva adding a record 243 for the third wicket. Jayasuriya returned to his best form with a sparkling 213 from just 278 deliveries. In posting a stylish 152 de Silva became the first Sri Lankan to pass 5000 Test runs.

England trailed by 146 and when Muralidaran removed Butcher and Hick late on day four the home side was going to have a battle to save the match. When Ramprakash ran out Stewart the game opened up for Sri Lanka. Muralidaran kept weaving his magic before Gough joined Ramprakash with England 8 for 127. Defiantly he resisted for over two and half hours. Ramprakash's resistance ended after more than four hours when he was caught at short leg.

Muralidaran finished with nine second innings wickets. His match figures of 16 for 220 where the fifth best in Test history.

PAKISTAN v AUSTRALIA 1998-99

Arbab Niaz Stadium, Peshawar
15, 16, 17, 18, 19 October 1998
Match Drawn

Australia 4 for 599 dec. (M.A. Taylor 334 not out, J.L Langer 116, R.T. Ponting 76 not out) and 5 for 289 (M. A. Taylor 92); Pakistan 9 for 580 dec. (Ijaz Ahmed 155, Saeed Anwar 126, Inzamamul Haq 97)

This match, played on a flat, evenly grassed pitch that hardly changed over the five days, will always be remembered for Taylor's 334 not out.

Right from the start of his innings the Australian captain was in superb form and played as well as he ever had in his ten year Test career.

With Langer he put on 279 for the second-wicket, a new record for any wicket in Australia-Pakistan Tests. At the end of the second day Taylor had batted for 12 hours faced 564 deliveries hit 32 fours and a six. Ijaz Ahmed, fielding at square leg, had stopped a forcing stroke off the last ball of the day.

To the surprise of most pundits Taylor declared the next morning. He had sacrificed the chance to break Bradman's Australian record score of 334 and Lara's world mark of 375. To his credit Taylor was more interested in winning the Test.

Given such a benign pitch Pakistan replied strongly with both Ijaz Ahmed and Saeed Anwar compiling centuries and Inzamam 97. Taylor's second innings of 92 gave him a match aggregate of 426 second only to Gooch against India in 1990.

Bradman later personally thanked Taylor for not exceeding his record.

INDIA v PAKISTAN 1998-99

M.A. Chidambaram Stadium, Chennai
28, 29, 30, 31 January 1999
Pakistan won by 12 runs

Pakistan 238 (Moin Khan 60, Yousuf Youhana 53, A. Kumble 6 for 70) and 286 (Shahid Afridi 141, Inzamamul Haq 51, B.K.V. Prasad 6 for 33); India 254 (S.C. Ganguly 54, R.Dravid 53, Saqlain Mushtaq 5 for 94) and 258 (S.R. Tendulkar 136, N.R. Mongia 52, Saqlain Mushtaq 5 for 93)

This was the first Test between these two countries for nine years and the first time in India for twelve.

After winning the toss Pakistan was soon in trouble at 5 for 91 before half centuries from Moin Khan and Yousuf Youhana gave the innings some respectability. Kumble polished off the tail to finish with 6 for 70.

India's reply was not much better with only Ganguly and Dravid reaching fifty. Tendulkar was Saqlain Mushtaq's first of ten wickets for the match, when he holed out to backward point on the third ball he faced.

Shahid Afridi took the last three wickets to fall to restrict India's lead to sixteen. He then dominated the third day, compiling his maiden Test century in just his second match. For a player with a reputation as a hard-hitting one day batsman he showed admirable restraint to bat for more than five hours. Prasad then produced an amazing spell of five wickets from 18 balls, without conceding a run as Pakistan lost its last 6 wickets for eleven.

India required 271 to pull off an unlikely victory and after slumping to 5 for 82 all hope appeared gone. Tendulkar received admirable support from wicketkeeper Mongia and they added 136 for the sixth wicket before Mongia fell at 218. Joshi joined Tendulkar and together they took the home team to within 17 of victory before Tendulkar holed out in the deep off Saqlain Mushtaq. The cagey spinner picked up a second five wicket haul to win the match for Pakistan and was most unlucky not to be named Man of the Match.

INDIA v PAKISTAN 1998-99

Feroz Shah Kotla, Delhi
4, 5, 6, 7, February, 1999
India won by 212 runs

India 252 (M.Azharuddin 67, S. Ramesh 60, Saqlain Mushtaq 5 for 94) and 339 (S.Ramesh 96, S.C. Ganguly 62 not out, Saqlain Mushtaq 5 for 122); Pakistan 172 and 207 (Saeed Anwar 69, A. Kumble 10 for 74).

This match belonged to India's leg spinner Kumble who became just the second bowler to take all ten wickets in an innings in 122 years of Test Cricket. Laker against Australia at Old Trafford in 1956 had been the first.

After Pakistan had been set a formidable 420 for victory Kumble had bowled six overs before lunch for 27 runs, without taking a wicket. After the interval he operated from the Pavilion end and sent down 20.3 overs in claiming 10 for 47.

At the end of his 26th over he had taken all nine and was on a hat-trick.

It has been suggested that the Indian captain Azharuddin, instructed Srinath to bowl wide of the stumps to give Kumble the chance to get the last wicket. Wasim Akram survived the hat-trick but was caught at short leg off Kumble's third ball. The leg spinner had all ten, and fourteen for the match.

Saqlain Mushtaq once again carried Pakistan's attack and became just the third bowler to take ten wickets in a Test in successive matches.

India's comprehensive victory was their first against Pakistan since 1979/1980 and enabled them to level the series.

WEST INDIES v AUSTRALIA 1998-99

Queen's Park Oval, Port-of-Spain, Trinidad
5, 6, 7, 8 March, 1999
Australia won by 312 runs.

Australia 269 (G.S. Blewett 58) and 261 (M.J. Slater 106); West Indies 167 (B.C. Lara 62, D.R.E. Joseph 50, G. D. Mc Grath 5 for 50) and 51 (G.D. McGrath 5 for 28)

West Indies second innings score of 51 was their lowest in 71 years of Test cricket and the winning margin of 312 was their third largest defeat by a runs margin.

By selecting both leg spinners, Warne and MacGill, Australia's new captain, S. Waugh, had no choice but to bat after calling correctly. Runs were hard to score with Gillespie and McGrath's 66 for the tenth wicket the best partnership of the innings. When Walsh trapped Healy in front he became the third bowler to reach 400 Test wickets. (Sir Richard Hadlee and Kapil Dev being the other two.)

West Indies found it even tougher to score with only debutant, Joseph, and Lara making worthwhile contributions. They put on 88 for the third wicket. With a lead of just over one hundred Slater grafted the only century of the match to leave the visitors well placed to draw first blood in the four Test series.

No one could have foreseen the dismal display of the home team. Only Jacobs reached double figures as West Indies was dismissed in 19.1 overs. McGrath returned match figures of 10 for 78, his first ten wicket haul in Tests.

The West Indies had lost their last 17 wickets for 69. The total of 11 ducks in the match equalled the Test record.

WEST INDIES v AUSTRALIA 1998-99

Kensington Oval, Bridgetown, Barbados
26, 27, 28, 29, 30 March, 1999
West Indies won by 1 wicket

Australia 490 (S.R. Waugh 199, R.T. Ponting 104, J.L. Langer 51) and 146 (C.A. Walsh 5 for 39); West Indies 329 (S.L. Camp bell 105, R.D. Jacobs 68) and 9 for 311 (B.C. Lara 153 not out, G.D. McGrath 5 for 92)

This will certainly be regarded as one of the greatest Test matches ever played.The West Indies amazing revival continuing thanks to its captain, Lara, and fast bowling giants, Ambrose and Walsh.

S. Waugh won his third toss for the series and was the backbone of Australia's commanding total of 490. With Ponting, he added a record 281 for the fifth wicket. Langer had provided valuable assistance in a century fourth wicket stand after Walsh and Ambrose had the visitors in early trouble at 3 for 36.

When the home side was 6 for 98 early on the third day it looked likely that they could be forced to follow-on. However, Campbell and Jacobs played with admirable application to post a 153 run partnership to avoid that possibility.

Walsh and Ambrose bowled West Indies back into the match with their typical sustained hostility. They were assisted by a lamentable Australian batting performance. Warne's 32 being top score. With a victory target of 308 West Indies had an outside chance. They started the final day 3 for 85 with Lara on 2. The skipper was the one man capable of pulling off the win although at 5 for 105 early on day five a West Indies victory seemed unlikely. Adams then helped Lara get to within 70 of victory but with 8 wickets lost and 60 still needed Australia looked certain winners. Ambrose stayed at the crease for 82 minutes while a further 54 runs were added. Last man Walsh survived five deliveries before Lara drove Gillespie to the cover boundary and a remarkable West Indies victory.

After being dismissed for a record low score of 51 in the first Test West Indies now led the four match series 2-1.

AUSTRALIA v PAKISTAN 1999-2000

Bellerive Oval, Hobart
18, 19, 20, 21, 22 November, 1999
Australia won by 4 wickets

Pakistan 222 (Mohammad Wasim 91) and 392 (Inzamamul Haq 118, Ijaz Ahmed 82, Saeed Anwar 78, S.K. Warne 5 for 110); Australia 246 (M.J. Slater 97, J.L. Langer 59, Saqlain Mushtaq 6 for 46) and 6 for 369 (A.C. Gilchrist 149 not out, J.L. Langer 127)

Australia achieved a memorable victory by scoring the third-highest fourth innings total to win a Test match.

After being sent in, Pakistan was dismissed for a modest 222 on the first day, Mohammad Wasim's 91, being the major contribution. Australia's reply was not much better although at 1 for 191 it looked as if the home side would gain a sizable first innings lead. Slater, Blewett and Langer had worked hard against hostile pace bowling from Wasim Akram, Shoaib Akhtar and Waqar Younis to establish Australia's sound position before spinner Saqlain Mushtaq ripped through the home side's line-up. Australia lost 9 for 55 as Saqlain captured 6 for 46.

Pakistan's top-order found batting conditions more comfortable in the second innings. A century from Inzamamul Haq, 82 from Ijaz Ahmed and 78 from Saeed Anwar placed the visitors in a winning position.

Needing 369 for victory Australia was soon in trouble at 3 for 81 and 5 for 126. Ponting, on his home ground, had been dismissed for a pair and his third nought in a row at Bellerive.

The home side started the final day requiring 181 to win with their last recognised batsmen, Langer and Gilchrist at the crease. In the first hour, Australian Umpire Parker, turned down a caught behind appeal on Langer from Wasim Akram's bowling. The Pakistan captain was visibly distressed by the decision. Umpire Parker had apologised to Langer the previous day for giving him wrongly out in the first innings. That was as close as the visitors came to achieving a breakthrough. Langer and Gilchrist put on 238 for the sixth wicket, a record for all countries against Pakistan. Gilchrist, playing in just his second Test match, gave a superb display of controlled aggressive batting to ensure the Australian win and an unbeatable lead in the series.

SOUTH AFRICA v ENGLAND 1999-2000

Centurion Park, Pretoria
14, 15 (no play), 16 (no play), 17 (no play), 18 January, 2000
England won by 2 wickets

South Africa 8 for 248 dec. (L. Klusener 61 not out) and innings forfeited; England innings forfeited and 8 for 251 (A.J. Stewart 73, M.P. Vaughan 69)

This was a history-making Test match as for the first time in Test cricket innings were forfeited.

South Africa had been sent in on a lively pitch under overcast skies and with only 45 overs play possible had reached 6 for 155. England's pace quartet, Gough, Caddick, Mullaly and Silverwood failed to exploit the conditions by bowling too short.

Unseasonal rain prevented play on the next three days. Before play started on the final day Cronje, the South African skipper, sought out his opposite number Hussain and suggested they 'make a game of it.' His offer was a target of 255 from 73 overs, on the basis that South Africa could score another 100 runs from 30 overs, followed by a double forfeiture of innings – England's first and South Africa's second. Hussain originally declined as he was concerned about the state of the pitch. However, he agreed to Cronje's offer after ten overs play on the final morning upon seeing how well the pitch was playing.

The equation changed slightly with England being set 249 from 76 overs. Stylish half centuries from Stewart and Vaughan took England close to victory before Gough hit the winning boundary with five balls remaining.

The cricket world was full of praise for Cronje's iniative with Hussain saying 'It was a very special thing that Hansie did and I hope he gets the credit he deserves. It certainly was a great finish to be part of.'

Five months after the match Cronje admitted receiving 53,000 Rand and a leather jacket from a bookmaker, who had urged him to initiate a positive result, rather than let the match finish in a draw. History would record that this win was the first Test in which match fixing was proven.

WEST INDIES v PAKISTAN 1999-2000

Recreation Ground, St. John's, Antigua
25, 26, 27, 28, 29 May 2000
West Indies won by 1 wicket

Pakistan 269 (Yousuf Youhana 103 not out, Inzamamul Haq 55, C.A. Walsh 5 for 83) and 219 (Inzamamul Haq 68); West Indies 273 (S. Chanderpaul 89, J.C. Adams 60, Wasim Akram 6 for 61) and 9 for 216 (W.W. Hinds 63, Wasim Akram 5 for 49)

West Indies won a home Test by the lowest possible margin, by wickets, for the second time in a year. However, unlike the win in Bridgetown against Australia, where the captain Lara was the hero, this time it was the new skipper, Adams, who guided his team to victory.

After being sent in Pakistan scored a modest 269. The consistent Yousuf Youhana top scored with his second century of the series while Pakistan's premier batsman Inzamamul Haq made 55. Leading Test wicket taker, Walsh, captured five wickets in an innings for the 19th time.

West Indies lead was restricted to just 4 runs after an inspired spell of bowling from Wasim Akram who claimed 6 for 4 from 28 deliveries and 5 for 1 from 22. The home team collapsing from 3 for 218 to be all out for 273.

Pakistan's second effort with the bat was disappointing although Inzamam, who top-scored with 68, was fined for lingering after being given out caught behind.

Despite missing Lara, 216 seemed a less than formidable target for the home side, but Wasim Akram had other ideas. His second five wicket haul reduced West Indies to 9 for 197.

Two umpiring decisions then appeared to go against the visitors. An appeal for a catch behind off Adams was turned down, Wasim Akram the unlucky bowler, while a claim for a bat-pad dismissal of Walsh off Saqlain Mushtaq was declined by Umpire Cowie of New Zealand. To make matters worse Saqlain bungled two run-out chances, the second with both Adams and Walsh stranded at the striker's end only for Saqlain to fail to gather the return.

Adams had occupied the crease for five and half hours in scoring 48 to guide his team home on a day that Antigua's favourite son, Sir Vivian Richards, was invested.

ENGLAND v WEST INDIES 2000

Lord's, London
29, 30 June, 1 July 2000
England won by 2 wickets
West Indies 267 (S.L. Campbell 82, W.W. Hinds 59) and 54 (A.R. Caddick 5 for 16); England 134 and 8 for 191 (C.A. Walsh 6 for 74).

England won a thrilling encounter just after 7pm, on the third day in a game that holds a unique place in Test cricket history. It is the only match in which part of all four innings occurred on the one day.

Acting captain, Stewart, sent the West Indies into bat under leaden skies. When the visitors had reached 1 for 162 shortly before tea the decision looked to have backfired. However, Gough and Cork with four wickets apiece bowled England back into the match. Caddick dismissed Walsh in the first over on the second day to restrict West Indies to a modest total of 267.

England's reply was deplorable! Only Stewart, White and Hick reached twenty as the home side succumbed, yet again, to the pace and hostility of Ambrose and Walsh, who both captured four wickets.

Stewart read the riot act in the England dressing room after the dismal batting display. His team's response was emphatic. West Indies was dismissed for just 54 with only Jacobs reaching double-figures. This was West Indies third lowest total in Tests and their lowest against England. Caddick bowled unchanged to capture 5 for 16 from 13 overs.

The target of 188 did not seem much but on a bouncy pitch and against two great campaigners it was never going to be easy. Atherton and Vaughan grafted their way cautiously through the morning session with every run being cheered as if it was the winner. Atherton top scored with 45, while Vaughan 41 was next best but after their departure the visitors got back on top and at 6 for 140 and 8 for 160 England was in real trouble.

The unlikely hero was Cork, who improvised his way to a match winning 33 not out and with admirable support from Caddick and Gough got England over the line in a nail biting finish.

AUSTRALIA v WEST INDIES 2000-01

W.A.C.A Ground, Perth
1, 2, 3, December 2000
Australia won by an innings and 27 runs
West Indies 196 (R.D. Jacobs 96 not out, W.W. Hinds 50) and 173 (B. Lee 5 for 61); Australia 8 for 396 dec. (M.E. Waugh 119, M.L. Hayden 69, A.C. Gilchrist 50)

This was a match made memorable for McGrath's hat-trick and Australia's record breaking 12th consecutive win.

After being sent in West Indies were reeling at 5 for 22 within the first hour's play including the McGrath hat-trick. The Australian spearhead removed Campbell, Lara and Adams to join Hughes, Fleming and Warne among recent Australian bowlers with Test hat-tricks. Jacobs and Hinds did offer some resistance but 196 was a disappointing total.

Australia declared with a lead of 200 runs after another elegant century from M. Waugh and contrasting half centuries from the watchful Hayden and the belligerent Gilchrist.

It was Lee who did most of the damage in West Indies' second innings as the visitors were bowled out for under 200 for the second time in the match.

Australia's 12th consecutive victory broke the record established by the West Indies in the mid 1980's. One of the champions of that team, Sir Vivian Richards, was among the first to congratulate the Australians.

INDIA v AUSTRALIA 2000-01

Wankhede Stadium, Mumbai
27, 28 February, 1 March 2001
Australia won by 10 wickets
India 176 (S. R. Tendulkar 76) and 219 (S.R. Tendulkar 65);
Australia 349 (A.C. Gilchrist 122, M.L. Hayden 119) and 0 for 47.

Australia was determined to win its first series in India since Lawry's team was successful in 1969-70. It made the perfect start with a comprehensive 10 wicket victory to take its total to 16 consecutive wins.

The Australia captain's bold decision to send India into bat paid dividends with the home side being dismissed for a disappointing 176. McGrath was at his miserly best conceding only one run per over while Warne enjoyed the first day conditions to claim 4 for 47. Tendulkar was the only Indian batsman to show his true form.

Early on the second day Australia was in deep trouble at 5 for 99 before Gilchrist joined Hayden. They put on 197 for the sixth wicket with Gilchrist reaching 122 off just 112 balls with 15 fours and four sixes. Hayden's 119 came from 172 deliveries with 18 boundaries and a six.

India's second innings was only a little better than the first. Once again Tendulkar was the only batsman to reach fifty although Ramesh 44 and Dravid 39 did offer some resistance. Tendulkar was out to a sensational catch by Ponting. He pulled a short ball from M. Waugh that hit Langer, who was fielding at short leg and stayed in the air long enough for Ponting to make the catch. In the match Agarkar was dismissed for his seventh duck in consecutive innings against Australia.

Hayden and Slater had no trouble scoring the 47 needed for victory on the third afternoon.

INDIA v AUSTRALIA 2000-01

Eden Gardens, Kolkata
11, 12, 13, 14, 15 March 2001
India won by 171 runs
Australia 445 (S.R. Waugh 110, M.L. Hayden 97, J.L. Langer 58, Harbhajan Singh 7 for 123) and 212 (M.L. Hayden 67, Harbhajan Singh 6 for 73); India 171 (V.V.S. Laxman 59) and 7 for 657 dec. (V.V.S. Laxman 281, R. Dravid 180)

This was one of the greatest Test matches ever played and featured one of the finest fightbacks in the history of the game. It was only the third time that a team had won after being asked to follow-on. That decision, in this writer's opinion, was the greatest misjudgement made by an Australian captain in the history of Test cricket. The game included several milestones for India. Laxman's 281 was a new record score while Harbhajan captured India's first hat-trick.

All that seemed a long way off as Australia cruised to 1 for 193 after winning the toss. Hayden again played with great responsibility and received admirable support from Slater and Langer. In was just after tea when Harbhajan struck, removing Ponting and Gilchrist leg before, with Warne going next ball caught at short leg. The twenty year old spinner had a hat-trick. On the second morning the Australian tail wagged. Gillespie and McGrath helping S. Waugh to reach his 25th Test century. The last two wickets had added 176.

India's reply was a disappointing 171. McGrath was again at his miserly best with Gillespie, Kasprowicz and Warne providing excellent support. On the third morning Laxman added 43 with Raju and Prasad and his good form prompted Ganguly to promote him to number three in the order for the second innings.

At the end of the third day India trailed by 20 runs with 6 second innings wickets in hand. Laxman, who had just reached his century, was batting with Dravid. This pair batted throughout the fourth day adding 335 from 90 overs. They were finally separated after a stand of 376, the second best partnership ever for India.

When Ganguly declared on the final morning Australia was left to bat for 75 overs to save the match or to score 384 to win. Slater and Hayden negotiated 23 overs but after Slater fell to Harbhajan wickets fell at regular intervals. The young off spinner had bowled India to a remarkable victory with 6 overs to spare. He finished the match with 13 for 196.

India had kept the series alive.

INDIA v AUSTRALIA 2000-01

Chidambaram Stadium, Chennai
18, 19, 20, 21, 22 March 2001
India won by 2 wickets
Australia 391 (M.L. Hayden 203, M.E. Waugh 70, Harbhajan Singh 7 for 133) and 264 (M.E. Waugh 57, Harbhajan Singh 8 for 84); India 501 (S.R. Tendulkar 126, S.S. Das 84, R. Dravid 81, V.V.S. Laxman 65, S. Ramesh 61) and 8 for 155 (V.V.S. Laxman 66)

The deciding Test of this enthralling series provided another memorable finish with both teams holding hope of victory at various stages.

The bare pitch prompted the teams to alter the balance of their attacks. Miller played for Australia while Bahutule and Kulkarni came into the Indian line-up giving them three spinners.

Australia won the toss for the third time in the series and once again relied on Hayden to provide the platform for a competitive total. The in-form opener was last man out for 203. His innings included 6 sixes, the most by an Australian in a Test innings. The Australian captain, S. Waugh, became the sixth batsman in Test history to be given out handled the ball. Harbhajan captured 6 for 26 as Australia tumbled from 3 for 340 to be all out for 391.

Five of India's top six batsman scored half centuries as they produced their most even batting performance of the series. Only Ganguly, 22, failed to reach fifty. Tendulkar was at his elegant best top scoring with 126. Warne was treated roughly, finishing with 2 for 140 from 42 overs.

Trailing by 110 Australia's openers worked hard to erase the deficit. Hayden's relative failure, he was dismissed for 35, was the breakthrough India needed and although most of the Australian top order got a start no one got the big score the team needed. This time Harbhajan took the last 6 wickets for 15 to finish with career best figures of 8 for 84 and 15 for 217 for the match.

With just 155 required India was cruising towards victory at 2 for 101 and Laxman and Tendulkar in full flight. However, some fine bowling from Miller, Gillespie and McGrath gave Australia a glimmer of hope. Fittingly it was Man of the Series, Harbhajan, who scored the winning runs.

India had regained the Border-Gavaskar Trophy while Australia had to wait for that elusive series victory in India.

SOUTH AFRICA v AUSTRALIA 2001-2002

Newlands, Cape Town
8, 9, 10, 11, 12 March 2002
Australia won by 4 wickets

South Africa 239 (A.J. Hall 70) and 473 (N.D. McKenzie 99, G. Kirsten 87, J.H Kallis 73, G.C. Smith 68, S.K. Warne 6 for 161); Australia 382 (A.C. Gilchrist 138 not out, M.L. Hayden 63, S.K. Warne 63) and 6 for 334 (R.T Ponting 100 not out, M.L. Hayden 96, J.L. Langer 58)

South Africa had been crushed in the first match of the series so introduced three new caps amongst the four changes for the second test.

Initially, it appeared if nothing much had changed as the home team slumped to 6 for 92 on the first afternoon. However, one of the new caps, Hall, scored a feisty 70 to give some credibility to the innings. When Australia's middle order collapsed mid-afternoon on the second day they still trailed by 54 with four wickets in hand. But Gilchrist, who had smashed a double century in the first Test came to the rescue again. He finished 138 not out and with Warne, who was playing his 100th test, added 132 for the seventh wicket.

South Africa batted with far more determination in the second innings. Four of the top six posted half-centuries. McKenzie top scored with 99. He was brilliantly run out by Martyn. Warne's marathon spell of 70 overs yielded six wickets.

Australia's target of 331 was the tenth highest in Test history. Langer and Hayden laid the foundation for victory with a century opening stand. Hayden and Ponting consolidated before Ponting guided the visitor's home. He hit Adams for six with three needed which brought up another timely century for Australia's number three.

NEW ZEALAND v ENGLAND 2001-2002

Lancaster Park, Christchurch
13, 14, 15, 16 March 2002
England won by 98 runs

England 228 (N. Hussain 106) and 6 for 468 dec. (G.P. Thorpe 200 not out, A. Flintoff 137); New Zealand 147 (M.J. Hoggard 7 for 63) and 451 (N.J. Astle 222, M.H. Richardson 76, A.R. Caddick 6 for 122).

Even though England had a relatively easy victory this Test will always be remembered as Astle's match.

England batted first after Hussain called correctly and Cairns then proceeded to remove Trescothick and Butcher in his first over without a run on the board. The skipper's tenth Test century was the only shinning light in a dismal England batting performance. Unfortunately for New Zealand Cairns limped off with an injured right knee after bowling fifteen overs.

Hussain's skill with the bat was matched by Hoggard's superb spell of sharp, swing bowling which netted him 7 for 63 and gave the visitors a first innings lead of 81.

With half the team out England's lead was only 187 but that was the cue for Thorpe and Flintoff to smash the depleted Kiwi attack to all points of the compass. Thorpe posted his double-century from 231 deliveries while Flintoff, whose previous best effort in Test cricket was 42 reached his maiden Test hundred from 114 balls. Their partnership of 281 was a new record for England against all countries. When Flintoff departed the game appeared to be well out of New Zealand's reach.

Richardson and Fleming had made useful contributions to the top order but when the injured Cairns hobbled out at number eleven the home team still needed 217 to win with Astle on 134. He had reached his century from 114 deliveries but that gave no indication of what was to follow. With some of the cleanest hitting ever seen in Test cricket he raced from 101 to 200 in only 39 balls. His was the fastest double-century in Test history coming from just 153 deliveries. Australia's Gilchrist had set the previous best of 212 in South Africa just three weeks before Astle's onslaught. He was eventually dismissed for 222 leaving the Kiwis 98 short of the victory target.

ENGLAND v INDIA 2002

Headingley, Leeds
22, 23, 24, 25, 26 August 2002
India won by an innings and 46 runs

India 8 for 628 dec. (S.R. Tendulkar 193, R. Dravid 148, S.C. Ganguly 128, S.B. Bangar 68); England 273 (A.J. Stewart 78 not out, M.P. Vaughan 61) and 309 (N. Hussain 110).

This was the third match in a four test series with the hosts holding a 1 nil lead.

India defied convention by picking two spinners for the seamer friendly Headingley pitch and the Indian captain Ganguly continued the defiance by deciding to bat after calling correctly.

The decision was vindicated by the visitor's superb batting which resulted in three of the top order scoring centuries before the declaration was made on the third morning, with the total over 600. Dravid and Bangar played with the utmost care on the first day allowing Tendulkar and Ganguly to play with more freedom on the second. They scored 96 from the first 11 overs of the third new ball, and added a record 249 for the fourth wicket. It was India's highest total against England.

Only Stewart and Vaughan, who both scored half centuries, offered any real resistance to the Indian attack. The follow-on was enforced with England trailing by 355. The decision to play the two spinners paid dividends; both Kumble and Harbhajan took three wickets.

The home team's second innings effort was only marginally better than the first although at the end of the fourth day with skipper, Hussain 90 and Stewart 40, there was a glimmer of hope that the match could be saved. But it was not to be with Hussain falling shortly after reaching his century and then Flintoff and Stewart going two runs later. The Indian spinners picked up five second innings wickets. Eleven for the match justified the gamble and ensured the series was tied-up.

PAKISTAN v AUSTRALIA 2002-03

P. Saravanamuttu Stadium, Colombo
3, 4, 5, 6, 7, October 2002
Australia won by 41 runs.

Australia 467 (R.T. Ponting 141, J.L. Langer 72, D.R. Martyn 67, A.C. Gilchrist 66 not out, M.E. Waugh 55) and 127 (Shoaib Akhtar 5 for 21); Pakistan 279 (Faisal Iqbal 83, Rashid Latif 66, Younis Khan 58, S.K. Warne 7 for 94) and 274 (Taufeeq Umar 88, Younis Khan 51)

This series was played at a neutral venue because of Pakistan's proximity to Afghanistan and the aftermarth of the Karachi suicide bombing that had cut short New Zealand's tour in May. Colombo was chosen for the first Test and Sharjah for the last two.

Despite the Australian captain's pre-match concern regarding the pitch it played remarkably well. Ponting was the major contributor, with 141 of Australia's formidable 467. Langer, Martyn, Gilchrist and M. Waugh all contributed half centuries. The total may have been greater but for some inspired reverse swing by Shoaib Akhtar. Australia's last five wickets fell for just 10 runs.

Pakistan avoided the follow-on after a determined sixth wicket partnership between Faisal Iqbal and Rashid Latif, which added 103. Warne was at his tantalising best in claiming 7 for 94.

Australia's lead had reached 249 with all ten wickets in hand when Shoaib Akhtar struck. Bowling with lighting pace he dismissed Ponting and the Waugh brothers in four balls before knocking over Gilchrist in his next over. Australia lost 10 for 66 to be dismissed for 127 leaving Pakistan with a target of 316.

When rain washed out the final session of the fourth day Pakistan needed 137 to win with seven wickets in hand. After reaching his second half-century of the match Younis Khan was trapped in front by Warne and then McGrath and Gillespie ripped through the lower order with the new ball. Warne picked up four second innings wickets to finish with eleven for the match.

The relatively inexperienced Pakistan team had nearly pulled off a major upset while the uncompromising Australians had to dig deep to win the Test.

WEST INDIES v AUSTRALIA 2002-03

Recreation Ground, St John's, Antigua
9, 10, 11, 12, 13, May 2003
West Indies won by 3 wickets

Australia 240 (J.J.C. Lawson 7 for 78) and 417 (M.L. Hayden 177, J.L. Langer 111); West Indies 240 (B.C. Lara 68) and 7 for 418 (R.K. Sarwan 105, S. Chanderpaul 104, B.C. Lara 60)

Australia entered the final match of the series three nil up and looking for its first clean sweep in the Caribbean.

The Test was played on the fastest and bounciest pitch of the series. Lawson made the most of the conditions to return career best figures of 7 for 78 as Australia was dismissed for a modest 240. However, by the fourth day, he had been reported to the I.C.C by match referee Procter, for a suspect action.

West Indies also scored 240, the seventh time first-innings scores had been equal in Test history. During his innings of 68, Lara argued furiously with the Australians, particularly the captain, S. Waugh.

With openers Langer and Hayden both scoring centuries and Lawson not bowling because of a back strain Australia looked likely to score in excess of 500 in its second innings but Dillon bowled tirelessly to capture 4 for 112 from 29 overs.

Nevertheless, the target of 418 looked beyond West Indies although the home team had over two days in which to score the required runs. The record fourth innings score to win a Test had been India's 406 at Port-of-Spain in 1975-76.

When Lee dismissed Sarwan and Jacobs with successive deliveries Australia was in the box set. West Indies needed 130 with four wickets in hand. Sarwan had scored a superb century and been involved in an angry verbal exchange with McGrath. However, Chanderpaul and Banks then batted through until stumps with the home side requiring 47 with four wickets in hand.

Chanderpaul fell after the addition of 1 run but Banks and Drakes got the West Indies home. A new record run chase had been achieved which prevented an Australian clean sweep.

ENGLAND v SOUTH AFRICA 2003

Kennington Oval, London
4, 5, 6, 7, 8 September 2003
England won by 9 wickets

South Africa 484 (H.H. Gibbs 183, G. Kirsten 90, J.H. Kallis 66, S.M. Pollock 66 not out) and 229; England 9 for 604 dec. (M.E. Trescothick 219, G.P Thorpe 124, A. Flintoff 95) and 1 for 110 (M.E. Trescothick 69 not out)

This was the final Test of a five match series with South Africa leading two one.

Gibbs and Kirsten batted South Africa into a formidable position on the first day with a second wicket partnership of 227. Gibbs reached his century with 20 fours and a six. (Only Flintoff had done better.) The visitors total of 484 should have been higher – there were three run-outs including Smith and Kallis, who was backing up at the bowler's end.

Thorpe, playing his first Test for over a year, joined Trescothick with England 2 for 78. They added 268 for the third wicket to restore England's position. Flintoff put the icing on the cake with a swashbuckling 95. In a partnership of 99 for the ninth wicket Harmison scored three.

In the second innings five South Africans scored at least 25 but no one reached fifty and they were bowled out for 229. Harmison and Bicknell both claimed four wickets. Bicknell had been recalled for the previous match after an absence of more than ten years.

England polished off the 110 required in the 23rd over. The match provided a fitting finale to the England match record holder, Alec Stewart, who retired after 133 Tests.

AUSTRALIA v ZIMBABWE 2003-04

W.A.C.A. Ground, Perth
9, 10, 11, 12, 13 October 2003
Australia won by an innings and 175 runs

Australia 6 for 735 dec. (M.L. Hayden 380, A.C. Gilchrist 113 not out, S.R. Waugh 78, D. R. Martyn 53); Zimbabwe 239 (T.R. Gripper 53) and 321 (H.H. Streak 71 not out, M.A. Vermeulen 63, S.M. Ervine 53)

This was the first Test played by Zimbabwe on Australian soil.

Streak sent the home side in on an unusually batsman- friendly Perth pitch. The first two sessions gave no indication of what was to come with Hayden on 76 at tea. His hundred was posted in just over five hours from 210 balls. From that point he increased the tempo moving from 100 to 150 in just 32 deliveries. At the end of the first day Hayden was 183 with Australia 3 for 368.

At the start of the second day his immediate goal was 203, his previous best Test score at Chennai in 2001. When that milestone was passed he moved onto a triple century. Hayden had become the fifth Australian to score 300 in a Test innings. He gave his first chance at 335, after he had passed Bradman and Taylor's Australian record score of 334, when Gripper dropped a skied ball at deep mid wicket.

Hayden eventually broke Lara's previous record of 375 three balls before tea and fell to Gripper three balls after the interval for 380. He had faced 437 balls and hit 38 fours and 11 sixes. Another superb Gilchrist century was completely overshadowed by Hayden's exploits.

The visitors were not able to cope with Australia's attack, even though it was without both McGrath and Warne, and the home team wrapped up the match early on the final day.

AUSTRALIA v INDIA 2003-04

Sydney Cricket Ground
2, 3, 4, 5, 6 January 2004
Match Drawn

India 7 for 705 dec. (S.R. Tendulkar 241 not out, V.V. S. Laxman 178, V. Sehwag 72, P.A. Patel 62) and 2 for 211 dec. (R. Dravid 91 not out, S.R. Tendulkar 60 not out); Australia 474 (S.M. Katich 125, J.L. Langer 117, M.L. Hayden 67, A. Kumble 8 for 141) and 6 for 357 (S.R. Waugh 80, S.M. Katich 77 not out).

This was the final match of a four Test series that stood one all. It was also the last of the record 168 Tests played by the Australian captain S. Waugh.

Ganguly called correctly, India proceded to dominate with the bat on a magnificent pitch. Tendulkar made the Australians pay for his earlier run of outs with a disciplined double century. He refused to play any flashy off-side strokes, thus 188 of his runs came on the leg side. Laxman relished the Sydney conditions again and with Tendulkar added 353 for the fourth wicket. Without McGrath and Warne Australia's attack really struggled. India continued batting on the third day until the score reached 700 and Lee had conceded more than 200 runs. India's total of 705 was their highest ever Test score and the second highest conceded by Australia.

Langer and Katich scored centuries in Australia's reply and Waugh a cameo of 40 but the feeling was that he would get a second innings later in the match. Kumble's skill and persistence was rewarded with an 8 wicket haul.

Ganguly did not enforce the follow-on, batting again to put the match out of Australia's reach. Tendulkar took his match aggregate to 301 without being dismissed.

Waugh's last innings included 15 sparkling boundaries in a knock of 80 that prevented India from winning the match and the series. With the series tied India retained the Border-Gavaskar Trophy.

The aggregate attendance of 181,063 was the second highest ever for a Sydney Test match. The Ashes Test of 1946-47 was greater but that was played over six days.

SRI LANKA v AUSTRALIA 2003-04

Asgiriya Stadium, Kandy
16, 17, 18, 19, 20 March 2004
Australia won by 27 runs

Australia 120 (M.L. Hayden 54) and 442 (D.R. Martyn 161, A.C. Gilchrist 144, M.Muralidaran 5 for 173); Sri Lanka 211 (W.P.U.J.C. Vaas 68 not out, S.K. Warne 5 for 65) and 324 (S.T. Jayasuriya 131, S.K. Warne 5 for 90).

On a pitch that offered the faster bowlers some movement off the seam Australia chose to bat first. Only Hayden, 54, scored more than 18. The total of 120 was Australia's lowest ever score against Sri Lanka and their worst since the 104 against England at Kennington Oval in 1997. Zoysa and Muralidaran both picked up four wickets.

Sri Lanka's batsmen failed to capitalise on the good work of their bowlers. By stumps they were 7 for 92. Sri Lanka's batting had been no better than the visitors. On the second morning Vaas, with the assistance of Lokuarachchi and Muralidaran gave the home team a lead of 91. Vaas and Muralidaran putting on 79 for the last wicket, a new record for Sri Lanka. Warne picked up another 5 wicket haul while Kasprowicz got 4.

At 2 for 26 Australia was in trouble but the out-of-form Gilchrist, promoted to number three because of the captain's ricked back, produced another brilliant century. After scores of 4, 0 and 0 earlier in the series, he added 200 with Martyn for the third wicket. Martyn was at the crease for nearly nine hours while 416 runs were scored. His patient, career-high innings gave the visitors some hope.

Sri Lanka required 352 to win the Test and level the series. For part of the fourth afternoon Jayasuriya looked likely to do it off his own bat as he raced to a run-a-ball century, however, his dismissal turned the game back in Australia's favour.

At the start of the final day the home team needed 51 runs with 3 wickets in hand. In the third over, Vaas was caught in the deep to snuff out Sri Lanka's quest. Warne captured 5 wickets in an innings. This was the fourth time he had achieved this in four innings of a series. Gillespie picked up four.

Australia's ability under pressure again proved the difference as they took an unbeatable 2 nil lead in the series.

WEST INDIES v ENGLAND 2003-04

Recreation Ground, St John's, Antigua
10, 11, 12, 13, 14 April 2004
Match Drawn

West Indies 5 for 751 dec. (B.C. Lara 400 not out, R.D. Jacobs 107 not out, R.R. Sarwan 90, C.H. Gayle 69); England 285 (A. Flintoff 102 not out, M.A. Butcher 52) and 5 for 422 (M.P. Vaughan 140, M.E. Trescothick 88, M.A. Butcher 61, N. Hussain 56)

Lara reclaimed his position as the scorer of Test cricket's highest innings from Australia's Hayden, who had made 380 against Zimbabwe in October 2003. In doing so, Lara become the first man to reach 400 in a Test innings. It was almost ten years to the day and on the same ground, that Lara had first secured the Test individual record score from Sir Garfield Sobers.

West Indies entered the match 3 nil down in the series. They were determined to avoid their first whitewash in a home series, as they had been able to do twelve months earlier against Australia. Lara was averaging 16 with a highest score of 36 and his captaincy was again under critical scrutiny.

On a belter of a pitch that had been prepared under the supervision of the former fast bowling great, Andy Roberts, Lara came to the crease with 33 runs on the board. In all, he batted for two minutes short of 13 hours and faced 582 balls, hitting four sixes and 43 fours. In the innings of 375 he had faced 538 deliveries hitting 45 boundaries and no sixes.

Lara was 234 when he was joined by the experienced wicketkeeper-batsman Jacobs. Together they put on 282, a sixth wicket record for West Indies. Lara lifted Batty over long-on for six to bring himself level with Hayden's 380. He swept the next ball to the fine-leg boundary to regain the record, becoming the first batsman to have held it twice. When the declaration was made England had conceded more than 750 in a Test innings for the first time.

A gritty century from Flintoff was not enough to avoid the follow-on but the visitors saved their best batting of the series to last and were able to comfortably hold on to draw the match and retain the Wisden Trophy.

INDIA v AUSTRALIA 2004-05

Vidarbha Cricket Association Ground, Nagpur
26, 27, 28, 29 October, 2004
Australia won by 342 runs

Australia 398 (D.R. Martyn 114, M.J. Clarke 91, D.S. Lehmann 70) and 5 for 329 dec. (S.M. Katich 99, D.R. Martyn 97, M.J. Clarke 73); India 185 (M.Kaif 55, J.N. Gillespie 5 for 56) and 200 (V. Sehwag 58)

Against the wishes of the Indian captain, Ganguly, a grassy pitch had been prepared for this third Test. It transpired that Ganguly, with an injury, and Harbhajan Singh, an illness, withdrew from the team on the morning of the match.

Australia took full advantage of winning the toss to compile 398. Martyn scored another elegant century and received great support from Lehmann and the youthful Clarke.

Despite the return of Tendulkar the Indian line-up could not handle the superb bowling of Australia's new ball combination, McGrath and Gillespie. Just as they had earlier in the series, the visitors adopted a sensible conservative approach. Unlike the previous tour, they did not enforce the follow-on. Katich, Martyn and Clarke all scored freely to allow the declaration to be made on the fourth morning.

India's victory target was 543. Again the home team's batting succumbed to the Australian pace bowlers. Gillespie claimed 4 wickets, making nine for the match while McGrath and Kasprowicz got 2 apiece. Tendulkar, Dravid and Laxman scored just 6 runs between them.

Australia had completely outplayed their hosts to win a series for the first time in India since 1969-70 and regain the Border–Gavaskar Trophy.

WEST INDIES v SOUTH AFRICA 2004-05

Recreation Ground, St John's, Antigua
29, 30 April, 1, 2, 3, May 2005
Match Drawn

South Africa 6 for 588 dec. (J.H. Kallis 147, A.G. Prince 131, G.C. Smith 126, A.B. de Villiers 114) and 1 for 127 (H.H. Dippenaar 56 not out, G.C. Smith 50 not out); West Indies 747 (C.H. Gayle 317, R.R. Sarwan 127, S. Chanderpaul 127, D.J.J. Bravo 107)

Antigua's Recreation Ground pitch must be the most batsman-friendly in Test Cricket. It was at its friendliest for the final Test of a four match series with the visitors holding a two nil lead.

Smith and de Villiers shared an opening stand of 245 before Kallis and Prince established a fifth wicket record partnership of 267 for South Africa. Kallis passed G. Kirsten as South Africa's leading Test run scorer and his innings of 147 was his 22nd Test century, one more than Kirsten.

Gayle's mighty 317 passed Bradman's 299 not out as the highest innings against South Africa. With Sarwan he added 331 for the second wicket. Bravo's maiden Test century was the eighth of the match, the most ever in a Test. He was dismissed by the wicketkeeper Boucher as all eleven South Africans bowled in West Indies' innings. This was the fourth occasion this had occurred in a Test.

As the match was petering out to a tame draw, Bravo accused South African captain, Smith, of racism. The charge was dismissed by match referee, Crowe, with Smith demanding an apology and threatening legal action.

SRI LANKA v SOUTH AFRICA 2006-07

Sinhalese Sports Club, Colombo
27, 28, 29, 30, 31 July, 2006
Sri Lanka won by an innings and 153 runs

South Africa 169 (A.B. de Villiers 65) and 434 (J.A. Rudolph 90, M.V. Boucher 85, A.J. Hall 64, A. G. Prince 61, M. Muralidaran 6 for 131); Sri Lanka 5 for 756 dec. D.P.M.D. Jayawardene 374, K.C. Sangakkara 287)

This was the first Test of a two match series and will always be remembered for the all-time record partnership in Test cricket.

South Africa's new skipper, Prince, won the toss and had no hesitation in batting first on a slow pitch. Excellent swing bowling from Fernando and the usual crafty fare from Muralidaran restricted South Africa to a disappointing 169. Fernando and Muralidaran captured four wickets apiece.

After the Sri Lankan openers Tharanga and Jayasuriya fell cheaply, Sangakkara and M. Jayawardene posted half-centuries by stumps to reduce the deficit to 41. Sangakkara and Jayawardene batted throughout the second day. Both batsmen reached their double centuries in the final session, and by the close the partnership had produced 471 runs.

They continued in similar fashion until after lunch on the third day. Sangakkara was finally dismissed for 287 in a new Test best ever partnership of 624. Jayasuriya and Mahanama had scored 576 for Sri Lanka against India in 1997–98. Jayawardene went on to pass Jayasuriya's 340 as the highest score by a Sri Lankan batsman in a Test innings, before he was out for 374 – just 26 runs short of Lara's record Test score of 400 not out.

South Africa batted with more determination in its second innings but was not able to survive for more than two days against the wily Muralidaran, who took ten wickets in a Test for the seventeenth time.

A comfortable win to Sri Lanka in a memorable record-breaking match.

SRI LANKA v SOUTH AFRICA 2006-07

P. Saravanamuttu Stadium, Colombo
4, 5, 6, 7, 8, August 2006
Sri Lanka won by 1 wicket

South Africa 361 (A.B. de Villers 95, A.G. Prince 86, S.M. Pollock 57 not out, M.Muralidaran 5 for 128) and 311 (H.H. Gibbs 92, M.V. Boucher 65, M. Muralidaran 7 for 97); Sri Lanka 321 (W.P.U.J.C. Vaas 64, C.K. Kapugedera 63, M.F. Maharoof 56, D.W. Steyn 5 for 82) and 9 for 352 (D.P.M.D. Jayawardene 123, Jayasuriya 73)

Both teams were able to include their most experienced fast bowlers – Pollock for South Africa and Vaas for Sri Lanka.

After a poor start, South Africa recovered from 1 for 0, 2 for 4 and 3 for 31 to reach 361. Skipper, Prince 86, and de Villiers 95 led the way, while Pollock hit lustily at the end. Muralidaran picked up his 55th five wicket haul in an innings.

Sri Lanka struggled in reply although the lower order fought back well. The home team recovered from 5 for 86 to reach 321.

With a lead of 40, South Africa worked hard to consolidate its position. Gibbs returned to form with a patient 92 while keeper Boucher scored 65. However, Muralidaran was able to weave his magic again with the wily off-spinner picking up 7 second innings wickets. It was his 18th ten wicket haul in a Test.

Sri Lanka required 352 in five sessions. Jayasuriya got them off to a flying start with a run-a-ball 73 before the skipper, M. Jayawardene, played with great responsibility to post his 16th Test century. Fortunes fluctuated on the final day before Sri Lanka reached the target with the last pair, Maharoof and Malinga, at the crease.

It was a new record fourth innings score for Sri Lanka to win a Test and gave them a 2–0 series win.

SRI LANKA v SOUTH AFRICA 2006-07 (First Test)

Sinhalese Sports Club Ground, Colombo, July 27, 28, 29, 30, 31, 2006. Sri Lanka won by an innings & 153 runs.

SOUTH AFRICA

H.H.Gibbs	b Fernando	19	(7)	c & b Muralidaran	18
A.J.Hall	b Fernando	17	(2)	lbw b Muralidaran	64
J.A.Rudolph	c H.A.P.W.Jayawardene b Maharoof	29	(1)	c Kapugedera b Fernando	90
H.M.Amla	st H.A.P.W.Jayawardene b Muralidaran	19	(3)	lbw b Fernando	2
A.G.Prince*	c H.A.P.W.Jayawardene b Maharoof	1	(4)	c D.P.M.D.Jayawardene b Muralidaran	61
A.B.de Villiers	c Kapugedera b Muralidaran	65	(5)	lbw b Muralidaran	24
M.V.Boucher†	c Jayasuriya b Muralidaran	4	(6)	c & b Jayasuriya	85
N.Boje	lbw b Muralidaran	5	(8)	not out	33
A.Nel	lbw b.Fernando	0	(9)	b Muralidaran	0
D.W.Steyn	b.Fernando	0	(10)	b Muralidaran	4
M.Ntini	not out	0	(11)	b Malinga	16
Extras	(B 4, LB 6)	10		(B 11, LB 4, NB 20, W 2)	37
Total		**169**			**434**

SRI LANKA

W.U.Tharanga	c Boucher b Steyn	7
S.T.Jayasuriya	lbw b Steyn	4
K.C.Sangakkara	c Boucher b Hall	287
D.P.M.D.Jayawardene*	b Nel	374
T.M.Dilshan	lbw b Steyn	45
C.K.Kapugedera	not out	1
H.A.P.W.Jayawardene†		
M.F.Maharoof		
S.L.Malinga		
C.R.D.Fernando		
M.Muralidaran		
Extras	(B 17, LB 5, NB 8, W 8)	38
Total	**5 wickets declared**	**756**

SRI LANKA	O	M	R	W		O	M	R	W
Malinga	10	2	38	0	Malinga	16.2	0	85	1
Maharoof	9	1	32	2	Maharoof	15	3	48	0
Fernando	13	2	48	4	Fernando	24	6	69	2
Muralidaran	18.2	6	41	4	Muralidaran	64	11	131	6
					Dilshan	4	1	10	0
					Jayasuriya	34	8	76	1

SOUTH AFRICA	O	M	R	W	O	M	R	W
Ntini	31	3	97	0				
Steyn	26	1	129	3				
Nel	25.1	2	114	1				
Hall	25	2	99	1				
Boje	65	5	221	0				
Rudolph	7	0	45	0				
Prince	2	0	7	0				
de Villiers	4	0	22	0				

FALL OF WICKETS

Wkt	SA 1st	SL 1st	SA 2nd	SL 2nd
1st	32	6	165	-
2nd	45	14	171	-
3rd	78	638	185	-
4th	80	751	234	-
5th	112	756	312	-
6th	128	-	350	-
7th	148	-	401	-
8th	151	-	404	-
9th	151	-	412	-
10th	169	-	434	-

Umpires: M.R.Benson and B.F.Bowden.

SRI LANKA v SOUTH AFRICA 2006-07 (Second Test)

P.Saravanamuttu Stadium, Colombo, August 4, 5, 6, 7, 8, 2006. Sri Lanka won by 1 wicket.

SOUTH AFRICA

H.H.Gibbs	lbw b Vaas	0	(1)	c Jayasuriya b Muralidaran	92
A.J.Hall	c Dilshan b Malinga	0	(2)	c H.A.P.W.Jayawardene b Maharoof	32
J.A.Rudolph	b Malinga	13	(3)	run out (Kapugedera)	15
H.M.Amla	lbw b Muralidaran	40	(4)	run out (Kapugedera)	8
A.G.Prince*	c H.A.P.W.Jayawardene b Muralidaran	86	(5)	c & b Muralidaran	17
A.B.de Villiers	c H.A.P.W.Jayawardene b Malinga	95	(6)	c Dilshan b Muralidaran	33
M.V.Boucher†	b Muralidaran	32	(7)	c .Dilshan b Muralidaran	65
S.M.Pollock	not out	57	(8)	c Tharanga b Muralidaran	14
N.Boje	c Sangakkara b Maharoof	11	(9)	c H.A.P.W.Jayawardene b Muralidaran	15
D.W.Steyn	c Jayasuriya b Muralidaran	6	(10)	lbw b M.Muralidaran	0
M.Ntini	c Maharoof b Muralidaran	13	(11)	not out	5
Extras	(NB 8)	8		(B 9, LB 4, NB 1, W 1)	15
Total		**361**			**311**

SRI LANKA

W.U.Tharanga	c Boje b Ntini	2	(1)	c Gibbs b Ntini	0
S.T.Jayasuriya	c Gibbs b Ntini	47	(2)	c Amla b Boje	73
K.C.Sangakkara	c Amla b Ntini	14	(3)	c Amla b Pollock	39
D.P.M.D.Jayawardene*	c Boucher b Steyn	13	(4)	c Gibbs b Boje	123
T.M.Dilshan	b Ntini	4	(5)	c Gibbs b Boje	18
C.K.Kapugedera	b Boje	63	(6)	c de Villiers b Boje	13
H.A.P.W.Jayawardene†	b Steyn	42	(7)	lbw b Hall	30
M.F.Maharoof	b Steyn	56	(8)	not out	29
W.P.U.J.C.Vaas	c Boucher b Steyn	64	(9)	c de Villiers b Hall	4
S.L.Malinga	not out	8	(11)	not out	1
M.Muralidaran	c Hall b Steyn	0	(10)	b Hall	2
Extras	(LB 1, NB 5, W 2)	8		(B 4, LB 8, NB 4, W 4)	20
Total		**321**		**9 wickets**	**352**

SRI LANKA	O	M	R	W		O	M	R	W		FALL OF WICKETS			
Vaas	18	4	71	1	Vaas	19	4	53	0		SA	SL	SA	SL
Malinga	18	4	81	3	Malinga	12	1	55	0	Wkt	1st	1st	2nd	2nd
Muralidaran	33.5	2	128	5	Maharoof	21	3	53	1	1st	0	16	76	12
Maharoof	15	2	52	1	Muralidaran	46.5	12	97	7	2nd	4	43	119	94
Jayasuriya	5	0	29	0	Jayasuriya	9	0	40	0	3rd	31	74	131	121
										4th	70	85	161	164
SOUTH AFRICA	O	M	R	W		O	M	R	W	5th	231	86	206	201
Ntini	21	3	84	4	Ntini	7.2	2	13	1	6th	256	191	207	279
Steyn	13.1	1	82	5	Steyn	22.4	2	81	0	7th	273	191	235	341
Pollock	16	4	52	0	Boje	39.3	11	111	4	8th	307	308	280	348
Hall	15	7	31	0	Pollock	19	2	60	1	9th	327	317	282	350
Boje	20	6	71	1	Hall	25	3	75	3	10th	361	321	311	-

Umpires: Aleem Dar and B.F.Bowden

Part 2

Test Cricket Lists

From great cricketing families to unusual dismissals; from cricketers who batted right-handed and bowled left-armed, to games that were abandoned without a ball being bowled. This section is full of fascinating Test trivia to interest and astound all cricket buffs.

FIRSTS

First ball bowled in Test cricket — by A.Shaw (England) v Australia from eastern end at Melbourne in 1876-77.

First run in Test cricket — C.Bannerman (Australia) from the second ball of A.Shaw's first over (above).

First wicket taken in Test cricket — by A.Hill (England) when he clean-bowled N.Thompson (Australia) at Melbourne in 1876-77. (The 4th over bowled in Test cricket).

First 5 wickets in an innings haul — W.E.Midwinter (Australia) 5 for 78 v England at Melbourne in 1876-77.

First 10 wickets in match haul — F.R.Spofforth (Australia) 6 for 48 and 7 for 62 v England at Melbourne in 1878-79.

First catch taken in Test cricket — A.Hill (England) caught Australian batsman T.P.Horan at third man, England v Australia at Melbourne in 1876-77.

First stumping completed in Test cricket — J.M.Blackham (Australia) stumped England's A.Shaw for 2 in the 2nd innings of the first-ever Test match at Melbourne in 1876-77.

First boundary hit — by T.P.Horan (Australia) v England at Melbourne in 1876-77 (a snick through slips).

First 100 partnership — W.G.Grace (152) and A.P.Lucas (55) put on 120 for England's 2nd wicket v Australia at The Oval in 1880.

First century — C.Bannerman (Australia) 165 retired hurt v England at Melbourne in 1876-77. His brother A.C.Bannerman was the first to score a Test ninety. He made 94 v England in the first innings of the Third Test at Sydney in 1882-83 – the twelfth Test ever played. He scored a second ninety (91) in Tests and did not score a century in his 50 Test innings. However, he was the first Australian to score 1000 Test runs and the second player, after England's A.Shrewsbury, to reach that milestone. Shrewsbury reached 1000 runs in the First Test at Lord's in 1893 and Bannerman reached it in the Second Test at The Oval.

It was similarly a close race to 100 Test wickets. England's J.Briggs was the first to reach this mark, in the Fourth Test against Australia at Sydney in 1894-95. He took four wickets in Australia's only innings — the last of these (A.H.Jarvis), which was the second-last of Australia's to fall, was his 100th. In England's first innings C.T.B.Turner took three wickets — the last of these (R.Peel) being his 100th.

First to score fifty in each innings — 52 and 63 G.Ulyett (England) v Australia at Melbourne in 1876-77. (Ulyett, at Melbourne, in 1881-82 became the first to score a century and a 50 in the same Test.)

First Hat-trick in Test cricket — F.R.Spofforth (Australia) in dismissing England batsmen V.P.F.A.Royle (bowled), F.A.McKinnon (bowled) and T.Emmett (caught by T.P.Horan) at Melbourne in 1878-79.

First batsman to carry his bat through a completed innings — A.B.Tancred (South Africa) 26* from a team total of 47 against England at Cape Town in 1888-89.

First player to take eight wickets in a Test innings and finish on the losing side was G.A.Lohmann — 8 for 58 for England v Australia at Sydney in 1891-92. (In the same Test, J.Briggs became the first player to take a hat-trick and finish on the losing side.)

First declaration in Test cricket — A.E.Stoddart (England) 8 for 234 v Australia at Lord's in 1893. (The match was drawn).

First player to score a century on his Test debut in two countries — H.Graham (Australia) 107 v England at Lord's in 1893 and 105 v England at Sydney in 1894-95.

First century before lunch — K.S.Ranjitsinhji (England) v Australia at Manchester in 1896. 'Ranji', the first Indian to play Test cricket, added 113 runs to his overnight score of 41 and finished not out on 154 in his First Test.

First six (without overthrows) in a Test — J.Darling (Australia) v England at Adelaide in 1897-98. To be a six in those early days the ball had to be hit out of the ground and not merely over the boundary.

First bowler to be 'no-balled' for throwing — E.Jones (Australia) — called by umpire J.Phillips in the match against England played at Melbourne in 1897-98.

First player to take 13 wickets in a Test and finish on the losing side was S.F.Barnes — 13 for 163 (6 for 42 and 7 for 121) England v Australia at Melbourne in 1901-02.

First Sunday Test match play — India v England 1933-34 at Bombay (First Test).

Australia defeated England 3 matches to 2 in 1936-37. This is the only time a country had won a Test series after losing the first two matches.

The Third Test at Melbourne in 1946-47 between Australia and England was the first drawn match in Australia since 1881-82. (All Tests in Australia from 1882-83 to 1936-37 were played to a finish.)

The first time an extra day was added to a Test match was New Zealand v England at Christchurch in 1946-47, after the third had been washed out but rain prevented play on the extra day also.

The first time Test cricket was played on Christmas Day was in the Third Test between Australia and West Indies at Adelaide in 1951-52.

First Test match streaker — Michael Angelow on the fourth day of the England v Australia Second Test at Lord's in August 1975. He did it to win a bet but lost the proceeds to the magistrate in court on the next day.

First U.S. President to watch a Test match — Dwight D.Eisenhower — Pakistan v Australia at Karachi 1959-60.

First batsman to wear a protective helmet in a Test — D.L.Amiss England v West Indies at The Oval in 1976.

First player to be given out by the 'TV umpire' — S.R.Tendulkar, run out, India v South Africa at Durban in 1992-93. This was the first Test in which television replays monitored by a third umpire were called upon to adjudicate in close decisions.

First instance of five penalty runs being awarded in a Test — to West Indies (first innings) against Australia at Adelaide in 2000-1, when the ball hit a helmet lying on the ground behind the wicket-keeper (A.C.Gilchrist).

First player to score a century on his first Test appearance against his first three opponents was A.J.Strauss (England). He scored 112 v New Zealand at Lord's in 2004; 137 v West Indies at Lord's in 2004; and 126 v South Africa at Port Elizabeth in 2004-05.

First instance of a team being awarded a Test — Pakistan v England at the Oval, 2006. On the fourth day, the umpires deemed that the condition of the ball had been changed and awarded 5 penalty runs under Law 42.3(d). After tea, the Umpires and English batsmen took the field, but the Pakistan team remained in their dressing room in protest. The umpires finally awarded the game to England under Law 22.3(a).

SOME NOTABLE FIRSTS AND LASTS

L.Hone was the first player to represent England in a Test without playing for a country — England v Australia in 1878-79.

D.C.H.Townsend was the last player to represent England in a Test match without having played for a first-class county — England v West Indies 1934-35.

First former Test cricketer to umpire in a Test — James Lillwhite, jr, Australia v England at Melbourne in 1881-82. This was the first Test in which 1000 runs were scored. This Test also saw Australia's first Test century partnership — 107 for the 5th wicket by T.P.Horan and G.Giffen.

Gloucestershire-born W.E.Midwinter was the first cricketer to have played for and against Australia in Test matches. Midwinter played 8 times for Australia against England 1876-77 (2), 1882-83 (1), 1884 (3), 1886-87 (2). He played 4 times for England v Australia in 1881-82.

South African-born K.C.Wessels is the last player to play for and against Australia in Test cricket. He represented Australia in 24 Tests between 1982-83 and 1985-86, and South Africa in 16 Tests between 1991-92 and 1994. (Uniquely, he scored a hundred on debut v England for both countries —162 for Australia (Brisbane[2]) 1982-83 and 105 for South Africa (Lord's) 1994.)

In the Second Test at Melbourne in 1882-83, W.Bates achieved the first hat-trick for England when he dismissed P.S.McDonnell, G.Giffen and G.J.Bonnor in Australia's first innings. He became the first player to score a fifty and take 10 or more wickets in the same Test. (55 runs; 26.2-14-28-7 and 33-14-74-7.) This was the first Test to be won by an innings.

The first double century in Test cricket was scored by the Australian captain W.L.Murdoch (211) v England at The Oval in 1884.

P.S.McDonnell (Australia) was the first batsman to score two centuries in successive Test innings. He scored 103 in his only innings of the Third Test against England at The Oval in 1884, and then 124 in the first innings of the First Test of the 1884-85 series at Adelaide (also the first Test played in that City). In his second innings of that Test he was unlucky not to become the first player to score a hundred in each innings of a Test. He was run out for 83 when his partner, G.Giffen, suffering from lumbago, refused what would normally have been a perfectly reasonable call.

S.Morris (Australia) was the first black man to play in a Test match — v England at Melbourne in 1884-85. Morris was born in Hobart of West Indian parents and when the 11 players from the First Test at Adelaide demanded 50% of the gate money for the Second Test and were refused by officials Morris got his chance — he scored 4 and 10* and took 2 for 73 in his only Test.

A.Shrewsbury (England) became the first batsman to score 1000 runs in Test cricket, at Lord's in 1893.

A.Coningham was the first bowler to take a wicket (A.C.MacLaren) with his first ball in Test cricket — Australia v England at Melbourne in 1894-95.

J.Briggs (England) became the first player to take 100 Test wickets, at Sydney in the Fourth Test in 1894-95. In the same match C.T.B.Turner became the first Australian bowler to capture 100 Test wickets.

The first bowler to take 9 wickets in a Test innings was G.A.Lohmann for England v South Africa at Johannesburg in 1895-96 — 14.2-6-28-9.

J.Darling (Australia) was the first left-hander to score a hundred in a Test match with 101 against England at Sydney in 1897-98. In the 1897-98 series Darling became the first batsman to score three centuries in the same series and the first to aggregate 500 runs in the same series.

W.Bardsley (Australia) was the first batsman to score a century in each innings of a Test match — 136 and 130 v England at The Oval in 1909.

Rt. Rev.D.S.Sheppard (later Baron Sheppard, Bishop of Liverpool) was the first ordained minister to play Test Cricket — England v Australia at Manchester in 1956.

A.Sandham (England) was the first batsman to score 300 in a Test innings — 325 v West Indies at Kingston in 1929-30.

A.K.Davison (Australia) was the first male player to complete the match double of 100 runs and 10 wickets in a Test — 44 and 80 runs; 30-2-135-5 and 24.6-4-87-6 bowling v West Indies at Brisbane in 1960-61. E.R. (Betty) Wilson had previously performed the feat with eleven wickets and 100 runs (12 and 100 runs; 10.3-4-7-7, including the hat-trick, and 19-14-9-4, for Australia v England at St Kilda in a women's Test in 1957-58).

In 1997-98 at Rawalpindi, Ali Naqvi and Azhar Mahmood (Pakistan) v South Africa, provided the first instance of two batsmen scoring a hundred on debut in the same innings.

SOME NOTABLE DEBUTS

1. J.E.Barrett became the first Australian player to carry his bat through a completed innings in a Test against England. Barrett scored 67* in Australia's second innings (176) at Lord's in 1890 — his first Test match.
2. F.Martin (England) took twelve wickets in his first Test appearance, v Australia at the Oval in 1890. His figures were 6 for 50 and 6 for 52.
3. A.E.Trott (Australia), in his first Test, played against England at the Adelaide Oval in January 1895, scored 110 runs (38* and 72*) without being dismissed and bowled unchanged throughout the second innings taking 8 wickets for 43 runs.
4. R.A.Duff (Australia), in his first Test, played against England at Melbourne in 1901-02, top-scored in the first innings with 32 and again in the second with 104. He also shared in the first hundred partnership for the tenth wicket with W.W.Armstrong who was also playing in his first Test.
5. E.G.Arnold (England) took the wicket of the great Victor Trumper with his first delivery in a Test match, at Sydney in 1903-04.
6. R.E.Foster (England) making his debut v Australia at Sydney in 1903-04, after an uncertain start, helped himself to a glorious 287, with 38 boundaries in 420 minutes. Foster added 192 for the fifth wicket with G.H.Hirst, 115 for the 9th with R.E.Relf, and 130 for the 10th with W.Rhodes, the latter being scored in an amazing 66 minutes.
7. A.Warren (England) took five wickets for 57 in the first innings v Australia at Leeds in 1905 in his only Test match.
8. G.Gunn (England), on holidays in Australia for health reasons in 1907-08, was called into the injury-hit England side for the Sydney Test. Playing his very first innings on Australian soil — and his first Test match innings — Gunn hit a brilliant 119 in $2^1/_2$ hours and followed up with 74 in the second innings.
9. H.L.Collins (Australia) began his Test career with consecutive scores of 70 and 104 (Sydney) 64 (Melbourne) and 162 (Adelaide) — v England in 1920-21.
10. G.M.Parker, a South African cricketer playing Bradford League cricket during the South African tour of England in 1924, was called up to play for his country in the First Test at Birmingham although not a member of the touring party. He took 6 wickets for 152 in England's only innings.
11. C.V.Grimmett (Australia) took eleven wickets in his first Test. Playing against England at Sydney during 1924-25 he captured 5 for 45 in the first innings and 6 for 37 in the second.
12. W.R.Hammond (England) scored 51 runs and took 5 wickets in his first Test — v South Africa at Johannesburg 1927-28.
13. M.J.C.Allom (England), in his first Test, against New Zealand at Christchurch in 1930, took four wickets in five balls, including the hat-trick.
14. H.D.Smith (New Zealand) bowled E.Paynter (England) with his first ball in Test cricket — his only wicket in his only Test at Christchurch in 1932-33.
15. C.S.Marriott (England) took eleven wickets in his first and only Test — v West Indies at The Oval in 1933.
16. A.V.Bedser (England) took eleven wickets in each of his first two Test matches. In his first, against India at Lord's in June 1946 he took 7 for 49 and 4 for 96. In his second appearance the following month, at Manchester, he captured 4 for 41 and 7 for 52.

17. J.C.Laker (England), playing against West Indies at Bridgetown in 1947-48, took 7 for 103 in his first Test innings.

18. H.H.H.Johnson (West Indies) played in his first Test at the age of 37, when he appeared against England at Kingston in 1947-48. He took 5 for 41 in the first innings and 5 for 55 in the second.

19. A.L.Valentine (West Indies) making his debut in the match v England at Manchester in 1950, took the first eight wickets to fall (8 for 104).

20. A.T.W.Grout (Australia) keeping wickets against South Africa in his first Test in 1957-58, set a then World Test record of six catches in an innings, at Johannesburg.

21. C.A.Milton (England) played his first Test against New Zealand at Leeds in 1958. He scored 104* in England's only innings and became the first English player to be on the ground throughout an entire Test match — although there was no play on the first two days.

22. J.D.F.Larter (England) v Pakistan at The Oval in 1962, took nine wickets in his first Test.

23. H.B.Taber (Australia), playing against South Africa at Johannesburg in 1966-67, caught seven and stumped one, a 'bag' never equalled by a wicket-keeper in his first Test.

24. B.R.Taylor (New Zealand) is the only Test player to make 100 and take five wickets in an innings on debut. He scored 105 and took 5 for 86 v India at Calcutta in 1964-65.

25. L.G.Rowe (West Indies) made history by scoring 214 and 100* in his first Test match v New Zealand at Kingston in 1971-72. Rowe is one of only two batsmen to score 100 in each innings on his Test debut (Yasir Hameed, Pakistan is the other player), and only one of six players (R.E.Foster, England; D.S.B.P.Kuruppu, Sri Lanka; M.S.Sinclair, New Zealand and J.A.Rudolph, South Africa being the others) to make a double-century on debut.

26. R.A.L.Massie (Australia), with an astonishing display of swing-bowling in overcast conditions, demolished England in the Lord's Test of 1972, taking 8 for 53 and 8 for 84 for an Australian record Test match bag of 16 wickets.

27. P.J.Petherick (New Zealand) took a hat-trick in his first Test — played against Pakistan at Lahore in October 1976. In the same match Javed Miandad scored 163 and 25* in his first Test.

28. J.K.Lever (England) scored 53 and took 7 for 46 and 3 for 24 in his first Test match, against India at Delhi in 1976-77.

29. Yajurvindra Singh (India) equalled two Test records in his first Test. Playing against England in Bangalore in the Fourth Test in 1976-77 he took five catches in the first innings and a total of seven for the match — both records for non wicket-keepers.

30. B.M.Laird (92 and 75) scored 167 runs for Australia v West Indies at Brisbane in 1979-80 — the highest aggregate without a century by a player on debut.

30. M.Azharuddin (India) began his Test career with 110 at Calcutta, 48 and 105 at Madras, and 122 and 54* at Kanpur — all against England in 1984-85.

31. D.S.B.P.Kuruppu (Sri Lanka), achieved the rare feat of being on the field throughout his maiden Test. He took 776 minutes to reach his double century — the then slowest 200 in first class cricket — and batted for 777 minutes for his 201* v New Zealand at Colombo 1986-87.

32. N.D.Hirwani (India), exacting great turn on an under-prepared pitch, exploited the weakness of West Indies batsmen against spin to take 8 for 61 and 8 for 75 at Madras in 1987-88 to establish an Indian record for wickets in a Test.

33. A.I.C.Dodemaide (Australia), brought in as a late replacement for the injured B.A.Reid scored 50 in his first innings and took 6 for 58 in the second innings v New Zealand at Melbourne in 1987-88.

34. When A.C.Hudson scored 163 and 0 v West Indies at Bridgetown in 1991-92, he became the first South African to score a century on Test debut and the first player to score a 'ton' and a 'duck' in his first Test.

35. D.L.Houghton (Zimbabwe) emulated the feat of C.Bannerman (Australia v England at Melbourne 1876-77) by scoring a century (121) in his country's inaugural Test — v India at Harare in 1992-93.

36. D.W.Fleming (Australia) captured 4 for 75 and 3 for 86, including the hat-trick, v Pakistan at Rawalpindi in 1994-95.

37. G.S.Blewett (Australia) followed his 102* and 12 v England at Adelaide in 1994-95 with 20 + 115 at Perth. (He also scored 7 and 125 in his next Test against England, at Birmingham in 1997).

38. C.I.Dunusinghe (Sri Lanka) scored 11 and 91 v New Zealand at Napier in 1994-95 as well as taking 7 catches behind the stumps.

39. D.G.Cork (England) captured 7 for 43 on his Test debut, v West Indies at Lord's in 1995.

40. S.Ganguly (India) became the third player to score a century in his first two Test innings, when he scored 131 at Lord's and 136 and 48 at Nottingham v England in 1996.

41. N.M.Kulkarni (India) on his Test debut v Sri Lanka at R.Premadasa Stadium, Colombo, quickly learnt how hard Test cricket can be. He dismissed M.S.Atapattu with his first ball in Test cricket. But this was his only success and he finished with 1 for 195!

41. Aminul Islam (Bangladesh) copied C.Bannerman and D.L.Houghton by scoring a century (145) in his country's inaugural Test — v India at Dhaka in 2000-01.

CENTURY ON DEBUT

Player	1st	2nd	Match Particulars			Venue	Series
C.Bannerman	165#	4	Australia	v	England	Melbourne	1876-77
W.G.Grace	152	9*	England	v	Australia	The Oval	1880
H.Graham	107	-	Australia	v	England	Lord's	1893
K.S.Ranjitsinhji	62	154*	England	v	Australia	Manchester	1896
P.F.Warner	21	132*	England	v	South Africa	Johannesburg[1]	1898-99
R.A.Duff †	32	104	Australia	v	England	Melbourne	1901-02
R.E.Foster	287	19	England	v	Australia	Sydney	1903-04
G.Gunn	119	74	England	v	Australia	Sydney	1907-08
M.J.Hartigan	48	116	Australia	v	England	Adelaide	1907-08
H.L.Collins	70	104	Australia	v	England	Sydney	1920-21
W.H.Ponsford †Ω	110	27	Australia	v	England	Sydney	1924-25
A.Jackson	164	36	Australia	v	England	Adelaide	1928-29
G.A.Headley	21	176	West Indies	v	England	Bridgetown	1929-30
J.E.Mills	117	7	New Zealand	v	England	Wellington	1929-30
Nawab of Pataudi, sr	102	-	England	v	Australia	Sydney	1932-33
N.B.Amarnath Δ	38	118	India	v	England	Bombay[1]	1933-34
B.H.Valentine	136	-	England	v	India	Bombay[1]	1933-34
P.A.Gibb	93	106	England	v	South Africa	Johannesburg[1]	1938-39
S.C.Griffith	140	4	England	v	West Indies	Port-of-Spain	1947-48
A.G.Ganteaume §	112	-	West Indies	v	England	Port-of-Spain	1947-48
J.W.Burke	12	101*	Australia	v	England	Adelaide	1950-51
P.B.H.May	138	-	England	v	South Africa	Leeds	1951
R.H.Shodhan	110	-	India	v	Pakistan	Calcutta	1952-53
B.H.Pairaudeau	115	-	West Indies	v	India	Port-of-Spain	1952-53
O.G.Smith	44	104	West Indies	v	Australia	Kingston	1954-55
A.G.Kripal Singh	100*	-	India	v	New Zealand	Hyderabad	1955-56
C.C.Hunte	142	11	West Indies	v	Pakistan	Bridgetown	1957-58
C.A.Milton	104*	-	England	v	New Zealand	Leeds	1958
A.A.Baig	26	112	India	v	England	Manchester	1959
Hanumant Singh	105	23	India	v	England	Delhi	1963-64
Khalid Ibadulla	166	3	Pakistan	v	Australia	Karachi[1]	1964-65
B.R.Taylor	105	0*	New Zealand	v	India	Calcutta	1964-65
K.D.Walters Ω	155	-	Australia	v	England	Brisbane[2]	1965-66
J.H.Hampshire	107	5	England	v	West Indies	Lord's	1969
G.R.Viswanath	0	137	India	v	Australia	Kanpur	1969-70
G.S.Chappell †#	108	-	Australia	v	England	Perth	1970-71
L.G.Rowe	214	100*	West Indies	v	New Zealand	Kingston	1971-72
A.I.Kallicharran Ω	100*	-	West Indies	v	New Zealand	Georgetown	1971-72
R.E.Redmond §	107	56	New Zealand	v	Pakistan	Auckland	1972-73
F.C.Hayes	16	106*	England	v	West Indies	The Oval	1973
C.G.Greenidge	93	107	West Indies	v	India	Bangalore	1974-75
L.Baichan	20	105*	West Indies	v	Pakistan	Lahore[2]	1974-75
G.J.Cosier	109	-	Australia	v	West Indies	Melbourne	1975-76
S.Amarnath Δ	124	-	India	v	New Zealand	Auckland	1975-76
Javed Miandad	163	25*	Pakistan	v	New Zealand	Lahore[2]	1976-77

A.B.Williams	10	100	West Indies	v	Australia	Georgetown	1977-78
D.M.Wellham	24	103	Australia	v	England	The Oval	1981
Saleem Malik	12	100*	Pakistan	v	Sri Lanka	Karachi[1]	1981-82
K.C.Wessels	162	46	Australia	v	England	Brisbane[2]	1982-83
W.B.Phillips	159	-	Australia	v	Pakistan	Perth	1983-84
M.Azharuddin †¶	110	-	India	v	England	Calcutta	1984-85
D.S.B.P.Kuruppu	201*	-	Sri Lanka	v	New Zealand	Colombo (CCC)	1986-87
M.J.Greatbatch	11	107*	New Zealand	v	England	Auckland	1987-88
M.E.Waugh	138	23	Australia	v	England	Adelaide	1990-91
A.C.Hudson	163	0	South Africa	v	West Indies	Bridgetown	1991-92
R.S.Kaluwitharana	132*	4	Sri Lanka	v	Australia	Colombo (SSC)	1992-93
D.L.Houghton #	121	41*	Zimbabwe	v	India	Harare	1992-93
P.K.Amre	103	-	India	v	South Africa	Durban[2]	1992-93
G.P.Thorpe	6	114*	England	v	Australia	Nottingham	1993
G.S.Blewett Ω	102*	12	Australia	v	England	Adelaide	1994-95
S.C.Ganguly Ω	131	-	India	v	England	Lord's	1996
Mohammad Wasim	0	109*	Pakistan	v	New Zealand	Lahore[2]	1996-97
Ali Naqvi ∑	115	19	Pakistan	v	South Africa	Rawalpindi[2]	1997-98
Azhar Mahmood ∑	128*	50*	Pakistan	v	South Africa	Rawalpindi[2]	1997-98
M.S.Sinclair	214	-	New Zealand	v	West Indies	Wellington	1999-2000
Younis Khan	12	107	Pakistan	v	Sri Lanka	Rawalpindi[2]	1999-2000
Aminul Islam	145	6	Bangladesh	v	India	Dhaka	2000-01
H.Masakadza	9	119	Zimbabwe	v	West Indies	Harare	2001-02
T.T.Samaraweera	103*	-	Sri Lanka	v	India	Colombo (SSC)	2001-02
Taufeeq Umar	104	-	Pakistan	v	Bangladesh	Multan[2]	2001-02
Mohammad Ashraful	26	114	Bangladesh	v	Sri Lanka	Colombo (SSC)	2001-02
V.K.Sehwag	105	31	India	v	South Africa	Bloemfontein	2001-02
L.Vincent	104	54	New Zealand	v	Australia	Perth	2001-02
S.B.Styris	107	69*	New Zealand	v	West Indies	St George's	2002-03
J.A.Rudolph	222*	-	South Africa	v	Bangladesh	Chittagong	2002-03
Yasir Hameed	170	105	Pakistan	v	Bangladesh	Karachi[1]	2003-04
D.R.Smith	20	105*	West Indies	v	South Africa	Cape Town	2003-04
A.J.Strauss #	112	83	England	v	New Zealand	Lord's	2004
M.J.Clarke	151	17	Australia	v	India	Bangalore	2004-05
A.N.Cook	60	104*	England	v	India	Nagpur	2005-06

§ Only Test. † Duff, Ponsford, Chappell and Azharuddin also scored a century in their last Test (Chappell also scored a century in each innings of his first Test as captain). Ω Ponsford, Walters, Kallicharran, Blewett and Ganguly also scored a century in their second Test. ¶ Azharuddin scored a century in each of his first three Tests. ∆ N.B. and S.Amarnath provide the only instance of a father and son scoring a century on debut. ∑ Ali Naqvi and Azhar Mahmood achieved the feat in the same innings. # Chappell, Houghton and Strauss also scored hundreds on their debut as captain.

FIVE WICKETS IN AN INNINGS ON DEBUT

Player	1st	2nd	Match Particulars			Venue	Series
W.E.Midwinter	5/78	1/23	Australia	v	England	Melbourne	1876-77
A.Shaw	3/51	5/38	England	v	Australia	Melbourne	1876-77
T.K.Kendall	1/54	7/55	Australia	v	England	Melbourne	1876-77
F.Morley	5/56	3/90	England	v	Australia	The Oval	1880
W.H.Cooper	3/80	6/120	Australia	v	England	Melbourne	1881-82
R.Peel	3/68	5/51	England	v	Australia	Adelaide	1884-85
C.T.B.Turner	6/15	2/53	Australia	v	England	Sydney	1886-87
J.J.Ferris	4/27	5/76	Australia	v	England	Sydney	1886-87
C.A.Smith	5/19	2/42	England	v	South Africa	Port Elizabeth	1888-89
A.Rose-Innes	5/73	0/16	South Africa	v	England	Port Elizabeth	1888-89
W.H.Ashley	7/95	-	South Africa	v	England	Cape Town	1888-89
F.Martin	6/50	6/52	England	v	Australia	The Oval	1890

R.W.McLeod	5/53	1/39	Australia	v	England	Melbourne	1891-92
W.H.Lockwood	6/101	-	England	v	Australia	Lord's	1893
T.Richardson	5/49	5/107	England	v	Australia	Manchester	1893
A.E.Trott	0/9	8/43	Australia	v	England	Adelaide	1894-95
J.Middleton	5/64	4/66	South Africa	v	England	Port Elizabeth	1895-96
G.A.Rowe	5/115	-	South Africa	v	England	Johannesburg[1]	1895-96
C.Heseltine	0/29	5/38	England	v	South Africa	Johannesburg[1]	1895-96
M.A.Noble	1/31	6/49	Australia	v	England	Melbourne	1897-98
W.M.Bradley	5/67	1/82	England	v	Australia	Manchester	1899
S.F.Barnes	5/65	1/74	England	v	Australia	Sydney	1901-02
L.C.Braund	2/40	5/61	England	v	Australia	Sydney	1901-02
J.V.Saunders	4/119	5/43	Australia	v	England	Sydney	1901-02
A.Warren	5/57	1/56	England	v	Australia	Leeds	1905
W.S.Lees	5/34	3/74	England	v	South Africa	Johannesburg[1]	1905-06
J.A.D.O'Connor	3/110	5/40	Australia	v	England	Adelaide	1907-08
D.W.Carr	5/146	2/136	England	v	Australia	The Oval	1909
G.H.T.Simpson-Hayward	6/43	2/59	England	v	South Africa	Johannesburg[1]	1909-10
H.V.Hordern	3/39	5/66	Australia	v	South Africa	Melbourne	1910-11
F.R.Foster	2/105	5/92	England	v	Australia	Sydney	1911-12
G.G.Macaulay	2/19	5/64	England	v	South Africa	Cape Town	1922-23
A.E.Hall	4/49	7/63	South Africa	v	England	Cape Town	1922-23
G.M.Parker	6/152	-	South Africa	v	England	Birmingham	1924
C.V.Grimmett	5/45	6/37	Australia	v	England	Sydney	1924-25
W.R.Hammond	0/21	5/36	England	v	South Africa	Johannesburg[1]	1927-28
H.L.E.Promnitz	5/58	0/14	South Africa	v	England	Johannesburg[1]	1927-28
G.F.Bissett	5/37	3/99	South Africa	v	England	Cape Town	1927-28
T.W.Wall	3/123	5/66	Australia	v	England	Melbourne	1928-29
A.J.Bell	6/99	0/60	South Africa	v	England	Lord's	1929
M.J.C.Allom	5/38	3/17	England	v	New Zealand	Christchurch	1929-30
Mahomed Nissar	5/93	1/42	India	v	England	Lord's	1932
J.Langridge	0/23	7/56	England	v	West Indies	Manchester	1933
C.S.Marriott	5/37	6/59	England	v	West Indies	The Oval	1933
K.Farnes	5/102	5/77	England	v	Australia	Nottingham	1934
C.I.J.Smith	0/8	5/16	England	v	West Indies	Bridgetown	1934-35
F.A.Ward	2/138	6/102	Australia	v	England	Brisbane[2]	1936-37
N.Gordon	5/103	2/59	South Africa	v	England	Johannesburg[1]	1938-39
R.T.D.Perks	5/100	1/99	England	v	South Africa	Durban[2]	1938-39
W.H.Copson	5/85	4/67	England	v	West Indies	Lord's	1939
A.V.Bedser	7/49	4/96	England	v	India	Lord's	1946
R.Pollard	5/24	2/63	England	v	India	Manchester	1946
† I.W.G.Johnson	6/42	2/92	Australia	v	England	Sydney	1946-47
L.Tuckett	5/68	1/127	South Africa	v	England	Nottingham	1947
J.C.Laker	7/103	2/95	England	v	West Indies	Bridgetown	1947-48
H.H.H.Johnson	5/41	5/55	West Indies	v	England	Kingston	1947-48
C.N.McCarthy	0/20	6/43	South Africa	v	England	Durban[2]	1948-49
T.E.Bailey	6/118	0/51	England	v	New Zealand	Leeds	1949
G.F.Cresswell	6/168	-	New Zealand	v	England	The Oval	1949
M.G.Melle	5/113	1/58	South Africa	v	Australia	Johannesburg[2]	1949-50
A.L.Valentine	8/104	3/100	West Indies	v	England	Manchester	1950
R.Berry	5/63	4/53	England	v	West Indies	Manchester	1950
A.M.Moir	6/155	-	New Zealand	v	England	Christchurch	1950-51
D.E.J.Ironside	5/51	3/37	South Africa	v	New Zealand	Johannesburg[2]	1953-54
R.Appleyard	5/51	2/72	England	v	Pakistan	Nottingham	1954
P.S.Heine	5/60	1/87	South Africa	v	England	Lord's	1955
I.Meckiff	5/125	3/52	Australia	v	South Africa	Johannesburg[3]	1957-58
J.O.Taylor	5/109	-	West Indies	v	Pakistan	Port-of-Spain	1957-58
V.V.Kumar	5/64	2/68	India	v	Pakistan	Delhi	1960-61

G.D.McKenzie	1/81	5/37	Australia	v	England	Lord's	1961
P.S.Pollock	3/61	6/38	South Africa	v	New Zealand	Durban[2]	1961-62
S.F.Burke	6/128	5/68	South Africa	v	New Zealand	Cape Town	1961-62
L.A.King	5/46	2/18	West Indies	v	India	Kingston	1961-62
L.J.Coldwell	3/25	6/85	England	v	Pakistan	Lord's	1962
J.D.F.Larter	5/57	4/88	England	v	Pakistan	The Oval	1962
Arif Butt	6/89	1/29	Pakistan	v	Australia	Melbourne	1964-65
B.R.Taylor	5/86	-	New Zealand	v	India	Calcutta	1964-65
S.Abid Ali	6/55	1/61	India	v	Australia	Adelaide	1967-68
J.N.Shepherd	5/104	-	West Indies	v	England	Manchester	1969
Mohammad Nazir	7/99	0/15	Pakistan	v	New Zealand	Karachi[1]	1969-70
K.Shuttleworth	0/81	5/47	England	v	Australia	Brisbane[2]	1970-71
D.K.Lillee	5/84	0/40	Australia	v	England	Adelaide	1970-71
R.A.L.Massie	8/84	8/53	Australia	v	England	Lord's	1972
G.Dymock	2/77	5/58	Australia	v	New Zealand	Adelaide	1973-74
P.H.Edmonds	5/28	1/64	England	v	Australia	Leeds	1975
J.K.Lever	7/46	3/24	England	v	India	Delhi	1976-77
I.T.Botham	5/74	0/60	England	v	Australia	Nottingham	1977
M.F.Malone	5/63	1/14	Australia	v	England	The Oval	1977
R.M.Hogg	6/74	1/35	Australia	v	England	Brisbane[2]	1978-79
D.R.Doshi	6/103	2/64	India	v	Australia	Madras[1]	1979-80
T.M.Alderman	4/68	5/62	Australia	v	England	Nottingham	1981
T.G.Hogan	1/50	5/66	Australia	v	Sri Lanka	Kandy	1982-83
N.G.B.Cook	5/35	3/90	England	v	New Zealand	Lord's	1983
A.K.Kuruppuarachchi	5/44	2/41	Sri Lanka	v	India	Colombo(CCC)	1985-86
P.L.Taylor	6/78	2/76	Australia	v	England	Sydney	1986-87
A.I.C.Dodemaide	1/48	6/58	Australia	v	New Zealand	Melbourne	1987-88
N.D.Hirwani	8/61	8/75	India	v	West Indies	Madras[1]	1987-88
N.A.Mallender	3/72	5/50	England	v	Pakistan	Leeds	1992
P.M.Such	6/67	2/78	England	v	Australia	Manchester	1993
D.G.Cork	1/72	7/43	England	v	West Indies	Lord's	1995
Shahid Nazir	5/53	2/45	Pakistan	v	Zimbabwe	Sheikhupura	1996-97
L.Klusener	0/75	8/64	South Africa	v	India	Calcutta	1996-97
Mohammad Zahid	4/64	7/66	Pakistan	v	New Zealand	Rawalpindi[2]	1996-97
F.A.Rose	6/100	1/23	West Indies	v	India	Kingston	1996-97
S.H.Cook	2/36	5/39	Australia	v	New Zealand	Perth	1997-98
P.J.Wiseman	2/61	5/82	New Zealand	v	Sri Lanka	Colombo(RPS)	1997-98
Shahid Afridi	5/52	0/49	Pakistan	v	Australia	Karachi[1]	1998-99
U.D.U.Chandana	6/179	-	Sri Lanka	v	Pakistan	Dhaka	1998-99
N.O.Perry	1/79	5/70	West Indies	v	Australia	Kingston	1998-99
B.Lee	5/47	2/31	Australia	v	India	Melbourne	1999-2000
Naimur Rahman	6/132	0/22	Bangladesh	v	India	Dhaka	2000-01
Mohammad Sami	3/70	5/36	Pakistan	v	New Zealand	Auckland	2000-01
A.M.Blignaut	5/73	3/37	Zimbabwe	v	Bangladesh	Bulawayo[2]	2000-01
Manjural Islam	6/81	-	Bangladesh	v	Zimbabwe	Bulawayo[2]	2000-01
J.M.Anderson	5/73	0/65	England	v	Zimbabwe	Lord's	2003
R.L.Johnson	6/33	0/67	England	v	Zimbabwe	Chester-le-Street	2003
F.H.Edwards	5/36	1/54	West Indies	v	Sri Lanka	Kingston	2002-03
R.J.Kirtley	2/80	6/34	England	v	South Africa	Nottingham	2003
Shabbir Ahmed	3/61	5/48	Pakistan	v	Bangladesh	Karachi[1]	2003-04
# S.M.Katich	0/25	6/65	Australia	v	Zimbabwe	Sydney	2003-04
C.K.Langeveldt	5/46	0/50	South Africa	v	England	Cape Town	2004-05
S.R.Clark	5/55	4/34	Australia	v	South Africa	Cape Town	2005-06

† 3rd Test, but did not bowl in 1st or 2nd Test. # 2nd Test, but did not bowl in 1st Test. § J.J.Ferris (6/54 and 7/37 v South Africa at Cape Town 1891-92) and A.E.Trott (4/61 and 5/49 v South Africa at Johannesburg[1] 1898-99) also took five wickets in an innings on debut for England, having previously achieved the feat for Australia. A.J.Traicos took 5/86 on debut for Zimbabwe v India at Harare (1992-93) after having played for South Africa.

TEN WICKETS IN MATCH ON DEBUT

12/102(6/50 + 6/52)	F.Martin	England	v	Australia	The Oval	1890
10/156(5/49 + 5/107)	T.Richardson	England	v	Australia	Manchester	1893
11/112(4/49 + 7/63)	A.E.Hall	South Africa	v	England	Cape Town	1922-23
11/82(5/45 + 6/37)	C.V.Grimmett	Australia	v	England	Sydney	1924-25
11/96(5/37 + 6/59)	C.S.Marriott †	England	v	West Indies	The Oval	1933
10/179(5/102 + 5/77)	K.Farnes	England	v	Australia	Nottingham	1934
11/145(7/49 + 4/96)	A.V.Bedser	England	v	India	Lord's	1946
10/96(5/41 + 5/55)	H.H.H.Johnson	West Indies	v	England	Kingston	1947-48
11/204(8/104 + 3/100)	A.L.Valentine	West Indies	v	England	Manchester	1950
11/196(6/128 + 5/68)	S.F.Burke	South Africa	v	New Zealand	Cape Town	1961-62
16/137(8/84 + 8/53)	R.A.L.Massie	Australia	v	England	Lord's	1972
10/70(7/46 + 3/24)	J.K.Lever	England	v	India	Delhi	1976-77
16/136(8/61 + 8/75)	N.D.Hirwani	India	v	West Indies	Madras[1]	1987-88
11/130(7/52 + 4/78)	Mohammad Zahid	Pakistan	v	New Zealand	Rawalpindi[2]	1996-97

† His only Test.

WICKET WITH FIRST BALL IN TEST CRICKET

Bowler	Batsman dismissed					
A.Coningham	A.C.MacLaren	Australia	v	England	Melbourne	1894-95
W.M.Bradley	F.J.Laver	England	v	Australia	Manchester	1899
E.G.Arnold	V.T.Trumper	England	v	Australia	Sydney	1903-04
G.G.Macaulay	G.A.L.Hearne	England	v	South Africa	Cape Town	1922-23
M.W.Tate	M.J.Susskind	England	v	South Africa	Birmingham	1924
M.Henderson	E.W.Dawson	New Zealand	v	England	Christchurch	1929-30
H.D.Smith	E.Paynter	New Zealand	v	England	Christchurch	1932-33
T.F.Johnson	W.W.Keeton	West Indies	v	England	The Oval	1939
R.Howorth	D.V.Dyer	England	v	South Africa	The Oval	1947
Intikhab Alam	C.C.McDonald	Pakistan	v	Australia	Karachi[1]	1959-60
R.K.Illingworth	P.V.Simmons	England	v	West Indies	Nottingham	1991
N.M.Kulkarni	M.S.Atapattu	India	v	Sri Lanka	Colombo (RPS)	1997-98
M.K.G.C.P.Lakshitha	Tushar Imran	Sri Lanka	v	Bangladesh	Colombo (SSC)	2002-03

WICKET IN FIRST OVER IN TEST CRICKET

Ball	Bowler	Batsman dismissed				
1st	A.Coningham	A.C.MacLaren	Australia	v England	Melbourne	1894-95
1st	W.M.Bradley	F.J.Laver	England	v Australia	Manchester	1899
1st	E.G.Arnold	V.T.Trumper	England	v Australia	Sydney	1903-04
1st	G.G.Macaulay	G.A.L.Hearne	England	v South Africa	Cape Town	1922-23
1st	M.W.Tate	M.J.Susskind	England	v South Africa	Birmingham	1924
1st	M.Henderson	E.W.Dawson	New Zealand	v England	Christchurch	1929-30
1st	H.D.Smith	E.Paynter	New Zealand	v England	Christchurch	1932-33
1st	T.F.Johnson	W.W.Keeton	West Indies	v England	The Oval	1939
1st	R.Howorth	D.V.Dyer	England	v South Africa	The Oval	1947
1st	Intikhab Alam	C.C.McDonald	Pakistan	v Australia	Karachi[1]	1959-60
1st	R.K.Illingworth	P.V.Simmons	England	v West Indies	Nottingham	1991
1st	N.M.Kulkarni	M.S.Atapattu	India	v Sri Lanka	Colombo (RPS)	1997-98
1st	M.K.G.C.P.Lakshitha	Tushar Imran	Sri Lanka	v Bangladesh	Colombo (SSC)	2002-03
2nd	G.A.Rowe	T.C.OBrien	South Africa	v England	Johannesburg[1]	1895-96
2nd	W.Barber	H.B.Cameron	England	v South Africa	Leeds	1935
2nd	J.H.Cameron	H.Gimblett	West Indies	v England	Lord's	1939
2nd	C.L.McCool	D.A.N.McRae	Australia	v New Zealand	Wellington	1945-46
2nd	G.W.A.Chubb	J.T.Ikin	South Africa	v England	Nottingham	1951
2nd	R.Appleyard	Hanif Mohammad	England	v Pakistan	Nottingham	1954
2nd	F.M.Misson	C.C.Hunte	Australia	v West Indies	Melbourne	1960-61

2nd	P.I.Philpott	C.C.Hunte	Australia	v West Indies	Kingston	1964-65
2nd	B.A.G.Murray	S.Abid Ali	New Zealand	v India	Wellington	1967-68
2nd	G.Dymock	J.M.Parker	Australia	v New Zealand	Adelaide	1973-74
2nd	K.H.R.K.Fernando	G.C.Smith	Sri Lanka	v South Africa	Johannesburg[3]	2002-03
3rd	I.W.G.Johnson	L.Hutton	Australia	v England	Sydney	1946-47
3rd	R.O.Jenkins	E.A.B.Rowan	England	v South Africa	Durban[2]	1948-49
3rd	M.S.Hardikar	R.B.Kanhai	India	v West Indies	Bombay[2]	1958-59
3rd	P.D.Lashley	G.Boycott	West Indies	v England	Leeds	1966
3rd	E.W.Freeman	S.Abid Ali	Australia	v India	Brisbane[2]	1967-68
3rd	K.Thompson	F.M.Engineer	New Zealand	v India	Wellington	1967-68
3rd	M.Hendrick	E.D.Solkar	England	v India	Manchester	1974
3rd	B.P.Bracewell	G.A.Gooch	New Zealand	v England	The Oval	1978
3rd	A.K.Kuruppuarachchi	Mudassar Nazar	Sri Lanka	v Pakistan	Colombo (CCC)	1985-86
3rd	G.A.Hick	P.V.Simmons	England	v West Indies	Lord's	1991
3rd	C.A.Lambert	M.R.Ramprakash	West Indies	v England	The Oval	1991
3rd	D.K.Liyanage	T.M.Moody	Sri Lanka	v Australia	Colombo (RPS)	1992-93
3rd	H.K.Olonga	Saeed Anwar	Zimbabwe	v Pakistan	Harare	1994-95
3rd	U.Afzaal	A.C.Gilchrist	England	v Australia	The Oval	2001
3rd	† R.L.Johnson	M.A.Vermeulen	England	v Zimbabwe	Chester-le-Street	2003
3rd	G.J.Batty	Alok Kapali	England	v Bangladesh	Dhaka	2003-04
3rd	T.Taibu	S.T.Jayasuriya	Zimbabwe	v Sri Lanka	Harare	2003-04
3rd	M.A.Hauritz	A.Kumble	Australia	v India	Mumbai[3]	2004-05
3rd	J.S.Patel	G.C.Smith	New Zealand	v South Africa	Cape Town	2005-06
4th	G.L.Weir	G.B.Legge	New Zealand	v England	Wellington	1929-30
4th	D.V.P.Wright	J.H.W.Fingleton	England	v Australia	Nottingham	1938
4th	F.W.Freer	C.Washbrook	Australia	v England	Sydney	1946-47
4th	A.M.B.Rowan	L.Hutton	South Africa	v England	Nottingham	1947
4th	J.C.Laker	C.L.Walcott	England	v West Indies	Bridgetown	1947-48
4th	H.J.Rhodes	Pankaj Roy	England	v India	Leeds	1959
4th	D.A.J.Holford	F.J.Titmus	West Indies	v England	Manchester	1966
4th	D.S.Steele	A.A.Mallett	England	v Australia	Lord's	1975
4th	J.E.Emburey	B.A.Edgar	England	v New Zealand	Lord's	1978
4th	E.E.Hemmings	Javed Miandad	England	v Pakistan	Birmingham	1982
4th	C.S.Cowdrey	Kapil Dev	England	v India	Bombay[3]	1984-85
4th	F.S.Ahangama	M.Azharuddin	Sri Lanka	v India	Colombo (SSC)	1985-86
4th	W.V.Raman	C.A.Walsh	India	v West Indies	Madras[1]	1987-88
4th	J.C.Adams	W.J.Cronje	West Indies	v South Africa	Bridgetown	1991-92
4th	S.G.Peall	Aamer Sohail	Zimbabwe	v Pakistan	Karachi[2]	1993-94
4th	Shahid Nazir	A.D.R.Campbell	Pakistan	v Zimbabwe	Sheikhupura	1996-97
4th	B.Lee	S.Ramesh	Australia	v India	Melbourne	1999-2000
4th	Mohammad Sami	M.D.Bell	Pakistan	v New Zealand	Auckland	2000-01
4th	W.W.Hinds	J.H.Kallis	West Indies	v South Africa	Port-of-Spain	2000-01
4th	J.A.Rudolph	N.Hussain	South Africa	v England	Leeds	2003
5th	G.H.T.Simpson-Hayward	J.W.Zulch	England	v South Africa	Johannesburg[1]	1909-10
5th	S.A.Banerjee	D.S.Atkinson	India	v West Indies	Calcutta	1948-49
5th	L.J.Coldwell	Imtiaz Ahmed	England	v Pakistan	Lord's	1962
5th	B.W.Yuile	E.R.Dexter	New Zealand	v England	Auckland	1962-63
5th	A.A.Mallett	M.C.Cowdrey	Australia	v England	The Oval	1968
5th	G.A.Chevalier	A.P.Sheahan	South Africa	v Australia	Cape Town	1969-70
5th	R.D.Jackman	C.G.Greenidge	England	v West Indies	Bridgetown	1980-81
5th	C.Sharma	Mohsin Khan	India	v Pakistan	Lahore[2]	1984-85
5th	D.Gough	M.J.Greatbatch	England	v New Zealand	Manchester	1994
5th	R.C.Irani	M.Azharuddin	England	v India	Birmingham	1996
5th	M.R.C.N.Bandaratilake	M.J.Horne	Sri Lanka	v New Zealand	Colombo (RPS)	1997-98
5th	C.R.Miller	Saleem Malik	Australia	v Pakistan	Rawalpindi[2]	1998-99
5th	V.C.Drakes	Anwar Hossain	West Indies	v Bangladesh	Dhaka	2002-03

6th	D.P.B.Morkel	P.Holmes	South Africa	v England	Johannesburg[1]	1927-28
6th	E.W.Clark	R.H.Catterall	England	v South Africa	The Oval	1929
6th	L.O.Fleetwood-Smith	K.G.Viljoen	Australia	v South Africa	Durban[2]	1949-50
6th	G.Pullar	F.M.M.Worrell	England	v West Indies	Port-of-Spain	1959-60
6th	V.V.Kumar	Imtiaz Ahmed	India	v Pakistan	Delhi	1960-61
6th	M.W.W.Selvey	R.C.Fredericks	England	v West Indies	Manchester	1976
6th	D.R.Pringle	Yashpal Sharma	England	v India	Lord's	1982
6th	Fazl-e-Akbar	G.Kirsten	Pakistan	v South Africa	Durban[2]	1997-98
7th	R.A.Gaunt	R.J.Westcott	Australia	v South Africa	Durban[2]	1957-58
7th	A.L.Mann	G.R.Viswanath	Australia	v India	Brisbane[2]	1977-78
?	M.Leyland	G.Challenor	England	v West Indies	The Oval	1928
?	B.Sutcliffe	A.Wharton	New Zealand	v England	Leeds	1949
?	E.W.Dempster	D.J.McGlew	New Zealand	v South Africa	Auckland	1952-53
?	A.F.Lissette	A.P.Binns	New Zealand	v West Indies	Dunedin	1955-56
?	L.A.King	M.L.Jaisimha	West Indies	v India	Kingston	1961-62

† R.L.Johnson also took a wicket with his 4th ball in Test cricket.
? Exact ball unknown.

FIRST CLASS DEBUT ON TEST DEBUT

J.R.Hodges	Australia	v	England	Melbourne	1876-77
T.K.Kendall	Australia	v	England	Melbourne	1876-77
C.J.Coventry	England	v	South Africa	Port Elizabeth	1888-89
O.R.Dunell	South Africa	v	England	Port Elizabeth	1888-89
C.E.Finlason	South Africa	v	England	Port Elizabeth	1888-89
B.A.F.Grieve	England	v	South Africa	Port Elizabeth	1888-89
P.Hutchinson	South Africa	v	England	Port Elizabeth	1888-89
G.A.Kempis	South Africa	v	England	Port Elizabeth	1888-89
W.H.Milton	South Africa	v	England	Port Elizabeth	1888-89
A.E.Ochse	South Africa	v	England	Port Elizabeth	1888-89
A.Rose-Innes	South Africa	v	England	Port Elizabeth	1888-89
F.W.Smith	South Africa	v	England	Port Elizabeth	1888-89
R.B.Stewart	South Africa	v	England	Port Elizabeth	1888-89
A.B.Tancred	South Africa	v	England	Port Elizabeth	1888-89
C.H.Vintcent	South Africa	v	England	Port Elizabeth	1888-89
W.H.Ashley	South Africa	v	England	Cape Town	1888-89
J.E.P.McMaster	England	v	South Africa	Cape Town	1888-89
W.H.M.Richards	South Africa	v	England	Cape Town	1888-89
N.H.C.D.Theunissen	South Africa	v	England	Cape Town	1888-89
G.Cripps	South Africa	v	England	Cape Town	1891-92
J.F.du Toit	South Africa	v	England	Cape Town	1891-92
C.G.Fichardt	South Africa	v	England	Cape Town	1891-92
E.A.Halliwell	South Africa	v	England	Cape Town	1891-92
A.M.Miller	England	v	South Africa	Port Elizabeth	1895-96
J.T.Willoughby	South Africa	v	England	Port Elizabeth	1895-96
W.H.B.Frank	South Africa	v	England	Johannesburg[1]	1895-96
G.H.Shepstone	South Africa	v	England	Johannesburg[1]	1895-96
A.G.Archer	England	v	South Africa	Cape Town	1898-99
G.E.Vivian	New Zealand	v	India	Calcutta	1964-65
U.Ranchod	Zimbabwe	v	India	Delhi	1992-93
Mashrafe Bin Mortaza	Bangladesh	v	Zimbabwe	Dhaka	2001-02
Yasir Ali	Pakistan	v	Bangladesh	Multan[2]	2003-04
Nazmul Hossain	Bangladesh	v	India	Chittagong	2004-05

RAPID RISES

1. In the first-ever Test at Melbourne 1876-77, J.R.Hodges and T.K.Kendall made their first-class debuts on their first Test appearance.
2. L.Hone, of Ireland, kept wicket for England v Australia in 1878-79. Hone never appeared in English county cricket. (This was his 3rd first-class match.)
3. G.J.Bonnor (Australia) was selected to tour England in 1880 without ever having played a first-class game.
4. Joseph Emile Patrick McMaster (England) deserves his spot in the record books. His Test appearance for England v South Africa in 1888-89 was his only match in first-class cricket. As he scored a duck, McMaster must be the only cricketer of Test match status who has never scored a run in his entire first-class career.
5. B.A.F.Grieve (England) appeared in only three first-class matches, of which two (v South Africa 1888-89) were Test matches.
6. T.R.McKibbin (Australia) played against England in 1894-95 in what was his sixth first-class match. J.J.Ferris, J.Darling, A.G.Fairfax, E.L.a'Beckett, D.G.Bradman, W.J.O'Reilly, J.R.Thomson, I.C.Davis and G.M.Wood were other Australians to make their Test debuts within ten matches of their first-class debut.
7. S.F.Barnes (England) was selected to tour Australia in 1901-02 after only six first-class games, in which he took 13 wickets.
8. D.W.Carr (England) in 1909 — aged 37 — played his first first-class game for Kent on May 27. He was chosen for Gentlemen v Players on July 8, made his debut in county cricket on July 29, and appeared for England v Australia on August 9. It was his seventh first-class game and he had risen to Test honours within ten weeks of his first-class debut.
9. G.N.Francis (West Indies) had never played a first-class game before touring England in 1923. (No Tests were played that year).
10. G.M.Parker (South Africa) came into the South African Test side (v England at Birmingham in 1924) from the Bradford League for only his second first-class match. He played in one more Test in that series — his entire first-class career comprised three games, two of which were Tests.
11. I.A.R.Peebles (England) played for his country v South Africa at Johannesburg in 1927-28, before he had made his debut in county cricket.
12. A.G.Chipperfield (Australia) was selected to tour England in 1934 after only three first-class games.
13. A.L.Valentine and S.Ramadhin (West Indies) were selected to tour England in 1950 after each had played in only two first-class games.
14. Edric Leadbeater (England) was flown out to India as a replacement for A.E.G.Rhodes during the 1951-52 tour of India. He played his first Test before being capped for his county.
15. J.E.F.Beck (South Africa 1953-54) and J.C.Alabaster (India 1955-56) were chosen for New Zealand tours without having made a first-class appearance and made their Test debuts after five and one match respectively.
16. C.C.Griffith (West Indies) was chosen for his first Test v England at Port-of-Spain in 1959-60, after only one first-class match.
17. G.E.Vivian (New Zealand) was selected to tour India, Pakistan and England in 1965 without having appeared in a first-class match. He made his first-class debut in the Test v India at Calcutta in 1964-65.
18. M.D.Marshall (West Indies) was selected for the tour of India 1978-79 after only one first-class appearance and played in his first Test (v India at Bombay) after only three matches.
19. A.Ranatunga (Sri Lanka) made his first-class debut v the touring English team in February 1982 and made his Test debut in his next game a week later.
20. Wasim Akram (Pakistan) was selected to tour New Zealand in 1984-85 after two first-class games and made his Test debut at Auckland in his fourth match.
21. G.F.Labrooy (Sri Lanka) was chosen to tour India in 1986-87 without any first-class experience and made his Test debut in only his second game.
22. U.Ranchod was chosen for Zimbabwe's first Test tour, to India in 1992-93, without having played in a first class match. He made his first class debut in the only Test played.
23. Saleem Elahi (Pakistan) made his first-class debut on the tour of Australia in 1995-96 and his Test debut in his third first-class match. He had made his Limited Over International debut two months earlier (scoring a century).

A NOTABLE UMPIRING DEBUT

Umpire W.E.Alley, standing in his first Test match — England v India at Birmingham in 1974 — was given little time to settle in. He was required to make a decision about the first ball of the match. His verdict? S.M.Gavaskar — out — caught behind by Knott, bowled Arnold.

INGLORIOUS DEBUTS

1. M.Leyland was dismissed for a duck during England's only innings in the Third Test against West Indies at The Oval in 1928 — his first appearance for his country.
2. D.G.Bradman scored only 18 and 1 in his debut in the First Test against England at Brisbane in the 1928-29 season. He was subsequently dropped from the team for the Second Test but reinstated for the third, scoring 79 and 112.
3. L.Hutton (England) scored a duck and 1 in his debut Test match, v New Zealand at Lord's in 1937. In his second match, at Manchester, he made 100 and 14.
4. I.M.Chappell (Australia) made a modest 11 runs and bowled 26 overs without a wicket in his debut Test against Pakistan at Melbourne in 1964-65.
5. New Zealand batsman J.M.Parker fractured a bone in his hand whilst fielding against Pakistan at Wellington in 1973 and was unable to bat in his debut match.
6. G.A.Gooch (England) recorded a pair of ducks in his first Test which was against Australia at Birmingham in 1975.
7. In 1991-92, S.K.Warne (Australia) took 1/150 v India at Sydney on his Test debut.
8. O.A.C.Banks (West Indies) took 3 for 204 on his Test debut v Australia at Bridgetown in 2002-03 — the most runs conceded by a player on his Test debut.

GREAT CRICKETING FAMILIES

1. Gregory (Australia). The family produced four Test cricketers, two of whom (Dave and Syd) captained Australia. Father of the clan was Edward William who played in Sydney in the 1820's. Four of his children played cricket for NSW — Dave (Australia's first captain), Ned, Charlie and Arthur. Ned's sons were Syd and Charles (who scored the first triple century in a first-class game in Australia). Jack, who arrived on the scene in the 1920's, was the grandson of Edward William — a cricket star a century after his grandfather.
2. Bannerman (Australia). Elder brother Charles faced the first ball bowled in Test cricket, scored the first run, the first 50 and the first 100. He was also the first Australian to make a century in England, New Zealand and Canada. Younger brother Alec scored the first run in a Test on English soil.
3. Amarnath (India). Father Lala and son Surinder are the only father-son combination to record a hundred on their Test debuts. Second son Mohinder narrowly missed becoming one of the few to score a century in each innings when he made 90 and 100 against Australia in Perth in 1977-78.
4. Mohammad (Pakistan). At least one Mohammad brother represented Pakistan in 100 of that country's first 101 Tests in 27 years of Test cricket between 1952-80. A fifth brother — Raees — was once Pakistan's 12th man against India (1954-55). Three brothers — Hanif, Mushtaq and Sadiq — all played together in one Test (v New Zealand 1969) and all batted and bowled during the match. Between them Hanif, Mushtaq, Sadiq and Wazir aggregated almost 11,000 Test runs with 29 centuries. They have also held 115 catches and taken 80 wickets. Hanif's son, Shoaib also played in 45 Tests, scoring 2705 runs with 7 centuries, holding 22 catches and taking 5 wickets.
5. Chappell (Australia). Grandsons of Victor Richardson, Ian, Greg and Trevor represent only the fourth set of three brothers to appear in Test cricket. Ian and Greg captained Australia more than 50 times, are the only brothers to score centuries in each innings of the same Test, and were the first brothers to score a century in the same Test. They were the first brothers who have each scored over 5,000 Test runs.
6. Waugh (Australia). Steve and Mark — the first set of twins to play Test cricket — became the first set of brothers to play together in more than 50 Tests and the second set of brothers (after the Chappells) to each score over 5000 Test runs.
7. Flower (Zimbabwe). Andrew and Grant were the leading batsmen for Zimbabwe. They are the only players to score over 3000 runs for Zimbabwe and scored 18 of the 37 Test hundreds scored during their playing career. Grant played in Zimbabwe's first 67 Tests and, with brother Andy are only the second pair of brothers to score a hundred in each innings of a Test.

RELATED TEST PLAYERS

FATHER AND SON AND GRANDSON

G.A. and R.G.A.Headley (West Indies) and D.W.Headley (England)

M.Jahangir Khan (India) and Majid Khan (Pakistan) and Bazid Khan (Pakistan)

FATHER AND TWO SONS

N.B.Amarnath and his sons M. and S. (India)

W.A.Hadlee and his sons D.R. and R.J. (New Zealand)

FATHERS AND SONS

N.B. & M., S.Amarnath (India)
W.M. & R.W.Anderson (New Zealand)
W.P. & G.E.Bradburn (New Zealand)
A.R. & M.A.Butcher (England)
B.L. & C.L.Cairns (New Zealand)
M.C. & C.S.Cowdrey (England)
D.K. & A.D.Gaekwad (India)
E.J. & E.S.Gregory (Australia)
W.A. & D.R., R.J.Hadlee (New Zealand)
J.Hardstaff, sr & J.Hardstaff, jr (England)
P.G.Z. & C.Z.Harris (New Zealand)
G.A. & R.G.A.Headley (West Indies)
R.G.A.Headley (West Indies) & D.W.Headley (England)
F.Hearne (England and South Africa) and G.A.L.Hearne (South Africa)
L. & R.A.Hutton (England)
I.J. & S.P.Jones (England)
H.S. & H.H.Kanitkar (India)
J.D. & D.T.Lindsay (South Africa)
V.L. & S.V.Manjrekar (India)
M.H. & A.V.Mankad (India)
F.T. & F.G.Mann (England)
Hanif Mohammad & Shoaib Mohammad (Pakistan)
Majid Khan & Bazid Khan (Pakistan)
Nazar Mohammad & Mudassar Nazar (Pakistan)
A.W. & A.D.Nourse (South Africa)
J.H. & J.M.Parks (England)
Nawab of Pataudi, sr (England and India) & Nawab of Pataudi, jr (India)
P.M. & S.M.Pollock (South Africa)
Pankaj & Pranab Roy (India)
O.C. & A.P.H.Scott (West Indies)
M.J. & A.J.Stewart (England)
F.W. & M.W.Tate (England)
C.L. & D.C.H.Townsend (England)
L.R. & L.Tuckett (South Africa)
H.G. & G.E.Vivian (New Zealand)
S.Wazir Ali (India) & Khalid Wazir (Pakistan)
E.D.Weekes & D.A.Murray (West Indies)
Yograj Singh & Yuvraj Singh (India)

FOUR BROTHERS

Hanif, Mushtaq, Sadiq & Wazir Mohammad (Pakistan)
Hanif, Mushtaq and Sadiq all played against New Zealand at Karachi[1] in 1969-70

THREE BROTHERS

G.S., I.M. & T.M.Chappell (Australia)

E.M., G.F. & W.G.Grace (England)
All three Grace brothers played against Australia at The Oval in 1880.

Manzoor Elahi, Saleem Elahi & Zahoor Elahi (Pakistan)
A., F. & G.G.Hearne (England) - F.Hearne also played for South Africa
A. & G.G.Hearne (E) & F.Hearne (SA) all played in the match between South Africa and England at Cape Town in 1891-92.

A., D. & S.Ranatunga (Sri Lanka)

A.B., L.J. & V.M.Tancred (South Africa)

TWO BROTHERS

Australia

K.A. and R.G.Archer
A.C. and C.Bannerman
J. and R.Benaud
G. and W.F.Giffen
D.W. and E.J.Gregory
M.R. and R.N.Harvey
C.E. and R.W.McLeod
A.E. and G.H.S.Trott
H. and J.W.Trumble
M.E. and S.R.Waugh (twins)

England

A.E.R. and A.H.H.Gilligan
A.W. and I.A.Greig
G. and J.R.Gunn
A.J. and B.C.Hollioake
D.W. and P.E.Richardson
C.L. and R.A.Smith
C.T. and G.B.Studd
G.E. and J.T.Tyldesley
C.E.M. and E.R.Wilson

South Africa

P.A.M. and R.H.M.Hands
G. and P.N.Kirsten
A.J. and D.B.Pithey
P.M. and R.G.Pollock
A.R. and W.H.M.Richards
A.M.B. and E.A.B.Rowan
S.D. and S.J.Snooke
G.L. and L.E.Tapscott
D. and H.W.Taylor
H.F. and W.W.Wade

West Indies

D.S. and E.S.Atkinson
F.J. and J.H.Cameron
C.M. and R.J.Christiani
B.A. and C.A.Davis
G.C. and R.S.Grant
N.E. and R.E.Marshall
M.N. and R.G.Samuels
E.L. and W.H.St Hill
J.B. and V.H.Stollmeyer
P.T.Collins and F.H.Edwards

New Zealand

B.P. and J.G.Bracewell
J.J. and M.D.Crowe
D.R. and R.J.Hadlee
M.N. and R.G.Hart
P.A. and M.J.Horne
G.P. and H.J.Howarth
J.M. and N. M.Parker
H.J.H. and J.A.H.Marshall (twins)

India

M. and S.Amarnath
L.Amar Singh and L.Ramji
A L. and M.L.Apte
B P. and S.P.Gupte
A G Kripal Singh and
A G Milkha Singh
C.K. and C.S.Nayudu
S Nazir Ali and S.Wazir Ali

Pakistan

Azmat Rana and Shafqat Rana
Humayun Farhat and Imran Farhat
Moin Khan and Nadeem Khan
Pervez Sajjad and Waqar Hassan
Rameez Raja and Wasim Raja
Saeed Ahmed and Younis Ahmed

Sri Lanka

L.W. and S.M.S.Kaluperuma
D.P. and T.T.Samaraweera
M.S. and S.Wettimuny

Zimbabwe

A. and G.W.Flower
G.J. and J.A.Rennie
B.C. and P.A.Strang
The Flower, Rennie and Strang brothers played for Zimbabwe against New Zealand at Harare in 1997-98.

TEST CRICKETERS WHO BATTED RIGHT-HANDED AND BOWLED LEFT-ARMED

Australia

M.J.Bennett
N.W.Bracken
R.J.Bright
M.J.Clarke
H.L.Collins
A.R.Dell
L.O.Fleetwood-Smith
J.B.Gannon
T.G.Hogan
R.J.Inverarity
B.P.Julian
C.G.Macartney
I.Meckiff
D.J.Sincock
E.R.H.Toshack
M.R.Whitney
W.J.Whitty

England

J.C.Balderstone
R.G.Barlow
C.Blythe
J.B.Bolus
J.Briggs
H.R.Bromley-Davenport
S.J.E.Brown
D.B.Carr
D.C.S.Compton
C.Cook
G.Cook
N.G.B.Cook
P.H.Edmonds
F.R.Foster
A.F.Giles
M.J.Hilton
G.H.Hirst
J.L.Hopwood
J.Iddon
R.K.Illingworth
I.J.Jones
J.K.Lever
G.A.R.Lock
B.W.Luckhurst
A.D.Mullally
G.A.E.Paine
C.W.L.Parker
M.M.Patel
W.Rhodes
F.E.Rumsey
A.M.Smith
D.S.Steele
P.C.R.Tufnell
D.L.Underwood
H.Verity
W.Voce
A.Waddington
P.M.Walker
J.C.White
H.I.Young
J.A.Young

South Africa

P.R.Adams
W.H.Ashley

H.V.Baumgartner
C.P.Carter
G.A.Chevalier
C.E.Eksteen
M.K.Elgie
A.E.Hall
C.W.Henderson
G.A.Kempis
M.J.Macaulay
A.H.McKinnon
Q.McMillan
N.B.F.Mann
J.B.Plimsoll
N.A.Quinn
A.Rose-Innes
G.A.Rowe
P.C.Strydon
P.L.van der Merwe
C.M.Willoughby

West Indies
M.R.Bynoe
G.M.Carew
P.T.Collins
B.D.Julien
R.R.Jumadeen
N.C.McGarrell
S.Shivnarine
A.L.Valentine
F.M.M.Worrell

New Zealand
G.I.Allott
S.L.Boock
T.B.Burtt
M.E.Chapple
R.O.Collinge
F.E.Fisher
N.Gallichan
E.J.Gray
A.F.Lissette
J.F.M.Morrison
J.Newman
D.R.O'Sullivan
D.G.Sewell
G.B.Troup
B.W.Yuile

India
B.S.Bedi
R.J.D.Jamshedji
Maninder Singh
M.H.Mankad
Mushtaq Ali
A.Nehra
R.G.Patel
A.K.Sharma
R.J.Shastri
K.K.Tarapore
S.L.Venkatapathy Raju
Zaheer Khan

Pakistan
Farrukh Zamman
Ijaz Ahmed[1]
Kabir Khan
Liaqat Ali
Mufasir-ul-Haq
Nadeem Ghauri
Nadeem Khan
Pervez Sajjad
Salim Jaffer
Shujauddin

Sri Lanka
S.D.Anurasiri
M.R.C.N.Bandaratilake
W.R.S.de Silva
D.Hettiarachchi
S.Jeganathan
A.K.Kuruppuarachchi
A.N.Ranasinghe
K.J.Silva
R.G.C.E.Wijesuriya
P.K.Wijetunge

Zimbabwe
D.H.Brain
G.W.Flower
M.P.Jarvis
B.C.Strang

Bangladesh
Enamul Haque[2]
Tapash Baisya

TEST CRICKETERS WHO BATTED LEFT-HANDED AND BOWLED RIGHT-ARMED

Australia
J.Angel
D.D.Blackie
I.W.Callen
S.H.Cook
R.M.Cowper
A.C.Dale
L.S.Darling
M.T.G.Elliott

S.H.Emery
R.A.Gaunt
J.M.Gregory
R.N.Harvey
M.L.Hayden
T.V.Hohns
W.P.Howell
J.L.Langer
T.J.Laughlin
E.L.McCormick
K.D.Mackay
T.R.McKibbin
R.W.McLeod
A.L.Mann
R.W.Marsh
R.L.A.Massie
G.R.J.Matthews
L.C.Mayne
J.D.A.O'Connor
W.J.O'Reilly
G.F.Rorke
B.K.Shepherd
M.A.Taylor
P.L.Taylor
T.R.Veivers
K.C.Wessels
S.Young

England
J.M.Anderson
R.W.Barber
J.Birkenshaw
B.C.Broad
M.A.Butcher
D.B.Close
G.R.Dilley
J.H.Edrich
R.M.Ellison
J.A.Flavell
G.Fowler
D.I.Gower
G.M.Hamilton
K.Higgs
J.T.Ikin
S.P.Jones
M.S.Nichols
C.M.Old
P.H.Parfitt
R.T.D.Perks
J.S.E.Price
G.Pullar
P.E.Richardson
C.P.Schofield
T.F.Smailes
J.B.Statham
R.Subba Row
R.Tattersall
G.P.Thorpe
C.L.Townsend
M.E.Trescothick
D.W.White

South Africa
A.C.Dawson
G.Kirsten
L.Klusener
J.F.W.Nicolson
A.W.Nourse
R.G.Pollock
J.A.Rudolph
G.C.Smith
K.C.Wessels

West Indies
C.E.L.Ambrose
M.C.Carew
S.Chanderpaul
N.Deonarine
C.H.Gayle
J.D.C.Goddard
H.A.Gomes
W.W.Hinds
A.B.Howard
A.I.Kallicharran
C.B.Lambert
B.C.Lara
P.D.Lashley
C.H.Lloyd
M.A.M.McLean
C.A.McWatt
M.V.Nagamootoo
G.C.Shillingford
D.S.Smith

New Zealand
V.R.Brown
D.C.Cleverley
G.F.Cresswell
B.A.Edgar
M.J.Greatbatch
R.J.Hadlee
C.Z.Harris
E.G.McLeod
L.S.M.Miller
B.D.Morrison
J.D.P.Oram
G.W.F.Overton
J.F.Reid
I.M.Sinclair
M.C.Snedden
B.R.Taylor

R.G.Twose
J.T.C.Vaughan
G.E.Vivian
J.G.Wright

India
S.Amarnath
N.J.Contractor
G.Gambir
S.C.Ganguly
H.H.Kanitkar
A.G.Milka Singh
S.V.Nayak
A.M.Pai
S.Ramesh
R.R.Singh

Pakistan
Abdul Hafeez
Imran Farhat
Mohammad Asif
Sadiq Mohammad
Shadab Kabir
Taufeeq Umar
Wasim Raja

Sri Lanka
F.S.Ahangama
R.P.Arnold
E.A.R.de Silva
A.P.Gurusinha
R.S.Kalpage
D.K.Liyanage
M.A.W.R.Madurasinghe
J.Mubarak
M.N.Nawaz
A.Ranatunga
S.Ranatunga
J.R.Ratnayeke
H.P.Tillekeratne
K.P.J.Warnaweera

Zimbabwe
A.M.Blignaut
A.D.R.Campbell
S.M.Ervine
A.Flower
N.C.Johnson
S.G.Peall
B.G.Rogers
A.H.Shah

Bangladesh
Faisal Hossain

TEST CRICKETERS WHO HAVE BEEN KNIGHTED

Australia
D.G.Bradman

England
Sir George Oswald Browning Allen
Sir Alec Victor Bedser
Sir Michael Colin Cowdrey
Sir John Berry Hobbs
Sir Leonard Hutton
Sir Francis Stanley Jackson
Sir Henry Dudley Gresham Leveson Gower
Sir Timothy Carew O'Brien
Sir Charles Aubrey Smith
Sir Pelham Francis Warner

South Africa
Sir Murray Bissett
Sir William Henry Milton

West Indies
Sir Learie Nicholas Constantine
Sir Clive Hubert Lloyd
Sir Isaac Vivian Alexander Richards
Sir Garfield St Auburn Sobers
Sir Frank Mortimor Maglinne Worrell
Sir Clyde Leopold Walcott
Sir Everton de Courcy Weekes

New Zealand
Sir Richard John Hadlee
Sir Jack Newman

India
Sir Gajapatairaj Vijaya Anada, The Maharajkumar of Vizianagram.

The following were made life peers:
Baron Constantine of Maraval and Nelson.
Baron Cowdrey of Tonbridge
Lord Harris
Lord Hawke
Baron David Stuart Sheppard (Bishop of Liverpool)

CRICKETERS' ROLL OF HONOUR — TEST CRICKETERS KILLED IN THE BOER WAR, WORLD WAR I AND WORLD WAR II

Boer War
J.J.Ferris (Australia/England)

World War I

A.Cotter (Australia)
C.Blythe (England)
K.L.Hutchings (England)
R.M.H.Hands (South Africa)
E.B.Lundie (South Africa)
R.O.Schwarz (South Africa)
G.C.White (South Africa)

World War II

R.G.Gregory (Australia)
K.Farnes (England)
G.B.Legge (England)
G.G.Macaulay (England)
M.J.L.Turnbull (England)
H.Verity (England)
A.W.Briscoe (South Africa)
A.B.C.Langton (South Africa)
D.A.R.Moloney (New Zealand

HIGHEST SCORES FOR EACH BATTING POSITION

No							
1	364	L.Hutton	England	v	Australia	The Oval	1938
2	380	M.L.Hayden	Australia	v	Zimbabwe	Perth	2003-04
3	400*	B.C.Lara	West Indies	v	England	St John's	2003-04
4	374	D.P.M.D.Jayawardene	Sri Lanka	v	South Africa	Colombo (SSC)	2006-07
5	329	Inzamamul Haq	Pakistan	v	New Zealand	Lahore[2]	2001-02
6	304	D.G.Bradman	Australia	v	England	Leeds	1934
7	250	K.D.Walters	Australia	v	New Zealand	Christchurch	1976-77
8	270	D.G.Bradman	Australia	v	England	Melbourne	1936-37
9	257*	Wasim Akram	Pakistan	v	Zimbabwe	Sheikhupura	1996-97
10	173	I.D.S.Smith	New Zealand	v	India	Auckland	1989-90
11	117	W.W.Read	England	v	Australia	The Oval	1884
12	75	Zaheer Khan	India	v	Bangladesh	Dhaka	2004-05

NUMBER TEN TOP SCORING IN A COMPLETED INNINGS

117	346	W.W.Read	England	v	Australia	The Oval	1884
51*	181	T.W.Garrett	Australia	v	England	Sydney	1884-85
17	53	J.Briggs	England	v	Australia	Lord's	1888
104	353	R.A.Duff	Australia	v	England	Melbourne	1901-02
41*	182	A.S.Kennedy	England	v	South Africa	Johannesburg	1922-23
76	294	G.G.Macaulay	England	v	Australia	Leeds	1926
41	158	N.B.F.Mann	South Africa	v	Australia	Port Elizabeth	1949-50
17	72	P.S.Heine	South Africa	v	England	Johannesburg[3]	1956-57
41*	161	A.M.Moir	New Zealand	v	England	The Oval	1958
35*	200	Afaq Hussain	Pakistan	v	England	Lahore[2]	1961-62
48*	258	S.A.Durani	India	v	West Indies	Bridgetown	1961-62
53	174	G.A.R.Lock	England	v	West Indies	Leeds	1963
26*	138	R.W.Blair	New Zealand	v	South Africa	Dunedin	1963-64
42	194	V.A.Holder	West Indies	v	New Zealand	Port-of-Spain	1971-72
42	184	R.A.L.Massie	Australia	v	Pakistan	Sydney	1972-73
63*	207	Madan Lal	India	v	West Indies	Kanpur	1983-84
90	343	Sarfraz Nawaz	Pakistan	v	England	Lahore[2]	1983-84
83*	293	J.G.Bracewell	New Zealand	v	Australia	Sydney	1985-86
38	224	S.K.Sharma	India	v	England	Lord's	1990
65	255	C.C.Lewis	England	v	West Indies	Birmingham	1991
29*	111	C.J.McDermott	Australia	v	South Africa	Sydney	1993-94
22	119	G.P.Wickramasinghe	Sri Lanka	v	India	Ahmedabad	1993-94
17*	114	J.Srinath	India	v	West Indies	Chandigarh	1994-95
108	364	P.L.Symcox	South Africa	v	Pakistan	Johannesburg[3]	1997-98
46	107	S.B.Doull	New Zealand	v	England	Birmingham	1999
20	83	J.Srinath	India	v	New Zealand	Mohali	1999-00
37*	123	B.C.Strang	Zimbabwe	v	England	Lord's	2000
29	125	N.A.M.McLean	West Indies	v	England	The Oval	2000

39	184	D.Gough	England	v	Australia	The Oval	2001
24*	109	Enamul Hoque	Bangladesh	v	Zimbabwe	Dhaka	2001-02
48	284	Tapash Baisya	Bangladesh	v	West Indies	Kingston	2004
66	262	Tapash Baisya	Bangladesh	v	New Zealand	Chittagong	2004-05

NUMBER ELEVEN TOP SCORING IN A COMPLETED INNINGS

50	163	F.R.Spofforth	Australia	v	England	Melbourne	1884-85
16	44	T.R.McKibbin	Australia	v	England	The Oval	1896
62*	333	A.E.E.Vogler	South Africa	v	England	Cape Town	1905-06
30*	199	Asif Masood	Pakistan	v	West Indies	Lahore[2]	1974-75
34	215	A.M.J.G.Amerasinghe	Sri Lanka	v	New Zealand	Kandy	1983-84
31	124	Talha Jubair	Bangladesh	v	India	Chittagong	2004-05
42	304	S.J.Harmison	England	v	South Africa	Cape Town	2004-05

HIGHEST SCORE AT THE FALL OF EACH WICKET

1st	413	India (3d-537)	v	New Zealand	Madras[2]	1955-56
2nd	615	Sri Lanka (6d-952)	v	India	Colombo (RPS)	1997-98
3rd	638	Sri Lanka (5d-756)	v	South Africa	Colombo (SSC)	2006-07
4th	790	Sri Lanka (6d-952)	v	India	Colombo (RPS)	1997-98
5th	921	Sri Lanka (6d-952)	v	India	Colombo (RPS)	1997-98
6th	924	Sri Lanka (6d-952)	v	India	Colombo (RPS)	1997-98
7th	876	England (7d-903)	v	Australia	The Oval	1938
8th	813	England (849)	v	West Indies	Kingston	1929-30
9th	821	England (849)	v	West Indies	Kingston	1929-30
10th	849	England (849)	v	West Indies	Kingston	1929-30

LOWEST SCORE AT THE FALL OF EACH WICKET

1st	0	Numerous instances				
2nd	0	{Numerous instances				
		{Australia(7d-32)	v	England	Brisbane[2]	1950-51
3rd	0	{India (165)	v	England	Leeds	1952
		{Zimbabwe (174)	v	Sri Lanka	Harare	1999-2000
		{Pakistan (245)	v	India	Karachi[1]	2005-06
4th	0	India (165)	v	England	Leeds	1952
5th	6	India (98)	v	England	The Oval	1952
6th	7	Australia (70)	v	England	Manchester	1888
7th	14	Australia (44)	v	England	The Oval	1896
8th	19	Australia (44)	v	England	The Oval	1896
9th	25	Australia (44)	v	England	The Oval	1896
10th	26	New Zealand (26)	v	England	Auckland	1954-55

MOST RUNS ADDED DURING A BATSMAN'S INNINGS

runs	Batsman (Score)	Match particulars				
770	L.Hutton (364)	England	v	Australia	The Oval	1938
742	D.P.M.D.Jayawardene (374)	Sri Lanka	v	South Africa	Colombo (SSC)	2006-07
735	M.L.Hayden (380)	Australia	v	Zimbabwe	Perth	2003-04
720	A.Sandham (325)	England	v	West Indies	Kingston	1929-30
718	B.C.Lara (400*)	West Indies	v	England	Bridgetown	2003-04
703	G.S.Sobers (365*)	West Indies	v	Pakistan	Kingston	1957-58
646	R.B.Simpson (311)	Australia	v	England	Manchester	1964
641	G.A.Gooch (333)	England	v	India	Lord's	1990
626	Hanif Mohammad (337)	Pakistan	v	West Indies	Bridgetown	1957-58
615	S.T.Jayasuriya (340)	Sri Lanka	v	India	Colombo (RPS)	1997-98

SIDE SCORING SAME TOTAL IN EACH INNINGS

Team		Opponent	Venue	Season
New Zealand (172 + 172)	v	South Africa (8d-524)	Wellington	1952-53
New Zealand (208 + 208)	v	West Indies (404 + 1-13)	Wellington	1955-56
India (136 + 136)	v	Australia (177 + 9d-189)	Calcutta	1956-57
India (201 + 201)	v	Australia (406)	Sydney	1980-81
Pakistan (230 + 3-230)	v	New Zealand (267 + 189)	Hyderabad	1984-85
New Zealand (161 + 161)	v	Australia (6d-544)	Hobart	1993-94
West Indies (189 + 4-189)	v	Sri Lanka (223 + 152)	St John's	1996-97
Sri Lanka (306 + 306)	v	South Africa (418 + 264)	Cape Town	1997-98
Bangladesh (148 + 148)	v	Pakistan (9d-465)	Chittagong	2001-02
India (407 + 9d-407)	v	Pakistan (393 + 226)	Kolkata	2004-05

BOTH TEAMS SCORING SAME TOTAL IN FIRST INNINGS

Team		Opponent	Venue	Season
South Africa (199)	v	England (199)	Durban[1]	1909-10
West Indies (222)	v	India (222)	Kanpur	1958-59
Pakistan (402)	v	New Zealand (402)	Auckland	1972-73
Australia (7d-428)	v	West Indies (428)	Kingston	1972-73
England (390)	v	India (390)	Birmingham	1986
West Indies (5d-593)	v	England (593)	St John's	1993-94
Australia (240)	v	West Indies (240)	St John's	2002-03

TWENTY BOWLERS IN A MATCH

South Africa (7d-501 + 346)	v	England (442 + 0-15)	Cape Town	1964-65

ELEVEN BOWLERS IN AN INNINGS

England	v	Australia (551)	The Oval	1884
Australia	v	Pakistan (2-382)	Faisalabad	1979-80
India	v	West Indies (9d-629)	St John's	2001-02
South Africa	v	West Indies (747)	St John's	2004-05

LONGEST MATCHES

10 days	South Africa	v	England	Durban[2]	1938-39
9 days	West Indies	v	England	Kingston	1929-30
8 days	Australia	v	England	Melbourne	1928-29

MOST OVERS BOWLED IN AN INNINGS

Overs	Bowled by (innings)		Opponent (score)	Venue	Series
335.2	Australia (1st)	v	England (7d-903)	The Oval	1938
319.0	West Indies (2nd)	v	Pakistan (8d-657)	Bridgetown	1957-58
311.0	England (1st)	v	Australia (551)	The Oval	1884
304.1	Australia (1st)	v	England (434)	The Oval	1886
293.1	Australia (1st)	v	England (611)	Manchester	1964
274.1	England (1st)	v	Australia (279)	Melbourne	1884-85
273.7	England (1st)	v	Australia (491)	Melbourne	1928-29
272.5	Australia (1st)	v	England (636)	Sydney	1928-29
271.0	India (1st)	v	Sri Lanka (6d-952)	Colombo (RPS)	1997-98
268.0	West Indies (1st)	v	New Zealand (3d-543)	Georgetown	1971-72
259.0	Australia (1st)	v	England (353)	Lord's	1886
258.2	West Indies (1st)	v	England (849)	Kingston	1929-30
258.0	West Indies (2nd)	v	England (4d-583)	Birmingham	1957
256.5	England (1st)	v	Australia (695)	The Oval	1930
255.5	England (1st)	v	Australia (8d-656)	Manchester	1964

248.0	India (1st)	v	West Indies (9d-629)	St John's	2001-02
245.4	West Indies (1st)	v	Australia (8d-758)	Kingston	1954-55
245.2	West Indies (2nd)	v	England (436)	Nottingham	1950
243.2	Australia (1st)	v	England (369)	Adelaide	1884-85
241.5	New Zealand (1st)	v	India (7d-531)	Delhi	1955-56
241.3	India (1st)	v	West Indies (475)	Bridgetown	1961-62
240.0	England (1st)	v	South Africa (9d-483)	Nottingham	1951
239.4	England (1st)	v	West Indies (8d-563)	Bridgetown	1959-60
237.2	Australia (2nd)	v	England (308)	Melbourne	1881-82
237.0	England (1st)	v	Australia (320)	Melbourne	1881-82
235.5	West Indies (1st)	v	Australia (668)	Bridgetown	1954-55
235.3	England (1st)	v	South Africa (538)	Leeds	1951
235.2	South Africa (1st)	v	West Indies (747)	St John's	2004-05
233.5	Pakistan (1st)	v	England (507)	Karachi[1]	1961-62
233.5	Australia (2nd)	v	England (538)	The Oval	1975
232.0	England (1st)	v	Australia (6d-729)	Lord's	1930
231.0	Australia (1st)	v	England (524)	Sydney	1932-33
227.3	New Zealand (1st)	v	England (439)	Auckland	1983-84
227.0	Pakistan (1st)	v	England (545)	The Oval	1974
227.0	Pakistan (1st)	v	India (9d-539)	Madras[2]	1960-61
226.2	South Africa (2nd)	v	England (551)	Nottingham	1947

COMPLETE SIDE DISMISSED TWICE IN A DAY

					Day	
India	(58 + 82)	v	England	Manchester	3rd	1952
Zimbabwe	(59 + 99)	v	New Zealand	Harare	2nd	2005-06

MATCHES COMPLETED IN TWO DAYS

England	(101 + 77)	v	Australia	(63 + 122)	The Oval	1882
England	(53 + 62)	v	Australia	(116 + 60)	Lord's	1888
England	(317)	v	Australia	(80 + 100)	The Oval	1888
England	(172)	v	Australia	(81 + 70)	Manchester	1888
South Africa	(84 + 129)	v	England	(148 + 2-67)	Port Elizabeth	1888-89
South Africa	(47 + 43)	v	England	(292)	Cape Town	1888-89
England	(100 + 8-95)	v	Australia	(92 + 102)	The Oval	1890
South Africa	(93 + 30)	v	England	(185 + 226)	Port Elizabeth	1895-96
South Africa	(115 + 117)	v	England	(265)	Cape Town	1895-96
England	(176 + 0-14)	v	South Africa	(95 + 93)	The Oval	1912
Australia	(448)	v	South Africa	(265 + 95)	Manchester	1912
England	(112 + 147)	v	Australia	(232 + 0-30)	Nottingham	1921
Australia	(8d-328)	v	West Indies	(99 + 107)	Melbourne	1930-31
South Africa	(157 + 98)	v	Australia	(439)	Johannesburg[1]	1935-36
New Zealand	(42 + 54)	v	Australia	(8d-199)	Wellington	1945-46
England	(272)	v	West Indies	(172 + 61)	Leeds	2000
Pakistan	(59 + 53)	v	Australia	(310)	Sharjah	2002-03
South Africa	(3d-340)	v	Zimbabwe	(54 + 265)	Cape Town	2004-05
New Zealand	(9d-452)	v	Zimbabwe	(59 + 99)	Harare	2005-06

SHORTEST COMPLETED TESTS (BY BALLS BOWLED)

Balls	Runs	Wkts	Match particulars			Venue	Series
656	234	29	Australia	v	South Africa	Melbourne	1931-32
672	309	29	West Indies	v	England	Bridgetown	1934-35
788	323	30	England	v	Australia	Manchester	1888
792	291	40	England	v	Australia	Lord's	1888

796	382	30	South Africa	v	England	Cape Town	1888-89
815	378	30	England	v	South Africa	The Oval	1912
872	295	28	New Zealand	v	Australia	Wellington	1945-46
883	499	16	South Africa	v	England	Centurion	1999-2000
893	422	29	Pakistan	v	Australia	Sharjah	2002-03
911	421	28	Australia	v	England	Sydney	1894-95
940	659	23	South Africa	v	Zimbabwe	Cape Town	2004-05
941	505	30	England	v	West Indies	Leeds	2000
976	423	40	England	v	South Africa	Leeds	1907
983	467	31	West Indies	v	Australia	Port-of-Spain	1994-95
1006	534	40	South Africa	v	England	Port Elizabeth	1895-96
1014	428	32	South Africa	v	England	Port Elizabeth	1888-89
1034	450	34	Australia	v	England	Brisbane[2]	1950-51
1034	536	29	England	v	West Indies	Birmingham	1995
1041	482	30	New Zealand	v	England	Christchurch	1983-84
1049	392	40	England	v	Australia	The Oval	1896
1050	534	28	Australia	v	West Indies	Melbourne	1930-31
1056	440	29	Sri Lanka	v	Pakistan	Kandy	1985-86

SHORTEST INNINGS (BY BALLS BOWLED)

Balls	Bowled by (inns)		Opponent (Score)	Venue	Series
75	England (1st)	v	South Africa (30)	Birmingham	1924
94	England (2nd)	v	South Africa (30)	Port Elizabeth	1895-96
94	Australia (1st)	v	England (61)	Melbourne	1901-02
99	England (2nd)	v	Australia (58)	Brisbane[2]	1936-37
102	England (2nd)	v	India (42)	Lord's	1974
108	England (2nd)	v	Australia (8-35)	Manchester	1953
113	England (1st)	v	Australia (53)	Lord's	1896
114	England (2nd)	v	South Africa (35)	Cape Town	1898-99
114	England (2nd)	v	South Africa (43)	Cape Town	1888-89
115	West Indies (2nd)	v	England (46)	Port-of-Spain	1993-94
115	Australia (2nd)	v	West Indies (51)	Port-of-Spain	1998-99
118	England (2nd)	v	Australia (60)	Lord's	1888
125	England (2nd)	v	Australia (70)	Manchester	1888
128	Australia (1st)	v	Pakistan (62)	Perth	1981-82
130	England (2nd)	v	Australia (44)	The Oval	1896
130	England (1st)	v	India (58)	Manchester	1952
132	Australia (2nd)	v	South Africa (85)	Johannesburg[1]	1902-03
136	England (2nd)	v	Australia (65)	The Oval	1912
137	Australia (2nd)	v	England (101)	Melbourne	1903-04
138	England (1st)	v	Australia (36)	Birmingham	1902
140	Australia (1st)	v	South Africa (36	Melbourne	1931-32
143	Australia (1st)	v	England (45)	Sydney	1886-87
149	Australia (2nd)	v	Pakistan (53)	Sharjah	2002-03
151	England (1st)	v	Australia (42)	Sydney	1887-88
153	England (2nd)	v	Australia (66)	Brisbane[1]	1928-29
153	England (2nd)	v	West Indies (47)	Kingston	2003-04
153	Pakistan (2nd)	v	West Indies (53)	Faisalabad	1986-87
154	Australia (2nd)	v	England (77)	Sydney	1884-85

TEAM UNCHANGED THROUGHOUT A SERIES

			Venue		Tests
England	v	Australia	Australia	1884-85	5
South Africa	v	England	South Africa	1905-06	5
West Indies	v	Australia	West Indies	1990-91	5
England	v	Australia	Australia	1881-82	4

Australia	v	West Indies	West Indies	1994-95	4
Australia	v	England	England	1884	3
Australia	v	England	England	1893	3
Pakistan	v	New Zealand	Pakistan	1964-65	3
India	v	England	England	1971	3
Australia	v	New Zealand	New Zealand	1981-82	3
India	v	England	India	1992-93	3
India	v	Sri Lanka	India	1993-94	3
South Africa	v	Australia	South Africa	1993-94	3
Australia	v	Pakistan	Australia	1995-96	3
Australia	v	South Africa	South Africa	1996-97	3
England	v	Pakistan	Pakistan	1999-2000	3
Australia	v	New Zealand	Australia	2001-02	3
Australia	v	South Africa	South Africa	2001-02	3
England	v	New Zealand	New Zealand	2001-02	3
Australia	v	South Africa	South Africa	2005-06	3

MOST PLAYERS ENGAGED BY ONE SIDE IN A SERIES

				Venue	
30 in 5 Tests	England	v	Australia	England	1921
29 in 6 Tests	England	v	Australia	England	1989
28 in 5 Tests	Australia	v	England	Australia	1884-85
27 in 4 Tests	West Indies	v	England	West Indies	1929-30
26 in 5 Tests	India	v	Pakistan	India	1952-53
25 in 4 Tests	England	v	West Indies	England	1950
25 in 5 Tests	England	v	Australia	England	1909
25 in 5 Tests	England	v	South Africa	England	1935
25 in 5 Tests	England	v	South Africa	England	1955

South Africa used 20 players in the 3-match rubber of 1895-96 against England in South Africa.

MOST WICKETS BEFORE LUNCH

						Day
18	Australia (2-32 to 81 + 70)	v	England	Manchester	1888	2nd

NO BATSMAN REACHING DOUBLE FIGURES IN A COMPLETED INNINGS

South Africa (30 - highest score 7)	v	England	Birmingham	1924

ELEVEN BATSMEN REACHING DOUBLE FIGURES IN AN INNINGS

					Lowest Score
England (475)	v	Australia	Melbourne	1894-95	11
South Africa (385)	v	England	Johannesburg[2]	1905-06	10
England (636)	v	Australia	Sydney	1928-29	11
South Africa (358)	v	Australia	Melbourne	1931-32	10*
Australia (8d-575)	v	India	Melbourne	1947-48	11
India (397)	v	Pakistan	Calcutta	1952-53	11
India (359)	v	New Zealand	Dunedin	1967-68	12
India (9d-524)	v	New Zealand	Kanpur	1976-77	10*
Australia (471)	v	Sri Lanka	Colombo (SSC)	1992-93	10*
England (470)	v	West Indies	The Oval	2004	10

NO WICKETS IN A FULL DAY'S PLAY

				Day	
England (0-283)	v	Australia	Melbourne	3rd	1924-25
West Indies (6-187 to 6-494)	v	Australia	Bridgetown	4th	1954-55
India (0-234)	v	New Zealand	Madras[2]	1st	1955-56
West Indies (1-147 to 1-504)	v	Pakistan	Kingston	3rd	1957-58
West Indies (3-279 to 3-486) §	v	England	Bridgetown	5th	1959-60

West Indies (2-81 to 2-291)	v	England	Kingston	3rd	1959-60
Australia (0-263)	v	West Indies	Bridgetown	1st	1964-65
West Indies (7-310 to 7d-365)	v	New Zealand (0-163)	Georgetown	3rd	1971-72
India (1-70 to 1d-361)	v	West Indies 0-15)	Calcutta	4th	1978-79
India (2-178 to 2-395)	v	England	Madras[2]	2nd	1981-82
Sri Lanka (3-83 to 3-323)	v	Pakistan	Colombo (PSS)	5th	1985-86
India (5-291 to 5-517)	v	Australia (0-9)	Bombay[3]	4th	1986-87
Australia (0-301)	v	England	Nottingham	1st	1989
Australia (4-191 to 4-479)	v	South Africa	Johannesburg[3]	3rd	1996-97
Sri Lanka (1-39 to 1-322) †	v	India	Colombo (RPS)	3rd	1997-98
Sri Lanka (1-322 to 1-587) †	v	India	Colombo (RPS)	4th	1997-98
West Indies (4-37 to 4-377) #	v	Australia	Kingston	2nd	1998-99
India (4-254 to 4-589)	v	Australia	Kolkata	4th	2000-01
South Africa (2-84 to 2-364)	v	Bangladesh	Chittagong	2nd	2002-03
Sri Lanka (2-128 to 2-485)	v	South Africa	Colombo (SSC)	2nd	2006-07

† S.T.Jayasuriya (340) and R.S.Mahanama (225) added 576 for the 2nd wicket in the longest partnership in Test cricket (753 minutes) and remain the only pair of batsmen to bat throughout two consecutive days of Test cricket. Although § G.S.Sobers (226) and F.M.M.Worrell (197) also batted throughout two consecutive days, the final hour of the fourth day was lost to rain and a rest day intervened. # P.T.Collins retired hurt at 4/56.*

The following pairs of batsmen also batted throughout one full day's play in the above matches: J.B.Hobbs & H.Sutcliffe (1924-25), D.S.Atkinson & C.C.Depeiza (1954-55), M.H.Mankad & Pankaj Roy (1955-56), C.C.Hunte & G.S.Sobers (1957-58) W.M.Lawry & R.B.Simpson (1964-65), G.R.Viswanath & Yashpal Sharma (1981-82), A.P.Gurusinha & A.Ranatunga (1985-86), G.R.Marsh & M.A.Taylor (1989), S.R.Waugh & G.S.Blewett (1996-97); V.V.S.Laxman & R.S.Dravid (2000-01) and J.A.Rudolph & H.H.Dippenaar (2002-03) and K.C.Sangakkara & D.P.M.D.Jayawardene (2006-07).

MOST WICKETS IN ONE DAY

						Day
27-157	England (3-18 to 53 + 62)	v	Australia (60)	Lord's	1888	2nd
25-221	Australia (112 + 5-48)	v	England (61)	Melbourne	1901-02	1st
24-255	England (1-69 to 145 + 5-60)	v	Australia (119	The Oval	1896	2nd
22-197	Australia (92 + 2-5)	v	England (100)	The Oval	1890	1st
22-207	Australia (82 + 2-0)	v	West Indies (105)	Adelaide	1951-52	1st
22-195	England (7-292 to 9d-347)	v	India (58 + 82)	Manchester	1952	3rd
22-284	India (8-92 to 99 + 154)	v	New Zealand (94 + 0-24)	Hamilton	2002-03	3rd
21-278	England (185 + 1-0)	v	South Africa (93)	Port Elizabeth	1895-96	1st
21-236	England (126 + 1-3)	v	New Zealand (107)	Birmingham	1999	2nd
21-188	West Indies (9-267 to 267 + 54)	v	England (134 + 0-0)	Lord's	2000	2nd
20-220	Australia (4-323 to 369)	v	West Indies (107† + 5-67)	Sydney	1930-31	3rd
20-293	India (0-5 to 205)	v	Australia (93)	Mumbai[3]	2004-05	3rd

† One batsman absent hurt.

ONLY FOUR BOWLERS IN AN INNINGS OF OVER 400 RUNS

Australia	v	England (8d-403)	The Oval	1921
South Africa	v	England (8-421)	The Oval	1924
New Zealand	v	England (482)	The Oval	1949
England	v	Australia (426)	Sydney	1950-51
India	v	England (9d-419)	Lord's	1979
India	v	Australia (528)	Adelaide	1980-81
Australia	v	England (404)	Manchester	1981
England	v	India (428)	Bangalore	1981-82
Sri Lanka	v	Pakistan (7d-500)	Lahore[2]	1981-82
Pakistan	v	Australia (6d-454)	Sydney	1983-84
Australia	v	West Indies (8d-468)	Port-of-Spain	1983-84
Australia	v	West Indies (498)	St John's	1983-84

Australia	v	West Indies (416)	Perth	1984-85
Australia	v	England (456)	Nottingham	1985
Pakistan	v	England (447)	Manchester	1987
New Zealand	v	India (482)	Auckland	1989-90
England	v	West Indies (446)	Bridgetown	1989-90
England	v	West Indies (446)	St John's	1989-90
England	v	Australia (408)	Birmingham	1993
Pakistan	v	Australia (455)	Lahore[2]	1994-95
Pakistan	v	South Africa (403)	Rawalpindi[2]	1997-98
England	v	New Zealand (451)	Christchurch	2001-02
Pakistan	v	India (516)	Mohali	2004-05
Australia	v	England (407)	Birmingham	2005

TEN BATSMEN CAUGHT IN AN INNINGS

Australia	v	England	Melbourne	1903-04
South Africa	v	Australia	Melbourne	1931-32
England	v	South Africa	Durban[2]	1948-49
New Zealand	v	England	Leeds	1949
England	v	Pakistan	The Oval	1954
England	v	Australia	Melbourne	1958-59
West Indies	v	Australia	Sydney	1960-61
New Zealand	v	India	Wellington	1967-68
New Zealand	v	West Indies	Auckland	1968-69
New Zealand	v	India	Bombay[2]	1969-70
India	v	West Indies	Port-of-Spain	1970-71
India	v	England	Lord's	1971
Australia	v	England	Nottingham	1972
England	v	India	Madras[1]	1972-73
England	v	West Indies	Lord's	1973
Australia	v	New Zealand	Auckland	1973-74
New Zealand	v	Pakistan	Auckland	1978-79
§ England	v	Australia	Brisbane[2]	1982-83
England	v	Australia	Melbourne	1982-83
India	v	West Indies	Bridgetown	1982-83
West Indies	v	India	Bridgetown	1982-83
Sri Lanka	v	Australia	Kandy	1982-83
England	v	New Zealand	Christchurch	1987-88
England	v	West Indies	The Oval	1988
India	v	New Zealand	Hyderabad	1988-89
Pakistan	v	India	Karachi[1]	1989-90
West Indies	v	Australia	Bridgetown	1990-91
Australia	v	India	Perth	1991-92
India	v	Australia	Perth	1991-92
India	v	South Africa	Port Elizabeth	1992-93
West Indies	v	England	Bridgetown	1993-94
Sri Lanka	v	Zimbabwe	Harare	1994-95
Pakistan	v	Zimbabwe	Harare	1994-95
New Zealand	v	Sri Lanka	Napier	1994-95
West Indies	v	Australia	Bridgetown	1994-95
West Indies	v	Australia	Port-of-Spain	1994-95
New Zealand	v	England	Wellington	1996-97
India	v	West Indies	Georgetown	1996-97
West Indies	v	England	Bridgetown	1997-98
South Africa	v	West Indies	Centurion	1998-99
Pakistan	v	West Indies	St John's	1999-2000

West Indies	v	Australia	Melbourne	2000-01
South Africa	v	Sri Lanka	Cape Town	2000-01
Australia	v	India	Mumbai[3]	2000-01
New Zealand	v	Pakistan	Hamilton	2000-01
South Africa	v	West Indies	Kingston	2000-01
New Zealand	v	Australia	Perth	2001-02
South Africa	v	Australia	Durban[2]	2001-02
New Zealand	v	West Indies	Auckland	2005-06

§ Australia held nine catches in England's second innings. This is the only occasion where a side has held 19 catches in a Test.

MOST BATSMEN CAUGHT IN A MATCH

33	Australia (15)	v	India (18)	Perth	1991-92
32	England (15)	v	Pakistan (17)	Leeds	1971
32	New Zealand (18)	v	Pakistan (14)	Auckland	1993-94
32	Zimbabwe (15)	v	Pakistan (17)	Harare	1994-95
31	India (13)	v	New Zealand (18)	Bombay[2]	1969-70
31	New Zealand (14)	v	Australia (17)	Auckland	1973-74
31	West Indies (18)	v	Pakistan (13)	Kingston	1976-77
31	West Indies (18)	v	England (13)	Bridgetown	1993-94
30	England (14)	v	India (16)	Lord's	1971
30	England (15)	v	Australia (15)	The Oval	1993
30	India (16)	v	West Indies (14)	Bombay[3]	1994-95
30	West Indies (17)	v	South Africa (13)	Kingston	2000-01

MOST BATSMEN CAUGHT AND BOWLED IN AN INNINGS

4	Australia	v	England	Lord's	1890
4	Australia	v	New Zealand	Sydney	1985-86
3	England	v	Australia	Melbourne	1884-85
3	England	v	South Africa	Port Elizabeth	1888-89
3	Australia	v	England	Sydney	1891-92
3	England	v	Australia	Sydney	1907-08
3	Australia	v	South Africa	Adelaide	1931-32
3	Australia	v	West Indies	Adelaide	1960-61
3	India	v	England	Kanpur	1961-62
3	Pakistan	v	England	Leeds	1962
3	England	v	New Zealand	Auckland	1970-71
3	Zimbabwe	v	New Zealand	Auckland	1995-96
3	South Africa	v	England	Johannesburg[3]	1995-96
3	New Zealand	v	Sri Lanka	Dunedin	1996-97

MOST BATSMEN CAUGHT AND BOWLED IN A MATCH

6	Australia	v	England	Lord's	1890
5	Australia	v	England	Melbourne	1903-04
5	England	v	Australia	Nottingham	1905
5	Australia	v	South Africa	Cape Town	1935-36
5	West Indies	v	Australia	Adelaide	1960-61
5	New Zealand	v	India	Nagpur	1969-70

MOST BATSMEN BOWLED IN AN INNINGS

9	South Africa	v	England	Cape Town	1888-89
8	Australia	v	England	Sydney	1886-87
8	England	v	Australia	Sydney	1886-87
8	Australia	v	England	The Oval	1890
8	South Africa	v	England	Port Elizabeth	1895-96
8	South Africa	v	England	Birmingham	1929
8	South Africa	v	Australia	Adelaide	1931-32
8	England	v	New Zealand	Wellington	1950-51

MOST BATSMEN BOWLED IN A MATCH

23	England (9)	v	Australia (14)	Sydney	1886-87
23	South Africa (14)	v	England (9)	Port Elizabeth	1895-96
22	South Africa (11)	v	England (11)	Cape Town	1898-99
21	England (10)	v	Australia (11)	The Oval	1882
20	South Africa (5)	v	England (15)	Cape Town	1888-89
20	England (10)	v	Australia (10)	The Oval	1896
20	England (13)	v	South Africa (7)	Lord's	1912
19	South Africa (10)	v	England (9)	Cape Town	1905-06
19	Australia (9)	v	England (10)	Melbourne	1907-08
19	England (10)	v	South Africa (9)	Leeds	1912
18	England (8)	v	India (10)	Lord's	1932
18	New Zealand (8)	v	England (10)	Wellington	1950-51
18	Australia (9)	v	England (9)	Melbourne	1954-55
18	New Zealand (13)	v	England (5)	Dunedin	1954-55

MOST BATSMEN RUN OUT IN AN INNINGS

4	India	v	Pakistan	Peshawar[1]	1954-55
4	Australia	v	West Indies	Adelaide	1968-69

There are 26 instances of 3 run outs in an innings.

MOST BATSMEN RUN OUT IN A MATCH

7	Australia (3)	v	Pakistan (4)	Melbourne	1972-73
6	Australia (2)	v	England (4)	Adelaide	1901-02
6	Australia (4)	v	South Africa (2)	Melbourne	1910-11
6	Australia (5)	v	England (1)	Sydney	1920-21
6	England (2)	v	South Africa (4)	Leeds	1924
6	West Indies (3)	v	India (3)	Georgetown	1970-71
6	England (3)	v	New Zealand (3)	The Oval	1983
6	England (4)	v	Pakistan (2)	Birmingham	1987
6	Zimbabwe (3)	v	New Zealand (3)	Bulawayo[2]	1997-98

MOST BATSMEN LBW IN AN INNINGS

7	Zimbabwe	v	England	Chester-le-Street	2003
7	New Zealand	v	Australia	Christchurch	2004-05
6	England	v	South Africa	Leeds	1955
6	England	v	West Indies	Kingston	1959-60
6	England	v	Pakistan	Karachi[1]	1977-78
6	West Indies	v	England	Kingston	1985-86
6	Pakistan	v	Australia	Melbourne	1989-90
6	India	v	Sri Lanka	Chandigarh	1990-91
6	Pakistan	v	Sri Lanka	Faisalabad	1991-92
6	New Zealand	v	Pakistan	Hamilton	1992-93
6	South Africa	v	Australia	Durban[2]	1993-94

6	West Indies	v	India	Mohali	1994-95
6	West Indies	v	Australia	Bridgetown	1998-99
6	West Indies	v	Pakistan	Sharjah	2001-02

MOST BATSMEN LBW IN A MATCH

17	West Indies (8)	v	Pakistan (9)	Port-of-Spain	1992-93
15	Pakistan (5)	v	New Zealand (10)	Lahore[2]	1996-97
15	West Indies (9)	v	Australia (6)	Port-of-Spain	1998-99
14	Pakistan (8)	v	Sri Lanka (6)	Faisalabad	1991-92
14	West Indies (9)	v	Australia (5)	Bridgetown	1998-99
14	England (8)	v	West Indies (6)	The Oval	2000
13	New Zealand (8)	v	England (5)	Auckland	1991-92
13	Pakistan (4)	v	New Zealand (9)	Rawalpindi[2]	1996-97
13	India (6)	v	South Africa (7)	Ahmedabad	1996-97
13	New Zealand (11)	v	Australia (2)	Christchurch	2004-05
12	New Zealand (5)	v	West Indies (7)	Dunedin	1979-80
12	England (9)	v	West Indies (3)	Lord's	1984
12	Pakistan (5)	v	West Indies (7)	Faisalabad	1986-87
12	New Zealand (8)	v	Pakistan (4)	Hamilton	1992-93
12	Pakistan (8)	v	Zimbabwe (4)	Rawalpindi[2]	1993-94
12	Pakistan (6)	v	India (6)	Chennai[1]	1998-99
12	West Indies (4)	v	Zimbabwe (8)	Port-of-Spain	1999-2000
12	Sri Lanka (5)	v	Australia (7)	Kandy	2003-04
12	Bangladesh (7)	v	Australia (5)	Fatullah	2005-06

MOST BATSMEN STUMPED IN AN INNINGS

5	West Indies	v	India (K.S.More)	Madras[1]	1987-88
4	England	v	Australia (W.A.S.Oldfield)	Melbourne	1924-25
4	England	v	India (P.Sen)	Madras[1]	1951-52
3	England	v	Australia (A.H.Jarvis)	Sydney	1894-95
3	South Africa	v	Australia (J.J.Kelly)	Cape Town	1902-03
3	Australia	v	England (A.F.A.Lilley)	Sydney	1903-04
3	Australia	v	South Africa (P.W.Sherwell)	Sydney	1910-11
3	England	v	Australia (H.Carter)	Melbourne	1920-21
3	Australia	v	South Africa (T.A.Ward)	Johannesburg1	1921-22
3	West Indies	v	Australia (W.A.S.Oldfield)	Adelaide	1930-31
3	England	v	Australia (W.A.S.Oldfield)	Brisbane2	1936-37
3	England	v	Australia (D.Tallon)	Sydney	1946-47
3	South Africa	v	Australia (R.A.Saggers)	Cape Town	1949-50
3	West Indies	v	Australia (G.R.A.Langley)	Brisbane2	1951-52
3	West Indies	v	Australia (G.R.A.Langley)	Georgetown	1954-55
3	Australia	v	England (A.P.E.Knott)	Leeds	1968
3	South Africa	v	Sri Lanka (P.B.Dassanayake)	Colombo (SSC)	1993-94
3	Australia	v	Sri Lanka (R.S.Kaluwitharana)	Cairns	2004-05
3	Australia	v	Pakistan (Kamran Akmal)	Sydney	2004-05

MOST BATSMEN STUMPED IN A MATCH

6	Australia	v	England	Sydney	1894-95
6	India	v	England	Madras[1]	1951-52
6	West Indies	v	India (all by K.S.More)	Madras[1]	1987-88
5	Australia	v	England	Sydney	1924-25
5	Australia	v	Sri Lanka	Cairns	2004-05

There are 20 instances of 4 stumpings in a match.

TEST CAREERS WHICH ENDED IN TRAGEDY

1. F.Morley (England). A left-arm fast bowler Fred Morley was a member of Hon.Ivo Bligh's team that sailed to Australia for the 1882-83 season. Morley was apparently hurt in a collision at sea on the voyage out but carried on throughout the tour nursing a broken rib. Upon his return to England his health deteriorated and he died the following year.
2. G.B.Street (England). A good county wicket-keeper and useful tail-end batsmen, George Street played one Test for England against South Africa in 1922-23. Tragically he was killed in a motorcycle accident just before the 1924 season.
3. H.B.Cameron (South Africa). 'Jock' Cameron was a wicket-keeper and gifted batsman who captained his country in 9 Tests. He contracted enteric fever on the voyage home from the 1935 tour of England and died at the age of 30, ten weeks after playing in his final Test.
4. N.B.F.Mann (South Africa). 'Tufty' Mann was a versatile middle-order batsman and left-arm spinner who played in 19 Tests between 1947 and 1951, He died in 1952, aged 31, after an abdominal operation.
5. O.G.Smith (West Indies). 'Collie' Smith was a versatile all rounder who died of injuries received in a car accident in England in 1959. He had played in 26 Tests for 1331 runs at 31.69 and 48 wickets at 33.85.
6. K.J.Wadsworth (New Zealand). One of his country's finest wicket-keepers, Ken Wadsworth died of cancer at the age of 29, at the peak of his career.

RETIRED HURT

W.Bates (England) — In a short but brilliant career Billy Bates represented England 15 times scoring 656 runs and taking 50 wickets in the late 1880's. His career came to an abrupt end in Melbourne in 1887 when struck in the eye at net practice. He suffered permanent damage to his sight, forcing his retirement.

J.Briggs (England) — A regular member of the England team during the late 1880's, Briggs scored over 800 runs and took 118 wickets. During a Test against Australia in 1899 he was struck over the heart by a ball while fielding, and suffered what was believed to be an epileptic fit. He retired from the game and although he attempted a first-class come-back the following year, his Test career was over.

J.J.Kelly (Australia) — A useful batsman and outstanding wicket-keeper Kelly played 36 Tests for Australia around the turn of the Century. He retired from first-class cricket after his last tour of England because of the effects of a damaged finger and a blow over the heart by a ball in a Test at Manchester.

R.K.Oxenham (Australia) — An excellent all-rounder Oxenham represented his country in seven Tests in the late twenties and thirties. He was seriously injured in a car accident in 1937 and never fully recovered. He died in 1939.

G.F.Rorke (Australia) — A big man, Gordon Rorke played four Tests for Australia and was a very effective fast bowler in Sheffield Shield cricket. His Test career was unfortunately cut short in 1959-60 when he contracted hepatitis on a tour of India.

G.B.Stevens (Australia) — An opening batsmen, Gavin Stevens played four Tests for Australia in 1959-60. He dehydrated badly from the same strain of hepatitis that G.F.Rorke picked up. He lost two stones in weight and was sent home early from the sub-continent, and never played first-class cricket again.

N.J.Contractor (India) — An opening bat and occasional medium-pace bowler, Nari Contractor captained India on twelve occasions. During a match against Barbados, on the 1961-62 tour of the West Indies, Contractor was hit on the head by a ball from C.C.Griffith. His skull was fractured and he remained gravely ill for some days. Fortunately he recovered but never again played international cricket.

I.J.Jones (England) — A Welshman, Jeff Jones represented England on 15 occasions taking 44 wickets as a fast bowler. In May 1968, yet to reach his peak, he tore the ligaments in his elbow and from then on was a spent force in top cricket.

C.Milburn (England) — One of the most punishing batsmen seen on the Test arena for many years 'Ollie' Milburn was involved in a car accident in 1969 which cost him his left eye. He was aged 28. In his last Test innings he had scored 139 v Pakistan at Karachi in 1968-69. He made 0 + 94 on his debut v West Indies at Manchester in 1966. He attempted a county come-back in 1973 but to all intents and purposes his career was finished by the crash.

R.C.Motz (New Zealand) — One of New Zealand's most successful Test bowlers — taking exactly 100 Test wickets — Motz was forced to retire from first-class cricket when it was discovered he had been bowling for some time with a displaced vertebra.

M.F.Kent (Australia) — Kent opened the batting for Australia on the 1981 tour of England. He suffered a back strain which degenerated so badly that he was forced to retire from all grades of cricket.

TEST CRICKETERS WHO WERE RHODES SCHOLARS

C.B.Van Ryneveld	South Africa
J.P.Duminy	South Africa
P.A.M.Hands	South Africa
R.H.M.Hands	South Africa
H.G.Owen-Smith	South Africa
D.B.Pithey	South Africa
J.A.Dunning	New Zealand

TEST CRICKET CAPTAINS BORN ABROAD

Australia

P.S.McDonnell	England
T.P.Horan	Ireland

England

Lord Harris	West Indies
P.F.Warner	West Indies
F.L.Fane	Ireland
D.R.Jardine	India
G.O.B.Allen	Australia
F.R.Brown	Peru
D.B.Carr	Germany
M.C.Cowdrey	India
E.R.Dexter	Italy
A.R.Lewis	Wales
M.H.Denness	Scotland
A.W.Greig	South Africa
A.J.Lamb	South Africa
N.Hussain	India
A.J.Strauss	South Africa

South Africa

W.H.Milton	England
E.A.Halliwell	England
F.Mitchell	England

West Indies

G.A.Headley	Panama

Pakistan

A.H.Kardar	India
Fazal Mahmood	India
Imtiaz Ahmed	India
Javed Burki	India
Hanif Mohammad	India
Intikhab Alam	India
Saeed Ahmed	India
Majid J.Khan	India
Mushtaq Mohammad	India
Asif Iqbal	India
Majid Khan	India

Zimbabwe

A.Flower	South Africa

TEST CRICKETERS WHO WERE TEST UMPIRES

Australia

C.Bannerman
G.Coulthard
T.W.Garrett *
P.G.McShane #
H.H.Massie ¶
A.J.Richardson
J.P.F.Travers

* T.W.Garrett, who was playing in the game, replaced umpire Hodges after tea on the last day, Australia v England Melbourne 1884-85.

P.G.McShane played and umpired in the same series Australia v England 1884-85.

¶ H.H.Massie substituted for E.H.Elliott, Australia v England, Sydney 1884-85.

England

R.G.Barlow
M.R.Benson
J.Birkenshaw
L.C.Braund
H.R.Butt
J.F.Crapp
A.Dolphin
H.Elliott
A.E.Fagg
W.Gunn †
J.H.Hampshire
J.Hardstaff sr
F.Hearne
A.Hill
J.W.Hitch
J.Lillywhite
N.A.Mallender
A.S.M.Oakman §
N.Oldfield
K.E.Palmer
W.F.F.Price
M.Sherwin
E.J.Smith
G.J.Thompson
P.Willey
H.Young

† W.Gunn replaced umpire (Swift) injured in the England v Australia Test at (Sydney) 1886-87. (He was playing in the Test.)

§ A.S.M.Oakman deputised for H.D.Bird (injured back) after tea on the 3rd day of the 1st Test England v Australia Birmingham 1975.

West Indies
E.E.Achong
G.E.Gomez

South Africa
W.W.Wade

New Zealand
J.Cowie
E.W.T.Tindill

India
S.Venkataraghavan

Pakistan
Javed Akhtar
Mohammad Nazir
Nadeem Ghauri

Sri Lanka
E.A.R.de Silva

PLAYERS WHO HAVE OPENED THE BATTING AND BOWLING IN THE SAME MATCH (First innings only apply for this record)

Australia
G.Giffen	v England, Sydney 1882-83
G.E.Palmer	v England, Sydney 1884-85
W.Bruce	v England, Melbourne 1884-85
C.T.B.Turner	v England, Lord's 1890
C.T.B.Turner	v England, The Oval 1890
G.H.S.Trott	v England, Sydney 1894-95
G.H.S.Trott	v England, Melbourne 1894-95
W.W.Armstrong	v South Africa, Johannesburg 1902-03
V.T.Trumper	v South Africa, Johannesburg, 1902-03
M.A.Noble	v England, Sydney 1907-08
F.J.Laver	v England, Lord's 1909
C.Kelleway	v England, Melbourne 1911-12
J.M.Gregory	v South Africa, Durban 1921-22

England
A.Shaw	v Australia, Melbourne 1876-77
G.Ulyett	v Australia, Melbourne 1878-79
C.T.Studd	v Australia, Melbourne 1882-83
R.G.Barlow	v Australia, Sydney 1882-83
G.Ulyett	v Australia, Sydney 1884-85
G.Ulyett	v South Africa, Cape Town 1888-89
G.A.Lohmann	v South Africa, Port Elizabeth 1895-96
G.L.Jessop	v Australia, Melbourne 1901-02
J.B.Hobbs	v South Africa, Johannesburg 1909-10
J.B.Hobbs	v South Africa, Durban 1909-10
J.B.Hobbs	v South Africa, Cape Town 1909-10
M.W.Tate	v Australia, Adelaide 1924-25
W.R.Hammond	v South Africa, Cape Town 1930-31
W.R.Hammond	v South Africa, Durban 1930-31
R.E.S.Wyatt	v West Indies, Port-of-Spain 1934-35
R.E.S.Wyatt	v West Indies, Georgetown 1934-35
R.E.S.Wyatt	v South Africa, Lord's 1935
W.J.Edrich	v South Africa, Johannesburg 1938-39
T.E.Bailey	v West Indies, Kingston 1953-54
T.E.Bailey	v Australia, Sydney 1954-55
T.E.Bailey	v South Africa, Port Elizabeth 1956-57

South Africa
A.Rose-Innes	v England, Cape Town 1888-89
J.H.Sinclair	v England, Johannesburg 1895-96
G.A.Faulkner	v England, The Oval 1907
D.J.Meintjes	v England, Johannesburg 1922-23
T.L.Goddard	v England, Nottingham 1955
T.L.Goddard	v England, The Oval 1955
T.L.Goddard	v Australia, Cape Town 1957-58

West Indies
F.M.M.Worrell	v England, Georgetown 1953-54
F.M.M.Worrell	v England, Nottingham 1957
F.M.M.Worrell	v England, Leeds 1957
F.M.M.Worrell	v England, The Oval 1957
W.W.Hinds	v Zimbabwe, Bulayawo, 2003-04

India
Pankaj Roy	v West Indies, Delhi 1958-59
M.L.Jaisimha	v England, Delhi 1961-62
M.L.Jaisimha	v England, Madras 1961-62
M.L.Jaisimha	v England, Delhi 1963-64
M.L.Jaisimha	v England, Kanpur 1963-64
M.L.Jaisimha	v Australia, Madras 1964-65
M.L.Jaisimha	v Australia, Bombay 1964-65
M.L.Jaisimha	v Australia, Calcutta 1964-65
M.L.Jaisimha	v New Zealand, Calcutta 1964-65
M.L.Jaisimha	v New Zealand, Bombay 1964-65
M.L.Jaisimha	v New Zealand, Madras 1964-65
M.L.Jaisimha	v New Zealand, Delhi 1964-65
M.L.Jaisimha	v West Indies, Bombay 1966-67
B.K.Kunderan	v England, Birmingham 1967
S.Abid Ali	v New Zealand, Wellington 1967-68
S.Abid Ali	v New Zealand, Bombay 1969-70
S.Abid Ali	v New Zealand, Nagpur 1969-70
S.Abid Ali	v New Zealand, Hyderabad 1969-70
S.Abid Ali	v West Indies, Kingston 1970-71
S.Abid Ali	v West Indies, Port-of-Spain 1970-71
S.M.Gavaskar	v England, Madras 1972-73
E.D.Solkar	v England, Manchester 1974
M.Amarnath	v England, Madras 1976-77
S.M.Gavaskar	v England, Bombay 1976-77
S.M.Gavaskar	v Australia, Melbourne 1977-78
S.M.Gavaskar	v Pakistan, Lahore 1978-79
M.Prabhakar	v New Zealand, Napier 1989-90
M.Prabhakar	v New Zealand, Auckland 1989-90
M.Prabhakar	v Sri Lanka, Chandigarh 1990-91
M.Prabhakar	v South Africa, Cape Town 1992-93

M.Prabhakar v England, Calcutta, 1992-93
M.Prabhakar v England, Madras, 1992-93
M.Prabhakar v England, Bombay, 1992-93
M.Prabhakar v Zimbabwe, Delhi, 1992-93
M.Prabhakar v Sri Lanka, Colombo (SSC), 1993-94
M.Prabhakar v Sri Lanka, Colombo (PSS), 1993-94
M.Prabhakar v Sri Lanka, Lucknow, 1993-94
M.Prabhakar v Sri Lanka, Bangalore, 1993-94
M.Prabhakar v Sri Lanka, Motera, 1993-94
M.Prabhakar v West Indies, Bombay, 1994-95
M.Prabhakar v West Indies, Nagpur, 1994-95
M.Prabhakar v West Indies, Mohali, 1994-95
M.Prabhakar v New Zealand, Bangalore, 1994-95
M.Prabhakar v New Zealand, Cuttack, 1994-95
M.Prabhakar v New Zealand, Bangalore, 1995-96
M.Prabhakar v New Zealand, Cuttack, 1995-96

Pakistan

Mudassar Nazar v New Zealand, Lahore 1984-85
Mudassar Nazar v New Zealand, Hyderabad 1984-85
Mudassar Nazar v New Zealand, Karachi 1984-85
Mudassar Nazar v New Zealand, Wellington 1984-85
Mudassar Nazar v England, Lahore 1987-88
Mudassar Nazar v England, Faisalabad 1987-88
Mudassar Nazar v Australia, Karachi 1988-89
Mudassar Nazar v Australia, Faisalabad 1988-89
Mudassar Nazar v Australia, Lahore 1988-89

Sri Lanka

B.Warnapura v England, Colombo 1981-82
J.R.Ratnayeke v India, Nagpur 1986-87
J.R.Ratnayeke v India, Calcutta 1986-87

CALENDAR YEAR TEST RECORDS

BATSMEN WITH 1000 RUNS IN THE CALENDAR YEAR

Player (Country)	Year	Tests	I	NO	Runs	HS	Avge	100	50
I.V.A.Richards (W)	1976	11	19	0	1710	291	90.00	7	5
S.M.Gavaskar (I)	1979	18	27	1	1555	221	59.80	5	8
R.T.Ponting (A)	2003	11	18	3	1503	257	100.20	6	4
M.P.Vaughan (E)	2002	14	26	2	1481	197	61.70	6	2
J.L.Langer (A)	2004	14	27	0	1481	215	54.85	5	4
R.T.Ponting (A)	2005	14	26	5	1444	207	68.76	6	5
S.R.Tendulkar (I)	2002	16	26	1	1392	193	55.68	4	5
M.L.Hayden (A)	2001	14	25	3	1391	203	63.22	5	5
G.R.Viswanath (I)	1979	17	26	3	1388	179	60.34	5	6
R.B.Simpson (A)	1964	14	26	3	1381	311	60.04	3	7
D.L.Amiss (E)	1974	13	22	2	1379	262*	68.95	5	3
R.S.Dravid (I)	2002	16	26	3	1357	217	59.00	5	5
D.R.Martyn (A)	2004	14	26	2	1353	161	56.37	6	5
B.C.Lara (W)	2003	10	19	1	1344	209	74.66	5	5
M.E.Trescothick (E)	2005	13	24	0	1323	194	55.12	4	4
M.L.Hayden (A)	2003	12	21	4	1312	380	77.17	5	3
S.M.Gavaskar (I)	1983	18	32	4	1310	236*	46.78	5	5
J.H.Kallis (SA)	2004	11	21	5	1288	162	80.50	5	7
S.T.Jayasuriya (SL)	1997	11	19	0	1271	340	66.89	3	7
G.A.Gooch (E)	1990	9	17	1	1264	333	79.00	4	5
D.C.Boon (A)	1993	16	25	5	1241	164*	62.05	4	7
B.C.Lara (W)	1995	12	20	2	1222	179	67.88	4	6
A.J.Stewart (E)	1998	16	31	3	1222	164	43.64	2	7
P.A.de Silva (SL)	1997	11	19	3	1220	168	76.25	7	2
M.A.Taylor (A)	# 1989	11	20	1	1219	219	64.15	4	5
G.C.Smith (SA)	2003	12	19	0	1198	277	63.05	4	2
G.S.Sobers (W)	1958	7	12	3	1193	365*	132.55	5	3
M.L.Hayden (A)	2005	14	27	3	1192	138	49.66	4	3
B.C.Lara W)	2004	12	21	1	1178	400*	58.90	3	4
D.B.Vengsarkar (I)	1979	18	27	4	1174	146*	51.04	5	6
K.J.Hughes (A)	1979	15	28	4	1163	130*	48.45	2	8
M.L.Hayden (A)	2002	11	17	1	1160	197	72.50	6	3
D.C.S.Compton (E)	1947	9	15	1	1159	208	82.78	6	3

H.H.Gibbs (SA)	2003	12	19	1	1156	228	64.22	4	3
B.C.Lara (W)	2001	9	18	0	1151	221	63.94	3	4
C.G.Greenidge (W)	1984	14	22	4	1149	223	63.83	4	3
V.K.Sehwag (I)	2004	12	19	1	1141	309	63.38	3	4
M.A.Atherton (E)	1994	13	23	0	1136	144	49.39	4	5
C.H.Gayle (W)	2004	12	22	1	1135	141	54.04	4	7
S.T.Jayasuriya (SL)	2004	11	20	0	1130	253	56.50	4	3
M.A.Atherton (E)	1995	13	24	1	1129	185*	49.08	2	7
H.H.Gibbs (SA)	2001	13	22	1	1124	196	53.52	3	6
M.J.Hayden (A)	2004	14	27	1	1123	132	43.19	3	6
Yousuf Youhana (P)	2006	8	14	1	1123	202	86.38	5	2
J.H.Kallis (SA)	2001	13	23	7	1120	189*	70.00	2	7
K.C.Sangakkara (SL)	2004	11	20	0	1114	270	55.70	3	5
M.A.Taylor (A)	1998	12	22	3	1112	334*	58.52	3	4
M.A.Taylor (A)	1993	15	23	2	1106	170	52.66	4	4
D.M.Jones (A)	1989	11	18	3	1099	216	73.26	4	4
A.R.Border (A)	1985	11	20	3	1099	196	64.64	4	2
I.T.Botham (E)	1982	14	22	0	1095	208	49.77	3	6
K.W.R.Fletcher (E)	1973	13	22	4	1090	178	60.55	2	9
Inzamamul Haq (P)	2000	12	19	1	1090	142	60.55	4	6
S.R.Tendulkar (I)	1999	10	19	3	1088	217	68.00	5	4
M.Amarnath (I)	1983	14	24	1	1077	120	46.82	4	7
A.R.Border (A)	1979	14	27	3	1073	162	44.70	3	6
B.C.Lara (W)	2005	8	15	0	1069	226	71.26	5	0
G.S.Blewett (A)	1997	15	25	0	1067	214	42.68	2	6
S.Chanderpaul (W)	2002	14	22	6	1065	140	66.56	4	6
R.T.Ponting (A)	2002	11	16	1	1064	154	70.93	5	2
D.I.Gower (E)	1982	14	25	2	1061	114	46.13	1	8
C.Hill (A)	1902	12	21	2	1060	142	55.78	2	7
D.I.Gower (E)	1986	14	25	1	1059	136	44.12	2	6
W.M.Lawry (A)	1964	14	27	2	1056	157	42.24	2	6
D.P.M.D.Jayawardene (SL)	2001	13	19	0	1053	150	55.42	4	4
M.J.Slater (A)	1999	14	25	2	1051	169	45.69	3	4
R.S.Dravid (I)	2006	10	18	4	1046	146	74.71	3	7
A.Flower (Z)	2000	9	16	3	1045	232*	80.38	3	5
S.M.Gavaskar (I)	1978	9	15	2	1044	205	80.30	4	4
G.A.Gooch (E)	1991	9	17	1	1040	174	65.00	3	5
W.J.Cronje (SA)	1998	14	24	2	1040	126	47.27	1	9
K.F.Barrington (E)	1963	12	22	2	1039	132*	51.95	3	5
E.R.Dexter (E)	1962	11	15	1	1038	205	74.14	2	6
M.E.Waugh (A)	1998	12	22	6	1034	153*	64.62	4	3
K.F.Barrington (E)	1961	10	17	4	1032	172	79.38	4	5
Mohsin Khan (P)	1982	10	17	3	1029	200	73.50	4	4
D.G.Bradman (A)	1948	8	13	4	1025	201	113.88	5	2
S.M.Gavaskar (I)	1976	11	20	1	1024	156	53.89	4	4
A.B.de Villiers (SA)	2005	11	19	0	1008	178	53.05	3	5
R.R.Sarwan (W)	2004	12	21	1	1005	261*	50.25	3	4
M.E.Trescothick (E)	2004	13	26	3	1004	132	43.65	4	3
S.R.Tendulkar (I)	2001	10	18	2	1003	155	62.68	3	6
M.E.Trescothick (E)	2003	13	24	3	1003	219	47.76	2	6
A.R.Border (A)	1986	11	19	3	1000	140	62.50	5	3
S.R.Tendulkar (I)	1997	12	17	1	1000	169	62.50	4	3

 # Taylor achieved the feat in his debut calendar year.

5 M.L.Hayden(A), B.C.Lara(W)
4 S.M.Gavaskar(I), S.R.Tendulkar(I)
3 A.R.Border(A), R.T.Ponting(A), M.A.Taylor(A), M.E.Trescothick(E)

2 M.A.Atherton(E), K.F.Barrington(E), R.S.Dravid(I), H.H.Gibbs(SA), G.A.Gooch(E), D.I.Gower(E), S.T.Jayasuriya(SL), J.H.Kallis(SA)

1 M.Amarnath(I), D.L.Amiss(E), G.S.Blewett(A), D.C.Boon(A), I.T.Botham(E), D.G.Bradman(A), S.Chanderpaul(W), D.C.S.Compton(E), W.J.Cronje(SA), P.A.de Silva(SL), A.B.de Villiers(SA), E.R.Dexter(E), R.S.Dravid(I), K.W.R.Fletcher(E), A.Flower(Z), C.H.Gayle(W), C.G.Greenidge(W), C.Hill(A), K.J.Hughes(A), Inzamamul Haq(P), D.P.M.D.Jayawardene(SL), D.M.Jones(A), J.L.Langer(A), W.M.Lawry(A), D.R.Martyn(A), Mohsin Khan(P), I.V.A.Richards(W), K.C.Sangakkara(SL), R.R.Sarwan(W), V.K.Sehwag(I), R.B.Simpson(A), M.J.Slater(A), G.C.Smith(SA), G.S.Sobers(W), A.J.Stewart(E), M.P.Vaughan(E), D.B.Vengsarkar(I), G.R.Viswanath(I), M.E.Waugh(A) Yousuf Youhana(P)

FIFTY WICKETS IN A CALENDAR YEAR *# includes one match in which player did not bowl.*

Player (Country)	Year	Tests	Balls	Mdns	Runs	Wkts	Avge	5w	10w	Best
S.K.Warne (A)	2005	14	4150	134	2043	90	22.70	6	2	6/46
D.K.Lillee (A)	1981	13	3710	162	1781	85	20.95	5	2	7/83
M.Muralidaran (SL)	2001	12	4688	216	1698	80	21.22	7	4	8/87
A.A.Donald (SA)	1998	14	3232	135	1571	80	19.63	7	0	6/88
J.Garner (W)	1984	15	3620	149	1603	77	20.81	4	0	6/60
M.Muralidaran (SL)	2000	10	3740	147	1463	75	19.50	7	3	7/84
Kapil Dev (I)	1983	18	3469	112	1738	75	23.17	5	1	9/83
Kapil Dev (I)	1979	18	3651	147	1720	74	23.24	5	0	6/63
A.Kumble (I)	2004	12	3680	126	1838	74	24.83	6	2	8/141
M.D.Marshall (W)	1984	13	3251	121	1471	73	20.15	9	1	7/53
S.K.Warne (A)	1993	16	5054	316	1697	72	23.56	2	0	6/31
G.D.McKenzie (A)	1964	14	4106	119	1737	71	24.46	4	1	7/153
S.K.Warne (A)	1994	10	3773	217	1274	70	18.20	6	2	8/71
S.K.Warne (A)	2004	12	3472	123	1685	70	24.07	5	2	6/125
S.M.Pollock (SA)	1998	14	3592	165	1411	69	20.44	6	0	7/87
M.Muralidaran (SL)	1998	8	3302	162	1258	68	18.50	6	2	9/65
G.D.McGrath (A)	2001	14	3508	196	1473	68	21.66	4	0	7/76
S.K.Warne (A)	1997	15	4091	194	1661	68	24.42	2	0	6/48
S.K.Warne (A)	2002	10	2874	109	1310	67	19.55	3	1	7/94
G.D.McGrath (A)	1999	14	3364	169	1425	67	21.26	4	1	5/28
S.J.Harmison (E)	2004	13	3161	115	1603	67	23.92	3	0	7/12
C.A.Walsh (WI)	2000	14	3501	184	1234	66	18.69	4	1	6/74
S.F.Barnes (E)	1912	# 10	2394	106	959	64	14.98	8	3	8/29
R.J.Hadlee (N)	1985	10	2588	102	1116	64	17.43	6	2	9/52
I.T.Botham (E)	1978	12	2757	91	1160	63	18.41	6	1	8/34
G.D.McGrath (A)	1997	13	3113	151	1347	63	21.38	4	0	8/38
Harbhajan Singh (I)	2002	13	3567	132	1463	63	23.22	5	0	7/48
Imran Khan (P)	1982	9	2359	112	824	62	13.29	5	2	8/58
F.S.Trueman (E)	1963	11	2563	90	1061	62	17.11	6	2	7/44
C.A.Walsh (W)	1995	12	3051	111	1347	62	21.72	4	1	7/37
I.T.Botham (E)	1981	12	3338	136	1590	62	25.64	4	1	6/95
A.Flintoff (E)	2005	13	2990	84	1553	61	25.45	1	0	5/78
M.Muralidaran (SL)	2006	9	2966	113	1304	73	17.86	8	4	8/70
M.D.Marshall (W)	1988	10	2477	83	1072	60	17.86	4	1	7/22
Harbhajan Singh (I)	2001	12	3424	133	1557	60	25.95	6	2	8/84
G.D.McGrath (A)	2005	12	3036	145	1310	59	22.20	3	0	6/115
M.Ntini (SA)	2003	12	2814	106	1566	59	26.54	4	1	5/75
W.P.U.J.C.Vaas (SL)	2001	12	2935	124	1324	58	22.82	3	1	7/71
A.R.C.Fraser (E)	1998	14	2909	116	1327	58	22.87	5	2	8/53
M.J.Hoggard (E)	2005	13	2453	61	1514	58	26.10	3	1	7/61
S.K.Warne (A)	2001	13	3501	113	1809	58	31.19	4	1	7/165
R.G.D.Willis (E)	1978	14	2921	94	1056	57	18.52	4	0	5/32
M.G.Hughes (A)	1993	12	3033	127	1448	57	25.40	2	0	5/64

S.C.G.MacGill (A)	2003	11	3148	107	1688	57	29.61	4	1	5/56
C.J.McDermott (A)	1991	9	2416	84	1188	56	21.21	4	1	8/97
Waqar Younis (P)	1993	7	1626	59	838	55	15.23	6	1	7/91
M.Muralidaran (SL)	2002	8	2836	140	979	55	17.80	5	1	5/39
R.Benaud (A)	1959	9	3248	177	1031	55	18.74	4	0	5/76
S.M.Pollock (SA)	2001	13	3126	166	1176	55	21.38	4	1	6/30
J.N.Gillespie (A)	2004	14	3087	130	1369	55	24.89	1	0	5/56
A.A.Mailey (A)	1921	# 10	2849	63	1567	55	28.49	4	2	9/121
M.D.Marshall (W)	1983	11	2371	99	1119	54	20.72	2	0	6/37
T.M.Alderman (A) †	1981	9	2672	105	1222	54	22.62	4	0	6/135
A.Kumble (I)	1999	10	3491	160	1461	54	27.05	4	2	10/74
H.Trumble (A)	1902	8	2520	140	994	53	18.75	4	2	8/65
M.A.Holding (W)	1976	11	2305	88	1080	53	20.37	4	1	8/92
M.H.Mankad (I)	1952	10	3512	218	1170	53	22.07	5	2	8/52
J.Garner (W)	1980	13	2758	139	897	52	17.25	1	0	6/56
G.D.McGrath (A)	1995	10	2319	92	1138	52	21.88	4	0	6/47
R.G.D.Willis (E)	1982	13	2428	72	1236	52	23.76	2	0	6/101
S.K.Warne (A)	1995	12	3051	156	1254	52	24.11	1	1	7/23
B.S.Chandrasekhar (I)	1976	11	3139	108	1458	52	28.03	3	0	6/94
M.A.Noble (A)	1902	12	2208	100	989	51	19.39	6	2	7/17
Saqlain Mushtaq (P)	2002	11	2649	82	1248	51	24.47	2	1	7/66
J.M.Gregory (A)	1921	12	2702	84	1292	51	25.33	3	0	7/69
Zaheer Khan (I)	2002	15	2875	108	1479	51	29.00	2	0	5/29
T.M.Alderman (A)	1989	10	2414	106	1019	50	20.38	6	1	6/128
R.G.D.Willis (E)	1977	11	2146	58	1108	50	22.16	5	0	7/78

The following players have taken 50 wickets in a calendar year:

8 S.K.Warne(A)
4 G.D.McGrath(A)
5 M.Muralidaran(SL)
3 M.D.Marshall(W), R.G.D.Willis(E)
2 T.M.Alderman(A), I.T.Botham(E), J.Garner(W), Harbhajan Singh(I), Kapil Dev(I), A.Kumble(I), S.M.Pollock(SA), C.A.Walsh(W)
1 S.F.Barnes(E), R.Benaud(A), B.S.Chandrasekhar(I), A.A.Donald(SA), A.Flintoff(E), A.R.C.Fraser(E), J.N.Gillespie(A), J.M.Gregory(A), R.J.Hadlee(N), S.J.Harmison(E), M.J.Hoggard(E), M.A.Holding(W), M.G.Hughes(A), Imran Khan(P), D.K.Lillee(A), C.J.McDermott(A), S.C.G.MacGill(A), G.D.McKenzie(A), A.A.Mailey(A), M.H.Mankad(I), M.A.Noble(A), M.Ntini(SA), Saqlain Mushtaq(P), F.S.Trueman(E), H.Trumble(A), W.P.U.J.C.Vaas(SL), Waqar Younis(P), Zaheer Khan(I)

WICKET-KEEPERS WITH 30 DISMISSALS IN THE CALENDAR YEAR

Player	Country	Year	Tests	C	S	Dismissals
I.A.Healy	Australia	1993	16	58	9	67
M.V.Boucher	South Africa	1998	13	65	2	67
A.C.Gilchrist	Australia	2004	14	58	8	66
I.A.Healy	Australia	1997	15	55	4	59
R.D.Jacobs	West Indies	2000	14	55	2	57
A.C.Gilchrist	Australia	2001	14	52	5	57
P.J.L.Dujon	West Indies	1984	15	54	1	55
R.W.Marsh	Australia	1981	13	52	1	53
G.O.Jones	England	2005	13	50	1	51
A.C.Gilchrist	Australia	2003	12	43	7	50
A.C.Gilchrist	Australia	2005	14	45	3	48
A.C.Gilchrist	Australia	2002	11	44	3	47
M.V.Boucher	South Africa	2001	13	44	1	45
R.W.Taylor	England	1978	14	43	1	44
R.W.Marsh	Australia	1982	12	42	1	43

Keith Miller, Australia's greatest all-rounder, batting in characteristically aggressive style at the peak of his career.

On day two of the first Test between New Zealand and Pakistan in Hamilton in 2003, Stephen Fleming drives the ball to the boundary for four.

The great New Zealand bowler Sir Richard Hadlee claims one of his ten wickets in the third Test against Australia in Melbourne, December 1987.

A dashing Brian Lara on his way to 83 for the West Indies against New Zealand at Napier in 2006.

ORDER YOUR CD UPDATES NOW!
Statistics you won't find anywhere else
Receive your first update FREE when you subscribe for four quarterly updates
Stay on the ball throughout the Test year!
For further details, go to our website: www.fivemile.com.au

M.V.Boucher	South Africa	2003	12	38	5	43
M.V.Boucher	South Africa	2005	11	41	1	42
Kamran Akmal	Pakistan	2005	9	33	8	41
A.J.Stewart	England	1998	16	41	0	41
R.W.Marsh	Australia	1975	10	38	2	40
R.W.Taylor	England	1982	14	40	0	40
R.C.Russell	England	1990	12	39	1	40
P.J.L.Dujon	West Indies	1991	10	40	0	40
A.C.Gilchrist	Australia	2000	8	38	2	40
A.P.E.Knott	England	1974	14	37	2	39
D.L.Murray	West Indies	1976	12	37	2	39
A.J.Stewart	England	1997	9	37	2	39
M.V.Boucher	South Africa	2000	11	37	2	39
G.O.Jones	England	2006	8	37	2	39
A.C.Parore	New Zealand	1999	13	38	1	39
A.P.E.Knott	England	1971	11	34	4	38
S.M.H.Kirmani	India	1983	18	35	3	38
P.J.L.Dujon	West Indies	1988	12	37	1	38
M.V.Boucher	South Africa	2002	9	38	0	38
R.W.Marsh	Australia	1974	9	36	1	37
I.A.Healy	Australia	1994	9	35	2	37
K.C.Sangakkara	Sri Lanka	2001	13	34	3	37
M.S.Dhoni	India	2006	10	33	4	37
A.T.W.Grout	Australia	1961	9	33	3	36
I.A.Healy	Australia	1995	12	32	5	36
I.A.Healy	Australia	1998	12	34	2	36
R.D.Jacobs	West Indies	2002	12	33	3	36
K.J.Wright	Australia	1979	10	31	4	35
P.J.L.Dujon	West Indies	1983	11	34	1	35
Wasim Bari	Pakistan	1983	11	32	3	35
D.J.Richardson	South Africa	1994	10	35	0	35
I.A.Healy	Australia	1991	10	34	0	34
M.V.Boucher	South Africa	1999	10	34	0	34
G.O.Jones	England	2004	10	32	2	34
A.T.W.Grout	Australia	1964	11	32	1	33
R.W.Marsh	Australia	1977	10	33	0	33
Wasim Bari	Pakistan	1979	9	31	2	33
S.J.Rhodes	England	1994	8	30	3	33
J.R.Murray	West Indies	1995	9	33	0	33
R.C.Russell	England	1995	7	30	3	33
R.D.Jacobs	West Indies	2004	10	30	3	33
Kamran Akmal	Pakistan	2006	9	29	4	33
P.R.Downton	England	1985	9	31	1	32
R.D.Jacobs	West Indies	1999	8	30	2	32
A.C.Parore	New Zealand	2000	32	29	3	32
K.C.Sangakkara	Sri Lanka	2002	9	29	3	32
T.G.Evans	England	1957	9	29	2	31
J.M.Parks	England	1966	10	28	3	31
S.M.H.Kirmani	India	1979	14	27	4	31
D.J.Richardson	South Africa	1997	8	29	2	31
A.T.W.Grout	Australia	1959	8	24	6	30
A.P.E.Knott	England	1973	13	30	0	30
M.V.Boucher	South Africa	2006	9	30	0	30
J.R.Murray	West Indies	1993	7	29	1	30
D.J.Richardson	South Africa	1995	8	30	0	30
R.D.Jacobs	West Indies	2001	10	29	1	30

The following wicket-keepers have made 30 dismissals in a calendar year:

8 M.V.Boucher(SA),
6 A.C.Gilchrist(A), I.A.Healy(A),
5 R.D.Jacobs(W), R.W.Marsh(A),
4 P.J.L.Dujon(W),
3 A.T.W.Grout(A), G.O.Jones(E), A.P.E.Knott(E), D.J.Richardson(SA),
2 Kamran Akmal(P), S.M.H.Kirmani(I), J.R.Murray(W), A.C.Parore(N), R.C.Russell(E), K.C.Sangakkara(SL), A.J.Stewart(E), R.W.Taylor(E), Wasim Bari(P),
1 M.S.Dhoni(I), P.R.Downton(E), T.G.Evans(E), Kamran Akmal(P), D.L.Murray(W), J.M.Parks(E), S.J.Rhodes(E), K.J.Wright(A),

PLAYERS WITH 15 CATCHES IN THE CALENDAR YEAR

Player	Country	Year	Tests	C
S.P.Fleming	New Zealand	1997	10	28
J.M.Gregory	Australia	1921	12	27
M.A.Taylor	Australia	1997	15	27
R.S.Dravid	India	2004	12	26
R.B.Simpson	Australia	1964	14	26
M.E.Waugh	Australia	1999	14	26
R.S.Dravid	India	2002	16	26
R.T.Ponting	Australia	2001	14	25
M.A.Taylor	Australia	1993	15	25
M.A.Taylor	Australia	1995	12	24
M.E.Waugh	Australia	2001	14	24
D.P.M.D.Jayawardene	Sri Lanka	2004	11	23
M.L.Hayden	Australia	2003	12	23
A.W.Greig	England	1974	13	23
S.L.Campbell	West Indies	2000	14	22
I.M.Chappell	Australia	1974	9	21
I.T.Botham	England	1979	9	20
G.C.Smith	South Africa	2005	11	20
G.A.Hick	England	1994	13	20
M.E.Trescothick	England	2003	13	20
G.S.Chappell	Australia	1974	9	19
G.R.J.Roope	England	1978	9	19
M.D.Crowe	New Zealand	1985	10	19
A.L.Logie	West Indies	1988	12	19
M.Azharuddin	India	1997	12	19
M.A.Taylor	Australia	1998	12	19
D.P.M.D.Jayawardene	Sri Lanka	2001	13	19
M.L.Hayden	Australia	2005	14	19
G.S.Blewett	Australia	1997	15	19
W.R.Endean	South Africa	1953	7	18
M.Azharuddin	India	1994	7	18
G.R.J.Roope	England	1973	8	18
L.C.Braund	England	1902	9	18
R.N.Harvey	Australia	1959	9	18
R.B.Simpson	Australia	1961	9	18
A.R.Border	Australia	1980	10	18
A.R.Border	Australia	1981	10	18
S.P.Fleming	New Zealand	1999	10	18
B.C.Lara	West Indies	2003	10	18
M.E.Trescothick	England	2004	13	18
M.E.Trescothick	England	2005	13	18
C.H.Gayle	West Indies	2002	14	18
J.H.Kallis	South Africa	1998	15	18

I.M.Chappell	Australia	1969	8	17
M.E.Waugh	Australia	2000	8	17
B.A.Young	New Zealand	1994	9	17
J.M.Brearley	England	1977	10	17
R.S.Dravid	India	2006	10	17
A.W.Greig	England	1977	10	17
J.M.Brearley	England	1978	10	17
R.P.Arnold	Sri Lanka	2000	10	17
V.V.S.Laxman	India	2001	10	17
G.A.Gooch	England	1986	11	17
D.C.Boon	Australia	1989	11	17
M.E.Trescothick	England	2003	11	17
S.K.Warne	Australia	2004	12	17
Yousuf Youhana	Pakistan	2000	12	17
I.T.Botham	England	1981	13	17
S.S.Das	India	2001	13	17
M.L.Hayden	Australia	2004	14	17
C.H.Lloyd	West Indies	1984	14	17
G.B.Hole	Australia	1953	7	16
Taufeeq Umar	Pakistan	2003	7	16
S.P.Fleming	New Zealand	2002	8	16
M.E.Waugh	Australia	1991	9	16 #
R.S.Mahanama	Sri Lanka	1997	9	16
G.S.Chappell	Australia	1975	10	16
G.S.Chappell	Australia	1980	10	16
I.V.A.Richards	West Indies	1980	11	16
I.V.A.Richards	West Indies	1981	11	16
H.H.Gibbs	South Africa	2005	11	16
A.R.Border	Australia	1985	12	16
R.S.Dravid	India	2001	13	16
N.D.McKenzie	South Africa	2001	13	16
A.Flintoff	England	2004	13	16
M.E.Waugh	Australia	1993	15	16
D.B.Vengsarkar	India	1979	18	16
A.L.Wadekar	India	1968	7	15
M.E.Waugh	Australia	2002	7	15
K.R.Stackpole	Australia	1969	8	15
M.C.Cowdrey	England	1957	9	15
W.R.Hammond	England	1928	10	15
J.J.Crowe	New Zealand	1985	10	15
C.L.Hooper	West Indies	1991	10	15
D.P.M.D.Jayawardene	Sri Lanka	2000	10	15
M.A.Atherton	England	2001	10	15
C.H.Gayle	West Indies	2001	10	15
R.T.Ponting	Australia	2002	11	15
S.M.Pollock	South Africa	2003	11	15
J.H.Kallis	South Africa	2001	13	15
S.M.Pollock	South Africa	2001	13	15
M.H.Denness	England	1974	14	15
S.K.Warne	Australia	2005	14	15
A.R.Border	Australia	1993	16	15
S.C.Ganguly	India	2002	16	15

 # Waugh achieved the feat in his debut calendar year.

The following fielders have taken 15 catches in a calendar year the most times:

6 M.E.Waugh(A),
4 A.R.Border(A), R.S.Dravid(I), M.A.Taylor(A), M.E.Trescothick(E),

3 G.S.Chappell(A), R.S.Dravid(I), S.P.Fleming(N), M.L.Hayden(A), D.P.M.D.Jayawardene(SL),
2 M.Azharuddin(I), I.T.Botham(E), J.M.Brearley(E), I.M.Chappell(A), C.H.Gayle(W), A.W.Greig(E), J.H.Kallis(SA), S.M.Pollock(SA), R.T.Ponting(A), I.V.A.Richards(W), G.R.J.Roope(E), R.B.Simpson(A), S.K.Warne(A),
1 R.P.Arnold(SL), M.A.Atherton(E), G.S.Blewett(A), D.C.Boon(A), L.C.Braund(E), S.L.Campbell(W), M.C.Cowdrey(E), J.J.Crowe(N), M.D.Crowe(N), S.S.Das(I), M.H.Denness(E), W.R.Endean(SA), A.Flintoff(E), S.C.Ganguly(I), H.H.Gibbs(SA), G.A.Gooch(E), J.M.Gregory(A), W.R.Hammond(E), R.N.Harvey(A), G.A.Hick(E), G.B.Hole(A), C.L.Hooper(W), B.C.Lara(W), V.V.S.Laxman(I), C.H.Lloyd(W), A.L.Logie(W), N.D.McKenzie(SA), R.S.Mahanama(SL), G.C.Smith(SA), K.R.Stackpole(A), Taufeeq Umar(P), D.B.Vengsarkar(I), A.L.Wadekar(I), B.A.Young(N), Yousuf Youhana(P),

MOST RUNS OFF ONE BALL

8 – E.H.Hendren (169) England v Australia, Brisbane 1928-29 (four boundary overthrows).

8 – J.G.Wright (44) New Zealand v Australia, Melbourne 1980-81 (four boundary overthrows).

8 – B.C.Lara (196) West Indies v South Africa, Port-of-Spain 2004-05 (Lara ran three before a return from the field hit a helmet lying behind the stumps for five penalty runs).

7 – A.Sandham (325) England v West Indies, Kingston 1929-30 (four boundary overthrows).

7 – A.P.E.Knott (116) England v West Indies, Leeds 1976 (one, plus two overthrows, plus four boundary overthrows).

7 – Majid Khan (74) Pakistan v Australia, Melbourne 1981-82 (ran four plus three overthows).

7 – H.K.Olonga (24) Zimbabwe v South Africa, Bloemfontein, 1999-2000 (five penalty runs plus two overthrows when S.M.Pollock's return struck a fielder's helmet, which was lying behind the wicket-keeper).

GAMES ABANDONED WITHOUT A BALL BEING BOWLED

England v Australia, Manchester 1890 — Rain washed out play on each day.

England v Australia, Manchester 1938 — Rain washed out play on each day.

Australia v England, Melbourne 1970-71 — This game, originally scheduled as the Third Test of the series, was abandoned after solid rain on the first three days. A replacement Test, becoming a historic Seventh Test of the series, was arranged to replace the washed-out game.

West Indies v England, Georgetown 1980-81 — Two days before this match was due to start, England bowler R.D.Jackman (who had been flown out to replace the injured R.G.D.Willis) had his visitor's permit revoked by the Guyanese Government, and was ordered to leave the country. This was because he had spent several English winters in South Africa (as, incidentally, had several other members of the English team). M.C.C. Manager A.C.Smith then issued a statement saying that England would not play this Second Test of the series 'as it is no longer possible for the Test team to be chosen without restrictions being imposed.' The game was then abandoned.

Sri Lanka v New Zealand, Kandy (2nd Test) & Sinhalese Sports Club, Colombo (3rd Test), 1986-87 — Abandoned following intensive political unrest.

New Zealand v Pakistan, Dunedin 1988-89 — Heavy sweeping rain caused the match to be called off on the third day.

West Indies v England, Georgetown 1989-90 — Torrential rain, falling nightly for five days, left the ground under water, and a contentiously early decision to abandon the match was made on the rest day.

Sri Lanka v Pakistan, Sinhalese Sports Club Ground, Colombo, 1994-95 — Cancelled due to post-election curfew.

Pakistan v Zimbabwe, Faisalabad, 1998-99 — Abandoned on the fifth day because of fog.

New Zealand v India, Dunedin, 1998-99 — Abandoned on the third day because of rain.

South Africa v India — Centurion, 2001-02. This Test was awarded to South Africa, by the I.C.C. after the Board of Control of Cricket in India refused to allow their team to play under appointed match referee M.H.Denness. After intervention by the Indian government, the South African government instructed the United Cricket Board of South Africa to play a five day Test and to replace Denness. The I.C.C. said that the match would not be officially recognised as a Test as it was not played under the auspices of I.C.C. and withdrew the umpire it had appointed (G.Sharp).

FAVOURITE GROUNDS

1. J.B.Hobbs (England) scored 1178 runs avge. 69.29 at Melbourne — 83 and 28; 57 and 0 (1907-08); 6 and 126*; 178 (1911-12); 122 and 20; 27 and 13 (1920-21); 154 and 22; 66 (1924-25); 20 and 49; 142 and 65 (1928-29).
2. H.Sutcliffe (England) scored 724 runs avge. 103.50 at Melbourne — 176 and 127; 143 (1924-25); 58 and 135 (1928-29); 52 and 33 (1932-33).
3. W.R.Hammond (England) scored 808 runs avge. 161.60 at Sydney — 251 (1928-29); 112; 101 and 75* (1932-33); 231* (1936-37); 1 and 37 (1946-47).
4. D.G.Bradman (Australia) scored 1671 runs avge. 128.53 at Melbourne — 79 and 112; 123 and 37* (1928-29); 152 (1930-31); 2 and 167 (1931-32); 0 and 103* (1932-33); 13 and 270; 169 (1936-37); 79 and 49 (1946-47); 132 and 127*; 57 retired hurt (1947-48).
5. D.G.Bradman (Australia) scored 963 runs avge. 192.60 at Leeds — 334 (1930); 304 (1934); 103 and 16 (1938); 33 and 173* (1948).
6. L.Hutton (England) scored 1521 runs avge. 89.47 at The Oval — 12 (1937); 364 (1938); 73 and 165* (1939); 25 (1946); 83 and 36 (1947); 30 and 64 (1948); 206 (1949); 20* and 2 (1950); 28 and 27 (1951); 86 (1952); 82 and 17 (1953); 14 and 5 (1954).
7. D.C.S.Compton (England) scored 955 runs avge. 95.50 at Nottingham — 102 (1938); 65 and 163 (1947); 19 and 184 (1948); 112 and 5 (1951); 0 (1953); 278 (1954); 27 (1955).
8. E.D.Weekes (West Indies) scored 1074 runs avge. 97.63 at Port-of-Spain — 30 and 20 (1947-48); 207; 161 and 55*(1952-53); 206 and 1 (1953-54); 139 and 87* (1954-55); 78 and 24; 51 and 9 (1957-58).
9. G.S.Sobers (West Indies) scored 1354 runs avge. 104.15 at Kingston — 14* and 26 (1953-54); 35* and 64 (1954-55); 365* (1957-58); 147 and 19 (1959-60); 153; 104 and 50 (1961-62); 30 and 27 (1964-65); 0 and 113* (1967-68); 44 and 93 (1967-68); 44 and 93 (1970-71); 13* (1971-72); 57 (1973-74).
10. W.M.Lawry (Australia) scored 1023 runs avge. 78.69 at Melbourne — 52 and 57 (1962-63); 157 and 20 (1963-64); 41 and 19 (1964-65); 88 and 78; 108 (1965-66); 100 (1967-68); 205 (1968-69); 56 and 42 (1970-71).
11. S.M.Gavaskar (India) scored 793 runs avge 113.28 at Port-of-Spain — 64 and 67*; 124 and 220 (1970-71); 156; 26 and 10 (1975-76); 1 and 32 (1982-83).
12. G.S.Chappell (Australia) scored 1006 runs avge. 111.78 at Brisbane (Woolloongabba) — 58 and 71 (1974-75); 123 and 109* (1975-76); 74 and 124 (1979-80); 35 (1980-81); 201 (1981-82); 53 and 8 (1982-83); 150* (1983-84).
13. Zaheer Abbas (Pakistan) scored 1093 runs avge. 99.36 at Lahore — 18 and 33 (1974-75); 15 and 15 (1976-77); 235* and 34* (1978-79); 134 (1981-82); 52 (v Australia 1982-83); 215; 13 (v India 1982-83); 82* and 5 (1983-84); 168* (v India 1984-85); 43 and 31 (v New Zealand 1984-85).
14. Javed Miandad (Pakistan) scored 1068 runs avge. 56.21 at Faisalabad — 154* and 6* (1978-79); 106* (1979-80); 50 and 22 (1980-81); 18 and 36 (1981-82); 6 (v Australia 1982-83); 126; 16 (v India 1982-83); 203* (1985-86); 1 and 30 (1986-87); 19 (1987-88); 43 and 107 (1988-89); 13 (1989-90); 25 and 55 (v New Zealand 1990-91); 7 and 9 (v West Indies 1990-91); 14 and 2 (1991-92).
15. A.R.Border (Australia) scored 1415 runs avge. 58.95 at Adelaide — 11 and 1 (1978-79); 54 and 24 (1979-80); 57 and 7 (1980-81); 78 and 126 (1981-82); 26 (1982-83); 117* and 66 (1983-84); 21 and 18 (1984-85); 49 (1985-86); 70 and 100* (1986-87); 205 (1987-88); 64 and 6* (1988-89); 13 and 8 (1989-90); 12 and 83* (1990-91); 0 and 91* (1991-92); 19 + 1 (1992-93); 84 + 4 (1993-94).
16. M.D.Crowe (New Zealand) scored 1123 runs avge. 70.18 at Wellington — 9 (1981-82); 13 and 100 (1983-84); 37 and 33 (1984-85); 19 (1985-86); 3 and 119 (1986-87); 143 (1987-88); 174 and 0 (1988-89); 30 and 299 (1989-90); 30 and 13* (1991-92); 98 and 3 (1992-93).
17. D.C.Boon (Australia) scored 1127 runs avge. 62.61 at Sydney — 49 (1984-85); 0 and 81 (v New Zealand 1985-86); 131 and 25 (v India 1985-86); 12 and 184* (v England) (1987-88); 149 and 10 (1988-89); 97 and 29 (1990-91); 129* and 7 (1991-92); 76 + 63* (1992-93); 50 + 38 (1993-94); 3 + 17 (1994-95); 16 + 6 (1995-96).

ONE THOUSAND RUNS AT A TEST GROUND

Player	Country	Ground	M	I	NO	Runs	HS	Avge	100s	50s	0s
A.R.Border	Aust	Adelaide	16	29	5	1415	205	58.95	4	9	1
S.R.Waugh	Aust	Adelaide	15	26	2	1056	170	44.00	3	4	1
J.L.Langer	Aust	Adelaide	10	18	1	1040	215	61.17	3	4	0
J.G.Wright	NZ	Auckland	15	29	2	1060	130	39.25	3	5	1
S.M.Gavaskar	India	Bombay[3]	11	20	0	1122	205	56.10	5	3	0
B.C.Lara	WI	Bridgetown	15	27	2	1339	176	53.56	3	7	0
D.L.Haynes	WI	Bridgetown	13	25	5	1210	145	60.50	4	6	1
G.S.Chappell	Aust	Brisbane[2]	7	11	2	1006	201	111.77	5	4	0
J.H.Kallis	SA	Cape Town	12	18	2	1123	149	70.18	4	6	0
D.P.M.D.Jayawardene	SL	Colombo,SSC	17	26	2	1740	374	72.50	6	4	0
S.T.Jayasuriya	SL	Colombo,SSC	22	37	3	1542	199	45.35	2	10	1
P.A.de Silva	SL	Colombo,SSC	16	28	4	1257	146	52.37	5	2	0
H.P.Tillakaratne	SL	Colombo,SSC	16	24	9	1106	204*	73.73	3	4	1
G.Kirsten	SA	Durban[2]	11	18	2	1048	275	65.50	3	4	1
Javed Miandad	Pak	Faisalabad	15	23	4	1068	203*	56.21	5	2	0
D.P.M.D.Jayawardene	SL	Galle	11	16	2	1176	237	84.00	3	6	0
A.Flower	Zim	Harare	20	35	5	1535	199*	51.16	4	6	1
G.W.Flower	Zim	Harare	21	37	1	1218	201*	33.83	3	5	3
Javed Miandad	Pak	Karachi[1]	17	25	1	1393	211	58.04	3	8	0
G.S.Sobers	WI	Kingston	11	18	5	1354	365*	104.15	5	4	1
B.C.Lara	WI	Kingston	11	18	1	1075	213	63.23	3	6	3
Javed Miandad	Pak	Lahore[2]	17	23	3	1122	163	56.10	3	3	0
Zaheer Abbas	Pak	Lahore[2]	10	15	4	1093	235*	99.36	4	2	0
G.A.Gooch	Eng	Lord's	21	39	1	2015	333	53.02	6	5	2
A.J.Stewart	Eng	Lord's	20	37	4	1476	124*	44.72	3	8	2
D.I.Gower	Eng	Lord's	17	30	2	1241	108	44.32	2	8	1
G.Boycott	Eng	Lord's	16	29	3	1189	128*	45.73	3	6	1
S.M.Gavaskar	India	Madras[1]	12	21	4	1018	236*	59.88	3	3	1
D.G.Bradman	Aust	Melbourne	11	17	4	1671	270	128.53	9	3	1
S.R.Waugh	Aust	Melbourne	17	30	6	1284	131*	53.50	3	6	0
A.R.Border	Aust	Melbourne	20	36	3	1272	163	38.54	4	5	3
G.S.Chappell	Aust	Melbourne	17	31	4	1257	121	46.55	4	9	4
J.B.Hobbs	Eng	Melbourne	10	18	1	1178	178	69.29	5	4	1
W.M.Lawry	Aust	Melbourne	8	13	0	1023	205	78.69	4	5	0
M.A.Atherton	Eng	Nottingham	11	19	1	1083	160	60.16	5	3	2
R.B.Kanhai	WI	Port-of-Spain	16	31	3	1212	153	43.28	4	4	1
E.D.Weekes	WI	Port-of-Spain	7	13	2	1074	207	97.63	4	4	0
C.H.Lloyd	WI	Port-of-Spain	16	28	2	1035	143	39.80	2	7	1
I.V.A.Richards	WI	Port-of-Spain	14	21	0	1015	177	48.33	3	4	1
B.C.Lara	WI	St John's	13	20	1	1632	400*	85.89	4	6	1
A.R.Border	Aust	Sydney	17	29	8	1177	89	56.04	0	11	0
G.S.Chappell	Aust	Sydney	12	22	4	1150	204	63.88	4	3	2
D.C.Boon	Aust	Sydney	11	21	3	1127	184*	62.61	4	4	1
S.R.Waugh	Aust	Sydney	17	25	1	1084	103	45.16	3	7	3
R.T.Ponting	Aust	Sydney	10	17	5	1081	207	90.08	5	3	0
L.Hutton	Eng	The Oval	12	19	2	1521	364	89.47	4	5	0
G.A.Gooch	Eng	The Oval	12	22	1	1097	196	52.23	1	9	3
M.D.Crowe	NZ	Wellington	10	17	1	1123	299	70.18	5	1	1
J.G.Wright	NZ	Wellington	13	23	2	1005	138	47.85	3	4	1

FIFTY WICKETS AT A TEST GROUND

Player	Country	Ground	M	Balls	Mdns	Runs	Wkts	Avge	5w	10w	Best
Warne,SK	Aus	Adelaide	12	3555	156	1489	51	29.19	2	0	6/80
Walsh,CA	WI	Bridgetown	12	3024	114	1342	53	25.32	3	0	5/22
Ambrose,CEL	WI	Bridgetown	13	3399	155	1421	52	27.32	2	1	7/45
Warne,SK	Aus	Brisbane[2]	10	3062	155	1232	64	19.25	3	2	8/71
McGrath.GD	Aus	Brisbane[2]	12	2985	138	1311	58	22.60	3	1	6/17
Hadlee,RJ	NZ	Christchurch	14	3679	112	1635	76	21.51	6	0	7/116
Muralidran,M	SL	Colombo(SSC)	20	7553	328	2893	134	21.59	10	3	8/87
Vaas,WPUJC	SL	Colombo(SSC)	17	3818	152	1696	75	22.61	4	1	7/71
Muralidaran,M	SL	Galle	11	4343	213	1405	87	16.14	10	4	7/46
Streak,HH	Zim	Harare	18	4340	199	1847	77	23.98	2	0	6/90
Muralidaran,M	SL	Kandy	14	4446	229	1653	96	17.21	8	4	9/51
Vaas,WPUJC	SL	Kandy	13	2513	113	995	51	19.49	1	0	6/22
Abdul Qadir	Pak	Karachi[1]	13	3655	128	1571	59	26.62	5	1	5/44
Imran Khan	Pak	Karachi[1]	11	2406	100	938	51	18.39	2	1	8/60
Imran Khan	Pak	Lahore[2]	11	2443	93	937	56	16.73	3	1	8/58
Abdul Qadir	Pak	Lahore[2]	12	3099	105	1348	51	26.43	3	2	9/56
Botham,IT	Eng	Lord's	15	3194	125	1693	69	24.53	8	1	8/34
Trueman,FS	Eng	Lord's	12	3087	113	1394	63	22.12	5	1	6/31
Bedser,AV	Eng	Manchester	7	1816	88	686	51	13.45	5	2	7/52
Lillee,DK	Aust	Melbourne	14	3833	105	1798	82	21.92	7	4	7/83
Ambrose,CEL	WI	Port-of-Spain	12	2770	142	877	66	13.28	6	1	6/24
Walsh,CA	WI	Port-of-Spain	14	3345	147	1181	57	20.71	1	0	6/61
Gibbs,LR	WI	Port-of-Spain	13	4754	239	1646	52	31.65	2	0	6/108
Warne,SK	Aus	Sydney	12	3702	155	1637	56	29.23	4	2	7/56
Botham,IT	Eng	The Oval	11	2615	90	1379	52	26.51	2	1	6/125
Hadlee,RJ	NZ	Wellington	12	2623	90	1075	53	20.28	3	2	7/23

BATTING CURIOSITIES

1. A.C.Bannerman (Australia v England, Sydney in 1891-92) scored off only five of 208 balls bowled to him by W.Attewell. Attewell bowled 46 overs (6-ball), 24 of which were maidens, for figures of 1 for 43. Bannerman batted 421 minutes for his 91.

2. There have been ten instances of all eleven batsmen reaching double figures in an innings of a Test match. On each occasion a team score of over 350 has been recorded. The first instance was by England v Australia at Melbourne in 1894-95 and the most recent instance was by England v West Indies at The Oval in 2004.

3. C.Hill (Australia) is the only batsman to be dismissed for three consecutive nineties: 99 (2nd innings 2nd Test) 98 and 97 (3rd Test) against England in 1901-02. In this series Hill also became the first player to score 500 runs in a series without making a century. His scores were 46 and 0, 15 and 99, 98 and 97, 21 and 30, 28 and 87. In his career Hill made the following nervous nineties scores: 96, 99, 98, 97, 91*, 98.

   The only other batsmen to score 500 runs in a series without making a century are: C.C.Hunte (West Indies) against Australia in 1964-65 — 41 and 81, 89 and 53, 31 and 38, 75 and 31, 1 and 60*; M.A.Atherton (England) against Australia in 1993 — 19 and 25, 80 and 99, 11 and 9, 55 and 63, 72 and 28, 50 and 42; G.P.Thorpe (England) against West Indies in 1995 — 20 and 61, 52 and 42, 30 and 0, 94 and 0, 19 and 76, 74 and 38.

4. R.E.Foster's score of 287 at Sydney in the First Test of the 1903-04 series is the highest score by any player in his first Test. He was the first player to share in three century partnerships in the same innings.

5. In the first Test of the Triangular Tournament at Manchester in 1912 T.A.Ward (South Africa) bagged a 'king pair'. He was the third victim of T.J.Matthews's two hat-tricks and was dismissed twice on the one day (May 28).

6. In the Second Test, South Africa v Australia at Johannesburg in 1921-22, A.W.Nourse (South Africa) became the oldest player to score a maiden Test century at 43 years 294 days.

7. Only once has an innings been completed without a single batsman reaching double figures. This was when South Africa was all out for 30 v England at Birmingham in 1924 — the highest score was 7 and there were 11 extras.

8. R.A.Duff and W.H.Ponsford (Australia) scored a century in their first and last Tests against England.

9. At Lord's in 1926 W.Bardsley carried his bat in scoring 193*. At 42 years 201 days he is the oldest to score a century for Australia against England.

10. C.F.Root (England) played in three Test matches during his career — and failed to get a hit in any of them. (All v Australia in 1926.)

11. M.Leyland and R.Subba Row (England) scored a century in their first and last Tests against Australia.

12. G.A.Headley (West Indies) with scores of 176, 114, 112, 223 was the first batsman to score four Test hundreds before turning 21. S.R.Tendulkar (India) passed this record by scoring six Test centuries before his 21st birthday.

13. G.C.Grant (West Indies) against Australia at Adelaide in 1930-31 with scores of 53* and 71* was the first batsman to score a fifty not out in each innings of a Test.

14. C.S.Nayudu (India v England, Calcutta in 1933-34) played only four scoring strokes in a stay of 145 minutes — a six, two fours and a single.

15. In 1932 the Nawab of Pataudi, sr. scored a century in his first Test against Australia. Thirty-two years later his son achieved the same distinction.

16. W.J.Edrich (England) who batted on 63 occasions for his country at an average of 40.00 had an incredible run of failures during 1938 and 1939. In consecutive innings he scored 5, 0, 10, 12, 28, 12, 4, 10, 0, 6 and 1. In his next he notched up 219.

17. W.J.Edrich (England) played two innings before lunch on the third day of the Test v South Africa at Nottingham in 1947. He had been not out at the start of play, and came in at number three when England followed-on.

18. A.G.Ganteaume (West Indies) scored 112 in his only Test innings at Port-of-Spain against England, 1947-48.

19. A.R.Morris (Australia) batted at one end and D.G.Bradman and I.W.G.Johnson at the other for 100 minutes (v England at The Oval, 1948) before the first single was scored and the batsmen changed ends.

20. Three batsmen in the Australian team v England at Nottingham in 1953 scored 237 out of 244 runs from the bat in Australia's first innings of 249. A.R.Morris hit 67, A.L.Hassett 115, and K.R.Miller 55, Morris and Hassett sharing a stand of 122 for the second wicket and Hassett and Miller one of 109 for the fourth. Next highest score was 4.

21. In the Second Test between South Africa and New Zealand, 1953-54, two New Zealand batsmen retired hurt before scoring. Both had been hit by balls from N.A.T.Adcock — B.Sutcliffe on the head and L.S.M.Miller on the chest. Both returned later — Sutcliffe scoring 80*, including seven sixes, and Miller 14.

22. Each batsman to go to the crease in the India v New Zealand Test at Delhi in 1955-56 reached double figures. Highest of the 15 who batted was 230*, lowest 10*.

23. In the West Indies first innings of the Fourth Test against England played at Leeds 1957, F.C.M.Alexander, who went in at the fall of the seventh wicket, was not called upon to face a single ball. F.S.Trueman took a wicket with the last ball of the over and in the next P.J.Loader took a hat-trick to dismiss the last three batsmen and end the innings. Four wickets fell in consecutive balls.

24. In the First Test of the 1957-58 rubber between West Indies and Pakistan, played at Bridgetown, Pakistan scored 106 in its first innings and 8d-657 in its second — a difference of 551 between the two innings.

25. At Durban in 1964-65 K.F.Barrington (England) became the first batsman to score a Test hundred in all seven Test-playing countries. (Since Barrington's retirement Sri Lanka was granted Test status and played its First Test in 1982; Zimbabwe in 1992-93 and Bangladesh in 2000-01. R.S.Dravid (India) is the only player to have scored hundreds in ten different countries.)

26. At Bridgetown in 1964-65 Australia's W.M.Lawry (210) and R.B.Simpson (201) became the first opening pair to score double centuries in the same Test innings.

27. M.C.Cowdrey (England) became the first cricketer to play 100 Tests, England v Australia Birmingham 1968. He duly celebrated this feat by scoring 104.

28. I.M.Chappell, Australia, (165) scored the 1000th Test hundred – for Australia against the West Indies at Melbourne 1968-69. It was scored in the 643rd match.

29. G.M.Turner (New Zealand) became the youngest player to carry his bat through a completed Test innings. Turner was 22 years 63 days when he scored scored 43* at Lord's in 1969.

30. In South Africa's last official Test series against Australia before their 22 year isolation, B.A.Richards became

the only batsman to score 500 runs in his first rubber for South Africa (508 runs, average 72.57).

31. The record aggregate for a batsman playing in his first rubber is 774 (average 154.80) scored by S.M.Gavaskar, India v West Indies 1970-71.

32. The first time brothers scored centuries in the same innings of a Test was at The Oval in 1972. I.M.Chappell (118) and G.S.Chappell (113), Australia v England.

33. R.E.Redmond (New Zealand) scored 107 and 56 in his only Test match at Auckland against Pakistan 1972-73. (see also A.G.Ganteaume above.)

34. The first time brothers scored centuries in each innings of the same Test was at Wellington in 1973-74. I.M.Chappell (145 and 121) and G.S.Chappell (247* and 133) against New Zealand.

35. G.S.Chappell (Australia) became the first player to score centuries in each innings of his first Test as Captain. 123 and 109* against West Indies at Brisbane 1975-76.

36. When S.Amarnath (India) scored 124 against New Zealand at Auckland in 1975-76 he became the first player to emulate his father by scoring a century in his first Test. N.B.('Lala')Amarnath 118 against England 1933-34.

37. The record number of runs scored in Tests in a calendar year was achieved by I.V.A.Richards (West Indies) in 1976 with 1710 runs (average 90.00).

38. In the Second Test at Kanpur in 1976-77 India scored 524 against New Zealand. This is the highest total in Test cricket in which no batsman has scored a century.

39. At Leeds, in 1977 G.Boycott (England) became the first batsman to score his 100th first-class century in a Test match when he scored 191 against Australia.

40. The highest aggregate by a batsman in his debut calendar year is 1219 (average 64.15) by M.A.Taylor (Australia) in 1989.

41. M.E.Waugh and S.R.Waugh (Australia) provided the first instance in Test cricket of twins playing in the same Test — v West Indies at Port-of-Spain 1990-91.

42. Waqar Younis on his debut as captain took 7 for 91 and 6 for 44 for Pakistan v Zimbabwe at the Karachi Defence Stadium in 1993-94. His match figures of 13 for 135 are the second best figures by a captain in a Test.

43. During the 1999-2000 Adelaide Test, A.Kumble (India) — at that time the only bowler to have taken five wickets in an innings against the other eight Test playing countries — bowled to S.R.Waugh (Australia) — at that time the only batsman to have scored a century against the other eight Test playing countries.

44. When M.Muralidaran (Sri Lanka) took 5 for 13 v Bangladesh at the Sinhalese Sports Club ground in Colombo in 2001-02, he became the first player to take five wickets in an innings against the other nine Test playing countries.

45. The 2001-02 Kandy Test between Sri Lanka and West Indies saw three bowlers used to complete one over. M.Dillon had abdominal pains after 2 balls of his 3rd over and was replaced by C.E.L.Stuart. Stuart was banned from bowling for the remainder of the innings after bowling 2 high full-pitched deliveries, both of which were called no-balls, in his first 3 balls. C.H.Gayle bowled the final 3 balls of the over.

46. When G.Kirsten (South Africa) scored 150 v Bangladesh at East London in 2002-03 he became the first player to score a Test hundred against the other nine Test playing countries. S.R.Waugh was the second person to achieve this feat (and the only one to make at least one score of 150 against each opponent). S.R.Tendulkar, R.S.Dravid (India). M.S.Atapattu (Sri Lanka), B.C.Lara (West Indies), R.T.Ponting (Australia) and A.C.Gilchrist (Australia) have since joined them.

ATTENDANCE RECORDS

Single day — 90,800 spectators spectators watched the second day (February 11) of the Fifth Test Australia v West Indies at Melbourne 1960-61.

Match — The 3rd Test at Melbourne 1936-37 attracted 350,534 spectators, the record confirmed crowd for any cricket match. The Test was played on January 1, 2, 4, 5, 6, 7. (Note: At the 4th Test at Calcutta 1981-82, it was estimated that about 394,000 attended the five days of the match. However, no official crowd figures were kept.)

Series — The five matches in the 1936-37 series Australia v England attracted 943,000 spectators, the biggest attendance for any Test rubber.

BATSMEN WHO SCORED THEIR ONE AND ONLY TEST CENTURY IN THEIR DEBUT MATCH

C.Bannerman (Australia) 165* v England, 1876-77
P.F.Warner (England) 132* v South Africa, 1898-99
R.E.Foster (England) 287 v Australia, 1903-04
R.J.Hartigan (Australia) 116 v England, 1907-08
A.Jackson (Australia) 164 v England, 1928-29
J.E.Mills (New Zealand) 117 v England, 1929-30
Nawab of Pataudi sr (England) 102 v Australia, 1932-33
N.B.Amarnath (India) 118 v England, 1933-34
S.C.Griffith (England) 140 v West Indies, 1947-48
A.G.Ganteaume (West Indies) 112 v England, 1947-48
R.H.Shodhan (India) 110 v Pakistan, 1952-53
B.H.Pairaudeau (West Indies) 115 v India, 1952-53
A.G.Kripal Singh (India) 100* v New Zealand, 1955-56
C.A.Milton (England) 104* v New Zealand, 1958
A.A.Baig (India) 112 v England, 1959
Hanumant Singh (India) 105 v England, 1963-64
Khalid Ibadulla (Pakistan) 166 v Australia, 1964-65
J.H.Hampshire (England) 107 v West Indies, 1969
R.E.Redmond (New Zealand) 107 v Pakistan, 1973
F.C.Hayes (England) 106* v West Indies, 1973
L.Baichan (West Indies) 105* v Pakistan, 1974-75
S.Amarnath (India) 124 v New Zealand, 1975-76
A.B.Williams (West Indies) 100 v Australia, 1977-78
D.M.Wellham (Australia) 103 v England, 1981
D.S.B.P.Kuruppu (Sri Lanka) 201* v New Zealand, 1986-87
P.K.Amre (India) 103 v South Africa, 1992-93
Ali Naqvi (Pakistan) 115 v South Africa 1997-98
Aminul Islam (Bangladesh) 145 v India 2000-01
D.R.Smith (West Indies) 105*v South Africa 2003-04
A.N.Cook (England) 104* v India 2005-06

SIXES TO WIN TEST MATCHES

Batsman	Bowler	Match particulars				
E.Paynter (14*)	S.J.McCabe	England	v	Australia	Brisbane[2]	1932-33
W.R.Hammond (75*)	P.K.Lee	England	v	Australia	Sydney	1932-33
W.R.Hammond (29*)	E.A.Martindale	England	v	West Indies	Bridgetown	1934-35
W.Watson (17*)	E.D.Weekes	England	v	West Indies	Georgetown	1953-54
H.R.Lance (28*)	I.M.Chappell	South Africa	v	Australia	Port Elizabeth	1966-67
Javed Miandad (25*)	P.J.Petherick	Pakistan	v	New Zealand	Lahore[2]	1976-77
A.Turner (20*)	E.J.Chatfield	Australia	v	New Zealand	Auckland	1976-77
Zaheer Abbas (34*)	G.R.Viswanath	Pakistan	v	India	Lahore[2]	1978-79
R.J.Hadlee (6*)	B.Yardley	New Zealand	v	Australia	Auckland	1981-82
Mohsin Khan (14*)	K.J.Hughes	Pakistan	v	Australia	Karachi[1]	1982-83
P.J.L.Dujon (17*)	M.Amarnath	West Indies	v	India	Kingston	1982-83
R.J.Hadlee (17*)	J.R.Ratnayeke	New Zealand	v	Sri Lanka	Wellington	1982-83
Kapil Dev (23*)	P.H.Edmonds	India	v	England	Lord's	1986
A.L.Logie (6*)	M.Venkatarama	West Indies	v	India	Kingston	1988-89
I.V.A.Richards (73*)	R.K.Illingworth	West Indies	v	England	Birmingham	1991
S.T.Jayasuriya (6*)	P.C.R.Tufnell	Sri Lanka	v	England	Colombo (SSC)	1992-93
Rashid Latif (13*)	S.A.Thomson	Pakistan	v	New Zealand	Auckland	1993-94
I.A.Healy (10*)	W.J.Cronje	Australia	v	South Africa	Port Elizabeth	1996-97
C.L.Hooper (6*)	M.Muralidaran	West Indies	v	Sri Lanka	St John's	1996-97
Harbhajan Singh (14*)	H.H.Streak	India	v	Zimbabwe	Delhi	2001-02
R.T.Ponting (100*)	P.R.Adams	Australia	v	South Africa	Cape Town	2001-02
M.V.Boucher (8*)	M.E.Waugh	South Africa	v	Australia	Durban[2]	2001-02
S.P.Fleming (31*)	N.Boje	New Zealand	v	South Africa	Auckland	2003-04
R.T.Ponting (62*)	Danish Kaneria	Australia	v	Pakistan	Melbourne	2004-05

REACHING CENTURY WITH A SIX

Batsman	Bowler					
J.Darling (178)	J.Briggs	Australia	v	England	Adelaide	1897-98
E.H.Bowley (109)	W.E.Merritt	England	v	New Zealand	Auckland	1929-30
P.R.Umrigar (130)	S.Ramadhin	India	v	West Indies	Port-of-Spain	1952-53
P.L.Winslow (108)	G.A.R.Lock	South Africa	v	England	Manchester	1955
K.F.Barrington (132*)	R.B.Simpson	England	v	Australia	Adelaide	1962-63

J.H.Edrich (103)	P.I.Philpott	England	v	Australia	Sydney	1965-66
K.F.Barrington (115)	T.R.Veivers	England	v	Australia	Melbourne	1965-66
D.T.Lindsay (131)	D.A.Renneberg	South Africa	v	Australia	Johannesburg[3]	1966-67
K.F.Barrington (143)	L.R.Gibbs	England	v	West Indies	Port-of-Spain	1967-68
B.R.Taylor (124)	R.M.Edwards	New Zealand	v	West Indies	Auckland	1968-69
J.Benaud (142)	Intikhab Alam	Australia	v	Pakistan	Melbourne	1972-73
K.R.Stackpole (142)	M.L.C.Foster	Australia	v	West Indies	Kingston	1972-73
J.H.Edrich (100*)	B.S.Bedi	England	v	India	Manchester	1974
K.D.Walters (103)	R.G.D.Willis	Australia	v	England	Perth	1974-75
D.L.Amiss (179)	B.S.Chandrasekhar	England	v	India	Delhi	1976-77
I.C.Davis (105)	Salim Altaf	Australia	v	Pakistan	Adelaide	1976-77
R.B.McCosker (107)	R.G.D.Willis	Australia	v	England	Nottingham	1977
Haroon Rashid (108)	G.Miller	Pakistan	v	England	Hyderabad	1977-78
Javed Miandad (154*)	B.S.Bedi	Pakistan	v	India	Faisalabad	1978-79
Kapil Dev (126*)	N.Phillip	India	v	West Indies	Delhi	1978-79
I.T.Botham (137)	Kapil Dev	England	v	India	Leeds	1979
C.L.King (100*)	G.P.Howarth	West Indies	v	New Zealand	Christchurch	1979-80
J.G.Wright (110)	D.R.Doshi	New Zealand	v	India	Auckland	1980-81
I.T.Botham (118)	M.R.Whitney	England	v	Australia	Manchester	1981
Imran Khan (117)	Kapil Dev	Pakistan	v	India	Faisalabad	1982-83
L.R.D.Mendis (105)	D.R.Doshi	Sri Lanka	v	India	Madras[1]	1982-83
D.L.Haynes (145)	T.M.Alderman	West Indies	v	Australia	Bridgetown	1983-84
G.R.J.Matthews (115)	V.R.Brown	Australia	v	New Zealand	Brisbane[2]	1985-86
P.A.de Silva (122)	Imran Khan	Sri Lanka	v	Pakistan	Faisalabad	1985-86
Imran Khan (135*)	N.S.Yadav	Pakistan	v	India	Madras[1]	1986-87
M.D.Crowe (104)	C.G.Butts	New Zealand	v	West Indies	Auckland	1986-87
Ijaz Ahmed (105)	Maninder Singh	Pakistan	v	India	Ahmedabad	1986-87
D.L.Haynes (112*)	N.D.Hirwani	West Indies	v	India	Bridgetown	1988-89
C.C.Lewis (117)	S.L.Venkatapathy Raju	England	v	India	Madras[1]	1992-93
D.L.Haynes (125)	Asif Mujtaba	West Indies	v	Pakistan	Bridgetown	1992-93
C.L.Hooper (178*)	Nadeem Khan	West Indies	v	Pakistan	St John's	1992-93
P.A.de Silva (148)	A.Kumble	Sri Lanka	v	India	Colombo (PSS)	1993-94
P.A.de Silva (127)	Mushtaq Ahmed	Sri Lanka	v	Pakistan	Colombo (PSS)	1994-95
S.R.Tendulkar (179)	C.A.Walsh	India	v	West Indies	Nagpur	1994-95
R.G.Samuels (125)	D.N.Patel	West Indies	v	New Zealand	St John's	1995-96
S.R.Tendulkar (122)	M.M.Patel	India	v	England	Birmingham	1996
Wasim Akram (257*)	P.A.Strang	Pakistan	v	Zimbabwe	Sheikhupura	1996-97
N.Hussain (113)	H.H.Streak	England	v	Zimbabwe	Bulawayo[2]	1996-97
B.C.Lara (103)	A.Kumble	West Indies	v	India	St John's	1996-97
M.Azharuddin (163*)	G.R.Robertson	India	v	Australia	Calcutta	1997-98
C.D.McMillan (139)	A.R.Whittall	New Zealand	v	Zimbabwe	Wellington	1997-98
Saeed Anwar (126)	M.E.Waugh	Pakistan	v	Australia	Peshawar[2]	1998-99
D.P.M.D.Jayawardene	Harbhajan Singh	Sri Lanka	v	India	Colombo (SSC)	1998-99
S.R.Tendulkar (126)	C.R.Miller	India	v	Australia	Chennai[1]	2000-01
M.P.Vaughan (120)	Abdul Razzaq	England	v	Pakistan	Manchester	2001
H.H.Gibbs (107)	Zaheer Khan	South Africa	v	India	Bloemfontein	2001-02
J.L.Langer (116)	C.W.Henderson	Australia	v	South Africa	Adelaide	2001-02
R.T.Ponting (100*)	P.R.Adams	Australia	v	South Africa	Cape Town	2001-02
R.D.Jacobs (118)	V.V.S.Laxman	West Indies	v	India	St Johns	2001-02
Imran Nazir (127)	C.Z.Harris	Pakistan	v	New Zealand	Lahore[2]	2001-02
M.L.Hayden (119)	Danish Kaneria	Australia	v	Pakistan	Sharjah	2002-03
R.T.Ponting (150)	Saqlain Mushtaq	Australia	v	Pakistan	Sharjah	2002-03
S.R.Waugh (103*)	Danish Kaneria	Australia	v	Pakistan	Sharjah	2002-03
J.L.Langer (250)	R.J.K.Dawson	Australia	v	England	Melbourne	2002-03
M.L.Hayden (101*)	G.M.Ewing	Australia	v	Zimbabwe	Sydney	2003-04
M.E.Trescothick (113)	Mohammad Rafique	England	v	Bangladesh	Dhaka	2003-04

R.S.Dravid (233)	J.N.Gillespie	India	v	Australia	Adelaide	2003-04
B.C.Lara (115)	J.H.Kallis	West Indies	v	South Africa	Cape Town	2003-04
V.K.Sehwag (309) §	Shoaib Akhtar	India	v	Pakistan	Lahore[2]	2003-04
S.P.Fleming (117)	M.J.Saggers	New Zealand	v	England	Nottingham	2004
D.R.Martyn (104)	A.Kumble	Australia	v	India	Chennai[1]	2004-05
S.T.Jayasuriya (253) †	Danish Kaneria	Sri Lanka	v	Pakistan	Faisalabad	2004-05
A.C.Gilchrist (113)	Shahid Afridi	Australia	v	Pakistan	Sydney	2004-05
B.C.Lara (130)	Danish Kaneria	West Indies	v	Pakistan	Bridgetown	2004-05
K.P.Pietersen (100)	Shoaib Akhtar	England	v	Pakistan	Faisalabad	2005-06
Shahid Afridi (156)	I.K.Pathan	Pakistan	v	India	Faisalabad	2005-06
Yousuf Youhana (192)	S.J.Harmison	Pakistan	v	England	Leeds	2006

Note: F.S.Jackson (103 England v Australia, The Oval , 1893 brought up his 100 with a hit over the boundary. However, under the Laws in force at the time, he was only awarded four runs for the stroke. R.N.Harvey (153) reached his 100 with an all-run five from the bowling of N.B.Amarnath - Australia v India at Melbourne 1947-78. § Sehwag brought up his 300 with a six off Saqlain Mushtaq. † Jayasuriya brought up his 200 with a six off Shoaib Akhtar.

MOST RUNS FROM STROKES WORTH FOUR OR MORE IN AN INNINGS

runs	6s	5s	4s							
238	5	-	52	J.H.Edrich	310*	England	v	New Zealand	Leeds	1965
223	11	1	38	M.L.Hayden	380	Australia	v	Zimbabwe	Perth	2003-04
206	9	-	38	Inzamamul Haq	329	Pakistan	v	New Zealand	Lahore[2]	2001-02
201	4	1	43	B.C.Lara	400*	West Indies	v	England	St John's	2003-04
196	10	-	34	W.R.Hammond	336*	England	v	New Zealand	Auckland	1932-33
194	1	-	47	V.K.Sehwag	254	India	v	Pakistan	Lahore[2]	2005-06
192	6	-	39	V.K.Sehwag	309	India	v	Pakistan	Multan[2]	2003-04
190	3	-	43	G.A.Gooch	333	England	v	India	The Oval	1990
184	-	-	46	D.G.Bradman	334	Australia	v	England	Leeds	1930
180	2	-	43	D.G.Bradman	304	Australia	v	England	Leeds	1934
180	-	-	45	B.C.Lara	375	West Indies	v	England	St John's	1993-94
178	11	-	28	N.J.Astle	222	New Zealand	v	England	Christchurch	2001-02
178	1	-	43	D.P.M.D.Jayawardene	374	Sri Lanka	v	South Africa	Colombo (SSC)	2006-07
177	-	1	43	R.G.Pollock	274	South Africa	v	Australia	Durban[2]	1969-70
176	-	-	44	V.V.S.Laxman	281	India	v	Australia	Kolkata	2000-01
168	-	-	42	R.B.Kanhai	256	West Indies	v	India	Calcutta	1958-59
166	1	-	40	D.L.Amiss	262*	England	v	West Indies	Kingston	1973-74
166	3	-	37	C.H.Gayle	317	West Indies	v	South Africa	St John's	2004-05
160	-	-	40	P.A.de Silva	267	Sri Lanka	v	New Zealand	Wellington	1990-91
160	12	-	22	Wasim Akram	257*	Pakistan	v	Sri Lanka	Sheikhupura	1996-97
158	3	-	35	D.L.Houghton	266	Zimbabwe	v	Sri Lanka	Bulawayo[2]	1994-95
157	-	1	38	G.S.Sobers	365*	West Indies	v	Pakistan	Kingston	1957-58
156	2	-	36	S.T.Jayasuriya	340	Sri Lanka	v	India	Colombo (RPS)	1997-98
156	2	-	36	K.C.Sangakkara	270	Sri Lanka	v	Zimbabwe	Bulawayo[2]	2003-04
156	4	-	33	S.T.Jayasuriya	253	Sri Lanka	v	Pakistan	Faisalabad	2004-05
152	2	-	35	F.M.M.Worrell	261	West Indies	v	England	Nottingham	1957
152	-	-	38	Zaheer Abbas	274	Pakistan	v	England	Birmingham	1971
152	-	-	38	I.V.A.Richards	291	West Indies	v	England	The Oval	1976
152	-	-	38	B.C.Lara	277	West Indies	v	Australia	Sydney	1992-93
152	-	-	38	N.Hussain	207	England	v	Australia	Birmingham	1997
152	6	-	29	H.H.Gibbs	228	South Africa	v	Pakistan	Cape Town	2002-03
150	1	-	36	L.G.Rowe	302	West Indies	v	England	Bridgetown	1973-74
150	3	-	33	K.C.Sangakkara	230	Sri Lanka	v	Pakistan	Lahore[2]	2001-02
150	1	-	36	M.S.Atapattu	249	Sri Lanka	v	Zimbabwe	Bulawayo[2]	2003-04

FEWEST BOUNDARIES IN AN INNINGS

Runs	Fours						
77	0	G.Boycott	England	v	Australia	Perth	1978-79
67	0	E.A.B.Rowan	South Africa	v	England	Durban[2]	1938-39
120	2	P.A.Gibb	England	v	South Africa	Durban[2]	1938-39
118	2	G.P.Thorpe	England	v	Pakistan	Lahore	2000-01
94	2	K.F.Barrington	England	v	Australia	Sydney	1962-63
105*	3	H.P.Tillakaratne	Sri Lanka	v	West Indies	Galle	2001-02
104	3	Mohsin Khan	Pakistan		England	Lahore[2]	1983-84
102	3	W.M.Woodfull	Australia	v	England	Melbourne	1928-29
100	3	G.M.Wood	Australia	v	Pakistan	Melbourne	1981-82
161	5	W.M.Woodfull	Australia	v	South Africa	Melbourne	1931-32
144*	5	D.G.Bradman	Australia	v	England	Nottingham	1938

G.Boycott's innings included one four but it was all-run and included two runs from an overthrow.

MOST RUNS OFF ONE OVER

EIGHT-BALLS

25 (66061600)	B.Sutcliffe/R.W.Blair (off H.J.Tayfield)	New Zealand v South Africa	Johannesburg[2]	1953-54
24 (2x6, 3x4)	J.F.M.Morrison (off Imran Khan)	New Zealand v Pakistan	Karachi[1]	1976-77
22 (42444004)	P.G.van der Bijl (off D.P.V.Wright)	South Africa v England	Durban[2]	1938-39
22 (44422204)	R.C.Fredericks (off G.J.Gilmour)	West Indies v Australia	Perth	1975-76
22 (?)	Javed Miandad/Wasim Raja (off B.P.Bracewell)	Pakistan v New Zealand	Christchurch	1978-79
21 (44442300)	V.Y.Richardson (off J.W.H.T.Douglas)	Australia v England	Melbourne	1924-25
21 (34144104)	R.N.Harvey/C.L.McCool (off J.C.Watkins)	Australia v South Africa	Cape Town	1949-50
21 (10206444)	K.R.Miller/R.R.Lindwall (off S.Ramadhin)	Australia v West Indies	Brisbane[2]	1951-52
21 (14466000)	E.J.Barlow/R.G.Pollock (off R.B.Simpson)	South Africa v Australia	Adelaide	1963-64
21 (3x6?)	I.M.Chappell of Intikhab Alam	Australia v Pakistan	Adelaide	1972-73
21 (34200444)	G.J.Cosier/G.S.Chappell (off Saleem Altaf)	Australia v Pakistan	Melbourne	1976-77
21 (04614222)	J.R.Thomson/A.G.Hurst (off S.Madan Lal)	Australia v India	Brisbane[2]	1977-78
20 (44404004)	K.D.Walters (off G.S.Sobers)	Australia v West Indies	Sydney	1968-69
20 (6246020X)	G.D.McKenzie (off G.S.Sobers)	Australia v West Indies	Sydney	1968-69
20 (?)	I.M.Chappell/R.Edwards (off Intikhab Alam)	Australia v Pakistan	Adelaide	1972-73
20 (?)	R.W.Marsh (off Asif Iqbal)	Australia v Pakistan	Adelaide	1972-73
20 (44444?)	R.E.Redmond (off Majid Khan)	New Zealand v Pakistan	Auckland	1972-73
20 (044440400)	A.I.Kallicharran (off Asif Masood)	West Indies v Pakistan	Karachi[1]	1974-75
20 (20**4**404402)	R.C.Fredericks (off J.R.Thomson)	West Indies v Australia	Perth	1975-76
20 (64442000)	Zaheer Abbas (off K.J.O'Keeffe)	Pakistan v Australia	Adelaide	1976-77
20 (00444440)	D.W.Hookes (off A.W.Greig)	Australia v England	Melbourne	1976-77

SIX-BALLS L: 1 leg-bye; (**bold:** no-ball; <u>B4:</u> 4 byes; <u>B2:</u> 2 byes; X: wicket)

28 (466444)	B.C.Lara (off R.J.Peterson)	West Indies v South Africa	Johannesburg[3]	2003-04
27 (666621)	Shahid Afridi (off Harbhajan Singh)	Pakistan v India	Lahore[2]	2005-06
26 (444446)	C.D.McMillan (off Younis Khan)	New Zealand v Pakistan	Hamilton	2000-01

25 (462660L)	A.M.E.Roberts (off I.T.Botham)	West Indies v England	Port-Of-Spain	1980-81
25 (666**L**410)	N.J.Astle/C.L.Cairns (off A.R.Caddick)	New Zealand v England	Christchurch	2001-02
25 (4444440)	R.R.Sarwan (off M.M.Patel)	West Indies v India	Bassaterre	2005-06
25 (44444**4**0)	R.R.Sarwan (off M.M.Patel)	West Indies v India	Bassaterre	2005-06
24 (44**4**0444)	S.M.Patil (off R.G.D.Willis)	India v England	Manchester	1982
24 (464604)	I.T.Botham (off D.A.Stirling)	England v New Zealand	The Oval	1986
24 (244266)	I.D.S.Smith (off A.S.Wassan)	New Zealand v India	Auckland	1989-90
24 (006666)	Kapil Dev (off E.E.Hemmings)	India v England	Lord's	1990
24 (444426)	Yousuf Youhana (off N.Boje)	Pakistan v South Africa	Cape Town	2002-03
24 (444444)	C.H.Gayle (off M.J.Hoggard)	West Indies v England	The Oval	2004
24 (B2260646)	A.M.Blignaut (off N.Boje)	Zimbabwe v South Africa	Cape Town	2004-05
23 (106646)	Azhar Mahmood/Mushtaq Ahmed (off P.L.Symcox)	Pakistan v South Africa	Rawalpindi[2]	1997-98
23 (6461**n**2**n**2)	G.A.Hick/M.R.Ramprakash (off J.N.Gillespie)	England v Australia	Perth	1998-99
23 (6**24**11106)	N.J.Astle/C.L.Cairns (off M.J.Hoggard)	New Zealand v England	Christchurch	2001-02
23 (466412)	S.C.Ganguly/S.R.Tendulkar (off A.F.Giles)	India v England	Leeds	2002
23 (44261**1**4)	G.C.Smith/A.B.de Villiers (off A.G.Cremer)	Zimbabwe v South Africa	Cape Town	2004-05
22 (116626)	M.W.Tate/W.Voce (off A.E.Hall)	England v South Africa	Johannesburg[1]	1930-31
22 (064066)	R.C.Motz (off D.A.Allen)	New Zealand v England	Dunedin	1965-66
22 (664420)	R.C.Motz (off E.A.S.Prasanna)	New Zealand v India	Dunedin	1967-68
22 (006664)	S.T.Clarke (off Mohammad Nazir)	West Indies v Pakistan	Faisalabad	1979-80
22 (613642)	I.T.Botham/C.J.Tavare (off D.K.Lillee)	England v Australia	Manchester	1981
22 (046444)	K.Srikkanth (off R.G.Holland)	India v Australia	Sydney	1985-86
22 (224644)	I.T.Botham (off M.G.Hughes)	England v Australia	Brisbane[2]	1986-87
22 (440446)	P.A.J.DeFreitas (off C.J.McDermott)	England v Australia	Adelaide	1994-95
22 (4444**nn**04)	Aamer Sohail (off D.H.Brain)	Pakistan v Zimbabwe	Bulawayo[2]	1994-95
22 (040666)	W.J.Cronje (off M.Muralidaran)	South Africa v Sri Lanka	Centurion	1997-98
22 (04**44nn**1104)	R.G.Twose/C.D.McMillan (off S.C.Ganguly)	New Zealand v India	Hamilton	1998-99
22 (460444)	B.C.Lara (off A.C.Dale)	West Indies v Australia	St John's	1998-99
22 (606460)	A.C.Gilchrist (off M.A.Butcher)	Australia v England	Birmingham	2001
22 (446044)	Shoaib Malik (off H.M.RK.B.Herath)	Pakistan v Sri Lanka	Karachi[1]	2004-05
22 (46**n**1**4**401)	A.C.Gilchrist/S.M.Katich (off M.J.Hoggard)	Australia v England	Nottingham	2005
22 (1**n**40664)	Inzamamul Haq/Shahid Afridi (off I.K.Pathan)	India v Pakistan	Faisalabad	2005-06
22 (166261)	A.C.Gilchrist/A.Symonds (off N.Boje)	Australia v South Africa	Cape Town	2005-06
22 (424444)	A.C.Gilchrist (off A.Nel)	Australia v South Africa	Durban[2]	2005-06
21 (124464)	J.H.Sinclair/C.M.H.Hathorn (off A.J.Y.Hopkins)	South Africa v Australia	Cape Town	1902-03
21 (122466)	D.G.Bradman/S.G.Barnes (off J.C.Laker)	Australia v England	Lord's	1948
21 (660612)	B.S.Bedi/B.S.Chandrasekhar (off P.J.Petherick)	India v New Zealand	Kanpur	1976-77
21 (**4**144044)	M.Amarnath/S.M.Gavaskar (off Sikander Bakht)	India v Pakistan	Karachi[1]	1978-79
21 (640461)	Imran Khan (off Kapil Dev)	Pakistan v India	Faisalabad	1982-83
21 (144444)	A.Kumble/M.Azharuddin (off L.Klusener)	India v South Africa	Calcutta	1996-97
21 (044661)	Harbhajan Singh (off R.R.Sarwan)	India v West Indies	Kolkata	2002-03

21 (2444L**4**11)	R.T.Ponting/M.L.Hayden (off A.M.Blignaut)	Australia v Zimbabwe	Sydney	2003-04
21 (421644)	D.R.Martyn/M.J.Clarke (off A.B.Agarkar)	Australia v India	Nagpur	2004-05
21 (064641)	N.B.Mahwire (off C.S.Martin)	Zimbabwe v New Zealand	Bulawayo[2]	2005-06
21 (066L2261)	Mohammad Rafique (off S.K.Warne)	Bangladesh v Australia	Chittagong[2]	2005-06
21 (66**4**X04)	Shahid Afridi/Kamran Akmal (off M.J.Hoggard)	Pakistan v England	Faisalabad	2005-06
20 (664400)	E.A.V.Williams (off J.C.Laker)	West Indies v England	Bridgetown	1947-48
20 (604046)	A.K.Davidson (off D.A.Allen)	Australia v England	Manchester	1961
20 (44444?)	D.T.Lindsay (off J.W.Gleeson)	South Africa v Australia	Port Elizabeth	1969-70
20 (444620)	D.L.Haynes (off J.R.Thomson)	West Indies v Australia	Port-of-Spain	1977-78
20 (460406)	Yashpal Sharma (off P.R.Sleep)	India v Australia	New Delhi	1979-80
20 (446420)	S.M.Patil (off Jalaluddin)	India v Pakistan	Lahore[2]	1982-83
20 (?)	N.S.Sidhu (off E.J.Gray)	India v New Zealand	Bangalore	1988-89
20 (1**nn**0**nn**13**n**30**nn4**1)	S.K.Warne/I.A.Healy (off C.E.L.Ambrose)	Australia v West Indies	Perth	1996-97
20 (044624)	M.Muralidaran (off H.T.Davis)	Sri Lanka v New Zealand	Dunedin	1996-97
20 (444044)	A.C.Gilchrist (off Mushtaq Ahmed)	Australia v Pakistan	Brisbane[2]	1999-2000
20 (242624)	A.C.Gilchrist (off N.D.McKenzie)	Australia v South Africa	Johannesburg[2]	2001-02
20 (262244)	A.C.Gilchrist (off P.R.Adams)	Australia v South Africa	Cape Town	2001-02
20 (004664)	N.J.Astle (off A.R.Caddick)	New Zealand v England	Christchurch	2001-02
20 (440066)	S.R.Waugh (off Danish Kaneria)	Australia v Pakistan	Sharjah	2002-03
20 (444440)	M.E.Trescothick (off M.Ntini)	England v South Africa	Birmingham	2003
20 (644420)	A.Flintoff (off S.M.Pollock)	England v South Africa	Lord's	2003
20 (644060)	J.L.Langer (off A.Kumble)	Australia v India	Adelaide	2003-04
20 (242606)	M.Muralidaran (off A.F.Giles)	Sri Lanka v England	Colombo (SSC)	2003-04
20 (0444B44)	S.T.Jayasuriya (off Shoaib Akhtar)	Sri Lanka v Pakistan	Faisalabad	2004-05
20 (0**6**06**1**4n0)	A.Flintoff/S.P.Jones (off M.S.Kasprowicz)	England v Australia	Birmingham	2005
20 (462440)	Shoaib Akhtar (off Zaheer Khan)	India v Pakistan	Faisalabad	2005-06

MOST SIXES OFF CONSECUTIVE BALLS

FOUR	Kapil Dev (77*) off E.E.Hemmings	India	v	England	Lord's	1990
	Shahid Afridi (off Harbhajan Singh)	Pakistan	v	India	Lahore[2]	2005-06
THREE	W.R.Hammond (336*) off J.Newman	England	v	New Zealand	Auckland	1932-33
	S.T.Clarke (35*) off Mohammad Nazir	West Indies	v	Pakistan	Faisalabad	1980-81
	W.J.Cronje (82) off M.Muralidaran	South Africa	v	Sri Lanka	Centurion	1997-98
	S.K.Warne (86) off Mushtaq Ahmed	Australia	v	Pakistan	Brisbane[2]	1999-2000
	N.J.Astle (222) off A.R.Caddick	New Zealand	v	England	Christchurch	2001-02
	J.H.Kallis (54) off A.G.Cremer	South Africa	v	Zimbabwe	Cape Town	2004-05

MOST FOURS OFF CONSECUTIVE BALLS

SIX	C.H.Gayle (105) off M.J.Hoggard	England	v	England	The Oval	2004
	R.R.Sarwan (116) off M.M.Patel	West Indies	v	India	Bassaterre	2005-06
FIVE	D.T.Lindsay (60) off J.W.Gleeson	South Africa	v	Australia	Port Elizabeth	1969-70
	R.E.Redmond (107) off Majid Khan	New Zealand	v	Pakistan	Auckland	1972-73
	D.W.Hookes (56) off A.W.Greig	Australia	v	England	Melbourne	1976-77
	M.Azharuddin (109) off L.Klusener	India	v	South Africa	Calcutta	1996-97
	M.E.Trescothick (52*) off M.Ntini	England	v	South Africa	Birmingham	2003

MOST SIXES IN AN INNINGS

TWELVE	Wasim Akram (257*)	Pakistan	v	Sri Lanka	Sheikhupura	1996-97
ELEVEN	N.J.Astle (222)	New Zealand	v	England	Christchurch	2001-02
	M.L.Hayden (380)	Australia	v	Zimbabwe	Perth	2003-04

TEN	W.R.Hammond (336*)	England	v	New Zealand	Auckland	1932-33
NINE	C.L.Cairns (120)	New Zealand	v	Zimbabwe	Auckland	1995-96
	Inzamamul Haq (329)	Pakistan	v	New Zealand	Lahore[2]	2001-02
EIGHT	N.S.Sidhu (124)	India	v	Sri Lanka	Lucknow[2]	1993-94
	A.C.Gilchrist (204*)	Australia	v	South Africa	Johannesburg[3]	2001-02
SEVEN	B.Sutcliffe (80*)	New Zealand	v	South Africa	Johannesburg[2]	1953-54
	I.V.A.Richards (110*)	West Indies	v	England	St John's	1985-86
	C G.Greenidge (213)	West Indies	v	New Zealand	Auckland	1986-87
	C.L.Cairns (158)	New Zealand	v	South Africa	Wellington	2003-04
	A.Flintoff (167)	England	v	West Indies	Birmingham	2004
	K.P.Pietersen (158)	England	v	Australia	The Oval	2005
	Shahid Afridi (103)	Pakistan	v	India	Lahore[2]	2005-06
SIX	J.H.Sinclair (104)	South Africa	v	Australia	Cape Town	1902-03
	I.V.A.Richards (192*)	West Indies	v	India	Delhi	1974-75
	Haroon Rashid (108)	Pakistan	v	England	Hyderabad	1977-78
	I.T.Botham (118)	England	v	Australia	Manchester	1981
	R.J.Shastri (121*)	India	v	Australia	Bombay[3]	1986-87
	W.J.Cronje (82)	South Africa	v	Sri Lanka	Centurion	1997-98
	C.D.McMillan (142)	New Zealand	v	Sri Lanka	Colombo (RPS)	1997-98
	J.N.Rhodes (102*)	South Africa	v	West Indies	Centurion	1998-99
	C.L.Cairns (69)	New Zealand	v	Australia	Wellington	1999-2000
	Wasim Akram (100)	Pakistan	v	Sri Lanka	Galle	2000-01
	M.L.Hayden (203)	Australia	v	India	Chennai[1]	2000-01
	S.T.Jayasuriya (145)	Sri Lanka	v	Bangladesh	Colombo (PSS)	2002-03
	H.H.Gibbs (228)	South Africa	v	Pakistan	Cape Town	2002-03
	V.K.Sehwag (309)	India	v	Pakistan	Multan[2]	2003-04
	A.M.Blignaut (61)	Zimbabwe	v	South Africa	Cape Town	2004-05
	A.C.Gilchrist (121)	Australia	v	New Zealand	Christchurch	2004-05
	Shahid Afridi (122)	Pakistan	v	West Indies	Bridgetown	2004-05
	Shahid Afridi (92)	Pakistan	v	England	Faisalabad	2005-06
	A.Symonds (72)	Australia	v	South Africa	Melbourne	2005-06
	Shahid Afridi (156)	Pakistan	v	India	Faisalabad	2005-06
	A.C.Gilchrist (144)	Australia	v	Bangladesh	Fatullah	2005-06
	Mohammad Rafique	Bangladesh	v	Australia	Chittagong[2]	2005-06
FIVE	S.J.E.Loxton (93)	Australia	v	England	Leeds	1948
	E.R.Dexter (172)	England	v	Pakistan	The Oval	1962
	J.H.Edrich (310*)	England	v	New Zealand	Leeds	1965
	D.T.Lindsay (182)	South Africa	v	Australia	Johannesburg[3]	1966-67
	G.T.Dowling (239)	New Zealand	v	India	Christchurch	1967-68
	B.R.Taylor (124)	New Zealand	v	West Indies	Auckland	1968-69
	I.T.Botham (137)	England	v	India	Leeds	1979
	A.R.Border (153)	Australia	v	Pakistan	Lahore[2]	1979-80
	I.T.Botham (66)	England	v	India	Delhi	1981-82
	Imran Khan (117)	Pakistan	v	India	Faisalabad	1982-83
	M.A.Holding (59)	West Indies	v	England	Leeds	1984
	Imran Khan (135*)	Pakistan	v	India	Madras[1]	1986-87
	Wasim Akram (62)	Pakistan	v	India	Madras[1]	1986-87
	Javed Miandad (271)	Pakistan	v	New Zealand	Auckland	1988-89
	P.A.de Silva (123)	Sri Lanka	v	New Zealand	Auckland	1990-91
	M.J.Slater (219)	Australia	v	Sri Lanka	Perth	1995-96
	A.C.Gilchrist (152)	Australia	v	England	Birmingham	2001
	J.H.Kallis (157*)	South Africa	v	Zimbabwe	Harare	2001-02
	R.D.Jacobs (118)	West Indies	v	India	St John's	2001-02
	A.Flintoff (142)	England	v	South Africa	Lord's	2003
	V.K.Sehwag (195)	India	v	Australia	Melbourne	2003-04
	J.H.Kallis (130*)	South Africa	v	West Indies	Cape Town	2003-04

A.C.Gilchrist (113)	Australia	v	Pakistan	Sydney	2004-05
J.H.Kallis (54)	South Africa	v	Zimbabwe	Cape Town	2004-05
A.C.Gilchrist (162)	Australia	v	New Zealand	Wellington	2004-05
A.Flintoff (68)	England	v	Australia	Birmingham	2005

MOST SIXES IN CAREER

6s	6s per Test	Player (Country)	Tests	Career Runs	runs in 6s	%
89	1.06	A.C.Gilchrist (A)#	84	5029	534	10.62
87	1.40	C.L.Cairns (NZ)	62	3320	522	15.72
84	0.69	I.V.A.Richards (WI)	121	8540	504	5.90
81	0.64	B.C.Lara (WI)#	127	11464	486	4.24
76	0.92	M.L.Hayden (A)#	83	7138	444	6.22
70	1.17	A.Flintoff (E)#	60	3076	420	13.65
70	0.64	C.H.Lloyd (WI)	110	7515	426	6.71
67	0.66	I.T.Botham (E)	102	5200	402	7.73
67	0.62	C.G.Greenidge (WI)	108	7558	402	5.32
63	0.62	C.L.Hooper (WI)	102	5762	378	6.56
61	0.47	Kapil Dev (I)	131	5248	366	6.97
57	0.56	Wasim Akram (P)	102	2898	342	11.80
57	0.55	R.T.Ponting (A)#	104	8692	342	3.93
56	0.53	S.T.Jayasuriya (SL)#	105	6745	336	4.98
55	0.63	Imran Khan (P)	88	3807	330	8.67
54	0.98	C.D.McMillan (NZ)#	55	3116	324	10.40
54	0.53	J.H.Kallis (SA)#	101	7950	330	4.15
50	1.92	Shahid Afridi (P)#	26	1683	300	17.83
48	0.52	P.A.de Silva (SL)	93	6361	288	4.53
48	0.39	Javed Miandad (P)	124	8832	288	3.26
47	0.42	Inzamamul Haq (P)#	112	8497	282	3.32
46	0.58	H.H.Gibbs (SA)#	79	5728	276	4.82
44	0.63	Yousuf Youhana (P)#	70	5737	264	4.60
42	0.55	M.E.Trescothick (E)#	76	5825	252	4.33
41	0.85	V.K.Sehwag (I)#	48	4013	246	6.13
41	0.47	S.C.Ganguly (I)#	88	5215	246	4.72
41	0.32	M.E.Waugh (A)	128	8029	246	3.06
41	0.31	S.R.Tendulkar (I)#	132	10469	246	2.35
40	0.43	A.Ranatunga (SL)	93	5105	240	4.70
40	0.40	J.L.Langer (A)#	99	7371	240	3.26
39	0.49	N.J.Astle (NZ)#	79	4650	234	5.03
38	0.75	N.S.Sidhu (I)	51	3202	228	7.12
36	0.60	M.A.Holding (WI)	60	910	216	23.74
35	0.25	S.K.Warne (A)#	139	2946	204	6.92
33	1.27	Mohammad Rafique (B)#	26	982	198	20.16
33	0.57	J.R.Reid (NZ)	58	3428	198	5.78
33	0.49	W.J.Cronje (SA)	68	3714	198	5.33
33	0.38	R.J.Hadlee (NZ)	86	3124	198	6.34
32	0.34	G.S.Sobers (WI)	93	8032	192	2.39
32	1.78	K.P.Pietersen (E)#	18	1597	192	12.02
31	0.31	S.M.Pollock (SA)#	101	3444	192	5.57
31	0.37	D.P.M.D.Jayawardene (SL)#	83	6253	186	2.97
30	0.49	C.H.Gayle (WI)#	61	4089	180	4.40
30	0.41	M.J.Slater (A)	74	5312	180	3.39
28	0.65	B.L.Cairns (NZ)	43	928	168	18.10
28	0.51	K.R.Miller (A)	55	2958	168	5.68
28	0.18	A.R.Border (A)	156	11174	168	1.50
27	0.47	Wasim Raja (P)	57	2821	162	5.74
27	0.39	Moin Khan (P)	69	2741	162	5.91

27	0.39	K.J.Hughes (A)	70	4415	162	3.67
27	0.35	M.D.Crowe (NZ)	77	5444	162	2.98
27	0.33	K.F.Barrington (E)	82	6806	162	2.38
26	0.31	W.R.Hammond (E)	85	7249	156	2.15
26	0.21	S.M.Gavaskar (I)	125	10122	156	1.54
25	0.37	F.S.Trueman (E)	67	981	150	15.29
25	0.36	D.J.Cullinan (SA)	70	4554	150	3.29
25	0.21	G.A.Gooch (E)	118	8900	150	1.69

BOUNDARY CURIOSITIES

1. E.H.Hendren (England) v Australia at the Exhibition Ground, Brisbane in 1928-29 scored an eight (including 4 overthrows) from the bowling of P.M.Hornibrook.

2. W.Voce (England) v South Africa at Johannesburg in 1930-31 hit three sixes from four balls bowled by A.E.Hall.

3. W.R.Hammond (England) v New Zealand at Auckland in 1932-33 hit three successive sixes from the bowling of J.Newman. He took his overnight score from 41 not out to 336 not out on the second day.

4. K.H.Weekes (West Indies) v England at The Oval in 1939 scored four successive fours from the bowling of R.T.D.Perks.

5. B.Sutcliffe (New Zealand) v South Africa at Johannesburg in 1953-54 hit four sixes (three in four balls) from one eight-ball over bowled by H.J.Tayfield.

6. G.S.Sobers (West Indies) v Australia at Bridgetown in 1954-55 hit 10 fours in an innings of 43, his other scoring shots consisting of three singles.

7. F.S.Trueman (England) v West Indies at Lord's in 1957 hit three sixes from one six-ball over bowled by S.Ramadhin.

8. J.H.Edrich (England) v New Zealand at Leeds in 1965 scored 238 in boundary hits (5 sixes and 52 fours) in an innings of 310*. Edrich was the first batsman to accumulate more than 200 runs through boundaries in a Test innings.

9. R.C.Motz (New Zealand) v England at Dunedin in 1965-66 hit three sixes from five balls bowled by D.A.Allen.

10. D.T.Lindsay (South Africa) v Australia at Port Elizabeth in 1969-70 scored five consecutive fours from the bowling of J.W.Gleeson.

11. Intikhab Alam (Pakistan) hit 11 fours in his score of 48 v Australia at Melbourne in 1972-73.

12. R.E.Redmond (New Zealand) v Pakistan at Auckland in 1972-73 scored five consecutive fours from the bowling of Majid J.Khan.

13. D.W.Hookes (Australia), on his Test debut, v England at Melbourne in 1976-77, hit five successive fours in an over from the bowling of A.W.Greig.

14. B.L.Cairns (New Zealand) hit three sixes in one over from the bowling of D.R.Parry v West Indies at Dunedin in 1979-80.

15. I.V.A.Richards (West Indies) in making 145 v England at Lord's in 1980 hit 106 runs in boundaries — 25 fours and one six.

16. S.T.Clarke (West Indies) v Pakistan at Faisalabad in 1980-81 hit three sixes from three successive balls bowled by Mohammad Nazir.

17. K.J.Hughes (Australia) scored 117 and 84 in the Ashes Centenary Test at Lord's in 1980. In addition to batting on each day of the Test, he, uniquely, hit a six on each day.

18. A.M.E.Roberts (West Indies) v England at Port-of-Spain in 1980-81 hit 3 sixes and a four from five balls bowled by I.T.Botham.

19. S.M.Patil (India) v England at Manchester in 1982 scored six boundaries off one over bowled by R.G.D.Willis.

20. Kapil Dev (India) at Lord's v England in 1982 scored 70 runs from boundaries in an innings of 89. He hit 13 fours and three sixes.

21. Kapil Dev (India) at Lord's v England in 1990 hit four successive sixes off the last four balls of an over from E.E.Hemmings to avoid the follow-on.

22. C.D.McMillan (New Zealand) hit a then record 26 from Younis Khan's only over (444446). He then hit a 4 from the next delivery he faced to give him a record 7 consecutive boundaries — New Zealand v Pakistan at Hamilton 2000-01.

23. N.J.Astle (New Zealand) scored 222 off 168 balls, with 11 sixes and 29 fours, in New Zealand's second innings v England at Christchurch in 2001-02, including 139 runs between tea and stumps (83*-222). His 50 came off 54 balls, 100 off 114 balls, 150 136 balls and 200 off 153 balls. In addition to making the highest

score for New Zealand v England, he hit a record number of sixes in an innings for New Zealand; the fastest 200 in Tests by balls, and the [then] highest score by an individual for a losing team. With C.L.Cairns he hit 23 off M.J.Hoggard's 23rd over (6**24**11106); he scored 20 off A.R.Caddick's 25th over (004664); with C.L.Cairns he hit 25 off A.R.Caddick's 26th over (666**L**410). He added 118 for the tenth wicket with C.L.Cairns. (L signifies leg-bye; **bold** signifies off a **no-ball**).

24. B.C.Lara (West Indies) playing against South Africa at Johannesburg in 2003-04, scored 28 (466444) off the 13th over by R.J.Peterson — the last over on the third day.

25. C.H.Gayle (West Indies) v England at The Oval in 2004, struck fours off all six balls of M.J.Hoggard's second over (the third over of the innings).

MOST RUNS IN A MATCH

456	G.A.Gooch (333 + 123)	England	v	India	Lord's	1990
426	M.A.Taylor (334* + 92)	Australia	v	Pakistan	Peshawar[2]	1998-99
400	B.C.Lara (400*)	West Indies	v	England	Bridgetown	2003-04
380	G.S.Chappell (247* + 133)	Australia	v	New Zealand	Wellington	1973-74
380	M.L.Hayden (380)	Australia	v	Zimbabwe	Perth	2003-04
375	A.Sandham (325 + 50)	England	v	West Indies	Kingston	1929-30
375	B.C.Lara (375)	West Indies	v	England	Bridgetown	1993-94
374	D.P.M.D.Jayawardene	Sri Lanka	v	South Africa	Colombo (SSC)	2006-07
365	G.S.Sobers (365*)	West Indies	v	Pakistan	Kingston	1957-58
364	L.Hutton (364)	England	v	Australia	The Oval	1938
362	G.C.Smith (277 + 85)	South Africa	v	England	Birmingham	2003
354	Hanif Mohammad (17 + 337)	Pakistan	v	West Indies	Bridgetown	1957-58
351	B.C.Lara (221 + 130)	West Indies	v	Sri Lanka	Colombo (SSC)	2001-02
351	Younis Khan (267 + 84*)	Pakistan	v	India	Bangalore	2004-05

The most for the other countries are as follows:

344	S.M.Gavaskar (124 + 220)	India	v	West Indies	Port-of-Spain	1970-71
343	S.P.Fleming (274* + 69*)	New Zealand	v	Sri Lanka	Colombo (PSS)	2002-03
341	A.Flower (142 + 199*)	Zimbabwe	v	South Africa	Harare	2001-02
340	S.T.Jayasuriya (340)	Sri Lanka	v	India	Colombo (RPS)	1997-98
184	Habibul Bashar (108 + 76)	Bangladesh	v	Zimbabwe	Chittagong	2001-02

PROGRESS OF LEADING RUN SCORERS IN TESTS

Player (Country)	runs	date
C.Bannerman (Australia	1	15 Mar 1877
G.Ulyett (England)	240	31 Dec 1881
W.L.Murdoch (Australia	677	11 Aug 1884
A.Shrewsbury (England)	861	12 Aug 1886
A.Shrewsbury (England)	1000	17 July 1893
J.Darling (Australia)	1278	23 January 1902
A.C.MacLaren (England)	1297	3 March 1902
C.Hill (Australia)	1495	24 July 1902
A.C.MacLaren (England)	1518	26 July 1902
C.Hill (Australia)	1542	12 August 1902
J.B.Hobbs (England)	3413	22 December 1924
W.R.Hammond (England)	5411	26 June 1937
M.C.Cowdrey (England)	7250	29 November 1971
G.S.Sobers (West Indies)	7460	26 March 1972
G.Boycott (England)	8033	23 December 1981
S.M.Gavaskar (India)	8115	13 November 1983
A.R.Border (Australia)	10123	26 February 1993
B.C.Lara (West Indies)	11174	25 March 2006

† 'runs' denotes the number of runs at the time of setting the new record; 'date' is the date the new record was set.

BATTED ON EACH DAY OF A FIVE-DAY MATCH

M.L.Jaisimha	20*	74	India	v	Australia	Calcutta	1959-60
G.Boycott	107	80*	England	v	Australia	Nottingham	1977
# K.J.Hughes	117	84	Australia	v	England	Lord's	1980
A.J.Lamb	23	110	England	v	West Indies	Lord's	1984
R.J.Shastri	111	7*	India	v	England	Calcutta	1984-85
A.Flintoff	70	51	England	v	India	Mohali	2005-06

 # Hughes hit a six on each day.

FAMOUS BATSMEN WHO SCORED A DUCK IN THEIR FIRST TEST INNINGS

It's been said of some cricketers, 'he batted so badly he was lucky to make a duck' and, on occasions, this applies equally to batsmen of proven ability as to their less-accomplished colleagues. One occasion which seems to have overawed a number of otherwise reliable batters is their first Test innings and below is a list of some who failed this, their first big test. The score on their second appearance is shown in brackets.

Hon.I.F.W.Bligh §	England	v Australia	Melbourne	1882-83	(3)
E.S.Gregory	Australia	v England	Lord's	1890	(9)
J.Darling	Australia	v England	Sydney	1894-95	(53)
V.T.Trumper	Australia	v England	Nottingham	1899	(11)
G.E.Tyldesley	England	v Australia	Nottingham	1921	(7)
R.E.S.Wyatt	England	v South Africa	Johannesburg	1927-28	(2)†
M.Leyland	England	v West Indies	The Oval	1928	(137)†
L.Hutton	England	v New Zealand	Lord's	1937	(1)
G.E.Gomez	West Indies	v England	Manchester	1939	(11)
D.B.Close	England	v New Zealand	Manchester	1949	(0)†
J.G.Leggatt	New Zealand	v West Indies	Auckland	1951-52	(6*)
K.F.Barrington	England	v South Africa	Nottingham	1955	(34)†
M.J.K.Smith	England	v New Zealand	Birmingham	1958	(7)
C.Milburn	England	v West Indies	Manchester	1966	(94)
A.P.E.Knott	England	v Pakistan	Nottingham	1967	(28)†
K.W.R.Fletcher	England	v Australia	Leeds	1968	(23*)
G.M.Turner	New Zealand	v West Indies	Auckland	1968-69	(40)
G.R.Viswanath	India	v Australia	Kanpur	1969-70	(137)
A.R.Lewis §	England	v India	Delhi	1972-73	(70*)
G.A.Gooch	England	v Australia	Birmingham	1975	(0)
J.M.Brearley	England	v West Indies	Nottingham	1976	(17)
M.S.Atapattu	Sri Lanka	v India	Chandigarh	1990-91	(0)
Saeed Anwar	Pakistan	v West Indies	Faisalabad	1990-91	(0)
M.T.G.Elliott	Australia	v West Indies	Brisbane[2]	1996-97	(21)

§ Captained England on first Test appearance. † not in the same match.

OVER 60% OF A COMPLETED INNINGS TOTAL

67.34	C.Bannerman	165*/245	Australia	v	England	Melbourne	1876-77
66.85	M.J.Slater	123/184	Australia	v	England	Sydney	1998-99
63.98	V.V.S.Laxman	167/261	India	v	Australia	Sydney	1999-2000
63.50	C.G.Greenidge	134/211	West Indies	v	England	Manchester	1976
63.41	A.P.Gurusinha	52*/82	Sri Lanka	v	India	Chandigarh	1990-91
62.89	J.R.Reid	100/159	New Zealand	v	England	Christchurch	1962-63
61.87	S.M.Nurse	258/417	West Indies	v	New Zealand	Christchurch	1968-69
61.85	M.Amarnath	60/97†	India	v	West Indies	Kingston	1975-76
61.11	G.N.Yallop	121/198	Australia	v	England	Sydney	1978-79
61.11	G.A.Gooch	154*/252	England	v	West Indies	Leeds	1991
60.65	V.T.Trumper	74/122	Australia	v	England	Melbourne	1903-04

60.26	H.A.Gomes	91/151	West Indies	v	India	Madras[1]	1978-79
60.19	J.T.Tyldesley	62/103	England	v	Australia	Melbourne	1903-04
60.00	Kapil Dev	129/215	India	v	South Africa	Port Elizabeth	1992-93

† Five men were absent hurt. D.L.Houghton (266) scored 62.29% of Zimbabwe's total of 462 for 9 declared against Sri Lanka at Bulawayo[2] in 1994-95. D.L.Amiss (262) scored 60.64% of England's total of 432 for 9 against West Indies at Kingston in 1973-74)*

FAMOUS BATSMEN WHO BAGGED A TEST MATCH PAIR

Australia	Runs	Avge	HS	100s
A.C.Bannerman	1108	23.08	94	0
R.Benaud	2201	24.45	122	3
A.R.Border	11174	50.56	205	27
J.Darling	1657	28.56	178	3
R.Edwards	1171	40.37	170*	2
J.H.W.Fingleton	1189	42.46	136	5
A.C.Gilchrist	5029	49.79	204*	16
E.S.Gregory	2282	24.53	201	4
R.N.Harvey	6149	48.41	205	21
I.A.Healy	4356	27.39	161*	4
D.W.Hookes	1306	34.36	143*	1
K.J.Hughes	4415	37.41	213	9
D.M.Jones	3631	46.55	216	11
J.L.Langer	6607	46.52	250	21
P.S.McDonnell	950	28.78	147	3
R.W.Marsh	3633	26.51	132	3
M.A.Noble	1997	30.25	133	1
R.T.Ponting	8692	58.33	257	31
V.Y.Richardson	706	23.53	138	1
K.R.Stackpole	2807	37.42	207	7
M.A.Taylor	7525	43.49	334*	19
V.T.Trumper (3 'ducks' in a row)	3163	39.04	214*	8
M.E.Waugh (twice)	8029	41.81	153*	20
G.M.Wood	3374	31.83	172	9

England	Runs	Avge	HS	100s
D.L.Amiss (twice)	3612	46.30	262*	11
M.A.Atherton (twice)	7728	37.69	185*	16
T.E.Bailey	2290	29.74	134*	1
I.T.Botham	5200	33.54	208	14
M.A.Butcher	4288	34.58	173*	8
A.Flintoff (twice)	3077	35.36	167	5
G.A.Gooch	8900	42.58	333	20
G.A.Hick	3383	31.32	178	6
N.Hussain	5764	37.18	207	14
A.P.E.Knott	4389	32.75	135	5
B.W.Luckhurst	1298	36.05	131	4
G.Pullar	1974	43.86	175	4
M.J.K.Smith	2278	31.61	121	3
A.J.Stewart	8463	39.54	190	15
G.P.Thorpe	6744	44.66	200*	16
R.A.Woolmer	1059	33.09	149	3

South Africa	Runs	Avge	HS	100s
W.R.Endean	1630	33.95	162*	3
G.Kirsten	7289	45.27	275	21
D.J.McGlew	2440	42.06	255*	7

West Indies	Runs	Avge	HS	100s
F.C.M.Alexander	961	30.03	108	1
J.C.Adams	3012	41.26	208*	6
K.L.T.Arthurton	1382	30.71	157*	2
P.J.L.Dujon	3322	31.94	139	5
C.H.Gayle (twice)	4089	38.94	317	7
C.G.Greenidge	7558	44.72	226	19
R.D.Jacobs (twice)	2577	28.01	118	3
A.I.Kallicharran (twice)	4399	44.43	187	12
A.L.Logie	2470	35.79	130	2
D.L.Murray	1993	22.90	91	0
C.A.Roach (twice)	952	30.70	209	2
R.R.Sarwan (twice)	4207	39.31	261*	9
O.G.Smith	1331	31.69	168	4
J.S.Solomon	1326	34.00	100*	1
E.D.Weekes	4455	58.61	207	15
F.M.M.Worrell	3860	49.48	261	9

New Zealand	Runs	Avge	HS	100s
J.V.Coney	2668	37.57	174*	3
S.P.Fleming	6545	40.15	274*	9
T.W.Jarvis	625	29.76	182	1
I.D.S.Smith	1815	25.56	173	2
J.G.Wright	4964	37.61	185	12

India	Runs	Avge	HS	100s
M.Amarnath (twice in run of 0 + 0, 1 + 0, 0 + 0)	4378	42.50	138	11
F.M.Engineer	2611	31.08	121	2
V.S.Hazare	2192	47.65	164*	7
M.L.Jaisimha	2056	30.68	129	3
V.V.S.Laxman	4447	43.17	281	9
Pankaj Roy	2442	32.56	173	5
G.S.Ramchand	1180	24.58	109	2
D.N.Sardesai	2001	39.23	212	5
D.B.Vengsarkar	6868	42.13	166	17
Yashpal Sharma	1606	33.45	140	2

Pakistan	Runs	Avge	HS	100s
Aamer Sohail	2823	35.28	205	5
Imtiaz Ahmed	2079	29.28	209	3
Javed Burki	1341	30.47	140	3
Majid Khan	3930	38.91	167	8

	Runs	Avge	HS	100s
Mudassar Nazar	4114	38.09	231	10
Saeed Anwar	4052	45.52	188*	11
Saleem Malik	5768	43.69	237	15
Taufeeq Umar	1729	39.29	135	4
Wazir Mohammad	801	27.62	189	2

Sri Lanka	Runs	Avge	HS	100s
R.P.Arnold	1821	28.01	123	3
M.S.Atapattu (4 pairs)	5330	38.90	249	16
A.Ranatunga	2023	34.87	135*	3

Zimbabwe	Runs	Avge	HS	100s
G.W.Flower	3457	29.54	201*	6

Bangladesh	Runs	Avge	HS	100s
Habibul Bashar	2838	34.61	113	3
Mohammad Ashraful	1511	29.05	158*	3

NOUGHT AND A CENTURY IN THE SAME MATCH *(§ in first Test)*

AUSTRALIA	Scores		Opponents		
W.L.Murdoch	0	153*	England	The Oval	1880
G.H.S.Trott	0	143	England	Lord's	1896
C.Hill	188	0	England	Melbourne	1897-98
D.G.Bradman	0	103*	England	Melbourne	1932-33
J.H.W.Fingleton	100	0	England	Brisbane[2]	1936-37
D.G.Bradman	138	0	England	Nottingham	1948
S.G.Barnes	0	141	England	Lord's	1948
R.N.Harvey	122	0	England	Manchester	1953
I.R.Redpath	0	132	West Indies	Sydney	1968-69
I.M.Chappell	138	0	India	Delhi	1969-70
I.C.Davis	105	0	Pakistan	Adelaide	1976-77
R.B.McCosker	0	105	Pakistan	Melbourne	1976-77
C.S.Serjeant	0	124	West Indies	Georgetown	1977-78
G.N.Yallop	0	114	England	Manchester	1981
G.R.Marsh	118	0	New Zealand	Auckland	1985-86
D.C.Boon	103	0	England	Adelaide	1986-87
M.E.Waugh	139*	0	West Indies	St John's	1990-91
J.L.Langer	121	0	India	Brisbane[2]	2003-04
R.T.Ponting	242	0	India	Adelaide	2003-04
A.C.Gilchrist	0	144	Sri Lanka	Kandy	2003-04
M.L.Hayden	0	102	South Africa	Durban[2]	2005-06

ENGLAND	Scores		Opponents		
L.C.Braund	102	0	Australia	Sydney	1903-04
J.T.Tyldesley	0	100	Australia	Leeds	1905
G.Gunn	122*	0	Australia	Sydney	1907-08
F.E.Woolley	0	123	Australia	Sydney	1924-25
G.B.Legge	196	0	New Zealand	Auckland	1929-30
D.C.S.Compton	145*	0	Australia	Manchester	1948
L.Hutton	101	0	New Zealand	Leeds	1949
P.B.H.May	0	112	South Africa	Lord's	1955
M.C.Cowdrey	119	0	West Indies	Port-of-Spain	1959-60
Rev.D.S.Sheppard	0	113	Australia	Melbourne	1962-63
M.C.Cowdrey	101	0	West Indies	Kingston	1967-68
D.L.Amiss	158	0	Pakistan	Hyderabad	1972-73
D.W.Randall	0	150	Australia	Sydney	1978-79
I.T.Botham	0	118	Australia	Manchester	1981
G.Boycott	137	0	Australia	The Oval	1981
M.W.Gatting	100	0	Australia	Adelaide	1986-87
D.I.Gower	100	0	Australia	Melbourne	1990-91
C.C.Lewis	0	117	India	Madras[1]	1992-93
M.A.Atherton	144	0	West Indies	Georgetown	1993-94

M.W.Gatting	117	0	Australia	Adelaide	1994-95
G.P.Thorpe	123	0	Australia	Perth	1994-95
N.Hussain	113	0	Zimbabwe	Bulawayo[2]	1996-97
G.A.Hick	107	0	Sri Lanka	The Oval	1998
A.Flintoff	0	137	New Zealand	Christchurch	2001-02
M.P.Vaughan	0	183	Australia	Sydney	2002-03
A.J.Strauss	147	0	South Africa	Johannesburg[3]	2004-05
I.R.Bell	115	0	Pakistan	Faisalabad	2005-06
SOUTH AFRICA	Scores		Opponents		
J.H.Sinclair	0	104	Australia	Cape Town	1902-03
G.A.Faulkner	122*	0	Australia	Manchester	1912
R.H.Catterall	0	120	England	Birmingham	1924
A.D.Nourse	0	231	Australia	Johannesburg[1]	1935-36
E.J.Barlow	114	0	Australia	Brisbane[2]	1963-64
A.C.Hudson §	163	0	West Indies	Bridgetown	1991-92
G.Kirsten	103	0	India	Cape Town	1996-97
D.J.Cullinan	103	0	Sri Lanka	Centurion	1997-98
D.J.Cullinan	168	0	West Indies	Cape Town	1998-99
H.H.Gibbs	120	0	New Zealand	Wellington	1998-99
M.V.Boucher	0	108	England	Durban[2]	1998-99
J.A.Rudolph	101	0	West Indies	Cape Town	2003-04
J.H.Kallis	0	109*	West Indies	Georgetown	2004-05
WEST INDIES	Scores		Opponents		
I.Barrow	105	0	England	Manchester	1933
F.C.M.Alexander	0	108	Australia	Sydney	1960-61
S.M.Nurse	201	0	Australia	Bridgetown	1964-65
G.S.Sobers	0	113*	England	Kingston	1967-68
C.A.Davis	103	0	England	Lord's	1969
G.S.Sobers	132	0	India	Port-of-Spain	1970-71
A.I.Kallicharran	0	103*	India	Port-of-Spain	1975-76
R.C.Fredericks	0	138	England	Lord's	1976
D.L.Haynes	0	122	New Zealand	Christchurch	1979-80
C.L.King	0	100*	New Zealand	Christchurch	1979-80
I.V.A.Richards	0	182*	England	Bridgetown	1980-81
I.V.A.Richards	208	0	Australia	Melbourne	1984-85
D.L.Haynes	0	109	England	Bridgetown	1989-90
R.B.Richardson	104	0	England	Birmingham	1991
K.L.T.Arthurton	157*	0	Australia	Brisbane[2]	1992-93
C.L.Hooper	0	106	Pakistan	Karachi[1]	1997-98
S.Chanderpaul	118	0	England	Georgetown	1997-98
S.L.Campbell	170	0	New Zealand	Hamilton	1998-99
D.Ganga	0	113	Australia	Georgetown	2002-03
S.Chanderpaul	0	109	South Africa	Durban[2]	2003-04
B.C.Lara	153	0	Pakistan	Kingston	2004-05
NEW ZEALAND	Scores		Opponents		
G.T.Dowling	129	0	India	Bombay[2]	1964-65
B.F.Hastings	0	117*	West Indies	Christchurch	1968-69
M.D.Crowe	174	0	Pakistan	Wellington	1988-89
J.G.Wright	116	0	England	Wellington	1991-92
M.D.Crowe	0	107	Sri Lanka	Colombo (SSC)	1992-93
C.D.McMillan	0	142	Sri Lanka	Colombo (RPS)	1997-98
S.P.Fleming	192	0	Pakistan	Hamilton	2003-04
INDIA	Scores		Opponents		
M.H.Mankad	111	0	Australia	Melbourne	1947-48

Pankaj Roy	140	0	England	Bombay[2]	1951-52
V.L.Manjrekar	133	0	England	Leeds	1952
M.L.Apte	0	163*	West Indies	Port-of-Spain	1952-53
V.L.Manjrekar	108	0	England	Madras[2]	1963-64
G.R.Viswanath §	0	137	Australia	Kanpur	1969-70
S.M.Gavaskar	0	118	Australia	Melbourne	1977-78
D.B.Vengsarkar	0	103	England	Lord's	1979
N.S.Sidhu	116	0	West Indies	Kingston	1988-89
M.Azharuddin	0	109	Pakistan	Faisalabad	1989-90
N.R.Mongia	152	0	Australia	Delhi	1996-97
S.R.Tendulkar	0	136	Pakistan	Chennai[1]	1998-99
S.R.Tendulkar	117	0	West Indies	Port-of-Spain	2001-02
V.K.Sehwag	106	0	England	Nottingham	2002

PAKISTAN	Scores		Opponents		
Imtiaz Ahmed	209	0	New Zealand	Lahore[1]	1955-56
Imtiaz Ahmed	122	0	West Indies	Kingston	1957-58
Hanif Mohammad	160	0	India	Bombay[2]	1960-61
Javed Burki	140	0	England	Dacca	1961-62
Asif Iqbal	0	152*	Australia	Adelaide	1976-77
Sadiq Mohammad	105	0	Australia	Melbourne	1976-77
Asif Iqbal	0	104	India	Faisalabad	1978-79
Ijaz Ahmed	122	0	Australia	Faisalabad	1988-89
Mohammad Wasim §	0	109*	New Zealand	Lahore[2]	1996-97
Saeed Anwar	0	188*	India	Calcutta	1998-99
Shahid Afridi	107	0	West Indies	Sharjah	2001-02
Younis Khan	147	0	India	Kolkata	2004-05

SRI LANKA	Scores		Opponents		
A.Ranatunga	127	0	Australia	Colombo (SSC)	1992-93
P.A.de Silva	0	105	Pakistan	Faisalabad	1994-95
H.P.Tillakaratne	115	0	Pakistan	Faisalabad	1994-95
T.M.Dilshan	163*	0	Zimbabwe	Harare	1999-2000
M.S.Atapattu	120	0	South Africa	Kandy	2000-01

ZIMBABWE	Scores		Opponents		
M.W.Goodwin	0	166*	Pakistan	Bulawayo[2]	1997-98

BANGLADESH	Scores		Opponents		
Javed Omar	119	0	Pakistan	Peshawar[2]	2003-04

FIRST THREE BATSMEN SCORING CENTURIES

England (2d-531)	v South Africa (J.B.Hobbs 211; H.Sutcliffe 122; F.E.Woolley 134*)	Lord's	1924
Australia (9d-600)	v West Indies (C.C.McDonald 110; A.R.Morris 111; R.N.Harvey 133)	Port-of-Spain	1954-55
Australia (6d-650)	v West Indies (W.M.Lawry 210; R.B.Simpson 201; R.M.Cowper 102)	Bridgetown	1964-65
India (4d-600)	v Australia (S.M.Gavaskar 172; K.Srikkanth 116; M.Amarnath 138)	Sydney	1985-86
Australia (4d-632)	v England (M.A.Taylor 111; M.J.Slater 152; D.C.Boon 164*)	Lord's	1993
South Africa (3d-600)	v Zimbabwe (H.H.Gibbs 147; G.Kirsten 220; J.H.Kallis 157*)	Harare	2001-02
New Zealand (6d-630)	v India (M.H.Richardson 145, L.Vincent 106, S.B.Styris 119)	Mohali	2003-04

PLAYER DISMISSED FROM THE FIRST BALL OF A TEST *† on debut. § in his last Test.*

Batsman	Bowler					
A.C.MacLaren	A.Coningham †	England	v	Australia	Melbourne	1894-95
T.W.Hayward	A.E.E.Vogler	England	v	South Africa	The Oval	1907
W.Bardsley	M.W.Tate	Australia	v	England	Leeds	1926
H.Sutcliffe	F.T.Badcock	England	v	New Zealand	Christchurch	1932-33
T.S.Worthington	E.L.McCormick	England	v	Australia	Brisbane^2	1936-37
C.C.Hunte	Fazal Mahmood	West Indies	v	Pakistan	Port-of-Spain	1957-58
E.J.Barlow	G.D.McKenzie	South Africa	v	Australia	Durban^2	1966-67
R.C.Fredericks	S.Abid Ali	West Indies	v	India	Port-of-Spain	1970-71
K.R.Stackpole §	R.J.Hadlee	Australia	v	New Zealand	Auckland	1973-74
S.M.Gavaskar	G.G.Arnold	India	v	England	Birmingham	1974
S.S.Naik §	A.M.E.Roberts	India	v	West Indies	Calcutta	1974-75
J.F.M.Morrison	G.G.Arnold	New Zealand	v	England	Christchurch	1974-75
Mohsin Khan	Kapil Dev	Pakistan	v	India	Jullundur	1983-84
S.M.Gavaskar	M.D.Marshall	India	v	West Indies	Calcutta	1983-84
S.M.Gavaskar	Imran Khan	India	v	Pakistan	Jaipur	1986-87
W.V.Raman	R.J.Hadlee	India	v	New Zealand	Napier	1989-90
S.J.Cook †	Kapil Dev	South Africa	v	India	Durban^2	1992-93
G.Kirsten	C.E.L.Ambrose	South Africa	v	West Indies	Cape Town	1998-99
S.T.Jayasuriya	G.D.McGrath	Sri Lanka	v	Australia	Galle	1999-2000
L.V.Garrick †	A.A.Donald	West Indies	v	South Africa	Kingston	2000-01
S.S.Das	M.Dillon	India	v	West Indies	Bridgetown	2001-02
Hannan Sarkar	P.T.Collins	Bangladesh	v	West Indies	Dhaka	2002-03
Hannan Sarkar	P.T.Collins	Bangladesh	v	West Indies	Gros Islet	2003-04
Hannan Sarkar	P.T.Collins	Bangladesh	v	West Indies	Kingston	2003-04

LONGEST INNINGS FOR EACH COUNTRY

For	Min		Opponents		
Australia	762	R.B.Simpson (311)	England	Manchester	1964
England	797	L.Hutton (364)	Australia	The Oval	1938
South Africa	878	G.Kirsten (275)	England	Durban^2	1999-2000
West Indies	778	B.C.Lara (400*)	England	St John's	2003-04
New Zealand	704	G.M.Turner (259)	West Indies	Georgetown	1971-72
India	740	R.S.Dravid (270)	Pakistan	Rawalpindi^2	2003-04
Pakistan	970	Hanif Mohammad (337)	West Indies	Bridgetown	1957-58
Sri Lanka	799	S.T.Jayasuriya (340)	India	Colombo (RPS)	1997-98
Zimbabwe	675	D.L.Houghton (266)	Sri Lanka	Bulawayo^2	1994-95
Bangladesh	535	Aminul Islam (145)	India	Dhaka	2000-01

PARTNERSHIP FEATS

1. J.B.Hobbs and H.Sutcliffe (England) shared four century opening stands v Australia in 1924-25. Three of these were recorded in the first three innings in which they partnered each other.

2. H.Sutcliffe (England) v Australia at Sydney 1932-33 shared in century stands for the first three wickets.

3. F.E.Woolley shared in 12 century partnerships in Tests, with 11 different partners. E.H.Hendren is the only player to share in two.

4. L.Hutton and C.Washbrook (England) shared three consecutive opening stands of over 100 v Australia 1946-47.

5. R.S.Modi and V.S.Hazare (India) shared three consecutive century stands for the third wicket v West Indies 1948-49.

6. C.G.Greenidge partnered D.L.Haynes in sixteen century opening stands for the West Indies.

7. J.B.Hobbs (England) shared in 24 century opening stands; M.A.Atherton (England) 23; S.M.Gavaskar (India) and C.G.Greenidge (West Indies) in 22; H.Sutcliffe (England) 21; G.Boycott (England) 20.

8. G.Boycott, B.W.Luckhurst and J.H.Edrich (England) figured in four successive opening stands of more than 100 v Australia in 1970-71. In eight successive innings these pairs registered six century opening stands.

9. R.T.Ponting (Australia) figured in 26 century partnerships for the second wicket; R.S.Dravid (India) 22, I.M.Chappell (Australia), J.L.Langer (Australia) and S.M.Gavaskar (India) 18.

10. Batsmen who have featured in the most century partnerships are — S.R.Waugh (Australia) 64; A.R.Border (Australia) 63; R.S.Dravid and S.R.Tendulkar (India) and B.C.Lara (West Indies) 59; S.M.Gavaskar (India) 58; R.T.Ponting (Australia) 56; Javed Miandad (Pakistan) 50; J.L.Langer (Australia) 48; G.Boycott (England) and M.E.Waugh (Australia) 47; C.G.Greenidge (West Indies) 46; G.Kirsten (South Africa) 45; M.A.Atherton (England), G.S.Chappell (Australia) and I.V.A.Richards (West Indies) 44; M.L.Hayden (Australia) and G.S.Sobers (West Indies) 43; D.C.Boon (Australia) and M.C.Cowdrey (England) 42; G.A.Gooch (England) L.Hutton (England), Inzamamul Haq (Pakistan) and C.H.Lloyd (West Indies) 41.

CENTURIES BY TAIL-ENDERS

(lower than No. 8 in order)

1. W.W.Read (England). Read batted No. 10 in the match v Australia at The Oval in 1884, and in the second innings came in with England facing defeat at 8 for 181. It was said that Read was in a towering rage at his captain's decision to place him so low in the order, and he made his point with a brilliant 117 in two hours, during which time he added 151 with W.H.Scotton (90 in $5^3/_4$ hours).

2. R.A.Duff (Australia). Batted at No. 6 in the first innings of the Second Test against England at Melbourne in 1901-02 but was held back to No. 10 in the second innings. Duff scored 104 and shared in a tenth wicket partnership of 120 with fellow debutant W.W.Armstrong.

3. C.Hill (Australia). Suffering from influenza, Hill joined R.J.Hartigan, batting at No. 9 in his Test debut v England at Adelaide in 1907-08, when Australia in their second innings led by only 102 with 7 wickets down. Hill made 160 as the two defied the English bowling and the 107°F heat to put on 243 for the eighth wicket (of which Hartigan's share was 116). Their record stand enabled Australia to win the match.

4. J.M.Gregory (Australia). After taking 7 for 69 earlier in the match v England at Melbourne in 1920-21, Gregory, batting at No. 9, joined C.E.Pellew with Australia 7 for 282 in their second innings. Together they put on 173, Gregory's share being exactly 100.

5. G.O.B.Allen (England). Batting at No. 9, Allen joined wicket-keeper L.E.G.Ames with England 7 for 190 in their first innings v New Zealand at Lord's in 1931. The two added 246 runs, with Allen making 122.

6. R.R.Lindwall (Australia). Batting at No. 9 in Australia's second innings v England at Melbourne in 1946-47, Lindwall joined wicket-keeper D.Tallon with Australia 7 for 341. These two then shared a blistering partnership, adding 154 in 88 minutes of brilliant hitting, Lindwall making 100 (one six and 13 fours) in 109 minutes.

7. J.T.Murray (England). Batting at No. 9 in England's only innings v West Indies at The Oval 1966, Murray (112) joined T.W.Graveney with England 7 for 166 in reply to West Indies's 268. This pair then added 217 for the eighth wicket to take England to the lead. Then a tenth wicket stand of 128 by K.Higgs and J.A.Snow helped gain an innings victory.

8. Asif Iqbal (Pakistan). Batting at No. 9 in Pakistan's second innings v England at The Oval in 1967, Asif (146) was joined by Intikhab Alam with Pakistan 8 for 65 and still 139 in arrears. They added 190 for a then Test record ninth wicket.

9. I.D.S.Smith (New Zealand). Batting at No. 9 in New Zealand's first innings v India at Auckland in 1989-90, Smith joined R.J.Hadlee with the score 7 for 131. He then added 101 with Hadlee for the eighth wicket and 136 for the ninth wicket with M.C.Snedden. His innings of 173 included 24 (244266) off an over from A.S.Wassan.

10. L.Klusener (South Africa). Batting at No 9. in South Africa's first innings v India at Cape Town in 1996-97, Klusener (102 not out, 100 balls) shared in an unbroken South African record eighth wicket stand of 147 with B.M.McMillan.

11. P.L.Symcox (South Africa). Batting at No 10. in South Africa's first innings v Pakistan in 1997-98 at Johannesburg, Symcox joined M.V.Boucher with the score on 8 for 166. He scored his maiden Test century (108) as they then proceeded to add a world record 195 for the ninth wicket to break the previous record held by Asif Iqbal and Intikhab Alam (see above) Symcox was relegated to twelfth man for the next Test.

12. S.M.Pollock (South Africa). Coming in at No. 9 with South Africa 7 down for 204 in the first innings, Pollock made 111 as he added a South African record 150 for the eighth wicket with N.D.McKenzie, v Sri Lanka at Centurion in 2000-01.

13. S.M.Pollock (South Africa). Batting at No. 9 in South Africa's first innings, Pollock (106*) came in with the score 7 for 307. He was joined by A.A.Donald at 8 for 315 and the pair added 132 for the ninth wicket v West Indies at Bridgetown in 2000-01.

14. A.C.Parore (New Zealand). Playing against Australia at Perth in 2001-02, Parore came in at 7 for 281 in the first innings. Scoring 110, he added 253 for the eighth wicket with N.J.Astle.

15. D.L.Vettori (New Zealand). Batting at No. 9 in New Zealand's first innings v Pakistan at Hamilton in 2003-04, Vettori (137 not out) came in at 7 for 314 and added 125 for the eighth wicket with his captain S.P.Fleming and 100 for the ninth wicket with D.R.Tuffey.

16. Mohammad Rafique (Bangladesh). Batting at No. 9 in Bangladesh's first innings v West Indies at Gros Islet in 2003-04, Mohammad came in with Test minnow Bangladesh 7 down for 250. He made 111 and was last man out at 416.

17. J.E.C.Franklin (New Zealand). Batting at No. 9 in New Zealand's first innings v South Africa at Cape Town in 2005-06, Franklin came in at 7 for 279 and added a record 256 for the eighth wicket with his captain S.P.Fleming.

GOOD EFFORTS BY 'NIGHT-WATCHMEN'

1. H.Carter (Australia) v England at Adelaide 1911-12 went in to bat late on the third day with Australia 1 for 86 in the second innings. He scored 71 and shared in a 124 runs stand for the fourth wicket with C.Hill.

2. H.Larwood (England) v Australia at Sydney 1932-33 went in to bat late on the second evening when England were 2 for 153. The Australian bowlers did not see his back until the score had reached 310, of which Larwood's share in 135 minutes was a grand 98. His innings was ended by a catch to Bert Ironmonger, not noted as a safe catcher — he held only three in 14 Test matches.

3. A.V.Bedser (England) v Australia at Leeds 1948 came in late on the first day with England 2 for 268. The following morning he defied the Australian attack of R.R.Lindwall, K.R.Miller, W.A.Johnston, E.R.H.Toshack and I.W.G.Johnson to make his highest Test score — 79 — and help add 155 for the third wicket with W.J.Edrich.

4. Nasim-ul-Ghani (Pakistan) v England at Lord's 1962. Normally batting at No. 8, Nasim was promoted two places and sent in as night-watchman when Pakistan were 4 for 77 in their second innings. He stayed to score 101 and shared in a Pakistan record fifth wicket partnership of 197 with Javed Burki — a record which still stands. Nasim's century was his first in first-class cricket and the first by a Pakistan batsman in England.

5. A.P.E.Knott (England) v Australia at Brisbane 1970-71 was sent in as night-watchman with England 1 for 92 late on the second day. He stayed long enough to score 73.

6. A.L.Mann (Australia) v India at Perth 1977-78, came in with the score at 1 for 13 late on the fourth day, having batted at No. 8 in the first innings. The following day Mann proceeded to score 105 out of a total of 8 for 342, sharing a partnership of 139 for the third wicket with P.M.Toohey. Mann's other seven Test innings in a four Test career netted a mere 84 runs. (In the first innings wicket-keeper S.J.Rixon was sent in as night-watchman with Australia 4 for 149 and scored 50 while sharing a fifth wicket stand of 101 with R.B.Simpson).

7. D.R.Parry (West Indies) v Australia at Georgetown 1977-78 was sent in with West Indies 2 for 95 in their second innings. He went on to score 51 — his only Test fifty.

8. Wasim Bari (Pakistan) v India at Lahore 1978-79 was sent in as night-watchman when the score was 1 for 19. He scored a Test career highest score of 85 sharing in a second wicket stand of 115 with Majid J.Khan and was dismissed when the score was 3 for 161.

9. R.R.Jumadeen (West Indies) v India at Kanpur 1978-79 came in late on the third day when the score was 2 for 134 and stayed long enough to score his only Test half-century (56) and share a third wicket stand of 129 with S.F.A.F.Bacchus.

10. S.M.H.Kirmani (India) v Australia at Bombay 1979-80 (6th Test) came in late on the first day to act as night-watchman when India was 3 for 231. 0* overnight, Kirmani (in the side as a wicket-keeper) batted for the remainder of the innings until India declared at 8 for 458. He scored 101* in five hours, adding 127 with K.D.Ghavri for the eighth wicket. (In the First Test at Madras Kirmani had been sent in late on the second day with India 1 for 80 and scored 57, adding 99 for the fourth wicket with D.B.Vengsarkar.)

11. Iqbal Qasim (Pakistan) v Sri Lanka at Karachi 1981-82 came in late on the third day to act as night-watchman with Pakistan 1 for 16 in the second innings. He scored his highest Test score of 56 before he was dismissed at 3 for 107.

12. E.E.Hemmings (England) v Australia at Sydney 1982-83 came in late on the fourth day with England 1 for 3 in the second innings. He batted for 226 minutes to record his highest Test score of 95.

13. W.W.Davis (West Indies) v England at Manchester 1984 came in late on the first day when the score was 5 for 267. He scored 77 sharing in a sixth wicket stand of 170 with C.G.Greenidge.

14. C.Sharma (India) v Australia at Adelaide 1985-86 came in late on the second day with India 1 for 97 scored 54 as night-watchman.

15. Saleem Yousuf (Pakistan) v West Indies at Faisalabad 1986-87 came in late on the second day with Pakistan 2 for 19 in the second innings. He scored 61 adding 94 for the third wicket with Qasim Omar.

16. B.N.French (England) v Pakistan at Manchester 1987 came in late on the first day with the score 3 for 133. He scored 59 whilst adding 113 for the fourth wicket with R.T.Robinson.

17. R.C.Russell (England) v Sri Lanka at Lord's 1988, making his Test debut, was sent in late on the first day as night-watchman with the score at 1 for 40. He scored 94 and shared in a second wicket stand of 131 with G.A.Gooch.

18. R.C.Russell (England) v West Indies at Bridgetown 1989-90, was sent in late on the fourth day with the score at 3 for 10 in England's second innings. He was sixth out for 55 when the score was 166.

19. P.L.Taylor (Australia) v New Zealand at Wellington 1989-90, was sent in as night-watchman late on the third day with Australia 2 for 54. He top-scored with 87 and added 103 for the fourth wicket with A.R.Border.

20. I.A.Healy (Australia) v England at Sydney 1990-91, came in as night-watchman late on the fourth day with Australia 1 for 21 in the second innings. He went on to top-score in the innings with 69.

21. W.K.M.Benjamin (West Indies) v Australia at Kingston in 1994-95, came in as night-watchman late on the third day, with the score 3 for 46 in the second innings. He went on to top-score with 51.

22. P.L.Symcox (South Africa) v Pakistan at Faisalabad in 1997-98, came in as night-watchman late on the second day with the score 2 for 21 in the second innings. He went on to top-score with 55.

23. A.J.Tudor (England) came in as night-watchman late on the second day v New Zealand at Birmingham in 1999, with the score 1 for 3. He remained 99 not out as England won by seven wickets.

24. M.V.Boucher (South Africa) came in as night-watchman late on the second day v Zimbabwe at Harare in 1999-2000 with the score 4 for 205, and went on to top-score in the innings with 125.

25. M.V.Boucher (South Africa) came in as night-watchman late on the fourth day v England at Durban in 1999-2000, with the score 4 for 244. He scored 108 and added 192 for the fifth wicket with G.Kirsten.

26. N.Boje (South Africa) v India at Bangalore in 1999-2000, came in as night-watchman late on the first day, with the score 1 for 10. He made a career high of 85 while adding 161 for the second wicket with G.KIrsten.

27. T.J.Friend (Zimbabwe) v Sri Lanka at the Sinhalese Sports Club ground in Colombo, in 2001-02, came in as night-watchman late on the third day, with the score two for 59. He top scored with 44.

28. J.N.Gillespie (Australia) v India at Chennai in 2004-05, came in as night-watchman late on the third day, with the score 4 for 145. Although he only made 26, he added 139 for the fifth wicket with D.R.Martyn.

29. J.N.Gillespie (Australia) v Bangladesh at Chittagong in 2005-06 sent in as night-watchman late on the second day, with the score 1 for 67. He made a maiden first class hundred and went on to 201* — the highest score by a night-watchman. He added 320 for the fourth wicket with M.E.K.Hussey.

HIGHEST SCORES BY A NUMBER 11

75 Zaheer Khan (India) v Bangladesh, Dhaka 2004-05

68* R.O.Collinge (New Zealand) v Pakistan, Auckland 1972-73. (Added 151 for the 10th wicket with B.F.Hastings, 110, a record for Test cricket.)

62* A.E.E.Vogler (South Africa) v England, Cape Town 1905-06.

61 G.D.McGrath (Australia) v New Zealand, Brisbane 2004-05. (Added 114 for the 10th wicket with J.N.Gillespie, 54*.)

60* Wasim Bari (Pakistan) v West Indies, Bridgetown 1976-77

59* J.A.Snow (England) v West Indies, The Oval 1966.

59 Mushtaq Ahmed (Pakistan) v South Africa, Rawalpindi 1997-98. (Added 151 for the 10th wicket with Azhar Mahmood, 128*, equal record for Test cricket.)

52 R.M.Hogg (Australia) v West Indies, Georgetown 1984-85.

50* W.W.Hall (West Indies) v India, Port-of-Spain 1961-62.

50 F.R.Spofforth (Australia) v England, Melbourne 1884-85.

50 Ghulam Ahmed (India) v Pakistan, Delhi 1952-53.

SLOW SCORING MEMORABILIA

Fourteen consecutive (four-ball) maiden overs were bowled to A.C.Bannerman and W.L.Murdoch (Australia) during their second wicket partnership v England at Melbourne 1882-83.

A.C.Bannerman (Australia) scored 19 runs in 200 minutes during the match v England at Sydney 1886-87.

Bannerman made 15* in two hours in the first innings and 4 in 80 minutes in the second.

Fifty-eight maiden overs were included in Australia's total of 175 in 325 minutes v England at Manchester, 1921.

B.Mitchell, on debut for South Africa v England at Birmingham in 1929 made a combined total of 149 in 575 minutes — 88 in 420 minutes and 61* in 155 minutes.

England scored only 37 runs in the pre-lunch session v Australia at Adelaide 1932-33.

P.G.van der Bijl (125) for South Africa v England at Durban in 1938-39 did not hit his first boundary until he had been at the wicket for three hours. The first four of the South African innings came after 130 minutes.

England took 972 minutes and 1723 balls to score 442 runs v Australia at Leeds in 1953 — 167 in 386 minutes (658 balls) and 275 in 586 minutes (1065 balls).

England scored only 27 (39 overs) before lunch on the 3rd day v West Indies at Bridgetown 1953-54. The new ball (then taken after 65 overs) arrived with the score at 77.

Hanif Mohammad scored 59 runs in 337 minutes for the match v England at Lord's 1954 — 20 in 197 minutes and 39 in 140 minutes.

New Zealand had scored only 24 at lunch (after 90 minutes) on the first day of the match v England at Dunedin 1954-55. The total for the day was 125 in 292 minutes.

New Zealand scored only 69 off 90 six-ball overs (56 maidens) v Pakistan at Dacca 1955-56.

I.D.Craig (Australia) scored 38 in $4^1/_2$ hours spread over 4 days v England, Manchester 1956.

New Zealand scored 6 for 32 and 3 for 37 in two pre-lunch sessions v England at Birmingham 1958.

England scored only 19 runs before lunch (90 minutes) v Australia at Brisbane 1958-59, taking an overnight score of 2 for 92 to 4 for 114. T.E.Bailey scored 8 of the 19 runs in the session.

T.E.Bailey (England) in the First Test v Australia, Brisbane 1958-59 scored 68 runs in 458 minutes — less than nine runs an hour. He took 357 minutes to reach fifty and scored off only 40 of the 425 balls bowled to him.

Pakistan scored 24 before lunch v Australia at Karachi 1959-60. The innings of 8 (dec.) for 194 lasted 8 hours.

M.L.Jaisimha (India) v Australia at Calcutta 1959-60 batted through a whole day's play, taking his overnight score of 0* to 59*.

C.J.Tavare (England) v Pakistan at Lord's in 1982 took 350 minutes to reach fifty (only T.E.Bailey —see above — has taken longer to bring up a first class fifty). He took 67 minutes to score his first run and spent 60 minutes with his score on 24 — the first player in any form of cricket to fail to score during two separate hours of an innings.

In the Perth Test v Australia in 1982-83, C.J.Tavare (England) spent 90 minutes in the first innings on 66 and took 63 minutes in the second innings to score his first run.

COURAGEOUS PERFORMANCES

1. E.Paynter (England) hospitalised with acute tonsillitis during the Fourth Test against Australia in 1932-33, insisted on taking his place at the crease where he stayed for four hours scoring 83 runs. In the second innings he struck a six which won the match and regained the Ashes for England.
2. A.D.Nourse (South Africa) batted for 550 minutes to score 208 in the First Test v England at Nottingham in 1951 — with a broken thumb.
3. On the second day of the Second Test against South Africa at Johannesburg in 1953-54, B.Sutcliffe (New Zealand) was struck on the head by a ball from N.A.T.Adcock and retired hurt (0) with the score at 2 for 9. He resumed at 6 for 81 and hit seven sixes and four fours, scoring 80 out of 106 in 112 minutes. At the fall of the ninth wicket he was joined by R.W.Blair, who, the previous day, had learnt of the death of his fiancee in a train disaster in New Zealand. As Blair walked slowly to the crease the crowd stood in silence.
4. W.M.Lawry (Australia) had ten stitches inserted in a head wound caused by a fast rising ball from P.M.Pollock in the Third Test against South Africa at Durban in 1966-67. He returned to the crease and top-scored with 44 out of the first innings total of 147.
5. During the First Test at Dunedin, of the 1967-68 New Zealand v India series R.B.Desai (India) had his jaw fractured by a rising ball from R.C.Motz but went on to score 32* in a tenth wicket partnership of 57 with B.S.Bedi.
6. During the Second Test of the 1970-71 Australia v England rubber at Perth, English batsman B.W.Luckhurst damaged his thumb early in his innings but carried on to score 131 runs. In the Fifth Test, played a little over a month later at Melbourne, Luckhurst's left little

finger was fractured early in his innings and on this occasion he scored 109 runs.

7. A.R.Border (Australia), despite batting in considerable pain from a broken finger during the 1981 series v England, scored in succession 123*, 106* and 84, batting in all for 15 hours and two minutes before losing his wicket.
8. R.B.McCosker (Australia). In the Centenary Test between Australia and England played at Melbourne in March 1977 McCosker suffered a fractured jaw whilst batting in the first innings. He returned to the crease, however, his face swathed in bandages to help Australia to a second innings total of 9 (dec.) for 419.
9. S.M.Patil (India). Playing in the First Test against Australia 1980-81, Patil was knocked unconscious by a bouncer from L.S.Pascoe. Three weeks later at Adelaide in the Second Test he scored 174 in 301 minutes.

SHORTEST TEAM TEST MATCH INNINGS

1. 50 minutes — South Africa, all out for 30 in 12.3 overs (6-ball) v England at Birmingham 1924.
2. 80 minutes — England, all out for 45 in 35.3 overs (4-ball) v Australia at Sydney 1886-87.
3. 90 minutes — Australia, all out for 30 in 23 overs (6-ball) v England at Birmingham 1902.
4. 225 minutes — India, all out twice in one day for 58 (21.4 6-ball overs) and 82 (37.3 overs) v England at Manchester 1952.
5. 339 minutes — Zimbabwe, all out twice in one day for 59 (29.4 overs) and 99 (49.5 overs) v New Zealand at Harare 2005-06.

UNUSUAL DISMISSALS

1. S.P.Jones (Australia) playing against England in the 1882 Ashes Test at The Oval was run out by W.G.Grace when, after completing a run, he left his crease to pat the pitch down. This was said to so infuriate F.R.Spofforth, that he bowled like a man possessed, and taking 7 for 44 in England's second innings was instrumental in gaining Australia's first-ever win in a Test on English soil.
2. S.J.Snooke for South Africa v England at Durban in 1909-10 was stumped for 53 by N.C.Tufnell, who was keeping wicket as a substitute in place of H.Strudwick (injured).
3. A.Ducat had scored 3 for England v Australia at Leeds 1921 when the shoulder of his bat was broken by an express delivery from E.A.McDonald. The broken piece of the bat knocked off a bail and the ball was caught by J.M.Gregory. (The umpire's decision, incidentally, was 'out caught'.)
4. J.W.Zulch (South Africa) in the Second Test against Australia played at Johannesburg in 1921-22 was given out hit wicket when a splinter of wood from his bat, dislodged by a ball from E.A.McDonald removed the bails.
5. W.H.Brann for South Africa v England at Cape Town in 1922-23 was given 'not out' for a catch at the wicket from the bowling of G.G.Macaulay — who then appealed for lbw and had the appeal granted.
6. Mushtaq Ali, batting for India v England at Manchester in 1936, was run out when a ball hit by his partner, V.M.Merchant, hit the back of Mushtaq Ali's bat and deflected to mid-off where A.E.Fagg fielded and threw down the non-striker's wicket with Mushtaq Ali out of his ground.
7. D.G.Bradman (Australia) was batting against India at Brisbane in 1947-48 when he played back so far to N.B.Amarnath that the downward swing of his bat broke the wicket from behind. Bradman was out hit wicket to Amarnath for 185.
8. W.A.Brown (Australia) was run out by the bowler, M.H.Mankad, when batting for Australia v India at Sydney 1947-48. Brown had been backing up too far and Mankad removed the bails as he ran in to bowl. Mankad did not deliver a warning as he had been involved in a similar incident with Brown only four weeks before in the match between an Australian XI and the touring Indian team.
9. L.Hutton (England) was dismissed for 'obstructing the field' v South Africa at The Oval, 1951. A delivery hit Hutton's bat handle or hand and lobbed into the air where wicket-keeper W.R.Endean prepared to take the catch. Hutton, however, hit the ball away as it fell (with the intention of preventing it hitting his wicket) and upon appeal was given out.
10. Ironically, W.R.Endean (South Africa) became the first batsman to be given out 'handled the ball' v England at Cape Town in 1956-57, when a ball from J.C.Laker rose sharply and Endean palmed it away with his hand in hockey goalkeeper style.
11. West Indian batsman J.S.Solomon was adjudged out hit wicket when his cap fell off dislodging the bails during the Second Test of the 1960-61 series against Australia at Melbourne.
12. Pervez Sajjad (Pakistan) was stumped by B.E.Congdon (New Zealand) at Lahore 1964-65. Congdon was sub-

stituting as wicket-keeper for A.E.Dick, who had been injured.

13. B.L.d'Oliveira (England). In the Second Test v West Indies played at Lord's in 1966 England's J.M.Parks and B.L.d'Oliveira were batting together in the first innings. Parks, facing W.W.Hall, drove a ball back down the pitch which rebounded off d'Oliveira's boot onto the stumps whilst he was out of his crease. Thinking he was run out d'Oliveira 'walked' whereupon Hall picked up the ball and removed a stump with the hand holding the ball, thus correctly completing the dismissal. Had the batsman stood his ground he would not have been out as no fielder had touched the ball when the wicket was first broken.

14. I.R.Redpath (Australia) was run out, when backing-up too far, by bowler C.C.Griffith (West Indies) at Adelaide 1968-69. Redpath had been involved in a similar incident some time before. (Interestingly, I.M.Chappell was caught out of his ground in the same way by bowler D.A.J.Holford only minutes later, but in this instance the bowler refrained from removing the bails.)

15. D.W.Randall (England) was run out, when backing-up too far, by bowler E.J.Chatfield (New Zealand) in the Test at Christchurch 1977-78.

16. R.M.Hogg (Australia) when batting against Pakistan at Melbourne 1978-79, had run a single and then, between deliveries, walked up the pitch to prod down some loose turf. However, the ball was still in the possession of a fielder, Javed Miandad, who put down the stumps with Hogg yards down the wicket to run the batsman out for 9.

17. Sikander Bakht (Pakistan) was run out, when backing-up too far, by bowler A.G.Hurst (Australia) at Perth 1978-79.

18. A.M.J.Hilditch (Australia) when batting against Pakistan at Perth, 1978-79, took pity on the perspiring fast bowler Sarfraz Nawaz and bent down and collected the ball by his feet at the bowler's end, and handed it to Sarfraz. Instead of thanking Hilditch, the bowler appealed for 'handled the ball' and the umpire had no option but to uphold the appeal.

19. Moin Khan (Pakistan) when batting against Australia at Karachi, 1982-83, defended a ball from J.R.Thomson and instinctively knocked it away with his hand when it rebounded towards his stumps and became the third player to be dismissed 'handled the ball'.

20. D.L.Haynes (West Indies) when batting against India at Bombay, 1983-84, played a ball from Kapil Dev, which took the inside edge, hit his pads and rolled slowly towards the stumps. He brushed it away with his glove to become the fourth player to be dismissed 'handled the ball'.

21. D.M.Jones (Australia) v West Indies at Georgetown 1990-91 was bowled by a no-ball from C.A.Walsh. Because of his helmet and the noise from the crowd, he did not hear the umpire's call and started to walk off the field. C.L.Hooper grabbed the ball and snatched up a stump with the hand holding the ball. The umpire then, incorrectly, gave the batsman out. The laws of cricket had been changed in 1980 so that the umpire can call back a batsman leaving the ground under a misapprehension that he had been dismissed. [It should be noted that at Port-of-Spain in 1973-74 A.W.Greig (England) ran out I.A.Kallicharran when, after B.D.Julien played the last ball of the second day's play down the pitch Greig picked up the ball and seeing Kallicharran out of his ground, threw down the non-striker's wicket and appealed. Umpire D.Sang Hue ruled Kallicharran 'run out'. That evening lengthy off-field discussions between the captains, officials and umpires led to the appeal being withdrawn in the interests of cricket.]

22. G.A.Gooch (England v Australia, Manchester, 1993) became the fifth player to be out 'handled the ball' when, after playing a ball from M.G.Hughes down into his crease, he knocked it away with his right glove when it bounced up and was about to fall on his stumps.

A FEW SURPRISE SELECTIONS

1. E.J.K.Burn (Australia) was selected in the 1890 Australian team to England as the second wicket-keeper. It was only when the team was assembled in Adelaide that it became known that Burn had never kept wickets in his life!

2. S.F.Barnes (England) was selected to tour Australia in 1901-02, mainly at the instigation of A.C.McLaren. Barnes, then a professional with Burnley in the Lancashire League, had taken only 9 wickets in first-class cricket — but then proceeded to take 19 wickets in his first two Tests on the way to becoming recognised as one of the greatest bowlers the world has ever seen.

3. Australian selectors had a "double" selection bonanza in 1907-08 when they brought J.D.A.O'Connor and M.J.Hartigan into the side for the Adelaide Test against England. Hartigan scored 48 and 116 (sharing in a record stand of 243 with C.Hill after Australia had been 7 for 180) and O'Connor bowled Australia to victory with 5 for 40 in the vital fourth innings of the match.

4. W.Rhodes (England) was brought back into the England team for the vital Fifth Test of the 1926 series

against Australia aged 48! With England needing a win to regain the Ashes, Rhodes bowled them to victory with 2 for 35 and 4 for 44.

5. A.L.Valentine (West Indies) was taken to England in 1950 after only two first-class matches in which he had taken two wickets for 190 runs.

6. S.Ramadhin (West Indies) was pulled out of Trinidad club cricket to tour England in 1950, a tour on which he and A.L.Valentine mystified the best batsmen in England, on the way to becoming Test greats. Ramadhin, like Valentine, had played only two games of first-class cricket — both on matting.

7. J.E.F.Beck (New Zealand) had played only club cricket and never appeared in a first-class match when chosen to tour South Africa in 1953-54. He was run out for 99 at Cape Town in his second Test match.

8. G.S.Sobers (West Indies) was called into the Test side (to replace the injured A.L.Valentine) v England at Kingston in 1953-54 after playing in only second first-class matches.

9. For the series against Australia in 1956 the English selectors pulled off three of the most amazing selections in history — and all worked!

   For the Third Test at Leeds, they included 41 year old C.Washbrook, who had not played Test cricket for 5 years. Coming in to bat with the score at 3 for 17, Washbrook made 98 and shared in a stand of 177 with P.B.H.May.

   For the next Test at Manchester, the Rev. David Sheppard was included. Because of clerical duties, he had played only 4 innings that year for Sussex — but promptly made 113 to help England win the Test.

   For The Oval Test, the selectors brought in Denis Compton — 18 years after he had played his first Test and not long after he had undergone an operation for the removal of a knee-cap. Compton completed the 'hat-trick' for the selectors with scores of 94 and 35*.

10. J.R.Watkins (Australia) — After A.A.Mallett had announced his unavailability for the forthcoming tour of the West Indies the Australian selectors chose Watkins for the Test against Pakistan at Sydney in 1972-73, although his first-class record for New South Wales was not particularly distinguished. In the second innings he made a fine 36 and shared in a stand of 83 with R.A.L.Massie after Australia had collapsed to 8 for 101 — but with the ball, delivered probably the six most inaccurate overs ever bowled at Sydney.

11. M.R.Whitney (Australia) was in England to play League cricket, and appear occasionally for Gloucestershire, when he was brought into the Australian Test team in 1981 after injuries to G.F.Lawson and R.M.Hogg. (Whitney had previously made 4 appearances for New South Wales.)

12. P.L.Taylor (Australia) was selected for the Fifth Test against England at Sydney 1986-87 after only six first-class matches — only one of them during that season. There was speculation in the media that the selectors had chosen the wrong Taylor. M.A.Taylor, an opening batsmen for New South Wales, had experienced a successful debut in first-class cricket the previous season. P.L.Taylor, bowling off-spin, took a career-best 6 for 78 and 2 for 76 as well as scoring a crucial 42 runs in Australia's second innings as Australia won their first Test against England since June 1985.

UNUSUAL INCIDENTS

1. G.J.Bonnor (Australia) in making 87 v England at Sydney 1882-83 was dropped 8 (eight!) times. A.G.Steel dropped four of the chances, when Bonnor was 2, 17, 24 and 80. When England batted, Steel himself was dropped 4 times — but went on to make 135*.

2. In the England v Australia series in Australia in 1936-37, Middlesex captain R.W.V.Robins played under the leadership of his county vice-captain, G.O.B.Allen. A similar situation occurred in 1980 when Somerset captain B.C.Rose played under the leadership of Somerset vice-captain I.T.Botham for England v West Indies and 1995 when Lancashire captain M.Watkinson played under the leadership of his county colleague M.A.Atherton v West Indies and v South Africa.

3. In the Seventh Test Australia v England at Sydney 1970-71, England nearly became the first team to forfeit a Test. England paceman J.A.Snow felled Australian tail-ender T.J.Jenner with a bouncer, and became involved in a war of words with umpire L.P.Rowan when warned for 'intimidatory' bowling. R.Illingworth, England's captain, joined in, and the crowd began to boo and hiss. Cans came flying onto the field and, when Snow was sent to field right on the fine-leg boundary, a drunken spectator leaned over the fence and grabbed his arm.

   Illingworth immediately motioned his team from the ground, and it was only the umpires' advice that if they did not return they would forfeit the match that persuaded Illingworth to resume.

4. In the India v Australia Test at Bangalore 1979-80, Australian pace-bowler R.M.Hogg, becoming upset with the feather-bed pitch and with his own spate of no-balls (7 in 5 overs), kicked down the stumps at the bowler's end. His captain, K.J.Hughes tendered an immediate apology to the umpire, an action which Hogg replicated at the end of play.

5. In the Australia v England Test at Perth in 1979-80, Australian batsman D.K.Lillee, not out overnight, continued his innings the next morning using an aluminium bat (which he had used once previously). After two balls had been played (rather noisily), England captain J.M.Brearley complained to the umpires that the aluminium bat was damaging the ball! The umpires then requested that Lillee change his bat, but Lillee, quite within his rights, refused, arguing heatedly with Brearley. Finally, the umpires ordered him off for a replacement, but after stalking from the ground, Lillee re-appeared — still carrying his aluminium bat. Still more argument ensued, and eventually Lillee threw the bat away in disgust, accepted a willow replacement, and the game was allowed to continue.

6. In the New Zealand v West Indies Test at Christchurch 1979-80, West Indian fast-bowler C.E.H.Croft took bad sportsmanship to the brink. After being no-balled and showing his displeasure several times, Croft ran in very close to the umpire (F.R.Goodall) — so close that the batsman could not see him — and shouldered Goodall heavily. Croft was later suspended for his actions, but the West Indians were so upset about Goodall's umpiring that they refused to take the field after tea on the third day unless he was replaced. They were finally persuaded to resume, 12 minutes late.

7. M.A.Holding, West Indies v New Zealand, Dunedin 1979-80, replicated the behaviour of R.M.Hogg (above) by kicking down the stumps at the batsman's end after having an appeal disallowed.

8. The start of the Pakistan v West Indies Test at Multan in 1980-81 was delayed because of the late arrival of one of the umpires.

9. In the match West Indies v Pakistan at Multan in 1980-81, bowler S.T.Clarke (West Indies) was bombarded by a shower of oranges, and a brick, thrown from the crowd as he fielded on the fine-leg fence. Enraged, Clarke picked up the brick and threw it back into the crowd, injuring a young student. Play was immediately held up, and only West Indies vice-captain A.I.Kallicharran's calming plea, on bended knee in front of the grandstand, restored order in the angry crowd. Clarke was later suspended for three matches by the West Indies Cricket Board of Control.

10. When given out lbw v Australia at Melbourne 1980-81, Indian captain S.M.Gavaskar indicated that the ball had hit his pad and was so angry at the decision that he ordered his batting partner, C.P.S.Chauhan, to accompany him from the field of play and forfeit the match! Both players were only metres inside the boundary when India's manager, Wing-Commander Durani, intervened and ordered Chauhan back to the crease. The following day Kapil Dev and D.R.Doshi bowled India to victory as Australia was dismissed for 83 chasing a target of 143.

11. West Indies v England at St John's 1980-81 opened the Test by scoring 45 from the first seven overs — made up of 11 fours and a single.

12. An off-field explosion held up play in the Second Test Pakistan v England at Faisalabad 2005-06. While the players were milling around the field, Shahid Afridi walked down the pitch and dug the spikes on his boots into both ends of the pitch.

CAPTAINCY CURIOSITIES

C.A.Smith (England) captained his country at his only appearance in a Test match — against South Africa at Port Elizabeth in 1888-89. Smith, later knighted, was afterwards famous as a Hollywood film actor.

P.W.Sherwell (South Africa) captained his country in his first Test appearance, against England at Johannesburg, 1905-06.

H.M.Taberer captained South Africa in his one and only Test match appearance when he led his country against England at Johannesburg in the First Test of 1902-03. For the Second Test less than a week later J.H.Anderson led South Africa in his only Test appearance.

N.Betancourt captained West Indies in his only Test match played against England in the 1929-30.

In the Fourth Test between West Indies and England played at Kingston in 1934-35 both captains were forced off the field through injury. England's R.E.S.Wyatt suffered a broken jaw and West Indies's C.G.Grant retired with an ankle injury.

During the 3rd Test at Birmingham, 1968, England captain, M.C.Cowdrey, pulled a muscle in his right leg and the Australian captain, W.M.Lawry, had his right-hand little finger fractured. As a result, T.W.Graveney and B.N.Jarman were given their only opportunity to captain their national teams, in the Fourth Test at Leeds.

During his period as captain of England (12 matches from June 1980 to July 1981) I.T.Botham scored 276 runs at an average of 13.80 and took 35 wickets at 32.00 average. Compare these figures to his pre-captaincy career statistics of 1336 runs at 40.48 and 139 wickets at 18.52 in 25 matches.

In the Third Test, Australia v India at Melbourne, 2003-04, Australian captain, S.R.Waugh, retired hurt in the second innings, on 0* at 4 for 373 and resumed at 5 for 437, after being struck on his elbow by a ball from A.B.Agarkar. The Indian captain, S.C.Ganguly, retired hurt in the second innings, on 16* at 2 for 39 and resumed at 4 for 160, after being struck on the back of the head by a ball from B.A.Williams.

ODDMENTS

1. In the Second Test match between Australia and England, played at the Melbourne Cricket Ground in 1876-77, Australian batsman T.J.D.Kelly hit eight consecutive fours in the second innings and C.Bannerman scored 30 in 15 minutes. Despite these spirited efforts Australia lost by four wickets.
2. An Australian team advertised for opponents. This unique event occurred during the visit of the Australians to England in 1880. Apparently, it was not certain until the late spring of that year that the Australians would be touring and consequently the county programmes had already been drawn up. The Australians therefore found the large part of their tour consisted of fixtures with local clubs in the North and Midlands, usually against odds. It was during this period that the team took out newspaper advertisements for opponents.

   Finally, at the end of August, and mainly through the efforts of one man, C.W.Alcock, that a match against a representative English team was organised — this became the first of all Test matches on English soil.
3. In the First Test of the 1881-82 season between Australia and England, played at Melbourne, W.E.Midwinter made his debut for England having played for Australia in the first two Tests between the two countries. (In the same match T.P.Horan and G.Giffen scored Australia's first-ever century partnership: 107 for the fifth wicket.)
4. W.L.Murdoch of Australia scored the first double century in Test cricket when he knocked up 211 against England at The Oval during the Third Test in 1884. In the same match all eleven English players were called upon to bowl whilst Australia scored 551 runs. The match was drawn.
5. In the Fifth Test between Australia and England at Melbourne during the 1884-85 season umpire G.J.Hodges refused to take the field after tea on the third day because of complaints made by some English players about his decisions. Australian player T.W.Garrett deputised for Hodges during the last session and the English manager J.Lillywhite took over on the last day. There is nothing in the records to indicate how Garrett performed in this unusual role.
6. Four players with the same surname played in the South Africa v England Test at Cape Town in 1891-92 — A., G.E., and J.T.Hearne for England, F.Hearne for South Africa.
7. W.Rhodes (England 1899 to 1929-30) in 98 innings and M.H.Mankad (India 1946 to 1958-59) in 72 innings in Test match cricket are the only two batsmen to bat in every position from 1 to 11 in their Test match careers.
8. In his debut Test match (v South Africa at Cape Town in 1922-23) G.G.Macaulay (England) took a wicket with his first ball, and made the winning hit when England won the match by one wicket.
9. The only occasion when one country has simultaneously played official Test matches in two different countries was in 1929-30 when England played New Zealand at Christchurch on 10, 11, 13 January and West Indies at Bridgetown on 11, 13, 14, 15, 16 January.
10. The most expensive miss? B.A.Barnett when keeping wicket for Australia v England at The Oval, 1938, missed stumping L.Hutton off L.O.Fleetwood-Smith when the batsman was 40. Hutton went on to make 364.
11. The appearance of a mouse on the field held up play for several minutes during the England v Pakistan Test at Birmingham in 1962.
12. A.S.M.Oakman, a former first class umpire, deputised for the first over of the third day of the Second Test England v West Indies, Birmingham, 1973. A.E.Fagg had refused to umpire because of dissent shown by R.B.Kanhai when an appeal for a catch by wicket-keeper D.L.Murray against G.Boycott was disallowed on the second afternoon.
13. A bomb alert at 2.42 p.m. on the third afternoon of the third Test between England and West Indies, at Lord's, 1973, resulted in 89 minutes being lost. The crowd was allowed onto the playing arena while the police searched for the bomb.
14. In the Pakistan v England Test at Lahore in 1977-78, England off-spinner G.A.Cope dismissed Abdul Qadir lbw and bowled Sarfraz Nawaz first ball. Iqbal Qasim then snicked the next delivery to J.M.Brearley, the English captain, at slip and the umpire confirmed the catch and Copes's hat-trick. However, Brearley indicated that the 'catch' had been taken on the bounce and Qasim was allowed to bat on. It would be difficult to get much closer to a Test hat-trick than Cope did on that day.
15. The second instance of all eleven players bowling in an innings occurred at Faisalabad in 1979-80 during the Second Test between Pakistan and Australia. The entire Australian team, including wicket-keeper R.W.Marsh, had a spell at the bowling crease during Pakistan's only innings. The match was drawn. Australia made 617 and Pakistan 2 for 382.

16. The first seven batsmen in Australia's batting order (A.M.J.Hilditch, G.M.Wood, A.R.Border, K.J.Hughes, G.N.Yallop, D.F.Whatmore and K.J.Wright) opened their score with a boundary in the First Test v India at Madras 1979-90.

PROGRESS OF LEADING WICKET-TAKERS IN TESTS

Player (Country)	wickets	date
A.Hill (England)	1	15 Mar 1877
J.Southerton (England	2	15 Mar 1877
A.Hill (England) - equalled	3	16 Mar 1877
W.E.Midwinter (Australia)	4	17 Mar 1877
A.Shaw (England)	6	17 Mar 1877
T.K.Kendall (Australia) - equalled	8	19 Mar 1877
T.K.Kendall (Australia)	9	31 Mar 1877
F.R.Spofforth (Australia)	15	4 Jan 1879
G.E.Palmer (Australia)	18	20 Feb 1882
F.R.Spofforth (Australia)	29	29 Aug 1882
G.E.Palmer (Australia)	33	1 Jan 1883
F.R.Spofforth (Australia)	46	29 Jan 1883
G.E.Palmer (Australia)	57	21 Jul 1884
F.R.Spofforth (Australia)	70	23 Feb 1885
J.Briggs (England)	95	12 Jan 1895
J.Briggs (England)	100	1 February 1895
C.T.B.Turner (Australia)	101	4 February 1895
J.Briggs (England)	102	1 March 1895
H.Trumble (Australia)	119	2 January1908
S.F.Barnes (England)	142	13 December 1913
C.V.Grimmett (Australia)	190	4 January 1936
A.V.Bedser (England)	217	24 July 1953
J.B.Statham (England)	237	26 January 1963
F.S.Trueman (England)	243	15 March 1963
L.R.Gibbs (West Indies)	308	31 January 1976
D.K.Lillee (Australia)	310	27 December 1981
I.T.Botham (England)	356	21 August 1986
R.J.Hadlee (New Zealand)	384	12 November 1988
Kapil Dev (India)	432	8 February 1994
C.A.Walsh (West Indies)	435	27 March 2000
M.Muralidaran (Sri Lanka)	520	8 May 2004
S.K.Warne (Australia)	533	15 October 2004

† 'wickets' denotes the number of wickets at the time of setting the new record; 'date' is the date the new record was set.

BOWLERS NO-BALLED FOR THROWING IN TEST MATCHES

E.Jones	Australia	v	England	Melbourne	1897-98

Once by umpire J.Phillips

G.A.R.Lock	England	v	West Indies	Kingston	1953-54

No-balled once.

G.M.Griffin	South Africa	v	England	Lord's	1960

11 times by umpire F.S.Lee. In England's only innings Griffin claimed the only Test hat-trick achieved for South Africa when he took the wickets of M.J.K.Smith, P.M.Walker and F.S.Trueman.

I.Meckiff	Australia	v	South Africa	Brisbane[2]	1963-64

4 times by umpire C.J.Egar in his only over.

Abid Ali — India v New Zealand — Christchurch — 1967-688
Once by umpire F.R.Goodall. He deliberately threw the ball in protest at the action of G.A.Bartlett who had not been 'called'.

S.M.H.Kirmani — India v West Indies — Bridgetown — 1982-83
His 2nd delivery in Test cricket gave West Indies a win by 10 wickets.

D.I.Gower — England v New Zealand — Nottingham — 1986
Deliberately threw the only ball he 'bowled' in the Test. The scores were level and New Zealand had 8 wickets in hand.

H.K.Olonga — Zimbabwe v Pakistan — Harare — 1994-95
On debut, Olonga took a wicket with his third ball before being no-balled in his 5th over by I.D.Robinson.

M.Muralidaran — Sri Lanka v Australia — Melbourne — 1995-96
7 times by umpire D.B.Hair. This is the only instance of a player being 'called' in a Test by the umpire at the bowler's end.

G.W.Flower — Zimbabwe v New Zealand — Bulawayo[2] — 2000-01
3 times by umpire D.B.Hair in his second over.

W.W.Hinds — West Indies v South Africa — St John's — 2004-05
Hinds deliberately over-stepped the bowling crease and threw a ball to South African captain, G.C.Smith. He was reported and fined his whole match fee for this behaviour.

(Although some recent record books and web sites state that Haseeb Ahsan was no-balled for throwing for Pakistan v India at Bombay in 1960-61, contemporary newspapers and tour books make no mention of his being called.)

BOWLING CURIOSITIES

1. J.Briggs (7 for 17 and 8 for 11) for England v South Africa at Cape Town in 1888-89 took all of his wickets unaided, bowling 14 and trapping one lbw.
2. W.W.Armstrong for Australia v England at Nottingham in 1905 bowled off-breaks wide outside leg stump in an attempt to slow the scoring. From 204 consecutive balls, the England batsmen scored from only 25. Of the remaining 179 balls, 19 only were played by the batsmen, the other 160 being allowed to go through to the wicket-keeper.
3. T.J.Matthews (Australia) took a hat-trick in each innings of the match Australia v South Africa at Manchester in 1912, the only instance of this type in all Test cricket history. These six wickets were the only ones taken by Matthews in the match, and constituted over one-third of his Test career 'bag'.
4. W.W.Armstrong (Australia) became the first man in Test history to bowl two consecutive overs when he did so against England at Manchester in 1921. England closed its innings on the second day but as the first day had been washed out, it was discovered that Australia was not left with sufficient batting time under the Laws as they then stood. After some confusion, the England innings was resumed and Armstrong, who had bowled the last over before the break, bowled the first one after it.
5. G.O.B.Allen (England) opened the bowling v Australia at Manchester in 1934 with a 13-ball over — three wides and four no-balls.
6. England's score of 7 (dec.) for 469 v South Africa at Durban in 1938-39 did not include a single maiden over (8-ball overs).
7. N.B.F.Mann (South Africa) — making his debut v England at Nottingham in 1947, bowled eight consecutive maiden overs before giving up his first run in Test cricket.
8. A.M.Moir (New Zealand) equalled the 1921 record of W.W.Armstrong by sending down two consecutive overs. Moir bowled the last over before tea in the Test v England at Wellington in 1950-51, and then the first over after tea.
9. H.J.Tayfield (South Africa) v New Zealand at Johannesburg in 1953-54 bowled 14 eight-ball overs, 7 of which were maidens, for figures of 6 for 13. There were only nine scoring shots made from 112 balls.
10. H.J.Tayfield (South Africa) v England at Durban 1956-57 bowled 16 consecutive (8-ball) maiden overs — he delivered 137 successive balls all told from which no runs were scored.
11. K.R.Miller (Australia) bowled unchanged before lunch on the first day v England at Melbourne 1954-55 for figures of 9-8-5-3. All five runs scored from Miller came in his fourth over.
12. S.Ramadhin (West Indies) v England at Lord's, 1950 bowled 10 consecutive maidens in the first innings and 11 consecutive in the second.

13. In the England v Australia Test at The Oval in 1882, English bowlers E.Peate and R.G.Barlow delivered 14 consecutive maidens in Australia's first innings of 63. Peate's return for the innings was 24 maidens in 38 overs, whilst Barlow's 31 overs included 22 maidens.

14. In the Third Test between West Indies and England played at Bridgetown in 1973-74 a total of 79 no-balls were bowled. With 20 runs scored off them the bowlers had given away almost a century.

15. In the six-match Test series between Australia and England played in Australia in 1970-71 not one lbw appeal was upheld against an Australian batsman.

16. L.R.Gibbs (West Indies) v India 1961-62 at Bridgetown. His second innings figures of 53.3 overs 37 maidens 38 runs 8 wickets included 15.3-4-14-6-8 in the final session of the match.

17. In the India v England Test played at Madras in 1963-64 R.G.Nadkarni bowled 21 consecutive maiden overs in the first innings but didn't take a wicket. His first innings figures were 32-27-5-0. In the second he took 2 for 6 off 6 overs (4 maidens).

18. H.Verity (England) bowled a Chinaman when he dismissed E.E.Achong (West Indies) in the Second Test at Manchester in 1933.

19. Because of an umpiring error, J.T.Sparling, New Zealand, bowled an 11-ball over (excluding no-balls and wides) in England's innings of the First Test at Auckland 1962-63.

20. At Lord's 1972, R.A.L.Massie, Australia, returned match figures of 16 for 137 — 32.5-7-84-8 and 27.2-9-53-8. At Madras 1987-88, N.D.Hirwani equalled this feat by taking 16 for 136 — 18.3-3-61-8 and 15.2-3-75-8. This is the record for any bowler in his first Test. A.E.Trott, A.L.Valentine and L.Klusener are the only other bowlers to have taken 8 wickets in an innings in their first Test.

MOST CONSECUTIVE MAIDENS

6-ball overs

21 R.G.Nadkarni, India v England, Madras 1963-64. (bowled 131 consecutive balls not scored from.)

15 M.C.Carew, West Indies v England, Port-of-Spain 1967-68. (90 consecutive balls not scored from.)

13 J.H.Wardle, England v South Africa, Nottingham 1955.

11 J.A.Young, England v Australia, Nottingham, 1948.

11 S.Ramadhin, West Indies v England, Lord's 1950.

10 S.Ramadhin, West Indies v England, Lord's 1950.

8-ball overs

16 H.J.Tayfield, South Africa v England, Durban 1956-57. (137 consecutive balls not scored from.)

9 H.J.Tayfield, South Africa v Australia, Melbourne 1952-53.

LONG BOWLING SPELLS

1. G.E.Palmer (53-36-68-7) and E.Evans (57-32-64-3) (Australia) together bowled unchanged for the entire English innings of 133 scored in 190 minutes — at Sydney 1881-82.

2. T.Richardson, for England v Australia at Manchester in 1896, bowled unchanged for three hours in the second innings to try and stave off an England defeat. Richardson, a pace bowler, delivered 42.3 overs, 16 maidens and took 6 for 76.

3. A.M.B.Rowan (South Africa) bowled unchanged for 46 six-ball overs v England at Leeds, 1947 for figures of 46-12-89-1.

4. Ghulam Ahmed, for India v Pakistan at Dacca 1954-55, bowled 40 overs unchanged on the first day, his figures being 40-8-84-4.

5. T.L.Goddard (South Africa) bowled 46 overs unchanged on the last day of the match v England at Leeds in 1955. His spell resulted in figures of 46-27-45-4.

6. H.J.Tayfield (South Africa) had an unchanged spell of 53.4-29-60-5 in the second English innings at The Oval in 1955.

7. T.R.Veivers (Australia) sent down 55 consecutive overs v England at Manchester in 1964. Veivers bowled 75 of the last 80 overs sent down from the City end.

GOOD BOWLING SPELLS

7 wickets for 1 run in 26 balls — Sarfraz Nawaz Pakistan v Australia, Melbourne 1978-79.

7 wickets for 1 run in 32 balls — C.E.L.Ambrose West Indies v Australia, Perth 1992-93.

7 wickets for 8 runs in 22 balls — J.C.Laker England v Australia, Manchester 1956.

6 wickets for 6 runs in 45 balls — S.Haigh England v South Africa, Cape Town 1898-99.

7 wickets for 17 runs in 46 balls — M.A.Noble Australia v England, Melbourne 1901-02.

8 wickets for 7 runs in 49 balls — G.A.Lohmann England v South Africa, Johannesburg 1895-96.

6 wickets for 7 runs in 29 balls — S.J.Pegler South Africa v England, Lord's 1912.

5 wickets for 1 run in 17 balls — G.R.Hazlitt Australia v England, The Oval 1912.

5 wickets for 7 runs in 31 balls — E.P.Nupen South Africa v England, Durban 1927-28.

6 wickets for 11 runs in 24 balls — E.P.Nupen South Africa v England, Johannesburg 1930-31.

6 wickets for 8 runs in 36 balls — H.Ironmonger Australia v South Africa, Melbourne 1931-32.

6 wickets for 9 runs in 56 balls — C.V.Grimmett Australia v South Africa, Adelaide 1931-32.

5 wickets for 1 run in 28 balls — I.T.Botham England v Australia, Birmingham 1981.

5 wickets for 2 runs in 19 balls — E.R.H.Toshack Australia v India, Brisbane 1947-48.

WIDES

Most by one bowler

14 Umar Gul Pakistan v England, Lords 2006

11 S.J.Harmison England v Pakistan, The Oval 2006

9 Kabir Khan Pakistan v South Africa, Johannesburg 1994-95 (also bowled 5 wides in 1st innings!).

8 B.J.T.Bosanquet England v Australia, Leeds 1905.

8 M.B.Owens New Zealand v Sri Lanka, Moratuwa 1992-93.

8 A.D.Mullally England v India, Lord's 1996.

6 M.A.Noble Australia v England, Leeds 1905.

6 J.R.Watkins Australia v Pakistan, Sydney 1972-73.

INEXPENSIVE ANALYSES

25-19-18-0	Fazal Mahmood	Pakistan	v	India	Dacca	1954-55
28-17-21-2	A.H.Kardar	Pakistan	v	New Zealand	Dacca	1955-56
30-19-20-2	Khan Mohammad	Pakistan	v	New Zealand	Dacca	1955-56
32-27-5-0	R.G.Nadkarni	India	v	England	Madras	1963-64
32-23-24-4	J.H.Wardle	England	v	South Africa	Nottingham	1955
36-23-27-3	J.C.Laker	England	v	New Zealand	Leeds	1958
45-28-48-4	A.L.Valentine	West Indies	v	England	Lord's	1950
45-26-42-6	K.D.Mackay	Australia	v	Pakistan	Dacca	1959-60
46-24-43-1	W.Attewell	England	v	Australia	Sydney	1891-92
46.1-20-42-1	G.E.Gomez	West Indies	v	India	Port-of-Spain	1952-53
46.3-24-42-6	Zulfiqar Ahmed	Pakistan	v	New Zealand	Karachi	1955-56
47-29-42-5	H.Ironmonger	Australia	v	South Africa	Brisbane	1931-32
47-28-39-3	C.V.Grimmett	Australia	v	England	Nottingham	1934
53-30-50-4	S.Ramadhin	West Indies	v	England	Bridgetown	1953-54
53.3-37-38-8	L.R.Gibbs	West Indies	v	India	Bridgetown	1961-62
54-38-43-4	B.W.Yuile	New Zealand	v	Pakistan	Auckland	1964-65
57-30-64-1	J.C.White	England	v	Australia	Melbourne	1928-29
61-34-71-1	M.H.Mankad	India	v	Pakistan	Peshawar	1954-55
61-32-51-3	W.Attewell	England	v	Australia	Melbourne	1891-92
62-37-69-4	T.L.Goddard	South Africa	v	England	Leeds	1955
62-35-61-1	D.S.Atkinson	West Indies	v	Pakistan	Bridgetown	1957-58
69-34-79-2	D.R.Doshi	India	v	New Zealand	Auckland	1980-81
71-47-79-3	A.L.Valentine	West Indies	v	England	Lord's	1950
72-43-86-6	S.Ramadhin	West Indies	v	England	Lord's	1950
76-47-58-4	M.H.Mankad	India	v	England	Delhi	1951-52
81-36-105-5	G.Geary	England	v	Australia	Melbourne	1928-29

All of the above instances were 6-ball overs.

EXPENSIVE ANALYSES

87-11-298-1	L.O.Fleetwood-Smith	Australia	v	England	The Oval	1938
80.2-13-266-5	O.C.Smith	West Indies	v	England	Kingston	1929-30
54-5-259-0	Khan Mohammad	Pakistan	v	West Indies	Kingston	1957-58

85.2-20-247-2	Fazal Mahmood	Pakistan	v	West Indies	Kingston	1957-58
70-10-229-1	S.L.Boock	New Zealand	v	Pakistan	Auckland	1988-89
82-17-228-5	M.H.Mankad	India	v	West Indies	Kingston	1952-53
64.2-8-226-6	B.S.Bedi	India	v	England	Lord's	1974
54-3-224-2	M.Muralidaran	Sri Lanka	v	Australia	Perth	1995-96
38.4-3-220-7	Kapil Dev	India	v	Pakistan	Faisalabad	
54-7-217-3	I.T.Botham	England	v	Pakistan	The Oval	1987
71-8-204-6	I.A.R.Peebles	England	v	Australia	The Oval	1930
75-16-202-3	M.H.Mankad	India	v	West Indies	Bombay	1948-49
84-19-202-6	Haseeb Ahsan	Pakistan	v	India	Madras	1960-61
65-5-221-0	N.Boje	South Africa	v	Sri Lanka	Colombo (SSC)	2006-07

LUCKY ESCAPES

J.R.Hodges forced H.Jupp (63) to play-on the first ball of the England first innings v Australia in the first-ever Test (Melbourne) 1876-77. However, umpire R.B.Terry was not watching and Jupp was allowed to bat on. He top-scored in the innings.

P.A.McAlister (28), when 9, played a ball from W.Rhodes on to his wicket without removing a bail — Australia v England (Adelaide) 1907-08

S.E.Gregory (32), when 18, had his wicket hit by a fast ball from F.R.Foster without a bail falling — Australia v England (Sydney) 1911-2.

J.M.Taylor, on his Test debut, played-on to a ball from J.W.Hearne, but no bail fell — Australia v England (Sydney) 1920-21.

H.Sutcliffe (194) when 43 played a ball from W.J.O'Reilly onto his stumps without dislodging a bail — England v Australia (Sydney) 1932-33.

R.B.Simpson (71), before he had scored, played a ball from F.S.Trueman onto his wickets without removing a bail — Australia v England (Brisbane[2]) 1962-63.

S.R.Waugh (55*) was given out caught by A.L.Logie from the bowling of M.D.Marshall when 28, by Umpire L.J.King, who reversed his decision when the fieldsman admitted to catching the ball on the half-volley — Australia v West Indies (Sydney) 1988-89.

P.V.Simmons (80) when on 4, in trying to stop the ball from rolling onto his wicket, accidently kicked it onto his stumps without dislodging a bail — West Indies v Australia (Perth) 1992-93.

In South Africa's 1st innings against Pakistan, at Faisalabad in 1997-98, P.L.Symcox, when his score was 56, was bowled by a ball from Mushtaq Ahmed. However, the ball passed between the middle and off stumps without dislodging a bail. Symcox went on to score 81 and share in an 8th wicket stand of 124 with G.KIrsten. South Africa went on to win the Test by 53 runs.

WICKET-KEEPING CURIOSITIES

In the first-ever Test between England and South Africa played at Port Elizabeth in March 1889 both wicket-keepers were at one stage off the field.

South Africa's W.H.Milton deputised for regular keeper F.W.Smith in the England second innings whilst M.P.Bowden filled in for H.Wood when the England keeper was unavailable.

Ironically deputy Milton was caught behind by deputy Bowden.

In the First Test England v New Zealand at Lord's 1986 four different players shared the wicket-keeping duties for England in the New Zealand first innings. The selected keeper, B.N.French was injured whilst batting. C.W.J.Athey kept wickets for the first two overs before handing over the gloves to R.W.Taylor (substitute). After a further 74 overs, R.J.Parks (substitute) took over the gloves until the end of the 140th over of the innings. B.N.French then returned and kept wicket for the remainder of the innings — viz one ball!

WICKET-KEEPERS WHO HAVE OPENED THE BOWLING IN A TEST MATCH

C.L.Walcott (West Indies) opened the bowling in England's second innings at Manchester in 1950 replacing the injured H.H.H.Johnson. R.J.Christiani deputised behind the stumps whilst Walcott bowled four overs without success.

Part 3

Test Match Results & Records

All the statistics, results and records for Test cricket since 1876.

Contents

Summary of International Tests

SUMMARY OF ALL INTERNATIONAL TEST MATCHES 1876-77 TO 2006

			won by											
	Opponent	Tests	A	E	SA	WI	NZ	I	P	SL	Z	B	Tied	Draw
Australia	v England	311	126	97	-	-	-	-	-	-	-	-	-	88
	v South Africa	77	44	-	15	-	-	-	-	-	-	-	-	18
	v West Indies	102	48	-	-	32	-	-	-	-	-	-	1	21
	v New Zealand	46	22	-	-	-	7	-	-	-	-	-	-	17
	v India	68	32	-	-	-	-	15	-	-	-	-	1	20
	v Pakistan	52	24	-	-	-	-	-	11	-	-	-	-	17
	v Sri Lanka	18	11	-	-	-	-	-	-	1	-	-	-	6
	v Zimbabwe	3	3	-	-	-	-	-	-	-	0	-	-	0
	v Bangladesh	4	4	-	-	-	-	-	-	-	-	0	-	0
England	v South Africa	130	-	54	26	-	-	-	-	-	-	-	-	50
	v West Indies	134	-	38	-	52	-	-	-	-	-	-	-	44
	v New Zealand	88	-	41	-	-	7	-	-	-	-	-	-	40
	v India	94	-	34	-	-	-	17	-	-	-	-	-	43
	v Pakistan	67	-	18	-	-	-	-	12	-	-	-	-	36
	v Sri Lanka	17	-	-	8	-	-	-	-	3	-	-	-	5
	v Zimbabwe	6	-	3	-	-	-	-	-	-	0	-	-	3
	v Bangladesh	4	-	4	-	-	-	-	-	-	-	0	-	0
South Africa	v New Zealand	33	-	-	18	-	4	-	-	-	-	-	-	11
	v West Indies	19	-	-	12	2	-	-	-	-	-	-	-	5
	v India	16	-	-	7	-	-	3	-	-	-	-	-	6
	v Sri Lanka	17	-	-	8	-	-	-	-	3	-	-	-	5
	v Pakistan	11	-	-	5	-	-	-	2	-	-	-	-	4
	v Zimbabwe	7	-	-	6	-	-	-	-	-	0	-	-	1
	v Bangladesh	4	-	-	4	-	-	-	-	-	-	0	-	0
West Indies	v New Zealand	35	-	-	-	10	9	-	-	-	-	-	-	16
	v India	82	-	-	-	30	-	11	-	-	-	-	-	41
	v Pakistan	41	-	-	-	14	-	-	13	-	-	-	-	14
	v Sri Lanka	10	-	-	-	2	-	-	-	5	-	-	-	3
	v Zimbabwe	6	-	-	-	4	-	-	-	-	0	-	-	2
	v Bangladesh	4	-	-	-	3	-	-	-	-	-	0	-	1
New Zealand	v India	44	-	-	-	-	9	14	-	-	-	-	-	21
	v Pakistan	45	-	-	-	-	6	-	21	-	-	-	-	18
	v Sri Lanka	22	-	-	-	-	8	-	-	4	-	-	-	10
	v Zimbabwe	13	-	-	-	-	7	-	-	-	0	-	-	6
	v Bangladesh	4	-	-	-	-	4	-	-	-	-	0	-	0
India	v Pakistan	56	-	-	-	-	-	8	12	-	-	-	-	36
	v Sri Lanka	26	-	-	-	-	-	10	-	3	-	-	-	13
	v Zimbabwe	11	-	-	-	-	-	7	-	-	2	-	-	2
	v Bangladesh	3	-	-	-	-	-	3	-	-	-	-	-	0
Pakistan	v Sri Lanka	32	-	-	-	-	-	-	15	7	-	-	-	10
	v Zimbabwe	14	-	-	-	-	-	-	8	-	2	-	-	4
	v Bangladesh	6	-	-	-	-	-	-	6	-	-	0	-	0
Sri Lanka	v Zimbabwe	15	-	-	-	-	-	-	-	10	0	-	-	5
	v Bangladesh	7	-	-	-	-	-	-	-	7	-	0	-	0
Zimbabwe	v Bangladesh	8	-	-	-	-	-	-	-	-	4	1	-	3
		1813	314	298	101	149	61	88	100	46	8	1	2	645

	Tests	Won	Lost	Drawn	Tied	Toss Won
Australia	681	314	178	187	2	341
England	852	298	245	309	-	341
South Africa	313	101	113	100	-	150
West Indies	433	149	136	147	1	232
New Zealand	330	61	130	139	-	167
India	400	88	129	182	1	205
Pakistan	324	100	85	139	-	154
Sri Lanka	165	46	62	57	-	84
Zimbabwe	83	8	49	26	-	49
Bangladesh	44	1	39	4	-	22
	1813	1166	1166	645	4	1813

The Grounds

TEST MATCH GROUNDS

The June 2006 Test between West Indies and India at Bassaterre lifted the number of Test match grounds to 94. Colombo has used four grounds, Johannesburg and Mumbai three apiece, whilst Brisbane, Bulawayo, Chennai, Durban, Karachi, Lahore, Lucknow, Multan, Peshawar, Rawalpindi and Chittagong each have two different grounds. For these fourteen cities the exact ground is denoted by a superscript numeral (e.g. Brisbane[1]) except for Colombo, where the ground is shown in brackets. This key to this numeral is given in the tables below. The tables show the full title, date of the first day's play and number of Tests staged for each ground.

Note: Where the name of a centre has been changed - Madras to Chennai, Bombay to Mumbai and Calcutta to Kolkata - the name in use at the time, has been listed.

Test Match Centres	Grounds	First Test Match Day	No.of Tests
AUSTRALIA	*9 grounds*		(349)
Adelaide	Adelaide Oval, North Adelaide	12 Dec 1884	64
Brisbane	[1]Exhibition Ground (1928-29 to 1930-31)	30 Nov 1928	2
	[2]Brisbane Cricket Ground, Woolloongabba	27 Nov 1931	48
Cairns	Bundaberg Rum Stadium	25 Jul 2003	2
Darwin	Marrara Oval, Marrara Sports Complex, Darwin	18 Jul 2003	2
Hobart	Bellerive Oval, Bellerive	16 Dec 1989	7
Melbourne	Melbourne Cricket Ground, Yarra Park, Jolimont	15 Mar 1877	98
Perth	Western Australia Cricket Association Ground, East Perth	11 Dec 1970	33
Sydney	Sydney Cricket Ground No.1, Moore Park, Sydney	17 Feb 1882	93
ENGLAND	*8 grounds*		(435)
Birmingham	County Cricket Ground, Edgbaston Road, Edgbaston	29 May 1902	42
Chester-le-Street	Riverside Complex, Ropery Lane	5 Jun 2003	2
Leeds	Headingley Cricket Ground, St Michael's Lane	29 Jun 1899	66
Lord's	Lord's Cricket Ground, St John's Wood Road, London	21 Jul 1884	111
Manchester	Old Trafford Cricket Ground, Stretford	†10 Jul 1884	71
Nottingham	Trent Bridge Ground, Bridgford Road	1 Jun 1899	53
Sheffield	Bramall Lane (New) Ground	3 Jul 1902	1
The Oval	Kennington Oval, London	6 Sep 1880	89
SOUTH AFRICA	*11 grounds*		(169)
Bloemfontein	Goodyear Park (formerly Springbok Park)	29 Oct 1999	3
Cape Town	Newlands	25 Mar 1889	40
Centurion	Centurion Park	16 Nov 1995	11
	(formerly Centurion Park, Verwoerdburg, Pretoria)		
Durban	[1]Lord's (1909-10 to 1921-22)	21 Jan 1910	4
	[2]Kingsmead	18 Jan 1923	33
East London	Buffalo Park	18 Oct 2002	1
Johannesburg	[1]Wanderers (1895-96 to 1938-39)	2 Mar 1896	22
	[2]Ellis Park (1948-49 to 1953-54)	27 Dec 1948	6
	[3]New Wanderers Stadium (Kent Park)	24 Dec 1956	28
Port Elizabeth	Crusaders Ground, St George's Park	12 Mar 1889	21
Potchefstroom	Sedgars Park (formerly North West Stadium)	25 Oct 2002	1
WEST INDIES	*9 grounds*		(197)
Basseterre, St Kitts	Warner Park, Basseterre, St Kitts	22 Jun 2006	1
Bridgetown, Barbados	Kensington Oval (Pickwick Cricket Club)	11 Jan 1930	43
Georgetown, Guyana	Bourda (Georgetown Cricket Club)	21 Feb 1930	30
Gros Islet, St Lucia	Beausejour Stadium	20 Jun 2003	3

Kingston, Jamaica	Sabina Park	3 Apr 1930	42
Kingstown, St Vincent	Arnos Vale Ground, Arnos Vale	20 Jun 1997	1
Port-of-Spain, Trinidad	Queen's Park Oval (St Clair Oval)	1 Feb 1930	55
St George's, Grenada	Queen's Park (New) Stadium	28 Jun 2002	1
St John's, Antigua	Antigua Recreation Ground	27 Mar 1981	21
NEW ZEALAND	*6 grounds*		(158)
Auckland	Eden Park	#14 Feb 1930	47
Christchurch	Jade Stadium (formerley Lancaster Park)	10 Jan 1930	39
Dunedin	Carisbrook	11 Mar 1955	10
Hamilton	Westpac Trust Bank (formerley Seddon, then Trust Bank) Park	22 Feb 1991	13
Napier	McLean Park	16 Feb 1979	5
Wellington	Basin Reserve	24 Jan 1930	45
INDIA	*19 grounds*		(207)
Ahmedabad	Sardar Patel (Gujarat) Stadium, Motera	12 Nov 1983	8
Bangalore	M.Chinnaswamy Stadium (Karnataka State Cricket Association Stadium)	22 Nov 1974	16
Chandigarh	Sector 16 Stadium	23 Nov 1990	1
Chennai	[1]M.A.Chidambaram Stadium (Chepauk)	10 Feb 1934	28
(formerly Madras)	[2]Nehru (Corporation) Stadium (1955-56 to 1964-65)	6 Jan 1956	9
Cuttack	Barabati Stadium	4 Jan 1987	2
Delhi	Feroz Shah Kotla Ground (Willingdon Pavillion)	10 Nov 1948	28
Hyderabad (Deccan)	Lal Bahadur Shastri Stadium (Fateh Maidan)	19 Nov 1955	3
Jaipur	Sawai Mansingh Stadium (Chogan Stadium)	21 Feb 1987	1
Jullundur	Burlton Park (B.S.Bedi Stadium/Gandhi Park)	24 Sep 1983	1
Kanpur	Green Park (Modi Stadium)	12 Jan 1952	19
Kolkata (formerly Calcutta)	Eden Gardens	5 Jan 1934	34
Lucknow	[1]University Ground (1952-53 only)	23 Oct 1952	1
	[2]K.D.Singh Babu Stadium (Central Sports Stadium)	19 Jan 1994	1
Mohali	Punjab Cricket Association Stadium	10 Dec 1994	6
Mumbai	[1]Gymkhana Ground (Espalanade Maidan/Azad Maidan) (1933-34 Only)	15 Dec 1933	1
(formerly	[2]Brabourne Stadium (1948-49 to 1972-73)	9 Dec 1948	17
Bombay)	[3]Wankhede Stadium	23 Jan 1975	21
Nagpur	Vidarbha (Madhya Pradesh) Cricket Association Ground	3 Oct 1969	10
PAKISTAN	*17 grounds*		(144)
Bahawalpur	Bahawal (Dring) Stadium	15 Jan 1955	1
Dacca	Dacca Stadium (now Banghabandhu Stadium, Bangladesh)	1 Jan 1955	7
Faisalabad	Iqbal Stadium (Lyallpur/National/City Stadium)	16 Oct 1978	24
Gujranwala	Jinnah (Municipal) Stadium	20 Dec 1991	1
Hyderabad (Sind)	Niaz Stadium	16 Mar 1973	5
Karachi	[1]National Stadium	26 Feb 1955	38
	[2]Defence Housing Authority (Defence Cricket) Stadium	1 Dec 1993	1
Lahore	[1]Bagh-e-Jinnah (Lahore Gymkhana, Lawrence Gardens) (1954-55 to 1958-59)	29 Jan 1955	3
	[2]Gaddafi (Lahore) Stadium	21 Nov 1959	37
Multan	[1]Ibn-e-Qasim Bagh (Old Fort) Stadium	30 Dec 1980	1
	[2]Multan Cricket Stadium	29 Aug 2001	4
Peshawar	[1]Peshawar (Services) Club Ground (1954-55 only)	13 Feb 1955	1
	[2]Arbab Niaz (Shahi Bagh) Stadium	8 Sep 1995	6
Rawalpindi	[1]Pindi Club Ground (Army Sports Ground) (1964-65 only)	27 Mar 1965	1
	[2]Rawalpindi Cricket Stadium	9 Dec 1993	8
Sheikhupura	Sheikhupura Stadium	17 Oct 1996	2
Sialkot	Jinnah Stadium	27 Oct 1985	4

SRI LANKA	*7 grounds*		(82)
Colombo	Colombo Cricket Club Ground, Maitland Crescent (CCC)	24 Mar 1984	3
	P.Saravanamuttu Stadium (Colombo Oval) (PSS)	17 Feb 1982	11
	R.Premadasa (Khettamara) Stadium (RPS)	28 Aug 1992	6
	Sinhalese Sports Club Ground, Maitland Place (SSC)	16 Mar 1984	28
Galle	Galle International Stadium (Esplanade)	3 Jun 1998	11
Kandy	Asgiriya Stadium	22 Apr 1983	19
Moratuwa	Tyrone Fernando (Moratuwa/De Zoysa) Stadium	8 Sep 1992	4
ZIMBABWE	*3 grounds*		(44)
Bulawayo	[1]Bulawayo Athletic Club (1992-93 only)	1 Nov 1992	1
	[2]Queens Sports Club	§ 18 Oct 1994	17
Harare	Harare (Salisbury) Sports Club	18 Oct 1992	26
BANGLADESH	*5 grounds*		(22)
Bogra	Shaheed Chandu Stadium (formerly Bogra District Stadium)	8 Mar 2006	1
Chittagong[1]	M.A.Aziz (Chittagong/Niaz) Stadium	15 Nov 2001	8
Chittagong[2]	Chittagong Divisional Stadium	28 Feb 2006	2
Dhaka	Bangabandhu National Stadium (Formerly Dacca Stadium)	12 Mar 1999	10
Fattullah	Narayanganj Osmani Stadium, Fattullah (formerly Fatullah Khan Saheb Osmani Stadium, Fatullah)	9 Apr 2006	1
#UNITED ARAB EMIRATES	*1 ground*		(4)
Sharjah	Sharjah Cricket Association Stadium	31 Jan 2002	4

 # Due to political unrest and security concerns, Pakistan played 'home' Tests against West Indies and Australia in Sharjah.

† Rain prevented play until 11 Jul 1884. # Rain prevented play until 17 Feb 1930. § Rain prevented play until 20 Oct 1994.

The 1890 and 1938 England v Australia, Third Tests at Manchester; the 1970-71 Australia v England, Third Test at Melbourne; the 1988-89 New Zealand v Pakistan, First Test at Dunedin; the 1989-90 West Indies v England, Second Test at Georgetown; 1989-99 Pakistan v Zimbabwe, Third Test at Faisalabad; 1998-99 New Zealand v India, First Test at Dunedin - all abandoned without a ball being bowled, plus the cancelled 1980-81 West Indies v England, Second Test at Georgetown; 1994-95 Sri Lanka v Pakistan, Second Test at Kandy; and 2001-02 Pakistan v New Zealand, Second Test at Karachi are excluded from these figures.

RECORD TOTALS FOR EACH TEST MATCH GROUND

AUSTRALIA

Centre		**Highest Total**			**Lowest Total**	
Adelaide	674	Australia v India	1947-48	82	Australia v West Indies	1951-52
Brisbane[1]	558	Australia v West Indies	1930-31	66	Australia v England	1928-29
Brisbane[2]	645	Australia v England	1946-47	58	Australia v England	1936-37
				58	India v Australia	1947-48
Cairns	556-4d	Australia v Bangladesh	2003-04	163	Bangladesh v Australia	2003-04
Darwin	407-7d	Australia v Bangladesh	2003-04	97	Bangladesh v Australia	2003-04
				97	Sri Lanka v Australia	2004-05
Hobart	558-8d	Australia v New Zealand	2001-02	149	West indies v Australia	2005-06
Melbourne	604	Australia v England	1936-37	36	South Africa v Australia	1931-32
Perth	735-6d	Australia v Zimbabwe	2003-04	62	Pakistan v Australia	1981-82
Sydney	705-7d	India v Australia	2003-04	42	Australia v England	1887-88

ENGLAND

Centre		**Highest Total**			**Lowest Total**	
Birmingham	633-5d	England v India	1979	30	South Africa v England	1924

Chester-le-Street	447-3d	England v Bangladesh	2005	94	Zimbabwe v England	2003
Leeds	653-4d	Australia v England	1993	61	West Indies v England	2000
Lord's	729-6d	Australia v England	1930	42	India v England	1974
Manchester	656-8d	Australia v England	1964	58	India v England	1952
Nottingham	658-8d	England v Australia	1938	88	South Africa v England	1960
Sheffield	289	Australia v England	1902	145	England v Australia	1902
The Oval	903-7d	England v Australia	1938	44	Australia v England	1896

SOUTH AFRICA

Centre		**Highest Total**			**Lowest Total**	
Bloemfontein	563	South Africa v India	2001-02	192	Zimbabwe v South Africa	1999-2000
Cape Town	620-7d	South Africa v Pakistan	2002-03	35	South Africa v England	1898-99
Centurion	604-6d	South Africa v West Indies	2003-04	119	Sri Lanka v South Africa	2000-01
Durban[1]	450	England v South Africa	1913-14	111	South Africa v England	1913-14
Durban[2]	658-9d	South Africa v West Indies	2003-04	66	India v South Africa	1996-97
East London	529-4d	South Africa v Bangladesh	2002-03	170	Bangladesh v South Africa	2002-03
Johannesburg[1]	491	South Africa v Australia	1935-36	85	South Africa v Australia	1902-03
Johannesburg[2]	608	England v South Africa	1948-49	79	New Zealand v South Africa	1953-54
Johannesburg[3]	652-7d	Australia v South Africa	2001-02	72	South Africa v England	1956-57
Port Elizabeth	549-7d	Australia v South Africa	1949-50	30	South Africa v England	1895-96
Potchefstroom	482-5d	South Africa v Bangladesh	2002-03	107	Bangladesh v South Africa	2002-03

WEST INDIES

Centre		**Highest Total**			**Lowest Total**	
Basseterre	581	West Indies v India	2005-06	362	India v West Indies	2005-06
Bridgetown	668	Australia v West Indies	1954-55	81	India v West Indies	1996-97
Georgetown	569	West Indies v Australia	1990-91	109	West Indies v Australia	1972-73
Gros Islet	588-8d	India v West Indies	2005-06	215	West Indies v India	2005-06
Kingston	849	England v West Indies	1929-30	47	West Indies v England	2003-04
Kingstown	343	West Indies v Sri Lanka	1996-97	147	West Indies v Sri Lanka	1996-97
Port-of-Spain	681-8d	West Indies v England	1953-54	46	England v West Indies	1993-94
St George's	470	West Indies v New Zealand	2002-03	373	New Zealand v West Indies	2002-03
St John's	751-5d	West Indies v England	2003-04	127	England v West Indies	1997-98

NEW ZEALAND

Centre		**Highest Total**			**Lowest Total**	
Auckland	621-5d	South Africa v New Zealand	1998-99	26	New Zealand v England	1954-55
Christchurch	580-9d	England v New Zealand	1991-92	65	New Zealand v England	1970-71
Dunedin	586-7d	New Zealand v Sri Lanka	1996-97	74	New Zealand v West Indies	1955-56
Hamilton	563	New Zealand v Pakistan	2003-04	93	New Zealand v Pakistan	1992-93
Napier	561	New Zealand v Sri Lanka	2004-05	109	New Zealand v Sri Lanka	1994-95
Wellington	671-4	New Zealand v Sri Lanka	1990-91	42	New Zealand v Australia	1945-46

INDIA

Centre		**Highest Total**			**Lowest Total**	
Ahmedabad	583-7d	India v New Zealand	1999-2000	103	India v West Indies	1983-84
Bangalore	570	Pakistan v India	2004-05	116	Pakistan v India	1986-87
Chandigarh	288	India v Sri Lanka	1990-91	82	Sri Lanka v India	1990-91
Chennai[1]	652-7d	England v India	1984-85	83	India v England	1976-77
Madras[2]	539-9d	India v Pakistan	1960-61	138	India v Australia	1959-60
Cuttack	400	India v Sri Lanka	1986-87	142	Sri Lanka v India	1986-87
Delhi	644-8d	West Indies v India	1958-59	75	India v West Indies	1987-88
Hyderabad	498-4d	India v New Zealand	1955-56	89	India v New Zealand	1969-70
Jaipur	465-8d	India v Pakistan	1986-87	341	Pakistan v India	1986-87
Jullundur	374	India v Pakistan	1983-84	337	Pakistan v India	1983-84
Kanpur	676-7	India v Sri Lanka	1986-87	105	Australia v India	1959-60

Kolkata	657-7d	India v Australia	2000-01	90	India v West Indies	1983-84
Lucknow[1]	331	Pakistan v India	1952-53	106	India v Pakistan	1952-53
Lucknow[2]	511	India v Sri Lanka	1993-94	174	Sri Lanka v India	1993-94
Mohali	630-6d	New Zealand v India	2003-04	83	India v New Zealand	1999-2000
Bombay[1]	438	England v India	1933-34	219	India v England	1933-34
Bombay[2]	629-6d	West Indies v India	1948-49	88	India v New Zealand	1964-65
Mumbai[3]	604-6d	West Indies v India	1974-75	93	Australia v India	2004-05
Nagpur	609-6d	India v Zimbabwe	2000-01	109	India v New Zealand	1969-70

PAKISTAN

Centre		**Highest Total**			**Lowest Total**	
Bahawalpur	312-9d	Pakistan v India	1954-55	235	India v Pakistan	1954-55
Dacca	439	England v Pakistan	1961-62	70	New Zealand v Pakistan	1955-56
Faisalabad	674-6	Pakistan v India	1984-85	53	West Indies v Pakistan	1986-87
Gujranwala	109-2	Pakistan v Sri Lanka	1991-92		no instance	
Hyderabad	581-3d	Pakistan v India	1982-83	189	India v Pakistan	1982-83
				189	New Zealand v Pakistan	1984-85
Karachi[1]	599-7d	Pakistan v India	2005-06	80	Australia v Pakistan	1956-57
Karachi[2]	423-8d	Pakistan v Zimbabwe	1993-94	134	Zimbabwe v Pakistan	1993-94
Lahore[1]	561	Pakistan v New Zealand	1955-56	104	Pakistan v West Indies	1958-59
Lahore[2]	699-5	Pakistan v India	1989-90	73	New Zealand v Pakistan	2001-02
Multan[1]	249	West Indies v Pakistan	1980-81	166	Pakistan v West Indies	1980-81
Multan[2]	675-5d	India v Pakistan	2003-04	134	Bangladesh v Pakistan	2001-02
Peshawar[1]	245	India v Pakistan	1954-55	182	Pakistan v India	1954-55
Peshawar[2]	599-4d	Australia v Pakistan	1998-99	96	Bangladesh v Pakistan	2003-04
Rawalpindi[1]	318	Pakistan v New Zealand	1964-65	79	New Zealand v Pakistan	1964-65
Rawalpindi[2]	600	India v Pakistan	2003-04	139	West Indies v Pakistan	1997-98
Sheikhupura	553	Pakistan v Zimbabwe	1996-97	375	Zimbabwe v Pakistan	1996-97
Sialkot	423-5d	Pakistan v Sri Lanka	1991-92	157	Sri Lanka v Pakistan	1985-86

SRI LANKA

Centre		**Highest Total**			**Lowest Total**	
Colombo (CCC)	459	New Zealand v Sri Lanka	1983-84	132	Pakistan v Sri Lanka	1985-86
Colombo (PSS)	541-9d	Sri Lanka v Bangladesh	2002-03	127	Australia v Pakistan	2002-03
Colombo (RPS)	952-6d	Sri Lanka v India	1996-97	86	Bangladesh v Sri Lanka	2005-06
Colombo (SSC)	756-5d	Sri Lanka v South Africa	2006-07	81	Sri Lanka v England	2000-01
Galle	600-8d	Pakistan v Sri Lanka	2000-01	79	Zimbabwe v Sri Lanka	2001-02
Kandy	514-4d	Australia v Sri Lanka	1982-83	71	Sri Lanka v Pakistan	1994-95
Moratuwa	337	Australia v Sri Lanka	1992-93	190	Sri Lanka v West Indies	1993-94

ZIMBABWE

Centre		**Highest Total**			**Lowest Total**	
Bulawayo[1]	325-3d	New Zealand v Zimbabwe	1992-93	219	Zimbabwe v New Zealand	1992-93
Bulawayo2	713-3d	Sri Lanka v Zimbabwe	2003-04	104	Zimbabwe v West Indies	2003-04
Harare	600-3d	South Africa v Zimbabwe	2001-02	59	Zimbabwe v New Zealand	2005-06

BANGLADESH

Centre		**Highest Total**			**Lowest Total**	
Bogra	316	Sri Lanka v Bangladesh	2005-06	201	Bangladesh v Sri Lanka	2005-06
Chittagong[1]	545-6d	New Zealand v Bangladesh	2004-05	124	Bangladesh v India	2004-05
Chittagong[2]	581-4d	Australia v Bangladesh	2005-06	181	Bangladesh v Sri Lanka	2005-06
Dhaka	594	Pakistan v Sri Lanka	1998-99	87	Bangladesh v West Indies	2002-03
Fattullah	427	Bangladesh v Australia	2005-06	148	Bangladesh v Australia	2005-06

UNITED ARAB EMIRATES

Centre		**Highest Total**			**Lowest Total**	
Sharjah	493	Pakistan v West Indies	2001-02	53	Pakistan v Australia	2002-03

HIGHEST INDIVIDUAL SCORE FOR EACH TEST MATCH GROUND

AUSTRALIA

Ground	Score	Batsman	Match	Season
Adelaide	299*	D.G.Bradman	Australia v South Africa	1931-32
Brisbane[1]	223	D.G.Bradman	Australia v West Indies	1930-31
Brisbane[2]	226	D.G.Bradman	Australia v South Africa	1931-32
Cairns	177	D.S.Lehmann	Australia v Bangladesh	2003-04
Darwin	110	D.S.Lehmann	Australia v Bangladesh	2003-04
Hobart	168	M.J.Slater	Australia v New Zealand	1993-94
Melbourne	307	R.M.Cowper	Australia v England	1965-66
Perth	380	M.L.Hayden	Australia v Zimbabwe	2003-04
Sydney	287	R.E.Foster	England v Australia	1903-04

ENGLAND

Ground	Score	Batsman	Match	Season
Birmingham	285*	P.B.H.May	England v West Indies	1957
Chester-le-Street	162*	M.E.Trescothick	England v Bangladesh	2005
Leeds	334	D.G.Bradman	Australia v England	1930
Lord's	333	G.A.Gooch	England v India	1990
Manchester	311	R.B.Simpson	Australia v England	1964
Nottingham	278	D.C.S.Compton	England v Pakistan	1954
Sheffield	119	C.Hill	Australia v England	1902
The Oval	364	L.Hutton	England v Australia	1938

SOUTH AFRICA

Ground	Score	Batsman	Match	Season
Bloemfontein	160	J.H.Kallis	South Africa v New Zealand	2000-01
Cape Town	262	S.P.Fleming	New Zealand v South Africa	2005-06
Centurion	192	H.H.Gibbs	South Africa v West Indies	2003-04
Durban[1]	119	J.W.H.T.Douglas	England v South Africa	1913-14
Durban[2]	275	G.Kirsten	South Africa v England	1999-2000
East London	200	G.C.Smith	South Africa v Bangladesh	2002-03
Johannesburg[1]	231	A.D.Nourse	South Africa v Australia	1935-36
Johannesburg[2]	195	C.Washbrook	England v South Africa	1948-49
Johannesburg[3]	214	G.S.Blewett	Australia v South Africa	1996-97
Port Elizabeth	196	H.H.Gibbs	South Africa v India	2001-02
Potchefstroom	160	G.Kirsten	South Africa v Bangladesh	2002-03

WEST INDIES

Ground	Score	Batsman	Match	Season
Basseterre	135	D.Ganga	West Indies v India	2005-06
Bridgetown	337	Hanif Mohammad	Pakistan v West Indies	1957-58
Georgetown	259	G.M.Turner	New Zealand v West Indies	1971-72
Gros Islet	209	B.C.Lara	West Indies v Sri Lanka	2002-03
Kingston	365*	G.S.Sobers	West Indies v Pakistan	1957-58
Kingstown	115	B.C.Lara	West Indies v Sri Lanka	1996-97
Port-of-Spain	220	S.M.Gavaskar	India v West Indies	1970-71
St George's	204	C.H.Gayle	West Indies v New Zealand	2002-03
St John's	400*	B.C.Lara	West Indies v England	2003-04

NEW ZEALAND

Ground	Score	Batsman	Match	Season
Auckland	336*	W.R.Hammond	England v New Zealand	1932-33
Christchurch	258	S.M.Nurse	West Indies v New Zealand	1968-69
Dunedin	267*	B.A.Young	New Zealand v Sri Lanka	1996-97
Hamilton	192	S.P.Fleming	New Zealand v Pakistan	2003-04
Napier	160	H.J.H.Marshall	New Zealand v Sri Lanka	2004-05
Wellington	299	M.D.Crowe	New Zealand v Sri Lanka	1990-91

Ground	Score	Batsman	Match	Season
INDIA				
Ahmedabad	222	R.S.Dravid	India v New Zealand	2003-04
Bangalore	267	Younis Khan	Pakistan v India	2004-05
Chandigarh	88	R.J.Shastri	India v Sri Lanka	1990-91
Chennai[1]	236*	S.M.Gavaskar	India v West Indies	1983-84
Madras[2]	231	M.H.Mankad	India v New Zealand	1955-56
Cuttack	166	D.B.Vengsarkar	India v Sri Lanka	1986-87
Delhi	230*	B.Sutcliffe	New Zealand v India	1955-56
Hyderabad	223	P.R.Umrigar	India v New Zealand	1955-56
Jaipur	125	R.J.Shastri	India v Pakistan	1986-87
Jullundur	201	A.D.Gaekwad	India v Pakistan	1983-84
Kanpur	250	S.F.A.F.Bacchus	West Indies v India	1978-79
Kolkata	281	V.V.S.Laxman	India v Australia	2000-01
Lucknow[1]	124*	Nazar Mohammad	Pakistan v India	1952-53
Lucknow[2]	142	S.R.Tendulkar	India v Sri Lanka	1993-94
Mohali	174*	J.C.Adams	West Indies v India	1994-95
Bombay[1]	136	B.H.Valentine	England v India	1933-34
Bombay[2]	223	M.H.Mankad	India v New Zealand	1955-56
Mumbai[3]	242*	C.H.Lloyd	West Indies v India	1974-75
Nagpur	232*	A.Flower	Zimbabwe v India	2000-01
PAKISTAN				
Bahawalpur	142	Hanif Mohammad	Pakistan v India	1954-55
Dacca	165	G.Pullar	England v Pakistan	1961-62
Faisalabad	253	S.T.Jayasuriya	Sri Lanka v Pakistan	2004-05
Gujranwala	51*	Rameez Raja	Pakistan v Sri Lanka	1991-92
Hyderabad	280*	Javed Miandad	Pakistan v India	1982-83
Karachi[1]	211	Javed Miandad	Pakistan v Australia	1988-89
Karachi[2]	81	Shoaib Mohammad	Pakistan v Zimbabwe	1993-94
Lahore[1]	217	R.B.Kanhai	Pakistan v India	1958-59
Lahore[2]	329	Inzamamul Haq	Pakistan v New Zealand	2001-02
Multan[1]	120*	I.V.A.Richards	West Indies v Pakistan	1980-81
Multan[2]	309	V.K.Sehwag	India v Pakistan	2003-04
Peshawar[1]	108	P.R.Umrigar	India v Pakistan	1954-55
Peshawar[2]	334*	M.A.Taylor	Australia v Pakistan	1998-99
Rawalpindi[1]	76	B.R.Taylor	New Zealand v Pakistan	1964-65
Rawalpindi[2]	270	R.S.Dravid	India v Pakistan	2003-04
Sheikhupura	257*	Wasim Akram	Pakistan v New Zealand	1996-97
Sialkot	117*	Moin Khan	Pakistan v Sri Lanka	1995-96
SRI LANKA				
Colombo (CCC)	201*	D.S.B.P.Kuruppu	Sri Lanka v New Zealand	1986-87
Colombo (PSS)	274*	S.P.Fleming	New Zealand v Sri Lanka	2002-03
Colombo (RPS)	340	S.T.Jayasuriya	Sri Lanka v India	1996-97
Colombo (SSC)	374	D.P.M.D.Jayawardene	Sri Lanka v South Africa	2006-07
Galle	237	D.P.M.D.Jayawardene	Sri Lanka v South Africa	2004-05
Kandy	223	M.S.Atapattu	Sri Lanka v Zimbabwe	1997-98
Moratuwa	153	R.S.Mahanama	Sri Lanka v New Zealand	1992-93
ZIMBABWE				
Bulawayo[1]	119	R.T.Latham	New Zealand v Zimbabwe	1992-93
Bulawayo[2]	270	K.C.Sangakkara	Sri Lanka v Zimbabwe	2003-04
Harare	220	G.Kirsten	South Africa v Zimbabwe	2001-02
BANGLADESH				
Bogra	165	W.U.Tharanga	Sri Lanka v Bangladesh	2005-06

Chittagong[1]	222*	J.A.Rudolph	South Africa v Bangladesh	2002-03
Chittagong[2]	201*	J.N.Gillespie	Australia v Bangladesh	2005-06
Dhaka	248*	S.R.Tendulkar	India v Bangladesh	2004-05
Fattullah	144	A.C.Gilchrist	Australia v Bangladesh	2005-06

UNITED ARAB EMIRATES

Sharjah	153	Younis Khan	Pakistan v West Indies	2001-02

MOST RUNS SCORED ON EACH TEST GROUND

Note: all instances of 1000 runs on a ground are shown

AUSTRALIA

Ground	Player	Country	M	I	NO	Runs	HS	Avge	100's	50's	0's
Adelaide	A.R.Border	Aust	16	29	5	1415	205	58.95	4	9	1
	S.R.Waugh	Aust	15	26	2	1056	170	44.00	3	4	1
	J.L.Langer	Aust	10	18	1	1040	215	61.17	3	4	0
Brisbane[1]	D.G.Bradman	Aust	2	3	0	242	223	80.66	1	0	0
Brisbane[2]	G.S.Chappell	Aust	7	11	2	1006	201	111.77	5	4	0
Cairns	M.L.Hayden	Aust	2	3	0	299	132	99.66	2	1	0
Darwin	D.S.Lehmann	Aust	2	3	0	218	110	72.66	1	2	0
Hobart	M.A.Taylor	Aust	4	7	1	405	123	67.50	2	1	0
Melbourne	D.G.Bradman	Aust	11	17	4	1671	270	128.53	9	3	1
	S.R.Waugh	Aust	17	30	6	1284	131*	53.50	3	6	0
	A.R.Border	Aust	20	36	3	1272	163	38.54	4	5	3
	G.S.Chappell	Aust	17	31	4	1257	121	46.55	4	9	4
	J.B.Hobbs	Eng	10	18	1	1178	178	69.29	5	4	1
	W.M.Lawry	Aust	8	13	0	1023	205	78.69	4	5	0
Perth	A.R.Border	Aus	16	26	3	931	125	40.48	2	6	2
Sydney	A.R.Border	Aust	17	29	8	1177	89	56.04	0	11	0
	G.S.Chappell	Aust	12	22	4	1150	204	63.88	4	3	2
	D.C.Boon	Aust	11	21	3	1127	184*	62.61	4	4	1
	S.R.Waugh	Aust	17	25	1	1084	103	45.16	3	7	3
	R.T.Ponting	Aust	10	17	5	1081	207	90.08	5	3	0

ENGLAND

Ground	Player	Country	M	I	NO	Runs	HS	Avge	100's	50's	0's
Birmingham	D.I.Gower	Eng	9	14	1	767	215	59.00	2	3	1
Chester-le-Street	M.E.Trescothick	Eng	2	2	0	194	151	97.00	1	0	0
Leeds	D.G.Bradman	Aust	4	6	1	963	334	192.60	4	0	0
Lord's	G.A.Gooch	Eng	21	39	1	2015	333	53.02	6	5	2
	A.J.Stewart	Eng	20	37	4	1476	124*	44.72	3	8	2
	D.I.Gower	Eng	17	30	2	1241	108	44.32	2	8	1
	G.Boycott	Eng	16	29	3	1189	128*	45.73	3	6	1
Manchester	D.C.S.Compton	Eng	8	13	3	818	158	81.80	3	4	1
Nottingham	M.A.Atherton	Eng	11	19	1	1083	160	60.16	5	3	2
Sheffield	C.Hill	Aust	1	2	0	137	119	68.50	1	0	0
The Oval	L.Hutton	Eng	12	19	2	1521	364	89.47	4	5	0
	G.A.Gooch	Eng	12	22	1	1097	196	52.23	1	9	3

SOUTH AFRICA

Ground	Player	Country	M	I	NO	Runs	HS	Avge	100's	50's	0's
Bloemfontein	J.H.Kallis	SA	3	5	1	326	160	81.50	1	2	0
Cape Town	J.H.Kallis	SA	12	18	2	1123	149	70.18	4	6	0
Centurion	J.H.Kallis	SA	10	15	3	678	136*	56.50	2	4	0
Durban[1]	J.B.Hobbs	Eng	3	5	0	366	97	73.20	0	5	0
Durban[2]	G.Kirsten	SA	11	18	2	1048	275	65.50	3	4	1
East London	G.C.Smith	SA	1	1	0	200	200	200.00	1	0	0
Johannesburg[1]	A.W.Nourse	SA	12	22	3	850	111	44.73	1	9	0

Johannesburg[2]	E.A.B.Rowan	SA	4	7	2	403	156*	80.60	1	3	0
Johannesburg[3]	W.J.Cronje	SA	9	17	0	683	122	40.17	1	2	0
Port Elizabeth	J.H.Kallis	SA	7	14	2	409	89*	34.08	0	4	2
Potchefstrom	G.Kirsten	SA	1	1	0	161	160	160.00	1	0	0
WEST INDIES											
Basseterre	D.Ganga	WI	1	2	1	201	135	201.00	1	1	0
Bridgetown	B.C.Lara	WI	15	27	2	1339	176	53.56	3	7	0
	D.L.Haynes	WI	13	25	5	1210	145	60.50	4	6	1
Georgetown	G.S.Sobers	WI	7	12	3	853	152	94.77	5	1	0
Gros Islet	B.C.Lara	WI	3	4	0	389	209	97.25	2	1	0
Kingston	G.S.Sobers	WI	11	18	5	1354	365*	104.15	5	4	1
	B.C.Lara	WI	12	20	1	1112	213	58.52	3	6	3
Kingstown	B.C.Lara	WI	1	2	0	116	115	58.00	1	0	0
Port-of-Spain	R.B.Kanhai	WI	16	31	3	1212	153	43.28	4	4	1
	E.D.Weekes	WI	7	13	2	1074	207	97.63	4	4	0
	C.H.Lloyd	WI	16	28	2	1035	143	39.80	2	7	1
	I.V.A.Richards	WI	14	21	0	1015	177	48.33	3	4	1
St George's	C.H.Gayle	WI	1	1	0	204	204	204.00	1	0	0
St John's	B.C.Lara	WI	14	22	1	1650	400*	78.57	4	6	2
NEW ZEALAND											
Auckland	J.G.Wright	NZ	15	29	2	1060	130	39.25	3	5	1
Christchurch	J.G.Wright	NZ	13	21	1	687	185	34.35	2	1	1
Dunedin	B.A.Young	NZ	2	3	2	351	267*	351.00	1	1	0
Hamilton	S.P.Fleming	NZ	11	19	1	682	192	37.88	1	4	2
Napier	J.G.Wright	NZ	2	2	1	201	113*	201.00	1	1	0
Wellington	M.D.Crowe	NZ	10	17	1	1123	299	70.18	5	1	1
	J.G.Wright	NZ	13	23	2	1005	138	47.85	3	4	1
INDIA											
Ahmedabad	S.R.Tendulkar	Ind	6	11	0	473	217	43.00	2	0	0
Bangalore	S.M.Gavaskar	Ind	8	12	1	600	172	54.54	2	3	2
Chandigarh	R.J.Shastri	Ind	1	1	0	88	88	88.00	0	1	0
Chennai[1]	S.M.Gavaskar	Ind	12	21	4	1018	236*	59.88	3	3	1
Madras[2]	V.L.Manjrekar	Ind	7	12	2	487	108	48.70	2	1	1
Cuttack	D.B.Vengsarkar	Ind	1	1	0	166	166	166.00	1	0	0
Delhi	D.B.Vengsarkar	Ind	8	12	2	671	159	67.10	4	1	0
Hyderabad	P.R.Umrigar	Ind	1	1	0	223	223	223.00	1	0	0
Jaipur	R.J.Shastri	Ind	1	1	0	125	125	125.00	1	0	0
Jullundur	A.D.Gaekwad	Ind	1	1	0	201	201	201.00	1	0	0
Kanpur	G.R.Viswanath	Ind	7	12	3	776	179	86.22	3	4	1
Kolkata	M.Azharuddin	Ind	7	9	1	860	182	107.50	5	2	0
Lucknow[1]	Nazar Mohammad	Pak	1	1	1	124	124*	-	1	0	0
Lucknow[2]	S.R.Tendulkar	Ind	1	1	0	142	142	142.00	1	0	0
Mohali	S.R.Tendulkar	Ind	6	9	1	455	126*	56.87	1	3	0
Bombay[1]	N.B.Amarnath	Ind	1	2	0	156	118	78.00	1	0	0
Bombay[2]	V.S.Hazare	Ind	4	7	2	629	155	125.80	4	0	0
Mumbai[3]	S.M.Gavaskar	Ind	11	20	0	1122	205	56.10	5	3	0
Nagpur	S.R.Tendulkar	Ind	7	10	2	683	201*	85.37	3	1	0
PAKISTAN											
Bahawalpur	Hanif Mohammad	Pak	1	1	0	142	142	142.00	1	0	0
Dacca	Hanif Mohammad	Pak	5	9	0	474	111	52.66	3	1	0
Faisalabad	Javed Miandad	Pak	15	23	4	1068	203*	56.21	5	2	0
Gujranwala	Rameez Raja	Pak	1	1	1	51	51*	-	0	1	0

Hyderabad	Javed Miandad	Pak	4	6	4	661	280*	330.50	3	2	0
Karachi[1]	Javed Miandad	Pak	17	25	1	1393	211	58.04	3	8	0
Karachi[2]	Aamer Sohail	Pak	1	2	0	92	63	46.00	0	1	0
Lahore[1]	Imtiaz Ahmed	Pak	3	6	0	314	209	52.33	1	1	1
Lahore[2]	Javed Miandad	Pak	17	23	3	1122	163	56.10	3	3	0
	Zaheer Abbas	Pak	10	15	4	1093	235*	99.36	4	2	0
Multan[1]	I.V.A.Richards	WI	1	2	1	132	120*	132.00	1	0	0
Multan[2]	Inzamamul Haq	Pak	4	7	2	455	138*	91.00	2	3	1
Peshawar[1]	P.R.Umrigar	Ind	1	2	1	111	108	111.00	1	0	0
Peshawar[2]	M.A.Taylor	Aust	1	2	1	426	334*	426.00	1	1	0
Rawalpindi[1]	B.R.Taylor	NZ	1	2	1	83	76	83.00	0	1	0
Rawalpindi[2]	Saeed Anwar	Pak	6	10	0	546	149	54.60	2	2	0
Sheikhupura	Wasim Akram	Pak	2	1	1	257	257*	-	1	0	0
Sialkot	Rameez Raja	Pak	3	4	0	184	98	46.00	0	2	0
SRI LANKA											
Colombo (CCC)	D.S.B.P.Kuruppu	SL	1	1	1	201	201*	-	1	0	0
Colombo (PSS)	P.A.de Silva	SL	6	10	0	688	206	68.80	3	2	0
Colombo (RPS)	S.T.Jayasuriya	SL	6	9	1	568	340	71.00	1	2	1
Colombo (SSC)	D.P.M.D.Jayawardene	SL	17	26	2	1740	374	72.50	6	4	0
	S.T.Jayasuriya	SL	22	37	3	1542	199	45.35	2	10	1
	P.A.de Silva	SL	16	28	4	1257	146	52.37	5	2	0
	H.P.Tillakaratne	SL	16	24	9	1106	204*	73.73	3	4	1
Galle	D.P.M.D.Jayawardene	SL	11	16	2	1176	237	84.00	3	6	0
Kandy	M.S.Atapattu	SL	12	21	3	850	223	47.22	3	1	3
Moratuwa	R.S.Mahanama	SL	4	6	0	295	153	49.16	1	2	0
ZIMBABWE											
Bulawayo[1]	M.J.Greatbatch	NZ	1	2	0	175	88	87.50	0	2	0
Bulawayo[2]	A.Flower	Zim	11	20	3	871	112	51.23	2	6	0
Harare	A.Flower	Zim	20	35	5	1535	199*	51.16	4	6	1
	G.W.Flower	Zim	21	37	1	1218	201*	33.83	3	5	3
BANGLADESH											
Bogra	W.U.Tharanga	SL	1	2	1	236	165	236.00	1	1	0
Chittagong[1]	Habibul Bashar	Ban	7	14	0	602	108	43.00	1	6	1
Chittagong[2]	J.N.Gillespie	Aus	1	1	1	201	201*	-	1	0	0
Dhaka	Habibul Bashar	Ban	8	16	0	404	71	25.25	0	4	2
Fattullah	Shahriar Nafees	Ban	1	2	0	171	138	85.50	1	0	0
SHARJAH											
Sharjah	Younis Khan	Pak	4	8	0	323	153	40.37	1	2	1

HIGHEST WICKET PARTNERSHIPS FOR EACH TEST GROUND

	Runs	Wkt			
AUSTRALIA					
Adelaide	341	3rd	E.J.Barlow, R.G.Pollock	South Africa v Australia	1963-64
Brisbane[1]	229	2nd	W.H.Ponsford, D.G.Bradman	Australia v West Indies	1930-31
Brisbane[2]	276	3rd	D.G.Bradman, A.L.Hassett	Australia v England	1946-47
Cairns	255	1st	J.L.Langer, M.L.Hayden	Australia v Sri Lanka	2004-05
Darwin	141	3rd	J.L.Langer, D.S.Lehmann	Australia v Bangladesh	2003-04
Hobart	260*	6th	D.M.Jones, S.R.Waugh	Australia v Sri Lanka	1989-90
Melbourne	346	6th	J.H.W.Fingleton, D.G.Bradman	Australia v England	1936-37
Perth	327	5th	J.L.Langer, R.T.Ponting	Australia v Pakistan	1999-2000
Sydney	405	5th	S.G.Barnes, D.G.Bradman	Australia v England	1946-47

ENGLAND					
Birmingham	411	4th	P.B.H.May, M.C.Cowdrey	England v West Indies	1957
Chester-le-Street	187*	4th	I.R.Bell, G.P.Thorpe	England v Bangladesh	2005
Leeds	388	4th	W.H.Ponsford, D.G.Bradman	Australia v England	1934
Lord's	370	3rd	W.J.Edrich, D.C.S.Compton	England v South Africa	1947
Manchester	267	3rd	M.P.Vaughan, G.P.Thorpe	England v Pakistan	2001
Nottingham	329	1st	G.R.Marsh, M.A.Taylor	Australia v England	1989
Sheffield	107	4th	C.Hill, S.E.Gregory	Australia v England	1902
The Oval	451	2nd	W.H.Ponsford, D.G.Bradman	Australia v England	1934
SOUTH AFRICA					
Bloemfontein	220	5th	S.R.Tendulkar, V.K.Sehwag	India v South Africa	2001-02
Cape Town	368	1st	G.C.Smith, H.H.Gibbs	South Africa v Pakistan	2002-03
Centurion	301	1st	G.C.Smith, H.H.Gibbs	South Africa v West Indies	2003-04
Durban[1]	143	4th	G.C.White, A.W.Nourse	South Africa v England	1909-10
Durban[2]	280	2nd	P.A.Gibb, W.J.Edrich	England v South Africa	1938-39
East London	272	2nd	G.C.Smith, G.Kirsten	South Africa v Bangladesh	2002-03
Johannesburg[1]	230	2nd	H.Sutcliffe, G.E.Tyldesley	England v South Africa	1927-28
Johannesburg[2]	359	1st	L.Hutton, C.Washbrook	England v South Africa	1948-49
Johannesburg[3]	385	5th	S.R.Waugh, G.S.Blewett	Australia v South Africa	1996-97
Port Elizabeth	187	3rd	A.R.Morris, R.N.Harvey	Australia v South Africa	1949-50
Potchefstroom	234	3rd	G.Kirsten, J.H.Kallis	South Africa v Bangladesh	2002-03
WEST INDIES					
Basseterre	203	2nd	D.Ganga, R.R.Sarwan	West Indies v India	2005-06
Bridgetown	399	4th	G.S.Sobers.F.M.M.Worrell	West Indies v England	1959-60
Georgetown	387	1st	G.M.Turner, T.W.Jarvis	New Zealand v West Indies	1971-72
Gros Islet	179	5th	R.S.Dravid, Mohammad Kaif	India v West Indies	2005-06
Kingston	446	2nd	C.C.Hunte, G.S.Sobers	West Indies v Pakistan	1957-58
Kingstown	97	4th	B.C.Lara, C.L.Hooper	West Indies v Sri Lanka	1996-97
Port-of-Spain	338	3rd	E.D.Weekes, F.M.M.Worrell	West Indies v England	1953-54
St George's	143	5th	C.H.Gayle, S.Chanderpaul	West Indies v New Zealand	2002-03
St John's	314	2nd	C.H.Gayle, R.R.Sarwan	West Indies v South Africa	2004-05
NEW ZEALAND					
Auckland	266	4th	M.H.Denness, K.W.R.Fletcher	England v New Zealand	1974-75
Christchurch	315*	2nd	H.H.Gibbs, W.J.Edrich	South Africa v New Zealand	1998-99
Dunedin	350	4th	Mushtaq Mohammad, Asif Iqbal	Pakistan v New Zealand	1972-73
Hamilton	276	1st	A.F.G.Griffith, S.L.Campbell	West Indies v New Zealand	1999-2000
Napier	195	2nd	J.G.Wright, G.P.Howarth	New Zealand v Pakistan	1978-79
Wellington	467	3rd	M.D.Crowe, A.H.Jones	New Zealand v Sri Lanka	1990-91
INDIA					
Ahmedabad	281	4th	S.R.Tendulkar, S.C.Ganguly	India v New Zealand	1999-2000
Bangalore	324	3rd	Younis Khan, Inzamamul Haq	Pakistan v India	2004-05
Chandigarh	76	2nd	R.J.Shastri, S.V.Manjrekar	India v Sri Lanka	1990-91
Chennai[1]	316	3rd	G.R.Viswanath, Yashpal Sharma	India v England	1981-82
Madras[2]	413	1st	M.H.Mankad, P.Roy	India v New Zealand	1955-56
Cuttack	111	6th	D.B.Vengsarkar, Kapil Dev	India v Sri Lanka	1986-87
Delhi	267	4th	C.L.Walcott, G.E.Gomez	West Indies v India	1948-49
Hyderabad	238	3rd	P.R.Umrigar, V.L.Manjrekar	India v New Zealand	1955-56
Jaipur	130	5th	M.Azharuddin, R.J.Shastri	India v Pakistan	1986-87
Jullundur	121	6th	A.D.Gaekwad, R.M.H.Binny	India v Pakistan	1983-84
Kanpur	272	6th	M.Azharuddin, Kapil Dev	India v Sri Lanka	1986-87
Kolkata	376	5th	V.V.S.Laxman, R.S.Dravid	India v Australia	2000-01
Lucknow[1]	63	1st	Nazar Mohammad, Hanif Mohammad	Pakistan v India	1952-53
	63	8th	Nazar Mohammad, Zulfiqar Ahmed	Pakistan v India	1952-53

Lucknow[2]	142	4th	S.R.Tendulkar, M.Azharuddin	India v Sri Lanka	1993-94
Mohali	231	1st	M.H.Richardson, L.Vincent	New Zealand v India	2003-04
Bombay[1]	186	3rd	N.B.Amarnath, C.K.Nayudu	India v England	1933-34
Bombay[2]	254	5th	K.W.R.Fletcher, A.W.Greig	England v India	1972-73
Mumbai[3]	298*	6th	D.B.Vengsarkar, R.J.Shastri	India v Australia	1986-87
Nagpur	249	3rd	R.S.Dravid, S.R.Tendulkar	India v Zimbabwe	2001-02

PAKISTAN

Bahawalpur	127	1st	Hanif Mohammad, Alimuddin	Pakistan v India	1954-55
Dacca	198	1st	G.Pullar, R.W.Barber	England v Pakistan	1961-62
Faisalabad	397	3rd	Qasim Omar, Javed Miandad	Pakistan v Sri Lanka	1985-86
Gujranwala	56	2nd	Rameez Raja, Zahid Fazal	Pakistan v Sri Lanka	1991-92
Hyderabad	451	3rd	Mudassar Nazar, Javed Miandad	Pakistan v India	1982-83
Karachi[1]	298	1st	Saeed Anwar, Ijaz Ahmed	Pakistan v West Indies	1997-98
Karachi[2]	95	1st	Aamer Sohail, Shoaib Mohammad	Pakistan v Zimbabwe	1993-94
Lahore[1]	308	7th	Waqar Hassan, Imtiaz Ahmed	Pakistan v New Zealand	1955-56
Lahore[2]	410	1st	V.K.Sehwag, R.S.Dravid	India v Pakistan	2005-06
Multan[1]	100	3rd	Majid Khan, Javed Miandad	Pakistan v West Indies	1980-81
Multan[2]	336	3rd	V.K.Sehwag, S.R.Tendulkar	India v Pakistan	2003-04
Peshawar[1]	91	3rd	P.R.Umrigar, V.L.Manjrekar	India v Pakistan	1954-55
Peshawar[2]	279	2nd	M.A.Taylor, J.L.Langer	Australia v Pakistan	1998-99
Rawalpindi[1]	114	2nd	Mohammad Ilyas, Saeed Ahmed	Pakistan v New Zealand	1964-65
Rawalpindi[2]	323	3rd	Aamer Sohail, Ijaz Ahmed	Pakistan v West Indies	1997-98
Sheikhupura	313	8th	Wasim Akram, Saqlain Mushtaq	Pakistan v Sri Lanka	1996-97
Sialkot	132	5th	Saleem Malik, Imran Khan	Pakistan v Sri Lanka	1991-92

SRI LANKA

Colombo (CCC)	246*	6th	J.J.Crowe, R.J.Hadlee	New Zealand v Sri Lanka	1986-87
Colombo (PSS)	280	5th	T.T.Samaraweera, T.M.Dilshan	Sri Lanka v Bangladesh	2005-06
Colombo (RPS)	576	2nd	S.T.Jayasuriya, R.S.Mahanama	Sri Lanka v India	1996-97
Colombo (SSC)	624	3rd	K.C.Sangakarra, D.P.M.D.Jayawardene	Sri Lanka v South Africa	2006-07
Galle	230	3rd	M.S.Atapattu, P.A.de Silva	Sri Lanka v England	2000-01
Kandy	335	1st	M.S.Atapattu, S.T.Jayasuriya	Sri Lanka v Pakistan	2000-01
Moratuwa	151	5th	K.R.Rutherford, C.Z.Harris	New Zealand v Sri Lanka	1992-93

ZIMBABWE

Bulawayo[1]	127	2nd	R.T.Latham, A.H.Jones	New Zealand v Zimbabwe	1992-93
Bulawayo[2]	438	2nd	M.S.Atapattu, K.C.Sangakkara	Sri Lanka v Zimbabwe	2003-04
Harare	281	1st	M.S.Atapattu, S.T.Jayasuriya	Sri Lanka v Zimbabwe	2004-05

BANGLADESH

Bogra	124	5th	W.U.Tharanga, D.P.M.D.Jayawardene	Sri Lanka v Bangladesh	2005-06
Chittagong[1]	429*	3rd	J.A.Rudolph, H.H.Dippenaar	South Africa v Bangladesh	2002-03
Chittagong[2]	320	4th	J.N.Gillespie, M.E.K.Hussey	Australia v Bangladesh	2005-06
Dhaka	352*	3rd	Ijaz Ahmed, Inzamamul Haq	Pakistan v Sri Lanka	1998-99
Fattullah	187	2nd	Shahriar Nafees, Habibul Bashar	Bangladesh v Australia	2005-06

UNITED ARAB EMIRATES

Sharjah	204	6th	Yousuf Youhana, Rashid Latif	Pakistan v West Indies	2001-02

BEST INNINGS BOWLING ANALYSIS FOR EACH TEST GROUND

AUSTRALIA

Adelaide	8/43	A.E.Trott	Australia v England	1894-95
Brisbane[1]	6/32	H.Larwood	England v Australia	1928-29
Brisbane[2]	9/52	R.J.Hadlee	New Zealand v Australia	1985-86
Cairns	5/56	S.C.G.MacGill	Australia v Bangladesh	2003-04
Darwin	7/39	M.S.Kasprowicz	Australia v Sri Lanka	2004-05
Hobart	6/31	S.K.Warne	Australia v New Zealand	1993-94
Melbourne	9/86	Sarfraz Nawaz	Pakistan v Australia	1978-79
Perth	8/24	G.D.McGrath	Australia v Pakistan	2004-05
Sydney	8/35	G.A.Lohmann	England v Australia	1886-87

ENGLAND

Birmingham	7/17	W.Rhodes	England v Australia	1902
Chester-le-Street	6/33	R.L.Johnson	England v Zimbawe	2003
Leeds	8/43	R.G.D.Willis	England v Australia	1981
Lord's	8/34	I.T.Botham	England v Pakistan	1978
Manchester	10/53	J.C.Laker	England v Australia	1956
Nottingham	8/70	M.Muralidaran	Sri Lanka v England	2006
Sheffield	6/49	S.F.Barnes	England v Australia	1902
The Oval	9/57	D.E.Malcolm	England v South Africa	1994

SOUTH AFRICA

Bloemfontein	6/56	S.M.Pollock	South Africa v India	2001-02
Cape Town	8/11	J.Briggs	England v South Africa	1888-89
Centurion	6/39	M.Zondeki	South Africa v Zimbabwe	2004-05
Durban[1]	7/56	S.F.Barnes	England v South Africa	1913-14
Durban[2]	8/69	H.J Tayfield	South Africa v England	1956-57
East London	5/19	M.Ntini	South Africa v Bangladesh	2002-03
Johannesburg[1]	9/28	G.A.Lohmann	England v South Africa	1895-96
Johannesburg[2]	6/13	H.J.Tayfield	South Africa v New Zealand	1953-54
Johannesburg[3]	9/113	H.J.Tayfield	South Africa v England	1956-57
Port Elizabeth	8/7	G.A.Lohmann	England v South Africa	1895-96
Potchefstroom	5/21	J.J.Kallis	South Africa v Bangladesh	2002-03

WEST INDIES

Basseterre	5/147	Harbhajan Singh	India v West Indies	2005-06
Bridgetown	8/38	L.R.Gibbs	West Indies v India	1961-62
Georgetown	7/44	I.W.Johnson	Australia v West Indies	1954-55
Gros Islet	5/66	C.D.Collymore	West Indies v Sri Lanka	2002-03
Kingston	7/12	S.J.Harmison	England v West Indies	2003-04
Kingstown	5/26	C.L.Hooper	West Indies v Sri Lanka	1996-97
Port-of-Spain	9/95	J.M.Noreiga	West Indies v India	1970-71
St George's	5/104	S.E.Bond	New Zealand v West Indies	2002-03
St John's	7/78	J.J.C.Lawson	West Indies v Australia	1994-95

NEW ZEALAND

Auckland	8/76	E.A.S.Prasanna	India v New Zealand	1975-76
Christchurch	7/47	P.C.R.Tufnell	England v New Zealand	1991-92
Dunedin	7/52	Intikhab Alam	Pakistan v New Zealand	1972-73
Hamilton	7/27	C.L.Cairns	New Zealand v West Indies	1999-2000
Napier	5/43	W.P.U.J.C.Vaas	Sri Lanka v New Zealand	1994-95
Wellington	7/23	R.J.Hadlee	New Zealand v India	1975-76

INDIA

Ahmedabad	9/83	Kapil Dev	India v West Indies	1983-84

Bangalore	7/27	Maninder Singh	India v Pakistan	1986-87
Chandigarh	6/12	S.L.Venkatapathy Raju	India v Sri Lanka	1990-91
Chennai[1]	8/55	M.H.Mankad	India v England	1951-52
Madras[2]	7/43	R.R.Lindwall	Australia v India	1956-57
Cuttack	6/59	N.D.Hirwani	India v New Zealand	1995-96
Delhi	10/74	A.Kumble	India v Pakistan	1998-99
Hyderabad	7/128	S.P.Gupte	India v New Zealand	1955-56
Jaipur	4/88	G.Sharma	India v Pakistan	1986-87
Jullundur	4/50	Wasim Raja	Pakistan v India	1983-84
Kanpur	9/69	J.M.Patel	India v Australia	1959-60
Kolkata	8/64	L.Klusener	South Africa v India	1996-97
Lucknow[1]	7/42	Fazal Mahmood	Pakistan v India	1952-53
Lucknow[2]	7/59	A.Kumble	India v Sri Lanka	1993-94
Mohali	6/27	D.J.Nash	New Zealand v India	1999-2000
Bombay[1]	5/55	M.S.Nichols	England v India	1933-34
Bombay[2]	7/157	B.S.Chandrasekhar	India v West Indies	1966-67
Mumbai[3]	7/48	I.T.Botham	England v India	1979-80
	7/48	Harbhajan Singh	India v West Indies	2002-03
Nagpur	7/51	Maninder Singh	India v Sri Lanka	1986-87
PAKISTAN				
Bahawalpur	6/74	P.R.Umrigar	India v Pakistan	1954-55
Dacca	6/21	Khan Mohammad	Pakistan v New Zealand	1955-56
Faisalabad	7/52	C.Pringle	New Zealand v Pakistan	1990-91
Gujranwala	1/27	G.P.Wickramasinghe	Sri Lanka v Pakistan	1991-92
Hyderabad	7/87	S.L.Boock	New Zealand v Pakistan	1984-85
Karachi[1]	8/60	Imran Khan	Pakistan v India	1982-83
Karachi[2]	7/91	Waqar Younis	Pakistan v Zimbabwe	1993-94
Lahore[1]	5/87	W.W.Hall	West Indies v Pakistan	1958-59
Lahore[2]	9/56	Abdul Qadir	Pakistan v England	1987-88
Multan[1]	5/62	Imran Khan	Pakistan v West Indies	1980-81
Multan[2]	6/42	Danish Kaneria	Pakistan v Bangladesh	2001-02
Peshawar[1]	5/63	S.P.Gupte	India v Pakistan	1954-55
Peshawar[2]	6/49	Shoaib Akhtar	Pakistan v Bangladesh	2003-04
Rawalpindi[1]	4/5	Pervez Sajjad	Pakistan v New Zealand	1964-65
Rawalpindi[2]	7/66	Mohammad Zahid	Pakistan v Zimbabwe	1996-97
Sheikhupura	5/53	Shahid Nazir	Pakistan v Zimbabwe	1996-97
Sialkot	8/83	J.R.Ratnayeke	Sri Lanka v Pakistan	1985-86
SRI LANKA				
Colombo (CCC)	5/29	R.J.Hadlee	New Zealand v Sri Lanka	1983-84
Colombo (PSS)	12/225	M.Muralidaran	Sri Lanka v South Africa	2006-07
Colombo (RPS)	6/18	M.Muralidaran	Sri Lanka v Bangladesh	2005-06
Colombo (SSC)	8/87	M.Muralidaran	Sri Lanka v India	2001-02
Galle	7/46	M.Muralidaran	Sri Lanka v England	2003-04
Kandy	9/51	M.Muralidaran	Sri Lanka v Zimbabwe	2001-02
Moratuwa	5/69	A.A.Donald	South Africa v Sri Lanka	1993-94
ZIMBABWE				
Bulawayo[1]	6/113	D.N.Patel	New Zealand v Zimbabwe	1992-93
Bulawayo[2]	8/109	P.A.Strang	Zimbabwe v New Zealand	2000-01
Harare	8/71	A.A.Donald	South Africa v Zimbabwe	1995-96
BANGLADESH				
Bogra	5/79	M.Muralidaran	Sri Lanka v Bangladesh	2005-06
Chittagong[1]	6/45	Enamul Haque[2]	Bangladesh v Zimbabwe	2004-05

Chittagong[2]	6/54	M.Muralidaran	Sri Lanka v Bangladesh	2005-06
Dhaka	7/77	Danish Kaneria	Pakistan v Bangladesh	2001-02
Fattullah	8/108	S.C.G.MacGill	Australia v Bangladesh	2005-06
UNITED ARAB EMIRATES				
Sharjah	5/24	Shoaib Akhtar	Pakistan v West Indies	2001-02

BEST MATCH BOWLING ANALYSIS FOR EACH TEST GROUND

AUSTRALIA				
Adelaide	14/199	C.V.Grimmett	Australia v South Africa	1931-32
Brisbane[1]	9/144	C.V.Grimmett	Australia v West Indies	1930-31
Brisbane[2]	15/123	R.J.Hadlee	New Zealand v Australia	1985-86
Cairns	10/133	S.C.G.MacGill	Australia v Bangladesh	2003-04
Darwin	7/54	M.S.Kasprowicz	Australia v Sri Lanka	2004-05
Hobart	9/67	S.K.Warne	Australia v New Zealand	1993-94
Melbourne	15/124	W.Rhodes	England v Australia	1903-04
Perth	13/217	M.G.Hughes	Australia v West Indies	1988-89
Sydney	12/87	C.T.B.Turner	Australia v England	1887-88
ENGLAND				
Birmingham	12/119	F.S.Trueman	England v West Indies	1963
Chester-le-Street	8/97	M.J.Hoggard	England v Bangladesh	2005
Leeds	15/99	C.Blythe	England v South Africa	1907
Lord's	16/137	R.A.L.Massie	Australia v England	1972
Manchester	19/90	J.C.Laker	England v Australia	1956
Nottingham	14/99	A.V.Bedser	England v Australia	1953
Sheffield	11/103	M.A.Noble	Australia v England	1902
The Oval	16/220	M.Muralidaran	Sri Lanka v England	1998
SOUTH AFRICA				
Bloemfontein	10/147	S.M.Pollock	South Africa v India	2001-02
Cape Town	15/28	J.Briggs	England v South Africa	1888-89
Centurion	10/145	M.Ntini	South Africa v New Zealand	2005-06
Durban[1]	14/144	S.F.Barnes	England v South Africa	1913-14
Durban[2]	13/173	C.V.Grimmett	Australia v South Africa	1935-36
East London	7/74	M.Ntini	South Africa v Bangladesh	2002-03
Johannesburg[1]	17/159	S.F.Barnes	England v South Africa	1913-14
Johannesburg[2]	8/61	H.J.Tayfield	South Africa v New Zealand	1953-54
Johannesburg[3]	13/192	H.J.Tayfield	South Africa v England	1956-57
Port Elizabeth	15/45	G.A.Lohmann	England v South Africa	1895-96
Potchefstroom	7/47	J.H.Kallis	South Africa v Bangladesh	2002-03
WEST INDIES				
Basseterre	6/186	Harbhajan Singh	India v West Indies	2005-06
Bridgetown	11/120	M.D.Marshall	West Indies v New Zealand	1984-85
Georgetown	11/121	Imran Khan	Pakistan v West Indies	1987-88
Gros Islet	7/96	R.R.Sarwan	West Indies v Bangladesh	2003-04
Kingston	11/134	C.D.Collymore	West Indies v Pakistan	2004-05
Kingstown	8/141	M.Muralidaran	Sri Lanka v West Indies	1996-97
Port-of-Spain	13/132	M.Ntini	South Africa v West Indies	2004-05
St George's	5/104	S.E.Bond	New Zealand v West Indies	2002-03
St John's	11/110	Wasim Akram	Pakistan v West Indies	1999-2000

NEW ZEALAND

Auckland	12/149	D.L.Vettori	New Zealand v Australia	1999-2000
Christchurch	12/97	D.L.Underwood	England v New Zealand	1970-71
Dunedin	11/102	R.J.Hadlee	New Zealand v West Indies	1979-80
Hamilton	10/100	C.L.Cairns	New Zealand v West Indies	1999-2000
Napier	10/90	W.P.J.U.C.Vaas	Sri Lanka v New Zealand	1994-95
Wellington	13/55	C.A.Walsh	West Indies v New Zealand	1994-95

INDIA

Ahmedabad	11/125	S.L.Venkatapathy Raju	India v Sri Lanka	1993-94
Bangalore	11/224	Harbhajan Singh	India v Australia	2004-05
Chandigarh	8/37	S.L.Venkatapathy Raju	India v Sri Lanka	1990-91
Chennai[1]	16/136	N.D.Hirwani	India v West Indies	1987-88
Madras[2]	11/122	R.G.Nadkarni	India v Australia	1964-65
Cuttack	6/59	N.D.Hirwani	India v New Zealand	1995-96
Delhi	14/149	A.Kumble	India v Pakistan	1998-99
Hyderabad	8/109	E.A.S.Prasanna	India v New Zealand	1969-70
Jaipur	4/88	G.Sharma	India v Pakistan	1986-87
Jullundur	4/50	Wasim Raja	Pakistan v India	1983-84
Kanpur	14/124	J.M.Patel	India v Australia	1959-60
Kolkata	13/132	J.Srinath	India v Pakistan	1998-99
Lucknow[1]	12/94	Fazal Mahmood	Pakistan v India	1952-53
Lucknow[2]	11/128	A.Kumble	India v Sri Lanka	1993-94
Mohali	9/171	L.Balaji	India v Pakistan	2004-05
Bombay[1]	8/108	M.S.Nichols	England v India	1933-34
Bombay[2]	11/235	B.S.Chandrasekhar	India v West Indies	1966-67
Mumbai[3]	13/106	I.T.Botham	England v India	1979-80
Nagpur	10/107	Maninder Singh	India v Sri Lanka	1986-87

PAKISTAN

Bahawalpur	7/124	Khan Mohammad	Pakistan v India	1954-55
Dacca	12/100	Fazal Mahmood	Pakistan v West Indies	1958-59
Faisalabad	12/130	Waqar Younis	Pakistan v New Zealand	1990-91
Gujranwala	1/27	G.P.Wickramasinghe	Sri Lanka v Pakistan	1991-92
Hyderabad	8/80	Imran Khan	Pakistan v India	1982-83
Karachi[1]	13/114	Fazal Mahmood	Pakistan v Australia	1956-57
Karachi[2]	13/135	Waqar Younis	Pakistan v Zimbabwe	1993-94
Lahore[1]	7/167	S.P.Gupte	India v Pakistan	1954-55
Lahore[2]	14/116	Imran Khan	Pakistan v Sri Lanka	1981-82
Multan[1]	5/89	Imran Khan	Pakistan v West Indies	1980-81
Multan[2]	12/94	Danish Kaneria	Pakistan v Bangladesh	2001-02
Peshawar[1]	6/115	S.P.Gupte	India v Pakistan	1954-55
Peshawar[2]	10/79	Shoaib Akhtar	Pakistan v Bangladesh	2003-04
Rawalpindi[1]	8/47	Pervez Sajjad	Pakistan v New Zealand	1964-65
Rawalpindi[2]	11/130	Mohammad Zahid	Pakistan v New Zealand	1996-97
Sheikhupura	7/98	Shahid Nazir	Pakistan v Zimbabwe	1996-97
Sialkot	9/95	Imran Khan	Pakistan v Sri Lanka	1985-86

SRI LANKA

Colombo (CCC)	10/102	R.J.Hadlee	New Zealand v Sri Lanka	1983-84
Colombo (PSS)	12/225	M.Muralidaran	Sri Lanka v South Africa	2006-07
Colombo (RPS)	9/60	M.Muralidaran	Sri Lanka v Bangladesh	2005-06
Colombo (SSC)	14/191	W.P.U.J.C.Vaas	Sri Lanka v West Indies	2001-02
Galle	13/171	M.Muralidaran	Sri Lanka v South Africa	2000-01
Kandy	13/115	M.Muralidaran	Sri Lanka v Zimbabwe	2001-02
Moratuwa	8/157	C.P.H.Ramanayake	Sri Lanka v Australia	1992-93

ZIMBABWE

Bulawayo[1]	7/173	D.N.Patel	New Zealand v Zimbabwe	1992-93
Bulawayo[2]	11/257	A.G.Huckle	Zimbabwe v New Zealand	1997-98
Harare	12/126	I.K.Pathan	India v Sri Lanka	2005-06

BANGLADESH

Bogra	7/141	M.Muralidaran	Sri Lanka v Bangladesh	2005-06
Chittagong[1]	12/170	D.L.Vettori	New Zealand v Bangladesh	2004-05
Chittagong[2]	9/141	M.Muralidaran	Sri Lanka v Bangladesh	2005-06
Dhaka	12/200	Enamul Haque[2]	Bangladesh v Zimbabwe	2004-05
Fattullah	9/138	S.C.G.MacGill	Australia v Bangladesh	2005-06

UNITED ARAB EMIRATES

Sharjah	8/24	S.K.Warne	Australia v Pakistan	2002-03

MOST WICKETS TAKEN ON EACH TEST GROUND

Note: all instances of 50 wickets on a ground are shown

AUSTRALIA

Ground	Player	Country	M	Balls	Mdns	Runs	Wkts	Avge	5w	10w	Best
Adelaide	Warne,SK	Aus	12	3555	156	1489	51	29.19	2	0	6/80
Brisbane[1]	Grimmett,CV	Aus	2	841	24	442	18	24.55	2	0	6/131
Brisbane[2]	Warne,SK	Aus	10	3062	155	1232	64	19.25	3	2	8/71
	McGrath.GD	Aus	12	2985	138	1311	58	22.60	3	1	6/17
Cairns	MacGill,SCG	Aus	1	264	12	133	10	13.30	2	1	5/56
	Chandana,UDU	SL	2	268	3	210	10	21.00	2	0	5/101
Darwin	McGrath,GD	Aus	2	324	19	106	11	9.63	1	0	5/37
Hobart	Warne,SK	Aus	6	1373	50	621	28	22.17	3	0	6/31
Melbourne	Lillee,DK	Aus	14	3833	105	1798	82	21.92	7	4	7/83
Perth	McGrath,GD	Aus	11	2718	134	1143	48	23.81	1	0	8/24
Sydney	Warne,SK	Aus	12	3702	155	1637	56	29.23	4	2	7/56

ENGLAND

Ground	Player	Country	M	Balls	Mdns	Runs	Wkts	Avge	5w	10w	Best
Birmingham	Trueman,FS	Eng	7	1709	55	798	39	20.46	3	1	7/44
Chester-le-Street	Harmison,SJ	Eng	2	364	10	201	12	16.75	1	0	5/38
Leeds	Trueman,FS	Eng	9	1764	66	795	44	18.06	2	1	6/30
Lord's	Botham,IT	Eng	15	3194	125	1693	69	24.53	8	1	8/34
	Trueman,FS	Eng	12	3087	113	1394	63	22.12	5	1	6/31
Manchester	Bedser,AV	Eng	7	1816	88	686	51	13.45	5	2	7/52
Nottingham	Bedser,AV	Eng	6	2289	111	829	41	20.22	4	1	7/44
Sheffield	Noble,MA	Aus	1	240	10	103	11	9.36	2	1	6/52
The Oval	Botham,IT	Eng	11	2615	90	1379	52	26.51	2	1	6/125

SOUTH AFRICA

Ground	Player	Country	M	Balls	Mdns	Runs	Wkts	Avge	5w	10w	Best
Bloemfontein	Pollock,SM	SA	3	814	50	332	21	15.81	2	1	6/56
Cape Town	Pollock,SM	SA	10	2169	100	897	46	19.50	2	0	6/30
Centurion	Ntini,M	SA	6	1184	60	699	37	18.89	3	1	5/49
Durban[1]	Barnes,SF	Eng	2	639	29	249	24	10.37	4	2	7/56
Durban[2]	Pollock,SM	SA	10	2245	116	837	38	22.02	2	0	6/50
East London	Ntini,M	SA	1	203	15	74	7	10.57	1	0	5/19
Johannesburg[1]	Nupen,EP	SA	8	2145	60	966	31	31.16	4	1	6/46
Johannesburg[2]	McCarthy,CN	SA	4	1145	13	525	15	35.00	1	0	5/114
Johannesburg[3]	Pollock,SM	SA	12	2614	119	1073	45	23.84	1	0	5/54
Port Elizabeth	Donald,AA	SA	7	1689	73	728	40	18.20	3	1	7/84
Potchefstrom	Kallis,JH	SA	1	105	5	47	7	6.71	1	0	5/21

WEST INDIES

Basseterre	Harbhajan Singh	WI	1	306	6	186	6	31.00	1	0	5/147
Bridgetown	Walsh,CA	WI	12	3024	114	1342	53	25.32	3	0	5/22
	Ambrose,CEL	WI	13	3399	155	1421	52	27.32	2	1	7/45
Georgetown	Gibbs,LR	WI	6	1867	112	578	28	20.64	3	0	6/29
Gros Islet	Sarwan,RR	WI	3	396	17	184	8	23.00	0	0	4/37
Kingston	Walsh,CA	WI	11	2219	91	897	48	18.68	2	1	6/62
Kingstown	Muralidaran,M	SL	1	318	14	141	8	17.62	1	0	5/113
Port-of-Spain	Ambrose,CEL	WI	12	2770	142	877	66	13.28	6	1	6/24
	Walsh,CA	WI	14	3345	147	1181	57	20.71	1	0	6/61
	Gibbs,LR	WI	13	4754	239	1646	52	31.65	2	0	6/108
St George's	Bond,SE	NZ	1	181	7	104	5	20.80	1	0	5/104
St John's	Ambrose,CEL	WI	11	2328	108	945	48	19.68	3	0	5/37

NEW ZEALAND

Auckland	Hadlee,RJ	NZ	13	3203	117	1463	45	32.51	3	0	6/105
Christchurch	Hadlee,RJ	NZ	14	3679	112	1635	76	21.51	6	0	7/116
Dunedin	Hadlee,RJ	NZ	2	636	36	212	19	11.15	3	1	6/51
Hamilton	Cairns,CL	NZ	8	1414	51	744	34	21.88	2	1	7/27
Napier	Morrison,DK	NZ	2	495	18	199	12	16.58	1	0	5/98
	Vaas,WPUJC	SL	2	573	22	253	12	21.08	2	1	5/43
Wellington	Hadlee,RJ	NZ	12	2623	90	1075	53	20.28	3	2	7/23

INDIA

Ahmedabad	Kumble,A	Ind	6	2326	110	886	35	25.31	3	1	7/116
Bangalore	Kumble,A	Ind	7	2194	65	1080	35	30.85	3	0	6/98
Chandigarh	Venkatapathy Raju,SL	Ind	1	323	38	37	8	4.62	1	0	6/12
Chennai[1]	Kumble,A	Ind	7	1738	71	776	45	17.24	5	1	7/48
Madras[2]	Nadkarni,RG	Ind	5	1253	103	275	20	13.75	2	1	6/91
Cuttack	Harwani,ND	Ind	1	186	12	59	6	9.83	1	0	6/59
	Maninder Singh	Ind	1	205	11	83	6	13.83	0	0	4/41
Delhi	Kumble,A	Ind	5	1952	94	742	48	15.45	4	2	10/74
Hyderabad	Prasanna,EAS	Ind	1	330	20	109	8	13.62	1	0	5/51
	Gupte,SP	Ind	1	568	42	156	8	19.50	1	0	7/128
Jaipur	Sharma,G	Ind	1	197	2	88	4	22.00	0	0	4/88
Jullundur	Wasim Raja	Pak	1	173	5	50	4	12.50	0	0	4/50
	Kapil Dev	Ind	1	204	8	89	4	22.25	0	0	4/80
Kanpur	Kapil Dev	Ind	7	1329	39	696	25	27.84	1	0	6/63
Kolkata	Kumble,A	Ind	7	2522	111	1038	35	29.65	2	1	7/63
Lucknow[1]	Fazal Mahmood	Pak	1	310	19	94	12	25.83	2	1	7/42
Lucknow[2]	Kumble,A	Ind	1	387	19	128	11	11.63	1	1	7/59
Mohali	Kumble,A	Ind	6	2026	91	934	27	34.59	1	0	6/81
Bombay[1]	Nichols,MS	Eng	1	283	15	108	8	13.50	1	0	5/55
Bombay[2]	Chandrasekhar,BS	Ind	5	1818	88	727	34	21.38	2	1	7/157
Mumbai[3]	Kumble,A	Ind	4	2192	101	832	38	21.89	1	0	5/90
Nagpur	Kumble,A	Ind	6	1929	92	844	29	29.10	2	0	5/63

PAKISTAN

Bahawalpur	Khan Mohammad	Pak	1	330	13	124	7	17.71	1	0	5/74
Dacca	Fazal Mahmood	Pak	4	1053	74	321	22	14.59	3	1	6/34
Faisalabad	Abdul Qadir	Pak	10	2711	94	1191	42	28.35	2	1	7/142
Gujranwala	Wickramasinghe,GP	SL	1	42	2	27	1	27.00	0	0	1/27
	Ratnayake,RJ	SL	1	78	3	39	1	39.00	0	0	1/39
Hyderabad	Abdul Qadir	Pak	3	981	36	395	16	24.68	2	0	6/44
Karachi[1]	Abdul Qadir	Pak	13	3655	128	1571	59	26.62	5	1	5/44
	Imran Khan	Pak	11	2406	100	938	51	18.39	2	1	8/60

Karachi[2]	Waqar Younis	Pak	1	336	15	135	13	10.38	2	1	7/91
Lahore[1]	Karhar,AH	Pak	2	384	23	93	7	13.28	0	0	3/47
	Gupte,SP	Ind	1	662	54	167	7	23.85	1	0	5/133
Lahore[2]	Imran Khan	Pak	11	2443	93	937	56	16.73	3	1	8/58
	Abdul Qadir	Pak	12	3099	105	1348	51	26.43	3	2	9/56
Multan[1]	Imran Khan	Pak	1	192	6	89	5	17.80	1	0	5/62
Multan[2]	Danish Kaneria	Pak	2	450	10	262	17	15.41	2	1	6/42
Peshawar[1]	Gupte,SP	Ind	1	459	38	115	6	19.16	1	0	5/63
	Mankad,MH	Ind	1	690	60	135	6	22.50	1	0	5/64
Peshawar[2]	Wasim Akram	Pak	3	664	26	273	20	13.65	2	0	5/53
	Shoaib Akhtar	Pak	3	712	18	376	20	18.80	2	1	6/49
Rawalpindi[1]	Pervez Sajjad	Pak	1	168	13	47	8	5.87	0	0	4/5
Rawalpindi[2]	Waqar Younis	Pak	5	1145	36	621	23	27.00	1	0	5/88
Sheikhupura	Saqlain Mushtaq	Pak	2	654	24	322	8	40.25	0	0	4/75
Sialkot	Imran Khan	Pak	3	513	16	240	14	17.14	1	0	5/40

SRI LANKA

Colombo (CCC)	Hadlee,RJ	NZ	2	461	21	204	14	14.57	2	1	5/29
Colombo (PSS)	Muralidran,M	SL	7	2329	94	983	42	23.40	4	1	7/97
Colombo (RPS)	Muralidran,M	SL	6	1815	69	761	33	23.06	4	0	6/18
Colombo (SSC)	Muralidran,M	SL	20	7553	328	2893	134	21.59	10	3	8/87
	Vaas,WPUJC	SL	17	3818	152	1696	75	22.61	4	1	7/71
Galle	Muralidaran,M	SL	11	4343	213	1405	87	16.14	10	4	7/46
Kandy	Muralidaran,M	SL	14	4446	229	1653	96	17.21	8	4	9/51
	Vaas,WPUJC	SL	13	2513	113	995	51	19.49	1	0	6/22
Moratuwa	Ramanayake,CPH	SL	2	559	15	241	11	21.90	1	0	5/82
	Muralidaran,M	SL	3	648	26	283	11	25.72	1	0	5/104

ZIMBABWE

Bulawayo[1]	Patel,DN	NZ	1	412	19	173	7	24.71	1	0	6/113
Bulawayo[2]	Streak,HH	Zim	14	2610	113	1199	37	32.40	1	0	5/70
Harare	Streak,HH	Zim	19	4532	209	1920	83	23.13	3	0	6/73

BANGLADESH

Bogra	Muralidaran,M	SL	1	263	9	141	7	20.14	1	0	5/79
Chittagong[1]	Mashrafe Bin Mortaza	Ban	5	958	40	466	17	27.41	0	0	4/60
	Mohammad Rafique	Ban	4	1366	53	563	17	33.11	1	0	5/65
Chittagong[2]	Muralidaran,M	SL	1	311	14	141	9	15.66	1	0	6/54
Dhaka	Mohammad Rafique	Ban	6	1802	92	698	23	30.34	2	0	6/77
Fattullah	MacGill,SCG	Aus	1	279	6	138	9	15.33	1	0	8/108
	Mohammad Rafique	Ban	1	422	15	160	9	17.77	1	0	5/62

SHARJAH

Sharjah	Warne,SK	Aus	2	414	19	154	16	9.62	1	0	5/74

Series by Series Records

• denotes batted first (Where a captain's name appears only once he was captain throughout the entire series).

AUSTRALIA v ENGLAND	Australia		England		Captains	
Venue and Result	1st	2nd	1st	2nd	Australia	England
1876-77 in Australia						
Melbourne-Australia 45 runs	•245	104	196	108	D.W.Gregory	J.Lillywhite
Melbourne-England 4 wkts	•122	259	261	6-122		
1878-79 in Australia						
Melbourne-Australia 10 wkts	256	0-19	•113	160	D.W.Gregory	Lord Harris
1880 in England						
The Oval-England 5 wkts	149	327	•420	5-57	W.L.Murdoch	Lord Harris
1881-82 in Australia						
Melbourne-Drawn	320	3-127	•294	308	W.L.Murdoch	A.Shaw
Sydney-Australia 5 wkts	197	5-169	•133	232		
Sydney-Australia 6 wkts	260	4-66	•188	134		
Melbourne-Drawn	300	-	•309	2-234		
1882 in England						
The Oval-Australia 7 runs	•63	122	101	77	W.L.Murdoch	A.N.Hornby
1882-83 in Australia						
Melbourne-Australia 9 wkts	•291	1-58	177	169	W.L.Murdoch	Hon.I.F.W.Bligh
Melbourne-England inn & 27 runs	114	153	•294	-		
Sydney-England 69 runs	218	83	•247	123		
Sydney-Australia 4 wkts	262	6-199	•263	197		
1884 in England						
Manchester-Drawn	182	-	•95	9-180	W.L.Murdoch	A.N.Hornby
Lord's-England inn & 5 runs	•229	145	379	-		Lord Harris
The Oval-Drawn	•551	-	346	2-85		Lord Harris
1884-85 in Australia						
Adelaide-England 8 wkts	•243	191	369	2-67	W.L.Murdoch	A.Shrewsbury
Melbourne-England 10 wkts	279	126	•401	0-7	T.P.Horan	
Sydney-Australia 6 runs	•181	165	133	207	H.H.Massie	
Sydney-Australia 8 wkts	309	2-40	•269	77	J.M.Blackham	
Melbourne-England inn & 98 runs	•163	125	386	-	T.P.Horan	
1886 in England						
Manchester-England 4 wkts	•205	123	223	6-107	H.J.H.Scott	A.G.Steel
Lord's-England inn & 106 runs	121	126	•353	-		
The Oval-England inn & 217 runs	68	149	•434	-		
1886-87 in Australia						
Sydney-England 13 runs	119	97	•45	184	P.S.McDonnell	A.Shrewsbury
Sydney-England 71 runs	84	150	•151	154		
1887-88 in Australia						
Sydney-England 126 runs	42	82	•113	137	P.S.McDonnell	W.W.Read
1888 in England						
Lord's-Australia 61 runs	•116	60	53	62	P.S.McDonnell	A.G.Steel
The Oval-England inn & 137 runs	•80	100	317	-		W.G.Grace

AUSTRALIA v ENGLAND (cont.) Venue and Result	Australia 1st	Australia 2nd	England 1st	England 2nd	Captains Australia	Captains England
Manchester-England inn & 21 runs	81	70	•172	-		W.G.Grace
1890 in England						
Lord's-England 7 wkts	•132	176	173	3-137	W.L.Murdoch	W.G.Grace
The Oval-England 2 wkts	•92	102	100	8-95		
Manchester-Abandoned	-	-	-	-		
1891-92 in Australia						
Melbourne-Australia 54 runs	•240	236	264	158	J.M.Blackham	W.G.Grace
Sydney-Australia 72 runs	•145	391	307	157		
Adelaide-England inn & 230 runs	100	169	•499			
1893 in England						
Lord's-Drawn	269	-	•334	8d-234	J.M.Blackham	A.E.Stoddart
The Oval-England inn & 43 runs	91	349	•483	-		W.G.Grace
Manchester-Drawn	•240	236	243	4-118		W.G.Grace
1894-95 in Australia						
Sydney-England 10 runs	•586	166	325	437	J.M.Blackham	A.E.Stoddart
Melbourne-England 94 runs	123	333	•75	475	G.Giffen	
Adelaide-Australia 382 runs	•238	411	124	143	G.Giffen	
Sydney-Australia inn & 147 runs	•284	-	65	72	G.Giffen	
Melbourne-England 6 wkts	•414	267	385	4-298	G.Giffen	
1896 in England						
Lord's-England 6 wkts	•53	347	292	4-111	G.H.S.Trott	W.G.Grace
Manchester-Australia 3 wkts	•412	7-125	231	305		
The Oval-England 66 runs	119	44	•145	84		
1897-98 in Australia						
Sydney-England 9 wkts	237	408	•551	1-96	G.H.S.Trott	A.C.MacLaren
Melbourne-Australia inn & 55 runs	•520	-	315	150		A.C.MacLaren
Adelaide-Australia inn & 13 runs	•573	-	278	282		A.E.Stoddart
Melbourne-Australia 8 wkts	•323	2-115	174	263		A.E.Stoddart
Sydney-Australia 6 wkts	239	4-276	•335	178		A.C.MacLaren
1899 in England						
Nottingham-Drawn	•252	8d-230	193	7-155	J.Darling	W.G.Grace
Lord's-Australia 10 wkts	421	0-28	•206	240		A.C.MacLaren
Leeds-Drawn	•172	224	220	0-19		A.C.MacLaren
Manchester-Drawn	196	7d-346	•372	3-94		A.C.MacLaren
The Oval-Drawn	352	5-254	•576	-		A.C.MacLaren
1901-02 in Australia						
Sydney-England inn & 124 runs	168	172	•464	-	J.Darling	A.C.MacLaren
Melbourne-Australia 229 runs	•112	353	61	175	J.Darling	
Adelaide-Australia 4 wkts	321	6-315	•388	247	J.Darling	
Sydney-Australia 7 wkts	299	3-121	•317	99	H.Trumble	
Melbourne-Australia 32 runs	•144	255	189	178	H.Trumble	
1902 in England						
Birmingham-Drawn	36	2-46	•9d-376	-	J.Darling	A.C.MacLaren
Lord's-Drawn	-	-	•2-102	-		
Sheffield-Australia 143 runs	•194	289	145	195		
Manchester-Australia 3 runs	•299	86	262	120		

AUSTRALIA v ENGLAND (cont.) Venue and Result	Australia 1st	Australia 2nd	England 1st	England 2nd	Captains Australia	Captains England
The Oval-England 1 wkt	•324	121	183	9-263		
1903-04 in Australia						
Sydney-England 5 wkts	•285	485	577	5-194	M.A.Noble	P.F.Warner
Melbourne-England 185 runs	122	111	•315	103		
Adelaide-Australia 216 runs	•388	351	245	278		
Sydney-England 157 runs	131	171	•249	210		
Melbourne-Australia 218 runs	•247	133	61	101		
1905 in England						
Nottingham-England 213 runs	221	188	•196	5d-426	J.Darling	Hon.F.S.Jackson
Lord's-Drawn	181	-	•282	5-151		
Leeds-Drawn	195	7-224	•301	5d-295		
Manchester-England inn & 80 runs	197	169	•446	-		
The Oval-Drawn	363	4-124	•430	6d-261		
1907-08 in Australia						
Sydney-Australia 2 wkts	300	8-275	•273	300	M.A.Noble	F.L.Fane
Melbourne-England 1 wkt	•266	397	382	9-282		F.L.Fane
Adelaide-Australia 245 runs	•285	506	363	183		F.L.Fane
Melbourne-Australia 308 runs	•214	385	105	186		A.O.Jones
Sydney-Australia 49 runs	•137	422	281	229		A.O.Jones
1909 in England						
Birmingham-England 10 wkts	•74	151	121	0-105	M.A.Noble	A.C.MacLaren
Lord's-Australia 9 wkts	350	1-41	•269	121		
Leeds-Australia 126 runs	•188	207	182	87		
Manchester-Drawn	•147	9d-279	119	3-108		
The Oval-Drawn	•325	5d-339	352	3-104		
1911-12 in Australia						
Sydney-Australia 146 runs	•447	308	318	291	C.Hill	J.W.H.T.Douglas
Melbourne-England 8 wkts	•184	299	265	2-219		
Adelaide-England 7 wkts	•133	476	501	3-112		
Melbourne-England inn & 225 runs	•191	173	589	-		
Sydney-England 70 runs	176	292	•324	214		
1912 in England						
Lord's-Drawn	7-282	-	•7d-310	-	S.E.Gregory	C.B.Fry
Manchester-Drawn	0-14	-	•203	-		
The Oval-England 244 runs	111	65	•245	175		
1920-21 in Australia						
Sydney-Australia 377 runs	•267	581	190	281	W.W.Armstrong	J.W.H.T.Douglas
Melbourne-Australia inn & 91 runs	•499	-	251	157		
Adelaide-Australia 119 runs	•354	582	447	370		
Melbourne-Australia 8 wkts	389	2-211	•284	315		
Sydney-Australia 9 wkts	392	1-93	•204	280		
1921 in England						
Nottingham-Australia 10 wkts	232	0-30	•112	147	W.W.Armstrong	J.W.H.T.Douglas
Lord's-Australia 8 wkts	342	2-131	•187	283		J.W.H.T Douglas
Leeds-Australia 219 runs	•407	7d-273	259	202		Hon.L.H.Tennyson
Manchester-Drawn	175	-	•4d-362	1-44		Hon.L.H.Tennyson
The Oval-Drawn	389	-	•8d-403	2-244		Hon.L.H.Tennyson

AUSTRALIA v ENGLAND (cont.)	Australia		England		Captains	
Venue and Result	1st	2nd	1st	2nd	Australia	England
1924-25 in Australia						
Sydney-Australia 193 runs	•450	452	298	411	H.L.Collins	A.E.R.Gilligan
Melbourne-Australia 81 runs	•600	250	479	290		
Adelaide-Australia 11 runs	•489	250	365	363		
Melbourne-England inn & 29 runs	269	250	•548	-		
Sydney-Australia 307 runs	•295	325	167	146		
1926 in England						
Nottingham-Drawn	-	-	•0-32	-	H.L.Collins	A.W.Carr
Lord's-Drawn	•383	5-194	3d-475	-	H.L.Collins	A.W.Carr
Leeds-Drawn	•494	-	294	3-254	W.Bardsley	A.W.Carr
Manchester-Drawn	•335	-	5-305	-	W.Bardsley	A.W.Carr
The Oval-England 289 runs	302	125	•280	436	H.L.Collins	A.P.F.Chapman
1928-29 in Australia						
Brisbane[1]-England 675 runs	122	66	•521	8d-342	J.Ryder	A.P.F.Chapman
Sydney-England 8 wkts	•253	397	636	2-16		A.P.F.Chapman
Melbourne-England 3 wkts	•397	351	417	7-332		A.P.F.Chapman
Adelaide-England 12 runs	369	336	•334	383		A.P.F.Chapman
Melbourne-Australia 5 wkts	491	5-287	•519	257		J.C.White
1930 in England						
Nottingham-England 93 runs	144	335	•270	302	W.M.Woodfull	A.P.F.Chapman
Lord's-Australia 7 wkts	6d-729	3-72	•425	375		A.P.F.Chapman
Leeds-Drawn	•566	-	391	3-95		A.P.F.Chapman
Manchester-Drawn	•345	-	8-251	-		A.P.F.Chapman
The Oval-Australia inn & 39 runs	695	-	•405	251		R.E.S.Wyatt
1932-33 in Australia						
Sydney-England 10 wkts	•360	164	524	0-1	W.M.Woodfull	D.R.Jardine
Melbourne-Australia 111 runs	•228	191	169	139		
Adelaide-England 338 runs	222	193	•341	412		
Brisbane[2]-England 6 wkts	•340	175	356	4-162		
Sydney-England 8 wkts	•435	182	454	2-168		
1934 in England						
Nottingham-Australia 238 runs	•374	8d-273	268	141	W.M.Woodfull	C.F.Walters
Lord's-England inn & 38 runs	284	118	•440	-		R.E.S.Wyatt
Manchester-Drawn	491	1-66	•9d-627	0d-123		R.E.S.Wyatt
Leeds-Drawn	584	-	•200	6-229		R.E.S.Wyatt
The Oval-Australia 562 runs	•701	327	321	145		R.E.S.Wyatt
1936-37 in Australia						
Brisbane[2]-England 322 runs	234	58	•358	256	D.G.Bradman	G.O.B.Allen
Sydney-England inn & 22 runs	80	324	•6d-426	-		
Melbourne-Australia 365 runs	•9d-200	564	9d-76	323		
Adelaide-Australia 148 runs	•288	433	330	243		
Melbourne-Australia inn & 200 runs	•604	-	239	165		
1938 in England						
Nottingham-Drawn	411	6-427	•8d-658	-	D.G.Bradman	W.R.Hammond
Lord's-Drawn	422	6-204	•494	8d-242		
Manchester-Abandoned	-	-	-	-		
Leeds-Australia 5 wkts	242	5-107	•223	123		
The Oval-England inn & 579 runs	201	123	•7d-903	-		

AUSTRALIA v ENGLAND (cont.)	Australia		England		Captains	
Venue and Result	1st	2nd	1st	2nd	Australia	England
1946-47 in Australia						
Brisbane[2]-Australia inn & 332 runs	•645	-	141	172	D.G.Bradman	W.R.Hammond
Sydney-Australia inn & 33 runs	8d-659	-	•255	371		W.R.Hammond
Melbourne-Drawn	•365	536	351	7-310		W.R.Hammond
Adelaide-Drawn	487	1-215	•460	8d-340		W.R.Hammond
Sydney-Australia 5 wkts	253	5-214	•280	186		N.W.D.Yardley
1948 in England						
Nottingham-Australia 8 wkts	509	2-98	•165	441	D.G.Bradman	N.W.D.Yardley
Lord's-Australia 409 runs	•350	7d-460	215	186		
Manchester-Drawn	221	1-92	•363	3d-174		
Leeds-Australia 7 wkts	458	3-404	•496	8d-365		
The Oval-Australia inn & 149 runs	389	-	•52	188		
1950-51 in Australia						
Brisbane[2]-Australia 70 runs	•228	7d-32	7d-68	122	A.L.Hassett	F.R.Brown
Melbourne-Australia 28 runs	•194	181	197	150		
Sydney-Australia inn &13 runs	426	-	•290	123		
Adelaide-Australia 274 runs	•371	8d-403	272	228		
Melbourne-England 8 wkts	•217	197	320	2-95		
1953 in England						
Nottingham-Drawn	•249	123	144	1-120	A.L.Hassett	L.Hutton
Lord's-Drawn	•346	368	372	7-282		
Manchester-Drawn	•318	8-35	276	-		
Leeds-Drawn	266	4-147	•167	275		
The Oval-England 8 wkts	•275	162	306	2-132		
1954-55 in Australia						
Brisbane[2]-Australia inn & 154 runs	•8d-601	-	190	257	I.W.G.Johnson	L.Hutton
Sydney-England 38 runs	228	184	•154	296	A.R.Morris	
Melbourne-England 128 runs	231	111	•191	279	I.W.G.Johnson	
Adelaide-England 5 wkts	•323	111	341	5-97	I.W.G.Johnson	
Sydney-Drawn	221	6-118	•7d-371	-	I.W.G.Johnson	
1956 in England						
Nottingham-Drawn	148	3-120	•8d-217	3d-188	I.W.G.Johnson	P.B.H.May
Lord's-Australia 185 runs	•285	257	171	186		
Leeds-England inn & 42 runs	143	140	•325	-		
Manchester-England inn & 170 runs	84	205	•459	-		
The Oval-Drawn	202	5-27	•247	3d-182		
1958-59 in Australia						
Brisbane[2]-Australia 8 wkts	186	2-147	•134	198	R.Benaud	P.B.H.May
Melbourne-Australia 8 wkts	308	2-42	•259	87		
Sydney-Drawn	357	2-54	•219	7d-287		
Adelaide-Australia 10 wkts	•476	0-36	240	270		
Melbourne-Australia 9 wkts	351	1-69	•205	214		
1961 in England						
Birmingham-Drawn	9d-516	-	•195	4-401	R.Benaud	M.C.Cowdrey
Lord's-Australia 5 wkts	340	5-71	•206	202	R.N.Harvey	M.C.Cowdrey
Leeds-England 8 wkts	•237	120	299	2-62	R.Benaud	P.B.H.May
Manchester-Australia 54 runs	•190	432	367	201	R.Benaud	P.B.H.May
The Oval-Drawn	494	-	•256	8-370	R.Benaud	P.B.H.May

AUSTRALIA v ENGLAND (cont.) Venue and Result	Australia 1st	Australia 2nd	England 1st	England 2nd	Captains Australia	Captains England
1962-63 in Australia						
Brisbane[2]-Drawn	•404	4d-362	389	6-278	R.Benaud	E.R.Dexter
Melbourne-England 7 wkts	•316	248	331	3-237		
Sydney-Australia 8 wkts	319	2-67	•279	104		
Adelaide-Drawn	•393	293	331	4-223		
Sydney-Drawn	349	4-152	•321	8d-268		
1964 in England						
Nottingham-Drawn	168	2-40	•8d-216	9d-193	R.B.Simpson	E.R.Dexter
Lord's-Drawn	•176	4-168	246	-		
Leeds-Australia 7 wkts	389	3-111	•268	229		
Manchester-Drawn	•8d-656	0-4	611	-		
The Oval-Drawn	379	-	•182	4-381		
1965-66 in Australia						
Brisbane[2]-Drawn	•6d-443	-	280	3-186	B.C.Booth	M.J K.Smith
Melbourne-Drawn	•358	426	558	0-5	R.B.Simpson	
Sydney-England inn & 93 runs	221	174	•488	-	B.C.Booth	
Adelaide-Australia inn & 9 runs	516	-	•241	266	R.B.Simpson	
Melbourne-Drawn	8d-543	-	•9d-485	3-69	R.B Simpson	
1968 in England						
Manchester-Australia 159 runs	•357	220	165	253	W.M.Lawry	M.C.Cowdrey
Lord's-Drawn	78	4-127	•7d-351	-	W.M.Lawry	M.C.Cowdrey
Birmingham-Drawn	222	1-68	•409	3d-142	W.M.Lawry	M.C.Cowdrey
Leeds-Drawn	•315	312	302	4-230	B.N.Jarman	T.W.Graveney
The Oval-England 226 runs	324	125	•494	181	W.M.Lawry	M.C.Cowdrey
1970-71 in Australia						
Brisbane[2]-Drawn	•433	214	464	1-39	W.M.Lawry	R.Illingworth
Perth-Drawn	440	3-100	•397	6d-287	W.M.Lawry	
Melbourne-Abandoned	-	-	-	-	W.M.Lawry	
Sydney-England 299 runs	236	116	•332	5d-319	W.M.Lawry	
Melbourne-Drawn	•9d-493	4d-169	392	0-161	W.M.Lawry	
Adelaide-Drawn	235	3-328	•470	4d-233	W.M.Lawry	
Sydney-England 62 runs	264	160	•184	302	I.M.Chappell	
1972 in England						
Manchester-England 89 runs	142	252	•249	234	I.M.Chappell	R.Illingworth
Lord's-Australia 8 wkts	308	2-81	•272	116		
Nottingham-Drawn	•315	4d-324	189	4-290		
Leeds-England 9 wkts	•146	136	263	1-21		
The Oval-Australia 5 wkts	399	5-242	•284	356		
1974-75 in Australia						
Brisbane[2]-Australia 166 runs	•309	5d-288	265	166	I.M.Chappell	M.H.Denness
Perth-Australia 9 wkts	481	1-23	•208	293		M.H.Denness
Melbourne-Drawn	241	8-238	•242	244		M.H.Denness
Sydney-Australia 171 runs	•405	4d-289	295	228		J.H.Edrich
Adelaide-Australia 163 runs	•304	5d-272	172	241		M.H.Denness
Melbourne-England inn & 4 runs	•152	373	529	-		M.H.Denness
1975 in England						
Birmingham-Australia inn & 85 runs	•359	-	101	173	I.M.Chappell	M.H.Denness
Lord's-Drawn	268	3-329	•315	7d-436		A.W.Greig

AUSTRALIA v ENGLAND (cont.)	Australia		England		Captains	
Venue and Result	1st	2nd	1st	2nd	Australia	England
Leeds-Drawn	135	3-220	•288	291		A.W.Greig
The Oval-Drawn	•9d-532	2-40	191	538		A.W.Greig
1976-77 in Australia (Centenary Test)						
Melbourne-Australia 45 runs	•138	9d-419	95	417	G.S.Chappell	A.W.Greig
1977 in England						
Lord's-Drawn	296	6-114	•216	305	G.S.Chappell	J.M.Brearley
Manchester-England 9 wkts	•297	218	437	1-82		
Nottingham-England 7 wkts	•243	309	364	3-189		
Leeds-England inn & 85 runs	103	248	•436	-		
The Oval-Drawn	385	-	•214	2-57		
1978-79 in Australia						
Brisbane[2]-England 7 wkts	•116	339	286	3-170	G.N.Yallop	J.M.Brearley
Perth-England 166 runs	190	161	•309	208		
Melbourne-Australia 103 runs	•258	167	143	179		
Sydney-England 93 runs	294	111	•152	346		
Adelaide-England 205 runs	164	160	•169	360		
Sydney-England 9 wkts	•198	143	308	1-35		
1979-80 in Australia						
Perth-Australia 138 runs	•244	337	228	215	G.S.Chappell	J.M.Brearley
Sydney-Australia 6 wkts	145	4-219	•123	237		
Melbourne-Australia 8 wkts	477	2-103	•306	273		
1980 in England (Centenary Test)						
Lord's-Drawn	•5d-385	4d-189	205	3-244	G.S.Chappell	I.T.Botham
1981 in England						
Nottingham-Australia 4 wkts	179	6-132	•185	125	K.J.Hughes	I.T.Botham
Lord's-Drawn	345	4-90	•311	8-265		I.T.Botham
Leeds-England 18 runs	•9-401	111	174	356		J.M.Brearley
Birmingham-England 29 runs	258	121	•189	219		J.M.Brearley
Manchester-England 103 runs	130	402	•231	404		J.M.Brearley
The Oval-Drawn	•352	9d-344	314	7-261		J.M.Brearley
1982-83 in Australia						
Perth-Drawn	9d-424	2-73	•411	358	K.J.Hughes	R.G.D.Willis
Brisbane[2]-Australia 7 wkts	341	3-190	•219	309		
Adelaide-Australia 8 wkts	•438	2-83	216	304		
Melbourne-England 3 runs	287	288	•284	294		
Sydney-Drawn	•314	382	237	7-314		
1985 in England						
Leeds-England 5 wkts	•331	324	533	5-123	A.R.Border	D.I.Gower
Lord's-Australia 4 wkts	425	6-127	•290	261		
Nottingham-Drawn	539	-	•456	2-196		
Manchester-Drawn	•257	5-340	9d-482	-		
Birmingham-England inn & 118 runs	•335	142	5d-595	-		
The Oval-England inn & 94 runs	241	129	•464	-		
1986-87 in Australia						
Brisbane[2]-England 7 wkts	248	282	•456	3-77	A.R.Border	M.W.Gatting
Perth-Drawn	401	4-197	•8d-592	8d-199		

AUSTRALIA v ENGLAND (cont.)	Australia		England		Captains	
Venue and Result	1st	2nd	1st	2nd	Australia	England
Adelaide-Drawn	•5d-514	3d-201	455	2-39		
Melbourne-England inn & 14 runs	•141	194	349	-		
Sydney-Australia 55 runs	•343	251	275	264		
1987-88 in Australia (Bicentennial Test)						
Sydney-Drawn	214	2-328	•425	-	A.R.Border	M.W.Gatting
1989 in England						
Leeds-Australia 210 runs	•7d-601	3d-230	430	191	A.R.Border	D.I.Gower
Lord's-Australia 6 wkts	528	4-119	•286	359		
Birmingham-Drawn	•424	2-158	242	-		
Manchester-Australia 9 wkts	447	1-81	•260	264		
Nottingham-Australia inn & 180 runs	•6d-602	-	255	167		
The Oval-Drawn	•468	4d-219	285	5-143		
1990-91 in Australia						
Brisbane[2]-Australia 10 wkts	152	0-157	•194	114	A.R.Border	A.J.Lamb
Melbourne-Australia 8 wkts	306	2-197	•352	150		G.A.Gooch
Sydney-Drawn	•518	205	8d-469	4-113		G.A.Gooch
Adelaide-Drawn	•386	6d-314	229	5-335		G.A.Gooch
Perth-Australia 9 wkts	307	1-120	•244	182		G.A.Gooch
1993 in England						
Manchester-Australia 179 runs	•289	5d-432	210	332	A.R.Border	G.A.Gooch
Lord's-Australia inn & 62 runs	•4d-632	-	205	365		G.A.Gooch
Nottingham-Drawn	373	6-202	•321	422		G.A.Gooch
Leeds-Australia inn & 148 runs	•4d-653	-	200	305		G.A.Gooch
Birmingham-Australia 8 wkts	408	2-120	•276	251		M.A.Atherton
The Oval-England 161 runs	303	229	•380	313		M.A.Atherton
1994-95 in Australia						
Brisbane[2]-Australia 184 runs	•426	8d-248	167	323	M.A.Taylor	M.A.Atherton
Melbourne-Australia 295 runs	•279	7d-320	212	92		
Sydney-Drawn	116	7-344	•309	2d-255		
Adelaide-England 106 runs	419	156	•353	328		
Perth-Australia 329 runs	•402	8d-345	295	123		
1997 in England						
Manchester-England 9 wkts	•118	477	9d-478	1-119	M.A.Taylor	M.A.Atherton
Lord's-Drawn	7d-213	-	•77	4d-266		
Nottingham-Australia 268 runs	•235	8d-395	162	200		
Leeds-Australia inn & 61 runs	9d-501	-	•172	268		
Birmingham-Australia 264 runs	•427	336	313	186		
The Oval-England 19 runs	220	104	•180	163		
1998-99 in Australia						
Brisbane[2]-Drawn	•485	3d-237	375	6-179	M.A.Taylor	A.J.Stewart
Perth-Australia 7 wkts	240	3-64	•112	191		
Adelaide-Australia 205 runs	•391	5d-278	227	237		
Melbourne-England 12 runs	270	244	•340	162		
Sydney-Australia 98 runs	•322	184	220	188		
2001 in England						
Birmingham-Australia inn & 118 runs	576	-	•294	164	S.R.Waugh	N.Hussain
Lord's-Australia 8 wkts	401	2-14	•187	227	S.R.Waugh	M.A.Atherton

AUSTRALIA v ENGLAND (cont.)	Australia		England		Captains	
Venue and Result	1st	2nd	1st	2nd	Australia	England
Manchester-Australia 7 wkts	190	3-158	•185	162	S.R.Waugh	M.A.Atherton
Leeds-England 6 wkts	•447	4d-176	309	4-315	A.C.Gilchrist	N.Hussain
The Oval-Australia inn & 25 runs	•4d-641	-	432	184	S.R.Waugh	N.Hussain
2002-03 in Australia						
Brisbane[2]-Australia 384 runs	•492	5d-296	325	79	S.R.Waugh	N.Hussain
Adelaide-Australia inn & 51 runs	9d-552	-	•342	159		
Perth-Australia inn & 48 runs	456	-	•185	223		
Melbourne-Australia 5 wkts	•6d-551	5-107	270	387		
Sydney-England 225 runs	363	226	•362	9d-452		
2005 in England						
Lord's-Australia 239 runs	•190	384	155	180	R.T.Ponting	M.P.Vaughan
Birmingham-England 2 runs	308	279	•407	182		
Manchester-Drawn	302	9-371	•444	6d-280		
Nottingham-England 3 wkts	218	387	•477	7-129		
The Oval-Drawn	367	0-4	•373	335		

Test Match Results Summary

AUSTRALIA v ENGLAND - in Australia

		Result			Melbourne			Sydney			Adelaide			Brisbane[1]			Brisbane[2]			Perth		
	Tests	A	E	D	A	E	D	A	E	D	A	E	D	A	E	D	A	E	D	A	E	D
1876-77	2	1	1	-	1	1	-	-	-	-	-	-	-	-	-	-	-	-	-	-	-	-
1878-79	1	1	-	-	1	-	-	-	-	-	-	-	-	-	-	-	-	-	-	-	-	-
1881-82	4	2	-	2	-	-	2	2	-	-	-	-	-	-	-	-	-	-	-	-	-	-
1882-83	4	2	2	-	1	1	-	1	1	-	-	-	-	-	-	-	-	-	-	-	-	-
1884-85	5	2	3	-	-	2	-	2	-	-	-	1	-	-	-	-	-	-	-	-	-	-
1886-87	2	-	2	-	-	-	-	-	2	-	-	-	-	-	-	-	-	-	-	-	-	-
1887-88	1	-	1	-	-	-	-	-	1	-	-	-	-	-	-	-	-	-	-	-	-	-
1891-92	3	2	1	-	1	-	-	1	-	-	-	1	-	-	-	-	-	-	-	-	-	-
1894-95	5	2	3	-	-	2	-	1	1	-	1	-	-	-	-	-	-	-	-	-	-	-
1897-98	5	4	1	-	2	-	-	1	1	-	1	-	-	-	-	-	-	-	-	-	-	-
1901-02	5	4	1	-	2	-	-	1	1	-	1	-	-	-	-	-	-	-	-	-	-	-
1903-04	5	2	3	-	1	1	-	-	2	-	1	-	-	-	-	-	-	-	-	-	-	-
1907-08	5	4	1	-	1	1	-	2	-	-	1	-	-	-	-	-	-	-	-	-	-	-
1911-12	5	1	4	-	-	2	-	1	1	-	-	1	-	-	-	-	-	-	-	-	-	-
1920-21	5	5	-	-	2	-	-	2	-	-	1	-	-	-	-	-	-	-	-	-	-	-
1924-25	5	4	1	-	1	1	-	2	-	-	1	-	-	-	-	-	-	-	-	-	-	-
1928-29	5	1	4	-	1	1	-	-	1	-	-	1	-	-	1	-	-	-	-	-	-	-
1932-33	5	1	4	-	1	-	-	-	2	-	-	1	-	-	-	-	-	1	-	-	-	-
1936-37	5	3	2	-	2	-	-	-	1	-	1	-	-	-	-	-	-	1	-	-	-	-
1946-47	5	3	-	2	-	-	1	2	-	-	-	-	1	-	-	-	1	-	-	-	-	-
1950-51	5	4	1	-	1	1	-	1	-	-	1	-	-	-	-	-	1	-	-	-	-	-
1954-55	5	1	3	1	-	1	-	-	1	1	-	1	-	-	-	-	1	-	-	-	-	-
1958-59	5	4	-	1	2	-	-	-	-	1	1	-	-	-	-	-	1	-	-	-	-	-
1962-63	5	1	1	3	-	1	-	1	-	1	-	-	1	-	-	-	-	-	1	-	-	-
1965-66	5	1	1	3	-	-	2	-	1	-	1	-	-	-	-	-	-	-	1	-	-	-
1970-71	6	-	2	4	-	-	1	-	2	-	-	-	1	-	-	-	-	-	1	-	-	1
1974-75	6	4	1	1	-	1	1	1	-	-	1	-	-	-	-	-	1	-	-	1	-	-
1976-77	1	1	-	-	1	-	-	-	-	-	-	-	-	-	-	-	-	-	-	-	-	-
1978-79	6	1	5	-	1	-	-	-	2	-	-	1	-	-	-	-	-	1	-	-	1	-
1979-80	3	3	-	-	1	-	-	1	-	-	-	-	-	-	-	-	-	-	-	1	-	-

		Result			Melbourne			Sydney			Adelaide			Brisbane[1]			Brisbane[2]			Perth		
	Tests	A	E	D	A	E	D	A	E	D	A	E	D	A	E	D	A	E	D	A	E	D
1982-83	5	2	1	2	-	1	-	-	-	1	1	-	-	-	-	-	1	-	-	-	-	1
1986-87	5	1	2	2	-	1	-	1	-	-	-	-	1	-	-	-	-	1	-	-	-	1
1987-88	1	-	-	1	-	-	-	-	-	1	-	-	-	-	-	-	-	-	-	-	-	-
1990-91	5	3	-	2	1	-	-	-	-	1	-	-	1	-	-	-	1	-	-	1	-	-
1994-95	5	3	1	1	1	-	-	-	-	1	-	1	-	-	-	-	1	-	-	1	-	-
1998-99	5	3	1	1	-	1	-	1	-	-	1	-	-	-	-	-	-	-	1	1	-	-
2002-03	5	4	1	-	1	-	-	-	1	-	1	-	-	-	-	-	1	-	-	1	-	-
	160	80	54	26	26	19	7	24	21	7	15	8	5	-	1	-	9	4	4	6	1	3

AUSTRALIA v ENGLAND - in England

		Result			The Oval			Manch.			Lord's			Notting.			Leeds			Birming.			Sheffield		
	Tests	A	E	D	A	E	D	A	E	D	A	E	D	A	E	D	A	E	D	A	E	D	A	E	D
1880	1	-	1	-	-	1	-	-	-	-	-	-	-	-	-	-	-	-	-	-	-	-	-	-	-
1882	1	1	-	-	1	-	-	-	-	-	-	-	-	-	-	-	-	-	-	-	-	-	-	-	-
1884	3	-	1	2	-	-	1	-	-	1	-	1	-	-	-	-	-	-	-	-	-	-	-	-	-
1886	3	-	3	-	-	1	-	-	1	-	-	1	-	-	-	-	-	-	-	-	-	-	-	-	-
1888	3	1	2	-	-	1	-	-	1	-	1	-	-	-	-	-	-	-	-	-	-	-	-	-	-
1890	2	-	2	-	-	1	-	-	-	-	-	1	-	-	-	-	-	-	-	-	-	-	-	-	-
1893	3	-	1	2	-	1	-	-	-	1	-	-	1	-	-	-	-	-	-	-	-	-	-	-	-
1896	3	1	2	-	-	1	-	1	-	-	-	1	-	-	-	-	-	-	-	-	-	-	-	-	-
1899	5	1	-	4	-	-	1	-	-	1	1	-	-	-	-	1	-	-	1	-	-	-	-	-	-
1902	5	2	1	2	-	1	-	1	-	-	-	-	1	-	-	-	-	-	-	-	-	1	1	-	-
1905	5	-	2	3	-	-	1	-	1	-	-	-	1	-	1	-	-	-	1	-	-	-	-	-	-
1909	5	2	1	2	-	-	1	-	-	1	1	-	-	-	-	-	1	-	-	-	1	-	-	-	-
1912	3	-	1	2	-	1	-	-	-	1	-	-	1	-	-	-	-	-	-	-	-	-	-	-	-
1921	5	3	-	2	-	-	1	-	-	1	1	-	-	1	-	-	1	-	-	-	-	-	-	-	-
1926	5	-	1	4	-	1	-	-	-	1	-	-	1	-	-	1	-	-	1	-	-	-	-	-	-
1930	5	2	1	2	1	-	-	-	-	1	1	-	-	-	1	-	-	-	1	-	-	-	-	-	-
1934	5	2	1	2	1	-	-	-	-	1	-	1	-	1	-	-	-	-	1	-	-	-	-	-	-
1938	4	1	1	2	-	1	-	-	-	-	-	-	1	-	-	1	1	-	-	-	-	-	-	-	-
1948	5	4	-	1	1	-	-	-	-	1	1	-	-	1	-	-	1	-	-	-	-	-	-	-	-
1953	5	-	1	4	-	1	-	-	-	1	-	-	1	-	-	1	-	-	1	-	-	-	-	-	-
1956	5	1	2	2	-	-	1	-	1	-	1	-	-	-	-	1	-	1	-	-	-	-	-	-	-
1961	5	2	1	2	-	-	1	1	-	-	1	-	-	-	-	-	-	1	-	-	-	1	-	-	-
1964	5	1	-	4	-	-	1	-	-	1	-	-	1	-	-	1	1	-	-	-	-	-	-	-	-
1968	5	1	1	3	-	1	-	1	-	-	-	-	1	-	-	-	-	-	1	-	-	1	-	-	-
1972	5	2	2	1	1	-	-	-	1	-	1	-	-	-	-	1	-	1	-	-	-	-	-	-	-
1975	4	1	-	3	-	-	1	-	-	-	-	-	1	-	-	-	-	-	1	1	-	-	-	-	-
1977	5	-	3	2	-	-	1	-	1	-	-	-	1	-	1	-	-	1	-	-	-	-	-	-	-
1980	1	-	-	1	-	-	-	-	-	-	-	-	1	-	-	-	-	-	-	-	-	-	-	-	-
1981	6	1	3	2	-	-	1	-	1	-	-	-	1	1	-	-	-	1	-	-	1	-	-	-	-
1985	6	1	3	2	-	1	-	-	-	1	1	-	-	-	-	1	-	1	-	-	1	-	-	-	-
1989	6	4	-	2	-	-	1	1	-	-	1	-	-	1	-	-	1	-	-	-	-	1	-	-	-
1993	6	4	1	1	-	1	-	1	-	-	1	-	-	-	-	1	1	-	-	1	-	-	-	-	-
1997	6	3	2	1	-	1	-	1	-	-	-	-	1	1	-	-	1	-	-	-	1	-	-	-	-
2001	5	4	1	-	1	-	-	-	-	-	1	-	-	1	-	-	-	1	-	1	-	-	-	-	-
2005	2	1	1	-	-	-	1	-	-	1	1	-	-	-	1	-	-	-	-	-	1	-	-	-	-
	151	46	43	62	6	15	13	7	7	14	14	5	14	7	4	9	8	7	8	3	5	4	1	-	-

Totals	311	126	97	88

Key to ground abbreviations: Manch. - Manchester; Notting. - Nottingham; Birming. - Birmingham. The matches abandoned without a ball being bowled at Manchester in 1890 and 1938 and at Melbourne in 1970-71 are excluded from these tables.

Highest Innings Totals

Australia in Australia	8d-659	Sydney	1946-47
Australia in England	6d-729	Lord's	1930
England in Australia	636	Sydney	1928-29
England in England	7d-903	The Oval	1938

Lowest Innings Totals

Australia in Australia	42	Sydney	1887-88
Australia in England	36	Birmingham	1902
England in Australia	45	Sydney	1886-87
England in England	52	The Oval	1948

Highest Match Aggregate	1753 for 40 wickets	Adelaide	1920-21
Lowest Match Aggregate	291 for 40 wickets	Lord's	1888

Highest Individual Innings

Australia in Australia	307	R.M.Cowper	Melbourne	1965-66
Australia in England	334	D.G.Bradman	Leeds	1930
England in Australia	287	R.E.Foster	Sydney	1903-04
England in England	364	L.Hutton	The Oval	1938

Most Runs in a Series

Australia in Australia	810 (av 90.00)	D.G.Bradman	1936-37
Australia in England	974 (av 139.14)	D.G.Bradman	1930
England in Australia	905 (av 113.12)	W.R.Hammond	1928-29
England in England	732 (av 81.33)	D.I.Gower	1985

Record Wicket Partnerships - Australia

1st	329	G.R.Marsh (138), M.A.Taylor(219)	Nottingham	1989
2nd	451	W.H.Ponsford (266), D.G.Bradman (244)	The Oval	1934
3rd	276	D.G.Bradman (187), A.L.Hassett (128)	Brisbane[2]	1946-47
4th	388	W H.Ponsford (181), D.G.Bradman (304)	Leeds	1934
5th	405	S.G.Barnes (234), D.G.Bradman (234)	Sydney	1946-47
6th	346	J.H.W Fingleton (136), D.G Bradman (270)	Melbourne	1936-37
7th	165	C.Hill (188), H.Trumble (46)	Melbourne	1897-98
8th	243	R.J.Hartigan (113), C.Hill (160)	Adelaide	1907-08
9th	154	S.E.Gregory (201), J.M.Blackham (74)	Sydney	1894-95
10th	127	J.M.Taylor (108), A.A.Mailey (46*)	Sydney	1924-25

Record Wicket Partnerships - England

1st	323	J.B.Hobbs (178), W.Rhodes (179)	Melbourne	1911-12
2nd	382	L.Hutton (364), M.Leyland (187)	The Oval	1938
3rd	262	W.R.Hammond (177), D.R.Jardine (98)	Adelaide	1928-29
4th	288	N.Hussain (207), G.P.Thorpe (138)	Birmingham	1997
5th	206	E.Paynter (216*), D.C.S.Compton (102)	Nottingham	1938
6th	215	L.Hutton (364), J.Hardstaff, jr (169*)	The Oval	1938
	215	G.Boycott (107), A.P.E.Knott (135)	Nottingham	1977
7th	143	F.E.Woolley (133*), J.Vine (36)	Sydney	1911-12
8th	124	E.H.Hendren (169), H.Larwood (70)	Brisbane[1]	1928-29
9th	151	W.H.Scotton (90), W.W.Read (117)	The Oval	1884
10th	130	R.E.Foster (287), W.Rhodes (40*)	Sydney	1903-04

Best Bowling in an Innings				
Australia in Australia	9/121	A.A.Mailey	Melbourne	1920-21
Australia in England	8/31	F.J.Laver	Manchester	1909
England in Australia	8/35	G.A.Lohmann	Sydney	1886-87
England in England	10/53	J.C.Laker	Manchester	1956
Best Bowling in a Match				
Australia in Australia	13/77	M.A.Noble	Melbourne	1901-02
Australia in England	16/137	R.A.L.Massie	Lord's	1972
England in Australia	15/124	W.Rhodes	Melbourne	1903-04
England in England	19/90	J.C.Laker	Manchester	1956
Most Wickets in a Series				
Australia in Australia	41 (av 12.85)		R.M.Hogg	1978-79
Australia in England	42 (av 21.26)		T.M.Alderman	1981
England in Australia	38 (av 23.18)		M.W.Tate	1924-25
England in England	46 (av 9.60)		J.C.Laker	1956

AUSTRALIA v SOUTH AFRICA	Australia		South Africa		Captains	
Venue and Result	1st	2nd	1st	2nd	Australia	South Africa
1902-03 in South Africa						
Johannesburg[1]-Drawn	296	7d-372	•454	4-101	J.Darling	H.M.Taberer
Johannesburg[1]-Australia 159 runs	•175	309	240	85		J.H.Anderson
Cape Town-Australia 10 wkts	•252	0-59	85	225		E.A.Halliwell
1910-11 in Australia						
Sydney-Australia inn &114 runs	•528	-	174	240	C.Hill	P.W.Sherwell
Melbourne-Australia 89 runs	•348	327	506	80		
Adelaide-South Africa 38 runs	465	339	•482	360		
Melbourne-Australia 530 runs	•328	578	205	171		
Sydney-Australia 7 wkts	•364	3-198	160	401		
1912 in England						
Manchester-Australia inn & 88 runs	•448	-	265	95	S.E.Gregory	F.Mitchell
Lord's-Australia 10 wkts	390	0-48	•263	173		F.Mitchell
Nottingham-Drawn	219	-	•329	-		L.J.Tancred
1921-22 in South Africa						
Durban[1]-Drawn	•299	7d-324	232	7-184	H.L.Collins	H.W.Taylor
Johannesburg[1]-Drawn	•450	0-7	243	8d-472		
Cape Town-Australia 10 wkts	396	0-1	•180	216		
1931-32 in Australia						
Brisbane[2]-Australia inn & 163 runs	•450	-	170	117	W.M.Woodfull	H.B.Cameron
Sydney-Australia inn & 155 runs	469	-	•153	161		
Melbourne-Australia 169 runs	•198	554	358	225		
Adelaide-Australia 10 wkts	513	0-73	•308	274		
Melbourne-Australia inn & 72 runs	153	-	•36	45		
1935-36 in South Africa						
Durban[2]-Australia 9 wkts	429	1-102	•248	282	V.Y.Richardson	H.F.Wade
Johannesburg[1]-Drawn	250	2-274	•157	491		
Cape Town-Australia inn & 78 runs	•8d-362	-	102	182		
Johannesburg[1]- Australia inn & 184 runs	439	-	•157	98		
Durban[2]-Australia inn & 6 runs	455	-	•222	227		

AUSTRALIA v SOUTH AFRICA (cont) Venue and Result	Australia 1st	Australia 2nd	South Africa 1st	South Africa 2nd	Captains Australia	Captains South Africa
1949-50 in South Africa						
Johannesburg^{2}-Australia inn & 85 runs	•413	-	137	191	A.L.Hassett	A.D.Nourse
Cape Town-Australia 8 wkts	•7d-526	2-87	278	333		
Durban^{2}-Australia 5 wkts	75	5-336	•311	99		
Johannesburg^{2}-Drawn	•8d-465	2-259	352	-		
Port Elizabeth-Australia inn & 259 runs	•7d-549	-	158	132		
1952-53 in Australia						
Brisbane^{2}-Australia 96 runs	•280	277	221	240	A.L.Hassett	J.E.Cheetham
Melbourne-South Africa 82 runs	243	290	•227	388		
Sydney-Australia inn & 38 runs	443	-	•173	232		
Adelaide-Drawn	•530	3d-233	387	6-177		
Melbourne-South Africa 6 wkts	•520	209	435	4-297		
1957-58 in South Africa						
Johannesburg^{3}-Drawn	368	3-162	•9d-470	201	I.D.Craig	D.J.McGlew
Cape Town-Australia inn & 141 runs	•449	-	209	99		C.B.van Ryneveld
Durban^{2}-Drawn	•163	7-292	384	-		C.B.van Ryneveld
Johannesburg^{3}-Australia 10 wkts	•401	0-1	203	198		C.B.van Ryneveld
Port Elizabeth-Australia 8 wkts	291	2-68	•214	144		C.B.van Ryneveld
1963-64 in Australia						
Brisbane^{2}-Drawn	•435	1d-144	346	1-13	R.Benaud	T.L.Goddard
Melbourne-Australia 8 wkts	447	2-136	•274	306	R.B.Simpson	
Sydney-Drawn	•260	9d-450	302	5-326	R.B.Simpson	
Adelaide-South Africa 10 wkts	•345	331	595	0-82	R.B.Simpson	
Sydney-Drawn	•311	270	411	0-76	R.B.Simpson	
1966-67 in South Africa						
Johannesburg^{3}-South Africa 233 runs	325	261	•199	620	R.B.Simpson	P.L.van der Merwe
Cape Town-Australia 6 wkts	•542	4-180	353	367		
Durban^{2}-South Africa 8 wkts	147	334	•300	2-185		
Johannesburg^{3}-Drawn	•143	8-148	9d-332	-		
Port Elizabeth-South Africa 7 wkts	•173	278	276	3-179		
1969-70 in South Africa						
Cape Town-South Africa 170 runs	164	280	•382	232	W.M.Lawry	A.Bacher
Durban^{2}-South Africa inn &129 runs	157	336	•9d-622	-		
Johannesburg^{3}-South Africa 307 runs	202	178	•279	408		
Port Elizabeth-South Africa 323 runs	212	246	•311	8d-470		
1993-94 in Australia						
Melbourne-Drawn	•7d-342	-	3-258	-	A.R.Border	K.C.Wessels
Sydney-South Africa 5 runs	292	111	•169	239		K.C.Wessels
Adelaide-Australia 191 runs	•7d-469	6d-124	273	129		W.J.Cronje
1993-94 in South Africa						
Johannesburg^{3}-South Africa 197 runs	248	256	•251	9d-450	A.R.Border	K.C.Wessels
Cape Town-Australia 9 wkts	435	1-92	•361	164		
Durban^{2}-Drawn	•269	4-297	422	-		

AUSTRALIA v SOUTH AFRICA (cont)	Australia		South Africa		Captains	
Venue and Result	1st	2nd	1st	2nd	Australia	South Africa
1996-97 in South Africa						
Johannesburg[3]-Australia inn & 196 runs	8d-628	-	•302	130	M.A.Taylor	W.J.Cronje
Port Elizabeth-Australia 2 wkts	108	8-271	•209	168		
Centurion-South Africa 8 wkts	•227	185	384	2-32		
1997-98 in Australia						
Melbourne-Drawn	•309	257	186	7-273	M.A.Taylor	W.J.Cronje
Sydney-Australia inn & 21 runs	421	-	•287	113		
Adelaide-Drawn	350	7-227	•517	6d-193		
2001-02 in Australia						
Adelaide-Australia 246 runs	•439	7d-307	274	128	S.R.Waugh	S.M.Pollock
Melbourne-Australia 9 wkts	487	1-10	•277	219		
Sydney-Australia 10 wkts	•554	0-54	154	452		
2001-02 in South Africa						
Johannesburg[3]-Australia inn & 360 runs	•7d-652	-	159	133	S.R.Waugh	M.V.Boucher
Cape Town-Australia 4 wkts	382	6-334	•239	473		
Durban[2]-South Africa 5 wkts	•315	186	167	5-340		
2005-06 in Australia						
Perth-Drawn	•258	8d-528	296	5-287	R.T.Ponting	G.C.Smith
Melbourne-Aust 184 runs	•355	7d-321	311	181		
Sydney-Aust 8 wkts	359	2-288	•9d-451	6d-194		
2005-06 in South Africa						
Cape Town-Australia 7 wkts	308	3-95	•205	197	R.T.Ponting	G.C.Smith
Durban[2]-Australia 112 runs	•369	4d-307	267	297		G.C.Smith
Johannesburg[3]-Australia 2 wkts	270	8-294	•303	258		J.H.Kallis

Test Match Results Summary

AUSTRALIA v SOUTH AFRICA - in Australia

		Result			Sydney			Melbourne			Adelaide			Brisbane[2]			Perth		
	Tests	A	SA	D	A	SA	D	A	SA	D	A	SA	D	A	SA	D	A	SA	D
1910-11	5	4	1	-	2	-	-	2	-	-	-	1	-	-	-	-	-	-	-
1931-32	5	5	-	-	1	-	-	2	-	-	1	-	-	1	-	-	-	-	-
1952-53	5	2	2	1	1	-	-	-	2	-	-	-	1	1	-	-	-	-	-
1963-64	5	1	1	3	-	-	2	1	-	-	-	1	-	-	-	1	-	-	-
1993-94	3	1	1	1	-	1	-	-	-	1	1	-	-	-	-	-	-	-	-
1997-98	3	1	-	2	1	-	-	-	-	1	-	-	1	-	-	-	-	-	-
2001-02	3	3	-	-	1	-	-	1	-	-	1	-	-	-	-	-	-	-	-
2005-06	3	2	-	1	1	-	-	1	-	-	-	-	-	-	-	-	-	-	1
	32	19	5	8	7	1	2	7	2	2	3	2	2	2	-	1	-	-	1

AUSTRALIA v SOUTH AFRICA - in South Africa

		Result			Jo'burg[1]			C.Town			Durban[1]			Durban[2]			Jo'burg[2]			P.Elizabeth			Jo'burg[3]			Centurion		
	Tests	A	S	D	A	S	D	A	S	D	A	S	D	A	S	D	A	S	D	A	S	D	A	S	D	A	S	D
1902-03	3	2	-	1	1	-	1	1	-	-	-	-	-	-	-	-	-	-	-	-	-	-	-	-	-	-	-	-
1921-22	3	1	-	2	-	-	1	1	-	-	-	-	1	-	-	-	-	-	-	-	-	-	-	-	-	-	-	-
1935-36	5	4	-	1	1	-	1	1	-	-	-	-	-	2	-	-	-	-	-	-	-	-	-	-	-	-	-	-
1949-50	5	4	-	1	-	-	-	1	-	-	-	-	-	1	-	-	1	-	1	1	-	-	-	-	-	-	-	-
1957-58	5	3	-	2	-	-	-	1	-	-	-	-	-	-	-	1	-	-	-	1	-	-	1	-	1	-	-	-
1966-67	5	1	3	1	-	-	-	1	-	-	-	-	-	-	1	-	-	-	-	-	1	-	-	1	1	-	-	-
1969-70	4	-	4	-	-	-	-	-	1	-	-	-	-	-	1	-	-	-	-	-	1	-	-	1	-	-	-	-
1993-94	3	1	1	1	-	-	-	1	-	-	-	-	-	-	-	1	-	-	-	-	-	-	-	1	-	-	-	-
1996-97	3	2	1	-	-	-	-	-	-	-	-	-	-	-	-	-	-	-	-	1	-	-	1	-	-	-	1	-
2001-02	3	2	1	-	-	-	-	1	-	-	-	-	-	-	1	-	-	-	-	-	-	-	1	-	-	-	-	-
2005-0	3	3	-	-	-	-	-	1	-	-	-	-	-	1	-	-	-	-	-	-	-	-	1	-	-	-	-	-
	42	23	10	9	2	-	3	9	1	-	-	-	1	4	3	2	1	-	1	3	2	-	4	3	2	-	1	-

AUSTRALIA v SOUTH AFRICA - in England

		Result			Manchester			Lord's			Nottingham		
	Tests	A	SA	D	A	SA	D	A	SA	D	A	SA	D
1912	3	2	-	1	1	-	-	1	-	-	-	-	1

Totals	77	44	15	18

Highest Innings Totals

Australia in Australia	578	Melbourne	1910-11
Australia in South Africa	7d-652	Johannesburg[3]	2001-02
South Africa in Australia	595	Adelaide	1963-64
South Africa in South Africa	9d-622	Durban[2]	1969-70

Lowest Innings Totals

Australia in Australia	111	Sydney	1993-94
Australia in South Africa	75	Durban[2]	1949-50
South Africa in Australia	36	Melbourne	1931-32
South Africa in South Africa	85	Johannesburg[1]	1902-03
	85	Cape Town	1902-03

Highest Match Aggregate	1646 for 40 wickets	Adelaide	1910-11
Lowest Match Aggregate	234 for 29 wickets	Melbourne	1931-32

Highest Individual Innings

Australia in Australia	299*	D.G.Bradman	Adelaide	1931-32
Australia in South Africa	214	G.S.Blewett	Johannesburg[3]	1996-97
South Africa in Australia	204	G.A.Faulkner	Melbourne	1910-11
South Africa in South Africa	274	R.G.Pollock	Durban[2]	1969-70

Most Runs in a Series

Australia in Australia	834 (av 92.66)	R.N.Harvey	1952-53
Australia in South Africa	660 (av 132.00)	R.N.Harvey	1949-50
South Africa in Australia	732 (av 73.20)	G.A.Faulkner	1910-11
South Africa in South Africa	606 (av 86.57)	D.T.Lindsay	1966-67

Record Wicket Partnerships - Australia

1st	233	J.H.W.Fingleton (112), W.A.Brown (121)	Cape Town	1935-36
2nd	275	C.C.McDonald (154), A.L.Hassett (163)	Adelaide	1952-53
3rd	242	C.Kelleway (102), W.Bardsley (164)	Lord's	1912
4th	169	M.A.Taylor (170), M.E.Waugh (84)	Melbourne	1993-94
5th	385	S.R.Waugh (160), G.S.Blewett (214)	Johannesburg[3]	1996-97
6th	317	D.R.Martyn (103), A.C.Gilchrist (204*)	Johannesburg[3]	2001-02
7th	160	R.Benaud (90), G.D.McKenzie (76)	Sydney	1963-64
8th	83	A.G.Chipperfield (109), C.V.Grimmett (15)	Durban[2]	1935-36
9th	78	D.G.Bradman (299*), W.J.O'Reilly (23)	Adelaide	1931-32
	78	K.D.Mackay (83*), I.Meckiff (26)	Johannesburg[3]	1957-58
10th	107	M.E.K.Hussey (122), G.D.McGrath (11*)	Melbourne	2005-06

Record Wicket Partnerships - South Africa

1st	176	D.J.McGlew (108), T.L.Goddard (90)	Johannesburg[3]	1957-58
2nd	173	L.J.Tancred (97), C.B.Llewellyn (90)	Johannesburg[1]	1902-03
3rd	341	E.J.Barlow (201), R.G.Pollock (175)	Adelaide	1963-64
4th	219	J.H.Kallis (111), A.G.Prince (119)	Sydney	2005-06
5th	129	J.H.B.Waite (59), W.R.Endean (77)	Johannesburg[3]	1957-58
6th	200	R.G.Pollock (274), H.R.Lance (61)	Durban[2]	1969-70
7th	221	D.T.Lindsay (182), P.L.van der Merwe (76)	Johannesburg[3]	1966-67
8th	124	A.W.Nourse (72), E.A.Halliwell (57)	Johannesburg[1]	1902-03
9th	85	R.G.Pollock (209), P.M.Pollock (41)	Cape Town	1966-67
10th	74	B.M.McMillan (87*), P.L.Symcox (54)	Adelaide	1997-98

Best Bowling in an Innings

Australia in Australia	7/56	S.K.Warne	Sydney	1993-94
Australia in South Africa	7/34	J.V.Saunders	Johannesburg[1]	1902-03
South Africa in Australia	7/81	H.J.Tayfield	Melbourne	1952-53
South Africa in South Africa	7/23	H.J.Tayfield	Durban[2]	1949-50

Best Bowling in a Match

Australia in Australia	14/199	C.V.Grimmett	Adelaide	1931-32
Australia in South Africa	13/173	C.V.Grimmett	Durban[2]	1935-36
South Africa in Australia	13/165	H.J.Tayfield	Melbourne	1952-53
South Africa in South Africa	10/116	C.B.Llewellyn	Johannesburg[1]	1902-03

Most Wickets in a Series

Australia in Australia	37 (av 17.08)	W.J.Whitty	1910-11
Australia in South Africa	44 (av 14.59)	C.V.Grimmett	1935-36
South Africa in Australia	30 (av 28.10)	H.J.Tayfield	1952-53
South Africa in South Africa	26 (av 16.23)	T.L.Goddard	1966-67
	26 (av 13.57)	M.J.Procter	1969-70

AUSTRALIA v WEST INDIES	Australia		West Indies		Captains	
Venue and Result	1st	2nd	1st	2nd	Australia	West Indies
1930-31 in Australia						
Adelaide-Australia 10 wkts	376	0-172	•296	249	W.M.Woodfull	G.C.Grant
Sydney-Australia inn & 172 runs	•369	-	107	90		
Brisbane[1]-Australia inn & 217 runs	•558	-	193	148		
Melbourne-Australia inn & 122 runs	8d-328	-	•99	107		
Sydney-West Indies 30 runs	224	220	•6d-350	5d-124		
1951-52 in Australia						
Brisbane[2]-Australia 3 wkts	226	7-236	•216	245	A.L.Hassett	J.D.C.Goddard

AUSTRALIA v WEST INDIES (cont.)	Australia		West Indies		Captains	
Venue and Result	1st	2nd	1st	2nd	Australia	West Indies
Sydney-Australia 7 wkts	517	3-137	•362	290	A.L.Hassett	J.D.C.Goddard
Adelaide-West Indies 6 wkts	•82	255	105	4-233	A.R.Morris	J.D.C.Goddard
Melbourne-Australia 1 wkt	216	9-260	•272	203	A.L.Hassett	J.D.C.Goddard
Sydney-Australia 202 runs	•116	377	78	213	A.L.Hassett	J.B.Stollmeyer
1954-55 in West Indies						
Kingston-Australia 9 wkts	•9d-515	1-20	259	275	I.W.G.Johnson	D.S.Atkinson
Port-of-Spain-Drawn	9d-600	-	•382	4-273		J.B.Stollmeyer
Georgetown-Australia 8 wkts	257	2-133	•182	207		J.B.Stollmeyer
Bridgetown-Drawn	•668	249	510	6-234		D.S.Atkinson
Kingston-Australia inn & 82 runs	8d-758	-	•357	319		D.S.Atkinson
1960-61 in Australia						
Brisbane[2]-Tied	505	232	•453	284	R.Benaud	F.M.M.Worrell
Melbourne-Australia 7 wkts	•348	3-70	181	233		
Sydney-West Indies 222 runs	202	241	•339	326		
Adelaide-Drawn	366	9-273	•393	6d-432		
Melbourne-Australia 2 wkts	356	8-258	•292	321		
1964-65 in West Indies						
Kingston-West Indies 179 runs	217	216	•239	373	R.B.Simpson	G.S.Sobers
Port-of-Spain-Drawn	516	-	•429	386		
Georgetown-West Indies 212 runs	179	144	•355	180		
Bridgetown-Drawn	•6d-650	4d-175	573	5-242		
Port-of-Spain-Australia 10 wkts	294	0-63	•224	131		
1968-69 in Australia						
Brisbane[2]-West Indies 125 runs	284	240	•296	353	W.M.Lawry	G.S.Sobers
Melbourne-Australia inn & 30 runs	510	-	•200	280		
Sydney-Australia 10 wkts	547	0-42	•264	324		
Adelaide-Drawn	533	9-339	•276	616		
Sydney-Australia 382 runs	•619	8d-394	279	352		
1972-73 in West Indies						
Kingston-Drawn	•7d-428	2d-260	428	3-67	I.M.Chappell	R.B.Kanhai
Bridgetown-Drawn	•324	2d-300	391	0-36		
Port-of-Spain-Australia 44 runs	•332	281	280	289		
Georgetown-Australia 10 wkts	341	0-135	•366	109		
Port-of-Spain-Drawn	•8d-419	7d-218	319	5-135		
1975-76 in Australia						
Brisbane[2]-Australia 8 wkts	366	2-219	•214	370	G.S.Chappell	C.H.Lloyd
Perth-West Indies inn & 87 runs	•329	169	585	-		
Melbourne-Australia 8 wkts	485	2-55	•224	312		
Sydney-Australia 7 wkts	405	3-82	•355	128		
Adelaide-Australia 190 runs	•418	7d-345	274	299		
Melbourne-Australia 165 runs	•351	3d-300	160	326		
1977-78 in West Indies						
Port-of-Spain-West Indies inn & 106 runs	•90	209	405	-	R.B.Simpson	C.H.Lloyd
Bridgetown-West Indies 9 wkts	•250	178	288	1-141		C.H.Lloyd
Georgetown-Australia 3 wkts	286	7-362	•205	439		A.I.Kallicharran
Port-of-Spain-West Indies 198 runs	290	94	•292	290		A.I.Kallicharran
Kingston-Drawn	•343	3d-305	280	9-258		A.I.Kallicharran

AUSTRALIA v WEST INDIES (cont.)	Australia		West Indies		Captains	
Venue and Result	1st	2nd	1st	2nd	Australia	West Indies
1979-80 in Australia						
Brisbane[2]-Drawn	•268	6d-448	441	3-40	G.S.Chappell	D L.Murray
Melbourne-West Indies 10 wkts	•156	259	397	0-22		C.H.Lloyd
Adelaide-West Indies 408 runs	203	165	•328	448		C.H.Lloyd
1981-82 in Australia						
Melbourne-Australia 58 runs	•198	222	201	161	G.S.Chappell	C H.Lloyd
Sydney-Drawn	267	4-200	•384	255		
Adelaide-West Indies 5 wkts	•238	386	389	5-239		
1983-84 in West Indies						
Georgetown-Drawn	•279	9d-273	230	0-250	K.J.Hughes	C.H.Lloyd
Port-of-Spain-Drawn	•255	9d-299	8d-468	-		I.V.A.Richards
Bridgetown-West Indies 10 wkts	•429	97	509	0-21		C.H.Lloyd
St John's-West Indies inn & 36 runs	•262	200	498	-		C.H.Lloyd
Kingston-West Indies 10 wkts	•199	160	305	0-55		C.H.Lloyd
1984-85 in Australia						
Perth-West Indies inn & 112 runs	76	228	•416	-	K.J.Hughes	C.H.Lloyd
Brisbane[2]-West Indies 8 wkts	•175	271	424	2-26	K.J.Hughes	
Adelaide-West Indies 191 runs	284	173	•356	7d-292	A.R.Border	
Melbourne-Drawn	298	8-198	•479	5d-186	A.R.Border	
Sydney-Australia inn & 55 runs	•9d-471	-	163	253	A.R.Border	
1988-89 in Australia						
Brisbane[2]-West Indies 8 wkts	•167	289	394	2-63	A.R.Border	I.V.A.Richards
Perth-West Indies 169 runs	8d-395	234	•449	9d-349		
Melbourne-West Indies 285 runs	242	114	•280	9d-361		
Sydney-Australia 7 wkts	401	3-82	•224	256		
Adelaide-Drawn	•515	4d-224	369	4-233		
1990-91 in West Indies						
Kingston-Drawn	371	-	•264	3-334	A.R.Border	I.V.A.Richards
Georgetown-West Indies 10 wkts	•348	248	569	0-31		
Port-of-Spain-Drawn	•294	3-123	227	-		
Bridgetown-West Indies 343 runs	134	208	•149	9d-536		
St John's-Australia 157 runs	•403	265	214	297		
1992-93 in Australia						
Brisbane[2]-Drawn	•293	308	371	8-133	A.R.Border	R.B.Richardson
Melbourne-Australia 139 runs	•395	196	233	219		
Sydney-Drawn	•9d-503	0-117	616	-		
Adelaide-West Indies 1 run	213	184	•252	146		
Perth-West Indies inn & 25 runs	•119	178	322	-		
1994-95 in West Indies						
Bridgetown-Australia 10 wkts	346	0-39	•195	189	M.A.Taylor	R.B.Richardson
St John's-Drawn	•216	7d-300	260	2-80		
Port-of-Spain-West Indies 9 wkts	•128	105	136	1-98		
Kingston-Australia inn & 53 runs	531	-	•265	213		
1996-97 in Australia						
Brisbane[2]-Australia 123 runs	•479	6d-217	277	296	M.A.Taylor	C.A.Walsh
Sydney-Australia 124 runs	•331	4d-312	304	215		
Melbourne-West Indies 6 wkts	•219	122	255	4-87		

AUSTRALIA v WEST INDIES (cont.)	Australia		West Indies		Captains	
Venue and Result	1st	2nd	1st	2nd	Australia	West Indies
Adelaide-Australia inn & 183 runs	517	-	•130	204		
Perth-West Indies 10 wkts	•243	194	384	0-57		
1998-99 in West Indies						
Bridgetown-Australia 312 runs	•269	261	167	51	S.R.Waugh	B.C.Lara
St John's-West Indies 10 wkts	•256	177	431	0-3		
Port-of-Spain-West Indies 1 wkt	•490	146	329	9-311		
Kingston-Australia 176 runs	•303	306	222	211		
2000-01 in Australia						
Brisbane[2]-Australia inn & 126 runs	332	-	•82	124	S.R.Waugh	J.C.Adams
Perth-Australia inn & 27 runs	8d-396	-	•196	173		
Adelaide-Australia 5 wkts	403	5-103	•391	141		
Melbourne-Australia 352 runs	•364	5d-262	165	109		
Sydney-Australia 6 wkts	452	4-174	•272	352		
2002-03 in West Indies						
Georgetown-Australia 9 wkts	489	1-147	•237	398	S.R.Waugh	B.C.Lara
Port-of-Spain-Australia 118 runs	•4d-576	3d-238	408	288		
Bridgetown-Australia 9 wkts	•9d-605	1-8	328	284		
St John's-West Indies 7 wkts	•240	417	240	7-418		
2005-06 in Australia						
Brisbane[2]-Australia 379 runs	•435	2d-383	210	129	R.T.Ponting	S.Chanderpaul
Hobart-Australia 9 wkts	406	1-78	•149	334		
Adelaide-Australia 7 wkts	428	3-182	•405	204		

Test Match Results Summary

AUSTRALIA v WEST INDIES - in Australia

		Result				Adelaide				Sydney				Brisbane[1]				Melbourne				Brisbane[2]				Perth				Hobart			
	Tests	A	W	D	T	A	W	D	T	A	W	D	T	A	W	D	T	A	W	D	T	A	W	D	T	A	W	D	T	A	W	D	T
1930-31	5	4	1	-	-	1	-	-	-	1	1	-	-	1	-	-	-	1	-	-	-	-	-	-	-	-	-	-	-	-	-	-	-
1951-52	5	4	1	-	-	-	1	-	-	2	-	-	-	-	-	-	-	1	-	-	-	1	-	-	-	-	-	-	-	-	-	-	-
1960-61	5	2	1	1	1	-	-	1	-	-	1	-	-	-	-	-	-	2	-	-	-	-	-	-	1	-	-	-	-	-	-	-	-
1968-69	5	3	1	1	-	-	-	1	-	2	-	-	-	-	-	-	-	1	-	-	-	-	1	-	-	-	-	-	-	-	-	-	-
1975-76	6	5	1	-	-	1	-	-	-	1	-	-	-	-	-	-	-	2	-	-	-	1	-	-	-	-	1	-	-	-	-	-	-
1979-80	3	-	2	1	-	-	1	-	-	-	-	-	-	-	-	-	-	-	1	-	-	-	-	1	-	-	-	-	-	-	-	-	-
1981-82	3	1	1	1	-	-	1	-	-	-	-	1	-	-	-	-	-	1	-	-	-	-	-	-	-	-	-	-	-	-	-	-	-
1984-85	5	1	3	1	-	-	1	-	-	1	-	-	-	-	-	-	-	-	-	1	-	-	1	-	-	-	1	-	-	-	-	-	-
1988-89	5	1	3	1	-	-	-	1	-	1	-	-	-	-	-	-	-	-	1	-	-	-	1	-	-	-	1	-	-	-	-	-	-
1992-93	5	1	2	2	-	-	1	-	-	-	-	1	-	-	-	-	-	1	-	-	-	-	-	1	-	-	1	-	-	-	-	-	-
1996-97	5	3	2	-	-	1	-	-	-	1	-	-	-	-	-	-	-	-	1	-	-	1	-	-	-	-	1	-	-	-	-	-	-
2000-01	5	5	-	-	-	1	-	-	-	1	-	-	-	-	-	-	-	1	-	-	-	1	-	-	-	1	-	-	-	-	-	-	-
2005-06	3	3	-	-	-	1	-	-	-	-	-	-	-	-	-	-	-	-	-	-	-	1	-	-	-	-	-	-	-	1	-	-	-
	60	33	18	8	1	5	5	3	-	10	2	2	-	1	-	-	-	10	3	1	-	5	3	2	1	1	5	-	-	1	-	-	-

AUSTRALIA v WEST INDIES - in West Indies

		Result				Kingston				Port-of-Spain				Georgetown				Bridgetown				St John's			
	Tests	A	W	D	T	A	W	D	T	A	W	D	T	A	W	D	T	A	W	D	T	A	W	D	T
1954-55	5	3	-	2	-	2	-	-	-	-	-	1	-	1	-	-	-	-	-	1	-	-	-	-	-
1964-65	5	1	2	2	-	-	1	-	-	1	-	1	-	-	1	-	-	-	-	1	-	-	-	-	-
1972-73	5	2	-	3	-	-	-	1	-	1	-	1	-	1	-	-	-	-	-	1	-	-	-	-	-
1977-78	5	1	3	1	-	-	-	1	-	-	2	-	-	1	-	-	-	-	1	-	-	-	-	-	-
1983-84	5	-	3	2	-	-	1	-	-	-	-	1	-	-	-	1	-	-	1	-	-	-	1	-	-
1990-91	5	1	2	2	-	-	-	1	-	-	-	1	-	-	1	-	-	-	1	-	-	1	-	-	-
1994-95	4	2	1	1	-	1	-	-	-	-	1	-	-	-	-	-	-	1	-	-	-	-	-	1	-
1998-99	4	2	2	-	-	-	1	-	-	1	-	-	-	-	-	-	-	-	1	-	-	1	-	-	-
2002-03	4	3	1	-	-	-	-	-	-	1	-	-	-	1	-	-	-	1	-	-	-	-	1	-	-
	42	15	14	13	-	3	3	3	-	4	3	5	-	4	2	1	-	2	4	3	-	2	2	1	-
Totals	102	48	32	21	1																				

Highest Innings Totals

Australia in Australia	619	Sydney	1968-69
Australia in West Indies	8d-758	Kingston	1954-55
West Indies in Australia	616	Adelaide	1968-69
West Indies in West Indies	573	Bridgetown	1964-65

Lowest Innings Totals

Australia in Australia	76	Perth	1984-85
Australia in West Indies	90	Port-of-Spain	1977-78
West Indies in Australia	78	Sydney	1951-52
West Indies in West Indies	51	Port-of-Spain	1998-99

Highest Match Aggregate	1764 for 39 wickets	Adelaide	1968-69
Lowest Match Aggregate	467 for 31 wickets	Port-of-Spain	1994-95

Highest Individual Innings

Australia in Australia	242	K.D.Walters	Sydney	1968-69
Australia in West Indies	210	W.M.Lawry	Bridgetown	1964-65
West Indies in Australia	277	B.C.Lara	Sydney	1992-93
West Indies in West Indies	226	C.G.Greenidge	Bridgetown	1990-91

Most Runs in a Series

Australia in Australia	702 (av 117.00)	G.S.Chappell	1975-76
Australia in West Indies	650 (av 108.33)	R.N.Harvey	1954-55
West Indies in Australia	537 (av 59.66)	D.L.Haynes	1988-89
West Indies in West Indies	827 (av 82.70)	C.L.Walcott	1954-55

Record Wicket Partnerships - Australia

1st	382	W.M.Lawry (210), R.B.Simpson (201)	Bridgetown	1964-65
2nd	298	W.M.Lawry (205), I.M.Chappell (165)	Melbourne	1968-69
3rd	316	R.T.Ponting (206), D.S.Lehmann (160)	Port-of-Spain	2002-03
4th	336	W.M.Lawry (151), K.D.Walters (242)	Sydney	1968-69
5th	281	S.R.Waugh (199), R.T.Ponting (104)	Bridgetown	1998-99
6th	206	K.R.Miller (137), R.G.Archer (98)	Bridgetown	1954-55
7th	134	R.Benaud (52), A.K.Davidson (80)	Brisbane[2]	1960-61
8th	137	R.Benaud (128), I.W.G.Johnson (27*)	Kingston	1954-55
9th	114	D.M.Jones (216), M.G.Hughes (72*)	Adelaide	1988-89
10th	97	T.G.Hogan (42*), R.M.Hogg (52)	Georgetown	1983-84

Record Wicket Partnerships - West Indies

1st	250*	C.G.Greenidge (120*), D.L.Haynes (103*)	Georgetown	1983-84
2nd	297	D.L.Haynes (111), R.B.Richardson (182)	Georgetown	1990-91
3rd	308	R.B.Richardson (154), I.V.A.Richards (178)	St John's	1983-84
4th	198	L.G.Rowe (107), A.I.Kallicharran (101)	Brisbane[2]	1975-76
5th	322	B.C.Lara (213), J.C.Adams (94)	Kingston	1998-99
6th	165	R.B.Kanhai (105), D.L.Murray (90)	Bridgetown	1972-73
7th	347	D.S.Atkinson (219), C.C.Depeiza (122)	Bridgetown	1954-55
8th	87	P.J.L.Dujon (70), C.E.L.Ambrose (53)	Port-of-Spain	1990-91
9th	122	D.A.J.Holford (80), J.L.Hendriks (37*)	Adelaide	1968-69
10th	56	J.Garner (60), C.E.H.Croft (2*)	Brisbane[2]	1979-80

Best Bowling in an Innings

Australia in Australia	8/71	G.D.McKenzie	Melbourne	1968-69
Australia in West Indies	7/44	I.W.G.Johnson	Georgetown	1954-55
West Indies in Australia	7/25	C.E.L.Ambrose	Perth	1992-93
West Indies in West Indies	7/78	J.J.C.Lawson	St John's	2002-03

Best Bowling in a Match

Australia in Australia	13/217	M.G.Hughes	Perth	1988-89
Australia in West Indies	10/78	G.D.McGrath	Port-of-Spain	1998-99
West Indies in Australia	11/107	M.A.Holding	Melbourne	1981-82
West Indies in West Indies	9/65	C.E.L.Ambrose	Port-of-Spain	1994-95

Most Wickets in a Series

Australia in Australia	33 (av 17.96)	C.V.Grimmett	1930-31
	33 (av 18.54)	A.K.Davidson	1960-61
Australia in West Indies	30 (av 16.93)	G.D.McGrath	1998-99
West Indies in Australia	33 (av 16.42)	C.E.L.Ambrose	1992-93
West Indies in West Indies	31 (av 16.87)	J.Garner	1983-84

AUSTRALIA v NEW ZEALAND	Australia		New Zealand		Captains	
Venue and Result	1st	2nd	1st	2nd	Australia	New Zealand
1945-46 in New Zealand						
Wellington-Australia inn & 103 runs	8d-199	-	•42	54	W.A.Brown	W.A.Hadlee
1973-74 in Australia						
Melbourne-Australia inn & 25 runs	•8d-462	-	237	200	I.M.Chappell	B.E.Congdon
Sydney-Drawn	162	2-30	•312	9d-305		
Adelaide-Australia inn & 57 runs	•477	-	218	202		
1973-74 in New Zealand						
Wellington-Drawn	•6d-511	8-460	484	-	I.M.Chappell	B.E.Congdon
Christchurch-New Zealand 5 wkts	•223	259	255	5-230		
Auckland-Australia 297 runs	•221	346	112	158		
1976-77 in New Zealand						
Christchurch-Drawn	•552	4d-154	357	8-293	G.S.Chappell	G.M.Turner
Auckland-Australia 10 wkts	377	0-28	•229	175		
1980-81 in Australia						
Brisbane[2]-Australia 10 wkts	305	0-63	•225	142	G.S.Chappell	G.P.Howarth
Perth-Australia 8 wkts	265	2-55	•196	121		M.G.Burgess
Melbourne-Drawn	•321	188	317	6-128		G.P.Howarth

AUSTRALIA v NEW ZEALAND (cont.)	Australia		New Zealand		Captains	
Venue and Result	1st	2nd	1st	2nd	Australia	New Zealand
1981-82 in New Zealand						
Wellington-Drawn	1-85	-	•7d-266	-	G.S.Chappell	G.P.Howarth
Auckland-New Zealand 5 wkts	•210	280	387	5-109		
Christchurch-Australia 8 wkts	•353	2-69	149	272		
1985-86 in Australia						
Brisbane[2]-New Zealand inn & 41 runs	•179	333	7d-553	-	A.R.Border	J.V.Coney
Sydney-Australia 4 wkts	227	6-260	•293	193		
Perth-New Zealand 6 wkts	•203	259	299	4-164		
1985-86 in New Zealand						
Wellington-Drawn	•435	-	6-379	-	A.R.Border	J.V.Coney
Auckland-Drawn	•364	7d-219	339	1-16		
Christchurch-New Zealand 8 wkts	•314	103	258	2-160		
1987-88 in Australia						
Brisbane[2]-Australia 9 wkts	305	1-97	•186	212	A.R.Border	J.J.Crowe
Adelaide-Drawn	496	-	•9d-485	7-182		
Melbourne-Drawn	357	9-230	•317	286		
1989-90 in Australia						
Perth-Drawn	•9d-521	-	231	7-322	A.R.Border	J.G.Wright
1989-90 in New Zealand						
Wellington-New Zealand 9 wkts	•110	269	202	1-181	A.R.Border	J.G.Wright
1992-93 in New Zealand						
Canterbury-Australia inn & 60 runs	•485	-	182	243	A.R.Border	M.D.Crowe
Wellington-Drawn	298	-	•329	7-210		
Auckland-New Zealand 5 wkts	•139	285	224	5-201		
1993-94 in Australia						
Perth-Drawn	•398	1d-323	9d-419	4-166	A.R.Border	M.D.Crowe
Hobart-Australia inn & 222 runs	•6d-544	-	161	161		K.R.Rutherford
Brisbane[2]-Australia inn & 96 runs	6d-607	-	•233	278		K.R.Rutherford
1997-98 in Australia						
Brisbane[2]-Australia 186 runs	•373	6d-294	349	132	M.A.Taylor	S.P.Fleming
Perth-Australia inn & 70 runs	461	-	•217	174		
Hobart-Drawn	•400	2d-138	6d-251	9-223		
1999-2000 in New Zealand						
Auckland-Australia 62 runs	•214	229	163	218	S.R.Waugh	S.P.Fleming
Wellington-Australia 6 wkts	419	4-177	•298	294		
Hamilton-Australia 6 wkts	252	4-212	•232	229		
2001-02 in Australia						
Brisbane[2]-Drawn	•9d-486	2d-84	8d-287	6-274	S.R.Waugh	S.P.Fleming
Hobart-Drawn	•8-558	-	7-243	-		
Perth-Drawn	351	7-381	•9d-534	9d-256		
2004-05 in Australia						
Brisbane[2]-Australia inn & 126 runs	585	-	•353	76	R.T.Ponting	S.P.Fleming
Adelaide-Australia 213 runs	•8d-575	2d-139	251	250		

AUSTRALIA v NEW ZEALAND (cont.)	Australia		New Zealand		Captains	
Venue and Result	1st	2nd	1st	2nd	Australia	New Zealand
2004-05 in New Zealand						
Christchurch-Australia 9 wkts	432	1-135	•433	131	R.T.Ponting	S.P.Fleming
Wellington-Drawn	•8d-570	-	244	3-48		
Auckland-Australia 9 wkts	383	1-166	•292	254		

Test Match Results Summary

AUSTRALIA v NEW ZEALAND - in Australia

		Result			Melbourne			Sydney			Adelaide			Brisbane²			Perth			Hobart		
	Tests	A	NZ	D	A	NZ	D	A	NZ	D	A	NZ	D	A	NZ	D	A	NZ	D	A	NZ	D
1973-74	3	2	-	1	1	-	-	-	-	1	1	-	-	-	-	-	-	-	-	-	-	-
1980-81	3	2	-	1	-	-	1	-	-	-	-	-	-	1	-	-	1	-	-	-	-	-
1985-86	3	1	2	-	-	-	-	1	-	-	-	-	-	-	1	-	-	1	-	-	-	-
1987-88	3	1	-	2	-	-	1	-	-	-	-	-	1	1	-	-	-	-	-	-	-	-
1989-90	1	-	-	1	-	-	-	-	-	-	-	-	-	-	-	-	-	-	1	-	-	-
1993-94	3	2	-	1	-	-	-	-	-	-	-	-	-	1	-	-	-	-	1	1	-	-
1997-98	3	2	-	1	-	-	-	-	-	-	-	-	-	1	-	-	1	-	-	-	-	1
2001-02	3	-	-	3	-	-	-	-	-	-	-	-	-	-	-	1	-	-	1	-	-	1
2004-05	2	2	-	-	-	-	-	-	-	-	1	-	-	1	-	-	-	-	-	-	-	-
	24	12	2	10	1	-	2	1	-	1	2	-	1	5	1	1	2	1	3	1	-	2

AUSTRALIA v NEW ZEALAND - in New Zealand

		Result			Wellington			Christchurch			Auckland			Hamilton		
	Tests	A	NZ	D	A	NZ	D	A	NZ	D	A	NZ	D	A	NZ	D
1945-46	1	1	-	-	1	-	-	-	-	-	-	-	-	-	-	-
1973-74	3	1	1	1	-	-	1	-	1	-	1	-	-	-	-	-
1976-77	2	1	-	1	-	-	-	-	-	1	1	-	-	-	-	-
1981-82	3	1	1	1	-	-	1	1	-	-	-	1	-	-	-	-
1985-86	3	-	1	2	-	-	1	-	-	1	-	1	-	-	-	-
1989-90	1	-	1	-	-	1	-	-	-	-	-	-	-	-	-	-
1992-93	3	1	1	1	-	-	1	1	-	-	-	1	-	-	-	-
1999-2000	3	3	-	-	1	-	-	-	-	-	1	-	-	1	-	-
2004-05	3	2	-	1	-	-	1	1	-	-	1	-	-	-	-	-
	22	10	5	7	2	1	5	3	1	2	4	3	-	1	-	-
Totals	46	22	7	17												

Highest Innings Totals

Australia in Australia	6d-607	Brisbane²	1993-94
Australia in New Zealand	8d-570	Wellington	2004-05
New Zealand in Australia	7d-553	Brisbane²	1985-86
New Zealand in New Zealand	484	Wellington	1973-74

Lowest Innings Totals

Australia in Australia	162	Sydney	1973-74
Australia in New Zealand	103	Auckland	1985-86
New Zealand in Australia	76	Brisbane²	2004-05
New Zealand in New Zealand	42	Wellington	1945-46

Highest Match Aggregate	1522 for 35 wickets	Perth	2001-02
Lowest Match Aggregate	295 for 28 wickets	Wellington	1945-46

Highest Individual Innings

Australia in Australia	215	J.L.Langer	Adelaide	2004-05
Australia in New Zealand	250	K.D.Walters	Christchurch	1976-77
New Zealand in Australia	188	M.D.Crowe	Sydney	1985-86
New Zealand in New Zealand	161	B.A.Edgar	Auckland	1981-82

Most Runs in a Series

Australia in Australia	320 (av 80.00)	J.L.Langer	2001-02
Australia in New Zealand	449 (av 89.80)	G.S.Chappell	1973-74
New Zealand in Australia	396 (av 66.00)	M.D.Crowe	1987-88
New Zealand in New Zealand	403 (av 100.75)	G.M.Turner	1973-74

Record Wicket Partnerships - Australia

1st	224	J.L.Langer (104), M.L.Hayden (136)	Brisbane[2]	2001-02
2nd	235	M.J.Slater (168), D.C.Boon (106)	Hobart	1993-94
3rd	264	I.M.Chappell (145), G.S.Chappell (247*)	Wellington	1973-74
4th	184	J.L.Langer (215), D.S.Lehmann (81)	Adelaide	2004-05
5th	213	G.M.Ritchie (92), G.R.J.Matthews (130)	Wellington	1985-86
6th	256	D.R.Martyn (165), A.C.Gilchrist (162)	Wellington	2004-05
7th	217	K.D.Walters (250), G.J.Gilmour (101)	Christchurch	1976-77
8th	135	A.C.Gilchrist (118), B.Lee (61)	Brisbane[2]	2001-02
9th	74	A.C.Gilchrist (60*), M.S.Kasprowicz (23)	Auckland	2004-05
10th	114	J.N.Gillespie (54*), G.D.McGrath (61)	Brisbane[2]	2004-05

Record Wicket Partnerships - New Zealand

1st	112	M.J.Greatbatch (61), J.G.Wright (72)	Wellington	1992-93
2nd	132	M.J.Horne (133), A.C.Parore (44)	Hobart	1997-98
3rd	224	J.F.Reid (108), M.D.Crowe (188)	Brisbane[2]	1985-86
4th	229	B.E.Congdon (132), B.F.Hastings (101)	Wellington	1973-74
5th	97	S.P.Fleming (71), C.D.McMillan (55)	Hobart	2001-02
6th	110	S.P.Fleming (60), C.L.Cairns (69)	Wellington	1999-2000
7th	132*	J.V.Coney (101*), R.J.Hadlee (81*)	Wellington	1985-86
8th	253	N.J.Astle (156*), A.C.Parore (110)	Perth	2001-02
9th	73	H.J.Howarth (60), D.R.Hadlee (37)	Christchurch	1976-77
10th	124	J.G.Bracewell (83*), S.L.Boock (37)	Sydney	1985-86

Best Bowling in an Innings

Australia in Australia	6/31	S.K.Warne	Hobart	1993-94
Australia in New Zealand	6/72	D.K.Lillee	Auckland	1976-77
New Zealand in Australia	9/52	R.J.Hadlee	Brisbane[2]	1985-86
New Zealand in New Zealand	7/87	D.L.Vettori	Auckland	1999-2000

Best Bowling in a Match

Australia in Australia	10/174	R.G.Holland	Sydney	1985-86
Australia in New Zealand	11/123	D.K.Lillee	Auckland	1976-77
New Zealand in Australia	15/123	R.J.Hadlee	Brisbane[2]	1985-86
New Zealand in New Zealand	12/149	D.L.Vettori	Auckland	1999-2000

Most Wickets in a Series

Australia in Australia	19 (av 25.05)	S.K.Warne	1997-98
Australia in New Zealand	18 (av 17.44)	B.Lee	1999-2000
	18 (av 15.72)	G.D.McGrath	2004-05
New Zealand in Australia	33 (av 12.15)	R.J.Hadlee	1985-86
New Zealand in New Zealand	17 (av 25.64)	R.O.Collinge	1973-74
	17 (av 16.94)	D.K.Morrison	1992-93

AUSTRALIA v INDIA	Australia		India		Captains	
Venue and Result	1st	2nd	1st	2nd	Australia	India
1947-48 in Australia						
Brisbane2-Australia inn & 226 runs	•8d-382	-	58	98	D.G.Bradman	N.B.Amarnath
Sydney-Drawn	107	-	•188	7-61		
Melbourne-Australia 233 runs	•394	4d-255	9d-291	125		
Adelaide-Australia inn & 16 runs	•674	-	381	277		
Melbourne-Australia inn & 177 runs	•8d-575	-	331	67		
1956-57 in India						
Madras2-Australia inn & 5 runs	319	-	•161	153	I.W.G.Johnson	P.R.Umrigar
Bombay2-Drawn	7d-523	-	•251	5-250	R.R.Lindwall	
Calcutta-Australia 94 runs	•177	9d-189	136	136	I.W.G.Johnson	
1959-60 in India						
Delhi-Australia inn & 127 runs	468	-	•135	206	R.Benaud	G.S.Ramchand
Kanpur-India 119 runs	219	105	•152	291		
Bombay2-Drawn	8d-387	1-34	•289	5d-226		
Madras2-Australia inn & 55 runs	•342	-	149	138		
Calcutta-Drawn	331	2-121	•194	339		
1964-65 in India						
Madras2-Australia 139 runs	•211	397	276	193	R.B.Simpson	Nawab of Pataudi, jr
Bombay2-India 2 wkts	•320	274	341	8-256		
Calcutta-Drawn	•174	1-143	235	-		
1967-68 in Australia						
Adelaide-Australia 146 runs	•335	369	307	251	R.B.Simpson	C.G Borde
Melbourne-Australia inn & 4 runs	529	-	•173	352	R.B.Simpson	Nawab of Pataudi, jr
Brisbane2-Australia 39 runs	•379	294	279	355	W M.Lawry	Nawab of Pataudi, jr
Sydney-Australia 144 runs	•317	292	268	197	W.M.Lawry	Nawab of Pataudi, jr
1969-70 in India						
Bombay2-Australia 8 wkts	345	2-67	•271	137	W.M.Lawry	Nawab of Pataudi, jr
Kanpur-Drawn	348	0-95	•320	7d-312		
Delhi-India 7 wkts	•296	107	223	3-181		
Calcutta-Australia 10 wkts	335	0-42	•212	161		
Madras1-Australia 77 runs	•258	153	163	171		
1977-78 in Australia						
Brisbane2-Australia 16 runs	•166	327	153	324	R.B.Simpson	B.S.Bedi
Perth-Australia 2 wkts	394	8-342	•402	9d-330		
Melbourne-India 222 runs	213	164	•256	343		
Sydney-India inn & 2 runs	•131	263	8d-396	-		
Adelaide-Australia 47 runs	•505	256	269	445		
1979-80 in India						
Madras1-Drawn	•390	7-212	425	-	K.J.Hughes	S.M.Gavaskar
Bangalore-Drawn	•333	3-77	5d-457	-		
Kanpur-India 153 runs	304	125	•271	311		
Delhi-Drawn	298	413	•7d-510	-		
Calcutta-Drawn	•442	6d-151	347	4-200		
Bombay3-India inn & 100 runs	160	198	•8d-458	-		
1980-81 in Australia						
Sydney-Australia inn & 4 runs	406	-	•201	201	G.S.Chappell	S.M.Gavaskar
Adelaide-Drawn	•528	7d-221	419	8-135		

AUSTRALIA v INDIA (cont.)	Australia		India		Captains	
Venue and Result	1st	2nd	1st	2nd	Australia	India
Melbourne-India 59 runs	419	83	•237	324		
1985-86 in Australia						
Adelaide-Drawn	•381	0-17	520	-	A.R.Border	Kapil Dev
Melbourne-Drawn	•262	308	445	2-59		
Sydney-Drawn	396	6-119	•4d-600	-		
1986-87 in India						
Madras[1]-Tied	•7d-574	5d-170	397	347	A.R.Border	Kapil Dev
Delhi-Drawn	•3d-207	-	3-107	-		
Bombay[3]-Drawn	•345	2-216	5d-517	-		
1991-92 in Australia						
Brisbane[2]-Australia 10 wkts	340	0-58	•239	156	A.R.Border	M.Azharuddin
Melbourne-Australia 8 wkts	349	2-128	•263	213		
Sydney-Drawn	•313	8-173	483	-		
Adelaide-Australia 38 runs	•145	451	225	333		
Perth-Australia 300 runs	•346	6d-367	272	141		
1996-97 in India						
Delhi-India 7 wkts	•182	234	361	3-58	M.A.Taylor	S.R.Tendulkar
1997-98 in India						
Chennai[1]-India 179 runs	328	168	•257	4d-418	M.A.Taylor	M.Azharuddin
Calcutta-India inn & 219 runs	•233	181	5d-633	-		
Bangalore-Australia 8 wkts	400	2-195	•424	169		
1999-2000 in Australia						
Adelaide-Australia 285 runs	•441	8d-239	285	110	S.R.Waugh	S.R.Tendulkar
Melbourne-Australia 180 runs	•405	5d-208	238	195		
Sydney-Australia inn & 141 runs	5d-552	-	•150	261		
2000-01 in India						
Mumbai[3]-Australia 10 wkts	349	0-47	•176	219	S.R.Waugh	S.C.Ganguly
Kolkata-India 171 runs	•445	212	171	7d-657		
Chennai[1]-India 2 wkts	•391	264	501	8-155		
2003-04 in Australia						
Brisbane[2]-Drawn	•323	3d-284	409	2-73	S.R.Waugh	S.C.Ganguly
Adelaide-India 4 wkts	•556	196	523	6-233		
Melbourne-Australia 9 wkts	558	1-97	•366	286		
Sydney-Drawn	474	6-357	•7d-705	2d-211		
2004-05 in India						
Bangalore-Australia 217 runs	•474	228	246	239	A.C.Gilchrist	S.C.Ganguly
Chennai[1]-Drawn	•235	369	376	0-19	A.C.Gilchrist	S.C.Ganguly
Nagpur-Australia 342 runs	•398	5d-329	185	200	A.C.Gilchrist	R.S.Dravid
Mumbai[3]-India 13 runs	203	93	•104	205	R.T.Ponting	R.S.Dravid

Test Match Results Summary

AUSTRALIA v INDIA - in Australia

		Result				Brisbane[2]				Sydney				Melbourne				Adelaide				Perth			
	Tests	A	I	D	T	A	I	D	T	A	I	D	T	A	I	D	T	A	I	D	T	A	I	D	T
1947-48	5	4	-	1	-	1	-	-	-	-	-	1	-	2	-	-	-	1	-	-	-	-	-	-	-
1967-68	4	4	-	-	-	1	-	-	-	1	-	-	-	1	-	-	-	1	-	-	-	-	-	-	-
1977-78	5	3	2	-	-	1	-	-	-	-	1	-	-	-	1	-	-	1	-	-	-	1	-	-	-
1980-81	3	1	1	1	-	-	-	-	-	1	-	-	-	-	1	-	-	-	-	1	-	-	-	-	-
1985-86	3	-	-	3	-	-	-	-	-	-	-	1	-	-	-	1	-	-	-	1	-	-	-	-	-
1991-92	5	4	-	1	-	1	-	-	-	-	-	1	-	1	-	-	-	1	-	-	-	1	-	-	-
1999-2000	3	3	-	-	-	-	-	-	-	1	-	-	-	1	-	-	-	1	-	-	-	-	-	-	-
2003-04	3	1	1	2	-	-	-	1	-	-	-	1	-	1	-	-	-	-	1	-	-	-	-	-	-
	32	20	4	8	-	4	-	1	-	3	1	4	-	6	2	1	-	5	1	2	-	2	-	-	-

AUSTRALIA v INDIA - in India

		Result				Madras[2]			Bombay[2]			Kolkata			Delhi			Kanpur			Bangalore			Madras[1]				Mumbai[3]			Nagpur		
	Tests	A	I	D	T	A	I	D	A	I	D	A	I	D	A	I	D	A	I	D	A	I	D	A	I	D	T	A	I	D	A	I	D
1956-57	3	2	-	1	-	1	-	-	-	-	1	1	-	-	-	-	-	-	-	-	-	-	-	-	-	-	-	-	-	-	-	-	-
1959-60	5	2	1	2	-	1	-	-	-	-	1	-	-	1	1	-	-	-	1	-	-	-	-	-	-	-	-	-	-	-	-	-	-
1964-65	3	1	1	1	-	1	-	-	-	1	-	-	-	1	-	-	-	-	-	-	-	-	-	-	-	-	-	-	-	-	-	-	-
1969-70	5	3	1	1	-	-	-	-	1	-	-	1	-	-	-	1	-	-	-	1	-	-	-	1	-	-	-	-	-	-	-	-	-
1979-80	6	-	2	4	-	-	-	-	-	-	-	-	-	1	-	-	1	-	1	-	-	-	1	-	-	1	-	-	1	-	-	-	-
1986-87	3	-	-	2	1	-	-	-	-	-	-	-	-	-	-	-	1	-	-	-	-	-	-	-	-	-	1	-	-	1	-	-	-
1996-97	1	-	1	-	-	-	-	-	-	-	-	-	-	-	-	1	-	-	-	-	-	-	-	-	-	-	-	-	-	-	-	-	-
1997-98	3	1	2			-	-	-	-	-	-		1	-	-	-	-	-	-	-	1	-	-	-	1	-	-	-	-	-	-	-	-
2000-01	3	1	2	-	-	-	-	-	-	-	-	-	1	-	-	-	-	-	-	-	-	-	-	-	1	-	-	1	-	-	-	-	-
2004-05	3	2	1	1	-	-	-	-	-	-	-	-	-	-	-	-	-	-	-	-	1	-	-	-	-	1	-	-	1	-	1	-	-
	36	12	11	12	1	3	-	-	1	1	2	2	2	3	1	2	2	-	2	1	2	-	1	1	2	2	1	1	2	1	1	-	-

Totals	68	32	15	20	1

Highest Innings Totals

Australia in Australia	674	Adelaide	1947-48
Australia in India	7d-574	Madras[1]	1986-87
India in Australia	7d-705	Sydney	2003-04
India in India	7d-657	Kolkata	2000-01

Lowest Innings Totals

Australia in Australia	83	Melbourne	1980-81
Australia in India	93	Mumbai[3]	2004-05
India in Australia	58	Brisbane[2]	1947-48
India in India	135	Delhi	1959-60

Highest Match Aggregate	1747 for 25 wickets	Sydney	2003-04
Lowest Match Aggregate	538 for 28 wickets	Brisbane[2]	1947-48

Highest Individual Innings

Australia in Australia	257	R.T.Ponting	Melbourne	2003-04
Australia in India	210	D.M.Jones	Madras[1]	1986-87
India in Australia	241*	S.R.Tendulkar	Sydney	2003-04
India in India	281	V.V.S.Laxman	Kolkata	2000-01

Most Runs in a Series

Australia in Australia	715 (av 178.75)	D.G.Bradman	1947-48
Australia in India	594 (av 59.40)	K.J.Hughes	1979-80
India in Australia	619 (av 123.80)	R.S.Dravid	2003-04
India in India	518 (av 74.00)	G.R.Viswanath	1979-80

Record Wicket Partnerships - Australia

1st	217	D.C.Boon (172), G.R.Marsh (116)	Sydney	1985-86
2nd	236	S.G.Barnes (112), D.G.Bradman (201)	Adelaide	1947-48
3rd	222	A.R.Border (162), K.J.Hughes (100)	Madras[1]	1979-80
4th	178	D.M.Jones (210), A.R.Border (106)	Madras[1]	1986-87
5th	239	S.R.Waugh (150), R.T.Ponting (125)	Adelaide	1999-2000
6th	197	M.L.Hayden (119), A.C.Gilchrist (122)	Mumbai[3]	2000-01
7th	108	S.R.Waugh (150), S.K.Warne (86)	Adelaide	1999-2000
8th	117	S.M.Katich (125), J.N.Gillespie (47)	Sydney	2003-04
9th	133	S.R.Waugh (110), J.N.Gillespie (46)	Kolkata	2000-01
10th	77	A.R.Border (163), D.R.Gilbert (10*)	Melbourne	1985-86

Record Wicket Partnerships - India

1st	192	S.M.Gavaskar (123), C.P.S.Chauhan (73)	Bombay[3]	1979-80
2nd	224	S.M.Gavaskar (172), M.Amarnath (138)	Sydney	1985-86
3rd	159	S.M.Gavaskar (115), G.R.Viswanath (131)	Delhi	1979-80
4th	353	S.R.Tendulkar (241*), V.V.S.Laxman (178)	Sydney	2003-04
5th	374	V.V.S.Laxman (281), R.S.Dravid (180)	Kolkata	2000-01
6th	298*	D.B.Vengsarkar (164*), R.J.Shastri (121*)	Bombay[3]	1986-87
7th	132	V.S.Hazare (145), H.R.Adhikari (51)	Adelaide	1947-48
8th	127	S.M.H.Kirmani (101*), K.D.Ghavri (86)	Bombay[3]	1979-80
9th	91	I.K.Pathan (55), Harbhajan Singh (42)	Bangalore	2004-05
10th	94	S.M.Gavaskar (166*), N.S.Yadav (41)	Adelaide	1985-86

Best Bowling in an Innings

Australia in Australia	7/27	M.R.Whitney	Perth	1991-92
Australia in India	7/43	R.R.Lindwall	Madras[2]	1956-57
India in Australia	8/106	Kapil Dev	Adelaide	1985-86
India in India	9/69	J.M.Patel	Kanpur	1959-60

Best Bowling in a Match

Australia in Australia	12/126	B.A.Reid	Melbourne	1991-92
Australia in India	12/124	A.K.Davidson	Kanpur	1959-60
India in Australia	12/104	B.S.Chandrasekhar	Melbourne	1977-78
India in India	15/217	Harbhajan Singh	Kolkata	2001-02

Most Wickets in a Series

Australia in Australia	31 (av 21.61)	C.J.McDermott	1991-92
Australia in India	29 (av 14 86)	A.K.Davidson	1959-60
	29 (av 19.58)	R.Benaud	1959-60
India in Australia	31 (av 23.87)	B.S.Bedi	1977-78
India in India	32 (av 17.03)	Harbhajan Singh	2001-02

AUSTRALIA v PAKISTAN	Australia		Pakistan		Captains	
Venue and Result	1st	2nd	1st	2nd	Australia	Pakistan
1956-57 in Pakistan						
Karachi[1]-Pakistan 9 wkts	•80	187	199	1-69	I.W.G.Johnson	A.H.Kardar
1959-60 in Pakistan						
Dacca-Australia 8 wkts	225	2-112	•200	134	R.Benaud	Fazal Mahmood
Lahore[2]-Australia 7 wkts	9d-391	3-123	•146	366		Imtiaz Ahmed
Karachi[1]-Drawn	257	2-83	•287	8d-194		Fazal Mahmood
1964-65 in Pakistan						
Karachi[1]-Drawn	352	2-227	•414	8d-279	R.B.Simpson	Hanif Mohammad
1964-65 in Australia						
Melbourne-Drawn	448	2-88	•287	326	R.B.Simpson	Hanif Mohammad
1972-73 in Australia						
Adelaide-Australia inn & 114 runs	585	-	•257	214	I.M.Chappell	Intikhab Alam
Melbourne-Australia 92 runs	•5d-441	425	8d-574	200		
Sydney-Australia 52 runs	•334	184	360	106		
1976-77 in Australia						
Adelaide-Drawn	454	6-261	•272	466	G.S.Chappell	Mushtaq Mohammad
Melbourne-Australia 348 runs	•8d-517	8d-315	333	151		
Sydney-Pakistan 8 wkts	•211	180	360	2-32		
1978-79 in Australia						
Melbourne-Pakistan 71 runs	168	310	•196	9d-353	G.N.Yallop	Mushtaq Mohammad
Perth-Australia 7 wkts	327	3-236	•277	285	K.J.Hughes	
1979-80 in Pakistan						
Karachi[1]-Pakistan 7 wkts	•225	140	292	3-76	G.S.Chappell	Javed Miandad
Faisalabad-Drawn	•617		2-382			
Lahore[2]-Drawn	•7d-407	8-391	9d-420	-		
1981-82 in Australia						
Perth-Australia 286 runs	•180	8d-424	62	256	G.S.Chappell	Javed Miandad
Brisbane[2]-Australia 10 wkts	9d-512	0-3	•291	223		
Melbourne-Pakistan inn & 82 runs	293	125	•8d-500	-		
1982-83 in Pakistan						
Karachi[1]-Pakistan 9 wkts	•284	179	9d-419	1-47	K.J.Hughes	Javed Miandad
Faisalabad-Pakistan inn & 3 runs	168	330	•6d-501	-		
Lahore[2]-Pakistan 9 wkts	•316	214	7d-467	1-64		
1983-84 in Australia						
Perth-Australia inn & 9 runs	•9d-436	-	129	298	K.J.Hughes	Zaheer Abbas
Brisbane[2]-Drawn	7d-506	-	•156	3-82		Zaheer Abbas
Adelaide-Drawn	•465	7-310	624	-		Zaheer Abbas
Melbourne-Drawn	555	-	•470	7-238		Imran Khan
Sydney-Australia 10 wkts	6d-454	0-35	•278	210		Imran Khan
1988-89 in Pakistan						
Karachi[1]-Pakistan inn & 188 runs	185	116	•9d-469	-	A.R.Border	Javed Miandad
Faisalabad-Drawn	321	3-67	•316	9d-378		
Lahore[2]-Drawn	•340	3d-161	233	8-153		

AUSTRALIA v PAKISTAN (cont.)	Australia		Pakistan		Captains	
Venue and Result	1st	2nd	1st	2nd	Australia	India
1989-90 in Australia						
Melbourne-Australia 92 runs	•223	8d-312	107	336	A.R.Border	Imran Khan
Adelaide-Drawn	341	6-233	•257	9d-387		
Sydney-Drawn	2-176	-	•199	-		
1994-95 in Pakistan						
Karachi[1]-Pakistan 1 wkt	•337	232	256	9-315	M.A.Taylor	Saleem Malik
Rawalpindi[2]-Drawn	•9d-521	1-14	260	537		
Lahore[2]-Drawn	455	-	•373	404		
1995-96 in Australia						
Brisbane[2]-Australia inn & 126 runs	•463	-	97	240	M.A.Taylor	Wasim Akram
Hobart-Australia 155 runs	•267	306	198	220		
Sydney-Pakistan 74 runs	257	172	•299	204		
1998-99 in Pakistan						
Rawalpindi[2]-Australia inn & 99 runs	513	-	•269	145	M.A.Taylor	Aamer Sohail
Peshawar[2]-Drawn	•4d-599	5-289	9d-580	-		
Karachi[1]-Drawn	280	390	252	4-262		
1999-2000 in Australia						
Brisbane[2]-Australia 10 wkts	575	0-74	•367	281	S.R.Waugh	Wasim Akram
Hobart-Australia 4 wkts	246	6-369	•222	392		
Perth-Australia inn & 20 runs	451	-	•155	276		
2002-03 in Sri Lanka & United Arab Emirates						
Colombo(PSS)-Australia 41 runs	•467	127	279	274	S.R.Waugh	Waqar Younis
Sharjah-Australia inn & 198 runs	310	-	•59	53		
Sharjah-Australia inn & 20 runs	•444	-	221	203		
2004-05 in Australia						
Perth-Aus 491 runs	•381	5d-361	179	72	R.T.Ponting	Inzamamul Haq
Melbourne-Aus 9 wkts	379	1-127	•341	163		Yousuf Youhana
Sydney-Aus 9 wkts	568	1-62	•204	325		Yousuf Youhana

Test Match Results Summary

AUSTRALIA v PAKISTAN - in Australia

		Result			Melbourne			Adelaide			Sydney			Perth			Brisbane[2]			Hobart		
	Tests	A	P	D	A	P	D	A	P	D	A	P	D	A	P	D	A	P	D	A	P	D
1964-65	1	-	-	1	-	-	1	-	-	-	-	-	-	-	-	-	-	-	-	-	-	-
1972-73	3	3	-	-	1	-	-	1	-	-	1	-	-	-	-	-	-	-	-	-	-	-
1976-77	3	1	1	1	1	-	-	-	-	1	-	1	-	-	-	-	-	-	-	-	-	-
1978-79	2	1	1	-	-	1	-	-	-	-	-	-	-	1	-	-	-	-	-	-	-	-
1981-82	3	2	1	-	-	1	-	-	-	-	-	-	-	1	-	-	1	-	-	-	-	-
1983-84	5	2	-	3	-	-	1	-	-	1	1	-	-	1	-	-	-	-	1	-	-	-
1989-90	3	1	-	2	1	-	-	-	-	1	-	-	1	-	-	-	-	-	-	-	-	-
1995-96	3	2	1	-	-	-	-	-	-	-	-	1	-	-	-	-	1	-	-	1	-	-
1999-2000	3	3	-	-	-	-	-	-	-	-	-	-	-	1	-	-	1	-	-	1	-	-
2004-05	3	3	-	-	1	-	-	-	-	-	1	-	-	1	-	-	-	-	-	-	-	-
	29	18	4	7	4	2	2	1	-	3	3	2	1	5	-	-	3	-	1	2	-	-

AUSTRALIA v PAKISTAN - in Pakistan

		Result			Karachi[1]			Dacca			Lahore[2]			Faisalabad			Rawalpindi[2]			Peshawar[2]		
	Tests	A	P	D	A	P	D	A	P	D	A	P	D	A	P	D	A	P	D	A	P	D
1956-57	1	-	1	-	-	1	-	-	-	-	-	-	-	-	-	-	-	-	-	-	-	-
1959-60	3	2	-	1	-	-	1	1	-	-	1	-	-	-	-	-	-	-	-	-	-	-
1964-65	1	-	-	1	-	-	1	-	-	-	-	-	-	-	-	-	-	-	-	-	-	-
1979-80	3	-	1	2	-	1	-	-	-	-	-	-	1	-	-	1	-	-	-	-	-	-
1982-83	3	-	3	-	-	1	-	-	-	-	-	1	-	-	1	-	-	-	-	-	-	-
1988-89	3	-	1	2	-	1	-	-	-	-	-	-	1	-	-	1	-	-	-	-	-	-
1994-95	3	-	1	2	-	1	-	-	-	-	-	-	1	-	-	-	-	-	1	-	-	-
1998-99	3	1	-	2	-	-	1	-	-	-	-	-	-	-	-	-	1	-	-	-	-	1
	20	3	7	10	-	5	3	1	-	-	1	1	3	-	1	2	1	-	1	-	-	1

AUSTRALIA v PAKISTAN - in Sri Lanka & United Arab Emirates

		Result			Colombo(PSS)			Sharjah		
	Tests	A	P	D	A	P	D	A	P	D
2002-03	3	3	-	-	1	-	-	2	-	-
Totals	52	24	11	17						

Highest Innings Totals

Australia in Australia	585	Adelaide	1972-73
Australia in Pakistan	617	Faisalabad	1979-80
Pakistan in Australia	624	Adelaide	1983-84
Pakistan in Pakistan	9d-580	Peshawar[2]	1998-99

Lowest Innings Totals

Australia in Australia	125	Melbourne	1981-82
Australia in Pakistan	80	Karachi[1]	1956-57
Pakistan in Australia	62	Perth	1981-82
Pakistan in Pakistan	134	Dacca	1959-60

Pakistan's lowest innings total is 53 at Sharjah in 2002-03.

Highest Match Aggregate	1640 for 33 wickets	Melbourne	1972-73
Lowest Match Aggregate	422 for 29 wickets	Sharjah	2002-03

Highest Individual Innings

Australia in Australia	268	G.N.Yallop	Melbourne	1983-84
Australia in Pakistan	334*	M.A.Taylor	Peshawar[2]	1998-99
Pakistan in Australia	158	Majid Khan	Melbourne	1972-73
Pakistan in Pakistan	237	Saleem Malik	Rawalpindi[2]	1994-95

Most Runs in a Series

Australia in Australia	554 (av 92.33)	G.N.Yallop	1983-84
Australia in Pakistan	513 (av 128.25)	M.A.Taylor	1998-99
Pakistan in Australia	390 (av 43.33)	Mohsin Khan	1983-84
Pakistan in Pakistan	557 (av 92.83)	Saleem Malik	1994-95

Record Wicket Partnerships - Australia

1st	269	M.J.Slater (169), G.S.Blewett (89)	Brisbane[2]	1999-2000
2nd	279	M.A.Taylor (334*), J.L.Langer (116)	Peshawar[2]	1998-99
3rd	203	G.N.Yallop (268), K.J.Hughes (94)	Melbourne	1983-84
4th	217	G.S.Chappell (235), G.N.Yallop (172)	Faisalabad	1979-80
5th	327	J.L.Langer (144), R.T.Ponting (197)	Perth	1999-2000
6th	238	J.L.Langer (127), A.C.Gilchrist (149*)	Hobart	1999-2000

7th	185	G.N.Yallop (268), G.R.J.Matthews (75)	Melbourne	1983-84
8th	117	G.J.Cosier (168), K.J.O'Keeffe (28*)	Melbourne	1976-77
9th	83	J.R.Watkins (36), R.A.L.Massie (42)	Sydney	1972-73
10th	86	S.K.Warne (86), S.A.Muller (6*)	Brisbane[2]	1999-2000

Record Wicket Partnerships - Pakistan

1st	249	Khalid Ibadulla (166), Abdul Kadir (95)	Karachi[1]	1964-65
2nd	233	Mohsin Khan (149), Qasim Omar (113)	Adelaide	1983-84
3rd	223*	Taslim Arif (210*), Javed Miandad (106*)	Faisalabad	1979-80
4th	192	Younis Khan (87), Yousuf Youhana (111)	Melbourne	2004-05
5th	186	Javed Miandad (131), Saleem Malik (77)	Adelaide	1983-84
6th	196	Saleem Malik (143), Aamer Sohail (105)	Lahore[2]	1994-95
7th	104	Intikhab Alam (64), Wasim Bari (72)	Adelaide	1972-73
8th	111	Majid Khan (110*), Imran Khan (56)	Lahore[2]	1979-80
9th	120	Saeed Anwar (145), Mushtaq Ahmed (26)	Rawalpindi[2]	1998-99
10th	87	Asif Iqbal (152*), Iqbal Qasim (4)	Adelaide	1976-77

Best Bowling in an Innings

Australia in Australia	8/24	G.D.McGrath	Perth	2004-05
Australia in Pakistan	7/75	L.F.Kline	Lahore[2]	1959-60
Pakistan in Australia	9/86	Sarfraz Nawaz	Melbourne	1978-79
Pakistan in Pakistan	7/49	Iqbal Qasim	Karachi[1]	1979-80

Best Bowling in a Match

Australia in Australia	11/77	S.K.Warne	Brisbane[2]	1995-96
Australia in Pakistan	10/111	R.J.Bright	Karachi[1]	1979-80
Pakistan in Australia	12/165	Imran Khan	Sydney	1976-77
Pakistan in Pakistan	13/114	Fazal Mahmood	Karachi[1]	1956-57

Most Wickets in a Series

Australia in Australia	24 (av 24.16)	G.F.Lawson	1983-84
Australia in Pakistan	18 (av 21.05)	R.Benaud	1959-60
	18 (av 28.00)	S.K.Warne	1994-95

Australia's highest aggregate in a Series is 27 (av 12.66) by S.K.Warne in Sri Lanka/United Arab Emirates in 2002-03.

Pakistan in Australia	19 (av 38.52)	Azeem Hafeez	1983-84
Pakistan in Pakistan	22 (av 25.54)	Abdul Qadir	1982-83

AUSTRALIA v SRI LANKA	Australia		Sri Lanka		Captains	
Venue and Result	1st	2nd	1st	2nd	Australia	Sri Lanka
1982-83 in Sri Lanka						
Kandy-Australia inn & 38 runs	•4d-514	-	271	205	G.S.Chappell	L.R.D.Mendis
1987-88 in Australia						
Perth-Australia inn & 108 runs	•455	-	194	153	A.R.Border	R.S.Madugalle
1989-90 in Australia						
Brisbane[2]-Drawn	•367	6-375	418	-	A.R.Border	A.Ranatunga
Hobart-Australia 173 runs	•224	5d-513	216	348		
1992-93 in Sri Lanka						
Colombo (SSC)-Australia 16 runs	•256	471	8d-547	164	A.R.Border	A.Ranatunga
Colombo (RPS)-Drawn	•247	6d-296	258	2-136		
Moratuwa-Drawn	•337	8-271	9d-274	-		

AUSTRALIA v SRI LANKA (cont.)	Australia		Sri Lanka		Captains	
Venue and Result	1st	2nd	1st	2nd	Australia	Sri Lanka
1995-96 in Australia						
Perth-Australia inn & 36 runs	5d-617	-	•251	330	M.A.Taylor	A.Ranatunga
Melbourne-Australia 10 wkts	•6d-500	0-41	233	307		A.Ranatunga
Adelaide-Australia 148 runs	•9d-502	6d-215	317	252		P.A.de Silva
1999-2000 in Sri Lanka						
Kandy-Sri Lanka 6 wkts	•188	140	234	4-95	S.R.Waugh	S.T.Jayasuriya
Galle-Drawn	228	-	•296	0-55		
Colombo (SSC)-Drawn	•342	-	4-61	-		
2003-04 in Sri Lanka						
Galle-Australia 197 runs	•220	8d-512	381	154	R.T.Ponting	H.P.Tillakaratne
Kandy-Australia 27 runs	•120	442	211	324		
Colombo (SSC)-Australia 121 runs	•401	375	407	248		
2004-05 in Australia						
Darwin-Australia inn & 149 runs	•207	201	97	162	A.C.Gilchrist	M.S.Atapattu
Cairns-Drawn	•517	9d-292	455	8-183	R.T.Ponting	

Test Match Results Summary

AUSTRALIA v SRI LANKA - in Australia

		Result			Perth			Brisbane[2]			Hobart			Melbourne			Adelaide			Darwin			Cairns		
	Tests	A	SL	D	A	SL	D	A	SL	D	A	SL	D	A	SL	D	A	SL	D	A	SL	D	A	SL	D
1987-88	1	1	-	-	1	-	-	-	-	-	-	-	-	-	-	-	-	-	-	-	-	-	-	-	-
1989-90	2	1	-	1	-	-	-	-	-	1	1	-	-	-	-	-	-	-	-	-	-	-	-	-	-
1995-96	3	3	-	-	1	-	-	-	-	-	-	-	-	1	-	-	1	-	-	-	-	-	-	-	-
2004-05	2	1	-	1	-	-	-	-	-	-	-	-	-	-	-	-	-	-	-	1	-	-	-	-	1
	7	6	-	2	2	-	-	-	-	1	1	-	-	1	-	-	1	-	-	1	-	-	-	-	1

AUSTRALIA v SRI LANKA - in Sri Lanka

		Result			Kandy			Colombo(SSC)			Colombo(RPS)			Moratuwa			Galle		
	Tests	A	SL	D	A	SL	D	A	SL	D	A	SL	D	A	SL	D	A	SL	D
1982-83	1	1	-	-	1	-	-	-	-	-	-	-	-	-	-	-	-	-	-
1992-93	3	1	-	2	-	-	-	1	-	-	-	-	1	-	-	1	-	-	-
1999-2000	3	-	1	2	-	1	-	-	-	1	-	-	-	-	-	-	-	-	1
2003-04	3	3	-	-	1	-	-	1	-	-	-	-	-	-	-	-	1	-	-
	10	5	1	4	1	1	-	2	-	1	-	-	1	1	-	1	1	-	1
Totals	17	11	1	6															

Highest Innings Totals

Australia in Australia	5d-617	Perth	1995-96
Australia in Sri Lanka	4d-514	Kandy	1982-83
Sri Lanka in Australia	418	Brisbane[2]	1989-90
Sri Lanka in Sri Lanka	8d-547	Colombo (SSC)	1992-93

Lowest Innings Totals

Australia in Australia	224	Hobart	1989-90
Australia in Sri Lanka	120	Kandy	2003-04
Sri Lanka in Australia	97	Darwin	2004-05
Sri Lanka in Sri Lanka	154	Galle	2003-04

Highest Match Aggregate	1447 for 37 wickets	Cairns	2004-05
Lowest Match Aggregate	657 for 32 wickets	Kandy	1999-2000

Highest Individual Innings

Australia in Australia	219	M.J.Slater	Perth	1995-96
Australia in Sri Lanka	166	J.L.Langer	Colombo (SSC)	2003-04
Sri Lanka in Australia	167	P.A.de Silva	Brisbane[2]	1989-90
Sri Lanka in Sri Lanka	137	A.P.Gurusinha	Colombo (SSC)	1992-93

Most Runs in a Series

Australia in Australia	362 (av 362.00)	S.R.Waugh	1995-96
Australia in Sri Lanka	375 (av 62.50)	D.S.Lehmann	2003-04
Sri Lanka in Australia	314 (av 104.66)	P.A.de Silva	1989-90
Sri Lanka in Sri Lanka	294 (av 49.00)	S.T.Jayasuriya	2003-04

Record Wicket Partnerships - Australia

1st	255	J.L.Langer (162), M.L.Hayden (117)	Cairns	2004-05
2nd	170	K.C.Wessels (141), G.N.Yallop (98)	Kandy	1982-83
3rd	200	A.C.Gilchrist (144), D.R.Martyn (161)	Kandy	2003-04
4th	206	D.R.Martyn (110), D.S.Lehmann (129)	Hobart	2003-04
5th	155*	D.W.Hookes (143*), A.R.Border (47*)	Kandy	1982-83
6th	260*	D.M.Jones (118*), S.R.Waugh (134*)	Hobart	1989-90
7th	129	G.R.J.Matthews (96), I.A.Healy (49)	Moratuwa	1992-93
8th	107	R.T.Ponting (96), J.N.Gillespie (41)	Kandy	1999-2000
9th	45	I.A.Healy (66*), S.K.Warne (24)	Colombo (SSC)	1992-93
10th	49	I.A.Healy (66*), M.R.Whitney (13)	Colombo (SSC)	1992-93

Record Wicket Partnerships - Sri Lanka

1st	134	M.S.Atapattu (118), S.T.Jayasuriya (71)	Colombo (SSC)	2003-04
2nd	138	M.S.Atapattu (133), K.C.Sangakkara (74)	Cairns	2004-05
3rd	125	S.T.Jayasuriya (125), S.Ranatunga (65)	Adelaide	1995-96
4th	230	A.P.Gurusinha (137), A.Ranatunga (127)	Colombo (SSC)	1992-93
5th	116	H.P.Tillakaratne (82), A.Ranatunga (48)	Moratuwa	1992-93
6th	96	A.P.Gurusinha (137), R.S.Kaluwitharana (132*)	Colombo (SSC)	1992-93
7th	144	P.A.de Silva (167), J.R.Ratnayeke (56)	Brisbane[2]	1989-90
8th	47	T.M.Dilshan (43), W.P.U.J.C.Vaas (45)	Kandy	2003-04
9th	46	H.D.P.K.Dharmasena (30), G.P.Wickramasinghe (28)	Perth	1995-96
10th	79	W.P.U.J.C.Vaas (68*), M.Muralidaran (43)	Kandy	2003-04

Best Bowling in an Innings

Australia in Australia	7/39	M.S.Kasprowicz	Darwin	2004-05
Australia in Sri Lanka	5/43	S.K.Warne	Galle	2003-04
Sri Lanka in Australia	6/66	R.J.Ratnayake	Hobart	1989-90
Sri Lanka in Sri Lanka	6/59	M.Muralidaran	Galle	2003-04

Best Bowling in a Match

Australia in Australia	8/156	M.G.Hughes	Hobart	1989-90
Australia in Sri Lanka	10/155	S.K.Warne	Kandy	2003-04
Sri Lanka in Australia	10/201	U.D.U.Chandana	Cairns	2004-05
Sri Lanka in Sri Lanka	11/222	M.Muralidaran	Galle	2003-04

Most Wickets in a Series

Australia in Australia	21 (av 20.85)	G.D.McGrath	1995-96
Australia in Sri Lanka	26 (av 20.03)	S.K.Warne	2003-04
Sri Lanka in Australia	12 (av 22.50)	U.D.U.Chandana	2004-05
Sri Lanka in Sri Lanka	28 (av 23.17)	M.Muralidaran	2003-04

AUSTRALIA v ZIMBABWE	Australia		Zimbabwe		Captains	
Venue and Result	1st	2nd	1st	2nd	Australia	Zimbabwe
1999-2000 in Zimbabwe						
Harare-Australia 10 wkts	422	0-5	•194	232	S.R.Waugh	A.D.R.Campbell
2003-04 in Australia						
Perth-Australia inn & 175 runs	•6d-735	-	239	321	S.R.Waugh	H.H.Streak
Sydney-Australia 9 wkts	403	1-172	•308	266		

Test Match Results Summary

AUSTRALIA v ZIMBABWE - in Australia

		Result			Perth			Sydney		
	Tests	A	Z	D	A	Z	D	A	Z	D
2002-03	2	2	-	-	1	-	-	1	-	-

AUSTRALIA v ZIMBABWE - in Zimbabwe

		Result			Harare		
	Tests	A	Z	D	A	Z	D
1999-2000	1	1	-	-	-	-	-
Totals	3	3	-	-			

Highest Innings Totals

Australia in Australia	6d-735	Perth	2003-04
Australia in Zimbabwe	422	Harare	1999-2000
Zimbabwe in Australia	321	Perth	2003-04
Zimbabwe in Zimbabwe	232	Harare	1999-2000

Lowest Innings Totals

Australia in Australia	403	Sydney	2003-04
Australia in Zimbabwe	422	Harare	1999-2000
Zimbabwe in Australia	239	Perth	2003-04
Zimbabwe in Zimbabwe	194	Harare	1999-2000

Highest Match Aggregate	1295 for 27 wickets	Perth	2003-04
Lowest Match Aggregate	853 for 32 wickets	Harare	1999-2000

Highest Individual Innings

Australia in Australia	380	M.L.Hayden	Perth	2003-04
Australia in Zimbabwe	151*	S.R.Waugh	Harare	1999-2000
Zimbabwe in Australia	71*	H.HStreak	Perth	2003-04
Zimbabwe in Zimbabwe	91	M.W.Goodwin	Harare	1999-2000

Most Runs in a Series

Australia in Australia	504 (250.50)	M.L.Hayden	2003-04
Australia in Zimbabwe	151 (av --.--)	S.R.Waugh	1999-2000
Zimbabwe in Australia	166 (41.50)	M.A.Vermeulen	2003-04
Zimbabwe in Zimbabwe	91 (av 45.50)	M.W.Goodwin	1999-2000

Record Wicket Partnerships - Australia

1st	43	J.L.Langer (26), M.L.Hayden (380)	Perth	2003-04
2nd	151*	M.L.Hayden (101*), R.T.Ponting (53*)	Sydney	2003-04
3rd	97	M.L.Hayden (380), D.R.Martyn (53)	Perth	2003-04
	97	R.T.Ponting (169), D.R.Martyn (32)	Sydney	2003-04

4th	207	M.L.Hayden (380), S.R.Waugh (78)	Perth	2003-04
5th	96	M.L.Hayden (380), D.S.Lehmann (30)	Perth	2003-04
6th	233	M.L.Hayden (380), A.C.Gilchrist (113*)	Perth	2003-04
7th	27	S.M.Katich (52), G.B.Hogg (13)	Sydney	2003-04
8th	114	S.R.Waugh (151*), D.W.Fleming (65)	Harare	1999-2000
9th	10	A.J.Bichel (5), B.Lee (6*)	Sydney	2003-04
10th	24	S.R.Waugh (151*), G.D.McGrath (13)	Harare	1999-2000

Record Wicket Partnerships - Zimbabwe

1st	61	D.D.Ebrahim (29), T.R.Gripper (53)	Perth	2003-04
2nd	98	T.R.Gripper (60), M.W.Goodwin (91)	Harare	1999-2000
3rd	99	M.A.Vermeulen (63, S.V.Carlisle (35)	Perth	2003-04
4th	48	S.V.Carlisle (118), C.B.Wishart (14)	Sydney	2003-04
5th	70	A.Flower (28), N.C.Johnson (75)	Harare	1999-2000
6th	67	S.V.Carlisle (118), H.H.Streak (14)	Sydney	2003-04
7th	31	T.Taibu (15), H.H.Streak (9)	Perth	2003-04
8th	83	S.M.Ervive (53), H.H.Streak (71*)	Perth	2003-04
9th	53	A.M.Blignaut (38*), R.W.Price (20)	Sydney	2003-04
10th	74	H.H.Streak (71*), R.W.Price (36)	Perth	2003-04

Best Bowling in an Innings

Australia in Australia	6/65	S.M.Katich	Sydney	2003-04
Australia in Zimbabwe	3/44	G.D.McGrath	Harare	1999-2000
Zimbabwe in Australia	6/121	R.W.Price	Sydney	2003-04
Zimbabwe in Zimbabwe	5/93	H.H.Streak	Harare	1999-2000

Best Bowling in a Match

Australia in Australia	6/90	S.M.Katich	Sydney	2003-04
Australia in Zimbabwe	6/90	G.D.McGrath	Harare	1999-2000
Zimbabwe in Australia	6/184	R.W.Price	Sydney	2003-04
Zimbabwe in Zimbabwe	5/93	H.H.Streak	Harare	1999-2000

Most Wickets in a Series

Australia in Australia	10 (av 25.50)	A.J.Bichel	2003-04
Australia in Zimbabwe	6 (av 15.00)	G.D.McGrath	1999-2000
	6 (av 22.83)	S.K.Warne	1999-2000
Zimbabwe in Australia	6 (av 61.83)	R.W.Price	2003-04
Zimbabwe in Zimbabwe	5 (av 18.60)	H.H.Streak	1999-2000

AUSTRALIA v BANGLADESH	Australia		Bangladesh		Captains	
Venue and Result	1st	2nd	1st	2nd	Australia	Bangladesh
2003-04 in Australia						
Darwin-Australia inn & 132 runs	7d-407	-	•97	178	S.R.Waugh	Khaled Mahmud
Cairns-Australia inn & 98 runs	4d-556	-	•295	163		
2005-06 in Bangladesh						
Fatullah-Australia 3 wkts	269	7-310	•427	148	R.T.Ponting	Habibul Bashar
Chittagong[2]-Australia inn & 80 runs	4d-581	-	•197	304		

Test Match Results Summary

AUSTRALIA v BANGLADESH - in Australia

		Result			Darwin			Cairns		
	Tests	A	B	D	A	B	D	A	B	D
2003-04	2	2	-	-	1	-	-	1	-	-

AUSTRALIA v BANGLADESH - in Bangladesh

		Result			Fatullah			Chittagong[2]		
	Tests	A	B	D	A	B	D	A	B	D
2005-06	2	2	-	-	1	-	-	1	-	-
Totals	4	4	-	-						

Highest Innings Totals

Australia in Australia	4d-556	Cairns	2003-04
Australia in Bangladesh	4d-581	Chittagong[2]	2005-06
Bangladesh in Australia	295	Cairns	2003-04
Bangladesh in Bangladesh	427	Fatullah	2005-06

Lowest Innings Totals

Australia in Australia	no instance		
Australia in Bangladesh	269	Fatullah	2005-06
Bangladesh in Australia	97	Darwin	2003-04
Bangladesh in Bangladesh	148	Fatullah	2005-06

Highest Match Aggregate	1154 for 37 wickets	Fatullah	2005-06
Lowest Match Aggregate	682 for 27 wickets	Darwin	2003-04

Highest Individual Innings

Australia in Australia	177	D.S.Lehmann	Cairns	2003-04
Australia in Bangladesh	201*	J.N.Gillespie	Chittagong[2]	2005-06
Bangladesh in Australia	76	Hannan Sarkar	Cairns	2003-04
Bangladesh in Bangladesh	138	Shahriar Nafees	Fatullah	2005-06

Most Runs in a Series

Australia in Australia	287 (av 143.50)	D.S.Lehmann	2003-04
Australia in Bangladesh	242 (av 80.33)	M.E.K.Hussey	2005-06
Bangladesh in Australia	166 (av 41.50)	Hannan Sarkar	2003-04
Bangladesh in Bangladesh	250 (av 62.50)	Shahriar Nafees	2005-06

Record Wicket Partnerships - Australia

1st	67	M.L.Hayden (29), P.A.Jaques (66)	Chittagong[2]	2005-06
2nd	109	M.L.Hayden (72), R.T.Ponting (118*)	Fatullah	2005-06
3rd	141	J.L.Langer (71), D.S.Lehmann (110)	Darwin	2003-04
4th	320	J.N.Gillespie (201*), M.E.K.Hussey (182)	Chittagong[2]	2005-06
5th	174*	S.R.Waugh (156*), M.L.Love (100*)	Cairns	2003-04
6th	69	S.R.Waugh (100*), A.C.Gilchrist (43)	Darwin	2003-04
7th	64	S.R.Waugh (100*), B.Lee (23)	Darwin	2003-04
8th	73	A.C.Gilchrist (144), J.N.Gillespie (26)	Fatullah	2005-06
9th	39	A.C.Gilchrist (144), S.R.Clark (0)	Fatullah	2005-06
10th	1	A.C.Gilchrist (144), S.C.G.MacGill (0*)	Fatullah	2005-06

Record Wicket Partnerships - Bangladesh

1st	51	Javed Omar (27), Shahriar Nafees (138)	Fatullah	2005-06
2nd	187	Shahriar Nafees (138), Habibul Bashar (76)	Fatullah	2005-06
3rd	27	Shariar Nafees (138), Rajin Saleh (67)	Fatullah	2005-06
4th	50	Shariar Nafees (79) Mohammad Ashraful (29)	Chittagong[2]	2005-06
5th	77	Rajin Saleh (33), Aftab Ahmed (17)	Fatullah	2005-06
6th	60	Sanwar Hossain (46), Khaled Mashud (44)	Cairns	2003-04
7th	27	Khaled Mashud (11), Khaled Mahmud (21)	Darwin	2003-04
8th	51	Khaled Mashud (44), Tapash Baisya (25)	Cairns	2003-04
9th	36	Khaled Mashud (34*), Abdur Razzak (15)	Chittagong[2]	2005-06
10th	69	Mohammad Rafique (65), Shahadat Hossain (3*)	Chittagong[2]	2005-06

Best Bowling in an Innings

Australia in Australia	5/56	S.C.G.MacGill	Cairns	2003-04
Australia in Bangladesh	8/108	S.C.G.MacGill	Fatullah	2005-06
Bangladesh in Australia	3/74	Mashrafe Bin Mortaza	Darwin	2003-04
Bangladesh in Bangladesh	5/62	Mohammad Rafique	Fatullah	2005-06

Best Bowling in a Match

Australia in Australia	10/133	S.C.G.MacGill	Cairns	2003-04
Australia in Bangladesh	9/138	S.C.G.MacGill	Fatullah	2005-06
Bangladesh in Australia	3/74	Mashrafe Bin Mortaza	Darwin	2003-04
Bangladesh in Bangladesh	9/160	Mohammad Rafique	Fatullah	2005-06

Most Wickets in a Series

Australia in Australia	17 (av 24.16)	S.C.G.MacGill	2003-04
Australia in Bangladesh	16 (av 18.81)	S.C.G.MacGill	2005-06
Bangladesh in Australia	4 (av 33.50)	Mashrafe Bin Mortaza	2003-04
Bangladesh in Bangladesh	11 (av 27.72)	Mohammad Rafique	2005-06

ENGLAND v SOUTH AFRICA	England		South Africa		Captains	
Venue and Result	1st	2nd	1st	2nd	England	South Africa
1888-89 in South Africa						
Port Elizabeth-England 8 wkts	148	2-67	•84	129	C.A.Smith	O.R.Dunell
Cape Town-England inn & 202 runs	•292	-	47	43	M.P.Bowden	W.H.Milton
1891-92 in South Africa						
Cape Town-England inn & 189 runs	369	-	•97	83	W.W.Read	W.H.Milton
1895-96 in South Africa						
Port Elizabeth-England 288 runs	•185	226	93	30	Sir T.C.O'Brien	E.A.Halliwell
Johannesburg[1]-England inn & 197 runs	•482	-	151	134	Lord Hawke	E.A.Halliwell
Cape Town-England inn & 33 runs	265	-	•115	117	Lord Hawke	A.R.Richards
1898-99 in South Africa						
Johannesburg[1]-England 32 runs	•145	237	251	99	Lord Hawke	M.Bisset
Cape Town-England 210 runs	•92	330	177	35		
1905-06 in South Africa						
Johannesburg[1]-South Africa 1 wkt	•184	190	91	9-287	P.F.Warner	P.W.Sherwell
Johannesburg[1]-South Africa 9 wkts	•148	160	277	1-33		
Johannesburg[1]-South Africa 243 runs	295	196	•385	5d-349		
Cape Town-England 4 wkts	198	6-160	•218	138		
Cape Town-South Africa inn & 16 runs	•187	130	333	-		
1907 in England						
Lord's-Drawn	•428	-	140	3-185	R.E.Foster	P.W.Sherwell
Leeds-England 53 runs	•76	162	110	75		
The Oval-Drawn	•295	138	178	5-159		
1909-10 in South Africa						
Johannesburg[1]-South Africa 19 runs	310	224	•208	345	H.D.G.Leveson Gower	S.J.Snooke
Durban[1]-South Africa 95 runs	199	252	•199	347	H.D.G.Leveson Gower	
Johannesburg[1]-England 3 wkts	322	7-221	•305	237	H.D.G.Leveson Gower	
Cape Town-South Africa 4 wkts	•203	178	207	6-175	F.L.Fane	
Cape Town-England 9 wkts	•417	1-16	103	327	F.L.Fane	
1912 in England						
Lord's-England inn & 62 runs	337	-	•58	217	C.B.Fry	F.Mitchell
Leeds-England 174 runs	•242	238	147	159		L.J.Tancred
The Oval-England 10 wkts	176	0-14	•95	93		L.J.Tancred
1913-14 in South Africa						
Durban[1]-England inn & 157 runs	450	-	•182	111	J.W.H.T.Douglas	H.W.Taylor
Johannesburg[1]-England inn & 12 runs	403	-	•160	231		
Johannesburg[1]-England 91 runs	•238	308	151	304		
Durban[1]-Drawn	163	5-154	•170	9d-305		
Port Elizabeth-England 10 wkts	411	0-11	•193	228		
1922-23 in South Africa						
Johannesburg[1]-South Africa 168 runs	182	218	•148	420	F.T.Mann	H.W.Taylor
Cape Town-England 1 wkt	183	9-173	•113	242		
Durban[2]-Drawn	•428	1-11	368	-		
Johannesburg[1]-Drawn	•244	6d-376	295	4-247		
Durban[2]-England 109 runs	•281	241	179	234		
1924 in England						
Birmingham-England inn & 18 runs	•438	-	30	390	A.E.R.Gilligan	H.W.Taylor

ENGLAND v SOUTH AFRICA (cont.) Venue and Result	England 1st	England 2nd	South Africa 1st	South Africa 2nd	Captains England	Captains South Africa
Lord's-England inn & 18 runs	2d-531	-	•273	240	A.E.R.Gilligan	
Leeds-England 9 wkts	•396	1-60	132	323	A.E.R.Gilligan	
Manchester-Drawn	-	-	•4-116	-	J.W.H.T.Douglas	
The Oval-Drawn	8-421	-	•342	-	A.E.R.Gilligan	
1927-28 in South Africa						
Johannesburg[1]-England 10 wkts	313	0-57	•196	170	R.T.Stanyforth	H.G.Deane
Cape Town-England 87 runs	•133	428	250	224	R.T.Stanyforth	
Durban[2]-Drawn	430	2-132	•246	8d-464	R.T.Stanyforth	
Johannesburg[1]-South Africa 4 wkts	•265	215	328	6-156	R.T.Stanyforth	
Durban[2]-South Africa 8 wkts	•282	118	7d-332	2-69	G.T.S.Stevens	
1929 in England						
Birmingham-Drawn	•245	4d-308	250	1-171	J C.White	H.G.Deane
Lord's-Drawn	•302	8d-312	322	5-90	J C.White	
Leeds-England 5 wkts	328	5-186	•236	275	J C.White	
Manchester-England inn & 32 runs	•7d-427	-	130	265	A.W.Carr	
The Oval-Drawn	•258	1-264	8d-492	-	A.W.Carr	
1930-31 in South Africa						
Johannesburg[1]-South Africa 28 runs	193	211	•126	306	A.P.F.Chapman	E.P.Nupen
Cape Town-Drawn	350	252	•8d-513	-		H.G.Deane
Durban[2]-Drawn	1d-223	-	•177	8-145		H.G.Deane
Johannesburg[1]-Drawn	•442	9d-169	295	7-280		H.B.Cameron
Durban[2]-Drawn	230	4-72	•252	7d-219		H.B.Cameron
1935 in England						
Nottingham-Drawn	•7d-384	-	220	1-17	R.E.S.Wyatt	H.F.Wade
Lord's-South Africa 157 runs	198	151	•228	7d-278		
Leeds-Drawn	•216	7d-294	171	5-194		
Manchester-Drawn	•357	6d-231	318	2-169		
The Oval-Drawn	6d-534	-	•476	6-287		
1938-39 in South Africa						
Johannesburg[1]-Drawn	•422	4d-291	390	1-108	W.R.Hammond	A.Melville
Cape Town-Drawn	•9d-559	-	286	2-201		
Durban[2]-England inn & 13 runs	•4d-469	-	103	353		
Johannesburg[1]-Drawn	•215	4-203	8d-349	-		
Durban[2]-Drawn	316	6-654	•530	481		
1947 in England						
Nottingham-Drawn	208	551	•533	1-166	N.W.D.Yardley	A.Melville
Lord's-England 10 wkts	•8d-554	0-26	327	252		
Manchester-England 7 wkts	478	3-130	•339	267		
Leeds-England 10 wkts	7d-317	0-47	•175	184		
The Oval-Drawn	•427	6d-325	302	7-423		
1948-49 in South Africa						
Durban[2]-England 2 wkts	253	8-128	•161	219	F.G.Mann	A.D.Nourse
Johannesburg[2]-Drawn	•608	-	315	2-270		
Cape Town-Drawn	•308	3d-276	356	4-142		
Johannesburg[2]-Drawn	•379	7d-253	9d-257	4-194		
Port Elizabeth-England 3 wkts	395	7-174	•379	3d-187		

ENGLAND v SOUTH AFRICA (cont.)	England		South Africa		Captains	
Venue and Result	1st	2nd	1st	2nd	England	South Africa
1951 in England						
Nottingham-South Africa 71 runs	9d-419	114	•9d-483	121	F.R.Brown	A.D.Nourse
Lord s-England 10 wkts	•311	0-16	115	211		
Manchester-England 9 wkts	211	1-142	•158	191		
Leeds-Drawn	505	-	•538	0-87		
The Oval-England 4 wkts	194	6-164	•202	154		
1955 in England						
Nottingham-England inn & 5 runs	•334	-	181	148	P.B.H.May	J.E.Cheetham
Lord's-England 71 runs	•133	353	304	111		J.E.Cheetham
Manchester-South Africa 3 wkts	•284	381	8d-521	7-145		D.J.McGlew
Leeds-South Africa 224 runs	191	256	•171	500		D.J.McGlew
The Oval-England 92 runs	•151	204	112	151		J.E.Cheetham
1956-57 in South Africa						
Johannesburg[3]-England 131 runs	•268	150	215	72	P.B.H.May	C.B.van Ryneveld
Cape Town-England 312 runs	•369	6d-220	205	72		D.J.McGlew
Durban[2]-Drawn	•218	254	283	6-142		C.B.van Ryneveld
Johannesburg[3]-South Africa 17 runs	251	214	•340	142		C.B.van Ryneveld
Port Elizabeth-South Africa 58 runs	110	130	•164	134		C.B.van Ryneveld
1960 in England						
Birmingham-England 100 runs	•292	203	186	209	M.C.Cowdrey	D.J.McGlew
Lord's-England inn & 73 runs	•8d-362	-	152	137		
Nottingham-England 8 wkts	•287	2-49	88	247		
Manchester-Drawn	•260	7d-153	229	0-46		
The Oval-Drawn	•155	9d-479	419	4-97		
1964-65 in South Africa						
Durban[2]-England inn & 104 runs	•5d-485	-	155	226	M J K.Smith	T L.Goddard
Johannesburg[3]-Drawn	•531	-	317	6-336		
Cape Town-Drawn	442	0 15	•7d-501	346		
Johannesburg[3]-Drawn	384	6-153	•6d-390	3d-307		
Port Elizabeth-Drawn	435	1-29	•502	4d-178		
1965 in England						
Lord's-Drawn	338	7-145	•280	248	M.J.K.Smith	P L.van der Merwe
Nottingham-South Africa 94 runs	240	224	•269	289		
The Oval-Drawn	202	4-308	•208	392		
1994 in England						
Lord's-South Africa 356 runs	180	99	•357	8d-278	M.A.Atherton	K.C.Wessels
Leeds-Drawn	•9d-477	5d-267	447	3-116		
The Oval-England 8 wkts	304	2-205	•332	175		
1995-96 in South Africa						
Centurion-Drawn	•9d-381	-	-	-	M.A.Atherton	W.J.Cronje
Johannesburg[3]-Drawn	200	5-351	•332	9d-346		
Durban[2]-Drawn	5-152	-	•225	-		
Port Elizabeth-Drawn	263	3-189	•428	9d-162		
Cape Town-South Africa 10 wkts	•153	157	244	0-70		

ENGLAND v SOUTH AFRICA (cont.) Venue and Result	England 1st	England 2nd	South Africa 1st	South Africa 2nd	Captains England	Captains South Africa
1998 in England						
Birmingham-Drawn	•462	8-170	343	-	A.J.Stewart	W.J.Cronje
Lord's-South Africa 10 wkts	110	264	•360	0-15		
Manchester-Drawn	183	9-369	•5d-552	-		
Nottingham-England 8 wkts	336	2-247	•374	208		
Leeds-England 23 runs	•230	240	252	195		
1999-2000 in South Africa						
Johannesburg[3]-South Africa inn & 21 runs	•122	260	9d-403	-	N.Hussain	W.J.Cronje
Port Elizabeth-Drawn	373	6-153	•450	4d-224		
Durban[2]-Drawn	•9d-366	-	156	7-572		
Cape Town-South Africa inn & 37 runs	•258	126	421	-		
Centurion-England 2 wkts	•0d-0	8-251	forfeited	8d-248		
2003 in England						
Birmingham-Drawn	408	1-110	•5d-594	4d-134	N.Hussain	G.C.Smith
Lord's-South Africa inn & 92 runs	•173	417	6d-682	-	M.P.Vaughan	
Nottingham-England 70 runs	•445	118	362	131	M.P.Vaughan	
Leeds-South Africa 191 runs	307	209	•342	365	M.P.Vaughan	
The Oval-England 9 wkts	9d-604	1-110	•484	229	M.P.Vaughan	
2004-05 in South Africa						
Port Elizabeth-Eng 7 wkts	425	3-145	•337	229	M.P.Vaughan	G.C.Smith
Durban[2]-Drawn	•139	7d-570	332	8-290		
Cape Town-South Africa 196 runs	163	304	•441	8d-222		
Johannesburg[3]-Eng 77 runs	•8d-411	9d-332	419	247		
Centurion-Drawn	359	4-73	•247	6d-296		

Test Match Results Summary

ENGLAND v SOUTH AFRICA - in England

		Result			Lord's			Leeds			The Oval			Birmingham			Manchester			Nottingham		
	Tests	E	SA	D	E	SA	D	E	SA	D	E	SA	D	E	SA	D	E	SA	D	E	SA	D
1907	3	1	-	2	-	-	1	1	-	-	-	-	1	-	-	-	-	-	-	-	-	-
1912	3	3	-	-	1	-	-	1	-	-	1	-	-	-	-	-	-	-	-	-	-	-
1924	5	3	-	2	1	-	-	1	-	-	-	-	1	1	-	-	-	-	1	-	-	-
1929	5	2	-	3	-	-	1	1	-	-	-	-	1	-	-	1	1	-	-	-	-	-
1935	5	-	1	4	-	1	-	-	-	1	-	-	1	-	-	-	-	-	1	-	-	1
1947	5	3	-	2	1	-	-	1	-	-	-	-	1	-	-	-	1	-	-	-	-	1
1951	5	3	1	1	1	-	-	-	-	1	1	-	-	-	-	-	1	-	-	-	1	-
1955	5	3	2	-	1	-	-	-	1	-	1	-	-	-	-	-	-	1	-	1	-	-
1960	5	3	-	2	1	-	-	-	-	-	-	-	1	1	-	-	-	-	1	1	-	-
1965	3	-	1	2	-	-	1	-	-	-	-	-	1	-	-	-	-	-	-	-	1	-
1994	3	1	1	1	-	1	-	-	-	1	1	-	-	-	-	-	-	-	-	-	-	-
1998	5	2	1	2	-	1	-	1	-	-	-	-	-	-	-	1	-	-	1	1	-	-
2003	5	2	2	1	-	1	-	-	1	-	1	-	-	-	-	1	-	-	-	1	-	-
	57	26	9	22	6	4	3	6	2	3	5	-	7	2	-	3	3	1	4	4	2	2

ENGLAND v SOUTH AFRICA (cont.)	England		South Africa		Captains	
Venue and Result	1st	2nd	1st	2nd	England	South Africa

ENGLAND v SOUTH AFRICA - in South Africa

		Result			P.Elizabeth			Cape Town			Johannesburg			Durban			Centurion		
	Tests	E	SA	D	E	SA	D	E	SA	D	E	SA	D	E	SA	D	E	SA	D
1888-89	2	2	-	-	1	-	-	1	-	-	-	-	-	-	-	-	-	-	-
1891-92	1	1	-	-	-	-	-	1	-	-	-	-	-	-	-	-	-	-	-
1895-96	3	3	-	-	1	-	-	1	-	-	1	-	-	-	-	-	-	-	-
1898-99	2	2	-	-	-	-	-	1	-	-	1	-	-	-	-	-	-	-	-
1905-06	5	1	4	-	-	-	-	1	1	-	-	3	-	-	-	-	-	-	-
1909-10	5	2	3	-	-	-	-	1	1	-	1	1	-	-	1	-	-	-	-
1913-14	5	4	-	1	1	-	-	-	-	-	2	-	-	1	-	1	-	-	-
1922-23	5	2	1	2	-	-	-	1	-	-	-	1	1	1	-	1	-	-	-
1927-28	5	2	2	1	-	-	-	1	-	-	1	1	-	-	1	1	-	-	-
1930-31	5	-	1	4	-	-	-	-	-	1	-	1	1	-	-	2	-	-	-
1938-39	5	1	-	4	-	-	-	-	-	1	-	-	2	1	-	1	-	-	-
1948-49	5	2	-	3	1	-	-	-	-	1	-	-	2	1	-	-	-	-	-
1956-57	5	2	2	1	-	1	-	1	-	-	1	1	-	-	-	1	-	-	-
1964-65	5	1	-	4	-	-	1	-	-	1	-	-	2	1	-	-	-	-	-
1995-96	5	-	1	4	-	-	1	-	1	-	-	-	1	-	-	1	-	-	1
1999-2000	5	1	2	2	-	-	1	-	1	-	-	1	-	-	-	1	1	-	-
2004-05	5	2	1	2	1	-	-	-	1	-	1	-	-	-	-	1	-	-	1
	73	28	17	28	5	1	3	9	4	5	8	9	9	5	2	10	1	-	2

Totals	130	54	26	50

Highest Innings Totals

England in England	9-604	The Oval	2003
England in South Africa	5-654	Durban[2]	1938-39
South Africa in England	6d-682	Lord's	2003
South Africa in South Africa	7-572	Durban[2]	1999-2000

Lowest Innings Totals

England in England	76	Leeds	1907
England in South Africa	92	Cape Town	1898-99
South Africa in England	30	Birmingham	1924
South Africa in South Africa	30	Port Elizabeth	1895-96

Highest Match Aggregate	1981 for 35 wickets	Durban[2]	1938-39
Lowest Match Aggregate	378 for 30 wickets	The Oval	1912

Highest Individual Innings

England in England	219	M.E.Trescothick	The Oval	2003
England in South Africa	243	E.Paynter	Durban[2]	1938-39
South Africa in England	277	G.C.Smith	Birmingham	2003
South Africa in South Africa	275	G.Kirsten	Durban[2]	1999-2000

Most Runs in a Series

England in England	753 (av 94.12)	D.C.S.Compton	1947
England in South Africa	656 (av 72.88)	A.J.Strauss	2004-05
South Africa in England	714 (av 79.33)	G.C.Smith	2003
South Africa in South Africa	625 (av 69.44)	J.H.Kallis	2004-05

ENGLAND v SOUTH AFRICA (cont.)	England		South Africa		Captains	
Venue and Result	1st	2nd	1st	2nd	England	South Africa

Record Wicket Partnerships - England

1st	359	L.Hutton (158), C.Washbrook (195)	Johannesburg[2]	1948-49
2nd	280	P.A.Gibb (120), W.J.Edrich (219)	Durban[2]	1938-39
3rd	370	W.J.Edrich (189), D.C.S.Compton (208)	Lord's	1947
4th	197	W.R.Hammond (181), L.E.G.Ames (115)	Cape Town	1938-39
5th	237	D.C.S.Compton (163), N.W.D.Yardley (99)	Nottingham	1947
6th	206*	K.F.Barrington (148*), J.M.Parks (108*)	Durban[2]	1964-65
7th	115	J.W.H.T.Douglas (119), M.C.Bird (61)	Durban[1]	1913-14
8th	154	C.W.Wright (71), H.R Bromley-Davenport (84)	Johannesburg[1]	1895-96
9th	99	A.Flintoff (95), S.J.Harmison (6*)	The Oval	2003
10th	92	C.A.G.Russell (111), A.E.R.Gilligan (39*)	Durban[2]	1922-23

Record Wicket Partnerships - South Africa

1st	338	G.C.Smith (277), H.H.Gibbs (179)	Birmingham	2003
2nd	257	G.C.Smith (259), G.Kirsten (108)	Lord's	2003
3rd	319	A.Melville (189), A.D.Nourse (149)	Nottingham	1947
4th	214	H.W.Taylor (121), H.G.Deane (93)	The Oval	1929
5th	192	G.Kirsten (275), M.V.Boucher (108)	Durban[2]	1999-2000
6th	171	J.H.B.Waite (113), P.L.Winslow (108)	Manchester	1955
7th	123	H.G.Deane (73), E.P.Nupen (69)	Durban[2]	1927-28
8th	150	G.Kirsten (130), M.Zondeki (59)	Leeds	2003
9th	137	E.L.Dalton (117), A.B.C.Langton (73*)	The Oval	1935
10th	103	H.G.Owen-Smith (129), A.J.Bell (26*)	Leeds	1929

Best Bowling in an Innings

England in England	9/57	D.E.Malcolm	The Oval	1994
England in South Africa	9/28	G.A.Lohmann	Johannesburg[1]	1895-96
South Africa in England	7/65	S.J.Pegler	Lord's	1912
South Africa in South Africa	9/113	H.J.Tayfield	Johannesburg[3]	1956-57

Best Bowling in a Match

England in England	15/99	C.Blythe	Leeds	1907
England in South Africa	17/159	S.F.Barnes	Johannesburg[1]	1913-14
South Africa in England	10/87	P.M.Pollock	Nottingham	1965
South Africa in South Africa	13/192	H.J.Tayfield	Johannesburg[3]	1956-57

Most Wickets in a Series

England in England	34 (av 8.29)	S F Barnes	1912
England in South Africa	49 (av 10.93)	S.F.Barnes	1913-14
South Africa in England	33 (av 19.79)	A.A.Donald	1998
South Africa in South Africa	37 (av 17.18)	H.J.Tayfield	1956-57

ENGLAND v WEST INDIES	England		West Indies		Captains	
Venue and Result	1st	2nd	1st	2nd	England	West Indies
1928 in England						
Lord's-England inn & 58 runs	•401	-	177	166	A.P.F.Chapman	R.K.Nunes
Manchester-England inn & 30 runs	351	-	•206	115		
The Oval-England inn & 71 runs	438	-	•238	129		

ENGLAND v WEST INDIES (cont.)	England		West Indies		Captains	
Venue and Result	1st	2nd	1st	2nd	England	West Indies
1929-30 in West Indies						
Bridgetown-Drawn	467	3-167	•369	384	Hon F.S.G.Calthorpe	E.L.G.Hoad
Port-of-Spain-England 167 runs	•208	8d-425	254	212		N.Betancourt
Georgetown-West Indies 289 runs	145	327	•471	290		M.P.Fernandes
Kingston-Drawn	•849	9d-272	286	5-408		R.K.Nunes
1933 in England						
Lord's-England inn & 27 runs	•296	-	97	172	D.R.Jardine	G.C.Grant
Manchester-Drawn	374	-	•375	225	D.R.Jardine	
The Oval-England inn & 17 runs	•312	-	100	195	R.E.S.Wyatt	
1934-35 in West Indies						
Bridgetown-England 4 wkts	7d-81	6-75	•102	6d-51	R.E.S.Wyatt	G.C.Grant
Port-of-Spain-West Indies 217 runs	258	107	•302	6d-280		
Georgetown-Drawn	•226	6d-160	184	5-104		
Kingston-West Indies inn & 161 runs	271	103	•7d-535	-		
1939 in England						
Lord's-England 8 wkts	5d-404	2-100	•277	225	W.R.Hammond	R.S.Grant
Manchester-Drawn	•7d-164	6d-128	133	4-43		
The Oval-Drawn	•352	3d-366	498	-		
1947-48 in West Indies						
Bridgetown-Drawn	253	4-86	•296	9d-351	K.Cranston	G.A.Headley
Port-of-Spain-Drawn	•362	275	497	3-72	G.O.B.Allen	G.E.Gomez
Georgetown-West Indies 7 wkts	111	263	•8d-297	3-78	G.O.B.Allen	J.D.C.Goddard
Kingston-West Indies 10 wkts	•227	336	490	0-76	G.O.B.Allen	J.D.C.Goddard
1950 in England						
Manchester-England 202 runs	•312	288	215	183	N.W.D.Yardley	J.D.C.Goddard
Lord's-West Indies 326 runs	151	274	•326	6d-425	N.W.D Yardley	
Nottingham-West Indies 10 wkts	•223	436	558	0-103	N.W.D.Yardley	
The Oval-West Indies inn & 56 runs	344	103	•503	-	F.R.Brown	
1953-54 in West Indies						
Kingston-West Indies 140 runs	170	316	•417	6d-209	L.Hutton	J.B.Stollmeyer
Bridgetown-West Indies 181 runs	181	313	•383	2d-292		
Georgetown-England 9 wkts	•435	1-75	251	256		
Port-of-Spain-Drawn	537	3-98	•8d-681	4d-212		
Kingston-England 9 wkts	414	1-72	•139	346		
1957 in England						
Birmingham-Drawn	•186	4d-583	474	7-72	P.B.H.May	J.D.C.Goddard
Lord's-England inn & 36 runs	424	-	•127	261		
Nottingham-Drawn	•6d-619	1-64	372	367		
Leeds-England inn & 5 runs	279	-	•142	132		
The Oval-England inn & 237 runs	•412	-	89	86		
1959-60 in West Indies						
Bridgetown-Drawn	•482	0-71	8d-563	-	P.B.H.May	F.C.M.Alexander
Port-of-Spain-England 256 runs	•382	9d-230	112	244	P.B.H.May	
Kingston-Drawn	•277	305	353	6-175	P.B.H.May	
Georgetown-Drawn	•295	8-334	8d-402	-	M.C.Cowdrey	
Port-of-Spain-Drawn	•393	7d-350	8d-338	5-209	M.C.Cowdrey	

ENGLAND v WEST INDIES (cont.)	England		West Indies		Captains	
Venue and Result	1st	2nd	1st	2nd	England	West Indies
1963 in England						
Manchester-West Indies 10 wkts	205	296	•6d-501	0-1	E.R.Dexter	F.M.M.Worrell
Lord's-Drawn	297	9-228	•301	229		
Birmingham-England 217 runs	•216	9d-278	186	91		
Leeds-West Indies 221 runs	174	231	•397	229		
The Oval-West Indies 8 wkts	•275	223	246	2-255		
1966 in England						
Manchester-West Indies inn & 40 runs	167	277	•484	-	M.J.K.Smith	G.S.Sobers
Lord's-Drawn	355	4-197	•269	5d-369	M.C.Cowdrey	
Nottingham-West Indies 139 runs	325	253	•235	5d-482	M.C.Cowdrey	
Leeds-West Indies inn & 55 runs	240	205	•9d-500	-	M.C.Cowdrey	
The Oval-England inn & 34 runs	527	-	•268	225	D.B.Close	
1967-68 in West Indies						
Port-of-Spain-Drawn	•568	-	363	8-243	M.C.Cowdrey	G.S.Sobers
Kingston-Drawn	•376	8-68	143	9d-391		
Bridgetown-Drawn	449	-	•349	6-284		
Port-of-Spain-England 7 wkts	404	3-215	•7d-526	2d-92		
Georgetown-Drawn	371	9-206	•414	264		
1969 in England						
Manchester-England 10 wkts	•413	0-12	147	275	R.Illingworth	G.S.Sobers
Lord's-Drawn	344	7-295	•380	9d-295		
Leeds-England 30 runs	•223	240	161	272		
1973 in England						
The Oval-West Indies 158 runs	257	255	•415	255	R.Illingworth	R.B.Kanhai
Birmingham-Drawn	305	2-182	•327	302		
Lord's-West Indies inn & 226 runs	233	193	•8d-652	-		
1973-74 in West Indies						
Port-of-Spain-West Indies 7 wkts	•131	392	392	3-132	M.H.Denness	R.B.Kanhai
Kingston-Drawn	•353	9-432	9d-583	-		
Bridgetown-Drawn	•395	7-277	8d-596	-		
Georgetown-Drawn	•448	-	4-198	-		
Port-of-Spain-England 26 runs	•267	263	305	199		
1976 in England						
Nottingham-Drawn	332	2-156	•494	5d-176	A.W.Greig	C.H.Lloyd
Lord's-Drawn	•250	254	182	6-241		
Manchester-West Indies 425 runs	71	126	•211	5d-411		
Leeds-West Indies 55 runs	387	204	•450	196		
The Oval-West Indies 231 runs	435	203	•8d-687	0d-182		
1980 in England						
Nottingham-West Indies 2 wkts	•263	252	308	8-209	I.T.Botham	C.H.Lloyd
Lord's-Drawn	•269	2-133	518	-		C.H.Lloyd
Manchester-Drawn	•150	7-391	260	-		C.H.Lloyd
The Oval-Drawn	•370	9d-209	265	-		C.H.Lloyd
Leeds-Drawn	•143	6d-227	245	-		I.V.A.Richards

ENGLAND v WEST INDIES (cont.)	England		West Indies		Captains	
Venue and Result	1st	2nd	1st	2nd	England	West Indies
1980-81 in West Indies						
Port-of-Spain-West Indies inn & 79 runs	178	169	•9-426	-	I.T.Botham	C.H.Lloyd
Georgetown-match cancelled	-	-	-	-		
Bridgetown-West Indies 298 runs	122	224	•265	7d-379		
St John's-Drawn	•271	3-234	9d-468	-		
Kingston-Drawn	•285	6d-302	442	-		
1984 in England						
Birmingham-West Indies inn & 180 runs	•191	235	606	-	D.I.Gower	C.H.Lloyd
Lord's-West Indies 9 wkts	•286	9d-300	245	1-344		
Manchester-West Indies 8 wkts	•270	159	302	2-131		
Leeds-West Indies inn & 64 runs	280	156	•500	-		
The Oval-West Indies 172 runs	190	346	162	202		
1985-86 in West Indies						
Kingston-West Indies 10 wkts	•159	152	307	0-5	D.I.Gower	I.V.A.Richards
Port-of-Spain-West Indies 7 wkts	•176	315	399	3-95		
Bridgetown-West Indies inn & 30 runs	189	199	•418	-		
Port-of-Spain-West Indies 10 wkts	•200	150	312	0-39		
St John's-West Indies 240 runs	310	170	•474	2d-246		
1988 in England						
Nottingham-Drawn	•245	3-301	9d-448	-	M.W.Gatting	I.V.A.Richards
Lord's-West Indies 134 runs	165	307	•209	397	J.E.Emburey	
Manchester-West Indies inn & 156 runs	•135	93	7d-384	-	J.E.Emburey	
Leeds-West Indies 10 wkts	•201	138	275	0-67	C.S.Cowdrey	
The Oval-West Indies 8 wkts	•205	202	183	2-226	G.A.Gooch	
1989-90 in West Indies						
Kingston-England 9 wkts	364	1-21	•164	240	G.A.Gooch	I.V.A.Richards
Georgetown-match abandoned	-	-	-	-	G.A.Gooch	I.V.A.Richards
Port-of-Spain-Drawn	288	5-120	•199	239	G.A.Gooch	D.L.Haynes
Bridgetown-West Indies 164 runs	358	191	•446	8d-267	A.J.Lamb	I.V.A.Richards
St John's-West Indies inn & 32 runs	•260	154	446	-	A.J.Lamb	I.V.A.Richards
1991 in England						
Leeds-England 115 runs	•198	252	173	162	G.A.Gooch	I.V.A.Richards
Lord's-Drawn	354	-	•419	2-12		
Nottingham-West Indies 9 wkts	•300	211	397	1-115		
Birmingham-West Indies 7 wkts	•188	255	292	3-157		
The Oval-England 5 wkts	•419	5-146	176	385		
1993-94 in West Indies						
Kingston- West Indies 8 wkts	•234	267	407	2-95	M.A.Atherton	R.B.Richardson
Georgetown-West Indies inn & 44 runs	•322	190	556	-		R.B.Richardson
Port-of-Spain-West Indies 147 runs	328	46	•252	269		R.B.Richardson
Bridgetown-England 208 runs	•355	7d-394	304	237		R.B.Richardson
St John's-Drawn	593	-	•5d-593	0-43		C.A.Walsh
1995 in England						
Leeds-West Indies 9 wkts	•199	208	282	1-129	M.A.Atherton	R.B.Richardson
Lord's-England 72 runs	•283	336	324	223		
Birmingham-West Indies inn & 64 runs	•147	89	300	-		
Manchester-England 6 wkts	437	4-94	•216	314		
Nottingham-Drawn	•440	9d-269	417	2-42		
The Oval-Drawn	•454	4-223	8d-692	-		

ENGLAND v WEST INDIES (cont.)	England		West Indies		Captains	
Venue and Result	1st	2nd	1st	2nd	England	West Indies
1997-98 in West Indies						
Kingston- Drawn	•3-17	-	-	-	M.A.Atherton	B.C.Lara
Port-of-Spain-West Indies 3 wkts	•214	257	191	7-282		
Port-of-Spain-England 3 wkts	145	7-225	•159	210		
Georgetown-West Indies 242 runs	170	137	•352	197		
Bridgetown-Drawn	•403	3d-233	262	2-112		
St John's-West Indies inn & 52 runs	•127	321	7d-500	-		
2000 in England						
Birmingham-West Indies inn & 93 runs	•179	125	397	-	N.Hussain	J.C.Adams
Lord's-England 2 wkts	134	8-191	•267	54	A.J.Stewart	
Manchester-Drawn	303	1-80	•157	7d-438	N.Hussain	
Leeds-England inn & 39 runs	272	-	•172	61	N.Hussain	
The Oval-England 158 runs	•281	217	125	215	N.Hussain	
2003-04 in West Indies						
Kingston- England 10 wkts	339	0-20	•311	47	M.P.Vaughan	B.C.Lara
Port-of-Spain-England 7 wkts	319	3-99	•208	209		
Bridgetown-England 8 wkts	226	2-93	•224	94		
St John's-Drawn	285	5-422	•5d-751	-		
2004 in England						
Lord's-England 210 runs	•568	5d-325	416	267	M.P.Vaughan	B.C.Lara
Birmingham-England 256 runs	•9d-566	248	336	222		
Manchester-England 7 wkts	300	3-231	•9d-395	165		
The Oval-England 10 wkts	•470	0-4	152	318		

Test Match Results Summary

ENGLAND v WEST INDIES - in England

		Result			Lord's			Manchester			The Oval			Nottingham			Birmingham			Leeds		
	Tests	E	WI	D	E	WI	D	E	WI	D	E	WI	D	E	WI	D	E	WI	D	E	WI	D
1928	3	3	-	-	1	-	-	1	-	-	1	-	-	-	-	-	-	-	-	-	-	-
1933	3	2	-	1	1	-	-	-	-	1	1	-	-	-	-	-	-	-	-	-	-	-
1939	3	1	-	2	1	-	-	-	-	1	-	-	1	-	-	-	-	-	-	-	-	-
1950	4	1	3	-	-	1	-	1	-	-	-	1	-	-	1	-	-	-	-	-	-	-
1957	5	3	-	2	1	-	-	-	-	-	1	-	-	-	-	1	-	-	1	1	-	-
1963	5	1	3	1	-	-	1	-	1	-	-	1	-	-	-	-	1	-	-	-	1	-
1966	5	1	3	1	-	-	1	-	1	-	1	-	-	-	1	-	-	-	-	-	1	-
1969	3	2	-	1	-	-	1	1	-	-	-	-	-	-	-	-	-	-	-	1	-	-
1973	3	-	2	1	-	1	-	-	-	-	-	1	-	-	-	-	-	-	1	-	-	-
1976	5	-	3	2	-	-	1	-	1	-	-	1	-	-	-	1	-	-	-	-	1	-
1980	5	-	1	4	-	-	1	-	-	1	-	-	1	-	1	-	-	-	-	-	-	1
1984	5	-	5	-	-	1	-	-	1	-	-	1	-	-	-	-	-	1	-	-	1	-
1988	5	-	4	1	-	1	-	-	1	-	-	1	-	-	-	1	-	-	-	-	1	-
1991	5	2	2	1	-	-	1	-	-	-	1	-	-	-	1	-	-	1	-	1	-	-
1995	6	2	2	2	1	-	-	1	-	-	-	-	1	-	-	1	-	1	-	-	1	-
2000	5	3	1	1	1	-	-	-	-	1	1	-	-	-	-	-	-	1	-	1	-	-
2004	4	4	-	-	1	-	-	1	-	-	1	-	-	-	-	-	1	-	-	-	-	-
	74	25	29	20	7	4	6	5	5	4	7	6	3	-	4	4	2	4	2	4	6	1

ENGLAND v WEST INDIES - in West Indies

		Result			Bridgetown			Port-of-Spain			Georgetown			Kingston			St John's		
	Tests	E	WI	D	E	WI	D	E	WI	D	E	WI	D	E	WI	D	E	WI	D
1929-30	4	1	1	2	-	-	1	1	-	-	-	1	-	-	-	1	-	-	-
1934-35	4	1	2	1	1	-	-	-	1	-	-	-	1	-	1	-	-	-	-
1947-48	4	-	2	2	-	-	1	-	-	1	-	1	-	-	1	-	-	-	-
1953-54	5	2	2	1	-	1	-	-	-	1	1	-	-	1	1	-	-	-	-
1959-60	5	1	-	4	-	-	1	1	-	1	-	-	1	-	-	1	-	-	-
1967-68	5	1	-	4	-	-	1	1	-	1	-	-	1	-	-	1	-	-	-
1973-74	5	1	1	3	-	-	1	1	1	-	-	-	1	-	-	1	-	-	-
1980-81	4	-	2	2	-	1	-	-	1	-	-	-	-	-	-	1	-	-	1
1985-86	5	-	5	-	-	1	-	-	2	-	-	-	-	-	1	-	-	1	-
1989-90	4	1	2	1	-	1	-	-	-	1	-	-	-	1	-	-	-	1	-
1993-94	5	1	3	1	1	-	-	-	1	-	-	1	-	-	1	-	-	-	1
1997-98	6	1	3	2	-	-	1	1	1	-	-	1	-	-	-	1	-	1	-
2003-04	4	3	-	1	1	-	-	1	-	-	-	-	-	1	-	-	-	-	1
	60	13	23	24	3	4	6	6	7	5	1	4	4	3	5	6	-	3	3
Totals	134	38	52	44															

Highest Innings Totals

England in England	6d-619	Nottingham	1957
England in West Indies	849	Kingston	1929-30
West Indies in England	8d-692	The Oval	1995
West Indies in West Indies	5d-751	St John's	2003-04

Lowest Innings Totals

England In England	71	Manchester	1976
England in West Indies	46	Port-of-Spain	1993-94
West Indies in England	54	Lord's	2000
West Indies in West Indies	47	Kingston	2003-04

Highest Match Aggregate	1815 for 34 wickets	Kingston	1929-30
Lowest Match Aggregate	309 for 29 wickets	Bridgetown	1934-35

Highest Individual Innings

England in England	285*	P.B.H.May	Birmingham	1957
England in West Indies	325	A.Sandham	Kingston	1929-30
West Indies in England	291	I.V.A.Richards	The Oval	1976
West Indies in West Indies	400*	B.C.Lara	St John's	2003-04

Most Runs in a Series

England in England	506 (av 42.16)	G.P.Thorpe	1995
England in West Indies	693 (av 115.50)	E.H.Hendren	1929-30
West Indies in England	829 (av 118.42)	I.V.A.Richards	1976
West Indies in West Indies	798 (av 99.75)	B.C.Lara	1993-94

Record Wicket Partnerships - England

1st	212	C.Washbrook (102), R.T.Simpson (94)	Nottingham	1950
2nd	291	A.J.Strauss (137), R.W.T.Key (221)	Lord's	2004
3rd	303	M.A.Atherton (135), R.A.Smith (175)	St John's	1993-94
4th	411	P.B.H.May (285*), M.C.Cowdrey (154)	Birmingham	1957
5th	150	A.J.Stewart (143), G.P.Thorpe (84)	Bridgetown	1993-94
6th	205	M.R.Ramprakash (154), G.P.Thorpe (103)	Bridgetown	1997-98
7th	197	M.J.K.Smith (96), J.M.Parks (101*)	Port-of-Spain	1959-60
8th	217	T.W.Graveney (165), J.T.Murray (112)	The Oval	1966
9th	109	G.A.R.Lock (89), P.I.Pocock (13)	Georgetown	1967-68
10th	128	K.Higgs (63), J.A.Snow (59*)	The Oval	1966

Record Wicket Partnerships - West Indies

1st	298	C.G.Greenidge (149), D.L.Haynes (167)	St John's	1989-90
2nd	287*	C.G.Greenidge (214*), H.A.Gomes (92*)	Lord's	1984
3rd	338	E.D.Weekes (206), F.M.M.Worrell (167)	Port-of-Spain	1953-54
4th	399	G.S.Sobers (226), F.M.M.Worrell (197*)	Bridgetown	1959-60
5th	265	S.M.Nurse (137), G.S.Sobers (174)	Leeds	1966
6th	282*	B.C.Lara (400*), R.D.Jacobs (107*)	St John's	2003-04
7th	155*†	G.S.Sobers (150*), B.D.Julien (121)	Lord's	1973
8th	99	C.A.McWatt (54), J.K.Holt (48*)	Georgetown	1953-54
9th	150	E.A.E.Baptiste (87*), M.A.Holding (69)	Birmingham	1984
10th	70	I.R.Bishop (44*), D.Ramnarine (19)	Georgetown	1997-98

† 231 runs were added for this wicket, G.S.Sobers retired ill and was replaced by K.D.Boyce after 155 had been scored.

Best Bowling in an Innings

England in England	8/103	I.T.Botham	Lord's	1984
England in West Indies	8/53	A.R.C.Fraser	Port-of-Spain	1997-98
West Indies in England	8/92	M.A.Holding	The Oval	1976
West Indies in West Indies	8/45	C.E.L.Ambrose	Bridgetown	1989-90

Best Bowling in a Match

England in England	12/119	F.S.Trueman	Birmingham	1963
England in West Indies	13/156	A.W.Greig	Port-of-Spain	1973-74
West Indies in England	14/149	M.A.Holding	The Oval	1976
West Indies in West Indies	11/84	C.E.L.Ambrose	Bridgetown	1993-94

Most Wickets in a Series

England in England	34 (av 17.47)	F.S.Trueman	1963
England in West Indies	27 (av 18.66)	J.A.Snow	1967-68
	27 (av 18.22)	A.R.C.Fraser	1997-98
West Indies in England	35 (av 12.65)	M.D.Marshall	1988
West Indies in West Indies	30 (av 14.26)	C.E.L.Ambrose	1997-98

ENGLAND v NEW ZEALAND

Venue and Result	England 1st	England 2nd	New Zealand 1st	New Zealand 2nd	Captains England	Captains New Zealand
1929-30 in New Zealand						
Christchurch-England 8 wkts	181	2-66	•112	131	A.H.H.Gilligan	T.C.Lowry
Wellington-Drawn	320	4-107	•440	4d-164		
Auckland-Drawn	•4d-330	-	1-96	-		
Auckland-Drawn	•540	3-22	387	-		
1931 in England						
Lord's-Drawn	454	5-146	•224	9d-469	D.R.Jardine	T.C.Lowry
The Oval-England inn & 26 runs	•4d-416	-	193	197		
Manchester-Drawn	•3-224	-	-	-		
1932-33 in New Zealand						
Christchurch-Drawn	•8d-560	-	223	0-35	D.R.Jardine	M.L.Page
Auckland-Drawn	7d-548	-	•158	0-16	R.E.S.Wyatt	
1937 in England						
Lord's-Drawn	•424	4d-226	295	8-175	R.W.V.Robins	M.L.Page
Manchester-England 130 runs	•9d-358	187	281	134		
The Oval-Drawn	7d-254	1-31	•249	187		

ENGLAND v NEW ZEALAND (cont.)	England		New Zealand		Captains	
Venue and Result	1st	2nd	1st	2nd	England	New Zealand
1946-47 in New Zealand						
Christchurch-Drawn	7d-265	-	•9d-345	-	W.R.Hammond	W.A.Hadlee
1949 in England						
Leeds-Drawn	•372	4d-267	341	2-195	F.G.Mann	W.A.Hadlee
Lord's-Drawn	•9d-313	5-306	484	-	F.G.Mann	
Manchester-Drawn	9d-440	-	•293	7-348	F.R.Brown	
The Oval-Drawn	482	-	•345	9d-308	F.R.Brown	
1950-51 in New Zealand						
Christchurch-Drawn	550	-	•8d-417	3-46	F.R.Brown	W.A.Hadlee
Wellington-England 6 wkts	227	4-91	•125	189		
1954-55 in New Zealand						
Dunedin-England 8 wkts	8d-209	2-49	•125	132	L.Hutton	G.O.Rabone
Auckland-England inn & 20 runs	246	-	•200	26		
1958 in England						
Birmingham-England 205 runs	•221	6d-215	94	137	P.B.H.May	J.R.Reid
Lord's-England inn & 148 runs	•269	-	47	74		
Leeds-England inn & 71 runs	2d-267	-	•67	129		
Manchester-England inn & 13 runs	9d-365	-	•267	85		
The Oval-Drawn	9d-219	-	•161	3-91		
1958-59 in New Zealand						
Christchurch-England inn & 99 runs	•374	-	142	133	P.B.H.May	J.R.Reid
Auckland-Drawn	7-311	-	•181	-		
1962-63 in New Zealand						
Auckland-England inn & 215 runs	•7d-562	-	258	89	E.R.Dexter	J.R.Reid
Wellington-England inn & 47 runs	8d-428	-	•194	187		
Christchurch-England 7 wkts	253	3-173	•266	159		
1965 in England						
Birmingham-England 9 wkts	•435	1-96	116	413	M.J.K.Smith	J.R.Reid
Lord's-England 7 wkts	307	3-218	•175	347		
Leeds-England inn & 187 runs	•4d-546	-	193	166		
1965-66 in New Zealand						
Christchurch-Drawn	•342	5d-201	347	8-48	M.J.K.Smith	M.E.Chapple
Dunedin-Drawn	8d-254	-	•192	9-147		B.W.Sinclair
Auckland-Drawn	222	4-159	•296	129		B.W.Sinclair
1969 in England						
Lord's-England 230 runs	•190	340	169	131	R.Illingworth	G.T.Dowling
Nottingham-Drawn	8d-451	-	•294	1-66		
The Oval-England 8 wkts	242	2-138	•150	229		
1970-71 in New Zealand						
Christchurch-England 8 wkts	231	2-89	•65	254	R.Illingworth	G.T.Dowling
Auckland-Drawn	•321	237	7d-313	0-40		
1973 in England						
Nottingham-England 38 runs	•250	8d-325	97	440	R.Illingworth	B.E.Congdon
Lord's-Drawn	•253	9-463	9d-551	-		
Leeds-England inn &1 run	419	-	•276	142		

ENGLAND v NEW ZEALAND (cont.)	England		New Zealand		Captains	
Venue and Result	1st	2nd	1st	2nd	England	New Zealand
1974-75 in New Zealand						
Auckland-England inn & 83 runs	•6d-593	-	326	184	M.H.Denness	B.E.Congdon
Christchurch-Drawn	2-272	-	•342	-		
1977-78 in New Zealand						
Wellington-New Zealand 72 runs	215	64	•228	123	G.Boycott	M.G.Burgess
Christchurch-England 174 runs	•418	4d-96	235	105		
Auckland-Drawn	429	-	•315	8-382		
1978 in England						
The Oval-England 7 wkts	279	3-138	•234	182	J.M.Brearley	M.G.Burgess
Nottingham-England inn &119 runs	•429	-	120	190		
Lord's-England 7 wkts	289	3-118	•339	67		
1983 in England						
The Oval-England 189 runs	•209	6d-446	196	270	R.G.D.Willis	G.P.Howarth
Leeds-New Zealand 5 wkts	•225	252	377	5-103		
Lord's-England 127 runs	•326	211	191	219		
Nottingham-England 165 runs	•420	297	207	345		
1983-84 in New Zealand						
Wellington-Drawn	463	0-69	•219	537	R.G.D.Willis	G.P.Howarth
Christchurch-New Zealand inn & 132 runs	82	93	•307	-		
Auckland-Drawn	439	-	•9d-496	0-16		
1986 in England						
Lord's-Drawn	•317	6d-295	342	2-41	M.W.Gatting	J.V.Coney
Nottingham-New Zealand 8 wkts	•256	230	413	2-77		
The Oval-Drawn	5d-388	-	•287	0-7		
1987-88 in New Zealand						
Christchurch-Drawn	•319	152	168	4-130	M.W.Gatting	J.J.Crowe
Auckland-Drawn	323	-	•301	7-350		J.J.Crowe
Wellington-Drawn	2-183	-	•6d-512	-		J.G.Wright
1990 in England						
Nottingham-Drawn	9d-345	-	•208	2-36	G.A.Gooch	J.G.Wright
Lord's-Drawn	•334	4d-272	9d-462	-		
Birmingham-England 114 runs	•435	158	249	230		
1991-92 in New Zealand						
Christchurch-England inn & 4 runs	•9d-580	-	312	264	G.A.Gooch	M.D.Crowe
Auckland-England 168 runs	•203	321	142	214		
Wellington-Drawn	•305	7d-359	9d-432	3-43		
1994 in England						
Nottingham-England inn & 90 runs	9d-567	-	•251	226	M.A.Atherton	K.R.Rutherford
Lord's-Drawn	281	8-254	•476	5d-211		
Birmingham-Drawn	•382	-	151	7-308		
1996-97 in New Zealand						
Auckland-Drawn	521	-	•390	9-248	M.A.Atherton	L.K.Germon
Wellington-England inn & 68 runs	383	-	•124	191		L.K.Germon
Christchurch-England 4 wkts	228	6-307	•346	186		S.P.Fleming

ENGLAND v NEW ZEALAND (cont.) Venue and Result	England 1st	England 2nd	New Zealand 1st	New Zealand 2nd	Captains England	Captains New Zealand
1999 in England						
Birmingham-England 7 wkts	126	3-211	•226	107	N.Hussain	S.P.Fleming
Lord's-New Zealand 9 wkts	•186	229	358	1-60		
Manchester-Drawn	•199	2-181	9d-496	-		
The Oval-New Zealand 83 runs	153	162	•236	162		
2001-02 in New Zealand						
Christchurch-England 98 runs	•228	6d-468	147	451	N.Hussain	S.P.Fleming
Wellington-Drawn	•280	4d-293	218	4-158		
Auckland-New Zealand 78 runs	160	233	•202	9d-269		
2004 in England						
Lord's-England 7 wkts	441	3-282	•386	336	M.E.Trescothick	S.P.Fleming
Leeds-England 9 wkts	526	1-45	•409	161	M.P.Vaughan	
Nottingham-England 4 wkts	319	6-284	•384	218	M.P.Vaughan	

Test Match Results Summary

ENGLAND v NEW ZEALAND - in England

		Result			Lord's			The Oval			Manchester			Leeds			Birmingham			Nottingham		
	Tests	E	NZ	D	E	NZ	D	E	NZ	D	E	NZ	D	E	NZ	D	E	NZ	D	E	NZ	D
1931	3	1	-	2	-	-	1	1	-	-	-	-	1	-	-	-	-	-	-	-	-	-
1937	3	1	-	2	-	-	-	-	-	1	1	-	-	-	-	-	-	-	-	-	-	-
1949	4	-	-	4	-	-	1	-	-	1	-	-	1	-	-	1	-	-	-	-	-	-
1958	5	4	-	1	1	-	-	-	-	1	1	-	-	1	-	-	1	-	-	-	-	-
1965	3	3	-	-	1	-	-	-	-	-	-	-	-	1	-	-	1	-	-	-	-	-
1969	3	2	-	1	1	-	-	1	-	-	-	-	-	-	-	-	-	-	-	-	-	1
1973	3	2	-	1	-	-	1	-	-	-	-	-	-	1	-	-	-	-	-	1	-	-
1978	3	3	-	-	1	-	-	1	-	-	-	-	-	-	-	-	-	-	-	1	-	-
1983	4	3	1	-	1	-	-	1	-	-	-	-	-	-	1	-	-	-	-	1	-	-
1986	3	-	1	2	-	-	1	-	-	1	-	-	-	-	-	-	-	-	-	-	1	-
1990	3	1	-	2	-	-	1	-	-	-	-	-	-	-	-	-	1	-	-	-	-	1
1994	3	1	-	2	-	-	1	-	-	-	-	-	1	-	-	-	-	-	-	1	-	-
1999	4	1	2	1	-	1	-	-	1	-	-	-	1	-	-	-	1	-	-	-	-	-
2004	3	3	-	-	1	-	-	-	-	-	-	-	-	1	-	-	-	-	-	1	-	-
	46	25	4	18	6	1	7	4	1	4	2	-	4	4	1	1	4	-	-	5	1	2

ENGLAND v NEW ZEALAND - in New Zealand

		Result			Christchurch			Wellington			Auckland			Dunedin		
	Tests	E	NZ	D	E	NZ	D	E	NZ	D	E	NZ	D	E	NZ	D
1929-30	4	1	-	3	1	-	-	-	-	1	-	-	2	-	-	-
1932-33	2	-	-	2	-	-	1	-	-	-	-	-	1	-	-	-
1946-47	1	-	-	1	-	-	1	-	-	-	-	-	-	-	-	-
1950-51	2	1	-	1	-	-	1	1	-	-	-	-	-	-	-	-
1954-55	2	2	-	-	-	-	-	-	-	-	1	-	-	1	-	-
1958-59	2	1	-	1	1	-	-	-	-	-	-	-	1	-	-	-
1962-63	3	3	-	-	1	-	-	1	-	-	1	-	-	-	-	-
1965-66	3	-	-	3	-	-	1	-	-	-	-	-	1	-	-	1
1970-71	2	1	-	1	1	-	-	-	-	-	-	-	1	-	-	-
1974-75	2	1	-	1	-	-	1	-	-	-	1	-	-	-	-	-
1977-78	3	1	1	1	1	-	-	-	1	-	-	-	1	-	-	-
1983-84	3	-	1	2	-	1	-	-	-	1	-	-	1	-	-	-
1987-88	3	-	-	3	-	-	1	-	-	1	-	-	1	-	-	-
1991-92	3	2	-	1	1	-	-	-	-	1	1	-	-	-	-	-
1996-97	3	2	-	1	1	-	-	1	-	-	-	-	1	-	-	-
2001-02	3	1	1	1	1	-	-	-	-	1	-	1	-	-	-	-
	41	16	3	22	7	1	6	2	1	5	4	1	9	1	-	1
Totals	88	41	7	40												

Highest Innings Totals

England in England	8d-567	Nottingham	1994
England in New Zealand	6d-593	Auckland	1974-75
New Zealand in England	9d-551	Lord's	1973
New Zealand in New Zealand	537	Wellington	1983-84

Lowest Innings Totals

England in England	126	Birmingham	1999
England in New Zealand	64	Wellington	1977-78
New Zealand in England	47	Lord's	1958
New Zealand in New Zealand	26	Auckland	1954-55

Highest Match Aggregate	1445 for 33 wickets	Lord's	2004
Lowest Match Aggregate	390 for 30 wickets	Lord's	1958

Highest Individual Innings

England in England	310*	J.H.Edrich	Leeds	1965
England in New Zealand	336*	W.R.Hammond	Auckland	1932-33
New Zealand in England	206	M.P.Donnelly	Lord's	1949
New Zealand in New Zealand	222	N.J.Astle	Christchurch	2001-02

Most Runs in a Series

England in England	469 (av 78.16)	L.Hutton	1949
England in New Zealand	563 (av 563.00)	W.R.Hammond	1932-33
New Zealand in England	462 (av 77.00)	M.P.Donnelly	1949
New Zealand in New Zealand	341 (av 85.25)	C.S.Dempster	1929-30

Record Wicket Partnerships - England

1st	223	G.Fowler (105), C.J.Tavaré (109)	The Oval	1983
2nd	369	J.H.Edrich (310*), K.F.Barrington (163)	Leeds	1965
3rd	245	J.Hardstaff, jr (114), W.R.Hammond (140)	Lord's	1937
4th	266	M H.Denness (188), K.W.R.Fletcher (216)	Auckland	1974-75
5th	242	W.R.Hammond (227), L.E.G.Ames (103)	Christchurch	1932-33
6th	281	G.P.Thorpe (200*), A.Flintoff (137)	Christchurch	2001-02

7th	149	A.P.E.Knott (104), P.Lever (64)	Auckland	1970-71
8th	246	L.E.G.Ames (137), G.O.B.Allen (122)	Lord's	1931
9th	163*	M.C.Cowdrey (128*), A.C.Smith (69*)	Wellington	1962-63
10th	59	A.P.E.Knott (49), N.Gifford (25*)	Nottingham	1973

Record Wicket Partnerships - New Zealand

1st	276	C.S.Dempster (136), J.E.Mills (117)	Wellington	1929-30
2nd	241	J.G.Wright (116), A.H.Jones (143)	Wellington	1991-92
3rd	210	B.A.Edgar (83), M.D.Crowe (106)	Lord's	1986
4th	155	M.D.Crowe (143), M.J.Greatbatch (68)	Wellington	1987-88
5th	180	M.D.Crowe (142), S.A.Thomson (69)	Lord's	1994
6th	141	M.D.Crowe (115), A.C.Parore (71)	Manchester	1994
7th	117	D.N.Patel (99), C.L.Cairns (61)	Christchurch	1991-92
8th	104	D.A.R.Moloney (64), A.W.Roberts (66*)	Lord's	1937
9th	118	J.V.Coney (174*), B.L.Cairns (64)	Wellington	1983-84
10th	118	N.J.Astle (222), C.L.Cairns (23*)	Christchurch	2001-02

Best Bowling in an Innings

England in England	7/32	D.L.Underwood	Lord's	1969
England in New Zealand	7/47	P.C.R.Tufnell	Christchurch	1991-92
New Zealand in England	7/74	B.L.Cairns	Leeds	1983
New Zealand in New Zealand	7/143	B.L.Cairns	Wellington	1983-84

Best Bowling in a Match

England in England	12/101	D.L.Underwood	The Oval	1969
England in New Zealand	12/97	D.L.Underwood	Christchurch	1970-71
New Zealand in England	11/169	D.J.Nash	Lord's	1994
New Zealand in New Zealand	10/100	R.J.Hadlee	Wellington	1977-78

Most Wickets in a Series

England in England	34 (av 7.47)	G.A.R.Lock	1958
England in New Zealand	19 (av 19.00)	D.Gough	1996-97
	19 (av 19.84)	A.R.Caddick	2001-02
New Zealand in England	21 (av 26.61)	R.J.Hadlee	1983
New Zealand in New Zealand	15 (av 19.53)	R.O.Collinge	1977-78
	15 (av 24.73)	R.J.Hadlee	1977-78

ENGLAND v INDIA	England		India		Captains	
Venue and Result	1st	2nd	1st	2nd	England	India
1932 in England						
Lord's-England 158 runs	•259	8d-275	189	187	D.R.Jardine	C.K.Nayudu
1933-34 in India						
Bombay[1]-England 9 wkts	438	1-40	•219	258	D.R.Jardine	C.K.Nayudu
Calcutta-Drawn	•403	2-7	247	237		
Madras[1]-England 202 runs	•335	7d-261	145	249		
1936 in England						
Lord's-England 9 wkts	134	1-108	•147	93	G.O.B.Allen	Maharaj Vizianagram
Manchester-Drawn	8d-571	-	•203	5-390		
The Oval-England 9 wkts	•8d-471	1-64	222	312		
1946 in England						
Lord's-England 10 wkts	428	0-48	•200	275	W.R.Hammond	Nawab of Pataudi, sr
Manchester-Drawn	•294	5d-153	170	9-152		
The Oval-Drawn	3-95	-	•331	-		

ENGLAND v INDIA (cont.) Venue and Result	England 1st	England 2nd	India 1st	India 2nd	Captains England	Captains India
1951-52 in India						
Delhi-Drawn	•203	6-368	6d-418	-	N.D.Howard	V.S.Hazare
Bombay[2]-Drawn	456	2-55	•9d-485	208	N.D.Howard	
Calcutta-Drawn	•342	5d-252	344	0-103	N.D.Howard	
Kanpur-England 8 wkts	203	2-76	•121	157	N.D.Howard	
Madras[1]-India inn & 8 runs	•266	183	9d-457	-	D.B.Carr	
1952 in England						
Leeds-England 7 wkts	334	3-128	•293	165	L.Hutton	V.S.Hazare
Lord's-England 8 wkts	537	2-79	•235	378		
Manchester-England inn & 207 runs	•9d-347	-	58	82		
The Oval-Drawn	•6d-326	-	98	-		
1959 in England						
Nottingham-England inn & 59 runs	•422	-	206	157	P.B.H.May	D.K.Gaekwad
Lord's-England 8 wkts	226	2-108	•168	165	P.B.H.May	P.Roy
Leeds-England inn & 173 runs	8d-483	-	•161	149	P.B.H.May	D.K.Gaekwad
Manchester-England 171 runs	•490	8d-265	208	376	M C Cowdrey	D.K.Gaekwad
The Oval-England inn & 27 runs	361	-	•140	194	M C Cowdrey	D.K.Gaekwad
1961-62 in India						
Bombay[2]-Drawn	•8d-500	5d-184	390	5-180	E.R.Dexter	N.J.Contractor
Kanpur-Drawn	244	5-497	•8d-467	-		
Delhi-Drawn	3-256	-	•466	-		
Calcutta-India 187 runs	212	233	•380	252		
Madras[2]-India 128 runs	281	209	•428	190		
1963-64 in India						
Madras[2]-Drawn	317	5-241	•7d-457	9d-152	M.J.K.Smith	Nawab of Pataudi, jr
Bombay[2]-Drawn	233	3-206	•300	8d-249		
Calcutta-Drawn	267	2-145	•241	7d-300		
Delhi-Drawn	451	-	•344	4 463		
Kanpur-Drawn	•8d-559	-	266	3-347		
1967 in England						
Leeds-England 6 wkts	•4d-550	4-126	164	510	D.B.Close	Nawab of Pataudi, jr
Lord's-England inn & 124 runs	386	-	•152	110		
Birmingham-England 132 runs	•298	203	92	277		
1971 in England						
Lord's-Drawn	•304	191	313	8-145	R.Illingworth	A.L.Wadekar
Manchester-Drawn	•386	3d-245	212	3-65		
The Oval-India 4 wkts	•355	101	284	6-174		
1972-73 in India						
Delhi-England 6 wkts	200	4-208	•173	233	A.R.Lewis	A.L.Wadekar
Calcutta-India 28 runs	174	163	•210	155		
Madras[1]-India 4 wkts	•242	159	316	6-86		
Kanpur-Drawn	397	-	•357	6-186		
Bombay[2]-Drawn	480	2-67	•448	5d-244		
1974 in England						
Manchester-England 113 runs	•9d-328	3d-213	246	182	M.H.Denness	A.L.Wadekar
Lord's-England inn & 285 runs	•629	-	302	42		
Birmingham-England inn & 78 runs	2d-459	-	•165	216		

ENGLAND v INDIA (cont.)	England		India		Captains	
Venue and Result	1st	2nd	1st	2nd	England	India
1976-77 in India						
Delhi-England inn & 25 runs	•381	-	122	234	A.W.Greig	B.S.Bedi
Calcutta-England 10 wkts	321	0-16	•155	181		
Madras[1]-England 200 runs	•262	9d-185	164	83		
Bangalore-India 140 runs	195	177	•253	9d-259		
Bombay[3]-Drawn	317	7-152	•338	192		
1979 in England						
Birmingham-England inn & 83 runs	•5d-633	-	297	253	J.M.Brearley	S.Venkataraghavan
Lord's-Drawn	9d-419	-	•96	4-318		
Leeds-Drawn	•270	-	6-223	-		
The Oval-Drawn	•305	8d-334	202	8-429		
1979-80 in India						
Bombay[3]-England 10 wkts	296	0-98	•242	149	J.M.Brearley	G.R.Viswanath
1981-82 in India						
Bombay[3]-India 138 runs	166	102	•179	227	K.W.R.Fletcher	S.M.Gavaskar
Bangalore-Drawn	•400	3-174	428	-		
Delhi-Drawn	•9d-476	0-68	487	-		
Calcutta-Drawn	•248	5d-265	208	3-170		
Madras[1]-Drawn	328	-	•4d-481	3-160		
Kanpur-Drawn	•9d-378	-	7-377	-		
1982 in England						
Lord's-England 7 wkts	•433	3-67	128	369	R.G.D.Willis	S.M.Gavaskar
Manchester-Drawn	•425	-	8-379	-		
The Oval-Drawn	•594	3d-191	410	3-111		
1984-85 in India						
Bombay[3]-India 8 wkts	•195	317	8d-465	2-51	D.I.Gower	S.M.Gavaskar
Delhi-England 8 wkts	418	2-127	•307	235		
Calcutta-Drawn	276	-	•7d-437	1-29		
Madras[1]-England 9 wkts	7d-652	1-35	•272	412		
Kanpur-Drawn	417	0-91	•8d-553	1d-97		
1986 in England						
Lord's-India 5 wkts	•294	180	341	5-136	D.I.Gower	Kapil Dev
Manchester-India 279 runs	102	128	•272	237	M.W.Gatting	
The Oval-Drawn	•390	235	390	5-174	M.W.Gatting	
1990 in England						
Lord's-England 247 runs	•4d-653	4d-272	454	224	G.A.Gooch	M.Azharuddin
Manchester-Drawn	•519	4d-320	432	6-343		
The Oval-Drawn	340	4d-477	•9d-606	-		
1992-93 in India						
Calcutta-India 8 wkts	163	286	•371	2-82	G.A.Gooch	M.Azharuddin
Madras[1]-India inn & 22 runs	286	252	•6d-560	-	A.J.Stewart	
Bombay[3]-India inn & 15 runs	•347	227	591		G.A.Gooch	
1996 in England						
Birmingham-England 8 wkts	313	2-121	•214	219	M.A.Atherton	M.Azharuddin
Lord's-Drawn	•344	9d-278	429	-		
Nottingham-Drawn	564	-	•521	211		

ENGLAND v INDIA (cont.)	England		India		Captains	
Venue and Result	1st	2nd	1st	2nd	England	India
2001-02 in India						
Mohali-India 10 wkts	•238	235	469	0-5	N.Hussain	S.C.Ganguly
Ahmedabad-Drawn	•407	257	291	3-198		
Bangalore-Drawn	•336	0-33	238	-		
2002 in England						
Lord's-England 170 runs	•487	6d-301	221	397	N.Hussain	S.C.Ganguly
Nottingham-Drawn	617	-	•357	8-424		
Leeds-India inn & 46 runs	273	309	•8d-628	-		
The Oval-Drawn	•515	0-114	508	-		
2005-06 in India						
Nagpur-Drawn	•393	3d-297	323	6-260	A.Flintoff	R.S.Dravid
Mohali-India 9 wkts	•300	181	338	1-144		
Bombay[3]-England 212 runs	•400	191	279	100		

Test Match Results Summary

ENGLAND v INDIA - in England

		Result			Lord's			Manchester			The Oval			Leeds			Nottingham			Birmingham		
	Tests	E	I	D	E	I	D	E	I	D	E	I	D	E	I	D	E	I	D	E	I	D
1932	1	1	-	-	1	-	-	-	-	-	-	-	-	-	-	-	-	-	-	-	-	-
1936	3	2	-	1	1	-	-	-	-	1	1	-	-	-	-	-	-	-	-	-	-	-
1946	3	1	-	2	1	-	-	-	-	1	-	-	1	-	-	-	-	-	-	-	-	-
1952	4	3	-	1	1	-	-	1	-	-	-	-	1	1	-	-	-	-	-	-	-	-
1959	5	5	-	-	1	-	-	1	-	-	1	-	-	1	-	-	-	-	-	-	-	-
1967	3	3	-	-	1	-	-	-	-	-	-	-	-	-	-	-	1	-	-	1	-	-
1971	3	-	1	2	-	-	1	-	-	1	-	1	-	-	-	-	-	-	-	-	-	-
1974	3	3	-	-	1	-	-	1	-	-	-	-	-	-	-	-	-	-	-	1	-	-
1979	4	1	-	3	-	-	1	-	-	-	-	-	1	-	-	1	-	-	-	1	-	-
1982	3	1	-	2	1	-	-	-	-	1	-	-	1	-	-	-	-	-	-	-	-	-
1986	3	-	2	1	-	1	-	-	-	-	-	-	-	-	1	-	-	-	-	-	-	1
1990	3	1	-	2	1	-	-	-	-	1	-	-	1	-	-	-	-	-	-	-	-	-
1996	3	1	-	2	1	-	-	-	-	-	-	-	-	-	-	-	-	-	1	-	-	1
2002	4	1	1	2	1	-	-	-	-	-	-	-	1	-	1	-	-	-	1	-	-	-
	45	23	4	18	11	1	2	3	-	5	2	1	6	3	2	1	1	-	2	3	-	2

ENGLAND v INDIA - in India

	Tests	Result E	Result I	Result D	Mumbai E I D	Calcutta E I D	Chennai E I D	Delhi E I D	Kanpur E I D	Bang. E I D	Mohali E I D	Ahmed. E I D	Nagpur E I D
1933-34	3	2	-	1	1 - -	- - 1	1 - -	- - -	- - -	- - -	- - -	- - -	- - -
1951-52	5	1	1	3	- - 1	- - 1	- 1 -	- - 1	1 - -	- - -	- - -	- - -	- - -
1961-62	5	-	2	3	- - 1	- 1 -	- 1 -	- - 1	- - 1	- - -	- - -	- - -	- - -
1963-64	5	-	-	5	- - 1	- - 1	- - 1	- - 1	- - 1	- - -	- - -	- - -	- - -
1972-73	5	1	2	2	- - 1	- 1 -	- 1 -	1 - -	- - 1	- - -	- - -	- - -	- - -
1976-77	5	3	1	1	- - 1	1 - -	1 - -	1 - -	- - -	- - 1	- - -	- - -	- - -
1979-80	1	1	-	-	1 - -	- - -	- - -	- - -	- - -	- - -	- - -	- - -	- - -
1981-82	6	-	1	5	- 1 -	- - 1	- - 1	- - 1	- - 1	- - 1	- - -	- - -	- - -
1984-85	5	2	1	2	- 1 -	- - 1	1 - -	1 - -	- - 1	- - -	- - -	- - -	- - -
1992-93	3	-	3	-	- 1 -	- 1 -	- 1 -	- - -	- - -	- - -	- - -	- - -	- - -
2001-02	3	-	1	2	- - -	- - -	- - -	- - -	- - -	- - 1	- 1 -	- - 1	- - -
2005-06	3	1	1	1	1 - -	- - -	- - -	- - -	- - -	- - -	- 1 -	- - -	- - 1
	49	11	13	25	2 3 5	1 3 5	3 4 2	3 - 4	1 - 5	- 1 2	- 2 -	- - 1	- - 1
Totals	94	34	17	43									

Key: Bang - Bangalore; Ahmed. - Ahmedabad.

Highest Innings Totals

England in England	4d-653	Lord's	1990
England in India	7d-652	Madras[1]	1984-85
India in England	8d-628	Leeds	2002
India in India	591	Bombay[3]	1992-93

Lowest Innings Totals

England in England	101	The Oval	1971
England in India	102	Bombay[3]	1981-82
India in England	42	Lord's	1974
India in India	83	Madras[1]	1976-77

Highest Match Aggregate	1614 for 30 wickets	Manchester	1990
Lowest Match Aggregate	482 for 31 wickets	Lord's	1936

Highest Individual Innings

England in England	333	G.A.Gooch	Lord's	1990
England in India	207	M.W.Gatting	Madras[1]	1984-85
India in England	221	S.M.Gavaskar	The Oval	1979
India in India	224	V.G.Kambli	Bombay[3]	1992-93

Most Runs in a Series

England in England	752 (av 125.33)	G.A.Gooch	1990
England in India	594 (av 99.00)	K.F.Barrington	1961-62
India in England	602 (av 100.33)	R.S.Dravid	2002
India in India	586 (av 83.71)	V.L.Manjrekar	1961-62

Record Wicket Partnerships - England

1st	225	G.A.Gooch(116), M.A.Atherton(131)	Manchester	1990
2nd	241	G.Fowler (201), M.W.Gatting (207)	Madras[1]	1984-85
3rd	308	G.A.Gooch(333), A.J.Lamb(139)	Lord's	1990
4th	266	W.R.Hammond (217), T.S.Worthington (128)	Oval	1936
5th	254	K.W.R.Fletcher (113), A.W.Greig (148)	Bombay[2]	1972-73
6th	171	I.T.Botham (114), R.W.Taylor (43)	Bombay[3]	1979-80
7th	125	D.W.Randall (126), P.H.Edmonds (64)	Lord's	1982

8th	168	R.Illingworth (107), P.Lever (88*)	Manchester	1971
9th	103	C.White (94*), M.J.Hoggard (32)	Nottingham	2002
10th	70	P.J.W.Allott (41*), R.G.D.Willis (28)	Lord's	1982

Record Wicket Partnerships - India

1st	213	S.M.Gavaskar (221), C.P.S.Chauhan (80)	The Oval	1979
2nd	192	F.M.Engineer (121), A.L.Wadekar (87)	Bombay[2]	1972-73
3rd	316†	G.R.Viswanath (222), Yashpal Sharma (140)	Madras[1]	1981-82
4th	249	S.R.Tendulkar (193), S.C.Ganguly (128)	Leeds	2002
5th	214	M.Azharuddin (110), R.J.Shastri (111)	Calcutta	1984-85
6th	130	S.M.H.Kirmani (43), Kapil Dev (97)	The Oval	1982
7th	235	R.J.Shastri (142), S.M.H.Kirmani (102)	Bombay[3]	1984-85
8th	128	R.J.Shastri (93), S.M.H.Kirmani (67)	Delhi	1981-82
	128	Mohammad Kaif (91), A.Kumble (58)	Nagpur	2005-06
9th	104	R.J.Shastri (93), S.Madan Lal (44)	Delhi	1981-82
10th	63	A.B.Agarkar (109*), A.Nehra (19)	Lord's	2002

† 415 runs were added for this wicket. D.B.Vengsarkar retired hurt after he had added 99 with Viswanath.

Best Bowling in an Innings

England in England	8/31	F.S.Trueman	Manchester	1952
England in India	7/46	J.K.Lever	Delhi	1976-77
India in England	6/35	L.Amar Singh	Lord's	1936
India in India	8/55	M.H.Mankad	Madras[1]	1951-52

Best Bowling in a Match

England in England	11/93	A.V.Bedser	Manchester	1946
England in India	13/106	I.T.Botham	Bombay[3]	1979-80
India in England	10/188	C.Sharma	Birmingham	1986
India in India	12/108	M.H.Mankad	Madras[1]	1951-52

Most Wickets in a Series

England in England	29 (av 13.31)	F.S.Trueman	1952
England in India	29 (av 17.55)	D.L.Underwood	1976-77
India in England	17 (av 34.64)	S.P.Gupte	1959
India in India	35 (av 18.91)	B.S.Chandrasekhar	1972-73

ENGLAND v PAKISTAN	England		Pakistan		Captains	
Venue and Result	1st	2nd	1st	2nd	England	Pakistan
1954 in England						
Lord's-Drawn	9d-117	-	•87	3-121	L.Hutton	A.H.Kardar
Nottingham-England inn &129 runs	6d-558	-	•157	272	D.S.Sheppard	
Manchester-Drawn	•8d-359	-	90	4-25	D.S.Sheppard	
The Oval-Pakistan 24 runs	130	143	•133	164	L.Hutton	
1961-62 in Pakistan						
Lahore[2]-England 5 wkts	380	5-209	•9d-387	200	E.R.Dexter	Imtiaz Ahmed
Dacca-Drawn	439	0-38	•7d-393	216		
Karachi[1]-Drawn	507	-	•253	8-404		
1962 in England						
Birmingham-England inn & 24 runs	•5d-544	-	246	274	E.R.Dexter	Javed Burki
Lord's-England 9 wkts	370	1-86	•100	355	E.R.Dexter	
Leeds-England inn & 117 runs	•428	-	131	180	M.C.Cowdrey	
Nottingham-Drawn	•5d-428	-	219	6-216	E.R.Dexter	
The Oval-England 10 wkts	•5d-480	0-27	183	323	E.R.Dexter	

ENGLAND v PAKISTAN (cont.)	England		Pakistan		Captains	
Venue and Result	1st	2nd	1st	2nd	England	Pakistan
1967 in England						
Lord's-Drawn	•369	9d-241	354	3-88	D.B.Close	Hanif Mohammad
Nottingham-England 10 wkts	8d-252	0-3	•140	114		
The Oval-England 8 wkts	440	2-34	•216	255		
1968-69 in Pakistan						
Lahore[2]-Drawn	•306	9d-225	209	5-203	M.C.Cowdrey	Saeed Ahmed
Dacca-Drawn	274	0-33	•246	6d-195		
Karachi[1]-Drawn	•7-502	-	-	-		
1971 in England						
Birmingham-Drawn	353	5-229	•7d-608	-	R.Illingworth	Intikhab Alam
Lord's-Drawn	•2d-241	0-117	148	-		
Leeds-England 25 runs	•316	264	350	205		
1972-73 in Pakistan						
Lahore[2]-Drawn	•355	7d-306	422	3-124	A.R.Lewis	Majid Khan
Hyderabad-Drawn	•487	6-218	9d-569	-		
Karachi[1]-Drawn	386	1-30	•6d-445	199		
1974 in England						
Leeds-Drawn	183	6-238	•285	179	M.H.Denness	Intikhab Alam
Lord's-Drawn	270	0-27	•9d-130	226		
The Oval-Drawn	545	-	•7d-600	4-94		
1977-78 in Pakistan						
Lahore[2]-Drawn	288	-	•9d-407	3-106	J.M.Brearley	Wasim Bari
Hyderabad-Drawn	191	1-186	•275	4d-259	J.M.Brearley	
Karachi[1]-Drawn	•266	5-222	281	-	G.Boycott	
1978 in England						
Birmingham-England inn & 57 runs	8d-452	-	•164	231	J.M.Brearley	Wasim Bari
Lord's-England inn &120 runs	•364	-	105	139		
Leeds-Drawn	7-119	-	•201	-		
1982 in England						
Birmingham-England 113 runs	•272	291	251	199	R.G.D.Willis	Imran Khan
Lord's-Pakistan 10 wkts	227	276	•8d-428	0-77	D.I.Gower	
Leeds-England 3 wkts	256	7-219	•275	199	R.G.D.Willis	
1983-84 in Pakistan						
Karachi[1]-Pakistan 3 wkts	•182	159	277	7-66	R.G.D.Willis	Zaheer Abbas
Faisalabad-Drawn	8d-546	-	•8d-449	4-137	D.I.Gower	
Lahore[2]-Drawn	•241	9d-344	343	6-217	D.I.Gower	
1987 in England						
Manchester-Drawn	•447	-	5-140	-	M.W.Gatting	Imran Khan
Lord's-Drawn	•368	-	-	-		
Leeds-Pakistan inn & 18 runs	•136	199	353	-		
Birmingham-Drawn	521	7-109	•439	205		
The Oval-Drawn	232	4-315	•708	-		
1987-88 in Pakistan						
Lahore[2]-Pakistan inn & 87 runs	•175	130	392	-	M.W.Gatting	Javed Miandad
Faisalabad-Drawn	•292	6d-137	191	1-51		
Karachi[1]-Drawn	•294	9-258	353	-		

ENGLAND v PAKISTAN (cont.) Venue and Result	England 1st	England 2nd	Pakistan 1st	Pakistan 2nd	Captains England	Captains Pakistan
1992 in England						
Birmingham-Drawn	7-459	-	•4d-448	-	G.A.Gooch	Javed Miandad
Lord's-Pakistan 2 wkts	•255	175	293	8-141		
Manchester-Drawn	390	-	•505	5d-239		
Leeds-England 6 wkts	320	4-99	•197	221		
The Oval-Pakistan 10 wkts	•207	174	380	0-5		
1996 in England						
Lord's-Pakistan 164 runs	285	243	•340	5d-352	M.A.Atherton	Wasim Akram
Leeds-Drawn	501	-	•448	7d-242		
The Oval-Pakistan 9 wickets	•326	242	8d-521	1-48		
2000-01 in Pakistan						
Lahore[2]-Drawn	•8d-480	4d-77	401	-	N.Hussain	Moin Khan
Faisalabad-Drawn	342	5-125	•316	3d-269		
Karachi[1]-England 6 wkts	388	4-176	•405	158		
2001 in England						
Lord's-England inn & 9 runs	•391	-	203	179	N.Hussain	Waqar Younis
Manchester-Pakistan 108 runs	357	261	•403	323	A.J.Stewart	
2005-06 in Pakistan						
Multan[2]-Pakistan 22 runs	418	175	•274	341	M.E.Trescothick	Inzamamul Haq
Faisalabad-Drawn	446	6-164	•462	9d-268	M.P.Vaughan	
Karachi[1]-Pakistan inn & 100 runs	•288	248	8d-636	-	M.P.Vaughan	
2006 in England						
Lord's-Drawn	•9d-528	8d-296	445	4-214	A.J.Strauss	Inzamamul Haq
Manchester-England inn & 120 runs	9d-461	-	•119	222		
Leeds-England 167 runs	•515	345	538	155		
The Oval-Match awarded to England	•173	4-298	504	-		

Test Match Results Summary

ENGLAND v PAKISTAN - in England

		Result			Lord's			Nottingham			Manchester			The Oval			Birmingham			Leeds		
	Tests	E	P	D	E	P	D	E	P	D	E	P	D	E	P	D	E	P	D	E	P	D
1954	4	1	1	2	-	-	1	1	-	-	-	-	1	-	1	-	-	-	-	-	-	-
1962	5	4	-	1	1	-	-	-	-	1	-	-	-	1	-	-	1	-	-	1	-	-
1967	3	2	-	1	-	-	1	1	-	-	-	-	-	1	-	-	-	-	-	-	-	-
1971	3	1	-	2	-	-	1	-	-	-	-	-	-	-	-	-	-	-	1	1	-	-
1974	3	-	-	3	-	-	1	-	-	-	-	-	-	-	-	1	-	-	-	-	-	1
1978	3	2	-	1	1	-	-	-	-	-	-	-	-	-	-	-	1	-	-	-	-	1
1982	3	2	1	-	-	1	-	-	-	-	-	-	-	-	-	-	1	-	-	1	-	-
1987	5	-	1	4	-	-	1	-	-	-	-	-	1	-	-	1	-	-	1	-	1	-
1992	5	1	2	2	-	1	-	-	-	-	-	-	1	-	1	-	-	-	1	1	-	-
1996	3	-	2	1	-	1	-	-	-	-	-	-	-	-	1	2	-	-	-	-	-	1
2001	2	1	1	-	1	-	-	-	-	-	-	1	-	-	-	-	-	-	-	-	-	-
2006	4	3	-	1	-	-	1	-	-	-	1	-	-	1	-	-	-	-	-	1	-	-
	43	17	8	18	3	3	6	2	-	1	1	1	3	3	3	2	3	-	3	5	1	3

ENGLAND v PAKISTAN - in Pakistan

		Result			Lahore[2]			Dacca			Karachi[1]			Hyderabad			Faisalabad			Multan[2]		
	Tests	E	P	D	E	P	D	E	P	D	E	P	D	E	P	D	E	P	D	E	P	D
1961-62	3	1	-	2	1	-	-	-	-	1	-	-	1	-	-	-	-	-	-	-	-	-
1968-69	3	-	-	3	-	-	1	-	-	-	-	-	1	-	-	1	-	-	-	-	-	-
1972-73	3	-	-	3	-	-	1	-	-	-	-	-	1	-	-	1	-	-	-	-	-	-
1977-78	3	-	-	3	-	-	1	-	-	1	-	-	1	-	-	-	-	-	-	-	-	-
1983-84	3	-	1	2	-	-	1	-	-	-	-	1	-	-	-	-	-	-	1	-	-	-
1987-88	3	-	1	2	-	1	-	-	-	-	-	-	1	-	-	-	-	-	1	-	-	-
2000-01	3	1	-	2	-	-	1	-	-	-	1	-	-	-	-	-	-	-	1	-	-	-
2005-06	3	-	2	1	-	1	-	-	-	-	-	-	-	-	-	-	-	-	1	-	1	-
	24	2	4	18	1	2	5	-	-	2	1	1	5	-	-	2	-	-	4	-	1	-
Totals	67	19	12	36																		

Highest Innings Totals

England in England	6d-558	Nottingham	1954
England in Pakistan	8d-546	Faisalabad	1983-84
Pakistan in England	708	The Oval	1987
Pakistan in Pakistan	8d-636	Lahore[2]	2005-06

Lowest Innings Totals

England in England	130	The Oval	1954
England in Pakistan	130	Lahore[2]	1987-88
Pakistan in England	87	Lord's	1954
Pakistan in Pakistan	158	Karachi[1]	2000-01

Highest Match Aggregate	1553 for 40 wickets	Leeds	2006
Lowest Match Aggregate	509 for 28 wickets	Nottingham	1967

Highest Individual Innings

England in England	278	D.C.S.Compton	Nottingham	1954
England in Pakistan	205	E.R.Dexter	Karachi[1]	1961-62
Pakistan in England	274	Zaheer Abbas	Birmingham	1971
Pakistan in Pakistan	223	Yousuf Youhana	Lahore[2]	2005-06

Most Runs in a Series

England in England	453 (av 90.60)	D.C.S.Compton	1954
England in Pakistan	449 (av 112.25)	D.I.Gower	1983-84
Pakistan in England	631 (av 90.14)	Yousuf Youhana	2006
Pakistan in Pakistan	431 (av 107.75)	Inzamamul Haq	2005-06

Record Wicket Partnerships - England

1st	198	G.Pullar (165), R.W.Barber (86)	Dacca	1961-62
2nd	248	M.C.Cowdrey (182), E.R.Dexter (172)	The Oval	1962
3rd	267	M.P.Vaughan (120), G.P.Thorpe (138)	Manchester	2001
4th	188	E.R.Dexter (205), P.H.Parfitt (111)	Karachi[1]	1961-62
5th	192	D.C.S.Compton (278), T.E.Bailey (36*)	Nottingham	1954
6th	166	G.P.Thorpe (118), C.White (93)	Lahore[2]	2000-01
7th	167	D.I.Gower (152), V.J.Marks (83)	Faisalabad	1983-84
8th	99	P.H.Parfitt (119), D.A.Allen (62)	Leeds	1962
9th	76	T.W.Graveney (153), F.S.Trueman (29)	Lord's	1962
10th	79	R.W.Taylor (54), R.G.D.Willis (28*)	Birmingham	1982

Record Wicket Partnerships - Pakistan

1st	173	Mohsin Khan (104), Shoaib Mohammad (80)	Lahore[2]	1983-84
2nd	291	Zaheer Abbas (274), Mushtaq Mohammad (100)	Birmingham	1971
3rd	363	Younis Khan (173), Yousuf Yoyhana (192)	Leeds	2006
4rd	180	Mudassar Nazar (114), Haroon Rashid (122)	Lahore[2]	1977-78
5th	322	Javed Miandad (153*), Saleem Malik (165)	Birmingham	1992
6th	197	Javed Burki (101), Nasim-ul-Ghani (101)	Lord's	1962
7th	269	Yousuf Youhana (223), Kamran Akmal (154)	Lahore[2]	2005-06
8th	112	Asif Mujtaba (51), Moin Khan (105)	Leeds	1996
9th	130	Hanif Mohammad (187*), Asif Iqbal (76)	Lord's	1967
10th	190	Asif Iqbal (146), Intikhab Alam (51)	The Oval	1967

Best Bowling in an Innings

England in England	8/34	I.T.Botham	Lord's	1978
England in Pakistan	7/66	P.H.Edmonds	Karachi[1]	1977-78
Pakistan in England	7/40	Imran Khan	Leeds	1987
Pakistan in Pakistan	9/56	Abdul Qadir	Lahore[2]	1987-88

Best Bowling in a Match

England in England	13/71	D.L.Underwood	Lord's	1974
England in Pakistan	11/83	N.G.B.Cook	Karachi[1]	1983-84
Pakistan in England	12/99	Fazal Mahmood	The Oval	1954
Pakistan in Pakistan	13/101	Abdul Qadir	Lahore[2]	1987-88

Most Wickets in a Series

England in England	22 (av 19.95)	F.S.Trueman	1962
England in Pakistan	17 (av 24.11)	A.F.Giles	2000-01
Pakistan in England	22 (av 25.31)	Waqar Younis	1992
Pakistan in Pakistan	30 (av 14.56)	Abdul Qadir	1987-88

ENGLAND v SRI LANKA	England		Sri Lanka		Captains	
Venue and Result	1st	2nd	1st	2nd	England	Sri Lanka
1981-82 in Sri Lanka						
Colombo (PSS)-England 7 wkts	223	3-171	•218	175	K.W.R.Fletcher	B.Warnapura
1984 in England						
Lord's-Drawn	370	-	•7d-491	7d-294	D.I.Gower	L.R.D.Mendis
1988 in England						
Lord's-England 7 wkts	429	3-100	•194	331	G.A.Gooch	R.S.Madugalle
1991 in England						
Lord's-England 137 runs	•282	3d-364	224	285	G.A.Gooch	P.A.de Silva
1992-93 in Sri Lanka						
Colombo (SSC)-Sri Lanka 5 wickets	•380	228	469	5-142	A.J.Stewart	A.Ranatunga
1998 in England						
The Oval-Sri Lanka 10 wkts	•445	181	591	0-37	A.J.Stewart	A.Ranatunga
2000-01 in Sri Lanka						
Galle-Sri Lanka inn & 28 run	253	189	•5d-470	-	N.Hussain	S.T.Jayasuriya
Kandy-England 3 wickets	387	7-161	•297	250		
Colombo (SSC)-England 4 wickets	249	6-74	•241	81		

ENGLAND v SRI LANKA (cont.) Venue and Result	England 1st	England 2nd	Sri Lanka 1st	Sri Lanka 2nd	Captains England	Captains Sri Lanka
2002 in England						
Lord's-Drawn	275	5d-529	•8d-555	1-42	N.Hussain	S.T.Jayasuriya
Birmingham-England inn & 111 runs	545	-	•162	272		
Manchester-England 10 wkts	•512	0-50	253	308		
2003-04 in Sri Lanka						
Galle-Drawn	235	9-210	•331	226	M.P.Vaughan	H.P.Tillakaratne
Kandy-Drawn	294	7-285	•382	7d-279		
Colombo (SSC)-Sri Lanka inn & 215 runs	•265	148	8d-628	-		
2006 in England						
Lord's-Drawn	•6d-551	-	192	9-537	A.Flintoff	D.P.M.D.Jayawardene
Birmingham-England 6 wkts	295	4-81	•141	231		
Nottingham-Sri Lanka 134 runs	229	190	•231	322		

Test Match Results Summary

ENGLAND v SRI LANKA - in England

	Tests	Result E	Result SL	Result D	Lord's E	Lord's SL	Lord's D	The Oval E	The Oval SL	The Oval D	Birmingham E	Birmingham SL	Birmingham D	Manchester E	Manchester SL	Manchester D	Nottingham E	Nottingham SL	Nottingham D
1984	1	-	-	1	-	-	1	-	-	-	-	-	-	-	-	-	-	-	-
1988	1	1	-	-	1	-	-	-	-	-	-	-	-	-	-	-	-	-	-
1991	1	1	-	-	1	-	-	-	-	-	-	-	-	-	-	-	-	-	-
1998	1	-	1	-	-	-	-	-	1	-	-	-	-	-	-	-	-	-	-
2002	3	2	-	1	-	-	1	-	-	-	1	-	-	1	-	-	-	-	-
2006	2	1	1	1	-	-	1	-	-	-	1	-	-	-	-	-	-	1	-
	10	5	2	3	2	-	3	-	1	-	2	-	-	1	-	-	-	1	-

ENGLAND v SRI LANKA - in Sri Lanka

	Tests	Result E	Result SL	Result D	Colombo (PSS) E	Colombo (PSS) SL	Colombo (PSS) D	Colombo (SSC) E	Colombo (SSC) SL	Colombo (SSC) D	Galle E	Galle SL	Galle D	Kandy E	Kandy SL	Kandy D
1981-82	1	1	-	-	1	-	-	-	-	-	-	-	-	-	-	-
1992-93	1	-	1	-	-	-	-	-	1	-	-	-	-	-	-	-
2000-01	3	2	1	-	-	-	-	1	-	-	-	1	-	1	-	-
2003-04	3	-	1	2	-	-	-	-	1	-	-	-	1	-	-	1
	8	3	3	2	1	-	-	1	2	-	-	1	1	1	-	1
Totals	18	8	5	5												

Highest Innings Totals

England in England	6d-551	Lord's	2006
England in Sri Lanka	387	Kandy	2000-01
Sri Lanka in England	591	The Oval	1998
Sri Lanka in Sri Lanka	8d-628	Colombo (SSC)	2003-04

Lowest Innings Totals

England in England	181	The Oval	1998
England in Sri Lanka	148	Colombo (SSC)	2003-04
Sri Lanka in England	162	Birmingham	2002
Sri Lanka in Sri Lanka	81	Colombo (PSS)	2000-01

Pakistan's captain Inzamamul Haq plays a shot against England in Lahore in 2005.

Herbert Sutcliffe scored a massive 194 runs for England against Australia at the SCG in 1932.

Jim Laker bowled a record-breaking spell against Australia at Old Trafford, Manchester, in 1956 where he took 10 for 153. He remains the only player to have taken 19 wickets in a Test.

In 1998, during the second Test against South Africa in Port Elizabeth, West Indies bowler Curtley Ambrose celebrates a dismissal.

Highest Match Aggregate		1401 for 24 wickets	Lord's	2002
Lowest Match Aggregate		645 for 36 wickets	Colombo (SSC)	2000-01

Highest Individual Innings

England in England	174	G.A.Gooch	Lord's	1991
England in Sri Lanka	128	R.A.Smith	Colombo (SSC)	1992-93
Sri Lanka in England	213	S.T.Jayasuriya	The Oval	1998
Sri Lanka in Sri Lanka	201*	M.S.Atapattu	Galle	2000-01

Most Runs in a Series

England in England	360 (av 72.00)	K.P.Pietersen	2006
England in Sri Lanka	269 (av 67.25)	G.P.Thorpe	2000-01
Sri Lanka in England	277 (av 55.40)	M.S.Atapattu	2002
Sri Lanka in Sri Lanka	334 (av 83.50)	D.P.M.D.Jayawardene	2003-04

Record Wicket Partnerships - England

1st	168	M.E.Trescothick (76), M.P.Vaughan (115)	Lord's	2002
2nd	202	M.E.Trescothick (161), M.A.Butcher (94)	Birmingham	2002
3rd	167	N.Hussain (109), G.P.Thorpe (59)	Kandy	2000-01
4th	128	G.A.Hick (107), M.R.Ramprakash (53)	The Oval	1998
5th	173	K.P.Pietersen (158), P.D.Collingwood (57)	Lord's	2006
6th	87	A.J.Lamb (107), R.M.Ellison (41)	Lord's	1984
	87	A.J.Stewart (54), C.White (39)	Kandy	2000-01
	87	A.Flintoff (77), G.J.Batty (14)	Colombo (SSC)	2003-04
7th	63	A.J.Stewart (113*), R.C.Russell (17)	Lord's	1991
8th	102	A.J.Stewart (123), A.F.Giles (45)	Manchester	2002
9th	53	M.R.Ramprakash (42), D.Gough (15)	The Oval	1998
10th	91	G.P.Thorpe (123), M.J.Hoggard (17*)	Birmingham	2002

Record Wicket Partnerships - Sri Lanka

1st	99	R.S.Mahanama (64), U.C.Hathurusingha (59)	Colombo (SSC)	1992-93
2nd	109	W.U.Tharanga (52), K.C.Sangakkara (65)	Lord's	2006
3rd	262	T.T.Samaraweera (142), D.P.M.D.Jayawardene (134)	Colombo (SSC)	2003-04
4th	153	D.P.M.D.Jayawardene (52), T.M.Dilshan (100)	Kandy	2003-04
5th	150	S.Wettimuny (190), L.R.D.Mendis(111)	Lord's	1984
6th	138	S.A.R.Silva (102*), L.R.D.Mendis (94)	Lord's	1984
7th	93	K.C.Sangakkara (95), H.D.P.K.Dharmasena (54)	Kandy	2000-01
8th	53	H.D.P.K.Dharmasena (54), W.P.U.J.C.Vaas (36)	Kandy	2000-01
9th	105	W.P.U.J.C.Vaas (50*), K.M.D.Kulasekara (64)	Lord's	2006
10th	64	J.R.Ratnayeke (59*), G.F.Labrooy (42)	Lord's	1988

Best Bowling in an Innings

England in England	7/70	P.A.J.DeFreitas	Lord's	1991
England in Sri Lanka	6/33	J.E.Emburey	Colombo (PSS)	1981-82
Sri Lanka in England	9/65	M.Muralidaran	The Oval	1998
Sri Lanka in Sri Lanka	7/46	M.Muralidaran	Galle	2003-04

Best Bowling in a Match

England in England	8/115	P.A.J.DeFreitas	Lord's	1991
England in Sri Lanka	8/95	D.L.Underwood	Colombo (PSS)	1981-82
Sri Lanka in England	16/220	M.Muralidaran	The Oval	1998
Sri Lanka in Sri Lanka	11/93	M.Muralidaran	Galle	2003-04

Most Wickets in a Series

England in England	14 (av 32.07)	M.J.Hoggard	2002
England in Sri Lanka	18 (av 29.94)	A.F.Giles	2003-04
Sri Lanka in England	24 (av 16.87)	M.Muralidaran	2006
Sri Lanka in Sri Lanka	26 (av 12.30)	M.Muralidaran	2003-04

ENGLAND v ZIMBABWE	England		Zimbabwe		Captains	
Venue and Result	1st	2nd	1st	2nd	England	Zimbabwe
1996-97 in Zimbabwe						
Bulawayo[2]-Drawn	406	6-204	•376	234	M.A.Atherton	A.D.R.Campbell
Harare-Drawn	•156	3-195	215	-		
2000 in England						
Lord's-England inn & 209 runs	415	-	•83	123	N.Hussain	A.Flower
Nottingham-Drawn	•374	147	4d-285	1-25		
2003 in England						
Lord's-England inn & 92 runs	•472	-	147	233	N.Hussain	H.H.Streak
Chester-le-Street-England inn & 69 runs	•416	-	94	253		

Test Match Results Summary

ENGLAND v ZIMBABWE - in England

	Tests	Result			Lord's			Nottingham			Chester-le-Street		
		E	Z	D	E	Z	D	E	Z	D	E	Z	D
2000	2	1	-	1	1	-	-	-	-	1	-	-	-
2003	2	2	-	-	1	-	-	-	-	-	1	-	-
Totals	4	3	-	1	1	-	-	-	-	1	1	-	-

ENGLAND v ZIMBABWE - in Zimbabwe

	Tests	Result			Bulawayo[2]			Harare		
		E	Z	D	E	SL	D	E	SL	D
1996-97	2	-	-	2	-	-	1	-	-	1
Totals	6	3	-	3						

Highest Innings Totals				
England in England	472		Lord's	2003
England in Zimbabwe	406		Bulawayo[2]	1996-97
Zimbawe in England	4d-285		Nottingham	2000
Zimbabwe in Zimbabwe	376		Bulawayo[2]	1996-97
Lowest Innings Totals				
England in England	147		Nottingham	2000
England in Zimbabwe	156		Harare	1996-97
Zimbawe in England	83		Lord's	2000
Zimbabwe in Zimbabwe	215		Harare	1996-97
Highest Match Aggregate	1220 for 36 wickets		Bulawayo[2]	1996-97
Lowest Match Aggregate	566 for 23 wickets		Harare	1996-97
Highest Individual Innings				
England in England	137	M.A.Butcher	Lord's	2003
England in Zimbabwe	113	N.Hussain	Bulawayo[2]	1996-97
Zimbabwe in England	148*	M.W.Goodwin	Nottingham	2000
Zimbabwe in Zimbabwe	112	A.Flower	Bulawayo[2]	1996-97
Most Runs in a Series				
England in England	225 (av 75.00)		M.A.Atherton	2000

England in Zimbabwe	241 (av 80.33)	A.J.Stewart	1996-97
Zimbabwe in England	178 (av 89.00)	M.W.Goodwin	2000
Zimbabwe in Zimbabwe	135 (av 45.00)	A.D.R.Campbell	1996-97

Record Wicket Partnerships - England

1st	121	M.A.Atherton (136), M.R.Ramprakash (56)	Nottingham	2000
2nd	137	N.V.Knight (96), A.J.Stewart (73)	Bulawayo[2]	1996-97
3rd	68	A.J.Stewart (48), N.Hussain (113)	Bulawayo[2]	1996-97
4th	149	G.A.Hick (101), A.J.Stewart (124*)	Lord's	2000
5th	148	N.Hussain (113), J.Crawley (112)	Bulawayo[2]	1996-97
6th	149	A.J.Stewart (68), A.McGrath (81)	Chester-le-Street	2003
7th	66	A.McGrath (69), A.F.Giles (52)	Lord's	2003
8th	32	C.P.Schofield (57), A.R.Caddick (13)	Nottingham	2000
	32	A.F.Giles (50), R.L.Johnson (24)	Chester-le-Street	2003
9th	66	A.F.Giles (52), M.J.Hoggard (19)	Lord's	2003
10th	28	J.P.Crawley (112), P.C.R.Tufnell (2*)	Bulawayo[2]	1996-97

Record Wicket Partnerships - Zimbabwe

1st	20	D.D.Ebrahim (68), M.A.Vermeulen (1)	Lord's	2003
2nd	127	G.W.Flower (43), A.D.R.Campbell (84)	Bulawayo[2]	1996-97
3rd	129	M.W.Goodwin (148*), N.C.Johnson (51)	Nottingham	2000
4th	122	M.W.Goodwin (148*), A.Flower (42)	Nottingham	2000
5th	30	A.Flower (112), A.C.Waller (15)	Bulawayo[2]	1996-97
6th	54	S.M.Ervine (34), T.J.Friend (65*)	Chester-le-Street	2003
7th	79	A.Flower (112), P.A.Strang (38)	Bulawayo[2]	1996-97
8th	41	A.Flower (112), H.H.Streak (19)	Bulawayo[2]	1996-97
9th	51	T.J.Friend (43), R.W.Price (26)	Lord's	2003
10th	31	B.C.Strang (37*), M.Mbangwa (8)	Lord's	2000

Best Bowling in an Innings

England in England	6/33	R.L.Johnson	Chester-le-Street	2003
England in Zimbabwe	4/40	D.Gough	Bulawayo[2]	1996-97
Zimbabwe in England	6/87	H.H.Streak	Lord's	2000
Zimbabwe in Zimbabwe	5/123	P.A.Strang	Bulawayo[2]	1996-97

Best Bowling in a Match

England in England	7/42	E.H.S.Giddins	Lord's	2000
England in Zimbabwe	6/137	P.C.R.Tufnell	Bulawayo[2]	1996-97
Zimbabwe in England	6/87	H.H.Streak	Lord's	2000
Zimbabwe in Zimbabwe	7/186	P.A.Strang	Bulawayo[2]	1996-97

Most Wickets in a Series

England in England	11 (av 20.27)	J.M.Anderson	2003
England in Zimbabwe	8 (av 22.25)	R.D.B.Croft	1996-97
Zimbawe in England	9 (av 20.22)	H.H.Streak	2000
Zimbabwe in Zimbabwe	10 (av 25.90)	P.A.Strang	1996-97

ENGLAND v BANGLADESH	England		Bangladesh		Captains	
Venue and Result	1st	2nd	1st	2nd	England	Bangladesh
2003-04 in Bangladesh						
Dhaka-England 7 wkts	295	3-164	•203	255	M.P.Vaughan	Khaled Mahmud
Chittagong[1]-England 329 runs	•326	5d-293	152	138		
2005 in England						
Lord's-England innings & 261 runs	•3d-528	-	108	159	M.P.Vaughan	Habibul Bashar
Chester-le-Street-Eng inn & 27 runs	3d-447	-	•104	316		

Test Match Results Summary

ENGLAND v BANGLADESH - in England

		Result			Lord's			Chester-le-Street		
	Tests	E	B	D	E	B	D	E	B	D
2005	2	2	-	-	1	-	-	1	-	-

ENGLAND v BANGLADESH - in Bangladesh

		Result			Dhaka			Chittagong[1]		
	Tests	E	B	D	E	B	D	E	B	D
2003-04	2	2	-	-	1	-	-	1	-	-
Totals	4	4	-	-						

Highest Innings Totals				
England in England		3d-528	Lord's	2005
England in Bangladesh		326	Chittagong[1]	2003-04
Bangladesh in England		306	Chester-le-Street	2005
Bangladesh in Bangladesh		255	Dhaka	2003-04
Lowest Innings Totals				
England in England		no instance		
England in Bangladesh		295	Dhaka	2003-04
Bangladesh in England		104	Chester-le-Street	2005
Bangladesh in Bangladesh		138	Chittagong[1]	2003-04
Highest Match Aggregate		917 for 33 wickets	Dhaka	2003-04
Lowest Match Aggregate		795 for 23 wickets	Lord's	2005
Highest Individual Innings				
England in England	194	M.E.Trescothick	Lord's	2005
England in Bangladesh	113	M.E.Trescothick	Dhaka	2003-04
Bangladesh in England	82*	Aftab Ahmed	Chester-le-Street	2005
Bangladesh in Bangladesh	59	Hannan Sarkar	Dhaka	2003-04
Most Runs in a Series				
England in England		345 (172.50)	M.E.Trescothick	2005
England in Bangladesh		208 (av 69.33)	M.P.Vaughan	2003-04
Bangladesh in England		155 (38.75)	Javed Omar	2005
Bangladesh in Bangladesh		114 (av 38.00)	Mushfiqur Rahman	2003-04

Record Wicket Partnerships - England

1st	148	M.E.Trescothick (194), A.J.Strauss (69)	Lord's	2005
2nd	255	M.E.Trescothick (194), M.P.Vaughan (120)	Lord's	2005
3rd	155	M.E.Trescothick (151), I.R.Bell (162*)	Chester-le-Street	2005
4th	187*	I.R.Bell (162*), G.P.Thorpe (66*)	Chester-le-Street	2005
5th	116	N.Hussain (76), R.Clarke (55)	Chittagong[1]	2003-04
6th	63	N.Hussain (76), C.M.WRead (37)	Chittagong[1]	2003-04
7th	41	G.P.Thorpe (64), G.J.Batty (19)	Dhaka	2003-04
8th	8	A.F.Giles (6), R.L.Johnson (6)	Chittagong[1]	2003-04
9th	5	A.F.Giles (6), M.J.Saggers (1)	Chittagong[1]	2003-04
10th	28	A.F.Giles (19), M.J.Hoggard (6*)	Dhaka	2003-04

Record Wicket Partnerships - Bangladesh

1st	50	Javed Omar (71), Nafis Iqbal (15)	Chester-le-Street	2005
2nd	108	Hannan Sarkar (59), Habibul Bashar (58)	Dhaka	2003-04
3rd	31	Javed Omar (22), Aftab Ahmed (20)	Lord's	2005
4th	24	Javed Omar (71), Habibul Bashar (63)	Chester-le-Street	2005
5th	70	Habibul Bashar (63), Khaled Mashud (25)	Chester-le-Street	2005
6th	60	Mushfiqur Rahman (34), Khaled Mahmud (51)	Dhaka	2003-04
7th	29	Mushfiqur Rahman (46*), Khaled Mahmud (18)	Dhaka	2003-04
8th	34	Khaled Mashud (51), Mohammad Rafique (32)	Dhaka	2003-04
9th	60	Aftab Ahmed (82*), Tapash Baisya (18)	Chester-le-Street	2005
10th	13	Mohammad Rafique (12*), Enamul Haque[2] (9)	Chittagong[1]	2003-04

Best Bowling in an Innings

England in England	5/38	S.J.Harmison	Chester-le-Street	2005
England in Bangladesh	5/35	S.J.Harmison	Dhaka	2003-04
Bangladesh in England	2/91	Mashrafe Bin Mortaza	Chester-le-Street	2005
Bangladesh in Bangladesh	4/60	Mashrafe Bin Mortaza	Chittagong[1]	2003-04

Best Bowling in a Match

England in England	8/97	M.J.Hoggard	Lord's	2005
England in Bangladesh	9/79	S.J.Harmison	Dhaka	2003-04
Bangladesh in England	2/91	Mashrafe Bin Mortaza	Chester-le-Street	2005
Bangladesh in Bangladesh	5/141	Mohammad Rafique	Dhaka	2003-04

Most Wickets in a Series

England in England	14 (av 12.92)	M.J.Hoggard	2003-04
England in Bangladesh	9 (av 8.77)	S.J.Harmison	2003-04
	9 (av 10.33)	R.L.Johnson	2003-04
	9 (av 22.66)	M.J.Hoggard	2003-04
Bangladesh in England	4 (av 49.50)	Mashrafe Bin Mortaza	2005
Bangladesh in Bangladesh	10 (av 31.00)	Mohammad Rafique	2003-04

SOUTH AFRICA v NEW ZEALAND	South Africa		New Zealand		Captains	
Venue and Result	1st	2nd	1st	2nd	South Africa	New Zealand
1931-32 in New Zealand						
Christchurch-South Africa inn & 12 runs	451	-	•293	146	H.B.Cameron	M.L.Page
Wellington-South Africa 8 wkts	410	2-150	•364	193		
1952-53 in New Zealand						
Wellington-South Africa inn & 180 runs	•8d-524	-	172	172	J.E.Cheetham	W.M.Wallace
Auckland-Drawn	•377	5d-200	245	2-31		
1953-54 in South Africa						
Durban[2]-South Africa inn & 58 runs	•9d-437	-	230	149	J.E.Cheetham	G.O.Rabone
Johannesburg[2]-South Africa 132 runs	•271	148	187	100		G.O.Rabone
Cape Town-Drawn	326	3-159	•505	-		G.O.Rabone
Johannesburg[2]-South Africa 9 wkts	•243	1-25	79	188		B.Sutcliffe
Port Elizabeth-South Africa 5 wkts	237	5-215	•226	222		B.Sutcliffe
1961-62 in South Africa						
Durban[2]-South Africa 30 runs	•292	149	245	166	D.J.McGlew	J.R.Reid
Johannesburg[3]-Drawn	•322	6d-178	223	4-165		
Cape Town-New Zealand 72 runs	190	335	•385	9d-212		
Johannesburg[3]-South Africa inn & 51 runs	464	-	•164	249		
Port Elizabeth-New Zealand 40 runs	190	273	•275	228		
1963-64 in New Zealand						
Wellington-Drawn	•302	2d-218	253	6-138	T.L.Goddard	J.R.Reid
Dunedin-Drawn	223	3-42	•149	138		
Auckland-Drawn	•371	5d-200	263	8-191		
1994-95 in South Africa						
Johannesburg[3]-New Zealand 137 runs	279	189	•411	194	W.J.Cronje	K.R.Rutherford
Cape Town-South Africa 8 wkts	226	2-153	•185	192		
Durban[2]-South Africa 7 wkts	440	3-89	•288	239		
1994-95 in New Zealand						
Auckland-South Africa 93 runs	•294	6d-308	328	181	W.J.Cronje	K.R.Rutherford
1998-99 in New Zealand						
Auckland-Drawn	•5d-621	-	352	3-244	W.J.Cronje	D.J.Nash
Christchurch-Drawn	1d-442	-	•168	1-127		
Wellington-South Africa 8 wkts	8d-498	2-16	•222	291		
2000-01 in South Africa						
Bloemfontein-South Africa 5 wkts	•9d-471	5-103	229	342	S.M.Pollock	S.P.Fleming
Port Elizabeth-South Africa 7 wkts	361	3-89	•298	148		
Johannesburg[3]-Drawn	3d-261		•200	-		
2003-04 in New Zealand						
Hamilton-Drawn	•459	4d-313	509	1-39	G.C.Smith	S.P.Fleming
Auckland-New Zealand 9 wkts	•296	349	595	1-53		
Wellington-South Africa 6 wkts	316	4-234	•297	252		
2005-06 in South Africa						
Centurion-South Africa 128 runs	•276	299	327	120	G.C.Smith	S.P.Fleming
Cape Town-Drawn	512	-	•8d-593	3-121		
Johannesburg[3]-South Africa 4 wkts	186	6-220	•119	283		

Test Match Results Summary

SOUTH AFRICA v NEW ZEALAND - in South Africa

		Result			Durban[2]			Johannesburg			Cape Town			P.Elizabeth			Bloemfontein			Centurion		
	Tests	SA	NZ	D	SA	NZ	D	SA	NZ	D	SA	NZ	D	SA	NZ	D	SA	N	D	-	-	-
1953-54	5	4	-	1	1	-	-	2	-	-	-	-	1	1	-	-	-	-	-	-	-	-
1961-62	5	2	2	1	1	-	-	1	-	1	-	1	-	-	1	-	-	-	-	-	-	-
1994-95	3	2	1	-	1	-	-	-	1	-	1	-	-	-	-	-	-	-	-	-	-	-
2000-01	3	2	-	1	-	-	-	-	-	1	-	-	-	1	-	-	1	-	-	-	-	-
2005-06	3	2	-	1	-	-	-	1	-	-	1	-	-	-	-	-	-	-	-	1	-	-
	19	12	3	4	3	-	-	4	1	2	2	1	1	2	1	-	1	-	-	1	-	-

SOUTH AFRICA v NEW ZEALAND - in New Zealand

		Result			Christchurch			Wellington			Auckland			Dunedin			Hamilton		
	Tests	SA	NZ	D	SA	NZ	D	SA	NZ	D	SA	NZ	D	SA	NZ	D	SA	N	D
1931-32	2	2	-	-	1	-	-	1	-	-	-	-	-	-	-	-	-	-	-
1952-53	2	1	-	1	-	-	-	1	-	-	-	-	1	-	-	-	-	-	-
1963-64	3	-	-	3	-	-	-	-	-	1	-	-	1	-	-	1	-	-	-
1994-95	1	1	-	-	-	-	-	-	-	-	1	-	-	-	-	-	-	-	-
1998-99	3	1	-	2	-	-	1	1	-	-	-	-	1	-	-	-	-	-	-
2003-04	3	1	1	1	-	-	-	1	-	-	-	1	-	-	-	-	1	-	-
	14	6	1	7	1	-	1	4	-	1	1	-	3	-	-	1	1	-	-
Totals	33	18	4	11															

Highest Innings Totals			
South Africa in South Africa	9d-471	Bloemfontein	2000-01
South Africa in New Zealand	5d-621	Auckland	1998-99
New Zealand in South Africa	8d-593	Cape Town	2005-06
New Zealand in New Zealand	595	Auckland	2003-04
Lowest Innings Totals			
South Africa in South Africa	148	Johannesburg[2]	1953-54
South Africa in New Zealand	223	Dunedin	1963-64
New Zealand in South Africa	79	Johannesburg[2]	1953-54
New Zealand in New Zealand	138	Dunedin	1963-64
Highest Match Aggregate	1320 for 25 wickets	Hamilton	2003-04
Lowest Match Aggregate	535 for 31 wickets	Johannesburg[2]	1953-54

Highest Individual Innings				
South Africa in South Africa	160	J.H.Kallis	Bloemfontein	2000-01
South Africa in New Zealand	275*	D.J.Cullinan	Auckland	1998-99
New Zealand in South Africa	262	S.P.Fleming	Cape Town	2005-06
New Zealand in New Zealand	170	S.B.Styris	Auckland	2003-04

Most Runs in a Series			
South Africa in South Africa	426 (av 60.85)	D.J.McGlew	1961-62
South Africa in New Zealand	427 (av 427.00)	D.J.Cullinan	1998-99
New Zealand in South Africa	546 (av 60.66)	J.R.Reid	1961-62
New Zealand in New Zealand	321 (av 80.25)	S.B.Styris	2003-04

Record Wicket Partnerships - South Africa

1st	196	J.A.J.Christy (103), B.Mitchell (113)	Christchurch	1931-32
2nd	315*	H.H.Gibbs (211*), J.H.Kallis (148*)	Christchurch	1998-99
3rd	183	G.Kirsten (128), D.J.Cullinan (275*)	Auckland	1998-99
4th	171	G.C.Smith (125*), G.Kirsten (76)	Wellington	2003-04
5th	141	D.J.Cullinan (275*), J.N.Rhodes (63)	Auckland	1998-99
6th	126*	D.J.Cullinan (275*), S.M.Pollock (69*)	Auckland	1998-99
7th	246	D.J.McGlew (255*), A.R.A.Murray (109)	Wellington	1952-53
8th	136	N.D.McKenzie (120), N.Boje (51)	Port Elizabeth	2000-01
9th	60	P.M.Pollock (54), N.A.T.Adcock (24)	Port Elizabeth	1961-62
10th	47	D.J.McGlew (28*), H.D.Bromfield (21)	Port Elizabeth	1961-62

Record Wicket Partnerships - New Zealand

1st	126	G.O.Rabone (56), M.E.Chapple (76)	Cape Town	1953-54
2nd	90	M.J.Horne (60), N.J.Astle (69*)	Auckland	1998-99
3rd	125	M.H.Richardson (45), S.B.Styris (170)	Auckland	2003-04
4th	171	B.W.Sinclair (138), S.N.McGregor (62)	Auckland	1963-64
5th	176	J.R.Reid (135), J.E.F.Beck (99)	Cape Town	1953-54
6th	100	H.G.Vivian (100), F.T Badcock (53)	Wellington	1931-32
7th	225	C.L.Cairns (158), J.D.P.Oram (90)	Auckland	2003-04
8th	256	S.P.Fleming (262), J.E.C.Franklin (122*)	Cape Town	2005-06
9th	69	C.F.W.Allcott (26), I.B.Cromb (51*)	Wellington	1931-32
10th	57	S.B.Doull (31*), R.P.de Groen (21)	Johannesburg[3]	1994-95

Best Bowling in an Innings

South Africa in South Africa	8/53	G.B.Lawrence	Johannesburg[3]	1961-62
South Africa in New Zealand	6/47	P.M.Pollock	Wellington	1963-64
New Zealand in South Africa	6/68	G.O.Rabone	Cape Town	1953-54
New Zealand in New Zealand	6/60	J.R.Reid	Dunedin	1963-64

Best Bowling in a Match

South Africa in South Africa	11/196	S.F.Burke	Cape Town	1961-62
South Africa in New Zealand	9/127	Q.McMillan	Christchurch	1931-32
New Zealand in South Africa	8/134	M.N.Hart	Johannesburg[3]	1994-95
New Zealand in New Zealand	11/180	C.S.Martin	Auckland	2003-04

Most Wickets in a Series

South Africa in South Africa	28 (av 18.28)	G.B.Lawrence	1961-62
South Africa in New Zealand	16 (av 20.18)	Q.McMillan	1931-32
New Zealand in South Africa	22 (av 20.63)	A.R.MacGibbon	1953-54
	22 (av 28.04)	J.C.Alabaster	1961-62
New Zealand in New Zealand	18 (av 16.66)	C.S.Martin	2003-04

SOUTH AFRICA v WEST INDIES	South Africa		West Indies		Captains	
Venue and Result	1st	2nd	1st	2nd	South Africa	West Indies
1991-92 in West Indies						
Bridgetown-West Indies 52 runs	345	148	•262	283	K.C.Wessels	R.B.Richardson
1998-99 in South Africa						
Johannesburg[3]-South Africa 4 wkts	268	6-164	•261	170	W.J.Cronje	B.C.Lara
Port Elizabeth-South Africa 178 runs	•245	195	121	141		
Durban[2]-South Africa 9 wkts	312	1-147	•198	259		
Cape Town-South Africa 149 runs	•8d-406	7d-226	212	271		
Centurion-South Africa 351 runs	•313	5d-399	144	217		

SOUTH AFRICA v WEST INDIES (cont.)	South Africa		West Indies		Captains	
Venue and Result	1st	2nd	1st	2nd	South Africa	West Indies
2000-01 in West Indies						
Georgetown-Drawn	332	2-142	•304	7d-333	S.M.Pollock	C.L.Hooper
Port-of-Spain-South Africa 69 runs	•286	287	342	162		
Bridgetown-Drawn	•454	9d-197	387	7-88		
St. John's-South Africa 82 runs	•247	7d-215	140	240		
Kingston-West Indies 130 runs	141	255	•225	301		
2003-04 in South Africa						
Johannesburg[3]-South Africa 189 runs	268	6-164	•261	170	G.C.Smith	B.C.Lara
Durban[2]-South Africa inn & 65 runs	9d-658	-	•264	329		
Cape Town-Drawn	•532	3d-335	427	5-354		
Centurion-South Africa 10 wkts	•6d-604	0-46	301	348		
2004-05 in West Indies						
Georgetown-Drawn	188	4-269	•5d-543	-	G.C.Smith	S.Chanderpaul
Port-of-Spain-South Africa 8 wkts	398	2-146	•347	194		
Bridgetown-S.Africa inn & 86 runs	9d-548	-	•296	166		
St. John's-Drawn	•6d-588	1-127	747	-		

Test Match Results Summary

SOUTH AFRICA v WEST INDIES - in South Africa

		Result			Johannesburg[3]			P.Elizabeth			Durban[2]			Cape Town			Centurion		
	Tests	SA	W	D	SA	W	D	SA	W	D	SA	W	D	SA	W	D	SA	W	D
1998-99	5	5	-	-	1	-	-	1	-	-	1	-	-	1	-	-	1	-	-
2003-04	4	3	-	1	1	-	-	-	-	-	-	-	-	-	-	1	1	-	-
	9	8	-	1	2	-	-	1	-	-	2	-	-	1	-	1	2	-	-

SOUTH AFRICA v WEST INDIES - in West Indies

		Result			Bridgetown			Georgetown			Port-of-Spain			St. John's			Kingston		
	Tests	SA	W	D	SA	W	D	SA	W	D	SA	W	D	SA	W	D	SA	W	D
1991-92	1	-	1	-	-	1	-	-	-	-	-	-	-	-	-	-	-	-	-
2000-01	5	2	1	2	-	-	1	-	-	1	1	-	-	1	-	-	-	1	-
2004-05	4	2	-	2	1	-	-	-	-	1	1	-	-	-	-	1	-	-	-
	10	4	2	4	1	1	1	-	-	2	2	-	-	1	-	1	-	1	-
Totals	19	12	2	5															

Highest Innings Totals			
South Africa in South Africa	9d-658	Durban[2]	2003-04
South Africa in West Indies	6d-588	St John's	2004-05
West Indies in South Africa	427	Cape Town	2003-04
West Indies in West Indies	747	St John's	2004-05
Lowest Innings Totals			
South Africa in South Africa	195	Port Elizabeth	1998-99
South Africa in West Indies	141	Kingston	2000-01
West Indies in South Africa	121	Port Elizabeth	1998-99
West Indies in West Indies	140	St John's	2000-01

Highest Match Aggregate		1648 for 28 wickets	Cape Town	2003-04
Lowest Match Aggregate		702 for 40 wickets	Port Elizabeth	1998-99

Highest Individual Innings

South Africa in South Africa	192	J.H.Kallis	Centurion	2003-04
South Africa in West Indies	178	A.B.de Villiers	Bridgetown	2004-05
West Indies in South Africa	202	B.C.Lara	Johannesburg[3]	2003-04
West Indies in West Indies	317	C.H.Gayle	St John's	2004-05

Most Runs in a Series

South Africa in South Africa	712 (av 178.00)	J.H.Kallis	2003-04
South Africa in West Indies	505 (av 84.16)	G.C.Smith	2004-05
West Indies in South Africa	531 (av 66.37)	B.C.Lara	2003-04
West Indies in West Indies	450 (av 90.00)	S.Chanderpaul	2004-05

Record Wicket Partnerships - South Africa

1st	301	G.C.Smith (139), H.H.Gibbs (192)	Centurion	2003-04
2nd	146	G.Kirsten (150), J.H.Kallis (50)	Georgetown	2000-01
3rd	251	H.H.Gibbs (142), J.H.Kallis (130*)	Cape Town	2003-04
4th	249	J.H.Kallis (177), G.Kirsten (137)	Durban[2]	2003-04
5th	267	J.H.Kallis (147), A.G.Prince (131)	St John's	2004-05
6th	92	J.N.Rhodes (64), S.M.Pollock (42)	Port Elizabeth	1998-99
7th	92	J.H.Kallis (83), M.V.Boucher (100)	Centurion	1998-99
8th	146	M.V.Boucher (122*), J.H.Kallis (73)	Cape Town	2003-04
9th	132	S.M.Pollock (106), A.A.Donald (37)	Bridgetown	2000-01
10th	41	R.J.Peterson (25), M.Ntini (22*)	Johannesburg[3]	2003-04

Record Wicket Partnerships - West Indies

1st	126	C.H.Gayle (116), D.Ganga (17)	Cape Town	2003-04
2nd	314	C.H.Gayle (317), R.R.Sarwan (127)	St John's	2004-05
3rd	160	S.Chanderpaul (75), B.C.Lara (79)	Durban[2]	1998-99
4th	284	W.W.Hinds (213), S.Chanderpaul (203*)	Georgetown	2004-05
5th	116	B.C.Lara (83), C.L.Hooper (74)	Bridgetown	2000-01
6th	130	S.Chanderpaul (127), D.J.J.Bravo (107)	St John's	2004-05
7th	81	R.D.Jacobs (78), N.A.M.McLean (33)	Centurion	1998-99
8th	65	R.D.Jacobs (69*), N.A.M.McLean (39)	Cape Town	1998-99
9th	71	R.D.Jacobs (93*), M.Dillon (21)	Port-of-Spain	2000-01
10th	64	R.D.Jacobs (69*), M.Dillon (36)	Cape Town	1998-99

Best Bowling in an Innings

South Africa in South Africa	5/43	S.M.Pollock	Port Elizabeth	1998-99
South Africa in West Indies	7/37	M.Ntini	Port-of-Spain	2004-05
West Indies in South Africa	7/84	F.A.Rose	Durban[2]	1998-99
West Indies in West Indies	6/34	C.E.L.Ambrose	Bridgetown	1991-92

Best Bowling in a Match

South Africa in South Africa	9/103	S.M.Pollock	Johannesburg[3]	1998-99
South Africa in West Indies	13/132	M.Ntini	Port-of-Spain	2004-05
West Indies in South Africa	8/79	C.E.L.Ambrose	Port Elizabeth	1998-99
West Indies in West Indies	8/81	C.E.L.Ambrose	Bridgetown	1991-92

Most Wickets in a Series

South Africa in South Africa	29 (av 16.65)	S.M.Pollock	1998-99
	29 (av 21.37)	M.Ntini	2003-04
South Africa in West Indies	20 (av 19.75)	J.H.Kallis	2000-01
	20 (av 23.20)	S.M.Pollock	2000-01
West Indies in South Africa	22 (av 18.90)	C.A.Walsh	1998-99
West Indies in West Indies	25 (av 19.68)	C.A.Walsh	2000-01

SOUTH AFRICA v INDIA	South Africa		India		Captains	
Venue and Result	1st	2nd	1st	2nd	South Africa	West Indies
1992-93 in South Africa						
Durban^2-Drawn	•254	3-176	277	-	K.C.Wessels	M.Azharuddin
Johannesburg^3-Drawn	•292	252	227	4-141		
Port Elizabeth-South Africa 9 wkts	275	1-155	•212	215		
Cape Town-Drawn	•9d-360	6d-130	276	1-29		
1996-97 in India						
Ahmedabad-India 64 runs	244	105	•223	190	W.J.Cronje	S.R.Tendulkar
Calcutta-South Africa 329 runs	•428	3d-367	329	137		
Kanpur-India 280 runs	177	180	•237	7d-400		
1996-97 in South Africa						
Durban^2-South Africa 328 runs	•235	259	100	66	W.J.Cronje	S.R.Tendulkar
Cape Town-South Africa 282 runs	•7d-529	6d-256	359	144		
Johannesburg^3-Drawn	321	8-228	•410	266		
1999-2000 in India						
Mumbai^3-South Africa 4 wkts	176	6-164	•225	113	W.J.Cronje	S.R.Tendulkar
Bangalore-South Africa Inn + 71 runs	479	-	•158	250		
2001-02 in South Africa						
Bloemfontein-South Africa 9 wkts	563	1-54	•379	237	S.M.Pollock	S.C.Ganguly
Port Elizabeth-Drawn	•362	5d-233	201	3-206		
2004-05 in India						
Kanpur-Drawn	•9d-210	4-169	466	-	G.C.Smith	S.C.Ganguly
Kolkata-India 8 wkts	•305	222	411	2-120		

Test Match Results Summary

SOUTH AFRICA v INDIA - in South Africa

		Result			Durban^2			Johannesburg^3			P.Elizabeth			Cape Town			Bloemfontein		
	Tests	SA	I	D	SA	I	D	SA	I	D	SA	I	D	SA	I	D	SA	I	D
1992-93	4	1	-	3	-	-	1	-	-	1	1	-	-	-	-	1	-	-	-
1996-97	3	2	-	1	1	-	-	-	-	1	-	-	-	1	-	-	-	-	-
2001-02	2	1	-	1	-	-	-	-	-	-	-	-	1	-	-	-	1	-	-
	9	4	-	5	1	-	1	-	-	2	1	-	1	1	-	1	1	-	-

SOUTH AFRICA v INDIA - in India

		Result			Ahmedabad			Calcutta			Kanpur			Mumbai^3			Bangalore		
	Tests	SA	I	D	SA	I	D	SA	I	D	SA	I	D	SA	I	D	SA	I	D
1996-97	3	1	2	-	-	1	-	1	-	-	-	1	-	-	-	-	-	-	-
1999-2000	2	2	-	-	-	-	-	-	-	-	-	-	-	1	-	-	1	-	-
2004-05	2	-	1	1	-	-	-	1	-	-	-	-	1	-	-	-	-	-	-
	7	3	3	1	-	1	-	2	-	-	-	1	1	1	-	-	1	-	-
Totals	16	7	3	6															

Highest Innings Totals

South Africa in South Africa	563	Bloemfontein	2001-02
South Africa in India	9d-510	Kanpur	2004-05
India in South Africa	410	Johannesburg[3]	1996-97
India in India	466	Kanpur	2004-05

Lowest Innings Totals

South Africa in South Africa	235	Durban[2]	1996-97
South Africa in India	105	Ahmedabad	1996-97
India in South Africa	66	Durban[2]	1996-97
India in India	113	Mumbai[3]	1999-2000

Highest Match Aggregate	1288 for 33 wickets	Cape Town	1996-97
Lowest Match Aggregate	660 for 40 wickets	Durban[2]	1996-97

Highest Individual Innings

South Africa in South Africa	196	H.H.Gibbs	Port Elizabeth	2001-02
South Africa in India	163	A.J.Hall	Kanpur	2004-05
India in South Africa	169	S.R.Tendulkar	Cape Town	1996-97
India in India	164	V.K.Sehwag	Kanpur	2004-05

Most Runs in a Series

South Africa in South Africa	316 (av 79.00)	H.H.Gibbs	2001-02
South Africa in India	322 (av 53.66)	G.Kirsten	1996-97
India in South Africa	277 (av 55.40)	R.S.Dravid	1996-97
India in India	388 (av 77.60)	M.Azharuddin	1996-97

Record Wicket Partnerships - South Africa

1st	236	A.C.Hudson (146), G.Kirsten (102)	Calcutta	1996-97
2nd	212	G.Kirsten (133), D.J.Cullinan (153*)	Calcutta	1996-97
3rd	130	J.H.Kallis (68), N.D.McKenzie (68)	Bloemfontein	2001-02
4th	105	H.H.Gibbs (196), H.H.Dippenaar (29)	Port Elizabeth	2001-02
5th	164	J.H.Kallis (95), L.Klusener (97)	Bangalore	1999-2000
6th	144	A.J.Hall (163), Z.de Bruyn (83)	Kanpur	2004-05
7th	121	L.Klusener (108), M.V.Boucher (47)	Bloemfontein	2001-02
8th	147*	B.M.McMillan (103*), L.Klusener (102*)	Cape Town	1996-97
9th	60	P.S.de Villiers (67*), A.A.Donald (17)	Ahmedabad	1996-97
10th	74	B.M.McMillan (51*), A.A.Donald (26)	Durban[2]	1996-97

Record Wicket Partnerships - India

1st	218	V.K.Sehwag (164), G.Gambhir (96)	Kanpur	2004-05
2nd	171	D.Dasgupta (63), R.S.Dravid (87)	Port Elizabeth	2001-02
3rd	60*	R.S.Dravid (47*), S.R.Tendulkar (32*)	Kolkata	2004-05
4th	145	R.S.Dravid (148), S.C.Ganguly (73)	Johannesburg[3]	1996-97
5th	220	S.R.Tendulkar (155), V.K.Sehwag (105)	Bloemfontein	2001-02
6th	222	S.R.Tendulkar (169), M.Azharuddin (115)	Cape Town	1996-97
7th	76	R.S.Dravid (148), J.Srinath (41)	Johannesburg[3]	1996-97
8th	161	M.Azharuddin (109), A.Kumble (88)	Calcutta	1996-97
9th	80	V.V.S.Laxman (89), A.Kumble (28)	Port Elizabeth	2001-02
10th	52	A.B.Agarkar (41*), M.Kartik (14)	Mumbai[3]	1999-2000

Best Bowling in an Innings

South Africa in South Africa	7/84	A.A.Donald	Port Elizabeth	1992-93
South Africa in India	8/64	L.Klusener	Calcutta	1996-97
India in South Africa	6/53	A.Kumble	Johannesburg[3]	1992-93
India in India	7/87	Harbhajan Singh	Kolkata	2004-05

Best Bowling in a Match

South Africa in South Africa	12/139	A.A.Donald	Port Elizabeth	1992-93
South Africa in India	8/139	L.Klusener	Calcutta	1996-97
	8/139	P.R.Adams	Kanpur	1996-97
India in South Africa	10/153	B.K.Venkatesh Prasad	Durban[2]	1996-97
India in India	9/141	Harbhajan Singh	Kolkata	2004-05

Most Wickets in a Series

South Africa in South Africa	20 (av 19.70)	A.A.Donald	1992-93
	20 (av 15.95)	A.A.Donald	1996-97
South Africa in India	14 (av 20.28)	P.R.Adams	1996-97
India in South Africa	18 (av 25.94)	A.Kumble	1992-93
	18 (av 28.72)	J.Srinath	1996-97
India in India	17 (av 25.94)	J.Srinath	1996-97

SOUTH AFRICA v SRI LANKA	South Africa		Sri Lanka		Captains	
Venue and Result	1st	2nd	1st	2nd	South Africa	Sri Lanka
1993-94 in Sri Lanka						
Moratuwa-Drawn	267	7-251	•331	6d-300	K.C.Wessels	A.Ranatunga
Colombo(SSC)-South Africa inn & 208 runs	495	-	•168	119		
Colombo(PSS)-Drawn	•316	4-159	9d-296	-		
1997-98 in South Africa						
Cape Town-South Africa 70 runs	•418	264	306	306	W.J.Cronje	A.Ranatunga
Centurion-South Africa 6 wkts	200	4-226	•303	122		
2000-01 in Sri Lanka						
Galle-Sri Lanka inn & 15 runs	238	269	•522	-	S.M.Pollock	S.T.Jayasuriya
Kandy-South Africa 7 runs	•253	231	308	169		
Colombo(SSC)-Drawn	•279	9d-241	258	4-195		
2000-01 in South Africa						
Durban-Drawn	•420	7d-140	216	6-149	S.M.Pollock	S.T.Jayasuriya
Cape Town-South Africa inn & 229 runs	7d-504	-	•95	180		
Centurion-South Africa inn & 7 runs	•378	-	119	252		
2002-03 in South Africa						
Johannesburg[3]-South Africa inn & 64 runs	386	-	•192	130	S.M.Pollock	S.T.Jayasuriya
Centurion-South Africa 3 wkts	448	7-124	•323	245		
2004-05 in Sri Lanka						
Galle-Drawn	486	9d-214	•376	3-203	G.C.Smith	M.S.Atapattu
Colombo(SSC)-Sri Lanka 313 runs	189	179	•470	4d-211		
2006-07 in Sri Lanka						
Colombo(SSC)-Sri Lanka inn & 153 runs	169	434	•5d-756	-	A.G.Prince	D.P.M.D.Jayawardene
Colombo(PSS)-Sri Lanka 1 wicket	•361	311	321	9-352		

Test Match Results Summary

SOUTH AFRICA v SRI LANKA - in South Africa

		Result			Cape Town			Centurion			Durban			Johannesburg[3]		
	Tests	SA	SL	D	SA	SL	D	SA	SL	D	SA	SL	D	SA	SL	D
1997-98	2	2	-	-	1	-	-	1	-	-	-	-	-	-	-	-
2000-01	3	2	-	1	1	-	-	1	-	-	-	-	1	-	-	-
2002-03	2	2	-	-	-	-	-	1	-	-	-	-	-	1	-	-
Total	7	6	-	1	2	-	-	3	-	-	-	-	1	1	-	-

SOUTH AFRICA v SRI LANKA - in Sri Lanka

		Result			Moratuwa			Colombo(SSC)			Colombo(PSS)			Galle			Kandy		
	Tests	SA	SL	D	SA	SL	D	SA	SL	D	SA	SL	D	SA	SL	D	SA	SL	D
1993-94	3	1	-	2	-	-	1	1	-	-	-	-	1	-	-	-	-	-	-
2000-01	3	1	1	1	-	-	-	-	-	1	-	-	-	-	1	-	1	-	-
2004-05	2	-	1	1	-	-	-	-	1	-	-	-	-	-	-	1	-	-	-
2006-07	2	-	2	-	-	-	-	-	1	-	-	1	-	-	-	-	-	-	-
	10	2	4	4	-	-	1	1	2	1	-	1	1	-	1	1	1	-	-
	8	2	2	4	-	-	1	-	1	1	-	-	1	-	1	1	1	-	-
Totals	17	8	4	5															

Highest Innings Totals			
South Africa in South Africa	7d-504	Cape Town	2000-01
South Africa in Sri Lanka	495	Colombo (SSC)	1993-94
Sri Lanka in South Africa	306 (twice)	Cape Town	1997-98
Sri Lanka in Sri Lanka	5d-756	Colombo (SSC)	2006-07

Lowest Innings Totals			
South Africa in South Africa	200	Centurion	1997-98
South Africa in Sri Lanka	169	Colombo (SSC)	2006-07
Sri Lanka in South Africa	95	Cape Town	2000-01
Sri Lanka in Sri Lanka	119	Colombo (SSC)	1993-94

Highest Match Aggregate	1359 for 25 wickets	Colombo (SSC)	2006-07
Lowest Match Aggregate	708 for 30 wickets	Johannesburg[3]	2002-03

Highest Individual Innings				
South Africa in South Africa	180	G.Kirsten	Durban[2]	2000-01
South Africa in Sri Lanka	122	W.J.Cronje	Colombo (SSC)	1993-94
Sri Lanka in South Africa	104*	H.P.Tillakaratne	Centurion	2002-03
Sri Lanka in Sri Lanka	374	D.P.M.D.Jayawardene	Colombo (SSC)	2006-07

Most Runs in a Series			
South Africa in South Africa	284 (av 71.00)	D.J.Cullinan	1997-98
South Africa in Sri Lanka	275 (av 68.75)	L.Klusener	2000-01
Sri Lanka in South Africa	235 (av 39.16)	K.C.Sangakkara	2000-01
Sri Lanka in Sri Lanka	367 (av 91.75)	K.C.Sangakkara	2004-05
Sri Lanka in Sri Lanka	510 (av 170.00)	D.P.M.D.Jayawardene	2006-07

Record Wicket Partnerships - South Africa

1st	165	J.A.Rudolph (90), A.J.Hall (64)	Colombo (SSC)	2006-07
2nd	108	G.C.Smith (65), H.H.Gibbs (51)	Colombo (SSC)	2004-05
3rd	140	H.H.Gibbs (92), J.H.Kallis (84)	Centurion	2002-03
4th	116	G.Kirsten (75*), W.J.Cronje (82)	Centurion	1997-98
5th	161	A.G.Prince (86), A.B.de Villiers (95)	Colombo (PSS)	2006-07
6th	86	D.J.Cullinan (112), M.V.Boucher (92)	Cape Town	2000-01
7th	124	L.Klusener (118*), M.V.Boucher (60)	Kandy	2000-01
8th	132	M.V.Boucher (63), S.M.Pollock (99*)	Centurion	2002-03
9th	150	N.D.McKenzie (103), S.M.Pollock (111)	Centurion	2000-01
10th	45	N.Boje (27), P.R.Adams (14*)	Kandy	2000-01

Record Wicket Partnerships - Sri Lanka

1st	193	M.S.Atapattu (54), S.T.Jayasuriya (148)	Galle	2000-01
2nd	103	S.T.Jayasuriya (85), R.P.Arnold (28)	Colombo (SSC)	2000-01
3rd	624	K.C.Sangakkara (287), D.P.M.D.Jayawardene (374)	Colombo (SSC)	2006-07
4th	118	R.S.Mahanama (50), A.Ranatunga (73)	Centurion	1997-98
5th	121	P.A.de Silva (68), A.Ranatunga (131)	Moratuwa	1993-94
6th	105	C.K.Kapugedera (630, H.A.P.W.Jayawardene (42)	Colombo (PSS)	2006-07
7th	103	A.Ranatunga (131), H.P.Tillakaratne (33*)	Moratuwa	1993-94
8th	43	P.A.de Silva (41), G.P.Wickramasinghe (21)	Centurion	1997-98
9th	170	D.P.M.D.Jayawardene (237), W.P.U.J.C.Vaas (69)	Galle	2004-05
10th	48	G.P.Wickramasinghe (51), M.Muralidaran (10)	Cape Town	1997-98

Best Bowling in an Innings

South Africa in South Africa	6/30	S.M.Pollock	Cape Town	2000-01
South Africa in Sri Lanka	5/48	B.N.Schultz	Colombo (SSC)	1993-94
Sri Lanka in South Africa	6/39	M.Muralidaran	Durban[2]	2000-01
Sri Lanka in Sri Lanka	7/84	M.Muralidaran	Galle	2000-01

Best Bowling in a Match

South Africa in South Africa	8/127	A.A.Donald	Centurion	1997-98
South Africa in Sri Lanka	9/106	B.N.Schultz	Colombo (SSC)	1993-94
Sri Lanka in South Africa	11/161	M.Muralidaran	Durban[2]	2000-01
Sri Lanka in Sri Lanka	13/171	M.Muralidaran	Galle	2000-01

Most Wickets in a Series

South Africa in South Africa	14 (av 18.35)	A.A.Donald	1997-98
South Africa in Sri Lanka	20 (av 16.30)	B.N.Schultz	1993-94
Sri Lanka in South Africa	16 (av 22.25)	M.Muralidaran	1997-98
Sri Lanka in Sri Lanka	26 (av 18.46)	M.Muralidaran	2000-01

SOUTH AFRICA v PAKISTAN	South Africa		Pakistan		Captains	
Venue and Result	1st	2nd	1st	2nd	South Africa	Pakistan
1994-95 in South Africa						
Johannesburg[3]-South Africa 324 runs	•460	7d-259	230	165	W.J.Cronje	Saleem Malik
1997-98 in Pakistan						
Rawalpindi[2]-Drawn	403	-	•456	6d-182	W.J.Cronje	Saeed Anwar
Sheikhupura-Drawn	•402	-	1-53	-		
Faisalabad-South Africa 53 runs	•239	214	308	92		

SOUTH AFRICA v PAKISTAN (cont.)	South Africa		Pakistan		Captains	
Venue and Result	1st	2nd	1st	2nd	South Africa	Pakistan
1997-98 in South Africa						
Johannesburg[3]-Drawn	•364	0-44	329	-	W.J.Cronje	Aamer Sohail
Durban[2]-Pakistan 29 runs	231	225	•259	226		Aamer Sohail
Port Elizabeth-South Africa 259 runs	•293	7d-206	106	134		Rashid Latif
2002-03 in South Africa						
Durban[2]-South Africa 10 wkts	•368	0-45	161	250	S.M.Pollock	Waqar Younis
Cape Town-South Africa inn & 142 runs	•7d-620	-	252	226		
2003-04 in Pakistan						
Lahore[2]-Pakistan 8 wkts	•320	241	401	2-164	G.C.Smith	Yousuf Youhana
Faisalabad-Drawn	•278	8d-371	348	6-242		Inzamamul Haq

Test Match Results Summary

SOUTH AFRICA v PAKISTAN - in South Africa

		Result			Johannesburg[3]			Durban[2]			Port Elizabeth			Cape Town		
	Tests	SA	P	D	SA	P	D	SA	P	D	SA	P	D	SA	P	D
1994-95	1	1	-	-	1	-	-	-	-	-	-	-	-	-	-	-
1997-98	3	1	1	1	-	-	1	-	1	-	1	-	-	-	-	-
2002-03	2	2	-	-	-	-	-	1	-	-	-	-	-	1	-	-
	6	4	1	1	1	-	1	1	1	-	1	-	-	1	-	-

SOUTH AFRICA v PAKISTAN - in Pakistan

		Result			Rawalpindi[2]			Sheikhupura			Faisalabad			Lahore[2]		
	Tests	SA	P	D	SA	P	D	SA	P	D	SA	P	D	SA	P	D
1997-98	3	1	-	2	-	-	1	-	-	1	1	-	-	-	-	-
2003-04	2	-	1	1	-	-	-	-	-	-	-	-	1	-	1	-
	5	1	1	3	-	-	1	-	-	1	1	-	1	-	1	-
Totals	11	5	2	4												

Highest Innings Totals			
South Africa in South Africa	7d-620	Cape Town	2002-03
South Africa in Pakistan	403	Rawalpindi[2]	1997-98
Pakistan in South Africa	329	Johannesburg[3]	1997-98
Pakistan in Pakistan	456	Rawalpindi[2]	1997-98
Lowest Innings Totals			
South Africa in South Africa	225	Durban[2]	1997-98
South Africa in Pakistan	214	Faisalabad	1997-98
Pakistan in South Africa	106	Port Elizabeth	1997-98
Pakistan in Pakistan	92	Faisalabad	1997-98
Highest Match Aggregate	1239 for 34 wickets	Faisalabad	2003-04
Lowest Match Aggregate	455 for 11 wickets	Sheikhupara	1997-98

Highest Individual Innings

South Africa in South Africa	228	H.H.Gibbs	Cape Town	2002-03
South Africa in Pakistan	118	G.Kirsten	Faisalabad	2003-04
Pakistan in South Africa	136	Azhar Mahmood	Johannesburg[3]	1997-98
Pakistan in Pakistan	128*	Azhar Mahmood	Rawalpindi[2]	1997-98
	128	Imran Farhat	Faisalabad	2003-04

Most Runs in a Series

South Africa in South Africa	264 (av 132.00)	H.H.Gibbs	2002-03
South Africa in Pakistan	271 (av 90.33)	G.Kirsten	2003-04
Pakistan in South Africa	327 (av 65.40)	Azhar Mahmood	1997-98
Pakistan in Pakistan	313 (av 78.25)	Taufiq Umar	2003-04

Record Wicket Partnerships - South Africa

1st	368	G.C.Smith (151), H.H.Gibbs (228)	Cape Town	2002-03
2nd	114	G.Kirsten (98), J.H.Kallis (61)	Rawalpindi[2]	1997-98
3rd	122	G.Kirsten (56), J.H.Kallis (105)	Durban[2]	2002-03
4th	108	H.H.Gibbs (98), G.Kirsten (54)	Faisalabad	2003-04
5th	90	G.Kirsten (118), J.H.Kallis (43)	Faisalabad	2003-04
6th	157	J.N.Rhodes (72), B.M.McMillan (113)	Johannesburg[3]	1994-95
7th	106	S.M.Pollock (48), D.J.Richardson (45*)	Rawalpindi[2]	1997-98
8th	124	G.Kirsten (100*), P.L.Symcox (81)	Faisalabad	1997-98
9th	195	M.V.Boucher (78), P.L.Symcox (108)	Johannesburg[3]	1997-98
10th	71	P.S.de Villiers (66*), A.A.Donald (15)	Durban[2]	1994-95

Record Wicket Partnerships - Pakistan

1st	137	Taufiq Umar (68), Imran Farhat (128)	Faisalabad	2003-04
2nd	116	Taufiq Umar (135), Younis Khan (46)	Cape Town	2002-03
3rd	121	Taufiq Umar (67), Inzamamul Haq (60)	Cape Town	2002-03
4th	93	Asif Mujtaba (26), Inzamamul Haq (95)	Johannesburg[3]	1994-95
5th	99	Asim Kamal (99), Shoaib Malik (47)	Lahore[2]	2003-04
6th	144	Inzamamul Haq (96), Moin Khan (80)	Johannesburg[3]	1997-98
7th	35	Saleem Malik (99), Wasim Akram (41)	Johannesburg[3]	1994-95
8th	40	Inzamamul Haq (95), Kabir Khan (10)	Johannesburg[3]	1994-95
9th	80	Azhar Mahmood (132), Shoaib Akhtar (6)	Johannesburg[3]	1997-98
10th	151	Azhar Mahmood (128*), Mushtaq Ahmed (59)	Rawalpindi[2]	1997-98

Best Bowling in an Innings

South Africa in South Africa	6/23	P.S.de Villiers	Johannesburg[3]	1997-98
South Africa in Pakistan	7/128	P.R.Adams	Lahore[2]	2003-04
Pakistan in South Africa	6/78	Mushtaq Ahmed	Durban[2]	1997-98
	6/78	Waqar Younis	Port Elizabeth	1997-98
Pakistan in Pakistan	5/46	Danish Kaneria	Lahore[2]	2003-04

Best Bowling in a Match

South Africa in South Africa	10/108	P.S.de Villiers	Johannesburg[3]	1994-95
South Africa in Pakistan	8/185	P.R.Adams	Lahore[2]	2003-04
Pakistan in South Africa	10/133	Waqar Younis	Port Elizabeth	1997-98
Pakistan in Pakistan	7/138	Mushtaq Ahmed	Faisalabad	1997-98

Most Wickets in a Series

South Africa in South Africa	16 (av 16.37)	A.A.Donald	1997-98
South Africa in Pakistan	10 (av 23.20)	S.M.Pollock	1997-98
	10 (av 34.20)	P.R.Adams	2003-04
Pakistan in South Africa	16 (av 22.12)	Waqar Younis	1997-98
Pakistan in Pakistan	14 (av 27.57)	Mushtaq Ahmed	1997-98

SOUTH AFRICA v ZIMBABWE	South Africa		Zimbabwe		Captains	
Venue and Result	1st	2nd	1st	2nd	South Africa	Zimbabwe
1995-96 in Zimbabwe						
Harare-South Africa 7 wkts	346	3-108	•170	283	W.J.Cronje	A.Flower
1999-2000 in South Africa						
Bloemfontein-South Africa inn & 13 runs	417	-	•192	212	W.J.Cronje	A.Flower
1999-2000 in Zimbabwe						
Harare-South Africa inn & 219 runs	9d-462	-	•102	141	W.J.Cronje	A.Flower
2001-02 in Zimbabwe						
Harare-South Africa 9 wkts	•3d-600	1-79	286	391	S.M.Pollock	H.H.Streak
Bulawayo[2]-Drawn	519	-	•9d-419	3-96		
2004-05 in South Africa						
Cape Town-South Africa inn & 21 runs	3d-340	-	•54	265	G.C.Smith	T.Taibu
Centurion-South Africa inn & 62 runs	7d-480	-	•269	149		

Test Match Results Summary

SOUTH AFRICA v ZIMBABWE - in South Africa

		Result			Bloemfontein			Cape Town			Centurion		
	Tests	SA	Z	D	SA	Z	D	SA	Z	D	SA	Z	D
1999-2000	1	1	-	-	1	-	-	-	-	-	-	-	-
2004-05	2	2	-	-	-	-	-	1	-	-	1	-	-
Totals	3	3	-	-	1	-	-	1	-	-	1	-	-

SOUTH AFRICA v ZIMBABWE - in Zimbabwe

		Result			Harare			Bulawayo[2]		
	Tests	SA	Z	D	SA	Z	D	SA	Z	D
1995-96	1	1	-	-	1	-	-	-	-	-
1999-2000	1	1	-	-	1	-	-	-	-	-
2001-02	2	1	-	1	1	-	-	-	-	1
	4	3	-	1	3	-	-	-	-	1
Totals	7	6	-	1						

Highest Innings Totals			
South Africa in South Africa	7d-480	Centurion	2004-05
South Africa in Zimbabwe	3d-600	Harare	2001-02
Zimbabwe in South Africa	269	Centurion	2004-05
Zimbabwe in Zimbabwe	9d-417	Harare	2001-02
Lowest Innings Totals			
South Africa in South Africa	417	Bloemfontein	1999-2000
South Africa in Zimbabwe	346	Harare	1995-96
Zimbabwe in South Africa	54	Cape Town	2004-05
Zimbabwe in Zimbabwe	102	Harare	1999-2000
Highest Match Aggregate	1356 for 24 wickets	Harare	2001-02
Lowest Match Aggregate	705 for 29 wickets	Harare	1999-2000

Highest Individual Innings

South Africa in South Africa	139*	A.G.Prince	Centurion	2004-05
South Africa in Zimbabwe	220	G.Kirsten	Harare	2001-02
Zimbabwe in South Africa	85	G.J.Whittall	Bloemfontein	1999-2000
	85	H.H.Streak	Centurion	2004-05
Zimbabwe in Zimbabwe	199*	A.Flower	Harare	2001-02

Most Runs in a Series

South Africa in South Africa	162 (av 81.00)	G.C.Smith	2004-05
South Africa in Zimbabwe	388 (av --.--)	J.H.Kallis	2001-02
Zimbabwe in South Africa	136 (av 68.00)	G.J.Whittall	1999-2000
Zimbabwe in Zimbabwe	422 (av 211.00)	A.Flower	2001-02

Record Wicket Partnerships - South Africa

1st	256	H.H.Gibbs (147), G.Kirsten (220)	Harare	2001-02
2nd	199	G.Kirsten (220), J.H.Kallis (157*)	Harare	2001-02
3rd	181	J.H.Kallis (189*), N.D.McKenzie (88)	Bulawayo[2]	2001-02
4th	100	J.H.Kallis (115), W.J.Cronje (58)	Harare	1999-2000
5th	60	A.C.Hudson (135), J.N.Rhodes (15)	Harare	1995-96
6th	119	A.G.Prince (139*), J.H.Kallis (58)	Centurion	2004-05
7th	142	A.G.Prince (139*), N.Boje (85)	Centurion	2004-05
8th	148	M.V.Boucher (125), S.M.Pollock (61)	Harare	1999-2000
9th	79	B.M.McMillan (98*), A.A.Donald (33)	Harare	1995-96
10th	54	M.V.Boucher (55*), P.R.Adams (20)	Bloemfontein	1999-2000

Record Wicket Partnerships - Zimbabwe

1st	152	A.D.R.Campbell (77), D.D.Ebrahim (71)	Bulawayo[2]	2001-02
2nd	51	M.H.Dekker (24), A.D.R.Campbell (28)	Harare	1995-96
3rd	98	D.D.Ebrahim (72), H.Masakadza (46)	Cape Town	2004-05
4th	186	H.Masakadza (85), A.Flower (199*)	Harare	2001-02
5th	97	A.Flower (63), G.J.Whittall (38)	Harare	1995-96
6th	17	A.Flower (123), G.J.Whittall (19)	Harare	2001-02
7th	58	E.Chigumbra (44), H.H.Streak (16)	Centurion	2004-05
8th	76	H.H.Streak (85), A.M.Blignaut (52)	Centurion	2004-05
9th	75	A.Flower (142), T.J.Friend (30)	Harare	2001-02
10th	47	A.Flower (199*), D.T.Hondo (6)	Harare	2001-02

Best Bowling in an Innings

South Africa in South Africa	6/39	M.Zondeki	Centurion	2004-05
South Africa in Zimbabwe	8/71	A.A.Donald	Harare	1995-96
Zimbabwe in South Africa	4/93	H.K.Olonga	Bloemfontein	1999-2000
Zimbabwe in Zimbabwe	5/101	B.C.Strang	Harare	1995-96

Best Bowling in a Match

South Africa in South Africa	9/105	M.Zondeki	Centurion	2004-05
South Africa in Zimbabwe	11/113	A.A.Donald	Harare	1995-96
Zimbabwe in South Africa	4/93	H.K.Olonga	Bloemfontein	1999-2000
Zimbabwe in Zimbabwe	5/105	A.C.I.Lock	Harare	1995-96

Most Wickets in a Series

South Africa in South Africa	14 (av 11.14)	S.M.Pollock	1999-2000
South Africa in Zimbabwe	11 (av 10.27)	A.A.Donald	1995-96
	11 (av 32.09)	C.W.Henderson	2001-02
Zimbabwe in South Africa	6 (av 32.00)	A.G.Cremer	2004-05
Zimbabwe in Zimbabwe	6 (av 46.33)	T.J.Friend	2001-02

SOUTH AFRICA v BANGLADESH	South Africa		Bangladesh		Captains	
Venue and Result	1st	2nd	1st	2nd	South Africa	Bangladesh
2002-03 in South Africa						
East London-South Africa inn & 107 runs	•4d-529	-	170	252	S.M.Pollock	Khaled Mashud
Potchefstroom-South Africa inn & 160 runs	5d-482	-	•215	107		
2002-03 in Bangladesh						
Chittagong[1]-South Africa inn & 60 runs	2d-470	-	•173	237	G.C.Smith	Khaled Mahmud
Dhaka-South Africa inn & 18 runs	•330	-	102	210		

Test Match Results Summary

SOUTH AFRICA v BANGLADESH - in South Africa

		Result			East London			Potchefstroom		
	Tests	SA	B	D	SA	B	D	SA	B	D
2002-03	2	2	-	-	1	-	-	1	-	-

SOUTH AFRICA v BANGLADESH - in Bangladesh

		Result			Chittagong[1]			Dhaka		
	Tests	SA	B	D	SA	B	D	SA	B	D
2002-03	2	2	-	-	1	-	-	1	-	-
Totals	4	4	-	-						

Highest Innings Totals				
South Africa in South Africa		4d-529	East London	2002-03
South Africa in Bangladesh		2d-470	Chittagong[1]	2002-03
Bangladesh in South Africa		252	East London	2002-03
Bangladesh in Bangladesh		237	Chittagong[1]	2002-03
Lowest Innings Totals				
South Africa in South Africa		no instance		
South Africa in Bangladesh		330	Dhaka	2002-03
Bangladesh in South Africa		107	Potchefstroom	2002-03
Bangladesh in Bangladesh		102	Dhaka	2002-03
Highest Match Aggregate		951 for 24 wickets	East London	2002-03
Lowest Match Aggregate		804 for 25 wickets	Potchefstroom	2002-03
Highest Individual Innings				
South Africa in South Africa	200	G.C.Smith	East London	2002-03
South Africa in Bangladesh	222*	J.A.Rudolph	Chittagong[1]	2002-03
Bangladesh in South Africa	71	Al Sahriar	East London	2002-03
Bangladesh in Bangladesh	75	Habibul Bashar	Chittagong[1]	2002-03
Most Runs in a Series				
South Africa in South Africa		310 (av 155.00)	G.Kirsten	2002-03
South Africa in Bangladesh		293 (293.00)	J.A.Rudolph	2002-03
Bangladesh in South Africa		146 (av 36.50)	Al Sahriar	2002-03
Bangladesh in Bangladesh		182 (av 45.50)	Habibul Bashar	2002-03

Record Wicket Partnerships - South Africa

1st	87	G.C.Smith (200), H.H.Gibbs (87)	East London	2002-03
2nd	272	G.C.Smith (200), G.Kirsten (150)	East London	2002-03
3rd	429*	J.A.Rudolph (222*), H.H.Dipenaar (178*)	Chittagong[1]	2002-03
4th	12	J.A.Rudolph (71), N.D.McKenzie (7)	East London	2002-03
5th	107	J.A.Rudolph (71), M.V.Boucher (71)	East London	2002-03
6th	49	M.V.Boucher (71), S.M.Pollock (41)	Potchefstroom	2002-03
7th	45	S.M.Pollock (41), R.J.Petersen (61)	Dhaka	2002-03
8th	30	R.J.Petersen (61), A.C.Dawson (10)	Dhaka	2002-03
9th	26	R.J.Petersen (61), P.R.Adams (9)	Dhaka	2002-03
10th	0	P.R.Adams (9), M.Ntini (0*)	Dhaka	2002-03

Record Wicket Partnerships - Bangladesh

1st	52	Hannan Sarkar (65), Al Sahariar (30)	Potchefstroom	2002-03
2nd	131	Javed Omar (71), Habibul Bashar (75)	Chittagong[1]	2002-03
3rd	66	Habibul Bashar (38), Sanwar Hossain (31)	East London	2002-03
4th	37	Sanwar Hossain (49), Khaled Mashud (33)	East London	2002-03
5th	22	Khaled Mashud (20), Rafiqul Islam (6)	Potchefstroom	2002-03
6th	35	Khaled Mashud (33), Alok Kapali (10)	East London	2002-03
7th	24	Alok Kapali (23), Mohammad Salim (26)	Dhaka	2002-03
8th	19	Mohammad Rafique (19), Tapash Baisya (10)	East London	2002-03
9th	16	Mohammad Salim (26), Tapash Baisya (8*)	Dhaka	2002-03
10th	26	Mohammad Salim (16*), Mashrafe Mortaza (20)	Chittagong[1]	2002-03

Best Bowling in an Innings

South Africa in South Africa	5/19	M.Ntini	East London	2002-03
South Africa in Bangladesh	5/37	P.R.Adams	Chittagong[1]	2002-03
Bangladesh in South Africa	2/108	Talha Jubair	East London	2002-03
Bangladesh in Bangladesh	6/77	Mohammad Rafique	Dhaka	2002-03

Best Bowling in a Match

South Africa in South Africa	7/47	J.H.Kallis	Potchefstroom	2002-03
South Africa in Bangladesh	10/106	P.R.Adams	Chittagong[1]	2002-03
Bangladesh in South Africa	2/108	Talha Jubair	East London	2002-03
Bangladesh in Bangladesh	6/77	Mohammad Rafique	Dhaka	2002-03

Most Wickets in a Series

South Africa in South Africa	12 (av 15.00)	M.Ntini	2002-03
South Africa in Bangladesh	12 (av 14.91)	P.R.Adams	2002-03
Bangladesh in South Africa	4 (av 54.25)	Talha Jubair	2002-03
Bangladesh in Bangladesh	6 (av 12.83)	Mohammad Rafique	2002-03

WEST INDIES v NEW ZEALAND	West Indies		New Zealand		Captains	
Venue and Result	1st	2nd	1st	2nd	West Indies	New Zealand
1951-52 in New Zealand						
Christchurch-West Indies 5 wkts	287	5-142	•236	189	J.D.C.Goddard	B.Sutcliffe
Auckland-Drawn	•6d-546	-	160	1-17		
1955-56 in New Zealand						
Dunedin-West Indies inn & 71 runs	353	-	•74	208	D.S.Atkinson	H.B.Cave
Christchurch-West Indies inn & 64 runs	•386	-	158	164		J.R.Reid
Wellington-West Indies 9 wkts	•404	1-13	208	208		J.R.Reid
Auckland-New Zealand 190 runs	145	77	•255	9d-157		J.R.Reid
1968-69 in New Zealand						
Auckland-West Indies 5 wkts	276	5-348	•323	8d-297	G.S.Sobers	G.T.Dowling
Wellington-New Zealand 6 wkts	•297	148	282	4-166		
Christchurch-Drawn	•417	-	217	6-367		
1971-72 in West Indies						
Kingston-Drawn	•4d-508	3d-218	386	6-236	G.S.Sobers	G.T.Dowling
Port-of-Spain-Drawn	341	5-121	•348	3d-288		G.T.Dowling
Bridgetown-Drawn	•133	8-564	422	-		B.E.Congdon
Georgetown-Drawn	•7d-365	0-86	3d-543	-		B.E.Congdon
Port-of-Spain-Drawn	•368	194	162	7-253		B.E.Congdon
1979-80 in New Zealand						
Dunedin-New Zealand 1 wkt	•140	212	249	9-104	C.H.Lloyd	G.P.Howarth
Christchurch-Drawn	•228	5d-447	460	-		
Auckland-Drawn	•220	9d-264	305	4-73		
1984-85 in West Indies						
Port-of-Spain-Drawn	•307	8d-261	262	6-187	I.V.A.Richards	G.P.Howarth
Georgetown-Drawn	•6d-511	6d-268	440	-		
Bridgetown-West Indies 10 wkts	336	0-10	•94	248		
Kingston-West Indies 10 wkts	•363	0-59	138	283		
1986-87 in New Zealand						
Wellington-Drawn	345	2-50	•228	5d-386	I.V.A.Richards	J.V.Coney
Auckland-West Indies 10 wkts	•9d-419	0-16	157	273		
Christchurch-New Zealand 5 wkts	•100	264	9d-332	5-33		
1994-95 in New Zealand						
Christchurch-Drawn	312	-	•8d-341	2-61	C.A.Walsh	K.R.Rutherford
Wellington-West Indies inn & 322 runs	•5d-660	-	216	122		
1995-96 in West Indies						
Bridgetown-West Indies 10 wkts	472	0-29	•195	305	C.A.Walsh	L.K.Germon
St John's-Drawn	•7d-548	184	437	5-130		
1999-2000 in New Zealand						
Hamilton-New Zealand 9 wkts	•365	97	393	1-70	B.C.Lara	S.P.Fleming
Wellington-New Zealand inn & 105 runs	179	234	•9d-518	-		
2001-02 in West Indies						
Bridgetown-New Zealand 204 runs	107	269	•337	243	C.L.Hooper	S.P.Fleming
St George's-Drawn	470	-	•373	5-256		

WEST INDIES v NEW ZEALAND (cont.)	West Indies		New Zealand		Captains	
Venue and Result	1st	2nd	1st	2nd	West Indies	New Zealand
2005-06 in New Zealand						
Auckland-New Zealand 27 runs	257	263	•275	272	S.Chanderpaul	S.P.Fleming
Wellington-New Zealand 10 wkts	372	0-36	•192	215		
Napier-Drawn	-	-	•4-256	-		

Test Match Results Summary

WEST INDIES v NEW ZEALAND - in West Indies

		Result			Kingston			Port-of-Spain			Bridgetown			Georgetown			St John's			St George's		
	Tests	WI	NZ	D	WI	NZ	D	WI	NZ	D	WI	NZ	D	WI	NZ	D	WI	NZ	D	WI	NZ	D
1971-72	5	-	-	5	-	-	1	-	-	2	-	-	1	-	-	1	-	-	-	-	-	-
1984-85	4	2	-	2	1	-	-	-	-	1	1	-	-	-	-	1	-	-	-	-	-	-
1995-96	2	1	-	1	-	-	-	-	-	-	1	-	-	-	-	-	-	-	1	-	-	-
2001-02	2	-	1	1	-	-	-	-	-	-	-	1	-	-	-	-	-	-	-	-	-	1
	13	3	1	9	1	-	1	-	-	3	2	1	1	-	-	2	-	-	1	-	-	1

WEST INDIES v NEW ZEALAND - in New Zealand

		Result			Christchurch			Auckland			Dunedin			Wellington			Hamilton			Napier		
	Tests	WI	NZ	D	WI	NZ	D	WI	NZ	D	WI	NZ	D	WI	NZ	D	WI	NZ	D	WI	NZ	D
1951-52	2	1	-	1	1	-	-	-	-	1	-	-	-	-	-	-	-	-	-	-	-	-
1955-56	4	3	1	-	1	-	-	-	1	-	1	-	-	1	-	-	-	-	-	-	-	-
1968-69	3	1	1	1	-	-	1	1	-	-	-	-	-	-	1	-	-	-	-	-	-	-
1979-80	3	-	1	2	-	-	1	-	-	1	-	1	-	-	-	-	-	-	-	-	-	-
1986-87	3	1	1	1	-	1	-	1	-	-	-	-	-	-	-	1	-	-	-	-	-	-
1994-95	2	1	-	1	-	-	1	-	-	-	-	-	-	1	-	-	-	-	-	-	-	-
1999-2000	2	-	2	-	-	-	-	-	-	-	-	-	-	-	1	-	-	1	-	-	-	-
2005-06	3	-	2	1	-	-	-	-	1	-	-	-	-	-	1	-	-	-	-	-	-	1
	22	7	8	7	2	1	3	2	2	2	1	1	-	2	3	1	-	1	-	-	-	1
Totals	35	10	9	16																		

Highest Innings Totals			
West Indies in West Indies	8-564	Bridgetown	1971-72
West Indies in New Zealand	5d-660	Wellington	1994-95
New Zealand in West Indies	3d-543	Georgetown	1971-72
New Zealand in New Zealand	9d-518	Wellington	1999-2000
Lowest Innings Totals			
West Indies in West Indies	107	Bridgetown	2001-02
West Indies in New Zealand	77	Auckland	1955-56
New Zealand in West Indies	94	Bridgetown	1984-85
New Zealand in New Zealand	74	Dunedin	1955-56
Highest Match Aggregate	1348 for 23 wickets	Kingston	1971-72
Lowest Match Aggregate	634 for 39 wickets	Auckland	1955-56

Highest Individual Innings				
West Indies in West Indies	214	L.G.Rowe	Kingston	1971-72
West Indies in New Zealand	258	S.M.Nurse	Christchurch	1968-69
New Zealand in West Indies	259	G.M.Turner	Georgetown	1971-72
New Zealand in New Zealand	214	M.S.Sinclair	Hamilton	1999-2000

Most Runs in a Series

West Indies in West Indies	487 (av 54.11)	R.C.Fredericks	1971-72
West Indies in New Zealand	558 (av 111.60)	S.M.Nurse	1968-69
New Zealand in West Indies	672 (av 98.00)	G.M.Turner	1971-72
New Zealand in New Zealand	328 (av 65.60)	M.D.Crowe	1986-87

Record Wicket Partnerships - West Indies

1st	276	A.F.G.Griffith (114), S.L.Campbell (170)	Hamilton	1999-2000
2nd	269	R.C.Fredericks (163), L.G.Rowe (214)	Kingston	1971-72
3rd	221	B.C.Lara (147), J.C.Adams (151)	Wellington	1994-95
4th	162	E.D.Weekes (123), O.G.Smith (64)	Dunedin	1955-56
	162	C.G.Greenidge (91), A.I.Kallicharran (75)	Christchurch	1979-80
5th	189	F.M.M.Worrell (100), C.L.Walcott (115)	Auckland	1951-52
6th	254	C.A.Davis (183), G.S.Sobers (142)	Bridgetown	1971-72
7th	143	D.S Atkinson (85), J.D.C.Goddard (83*)	Christchurch	1955-56
8th	83	I.V.A.Richards (105), M.D.Marshall (63)	Bridgetown	1984-85
9th	70	M.D.Marshall (63), J.Garner (37*)	Bridgetown	1984-85
10th	31	T.M.Findlay (44*), G.C.Shillingford (15)	Bridgetown	1971-72

Record Wicket Partnerships - New Zealand

1st	387	G.M.Turner (259), T.W.Jarvis (182)	Georgetown	1971-72
2nd	210	G.P.Howarth (84), J.J.Crowe (112)	Kingston	1984-85
3rd	241	J.G.Wright (138), M.D.Crowe (119)	Wellington	1986-87
4th	189	M.S.Sinclair (214), N.J.Astle (93)	Wellington	1999-2000
5th	144	N.J.Astle (125), J.T.C.Vaughan (24)	Bridgetown	1995-96
6th	220	G.M.Turner (223*), K.J.Wadsworth (78)	Kingston	1971-72
7th	143	M.D.Crowe (188), I.D.S.Smith (53)	Georgetown	1984-85
8th	136	B.E.Congdon (166*), R.S.Cunis (51)	Port-of-Spain	1971-72
9th	62*	V.Pollard (51*), R.S.Cunis (20*)	Auckland	1968-69
	62	B.B.McCullum (74), S.E.Bond (18*)	Auckland	2005-06
10th	45	D.K.Morrison (26*), R.J.Kennedy (22)	Bridgetown	1995-96

Best Bowling in an Innings

West Indies in West Indies	7/80	M.D.Marshall	Bridgetown	1984-85
West Indies in New Zealand	7/37	C.A.Walsh	Wellington	1994-95
New Zealand in West Indies	7/74	B.R.Taylor	Bridgetown	1971-72
New Zealand in New Zealand	7/27	C.L.Cairns	Hamilton	1999-2000

Best Bowling in a Match

West Indies in West Indies	11/120	M.D.Marshall	Bridgetown	1984-85
West Indies in New Zealand	13/55	C.A.Walsh	Wellington	1994-95
New Zealand in West Indies	10/124	E.J.Chatfield	Port-of-Spain	1984-85
New Zealand in New Zealand	11/102	R.J Hadlee	Dunedin	1979-80

Most Wickets in a Series

West Indies in West Indies	27 (av 18.00)	M.D.Marshall	1984-85
West Indies in New Zealand	20 (av 15.80)	S.Ramadhin	1955-56
New Zealand in West Indies	27 (av 17.70)	B.R.Taylor	1971-72
New Zealand in New Zealand	19 (av 19.00)	R.J Hadlee	1979-80

WEST INDIES v INDIA	West Indies		India		Captains	
Venue and Result	1st	2nd	1st	2nd	West Indies	India
1948-49 in India						
Delhi-Drawn	•631	-	454	6-220	J.D.C.Goddard	N.B.Amarnath
Bombay[2]-Drawn	•6d-629	-	273	3-333		
Calcutta-Drawn	•366	9d-336	272	3-325		
Madras[1]-West Indies inn & 193 runs	•582	-	245	144		
Bombay[2]-Drawn	•286	267	193	8-355		
1952-53 in West Indies						
Port-of-Spain-Drawn	438	0-142	•417	294	J.B.Stollmeyer	V.S.Hazare
Bridgetown-West Indies 142 runs	•296	228	253	129		
Port-of-Spain-Drawn	315	2-192	•279	7d-362		
Georgetown-Drawn	364	-	•262	5-190		
Kingston-Drawn	576	4-92	•312	444		
1958-59 in India						
Bombay[2]-Drawn	•227	4d-323	152	5-289	F.C.M.Alexander	P.R.Umrigar
Kanpur-West Indies 203 runs	•222	7d-443	222	240		Ghulam Ahmed
Calcutta-West Indies inn & 336 runs	•5d-614	-	124	154		Ghulam Ahmed
Madras[2]-West Indies 295 runs	•500	5d-168	222	151		M.H.Mankad
Delhi-Drawn	8d-644	-	•415	275		H.R.Adhikari
1961-62 in West Indies						
Port-of-Spain-West Indies 10 wkts	289	0-15	•203	98	F.M.M.Worrell	N.J.Contractor
Kingston-West Indies inn & 18 runs	8d-631	-	•395	218		N.J.Contractor
Bridgetown-West Indies inn & 30 runs	475	-	•258	187	-	Nawab of Pataudi, jr
Port-of-Spain-West Indies 7 wkts	•9d-444	3-176	197	422		Nawab of Pataudi, jr
Kingston-West Indies 123 runs	•253	283	178	235		Nawab of Pataudi, jr
1966-67 in India						
Bombay[2]-West Indies 6 wkts	421	4-192	•296	316	G.S.Sobers	Nawab of Pataudi, jr
Calcutta-West Indies inn & 45 runs	•390	-	167	178		
Madras[1]-Drawn	406	7-270	•404	323		
1970-71 in West Indies						
Kingston-Drawn	217	5-385	•387	-	G.S.Sobers	A.L.Wadekar
Port-of-Spain-India 7 wkts	•214	261	352	3-125		
Georgetown-Drawn	•363	3d-307	376	0-123		
Bridgetown-Drawn	•5d-501	6d-180	347	5-221		
Port-of-Spain-Drawn	526	8-165	•360	427		
1974-75 in India						
Bangalore-West Indies 267 runs	•289	6d-356	260	118	C.H.Lloyd	Nawab of Pataudi, jr
Delhi-West Indies inn & 17 runs	493	-	•220	256		S.Venkataraghavan
Calcutta-India 85 runs	240	224	•233	316		Nawab of Pataudi, jr
Madras[1]-India 100 runs	192	154	•190	256		Nawab of Pataudi, jr
Bombay[3]-West Indies 201 runs	•6d-604	3d-205	406	202		Nawab of Pataudi, jr
1975-76 in West Indies						
Bridgetown-West Indies inn & 97 runs	9d-488	-	•177	214	C.H.Lloyd	B.S.Bedi
Port-of-Spain-Drawn	•241	8-215	5d-402	-		
Port-of-Spain-India 6 wkts	•359	6d-271	228	4-406		
Kingston-West Indies 10 wkts	391	0-13	•6d-306	97		

WEST INDIES v INDIA (cont.)	West Indies		India		Captains	
Venue and Result	1st	2nd	1st	2nd	West Indies	India
1978-79 in India						
Bombay[3]-Drawn	493	-	•424	2-224	A.I.Kallicharran	S.M.Gavaskar
Bangalore-Drawn	•437	8-200	371	-		
Calcutta-Drawn	327	9-197	•300	1d-361		
Madras[1]-India 3 wkts	•228	151	255	7-125		
Delhi-Drawn	172	3-179	•8d-566	-		
Kanpur-Drawn	8-452	-	•7d-644	-		
1982-83 in West Indies						
Kingston-West Indies 4 wkts	254	6-173	•251	174	C.H.Lloyd	Kapil Dev
Port-of-Spain-Drawn	394	-	•175	7-469		
Georgetown-Drawn	•470	-	3-284	-		
Bridgetown-West Indies 10 wkts	486	0-1	•209	277		
St John's-Drawn	550	-	•457	5d-247		
1983-84 in India						
Kanpur-West Indies inn & 83 runs	•454	-	207	164	C.H.Lloyd	Kapil Dev
Delhi-Drawn	384	2-120	•464	233		
Ahmedabad-West Indies 138 runs	•281	201	241	103		
Bombay[3]-Drawn	393	4-104	•463	5d-173		
Calcutta-West Indies inn & 46 runs	377	-	•241	90		
Madras[1]-Drawn	•313	1-64	8d-451	-		
1987-88 in India						
Delhi-West Indies 5 wkts	127	5-276	•75	327	I.V.A.Richards	D.B.Vengsarkar
Bombay[3]-Drawn	337	1-4	•281	173		D.B.Vengsarkar
Calcutta-Drawn	•5d-530	2-157	565	-		D.B.Vengsarkar
Madras[1]-India 255 runs	184	160	•382	8d-217		R.J.Shastri
1988-89 in West Indies						
Georgetown-Drawn	•437	-	1-86	-	I.V.A.Richards	D.B.Vengsarkar
Bridgetown-West Indies 8 wkts	377	2-196	•321	251		
Port-of-Spain-West Indies 217 runs	•314	266	150	213		
Kingston-West Indies 7 wkts	384	3-60	•289	152		
1994-95 in India						
Bombay[3]-India 96 runs	243	266	•272	333	C.A.Walsh	M.Azharuddin
Nagpur-Drawn	428	5-132	•9d-546	7d-208		
Mohali-West Indies 243 runs	•443	3d-301	387	114		
1996-97 in West Indies						
Kingston-Drawn	•427	4d-241	349	2-99	C.A.Walsh	S.R.Tendulkar
Port-of-Spain-Drawn	296	6-299	436	-	C.A.Walsh	
Bridgetown-West Indies 38 runs	•298	140	319	81	B.C.Lara	
St John's-Drawn	•333	-	2-212	-	C.A.Walsh	
Georgetown-Drawn	3-145	-	•355	-	C.A.Walsh	
2001-02 in West Indies						
Georgetown-Drawn	•501	-	7-395	-	C.L.Hooper	S.C.Ganguly
Port-of-Spain-India 37 runs	245	275	•339	218		
Bridgetown-West Indies 10 wkts	394	0-5	•102	296		
St John's-Drawn	9d-629	-	•9d-513	-		
Kingston-West Indies 155 runs	•422	197	212	252		

WEST INDIES v INDIA (cont.)	West Indies		India		Captains	
Venue and Result	1st	2nd	1st	2nd	West Indies	India
2002-03 in India						
Bombay[3]-India inn & 112 runs	157	188	•9-457	-	C.L.Hooper	S.C.Ganguly
Chennai[1]-India 8 wkts	•167	229	316	2-81		
Kolkata-Drawn	497	-	•358	8-471		
2005-06 in West Indies						
St John's-Drawn	371	9-298	•241	6d-521	B.C.Lara	R.S.Dravid
Gros Islet-Drawn	215	7-294	•8d-588	-		
Basseterre-Drawn	•581	6d-172	362	4-298		
Kingston-India 49 runs	103	219	•200	171		

Test Match Results Summary

WEST INDIES v INDIA - in West Indies

		Result			P-O-Spain			Bridgetown			G'town			Kingston			St John's			Gros Islet			Basseterre		
	Tests	WI	I	D	WI	I	D	WI	I	D	WI	I	D	WI	I	D	WI	I	D	-	-	-	-	-	-
1952-53	5	1	-	4	-	-	2	1	-	-	-	-	1	-	-	1	-	-	-	-	-	-	-	-	-
1961-62	5	5	-	-	2	-	-	1	-	-	-	-	-	2	-	-	-	-	-	-	-	-	-	-	-
1970-71	5	-	1	4	-	1	1	-	-	1	-	-	1	-	-	1	-	-	-	-	-	-	-	-	-
1975-76	4	2	1	1	-	1	1	1	-	-	-	-	-	1	-	-	-	-	-	-	-	-	-	-	-
1982-83	5	2	-	3	-	-	1	1	-	-	-	-	1	1	-	-	-	-	1	-	-	-	-	-	-
1988-89	4	3	-	1	1	-	-	1	-	-	-	-	1	1	-	-	-	-	-	-	-	-	-	-	-
1996-97	5	1	-	4	-	-	1	1	-	-	-	-	1	-	-	1	-	-	1	-	-	-	-	-	-
2001-02	5	2	1	2	-	1	-	1	-	-	-	-	1	1	-	-	-	-	1	-	-	-	-	-	-
2005-06	4	-	1	3	-	-	-	-	-	-	-	-	-	-	1	-	-	-	1	-	-	1	-	-	1
	42	16	4	22	3	3	6	7	-	1	-	-	6	6	1	3	-	-	4	-	-	1	-	-	1

WEST INDIES v INDIA - in India

		Result			Delhi			Mumbai			Calcutta			Chennai			Kanpur			Bang.			Ahmed.			Nagpur			Mohali		
	Tests	WI	I	D	WI	I	D	WI	I	D	WI	I	D	WI	I	D	WI	I	D	WI	I	D	WI	I	D	WI	I	D	WI	I	D
1948-49	5	1	-	4	-	-	1	-	-	2	-	-	1	1	-	-	-	-	-	-	-	-	-	-	-	-	-	-	-	-	-
1958-59	5	3	-	2	-	-	1	-	-	1	1	-	-	1	-	-	1	-	-	-	-	-	-	-	-	-	-	-	-	-	-
1966-67	3	2	-	1	-	-	-	1	-	-	1	-	-	-	-	1	-	-	-	-	-	-	-	-	-	-	-	-	-	-	-
1974-75	5	3	2	-	1	-	-	1	-	-	-	1	-	-	1	-	-	-	-	1	-	-	-	-	-	-	-	-	-	-	-
1978-79	6	-	1	5	-	-	1	-	-	1	-	-	1	-	1	-	-	-	1	-	-	1	-	-	-	-	-	-	-	-	-
1983-84	6	3	-	3	-	-	1	-	-	1	1	-	-	-	-	1	1	-	-	-	-	-	1	-	-	-	-	-	-	-	-
1987-88	4	1	1	2	1	-	-	-	-	1	-	-	1	-	1	-	-	-	-	-	-	-	-	-	-	-	-	-	-	-	-
1994-95	3	1	1	1	-	-	-	-	1	-	-	-	-	-	-	-	-	-	-	-	-	-	-	-	-	-	-	1	1	-	-
2002-03	3	-	2	1	-	-	-	-	1	-	-	-	1	-	1	-	-	-	-	-	-	-	-	-	-	-	-	-	-	-	-
	40	14	7	19	2	-	4	2	1	6	3	1	4	2	4	2	2	-	1	1	-	1	1	-	-	-	-	1	1	-	-
Totals	82	30	11	41																											

Key to ground abbreviation: P-O-Spain - Port-of-Spain; G'town - Georgetown; Bang. - Bangalore; Ahmed. - Ahmedabad.

Highest Innings Totals

West Indies in West Indies	8d-631	Kingston	1961-62
West Indies in India	8d-644	Delhi	1958-59
India in West Indies	8d-588	Gros Islet	2005-06
India in India	7d-644	Kanpur	1978-79

Lowest Innings Totals

West Indies in West Indies	103	Kingston	2005-06
West Indies in India	127	Delhi	1987-88
India in West Indies	81	Bridgetown	1996-97
India in India	75	Delhi	1987-88

Highest Match Aggregate	1478 for 38 wickets	Port-of-Spain	1970-71
Lowest Match Aggregate	605 for 30 wickets	Port-of-Spain	1961-62

Highest Individual Innings

West Indies in West Indies	237	F.M.M.Worrell	Kingston	1952-53
West Indies in India	256	R.B.Kanhai	Calcutta	1958-59
India in West Indies	220	S.M.Gavaskar	Port-of-Spain	1970-71
India in India	236*	S.M.Gavaskar	Madras[1]	1983-84

Most Runs in a Series

West Indies in West Indies	716 (av 102.28)	E.D.Weekes	1952-53
West Indies in India	779 (av 111.28)	E.D.Weekes	1948-49
India in West Indies	774 (av 154.80)	S.M.Gavaskar	1970-71
India in India	732 (av 91.50)	S.M.Gavaskar	1978-79

Record Wicket Partnerships - West Indies

1st	296	C.G.Greenidge (154*), D.L.Haynes (136)	St John's	1982-83
2nd	255	E.D A.S.McMorris (125), R.B.Kanhai (158)	Kingston	1961-62
3rd	220	I V.A Richards (142), A.I.Kallicharran (93)	Bridgetown	1975-76
4th	267	C.L.Walcott (152), G.E.Gomez (101)	Delhi	1948-49
5th	293	C.L.Hooper (233), S.Chanderpaul (140)	Georgetown	2001-02
6th	250	C.H.Lloyd (242), D.L.Murray (91)	Bombay[3]	1974-75
7th	130	C.G.Greenidge (194), M.D.Marshall (92)	Kanpur	1983-84
8th	124	I.V.A Richards (192), K.D.Boyce (68)	Delhi	1974-75
9th	161	C.H.Lloyd (161*), A.M.E.Roberts (68)	Calcutta	1983-84
10th	98*	F.M.M.Worrell (73*), W.W.Hall (50*)	Port-of-Spain	1961-62

Record Wicket Partnerships - India

1st	201	S.B.Bangar (55), V.K.Sehwag (147)	Bombay[3]	2002-03
2nd	344*	S.M.Gavaskar (182*), D.B.Vengsarkar (157*)	Calcutta	1978-79
3rd	203	Wasim Jaffer (212), R.S.Dravid (62)	St John's	2005-06
4th	172	G.R.Viswanath (179), A.D.Gaekwad (102)	Kanpur	1978-79
5th	214	S.R.Tendulkar (176), V.V.S.Laxman (154*)	Kolkata	2002-03
6th	170	S.M.Gavaskar (236*), R.J.Shastri (72)	Madras[1]	1983-84
7th	217	V.V.S.Laxman (130), A.Ratra (115*)	St John's	2001-02
8th	120*	R.S.Dravid (144*), Saranddep Singh (39*)	Georgetown	2001-02
9th	143*	S.M.Gavaskar (236*), S.M.H.Kirmani (63*)	Madras[1]	1983-84
10th	64	J.Srinath (52*), S.L.Venkatapathy Raju (15)	Mohali	1994-95

Best Bowling in an Innings

West Indies in West Indies	9/95	J.M.Noreiga	Port-of-Spain	1970-71
West Indies in India	7/64	A.M.E.Roberts	Madras[1]	1974-75
India in West Indies	7/162	S.P.Gupte	Port-of-Spain	1952-53
India in India	9/83	Kapil Dev	Ahmedabad	1983-84

Best Bowling in a Match

West Indies in West Indies	11/89	M.D.Marshall	Port-of-Spain	1988-89
West Indies in India	12/121	A.M.E.Roberts	Madras[1]	1974-75
India in West Indies	8/118	Kapil Dev	Kingston	1982-83
India in India	16/136	N.D.Hirwani	Madras[1]	1987-88

Most Wickets in a Series

West Indies in West Indies	28 (av 29.57)	A.L.Valentine	1952-53
West Indies in India	33 (av 18.81)	M.D.Marshall	1983-84
India in West Indies	27 (av 29.22)	S.P.Gupte	1952-53
India in India	29 (av 18.51)	Kapil Dev	1983-84

WEST INDIES v PAKISTAN	West Indies		Pakistan		Captains	
Venue and Result	1st	2nd	1st	2nd	West Indies	Pakistan
1957-58 in West Indies						
Bridgetown-Drawn	•9d-579	0-28	106	8d-657	F.C.M.Alexander	A.H.Kardar
Port-of-Spain-West Indies 120 runs	•325	312	282	235		
Kingston-West Indies inn & 174 runs	3d-790	-	•328	288		
Georgetown-West Indies 8 wkts	410	2-317	•408	318		
Port-of-Spain-Pakistan inn & 1 run	•268	227	496	-		
1958-59 in Pakistan						
Karachi[1]-Pakistan 10 wkts	•146	245	304	0-88	F.C.M.Alexander	Fazal Mahmood
Dacca-Pakistan 41 runs	76	172	•145	144		
Lahore[1]-West Indies inn & 156 runs	•469	-	209	104		
1974-75 in Pakistan						
Lahore[2]-Drawn	214	4-258	•199	7d-373	C.H.Lloyd	Intikhab Alam
Karachi[1]-Drawn	493	0-1	•8d-406	256		
1976-77 in West Indies						
Bridgetown-Drawn	421	9-251	•435	291	C.H.Lloyd	Mushtaq Mohammad
Port-of-Spain-West Indies 6 wkts	316	4-206	•180	340		
Georgetown-Drawn	448	1-154	•194	540		
Port-of-Spain-Pakistan 266 runs	154	222	•341	9d-301		
Kingston-West Indies 140 runs	•280	359	198	301		
1980-81 in Pakistan						
Lahore[2]-Drawn	297	-	•369	7-156	C.H.Lloyd	Javed Miandad
Faisalabad-West Indies 156 runs	•235	242	176	145		
Karachi[1]-Drawn	169	-	•128	9-204		
Multan-Drawn	•249	5-116	166	-		
1986-87 in Pakistan						
Faisalabad-Pakistan 186 runs	248	53	•159	328	I.V.A.Richards	Imran Khan
Lahore[2]-West Indies inn & 10 runs	218	-	•131	77		
Karachi[1]-Drawn	•240	211	239	7-125		
1987-88 in West Indies						
Georgetown-Pakistan 9 wkts	•292	172	435	1-32	C.G.Greenidge	Imran Khan
Port-of-Spain-Drawn	•174	391	194	9-341	I.V.A.Richards	
Bridgetown-West Indies 2 wkts	306	8-268	•309	262	I.V.A.Richards	
1990-91 in Pakistan						
Karachi[1]-Pakistan 8 wkts	•216	181	345	2-98	D.L.Haynes	Imran Khan
Faisalabad-West Indies 7 wkts	195	3-130	•170	154		
Lahore[2]-Drawn	•294	173	122	6-242		
1992-93 in West Indies						
Port-of-Spain-West Indies 204 runs	•127	382	140	165	R.B.Richardson	Wasim Akram
Bridgetown-West Indies 10 wkts	•455	0-29	221	262		
St John's-Drawn	•438	4-153	326			

WEST INDIES v PAKISTAN (cont.) Venue and Result	West Indies 1st	West Indies 2nd	Pakistan 1st	Pakistan 2nd	Captains West Indies	Captains Pakistan
1997-98 in Pakistan						
Peshawar[2]-Pakistan inn & 19 runs	•151	211	381	-	C.A.Walsh	Wasim Akram
Rawalpindi[2]-Pakistan inn & 29 runs	•303	139	471	-		
Karachi[1]-Pakistan 10 wkts	•216	212	417	0-15		
1999-2000 in West Indies						
Georgetown-Drawn	7-222	-	•288	-	J.C.Adams	Moin Khan
Bridgetown-Drawn	398	4-132	•253	9d-419		
St John's-West Indies 1 wkt	273	9-216	•269	219		
2001-02 in United Arab Emirates						
Sharjah-Pakistan 170 runs	366	171	•493	6d-214	C.L.Hooper	Waqar Younis
Sharjah-Pakistan 244 runs	264	189	•472	225		
2004-05 in West Indies						
Bridgetown-West Indies 276 runs	•345	371	144	296	S.Chanderpaul	Younis Khan
Kingston-Pakistan 136 runs	404	143	•374	309		Inzamamul Haq

Test Match Results Summary

WEST INDIES v PAKISTAN - in West Indies

		Result			Bridgetown			Port-of-Spain			Kingston			Georgetown			St John's		
	Tests	WI	P	D	WI	P	D	WI	P	D	WI	P	D	WI	P	D	WI	P	D
1957-58	5	3	1	1	-	-	1	1	1	-	1	-	-	1	-	-	-	-	-
1976-77	5	2	1	2	-	-	1	1	1	-	1	-	-	-	-	1	-	-	-
1987-88	3	1	1	1	1	-	-	-	-	1	-	-	-	-	1	-	-	-	-
1992-93	3	2	-	1	1	-	-	1	-	-	-	-	-	-	-	-	-	-	1
1999-2000	3	1	-	2	-	-	1	-	-	-	-	-	-	-	-	1	1	-	-
2004-05	2	1	1	-	1	-	-	-	-	-	-	1	-	-	-	-	-	-	-
	21	10	4	7	3	-	3	3	2	1	2	1	-	1	1	2	1	-	1

WEST INDIES v PAKISTAN - in Pakistan

		Result			Karachi[1]			Dacca			Lahore			Faisalabad			Multan			Peshawar[2]			Rawalpindi[2]		
	Tests	W	P	D	W	P	D	W	P	D	W	P	D	W	P	D	W	P	D	W	P	D	W	P	D
1955-56	3	-	2	1	-	1	-	-	1	-	-	-	1	-	-	-	-	-	-	-	-	-	-	-	-
1958-59	3	1	2	-	-	1	-	-	1	-	1	-	-	-	-	-	-	-	-	-	-	-	-	-	-
1974-75	2	-	-	2	-	-	1	-	-	-	-	-	1	-	-	-	-	-	-	-	-	-	-	-	-
1980-81	4	1	-	3	-	-	1	-	-	-	-	-	1	1	-	-	-	-	1	-	-	-	-	-	-
1986-87	3	1	1	1	-	-	1	-	-	-	1	-	-	-	1	-	-	-	-	-	-	-	-	-	-
1990-91	3	1	1	1	-	1	-	-	-	-	-	-	1	1	-	-	-	-	-	-	-	-	-	-	-
1997-98	3	-	3	-	-	1	-	-	-	-	-	-	-	-	-	-	-	-	-	-	1	-	-	1	-
	18	4	7	7	-	3	3	-	1	-	2	-	3	2	1	-	-	-	1	-	1	-	-	1	-

WEST INDIES v PAKISTAN- in United Arab Emirates

		Result			Sharjah		
	Tests	WI	P	D	WI	P	D
2001-02	2	-	2	-	-	2	-
Totals	41	14	13	14			

Highest Innings Totals

West Indies in West Indies	3d-790	Kingston	1957-58
West Indies in Pakistan	493	Karachi[1]	1974-75
Pakistan in West Indies	8d-657	Bridgetown	1957-58
Pakistan in Pakistan	471	Rawalpindi[2]	1997-98

Lowest Innings Totals

West Indies in West Indies	127	Port-of-Spain	1992-93
West Indies in Pakistan	53	Faisalabad	1986-87
Pakistan in West Indies	106	Bridgetown	1957-58
Pakistan in Pakistan	77	Lahore[2]	1986-87

Highest Match Aggregate	1453 for 32 wickets	Georgetown	1957-58
Lowest Match Aggregate	426 for 29 wickets	Lahore[2]	1986-87

Highest Individual Innings

West Indies in West Indies	365	G.S.Sobers	Kingston	1957-58
West Indies in Pakistan	217	R.B.Kanhai	Lahore[1]	1958-59
Pakistan in West Indies	337	Hanif Mohammad	Bridgetown	1957-58
Pakistan in Pakistan	177	Inzamamul Haq	Rawalpindi[2]	1997-98

Most Runs in a Series

West Indies in West Indies	824 (av 137.33)	G.S.Sobers	1957-58
West Indies in Pakistan	364 (av 72.80)	I.V.A.Richards	1980-81
Pakistan in West Indies	628 (av 69.77)	Hanif Mohammad	1957-58
Pakistan in Pakistan	324 (av 108.00)	Aamer Sohail	1997-98

Record Wicket Partnerships - West Indies

1st	182	R.C.Fredericks (83), C.G.Greenidge (82)	Kingston	1976-77
2nd	446	C.C.Hunte (260), G.S.Sobers (365*)	Kingston	1957-58
3rd	169	D.L.Haynes (143*), B.C.Lara (96)	Port-of-Spain	1992-93
4th	188*	G.S Sobers (365*), C.L.Walcott (88*)	Kingston	1957-58
5th	185	E.D.Weekes (197), O.G Smith (78)	Bridgetown	1957-58
6th	151	C.H.Lloyd (157), D.L.Murray (52)	Bridgetown	1976-77
7th	74	S.Chanderpaul (46*), N.A.M.McLean (46)	Georgetown	1999-2000
8th	60	C.L.Hooper (178*) A.C.Cummins (14)	St John's	1992-93
9th	61*	P.J.L.Dujon (29*), W.K.M.Benjamin (40*)	Bridgetown	1987-88
10th	106	C.L.Hooper (178*), C.A.Walsh (30)	St John's	1992-93

Record Wicket Partnerships - Pakistan

1st	298	Aamer Sohail (160), Ijaz Ahmed (151)	Karachi[1]	1997-98
2nd	190	Shahid Afridi (107), Younis Khan (153)	Sharjah	2001-02
3rd	323	Aamer Sohail (160), Inzamamul Haq (177)	Rawalpindi[2]	1997-98
4th	174	Shoaib Mohammad (86), Saleem Malik (102)	Karachi[1]	1990-91
5th	115	Asim Kamal (55), Shahid Afridi (122)	Bridgetown	2004-05
6th	206	Inzamamul Haq (135), Abdur Razzaq (87)	Georgetown	1999-2000
7th	128	Wasim Raja (107*), Wasim Bari (58)	Karachi[1]	1974-75
8th	94	Saleem Malik (66), Saleem Yousuf (39)	Port-of-Spain	1987-88
9th	96	Inzamamul Haq (123), Nadeem Khan (25)	St John's	1992-93
10th	133	Wasim Raja (71), Wasim Bari (60*)	Bridgetown	1976-77

Best Bowling in an Innings

West Indies in West Indies	8/29	C.E.H.Croft	Port-of-Spain	1976-77
West Indies in Pakistan	5/33	M.D.Marshall	Lahore[2]	1986-87
Pakistan in West Indies	7/80	Imran Khan	Georgetown	1987-88
Pakistan in Pakistan	6/16	Abdul Qadir	Faisalabad	1986-87

Best Bowling in a Match

West Indies in West Indies	11/134	C.D.Collymore	Kingston	2004-05
West Indies in Pakistan	9/187	A.M.E.Roberts	Lahore[2]	1974-75
Pakistan in West Indies	11/110	Wasim Akram	St John's	1999-2000
Pakistan in Pakistan	12/100	Fazal Mahmood	Dacca	1959-60

Most Wickets in a Series

West Indies in West Indies	33 (av 20.48)	C E.H.Croft	1976-77
West Indies in Pakistan	17 (av 17.76)	C.E.H.Croft	1980-81
Pakistan in West Indies	25 (av 31.60)	Imran Khan	1976-77
Pakistan in Pakistan	21 (av 15.85)	Fazal Mahmood	1958-59
	21 (av 14.19)	Wasim Akram	1990-91

WEST INDIES v SRI LANKA	West Indies		Sri Lanka		Captains	
Venue and Result	1st	2nd	1st	2nd	West Indies	Sri Lanka
1993-94 in Sri Lanka						
Moratuwa-Drawn	•190	2-43	204	-	R.B.Richardson	A.Ranatunga
1996-97 in West Indies						
St John's-West Indies 6 wkts	189	4-189	•223	152	C.A.Walsh	A.Ranatunga
Arnos Vale-Drawn	•147	343	222	8-233		
2001-02 in Sri Lanka						
Galle-Sri Lanka 10 wkts	•448	144	9d-590	0-6	C.L.Hooper	S.T.Jayasuriya
Kandy-Sri Lanka 131 runs	191	190	•288	6d-224		
Colombo (SSC)-Sri Lanka 10 wkts	•390	262	9d-627	0-27		
2002-03 in West Indies						
Gros Islet-Drawn	354	0-126	•9d-477	-	B.C.Lara	H.P.Tillakaratne
Kingston-West Indies 7 wkts	191	3-212	•208	194		
2005-06 in Sri Lanka						
Colombo (SSC)-Sri Lanka 6 wkts	•285	113	227	4-175	S.Chanderpaul	M.S.Atapattu
Kandy-Sri Lanka 240 runs	148	137	•150	7d-375		

Test Match Results Summary

WEST INDIES v SRI LANKA - in West Indies

		Result			St John's			Arnos Vale			Gros Islet			Kingston		
	Tests	WI	SL	D	WI	SL	D	WI	SL	D	WI	SL	D	WI	SL	D
1996-97	2	1	-	1	1	-	-	-	-	1	-	-	-	-	-	-
2002-03	2	1	-	1	-	-	-	-	-	-	-	-	1	1	-	-
	4	2	-	2	1	-	-	-	-	1	-	-	1	1	-	-

WEST INDIES v SRI LANKA - in Sri Lanka

		Result			Moratuwa			Galle			Kandy			Colombo(SSC)		
	Tests	WI	SL	D	WI	SL	D	WI	SL	D	WI	SL	D	WI	SL	D
1993-94	1	-	-	1	-	-	1	-	-	-	-	-	-	-	-	-
2001-02	3	-	3	-	-	-	-	-	1	-	-	1	-	-	1	-
2005-06	2	-	2	-	-	-	-	-	-	-	-	1	-	-	1	-
	6	-	5	1	-	-	1	-	1	-	-	2	-	-	2	-
Totals	10	2	5	3												

Highest Innings Totals

West Indies in West Indies	9d-477	Gros Islet	2002-03
West Indies in Sri Lanka	448	Galle	2001-02
Sri Lanka in West Indies	8-233	Arnos Vale	1996-97
Sri Lanka in Sri Lanka	9d-627	Colombo (SSC)	2001-02

Lowest Innings Totals

West Indies in West Indies	147	Arnos Vale	1996-97
West Indies in Sri Lanka	113	Colombo (SSC)	2005-06
Sri Lanka in West Indies	152	St John's	1996-97
Sri Lanka in Sri Lanka	150	Kandy	2005-06

Highest Match Aggregate	1306 for 29 wickets	Colombo (SSC)	2001-02
Lowest Match Aggregate	437 for 22 wickets	Moratuwa	1993-94

Highest Individual Innings

West Indies in West Indies	209	B.C.Lara	Gros Islet	2002-03
West Indies in Sri Lanka	221	C.L.Hooper	Colombo (SSC)	2001-02
Sri Lanka in West Indies	118	M.S.Atapattu	Gros Islet	2002-03
Sri Lanka in Sri Lanka	204*	H.P.Tillakaratne	Colombo (SSC)	2001-02

Most Runs in a Series

West Indies in West Indies	299 (av 149.50)	B.C.Lara	2002-03
West Indies in Sri Lanka	688 (av 114.66)	B.C.Lara	2001-02
Sri Lanka in West Indies	211 (av 70.33)	M.S.Atapattu	2002-03
Sri Lanka in Sri Lanka	403 (av 403.00)	H.P.Tillakaratne	2001-02

Record Wicket Partnerships - West Indies

1st	160	S.L.Campbell (79), S.C.Williams (83)	St John's	1996-97
2nd	80	D.Ganga (47), R.R.Sarwan (88)	Galle	2001-02
3rd	194	R.R.Sarwan (69), B.C.Lara (221)	Colombo (SSC)	2001-02
4th	153	B.C.Lara (178), C.L.Hooper (69)	Galle	2001-02
5th	84	R.B.Richardson (51), C.L.Hooper (62)	Moratuwa	1993-94
6th	79	S.Chanderpaul (69), D.Ramdin (56)	Colombo (SSC)	2005-06
7th	136	B.C.Lara (209), O.A.C.Banks (50*)	Gros Islet	2002-03
8th	53	R.I.C..Holder (34), C.E.L.Ambrose (31)	Arnos Vale	1996-97
9th	44	S.Chanderpaul (48*), T.L.Best (27)	Colombo (SSC)	2005-06
10th	29*	O.A.C.Banks (50*), J.E.Taylor (9*)	Gros Islet	2002-03

Record Wicket Partnerships - Sri Lanka

1st	126*	M.S.Atapattu (50*), S.T.Jayasuriya (72*)	Gros Islet	2002-03
2nd	109	M.S.Atapattu (61), K.C.Sangakkara (140)	Galle	2001-02
3rd	162	K.C.Sangakkara (140), D.P.M.D.Jayawardene (99)	Galle	2001-02
4th	110	S.T.Jayasuriya (85), A.Ranatunga (42)	St John's	1996-97
5th	141	R.P.Arnold (65), H.P.Tillakaratne (204*)	Colombo (SSC)	2001-02
6th	165	H.P.Tillakaratne (204*), T.T.Samaraweera (87)	Colombo (SSC)	2001-02
7th	52	K.C.Sangakkara (75), W.P.U.J.C.Vaas (12*)	Kingston	2002-03
8th	54*	K.C.Sangakkara (157*), H.M.R.K.B.Herath (15*)	Kandy	2005-06
9th	42	H.P.Tillakaratne (204*), M.R.C.N.Bandaratilleke (25)	Colombo (SSC)	2001-02
10th	28	W.P.U.J.C.Vaas (38), R.A.P.Nissanka (12*)	Gros Islet	2002-03

Best Bowling in an Innings

West Indies in West Indies	7/57	C.D.Collymore	Kingston	2002-03
West Indies in Sri Lanka	5/25	D.B.Powell	Kandy	2005-06
Sri Lanka in West Indies	5/34	M.Muralidaran	St John's	1996-97
Sri Lanka in Sri Lanka	8/46	M.Muralidaran	Kandy	2005-06

Best Bowling in a Match

West Indies in West Indies	9/82	C.D.Collymore	Kingston	2002-03
West Indies in Sri Lanka	8/102	J.J.C.Lawson	Colombo (SSC)	2005-06
Sri Lanka in West Indies	8/106	M.Muralidaran	St John's	1996-97
Sri Lanka in Sri Lanka	14/191	W.P.U.J.C.Vaas	Colombo (SSC)	2001-02

Most Wickets in a Series

West Indies in West Indies	14 (av 11.35)	C.D.Collymore	2002-03
West Indies in Sri Lanka	11 (av 21.36)	J.J.C.Lawson	2005-06
Sri Lanka in West Indies	16 (av 15.43)	M.Muralidaran	1996-97
Sri Lanka in Sri Lanka	26 (av 15.46)	W.P.U.J.C.Vaas	2001-02

WEST INDIES v ZIMBABWE	West Indies		Zimbabwe		Captains	
Venue and Result	1st	2nd	1st	2nd	West Indies	Zimbabwe
1999-2000 in West Indies						
Port-of-Spain-West Indies 35 runs	•187	147	236	63	J.C.Adams	A.Flower
Kingston-West Indies 10 wkts	339	0-75	•308	102		
2001-02 in Zimbabwe						
Bulawayo[2]-W.Indies inn & 176 runs	6d-559	-	•155	228	C.L.Hooper	H.H.Streak
Harare-Drawn	347	1-98	•131	9d-563		
2003-04 in Zimbabwe						
Harare-Drawn	335	9-207	•9d-507	7d-200	B.C.Lara	H.H.Streak
Bulawayo[2]-W.Indies 128 runs	•481	128	377	104		

Test Match Results Summary

WEST INDIES v ZIMBABWE - in West Indies

		Result			Port-of-Spain			Kingston		
	Tests	W	Z	D	W	Z	D	W	Z	D
1999-2000	2	2	-	-	1	-	-	1	-	-

WEST INDIES v ZIMBABWE - in Zimbabwe

		Result			Bulawayo[2]			Harare		
	Tests	W	Z	D	W	Z	D	W	Z	D
2001-02	2	1	-	1	1	-	-	-	-	1
2003-04	2	1	-	1	1	-	-	-	-	1
	4	2	-	2	2	-	-	-	-	2
Totals	6	4	-	2						

Highest Innings Totals

West Indies in West Indies	339	Kingston	1999-2000
West Indies in Zimbabwe	6d-559	Bulawayo[2]	2001-02
Zimbabwe in West Indies	308	Kingston	1999-2000
Zimbabwe in Zimbabwe	9d-563	Harare	2001-02

Lowest Innings Totals

West Indies in West Indies	147	Port-of-Spain	1999-2000
West Indies in Zimbabwe	128	Bulawayo[2]	2003-04
Zimbabwe in West Indies	63	Port-of-Spain	1999-2000
Zimbabwe in Zimbabwe	104	Bulawayo[2]	2003-04

Highest Match Aggregate	1249 for 35 wickets	Harare	2003-04
Lowest Match Aggregate	633 for 40 wickets	Port-of-Spain	1999-2000

Highest Individual Innings

West Indies in West Indies	101*	J.C.Adams	Kingston	1999-2000
West Indies in Zimbabwe	191	B.C.Lara	Bulawayo[2]	2003-04
Zimbabwe in West Indies	113*	A.Flower	Port-of-Spain	1999-2000
	113	M.W.Goodwin	Kingston	1999-2000
Zimbabwe in Zimbabwe	127*	H.H.Streak	Harare	2003-04

Most Runs in a Series

West Indies in West Indies	145 (av 72.50)	J.C.Adams	1999-2000
West Indies in Zimbabwe	233 (av 116.50)	C.H.Gayle	2001-02
Zimbabwe in West Indies	194 (av 64.66)	A.Flower	1999-2000
Zimbabwe in Zimbabwe	202 (av 50.50)	A.D.R.Campbell	2001-02

Record Wicket Partnerships - West Indies

1st	214	D.Ganga (89), C.H.Gayle (175)	Bulawayo[2]	2001-02
2nd	100	D.Ganga (43), S.Chanderpaul (74)	Harare	2001-02
3rd	52	D.Ganga (73), B.C.Lara (29)	Harare	2003-04
4th	190	B.C.Lara (191), R.R.Sarwan (65)	Bulawayo[2]	2003-04
5th	100	C.L.Hooper (149), M.N.Samuels (42)	Bulawayo[2]	2001-02
6th	68	S.Chanderpaul (39), R.D.Jacobs (60*)	Harare	2003-04
7th	50	R.R.Sarwan (86), N.C.McGarrell (33)	Harare	2001-02
	50	S.Chanderpaul (36), V.C.Drakes (31)	Harare	2003-04
8th	148	J.C.Adams (101*), F.A.Rose (69)	Kingston	1999-2000
9th	26	M.Dillon (19), C.D.Collymore (16*)	Bulawayo[2]	2003-04
10th	26	W.W.Hinds (46*), C.A.Walsh (11)	Port-of-Spain	1999-2000
	26	C.D.Collymore (11*), F.H.Edwards (18)	Harare	2003-04

Record Wicket Partnerships - Zimbabwe

1st	164	D.D.Ebrahim (75), A.D.R.Campbell (103)	Bulawayo[2]	2001-02
2nd	91	A.D.R.Campbell (65), H.Masakadza (119)	Harare	2001-02
3rd	169	H.Masakadza (119), C.B.Wishart (93)	Harare	2001-02
4th	176	M.W.Goodwin (113), A.Flower (66)	Kingston	1999-2000
5th	42	C.B.Wishart (470, S.Matsikenyeri (57)	Harare	2003-04
6th	79	S.Matsikenyeri (57), T.Taibu (83)	Harare	2003-04
7th	154	H.H.Streak (83*), A.M.Blignaut (92)	Harare	2001-02
8th	168	T.Taibu (83), H.H.Streak (127*)	Harare	2003-04
9th	34	A.M.Blignaut (310, R.W.Price (35)	Bulwayo[2]	2003-04
10th	54	S.V.Carlisle (44), H.K.Olonga (22*)	Kingston	1999-2000

Best Bowling in an Innings

West Indies in West Indies	5/50	R.D.King	Arnos Vale	1999-2000
West Indies in Zimbabwe	5/133	F.H.Edwards	Harare	2003-04
Zimbabwe in West Indies	5/23	H.H.Streak	Port-of-Spain	1999-2000
Zimbabwe in Zimbabwe	6/73	R.W.Price	Harare	2003-04

Best Bowling in a Match

West Indies in West Indies	7/50	C.E.L.Ambrose	Port-of-Spain	1999-2000
West Indies in Zimbabwe	7/185	N.C.McGarrell	Harare	2001-02
Zimbabwe in West Indies	9/68	H.H.Streak	Port-of-Spain	1999-2000

Zimbabwe in Zimbabwe	10/161	R.W.Price	Harare	2001-02

Most Wickets in a Series

West Indies in West Indies	9 (av 14.88)	C.A.Walsh	1999-2000
	9 (av 17.00)	F.A.Rose	1999-2000
West Indies in Zimbabwe	12 (av 20.41)	N.C.McGarrell	2001-02
Zimbabwe in West Indies	9 (av 7.55)	H.H.Streak	1999-2000
Zimbabwe in Zimbabwe	19 (av 20.50)	R.W.Price	2003-04

WEST INDIES v BANGLADESH	West Indies		Bangladesh		Captains	
Venue and Result	1st	2nd	1st	2nd	West Indies	Bangladesh
2002-03 in Bangladesh						
Dhaka-West Indies inn & 310 runs	536	-	•139	87	C.L.Hooper	Khaled Mashud
Chittagong[1]-West Indies 7 wickets	296	3-111	•194	212		
2003-04 in West Indies						
Gros Islet-Drawn	352	0-113	•416	9d-271	B.C.Lara	Habibul Bashar
Kingston-West Indies inn & 99 runs	4d-559	-	•284	176		

Test Match Results Summary

WEST INDIES v BANGLADESH - in West Indies

		Result			Gros Islet			Kingston		
	Tests	W	B	D	W	B	D	W	B	D
2003-04	2	1	-	1	-	-	1	1	-	-

WEST INDIES v BANGLADESH - in Bangladesh

		Result			Dhaka			Chittagong[1]		
	Tests	W	B	D	W	B	D	W	B	D
2002-03	2	2	-	-	1	-	-	1	-	-
Totals	4	3	-	1						

Highest Innings Totals

West Indies in West Indies	4d-559	Kingston	2003-04
West Indies in Bangladesh	536	Dhaka	2002-03
Bangladesh in West Indies	416	Gros Islet	2003-04
Bangladesh in Bangladesh	212	Chittagong[1]	2002-03

Lowest Innings Totals

West Indies in West Indies	352	Gros Islet	2003-04
West Indies in Bangladesh	296	Chittagong[1]	2002-03
Bangladesh in West Indies	176	Kingston	2003-04
Bangladesh in Bangladesh	87	Dhaka	2002-03

Highest Match Aggregate	1152 for 29 wickets	Gros Islet	2003-04
Lowest Match Aggregate	762 for 30 wickets	Dhaka	2002-03

Highest Individual Innings

West Indies in West Indies	261*	R.R.Sarwan	Kingston	2003-04
West Indies in Bangladesh	119	R.R.Sarwan	Dhaka	2002-03
Bangladesh in West Indies	113	Habibul Bashar	Gros Islet	2003-04
Bangladesh in Bangladesh	85	Alok Kapali	Chittagong[1]	2002-03

Most Runs in a Series

West Indies in West Indies	301 (av 301.00)	R.R.Sarwan	2003-04
West Indies in Bangladesh	150 (av 150.00)	R.D.Jacobs	2002-03
Bangladesh in West Indies	235 (av 58.75)	Habibul Bashar	2003-04
Bangladesh in Bangladesh	139 (av 34.75)	Alok Kapali	2002-03

Record Wicket Partnerships - West Indies

1st	131	C.H.Gayle (51), W.W.Hinds (75)	Dhaka	2002-03
2nd	87	C.H.Gayle (141), R.R.Sarwan (40)	Gros Islet	2003-04
3rd	179	R.R.Sarwan (261*), B.C.Lara (53)	Kingston	2003-04
4th	176	R.R.Sarwan (119), M.N.Samuels (91)	Dhaka	2002-03
5th	262*	R.R.Sarwan (261*), S.Chanderpaul (101*)	Kingston	2003-04
6th	99	D.Ganga (63), R.D.Jacobs (59)	Chittagong[1]	2002-03
7th	38	R.D.Jacobs (59), V.C.Drakes (26)	Chittagong[1]	2002-03
8th	40	R.D.Jacobs (91*), D.B.Powell (16)	Dhaka	2002-03
9th	34	R.D.Jacobs (91*), P.T.Collins (13)	Dhaka	2002-03
10th	17	P.T.Collins (12*), J.J.C.Lawson (6)	Chittagong[1]	2002-03

Record Wicket Partnerships - Bangladesh

1st	44	Hannan Sarkar (13), Al Sahariar (34)	Chittagong[1]	2002-03
2nd	121	Javed Omar (32), Habibul Bashar (113)	Gros Islet	2003-04
3rd	50	Habibul Bashar (113), Rajin Saleh (26)	Gros Islet	2003-04
4th	120	Habibul Bashar (77), Manjural Islam[2] (35)	Kingston	2003-04
5th	26	Mohammad Ashraful (15), Alok Kapali (85)	Chittagong[1]	2002-03
6th	73	Alok Kapali (52), Khaled Mashud (22)	Dhaka	2002-03
7th	73	Alok Kapali (85), Enamul Haque[1] 11*)	Chittagong[1]	2002-03
8th	87	Mohammad Ashraful (81), Mohammad Rafique (111)	Gros Islet	2003-04
9th	74	Khaled Mashud (103*), Tapash Baisya (26)	Gros Islet	2003-04
10th	46	Mohammad Rafique (111), Tariq Aziz (6*)	Gros Islet	2003-04
	46	Tapash Baisya (48), Tareq Aziz (10*)	Kingston	2003-04

Best Bowling in an Innings

West Indies in West Indies	6/53	P.T.Collins	Kingston	2003-04
West Indies in Bangladesh	6/3	J.J.C.Lawson	Dhaka	2002-03
Bangladesh in West Indies	4/65	Mushfiqur Rahman	Gros Islet	2003-04
Bangladesh in Bangladesh	4/83	Tapash Baisya	Chittagong[1]	2002-03

Best Bowling in a Match

West Indies in West Indies	9/117	P.T.Collins	Kingston	2003-04
West Indies in Bangladesh	7/31	J.J.C.Lawson	Dhaka	2002-03
Bangladesh in West Indies	4/90	Mushfiqur Rahman	Gros Islet	2003-04
Bangladesh in Bangladesh	6/117	Tapash Baisya	Chittagong[1]	2002-03

Most Wickets in a Series

West Indies in West Indies	14 (av 17.28)	R.R.Sarwan	2003-04
West Indies in Bangladesh	12 (av 14.50)	P.T.Collins	2002-03
Bangladesh in West Indies	4 (av 54.25)	Mushfiqur Rahman	2003-04
	4 (av 55.25)	Mohammad Rafique	2003-04
Bangladesh in Bangladesh	8 (av 29.25)	Tapash Baisya	2002-03

NEW ZEALAND v INDIA	New Zealand		India		Captains	
Venue and Result	1st	2nd	1st	2nd	New Zealand	India
1955-56 in India						
Hyderabad-Drawn	326	2-212	•4d-498	-	H.B.Cave	Ghulam Ahmed
Bombay[2]-India inn & 27 runs	258	136	•8d-421	-		P.R.Umrigar
Delhi-Drawn	•2d-450	1-112	7d-531	-		P.R.Umrigar
Calcutta-Drawn	336	6-75	•132	7d-438		P.R.Umrigar
Madras[2]-India inn & 109 runs	209	219	•3d-537	-		P.R.Umrigar
1964-65 in India						
Madras[2]-Drawn	315	0-62	•397	2d-199	J.R.Reid	Nawab of Pataudi, jr
Calcutta-Drawn	•9d-462	9d-191	380	3-92		
Bombay[2]-Drawn	•297	8-80	88	5d-463		
Delhi-India 7 wkts	•262	272	8d-465	3-73		
1967-68 in New Zealand						
Dunedin-India 5 wkts	•350	208	359	5-200	B.W.Sinclair	Nawab of Pataudi, jr
Christchurch-New Zealand 6 wkts	•502	4-88	288	301	G.T.Dowling	
Wellington-India 8 wkts	•186	199	327	2-59	G.T.Dowling	
Auckland-India 272 runs	140	101	•252	5d-261	G.T.Dowling	
1969-70 in India						
Bombay[2]-India 60 runs	229	127	•156	260	G.T.Dowling	Nawab of Pataudi, jr
Nagpur-New Zealand 167 runs	•319	214	257	109		
Hyderabad-Drawn	•181	8d-175	89	7-67		
1975-76 in New Zealand						
Auckland-India 8 wkts	•266	215	414	2-71	G.M.Turner	S.M.Gavaskar
Christchurch-Drawn	403	-	•270	6-255		B.S.Bedi
Wellington-New Zealand inn & 33 runs	334	-	•220	81		B.S.Bedi
1976-77 in India						
Bombay[3]-India 162 runs	298	141	•399	4d-202	G.M.Turner	B.S.Bedi
Kanpur-Drawn	350	7-193	•9d-524	2d-208		
Madras[1]-India 216 runs	140	143	•298	5d-201		
1980-81 in New Zealand						
Wellington-New Zealand 62 runs	•375	100	223	190	G.P.Howarth	S.M.Gavaskar
Christchurch-Drawn	5-286	-	•255	-		
Auckland-Drawn	366	5-95	•238	284		
1988-89 in India						
Bangalore-India 172 runs	189	164	•9d-384	1d-141	J.G.Wright	D.B.Vengsarkar
Bombay[3]-New Zealand 136 runs	•236	279	234	145		
Hyderabad-India 10 wkts	•254	124	358	0-22		
1989-90 in New Zealand						
Christchurch-New Zealand 10 wkts	•459	0-2	164	296	J.G.Wright	M.Azharuddin
Napier-Drawn	1-178	-	•358	-		
Auckland-Drawn	•391	5d-483	482	0-149		
1993-94 in New Zealand						
Hamilton-Drawn	•187	7d-368	246	3-177	K.R.Rutherford	M.Azharuddin
1995-96 in India						
Bangalore-India 8 wkts	228	2-151	•145	233	L.K.Germon	M.Azharuddin
Chennai[1]-Drawn	-	-	•2-144	-		
Cuttack-Drawn	8-175	-	•8d-296	-		

NEW ZEALAND v INDIA (cont.)	New Zealand		India		Captains	
Venue and Result	1st	2nd	1st	2nd	New Zealand	India
1998-99 in New Zealand						
Wellington-New Zealand 4 wkts	352	6-215	•208	356	S.P.Fleming	M.Azharuddin
Hamilton-Drawn	•366	8d-464	416	2-249		
1999-2000 in India						
Mohali-Drawn	215	7-251	•83	3d-505	S.P.Fleming	S.R.Tendulkar
Kanpur-India 8 wkts	•256	155	330	2-83		
Ahmedabad-Drawn	308	2-252	•7d-583	5d-148		
2002-03 in New Zealand						
Wellington-New Zealand 10 wkts	247	0-36	•161	121	S.P.Fleming	S.C.Ganguly
Hamilton-New Zealand 4 wkts	94	6-160	•99	154		
2003-04 in India						
Ahmedabad-Drawn	340	6-272	•5d-500	6d-209	S.P.Fleming	S.C.Ganguly
Mohali-Drawn	•6d-630	-	424	4-136		

Test Match Results Summary

NEW ZEALAND v INDIA - in New Zealand

		Result			Dunedin			Christchurch			Wellington			Auckland			Napier			Hamilton		
	Tests	NZ	I	D	NZ	I	D	NZ	I	D	NZ	I	D	NZ	I	D	NZ	I	D	NZ	I	D
1967-68	4	1	3	-	-	1	-	1	-	-	-	1	-	-	1	-	-	-	-	-	-	-
1975-76	3	1	1	1	-	-	-	-	-	1	1	-	-	-	1	-	-	-	-	-	-	-
1980-81	3	1	-	2	-	-	-	-	-	1	1	-	-	-	-	1	-	-	-	-	-	-
1989-90	3	1	-	2	-	-	-	1	-	-	-	-	-	-	-	1	-	-	1	-	-	-
1993-94	1	-	-	1	-	-	-	-	-	-	-	-	-	-	-	-	-	-	-	-	-	1
1998-99	2	1	-	1	-	-	-	-	-	-	1	-	-	-	-	-	-	-	-	-	-	1
2002-03	2	2	-	-	-	-	-	-	-	-	1	-	-	-	-	-	-	-	-	1	-	-
	18	7	4	7	-	1	-	2	-	2	4	1	-	-	2	2	-	-	1	1	-	2

NEW ZEALAND v INDIA - in India

		Result			Hyder.			Mumbai			Delhi			Calc.			Chen.			Nagpur			Kanpur			Bang.			Cuttack			Mohali			Ahd.		
	Tests	N	I	D	N	I	D	N	I	D	N	I	D	N	I	D	N	I	D	N	I	D	N	I	D	N	I	D	N	I	D	N	I	D	N	I	D
1955-56	5	-	2	3	-	-	1	-	1	-	-	-	1	-	-	1	-	1	-	-	-	-	-	-	-	-	-	-	-	-	-	-	-	-	-	-	-
1964-65	4	-	1	3	-	-	-	-	-	1	-	1	-	-	-	1	-	-	1	-	-	-	-	-	-	-	-	-	-	-	-	-	-	-	-	-	-
1969-70	3	1	1	1	-	-	1	-	1	-	-	-	-	-	-	-	-	-	-	1	-	-	-	-	-	-	-	-	-	-	-	-	-	-	-	-	-
1976-77	3	-	2	1	-	-	-	-	1	-	-	-	-	-	-	-	-	1	-	-	-	-	-	-	1	-	-	-	-	-	-	-	-	-	-	-	-
1988-89	3	1	2	-	-	1	-	1	-	-	-	-	-	-	-	-	-	-	-	-	-	-	-	-	-	-	1	-	-	-	-	-	-	-	-	-	-
1995-96	3	-	1	2	-	-	-	-	-	-	-	-	-	-	-	-	-	-	1	-	-	-	-	-	-	1	-	-	-	-	1	-	-	-	-	-	-
1999-00	3	-	1	2	-	-	-	-	-	-	-	-	-	-	-	-	-	-	-	-	-	-	-	1	-	-	-	-	-	-	-	-	-	1	-	-	1
2003-04	2	-	-	2	-	-	-	-	-	-	-	-	-	-	-	-	-	-	-	-	-	-	-	-	-	-	-	-	-	-	-	-	-	1	-	-	1
	26	2	10	14	-	1	2	1	3	1	-	1	1	-	-	2	-	2	2	1	-	-	-	1	1	1	1	-	-	-	1	-	-	2	-	-	2
Totals	44	9	14	21																																	

Key to ground abbreviation: Hyder. - Hyderabad; Calc. - Calcutta; Chen. - Chennai.

Highest Innings Totals

New Zealand in New Zealand	502	Christchurch	1967-68
New Zealand in India	6d-630	Mohali	2003-04
India in New Zealand	482	Auckland	1989-90
India in India	7d-583	Ahmedabad	1999-2000

Lowest Innings Totals

New Zealand in New Zealand	94	Hamilton	2002-03
New Zealand in India	124	Hyderabad	1988-89
India in New Zealand	81	Wellington	1975-76
India in India	83	Mohali	1999-2000

Highest Match Aggregate	1505 for 25 wickets	Auckland	1989-90
Lowest Match Aggregate	507 for 36 wickets	Hamilton	2002-03

Highest Individual Innings

New Zealand in New Zealand	239	G.T.Dowling	Christchurch	1967-68
New Zealand in India	230*	B.Sutcliffe	Delhi	1955-56
India in New Zealand	192	M.Azharuddin	Auckland	1989-90
India in India	231	M.H.Mankad	Madras[2]	1955-56

Most Runs in a Series

New Zealand in New Zealand	471 (av 58.87)	G.T.Dowling	1967-68
New Zealand in India	611 (av 87.28)	B.Sutcliffe	1955-56
India in New Zealand	328 (av 46.86)	A.L.Wadekar	1967-68
India in India	526 (av 105.20)	M.H.Mankad	1955-56

Record Wicket Partnerships - New Zealand

1st	231	M.H.Richardson (145), L.Vincent (106)	Mohali	2003-04
2nd	155	G.T.Dowling (143), B.E.Congdon (58)	Dunedin	1967-68
3rd	222*	B.Sutcliffe (230*), J.R Reid (119*)	Delhi	1955-56
4th	160	R.G.Twose (87), C.D.McMillan (92)	Hamilton	1998-99
5th	140	C.D.McMillan (84), A.C.Parore (50)	Hamilton	1998-99
6th	137	C.D.McMillan (74*), C.L.Cairns (62)	Wellington	1998-99
7th	163	B.Sutcliffe (151*), B.R Taylor (105)	Calcutta	1964-65
8th	137	D.J.Nash (89*), D.L.Vettori (57)	Wellington	1998-99
9th	136	I.D.S.Smith (173), M.C.Snedden (22)	Auckland	1989-90
10th	61	J.T.Ward (35*), R.O.Collinge (34)	Madras[2]	1964-65

Record Wicket Partnerships - India

1st	413	M.H.Mankad (231), P.Roy (173)	Madras[2]	1955-56
2nd	204	S.M Gavaskar (116), S Amarnath (124)	Auckland	1975-76
3rd	238	P.R Umrigar (223), V.L.Manjrekar (118)	Hyderabad	1955-56
4th	281	S.R.Tendulkar (217), S.C.Ganguly (125)	Ahmedabad	1999-2000
5th	180	R.S.Dravid (222), S.C.Ganguly (100*)	Ahmedabad	2003-04
6th	193*	D.N Sardesai (200), Hanumant Singh (75*)	Bombay[3]	1964-65
7th	128	S.R.Tendulkar (88), K.S.More (73)	Napier	1989-90
8th	144	R.S.Dravid (190), J.Srinath (76)	Hamilton	1998-99
9th	105	S.M.H.Kirmani (88), B.S.Bedi (36)	Bombay[3]	1976-77
	105	S.M.H.Kirmani (78), N.S.Yadav (43)	Auckland	1980-81
10th	57	R.B.Desai (32*), B.S.Bedi (22)	Dunedin	1967-68

Best Bowling in an Innings

New Zealand in New Zealand	7/23	R.J.Hadlee	Wellington	1975-76
New Zealand in India	6/27	D.J.Nash	Mohali	1999-2000
India in New Zealand	8/76	E.A.S.Prasanna	Auckland	1975-76
India in India	8/72	S.Venkataraghavan	Delhi	1964-65

Best Bowling in a Match

New Zealand in New Zealand	11/58	R.J.Hadlee	Wellington	1975-76
New Zealand in India	10/88	R.J.Hadlee	Bombay[3]	1969-70
India in New Zealand	11/140	E.A.S.Prasanna	Auckland	1975-76
India in India	12/152	S.Venkataraghavan	Delhi	1964-65

Most Wickets in a Series

New Zealand in New Zealand	16 (av 27.87)	D.K.Morrison	1989-90
New Zealand in India	18 (av 14.00)	R.J.Hadlee	1988-89
India in New Zealand	24 (av 18.79)	E.A.S.Prasanna	1967-68
India in India	34 (av 19.17)	S.P.Gupte	1955-56

NEW ZEALAND v PAKISTAN	New Zealand		Pakistan		Captains	
Venue and Result	1st	2nd	1st	2nd	New Zealand	Pakistan
1955-56 in Pakistan						
Karachi[1]-Pakistan inn & 1 run	•164	124	289	-	H.B.Cave	A.H.Kardar
Lahore[1]-Pakistan 4 wkts	•348	328	561	6-117		
Dacca-Drawn	•70	6-69	6d-195	-		
1964-65 in New Zealand						
Wellington-Drawn	•266	7d-179	187	7-140	J.R.Reid	Hanif Mohammad
Auckland-Drawn	214	7-166	•226	207		
Christchurch-Drawn	202	5-223	•206	8d-309		
1964-65 in Pakistan						
Rawalpindi[1]-Pakistan inn & 64 runs	•175	79	318	-	J.R.Reid	Hanif Mohammad
Lahore[2]-Drawn	6d-482	-	•7d-385	8d-194		
Karachi[1]-Pakistan 8 wkts	•285	223	8d-307	2-202		
1969-70 in Pakistan						
Karachi[1]-Drawn	274	5-112	•220	8d-283	G.T.Dowling	Intikhab Alam
Lahore[2]-New Zealand 5 wkts	241	5-82	•114	208		
Dacca-Drawn	•273	200	7d-290	4-51		
1972-73 in New Zealand						
Wellington-Drawn	325	3-78	•357	6d-290	B.E.Congdon	Intikhab Alam
Dunedin-Pakistan inn & 166 runs	156	185	•6d-507	-		
Auckland-Drawn	402	3-92	•402	271		
1976-77 in Pakistan						
Lahore[2]-Pakistan 6 wkts	157	360	•417	4-105	G.M.Turner	Mushtaq Mohammad
Hyderabad-Pakistan 10 wkts	219	254	•8d-473	0-4	G.M.Turner	
Karachi[1]-Drawn	468	7-262	•9d-565	5d-290	J.M.Parker	
1978-79 in New Zealand						
Christchurch-Pakistan 128 runs	290	176	•271	6d-323	M.G.Burgess	Mushtaq Mohammad
Napier-Drawn	402	-	•360	3d-234		
Auckland-Drawn	•254	8d-281	359	0-8		
1984-85 in Pakistan						
Lahore[2]-Pakistan 6 wkts	•157	241	221	4-181	J.V.Coney	Zaheer Abbas
Hyderabad-Pakistan 7 wkts	•267	189	230	3-230		
Karachi[1]-Drawn	426	-	•328	5-308		
1984-85 in New Zealand						
Wellington-Drawn	•492	4-103	322	-	G.P.Howarth	Javed Miandad
Christchurch-New Zealand inn & 99 runs	9d-451	-	•169	183		
Dunedin-New Zealand 2 wkts	220	8-278	•274	223		
1988-89 in New Zealand						
Dunedin-Abandoned	-	-	-	-	J.G.Wright	Imran Khan
Wellington-Drawn	•447	8-186	7d-438	-		
Auckland-Drawn	403	3-99	•5d-616	-		

NEW ZEALAND v PAKISTAN (cont.)	New Zealand		Pakistan		Captains	
Venue and Result	1st	2nd	1st	2nd	New Zealand	Pakistan
1990-91 in Pakistan						
Karachi[1]-Pakistan inn & 43 runs	•196	194	6d-433	-	M.D.Crowe	Javed Miandad
Lahore[2]-Pakistan 9 wkts	•160	287	9d-373	1-77		
Faisalabad-Pakistan 65 runs	217	177	•102	357		
1992-93 in New Zealand						
Auckland-Pakistan 33 runs	264	93	•216	174	K.R.Rutherford	Javed Miandad
1993-94 in New Zealand						
Auckland-Pakistan 5 wkts	•242	110	215	5-141	K.R.Rutherford	Saleem Malik
Wellington-Pakistan inn & 12 runs	•175	361	5d-548	-		
Christchurch-New Zealand 5 wkts	200	5-324	•344	179		
1995-96 in New Zealand						
Christchurch-Pakistan 161 runs	286	195	•208	434	L.K.Germon	Wasim Akram
1996-97 in Pakistan						
Lahore[2]-New Zealand 44 runs	•155	311	191	231	L.K.Germon	Saeed Anwar
Rawalpindi[2]-Pakistan inn & 13 runs	•249	168	430	-		
2000-01 in New Zealand						
Auckland-Pakistan 161 runs	252	131	•346	5d-336	S.P.Fleming	Moin Khan
Christchurch-Drawn	•476	1d-196	8d-571	-		Moin Khan
Hamilton-New Zealand inn & 185 runs	4d-407	-	•104	118		Inzamamul Haq
2001-02 in Pakistan						
Lahore[2]-Pakistan inn & 324 runs	73	246	•643	-	S.P.Fleming	Waqar Younis
2003-04 in New Zealand						
Hamilton-Drawn	•563	8-96	463	-	S.P.Fleming	Inzamamul Haq
Wellington-Pakistan 7 wkts	•366	103	196	3-277		

Test Match Results Summary

NEW ZEALAND v PAKISTAN - in New Zealand

		Result			Wellington			Auckland			Christchurch			Dunedin			Napier			Hamilton		
	Tests	NZ	P	D	NZ	P	D	NZ	P	D	NZ	P	D	NZ	P	D	NZ	P	D	NZ	P	D
1964-65	3	-	-	3	-	-	1	-	-	1	-	-	1	-	-	-	-	-	-	-	-	-
1972-73	3	-	1	2	-	-	1	-	-	1	-	-	-	-	1	-	-	-	-	-	-	-
1978-79	3	-	1	2	-	-	-	-	-	1	-	1	-	-	-	-	-	-	1	-	-	-
1984-85	3	2	-	1	-	-	1	1	-	-	-	-	-	1	-	-	-	-	-	-	-	-
1988-89	2	-	-	2	-	-	1	-	-	1	-	-	-	-	-	-	-	-	-	-	-	-
1992-93	1	-	1	-	-	-	-	-	-	-	-	-	-	-	-	-	-	-	-	-	1	-
1993-94	3	1	2	-	-	-	1	-	-	1	1	-	-	-	-	-	-	-	-	-	-	-
1995-96	1	-	1	-	-	-	-	-	-	-	-	1	-	-	-	-	-	-	-	-	-	-
2000-01	3	1	1	1	-	-	-	-	1	-	-	-	1	-	-	-	-	-	-	1	-	-
2003-04	2	-	1	1	-	1	-	-	-	-	-	-	-	-	-	-	-	-	-	-	-	1
	24	4	8	12	-	1	5	1	1	5	1	2	2	1	1	-	-	-	1	1	1	1

NEW ZEALAND v PAKISTAN - in Pakistan

	Tests	Result			Karachi[1]			Lahore			Dacca			Rawalpindi[1]			Hyderabad			Faisalabad			Rawalpindi[2]		
		NZ	P	D	NZ	P	D	NZ	P	D	NZ	P	D	NZ	P	D	NZ	P	D	NZ	P	D	NZ	P	D
1955-56	3	-	2	1	-	1	-	-	1	-	-	-	1	-	-	-	-	-	-	-	-	-	-	-	-
1964-65	3	-	2	1	-	1	-	-	-	1	-	-	-	-	1	-	-	-	-	-	-	-	-	-	-
1969-70	3	1	-	2	-	-	1	1	-	-	-	-	1	-	-	-	-	-	-	-	-	-	-	-	-
1976-77	3	-	2	1	-	-	1	-	1	-	-	-	-	-	-	-	-	1	-	-	-	-	-	-	-
1984-85	3	-	2	1	-	-	1	-	1	-	-	-	-	-	-	-	-	1	-	-	-	-	-	-	-
1990-91	3	-	3	-	-	1	-	-	1	-	-	-	-	-	-	-	-	-	-	-	1	-	-	-	-
1996-97	2	1	1	-	-	-	-	1	-	-	-	-	-	-	-	-	-	-	-	-	-	-	-	1	-
2001-02	1	-	1	-	-	-	-	-	1	-	-	-	-	-	-	-	-	-	-	-	-	-	-	-	-
	21	2	13	6	-	3	3	2	5	1	-	-	2	-	1	-	-	2	-	-	1	-	-	1	-
Totals	45	6	21	18																					

Highest Innings Totals

New Zealand in New Zealand	563	Hamilton	2003-04
New Zealand in Pakistan	6d-482	Lahore[2]	1964-65
Pakistan in New Zealand	5d-616	Auckland	1988-89
Pakistan in Pakistan	643	Lahore[2]	2001-02

Lowest Innings Totals

New Zealand in New Zealand	93	Hamilton	1992-93
New Zealand in Pakistan	70	Dacca	1955-56
Pakistan in New Zealand	104	Hamilton	2000-01
Pakistan in Pakistan	102	Faisalabad	1990-91

Highest Match Aggregate	1585 for 31 wickets	Karachi[1]	1976-77
Lowest Match Aggregate	572 for 30 wickets	Rawalpindi[1]	1964-65

Highest Individual Innings

New Zealand in New Zealand	204*	M.S.Sinclair	Christchurch	2000-01
New Zealand in Pakistan	152	W.K.Lees	Karachi[1]	1976-77
Pakistan in New Zealand	271	Javed Miandad	Auckland	1988-89
Pakistan in Pakistan	329	Inzamamul Haq	Lahore[2]	2001-02

Most Runs in a Series

New Zealand in New Zealand	333 (av 83.25)	J.F.Reid	1984-85
New Zealand in Pakistan	296 (av 59.20)	J.R.Reid	1964-65
Pakistan in New Zealand	389 (av 194.50)	Javed Miandad	1988-89
Pakistan in Pakistan	507 (av 169.00)	Shoaib Mohammad	1990-91

Record Wicket Partnerships - New Zealand

1st	181	M.H.Richardson (106), M.D.Bell (105)	Hamilton	2000-01
2nd	195	J.G.Wright (88), G.P.Howarth (114)	Napier	1978-79
3rd	178	B.W.Sinclair (130), J.R.Reid (88)	Lahore[2]	1964-65
4th	147	C.D.McMillan (98), S.P.Fleming (51*)	Hamilton	2000-01
5th	183	M.G.Burgess (111), R.W.Anderson (92)	Lahore[2]	1976-77
6th	145	J.F.Reid (148), R.J.Hadlee (87)	Wellington	1984-85
7th	186	W.K.Lees (152), R.J.Hadlee (87)	Karachi[1]	1976-77
8th	125	S.P.Fleming (192), D.L.Vettori (137*)	Hamilton	2003-04
9th	99	D.L.Vettori (137*), D.R.Tuffey (35)	Hamilton	2003-04
10th	151	B.F.Hastings (110), R.O.Collinge (68*)	Auckland	1972-73

Record Wicket Partnerships - Pakistan

1st	172	Rameez Raja (78), Shoaib Mohammad (203*)	Karachi[1]	1990-91
2nd	262	Saeed Anwar (149), Ijaz Ahmed (125)	Rawalpindi[2]	1996-97
3rd	248	Shoaib Mohammad (112), Javed Miandad (271)	Auckland	1988-89
4th	350	Mushtaq Mohammad (201), Asif Iqbal (175)	Dunedin	1972-73
5th	281	Javed Miandad (163), Asif Iqbal (166)	Lahore[2]	1976-77
6th	217	Hanif Mohammad (203*), Majid Khan (80)	Lahore[2]	1964-65
7th	308	Waqar Hassan (189), Imtiaz Ahmed (209)	Lahore[1]	1955-56
8th	89	Anil Dalpat (52), Iqbal Qasim (45*)	Karachi[1]	1984-85
9th	78	Inzamamul Haq (329), Arif Butt (20)	Lahore[2]	2001-02
10th	65	Salahuddin (34*), Mohammad Farooq (47)	Rawalpindi[1]	1964-65

Best Bowling in an Innings

New Zealand in New Zealand	6/46	I.G.Butler	Wellington	2003-04
New Zealand in Pakistan	7/52	C.Pringle	Faisalabad	1990-91
Pakistan in New Zealand	7/52	Intikhab Alam	Dunedin	1972-73
Pakistan in Pakistan	7/66	Mohammad Zahid	Rawalpindi[2]	1996-97

Best Bowling in a Match

New Zealand in New Zealand	9/70	F.J.Cameron	Auckland	1964-65
New Zealand in Pakistan	11/152	C.Pringle	Faisalabad	1990-91
Pakistan in New Zealand	11/78	Shoaib Akhtar	Wellington	2003-04
Pakistan in Pakistan	12/130	Waqar Younis	Faisalabad	1990-91

Most Wickets in a Series

New Zealand in New Zealand	18 (av 23.00)	R.J.Hadlee	1978-79
New Zealand in Pakistan	17 (av 25.35)	S.L.Boock	1984-85
Pakistan in New Zealand	25 (av 17.24)	Wasim Akram	1993-94
Pakistan in Pakistan	29 (av 10.86)	Waqar Younis	1990-91

NEW ZEALAND v SRI LANKA	New Zealand		Sri Lanka		Captains	
Venue and Result	1st	2nd	1st	2nd	New Zealand	Sri Lanka
1982-83 in New Zealand						
Christchurch-New Zealand inn & 25 runs	•344	-	144	175	G.P.Howarth	D.S.de Silva
Wellington-New Zealand 6 wkts	201	4-134	•240	93		
1983-84 in Sri Lanka						
Kandy-New Zealand 165 runs	•276	8d-201	215	97	G.P.Howarth	L.R.D.Mendis
Colombo (SSC)-Drawn	198	4-123	•174	9d-289		
Colombo (CCC)-New Zealand inn & 61 runs	459	-	•256	142		
1986-87 in Sri Lanka						
Colombo (CCC)-Drawn	5-406	-	•9d-397	-	J.J.Crowe	L.R.D.Mendis
1990-91 in New Zealand						
Wellington-Drawn	•174	4-671	497	-	M.D.Crowe	A.Ranatunga
Hamilton-Drawn	•296	6d-374	253	6-344	M.D.Crowe	
Auckland-Drawn	317	5-261	•380	319	I.D.S.Smith	
1992-93 in Sri Lanka						
Moratuwa-Drawn	•288	5-195	6d-327	-	M.D.Crowe	A.Ranatunga
Colombo (SSC)-Sri Lanka 9 wkts	102	361	•394	1-70		

NEW ZEALAND v SRI LANKA (cont.)	New Zealand		Sri Lanka		Captains	
Venue and Result	1st	2nd	1st	2nd	New Zealand	Sri Lanka
1994-95 in New Zealand						
Napier-Sri Lanka 241 runs	109	185	•183	352	K.R.Rutherford	A.Ranatunga
Dunedin-Drawn	307	0-0	•233	411		
1996-97 in New Zealand						
Dunedin-New Zealand inn & 36 runs	•7d-586	-	222	328	S.P.Fleming	A.Ranatunga
Hamilton-New Zealand 120 runs	•222	273	170	205		
1997-98 in Sri Lanka						
Colombo (RPS)-New Zealand 167 runs	•305	6d-444	285	297	S.P.Fleming	A.Ranatunga
Galle-Sri Lanka inn & 16 runs	•193	114	323	-		
Colombo (SSC)-Sri Lanka 164 runs	193	131	•206	282		
2002-03 in Sri Lanka						
Colombo (PSS)-Drawn	•7d-505	5d-161	483	-	S.P.Fleming	H.P.Tillakaratne
Kandy-Drawn	•305	183	298	1-72		
2004-05 in New Zealand						
Hamilton-Drawn	•561	238	498	-	S.P.Fleming	M.S.Atapattu
Wellington-New Zealand inn & 38 runs	9d-522	-	•211	273		

Test Match Results Summary

NEW ZEALAND v SRI LANKA - in New Zealand

		Result			Christchurch			Wellington			Hamilton			Auckland			Napier			Dunedin		
	Tests	NZ	SL	D	NZ	SL	D	NZ	SL	D	NZ	SL	D	NZ	SL	D	NZ	SL	D	NZ	SL	D
1982-83	2	2	-	-	1	-	-	1	-	-	-	-	-	-	-	-	-	-	-	-	-	-
1990-91	3	-	-	3	-	-	-	-	-	1	-	-	1	-	-	1	-	-	-	-	-	-
1994-95	2	-	1	1	-	-	-	-	-	-	-	-	-	-	-	-	-	1	-	-	-	1
1996-97	2	2	-	-	-	-	-	-	-	-	1	-	-	-	-	-	-	-	-	1	-	-
2004-05	2	1	-	1	-	-	-	1	-	-	-	-	-	-	-	-	-	-	1	-	-	-
	11	5	1	5	1	-	-	2	-	1	1	-	1	-	-	1	-	1	1	1	-	1

NEW ZEALAND v SRI LANKA - in Sri Lanka

		Result			Kandy			Col(SSC)			Col(CCC)			Moratuwa			Col(RPS)			Galle			Col(PSS)		
	Tests	NZ	SL	D	NZ	SL	D	NZ	SL	D	NZ	SL	D	NZ	SL	D	NZ	SL	D	NZ	SL	D	-	-	-
1983-84	3	2	-	1	1	-	-	-	-	1	1	-	-	-	-	-	-	-	-	-	-	-	-	-	-
1986-87	1	-	-	1	-	-	-	-	-	-	-	-	1	-	-	-	-	-	-	-	-	-	-	-	-
1992-93	2	-	1	1	-	-	-	-	1	-	-	-	-	-	-	1	-	-	-	-	-	-	-	-	-
1997-98	3	1	2	-	-	-	-	-	1	-	-	-	-	-	-	-	1	-	-	-	1	-	-	-	-
2002-03	2	-	-	2	-	-	1	-	-	-	-	-	-	-	-	-	-	-	-	-	-	-	-	-	1
	11	3	3	5	1	-	1	-	2	1	1	-	1	-	-	1	1	-	-	-	1	-	-	-	1
Totals	22	8	4	10																					

Highest Innings Totals

New Zealand in New Zealand	4-671	Wellington	1990-91
New Zealand in Sri Lanka	7d-515	Colombo (PSS)	2002-03
Sri Lanka in New Zealand	498	Napier	2004-05
Sri Lanka in Sri Lanka	483	Colombo (PSS)	2002-03

Lowest Innings Totals

New Zealand in New Zealand	109	Napier	1994-95
New Zealand in Sri Lanka	102	Colombo (SSC)	1992-93
Sri Lanka in New Zealand	93	Wellington	1987-88
Sri Lanka in Sri Lanka	97	Kandy	1983-84
Highest Match Aggregate	1342 for 23 wickets	Wellington	1990-91
Lowest Match Aggregate	630 for 30 wickets	Galle	1997-98

Highest Individual Innings

New Zealand in New Zealand	299	M.D.Crowe	Wellington	1990-91
New Zealand in Sri Lanka	274*	S.P.Fleming	Colombo (PSS)	2002-03
Sri Lanka in New Zealand	267	P.A.de Silva	Wellington	1990-91
Sri Lanka in Sri Lanka	201*	D.S.B.P.Kuruppu	Colombo (CCC)	1986-87

Most Runs in a Series

New Zealand in New Zealand	513 (av 102.60)	A.H.Jones	1990-91
New Zealand in Sri Lanka	376 (av 188.00)	S.P.Fleming	2002-03
Sri Lanka in New Zealand	493 (av 98.60)	P.A.de Silva	1990-91
Sri Lanka in Sri Lanka	300 (av 60.00)	D.P.M.Jayawardene	1997-98

Record Wicket Partnerships - New Zealand

1st	161	T.J.Franklin (69), J.G.Wright (101)	Hamilton	1990-91
2nd	172	M.H.Richardson (85), S.P.Fleming (275*)	Colombo (PSS)	2002-03
3rd	467	A.H.Jones (188), M.D.Crowe (299)	Wellington	1990-91
4th	240	S.P.Fleming (175*), C.D.McMillan (142)	Colombo (RPS)	1997-98
5th	151	S.P.Fleming (275*), S.B.Styris (63)	Colombo (PSS)	2002-03
6th	246*	J.J.Crowe (120*), R.J.Hadlee (151*)	Colombo (CCC)	1986-87
7th	48	L.Vincent (224), J.E.C.Franlkin (15)	Wellington	2004-05
8th	98	L.Vincent (224), K.D.Mills (31)	Wellington	2004-05
9th	59	L.Vincent (224), P.J.Wiseman (32*)	Wellington	2004-05
10th	52	W.K.Lees (89), E.J.Chatfield (10*)	Christchurch	1982-83

Record Wicket Partnerships - Sri Lanka

1st	102	R.S.Mahanama (109), U.C.Hathurusingha (27)	Colombo (SSC)	1992-93
2nd	138	R.S.Mahanama (153), A.P.Gurusinha (43)	Moratuwa	1992-93
3rd	184	M.S.Atapattu (127), D.P.M.D.Jayawardene (141)	Napier	2004-05
4th	192	A.P.Gurusinha (127), H.P.Tillakaratne (108)	Dunedin	1994-95
5th	133	D.P.M.D.Jayawardene (58), H.P.Tillakaratne (144*)	Colombo (PSS)	2002-03
6th	109*§	R.S.Madugalle (89*), A.Ranatunga (37)	Colombo (CCC)	1983-84
	109	D.S.B.P.Kuruppu (201*), R.S.Madugalle (60)	Colombo (CCC)	1986-87
7th	137	R.S.Kaluwitharana (103), W.P.U.J.C.Vaas (57)	Dunedin	1996-97
8th	99	T.T.Samaraweera (73), U.D.U.Chandana (41)	Wellington	2004-05
9th	31	G.F.Labrooy (70*), R.J.Ratnayake (18)	Auckland	1990-91
	31	S.T.Jayasuriya (12*), R.J.Ratnayake (20)	Auckland	1990-91
10th	71	R.S.Kaluwitharana (88), M.Muralidaran (26*)	Colombo (SSC)	1997-98

§ 119 runs were added for this wicket, R.S.Madugalle retired hurt and was replaced by D.S.de Silva after 109 had been scored.

Best Bowling in an Innings

New Zealand in New Zealand	6/54	C.S.Martin	Wellington	2004-05
New Zealand in Sri Lanka	6/64	D.L.Vettori	Colombo (SSC)	1997-98
Sri Lanka in New Zealand	6/87	W.P.J.U.C.Vaas	Dunedin	1994-95
Sri Lanka in Sri Lanka	6/72	H.D.P.K.Dharmasena	Galle	1997-98

Best Bowling in a Match

New Zealand in New Zealand	9/130	D.L.Vettori	Hamilton	1996-97
New Zealand in Sri Lanka	10/102	R.J.Hadlee	Colombo (CCC)	1983-84
Sri Lanka in New Zealand	10/90	W.P.J.U.C.Vaas	Napier	1994-95
Sri Lanka in Sri Lanka	9/83	M.R.C.N.Bandaratilake	Galle	1997-98

Most Wickets in a Series

New Zealand in New Zealand	13 (av 36.61)	D.K.Morrison	1990-91
New Zealand in Sri Lanka	23 (av 10.00)	R.J.Hadlee	1983-84
Sri Lanka in New Zealand	16 (av 11.06)	W.P.J.U.C.Vaas	1994-95
Sri Lanka in Sri Lanka	19 (av 19.68)	M.Muralidaran	1997-98

NEW ZEALAND v ZIMBABWE	New Zealand		Zimbabwe		Captains	
Venue and Result	1st	2nd	1st	2nd	New Zealand	Zimbabwe
1992-93 in Zimbabwe						
Bulawayo[1]-Drawn	•3d-325	5d-222	219	1-197	M.D.Crowe	D.L.Houghton
Harare-New Zealand won by 177 runs	•335	5d-262	9d-283	137		
1995-96 in New Zealand						
Hamilton-Drawn	•8d230	5d222	196	6-208	L.K.Germon	A.Flower
Auckland-Drawn	•251	5d-441	9d-326	4-246		
1997-98 in Zimbabwe						
Harare-Drawn	207	8-304	•298	9d-311	S.P.Fleming	A.D.R.Campbell
Bulawayo[2]-Drawn	403	8-275	•461	8d-227		
1997-98 in New Zealand						
Wellington-New Zealand 10 wkts	411	0-20	•180	250	S.P.Fleming	A.D.R.Campbell
Auckland-New Zealand inn & 13 runs	460	-	•170	277		
2000-01 in Zimbabwe						
Bulawayo[2]-New Zealand 7 wkts	338	3-132	•350	119	S.P.Fleming	H.H.Streak
Harare-New Zealand 8 wkts	•465	2-74	166	370		
2000-01 in New Zealand						
Wellington-Drawn	•7d-487	4d-153	6d-340	2-60	S.P.Fleming	H.H.Streak
2005-06 in Zimbabwe						
Harare-New Zealand inn & 294 runs	•9d-452	-	59	99	S.P.Fleming	T.Taibu
Bulawayo[2]-New Zealand inn & 436 runs	484	-	•231	207		

Test Match Results Summary

NEW ZEALAND v ZIMBABWE - in New Zealand

		Result			Auckland			Hamilton			Wellington		
	Tests	NZ	Z	D	NZ	Z	D	NZ	Z	D	NZ	Z	D
1995-96	2	-	-	2	-	-	1	-	-	1	-	-	-
1997-98	2	2	-	-	1	-	-	-	-	-	1	-	-
2000-01	1	-	-	1	-	-	-	-	-	-	-	-	1
	5	2	-	3	1	-	1	-	-	1	1	-	1

NEW ZEALAND v ZIMBABWE - in Zimbabwe

		Result			Harare			Bulawayo[1]			Bulawayo[2]		
	Tests	NZ	Z	D	NZ	Z	D	NZ	Z	D	NZ	Z	D
1992-93	2	1	-	1	1	-	-	-	-	1	-	-	-
1997-98	2	-	-	2	-	-	1	-	-	-	-	-	1
2000-01	2	2	-	-	1	-	-	-	-	-	1	-	-
2005-06	2	2	-	-	1	-	-	-	-	-	1	-	-
	7	5	-	3	3	-	1	-	-	1	2	-	1
Totals	13	7	-	6									

Highest Innings Totals

New Zealand in New Zealand	7d-487	Wellington	2000-01
New Zealand in Zimbabwe	484	Bulawayo[2]	2005-06
Zimbabwe in New Zealand	6d-340	Wellington	2000-01
Zimbabwe in Zimbabwe	461	Bulawayo[2]	1997-98

Lowest Innings Totals

New Zealand in New Zealand	251	Auckland	1995-96
New Zealand in Zimbabwe	335	Harare	1992-93
Zimbabwe in New Zealand	170	Auckland	1997-98
Zimbabwe in Zimbabwe	59	Harare	2005-06

Highest Match Aggregate	1366 for 36 wickets	Bulawayo[2]	1997-98
Lowest Match Aggregate	610 for 29 wickets	Harare	2005-06

Highest Individual Innings

New Zealand in New Zealand	157	M.J.Horne	Auckland	1997-98
New Zealand in Zimbabwe	140	M.D.Crowe	Harare	1992-93
Zimbabwe in New Zealand	104+	D.L.Houghton	Auckland	1995-96
Zimbabwe in Zimbabwe	203*	G.J.Whittall	Bulawayo[2]	1997-98

Most Runs in a Series

New Zealand in New Zealand	227 (av 113.50)	C.D.McMillan	1997-98
New Zealand in Zimbabwe	249 (av 62.25)	M.D.Crowe	1992-93
Zimbabwe in New Zealand	166 (av 83.00)	D.L.Houghton	1995-96
Zimbabwe in Zimbabwe	387 (av 96.75)	G.J.Whittall	1997-98

Record Wicket Partnerships - New Zealand

1st	214	C.M.Spearman (112), R.G.Twose (94)	Auckland	1995-96
2nd	127	R.T.Latham (119), A.H.Jones (67*)	Bulawayo[1]	1992-93
3rd	137	L.Vincent (92), S.P.Fleming (65)	Bulawayo[2]	2005-06
4th	243	M.J.Horne (157), N.J.Astle (114)	Auckland	1997-98
5th	222	N.J.Astle (141), C.D.McMillan (142)	Wellington	2000-01
6th	120	S.P.Fleming (73), B.B.McCullum (111)	Harare	2005-06
7th	108	C.D.McMillan (139), D.J.Nash (41)	Wellington	1997-98
8th	144	C.L.Cairns (124), D.J.Nash (62)	Harare	2000-01
9th	78	A.C.Parore (32*), D.L.Vettori (49)	Bulawayo[2]	2000-01
10th	27	C.D.McMillan (88), S.B.Doull (6*)	Auckland	1997-98

Record Wicket Partnerships - Zimbabwe

1st	156	G.J.Rennie (57), G.W.Flower (151)	Harare	1997-98
2nd	107	K.J.Arnott (68), A.D.R.Campbell (52)	Harare	1992-93
3rd	70	A.Flower (39), G.J.Whittall (203*)	Bulawayo[2]	1997-98
4th	130	G.J.Rennie (93), A.Flower (79)	Wellington	2000-01
5th	131	A.Flower (65), G.J.Whittall (188*)	Harare	2000-01
6th	151	G.J.Whittall (188*), H.H.Streak (54)	Harare	2000-01
7th	91	G.J.Whittall (54), P.A.Strang (49)	Hamilton	1995-96
8th	94	A.D.R.Campbell (56), H.H.Streak (43*)	Wellington	1997-98
9th	46	G.J.Crocker (33), M.G.Burmester (17*)	Harare	1992-93
10th	40	G.J.Whittall (203*), E.Matambanadzo (4)	Bulawayo[2]	1997-98

Best Bowling in an Innings

New Zealand in New Zealand	5/71	C.S.Martin	Wellington	2000-01
New Zealand in Zimbabwe	6/50	D.N.Patel	Harare	1992-93
Zimbabwe in New Zealand	4/52	H.H.Streak	Hamilton	1995-96
Zimbabwe in Zimbabwe	8/109	P.A.Strang	Bulawayo[2]	2000-01

Best Bowling in a Match

New Zealand in New Zealand	8/85	S.B.Doull	Auckland	1997-98
New Zealand in Zimbabwe	10/99	S.E.Bond	Bulawayo[2]	2005-06
Zimbabwe in New Zealand	7/160	H.H.Streak	Auckland	1995-96
Zimbabwe in Zimbabwe	11/255	A.G.Huckle	Bulawayo[2]	1997-98

Most Wickets in a Series

New Zealand in New Zealand	11 (av 13.63)	S.B.Doull	1997-98
	11 (av 22.09)	C.L.Cairns	1997-98
New Zealand in Zimbabwe	15 (av 20.26)	D.N.Patel	1992-93
Zimbabwe in New Zealand	12 (av 22.33)	H.H.Streak	1995-96
Zimbabwe in Zimbabwe	16 (av 23.18)	A.G.Huckle	1997-98

NEW ZEALAND v BANGLADESH	New Zealand		Bangladesh		Captains	
Venue and Result	1st	2nd	1st	2nd	New Zealand	Bangladesh
2001-02 in New Zealand						
Hamilton-New Zealand inn & 52 runs	•9d-365	-	205	108	S.P.Fleming	Khaled Mashud
Wellington-New Zealand inn & 74 runs	6d-341	-	•132	135		
2004-05 in Bangladesh						
Dhaka-New Zealand inn & 99 runs	402	-	•177	126	S.P.Fleming	Khaled Mashud
Chittagong[1]-New Zealand inn & 101 runs	•6d-545	-	182	262		

Test Match Results Summary

NEW ZEALAND v BANGLADESH- in New Zealand

		Result			Hamilton			Wellington		
	Tests	NZ	Z	D	NZ	Z	D	NZ	Z	D
2001-02	2	2	-	-	1	-	-	1	-	-

BANGLADESH v NEW ZEALAND - in Bangladesh

		Result			Dhaka			Chittagong[1]		
	Tests	NZ	Z	D	NZ	Z	D	NZ	Z	D
2004-05	2	2	-	-	1	-	-	1	-	-
Totals	4	4	-	-						

Highest Innings Totals

New Zealand in New Zealand	9d-365	Hamilton	2000-01
New Zealand in Bangladesh	6d-545	Chittagong[1]	2004-05
Bangladesh in New Zealand	205	Hamilton	2000-01
Bangladesh in Bangladesh	177	Dhaka	2004-05

Lowest Innings Totals

New Zealand in New Zealand	no instance		
New Zealand in Bangladesh	402	Dhaka	2004-05
Bangladesh in New Zealand	108	Hamilton	2000-01
Bangladesh in Bangladesh	126	Dhaka	2004-05

Highest Match Aggregate	987 for 26 wickets	Chittagong[1]	2004-05
Lowest Match Aggregate	608 for 26 wickets	Wellington	2001-02

Highest Individual Innings

New Zealand in New Zealand	143	M.H.Richardson	Hamilton	2001-02
New Zealand in Bangladesh	202	S.P.Fleming	Chittagong[1]	2004-05
Bangladesh in New Zealand	61	Habibul Bashar	Hamilton	2001-02
Bangladesh in Bangladesh	67	Mohammad Ashraful	Dhaka	2004-05

Most Runs in a Series

New Zealand in New Zealand	226 (av 113.00)	M.H.Richardson	2001-02
New Zealand in Bangladesh	231 (av 115.50)	S.P.Fleming	2004-05
Bangladesh in New Zealand	100 (av 25.00)	Habibul Bashar	2001-02
Bangladesh in Bangladesh	94 (av 23.50)	Khaled Mashud	2004-05

Record Wicket Partnerships - New Zealand

1st	104	M.H.Richardson (83), M.J.Horne (38)	Wellington	2001-02
2nd	63	M.S.Sinclair (76), S.P.Fleming (29)	Dhaka	2004-05
3rd	10	M.H.Richardson (143), S.P.Fleming (4)	Hamilton	2001-02
4th	130	S.P.Fleming (61), C.D.McMillan (70)	Wellington	2001-02
5th	190	M.H.Richardson (83), C.D.McMillan (106)	Wellington	2001-02
6th	89	M.H.Richardson (143), C.L.Cairns (48)	Hamilton	2001-02
7th	71	B.B.McCullum (143), D.L.Vettori (23)	Dhaka	2004-05
8th	57	B.B.McCullum (143), J.E.C.Franklin (22)	Dhaka	2004-05
9th	20	B.B.McCullum (143), P.J.Wiseman (28)	Dhaka	2004-05
10th	31	P.J.Wiseman (28), I.G.Butler (15*)	Dhaka	2004-05

Record Wicket Partnerships - Bangladesh

1st	39	Javed Omar (15), Al Sahriar (53)	Hamilton	2001-02
2nd	32	Javed Omar (58), Aftab Ahmed (20)	Chittagong	2004-05
3rd	60	Habibul Bashar (61), Animul Islam (14)	Hamilton	2001-02
4th	115	Rajin Saleh (41), Mohammad Ashraful (67)	Dhaka	2004-05
5th	26	Habibul Bashar (61), Sanwar Hossain (45)	Hamilton	2001-02
	26	Javed Omar (58), Alok Kapali (13)	Chittagong	2004-05
6th	49	Rajin Saleh (35), Khaled Mashud (51)	Chittagong	2004-05
7th	38	Khaled Mashud (51), Mushfiqur Rahman (20)	Chittagong	2004-05
8th	39	Mushfiqur Rahman (15), Mohammad Rafique (32)	Chittagong	2004-05
9th	49	Khaled Mashud (19*), Mashrafe Mortaza (29)	Wellington	2001-02
10th	45	Tapash Baisya (66), Enamul Haque[2] (0*)	Chittagong	2004-05

Best Bowling in an Innings

New Zealand in New Zealand	7/53	C.L.Cairns	Hamilton	2001-02
New Zealand in Bangladesh	6/28	D.L.Vettori	Dhaka	2004-05
Bangladesh in New Zealand	8/108	Manjural Islam[1]	Wellington	2001-02
Bangladesh in Bangladesh	6/122	Mohammad Rafique	Dhaka	2004-05

Best Bowling in a Match

New Zealand in New Zealand	8/85	C.L.Cairns	Hamilton	2001-02
New Zealand in Bangladesh	12/170	D.L.Vettori	Chittagong	2004-05
Bangladesh in New Zealand	3/99	Manjural Islam[1]	Wellington	2001-02
Bangladesh in Bangladesh	6/122	Mohammad Rafique	Dhaka	2004-05

Most Wickets in a Series

New Zealand in New Zealand	13 (av 12.23)	C.L.Cairns	2001-02
New Zealand in Bangladesh	20 (av 11.20)	D.L.Vettori	2004-05
Bangladesh in New Zealand	5 (av 33.00)	Manjural Islam[1]	2001-02
Bangladesh in Bangladesh	9 (av 28.00)	Mohammad Rafique	2004-05

INDIA v PAKISTAN	India		Pakistan		Captains	
Venue and Result	1st	2nd	1st	2nd	India	Pakistan
1952-53 in India						
Delhi-India inn & 70 runs	•372	-	150	152	N.B.Amarnath	A.H.Kardar
Lucknow[1]-Pakistan inn & 43 runs	•106	182	331	-		
Bombay[2]-India 10 wkts	4d-387	0-45	•186	242		
Madras[1]-Drawn	6-175	-	•344	-		
Calcutta-Drawn	397	0-28	•257	7d-236		
1954-55 in Pakistan						
Dacca-Drawn	148	2-147	•257	158	M.H.Mankad	A.H.Kardar
Bahawalpur-Drawn	•235	5-209	9d-312	-		
Lahore[1]-Drawn	251	2-74	•328	5d-136		
Peshawar[1]-Drawn	245	1-23	•188	182		
Karachi[1]-Drawn	145	2-69	•162	5d-241		
1960-61 in India						
Bombay[2]-Drawn	9d-449	-	•350	4-166	N.J.Contractor	Fazal Mahmood
Kanpur-Drawn	404	-	•335	3-140		
Calcutta-Drawn	180	4-127	•301	3d-146		
Madras[2]-Drawn	9d-539	-	•8d-448	0-59		
Delhi-Drawn	•463	0-16	286	250		
1978-79 in Pakistan						
Faisalabad-Drawn	9d-462	0-43	•8d-503	4d-264	B.S.Bedi	Mushtaq Mohammad
Lahore[2]-Pakistan 8 wkts	•199	465	6d-539	2-182		
Karachi[1]-Pakistan 8 wkts	•344	300	9d-481	2-164		
1979-80 in India						
Bangalore-Drawn	416	-	•9d-431	2-108	S.M.Gavaskar	Asif Iqbal
Delhi-Drawn	126	6-364	•273	242	S.M.Gavaskar	
Bombay[3]-India 131 runs	•334	160	173	190	S.M.Gavaskar	
Kanpur-Drawn	•162	2-193	249	-	S.M.Gavaskar	
Madras[1]-India 10 wkts	430	0-78	•272	233	S.M.Gavaskar	
Calcutta-Drawn	•331	205	4d-272	6-179	G.R.Viswanath	
1982-83 in Pakistan						
Lahore[2]-Drawn	379	-	•485	1-135	S.M.Gavaskar	Imran Khan
Karachi[1]-Pakistan inn & 86 runs	•169	197	452	-		
Faisalabad-Pakistan 10 wkts	•372	286	652	0-10		
Hyderabad-Pakistan inn & 119 runs	189	273	•3d-581	-		
Lahore[2]-Drawn	3-235	-	•323	-		
Karachi[1]-Drawn	•8d-393	2-224	6d-420	-		
1983-84 in India						
Bangalore-Drawn	•275	0-176	288	-	Kapil Dev	Zaheer Abbas
Jullundur-Drawn	374	-	•337	0-16		
Nagpur-Drawn	•245	8d-262	322	1-42		
1984-85 in Pakistan						
Lahore[2]-Drawn	156	6-371	•9d-428	-	S.M.Gavaskar	Zaheer Abbas
Faisalabad-Drawn	•500	-	6-674	-		
1986-87 in India						
Madras[1]-Drawn	9d-527	-	•9d-487	3-182	Kapil Dev	Imran Khan
Calcutta-Drawn	•403	3d-181	229	5-179		
Jaipur-Drawn	•8d-465	2-114	341	-		

INDIA v PAKISTAN (cont.)	India		Pakistan		Captains	
Venue and Result	1st	2nd	1st	2nd	India	Pakistan
Ahmedabad-Drawn	323	-	•395	2-135		
Bangalore-Pakistan 16 runs	145	204	•116	249		
1989-90 in Pakistan						
Karachi[1]-Drawn	262	3-303	•409	5d-305	K.Srikkanth	Imran Khan
Faisalabad-Drawn	•288	7-398	9d-423	-		
Lahore[2]-Drawn	•509	-	5-699	-		
Sialkot-Drawn	•324	7-234	250	-		
1998-99 in India						
Chennai[1]-Pakistan 12 runs	254	258	•238	286	M.Azharuddin	Wasim Akram
Delhi-India 212 runs	•252	339	172	207		
1998-99 in India (Asian Test Championship)						
Calcutta-Pakistan 12 runs	223	232	•185	316	M.Azharuddin	Wasim Akram
2003-04 in Pakistan						
Multan[2]-India inn & 52 runs	•5d-675	-	407	216	R.S.Dravid	Inzamamul Haq
Lahore[2]-Pak 9 wkts	•287	241	489	1-40	R.S.Dravid	
Rawalpindi[2]-India inn & 131 runs	600	-	•224	245	S.C.Ganguly	
2004-05 in India						
Mohali-Drawn	516	1-85	•312	9d-496	S.C.Ganguly	Inzamamul Haq
Kolkata-India 195 runs	•407	9d-407	393	226		
Bangalore-Pakistan 168 runs	449	214	•570	2d-261		
2005-06 in Pakistan						
Lahore[2]-Drawn	1-410	-	•7d679	-	R.S.Dravid	Inzamamul Haq
Faisalabad-Drawn	603	0-21	•588	490		Inzamamul Haq
Karavhi[1]-Pak 341 runs	238	265	•245	7d-599		Younis Khan

Test Match Results Summary

INDIA v PAKISTAN - in India

		Result	Delhi	Luck.	Bomb.	Chennai	Calc.	Kanpur	Bang.	Jull.	Nagpur	Jaipur	Ahmed.	Mohali
	T	I P D	I P D	I P D	I P D	I P D	I P D	I P D	I P D	I P D	I P D	I P D	I P D	I P D
1952-53	5	2 1 2	1 - -	- 1 -	1 - -	- - 1	- - 1	- - -	- - -	- - -	- - -	- - -	- - -	- - -
1960-61	5	- - 5	- - 1	- - -	- - 1	- - 1	- - 1	- - 1	- - -	- - -	- - -	- - -	- - -	- - -
1979-80	6	2 - 4	- - 1	- - -	1 - -	1 - -	- - 1	- - 1	- - 1	- - -	- - -	- - -	- - -	- - -
1983-84	3	- - 3	- - -	- - -	- - -	- - -	- - -	- - -	- - 1	- - 1	- - 1	- - -	- - -	- - -
1986-87	5	- 1 4	- - -	- - -	- - -	- - 1	- - 1	- - -	- 1 -	- - -	- - -	- - 1	- - 1	- - -
1998-99	2	1 1 -	1 - -	- - -	- - -	- 1 -	- - -	- - -	- - -	- - -	- - -	- - -	- - -	- - -
1998-99	1	- 1 -	- - -	- - -	- - -	- - -	- 1 -	- - -	- - -	- - -	- - -	- - -	- - -	- - -
2004-05	3	1 1 1	- - -	- - -	- - -	- - -	1 - -	- - -	- 1 -	- - -	- - -	- - -	- - -	- - 1
	30	6 5 19	1 - 2	- 1 -	2 - 1	1 - 3	1 1 4	- - 2	- 2 2	- - 1	- - 1	- - 1	- - 1	- - 1

INDIA v PAKISTAN - in Pakistan

	T	Result	Dacca	Bah.	Lahore	Pesh.	Karachi[1]	Fais.	Hyd.	Sialkot	Multan	Rawal.
		I P D	I P D	I P D	I P D	I P D	I P D	I P D	I P D	I P D	I P D	I P D
1954-55	5	- - 5	- - 1	- - 1	- - 1	- - 1	- - 1	- - -	- - -	- - -	- - -	- - -
1978-79	3	- 2 1	- - -	- - -	- 1 -	- - -	- 1 -	- - 1	- - -	- - -	- - -	- - -
1982-83	6	- 3 3	- - -	- - -	- - 2	- - -	- 1 1	- 1 -	- 1 -	- - -	- - -	- - -
1984-85	2	- - 2	- - -	- - -	- - 1	- - -	- - -	- - 1	- - -	- - -	- - -	- - -
1989-90	4	- - 4	- - -	- - -	- - 1	- - -	- - 1	- - 1	- - -	- - 1	- - -	- - -
2003-04	3	2 1 -	- - -	- - -	- 1 -	- - -	- - -	- - -	- - -	- - -	1 - -	1 - -
2005-06	1	- - 1	- - -	- - -	- - 1	- - -	- 1 -	- - 1	- - -	- - -	- - -	- - -
	26	2 7 17	- - 1	- - 1	- 2 6	- - 1	- 3 3	- 1 4	- 1 -	- - 1	1 - -	1 - -
Totals	56	8 12 36										

Key to ground abbreviations: Luck. - Lucknow[1]; Bomb. - Mumbai; Calc. - Calcutta; Bang. - Bangalore; Jull. - Jullundur; Ahmed. - Ahmedabad; Bah. - Bahawalpur; Pesh. - Peshawar[1]; Fais. - Faisalabad; Hyd. - Hyderabad; Rawal. - Rawalpindi.

Highest Innings Totals

India in India	9d-539	Madras[2]	1960-61
India in Pakistan	5d-675	Multan[2]	2003-04
Pakistan in India	570	Bangalore	2004-05
Pakistan in Pakistan	5-699	Lahore[2]	1989-90

Lowest Innings Totals

India in India	106	Lucknow[1]	1952-53
India in Pakistan	145	Karachi[1]	1954-55
Pakistan in India	116	Delhi	1986-87
Pakistan in Pakistan	158	Dacca	1954-55

Highest Match Aggregate	1702 for 28 wickets	Faisalabad	2005-06
Lowest Match Aggregate	619 for 30 wickets	Lucknow[1]	1952-53

Highest Individual Innings

India in India	201	A.D.Gaekwad	Jullundur	1983-84
	201	V.K.Sehwag	Bangalore	2004-05
India in Pakistan	309	V.K.Sehwag	Multan[2]	2003-04
Pakistan in India	270	Younis Khan	Bangalore	2004-05
Pakistan in Pakistan	280*	Javed Miandad	Hyderabad	1982-83

Most Runs in a Series

India in India	544 (av 90.66)	V.K.Sehwag	2004-05
India in Pakistan	584 (av 73.00)	M.Amarnath	1982-83
Pakistan in India	508 (av 101.60)	Younis Khan	2004-05
Pakistan in Pakistan	761 (av 126.83)	Mudassar Nazar	1982-83

Record Wicket Partnerships - India

1st	410	V.K.Sehwag (254), R.S.Dravid (128*)	Lahore[2]	2005-06
2nd	197	R.S.Dravid (103), V.V.S.Laxman (90)	Faisalabad	2005-06
3rd	336	V.K.Sehwag (309), S.R.Tendulkar (194*)	Multan[2]	2003-04
4th	186	S.V.Manjrekar (218), R.J.Shastri (61)	Lahore[2]	1989-90
5th	200	S.M.Patil (127), R.J.Shastri (139)	Faisalabad	1984-85
6th	210	M.S.Dhoni (148), I.K.Pathan (90)	Faisalabad	2005-06
7th	155	R.M.H.Binny (83*), S.Madan Lal (74)	Bangalore	1983-84
8th	122	S.M.H.Kirmani (66), S.Madan Lal (54)	Faisalabad	1982-83
9th	149	P.G.Joshi (52*), R.B.Desai (85)	Bombay[2]	1960-61
10th	109	H.R.Adhikari (81*), Ghulam Ahmed (50)	Delhi	1952-53

Record Wicket Partnerships - Pakistan

1st	162	Hanif Mohammad (62), Imtiaz Ahmed (135)	Madras[2]	1960-61
2nd	250	Mudassar Nazar (199), Qasim Omar (210)	Faisalabad	1984-85
3rd	451	Mudassar Nazar (230), Javed Miandad (280*)	Hyderabad	1982-83
4th	287	Javed Miandad (126), Zaheer Abbas (168)	Faisalabad	1982-83
5th	213	Zaheer Abbas (186), Mudassar Nazar (119)	Karachi[1]	1982-83
6th	207	Saleem Malik (107), Imran Khan (117)	Faisalabad	1982-83
7th	184	Abdul Razzaq (71), Kamran Akmal (109)	Mohali	2004-05
8th	112	Imran Khan (135*), Wasim Akram (62)	Madras[1]	1986-87
9th	70	Yousuf Youhana (112), Shoaib Akhtar (4)	Multan[2]	2003-04
	70	Mohammad Sami (49), Fazl-e-Akbar (25)	Rawalpindi[2]	2003-04
10th	104	Zulfiqar Ahmed (63*), Amir Elahi (47)	Madras[1]	1952-53

Best Bowling in an Innings

India in India	10/74	A.Kumble	Delhi	1998-99
India in Pakistan	8/85	Kapil Dev	Lahore[2]	1982-83
Pakistan in India	8/69	Sikander Bakht	Delhi	1979-80
Pakistan in Pakistan	8/60	Imran Khan	Karachi[1]	1982-83

Best Bowling in a Match

India in India	14/149	A.Kumble	Delhi	1998-99
India in Pakistan	8/85	Kapil Dev	Lahore[2]	1982-83
Pakistan in India	12/94	Fazal Mahmood	Lucknow[1]	1952-53
Pakistan in Pakistan	11/79	Imran Khan	Karachi[1]	1982-83

Most Wickets in a Series

India in India	32 (av 17.68)	Kapil Dev	1979-80
India in Pakistan	24 (av 34.62)	Kapil Dev	1982-83
Pakistan in India	24 (av 26.70)	Sikander Bakht	1979-80
Pakistan in Pakistan	40 (av 13.95)	Imran Khan	1982-83

INDIA v SRI LANKA	India		Sri Lanka		Captains	
Venue and Result	1st	2nd	1st	2nd	India	Sri Lanka
1982-83 in India						
Madras[1]-Drawn	6d-566	7-135	•346	394	S.M.Gavaskar	B.Warnaweera
1985-86 in Sri Lanka						
Colombo (SSC)-Drawn	•218	251	347	4-61	Kapil Dev	L.R.D.Mendis
Colombo (PSS)-Sri Lanka 149 runs	244	198	•385	3d-206		
Kandy-Drawn	•249	5d-325	198	7-307		
1986-87 in India						
Kanpur-Drawn	7-676	-	•420	-	Kapil Dev	L.R.D.Mendis
Nagpur-India inn & 106 runs	6d-451	-	•204	141		
Cuttack-India inn & 67 runs	•400	-	191	142		
1990-91 in India						
Chandigarh-India inn & 8 runs	•288	-	82	198	M.Azharuddin	A.Ranatunga
1993-94 in Sri Lanka						
Kandy-Drawn	-	-	•3-24	-	M.Azharuddin	A.Ranatunga
Colombo (SSC)-India 235 runs	•366	4d-359	254	236		
Colombo (PSS)-Drawn	446	-	•351	6-352		

INDIA v SRI LANKA (cont.) Venue and Result	India 1st	India 2nd	Sri Lanka 1st	Sri Lanka 2nd	Captains India	Captains Sri Lanka
1993-94 in India						
Lucknow[2]-India inn & 119 runs	•511	-	218	174	M.Azharuddin	A.Ranatunga
Bangalore-India inn & 95 runs	•6d-541	-	231	215		
Ahmedabad-India inn & 17 runs	358	-	•119	222		
1997-98 in Sri Lanka						
Colombo (RPS)-Drawn	•8d-537	-	6d-952	-	S.R.Tendulkar	A.Ranatunga
Colombo (SSC)-Drawn	375	5-281	•332	7d-415		
1997-98 in India						
Mohali-Drawn	9d-515	-	•369	6-251	S.R.Tendulkar	A.Ranatunga
Nagpur-Drawn	•485	-	-	-		
Mumbai[3]-Drawn	•512	9d-181	361	7-166		
1998-99 in Sri Lanka (Asian Test Championship)						
Colombo (SSC)-Drawn	•7d-518	5-306	485	-	M.Azharuddin	A.Ranatunga
2001-02 in Sri Lanka						
Galle-Sri Lanka 10 wkts	•187	180	362	0-6	S.C.Ganguly	S.T.Jayasuriya
Kandy-India 7 wkts	232	3-264	•274	221		
Colombo(SSC)-Sri Lanka inn & 77 runs	•234	299	6d-610	-		
2005-06 in India						
Chennai[1]-Drawn	•167	-	4-168	-	R.S.Dravid	M.S.Atapattu
Delhi-India 199 runs	•290	6d-375	230	247		
Ahmedabad-India 259 runs	•398	9d-316	206	249	V.K.Sehwag	

Test Match Results Summary

INDIA v SRI LANKA - in India

		Result			Chennai			Kanpur			Nagpur			Cuttack			Chand.			Luck.			Banga.			Ahmed.			Mohali			Mumbai			Delhi		
	T	I	S	D	I	S	D	I	S	D	I	S	D	I	S	D	I	S	D	I	S	D	I	S	D	I	S	D	I	S	D	I	S	D	I	S	D
1982-83	1	-	-	1	-	-	1	-	-	-	-	-	-	-	-	-	-	-	-	-	-	-	-	-	-	-	-	-	-	-	-	-	-	-	-	-	-
1986-87	3	2	-	1	-	-	-	1	-	-	-	-	1	1	-	-	-	-	-	-	-	-	-	-	-	-	-	-	-	-	-	-	-	-	-	-	-
1990-91	1	1	-	-	-	-	-	-	-	-	-	-	-	-	-	-	-	-	1	-	-	-	-	-	-	-	-	-	-	-	-	-	-	-	-	-	-
1993-94	3	3	-	-	-	-	-	-	-	-	-	-	-	-	-	-	-	-	-	1	-	-	1	-	-	1	-	-	-	-	-	-	-	-	-	-	-
1997-98	3	-	-	3	-	-	-	-	-	-	-	-	1	-	-	-	-	-	-	-	-	-	-	-	-	-	-	-	-	-	1	-	-	1	-	-	-
2005-06	3	2	-	1	-	-	1	-	-	-	-	-	-	-	-	-	-	-	-	-	-	-	-	-	-	1	-	-	-	-	-	-	-	-	1	-	-
	14	8	-	6	-	-	1	1	-	-	-	-	2	1	-	-	-	-	1	1	-	-	1	-	-	2	-	-	-	-	1	-	-	1	1	-	-

INDIA v SRI LANKA - in Sri Lanka

		Result			Colombo(SSC)			Colombo(PSS)			Kandy			Colombo(RPS)			Galle		
	Tests	I	SL	D	I	SL	D	I	SL	D	I	SL	D	I	SL	D	I	SL	D
1985-86	3	-	1	2	-	-	1	-	1	-	-	-	1	-	-	-	-	-	-
1993-94	3	1	-	2	1	-	-	-	-	1	-	-	1	-	-	-	-	-	-
1997-98	2	-	-	2	-	-	1	-	-	-	-	-	-	-	-	1	-	-	-
1998-99	1	-	-	1	-	-	1	-	-	-	-	-	-	-	-	-	-	-	-
2001-02	3	1	2	-	-	1	-	-	-	-	1	-	-	-	-	-	-	1	-
	12	2	3	7	1	1	3	-	1	1	1	-	2	-	-	1	-	1	-
Totals	26	10	3	13															

Key to ground abbreviations: Chand. - Chandigarh; Luck. - Lucknow; Bang. - Bangalore; Ahmed. - Ahmedabad.

Highest Innings Totals

India in India	7-676	Kanpur	1986-87
India in Sri Lanka	8d-537	Colombo (RPS)	1997-98
Sri Lanka in India	420	Kanpur	1986-84
Sri Lanka in Sri Lanka	6d-952	Colombo (RPS)	1997-98

Lowest Innings Totals

India in India	167	Chennai[1]	2005-06
India in Sri Lanka	180	Galle	2001-02
Sri Lanka in India	82	Chandigarh	1990-91
Sri Lanka in Sri Lanka	198	Kandy	1985-86

Highest Match Aggregate	1489 for 14 wickets	Colombo (RPS)	1997-98
Lowest Match Aggregate	568 for 30 wickets	Chandigarh	1990-91

Highest Individual Innings

India in India	199	M.Azharuddin	Kanpur	1986-87
India in Sri Lanka	147	S.C.Ganguly	Colombo (SSC)	1997-98
Sri Lanka in India	110*	P.A.de Silva	Mohali	1997-98
Sri Lanka in Sri Lanka	340	S.T.Jayasuriya	Colombo (RPS)	1997-98

Most Runs in a Series

India in India	392 (av 98.00)	S.C.Ganguly	1997-98
India in Sri Lanka	290 (av 96.66)	S.R.Tendulkar	1997-98
Sri Lanka in India	282 (av 47.00)	R.S.Mahanama	1993-94
Sri Lanka in Sri Lanka	571 (av 190.33)	S.T.Jayasuriya	1997-98

Record Wicket Partnerships - India

1st	171	M.Prabhakar (94), N.S.Sidhu (104)	Colombo (SSC)	1993-94
2nd	232	S.Ramesh (143), R.S.Dravid (107)	Colombo (SSC)	1998-99
3rd	173	M.Amarnath (131), D.B.Vengsarkar (153)	Nagpur	1986-87
4th	256	S.C.Ganguly (173), S.R.Tendulkar (148)	Mumbai[3]	1997-98
5th	150	S.R.Tendulkar (139), S.C.Ganguly (147)	Colombo (SSC)	1997-98
6th	272	M.Azharuddin (199), Kapil Dev (163)	Kanpur	1986-87
7th	125	V.V.S.Laxman (104), I.K.Patahan (82)	Ahmedabad	2005-06
8th	70	Kapil Dev (78), L.Sivaramakrishnan (21)	Colombo (PSS)	1985-86
9th	89	S.C.Ganguly (109), A.Kuruvilla (35*)	Mohali	1997-98
10th	69*	A.Kumble (29*), Harbhajan Singh (40*)	Ahmedabad	2005-06

Record Wicket Partnerships - Sri Lanka

1st	159	S.Wettimuny (79), J.R.Ratnayeke (93)	Kanpur	1986-87
2nd	576	S.T.Jayasuriya (340), R.S.Mahanama (225)	Colombo (RPS)	1997-98
3rd	218	S.T.Jayasuriya (199), P.A.de Silva (120)	Colombo (SSC)	1997-98
4th	216	R.L.Dias (106), L.R.D.Mendis (124)	Kandy	1985-86
5th	144	R.S.Madugalle (103), A.Ranatunga (111)	Colombo (SSC)	1985-86
6th	103	P.A.de Silva (110*), H.D.P.K.Dharmasena (25)	Mohali	1997-98
7th	194*	H.P.Tillakaratne (136*), T.T.Samaraweera (103*)	Colombo (SSC)	2001-02
8th	48	P.A.de Silva (146), M.Muralidaran (39)	Colombo (RPS)	1997-98
9th	60	H.P.Tillakaratne (55), M.A.W.R.Madurasinghe (11)	Chandigarh	1990-91
10th	64	M.Muralidaran (67), P.D.R.L.Perera (6*)	Kandy	2001-02

Best Bowling in an Innings

India in India	7/51	Maninder Singh	Nagpur	1986-87
India in Sri Lanka	5/72	B.K.Venkatesh Prasad	Kandy	2001-02
Sri Lanka in India	7/100	M.Muralidaran	Delhi	2005-06
Sri Lanka in Sri Lanka	8/87	M.Muralidaran	Colombo (SSC)	2001-02

Best Bowling in a Match

India in India	11/125	S.L.Venkatapathy Raju	Ahmedabad	1993-94
India in Sri Lanka	8/172	A.Kumble	Colombo (SSC)	1993-94
Sri Lanka in India	8/201	H.D.P.K.Dharmasena	Mumbai[3]	1997-98
Sri Lanka in Sri Lanka	11/196	M.Muralidaran	Colombo (SSC)	2001-02

Most Wickets in a Series

India in India	20 (av 18.70)	A.Kumble	2005-06
India in Sri Lanka	14 (av 27.35)	C.Sharma	1985-86
Sri Lanka in India	16 (av 31.00)	M.Muralidaran	2005-06
Sri Lanka in Sri Lanka	23 (av 19.30)	M.Muralidaran	2001-02

INDIA v ZIMBABWE	India		Zimbabwe		Captains	
Venue and Result	1st	2nd	1st	2nd	India	Zimbabwe
1992-93 in Zimbabwe						
Harare-Drawn	307	-	•456	4-146	M.Azharuddin	D.L.Houghton
1992-93 in India						
Delhi-India inn & 13 runs	•7d-536	-	322	201	M.Azharuddin	D.L.Houghton
1998-99 in Zimbabwe						
Harare-Zimbabwe 61 runs	280	173	•221	293	M.Azharuddin	A.D.R.Campbell
2000-01 in India						
Delhi-India 7 wkts	4d-458	3-190	•9d-422	225	S.C.Ganguly	H.H.Streak
Nagpur-Drawn	•6d-609	-	382	6-503		
2001-02 in Zimbabwe						
Bulawayo[2]-India 8 wkts	318	2-184	•173	328	S.C.Ganguly	H.H.Streak
Harare-Zimbabwe 4 wkts	•237	234	315	6-157		
2001-02 in India						
Nagpur-India inn & 101 runs	7d-570	-	•287	182	S.C.Ganguly	S.V.Carlisle
Delhi-India 4 wkts	354	6-126	•329	146		
2005-06 in Zimbabwe						
Bulawayo[2]-India inn & 90 runs	554	-	•279	185	S.C.Ganguly	T.Taibu
Harare-India 10 wkts	366	0-19	•161	223		

Test Match Results Summary

INDIA v ZIMBABWE - in India

		Result			Delhi			Nagpur		
	Tests	I	Z	D	I	Z	D	I	Z	D
1992-93	1	1	-	-	1	-	-	-	-	-
2000-01	2	1	-	1	1	-	-	-	-	1
2001-02	2	2	-	-	1	-	-	1	-	-
	5	4	-	1	3	-	-	1	-	1

INDIA v ZIMBABWE - in Zimbabwe

		Result			Harare			Bulawayo[2]		
	Tests	I	Z	D	I	Z	D	I	Z	D
1992-93	1	-	-	1	-	-	1	-	-	-
1998-99	1	-	1	-	-	1	-	-	-	-
2001-02	2	1	1	-	-	1	-	1	-	-
2005-06	2	2	-	-	1	-	-	1	-	-
	6	3	2	1	1	2	1	2	-	-
Totals	11	7	2	2						

Highest Innings Totals

India in India	6d-609	Nagpur	2000-01
India in Zimbabwe	554	Bulawayo[2]	2005-06
Zimbabwe in India	6-503	Delhi	2000-01
Zimbabwe in Zimbabwe	456	Harare	1992-93

Lowest Innings Totals

India in India	354	Delhi	2001-02
India in Zimbabwe	173	Harare	1998-99
Zimbabwe in India	146	Delhi	2001-02
Zimbabwe in Zimbabwe	173	Bulawayo[2]	2001-02

Highest Match Aggregate	1494 for 22 wickets	Nagpur	2000-01
Lowest Match Aggregate	909 for 24 wickets	Harare	1992-93

Highest Individual Innings

India in India	227	V.G.Kambli	Delhi	1992-93
India in Zimbabwe	140	V.V.S.Laxman	Bulawayo[2]	2005-06
Zimbabwe in India	232*	A.Flower	Nagpur	2000-01
Zimbabwe in Zimbabwe	121	D.L.Houghton	Harare	1992-93

Most Runs in a Series

India in India	432 (av 432.00)	R.S.Dravid	2000-01
India in Zimbabwe	239 (av 79.66)	S.S.Das	2001-02
Zimbabwe in India	540 (av 270.00)	A.Flower	2000-01
Zimbabwe in Zimbabwe	187 (av 62.33)	A.Flower	2001-02

Record Wicket Partnerships - India

1st	88	G.Gambhir (46), V.K.Sehwag (44)	Bulawayo[2]	2005-06
2nd	155	S.S.Das (110), R.S.Dravid (162)	Nagpur	2000-01
3rd	249	R.S.Dravid (162), S.R.Tendulkar (201*)	Nagpur	2000-01
4th	128	V.V.S.Laxman (140), S.C.Ganguly (101)	Bulawayo[2]	2005-06
5th	120	S.C.Ganguly (136), V.K.Sehwag (74)	Delhi	2001-02
6th	96	S.R.Tendulkar (176), V.K.Sehwag (100*)	Nagpur	2001-02
7th	97	S.C.Ganguly (101), I.K.Patahn (52)	Bulawayo[2]	2005-06
8th	72	S.S.Dighe (47), Harbhajan Singh (66)	Bulawayo[2]	2001-02
9th	19	H.K.Badani (16*), J.Srinath (3)	Harare	2001-02
	19	I.K.Patahn (32), Harbhajan Singh (14*)	Harare	2005-06
10th	40	J.Srinath (23), Harbhajan Singh (15*)	Harare	1998-99

Record Wicket Partnerships - Zimbabwe

1st	138	G.J.Rennie (84), C.B.Wishart (63)	Harare	1998-99
2nd	106	S.V.Carlisle (77), A.D.R.Campbell (57)	Nagpur	2001-02
3rd	119	S.V.Carlisle (58), A.D.R.Campbell (70)	Delhi	2000-01
4th	209	A.D.R.Campbell (102), A.Flower (232*)	Nagpur	2000-01
5th	96	A.Flower (55), G.W.Flower (106*)	Nagpur	2000-01
6th	165	D.L.Houghton (121), A.Flower (59)	Harare	1992-93
7th	116	H.Masakadza (71), A.M.Blignaut (84*)	Harare	2005-06
8th	59	T.Taibu (71*), K.M.Dabengwa (35)	Bulawayo[2]	2005-06
9th	59	T.J.Friend (60), R.W.Price (18)	Nagpur	2001-02
10th	97*	A.Flower (183*), H.K.Olonga (11*)	Delhi	2000-01

Best Bowling in an Innings

India in India	6/62	Harbhajan Singh	Delhi	2001-02
India in Zimbabwe	7/59	I.K.Pathan	Harare	2005-06
Zimbabwe in India	5/182	R.W.Price	Nagpur	2001-02
Zimbabwe in Zimbabwe	6/73	H.H.Streak	Harare	2005-06

Best Bowling in a Match

India in India	9/141	J.Srinath	Delhi	2000-01
India in Zimbabwe	12/126	I.K.Pathan	Harare	2005-06
Zimbabwe in India	5/132	R.W.Price	Delhi	2001-02
Zimbabwe in Zimbabwe	7/115	H.H.Streak	Harare	2001-02

Most Wickets in a Series

India in India	16 (av 18.18)	A.Kumble	2001-02
India in Zimbabwe	21 (av 11.28)	I.K.Pathan	2005-06
Zimbabwe in India	10 (av 31.40)	R.W.Price	2001-02
Zimbabwe in Zimbabwe	10 (av 17.80)	H.H.Streak	2001-02

INDIA v BANGLADESH	India		Bangladesh		Captains	
Venue and Result	1st	2nd	1st	2nd	India	Bangladesh
2000-01 in Bangladesh						
Dhaka-India 9 wkts	429	1-64	•400	91	S.C.Ganguly	Naimur Rahman
2004-05 in Bangladesh						
Dhaka-India inn & 140 runs	526	-	•184	202	S.C.Ganguly	Habibul Bashar
Chittagong[1]-India inn & 83 runs	•540	-	333	124		

Test Match Results Summary

INDIA v BANGLADESH - in Bangladesh

		Result			Dhaka			Chittagong[1]		
	Tests	I	B	D	I	B	D	I	B	D
2000-01	1	1	-	-	1	-	-	-	-	-
2004-05	2	2	-	-	1	-	-	1	-	-
	3	3	-	-	2	-	-	1	-	-
Totals	3	3	-	-						

Highest Innings Totals

India in India	no instance		
India in Bangladesh	540	Chittagong[1]	2004-05
Bangladesh in India	no instance		
Bangladesh in Bangladesh	400	Dhaka	2000-01

Lowest Innings Totals

India in India	no instance		
India in Bangladesh	429	Dhaka	2000-01
Bangladesh in India	no instance		
Bangladesh in Bangladesh	91	Dhaka	2000-01

Highest Match Aggregate	997 for 30 wickets	Chittagong[1]	2004-05
Lowest Match Aggregate	912 for 30 wickets	Dhaka	2004-05

Highest Individual Innings

India in India		no instance		
India in Bangladesh	248*	S.R.Tendulkar	Dhaka	2004-05
Bangladesh in India		no instance		
Bangladesh in Bangladesh	158*	Mohammad Ashraful	Chittagong[1]	2004-05

Most Runs in a Series

India in India	no instance		
India in Bangladesh	284 (av 284.00)	S.R.Tendulkar	2004-05
Bangladesh in India	no instance		
Bangladesh in Bangladesh	221 (av 110.50)	Mohammad Ashraful	2004-05

Record Wicket Partnerships - India

1st	66	S.S.Das (29), S.Ramesh (58)	Dhaka	2000-01
2nd	259	G.Gambhir (139), R.S.Dravid (169)	Chittagong[1]	2004-05
3rd	51	R.S.Dravid (169), S.R.Tendulkar (36)	Chittagong[1]	2004-05
4th	164	S.R.Tendulkar (248*), S.C.Ganguly (71)	Dhaka	2004-05
5th	66	S.R.Tendulkar (248*), V.V.S.Laxman (32)	Dhaka	2004-05
6th	46	S.C.Ganguly (84), S.S.Karim (15)	Dhaka	2000-01
7th	121	S.C.Ganguly (84), S.B.Joshi (92)	Dhaka	2000-01
8th	56	S.B.Joshi (92), A.B.Agarkar (34)	Dhaka	2000-01
9th	75	S.C.Ganguly (88), Harbhajan Singh (47)	Chittagong[1]	2004-05
10th	133	S.R.Tendulkar (248*), Zaheer Khan (75)	Dhaka	2004-05

Record Wicket Partnerships - Bangladesh

1st	48	Nafis Iqbal (31), Javed Omar (10)	Chittagong[1]	2004-05
2nd	34	Shahriar Hossain (12), Habibul Bashar (71)	Dhaka	2000-01
3rd	66	Habibul Bashar (71), Aminul Islam (145)	Dhaka	2000-01
4th	70	Habibul Bashar (22), Mohammad Ashraful (158*)	Chittagong[1]	2004-05
5th	115	Mohammad Ashraful (158*), Aftab Ahmed (43)	Chittagong[1]	2004-05
6th	64	Nafis Iqbal (54), Manjural Islam[2] (69)	Dhaka	2004-05
7th	93	Aminul Islam (145), Khaled Mashud (32)	Dhaka	2000-01
8th	65	Mohammad Ashraful (60*), Mohammad Rafique (47)	Dhaka	2004-05
9th	69	Aminul Islam (145), Hasibul Hossain (28*)	Dhaka	2004-05
10th	40	Nazmul Hossain (8*), Talha Jubair (31)	Chittagong[1]	2004-05

Best Bowling in an Innings

India in India	no instance			
India in Bangladesh	6/51	I.K.Pathan	Dhaka	2004-05
Bangladesh in India	no instance			
Bangladesh in Bangladesh	6/132	Naimur Rahman	Dhaka	2000-01

Best Bowling in a Match

India in India	no instance			
India in Bangladesh	11/96	I.K.Pathan	Dhaka	2004-05
Bangladesh in India	no instance			
Bangladesh in Bangladesh	6/154	Naimur Rahman	Dhaka	2000-01

Most Wickets in a Series

India in India	no instance		
India in Bangladesh	18 (av 11.88)	I.K.Pathan	2004-05
Bangladesh in India	no instance		
Bangladesh in Bangladesh	6 (av 25.66)	Naimur Rahman	2000-01
	6 (av 44.83)	Mohammad Rafique	2004-05

PAKISTAN v SRI LANKA	Pakistan		Sri Lanka		Captains	
Venue and Result	1st	2nd	1st	2nd	Pakistan	Sri Lanka
1981-82 in Pakistan						
Karachi[1]-Pakistan 204 runs	•396	4d-301	344	149	Javed Miandad	B Warnapura
Faisalabad-Drawn	270	7-186	•454	8d-154		L. R. D. Mendis
Lahore[2]-Pakistan inn & 102 runs	7d-500	-	•240	158		B. Warnapura
1985-86 in Pakistan						
Faisalabad-Drawn	3-555	-	•479	-	Javed Miandad	L. R. D. Mendis
Sialkot-Pakistan 8 wkts	259	2-100	•157	200		
Karachi[1]-Pakistan 10 wkts	295	0-98	•162	230		
1985-86 in Sri Lanka						
Kandy-Pakistan inn & 20 runs	230	-	•109	101	Imran Khan	L. R. D. Mendis
Colombo (CCC)-Sri Lanka 149 runs	•132	172	273	2-32		
Colombo (PSS)-Drawn	318	-	•281	3-323		
1991-92 in Pakistan						
Sialkot-Drawn	5d-423	-	•270	5-137	Imran Khan	P.A.de Silva
Gujranwala-Drawn	•2-109	-	-	-		
Faisalabad-Pakistan 3 wkts	221	7-188	•240	165		
1994-95 in Sri Lanka						
Colombo (PSS)-Pakistan 301 runs	•390	4d-318	226	181	Saleem Malik	A.Ranatunga
Colombo (SSC)-Match cancelled						
Kandy-Pakistan inn & 52 runs	9d-357	-	71	234		
1995-96 in Pakistan						
Peshawar[2]-Pakistan inn & 40 runs	•9d-459	-	186	233	Rameez Raja	A.Ranatunga
Faisalabad-Sri Lanka 42 runs	333	209	•223	361		
Sialkot-Sri Lanka 144 runs	214	212	•232	9d-338		
1996-97 in Sri Lanka						
Colombo (RPS)-Drawn	378	-	•330	8-423	Rameez Raja	A.Ranatunga
Colombo (SSC)-Drawn	292	5-285	•331	4d-386		
1998-99 in Pakistan/Bangladesh (Asian Test Championship)						
Lahore[2]-Drawn	•398	8d-314	328	2-165	Wasim Akram	H.P.Tillakaratne
Dhaka-Pakistan inn & 175 runs	594	-	•231	188		P.A.de Silva

PAKISTAN v SRI LANKA (cont.)	Pakistan		Sri Lanka		Captains	
Venue and Result	1st	2nd	1st	2nd	Pakistan	Sri Lanka
1999-2000 in Pakistan						
Rawalpindi[2]-Sri Lanka 2 wkts	•182	390	353	8-220	Saeed Anwar	S.T.Jayasuriya
Peshawar[2]-Sri Lanka 57 runs	199	236	•268	224	Saeed Anwar	
Karachi[1]-Pakistan 222 runs	•256	421	227	228	Moin Khan	
1999-2000 in Sri Lanka						
Colombo (SSC)-Pakistan 5 wkts	266	5-131	•273	123	Moin Khan	S.T.Jayasuriya
Galle-Pakistan inn & 163 runs	8d-600	-	•181	256		
Kandy-Drawn	-	-	•5-467	-		
2001-02 in Pakistan (Asian Test Championship)						
Lahore[2]-Sri Lanka 8 wkts	•234	325	528	2-33	Moin Khan	S.T.Jayasuriya
2004-05 in Pakistan						
Faisalabad-Sri Lanka 201 runs	264	216	•243	438	Inzamamul Haq	M.S.Atapattu
Karachi[1]-Pakistan 6 wkts	478	4-139	•208	406		
2005-06 in Sri Lanka						
Colombo (SSC)-Drawn	176	4-337	•185	5d-448	Inzamamul Haq	D.P.M.D.Jayawardene
Kandy-Pakistan 8 wkts	170	2-183	•279	73		

Test Match Results Summary

PAKISTAN v SRI LANKA - in Pakistan

		Results			Karachi[1]			Faisalabad			Lahore[2]			Sialkot			Gujranwala			Peshawar[2]			Rawalpindi[2]		
	Tests	P	SL	D	P	SL	D	P	SL	D	P	SL	D	P	SL	D	P	SL	D	P	SL	D	P	SL	D
1981-82	3	2	-	1	1	-	-	-	-	1	1	-	-	-	-	-	-	-	-	-	-	-	-	-	-
1985-86	3	2	-	1	1	-	-	-	-	1	-	-	-	1	-	-	-	-	-	-	-	-	-	-	-
1991-92	3	1	-	2	-	-	-	1	-	-	-	-	-	-	-	1	-	-	1	-	-	-	-	-	-
1995-96	3	1	2	-	-	-	-	-	1	-	-	-	-	-	1	-	-	-	-	1	-	-	-	-	-
1998-99	1	-	-	1	-	-	-	-	-	-	-	-	1	-	-	-	-	-	-	-	-	-	-	-	-
1999-2000	3	1	2	-	1	-	-	-	-	-	-	-	-	-	-	-	-	-	-	-	1	-	-	1	-
2001-02	1	-	1	-	-	-	-	-	-	-	-	1	-	-	-	-	-	-	-	-	-	-	-	-	-
2004-05	2	1	1	-	1	-	-	-	1	-	-	-	-	-	-	-	-	-	-	-	-	-	-	-	-
	19	8	6	5	4	-	-	1	2	2	1	1	1	1	1	1	-	-	1	1	1	-	-	1	-

PAKISTAN v SRI LANKA - in Sri Lanka

		Result			Kandy			Col (CCC)			Col (PSS)			Col (SSC)			Col (RPS)			Galle		
	Tests	P	SL	D	P	SL	D	P	SL	D	P	SL	D	P	SL	D	P	SL	D	P	SL	D
1985-86	3	1	1	1	1	-	-	-	1	-	-	-	1	-	-	-	-	-	-	-	-	-
1994-95	2	2	-	-	1	-	-	-	-	-	1	-	-	-	-	-	-	-	-	-	-	-
1996-97	2	-	-	2	-	-	-	-	-	-	-	-	-	-	-	1	-	-	1	-	-	-
1999-2000	3	2	-	1	-	-	1	-	-	-	-	-	-	1	-	-	-	-	-	1	-	-
2005-06	2	1	-	1	1	-	-	-	-	-	-	-	-	-	-	1	-	-	-	-	-	-
	12	6	1	5	3	-	1	-	1	-	1	-	1	1	-	2	-	-	1	1	-	-

PAKISTAN v SRI LANKA - in Bangladesh

		Result			Dhaka		
	Tests	P	SL	D	P	SL	D
1998-99	1	1	-	-	1	-	-
Totals	32	15	7	10			

Highest Innings Totals

Pakistan in Pakistan	3-555	Faisalabad	1985-86
Pakistan in Sri Lanka	8d-600	Galle	2000-01
Sri Lanka in Pakistan	528	Lahore[2]	2001-02
Sri Lanka in Sri Lanka	5-467	Kandy	2000-01

Lowest Innings Totals

Pakistan in Pakistan	182	Rawalpindi[2]	1999-2000
Pakistan in Sri Lanka	132	Colombo (CCC)	1985-86
Sri Lanka in Pakistan	149	Karachi[1]	1981-82
Sri Lanka in Sri Lanka	71	Kandy	1994-95

Highest Match Aggregate	1294 for 29 wickets	Colombo (SSC)	1996-97
Lowest Match Aggregate	440 for 30 wickets	Kandy	1985-86

Highest Individual Innings

Pakistan in Pakistan	206	Qasim Omar	Faisalabad	1985-86
Pakistan in Sri Lanka	155	Saleem Malik	Colombo (SSC)	1996-97
Sri Lanka in Pakistan	253	S.T.Jayasuriya	Faisalabad	2004-05
Sri Lanka in Sri Lanka	207*	M.S.Atapattu	Kandy	2000-01

Note: Ijaz Ahmed scored 211 for Pakistan v Sri Lanka at Dhaka in 1998-99.

Most Runs in a Series

Pakistan in Pakistan	355 (av 71.00)	Inzamamul Haq	1999-2000
Pakistan in Sri Lanka	261 (av 87.00)	Saaed Anwar	1994-95
Sri Lanka in Pakistan	424 (av 106.00)	S.T.Jayasuriya	2004-05
Sri Lanka in Sri Lanka	432 (av 216.00)	P.A.de Silva	1996-97

Record Wicket Partnerships - Pakistan

1st	156	Wajahatullah Wasti (121*), Shahid Afridi (84)	Lahore[2]	1998-99
2nd	151	Mohsin Khan (129), Majid Khan (63)	Lahore[2]	1981-82
3rd	397	Qasim Omar (206), Javed Miandad (203*)	Faisalabad	1985-86
4th	178	Wajahatullah Wasti (133), Yousuf Youhana (83)	Lahore[2]	1998-99
5th	132	Saleem Malik (101), Imran Khan (93*)	Sialkot	1991-92
6th	124	Inzamamul Haq (138), Younis Khan (61)	Karachi[1]	1999-2000
7th	120	Younis Khan (116), Wasim Akram (100)	Galle	2000-01
8th	88	Moin Khan (70), Waqar Younis (39)	Karachi[1]	1999-2000
9th	145	Yousuf Khan (107), Wasim Akram (79)	Rawalpindi[2]	1999-2000
10th	90	Wasim Akram (78), Arshad Khan (9*)	Colombo (SSC)	2000-01

Record Wicket Partnerships - Sri Lanka

1st	335	M.S.Atapattu (207*). S.T.Jayasuriya (188)	Kandy	2000-01
2nd	217	S.Wettimuny (157), R.L.Dias (98)	Faisalabad	1981-82
3rd	176	U.C.Hathurusingha (83), P.A.de Silva (105)	Faisalabad	1995-96
4th	240*	A.P.Gurusinha (116*), A.Ranatunga (135*)	Colombo (PSS)	1985-86
5th	143	R.P.Arnold (123), R.S.Kaluwitharana (100)	Lahore[2]	1998-99
6th	121	A.Ranatunga (79), P.A.de Silva (122)	Faisalabad	1985-86
7th	131	H.P.Tillakaratne (83*), R.S.Kalpage (62)	Kandy	1994-95
8th	76	P.A.de Silva (138*), W.P.J.U.C.Vaas (17)	Colombo (SSC)	1996-97
9th	101	S.T.Jayasuriya (253), C.R.D.Fernando (1)	Faisalabad	2004-05
10th	73	H.P.Tillakaratne (55*), K.S.C.de Silva (27)	Dhaka	1998-99

Best Bowling in an Innings

Pakistan in Pakistan	8/58	Imran Khan	Lahore[2]	1981-82
Pakistan in Sri Lanka	6/34	Waqar Younis	Kandy	1994-95
Sri Lanka in Pakistan	8/83	J.R.Ratnayake	Sialkot	1985-86
Sri Lanka in Sri Lanka	6/98	M.Muralidaran	Colombo (RPS)	1996-97

Best Bowling in a Match

Pakistan in Pakistan	14/116	Imran Khan	Lahore[2]	1981-82
Pakistan in Sri Lanka	11/70	Mohammad Asif	Kandy	2005-06
Sri Lanka in Pakistan	10/148	M.Muralidaran	Peshawar[2]	1999-2000
Sri Lanka in Sri Lanka	8/168	M.Muralidaran	Colombo (PSS)	1999-2000

Most wickets in a Series

Pakistan in Pakistan	17 (av 15.94)	Imran Khan	1985-86
Pakistan in Sri Lanka	17 (av 10.76)	Mohammad Asif	2005-06
Sri Lanka in Pakistan	26 (av 19.84)	M.Muralidaran	1999-2000
Sri Lanka in Sri Lanka	12 (av 21.50)	H.D.P.K.Dharmasena	1994-95
	12 (av 25.50)	M.Muralidaran	2000-01

PAKISTAN v ZIMBABWE	Pakistan		Zimbabwe		Captains	
Venue and Result	1st	2nd	1st	2nd	Pakistan	Zimbabwe
1993-94 in Pakistan						
Karachi[2]-Pakistan 131 runs	•8d-423	3d-131	289	134	Waqar Younis	A.Flower
Rawalpindi[2]-Pakistan 52 runs	•245	248	254	187	Wasim Akram	
Lahore[2]-Drawn	•147	1-174	230	-	Wasim Akram	
1994-95 in Zimbabwe						
Harare-Zimbabwe inn & 64 runs	322	158	•4d-544	-	Saleem Malik	A.Flower
Bulawayo[2]-Pakistan 8 wkts	260	2-61	•174	146		
Harare-Pakistan 99 runs	•231	250	243	139		
1996-97 in Pakistan						
Sheikhupura-Drawn	553	-	•375	7-241	Wasim Akram	A.D.R.Campbell
Faisalabad-Pakistan 10 wkts	267	0-69	•133	200		
1997-98 in Zimbabwe						
Bulawayo[2]-Drawn	256	6-258	•321	4d-302	Rashid Latif	A.D.R.Campbell
Harare-Pakistan 3 wkts	354	7-192	•277	268		
1998-99 in Pakistan						
Peshawar[2]-Zimbabwe 7 wkts	•296	103	238	3-162	Aamer Sohail	A.D.R.Campbell
Lahore[2]-Drawn	325	-	•183	0-48		
2002-03 in Zimbabwe						
Harare-Pakistan 119 runs	•285	369	225	310	Waqar Younis	A.D.R.Campbell
Bulawayo[2]-Pakistan 10 wkts	403	0-57	•178	281		

Test Match Results Summary

PAKISTAN v ZIMBABWE - in Pakistan

		Result			Karachi[2]			Rawalpindi[2]			Lahore[2]			Sheikhupura			Faisalabad			Peshawar[2]		
	Tests	P	Z	D	P	Z	D	P	Z	D	P	Z	D	P	Z	D	P	Z	D	P	Z	D
1993-94	3	2	-	1	1	-	-	1	-	-	-	-	1	-	-	-	-	-	-	-	-	-
1996-97	2	1	-	1	-	-	-	-	-	-	-	-	-	-	-	1	1	-	-	-	-	-
1998-99	2	-	1	1	-	-	-	-	-	-	-	-	1	-	-	-	-	-	-	-	1	-
	7	3	1	3	1	-	-	1	-	-	-	-	2	-	-	1	1	-	-	-	1	-

PAKISTAN v ZIMBABWE - in Zimbabwe

		Result			Harare			Bulawayo[2]		
	Tests	P	Z	D	P	Z	D	P	Z	D
1994-95	3	2	1	-	1	1	-	1	-	-
1997-98	2	1	-	1	1	-	-	-	-	1
2002-03	2	2	-	-	1	-	-	1	-	-
	7	5	1	1	3	1	-	2	-	1
Totals	14	8	2	4						

Highest Innings Totals

Pakistan in Pakistan	553	Sheikhupura	1996-97
Pakistan in Zimbabwe	403	Bulawayo[2]	2002-03
Zimbabwe in Pakistan	375	Sheikhupura	1996-97
Zimbabwe in Zimbabwe	4d-544	Harare	1994-95

Lowest Innings Totals

Pakistan in Pakistan	103	Peshawar[2]	1998-99
Pakistan in Zimbabwe	158	Harare	1994-95
Zimbabwe in Pakistan	133	Faisalabad	1996-97
Zimbabwe in Zimbabwe	139	Harare	1994-95

Highest Match Aggregate	1189 for 40 wickets	Harare	2002-03
Lowest Match Aggregate	551 for 21 wickets	Lahore[2]	1993-94

Highest Individual Innings

Pakistan in Pakistan	257*	Wasim Akram	Sheikhupura	1996-97
Pakistan in Zimbabwe	192	Mohammad Wasim	Harare	1997-98
Zimbabwe in Pakistan	110	G.W.Flower	Sheikhupura	1996-97
Zimbabwe in Zimbabwe	201*	G.W.Flower	Harare	1994-95

Most Runs in a Series

Pakistan in Pakistan	292 (av 292.00)	Wasim Akram	1996-97
Pakistan in Zimbabwe	367 (av 73.40)	Inzamamul Haq	1994-95
Zimbabwe in Pakistan	205 (av 41.00)	A.D.R.Campbell	1996-97
Zimbabwe in Zimbabwe	300 (av 100.00)	M.W.Goodwin	1997-98

Record Wicket Partnerships - Pakistan

1st	95	Aamer Sohail (63), Shoaib Mohammad (81)	Karachi[2]	1993-94
2nd	118*	Shoaib Mohammad (53*), Asif Mujtaba (65*)	Lahore[2]	1993-94
3rd	180	Taufeeq Umar (111), Inzamamul Haq (112)	Harare	2002-03
4th	127	Younis Khan (52), Yousuf Youhana (159)	Bulawayo[2]	2002-03
5th	110	Yousuf Youhana (64), Moin Khan (97)	Bulawayo[2]	1997-98
6th	121	Yousuf Youhana (159), Kamran Akmal (56)	Bulawayo[2]	2002-03
7th	120	Inzamamul Haq (71), Wasim Akram (27)	Harare	1994-95

8th	313	Wasim Akram(257*), Saqlain Mushtaq (79)	Sheikhupura	1996-97
9th	147	Mohammad Wasim (192), Mushtaq Ahmed (57)	Harare	1997-98
10th	50*	Yousuf Youhana (120*), Waqar Younis (24*)	Lahore[2]	1998-99

Record Wicket Partnerships - Zimbabwe

1st	48*	G.J.Rennie (16*), G.W.Flower (17*)	Lahore[2]	1998-99
2nd	135	M.H.Dekker (68*), A.D.R.Campbell (75)	Rawalpindi[2]	1993-94
3rd	111	D.D.Ebrahim (69), G.W.Flower (69)	Harare	2002-03
4th	269	G.W.Flower (201*), A.Flower (156)	Harare	1994-95
5th	277*	M.W.Goodwin (166*), A.Flower (100*)	Bulawayo[2]	1997-98
6th	72	M.H.Dekker (68), H.H.Streak (29)	Rawalpindi[2]	1993-94
7th	131	G.W.Flower (110), P.A.Strang (106*)	Sheikhupura	1996-97
8th	110	G.J.Whittall (62), B.C.Strang (53)	Harare	1997-98
9th	87	P.A.Strang 106*), B.C..Strang (42)	Sheikhupura	1996-97
10th	29	E.A.Brandes (18), S.G.Peall (11*)	Rawalpindi[2]	1993-94

Best Bowling in an Innings

Pakistan in Pakistan	7/91	Waqar Younis	Karachi[2]	1993-94
Pakistan in Zimbabwe	7/66	Saqlain Mushtaq	Bulawayo[2]	2002-03
Zimbabwe in Pakistan	5/42	D.H.Brain	Lahore[2]	1993-94
Zimbabwe in Zimbabwe	6/90	H.H.Streak	Harare	1994-95

Best Bowling in a Match

Pakistan in Pakistan	13/135	Waqar Younis	Karachi[2]	1993-94
Pakistan in Zimbabwe	10/155	Saqlain Mushtaq	Bulawayo[2]	2002-03
Zimbabwe in Pakistan	8/114	H.H.Streak	Rawalpindi[2]	1993-94
Zimbabwe in Zimbabwe	9/105	H.H.Streak	Harare	1994-95

Most Wickets in a Series

Pakistan in Pakistan	27 (av 13.81)	Waqar Younis	1993-94
Pakistan in Zimbabwe	15 (av 21.53)	Saqlain Mushtaq	2002-03
Zimbabwe in Pakistan	13 (av 30.30)	E.A.Brandes	1993-94
Zimbabwe in Zimbabwe	22 (av 13.54)	H.H.Streak	1994-95

PAKISTAN v BANGLADESH	Pakistan		Bangladesh		Captains	
Venue and Result	1st	2nd	1st	2nd	Pakistan	Bangladesh
2001-02 in Pakistan						
Multan[2]-Pakistan inn & 264 runs	3d-546	-	•134	148	Waqar Younis	Naimur Rahman
2001-02 in Bangladesh						
Dhaka-Pakistan inn & 178 runs	9d-490	-	•160	152	Waqar Younis	Khaled Mashud
Chittagong[1]-Pakistan inn & 169 runs	9d-465	-	•148	148		
2003-04 in Pakistan						
Karachi[1]-Pakistan 7 wkts	316	3-217	•288	274	Rashid Latif	Khaled Mahmid
Peshawar[2]-Pakistan 9 wkts	295	1-165	•361	96		
Multan[2]-Pakistan 1 wkt	176	9-262	•281	154		

Test Match Results Summary

PAKISTAN v BANGLADESH - in Pakistan

		Result			Multan[2]			Karachi[1]			Peshawar[2]		
	Tests	P	B	D	P	B	D	P	B	D	P	B	D
2001-02	1	1	-	-	1	-	-	-	-	-	-	-	-
2003-04	3	3	-	-	1	-	-	1	-	-	1	-	-
	4	4	-	-	2	-	-	1	-	-	1	-	-

PAKISTAN v BANGLADESH - in Bangladesh

		Result			Dhaka			Chittagong[1]		
	Tests	P	B	D	P	B	D	P	B	D
2001-02	2	2	-	-	-	-	2	-	-	1
Totals	6	6	-	-						

Highest Innings Totals

Pakistan in Pakistan	3d-546	Multan[2]	2001-02
Pakistan in Bangladesh	9d-490	Dhaka	2001-02
Bangladesh in Pakistan	361	Peshawar[2]	2003-04
Bangladesh in Bangladesh	160	Dhaka	2001-02

Lowest Innings Totals

Pakistan in Pakistan	176	Multan[2]	2003-04
Pakistan in Bangladesh	no instance		
Bangladesh in Pakistan	96	Peshawar[2]	2003-04
Bangladesh in Bangladesh	148	Dhaka	2001-02

Highest Match Aggregate	1095 for 33 wickets	Karachi[1]	2003-04
Lowest Match Aggregate	761 for 29 wickets	Chittagong[1]	2001-02

Highest Individual Innings

Pakistan in Pakistan	170	Yasir Hameed	Karachi[1]	2003-04
Pakistan in Bangladesh	204*	Yousuf Youhana	Chittagong[1]	2001-02
Bangladesh in Pakistan	119	Javed Omar	Peshawar[2]	2003-04
Bangladesh in Bangladesh	53	Habibul Bashar	Dhaka	2001-02

Most Runs in a Series

Pakistan in Pakistan	373 (av 74.60)	Yasir Hameed	2003-04
Pakistan in Bangladesh	276 (av 276.00)	Yousuf Youhana	2001-02
Bangladesh in Pakistan	379 (av 63.16)	Habibul Bashar	2003-04
Bangladesh in Bangladesh	106 (av 26.50)	Habibul Bashar	2001-02

Record Wicket Partnerships - Pakistan

1st	168	Saeed Anwar (101), Taufeeq Umar (104)	Multan[2]	2001-02
2nd	134	Mohammad Hafeez (50), Yasir Hameed (105)	Karachi[1]	2003-04
3rd	80	Taufeeq Umar (104), Inzamamul Haq (105#)	Multan[2]	2001-02
4th	165*	Yousuf Youhana (102*), Abdur Razzaq (110*)	Multan[2]	2001-02
5th	64	Yousuf Youhana (64*), Rashid Latif (40)	Peshawar[2]	2003-04
6th	175	Abdur Razzaq (134), Rashid Latif (94)	Dhaka	2001-02
7th	67	Abdur Razzaq (134), Inzamamul Haq (43)	Dhaka	2001-02
8th	99	Yousuf Youhana (204*), Saqlain Mushtaq (7)	Chittagong[1]	2001-02
9th	52	Inzamamul Haq (138*), Umar Gul (5)	Multan[2]	2003-04
10th	18*	Yousuf Youhana (204*), Danish Kaneria (4*)	Chittagong[1]	2001-02

Record Wicket Partnerships - Bangladesh

1st	38	Mehrab Hossain (19), Mohammad Ashraful (22)	Dhaka	2001-02
2nd	167	Javed Omar (119), Habibul Bashar (97)	Peshawar[2]	2003-04
3rd	130	Javed Omar (119), Mohammad Ashraful (77)	Peshawar[2]	2001-02
4th	111	Habibul Bashar (108), Rajin Saleh (60)	Karachi[1]	2003-04
5th	69	Habibul Bashar (51), Sanwar Hossain (30)	Chittagong[1]	2001-02
6th	62	Rajin Saleh (60), Khaled Mashud (22)	Multan[2]	2003-04
7th	27	Aminul Islam (25), Khaled Mashud (28)	Chittagong[1]	2001-02
8th	45	Habibul Bashar (56*), Hasibul Hossain (31)	Multan[2]	2001-02
9th	27	Hasibul Hossain (18), Mohammad Sharif (13)	Multan[2]	2001-02
	27	Fahim Muntasir (33), Mohammad Sharif (11)	Dhaka	2001-02
10th	21	Khaled Mashud (28), Manjural Islam[1] (4*)	Chittagong[1]	2001-02

Best Bowling in an Innings

Pakistan in Pakistan	6/42	Danish Kaneria	Multan[2]	2001-02
Pakistan in Bangladesh	7/77	Danish Kaneria	Dhaka	2001-02
Bangladesh in Pakistan	5/36	Mohammad Rafique	Multan[2]	2003-04
Bangladesh in Bangladesh	4/98	Mohammad Sharif	Chittagong[1]	2001-02

Best Bowling in a Match

Pakistan in Pakistan	12/94	Danish Kaneria	Multan[2]	2001-02
Pakistan in Bangladesh	9/113	Danish Kaneria	Dhaka	2001-02
Bangladesh in Pakistan	7/116	Mohammad Rafique	Multan[2]	2003-04
Bangladesh in Bangladesh	4/98	Mohammad Sharif	Chittagong[1]	2001-02

Most Wickets in a Series

Pakistan in Pakistan	17 (av 20.05)	Shabbir Ahmed	2003-04
Pakistan in Bangladesh	13 (av 14.15)	Danish Kaneria	2001-02
Bangladesh in Pakistan	17 (av 23.82)	Mohammad Rafique	2003-04
Bangladesh in Bangladesh	6 (32.16)	Mohammad Sharif	2001-02

SRI LANKA v ZIMBABWE	Sri Lanka		Zimbabwe		Captains	
Venue and Result	1st	2nd	1st	2nd	Sri Lanka	Zimbabwe
1994-95 in Zimbabwe						
Harare-Drawn	•383	-	8-319	-	A.Ranatunga	A.Flower
Bulawayo²-Drawn	218	4-193	•9d-462	-		
Harare-Drawn	•402	3-89	375	-		
1996-97 in Sri Lanka						
Colombo (RPS)-Sri Lanka inn & 77 runs	•349	-	145	127	A.Ranatunga	A.D.R.Campbell
Colombo (SSC)-Sri Lanka 10 wkts	8d-350	0-30	•141	235		
1997-98 in Sri Lanka						
Kandy-Sri Lanka 8 wkts	•9d-469	2-10	140	338	A.Ranatunga	A.D.R.Campbell
Colombo (SSC)-Sri Lanka 5 wkts	225	5-326	•251	299		
1999-2000 in Zimbabwe						
Bulawayo²-Drawn	428	-	•286	3-136	S.T.Jayasuriya	A.Flower
Harare-Sri Lanka 6 wkts	432	4-38	•174	292		
Harare-Drawn	231	1-36	•218	7d-197		
2001-02 in Sri Lanka						
Colombo(SSC)-Sri Lanka inn & 166 runs	•6d-586	-	184	236	S.T.Jayasuriya	S.V.Carlisle
Kandy-Sri Lanka inn & 94 runs	505	-	•236	175		
Galle-Sri Lanka 315 runs	•418	2d-212	236	79		
2003-04 in Zimbabwe						
Harare-Sri Lanka inn & 240 runs	541	-	•199	102	M.S.Atapattu	T.Taibu
Bulawayo²-Sri Lanka inn & 254 runs	3d-713	-	•228	231		

Test Match Results Summary

SRI LANKA v ZIMBABWE - in Sri Lanka

		Result			Colombo (RPS)			Colombo (SSC)			Kandy			Galle		
	Tests	SL	Z	D	SL	Z	D	SL	Z	D	SL	Z	D	SL	Z	D
1996-97	2	2	-	-	1	-	-	1	-	-	-	-	-	-	-	-
1997-98	2	2	-	-	-	-	-	1	-	-	1	-	-	-	-	-
2001-02	3	3	-	-	-	-	-	1	-	-	1	-	-	1	-	-
	7	7	-	-	1	-	-	3	-	-	2	-	-	1	-	-

SRI LANKA v ZIMBABWE - in Zimbabwe

		Result			Harare			Bulawayo²		
	Tests	SL	Z	D	SL	Z	D	SL	Z	D
1994-95	3	-	-	3	-	-	2	-	-	1
1999-2000	3	1	-	2	1	-	1	-	-	1
2003-04	2	2	-	-	1	-	-	1	-	-
	8	3	-	5	2	-	3	1	-	2
Totals	15	10	-	5						

Highest Innings Totals

Sri Lanka in Sri Lanka	6d-586	Colombo (SSC)	2001-02
Sri Lanka in Zimbabwe	3d-713	Bulawayo²	2003-04
Zimbabwe in Sri Lanka	338	Kandy	1997-98
Zimbabwe in Zimbabwe	9-462	Bulawayo²	1994-95

Lowest Innings Totals

Sri Lanka in Sri Lanka	225	Colombo (RPS)	1997-98
Sri Lanka in Zimbabwe	218	Bulawayo[2]	1994-95
Zimbabwe in Sri Lanka	79	Galle	2001-02
Zimbabwe in Zimbabwe	102	Harare	2003-04

Highest Match Aggregate	1172 for 23 wickets	Bulawayo[2]	2003-04
Lowest Match Aggregate	621 for 30 wickets	Colombo (RPS)	1996-97

Highest Individual Innings

Sri Lanka in Sri Lanka	223	M.S.Atapattu	Kandy	1997-98
Sri Lanka in Zimbabwe	270	K.C.Sangakkara	Bulawayo[2]	2003-04
Zimbabwe in Sri Lanka	105*	A.Flower	Colombo (SSC)	1997-98
Zimbabwe in Zimbabwe	266	D.L.Houghton	Bulawayo[2]	1994-95

Most Runs in a Series

Sri Lanka in Sri Lanka	277 (av 92.33)	M.S.Atapattu	1997-98
Sri Lanka in Zimbabwe	419 (av 209.50)	M.S.Atapattu	2003-04
Zimbabwe in Sri Lanka	188 (av 62.66)	A.Flower	1997-98
Zimbabwe in Zimbabwe	466 (av 155.33)	D.L.Houghton	1994-95

Record Wicket Partnerships - Sri Lanka

1st	281	M.S.Atapattu (170), S.T.Jayasuriya (157)	Harare	2003-04
2nd	438	M.S.Atapattu (249), K.C.Sangakkara (270)	Bulawayo[2]	2003-04
3rd	140	M.S.Atapattu (223), P.A.de Silva (75)	Kandy	1997-98
4th	178	D.P.M.D.Jayawardene (91), T.M.Dilshan (163*)	Harare	1999-2000
5th	114	A.P.Gurusinha (88), H.P.Tillakaratne (116)	Colombo (SSC)	1996-97
6th	189*	P.A.de Silva (143*), A.Ranatunga (87*)	Colombo (SSC)	1997-98
7th	136*	T.T.Samaraweera (123*), W.P.U.J.C.Vaas (74*)	Colombo (SSC)	2001-02
8th	146	T.T.Samaraweera (76), U.D.U.Chandana (92)	Galle	2001-02
9th	39	M.F.Maharoof (40), D.N.T.Zoysa (28*)	Harare	2003-04
10th	45	D.N.T.Zoysa (28*), M.Muralidaran (26)	Harare	2003-04

Record Wicket Partnerships - Zimbabwe

1st	153	S.V.Carlisle (64), T.R.Gripper (83)	Galle	2001-02
2nd	40	G.J.Rennie (50), M.W.Goodwin (73)	Colombo (SSC)	1997-98
3rd	194	A.D.R.Campbell (99), D.L.Houghton (142)	Harare	1994-95
4th	121	D.L.Houghton (266), A.Flower (50)	Bulawayo[2]	1994-95
5th	101	M.W.Goodwin (48), A.Flower (129)	Harare	1999-2000
6th	100	D.L.Houghton (266), W.R.James (33)	Bulawayo[2]	1994-95
7th	125	A.Flower (129), G.J.Whittall (53*)	Harare	1999-2000
8th	84	D.L.Houghton (266), J.A.Rennie (19*)	Bulawayo[2]	1994-95
9th	43	J.A.Rennie (19*), S.G.Peall (30)	Bulawayo[2]	1994-95
10th	50	D.T.Hondo (19), T.Panyangara (32*)	Harare	2003-04

Best Bowling in an Innings

Sri Lanka in Sri Lanka	9/51	M.Muralidaran	Kandy	2001-02
Sri Lanka in Zimbabwe	7/116	K.R.Pushpakumara	Harare	1994-95
Zimbabwe in Sri Lanka	5/106	P.A.Strang	Colombo (RPS)	1996-97
Zimbabwe in Zimbabwe	4/70	G.J.Whittall	Harare	1994-95

Best Bowling in a Match

Sri Lanka in Sri Lanka	13/115	M.Muralidaran	Kandy	2001-02
Sri Lanka in Zimbabwe	8/73	D.N.T.Zoysa	Harare	2003-04
Zimbabwe in Sri Lanka	6/112	H.H.Streak	Colombo (SSC)	1997-98
Zimbabwe in Zimbabwe	5/129	H.H.Streak	Harare	1994-95

Most Wickets in a Series

Sri Lanka in Sri Lanka	30 (av 9.80)	M.Muralidaran	2001-02
Sri Lanka in Zimbabwe	14 (av 24.78)	W.P.U.J.C.Vaas	1999-2000
	14 (av 15.64)	M.Muralidaran	2003-04
Zimbabwe in Sri Lanka	10 (av 21.20)	H.H.Streak	1997-98
Zimbabwe in Zimbabwe	13 (av 23.38)	H.H.Streak	1994-95

SRI LANKA v BANGLADESH	Sri Lanka		Bangladesh		Captains	
Venue and Result	1st	2nd	1st	2nd	Sri Lanka	Bangladesh
2001-02 in Sri Lanka						
Colombo(SSC)-Sri Lanka inn & 137 runs	5d-555	-	•90	328	S.T.Jayasuriya	Naimur Rahman
2002-03 in Sri Lanka						
Colombo(PSS)-Sri Lanka inn & 196 runs	9d-541	-	•161	184	S.T.Jayasuriya	Khaled Mashud
Colombo(SSC)-Sri Lanka 288 runs	•373	2d-263	164	184		
2005-06 in Sri Lanka						
Colombo(RPS)-Sri Lanka inn & 96 runs	9d-370	-	•188	86	M.S.Atapattu	Habibul Bashar
Colombo(PSS)-Sri Lanka inn & 69 runs	•9d-457	-	191	197		
2005-06 in Bangladesh						
Chittagong^2-Sri Lanka 8 wkts	338	2-166	•319	181	D.P.M.D.Jayawardene	Habibul Bashar
Bogra-Sri Lanka 10 wkts	316	0-120	•234	201		

Test Match Results Summary

SRI LANKA v BANGLADESH - in Sri Lanka

		Result			Colombo(SSC)			Colombo(PSS)			Colombo(RPS)		
	Tests	SL	B	D	SL	B	D	SL	B	D	SL	B	D
2001-02	1	1	-	-	1	-	-	-	-	-	-	-	-
2002-03	2	2	-	-	1	-	-	1	-	-	-	-	-
2005-06	2	2	-	-	-	-	-	1	-	-	1	-	-
	5	5	-	-	2	-	-	2	-	-	1	-	-

SRI LANKA v BANGLADESH - in Bangladesh

		Result			Chittagong^2			Dhaka			Bogra		
	Tests	SL	B	D	SL	B	D	SL	B	D	SL	B	D
2005-06	2	2	-	-	1	-	-	-	-	-	1	-	-
	2	2	-	-	1	-	-	-	-	-	1	-	-
Totals	7	7	-	-									

Highest Innings Totals			
Sri Lanka in Sri Lanka	5d-555	Colombo (SSC)	2001-02
Sri Lanka in Bangladesh	338	Chittagong^2	2005-06
Bangladesh in Sri Lanka	328	Colombo (SSC)	2001-02
Bangladesh in Bangladesh	319	Chittagong^2	2005-06
Lowest Innings Totals			
Sri Lanka in Sri Lanka	373	Colombo (SSC)	2002-03
Sri Lanka in Bangladesh	338	Chittagong^2	2005-06
Bangladesh in Sri Lanka	86	Colombo (RPS)	2005-06
Bangladesh in Bangladesh	181	Chittagong^2	2005-06

Highest Match Aggregate		1004 for 32 wickets	Chittagong[2]	2005-06
Lowest Match Aggregate		644 for 29 wickets	Colombo (RPS)	2005-06

Highest Individual Innings

Sri Lanka in Sri Lanka	206	P.A.de Silva	Colombo (PSS)	2002-03
Sri Lanka in Bangladesh	165	W.U.Tharanga	Bogra	2005-06
Bangladesh in Sri Lanka	114	Mohammad Ashraful	Colombo (SSC)	2001-02
Bangladesh in Bangladesh	136	Mohammad Ashraful	Chittagong[2]	2005-06

Most Runs in a Series

Sri Lanka in Sri Lanka	254 (av 127.00)	T.M.Dilshan	2005-06
Sri Lanka in Bangladesh	297 (av 99.00)	W.U.Tharanga	2005-06
Bangladesh in Sri Lanka	140 (av 70.00)	Mohammad Ashraful	2001-02
Bangladesh in Bangladesh	183 (av 45.75)	Habibul Bashar	2005-06

Record Wicket Partnerships - Sri Lanka

1st	144	M.S.Atapattu (201), S.T.Jayasuriya (89)	Colombo (SSC)	2001-02
2nd	172	M.G.Vandort (140), M.N.Nawaz (78*)	Colombo (SSC)	2002-03
3rd	171	M.S.Atapattu (201), D.P.M.D.Jayawardene (150)	Colombo (SSC)	2001-02
4th	150	K.C.Sangakkara (75), P.A.de Silva (206)	Colombo (PSS)	2002-03
5th	280	T.T.Samaraweera (138), T.M.Dilshan (168)	Colombo (PSS)	2005-06
6th	117	T.T.Samaraweera (58), M.F.Maharoof (72)	Chittagong[2]	2005-06
7th	44	S.T.Jayasuriya (145), T.C.B.Fernando (31*)	Colombo (PSS)	2002-03
8th	53	W.P.U.J.C.Vaas (65), M.Muralidaran (24)	Colombo (PSS)	2005-06
9th	42	W.U.Tharanga (165), S.L.Malinga (12)	Bogra	2005-06
10th	64	T.C.B.Fernando (29*), M.K.G.C.P.Lakshitha (40)	Colombo (SSC)	2002-03

Record Wicket Partnerships - Bangladesh

1st	52	Javed Omar (35), Nafees Iqbal (26)	Bogra	2005-06
2nd	76	Nafees Iqbal (34), Habibul Bashar (29)	Chittagong[2]	2005-06
3rd	92	Habibul Bashar (84), Mohammad Ashraful (17)	Colombo (RPS)	2005-06
4th	75	Shahriar Nafees (51), Mohammad Ashraful (26)	Colombo (PSS)	2005-06
5th	126	Aminul Islam (56), Mohammad Ashraful (114)	Colombo (SSC)	2001-02
6th	96	Mohammad Ashraful (114), Naimur Rahman (48)	Colombo (SSC)	2001-02
7th	52	Habibul Bashar (73), Mohammad Rafique (64)	Bogra	2005-06
8th	37	Alok Kapali (39), Tapash Baisya (52*)	Colombo (SSC)	2002-03
9th	40	Tapash Baisya (52*), Manjural Islam[1] (0)	Colombo (SSC)	2002-03
10th	26	Khaled Mashud (26), Enamul Haque[2] (2*)	Colombo (PSS)	2005-06

Best Bowling in an Innings

Sri Lanka in Sri Lanka	6/18	M.Muralidaran	Colombo (RPS)	2005-06
Sri Lanka in Bangladesh	6/54	M.Muralidaran	Chittagong[2]	2005-06
Bangladesh in Sri Lanka	5/115	Mohammad Rafique	Colombo (RPS)	2005-06
Bangladesh in Bangladesh	5/86	Shahadat Hossain	Bogra	2005-06

Best Bowling in a Match

Sri Lanka in Sri Lanka	10/98	M.Muralidaran	Colombo (PSS)	2002-03
Sri Lanka in Bangladesh	9/141	M.Muralidaran	Chittagong[2]	2005-06
Bangladesh in Sri Lanka	5/115	Mohammad Rafique	Colombo (RPS)	2005-06
Bangladesh in Bangladesh	5/129	Shahadat Hossain	Bogra	2005-06

Most Wickets in a Series

Sri Lanka in Sri Lanka	14 (av 9.64)	M.Muralidaran	2005-06
Sri Lanka in Bangladesh	16 (av 17.62)	M.Muralidaran	2005-06
Bangladesh in Sri Lanka	6 (av 30.50)	Shahadat Hossain	2005-06
	6 (av 32.66)	Syed Rasel	2005-06
Bangladesh in Bangladesh	9 (av 27.88)	Shahadat Hossain	2005-06

ZIMBABWE v BANGLADESH	Zimbabwe		Bangladesh		Captains	
Venue and Result	1st	2nd	1st	2nd	Zimbabwe	Bangladesh
2000-01 in Zimbabwe						
Bulawayo[2]-Zimbabwe inn & 32 runs	457	-	•257	168	H.H.Streak	Naimur Rahman
Harare-Zimbabwe 8 wkts	9d-421	2-100	•244	266		
2001-02 in Bangladesh						
Dhaka-Drawn	431	-	•107	3-125	S.V.Carlisle	Naimur Rahman
Chittagong[1]-Zimbabwe 8 wkts	•7d-542	2-11	251	301		
2003-04 in Zimbabwe						
Harare-Zimbabwe 183 runs	•441	8d-242	331	169	H.H.Streak	Habibul Bashar
Bulawayo[2]-Drawn	2-210	-	•168	-		
2004-05 in Bangladesh						
Chittagong[1]-Bangladesh 226 runs	312	154	•488	9d-204	T.Taibu	Habibul Bashar
Dhaka-Drawn	•298	286	211	5-285		

Test Match Results Summary

ZIMBABWE v BANGLADESH - in Zimbabwe

		Result			Bulawayo[2]			Harare		
	Tests	Z	B	D	Z	B	D	Z	B	D
2000-01	2	2	-	-	1	-	-	1	-	-
2003-04	2	1	-	1	-	-	1	1	-	-
	4	3	-	1	1	-	1	2	-	-

ZIMBABWE v BANGLADESH - in Bangladesh

		Result			Dhaka			Chittagong[1]		
	Tests	Z	B	D	Z	B	D	Z	B	D
2001-02	2	1	-	1	-	-	1	1	-	-
2004-05	2	-	1	1	-	-	1	-	1	-
	4	1	1	2	-	-	2	1	1	-
Totals	8	4	1	3						

Highest Innings Totals			
Zimbabwe in Zimbabwe	457	Bulawayo[2]	2000-01
Zimbabwe in Bangladesh	7d-542	Chittagong[1]	2001-02
Bangladesh in Zimbabwe	331	Harare	2003-04
Bangladesh in Bangladesh	488	Chittagong[1]	2004-05
Lowest Innings Totals			
Zimbabwe in Zimbabwe	441	Harare	2003-04
Zimbabwe in Bangladesh	286	Dhaka	2004-05
Bangladesh in Zimbabwe	168	Bulawayo[2]	2000-01
	168	Bulawayo[2]	2003-04
Bangladesh in Bangladesh	107	Dhaka	2001-02
Highest Match Aggregate	1183 for 38 wickets	Harare	2003-04
Lowest Match Aggregate	663 for 23 wickets	Dhaka	2001-02

Highest Individual Innings

Zimbabwe in Zimbabwe	119	G.J.Whittall	Bulawayo[2]	2000-01
Zimbabwe in Bangladesh	153	T.Taibu	Dhaka	2004-05
Bangladesh in Zimbabwe	98	Mohammad Ashraful	Harare	2003-04
Bangladesh in Bangladesh	121	Nafis Iqbal	Dhaka	2004-05

Most Runs in a Series

Zimbabwe in Zimbabwe	238 (av 79.33)	G.J.Whittall	2000-01
Zimbabwe in Bangladesh	330 (av 110.00)	T.Taibu	2004-05
Bangladesh in Zimbabwe	191 (av 63.66)	Javed Omar	2000-01
Bangladesh in Bangladesh	249 (av 62.25)	Habibul Bashar	2001-02

Record Wicket Partnerships - Zimbabwe

1st	108	D.D.Ebrahim (41), T.R.Gripper (112)	Chittagong[1]	2001-02
2nd	129	T.R.Gripper (65), S.V.Carlisle (103*)	Bulawayo[2]	2003-04
3rd	76*	S.V.Carlisle (103*), G.W.Flower (37*)	Bulawayo[2]	2003-04
4th	149	G.J.Whittall (119), A.Flower (73)	Bulawayo[2]	2000-01
5th	150	B.R.M.Taylor (78), T.Taibu (153)	Dhaka	2004-05
6th	137	C.B.Wishart 94), D.A.Marillier (73)	Dhaka	2001-02
7th	119	T.Taibu (92), E.Chigumbura (71)	Chittagong[1]	2004-05
8th	108	H.H.Streak (65), T.J.Friend (81)	Dhaka	2001-02
9th	56	T.Taibu (153), D.T.Hondo (3)	Dhaka	2004-05
10th	14	B.A.Murphy (25), H.K.Olonga (2*)	Dhaka	2001-02

Record Wicket Partnerships - Bangladesh

1st	133	Javed Omar (43), Nafis Iqbal (121)	Dhaka	2004-05
2nd	122	Javed Omar (80), Habibul Bashar (76)	Chittagong[1]	2000-01
3rd	84	Javed Omar (62), Aminul Islam (84)	Bulawayo[2]	2000-01
4th	119	Habibul Bashar (94), Rajin Saleh (89)	Chittagong[1]	2004-05
5th	85	Rajin Saleh (49), Mohammad Ashraful (98)	Harare	2003-04
6th	97	Mohammad Ashraful (98), Mushafiqur Rahman (44)	Harare	2003-04
7th	69	Khaled Mashud (49), Mohammad Rafique (69)	Chittagong[1]	2004-05
8th	72	Mohammad Rafique (69), Mashrafe Bin Mortaza (48)	Chittagong[1]	2004-05
9th	35	Mashrafe Bin Mortza (26), Tapash Baisya (13)	Dhaka	2004-05
10th	46	Khaled Mashud (61), Manural Islam (1*)	Harare	2003-04

Best Bowling in an Innings

Zimbabwe in Zimbabwe	5/73	A.M.Blignaut	Bulawayo[2]	2000-01
Zimbabwe in Bangladesh	6/59	D.T.Hondo	Dhaka	2004-05
Bangladesh in Zimbabwe	6/81	Manjural Islam[1]	Bulawayo[2]	2000-01
Bangladesh in Bangladesh	7/95	Enamul Haque[2]	Dhaka	2004-05

Best Bowling in a Match

Zimbabwe in Zimbabwe	8/110	A.M.Blignaut	Bulawayo[2]	2000-01
Zimbabwe in Bangladesh	8/104	G.W.Flower	Chittagong[1]	2001-02
Bangladesh in Zimbabwe	6/81	Manjural Islam[1]	Bulawayo[2]	2000-01
Bangladesh in Bangladesh	12/200	Enamul Haque[2]	Dhaka	2004-05

Most Wickets in a Series

Zimbabwe in Zimbabwe	11 (av 15.81)	H.H.Streak	2000-01
Zimbabwe in Bangladesh	9 (av 25.22)	D.T.Hondo	2004-05
Bangladesh in Zimbabwe	7 (av 34.42)	Tapash Baisya	2003-04
Bangladesh in Bangladesh	18 (av 16.66)	Enamul Haque[2]	2004-05

The Teams

HIGHEST INNINGS TOTALS

952-6d	Sri Lanka	v	India	Colombo (RPS)	1997-98
903-7d	England	v	Australia	The Oval	1938
849	England	v	West Indies	Kingston	1929-30
790-3d	West Indies	v	Pakistan	Kingston	1957-58
758-8d	Australia	v	West Indies	Kingston	1954-55
756-5d	Sri Lanka	v	South Africa	Colombo (SSC)	2006-07
751-5d	West Indies	v	England	St John's	2003-04
747	West Indies	v	South Africa	St John's	2004-05
735-6d	Australia	v	Zimbabwe	Perth	2003-04
729-6d	Australia	v	England	Lord's	1930
713-3d	Sri Lanka	v	Zimbabwe	Bulawayo[2]	2003-04
708	Pakistan	v	England	The Oval	1987
705-7d	India	v	Australia	Sydney	2003-04
701	Australia	v	England	The Oval	1934
699-5	Pakistan	v	India	Lahore[2]	1989-90
695	Australia	v	England	The Oval	1930
692-8d	West Indies	v	England	The Oval	1995
687-8d	West Indies	v	England	The Oval	1976
682-6d	South Africa	v	England	Lord's	2003
681-8d	West Indies	v	England	Port-of-Spain	1953-54
679-7d	Pakistan	v	India	Lahore[2]	2005-06
676-7	India	v	Sri Lanka	Kanpur	1986-87
675-5d	India	v	Pakistan	Multan[2]	2003-04
674-6	Pakistan	v	India	Faisalabad	1984-85
674	Australia	v	India	Adelaide	1947-48
671-4	New Zealand	v	Sri Lanka	Wellington	1990-91
668	Australia	v	West Indies	Bridgetown	1954-55
660-5d	West Indies	v	New Zealand	Wellington	1994-95
659-8d	Australia	v	England	Sydney	1946-47
658-8d	England	v	Australia	Nottingham	1938
658-9d	South Africa	v	West Indies	Durban[2]	2003-04
657-7d	India	v	Australia	Kolkata	2000-01
657-8d	Pakistan	v	West Indies	Bridgetown	1957-58
656-8d	Australia	v	England	Manchester	1964
654-5	England	v	South Africa	Durban[2]	1938-39
653-4d	England	v	India	Lord's	1990
653-4d	Australia	v	England	Leeds	1993
652-7d	England	v	India	Madras[1]	1984-85
652-7d	Australia	v	South Africa	Johannesburg[3]	2001-02
652-8d	West Indies	v	England	Lord's	1973
652	Pakistan	v	India	Faisalabad	1982-83
650-6d	Australia	v	West Indies	Bridgetown	1964-65
645	Australia	v	England	Brisbane[2]	1946-47
644-7d	India	v	West Indies	Kanpur	1978-79
644-8d	West Indies	v	India	Delhi	1958-59
643	Pakistan	v	New Zealand	Lahore[2]	2001-02
641-4d	Australia	v	England	The Oval	2001
636-8d	Pakistan	v	England	Lahore[2]	2005-06
636	England	v	Australia	Sydney	1928-29
633-5d	England	v	India	Birmingham	1979
633-5d	India	v	Australia	Calcutta	1997-98
632-4d	Australia	v	England	Lord's	1993

631-8d	West Indies	v	India	Kingston	1961-62
631	West Indies	v	India	Delhi	1948-49
630-6d	New Zealand	v	India	Mohali	2003-04
629-6d	West Indies	v	India	Bombay[2]	1948-49
629-9d	West Indies	v	India	St John's	2001-02
629	England	v	India	Lord's	1974
628-8d	Australia	v	South Africa	Johannesburg[3]	1996-97
628-8d	India	v	England	Leeds	2002
628-8d	Sri Lanka	v	England	Colombo (SSC)	2002-03
627-9d	England	v	Australia	Manchester	1934
627-9d	Sri Lanka	v	West Indies	Colombo (SSC)	2001-02
624	Pakistan	v	Australia	Adelaide	1983-84
622-9d	South Africa	v	Australia	Durban[2]	1969-70
621-5d	South Africa	v	New Zealand	Auckland	1998-99
620-7d	South Africa	v	Pakistan	Cape Town	2002-03
620	South Africa	v	Australia	Johannesburg[3]	1966-67
619-6d	England	v	West Indies	Nottingham	1957
619	Australia	v	West Indies	Sydney	1968-69
617-5d	Australia	v	Sri Lanka	Perth	1995-96
617	Australia	v	Pakistan	Faisalabad	1979-80
617	England	v	India	Nottingham	2002
616-5d	Pakistan	v	New Zealand	Auckland	1988-89
616	West Indies	v	Australia	Adelaide	1968-69
614-5d	West Indies	v	India	Calcutta	1958-59
611	England	v	Australia	Manchester	1964
610-6	Sri Lanka	v	India	Colombo (SSC)	2001-02
609-6d	India	v	Zimbabwe	Nagpur	2000-01
608-7d	Pakistan	v	England	Birmingham	1971
608	England	v	South Africa	Johannesburg[2]	1948-49
607-6d	Australia	v	New Zealand	Hobart	1993-94
606-9d	India	v	England	The Oval	1990
606	West Indies	v	England	Birmingham	1984
606	West Indies	v	Australia	Sydney	1992-93
605-9d	Australia	v	West Indies	Bridgetown	2002-03
604-6d	West Indies	v	India	Bombay[3]	1974-75
604-6d	South Africa	v	West Indies	Centurion	2003-04
604-9d	England	v	South Africa	The Oval	2003
604	Australia	v	England	Melbourne	1936-37
603	India	v	Pakistan	Faisalabad	2005-06
602-6d	Australia	v	England	Nottingham	1989
601-7d	Australia	v	England	Leeds	1989
601-8d	Australia	v	England	Brisbane[2]	1954-55
600-3d	South Africa	v	Zimbabwe	Harare	2001-02
600-4d	India	v	Australia	Sydney	1985-86
600-7d	Pakistan	v	England	The Oval	1974
600-8d	Pakistan	v	Sri Lanka	Galle	2000-01
600-9d	Australia	v	West Indies	Port-of-Spain	1954-55
600	Australia	v	England	Melbourne	1924-25
600	India	v	Pakistan	Rawalpindi[2]	2003-04

The highest total for the other countries are:

563-9d	Zimbabwe	v	West Indies	Harare	2000-01
488	Bangladesh	v	Zimbabwe	Chittagong[1]	2004-05

BOTH TEAMS SCORING 600

Australia (8d-656)	v	England (611)	Manchester	1964

HIGHEST SECOND INNINGS TOTALS *First innings shown in brackets. § After following on.*

671-4	(174)	New Zealand	v	Sri Lanka	Wellington	1990-91
657-7d §	(171)	India	v	Australia	Kolkata	2000-01
657-8d §	(106)	Pakistan	v	West Indies	Bridgetown	1957-58
654-5	(316)	England	v	South Africa	Durban[2]	1938-39
620	(199)	South Africa	v	Australia	Johannesburg[3]	1966-67
616	(276)	West Indies	v	Australia	Adelaide	1968-69
599-7d	(245)	Pakistan	v	India	Karachi[1]	2005-06
583-4d	(186)	England	v	West Indies	Birmingham	1957
582	(354)	Australia	v	England	Adelaide	1920-21
581	(267)	Australia	v	England	Sydney	1920-21
578	(328)	Australia	v	South Africa	Melbourne	1910-11
572-7§	(156)	South Africa	v	England	Durban[2]	1999-2000
570-7d	(139)	England	v	South Africa	Durban[2]	2004-05
564-8	(133)	West Indies	v	New Zealand	Bridgetown	1971-72
564	(200-9d)	Australia	v	England	Melbourne	1936-37
563-9d	(131)	Zimbabwe	v	West Indies	Harare	2000-01
554	(198)	Australia	v	South Africa	Melbourne	1931-32
551 §	(208)	England	v	South Africa	Nottingham	1947

HIGHEST FOURTH INNINGS TOTALS

						Runs set in 4th innings
TO WIN						
418-7	West Indies	v	Australia	St John's	2002-03	418
406-4	India	v	West Indies	Port-of-Spain	1975-76	403
404-3	Australia	v	England	Leeds	1948	404
369-6	Australia	v	Pakistan	Hobart	1999-2000	369
362-7	Australia	v	West Indies	Georgetown	1977-78	359
348-5	West Indies	v	New Zealand	Auckland	1968-69	345
344-1	West Indies	v	England	Lord's	1984	342
342-8	Australia	v	India	Perth	1977-78	339
340-5	South Africa	v	Australia	Durban[2]	2001-02	335
336-5	Australia	v	South Africa	Durban[2]	1949-50	336
334-6	Australia	v	South Africa	Cape Town	2001-02	331
332-7	England	v	Australia	Melbourne	1928-29	332
326-5	Sri Lanka	v	Zimbabwe	Colombo (SSC)	1997-98	326
324-5	New Zealand	v	Pakistan	Christchurch	1993-94	323
317-2	West Indies	v	Pakistan	Georgetown	1957-58	317
315-4	England	v	Australia	Leeds	2001	315
315-6	Australia	v	England	Adelaide	1901-02	315
315-9	Pakistan	v	Australia	Karachi[1]	1994-95	314
311-9	West Indies	v	Australia	Bridgetown	1998-99	308
307-6	England	v	New Zealand	Christchurch	1996-97	305
307-7	Australia	v	Bangladesh	Fatullah	2005-06	307
TO TIE						
347	India	v	Australia	Madras[1]	1986-87	
TO LOSE						Losing Margin
451	New Zealand	v	England	Christchurch	2001-02	98
445	India	v	Australia	Adelaide	1977-78	47
440	New Zealand	v	England	Nottingham	1973	38
417	England	v	Australia	Melbourne	1976-77	45
411	England	v	Australia	Sydney	1924-25	193
402	Australia	v	England	Manchester	1981	103

397	India	v	England	Lord's	2002	170
376	India	v	England	Manchester	1959	171
370	England	v	Australia	Adelaide	1920-21	119
363	England	v	Australia	Adelaide	1924-25	11
355	India	v	Australia	Brisbane[2]	1967-68	39
352	West Indies	v	Australia	Sydney	1968-69	382
348	Sri Lanka	v	Australia	Hobart	1989-90	173
345	New Zealand	v	England	Nottingham	1983	165
339	Australia	v	South Africa	Adelaide	1910-11	38
336	Australia	v	England	Adelaide	1928-29	12
336	Pakistan	v	Australia	Melbourne	1989-90	92
335	Australia	v	England	Nottingham	1930	93
335	South Africa	v	New Zealand	Cape Town	1961-62	72
333	Australia	v	England	Melbourne	1894-95	94
333	India	v	Australia	Adelaide	1991-92	38
332	England	v	Australia	Manchester	1993	179
327	England	v	West Indies	Georgetown	1929-30	289
326	West Indies	v	Australia	Melbourne	1975-76	165
324	India	v	Australia	Brisbane[2]	1977-78	16
324	Sri Lanka	v	Australia	Kandy	2003-04	27
323	England	v	Australia	Melbourne	1936-37	365
323	England	v	Australia	Brisbane[2]	1994-95	184
316	England	v	West Indies	Kingston	1953-54	140
313	England	v	West Indies	Bridgetown	1953-54	181
310	Australia	v	Pakistan	Melbourne	1978-79	71
310	Zimbabwe	v	Pakistan	Harare	2002-03	119
307	England	v	West Indies	Lord's	1988	134
306	Sri Lanka	v	South Africa	Cape Town	1997-98	377
304	South Africa	v	England	Johannesburg[1]	1913-14	91
301	Pakistan	v	West Indies	Kingston	1976-77	140

TO DRAW						Runs set in 4th innings
654-5	England	v	South Africa	Durban[2]	1938-39	696
429-8	India	v	England	The Oval	1979	438
423-7	South Africa	v	England	The Oval	1947	451
408-5	West Indies	v	England	Kingston	1929-30	836
381-7	Australia	v	New Zealand	Perth	2001-02	440
371-9	Australia	v	England	Manchester	2005	423
364-6	India	v	Pakistan	Delhi	1979-80	390
357-6	Australia	v	India	Sydney	2003-04	443
355-8	India	v	West Indies	Bombay[2]	1948-49	361
354-5	West Indies	v	South Africa	Cape Town	2003-04	441
351-5	England	v	South Africa	Johannesburg[3]	1995-96	479
344-6	Sri Lanka	v	New Zealand	Hamilton	1990-91	418
344-7	Australia	v	England	Sydney	1994-95	449
343-6	India	v	England	Manchester	1990	408
341-9	Pakistan	v	West Indies	Port-of-Spain	1987-88	372
339-9	Australia	v	West Indies	Adelaide	1968-69	360
337-4	Pakistan	v	Sri Lanka	Colombo (SSC)	2005-06	458
335-5	England	v	Australia	Adelaide	1990-91	472
329-3	Australia	v	England	Lord's	1975	484
328-3	Australia	v	England	Adelaide	1970-71	469
326-5	South Africa	v	Australia	Sydney	1963-64	409
325-3	India	v	West Indies	Calcutta	1948-49	431
314-7	England	v	Australia	Sydney	1982-83	460
310-7	England	v	Australia	Melbourne	1946-47	551
308-4	England	v	South Africa	The Oval	1965	399

307-7	Sri Lanka	v	India	Kandy	1985-86	377
304-8	New Zealand	v	Zimbabwe	Harare	1997-98	403
303-3	India	v	Pakistan	Karachi[1]	1989-90	453

HIGHEST MATCH AGGREGATES - BOTH SIDES

Runs	Wkts						Days Played
1981	35	South Africa	v	England	Durban[2]	1938-39	§10
1815	34	West Indies	v	England	Kingston	1929-30	†9
1764	39	Australia	v	West Indies	Adelaide	1968-69	5
1753	40	Australia	v	England	Adelaide	1920-21	6
1747	25	Australia	v	India	Sydney	2003-04	5
1723	31	England	v	Australia	Leeds	1948	5
1702	28	Pakistan	v	India	Faisalabad	2005-06	5
1661	36	West Indies	v	Australia	Bridgetown	1954-55	6
1648	28	South Africa	v	West Indies	Cape Town	2003-04	5
1646	40	Australia	v	South Africa	Adelaide	1910-11	6
1644	38	Australia	v	West Indies	Sydney	1968-69	6
1640	24	West Indies	v	Australia	Bridgetown	1964-65	6
1640	33	Australia	v	Pakistan	Melbourne	1972-73	5
1619	40	Australia	v	England	Melbourne	1924-25	7
1614	30	England	v	India	Manchester	1990	5
1611	40	Australia	v	England	Sydney	1924-25	7
1603	28	England	v	India	Lord's	1990	5
1601	29	England	v	Australia	Lord's	1930	4
1585	31	Pakistan	v	New Zealand	Karachi[1]	1976-77	5
1576	35	England	v	West Indies	Lord's	2004	5
1562	37	Australia	v	England	Melbourne	1946-47	6
1554	35	Australia	v	England	Melbourne	1928-29	8
1553	40	England	v	Pakistan	Leeds	2006	5
1541	35	Australia	v	England	Sydney	1903-04	6
1528	24	West Indies	v	England	Port-of-Spain	1953-54	6
1522	35	New Zealand	v	Australia	Perth	2001-02	5
1514	40	Australia	v	England	Sydney	1894-95	6
1510	27	Australia	v	West Indies	Port-of-Spain	2002-03	5
1508	36	Australia	v	India	Adelaide	2003-04	5
1507	28	England	v	West Indies	The Oval	1976	5
1505	25	New Zealand	v	India	Auckland	1989-90	5
1502	29	Australia	v	England	Adelaide	1946-47	6
1553	40	England	v	Pakistan	Leeds	2006	5

§ No play on one day. † No play on two days.)

HIGHEST MATCH AGGREGATES - ONE SIDE

Runs	Wkts					
1121	19	England	v	West Indies	Kingston	1929-30
1078	18	Pakistan	v	India	Faisalabad	2005-06
1028	20	Australia	v	England	The Oval	1934
1013	18	Australia	v	West Indies	Sydney	1968-69
1011	20	South Africa	v	England	Durban[2]	1938-39

LOWEST MATCH AGGREGATES IN COMPLETED MATCHES - BOTH SIDES

Runs	Wkts						Days Played
234	29	Australia	v	South Africa	Melbourne	1931-32	§3
291	40	England	v	Australia	Lord's	1888	2
295	28	New Zealand	v	Australia	Wellington	1945-46	2
309	29	West Indies	v	England	Bridgetown	1934-35	3
323	30	England	v	Australia	Manchester	1888	2

363	40	England	v	Australia	The Oval	1882	2
374	40	Australia	v	England	Sydney	1887-88	†5
378	30	England	v	South Africa	The Oval	1912	2
382	30	South Africa	v	England	Cape Town	1888-89	2
389	38	England	v	Australia	The Oval	1890	2
390	30	England	v	New Zealand	Lord's	1958	3
392	40	England	v	Australia	The Oval	1896	3

§ No play on one day. † No play on two days.

LOWEST MATCH AGGREGATES IN A COMPLETED MATCH - ONE SIDE

Runs	Wkts					
81	20	South Africa	v	Australia	Melbourne	1931-32
90	20	South Africa	v	England	Cape Town	1888-89
96	20	New Zealand	v	Australia	Wellington	1945-46
112	19	Pakistan	v	Australia	Sharjah	2002-03
115	20	England	v	Australia	Lord's	1888
121	20	New Zealand	v	England	Lord's	1958
123	20	South Africa	v	England	Port Elizabeth	1895-96
124	20	Australia	v	England	Sydney	1887-88
137	18	England	v	Australia	Sydney	1894-95
140	20	India	v	England	Manchester	1952

LOWEST COMPLETED INNINGS TOTALS

26	New Zealand	v	England	Auckland	1954-55
30	South Africa	v	England	Port Elizabeth	1895-96
30	South Africa	v	England	Birmingham	1924
35	South Africa	v	England	Cape Town	1898-99
36	Australia	v	England	Birmingham	1902
36	South Africa	v	Australia	Melbourne	1931-32
42	Australia	v	England	Sydney	1887-88
42	New Zealand	v	Australia	Wellington	1945-46
42 §	India	v	England	Lord's	1974
43	South Africa	v	England	Cape Town	1888-89
44	Australia	v	England	The Oval	1896
45	England	v	Australia	Sydney	1886-87
45	South Africa	v	Australia	Melbourne	1931-32
46	England	v	West Indies	Port-of-Spain	1993-94
47	South Africa	v	England	Cape Town	1888-89
47	New Zealand	v	England	Lord's	1958
47	West Indies	v	England	Kingston	2003-04
51	West Indies	v	Australia	Port-of-Spain	1998-99
52	England	v	Australia	The Oval	1948
53	England	v	Australia	Lord's	1888
53	Australia	v	England	Lord's	1896
53	West Indies	v	Pakistan	Faisalabad	1986-87
53 §	Pakistan	v	Australia	Sharjah	2002-03
54	New Zealand	v	Australia	Wellington	1945-46
54	West Indies	v	England	Lord's	2000
54	Zimbabwe	v	South Africa	Cape Town	2004-05
58	South Africa	v	England	Lord's	1912
58 §	Australia	v	England	Brisbane[2]	1936-37
58	India	v	Australia	Brisbane[2]	1947-48
58	India	v	England	Manchester	1952
59	Pakistan	v	Australia	Sharjah	2002-03

59	Zimbabwe	v	New Zealand	Harare	2005-06
60	Australia	v	England	Lord's	1888
61	England	v	Australia	Melbourne	1901-02
61	England	v	Australia	Melbourne	1903-04
61	West Indies	v	England	Leeds	2000
62	England	v	Australia	Lord's	1888
62	Pakistan	v	Australia	Perth	1981-82
63	Australia	v	England	The Oval	1882
63	Zimbabwe	v	West Indies	Port-of-Spain	1999-2000
64	England	v	New Zealand	Wellington	1977-78
65 §	England	v	Australia	Sydney	1894-95
65	Australia	v	England	The Oval	1912
65	New Zealand	v	England	Christchurch	1970-71

§ One batsman absent hurt/ill.

The lowest completed innings total for the other countries are:

71	Sri Lanka	v	Pakistan	Kandy	1994-95
86	Bangladesh	v	Sri Lanka	Colombo (RPS)	2005-06

The following innings were closed at a low total:

32-7d	Australia	v	England	Brisbane[2]	1950-51
35-8	Australia	v	England	Manchester	1953
48-8	New Zealand	v	England	Christchurch	1965-66
51-6d	West Indies	v	England	Bridgetown	1934-35
61-7	India	v	Australia	Sydney	1947-48
66-7	Pakistan	v	England	Karachi[1]	1983-84
68-8	England	v	West Indies	Kingston	1967-68
72-7	West Indies	v	England	Birmingham	1957
75-6	New Zealand	v	India	Calcutta	1955-56
76-7	India	v	New Zealand	Hyderabad	1969-70
80-8	New Zealand	v	India	Bombay[2]	1964-65

DISMISSED FOR UNDER 100 IN BOTH INNINGS *(§ One batsman absent hurt/ill.)*

42	82	Australia	v	England	Sydney	1887-88
53	62	England	v	Australia	Lord's	1888
81	70	Australia	v	England	Manchester	1888
47	43	South Africa	v	England	Cape Town	1888-89
97	83	South Africa	v	England	Cape Town	1891-92
65 §	72 §	England	v	Australia	Sydney	1894-95
93	30	South Africa	v	England	Port Elizabeth	1895-96
95	93	South Africa	v	England	The Oval	1912
36	45	South Africa	v	Australia	Melbourne	1931-32
42	54	New Zealand	v	Australia	Wellington	1945-46
58	98	India	v	Australia	Brisbane[2]	1947-48
58	82	India	v	England	Manchester	1952
89 §	86 §	West Indies	v	England	The Oval	1957
47	74	New Zealand	v	England	Lord's	1958
82	93	England	v	New Zealand	Christchurch	1983-84
59	53 §	Pakistan	v	Australia	Sharjah	2002-03
59	99	Zimbabwe	v	New Zealand	Harare	2005-06

VICTORY AFTER BEING DISMISSED FOR UNDER 100 IN FIRST INNINGS

1st Inn	Winning team	Opponent	Venue	Series	Margin
45	England (+ 184)	Australia (119 + 97)	Sydney	1886-87	13 runs
63	Australia (+ 122)	England (101 + 77)	The Oval	1882	7 runs
75	England (+ 475)	Australia (123 + 333)	Melbourne	1894-95	94 runs
75	Australia (+5-336)	South Africa (311 + 99)	Durban2	1949-50	5 wkts

76	England (+ 162)	South Africa (110 + 75)	Leeds	1907	53 runs
91	South Africa (+ 9-287)	England (184 + 190)	Johannesburg[1]	1905-06	1 wkt
92	England (+ 330)	South Africa (177 + 35)	Cape Town	1898-99	210 runs
94	New Zealand (+ 6-160)	India (99 + 154)	Hamilton	2002-03	4 wkts

VICTORY AFTER FOLLOWING-ON

England (325 + 437)	beat	Australia (586 +166) by 10 runs	Sydney	1894-95
England (174 + 356)	beat	Australia (9d-401 + 111) by 12 runs	Leeds	1981
India (171 + 7d-657)	beat	Australia (445 + 212) by 171 runs	Kolkata	2000-01

VICTORY LOSING FEWEST WICKETS

TWO WICKETS				
England (2d-531)	v	South Africa (273 + 240)	Lord's	1924
England (2d-267)	v	New Zealand (67 + 129)	Leeds	1958
England (2d-459)	v	India (165 + 216)	Birmingham	1974
South Africa (2d-470)	v	Bangladesh (173 + 237)	Chittagong[1]	2002-03
THREE WICKETS				
India (3d-537)	v	New Zealand (209 + 219)	Madras[2]	1955-56
West Indies (3d-790)	v	Pakistan (328 + 288)	Kingston	1957-58
Pakistan (3d-581)	v	India (189 + 273)	Hyderabad	1982-83
Pakistan (3d-546)	v	Bangladesh (134 + 182)	Multan[2]	2001-02
Sri Lanka (3d-713)	v	Zimbabwe (228 + 231)	Bulawayo[2]	2003-04
South Africa (3d-340)	v	Zimbabwe (54 + 265)	Cape Town	2004-05
England (3d-528)	v	Bangladesh (108 + 159)	Lord's	2005
England (3d-447)	v	Bangladesh (104 + 316)	Chester-le-Street	2005

RESULTS BY NARROW MARGINS - TIE

Australia (505 + 232)	v	West Indies (453 + 284)	Brisbane[2]	1960-61
India (397 + 347)	v	Australia (7d-574 + 5d-170)	Madras[1]	1986-87

10th Wicket

RESULTS BY NARROW MARGINS - WON BY ONE WICKET

				Stand	
England (183 + 9-263)	v	Australia (324 + 121)	The Oval	15*	1902
South Africa (91 + 9-287)	v	England (184 + 190)	Johannesburg[1]	48*	1905-06
England (382 + 9-282)	v	Australia (266 + 397)	Melbourne	39*	1907-08
England (183 + 9-173)	v	South Africa (113 + 242)	Cape Town	5*	1922-23
Australia (216 + 9-260)	v	West Indies (272 + 203	Melbourne	38*	1951-52
New Zealand (249 + 9-104)	v	West Indies (140 + 212)	Dunedin	4*	1979-80
Pakistan (256 + 9-315)	v	Australia (337 + 232)	Karachi[1]	57*	1994-95
West Indies (329 + 9-311)	v	Australia (490 + 146)	Bridgetown	9*	1998-99
West Indies (273 + 9-216)	v	Pakistan (269 + 219)	St John's	22*	1999-2000
Pakistan (175 + 9-262)	v	Bangladesh (281 + 154)	Multan[2]	5*	2003-04
Sri Lanka (321 + 9-352)	v	South Africa (361 + 311)	Colombo(PSS)	2*	2006-07

RESULTS BY NARROW MARGINS - WON BY TWO WICKETS

England (100 + 8-95)	v	Australia (92 + 102)	The Oval	1890
Australia (300 + 8-275)	v	England (273 + 100)	Sydney	1907-08
§ England (253 + 8-128)	v	South Africa (161 + 219)	Durban[2]	1948-49
Australia (356 + 8-258)	v	West Indies (292 + 321)	Melbourne	1960-61
India (341 + 8-256)	v	Australia (320 + 274)	Bombay[2]	1964-65
Australia (394 + 8-342)	v	India (402 + 9d-330)	Perth	1977-78
West Indies (308+ 8-209)	v	England (263 + 252)	Nottingham	1980
New Zealand (220 + 8-278)	v	Pakistan (274 + 223)	Dunedin	1984-85
West Indies (306 + 8-268)	v	Pakistan (309 + 262)	Bridgetown	1987-88
Pakistan (293 + 8-141)	v	England (255 + 175)	Lord's	1992
Australia (108 + 8-271)	v	South Africa (209 + 168)	Port Elizabeth	1996-97

England (0d-0 + 8-251)	v	South Africa (8d-248 + forfeited)	Centurion	1999-2000
Sri Lanka (353 + 8-220)	v	Pakistan (182 + 390)	Rawalpindi[2]	1999-2000
England (134 + 8-191)	v	West Indies (267 + 54)	Lord's	2000
India (501 + 8-155)	v	Australia (391 + 264)	Chennai[1]	2000-01
Australia (270 + 8-294)	v	South Africa (303 + 258)	Johannesburg[3]	2005-06

§ England won by a leg bye off the last possible ball

RESULTS BY NARROW MARGINS - LESS THAN TWENTY RUNS

1	West Indies (252 + 146)	v	Australia (213 + 184)	Adelaide	1992-93
2	England (407 + 182)	v	Australia (308 + 279)	Birmingham	2005
3	Australia (299 + 86)	v	England (262 + 120)	Manchester	1902
3	England (284 + 294)	v	Australia (287 + 288)	Melbourne	1982-83
5	South Africa (169 + 239)	v	Australia (292 + 111)	Sydney	1993-94
6	Australia (182 + 165)	v	England (133 + 207)	Sydney	1884-85
7	Australia (63 + 122)	v	England (101 + 77)	The Oval	1882
7	South Africa (253 + 231)	v	Sri Lanka (308 + 169)	Kandy	2000-01
10	England (325 + 437)	v	Australia (586 + 166)	Sydney	1894-95
11	Australia (489 + 250)	v	England (365 + 363)	Adelaide	1924-25
12	England (334 + 383)	v	Australia (369 + 336)	Adelaide	1928-29
12	England (270 + 244)	v	Australia (340 + 162)	Melbourne	1998-99
12	Pakistan (238 + 286)	v	India (254 + 258)	Chennai[1]	1998-99
13	England (115 + 184)	v	Australia (119 + 97)	Sydney	1886-87
13	India (104 + 205)	v	Australia (203 + 93)	Mumbai[3]	2004-05
16	Australia (166 + 327)	v	India (153 + 324)	Brisbane[2]	1977-78
16	Pakistan (116 + 249)	v	India (145 + 204)	Bangalore	1986-87
16	Australia (256 + 471)	v	Sri Lanka (8d-547 + 164)	Colombo (SSC)	1992-93
17	South Africa (340 + 142)	v	England (251 + 214)	Johannesburg[3]	1956-57
18	England (174 + 356)	v	Australia (9d-401 + 111)	Leeds	1981
19	South Africa (208 + 345)	v	England (310 + 224)	Johannesburg[1]	1909-10
19	England (180 + 163)	v	Australia (220 + 104)	The Oval	1997

At Port-of-Spain in 1934-35, West Indies took England's last second innings wicket with the fifth ball of the last possible over to win by 217 runs.

RESULTS BY NARROW MARGINS - DRAWS

	Target	Total	Opponents		
India	361	355-8	West Indies	Bombay[2]	1948-49
England	234	228-9	West Indies	Lord's	1963
Australia	360	339-9	West Indies	Adelaide	1968-69
Australia	246	238-8	England	Melbourne	1974-75
India	438	429-8	England	The Oval	1979
Australia	247	230-9	New Zealand	Melbourne	1987-88
Pakistan	372	341-9	West Indies	Port-of-Spain	1987-88
England	205	204-6	Zimbabwe	Bulawayo[2]	1996-97
New Zealand	286	275-8	Zimbabwe	Bulawayo[2]	1997-98
New Zealand	288	223-9	Australia	Hobart	1997-98
New Zealand	284	274-6	Australia	Brisbane[2]	2001-02
Australia	423	371-9	England	Manchester	2005
West Indies	392	298-9	India	St John's	2005-06

GREATEST TEST VICTORIES BY AN INNINGS

Inns and 579 runs	England	v	Australia	The Oval	1938
Inns and 360 runs	Australia	v	South Africa	Johannesburg[3]	2001-02
Inns and 336 runs	West Indies	v	India	Calcutta	1958-59
Inns and 332 runs	Australia	v	England	Brisbane[2]	1946-47
Inns and 324 runs	Pakistan	v	New Zealand	Lahore[2]	2001-02
Inns and 322 runs	West Indies	v	New Zealand	Wellington	1994-95

Inns and 310 runs	West Indies	v	Bangladesh	Dhaka	2002-03
Inns and 294 runs	New Zealand	v	Zimbabwe	Harare	2005-06
Inns and 285 runs	England	v	India	Lord's	1974
Inns and 264 runs	Pakistan	v	Bangladesh	Multan[2]	2001-02
Inns and 261 runs	England	v	Bangladesh	Lord's	2005
Inns and 259 runs	Australia	v	South Africa	Port Elizabeth	1949-50
Inns and 254 runs	Sri Lanka	v	Zimbabwe	Bulawayo[2]	2003-04
Inns and 240 runs	Sri Lanka	v	Zimbabwe	Harare	2003-04
Inns and 237 runs	England	v	West Indies	The Oval	1957
Inns and 230 runs	England	v	Australia	Adelaide	1891-92
Inns and 229 runs	South Africa	v	Sri Lanka	Cape Town	2000-01
Inns and 226 runs	Australia	v	India	Brisbane[2]	1947-48
Inns and 226 runs	West Indies	v	England	Lord's	1973
Inns and 225 runs	England	v	Australia	Melbourne	1911-12
Inns and 222 runs	Australia	v	New Zealand	Hobart	1993-94
Inns and 219 runs	India	v	Australia	Calcutta	1997-98
Inns and 219 runs	South Africa	v	Zimbabwe	Harare	1999-2000
Inns and 217 runs	England	v	Australia	The Oval	1886
Inns and 217 runs	Australia	v	West Indies	Brisbane[1]	1930-31
Inns and 215 runs	England	v	New Zealand	Auckland	1962-63
Inns and 209 runs	England	v	Zimbabwe	Lord's	2000
Inns and 208 runs	South Africa	v	Sri Lanka	Colombo (SSC)	1993-94
Inns and 207 runs	England	v	India	Manchester	1952
Inns and 202 runs	England	v	South Africa	Cape Town	1888-89
Inns and 200 runs	Australia	v	England	Melbourne	1936-37

GREATEST TEST VICTORIES BY A RUN MARGIN

675 runs	England	v	Australia	Brisbane[1]	1928-29
562 runs	Australia	v	England	The Oval	1934
530 runs	Australia	v	South Africa	Melbourne	1910-11
491 runs	Australia	v	Pakistan	Perth	2004-05
425 runs	West Indies	v	England	Manchester	1976
409 runs	Australia	v	England	Lord's	1948
408 runs	West Indies	v	Australia	Adelaide	1979-80
384 runs	Australia	v	England	Brisbane[2]	2002-03
382 runs	Australia	v	England	Adelaide	1894-95
382 runs	Australia	v	West Indies	Sydney	1968-69
379 runs	Australia	v	West Indies	Brisbane[2]	2005-06
377 runs	Australia	v	England	Sydney	1920-21
365 runs	Australia	v	England	Melbourne	1936-37
356 runs	South Africa	v	England	Lord's	1994
352 runs	Australia	v	West Indies	Melbourne	2000-01
351 runs	South Africa	v	West Indies	Centurion	1998-99
348 runs	Australia	v	Pakistan	Melbourne	1976-77
343 runs	West Indies	v	Australia	Bridgetown	1990-91
342 runs	Australia	v	India	Nagpur	2004-05
341 runs	Pakistan	v	India	Karachi[1]	2005-06
338 runs	England	v	Australia	Adelaide	1932-33
329 runs	Australia	v	England	Perth	1994-95
329 runs	South Africa	v	India	Calcutta	1996-97
329 runs	England	v	Bangladesh	Chittagong[1]	2003-04
328 runs	South Africa	v	India	Durban[2]	1996-97
326 runs	West Indies	v	England	Lord's	1950
324 runs	South Africa	v	Pakistan	Johannesburg[3]	1994-95
323 runs	South Africa	v	Australia	Port Elizabeth	1969-70
322 runs	England	v	Australia	Brisbane[2]	1936-37

315 runs	Sri Lanka	v	Zimbabwe	Galle	2001-02
313 runs	Sri Lanka	v	South Africa	Colombo (SSC)	2004-05
312 runs	England	v	South Africa	Cape Town	1956-57
312 runs	Australia	v	West Indies	Port-of-Spain	1998-99
308 runs	Australia	v	England	Melbourne	1907-08
307 runs	Australia	v	England	Sydney	1924-25
307 runs	South Africa	v	Australia	Johannesburg[3]	1969-70
301 runs	Pakistan	v	Sri Lanka	Colombo (PSS)	1994-95
300 runs	Australia	v	India	Perth	1991-92

BATSMEN'S PARADISE (Over 60 runs per wicket)

Runs per Wkt	Runs-Wkts					
136.12	(1089-8)	Pakistan	v	India	Lahore[2]	2005-06
109.30	(1093-10)	India	v	New Zealand	Delhi	1955-56
106.35	(1489-14)	Sri Lanka	v	India	Colombo (RPS)	1997-98
99.40	(994-10)	West Indies	v	New Zealand	Georgetown	1971-72
86.87	(695-8)	New Zealand	v	England	Wellington	1987-88
86.00	(1462-17)	West Indies	v	South Africa	St John's	2004-05
83.25	(999-12)	Pakistan	v	Australia	Faisalabad	1979-80
82.27	(905-11)	England	v	Pakistan	Birmingham	1992
81.93	(1229-15)	West Indies	v	England	St John's	1993-94
81.55	(1468-18)	Pakistan	v	Australia	Peshawar[2]	1998-99
80.53	(1208-15)	Pakistan	v	India	Lahore[2]	1989-90
79.53	(1034-13)	Pakistan	v	Sri Lanka	Faisalabad	1985-86
78.25	(1252-16)	India	v	West Indies	Calcutta	1987-88
73.37	(1174-16)	Pakistan	v	India	Faisalabad	1984-85
73.06	(1096-15)	India	v	West Indies	Kanpur	1978-79
72.90	(1458-20)	West Indies	v	England	St John's	2003-04
70.61	(1271-18)	England	v	Australia	Manchester	1964
69.88	(1747-25)	Australia	v	India	Sydney	2003-04
68.33	(1640-24)	West Indies	v	Australia	Bridgetown	1964-65
67.90	(1494-22)	India	v	Zimbabwe	Nagpur	2000-01
67.61	(1217-18)	New Zealand	v	South Africa	Auckland	1998-99
66.95	(1406-21)	West Indies	v	Pakistan	Kingston	1957-58
65.42	(1243-19)	New Zealand	v	Pakistan	Christchurch	2000-01
65.35	(1307-20)	England	v	Australia	Manchester	1934
65.00	(1235-19)	India	v	West Indies	Bombay[2]	1948-49
64.75	(1036-16)	India	v	New Zealand	Hyderabad	1955-56
64.52	(1226-19)	Australia	v	West Indies	Sydney	1992-93
64.47	(1096-17)	India	v	Sri Lanka	Kanpur	1986-87
63.66	(1528-24)	West Indies	v	England	Port-of-Spain	1953-54
63.44	(1142-18)	West Indies	v	India	St John's	2001-02
63.41	(1078-17)	India	v	Australia	Bombay[3]	1986-87
62.33	(1496-24)	England	v	Australia	Nottingham	1938
62.30	(1246-20)	England	v	South Africa	Birmingham	2003
62.22	(1369-22)	England	v	West Indies	The Oval	1995
62.11	(1118-18)	New Zealand	v	Pakistan	Auckland	1988-89
62.00	(1116-18)	West Indies	v	England	Bridgetown	1959-60
61.86	(1423-23)	England	v	India	The Oval	1990
61.52	(1042-17)	India	v	Pakistan	Madras[2]	1960-61
61.41	(737-12)	New Zealand	v	South Africa	Christchurch	1998-99
60.94	(1158-12)	India	v	England	Kanpur	1984-85
60.78	(1702-28)	Pakistan	v	India	Faisalabad	2005-06
60.62	(1455-24)	New Zealand	v	Australia	Wellington	1973-74
60.57	(1272-21)	Pakistan	v	India	Faisalabad	1978-79
60.45	(1209-20)	Australia	v	England	Adelaide	1986-87
60.20	(1505-25)	New Zealand	v	India	Auckland	1989-90

MOST CENTURIES IN A MATCH (BOTH TEAMS)

8	West Indies (4)	v	South Africa (4)	St John's	2004-05
7	England (4)	v	Australia (3)	Nottingham	1938
7	West Indies (2)	v	Australia (5)	Kingston	1954-55
7	South Africa (4)	v	West Indies (3)	Cape Town	2003-04
6	Australia (4)	v	England (2)	Adelaide	1920-21
6	Australia (3)	v	England (3)	Sydney	1924-25
6	Australia (4)	v	England (2)	Melbourne	1928-29
6	South Africa (3)	v	England (3)	Durban[2]	1938-39
6	Australia (3)	v	India (3)	Adelaide	1947-48
6	West Indies (3)	v	India (3)	Kingston	1952-53
6	West Indies (3)	v	Australia (3)	Port-of-Spain	1954-55
6	Australia (4)	v	West Indies (2)	Sydney	1968-69
6	Australia (4)	v	Pakistan (2)	Melbourne	1972-73
6	New Zealand (2)	v	Australia (4)	Wellington	1973-74
6	West Indies (4)	v	India (2)	St John's	1982-83
6	Australia (3)	v	Pakistan (3)	Adelaide	1983-84
6	England (4)	v	India (2)	Lord's	1990
6	England (4)	v	India (2)	Manchester	1990
6	Sri Lanka (3)	v	India (3)	Colombo (RPS)	1997-98
6	Sri Lanka (3)	v	India (3)	Colombo (SSC)	1997-98
6	India (3)	v	Zimbabwe (3)	Nagpur	2000-01
6	West Indies (2)	v	Australia (4)	Port-of-Spain	2002-03
6	India (2)	v	New Zealand (4)	Mohali	2003-04
6	Pakistan (4)	v	India (2)	Lahore[2]	2005-06
6	Pakistan (4)	v	India (2)	Faislabad	2005-06

MOST CENTURIES IN AN INNINGS

5	Australia (8d-758)	v	West Indies	Kingston	1954-55
5	Pakistan (3d-546)	v	Bangladesh	Multan[2]	2001-02
4	England (8d-658)	v	Australia	Nottingham	1938
4	West Indies (631)	v	India	Delhi	1948-49
4	Pakistan (652)	v	India	Faisalabad	1982-83
4	West Indies (550)	v	India	St John's	1982-83
4	Pakistan (8d-600)	v	Sri Lanka	Galle	2000-01
4	Sri Lanka (6d-610)	v	India	Colombo (SSC)	2001-02
4	New Zealand (9d-534)	v	Australia	Perth	2001-02
4	New Zealand (6d-630)	v	India	Mohali	2003-04
4	South Africa (6d-588)	v	West Indies	St John's	2004-05
4	West Indies (747)	v	South Africa	St John's	2004-05
4	Pakistan (7d-679)	v	India	Lahore[2]	2005-06

MOST CENTURIES IN A SERIES (ONE TEAM)

				Venue		Tests
12	Australia	v	West Indies	West Indies	1954-55	5
12	Pakistan	v	India	Pakistan	1982-83	6
12	South Africa	v	West Indies	South Africa	2003-04	4
11	England	v	South Africa	South Africa	1938-39	5
11	West Indies	v	India	India	1948-49	5
11	Australia	v	South Africa	South Africa	1949-50	5
11	India	v	West Indies	India	1978-79	6

MOST CENTURIES IN A SERIES (BOTH TEAMS)

				Venue		Tests
21	West Indies (9)	v	Australia (12)	West Indies	1954-55	5
20	South Africa (12)	v	West Indies (8)	South Africa	2003-04	4
17	Australia (9)	v	England (8)	Australia	1928-29	5
17	South Africa (6)	v	England (11)	South Africa	1938-39	5
17	Pakistan (12)	v	India (5)	Pakistan	1982-83	6
17	West Indies (9)	v	South Africa (8)	West Indies	2004-05	4
16	India (5)	v	West Indies (11)	India	1948-49	5
16	Australia (10)	v	West Indies (6)	Australia	1968-69	5
16	Australia (10)	v	West Indies (6)	Australia	1975-76	6
15	Australia (10)	v	England (5)	Australia	1946-47	5
15	England (9)	v	India (6)	England	1990	3
15	Pakistan (10)	v	India (5)	Pakistan	2005-06	3

WINNING EVERY TEST IN A SERIES (Minimum: 4 matches)

			Venue		Tests
Australia	v	England	Australia	1920-21	5
Australia	v	South Africa	Australia	1931-32	5
England	v	India	England	1959	5
West Indies	v	India	West Indies	1961-62	5
Australia	v	India	Australia	1967-68	4
South Africa	v	Australia	South Africa	1969-70	4
West Indies	v	England	England	1984	5
West Indies	v	England	West Indies	1985-86	5
South Africa	v	West Indies	South Africa	1998-99	5
Australia	v	West Indies	Australia	2000-01	5
England	v	West Indies	England	2004	4

Australia (v West Indies 1975-76) England (v Australia 1978-79) won 6-match series in Australia by 5 Tests to 1.

MOST CONSECUTIVE WINS

16	Australia	Harare	1999-2000	to	Mumbai[3]	2000-01
11	West Indies	Bridgetown	1983-84	to	Adelaide	1984-85
9	Sri Lanka	Colombo (SSC)	2001-02	to	Lahore[2]	2001-02
9	South Africa	Durban[2]	2001-02	to	Dhaka	2002-03
8	Australia	Sydney	1920-21	to	Leeds	1921
8	England	Lord's	2004	to	Port Elizabeth	2004-05
7	England	Melbourne	1884-85	to	Sydney	1887-88
7	England	Lord's	1928	to	Adelaide	1928-29
7	West Indies	Bridgetown	1984-85	to	St John's	1985-86
7	West Indies	Lord's	1988	to	Melbourne	1988-89
7	Australia	Colombo (PSS)	2002-03	to	Melbourne	2002-03
7	Australia	Brisbane[2]	2004-05	to	Lord's	2005
7	Australia	Melbourne	2005-06	to	Chittagong[2]	2005-06
6	England	The Oval	1888	to	The Oval	1890
6	England	Leeds	1957	to	Manchester	1958
6	West Indies	Port-of-Spain	1961-62	to	Manchester	1963
6	Pakistan	Manchester	2001	to	Sharjah	2001-02

DRAWING EVERY TEST IN A FIVE-MATCH SERIES

Pakistan	v	India	1954-55
India	v	Pakistan	1960-61
India	v	England	1963-64
West Indies	v	New Zealand	1971-72

MOST CONSECUTIVE MATCHES WITHOUT DEFEAT

27	West Indies	Sydney	1981-82	to	Melbourne	1984-85
26	England	Lord's	1968	to	Manchester	1971
25	Australia	Wellington	1945-46	to	Adelaide	1950-51
18	England	Christchurch	1958-59	to	Birmingham	1961
18	Australia	Galle	1999-2000	to	Mumbai[3]	2000-01
17	Australia	Madras[2]	1956-57	to	Delhi	1959-60
17	India	Kandy	1985-86	to	Ahmedabad	1986-87
16	Australia	Sydney	1920-21	to	Adelaide	1924-25
16	Pakistan	Karachi[1]	1986-87	to	Port-of-Spain	1987-88
15	England	Melbourne	1911-12	to	Port Elizabeth	1913-14
15	Pakistan	Wellington	1972-73	to	Adelaide	1976-77
15	India	Lord's	1979	to	Calcutta	1979-80
15	West Indies	Christchurch	1979-80	to	Kingston	1980-81
14	Australia	Sydney	1988-89	to	Sydney	1989-90
14	India	Cape Town	1992-93	to	Nagpur	1994-95
14	South Africa	Johannesburg[3]	1998-99	to	Cape Town	1999-2000
13	India	Port-of-Spain	1952-53	to	Madras[2]	1955-56
13	Australia	The Oval	1972	to	Wellington	1973-74
13	England	Kingston	2003-04	to	Durban[2]	2004-05
12	England	The Oval	1938	to	The Oval	1946
12	Pakistan	Manchester	1954	to	Bridgetown	1957-58
12	England	The Oval	1966	to	Georgetown	1967-68
12	Pakistan	Karachi[1]	1982-83	to	Nagpur	1983-84
12	Australia	St John's	1990-91	to	Sydney	1992-93
12	South Africa	Kandy	2000-01	to	St John's	2000-01

MOST CONSECUTIVE DEFEATS

21	Bangladesh	Chittagong[1]	2001-02	to	Harare	2003-04
11	Zimbabwe	Colombo (SSC)	2001-02	to	Sydney	2003-04
8 †	South Africa	Port Elizabeth	1888-89	to	Cape Town	1898-99
8	England	Sydney	1920-21	to	Leeds	1921
8	West Indies	Kingston	2005-06	to	Wellington	2005-06
8	Bangladesh	Lord's	2005	to	Chittagong[2]	2005-06
7	Australia	Melbourne	1884-85	to	Sydney	1887-88
7	England	Lord's	1950	to	Adelaide	1950-51
7	India	Leeds	1967	to	Sydney	1967-68
7	England	Kingston	1985-86	to	Leeds	1986
7	England	The Oval	1992	to	Lord's	1993
7	West Indies	Leeds	2000	to	Sydney	2000-01
6	South Africa	Melbourne	1910-11	to	Lord's	1912
6	New Zealand	Johannesburg[2]	1953-54	to	Lahore[1]	1955-56
6	India	Nottingham	1959	to	Delhi	1959-60
6	Australia	Bridgetown	1983-84	to	Adelaide	1984-85
6	West Indies	Johannesburg[3]	1998-99	to	Port-of-Spain	1998-99

† South Africa's first 8 Tests

MOST CONSECUTIVE MATCHES WITHOUT VICTORY

44 †	New Zealand	Christchurch	1929-30	to	Wellington	1955-56
34 #	Bangladesh	Dhaka	2000-01	to	Chittagong[1]	2004-05
31	India	Bangalore	1981-82	to	Faisalabad	1984-85
28	South Africa	Leeds	1935	to	Port Elizabeth	1949-50
24	India	Lord's	1932	to	Kanpur	1951-52
23	New Zealand	Auckland	1962-63	to	Dunedin	1967-68
22	Pakistan	Lahore[1]	1958-59	to	Christchurch	1964-65
21	Sri Lanka	Colombo (PSS)	1985-86	to	Moratuwa	1992-93

20	West Indies	Wellington	1968-69	to	Port-of-Spain	1972-73
19	Zimbabwe	Bulawayo[2]	1994-95	to	Harare	1997-98
18	New Zealand	Dacca	1969-70	to	Wellington	1973-74
18	England	Sydney	1986-87	to	The Oval	1988
16	South Africa	Melbourne	1910-11	to	Cape Town	1921-22
16	Pakistan	Lord's	1967	to	Wellington	1972-73
16	Zimbabwe	Lahore[2]	1998-99	to	Wellington	2000-01
15	Sri Lanka	Kandy	1993-94	to	Harare	1994-95
15	New Zealand	Durban[2]	1994-95	to	St John's	1995-96
14	India	Madras[2]	1956-57	to	Delhi	1959-60
14	Australia	Perth	1985-86	to	Melbourne	1986-87
14	India	Georgetown	1988-89	to	The Oval	1990
13	India	Madras[1]	1952-53	to	Hyderabad	1955-56
13	England	Wellington	1983-84	to	Bombay[3]	1984-85
13	Sri Lanka	Colombo (PSS)	1981-82	to	Colombo (SSC)	1985-86
13	New Zealand	Nottingham	1990	to	Bulawayo[1]	1992-93
13	Sri Lanka	Kandy	1993-94	to	Harare	1994-95
13	India	Durban[2]	1996-97	to	Mumbai[3]	1997-98
13	Zimbabwe	Colombo (SSC)	2001-02	to	Bulawayo[2]	2003-04
13	West Indies	Kingston	2004-05	to	Kingston	2005-06
12	South Africa	Cape Town	1922-23	to	Durban[2]	1927-28
12	England	Leeds	1963	to	The Oval	1964
12	England	Nottingham	1980	to	Lord's	1981

† New Zealand's first 44 Tests. # Bangladesh's first 34 Tests.

MOST CONSECUTIVE DRAWS

10	West Indies	Georgetown	1970-71	to	Bridgetown	1972-73
9	India	Port-of-Spain	1952-53	to	Hyderabad	1955-56
9	India	Calcutta	1959-60	to	Delhi	1961-62
9	New Zealand	Wellington	1963-64	to	Bombay[2]	1964-65
9	Pakistan	Auckland	1972-73	to	Karachi[1]	1974-75

MOST RUNS IN ONE DAY - BY ONE TEAM

						Day
509-9	Sri Lanka (0-32 to 9-541)	v	Bangladesh	Colombo (PSS)	2002-03	2nd
503-2	England (0-28 to 2d-531)	v	South Africa	Lord's	1924	2nd
494-6	Australia (6-496)	v	South Africa	Sydney	1910-11	1st
475-2	Australia (2-475)	v	England	The Oval	1934	1st
471-8	England (8d-471)	v	India	The Oval	1936	1st
458-3	Australia (3-458)	v	England	Leeds	1930	1st
455-1	Australia (3-93 to 4-494)	v	England	Leeds	1934	2nd
452-9	New Zealand (9d-452)	v	Zimbabwe	Harare	2005-06	1st
451-10	South Africa (451)	v	New Zealand	Christchurch	1931-32	2nd
450-10	Australia (450)	v	South Africa	Johannesburg[1]	1921-22	1st
449-7	Sri Lanka (7-449)	v	Bangladesh	Colombo (PSS)	2005-06	1st
448-10	Australia (448)	v	South Africa	Manchester	1912	1st
445-3	South Africa (3-445)	v	Pakistan	Cape Town	2002-03	1st
437-4	England (2-121 to 6d-558)	v	Pakistan	Nottingham	1954	2nd
437-9	West Indies (9-437)	v	England	Leeds	1976	1st
435-4	England (4-435)	v	Australia	The Oval	1899	1st
432-4	England (4-432)	v	New Zealand	The Oval	1949	2nd
428-3	Australia (3-428)	v	West Indies	Brisbane[1]	1930-31	1st
428-6	Australia (1-48 to 7-476)	v	South Africa	Melbourne	1910-11	3rd
428-7	South Africa (7-428)	v	Australia	Johannesburg[1]	1902-03	1st
428-10	England (428)	v	South Africa	Lord's	1907	1st
427-7	England (7-427)	v	South Africa	Manchester	1929	1st
425-1	Sri Lanka (0-18 to 1-443)	v	Zimbabwe	Bulawayo[2]	2003-04	2nd

MOST RUNS IN ONE DAY - BY BOTH TEAMS

						Day
588-6	England (2-173 to 8d-571)	v	India (0-190)	Manchester	1936	2nd
522-2	England (0-28 to 2d-531)	v	South Africa (0-19)	Lord's	1924	2nd
508-8	England (4-313- to 6d-534)	v	South Africa (6-287)	The Oval	1935	3rd
496-4	England (2-121 to 6d-558)	v	Pakistan (0-59)	Nottingham	1954	2nd
492-8	South Africa (6-297 to 476)	v	England (4-313)	The Oval	1935	2nd
491-7	New Zealand (9-312 to 341 & 2-195)	v	England (4d-267)	Leeds	1949	3rd
482-11	Australia (4-331 to 5d-552)	v	India (261)	Sydney	1999-2000	3rd
475-8	England (3-269 to 3d-447)	v	Bangladesh (8-297)	Chester-le-Street	2005	2nd
473-4	South Africa (5-283 to 8d-492)	v	England (1-264)	The Oval	1929	3rd
471-9	Australia (3-162 to 389)	v	England (2-244)	The Oval	1921	3rd
469-7	West Indies (6-395 to 498)	v	England (3d-366)	The Oval	1939	3rd
467-10	South Africa (451)	v	New Zealand (0-16)	Christchurch	1931-32	2nd
464-11	Australia (448)	v	South Africa (1-16)	Manchester	1912	1st
459-11	New Zealand (5-186 to 8d-287 & 6-274)	v	Australia (2d-84)	Brisbane[2]	2001-02	5th
458-12	Australia (3-239 to 8d-394)	v	West Indies (7-303)	Sydney	1968-69	5th
457-6	New Zealand (8-320 to 345)	v	England (4-432)	The Oval	1949	2nd
455-10	England (4-135 to 428)	v	India (4-162)	Lord's	1946	2nd
454-9	New Zealand (2-161 to 9d-469)	v	England (5-146)	Lord's	1931	3rd
450-16	Australia (2-86 to 390)	v	South Africa (8-146)	Lord's	1912	2nd
446-4	Australia (3-368 to 6d-735)	v	Zimbabwe (1-79)	Perth	2003-04	2nd
442-12	New Zealand (364)	v	South Africa (2-78)	Wellington	1931-32	1st
439-7	England (4-278 to 551)	v	South Africa (1-166)	Nottingham	1947	4th
437-7	England (5-313 to 9d-566)	v	West Indies (2-184)	Birmingham	2004	2nd
433-4	England (2-63 to 6d-468)	v	New Zealand (0-28)	Christchurch	2001-02	3rd
431-17	South Africa (4-204 to 302 & 1-8)	v	England (6d-325)	The Oval	1947	3rd
430-7	England (1-188 to 3d-528)	v	Bangladesh (5-90)	Lord's	2005	2nd
429-6	England (1-127 to 7d-548)	v	New Zealand (0-8)	Auckland	1932-33	2nd
427-12	England (294)	v	Australia (2-133)	Birmingham	2001	1st
426-5	England (4d-330)	v	New Zealand (1-96)	Auckland	1929-30	3rd
425-5	England (7-190 to 454)	v	New Zealand (2-161)	Lord's	1931	2nd
425-11	England (5-363 to 9d-440)	v	New Zealand (7-348)	Manchester	1949	3rd

FEWEST RUNS IN A FULL DAY'S PLAY

						Day
95-12	Australia (80 all out)	v	Pakistan (2-15)	Karachi[1]	1956-57	1st
104-5	Pakistan (5-104)	v	Australia	Karachi[1]	1959-60	4th
106-8	England (2-92 to 198 all out)	v	Australia	Brisbane[2]	1958-59	4th
112-5	Australia (6-138 to 187 all out)	v	Pakistan (1-63)	Karachi[1]	1956-57	4th
115-18	Australia (7-116 to 165 all out & 5-66)	v	Pakistan	Karachi[1]	1988-89	4th
117-5	India (5-117)	v	Australia	Madras[2]	1956-57	1st
117-4	New Zealand (0-6 to 1-123)	v	Sri Lanka	Colombo (SSC)	1983-84	5th
122-8	England (9-110 to 110)	v	South Africa (7-122)	Port Elizabeth	1956-57	3rd
122-6	Australia (6-156 to 186)	v	England (2-92)	Brisbane[1]	1958-59	3rd
122-15	Australia (6-282 to 306 & 1-9)	v	England (87)	Melbourne	1958-59	4th
122-14	Australia (4-243 to 258)	v	England (8-107)	Melbourne	1978-79	2nd
123-9	England (2-123 to 191)	v	Pakistan (1-55)	Hyderabad	1977-78	3rd
124-7	Pakistan (4-74 to 134)	v	Australia (1-64)	Dacca	1959-60	4th
124-6	India (6-226 to 291)	v	Australia (2-59)	Kanpur	1959-60	4th
127-8	India (3-162 to 245)	v	Pakistan (1-44)	Peshawar[1]	1954-55	3rd
127-8	West Indies (2-291 to 353)	v	England (0-65)	Kingston	1959-60	4th
128-7	England (2-53 to 9-181)	v	West Indies	Bridgetown	1953-54	3rd
129-6	Pakistan (6-129)	v	India	Peshawar[1]	1954-55	1st
129-11	India (1-46 to 149 & 2-26)	v	Australia	Madras[2]	1959-60	3rd
130-14	South Africa (7-200 to 243)	v	New Zealand (78 & 1-8)	Johannesburg[2]	1953-54	2nd
130-6	India (5-115 to 148)	v	Pakistan (1-97)	Dacca	1954-55	3rd
130-8	West Indies (7-349 to 386)	v	New Zealand (5-93)	Christchurch	1955-56	2nd

130-4	Pakistan (4-130)	v	India	Ahmedabad	1986-87	1st
134-9	England (1-333 to 439)	v	Pakistan (0-28)	Dacca	1961-62	4th
136-14	South Africa (5-138 to 164)	v	England (9-110)	Port Elizabeth	1956-57	2nd
136-6	New Zealand (0-9 to 6-145)	v	India	Bangalore	1988-89	3rd
138-6	Australia (6-138)	v	Pakistan	Karachi[1]	1956-57	3rd
138-5	South Africa (5-138)	v	England	Port Elizabeth	1956-57	1st
140-5	New Zealand (1-8 to 6-148)	v	South Africa	Johannesburg[2]	1953-54	3rd

TWENTY-FIVE OR MORE BYES IN AN INNINGS

37	Australia (327)	v	England	The Oval	1934
33	India (390)	v	England	Bombay[2]	1961-62
33	West Indies (9d-391)	v	England	Kingston	1967-68
31	New Zealand (387)	v	England	Auckland	1929-30
31	Pakistan (366)	v	Australia	Lahore[2]	1959-60
30	England (417)	v	South Africa	Cape Town	1909-10
30	South Africa (329)	v	Australia	Nottingham	1912
30	England (327)	v	West Indies	Georgetown	1929-30
30	New Zealand (189)	v	England	Wellington	1950-51
29	India (378)	v	England	Lord's	1952
29	England (559)	v	India	Kanpur	1952
29	Pakistan (291)	v	West Indies	Bridgetown	1976-77
28	India (372)	v	Pakistan	Delhi	1952-53
28	Sri Lanka (6-952)	v	India	Colombo (RPS)	1997-98
26	Australia (476)	v	England	Adelaide	1911-12
25	South Africa (327)	v	England	Cape Town	1909-10
25	England (450)	v	South Africa	Durban[1]	1913-14
25	West Indies (288)	v	Australia	Port-of-Spain	2002-03
25	South Africa (6d-682)	v	England	Lord's	2003
25	England (526)	v	New Zealand	Leeds	2004

TWENTY-FIVE OR MORE LEG BYES IN AN INNINGS

31	England (515)	v	India	The Oval	2002
30	West Indies (5d-411)	v	England	Manchester	1976
29	England (415)	v	Zimbabwe	Lord's	2000
28	New Zealand (307)	v	Sri Lanka	Dunedin	1994-95
28	New Zealand (6d-630)	v	India	Mohali	2003-04
28	Australia (8d-512)	v	Sri Lanka	Galle	2003-04
28	England (339)	v	West Indies	Kingston	2003-04
27	England (5d-633)	v	India	Birmingham	1979
27	England (336)	v	West Indies	Lord's	1995
27	England (472)	v	Zimbabwe	Lord's	2003
26	England (8d-452)	v	Pakistan	Birmingham	1978
26	England (462)	v	South Africa	Birmingham	1998
26	Pakistan (407)	v	India	Multan[2]	2003-04
25	Australia (394)	v	India	Perth	1977-78
25	West Indies (509)	v	Australia	Bridgetown	1983-84
25	West Indies (6d-268)	v	New Zealand	Georgetown	1984-85
25	India (565)	v	West Indies	Calcutta	1987-88
25	India (429)	v	England	Lord's	1996
25	West Indies (284)	v	Australia	Bridgetown	2002-03
25	India (338)	v	England	Mohali	2005-06

THIRTY-FIVE OR MORE NO BALLS IN AN INNINGS *(only no-balls included in extras)*

40	England (310)	v	West Indies	St John's	1985-86
40	Australia (515)	v	West Indies	Adelaide	1988-89
39	Pakistan (325)	v	Sri Lanka	Lahore[2]	2001-02
38	Pakistan (435)	v	West Indies	Georgetown	1987-88
37	Australia (234) *(2nd innings)*	v	West Indies	Perth	1988-89
36	England (7d-394)	v	West Indies	Bridgetown	1993-94
36	Zimbabwe (8-319)	v	Sri Lanka	Harare	1994-95
36	South Africa (460)	v	Pakistan	Johannesburg[3]	1994-95
35	West Indies (8d-596)	v	England	Bridgetown	1973-74
35	England (309)	v	Australia	Brisbane[2]	1982-83
35	Australia (8d-395) *(1st innings)*	v	West Indies	Perth	1988-89
35	New Zealand (4-671)	v	Sri Lanka	Wellington	1990-91
35	England (419)	v	West Indies	The Oval	1991
35	England (390)	v	Pakistan	Manchester	1992
35	Australia (9d-501)	v	England	Leeds	1997
35	England (425)	v	South Africa	Port Elizabeth	2004-05

TEN OR MORE WIDES IN AN INNINGS

18	England (330)	v	West Indies	Manchester	2004
16	England (374)	v	Zimbabwe	Nottingham	2000
15	India (288)	v	Pakistan	Faisalabad	1989-90
15	England (260)	v	West Indies	St John's	1989-90
15	South Africa (7d-259)	v	Pakistan	Johannesburg[3]	1994-95
15	England (9d-528)	v	Pakistan	Lord's	2006
13	Pakistan (164)	v	England	Birmingham	1978
13	England (227)	v	Pakistan	Lord's	1982
13	England (568)	v	West Indies	Lord's	2004
13	Pakistan (9d-496)	v	India	Mohali	2004-05
12	India (6d-306)	v	West Indies	Kingston	1975-76
12	India (234)	v	Zimbabwe	Harare	2000-01
12	South Africa (6d-604) *(1st innings)*	v	West Indies	Centurion	2003-04
11	England (288)	v	Australia	Leeds	1975
11	England (5d-633)	v	India	Birmingham	1979
11	England (521)	v	Pakistan	Birmingham	1987
11	Pakistan (369)	v	Zimbabwe	Harare	2002-03
11	England (408)	v	South Africa	Birmingham	2003
11	Pakistan (463)	v	New Zealand	Hamilton	2003-04
11	Pakistan (504)	v	England	The Oval	2006
10	England (277)	v	West Indies	Kingston	1959-60
10	England (252)	v	West Indies	Nottingham	1980
10	England (370)	v	West Indies	The Oval	1980
10	India (371)	v	England	Calcutta	1992-93
10	India (366)	v	Sri Lanka	Colombo (SSC)	1993-94
10	India (429)	v	England	Lord's	1996
10	South Africa (0-46) *(2nd innings)*	v	West Indies	Centurion	2003-04
10	South Africa (8d-222)	v	England	Cape Town	2004-05
10	India (214)	v	Pakistan	Bangalore	2004-05

FIFTY OR MORE EXTRAS IN AN INNINGS

71 (b21, lb8, nb38, w4)	Pakistan (435)	v	West Indies	Georgetown	1987-88
68 (b29, lb11, nb28)	Pakistan (291)	v	West Indies	Bridgetown	1976-77
65 (b10, lb18, nb36, w1)	Zimbabwe (8-319)	v	Sri Lanka	Harare	1994-95
64 (b12, lb25, nb27)	India (565)	v	West Indies	Calcutta	1987-88
64 (b4, lb18, nb36, w6)	South Africa (460)	v	Pakistan	Johannesburg[3]	1994-95

64 (b18, lb11, nb34, w1)	England (437)	v	West Indies	Manchester	1995
64 (b25, lb21, nb13, w5)	South Africa (6d-682)	v	England	Lord's	2003
62 (b16, lb10, nb31, w5)	South Africa 386)	v	Sri Lanka	Johannesburg[3]	2002-03
62 (b25, lb21, nb13, w3)	England (526)	v	New Zealand	Leeds	2003
61 (b17, lb17, nb25, w2)	Pakistan (9-341)	v	West Indies	Port-of-Spain	1987-88
61 (b6, lb23, nb29, w3)	Australia (6d-602)	v	England	Nottingham	1989
61 (b14, lb27, nb17, w3)	England (472)	v	Zimbabwe	Lord's	2003
60 (b4, lb27, nb18, w11)	England (5d-633)	v	India	Birmingham	1979
60 (b7, lb28, nb18, w7)	England (339)	v	West Indies	Kingston	2003-04
59 (b20, lb11, nb27, w1)	England (315)	v	West Indies	Port-of-Spain	1985-86
58 (lb18, nb40)	Australia (515)	v	West Indies	Adelaide	1988-89
58 (lb23, nb34, w1)	Australia (471)	v	Sri Lanka	Colombo (SSC)	1992-93
58 (b28, lb9, nb14, w7)	Sri Lanka (6-952)	v	India	Colombo (RPS)	1997-98
58 (b4, lb12, nb33, w9)	New Zealand (563)	v	Pakistan	Hamilton	2004-05
57 (b31, lb16, nb10)	New Zealand (387)	v	England	Auckland	1929-30
57 (b7, lb21, nb19, w10)	England (370)	v	West Indies	The Oval	1980
57 (b16, lb14, nb26, w1)	India (463)	v	West Indies	Bombay[3]	1983-84
57 (lb21, nb35, w1)	England (425)	v	South Africa	Port Elizabeth	2004-05
55 (b6, lb11, nb32, w6)	Australia (345)	v	England	Lord's	1981
55 (b2, lb16, nb22, w15)	India (288)	v	Pakistan	Faisalabad	1989-90
55 (b16, lb22, nb12, w5)	England (4-477)	v	India	The Oval	1990
55 (b11, lb25, nb9, w10)	India (429)	v	England	Lord's	1996
54 (b7, lb13, nb34)	India (8d-566)	v	West Indies	Delhi	1978-79
54 (b8, lb10, nb35, w1)	England (419)	v	West Indies	The Oval	1991
54 (b9, lb10, nb35)	Australia (9d-501)	v	England	Leeds	1997
54 (b18, lb26, nb2, w2)	England (462)	v	South Africa	Birmingham	1998
54 (b12, lb2, nb39, w1)	Pakistan (325)	v	Sri Lanka	Lahore[2]	2001-02
53 (b20, lb8, nb21, w4)	India (487)	v	England	Delhi	1981-82
53 (b6, lb17, nb28, w2)	West Indies (606)	v	England	Birmingham	1984
53 (b17, lb6, nb28, w2)	Australia (248)	v	West Indies	Georgetown	1990-91
53 (b8, lb8, nb35, w2)	England (390)	v	Pakistan	Manchester	1992
53 (b13, lb9, nb25, w6)	Pakistan (471)	v	West Indies	Rawalpindi[2]	1997-98
53 (b19, lb6, nb17, w11)	England (408)	v	South Africa	Birmingham	2003
53 (b21, lb28, nb3, w1)	New Zealand (6d-630)	v	India	Mohali	2003-04
53 (b9, lb22, nb16, w1, p5)	South Africa (9d-510)	v	India	Kanpur	2004-05
52 (b12, lb7, nb33)	New Zealand (468)	v	Pakistan	Karachi[1]	1976-77
52 (b19, lb13, nb10, w10)	England (252)	v	West Indies	Nottingham	1980
52 (b8, lb8, nb35, w1)	England (309)	v	Australia	Brsbane[2]	1982-83
52 (b1, lb24, nb16, w11)	England (521)	v	Pakistan	Birmingham	1987
52 (b4, lb23, nb21, w4)	Australia (371)	v	West Indies	Kingston	1990-91
52 (b9, lb20, nb23)	England (593)	v	West Indies	Port-of-Spain	1993-94
52 (b17, lb20, nb2, w13)	Pakistan (9d-496)	v	India	Mohali	2004-05
51 (b10, lb20, nb21)	India (7-469)	v	West Indies	Port-of-Spain	1982-83
51 (b5, lb6, nb40)	England (310)	v	West Indies	St John's	1985-86
51 (b14, lb9, nb25, w3)	England (358)	v	West Indies	Bridgetown	1989-90
51 (b12, lb31, nb7, w1)	England (515)	v	India	The Oval	2002
50 (b37, lb8, nb4, w1)	Australia (327)	v	England	The Oval	1934
50 (b22, lb19, nb8, w1)	England (7d-903)	v	Australia	The Oval	1938
50 (b11, lb8, nb29, w2)	India (6d-566)	v	Sri Lanka	Madras[1]	1982-83
50 (b13, lb9, nb28)	India (8d-393)	v	Pakistan	Karachi[1]	1982-83
50 (b13, lb11, nb26)	England (464)	v	Australia	The Oval	1985
50 (b8, lb6, nb36)	England (7d-394)	v	West Indies	Bridgetown	1993-94
50 (b18, lb18, nb14)	England (564)	v	India	Nottingham	1996
50 (b4, lb14, nb32)	England (342)	v	Pakistan	Faisalabad	2000-01
50 (b14, lb13, nb18, w5)	India (8d-628)	v	England	Leeds	2002

ONE HUNDRED EXTRAS IN A MATCH

173 (b37, lb31, nb103, w2)	West Indies	v	Pakistan	Bridgetown	1976-77
149 (b25, lb34, nb90)	Australia	v	West Indies	Perth	1988-89
140 (b20, lb48, nb71, w1)	Australia	v	West Indies	Adelaide	1988-89
140 (b34, lb52, nb47, w7)	England	v	New Zealand	Lord's	2004
137 (b30, lb54, nb35, w18)	England	v	West Indies	Lord's	2004
136 (b28, lb29, nb75, w4)	West Indies	v	Australia	Georgetown	1990-91
135 (b52, lb35, nb35, w13)	West Indies	v	Australia	Port-of-Spain	2002-03
134 (b22, lb31, nb78, w3)	West Indies	v	Australia	Bridgetown	1998-99
129 (b18, lb35, nb54, w22)	South Africa	v	Pakistan	Johannesburg[3]	1994-95
127 (b22, lb38, nb62, w5)	West Indies	v	England	Bridgetown	1989-90
124 (b21, lb36, nb63, w4)	West Indies	v	England	St John's	1985-86
124 (b9, lb70, nb35, w10)	England	v	South Africa	Leeds	2003
122 (b19, lb33, nb58, w12)	England	v	West Indies	Leeds	1976
122 (b31, lb39, nb37, w15)	England	v	India	The Oval	1990
122 (b11, lb31, nb69, w11)	England	v	Sri Lanka	Lord's	2002
122 (b22, lb23, nb64, w13)	England	v	Australia	Manchester	2005
120 (b4, lb43, nb68, w5)	Sri Lanka	v	Australia	Colombo (SSC)	1992-93
119 (b25, lb27, nb66, w1)	West Indies	v	South Africa	Bridgetown	1991-92
118 (b19, lb49, nb48, w2)	West Indies	v	India	Port-of-Spain	1988-89
117 (b41, lb43, nb33)	India	v	West Indies	Bombay[3]	1994-95
117 (b40, lb36, nb41)	Pakistan	v	Sri Lanka	Sialkot	1995-96
117 (b33, lb38, nb45, w1)	West Indies	v	England	Port-of-Spain	1997-98
117 (b34, lb38, nb30, w15)	India	v	Pakistan	Mohali	2004-05
115 (b16, lb24, nb65, w10)	Australia	v	India	Sydney	2003-04
114 (b53, lb30, nb25, w6)	West Indies	v	Australia	Bridgetown	1964-65
114 (b25, lb62, nb26, w1)	England	v	Sri Lanka	Lord's	1991
114 (b7, lb30, nb67, w10)	Australia	v	West Indies	Perth	1996-97
113 (b26, lb32, nb54, w1)	Pakistan	v	West Indies	Lahore[2]	1990-91
113 (b5, lb36, nb71, w1)	New Zealand	v	Sri Lanka	Auckland	1990-91
113 (b11, lb27, nb75)	Pakistan	v	Sri Lanka	Karachi[1]	1999-2000
112 (b7, lb39, nb54, w12)	England	v	West Indies	The Oval	1980
112 (b11, lb32, nb39, w30)	Pakistan	v	India	Faisalabad	1989-90
112 (b9, lb22, nb81)	West Indies	v	England	Bridgetown	1993-94
112 (b36, lb29, nb33, w9, p5)	England	v	South Africa	Lord's	2003
112 (b28, lb31, nb28, w25)	England	v	West Indies	Manchester	2004
112 (b4, lb40, nb57, w6, p5)	South Africa	v	England	Port Elizabeth	2004-05
111 (b10, lb23, nb68, w10)	Australia	v	West Indies	Brisbane[2]	1988-89
111 (b13, lb24, nb75, w9)	Pakistan	v	Sri Lanka	Lahore[2]	2001-02
110 (b27, lb41, nb27, w15)	England	v	West Indies	Nottingham	1980
110 (b23, lb36, nb50, w1)	Pakistan	v	West Indies	Karachi[1]	1990-91
110 (b9, lb33, nb62, w6)	India	v	Pakistan	Calcutta	1998-99
110 (b46, lb38, nb26)	India	v	New Zealand	Mohali	1999-2000
110 (b7, lb36, nb57, w10)	West Indies	v	India	St John's	2005-06
109 (b16, lb33, nb59, w1)	New Zealand	v	India	Christchurch	1967-68
109 (b25, lb49, nb16, w19)	England	v	Pakistan	Lord's	1982
109 (b19, lb24, nb62, w4)	England	v	West Indies	The Oval	1991
109 (b29, lb33, nb37, w10)	India	v	Pakistan	Kolkata	2004-05
108 (b23, lb25, nb59, w1)	India	v	Australia	Delhi	1979-80
108 (b9, lb47, nb48, w4)	England	v	Australia	Nottingham	1989
108 (b17, lb33, nb46, w12)	South Africa	v	West Indies	Cape Town	2003-04
107 (b36, lb42, nb29)	Australia	v	England	Melbourne	1970-71
107 (b51, lb38, nb17, w1)	West Indies	v	Australia	Port-of-Spain	1972-73
107 (b10, lb18, nb79)	West Indies	v	England	Bridgetown	1973-74
107 (b22, lb35, nb39, w11)	England	v	Pakistan	Leeds	2006
106 (b26, lb39, nb38, w3)	Australia	v	England	Perth	1986-87

106 (b36, lb32, nb32, w6)	India	v	Sri Lanka	Mohali	1997-98
106 (b35, lb22, nb41, w8)	West Indies	v	Australia	Georgetown	2002-03
106 (b15, lb 29, nb47, w15)	Pakistan	v	India	Lahore[2]	2005-06
105 (b26, lb36, nb42, w1)	West Indies	v	England	Kingston	1973-74
105 (b27, lb39, nb36, w3)	Pakistan	v	India	Karachi[1]	1978-79
105 (b47, lb42, nb12, w4)	Pakistan	v	West Indies	Karachi[1]	1986-87
105 (b27, lb37, nb39, w2)	West Indies	v	Pakistan	Port-of-Spain	1987-88
105 (b16, lb34, nb52, w3)	South Africa	v	England	Johannesburg[3]	1995-96
105 (b28, lb31, nb32, w14)	South Africa	v	West Indies	Johannesburg[3]	2003-04
105 (b4, lb20, nb60, w21)	New Zealand	v	Pakistan	Hamilton	2003-04
105 (b29, lb27, nb29, w20)	India	v	Pakistan	Bangalore	2004-05
105 (b26, lb25, nb51, w3)	England	v	Australia	Birmingham	2005
104 (b28, lb32, nb35, w9)	England	v	West Indies	The Oval	1976
104 (b30, lb36, nb38)	West Indies	v	New Zealand	Port-of-Spain	1984-85
104 (b26, lb25, nb47, w6)	Pakistan	v	New Zealand	Lahore[2]	1990-91
104 (b25, lb41, nb28, w10)	England	v	India	Lord's	1996
104 (b40, lb28, nb34, w2)	India	v	Pakistan	Delhi	1998-99
104 (b26, lb37, nb40, w1)	England	v	India	The Oval	2002
103 (b20, lb43, nb32, w8)	West Indies	v	New Zealand	Georgetown	1984-85
103 (b22, lb33, nb42, w6)	India	v	West Indies	Mohali	1994-95
103 (b23, lb23, nb50, w7)	England	v	West Indies	Manchester	1995
103 (b29, lb26, nb41, w2, p5)	India	v	Australia	Calcutta	2000-01
102 (b24, lb29, nb48, w1)	West Indies	v	England	Georgetown	1997-98
102 (b14, lb47, nb34, w7)	Australia	v	England	Melbourne	2002-03
102 (b23, lb37, nb35, w7)	Australia	v	England	Sydney	2002-03
102 (b3, lb39, nb53, w7)	Pakistan	v	South Africa	Lahore[2]	2003-04
101 (b12, lb43, nb32, w14)	England	v	India	Birmingham	1979
101 (b18, lb39, nb44)	India	v	West Indies	Calcutta	1987-88
101 (b2, lb44, nb50, w5)	England	v	West Indies	Nottingham	1991
101 (b31, lb36, nb28, w1, p5)	India	v	South Africa	Kanpur	2004-05
101 (b21, lb36, nb25, w19)	South Africa	v	England	Cape Town	2004-05
100 (b65, lb22, nb12, w1)	West Indies	v	England	Kingston	1967-68
100 (b15, lb30, nb42, w13)	England	v	Australia	Leeds	1981
100 (b27, lb19, nb50, w4)	West Indies	v	Pakistan	Georgetown	1987-88
100 (b19, lb35, nb40, w6)	West Indies	v	Australia	Kingston	1990-91
100 (b25, lb47, nb16, w12)	England	v	Australia	Nottingham	1993
100 (b25, lb31, nb36, w8)	England	v	India	Nottingham	1996

UNUSUAL DISMISSALS – STUMPED BY A SUBSTITUTE

S.J.Snooke by N.C.Tufnell (sub for H.Strudwick)	South Africa	v	England	Durban[1]	1909-10
Pervez Sajjad by B.E.Congdon (sub for A.E.Dick)	Pakistan	v	New Zealand	Lahore[1]	1964-65

UNUSUAL DISMISSALS – RUN OUT BY THE BOWLER

(while backing up before the ball had been bowled)

W.A.Brown (18) by M.H.Mankad	Australia	v	India	Sydney	1947-48
I.R.Redpath (9) by C.C.Griffith	Australia	v	West Indies	Adelaide	1968-69
D.W Randall (13) by E.J.Chatfield	England	v	New Zealand	Christchurch	1977-78
Sikander Bakht (0) by A.G.Hurst	Pakistan	v	Australia	Perth	1978-79

UNUSUAL DISMISSALS – OBSTRUCTING THE FIELD

L.Hutton (27)	England	v	South Africa	The Oval	1951

Aravinda de Silva on his way to a score of 167 at the Gabba in Brisbane in 1989 – the highest innings score by a Sri Lankan against Australia.

Sachin Tendulkar blocks during the fourth Test between Australia and India in Mumbai in 2004.

The West Indies' Clive Lloyd made 121 against Australia in Adelaide during the 1979/80 series.

Australian batsman Michael Hussey pulls the ball for four runs against South Africa in Johannesburg, April 2006. This talented young player brought up his 1000th Test run just 166 days from debut, breaking the old record by a mammoth 61 days.

UNUSUAL DISMISSALS – HANDLED THE BALL

W.R.Endean (3)	South Africa	v	England	Cape Town	1956-57
A.M.J.Hilditch (29)	Australia	v	Pakistan	Perth	1978-79
Mohsin Khan (58)	Pakistan	v	Australia	Karachi[1]	1982-83
D.L.Haynes (55)	West Indies	v	India	Bombay[3]	1983-84
G.A.Gooch (133)	England	v	Australia	Manchester	1993
S.R.Waugh (47)	Australia	v	India	Chennai[1]	2000-01
M.P.Vaughan (64)	England	v	India	Bangalore	2001-02

UNUSUAL DISMISSALS – RETIRED OUT

M.S.Atapattu (201)	Sri Lanka	v	Bangladesh	Colombo (SSC)	2001-02
D.P.M.D.Jayawardene (150)	Sri Lanka	v	Bangladesh	Colombo (SSC)	2001-02

UNUSUAL DISMISSALS – BATSMAN STUMPED IN EACH INNINGS OF A TEST

A.N.Hornby	England	v	Australia	Manchester	1884
R.Peel	England	v	Australia	Sydney	1894-95
T.W.Hayward	England	v	South Africa	Leeds	1907
C.Newberry	South Africa	v	England	Johannesburg[1]	1913-14
R.H.M.Hands	South Africa	v	England	Port Elizabeth	1913-14
C.H.Parkin	England	v	Australia	Adelaide	1920-21
I.M.Barrow	West Indies	v	Australia	Brisbane[1]	1930-31
W.R.Hammond	England	v	South Africa	Durban[2]	1938-39
W.Place	England	v	West Indies	Kingston	1947-48
H.J.Tayfield	South Africa	v	Australia	Port Elizabeth	1949-50
F.M.M.Worrell	West Indies	v	England	Manchester	1950
M.J.Hilton	England	v	India	Madras[1]	1951-52
R.J.Christiani	West Indies	v	India	Bridgetown	1952-53
B.Sutcliffe	New Zealand	v	West Indies	Christchurch	1955-56
P.J.L.Dujon	West Indies	v	India	Madras[1]	1987-88
M.A.Butcher	England	v	Sri Lanka	Kandy	2003-04
U.D.A.Chandana	Sri Lanka	v	Australia	Cairns	2004-05
C.B.Mpofu	Zimbabwe	v	New Zealand	Harare	2005-06

UNUSUAL DISMISSALS – BATSMAN RUN OUT IN EACH INNINGS OF A TEST

P.A.McAlister	Australia	v	England	Melbourne	1907-08
C.Kelleway	Australia	v	South Africa	Melbourne	1910-11
J.Ryder	Australia	v	England	Sydney	1920-21
J.Trim	West Indies	v	Australia	Melbourne	1951-52
J.B.Stollmeyer	West Indies	v	England	Bridgetown	1953-54
I.Meckiff	Australia	v	West Indies	Brisbane[2]	1960-61
J.S.Solomon	West Indies	v	Australia	Melbourne	1960-61
S.N.McGregor	New Zealand	v	South Africa	Dunedin	1963-64
R.M.Edwards	West Indies	v	New Zealand	Wellington	1968-69
C.H.Lloyd	West Indies	v	India	Kingston	1970-71
J.A.Jameson	England	v	India	The Oval	1971
Zaheer Abbas	Pakistan	v	Australia	Melbourne	1972-73
A.R.Border	Australia	v	Pakistan	Melbourne	1981-82
M.A.Taylor	Australia	v	West Indies	Adelaide	1988-89
Wasim Akram	Pakistan	v	West Indies	Faisalabad	1990-91
M.A.Taylor	Australia	v	England	Adelaide	1990-91
I.A.Healy	Australia	v	West Indies	Georgetown	1990-91
A.H.Jones	New Zealand	v	Pakistan	Christchurch	1993-94

J.Angel	Australia	v	England	Perth	1994-95
A.C.Parore	New Zealand	v	Sri Lanka	Hamilton	1996-97
W.J.Cronje	South Africa	v	West Indies	Port Elizabeth	1998-99
I.A.Healy	Australia	v	West Indies	Kingston	1998-99
M.S.Atapattu	Sri Lanka	v	Zimbabwe	Harare	1999-2000
S.P.Fleming	New Zealand	v	Zimbabwe	Wellington	2000-01

UNUSUAL DISMISSALS – NON-STRIKER RUN OUT FROM DEFLECTION OFF BOWLER WHILE BACKING UP

Player	Bowler	Striker	Match Particulars		
B.F.Butcher	G.A.R.Lock	G.S.Sobers	West Indies v England	The Oval	1963
D.C.Boon	P.W.Jarvis	D.M.Jones	Australia v England	Birmingham	1989
D.L.Haynes	M.G.Hughes	C.G.Greenidge	West Indies v Australia	St John's	1990-91
S.R.Waugh	D.L.Vettori	A.C.Gilchrist	Australia v New Zealand	Perth	2001-02
A.Flintoff	W.P.U.J.C.Vaas	A.J.Stewart	England v Sri Lanka	Manchester	2002
J.L.Langer	Danish Kaneria	M.L.Hayden	Australia v Pakistan	Sharjah	2002-03
H.H.Streak	S.J.Harmison	T.J.Friend	Zimbabwe v England	Chester-le-Street	2003
J.H.Kallis	A.F.Giles	S.M.Pollock	South Africa v England	The Oval	2003
Rajin Saleh	Yasir Ali	Khaled Mashud	Pakistan v Bangladesh	Multan[2]	2003-04
Harbhajan Singh	I.G.Butler	V.V.S.Laxman	India v New Zealand	Mohali	2003-04
W.P.U.J.C.Vaas	A.F.Giles	U.D.U.Chandana	Sri Lanka v England	Colombo (SSC)	2003-04
N.J.Astle	S.T.Jayasuriya	L.Vincent	New Zealand v Sri Lanka	Napier	2004-05
J.M.How	I.D.R.Bradshaw	H.J.H.Marshall	New Zealand v West Indies	Auckland	2005-06

Batting

SIX THOUSAND RUNS IN TESTS

Player (Country)	M	I	runs	A	E	SA	W	N	I	P	SL	Z	B
				Opponent									
B.C.Lara (W)	127	225	**11464**	2815	2983	1715	-	704	1002	725	1125	222	173
A.R.Border (A)	156	265	**11174**	-	3548	298	2052	1500	1567	1666	543	-	-
S.R.Waugh (A)	168	260	**10927**	-	3200	1147	2192	1117	1090	934	701	290	256
S.R.Tendulkar (I)	132	211	**10469**	1849	1766	1003	1328	1062	-	916	1313	918	302
S.M.Gavaskar (I)	125	214	**10122**	1550	2483	-	2749	651	-	2089	600	-	-
R.S.Dravid (I)	103	174	**9026**	1480	1220	829	1408	1004	-	1045	832	979	229
G.A.Gooch (E)	118	215	**8900**	2632	-	139	2197	1148	1725	683	376	-	-
Javed Miandad (P)	124	189	**8832**	1797	1329	-	834	1919	2228	-	582	143	-
R.T.Ponting (A)	104	173	**8692**	-	1402	1535	1372	808	1253	1061	711	290	260
I.V.A.Richards (W)	121	182	**8540**	2266	2869	-	-	387	1927	1091	-	-	-
Inzamamul Haq (P)	112	185	**8497**	784	1584	495	1007	1059	833	-	1559	772	404
A.J.Stewart (E)	133	235	**8463**	1810	-	1433	1476	1145	569	994	536	483	-
D.I.Gower (E)	117	204	**8231**	3269	-	-	1149	1051	1391	1185	186	-	-
G.S.Sobers (W)	93	160	**8032**	1510	3214	-	-	404	1920	984	-	-	-
M.E.Waugh (A)	128	209	**8029**	-	2204	1135	1858	766	698	933	345	90	-
J.H.Kallis (SA)	101	170	**7950**	1105	1412	-	1856	1010	579	456	639	679	214
M.A.Atherton (E)	115	212	**7728**	1900	-	1315	1587	1088	689	746	144	259	-
M.C.Cowdrey (E)	114	188	**7624**	2433	-	1021	1751	1133	653	633	-	-	-
C.G.Greenidge (W)	108	185	**7558**	1819	2318	-	-	882	1678	861	-	-	-
M.A.Taylor (A)	104	186	**7525**	-	2496	746	984	666	675	1347	611	-	-
C.H.Lloyd (W)	110	175	**7515**	2211	2120	-	-	234	2344	606	-	-	-
D.L.Haynes (W)	116	202	**7487**	2233	2392	81	-	843	990	928	20	-	-
D.C.Boon (A)	107	190	**7422**	-	2237	433	1437	1187	1204	431	493	-	-
J.L.Langer (A)	99	171	**7371**	-	1355	768	1093	1249	1047	1139	502	80	72
G.Kirsten (SA)	101	176	**7289**	1134	1608	-	759	951	720	838	639	330	310
W.R.Hammond (E)	85	140	**7249**	2852	-	2188	639	1015	555	-	-	-	-
M.L.Hayden (A)	83	148	**7138**	-	1048	1369	1237	626	1244	374	571	501	168
G.S.Chappell (A)	87	151	**7110**	-	2619	-	1400	1076	368	1581	66	-	-
D.G.Bradman (A)	52	80	**6996**	-	5028	806	447	-	715	-	-	-	-
L.Hutton (E)	79	138	**6971**	2428	-	1564	1661	777	522	19	-	-	-
D.B.Vengsarkar (I)	116	185	**6868**	1304	1589	-	1596	440	-	1284	655	-	-
K.F.Barrington (E)	82	131	**6806**	2111	-	989	1042	594	1355	715	-	-	-
S.T.Jayasuriya (SL)	105	178	**6745**	592	731	857	562	414	938	1490	0	730	378
G.P.Thorpe (E)	100	179	**6744**	1235	-	897	1740	905	283	671	699	70	244
S.P.Fleming (N)	102	173	**6545**	680	932	918	703	-	620	665	1091	640	296
S.Chanderpaul (W)	97	166	**6508**	768	1305	1072	-	527	1558	718	154	259	147
P.A.de Silva (SL)	93	159	**6361**	803	739	461	228	785	1252	1475	-	412	206
D.P.M.D.Jayawardene (SL)	82	136	**6250**	414	1107	1472	422	560	882	656	-	420	317
R.B.Kanhai (W)	79	137	**6227**	1694	2267	-	-	-	1693	573	-	-	-
M.Azharuddin (I)	99	147	**6215**	780	1278	779	539	796	-	769	1215	59	-
R.N.Harvey (A)	79	137	**6149**	-	2416	1625	1054	-	775	279	-	-	-
G.R.Viswanath (I)	91	155	**6080**	1538	1880	-	1455	585	-	611	11	-	-

TWO THOUSAND RUNS IN TESTS

AUSTRALIA	Tests	I	NO	Runs	HS	Avge	100s	50s
A.R.Border	156	265	44	11174	205	50.56	27	63
S.R.Waugh	168	260	46	10927	200	51.06	32	50
R.T.Ponting	104	173	24	8692	257	58.33	31	33
M.E.Waugh	128	209	17	8029	153*	41.81	20	47
M.A.Taylor	104	186	13	7525	334*	43.49	19	40

D.C.Boon	107	190	20	7422	200	43.65	21	32
J.L.Langer	99	171	10	7371	250	45.78	22	29
M.L.Hayden	83	148	12	7138	380	52.48	25	25
G.S.Chappell	87	151	19	7110	247*	53.86	24	31
D.G.Bradman	52	80	10	6996	334	99.94	29	13
R.N.Harvey	79	137	10	6149	205	48.41	21	24
K.D.Walters	74	125	14	5357	250	48.26	15	33
I.M.Chappell	75	136	10	5345	196	42.42	14	26
M.J.Slater	74	131	7	5312	219	42.83	14	21
W.M.Lawry	67	123	12	5234	210	47.15	13	27
A.C.Gilchrist	84	119	18	5029	204*	49.79	16	21
R.B.Simpson	62	111	7	4869	311	46.81	10	27
I.R.Redpath	66	120	11	4737	171	43.45	8	31
K.J.Hughes	70	124	6	4415	213	37.41	9	22
D.R.Martyn	65	106	14	4361	165	47.40	13	23
I.A.Healy	119	182	23	4356	161*	27.39	4	22
R.W.Marsh	96	150	13	3633	132	26.51	3	16
D.M.Jones	52	89	11	3631	216	46.55	11	14
A.R.Morris	46	79	3	3533	206	46.48	12	12
C.Hill	49	89	2	3412	191	39.21	7	19
G.M.Wood	59	112	6	3374	172	31.83	9	12
V.T.Trumper	48	89	8	3163	214*	39.04	8	13
C.C.McDonald	47	83	4	3107	170	39.32	5	17
A.L.Hassett	43	69	3	3073	198*	46.56	10	11
K.R.Miller	55	87	7	2958	147	36.97	7	13
S.K.Warne	139	192	16	2946	99	16.73	0	11
W.W.Armstrong	50	84	10	2863	159*	38.68	6	8
G.R.Marsh	50	93	7	2854	138	33.18	4	15
K.R.Stackpole	43	80	5	2807	207	37.42	7	14
N.C.O'Neill	42	69	8	2779	181	45.55	6	15
G.N.Yallop	39	70	3	2756	268	41.13	8	9
S.J.McCabe	39	62	5	2748	232	48.21	6	13
G.S.Blewett	46	79	4	2552	214	34.02	4	15
W.Bardsley	41	66	5	2469	193*	40.47	6	14
W.M.Woodfull	35	54	4	2300	161	46.00	7	13
P.J.P.Burge	42	68	8	2290	181	38.16	4	12
E.S.Gregory	58	100	7	2282	201	24.53	4	8
R.Benaud	63	97	7	2201	122	24.45	3	9
C.G.Macartney	35	55	4	2131	170	41.78	7	9
W.H.Ponsford	29	48	4	2122	266	48.22	7	6
R.M.Cowper	27	46	2	2061	307	46.84	5	10

ENGLAND	Tests	I	NO	Runs	HS	Avge	100s	50s
G.A.Gooch	118	215	6	8900	333	42.58	20	46
A.J.Stewart	133	235	21	8463	190	39.54	15	45
D.I.Gower	117	204	18	8231	215	44.25	18	39
G.Boycott	108	193	23	8114	246*	47.72	22	42
M.A.Atherton	115	212	7	7728	185*	37.69	16	46
M.C.Cowdrey	114	188	15	7624	182	44.06	22	38
W.R.Hammond	85	140	16	7249	336*	58.45	22	24
L.Hutton	79	138	15	6971	364	56.67	19	33
K.F.Barrington	82	131	15	6806	256	58.67	20	35
G.P.Thorpe	100	179	28	6744	200*	44.66	16	39
M.E.Trescothick	76	143	10	5825	219	43.79	14	29
D.C.S.Compton	78	131	15	5807	278	50.06	17	28
N.Hussain	95	171	16	5764	207	37.18	14	33

J.B.Hobbs	61	102	7	5410	211	56.94	15	28
I.T.Botham	102	161	6	5200	208	33.54	14	22
J.H.Edrich	77	127	9	5138	310*	43.54	12	24
T.W.Graveney	79	123	13	4882	258	44.38	11	20
A.J.Lamb	79	139	10	4656	142	36.09	14	18
M.P.Vaughan	64	115	9	4587	197	43.27	15	14
H.Sutcliffe	54	84	9	4555	194	60.73	16	23
P.B.H.May	66	106	9	4537	285*	46.77	13	22
E.R.Dexter	62	102	8	4502	205	47.89	9	27
M.W.Gatting	79	138	14	4409	207	35.55	10	21
A.P.E.Knott	95	149	15	4389	135	32.75	5	30
M.A.Butcher	71	131	7	4288	173*	34.58	8	23
R.A.Smith	62	112	15	4236	175	43.67	9	28
A.W.Greig	58	93	4	3599	148	40.43	8	20
E.H.Hendren	51	83	9	3525	205*	47.63	7	21
G.A.Hick	65	114	6	3383	178	31.32	6	18
F.E.Woolley	64	98	7	3283	154	36.07	5	23
K.W.R.Fletcher	59	96	14	3272	216	39.90	7	19
A.Flintoff	61	98	11	3077	167	35.36	5	22
M.Leyland	41	65	5	2764	187	46.06	9	10
A.J.Strauss	31	58	2	2597	147	46.37	10	7
C.Washbrook	37	66	6	2569	195	42.81	6	12
B.L.D'Oliveira	44	70	8	2484	158	40.06	5	15
D.W.Randall	47	79	5	2470	174	33.37	7	12
W.J.Edrich	39	63	2	2440	219	40.00	6	13
T.G.Evans	91	133	14	2439	104	20.49	2	8
L.E.G.Ames	47	72	12	2434	149	40.56	8	7
M.R.Ramprakash	52	92	6	2350	154	27.32	2	12
W.Rhodes	58	98	21	2325	179	30.19	2	11
T.E.Bailey	61	91	14	2290	134*	29.74	1	10
M.J.K.Smith	50	78	6	2278	121	31.63	3	11
P.E.Richardson	34	56	1	2061	126	37.47	5	9

SOUTH AFRICA	Tests	I	NO	Runs	HS	Avge	100s	50s
J.H.Kallis	101	170	27	7950	189*	55.59	24	40
G.Kirsten	101	176	15	7289	275	45.27	21	34
H.H.Gibbs	79	135	6	5728	228	44.40	14	22
D.J.Cullinan	70	114	11	4555	275*	44.22	14	20
G.C.Smith	47	82	5	3879	277	50.37	11	14
W.J.Cronje	68	111	9	3714	135	36.41	6	23
M.V.Boucher	95	134	17	3565	125	30.47	4	23
S.M.Pollock	102	147	37	3515	111	31.95	2	15
B.Mitchell	42	80	9	3471	189*	48.88	8	21
A.D.Nourse	34	62	7	2960	231	53.81	9	14
H.W.Taylor	42	76	4	2936	176	40.77	7	17
J.N.Rhodes	52	80	9	2532	117	35.66	3	17
E.J.Barlow	30	57	2	2516	201	45.74	6	15
T.L.Goddard	41	78	5	2516	112	34.46	1	18
D.J.McGlew	34	64	6	2440	255*	42.06	7	10
J.H.B.Waite	50	86	7	2405	134	30.44	4	16
R.G.Pollock	23	41	4	2256	274	60.97	7	11
A.W.Nourse	45	83	8	2234	111	29.78	1	15
R.A.McLean	40	73	3	2120	142	30.28	5	10
N.D.McKenzie	41	65	4	2028	120	33.24	2	13
J.A.Rudolph	35	63	7	2028	222*	36.21	5	8
A.C.Hudson	35	63	3	2007	163	33.45	4	13

WEST INDIES	Tests	I	NO	Runs	HS	Avge	100s	50s
B.C.Lara	127	225	6	11464	400*	52.34	32	47
I.V.A.Richards	121	182	12	8540	291	50.23	24	45
G.S.Sobers	93	160	21	8032	365*	57.78	26	30
C.G.Greenidge	108	185	16	7558	226	44.72	19	34
C.H.Lloyd	110	175	14	7515	242*	46.67	19	39
D.L.Haynes	116	202	25	7487	184	42.29	18	39
S.Chanderpaul	98	168	22	6531	203*	44.73	14	38
R.B.Kanhai	79	137	6	6227	256	47.53	15	28
R.B.Richardson	86	146	12	5949	194	44.39	16	27
C.L.Hooper	102	173	15	5762	233	36.46	13	27
E.D.Weekes	48	81	5	4455	207	58.61	15	19
A.I.Kallicharran	66	109	10	4399	187	44.43	12	21
R.C.Fredericks	59	109	7	4334	169	42.49	8	26
R.R.Sarwan	63	114	7	4207	261*	39.31	9	26
C.H.Gayle	61	108	3	4089	317	38.94	7	25
F.M.M.Worrell	51	87	9	3860	261	49.48	9	22
C.L.Walcott	44	74	7	3798	220	56.68	15	14
P.J.L.Dujon	81	115	11	3322	139	31.94	5	16
C.C.Hunte	44	78	6	3245	260	45.06	8	13
H.A.Gomes	60	91	11	3171	143	39.63	9	13
B.F.Butcher	44	78	6	3104	209*	43.11	7	16
J.C.Adams	54	90	17	3012	208*	41.26	6	14
S.L.Campbell	52	93	4	2882	208	32.38	4	18
W.W.Hinds	45	80	2	2608	213	33.43	5	14
R.D.Jacobs	65	112	20	2577	118	28.01	3	14
S.M.Nurse	29	54	1	2523	258	47.60	6	10
A.L.Logie	52	78	9	2470	130	35.79	2	16
G.A.Headley	22	40	4	2190	270*	60.83	10	5
J.B.Stollmeyer	32	56	5	2159	160	42.33	4	12
L.G.Rowe	30	49	2	2047	302	43.55	7	7

NEW ZEALAND	Tests	I	NO	Runs	HS	Avge	100s	50s
S.P.Fleming	102	173	10	6545	274*	40.15	9	41
M.D.Crowe	77	131	11	5444	299	45.36	17	18
J.G.Wright	82	148	7	5334	185	37.82	12	23
N.J.Astle	79	133	10	4650	222	37.80	11	24
B.E.Congdon	61	114	7	3448	176	32.22	7	19
J..R.Reid	58	108	5	3428	142	33.28	6	22
C.L.Cairns	62	104	5	3320	158	33.53	5	22
R.J.Hadlee	86	134	19	3124	151*	27.16	2	15
C.D.McMillan	55	91	10	3116	142	38.46	6	19
G.M.Turner	41	73	6	2991	259	44.64	7	14
A.H.Jones	39	74	8	2922	186	44.27	7	11
A.C.Parore	78	128	19	2865	110	26.28	2	14
M.H.Richardson	38	65	3	2776	145	44.77	4	19
B.Sutcliffe	42	76	8	2727	230*	40.10	5	15
M.G.Burgess	50	92	6	2684	119*	31.20	5	14
J.V.Coney	52	85	14	2668	174*	37.57	3	16
G.P.Howarth	47	83	5	2531	147	32.44	6	11
K.R.Rutherford	56	99	8	2463	107*	27.06	3	15
G.T.Dowling	39	77	3	2306	239	31.16	3	11
D.L.Vettori	70	100	15	2128	137*	25.03	2	11
B.A.Young	35	68	4	2051	267*	32.04	2	12
M.J.Greatbatch	41	71	5	2021	146*	30.62	3	10

INDIA	Tests	I	NO	Runs	HS	Avge	100s	50s
S.R.Tendulkar	132	211	22	10469	248*	55.39	35	41
S.M.Gavaskar	125	214	16	10122	236*	51.12	34	45
R.S.Dravid	103	174	22	9026	270	59.38	23	46
D.B.Vengsarkar	116	185	22	6868	166	42.13	17	35
M.Azharuddin	99	147	9	6215	199	45.03	22	21
G.R.Viswanath	91	155	10	6080	222	41.93	14	35
Kapil Dev	131	184	15	5248	163	31.05	8	27
S.C.Ganguly	88	140	12	5215	173	40.74	12	25
V.V.S.Laxman	77	124	14	4704	281	42.76	10	25
M.Amarnath	69	113	10	4378	138	42.50	11	24
V.K.Sehwag	48	79	3	4013	309	52.80	12	12
R.J.Shastri	80	121	14	3830	206	35.79	11	12
P.R.Umrigar	59	94	8	3631	223	42.22	12	14
V.L.Manjrekar	55	92	10	3208	189*	39.12	7	15
N.S.Sidhu	51	78	2	3202	201	42.13	9	15
C.G.Borde	55	97	11	3061	177*	35.59	5	18
Nawab of Pataudi, jr	46	83	3	2793	203*	34.91	6	16
S.M.H.Kirmani	88	124	22	2759	102	27.04	2	12
F.M.Engineer	46	87	3	2611	121	31.08	2	16
Pankaj Roy	43	79	4	2442	173	32.56	5	9
V.S.Hazare	30	52	6	2192	164*	47.65	7	9
A.L.Wadekar	37	71	3	2113	143	31.07	1	14
M.H.Mankad	44	72	5	2109	231	31.47	5	6
C.P.S.Chauhan	40	68	2	2084	97	31.57	-	16
K.Srikkanth	43	72	3	2062	123	29.88	2	12
M.L.Jaisimha	39	71	4	2056	129	30.68	3	12
S.V.Manjrekar	37	61	6	2043	218	37.14	4	9
A.Kumble	110	140	27	2025	88	17.92	0	4
D.N.Sardesai	30	55	4	2001	212	39.23	5	9

PAKISTAN	Tests	I	NO	Runs	HS	Avge	100s	50s
Javed Miandad	124	189	21	8832	280*	52.57	23	43
Inzamamul Haq	112	185	20	8497	329	51.49	25	44
Saleem Malik	103	154	22	5768	237	43.69	15	29
Yousuf Youhana	70	117	9	5737	223	53.12	19	25
Zaheer Abbas	78	124	11	5062	274	44.79	12	20
Mudassar Nazar	76	116	8	4114	231	38.09	10	17
Saeed Anwar	55	91	2	4052	188*	45.52	11	25
Majid Khan	63	106	5	3930	167	38.91	8	19
Hanif Mohammad	55	97	8	3915	337	43.98	12	15
Younis Khan	47	83	4	3884	267	49.16	12	15
Imran Khan	88	126	25	3807	136	37.69	6	18
Mushtaq Mohammad	57	100	7	3643	201	39.17	10	19
Asif Iqbal	58	99	7	3575	175	38.85	11	12
Ijaz Ahmed	60	92	4	3315	211	37.67	12	12
Saeed Ahmed	41	78	4	2991	172	40.41	5	16
Wasim Akram	102	147	19	2899	257*	22.64	3	7
Aamer Sohail	47	83	3	2866	205	35.82	5	14
Rameez Raja	57	94	5	2833	122	31.83	2	22
Wasim Raja	57	92	14	2821	125	36.16	4	18
Moin Khan	69	104	8	2741	137	28.55	4	15
Mohsin Khan	48	79	6	2709	200	37.10	7	9
Shoaib Mohammad	45	68	7	2705	203*	44.34	7	13
Sadiq Mohammad	41	74	2	2579	166	35.81	5	10
Imtiaz Ahmed	41	72	1	2079	209	29.28	3	11

SRI LANKA	Tests	I	NO	Runs	HS	Avge	100s	50s
S.T.Jayasuriya	105	178	14	6745	340	41.12	14	30
P.A.de Silva	93	159	11	6361	267	42.98	20	22
D.P.M.Jayawardene	83	136	10	6253	374	49.62	16	29
M.S.Atapattu	88	152	15	5330	249	38.90	16	15
A.Ranatunga	93	155	12	5105	135	35.69	4	38
K.C.Sangakkara	62	103	5	4796	287	48.93	10	22
H.P.Tillakaratne	83	131	25	4545	204*	42.87	11	20
R.S.Mahanama	52	89	1	2576	225	29.27	4	11
W.P.U.J.C.Vaas	94	136	26	2503	74*	22.75	0	11
A.P.Gurusinha	41	70	7	2452	143	38.92	7	8
T.T.Samaraweera	39	58	8	2089	142	41.78	5	13
T.M.Dilshan	39	63	7	2056	168	36.71	4	9

1000 runs for Zimbabwe:

ZIMBABWE	Tests	I	NO	Runs	HS	Avge	100s	50s
A.Flower	63	112	19	4794	232*	51.54	12	27
G.W.Flower	67	123	6	3457	201*	29.54	6	15
A.D.R.Campbell	60	109	4	2858	103	27.21	2	18
G.J.Whittall	46	82	7	2207	203*	29.42	4	10
H.H.Streak	65	107	18	1990	127*	22.36	1	11
S.V.Carlisle	37	66	6	1615	118	26.91	2	8
D.L.Houghton	22	36	2	1466	266	43.11	4	4
M.W.Goodwin	19	37	4	1414	166*	42.84	3	8
T.Taibu	24	46	3	1273	153	29.60	1	9
D.D.Ebrahim	29	55	1	1225	94	22.68	0	10
C.B.Wishart	27	50	1	1098	114	22.40	1	5
G.J.Rennie	23	46	1	1023	93	22.73	0	7

500 runs for Bangladesh:

BANGLADESH	Tests	I	NO	Runs	HS	Avge	100s	50s
Habibul Bashar	42	83	1	2838	113	34.61	3	24
Javed Omar	35	70	1	1525	119	22.10	1	6
Mohammad Ashraful	33	65	3	1511	158*	29.05	3	6
Khaled Mashud	41	79	9	1361	103*	19.44	1	3
Mohammad Rafique	26	47	5	982	111	23.38	1	4
Rajin Saleh	17	33	1	930	89	29.06	0	6
Al Sahariar	15	30	0	683	70	22.76	0	4
Hannan Sarkar	17	33	0	662	76	20.06	0	5
Alok Kapali	17	34	1	584	85	17.69	0	2
Aminul Islam	13	26	1	530	145	21.20	1	2
Nafees Iqbal	11	22	0	518	121	23.54	1	2

FIVE HUNDRED RUNS IN A TEST SERIES *(§ first Test series. # last Test series. † only Test Series)*

AUSTRALIA	Opp	Season	Tests	I	NO	Runs	HS	Avge	100s	50s
D.G.Bradman	ENG	1930	5	7	0	974	334	139.14	4	0
M.A.Taylor	ENG	1989	6	11	1	839	219	83.90	2	5
R.N.Harvey	SA	1952-53	5	9	0	834	205	92.66	4	3
D.G.Bradman	ENG	1936-37	5	9	0	810	270	90.00	3	1
D.G.Bradman	SA	1931-32	5	5	1	806	299*	201.50	4	0
D.G.Bradman	ENG	1934	5	8	0	758	304	94.75	2	1
D.G.Bradman	IND	1947-48	5	6	2	715	201	178.75	4	1
R.T.Ponting	IND	2003-04	4	8	1	706	257	100.85	2	2
G.S.Chappell	WI	1975-76	6	11	5	702	182*	117.00	3	3
K.D.Walters	WI	1968-69	4	6	0	699	242	116.50	4	2
A.R.Morris	ENG	1948	5	9	1	696	196	87.00	3	3

D.G.Bradman	ENG	1946-47	5	8	1	680	234	97.14	2	3
W.M.Lawry	WI	1968-69	5	8	0	667	205	83.38	3	2
V.T.Trumper	SA	1910-11	5	9	2	661	214*	94.42	2	2
R.N.Harvey	SA	1949-50	5	8	3	660	178	132.00	4	1
R.N.Harvey	WI	1954-55	5	7	1	650	204	108.33	3	1
K.R.Stackpole	ENG	1970-71	6	12	0	627	207	52.25	2	2
M.J.Slater	ENG	1994-95	5	10	0	623	176	62.30	3	1
G.S.Chappell	ENG	1974-75	6	11	0	608	144	55.27	2	5
A.R.Border	ENG	1985	6	11	2	597	196	66.33	2	1
K.J.Hughes	IND	1979-80	6	12	2	594	100	59.40	1	5
W.M.Lawry	ENG	1965-66	5	7	0	592	166	84.57	3	2
I.R.Redpath	WI	1975-76	6	11	0	575	103	52.27	3	2
V.T.Trumper	ENG	1903-04	5	10	1	574	185*	63.77	2	3
W.Bardsley	SA	1910-11	5	9	0	573	132	63.66	1	5
W.H.Ponsford #	ENG	1934	4	7	1	569	266	94.83	2	1
D.M.Jones	ENG	1989	6	9	1	566	157	70.75	2	3
H.L.Collins §	ENG	1920-21	5	9	0	557	162	61.88	2	3
D.C.Boon	IND	1991-92	5	9	2	556	135	79.42	3	1
M.T.G.Elliott	ENG	1997	6	10	0	556	199	55.60	2	2
D.C.Boon	ENG	1993	6	10	2	555	164*	69.37	3	1
G.N.Yallop	PAK	1983-84	5	6	0	554	268	92.33	2	1
M.E.Waugh	ENG	1993	6	10	1	550	137	61.11	1	5
M.L.Hayden	IND	2000-01	3	6	1	549	203	109.80	2	2
I.M.Chappell	WI	1968-69	5	8	0	548	165	68.50	2	3
I.M.Chappell	WI	1972-73	5	9	2	542	109	77.42	2	3
J.M.Taylor	ENG	1924-25	5	10	0	541	108	54.10	1	4
R.B.Simpson	IND	1977-78	5	10	0	539	176	53.90	2	2
J.Darling	ENG	1897-98	5	8	0	537	178	67.12	3	0
A.R.Border	ENG	1981	6	12	3	533	123*	59.22	2	3
B.C.Booth	SA	1963-64	4	7	1	531	169	88.50	2	3
D.C.Boon	ENG	1990-91	5	9	2	530	121	75.71	1	3
R.T.Ponting	WI	2002-03	3	5	1	523	206	130.75	3	0
N.C.O'Neill	WI	1960-61	5	10	0	522	181	52.20	1	3
C.Hill	ENG	1901-02	5	10	0	521	99	52.10	0	4
A.R.Border	IND	1979-80	6	12	0	521	162	49.63	1	3
A.R.Border	WI	1983-84	5	10	3	521	100*	74.42	1	4
C.C.McDonald	ENG	1958-59	5	9	1	519	170	64.87	2	1
R.T.Ponting	SAF	2005-06	3	6	1	515	143*	103.00	3	2
M.A.Taylor	PAK	1998-99	3	5	1	513	334*	128.25	1	2
W.A.Brown	ENG	1938	4	8	1	512	206*	73.14	2	1
D.M.Jones	ENG	1986-87	5	10	1	511	184*	56.77	1	3
D.G.Bradman #	ENG	1948	5	9	2	508	173*	72.57	2	1
S.R.Waugh	ENG	1989	6	8	4	506	177*	126.50	2	1
K.C.Wessels	WI	1984-85	5	9	0	505	173	56.11	1	4
A.R.Morris §	ENG	1946-47	5	8	1	503	155	71.85	3	1
M.L.Hayden	ZIM	2003-04	2	3	1	501	380	250.50	2	0

ENGLAND	Opp	Season	Tests	I	NO	Runs	HS	Avge	100s	50s
W.R.Hammond	AUS	1928-29	5	9	1	905	251	113.12	4	0
D.C.S.Compton	SA	1947	5	8	0	753	208	94.12	4	2
G.A.Gooch	IND	1990	3	6	0	752	333	125.33	3	2
H.Sutcliffe	AUS	1924-25	5	9	0	734	176	81.56	4	2
D.I.Gower	AUS	1985	6	9	0	732	215	81.33	3	1
E.H.Hendren	WI	1929-30	4	8	2	693	205*	115.50	2	5
L.Hutton	WI	1953-54	5	8	1	677	205	96.71	2	3
G.A.Gooch	AUS	1993	6	12	0	673	133	56.08	2	4

D.L.Amiss	WI	1973-74	5	9	1	663	262*	82.87	3	0
J.B.Hobbs	AUS	1911-12	5	9	1	662	187	82.75	3	1
G.Boycott	AUS	1970-71	5	10	3	657	142*	93.85	2	5
A.J.Strauss	SA	2004-05	5	10	1	656	147	72.88	3	1
E.Paynter #	SA	1938-39	5	8	0	653	243	81.62	3	2
J.H.Edrich	AUS	1970-71	6	11	2	648	130	72.00	2	4
M.P.Vaughan	AUS	2002-03	5	10	0	633	183	63.30	3	0
M.P.Vaughan	IND	2002	4	7	1	615	197	102.50	3	1
W.R.Hammond	SA	1938-39	5	8	1	609	181	87.00	3	2
K.F.Barrington	IND	1961-62	5	9	3	594	172	99.00	3	1
A.Sandham #	WI	1929-30	4	8	0	592	325	74.00	2	2
K.F.Barrington	AUS	1962-63	5	10	2	582	132	72.75	2	3
P.B.H.May	SA	1955	5	9	1	582	117	72.75	2	3
L.Hutton	SA	1948-49	5	9	0	577	158	64.11	2	2
M.W.Gatting	IND	1984-85	5	9	3	575	207	95.83	2	1
J.B.Hobbs	AUS	1924-25	5	9	0	573	154	63.66	3	2
W.R.Hammond	NZ	1932-33	2	2	1	563	336*	64.49	2	0
D.C.S.Compton	AUS	1948	5	10	1	562	184	62.44	2	2
J.H.Edrich	AUS	1968	5	9	0	554	164	61.55	1	4
R.A.Smith	AUS	1989	5	10	1	553	143	61.44	2	3
M.A.Atherton	AUS	1993	6	12	0	553	99	46.08	0	6
W.J.Edrich	SA	1947	4	6	1	552	191	110.40	2	2
C.Washbrook	SA	1948-49	5	9	0	542	195	60.22	1	2
J.B.Hobbs	SA	1909-10	5	9	1	539	187	67.37	1	4
M.C.Cowdrey	WI	1967-68	5	8	0	534	148	66.75	2	4
L.Hutton	AUS	1950-51	5	10	4	533	156*	88.83	1	4
K.F.Barrington	AUS	1964	5	8	1	531	256	75.85	1	2
M.W.Gatting	AUS	1985	6	9	3	527	160	87.83	2	3
E.R.Dexter	WI	1959-60	5	9	1	526	136*	65.75	2	2
G.E.Tyldesley	SA	1927-28	5	9	1	520	122	65.00	2	3
W.R.Hammond	SA	1930-31	5	9	1	517	136*	64.62	1	4
H.Sutcliffe	SA	1929	5	9	1	513	114	64.12	4	0
M.A.Atherton	WI	1993-94	5	9	0	510	144	56.66	2	2
K.F.Barrington	SA	1964-65	5	7	2	508	148*	101.60	2	2
G.P.Thorpe	WI	1995	6	12	0	506	94	42.16	0	5
J.B.Hobbs	AUS	1920-21	5	10	0	505	123	50.50	2	1

SOUTH AFRICA	Opp	Season	Tests	I	NO	Runs	HS	Avge	100s	50s
G.A.Faulkner	AUS	1910-11	5	10	0	732	204	73.20	2	5
G.C.Smith	ENG	2003	5	9	0	714	277	79.33	2	1
J.H.Kallis	WI	2003-04	4	6	2	712	177	178.00	4	1
J.H.Kallis	ENG	2004-05	5	10	1	625	162	69.44	3	2
A.D.Nourse	ENG	1947	5	9	0	621	149	69.00	2	5
D.T.Lindsay	AUS	1966-67	5	7	0	606	182	86.57	3	1
E.J.Barlow	AUS	1963-64	5	10	2	603	201	75.37	3	1
B.Mitchell	ENG	1947	5	10	1	597	189*	66.33	2	3
H.H.Gibbs	WI	2003-04	4	7	2	583	192	116.60	3	1
H.W.Taylor	ENG	1922-23	5	9	0	582	176	64.66	3	2
K.C.Bland	ENG	1964-65	5	10	2	572	144*	71.50	1	4
A.Melville	ENG	1947	5	10	1	569	189	63.22	3	1
E.J.Barlow	ENG	1964-65	5	10	0	558	138	55.80	1	4
G.A.Faulkner	ENG	1909-10	5	10	1	545	123	60.55	1	3
R.G.Pollock	AUS	1966-67	5	9	2	537	209	76.71	2	2
A.D.Nourse	ENG	1948-49	5	10	3	536	129*	76.57	2	2
A.D.Nourse	AUS	1935-36	5	10	1	518	231	57.55	1	2
R.G.Pollock #	AUS	1969-70	4	7	0	517	274	73.85	1	3

	Opp	Season	Tests	I	NO	Runs	HS	Avge	100s	50s
E.A.B.Rowan #	ENG	1951	5	10	1	515	236	57.22	1	3
H.W.Taylor	ENG	1913-14	5	10	0	508	109	35.10	1	3
B.A.Richards †	AUS	1969-70	4	7	0	508	140	72.57	2	2
G.C.Smith	WI	2004-05	4	7	1	505	148	84.16	3	1

WEST INDIES	Opp	Season	Tests	I	NO	Runs	HS	Avge	100s	50s
I.V.A.Richards	ENG	1976	4	7	0	829	291	118.42	3	2
C.L.Walcott	AUS	1954-55	5	10	0	827	155	82.70	5	2
G.S.Sobers	PAK	1957-58	5	8	2	824	365*	137.33	3	3
B.C.Lara	ENG	1993-94	5	8	0	798	375	99.75	2	2
E.D.Weekes	IND	1948-49	5	7	0	779	194	111.28	4	2
B.C.Lara	ENG	1995	6	10	1	765	179	85.00	3	3
G.S.Sobers	ENG	1966	5	8	1	722	174	103.14	3	2
E.D.Weekes	IND	1952-53	5	8	1	716	207	102.28	3	2
G.S.Sobers	ENG	1959-60	5	8	1	709	226	101.28	3	1
G.A.Headley §	ENG	1929-30	4	8	0	703	223	87.87	4	0
C.L.Walcott	ENG	1953-54	5	10	2	698	220	87.25	3	3
B.C.Lara	SL	2001-02	3	6	0	688	221	114.66	3	1
C.H.Lloyd	IND	1974-75	5	9	1	636	242*	79.50	2	1
C.C.Hunte §	PAK	1957-58	5	9	1	622	260	79.75	3	0
R.B.Richardson	IND	1988-89	4	7	0	619	194	88.42	2	3
L.G.Rowe	ENG	1973-74	5	7	0	616	302	88.00	3	0
G.S.Sobers	IND	1970-71	5	10	2	597	178*	74.62	3	1
C.G.Greenidge	ENG	1976	5	10	1	592	134	65.66	3	2
C.L.Hooper	IND	2001-02	5	7	0	579	233	82.71	3	1
C.G.Greenidge	ENG	1984	5	8	1	572	223	81.71	2	0
S.Chanderpaul	IND	2001-02	5	7	3	562	140	140.50	3	3
S.M.Nurse †	NZ	1968-69	3	5	0	558	258	111.60	2	1
G.S.Sobers	IND	1958-59	5	8	2	557	198	92.83	3	0
I.V.A.Richards	IND	1975-76	4	7	0	556	177	92.66	3	1
C.C.Hunte	AUS	1964-65	5	10	1	550	89	61.11	0	6
B.C.Lara	AUS	1998-99	4	7	1	546	213	91.00	3	1
G.S.Sobers	ENG	1967-68	5	9	3	545	152	90.83	2	2
F.M.M.Worrell	ENG	1950	4	6	0	539	261	89.33	2	1
R.B.Kanhai	IND	1958-59	5	8	0	538	256	67.25	1	2
A.I.Kallicharran	IND	1978-79	6	10	1	538	187	59.77	1	3
D.L.Haynes	AUS	1988-89	5	10	1	537	143	59.66	2	2
C.G.Greenidge	PAK	1976-77	5	10	0	536	100	53.60	1	4
R.B.Kanhai	ENG	1967-68	5	10	1	535	153	59.44	2	1
B.C.Lara	AUS	2002-03	4	8	0	533	164	66.62	2	3
B.C.Lara	SA	2003-04	4	8	0	531	202	66.37	2	2
C.A.Davis	IND	1970-71	4	8	4	529	125*	132.25	2	3
R.B.Richardson	AUS	1988-89	5	10	1	528	122	58.66	2	2
J.C.Adams	IND	1994-95	3	6	3	520	174*	173.33	2	2
R.C.Fredericks	ENG	1976	5	10	1	517	138	57.44	2	3
R.B.Kanhai	AUS	1960-61	5	10	0	503	117	50.30	2	2
S.M.Nurse	ENG	1966	5	8	0	501	137	62.65	1	4
B.C.Lara	ENG	2003-04	4	7	1	500	400*	83.33	1	0

NEW ZEALAND	Opp	Season	Tests	I	NO	Runs	HS	Avge	100s	50s
G.M.Turner	WI	1971-72	5	8	1	672	259	96.00	2	2
B.Sutcliffe	IND	1955-56	5	9	2	611	230*	87.28	2	1
J.R.Reid	SA	1961-62	5	10	1	546	142	60.66	1	4
B.E.Congdon	WI	1971-72	5	8	2	531	166*	88.50	2	3
A.H.Jones	SL	1990-91	3	6	1	513	186	102.60	3	1

INDIA	Opp	Season	Tests	I	NO	Runs	HS	Avge	100s	50s
S.M.Gavaskar §	WI	1970-71	4	8	3	774	220	154.80	4	3
S.M.Gavaskar	WI	1978-79	6	9	1	732	205*	91.50	4	1
D.N.Sardesai	WI	1970-71	5	8	0	642	212	80.25	3	1
R.S.Dravid	ENG	2002	4	6	0	602	217	100.33	3	1
M.Amarnath	WI	1982-83	5	9	0	598	117	66.44	2	4
V.L.Manjrekar	ENG	1961-62	5	8	1	586	189*	83.71	1	4
M.Amarnath	PAK	1982-83	6	10	2	584	120	73.00	3	3
S.V.Manjrekar	PAK	1989-90	4	7	1	569	218	94.83	2	3
G.R.Viswanath	WI	1974-75	5	10	1	568	139	63.11	1	3
R.S.Modi	WI	1948-49	5	10	0	560	112	56.00	1	5
P.R.Umrigar	WI	1952-53	5	10	1	560	130	62.22	2	4
V.K.Sehwag	PAK	2004-05	3	6	0	544	201	90.66	2	1
V.S.Hazare	WI	1948-49	5	10	2	543	134*	67.87	2	3
S.M.Gavaskar	ENG	1979	4	7	0	542	221	77.42	1	4
S.M.Gavaskar	PAK	1979-80	6	11	1	529	166	52.90	1	2
M.H.Mankad	NZ	1955-56	4	5	0	526	231	105.20	2	0
B.K.Kunderan	ENG	1963-64	5	10	0	525	192	52.50	2	1
G.R.Viswanath	AUS	1979-80	6	8	1	518	161*	74.00	2	2
S.M.Gavaskar	WI	1983-84	6	11	1	505	236*	50.50	2	1
V.V.S.Laxman	AUS	2000-01	3	6	0	503	281	83.83	1	3
S.M.Gavaskar	ENG	1981-82	6	9	1	500	172	62.50	1	3

PAKISTAN	Opp	Season	Tests	I	NO	Runs	HS	Avge	100s	50s
Mudassar Nazar	IND	1982-83	6	8	2	761	231	126.83	4	1
Zaheer Abbas	IND	1982-83	6	6	1	650	215	130.00	3	0
Yousuf Youhana	ENG	2006	3	7	0	631	202	90.14	3	0
Hanif Mohammad	WI	1957-58	5	9	0	628	337	39.10	1	3
Javed Miandad	IND	1982-83	6	6	1	594	280*	118.88	2	1
Zaheer Abbas	IND	1978-79	3	5	2	583	235	174.33	2	1
Saleem Malik	AUS	1994-95	3	6	0	557	237	92.83	2	1
Younis Khan	IND	2005-06	3	5	0	553	199	110.60	2	2
Majid Khan	WI	1976-77	5	10	0	530	167	53.00	1	3
Wasim Raja	WI	1976-77	5	10	1	517	117*	57.44	1	5
Saeed Ahmed §	WI	1957-58	5	9	0	508	150	56.44	1	4
Younis Khan	IND	2004-05	3	6	1	508	267*	101.60	2	1
Shoaib Mohammad	NZ	1990-91	3	5	2	507	203*	169.00	3	0
Javed Miandad §	NZ	1976-77	3	5	1	504	206	126.00	2	1

Most runs in a Test series for the other countries:

SRI LANKA	Opp	Season	Tests	I	NO	Runs	HS	Avge	100s	50s
S.T.Jayasuriya	IND	1997-98	2	3	0	571	340	190.33	2	0
D.P.M.D.Jayawardene	SAF	2006-07	2	3	0	510	374	170.00	2	0
P.A.de Silva	NZ	1990-91	3	5	0	493	267	98.60	2	1
P.A.de Silva	PAK	1996-97	2	4	2	432	168	216.00	3	0
S.T.Jayasuriya	PAK	2004-05	2	4	0	424	253	106.00	2	0
M.S.Atapattu	ZIM	2003-04	2	2	0	419	249	209.50	2	0
H.P.Tillakaratne	WI	2001-02	3	4	3	403	204*	403.00	2	1

ZIMBABWE	Opp	Season	Tests	I	NO	Runs	HS	Avge	100s	50s
A.Flower	IND	2000-01	2	4	2	540	232*	270.00	2	2
D.L.Houghton	SL	1994-95	3	3	0	466	266	155.33	2	1
A.Flower	SA	2001-02	2	4	2	422	199*	211.00	2	1
A.Flower	SL	1999-2000	3	6	2	388	129	97.00	1	3
G.W.Flower	NZ	1997-98	2	4	0	387	151	96.75	2	1
T.Taibu	BAN	2004-05	2	4	1	330	153	110.00	1	2
M.W.Goodwin	PAK	1997-98	2	4	1	300	166*	100.00	1	2

BANGLADESH	Opp	Season	Tests	I	NO	Runs	HS	Avge	100s	50s
Habibul Bashar	PAK	2003-04	3	6	0	379	108	63.16	1	3
Shahriar Nafees	AUS	2005-06	2	4	0	250	138	62.50	1	1
Habibul Bashar	ZIM	2001-02	2	4	0	249	108	62.25	1	2
Habibul Bashar	WI	2003-04	2	4	0	235	113	58.75	1	1
Mohammad Ashraful	IND	2004-05	2	4	2	221	158*	110.50	1	1
Nafis Iqbal	ZIM	2004-05	2	4	0	205	121	51.25	1	1

MOST RUNS IN A TEST SERIES FOR A LOSING TEAM *(§ first Test series. # last Test series.)*

Player	Opp	Season	Tests	I	NO	Runs	HS	Avge	100s	50s
C.L.Walcott (W)	AUS	1954-55	5	10	0	827	155	82.70	5	2
G.A.Faulkner (SA)	AUS	1910-11	5	10	0	732	204	73.20	2	5
G.S.Sobers (W)	ENG	1959-60	5	8	1	709	226	101.28	3	1
B.C.Lara (W)	SL	2001-02	3	6	0	688	221	114.66	3	1
G.A.Gooch (E)	AUS	1993	6	12	0	673	133	56.08	2	4
M.P.Vaughan (E)	AUS	2002-03	5	10	0	633	183	63.30	3	0
Yousuf Youhana (P)	ENG	2006	3	7	0	631	202	90.14	3	0
Hanif Mohammad (P)	WI	1957-58	5	9	0	628	337	39.10	1	3
K.R.Stackpole (A)	ENG	1970-71	6	12	0	627	207	52.25	2	2
J.H.Kallis (SA)	ENG	2004-05	5	10	1	625	162	69.44	3	2
A.D.Nourse (SA)	ENG	1947	5	9	0	621	149	69.00	2	5
B.Sutcliffe (N)	IND	1955-56	5	9	2	611	230*	87.28	2	1
M.Amarnath (I)	WI	1982-83	5	9	0	598	117	66.44	2	4
B.Mitchell (SA)	ENG	1947	5	10	1	597	189*	66.33	2	3
G.S.Sobers (W)	IND	1970-71	5	10	2	597	178*	74.62	3	1
A.R.Border (A)	ENG	1985	6	11	2	597	196	66.33	2	1
K.F.Barrington (E)	IND	1961-62	5	9	3	594	172	99.00	3	1
K.J.Hughes (A)	IND	1979-80	6	12	2	594	100	59.40	1	5
V.L.Manjrekar (I)	ENG	1961-62	5	8	1	586	189*	83.71	1	4
M.Amarnath (I)	PAK	1982-83	6	10	2	584	120	73.00	3	3
H.W.Taylor (SA)	ENG	1922-23	5	9	0	582	176	64.66	3	2
V.T.Trumper (A)	ENG	1903-04	5	10	1	574	185*	63.77	2	3
J.B.Hobbs (E)	AUS	1924-25	5	9	0	573	154	63.66	3	2
K.C.Bland (SA)	ENG	1964-65	5	10	2	572	144*	71.50	1	4
A.Melville (SA)	ENG	1947	5	10	1	569	189	63.22	3	1
G.R.Viswanath (I)	WI	1974-75	5	10	1	568	139	63.11	1	3
D.C.S.Compton (E)	AUS	1948	5	10	1	562	184	62.44	2	2
R.S.Modi (I)	WI	1948-49	5	10	0	560	112	56.00	1	5
P.R.Umrigar (I)	WI	1952-53	5	10	1	560	130	62.22	2	4
E.J.Barlow (SA)	ENG	1964-65	5	10	0	558	138	55.80	1	4
R.A.Smith (E)	AUS	1989	5	10	1	553	143	61.44	2	3
M.A.Atherton (E)	AUS	1993	6	12	0	553	99	46.08	0	6
M.L.Hayden (A)	IND	2000-01	3	6	1	549	203	109.80	2	2
G.S.Sobers (W)	ENG	1967-68	5	9	3	545	152	90.83	2	2
V.S.Hazare (I)	WI	1948-49	5	10	2	543	134*	67.87	2	3
S.M.Gavaskar (I)	ENG	1979	4	7	0	542	221	77.42	1	4
A.Flower (Z)	IND	2000-01	2	4	2	540	232*	270.00	2	2
J.B.Hobbs (E)	SA	1909-10	5	9	1	539	187	67.37	1	4
A.D.Nourse (SA)	ENG	1948-49	5	10	3	536	129*	76.57	2	2
R.B.Kanhai (W)	ENG	1967-68	5	10	1	535	153	59.44	2	1
L.Hutton (E)	AUS	1950-51	5	10	4	533	156*	88.83	1	4
A.R.Border (A)	ENG	1981	6	12	3	533	123*	59.22	2	3
B.C.Lara (W)	AUS	2002-03	4	8	0	533	164	66.62	2	3
K.F.Barrington (E)	AUS	1964	5	8	1	531	256	75.85	1	2
B.C.Lara (W)	SA	2003-04	4	8	0	531	202	66.37	2	2
Majid Khan (P)	WI	1976-77	5	10	0	530	167	53.00	1	3

C.A.Davis (W)	IND	1970-71	4	8	4	529	125*	132.25	2	3
S.M.Gavaskar (I)	PAK	1979-80	6	11	1	529	166	52.90	1	2
A.R.Border (A)	IND	1979-80	6	12	0	521	162	49.63	1	3
A.R.Border (A)	WI	1983-84	5	10	3	521	100*	74.42	1	4
A.D.Nourse (SA)	AUS	1935-36	5	10	1	518	231	57.55	1	2
W.R.Hammond (E)	SA	1930-31	5	9	1	517	136*	64.62	1	4
Wasim Raja (P)	WI	1976-77	5	10	1	517	117*	57.44	1	5
E.A.B.Rowan (SA) #	ENG	1951	5	10	1	515	236	57.22	1	3
D.M.Jones (A)	ENG	1986-87	5	10	1	511	184*	56.77	1	3
M.A.Atherton (E)	WI	1993-94	5	9	0	510	144	56.66	2	2
H.W.Taylor (SA)	ENG	1913-14	5	10	0	508	109	35.10	1	3
Saeed Ahmed (P) §	WI	1957-58	5	9	0	508	150	56.44	1	4
Younis Khan (P)	IND	2004-05	3	6	1	508	267*	101.60	2	1
G.P.Thorpe (E)	WI	1995	6	12	0	506	94	42.16	0	5
J.B.Hobbs (E)	AUS	1920-21	5	10	0	505	123	50.50	2	1
S.M.Gavaskar (I)	WI	1983-84	6	11	1	505	236*	50.50	2	1
K.C.Wessels (A)	WI	1984-85	5	9	0	505	173	56.11	1	4
R.B.Kanhai (W)	AUS	1960-61	5	10	0	503	117	50.30	2	2
B.C.Lara (W)	ENG	2003-04	4	7	1	500	400*	83.33	1	0

MOST CENTURIES

Player	Country	100	Inns	A	E	SA	W	N	I	P	SL	Z	B
S.R.Tendulkar	India	**35**	211	7	6	3	3	3	-	2	7	3	1
S.M.Gavaskar	India	**34**	214	8	4	-	13	2	-	5	2	-	-
B.C.Lara	West Indies	**32**	225	9	7	4	-	1	2	2	5	1	1
S.R.Waugh	Australia	**32**	260	-	10	2	7	2	2	3	3	1	2
R.T.Ponting	Australia	**31**	173	-	5	7	6	2	4	4	1	1	1
D.G.Bradman	Australia	**29**	80	-	19	4	2	-	4	-	-	-	-
A.R.Border	Australia	**27**	265	-	8	0	3	5	4	6	1	-	-
G.S.Sobers	West Indies	**26**	160	4	10	-	-	1	8	3	-	-	-
M.L.Hayden	Australia	**25**	148	-	4	6	5	1	3	1	3	1	0
Inzamamul Haq	Pakistan	**25**	185	1	5	0	4	3	3	-	5	2	2
G.S.Chappell	Australia	**24**	151	-	9	-	5	3	1	6	0	-	-
J.H.Kallis	South Africa	**24**	170	3	5	-	7	3	1	1	0	3	1
I.V.A.Richards	West Indies	**24**	182	5	8	-	-	1	8	2	-	-	-
R.S.Dravid	India	**23**	174	2	3	1	3	4	-	5	1	3	1
Javed Miandad	Pakistan	**23**	189	6	2	-	2	7	5	-	1	-	-
W.R.Hammond	England	**22**	140	9	-	6	1	4	2	-	-	-	-
M.Azharuddin	India	**22**	147	2	6	4	0	2	-	3	5	0	-
J.L.Langer	Australia	**22**	171	-	4	2	3	4	3	4	2	0	0
M.C.Cowdrey	England	**22**	188	5	-	3	6	2	3	3	-	-	-
G.Boycott	England	**22**	193	7	-	1	5	2	4	3	-	-	-
R.N.Harvey	Australia	**21**	137	-	6	8	3	-	4	0	-	-	-
G.Kirsten	South Africa	**21**	176	2	5	-	3	2	3	2	1	1	2
D.C.Boon	Australia	**21**	190	-	7	0	3	3	6	1	1	-	-
K.F.Barrington	England	**20**	131	5	-	2	3	3	3	4	-	-	-
P.A.de Silva	Sri Lanka	**20**	159	1	2	0	0	2	5	8	-	1	1
M.E.Waugh	Australia	**20**	209	-	6	4	4	1	1	3	1	0	-
G.A.Gooch	England	**20**	215	4	-	0	5	4	5	1	1	-	-
L.Hutton	England	**19**	138	5	-	4	5	3	2	0	-	-	-
C.H.Lloyd	West Indies	**19**	175	6	5	-	-	0	7	1	-	-	-
C.G.Greenidge	West Indies	**19**	185	4	7	-	-	2	5	1	-	-	-
M.A.Taylor	Australia	**19**	186	-	6	2	1	2	2	4	2	-	-
Yousuf Youhana	Pakistan	**19**	117	1	6	0	3	1	4	-	0	2	2
D.L.Haynes	West Indies	**18**	202	5	5	-	-	3	2	3	0	-	-
D.I.Gower	England	**18**	204	9	-	-	1	4	2	2	0	-	-
D.C.S.Compton	England	**17**	131	5	-	7	2	2	0	1	-	-	-

M.D.Crowe	New Zealand	**17**	131	3	5	0	3	-	1	2	2	1	-

Player	Country	100	Inns	A	E	SA	W	N	I	P	SL	Z	B
D.B.Vengsarkar	India	**17**	185	2	5	-	6	0	-	2	2	-	-
H.Sutcliffe	England	**16**	84	8	-	6	0	2	0	-	-	-	-
A.C.Gilchrist	Australia	**16**	119	-	2	2	1	4	2	2	1	1	1
R.B.Richardson	West Indies	**16**	146	9	4	0	-	1	2	0	0	-	-
M.S.Atapattu	Sri Lanka	**16**	152	2	2	1	1	1	2	1	-	5	1
G.P.Thorpe	England	**16**	179	3	-	2	3	4	0	2	2	0	0
M.A.Atherton	England	**16**	212	1	-	3	4	4	2	0	0	1	-
D.P.M.D.Jayawardene	Sri Lanka	**16**	136	0	4	5	0	4	1	0	-	1	1
C.L.Walcott	West Indies	**15**	74	5	4	-	-	1	4	1	-	-	-
E.D.Weekes	West Indies	**15**	81	1	3	-	-	3	7	1	-	-	-
J.B.Hobbs	England	**15**	102	12	-	2	1	-	-	-	-	-	-
M.P.Vaughan	England	**15**	115	4	-	1	3	0	3	1	2	0	1
K.D.Walters	Australia	**15**	125	-	4	0	6	3	1	1	-	-	-
R.B.Kanhai	West Indies	**15**	137	5	5	-	-	-	4	1	-	-	-
Saleem Malik	Pakistan	**15**	154	2	4	0	1	2	3	-	3	0	-
A.J.Stewart	England	**15**	235	1	-	1	3	4	0	2	2	2	-
D.J.Cullinan	South Africa	**14**	115	0	2	-	3	2	2	0	5	0	-
H.H.Gibbs	South Africa	**14**	135	1	3	-	3	2	2	1	0	1	1
M.J.Slater	Australia	**14**	131	-	7	0	1	2	0	3	1	0	-
I.M.Chappell	Australia	**14**	136	-	4	0	5	2	2	1	-	-	-
M.E.Trescothick	England	**14**	143	0	-	3	2	1	0	2	3	0	3
A.J.Lamb	England	**14**	139	1	-	-	6	3	3	0	1	-	-
G.R.Viswanath	India	**14**	155	4	4	-	4	1	-	1	0	-	-
I.T.Botham	England	**14**	161	4	-	-	0	3	5	2	0	-	-
S.Chanderpaul	West Indies	**14**	166	2	2	3	-	0	5	1	0	0	1
N.Hussain	England	**14**	171	2	-	3	1	2	4	0	1	1	-
S.T.Jayasuriya	Sri Lanka	**14**	178	2	1	1	0	0	3	4	-	2	1
D.R.Martyn	Australia	**13**	106	-	2	4	0	1	2	2	2	0	-
P.B.H.May	England	**13**	106	3	-	3	3	3	1	0	-	-	-
W.M.Lawry	Australia	**13**	123	-	7	1	4	-	1	0	-	-	-
C.L.Hooper	West Indies	**13**	173	1	3	0	-	0	5	3	0	1	-
V.K.Sehwag	India	**12**	79	2	1	2	2	1	-	4	-	0	0
A.R.Morris	Australia	**12**	79	-	8	2	1	-	1	-	-	-	-
Ijaz Ahmed	Pakistan	**12**	92	6	1	0	1	2	0	-	2	0	-
P.R.Umrigar	India	**12**	94	-	3	-	3	1	-	5	-	-	-
Hanif Mohammad	Pakistan	**12**	97	2	3	-	2	3	2	-	-	-	-
A.I.Kallicharran	West Indies	**12**	109	4	2	-	-	2	3	1	-	-	-
A.Flower	Zimbabwe	**12**	112	0	1	2	1	0	3	2	2	-	1
Zaheer Abbas	Pakistan	**12**	124	2	2	-	0	1	6	-	1	-	-
J.H.Edrich	England	**12**	127	7	-	0	1	3	1	0	-	-	-
S.C.Ganguly	India	**12**	140	1	3	0	0	3	-	0	3	2	0
J.G.Wright	New Zealand	**12**	148	2	4	-	1	-	3	1	1	-	-
Younis Khan	Pakistan	**12**	83	0	1	0	2	1	4	-	3	0	1
G.C.Smith	South Africa	**11**	82	0	2	-	5	1	0	1	0	1	1
D.L.Amiss	England	**11**	88	0	-	-	4	2	2	3	-	-	-
D.M.Jones	Australia	**11**	89	-	3	-	1	0	2	2	3	-	-
Saeed Anwar	Pakistan	**11**	91	3	1	1	0	2	1	-	2	0	1
Asif Iqbal	Pakistan	**11**	99	3	3	-	1	3	1	-	-	-	-
M.Amarnath	India	**11**	113	2	0	-	3	0	-	4	2	-	-
R.J.Shastri	India	**11**	121	2	4	0	2	0	-	3	0	0	-
T.W.Graveney	England	**11**	123	1	-	0	5	0	2	3	-	-	-
H.P.Tillakaratne	Sri Lanka	**11**	131	1	0	1	2	2	1	2	-	2	0
N.J.Astle	New Zealand	**11**	133	1	3	0	2	-	1	0	1	3	0
G.A.Headley	West Indies	**10**	40	2	8	-	-	-	-	-	-	-	-
A.L.Hassett	Australia	**10**	69	-	4	3	2	-	1	-	-	-	-

Mushtaq Mohammad	Pakistan	**10**	100	1	3	-	2	3	1	-	-	-	-
R.B.Simpson	Australia	**10**	111	-	2	1	1	-	4	2	-	-	-
Mudassar Nazar	Pakistan	**10**	116	0	3	-	0	1	6	-	0	-	-
V.V.S.Laxman	India	**10**	124	4	0	0	3	1	-	0	1	1	0
M.W.Gatting	England	**10**	138	4	-	-	0	1	3	2	0	-	-
K.C.Sangakkara	Sri Lanka	**10**	103	0	0	2	2	0	1	3	-	2	0
A.J.Strauss	England	**10**	58	2	-	3	1	1	1	2	0	-	0

The leading century-makers for Bangladesh are Habibul Bashar (3 in 83 innings) & Mohammad Ashraful (3 in 65 innings).

HIGHEST BATTING AVERAGES

(Qualification: 15 innings)

Player	Country	Tests	I	NO	Runs	HS	Avge	100s	50s
D.G.Bradman	Australia	52	80	10	6996	334	**99.94**	29	13
M.E.K.Hussey	Australia	11	19	4	1139	182	**75.93**	4	4
C.S.Dempster	New Zealand	10	15	4	723	136	**65.72**	2	5
S.G.Barnes	Australia	13	19	2	1072	234	**63.05**	3	5
R.G.Pollock	South Africa	23	41	4	2256	274	**60.97**	7	11
G.A.Headley	West Indies	22	40	4	2190	270*	**60.83**	10	5
H.Sutcliffe	England	54	84	9	4555	194	**60.73**	16	23
E.Paynter	England	20	31	5	1540	243	**59.23**	4	7
R.S.Dravid	India	103	174	22	9026	270	**59.38**	23	46
K.F.Barrington	England	82	131	15	6806	256	**58.67**	20	35
E.D.Weekes	West Indies	48	81	5	4455	207	**58.61**	15	19
K.S.Duleepsinhji	England	12	19	2	995	173	**58.52**	3	5
W.R.Hammond	England	85	140	16	7249	336*	**58.46**	22	24
R.T.Ponting	Australia	104	173	24	8692	257	**58.33**	31	33
G.S.Sobers	West Indies	93	160	21	8032	365*	**57.78**	26	30
J.B.Hobbs	England	61	102	7	5410	211	**56.94**	15	28
C.A.G.Russell	England	10	18	2	990	140	**56.87**	5	2
C.L.Walcott	West Indies	44	74	7	3798	220	**56.68**	15	14
L.Hutton	England	79	138	15	6971	364	**56.67**	19	33
J.H.Kallis	South Africa	101	170	27	7950	189*	**55.59**	24	40
S.R.Tendulkar	India	132	211	22	10469	248*	**55.39**	35	41
G.E.Tyldesley	England	14	20	2	990	122	**55.00**	3	6
A.N.Cook	England	9	16	2	761	127	**54.35**	3	3
C.A.Davis	West Indies	15	29	5	1301	183	**54.20**	4	4
V.G.Kambli	India	17	21	1	1084	227	**54.20**	4	3
G.S.Chappell	Australia	87	151	19	7110	247*	**53.86**	24	31
A.D.Nourse	South Africa	34	62	7	2960	231	**53.81**	9	14
Yousuf Youhana	Pakistan	70	117	9	5737	223	**53.12**	19	25
V.K.Sehwag	India	48	79	3	4013	309	**52.80**	12	12
B.C.Lara	West Indies	127	225	6	11464	400*	**52.34**	32	47
A.Melville	South Africa	11	19	2	894	189*	**52.58**	4	3
Javed Miandad	Pakistan	124	189	21	8832	280*	**52.57**	23	43
M.L.Hayden	Australia	83	148	12	7138	380	**52.48**	25	25
C.F.Walters	England	11	18	3	784	102	**52.26**	1	7
J.Ryder	Australia	20	32	5	1394	201*	**51.62**	3	9
A.Flower	Zimbabwe	63	112	19	4794	232*	**51.54**	12	27
Inzamamul Haq	Pakistan	112	185	20	8497	329	**51.49**	25	44
S.M.Gavaskar	India	125	214	12	10122	236*	**51.12**	34	45
S.R.Waugh	Australia	168	260	46	10927	200	**51.06**	32	50
A.R.Border	Australia	156	265	44	11174	205	**50.56**	27	63
G.C.Smith	South Africa	47	82	5	3879	277	**50.37**	11	14
I.V.A.Richards	West Indies	121	182	12	8540	291	**50.23**	24	45
D.C.S.Compton	England	78	131	15	5807	278	**50.06**	17	28

WORST BATTING AVERAGES *(Qualification: 1000 runs)*

Player	Country	Tests	I	NO	Runs	HS	Avge	100s	50s	0
Waqar Younis	PAK	87	120	21	1010	45	**10.20**	0	0	21
M.Muralidaran	SL	107	138	49	1093	67	**12.28**	0	1	27
C.E.L.Ambrose	WI	98	145	29	1439	53	**12.40**	0	1	26
J.Srinath	IND	67	92	21	1009	76	**14.21**	0	4	13
Abdul Qadir	PAK	67	77	11	1029	61	**15.59**	0	3	7
Wasim Bari	PAK	81	112	26	1366	85	**15.88**	0	6	19
R.W.Taylor	ENG	57	83	12	1156	97	**16.28**	0	3	10
M.G.Hughes	AUS	53	70	8	1032	72*	**16.64**	0	2	10
S.K.Warne	AUS	139	192	16	2946	99	**16.73**	0	11	34
Sarfraz Nawaz	PAK	55	72	13	1045	90	**17.71**	0	4	6
A.Kumble	IND	110	140	27	2025	88	**17.92**	0	4	13
I.W.G.Johnson	AUS	45	66	12	1000	77	**18.51**	0	6	10
J.N.Gillespie	AUS	71	93	28	1218	201*	**18.73**	1	2	13
M.D.Marshall	WI	81	107	11	1810	92	**18.85**	0	10	15
Khaled Mashud	BAN	41	79	9	1361	103*	**19.44**	1	3	11
S.Abid Ali	IND	29	53	3	1018	81	**20.36**	0	6	3
J.G.Bracewell	NZ	41	60	11	1001	110	**20.42**	1	4	13
T.G.Evans	ENG	91	133	14	2439	104	**20.49**	2	8	17
D.N.Patel	NZ	37	66	8	1200	99	**20.69**	0	5	10
A.F.Giles	ENG	52	77	12	1347	59	**20.72**	0	4	8
R.R.Lindwall	AUS	61	84	13	1502	118	**21.15**	2	5	9
K.J.Wadsworth	NZ	33	51	4	1010	80	**21.48**	0	5	5
B.Lee	AUS	53	58	11	1029	64	**21.89**	0	3	9
Javed Omar	BAN	35	70	1	1525	119	**22.10**	1	6	3
P.V.Simmons	WI	26	47	2	1002	110	**22.26**	1	4	4
Intkhab Alam	PAK	47	77	10	1493	138	**22.28**	1	8	10
F.J.Titmus	ENG	53	76	11	1449	84*	**22.29**	0	10	4
H.H.Streak	ZIM	65	107	18	1990	127*	**22.36**	1	11	15
C.B.Wishart	ZIM	27	50	1	1098	114	**22.40**	1	5	6
S.J.Snooke	SAF	26	46	1	1008	103	**22.40**	1	5	1
J.E.Emburey	ENG	64	96	20	1713	75	**22.53**	0	10	12
Wasim Akram	PAK	104	147	19	2898	257*	**22.64**	3	7	17
W.A.S.Oldfield	AUS	54	80	17	1427	65*	**22.65**	0	4	9
S.Madan Lal	IND	39	62	16	1042	74	**22.65**	0	5	7
D.D.Ebrahim	ZIM	29	55	1	1225	94	**22.68**	0	10	8
G.J.Rennie	ZIM	23	46	1	1023	93	**22.73**	0	7	5
W.P.U.J.C.Vaas	SL	94	136	26	2503	74*	**22.75**	0	11	9
J.M.Brearley	ENG	39	66	3	1442	91	**22.88**	0	9	6
D.L.Murray	WI	62	96	9	1993	91	**22.90**	0	11	7

THE TRIPLE HUNDREDS

Player	Score	Mins	Balls	6s/4s	Match particulars				
B.C.Lara	400*	778	582	4/43	West Indies	v	England	St John's	2003-04
M.L.Hayden	380	622	437	11/38	Australia	v	Zimbabwe	Perth	2003-04
B.C.Lara	375	766	538	0/45	West Indies	v	England	St John's	1993-94
D.P.M.D.Jayawardene	374	752	572	1/43	Sri Lanka	v	South Africa	Colombo (SSC)	2006-07
G.S.Sobers	365*	614		0/38	West Indies	v	Pakistan	Kingston	1957-58
L.Hutton	364	797	844	0/35	England	v	Australia	The Oval	1938
S.T.Jayasuriya	340	799	578	2/36	Sri Lanka	v	India	Colombo (RPS)	1997-98
Hanif Mohammad	337	973		0/24	Pakistan	v	West Indies	Bridgetown	1957-58
W.R.Hammond	336*	325	398	10/34	England	v	New Zealand	Auckland	1932-33
M.A.Taylor	334*	720	564	1/32	Australia	v	Pakistan	Peshawar[2]	1998-99
D.G.Bradman	334	378	446	0/46	Australia	v	England	Leeds	1930
G.A.Gooch	333	627	485	3/43	England	v	India	Lord's	1990

Inzamamul Haq	329	579	436	9/38	Pakistan	v	New Zealand	Lahore[2]	2001-02
A.Sandham	325	600		0/28	England	v	West Indies	Kingston	1929-30
C.H.Gayle	317	630	483	3/37	West Indies	v	South Africa	St John's	2004-05
R.B.Simpson	311	762	740	1/23	Australia	v	England	Manchester	1964
J.H.Edrich	310*	532	450	5/52	England	v	New Zealand	Leeds	1965
V.K.Sehwag	309	531	375	6/39	India	v	Pakistan	Multan[2]	2003-04
R.M.Cowper	307	727	589	0/20	Australia	v	England	Melbourne	1965-66
D.G.Bradman	304	430	466	2/44	Australia	v	England	Leeds	1934
L.G.Rowe	302	612	430	1/36	West Indies	v	England	Bridgetown	1973-74

THE DOUBLE HUNDREDS

299*	D.G.Bradman	Australia	v	South Africa	Adelaide	1931-32
299	M.D.Crowe	New Zealand	v	Sri Lanka	Wellington	1990-91
291	I.V.A.Richards	West Indies	v	England	The Oval	1976
287	R.E.Foster	England	v	Australia	Sydney	1903-04
287	K.C.Sangakkara	Sri Lanka	v	South Africa	Colombo(SSC)	2006-07
285*	P.B.H.May	England	v	West Indies	Birmingham	1957
281	V.V.S.Laxman	India	v	Australia	Kolkata	2000-01
280*	Javed Miandad	Pakistan	v	India	Hyderabad	1982-83
278	D.C.S.Compton	England	v	Pakistan	Nottingham	1954
277	B.C.Lara	West Indies	v	Australia	Sydney	1992-93
277	G.C.Smith	South Africa	v	England	Birmingham	2003
275*	D.J.Cullinan	South Africa	v	New Zealand	Auckland	1998-99
275	G.Kirsten	South Africa	v	England	Durban[2]	1999-2000
274*	S.P.Fleming	New Zealand	v	Sri Lanka	Colombo (PSS)	2002-03
274	R.G.Pollock	South Africa	v	Australia	Durban[2]	1969-70
274	Zaheer Abbas	Pakistan	v	England	Birmingham	1971
271	Javed Miandad	Pakistan	v	New Zealand	Auckland	1988-89
270*	G.A.Headley	West Indies	v	England	Kingston	1934-35
270	D.G.Bradman	Australia	v	England	Melbourne	1936-37
270	R.S.Dravid	India	v	Pakistan	Rawalpindi[2]	2003-04
270	K.C.Sangakkara	Sri Lanka	v	Zimbabwe	Bulawayo[2]	2003-04
268	G.N.Yallop	Australia	v	Pakistan	Melbourne	1983-84
267*	B.A.Young	New Zealand	v	Sri Lanka	Dunedin	1996-97
267	P.A.de Silva	Sri Lanka	v	New Zealand	Wellington	1990-91
267	Younis Khan	Pakistan	v	India	Bangalore	2004-05
266	W.H.Ponsford	Australia	v	England	The Oval	1934
266	D.L.Houghton	Zimbabwe	v	Sri Lanka	Bulawayo[2]	1994-95
262*	D.L.Amiss	England	v	West Indies	Kingston	1973-74
262	S.P.Fleming	New Zealand	v	South Africa	Cape Town	2005-06
261*	R.R.Sarwan	West Indies	v	Bangladesh	Kingston	2003-04
261	F.M.M.Worrell	West Indies	v	England	Nottingham	1950
260	C.C.Hunte	West Indies	v	Pakistan	Kingston	1957-58
260	Javed Miandad	Pakistan	v	England	The Oval	1987
259	G.M.Turner	New Zealand	v	West Indies	Georgetown	1971-72
259	G.C.Smith	South Africa	v	England	Lord's	2003
258	T.W.Graveney	England	v	West Indies	Nottingham	1957
258	S.M.Nurse	West Indies	v	New Zealand	Christchurch	1968-69
257*	Wasim Akram	Pakistan	v	Zimbabwe	Sheikhupura	1996-97
257	R.T.Ponting	Australia	v	India	Melbourne	2003-04
256	R.B.Kanhai	West Indies	v	India	Calcutta	1958-59
256	K.F.Barrington	England	v	Australia	Manchester	1964
255*	D.J.McGlew	South Africa	v	New Zealand	Wellington	1952-53
254	D.G.Bradman	Australia	v	England	Lord's	1930
254	V.K.Sehwag	India	v	Pakistan	Lahore[2]	2005-06
253	S.T.Jayasuriya	Sri Lanka	v	Pakistan	Faisalabad	2004-05

251	W.R.Hammond	England	v	Australia	Sydney	1928-29
250	K.D.Walters	Australia	v	New Zealand	Christchurch	1976-77
250	S.F.A.F.Bacchus	West Indies	v	India	Kanpur	1978-79
250	J.L.Langer	Australia	v	England	Melbourne	2002-03
249	M.S.Atapattu	Sri Lanka	v	Zimbabwe	Bulawayo[2]	2003-04
248*	S.R.Tendulkar	India	v	Bangladesh	Dhaka	2004-05
247*	G.S.Chappell	Australia	v	New Zealand	Wellington	1973-74
246*	G.Boycott	England	v	India	Leeds	1967
244	D.G.Bradman	Australia	v	England	The Oval	1934
243	E.Paynter	England	v	South Africa	Durban[2]	1938-39
242*	C.H.Lloyd	West Indies	v	India	Bombay[3]	1974-75
242	K.D.Walters	Australia	v	West Indies	Sydney	1968-69
242	D.P.M.D.Jayawardene	Sri Lanka	v	India	Colombo (SSC)	1998-99
242	R.T.Ponting	Australia	v	India	Adelaide	2003-04
241*	S.R.Tendulkar	India	v	Australia	Sydney	2003-04
240	W.R.Hammond	England	v	Australia	Lord's	1938
240	Zaheer Abbas	Pakistan	v	England	The Oval	1974
239	G.T.Dowling	New Zealand	v	India	Christchurch	1967-68
237	F.M.M.Worrell	West Indies	v	India	Kingston	1952-53
237	Saleem Malik	Pakistan	v	Australia	Rawalpindi[2]	1994-95
237	D.P.M.D.Jayawardene	Sri Lanka	v	South Africa	Galle	2004-05
236*	S.M.Gavaskar	India	v	West Indies	Madras[1]	1983-84
236	E.A.B.Rowan	South Africa	v	England	Leeds	1951
235*	Zaheer Abbas	Pakistan	v	India	Lahore[2]	1978-79
235	G.S.Chappell	Australia	v	Pakistan	Faisalabad	1979-80
234	D.G.Bradman	Australia	v	England	Sydney	1946-47
234	S.G.Barnes	Australia	v	England	Sydney	1946-47
233	C.L.Hooper	West Indies	v	India	Georgetown	2001-02
233	R.S.Dravid	India	v	Australia	Adelaide	2003-04
232*	A.Flower	Zimbabwe	v	India	Nagpur	2000-01
232	D.G.Bradman	Australia	v	England	The Oval	1930
232	S.J.McCabe	Australia	v	England	Nottingham	1938
232	I.V.A.Richards	West Indies	v	England	Nottingham	1976
232	K.C.Sangakkara	Sri Lanka	v	South Africa	Colombo (SSC)	2004-05
231*	W.R.Hammond	England	v	Australia	Sydney	1936-37
231	A.D.Nourse	South Africa	v	Australia	Johannesburg[1]	1935-36
231	M.H.Mankad	India	v	New Zealand	Madras[2]	1955-56
231	Mudassar Nazar	Pakistan	v	India	Hyderabad	1982-83
230*	B.Sutcliffe	New Zealand	v	India	Delhi	1955-56
230	K.C.Sangakkara	Sri Lanka	v	Pakistan	Lahore[2]	2001-02
228	H.H.Gibbs	South Africa	v	Pakistan	Cape Town	2002-03
227	W.R.Hammond	England	v	New Zealand	Christchurch	1932-33
227	V.G.Kambli	India	v	Zimbabwe	Delhi	1992-93
226	D.G.Bradman	Australia	v	South Africa	Brisbane[2]	1931-32
226	G.S.Sobers	West Indies	v	England	Bridgetown	1959-60
226	C.G.Greenidge	West Indies	v	Australia	Bridgetown	1990-91
226	B.C.Lara	West Indies	v	Australia	Adelaide	2005-06
225	R.B.Simpson	Australia	v	England	Adelaide	1965-66
225	R.S.Mahanama	Sri Lanka	v	India	Colombo (RPS)	1997-98
224	V.G.Kambli	India	v	England	Bombay[3]	1992-93
224	L.Vincent	New Zealand	v	Sri Lanka	Wellington	2004-05
223*	G.M.Turner	New Zealand	v	West Indies	Kingston	1971-72
223	G.A.Headley	West Indies	v	England	Kingston	1929-30
223	D.G.Bradman	Australia	v	West Indies	Brisbane[1]	1930-31
223	P.R.Umrigar	India	v	New Zealand	Hyderabad	1955-56
223	M.H.Mankad	India	v	New Zealand	Bombay[2]	1955-56

223	C.G.Greenidge	West Indies	v	England	Manchester	1984
223	M.S.Atapattu	Sri Lanka	v	Zimbabwe	Kandy	1997-98
223	J.L.Langer	Australia	v	India	Sydney	1999-2000
223	Yousuf Youhana	Pakistan	v	England	Lahore[2]	2005-06
222*	J.A.Rudolph	South Africa	v	Bangladesh	Chittagong[1]	2002-03
222	G.R.Viswanath	India	v	England	Madras[1]	1981-82
222	N.J.Astle	New Zealand	v	England	Christchurch	2001-02
222	R.S.Dravid	India	v	New Zealand	Ahmedabad	2003-04
221	S.M.Gavaskar	India	v	England	The Oval	1979
221	B.C.Lara	West Indies	v	Sri Lanka	Colombo (SSC)	2001-02
221	R.W.T.Key	England	v	West Indies	Lord's	2004
220	C.L.Walcott	West Indies	v	England	Bridgetown	1953-54
220	S.M.Gavaskar	India	v	West Indies	Port-of-Spain	1970-71
220	G.Kirsten	South Africa	v	Zimbabwe	Harare	2001-02
219	W.J.Edrich	England	v	South Africa	Durban[2]	1938-39
219	D.S.Atkinson	West Indies	v	Australia	Bridgetown	1954-55
219	M.A.Taylor	Australia	v	England	Nottingham	1989
219	M.J.Slater	Australia	v	Sri Lanka	Perth	1995-96
219	M.E.Trescothick	England	v	South Africa	The Oval	2003
218	S.V.Manjrekar	India	v	Pakistan	Lahore[2]	1989-90
217	W.R.Hammond	England	v	India	The Oval	1936
217	R.B.Kanhai	West Indies	v	Pakistan	Lahore[1]	1958-59
217	S.R.Tendulkar	India	v	New Zealand	Ahmedabad	1999-2000
217	R.S.Dravid	India	v	England	The Oval	2002
216*	E.Paynter	England	v	Australia	Nottingham	1938
216*	M.S.Atapattu	Sri Lanka	v	Zimbabwe	Bulawayo[2]	1999-2000
216	K.W.R.Fletcher	England	v	New Zealand	Auckland	1974-75
216	D.M.Jones	Australia	v	West Indies	Adelaide	1988-89
215	Zaheer Abbas	Pakistan	v	India	Lahore[2]	1982-83
215	D.I.Gower	England	v	Australia	Birmingham	1985
215	J.L.Langer	Australia	v	New Zealand	Adelaide	2004-05
214*	V.T.Trumper	Australia	v	South Africa	Adelaide	1910-11
214*	D.Lloyd	England	v	India	Birmingham	1974
214*	C.G.Greenidge	West Indies	v	England	Lord's	1984
214	L.G.Rowe	West Indies	v	New Zealand	Kingston	1971-72
214	G.S.Blewett	Australia	v	South Africa	Johannesburg[3]	1996-97
214	M.S.Sinclair	New Zealand	v	West Indies	Wellington	1999-2000
213	K.J.Hughes	Australia	v	India	Adelaide	1980-81
213	C.G.Greenidge	West Indies	v	New Zealand	Auckland	1986-87
213	S.T.Jayasuriya	Sri Lanka	v	England	The Oval	1998
213	B.C.Lara	West Indies	v	Australia	Kingston	1999-2000
213	W.W.Hinds	West Indies	v	South Africa	Georgetown	2004-05
212	D.G.Bradman	Australia	v	England	Adelaide	1936-37
212	D.N.Sardesai	India	v	West Indies	Kingston	1970-71
212	Wasim Jaffer	India	v	West Indies	St John's	2005-06
211*	H.H.Gibbs	South Africa	v	New Zealand	Christchurch	1999-2000
211	W.L.Murdoch	Australia	v	England	The Oval	1884
211	J.B.Hobbs	England	v	South Africa	Lord's	1924
211	Javed Miandad	Pakistan	v	Australia	Karachi[1]	1988-89
211	Ijaz Ahmed	Pakistan	v	Sri Lanka	Dhaka	1998-99
210*	Taslim Arif	Pakistan	v	Australia	Faisalabad	1979-80
210	W.M.Lawry	Australia	v	West Indies	Bridgetown	1964-65
210	Qasim Omar	Pakistan	v	India	Faisalabad	1984-85
210	D.M.Jones	Australia	v	India	Madras[1]	1986-87
210	G.A.Gooch	England	v	New Zealand	Nottingham	1994
210	G.Kirsten	South Africa	v	England	Manchester	1998

209*	B.F.Butcher	West Indies	v	England	Nottingham	1966
209	C.A.Roach	West Indies	v	England	Georgetown	1929-30
209	Imtiaz Ahmed	Pakistan	v	New Zealand	Lahore[1]	1955-56
209	R.G.Pollock	South Africa	v	Australia	Cape Town	1966-67
209	B.C.Lara	West Indies	v	Sri Lanka	Gros Islet	2002-03
208*	J.C.Adams	West Indies	v	New Zealand	St John's	1995-96
208	D.C.S.Compton	England	v	South Africa	Lord's	1947
208	A.D.Nourse	South Africa	v	England	Nottingham	1951
208	I.T.Botham	England	v	India	The Oval	1982
208	I.V.A.Richards	West Indies	v	Australia	Melbourne	1984-85
208	S.L.Campbell	West Indies	v	New Zealand	Bridgetown	1995-96
207*	M.S.Atapattu	Sri Lanka	v	Pakistan	Galle	2000-01
207	E.D.Weekes	West Indies	v	India	Port-of-Spain	1952-53
207	K.R.Stackpole	Australia	v	England	Brisbane[2]	1970-71
207	M.W.Gatting	England	v	India	Madras[1]	1984-85
207	N.Hussain	England	v	Australia	Birmingham	1997
207	R.T.Ponting	Australia	v	Pakistan	Sydney	2004-05
206*	W.A.Brown	Australia	v	England	Lord's	1938
206	M.P.Donnelly	New Zealand	v	England	Lord's	1949
206	L.Hutton	England	v	New Zealand	The Oval	1949
206	A.R.Morris	Australia	v	England	Adelaide	1950-51
206	E.D.Weekes	West Indies	v	England	Port-of-Spain	1953-54
206	Javed Miandad	Pakistan	v	New Zealand	Karachi[1]	1976-77
206	Qasim Omar	Pakistan	v	Sri Lanka	Faisalabad	1985-86
206	R.J.Shastri	India	v	Australia	Sydney	1991-92
206	P.A.de Silva	Sri Lanka	v	Bangladesh	Colombo (PSS)	2002-03
206	R.T.Ponting	Australia	v	West Indies	Port-of-Spain	2002-03
205*	E.H.Hendren	England	v	West Indies	Port-of-Spain	1929-30
205*	J.Hardstaff, jr	England	v	India	Lord's	1946
205	R.N.Harvey	Australia	v	South Africa	Melbourne	1952-53
205	L.Hutton	England	v	West Indies	Kingston	1953-54
205	E.R.Dexter	England	v	Pakistan	Karachi[1]	1961-62
205	W.M.Lawry	Australia	v	West Indies	Melbourne	1968-69
205	S.M.Gavaskar	India	v	West Indies	Bombay[3]	1978-79
205	A.R.Border	Australia	v	New Zealand	Adelaide	1987-88
205	Aamer Sohail	Pakistan	v	England	Manchester	1992
204*	M.S.Sinclair	New Zealand	v	Pakistan	Christchurch	2000-01
204*	H.P.Tillakaratne	Sri Lanka	v	West Indies	Colombo (SSC)	2001-02
204*	Yousuf Youhana	Pakistan	v	Bangladesh	Chittagong[1]	2001-02
204*	A.C.Gilchrist	Australia	v	South Africa	Johannesburg[3]	2001-02
204	G.A.Faulkner	South Africa	v	Australia	Melbourne	1910-11
204	R.N.Harvey	Australia	v	West Indies	Kingston	1954-55
204	G.S.Chappell	Australia	v	India	Sydney	1980-81
204	C.H.Gayle	West Indies	v	New Zealand	St Georges	2002-03
203*	Nawab of Pataudi, jr	India	v	England	Delhi	1963-64
203*	Hanif Mohammad	Pakistan	v	New Zealand	Lahore[2]	1964-65
203*	Javed Miandad	Pakistan	v	Sri Lanka	Faisalabad	1985-86
203*	Shoaib Mohammad	Pakistan	v	India	Lahore[2]	1989-90
203*	Shoaib Mohammad	Pakistan	v	New Zealand	Karachi[1]	1990-91
203*	G.J.Whittall	Zimbabwe	v	New Zealand	Bulawayo[2]	1997-98
203*	S.Chanderpaul	West Indies	v	South Africa	Georgetown	2004-05
203*	B.J.Hodge	Australia	v	South Africa	Perth	2005-06
203	H.L.Collins	Australia	v	South Africa	Johannesburg[1]	1921-22
203	D.L.Amiss	England	v	West Indies	The Oval	1976
203	M.L.Hayden	Australia	v	India	Chennai[1]	2000-01
202	Yousuf Youhana	Pakistan	v	England	Lord's	2006

202*	L.Hutton	England	v	West Indies	The Oval	1950
202	B.C.Lara	West Indies	v	South Africa	Johannesburg[3]	2003-04
202	S.P.Fleming	New Zealand	v	Bangladesh	Chittagong[1]	2004-05
201*	J.Ryder	Australia	v	England	Adelaide	1924-25
201*	D.S.B.P.Kuruppu	Sri Lanka	v	New Zealand	Colombo (CCC)	1986-87
201*	G.W.Flower	Zimbabwe	v	Pakistan	Harare	1994-95
201*	S.R.Tendulkar	India	v	Zimbabwe	Nagpur	2000-01
201*	M.S.Atapattu	Sri Lanka	v	England	Galle	2000-01
201*	J.N.Gillespie	Australia	v	Bangladesh	Chittagong[2]	2005-06
201	E.S.Gregory	Australia	v	England	Sydney	1894-95
201	D.G.Bradman	Australia	v	India	Adelaide	1947-48
201	E.J.Barlow	South Africa	v	Australia	Adelaide	1963-64
201	R.B.Simpson	Australia	v	West Indies	Bridgetown	1964-65
201	S.M.Nurse	West Indies	v	Australia	Bridgetown	1964-65
201	Mushtaq Mohammad	Pakistan	v	New Zealand	Dunedin	1972-73
201	G.S.Chappell	Australia	v	Pakistan	Brisbane[2]	1981-82
201	A.D.Gaekwad	India	v	Pakistan	Jullundur	1983-84
201	G.Fowler	England	v	India	Madras[1]	1984-85
201	N.S.Sidhu	India	v	West Indies	Port-of-Spain	1996-97
201	M.S.Atapattu	Sri Lanka	v	Bangladesh	Colombo (SSC)	2001-02
201	V.K.Sehwag	India	v	Pakistan	Bangalore	2004-05
200*	D.N.Sardesai	India	v	New Zealand	Bombay[2]	1964-65
200*	D.I.Gower	England	v	India	Birmingham	1979
200*	A.R.Border	Australia	v	England	Leeds	1993
200*	Inzamamul Haq	Pakistan	v	Sri Lanka	Dhaka	1998-99
200*	R.S.Dravid	India	v	Zimbabwe	Delhi	2000-01
200*	G.P.Thorpe	England	v	New Zealand	Christchurch	2001-02
200	W.R.Hammond	England	v	Australia	Melbourne	1928-29
200	Mohsin Khan	Pakistan	v	England	Lord's	1982
200	D.C.Boon	Australia	v	New Zealand	Perth	1989-90
200	S.R.Waugh	Australia	v	West Indies	Kingston	1994-95
200	G.C.Smith	South Africa	v	Bangladesh	East London	2002-03

Most scores of 200 & over:

12 D.G.Bradman(A)
8 B.C.Lara(W)
7 W.R.Hammond(E)
6 M.S.Atapattu(SL), Javed Miandad(P)
5 R.S.Dravid(I)
4 G.S.Chappell(A), S.M.Gavaskar(I), C.G.Greenidge(W), L.Hutton(E), R.T.Ponting(A), K.C.Sangakkara(SL), S.R.Tendulkar(I), Zaheer Abbas(P)
3 S.P.Fleming(N), S.T.Jayasuriya(SL), D.P.M.D.Jayawardene(SL), G.Kirsten(SA), J.L.Langer(A), I.V.A.Richards(W), V.K.Sehwag(I), R.B.Simpson(A), G.C.Smith(SA), Yousuf Youhana(P)
2 D.L.Amiss(E), A.R.Border(A), D.C.S.Compton(E), P.A.de Silva(SL), C.H.Gayle(W), H.H.Gibbs(SA), G.A.Gooch(E), D.I.Gower(E), Hanif Mohammad(P), R.N.Harvey(A), M.L.Hayden(A), G.A.Headley(W), Inzamamul Haq(P), D.M.Jones(A), V.G.Kambli(I), R.B.Kanhai(W), W.M.Lawry(A), M.H.Mankad(I), A.D.Nourse(SA), S.M.Nurse(W), E.Paynter(E), R.G.Pollock(SA), Qasim Omar(P), L.G.Rowe(W), D.N.Sardesai(I), Shoaib Mohammad(P), M.S.Sinclair(N), G.S.Sobers(W), M.A.Taylor(A), G.M.Turner(N), K.D.Walters(A), E.D.Weekes(W), F.M.M.Worrell(W)
1 Aamer Sohail(P), J.C.Adams(W), N.J.Astle(N), D.S.Atkinson(W), S.F.A.F.Bacchus(W), E.J.Barlow(SA), S.G.Barnes(A), K.F.Barrington(E), G.S.Blewett(A), D.C.Boon(A), I.T.Botham(E), G.Boycott(E), W.A.Brown(A), B.F.Butcher(W), S.L.Campbell(W), S.Chanderpaul(W), H.L.Collins(A), R.M.Cowper(A), M.D.Crowe(N), D.J.Cullinan(SA), E.R.Dexter(E), M.P.Donnelly(N), G.T.Dowling(N), J.H.Edrich(E), W.J.Edrich(E), G.A.Faulkner(SA), K.W.R.Fletcher(E), A.Flower(Z), G.W.Flower(Z), R.E.Foster(E), G.Fowler(E), A.D.Gaekwad(I), M.W.Gatting(E), A.C.Gilchrist(A), J.N.Gillespie(A), T.W.Graveney(E), E.S.Gregory(A), J.Hardstaff jr(E), E.H.Hendren(E), W.W.Hinds(W), J.B.Hobbs(A), B.J.Hodge(A),

C.L.Hooper(W), D.L.Houghton(Z), K.J.Hughes(A), C.C.Hunte(A), N.Hussain(E), Ijaz Ahmed(P), Imtiaz Ahmed(P), R.W.T.Key(E), D.S.B.P.Kuruppu(SL), V.V.S.Laxman(I), C.H.Lloyd(W), D.Lloyd(I), S.J.McCabe(A), D.J.McGlew(SA), R.S.Mahanama(SL), S.V.Manjrekar(I), P.B.H.May(E), Mohsin Khan(P), A.R.Morris(A), Mudassar Nazar(P), W.L.Murdoch(A), Mushtaq Mohammad(P), Nawab of Pataudi jr(I), W.H.Ponsford(A), C.A.Roach(W), E.A.B.Rowan(W), J.A.Rudolph(SA), J.Ryder(A), Saleem Malik(P), A.Sandham(E), R.R.Sarwan(W), R.J.Shastri(I), N.S.Sidhu(I), M.J.Slater(A), K.R.Stackpole(A), B.Sutcliffe(N), Taslim Arif(P), G.P.Thorpe(E), H.P.Tillakaratne(SL), M.E.Trescothick(E), V.T.Trumper(A), P.R.Umrigar(I), L.Vincent(N), G.R.Viswanath(I), C.L.Walcott(W), Wasim Akram(P), Wasim Jaffer(I), S.R.Waugh(A), G.J.Whittall(Z), G.N.Yallop(A), B.A.Young(N), Younis Khan(P)

MOST CENTURIES IN A SERIES

FIVE				
C.L Walcott	West Indies	v	Australia	1954-55
FOUR				
H.Sutcliffe	England	v	Australia	1924-25
W.R.Hammond	England	v	Australia	1928-29
H.Sutcliffe	England	v	South Africa	1929
G.A.Headley	West Indies	v	England	1929-30
D.G Bradman	Australia	v	England	1930
D.G Bradman	Australia	v	South Africa	1931-32
D.C.S.Compton	England	v	South Africa	1947
D.G Bradman	Australia	v	India	1947-48
E.D.Weekes	West Indies	v	India	1948-49
R.N.Harvey	Australia	v	South Africa	1949-50
R.N.Harvey	Australia	v	South Africa	1952-53
K.D.Walters	Australia	v	West Indies	1968-69
S.M.Gavaskar	India	v	West Indies	1970-71
S.M.Gavaskar	India	v	West Indies	1978-79
Mudassar Nazar	Pakistan	v	India	1982-83
J.H.Kallis	South Africa	v	West Indies	2003-04

MOST DOUBLE CENTURIES IN A SERIES

THREE				
D.G.Bradman	Australia	v	England	1930
TWO				
W.R.Hammond	England	v	Australia	1928-29
D.G.Bradman	Australia	v	South Africa	1931-32
W.R.Hammond	England	v	New Zealand	1932-33
D.G.Bradman	Australia	v	England	1934
D.G.Bradman	Australia	v	England	1936-37
M.H.Mankad	India	v	New Zealand	1955-56
G.M.Turner	New Zealand	v	West Indies	1971-72
I.V.A.Richards	West Indies	v	England	1976
C.G.Greenidge	West Indies	v	England	1984
G.C.Smith	South Africa	v	England	2003
R.T.Ponting	Australia	v	India	2003-04

MOST CENTURIES IN CONSECUTIVE INNINGS

FIVE			Opponents		
E.D.Weekes	West Indies	141	England	Kingston	1947-48
		128	India	Delhi	1948-49
		194	India	Bombay[2]	1948-49
		162)	India	Calcutta	1948-49
		101)			

Weekes was run out for 90 in his next innings (Madras[1] 1948-49).

FOUR			Opponents		
J.H.W.Fingleton	Australia	112	South Africa	Cape Town	1935-36
		108	South Africa	Johannesburg[1]	1935-36
		118	South Africa	Durban[2]	1935-36
		100	England	Brisbane[2]	1936-37
A.Melville	South Africa	103	England	Durban[2]	1938-39
		189)	England	Nottingham	1947
		104*)			
		117	England	Lord's	1947
R.S.Dravid	India	115	England	Nottingham	2002
		148	England	Leeds	2002
		217	England	The Oval	2002
		100#	West Indies	Mumbai[3]	2002-03
THREE			Opponents		
W.Bardsley	Australia	136)	England	The Oval	1909
		130)			
		132	South Africa	Sydney	1910-11
H.Sutcliffe	England	115	Australia	Sydney	1924-25
		176)	Australia	Melbourne	1924-25
		127)			
C.G.Macartney	Australia	133*	England	Lord's	1926
		151	England	Leeds	1926
		109	England	Manchester	1926
G.A.Headley	West Indies	270*	England	Kingston	1934-35
		106)	England	Lord's	1939
		107)			
A.R.Morris	Australia	155	England	Melbourne	1946-47
		122)	England	Adelaide	1946-47
		124*)			
D.C.S.Compton	England	163	South Africa	Nottingham	1947
		208	South Africa	Lord's	1947
		115	South Africa	Manchester	1947
D G Bradman	Australia	132)	India	Melbourne	1947-48
		127*)			
		201	India	Adelaide	1947-48
V.S.Hazare	India	122	West Indies	Bombay[2]	1948-49
		164*	England	Delhi	1951-52
		155	England	Bombay[2]	1951-52
E.D.Weekes	West Indies	123	New Zealand	Dunedin	1955-56
		103	New Zealand	Christchurch	1955-56
		156	New Zealand	Wellington	1955-56
G.S.Sobers	West Indies	365*	Pakistan	Kingston	1957-58
		125)	Pakistan	Georgetown	1957-58
		109*)			
P.R.Umrigar	India	117	Pakistan	Madras[2]	1960-61
		112	Pakistan	Delhi	1960-61
		147*	England	Kanpur	1961-62
G.Boycott	England	119*	Australia	Adelaide	1970-71
		121*	Pakistan	Lord's	1971
		112	Pakistan	Leeds	1971
S.M.Gavaskar	India	117*	West Indies	Bridgetown	1970-71
		124)	West Indies	Port-of-Spain	1970-71
		220)			
C G Greenidge	West Indies	134)	England	Manchester	1976
		101)			
		115	England	Leeds	1976

S.M.Gavaskar		111)	Pakistan	Karachi[1]	1978-79
		137)			
		205	West Indies	Bombay[3]	1978-79
Mudassar Nazar	Pakistan	231	India	Hyderabad	1982-83
		152*	India	Lahore[2]	1982-83
		152	India	Karachi[1]	1982-83
Zaheer Abbas	Pakistan	215	India	Lahore[2]	1982-83
		186	India	Karachi[1]	1982-83
		168	India	Faisalabad	1982-83
D.L.Haynes	West Indies	109	England	Bridgetown	1989-90
		167	England	St.Johns	1989-90
		117	Pakistan	Karachi[1]	1990-91
G.A.Gooch	England	333)	India	Lord's	1990
		123)			
		116	India	Manchester	1990
A.H.Jones	New Zealand	186	Sri Lanka	Wellington	1990-91
		122)	Sri Lanka	Hamilton	1990-91
		100*)			
V.G.Kambli	India	224	England	Bombay[3]	1992-93
		227	Zimbabwe	Delhi	1992-93
		125	Sri Lanka	Colombo (SSC)	1993-94
P.A.de Silva	Sri Lanka	168	Pakistan	Colombo (RPS)	1996-97
		138*)	Pakistan	Colombo (SSC)	1996-97
		103*)			
P.A.de Silva	Sri Lanka	125	India	Colombo (RPS)	1997-98
		146)	India	Colombo (SSC)	1997-98
		120)			
A.C.Gilchrist	Australia	113	Pakistan	Sydney	2004-05
		121	New Zealand	Christchurch	2004-05
		162	New Zealand	Wellington	2004-05

CARRYING BAT THROUGH A COMPLETED INNINGS

(§ on Test debut. # one or more batsmen absent or retired hurt)

AUSTRALIA	Score	Total	Opponents		
J.E.Barrett	67*	176 §	England	Lord's	1890
W.W.Armstrong	159*	309	South Africa	Johannesburg[1]	1902-03
W.Bardsley	193*	383	England	Lord's	1926
W.M.Woodfull	30*	66#	England	Brisbane[1]	1928-29
W.M.Woodfull	73*	193#	England	Adelaide	1932-33
W.A.Brown	206*	422	England	Lord's	1938
W.M.Lawry	49*	107	India	Delhi	1969-70
W.M.Lawry	60*	116#	England	Sydney	1970-71
I.R.Redpath	159*	346	New Zealand	Auckland	1973-74
D.C.Boon	58*	103	New Zealand	Auckland	1985-86
M.A.Taylor	169*	350	South Africa	Adelaide	1997-98

ENGLAND	Score	Total	Opponents		
R.Abel	132*	307	Australia	Sydney	1891-92
P.F.Warner	132*	237 §	South Africa	Johannesburg[1]	1898-99
L.Hutton	202*	344	West Indies	The Oval	1950
L.Hutton	156*	272	Australia	Adelaide	1950-51
G.Boycott	99*	215	Australia	Perth	1979-80
G.A.Gooch	154*	252	West Indies	Leeds	1991
A.J.Stewart	69*	175	Pakistan	Lord's	1992
M.A.Atherton	94*	228	New Zealand	Christchurch	1996-97

SOUTH AFRICA	Score	Total	Opponents		
A.B.Tancred	26*	47	England	Cape Town	1888-89
J.W.Zulch	43*	103	England	Cape Town	1909-10
T.L.Goddard	56*	99	Australia	Cape Town	1957-58
D.J.McGlew	127*	292	New Zealand	Durban[2]	1961-62
G.Kirsten	100*	239	Pakistan	Faisalabad	1997-98

WEST INDIES	Score	Total	Opponents		
F.M.M.Worrell	191*	372	England	Nottingham	1957
C.C.Hunte	60*	131	Australia	Port-of-Spain	1964-65
D.L.Haynes	88*	211	Pakistan	Karachi[1]	1986-87
D.L.Haynes	75*	176	England	The Oval	1991
D.L.Haynes	143*	382	Pakistan	Port-of-Spain	1992-93

NEW ZEALAND	Score	Total	Opponents		
G.M.Turner	43*	131	England	Lord's	1969
G.M.Turner	223*	386	West Indies	Kingston	1971-72

INDIA	Score	Total	Opponents		
S.M.Gavaskar	127*	286	Pakistan	Faisalabad	1982-83

PAKISTAN	Score	Total	Opponents		
Nazar Mohammad	124*	331	India	Lucknow[1]	1952-53
Mudassar Nazar	152*	323	India	Lahore[2]	1982-83
Saeed Anwar	188*	316	India	Calcutta	1998-99

SRI LANKA	Score	Total	Opponents		
S.Wettimuny	63*	144	New Zealand	Christchurch	1982-83
M.S.Atapattu	216*	428	Zimbabwe	Bulawayo[2]	1999-2000
R.P.Arnold	104*	231	Zimbabwe	Harare	1999-2000

ZIMBABWE	Score	Total	Opponents		
M.H.Dekker	68*	187	Pakistan	Rawalpindi[2]	1993-94
G.W.Flower	156*	321	Pakistan	Bulawayo[2]	1997-98

BANGLADESH	Score	Total	Opponents		
Javed Omar	85*	168#§	Zimbabwe	Bulawayo[2]	2000-01

CENTURY IN EACH INNINGS OF A MATCH *(† last Test)*

AUSTRALIA			Opponents		
W.Bardsley	136	130	England	The Oval	1909
A.R.Morris	122	124*	England	Adelaide	1946-47
D.G.Bradman	132	127*	India	Melbourne	1947-48
J.Moroney	118	101*	South Africa	Johannesburg[2]	1949-50
R.B.Simpson	153	115	Pakistan	Karachi[1]	1964-65
K.D.Walters	242	103	West Indies	Sydney	1968-69
I.M.Chappell	145	121	New Zealand	Wellington	1973-74
G.S.Chappell	247*	133	New Zealand	Wellington	1973-74
G.S.Chappell	123	109*	West Indies	Brisbane[2]	1975-76
A.R.Border	150*	153	Pakistan	Lahore[2]	1979-80
A.R.Border	140	114*	New Zealand	Christchurch	1985-86
D.M.Jones	116	121*	Pakistan	Adelaide	1989-90
S.R.Waugh	108	116	England	Manchester	1997
M.L.Hayden	197	103	England	Brisbane[2]	2002-03
M.L.Hayden	117	132	Sri Lanka	Cairns	2004-05
R.T.Ponting	149	104*	West Indies	Brisbane[2]	2005-06

R.T.Ponting	120	143*	South Africa	Sydney	2005-06
R.T.Ponting	103	116	South Africa	Durban[2]	2005-06
ENGLAND			Opponents		
C.A.G.Russell †	140	111	South Africa	Durban[2]	1922-23
H.Sutcliffe	176	127	Australia	Melbourne	1924-25
W.R.Hammond	119*	177	Australia	Adelaide	1928-29
H.Sutcliffe	104	109*	South Africa	The Oval	1929
E.Paynter	117	100	South Africa	Johannesburg[1]	1938-39
D.C.S.Compton	147	103*	Australia	Adelaide	1946-47
G.A.Gooch	333	123	India	Lord's	1990
A.J.Stewart	118	143	West Indies	Bridgetown	1993-94
M.P.Vaughan	103	101*	West Indies	Lord's	2004
M.E.Trescothick	105	107	West Indies	Birmingham	2004
SOUTH AFRICA			Opponents		
A.Melville	189	104*	England	Nottingham	1947
B.Mitchell	120	189*	England	The Oval	1947
G.Kirsten	102	133	India	Calcutta	1996-97
WEST INDIES			Opponents		
G.A.Headley	114	112	England	Georgetown	1929-30
G.A.Headley	106	107	England	Lord's	1939
E.D.Weekes	162	101	India	Calcutta	1948-49
C.L.Walcott	126	110	Australia	Port-of-Spain	1954-55
C.L.Walcott	155	110	Australia	Kingston	1954-55
G.S.Sobers	125	109*	Pakistan	Georgetown	1957-58
R.B.Kanhai	117	115	Australia	Adelaide	1960-61
L.G.Rowe	214	100*	New Zealand	Kingston	1971-72
C.G.Greenidge	134	101	England	Manchester	1976
B.C.Lara	221	130	Sri Lanka	Colombo (SSC)	2001-02
NEW ZEALAND			Opponents		
G.M.Turner	101	110*	Australia	Christchurch	1973-74
G.P.Howarth	122	102	England	Auckland	1977-78
A.H.Jones	122	100*	Sri Lanka	Hamilton	1990-91
INDIA			Opponents		
V.S.Hazare	116	145	Australia	Adelaide	1947-48
S.M.Gavaskar	124	220	West Indies	Port-of-Spain	1970-71
S.M.Gavaskar	111	137	Pakistan	Karachi[1]	1978-79
S.M.Gavaskar	107	182*	West Indies	Calcutta	1978-79
R.S.Dravid	190	103*	New Zealand	Wellington	1998-99
R.S.Dravid	110	135	New Zealand	Kolkata	2004-05
PAKISTAN			Opponents		
Hanif Mohammad	111	104	England	Dacca	1961-62
Javed Miandad	104	103*	New Zealand	Hyderabad	1984-85
Wajahatullah Wasti	133	121*	Sri Lanka	Lahore[2]	1998-99
Yasir Hameed	170	105	Bangladesh	Karachi[1]	2003-04
Inzamamul Haq	109	100*	England	Faisalabad	2005-06
SRI LANKA			Opponents		
L.R.D.Mendis	105	105	India	Madras[1]	1982-83
A.P.Gurusinha	119	102	New Zealand	Hamilton	1990-91
P.A.de Silva	138*	103*	Pakistan	Colombo (SSC)	1996-97
P.A.de Silva	146	120	India	Colombo (SSC)	1997-98

ZIMBABWE			Opponents		
G.W.Flower	104	151	New Zealand	Harare	1997-98
A.Flower	142	199*	South Africa	Harare	2001-02

CENTURY AND A NINETY IN A MATCH *(§ In first Test. † in last Test)*

AUSTRALIA			Opponents		
R.M.Cowper	92	108	India	Adelaide	1967-68
P.M.Toohey	122	97	West Indies	Kingston	1977-78
A.R.Border	98*	100*	West Indies	Port-of-Spain	1983-84
M.A.Taylor	334*	92	Pakistan	Peshawar[2]	1998-99
D.R.Martyn	114	97	India	Nagpur	2004-05
J.L.Langer	191	97	Pakistan	Perth	2004-05
ENGLAND			Opponents		
P.A.Gibb §	93	106	South Africa	Johannesburg[1]	1938-39
M.C.Cowdrey	114	97	West Indies	Kingston	1959-60
K.F.Barrington	101	94	Australia	Sydney	1962-63
A.P.E.Knott	101	96	New Zealand	Auckland	1970-71
G.Boycott	99	112	West Indies	Port-of-Spain	1973-74
M.A.Atherton	94*	118	New Zealand	Christchurch	1996-97
A.J.Strauss	126	94*	South Africa	Port Elizabeth	2004-05
SOUTH AFRICA			Opponents		
P.G.V.van der Bijl †	125	97	England	Durban[2]	1938-39
J.H.Kallis	92	150*	New Zealand	Hamilton	2003-04
H.H.Gibbs	161	98	England	Johannesburg[3]	2004-05
A.B.de Villiers	92	109	England	Centurion	2004-05
WEST INDIES			Opponents		
G.S.Sobers	152	92*	England	Georgetown	1967-68
S.M.Nurse	95	168	New Zealand	Auckland	1968-69
C.G.Greenidge §	93	107	India	Bangalore	1974-75
B.C.Lara	91	122	Australia	Port-of-Spain	2002-03
S.Chanderpaul	128*	97*	England	Lord's	2004
S.Chanderpaul	92	153*	Pakistan	Bridgetown	2004-05
NEW ZEALAND			Opponents		
M.H.Richardson	93	101	England	Lord's	2004
INDIA			Opponents		
C.G.Borde	109	96	West Indies	Delhi	1958-59
M.Amarnath	90	100	Australia	Perth	1977-78
PAKISTAN			Opponents		
Hanif Mohammad	104	93	Australia	Melbourne	1964-65
Zaheer Abbas	176	96	India	Faisalabad	1978-79
Mohsin Khan	94	101*	India	Lahore[2]	1982-83
Saeed Anwar	94	136	Sri Lanka	Colombo (PSS)	1993-94
SRI LANKA			Opponents		
L.R.D.Mendis	111	94	England	Lord's	1984
P.A.de Silva	96	123	New Zealand	Auckland	1990-91

NINETY IN EACH INNINGS OF A MATCH

AUSTRALIA			Opponents		
C.Hill	98	97	England	Adelaide	1901-02
ENGLAND			Opponents		
F.E.Woolley	95	93	Australia	Lord's	1921
WEST INDIES			Opponents		
C.G.Greenidge	91	96	Pakistan	Georgetown	1976-77
C.G.Greenidge	91	97	New Zealand	Christchurch	1979-80

HIGHEST MAIDEN TEST CENTURY

365*	G.S.Sobers	West Indies	v	Pakistan	Kingston	1957-58
311	R.B.Simpson	Australia	v	England	Manchester	1964
287	R.E.Foster	England	v	Australia	Sydney	1903-04
277	B.C.Lara	West Indies	v	Australia	Sydney	1992-93
274	Zaheer Abbas	Pakistan	v	England	Birmingham	1971
256	R.B.Kanhai	West Indies	v	India	Calcutta	1958-59
255*	D.J.McGlew	South Africa	v	New Zealand	Wellington	1952-53
251	W.R.Hammond	England	v	Australia	Sydney	1928-29
250	S.F.A.F.Bacchus	West Indies	v	India	Kanpur	1978-79
234	S.G.Barnes	Australia	v	England	Sydney	1946-47
231	A.D.Nourse	South Africa	v	Australia	Johannesburg[1]	1935-36
224	V.G.Kambli	India	v	England	Bombay[3]	1992-93
222*	J.A.Rudolph	South Africa	v	Bangladesh	Chittagong[1]	2002-03
221	R.W.T.Key	England	v	West Indies	Lord's	2004
219	W.J.Edrich	England	v	South Africa	Durban[2]	1938-39
219	D.S.Atkinson	West Indies	v	Australia	Bridgetown	1954-55
216*	E.Paynter	England	v	Australia	Nottingham	1938
214*	D.Lloyd	England	v	India	Birmingham	1974
214	L.G.Rowe	West Indies	v	New Zealand	Kingston	1971-72
214	M.S.Sinclair	New Zealand	v	West Indies	Wellington	1999-2000
211*	H.H.Gibbs	South Africa	v	New Zealand	Christchurch	1998-99
210*	Taslim Arif	Pakistan	v	Australia	Faisalabad	1979-80
210	D.M.Jones	Australia	v	India	Madras[1]	1986-87
209	Imtiaz Ahmed	Pakistan	v	New Zealand	Lahore[2]	1955-56
208	S.L.Campbell	West Indies	v	New Zealand	Bridgetown	1995-96
206	M.P.Donnelly	New Zealand	v	England	Lord's	1949
205	Aamer Sohail	Pakistan	v	England	Manchester	1992
203*	B.J.Hodge	Australia	v	South Africa	Perth	2005-06
201*	D.S.B.P.Kuruppu	Sri Lanka	v	New Zealand	Colombo (CCC)	1986-87
201*	G.W.Flower	Sri Lanka	v	Pakistan	Harare	1994-95
201*	J.N.Gillespie †	Australia	v	Bangladesh	Chittagong[2]	2005-06
201	E.S.Gregory	Australia	v	England	Sydney	1894-95
201	S.M.Nurse	West Indies	v	Australia	Bridgetown	1964-65
200*	D.N.Sardesai	India	v	New Zealand	Bombay[2]	1964-65
200	G.C.Smith	South Africa	v	Bangladesh	East London	2002-03

Note: Kanhai (217 v Pakistan, Lahore[1], 1958-59); Kambli (227 v Zimbabwe, Delhi, 1992-93); and Zaheer Abbas (240 v England, The Oval, 1974) also scored a double century as their 2nd hundred. † Gillespie scored his double century as a 'night watchman'.

MAIDEN FIRST-CLASS CENTURY IN A TEST MATCH

C.Bannerman § †	165*	Australia	v	England	Melbourne	1876-77
W.L.Murdoch	153*	Australia	v	England	The Oval	1880
P.S.McDonnell	147	Australia	v	England	Sydney	1881-82
H.Wood †	134*	England	v	South Africa	Cape Town	1891-92
H.Graham § ¶	107	Australia	v	England	Lord's	1893

A.J.L.Hill	124	England	v	South Africa	Cape Town	1895-96
J.H.Sinclair	106	South Africa	v	England	Cape Town	1898-99
P.W.Sherwell	115	South Africa	v	England	Lord's	1907
H.G.Owen-Smith	129	South Africa	v	England	Leeds	1929
C.A.Roach ¶	122	West Indies	v	England	Bridgetown	1929-30
S.C.Griffith §	140	England	v	West Indies	Port-of-Spain	1947-48
V.L.Manjrekar	133	India	v	England	Leeds	1952
C.C.Depeiza †	122	West Indies	v	Australia	Bridgetown	1954-55
P.L.Winslow	108	South Africa	v	England	Manchester	1955
S.N.McGregor	111	New Zealand	v	Pakistan	Lahore[1]	1955-56
F.C.M.Alexander †	108	West Indies	v	Australia	Sydney	1960-61
Nasim-ul-Ghani	101	Pakistan	v	England	Lord's	1962
B.R.Taylor § ¶	105	New Zealand	v	India	Calcutta	1964-65
B.D.Julien	121	West Indies	v	England	Lord's	1973
W.K.Lees	152	New Zealand	v	Pakistan	Karachi[1]	1976-77
Kapil Dev	126*	India	v	West Indies	Delhi	1978-79
S.Wettimuny	157	Sri Lanka	v	Pakistan	Faisalabad	1981-82
S.A.R.Silva	102*	Sri Lanka	v	England	Lord's	1984
D.S.B.P.Kuruppu §	201*	Sri Lanka	v	New Zealand	Colombo (CCC)	1986-87
R.C.Russell	128*	England	v	Australia	Manchester	1989
I.A.Healy ¢	102*	Australia	v	England	Manchester	1993
Azhar Mahmood §	128*	Pakistan	v	South Africa	Rawalpindi[2]	1997-98
Saqlain Mushtaq †	101*	Pakistan	v	New Zealand	Christchurch	2000-01
A.Ratra †	115*	India	v	West Indies	St John's	2001-02
M.N.Samuels	104	West Indies	v	India	Kolkata	2002-03
Mohammad Rafique †	111	Bangladesh	v	West Indies	Gros Islet	2003-04
Shahriar Nafees †	138	Bangladesh	v	Australia	Fatullah	2005-06
J.N.Gillespie †	201*	Australia	v	Bangladesh	Chittagong[2]	2005-06

§ On Test debut. † Only first-class century. ¶ H.Graham (105 v England, Sydney, 1894-95), C.A.Roach (209 v England, Georgetown, 1929-30) and B.R.Taylor (124 v West Indies, Auckland, 1968-69) also scored their 2nd first-class century in a Test match. ¢ I.A.Healy (113 v New Zealand, Perth, 1993-94, 161* v West Indies, Brisbane[2], 1996-97 & 134 v England, Brisbane[2] 1998-99) scored his only 4 first-class centuries in Test matches.*

HUNDRED IN LAST TEST MATCH

H.Wood	134*	-	England	v	South Africa	Cape Town	1891-92
A.J.L.Hill	124	-	England	v	South Africa	Cape Town	1895-96
R.A.Duff	146	-	Australia	v	England	The Oval	1905
J.Sharp	105	0*	England	v	Australia	The Oval	1909
C.A.G.Russell	140	111	England	v	South Africa	Durban	1922-23
G.B.Legge	196	0	England	v	New Zealand	Auckland	1929-30
A.Sandham	325	50	England	v	West Indies	Kingston	1929-30
F.R.Martin	123*	20	West Indies	v	Australia	Sydney	1930-31
W.H.Ponsford	266	22	Australia	v	England	The Oval	1934
M.Leyland	187	-	England	v	Australia	The Oval	1938
P.G.V.van der Bijl	125	97	South Africa	v	England	Durban[2]	1938-39
K.H.Weekes	137	-	West Indies	v	England	The Oval	1939
A.G.Ganteaume #	112	-	West Indies	v	England	Port-of-Spain	1947-48
W.Place	8	107	England	v	West Indies	Kingston	1947-48
V.M.Merchant	154	-	India	v	England	Delhi	1951-52
R.Subba Row	12	137	England	v	Australia	The Oval	1961
V.L.Manjrekar	19	102*	India	v	New Zealand	Madras[2]	1964-65
C.Milburn	139	-	England	v	Pakistan	Karachi[1]	1968-69
S.M.Nurse	258	-	West Indies	v	New Zealand	Christchurch	1968-69
B.A.Richards	81	126	South Africa	v	Australia	Port Elizabeth	1969-70
B.L.Irvine	25	102	South Africa	v	Australia	Port Elizabeth	1969-70
R.E.Redmond #	107	56	New Zealand	v	Pakistan	Auckland	1972-73
I.R.Redpath	101	70	Australia	v	West Indies	Melbourne	1975-76

G.S.Chappell	182	-	Australia	v	Pakistan	Sydney	1983-84
M.Azharuddin	9	102	India	v	South Africa	Bangalore	1999-2000
M.W.Goodwin	148*	1*	Zimbabwe	v	England	Nottingham	2000
Saeed Anwar	101	-	Pakistan	v	Bangladesh	Multan[2]	2001-02
P.A.de Silva	206	-	Sri Lanka	v	Bangladesh	Colombo (PSS)	2002-03
M.L.Love	100*	-	Australia	v	Bangladesh	Cairns	2003-04
N.Hussain	34	103*	England	v	New Zealand	Lord's	2004
Shoaib Malik †	13	148*	Pakistan	v	Sri Lanka	Colombo (SSC)	2005-06
J.N.Gillespie †	201*	-	Australia	v	Bangladesh	Chittagong[2]	2005-06
M.E.K.Hussey †	182	-	Australia	v	Bangladesh	Chittagong[2]	2005-06
D.P.M.D.Jayawardene †	13	123	Sri Lanka	v	South Africa	Colombo(PSS)	2006-07
Yousuf Youhana †	128	-	Pakistan	v	England	The Oval	2006

 # Only Test. † Current players.

YOUNGEST PLAYERS TO SCORE A CENTURY

Years	Days							
16	364	Mohammad Ashraful	114	Bangladesh	v	Sri Lanka	Colombo (SSC)	2001-02
17	82	Mushtaq Mohammad	101	Pakistan	v	India	Delhi	1960-61
17	112	S.R.Tendulkar	119*	India	v	England	Manchester	1990
17	354	H.Masakadza	119	Zimbabwe	v	West Indies	Harare	2001-02
18	156	Imran Nazir	131	Pakistan	v	West Indies	Bridgetown	1999-2000
18	251	Mushtaq Mohammad	100*	Pakistan	v	England	Nottingham	1962
18	256	S.R.Tendulkar	148*	India	v	Australia	Sydney	1991-92
18	285	S.R.Tendulkar	114	India	v	Australia	Perth	1991-92
18	328	Saleem Malik	100*	Pakistan	v	Sri Lanka	Karachi[1]	1981-82
18	335	Shahid Afridi	141	Pakistan	v	India	Chennai[1]	1998-99
19	26	Mohammad Ilyas	126	Pakistan	v	New Zealand	Karachi[1]	1964-65
19	108	Mohammad Wasim	109*	Pakistan	v	New Zealand	Lahore[2]	1996-97
19	119	Javed Miandad	163	Pakistan	v	New Zealand	Lahore[2]	1976-77
19	121	H.G.Vivian	100	New Zealand	v	South Africa	Wellington	1931-32
19	121	R.N.Harvey	153	Australia	v	India	Melbourne	1947-48
19	140	Javed Miandad	206	Pakistan	v	New Zealand	Karachi[1]	1976-77
19	152	A.Jackson	164	Australia	v	England	Adelaide	1928-29
19	192	A.P.Gurusinha	116*	Sri Lanka	v	Pakistan	Colombo (PSS)	1985-86
19	218	S.R.Tendulkar	111	India	v	South Africa	Johannesburg[3]	1992-93
19	264	Saleem Malik	107	Pakistan	v	India	Faisalabad	1982-83
19	290	R.N.Harvey	112	Australia	v	England	Leeds	1948
19	294	S.R.Tendulkar	165	India	v	England	Madras[1]	1992-93
19	318	R.G.Pollock	122	South Africa	v	Australia	Sydney	1963-64
19	332	R.G.Pollock	175	South Africa	v	Australia	Adelaide	1963-64
19	353	Nafis Iqbal	121	Bangladesh	v	Zimbabwe	Dhaka	2004-05
19	357	K.D.Walters	155	Australia	v	England	Brisbane[2]	1965-66
20	1	P.A.de Silva	122	Sri Lanka	v	Pakistan	Faisalabad	1985-86
20	3	Ijaz Ahmed	122	Pakistan	v	Australia	Faisalabad	1988-89
20	14	K.D.Walters	115	Australia	v	England	Melbourne	1965-66
20	19	D.C.S.Compton	102	England	v	Australia	Nottingham	1938
20	21	Kapil Dev	126*	India	v	West Indies	Delhi	1978-79
20	23	P.A.de Silva	105	Sri Lanka	v	Pakistan	Karachi[1]	1985-86
20	58	Hanif Mohammad	142	Pakistan	v	India	Bahawalpur	1954-55
20	70	Taufeeq Umar	104	Pakistan	v	Bangladesh	Multan[2]	2001-02
20	87	Salman Butt	108	Pakistan	v	Australia	Sydney	2004-05
20	96	S.R.Tendulkar	104*	India	v	Sri Lanka	Colombo (SSC)	1993-94
20	99	Mohammad Ashraful	158*	Bangladesh	v	India	Chittagong[1]	2004-05
20	105	Shahriar Nafees	138	Bangladesh	v	Australia	Fatullah	2005-06
20	129	D.G.Bradman	112	Australia	v	England	Melbourne	1928-29
20	131	A.A.Baig	112	India	v	England	Manchester	1959

20	136	Imran Nazir	127	Pakistan	v	New Zealand	Lahore[2]	2001-02
20	141	M.L.Apte	163*	India	v	West Indies	Port-of-Spain	1952-53
20	148	H.G.Owen-Smith	129	South Africa	v	England	Leeds	1929
20	150	A.Ratra	115*	India	v	West Indies	St John's	2001-02
20	154	Saeed Ahmed	150	Pakistan	v	West Indies	Georgetown	1957-58
20	197	D.G.Bradman	123	Australia	v	England	Melbourne	1928-29
20	201	Ali Naqvi	115	Pakistan	v	South Africa	Rawalpindi[2]	1997-98
20	227	Mohammad Wasim	192	Pakistan	v	Zimbabwe	Harare	1997-98
20	230	G.A.Headley	176	West Indies	v	England	Bridgetown	1929-30
20	240	J.W.Burke	101*	Australia	v	England	Adelaide	1950-51
20	249	R.J.Shastri	128	India	v	Pakistan	Karachi[1]	1982-83
20	253	V.L.Manjrekar	133	India	v	England	Leeds	1952
20	268	G.A.Headley	114	West Indies	v	England	Georgetown	1929-30
20	269	D.R.Smith	105*	West Indies	v	South Africa	Cape Town	2003-04
20	271	G.A.Headley	112	West Indies	v	England	Georgetown	1929-30
20	271	S.R.Tendulkar	142	India	v	Sri Lanka	Lucknow[2]	1993-94
20	281	G.R.Viswanath	137	India	v	Australia	Kanpur	1969-70
20	314	G.A.Headley	223	West Indies	v	England	Kingston	1929-30
20	317	C.Hill	188	Australia	v	England	Melbourne	1897-98
20	324	J.W.Hearne	114	England	v	Australia	Melbourne	1911-12
20	325	Hanif Mohammad	102	Pakistan	v	New Zealand	Dacca	1955-56
20	332	Saleem Malik	116	Pakistan	v	England	Faislabad	1984-85
20	337	R.J.Shastri	102	India	v	West Indies	St John's	1982-83
20	343	A.B.de Villiers	136*	South Africa	v	England	Centurion	2004-05
20	351	R.G.Pollock	137	South Africa	v	England	Port Elizabeth	1964-65

YOUNGEST PLAYERS TO SCORE A DOUBLE CENTURY

Years	Days							
19	141	Javed Miandad	206	Pakistan	v	New Zealand	Karachi[1]	1976-77
20	315	G.A.Headley	223	West Indies	v	England	Kingston	1929-30
21	33	V.G.Kambli	224	India	v	England	Bombay[3]	1992-93
21	54	V.G.Kambli	227	India	v	Zimbabwe	Delhi	1992-93
21	216	G.S.Sobers	365*	West Indies	v	Pakistan	Kingston	1957-58
21	259	G.C.Smith	200	South Africa	v	Bangladesh	East London	2002-03
21	277	D.P.M.D.Jayawardene	242	Sri Lanka	v	India	Colombo (SSC)	1998-99
21	282	S.M.Gavaskar	220	India	v	West Indies	Port-of-Spain	1970-71
21	307	D.G.Bradman	254	Australia	v	England	Lord's	1930
21	318	D.G.Bradman	334	Australia	v	England	Leeds	1930
21	355	D.G.Bradman	232	Australia	v	England	The Oval	1930

YOUNGEST PLAYERS TO SCORE A TRIPLE CENTURY

Years	Days							
21	216	G.S.Sobers	365*	West Indies	v	Pakistan	Kingston	1957-58
21	318	D.G.Bradman	334	Australia	v	England	Leeds	1930

OLDEST PLAYERS TO SCORE A CENTURY

Years	Days							
46	82	J.B.Hobbs	142	England	v	Australia	Melbourne	1928-29
45	241	J.B.Hobbs	159	England	v	West Indies	The Oval	1928
45	151	E.H.Hendren	132	England	v	Australia	Manchester	1934
43	294	A.W.Nourse	111	South Africa	v	Australia	Johannesburg[1]	1921-22
43	244	J.B.Hobbs	100	England	v	Australia	The Oval	1926
43	201	W.Bardsley	193*	Australia	v	England	Lord's	1926
43	194	J.B.Hobbs	119	England	v	Australia	Lord's	1926
42	61	F.E.Woolley	154	England	v	South Africa	Manchester	1929
42	35	J.B.Hobbs	119	England	v	Australia	Adelaide	1924-25

42	18	J.B.Hobbs	154	England	v	Australia	Melbourne	1924-25
42	6	J.B.Hobbs	115	England	v	Australia	Sydney	1924-25
42	6	E.A.B.Rowan	236	South Africa	v	England	Leeds	1951
41	360	R.B.Simpson	100	Australia	v	India	Adelaide	1977-78
41	318	R.B.Simpson	176	Australia	v	India	Perth	1977-78
41	266	W.W.Armstrong	123*	Australia	v	England	Melbourne	1920-21
41	264	T.W.Graveney	105	England	v	Pakistan	Karachi[1]	1968-69
41	242	H.W.Taylor	117	South Africa	v	England	Cape Town	1930-31
41	241	W.W.Armstrong	121	Australia	v	England	Adelaide	1920-21
41	213	W.W.Armstrong	158	Australia	v	England	Sydney	1920-21
41	197	J.B.Hobbs	211	England	v	South Africa	Lord's	1924
41	109	B.Sutcliffe	151*	New Zealand	v	India	Calcutta	1964-65
41	64	G.Boycott	105	England	v	India	Delhi	1981-82
41	21	E.H.Hendren	123	England	v	West Indies	Georgetown	1929-30
40	364	E.H.Hendren	205*	England	v	West Indies	Port-of-Spain	1929-30
40	315	G.A.Gooch	210	England	v	New Zealand	Nottingham	1994
40	312	G.Boycott	137	England	v	Australia	The Oval	1981
40	218	T.W.Graveney	118	England	v	West Indies	Port-of-Spain	1967-68
40	208	A.D.Nourse	208	South Africa	v	England	Nottingham	1951
40	184	E.A.B.Rowan	143	South Africa	v	Australia	Durban[2]	1949-50
40	162	G.Boycott	104*	England	v	West Indies	St John's	1980-81
40	105	H.W.Taylor	121	South Africa	v	England	The Oval	1929
40	85	C.H.Lloyd	114	West Indies	v	Australia	Brisbane[2]	1984-85
40	76	A.L.Hassett	115	Australia	v	England	Nottingham	1953
40	29	C.G.Macartney	109	Australia	v	England	Manchester	1926
40	22	V.J.Merchant	154	India	v	England	Delhi	1951-52
40	13	C.G.Macartney	151	Australia	v	England	Leeds	1926
40	8	T.W.Graveney	151	England	v	India	Lord's	1967
40	2	C.G.Macartney	133*	Australia	v	England	Lord's	1926

OLDEST PLAYERS TO SCORE A DOUBLE CENTURY

Years	Days							
42	7	E.A.B.Rowan	236	South Africa	v	England	Leeds	1951
41	197	J.B.Hobbs	211	England	v	South Africa	Lord's	1924
41	0	E.H.Hendren	205*	England	v	West Indies	Port-of-Spain	1929-30
40	316	G.A.Gooch	210	England	v	New Zealand	Nottingham	1994
40	208	A.D.Nourse	208	South Africa	v	England	Nottingham	1951
39	355	C.G.Greenidge	226	West Indies	v	Australia	Bridgetown	1990-91
39	349	A.Sandham	325	England	v	West Indies	Kingston	1929-30
39	149	D.G.Bradman	201	Australia	v	India	Adelaide	1947-48
38	270	M.H.Mankad	231	India	v	New Zealand	Madras[2]	1955-56
38	233	M.V.Mankad	223	India	v	New Zealand	Bombay[2]	1955-56
38	112	D.G.Bradman	234	Australia	v	England	Sydney	1946-47

OLDEST PLAYERS TO SCORE A MAIDEN CENTURY

Years	Days							
43	294	A.W.Nourse	111	South Africa	v	Australia	Johannesburg[1]	1921-22
39	256	E.H.Bowley	109	England	v	New Zealand	Auckland	1929-30
39	191	A.Sandham	152	England	v	West Indies	Bridgetown	1929-30
39	173	J.W.H.Makepeace	117	England	v	Australia	Melbourne	1920-21
39	163	E.A.B.Rowan	156*	South Africa	v	England	Johannesburg[2]	1948-49
39	84	P.N.Kirsten	104	South Africa	v	England	Leeds	1994
38	324	G.E.Tyldesley	122	England	v	South Africa	Johannesburg[1]	1927-28
38	98	H.Wood	134*	England	v	South Africa	Cape Town	1891-92
37	353	A.J.Richardson	100	Australia	v	England	Leeds	1926
37	308	P.L.Symcox	108	South Africa	v	Pakistan	Johannesburg[3]	1997-98

37	253	G.M.Carew	107	West Indies	v	England	Port-of-Spain	1947-48
37	138	F.R.Martin	123*	West Indies	v	Australia	Sydney	1930-31
37	22	R.Illingworth	113	England	v	West Indies	Lord's	1969
36	218	E.Paynter	216*	England	v	Australia	Nottingham	1938
35	262	G.Giffen	161	Australia	v	England	Sydney	1894-95
35	248	B.L.D'Oliveira	109	England	v	India	Leeds	1967
35	239	D.Denton	104	England	v	South Africa	Johannesburg[1]	1909-10
35	157	E.H.Hendren	132	England	v	South Africa	Leeds	1924
35	118	D.L.Houghton	121	Zimbabwe	v	India	Harare	1992-93
32	111	D.J.Richardson	111	South Africa	v	New Zealand	Cape Town	1994-95

DISTRIBUTION OF TEST MATCH CENTURIES

Conceded					Scored For						Total
By	A	E	SA	WI	NZ	I	P	SL	Z	B	Conceded
Australia	0	217	46	95	27	51	46	11	1	1	495
England	267	0	84	117	47	74	52	16	2	0	659
South Africa	87	108	0	18	14	12	8	11	2	0	260
West Indies	102	111	30	0	24	72	33	5	6	3	386
New Zealand	48	91	29	34	0	36	48	15	6	0	307
India	71	86	15	96	27	0	61	25	6	2	389
Pakistan	62	64	7	29	26	45	0	25	9	2	269
Sri Lanka	26	19	12	6	17	32	26	0	4	2	144
Zimbabwe	5	7	9	4	14	14	7	19	0	2	81
Bangladesh	9	5	7	5	4	3	12	8	6	0	59
Total Scored	677	708	239	404	200	339	293	135	42	12	3049

CENTURIES IN TEST CRICKET

§ Denotes century on first appearance against that country. Where known I have shown the batting time, balls faced and boundary details of the complete innings. The following abbreviations are used: m minutes; h minutes where time has been converted from hours e.g. 4¾ hours converts to 285h; a about; n nearly; > more than; ≥ just over; < less than; ≤ just under; Δ indicates that the ball was hit over the boundary but the match was played in Australia at a time when such hits were awarded only five runs, the ball having to be hit clear out of the ground for a six. Such sixes are indicated thus: !. The majority of this information was supplied by Dr Colin Clowes.

AUSTRALIA (677)			Time	Balls	6/4	Opponents		
Archer,RG	(1)	128	213m		2/19	West Indies	Kingston	1954-55
Armstrong,WW	(6)	159*			-/16	South Africa	Johannesburg[1]	1902-03
		133*	289m		2!/14	England	Melbourne	1907-08
		132	208m		-/13	South Africa	Melbourne	1910-11
		158	205m	209	-/17	England	Sydney	1920-21
		121	206m		-/11	England	Adelaide	1920-21
		123*	214m		-/9	England	Melbourne	1920-21
Badcock,CL	(1)	118	205m		-/15	England	Melbourne	1936-37
Bannerman,C	(1)	165* §	285h		-/18	England	Melbourne	1876-77
		(The first century in Test cricket)						
Bardsley,W	(6)	136)	228m	230	1/12	England	The Oval	1909
		130)	200m	250	-/10			
		132 §	150m		-/16	South Africa	Sydney	1910-11
		121	150m	157	2/11	South Africa	Manchester	1912
		164	216m	283	1/16	South Africa	Lord's	1912
		193*	398m		-/14	England	Lord's	1926
Barnes,SG	(3)	234	642m	661	-/17	England	Sydney	1946-47
		112	227m		1/6	India	Adelaide	1947-48

		141	227m	286	2/14	England	Lord's	1948
Benaud,J	(1)	142	211m	207	2/18	Pakistan	Melbourne	1972-73
Benaud,R	(3)	121	96m		2/18	West Indies	Kingston	1954-55
		122	220m		-/20	South Africa	Johannesburg[3]	1957-58
		100	186m		1/9	South Africa	Johannesburg[3]	1957-58
Blewett,GS	(4)	102* §	261m	180	-/12	England	Adelaide	1994-95
		115	202m	158	-/19	England	Perth	1994-95
		214 §	519m	420	-/33	South Africa	Johannesburg[3]	1996-97
		125	300m	228	1/19	England	Birmingham	1997
Bonnor,GJ	(1)	128	115m		3∆/14	England	Sydney	1884-85
Boon,DC	(21)	123 §	336m	255	-/14	India	Adelaide	1985-86
		131	345m	311	-/16	India	Sydney	1985-86
		122	332m	258	-/21	India	Madras[1]	1986-87
		103	305m	274	-/14	England	Adelaide	1986-87
		143	342m	255	-/15	New Zealand	Brisbane[2]	1987-88
		184*	492m	431	-/14	England	Sydney	1987-88
		149	479m	425	-/10	West Indies	Sydney	1988-89
		200	451m	326	-/28	New Zealand	Perth	1989-90
		121	368m	276	-/9	England	Adelaide	1990-91
		109*	388m	253	-/9	West Indies	Kingston	1990-91
		129*	444m	361	-/13	India	Sydney	1991-92
		135	465m	352	-/16	India	Adelaide	1991-92
		107	377m	304	-/14	India	Perth	1991-92
		111	325m	259	-/13	West Indies	Brisbane[2]	1992-93
		164*	471m	378	-/15	England	Lord's	1993
		101	257m	177	-/17	England	Nottingham	1993
		107	310m	225	-/17	England	Leeds	1993
		106	317m	242	-/9	New Zealand	Hobart	1993-94
		114	336m	220	-/10	Pakistan	Karachi[1]	1994-95
		131	378m	277	-/14	England	Melbourne	1994-95
		110	408m	312	-/11	Sri Lanka	Melbourne	1995-96
Booth,BC	(5)	112	217m		-/14	England	Brisbane[2]	1962-63
		103	348m		-/19	England	Melbourne	1962-63
		169 §	330m		-/19	South Africa	Brisbane[2]	1963-64
		102*	306m	235	-/5	South Africa	Sydney	1963-64
		117	315m		-/13	West Indies	Port-of-Spain	1964-65
Border,AR	(27)	105 §	373m	275	-/7	Pakistan	Melbourne	1978-79
		162 §	416m		1/24	India	Madras[1]	1979-80
		115	384m	296	-/13	England	Perth	1979-80
		150*)	397m		2/16	Pakistan	Lahore[2]	1979-80
		153)	214m		5/16			
		124	303m	265	-/12	India	Melbourne	1980-81
		123*	415m	356	-/17	England	Manchester	1981
		106*	290m	230	-/13	England	The Oval	1981
		126	336m	278	-/9	West Indies	Adelaide	1981-82
		118	347m	254	-/10	Pakistan	Brisbane[2]	1983-84
		117*	310m	208	-/11	Pakistan	Adelaide	1983-84
		100*	279m	269	-/12	West Indies	Port-of-Spain	1983-84
		196	450m	317	-/22	England	Lord's	1985
		146*	346m	333	-/13	England	Manchester	1985
		152*	458m	301	2/20	New Zealand	Brisbane[2]	1985-86
		163	410m	358	-/16	India	Melbourne	1985-86
		140)	386m	338	1/15	New Zealand	Christchurch	1985-86
		114*)	280m	201	-/10			
		106	252m	172	1/14	India	Madras[1]	1986-87
		125	372m	282	-/17	England	Perth	1986-87

		100*	303m	253	-/11	England	Adelaide	1986-87
		205	599m	485	-/20	New Zealand	Adelaide	1987-88
		113*	354m	237	-/13	Pakistan	Faisalabad	1988-89
		106	217m	164	-/16	Sri Lanka	Moratuwa	1992-93
		110	350m	274	1/5	West Indies	Melbourne	1992-93
		200*	565m	399	-/26	England	Leeds	1993
		105	275m	193	-/15	New Zealand	Brisbane[2]	1993-94
Bradman,DG	(29)	112	247m	281	-/7	England	Melbourne	1928-29
		123	217m	247	-/8	England	Melbourne	1928-29
		131	258m	287	-/10	England	Nottingham	1930
		254	339m	376	-/25	England	Lord's	1930
		334	378m	446	-/46	England	Leeds	1930
		232	408m	410	-/16	England	The Oval	1930
		223	297m		-/24	West Indies	Brisbane[1]	1930-31
		152	154m		-/13	West Indies	Melbourne	1930-31
		226 §	277m		-/22	South Africa	Brisbane[2]	1931-32
		112	155m		-/10	South Africa	Sydney	1931-32
		167	183m		-/18	South Africa	Melbourne	1931-32
		299*	396m		-/23	South Africa	Adelaide	1931-32
		103*	185m	146	-/7	England	Melbourne	1932-33
		304	430m	466	2/44	England	Leeds	1934
		244	316m	277	1/32	England	The Oval	1934
		270	458m	375	-/22	England	Melbourne	1936-37
		212	441m	393	-/14	England	Adelaide	1936-37
		169	223m		-/15	England	Melbourne	1936-37
		144*	363m	377	-/5	England	Nottingham	1938
		102*	147m	132	-/15	England	Lord's	1938
		103	176m	181	-/9	England	Leeds	1938
		187	318m	313	-/19	England	Brisbane[2]	1946-47
		234	393m	396	-/24	England	Sydney	1946-47
		185 §	288m		-/20	India	Brisbane[2]	1947-48
		132)	197m		-/8	India	Melbourne	1947-48
		127*)	178m		-/12			
		201	272m		1/21	India	Adelaide	1947-48
		138	288m	315	-/10	England	Nottingham	1948
		173*	255m	294	-/29	England	Leeds	1948
Brown,WA	(4)	105	199m	199	-/14	England	Lord's	1934
		121	207m	225	1/5	South Africa	Cape Town	1935-36
		133	320m	377	-/13	England	Nottingham	1938
		206*	370m	386	-/22	England	Lord's	1938
Burge,PJP	(4)	181	411m		-/22	England	The Oval	1961
		103	331m	293	-/9	England	Sydney	1962-63
		160	314m	307	-/24	England	Leeds	1964
		120	255m		-/12	England	Melbourne	1965-66
Burke,JW	(3)	101* §	245m		-/9	England	Adelaide	1950-51
		161	504m		-/15	India	Bombay[2]	1956-57
		189	578m		-/15	South Africa	Cape Town	1957-58
Chappell,GS	(24)	108 §	272m		-/10	England	Perth	1970-71
		131	372m		-/14	England	Lord's	1972
		113	272m		-/17	England	The Oval	1972
		116*	230m		-/12	Pakistan	Melbourne	1972-73
		106	255m		-/10	West Indies	Bridgetown	1972-73
		247*)	410m	356	1/30	New Zealand	Wellington	1973-74
		133)	186m	175	-/8			
		144	252m	209	-/16	England	Sydney	1974-75
		102	249m	177	-/11	England	Melbourne	1974-75

		123)	231m	232	2/15	West Indies	Brisbane[2]	1975-76
		109*)	161m	172	1/14			
		182*	366m	274	-/22	West Indies	Sydney	1975-76
		121	246m		-/9	Pakistan	Melbourne	1976-77
		112	282m	230	1/15	England	Manchester	1977
		124	376m	299	-/12	West Indies	Brisbane[2]	1979-80
		114	288m	213	-/14	England	Melbourne	1979-80
		235	441m		-/24	Pakistan	Faisalabad	1979-80
		204 §	408m	296	-/27	India	Sydney	1980-81
		201	417m	296	-/22	Pakistan	Brisbane[2]	1981-82
		176	257m	218	2/23	New Zealand	Christchurch	1981-82
		117	259m	174	2/11	England	Perth	1982-83
		115	239m	201	-/19	England	Adelaide	1982-83
		150*	334m	250	-/17	Pakistan	Brisbane[2]	1983-84
		182	526m	400	-/17	Pakistan	Sydney	1983-84
Chappell,IM	(14)	151	252m		-/21	India	Melbourne	1967-68
		117 §	247m		-/17	West Indies	Brisbane[2]	1968-69
		165	319m		-/16	West Indies	Melbourne	1968-69
		138	276m		-/21	India	Delhi	1969-70
		111	243m		-/12	England	Melbourne	1970-71
		104	326m		-/9	England	Adelaide	1970-71
		118	330m		-/20	England	The Oval	1972
		196	295m	243	4/21	Pakistan	Adelaide	1972-73
		106*	247m		-/15	West Indies	Bridgetown	1972-73
		109	302m		-/10	West Indies	Georgetown	1972-73
		145)	283m	268	1/17	New Zealand	Wellington	1973-74
		121)	199m	218	1/13			
		192	442m	367	-/17	England	The Oval	1975
		156	377m	261	-/19	West Indies	Perth	1975-76
Chipperfield,AG	(1)	109 §	171m	193	-/8	South Africa	Durban[2]	1935-36
Clarke,MJ	(2)	151 §	343m	249	4/18	India	Bangalore	2004-05
		141 §	297m	200	1/21	New Zealand	Brisbane[2]	2004-05
Collins,HL	(4)	104 §	219m	278	-/11	England	Sydney	1920-21
		162	258m		-/20	England	Adelaide	1920-21
		203	277m		-/26	South Africa	Johannesburg[1]	1921-22
		114	236m		-/9	England	Sydney	1924-25
Cosier,GJ	(2)	109 §	254m	186	-/13	West Indies	Melbourne	1975-76
		168	228m		-/20	Pakistan	Melbourne	1976-77
Cowper,RM	(5)	143	339m		-/18	West Indies	Port-of-Spain	1964-65
		102	183m		-/13	West Indies	Bridgetown	1964-65
		307	727m	589	-/20	England	Melbourne	1965-66
		108	212m		-/13	India	Adelaide	1967-68
		165	321m	346	-/13	India	Sydney	1967-68
Darling,J	(3)	101	195m		-/19	England	Sydney	1897-98
		178	285m		1!/26	England	Adelaide	1897-98
		160	175m		-/30	England	Sydney	1897-98
Davis,IC	(1)	105 §	229m		1/14	Pakistan	Adelaide	1976-77
Duff,RA	(2)	104 §	206m		-/11	England	Melbourne	1901-02
		146	197m		-/20	England	The Oval	1905
Dyson,J	(2)	102	292m	233	-/14	England	Leeds	1981
		127* §	377m	321	-/11	West Indies	Sydney	1981-82
Edwards,R	(2)	170*	344m		-/13	England	Nottingham	1972
		115	322m	252	-/6	England	Perth	1974-75
Elliott,MTG	(3)	112	240m	180	-/20	England	Lord's	1997
		199	450m	351	3/23	England	Leeds	1997
		114	338m	265	-/18	New Zealand	Hobart	1997-98

Favell,LE	(1)	101				India	Madras[2]	1959-60
Fingleton,JHW	(5)	112	191m	212	-/7	South Africa	Cape Town	1935-36
		108	132m	169	-/7	South Africa	Johannesburg[1]	1935-36
		118	224m	212	-/9	South Africa	Durban[2]	1935-36
		100	301m		-/6	England	Brisbane[2]	1936-37
		136	386m		-/6	England	Melbourne	1936-37
Giffen,G	(1)	161	254m		1Δ/22	England	Sydney	1894-95
Gilchrist,AC	(16)	149* §	268m	163	1/13	Pakistan	Hobart	1999-2000
		122	162m	112	4/15	India	Mumbai[3]	2000-01
		152	204m	143	5/20	England	Birmingham	2001
		118	242m	158	1/17	New Zealand	Brisbane[2]	2001-02
		204*	293m	213	8/19	South Africa	Johannesburg[3]	2001-02
		138*	172m	108	2/22	South Africa	Cape Town	2001-02
		133	121m	194	-/18	England	Sydney	2002-03
		101*	208m	101	2/11	West Indies	Port-of-Spain	2002-03
		113*	140m	94	4/12	Zimbabwe	Perth	2003-04
		144	252m	185	3/19	Sri Lanka	Kandy	2003-04
		104	165m	109	3/13	India	Bangalore	2004-05
		126	194m	151	4/13	New Zealand	Brisbane[2]	2004-05
		113	139m	120	5/14	Pakistan	Sydney	2004-05
		121	183m	126	6/12	New Zealand	Christchurch	2004-05
		162	220m	146	5/22	New Zealand	Wellington	2004-05
		144	294m	212	6/15	Bangladesh	Fatullah	2005-06
Gillespie,JN	(1)	201*	561m	425	2/26	Bangladesh	Chittagong[2]	2005-06
Gilmour,GJ	(1)	101	187m	146	1/20	New Zealand	Christchurch	1976-77
Graham,H	(2)	107 §	140m		-/12	England	Lord's	1893
		105	135m		-/14	England	Sydney	1894-95
Gregory,ES	(4)	201	243m		-/28	England	Sydney	1894-95
		103	160m		-/17	England	Lord's	1896
		117	195m		-/15	England	The Oval	1899
		112	122m		-/15	England	Adelaide	1903-04
Gregory,JM	(2)	100	137m		-/12	England	Melbourne	1920-21
		119	85m		2/19	South Africa	Johannesburg[1]	1921-22
		(Including the fastest Test century in 70 minutes)						
Hartigan,RJ	(1)	116 §	319m		-/18	England	Adelaide	1907-08
Harvey,RN	(21)	153	249m		-/11	India	Melbourne	1947-48
		112 §	188m	186	-/17	England	Leeds	1948
		178	237m	253	-/16	South Africa	Cape Town	1949-50
		151*	325m	361	-/14	South Africa	Durban[2]	1949-50
		100	133m	132	-/13	South Africa	Johannesburg[2]	1949-50
		116	130m	128	-/14	South Africa	Port Elizabeth	1949-50
		109	155m		-/16	South Africa	Brisbane[2]	1952-53
		190	361m		-/21	South Africa	Sydney	1952-53
		116	125m		-/14	South Africa	Adelaide	1952-53
		205	295m		-/19	South Africa	Melbourne	1952-53
		122	240m	248	-/11	England	Manchester	1953
		162	380m		-/17	England	Brisbane[2]	1954-55
		133	306m		-/20	West Indies	Kingston	1954-55
		133	242m		-/18	West Indies	Port-of-Spain	1954-55
		204	426m		1/24	West Indies	Kingston	1954-55
		140	244m		-/18	India	Bombay[2]	1956-57
		167	370m	325	-/16	England	Melbourne	1958-59
		114	240h		-/14	India	Delhi	1959-60
		102	287m		-/9	India	Bombay[2]	1959-60
		114	212m		-/18	England	Birmingham	1961
		154	326m		-/18	England	Adelaide	1962-63

Hassett,AL	(10)	128	394m	395	-/10	England	Brisbane[2]	1946-47
		198*	342m		-/16	India	Adelaide	1947-48
		137	352m	385	1/20	England	Nottingham	1948
		112 §	261m	283	-/7	South Africa	Johannesburg[2]	1949-50
		167	314m	314	1/14	South Africa	Port Elizabeth	1949-50
		132	381m		-/10	West Indies	Sydney	1951-52
		102	323m		-/10	West Indies	Melbourne	1951-52
		163	359m		-/15	South Africa	Adelaide	1952-53
		115	394m	315	-/9	England	Nottingham	1953
		104	296m	251	-/11	England	Lord's	1953
Hayden,ML	(25)	125	354m	226	1/15	West Indies	Adelaide	1996-97
		119 §	283m	172	1/18	India	Mumbai[3]	2000-01
		203	474m	320	6/15	India	Chennai[1]	2000-01
		136	251m	195	2/20	New Zealand	Brisbane[2]	2001-02
		131	261m	207	4/12	South Africa	Adelaide	2001-02
		138	290m	211	-/17	South Africa	Melbourne	2001-02
		105	240m	198	1/14	South Africa	Sydney	2001-02
		122	290m	189	2/18	South Africa	Johannesburg[3]	2001-02
		119	433m	255	1/9	Pakistan	Sharjah	2002-03
		197)	395m	268	2/25	England	Brisbane[2]	2002-03
		103)	217m	152	1/13			
		102	189m	149	3/10	England	Melbourne	2002-03
		100*	270m	180	-/10	West Indies	Port-of-Spain	2002-03
		177	343m	260	3/22	West Indies	St John's	2002-03
		380	622m	437	11/38	Zimbabwe	Perth	2003-04
		101*	140m	85	3/11	Zimbabwe	Sydney	2003-04
		136	260m	173	1/17	India	Melbourne	2003-04
		130 §	310m	211	2/12	Sri Lanka	Galle	2003-04
		117)	275m	184	2/14	Sri Lanka	Cairns	2004-05
		132)	277m	169	1/10			
		138	416m	303	-/18	England	The Oval	2005
		118	233m	163	2/10	West Indies	Brisbane[2]	2005-06
		110	265m	169	1/10	West Indies	Hobart	2005-06
		137	356m	242	2/17	South Africa	Melbourne	2005-06
		116	309m	217	-/12	South Africa	Durban[2]	2005-06
Healy,IA	(4)	102*	164m	133	-/12	England	Manchester	1993
		113*	262m	181	-/11	New Zealand	Perth	1993-94
		161*	356m	250	-/20	West Indies	Brisbane[2]	1996-97
		134	303m	229	-/14	England	Brisbane[2]	1998-99
Hendry,HSTL	(1)	112	233m	305	-/7	England	Sydney	1928-29
Hilditch,AMJ	(2)	113 §	339m	273	-/7	West Indies	Melbourne	1984-85
		119	245m	182	2/17	England	Leeds	1985
Hill,C	(7)	188	294m		-/21	England	Melbourne	1897-98
		135	240m		-/17	England	Lord's	1899
		119	145m		-/19	England	Sheffield	1902
		142 §	135m		1!/16	South Africa	Johannesburg[1]	1902-03
		160	254m		-/12	England	Adelaide	1907-08
		191	202m		-/18	South Africa	Sydney	1910-11
		100	<100m		-/13	South Africa	Melbourne	1910-11
Hodge,BJ	(1)	203*	469m	332	-/22	South Africa	Perth	2005-06
Hookes,DW	(1)	143* §	201m	152	2/17	Sri Lanka	Kandy	1982-83
Horan,TP	(1)	124	250m		-/7	England	Melbourne	1881-82
Hughes,KJ	(9)	129	481m	411	2/8	England	Brisbane[2]	1978-79
		100	278m		1/10	India	Madras[1]	1979-80
		130* §	376m	244	1/17	West Indies	Brisbane[2]	1979-80
		117	205m	213	3/14	England	Lord's	1980

		213	383m	301	-/21	India	Adelaide	1980-81
		106	271m	198	-/17	Pakistan	Perth	1981-82
		100*	266m	200	-/11	West Indies	Melbourne	1981-82
		137	379m	316	3/12	England	Sydney	1982-83
		106	269m	245	1/11	Pakistan	Adelaide	1983-84
Hussey,MEK	(4)	137	388m	234	-/19	West Indies	Hobart	2005-06
		133*	293m	215	3/13	West Indies	Adelaide	2005-06
		122	247m	203	4/14	South Africa	Melbourne	2005-06
		182	305m	203	1/21	Bangladesh	Chittagong[2]	2005-06
Iredale,FA	(2)	140	245m		-/17	England	Adelaide	1894-95
		108	220m		-/16	England	Manchester	1896
Jackson,AA	(1)	164 §	318m	331	-/15	England	Adelaide	1928-29
Jones,DM	(11)	210 §	502m	330	2/27	India	Madras[1]	1986-87
		184*	540m	421	1/12	England	Sydney	1986-87
		102 §	251m	174	-/13	Sri Lanka	Perth	1987-88
		216	538m	347	-/16	West Indies	Adelaide	1988-89
		157	391m	295	-/17	England	Birmingham	1989
		122	214m	180	-/17	England	The Oval	1989
		118*	252m	178	-/6	Sri Lanka	Hobart	1989-90
		116)	331m	239	-/7	Pakistan	Adelaide	1989-90
		121*)	260m	205	1/11			
		150*	395m	265	1/14	India	Perth	1991-92
		100*	281m	213	2/7	Sri Lanka	Colombo (RPS)	1992-93
Katich,SM	(2)	125	230m	166	-/17	India	Sydney	2003-04
		118 §	273m	229	1/20	New Zealand	Christchurch	2004-05
Kelleway,C	(3)	114	201m	244	-/5	South Africa	Manchester	1912
		102	196m	279	-/7	South Africa	Lord's	1912
		147	422m		-/13	England	Adelaide	1920-21
Kippax,AF	(2)	100	217m	255	-/9	England	Melbourne	1928-29
		146 §	229m		-/18	West Indies	Adelaide	1930-31
Langer,JL	(22)	116	362m	212	-/10	Pakistan	Peshawar[2]	1998-99
		179*	491m	351	-/13	England	Adelaide	1998-99
		127	396m	307	2/8	West Indies	St John's	1998-99
		127	425m	295	-/12	Pakistan	Hobart	1999-2000
		144	437m	286	-/17	Pakistan	Perth	1999-2000
		223	523m	355	-/30	India	Sydney	1999-2000
		122*	165m	122	-/19	New Zealand	Hamilton	1999-2000
		102#	260m	186	1/12	England	The Oval	2001
		104	317m	231	-/13	New Zealand	Brisbane[2]	2001-02
		123	198m	154	-/20	New Zealand	Hobart	2001-02
		116 §	332m	246	1/15	South Africa	Adelaide	2001-02
		126	276m	211	1/19	South Africa	Sydney	2001-02
		250	578m	407	1/30	England	Melbourne	2002-03
		146	377m	270	-/19	West Indies	Georgetown	2002-03
		111	238m	161	1/17	West Indies	St John's	2002-03
		121	325m	194	-/17	India	Brisbane[2]	2003-04
		117	194m	149	1/17	India	Sydney	2003-04
		166	405m	295	2/13	Sri Lanka	Colombo (SSC)	2003-04
		162	410m	285	-/22	Sri Lanka	Cairns	2004-05
		215	499m	257	3/25	New Zealand	Adelaide	2004-05
		191	413m	280	3/18	Pakistan	Perth	2004-05
		105	233m	146	2/11	England	The Oval	2005
Lawry,WM	(13)	130	369m		-/18	England	Lord's	1961
		102	270m		-/13	England	Manchester	1961
		157	329m		-/19	South Africa	Melbourne	1963-64
		106	281m	311	3/5	England	Manchester	1964

		210	544m		3/25	West Indies	Bridgetown	1964-65
		166	419m		1/23	England	Brisbane[2]	1965-66
		119	255m		1/9	England	Adelaide	1965-66
		108	369m		-/7	England	Melbourne	1965-66
		100	179m	186	-/8	India	Melbourne	1967-68
		135	447m		-/22	England	The Oval	1968
		105	286m		-/12	West Indies	Brisbane[2]	1968-69
		205	461m		1/12	West Indies	Melbourne	1968-69
		151	500m	367	-/12	West Indies	Sydney	1968-69
Lehmann,DS	(5)	160	305m	228	1/21	West Indies	Port-of-Spain	2002-03
		110 §	266m	221	1/10	Bangladesh	Darwin	2003
		177	260m	207	-/22	Bangladesh	Cairns	2003
		110 §	328m	250	-/10	Sri Lanka	Galle	2003-04
		153	358m	269	2/14	Sri Lanka	Colombo (SSC)	2003-04
Lindwall,RR	(2)	100	113m	90	1/13	England	Melbourne	1946-47
		118	159m		2/15	West Indies	Bridgetown	1954-55
Love,ML	(1)	100*	177m	154	-/7	Bangladesh	Cairns	2003
Loxton,SJE	(1)	101 §	144m	193	-/14	South Africa	Johannesburg[2]	1949-50
Lyons,JJ	(1)	134	165h		-/16	England	Sydney	1891-92
Macartney,CG	(7)	137	193m		-/16	South Africa	Sydney	1910-11
		170	244m	227	-/20	England	Sydney	1920-21
		115	186m	176	-/13	England	Leeds	1921
		116	114m		1/17	South Africa	Durban[1]	1921-22
		133*	205m		-/13	England	Lord's	1926
		151	170m		-/21	England	Leeds	1926
		109	178m		-/14	England	Manchester	1926
McCabe,SJ	(6)	187*	242m	233	-/25	England	Sydney	1932-33
		137	214m	205	-/22	England	Manchester	1934
		149	268m	266	-/6	South Africa	Durban[2]	1935-36
		189*	197m	232	-/29	South Africa	Johannesburg[1]	1935-36
		112	163m		-/16	England	Melbourne	1936-37
		232	235m	276	1/34	England	Nottingham	1938
McCool,CL	(1)	104*	183m	194	-/8	England	Melbourne	1946-47
McCosker,RB	(4)	127	372m	294	-/21	England	The Oval	1975
		109*	249m	267	-/7	West Indies	Melbourne	1975-76
		105	222m		-/10	Pakistan	Melbourne	1976-77
		107	371m	307	1/10	England	Nottingham	1977
McDonald,CC	(5)	154	316m		1/16	South Africa	Adelaide	1952-53
		110	257m		-/12	West Indies	Port-of-Spain	1954-55
		127	323m		-/11	West Indies	Kingston	1954-55
		170	487m	315	-/12	England	Adelaide	1958-59
		133	339m	249	-/7	England	Melbourne	1958-59
McDonnell,PS	(3)	147	250m		1Δ/16	England	Sydney	1881-82
		103	136m	168	-/14	England	The Oval	1884
		124	195m		-/9	England	Adelaide	1884-85
McLeod,CE	(1)	112	244m		-/4	England	Melbourne	1897-98
Mann,AL	(1)	105	184m		-/11	India	Perth	1977-78
Marsh,GR	(4)	118	346m	287	-/14	New Zealand	Auckland	1985-86
		101	370m	300	-/11	India	Bombay[3]	1986-87
		110 §	392m	311	-/12	England	Brisbane[2]	1986-87
		138	432m	382	-/15	England	Nottingham	1989
Marsh,RW	(3)	118 §	164m		4/10	Pakistan	Adelaide	1972-73
		132	305m	266	-/9	New Zealand	Adelaide	1973-74
		110*	297m	173	-/10	England	Melbourne	1976-77
Martyn,DR	(13)	105 §	222m	165	-/15	England	Birmingham	2001
		118	186m	135	-/18	England	Leeds	2001

		124*	294m	210	-/9	South Africa	Adelaide	2001-02
		117	225m	166	-/13	South Africa	Sydney	2001-02
		133	314m	207	-/17	South Africa	Johannesburg[3]	2001-02
		129 §	270m	214	1/16	Sri Lanka	Galle	2003-04
		161	536m	349	1/21	Sri Lanka	Kandy	2003-04
		104	278m	210	1/11	India	Chennai[1]	2004-05
		114	222m	165	1/16	India	Nagpur	2004-05
		100*	130m	121	-/11	Pakistan	Perth	2004-05
		142	370m	245	-/12	Pakistan	Melbourne	2004-05
		165	349m	287	-/24	New Zealand	Wellington	2004-05
		101	286m	208	1/13	South Africa	Johannesburg[3]	2005-06
Matthews,GRJ	(4)	115 §	229m	205	1/10	New Zealand	Brisbane[2]	1985-86
		100*	195m	152	2/9	India	Melbourne	1985-86
		130	306m	235	-/12	New Zealand	Wellington	1985-86
		128	242m	175	-/17	England	Sydney	1990-91
Miller,KR	(7)	141*	270m	198	1/9	England	Adelaide	1946-47
		145*	354m		1/6	England	Sydney	1950-51
		129	246m		-/15	West Indies	Sydney	1951-52
		109	292m	269	1/14	England	Lord's	1953
		147	346m		-/15	West Indies	Kingston	1954-55
		137	237m		-/22	West Indies	Bridgetown	1954-55
		109	328m		1/15	West Indies	Kingston	1954-55
Moody,TM	(2)	106 §	218m	179	-/12	Sri Lanka	Brisbane[2]	1989-90
		101 §	186m	149	-/9	India	Perth	1991-92
Moroney,J	(2)	118)	321m	334	-/13	South Africa	Johannesburg[2]	1949-50
		101*)	225m	197	-/17			
Morris,AR	(12)	155	364m	317	-/8	England	Melbourne	1946-47
		122)	268m	255	2/12	England	Adelaide	1946-47
		124*)	198m	171	-/12			
		100*	196m		-/7	India	Melbourne	1947-48
		105	209m	214	1/14	England	Lord's	1948
		182	291m	294	-/33	England	Leeds	1948
		196	406m	493	-/16	England	The Oval	1948
		111	267m	242	1/9	South Africa	Johannesburg[2]	1949-50
		157	301m	226	1/14	South Africa	Port Elizabeth	1949-50
		206	462m		-/23	England	Adelaide	1950-51
		153	419m		2/18	England	Brisbane[2]	1954-55
		111	322m		-/18	West Indies	Port-of-Spain	1954-55
Murdoch,WL	(2)	153*	330m		-/18	England	The Oval	1880
		211	484m	525	-/24	England	The Oval	1884
Noble,MA	(1)	133	287m		-/17	England	Sydney	1903-04
O'Neill,NC	(6)	134			-/17	Pakistan	Lahore[2]	1959-60
		163	360h		-/14	India	Bombay[2]	1959-60
		113			-/15	India	Calcutta	1959-60
		181 §	401m		-/22	West Indies	Brisbane[2]	1960-61
		117	200m		-/14	England	The Oval	1961
		100	171m		-/13	England	Adelaide	1962-63
Pellew,CE	(2)	116	203m		-/8	England	Melbourne	1920-21
		104	123m		-/14	England	Adelaide	1920-21
Phillips,WB	(2)	159 §	307m	240	-/20	Pakistan	Perth	1983-84
		120	227m	197	4/14	West Indies	Bridgetown	1983-84
Ponsford,WH	(7)	110 §	228m		-/8	England	Sydney	1924-25
		128	222m		-/6	England	Melbourne	1924-25
		110	159m	206	-/11	England	The Oval	1930
		183	348m		-/11	West Indies	Sydney	1930-31
		109	165m		-/12	West Indies	Brisbane[1]	1930-31

		181	387m	425	-/19	England	Leeds	1934
		266	460m	418	-/27	England	The Oval	1934
Ponting,RT	(31)	127 §	261m	202	1/19	England	Leeds	1997
		105 §	269m	208	-/14	South Africa	Melbourne	1997-98
		104	375m	290	-/10	West Indies	Bridgetown	1998-99
		105*	224m	171	-/11	Sri Lanka	Colombo (SSC)	1999-2000
		197	420m	288	-/22	Pakistan	Perth	1999-2000
		125	275m	198	-/15	India	Adelaide	1999-2000
		141*	262m	183	1/17	India	Sydney	1999-2000
		144	211m	154	3/20	England	Leeds	2001
		157*	309m	218	1/20	New Zealand	Hobart	2001-02
		100*	261m	160	1/16	South Africa	Cape Town	2001-02
		141	259m	163	-/23	Pakistan	Colombo (PSS)	2002-03
		150	395m	266	3/14	Pakistan	Sharjah	2002-03
		123	253m	195	2/12	England	Brisbane^2	2002-03
		154	269m	349	-/9	England	Adelaide	2002-03
		117	292m	195	-/18	West Indies	Georgetown	2002-03
		206	491m	362	1/24	West Indies	Port-of-Spain	2002-03
		113	300m	204	1/8	West Indies	Bridgetown	2002-03
		169	314m	249	2/23	Zimbabwe	Sydney	2003-04
		242	508m	352	-/31	India	Adelaide	2003-04
		257	590m	458	-/25	India	Melbourne	2003-04
		207	491m	332	-/30	Pakistan	Sydney	2004-05
		105	154m	110	4/13	New Zealand	Auckland	2004-05
		156	410m	275	1/16	England	Manchester	2005
		149	316m	213	-/15)	West Indies	Brisbane^2	2005-06
		104*	182m	158	-/8)			
		117	298m	198	-/13	South Africa	Melbourne	2005-06
		120	257m	174	1/12)	South Africa	Sydney	2005-06
		143*	201m	159	-/16)			
		103	320m	225	-/11)	South Africa	Durban^2	2005-06
		116	273m	187	2/12)			
		101	286m	208	1/13	South Africa	Johannesburg^3	2005-06
		118*	367m	253	-/13	Bangladesh	Fatullah	2005-06
Ransford,VS	(1)	143*	252m	260	-/21	England	Lord's	1909
Redpath,IR	(8)	132	267m	277	-/11	West Indies	Sydney	1968-69
		171	484m		-/14	England	Perth	1970-71
		135	277m		-/14	Pakistan	Melbourne	1972-73
		159*	348m	310	-/20	New Zealand	Auckland	1973-74
		105	344m	239	-/9	England	Sydney	1974-75
		102	320m	258	-/10	West Indies	Melbourne	1975-76
		103	220m	175	2/6	West Indies	Adelaide	1975-76
		101	325m	230	-/11	West Indies	Melbourne	1975-76
Richardson,AJ	(1)	100	186m		-/10	England	Leeds	1926
Richardson,VY	(1)	138	198m		-/13	England	Melbourne	1924-25
Rigg,KE	(1)	127 §	240m		-/12	South Africa	Sydney	1931-32
Ritchie,GM	(3)	106*	293m	216	3/9	Pakistan	Faisalabad	1982-83
		146	361m	308	-/16	England	Nottingham	1985
		128 §	389m	321	-/11	India	Adelaide	1985-86
Ryder,J	(3)	142	181m		-/12	South Africa	Cape Town	1921-22
		201*	385m		1/12	England	Adelaide	1924-25
		112	224m	219	1/6	England	Melbourne	1928-29
Scott,HJH	(1)	102	203m	216	-/15	England	The Oval	1884
Serjeant,CS	(1)	124	268m		1/18	West Indies	Georgetown	1977-78
Sheahan,AP	(2)	114	257m		-/20	India	Kanpur	1969-70
		127	275m	207	-/12	Pakistan	Melbourne	1972-73

Simpson,RB	(10)	311	762m	740	1/23	England	Manchester	1964
		153 §)	408m	361	-/12	Pakistan	Karachi[1]	1964-65
		115 §)	200m	192	-/15			
		201	414m		-/22	West Indies	Bridgetown	1964-65
		225	545m		1/18	England	Adelaide	1965-66
		153	386m		-/12	South Africa	Cape Town	1966-67
		103	232m		-/12	India	Adelaide	1967-68
		109	220m	170	-/8	India	Melbourne	1967-68
		176	391m	343	-/17	India	Perth	1977-78
		100	264m		-/6	India	Adelaide	1977-78
Slater,MJ	(14)	152	293m	263	-/18	England	Lord's	1993
		168	328m	235	-/17	New Zealand	Hobart	1993-94
		110	250m	155	-/14	Pakistan	Rawalpindi[2]	1994-95
		176	324m	244	-/25	England	Brisbane[2]	1994-95
		103	283m	236	-/10	England	Sydney	1994-95
		124	296m	231	-/13	England	Perth	1994-95
		219 §	460m	321	5/15	Sri Lanka	Perth	1995-96
		108	298m	236	1/11	Pakistan	Rawalpindi[2]	1998-99
		113	190m	138	1/13	England	Brisbane[2]	1998-99
		103	276m	191	1/8	England	Adelaide	1998-99
		123	271m	189	3/11	England	Sydney	1998-99
		106	285m	206	-/12	West Indies	Port-of-Spain	1998-99
		169	351m	271	1/25	Pakistan	Brisbane[2]	1999-2000
		143	278m	214	1/23	New Zealand	Wellington	1999-2000
Stackpole,KR	(7)	134	196m		2/18	South Africa	Cape Town	1966-67
		103 §	290m		-/14	India	Bombay[2]	1969-70
		207	454m		1/25	England	Brisbane[2]	1970-71
		136	410m		-/16	England	Adelaide	1970-71
		114	335m		-/10	England	Nottingham	1972
		142	265m		-/22	West Indies	Kingston	1972-73
		122 §	222m	191	-/13	New Zealand	Melbourne	1973-74
Taylor,JM	(1)	108	164m		-/8	England	Sydney	1924-25
Taylor,MA	(19)	136 §	394m	315	-/16	England	Leeds	1989
		219	551m	461	-/23	England	Nottingham	1989
		164 §	425m	334	2/17	Sri Lanka	Brisbane[2]	1989-90
		108	291m	291	-/12	Sri Lanka	Hobart	1989-90
		101 §	322m	240	-/11	Pakistan	Melbourne	1989-90
		101*	258m	227	-/8	Pakistan	Sydney	1989-90
		144	361m	277	-/12	West Indies	St John's	1990-91
		100	395m	303	-/9	India	Adelaide	1991-92
		124	325m	234	2/12	England	Manchester	1993
		111	323m	245	1/10	England	Lord's	1993
		142*	360m	255	-/8	New Zealand	Perth	1993-94
		170 §	495m	349	-/12	South Africa	Melbourne	1993-94
		113	364m	248	-/9	England	Sydney	1994-95
		123	356m	243	-/13	Pakistan	Hobart	1995-96
		129	396m	298	1/13	England	Birmingham	1997
		112	313m	258	-/10	New Zealand	Brisbane[2]	1997-98
		169*	524m	376	-/21	South Africa	Adelaide	1997-98
		102*	209m	193	-/17	India	Bangalore	1997-98
		334*	720m	564	1/32	Pakistan	Peshawar[2]	1998-99
Toohey,PM	(1)	122	313m	293	-/10	West Indies	Kingston	1977-78
Trott,G HS	(1)	143	210m		-/24	England	Lord's	1896
Trumper,VT	(8)	135*	195m		-/20	England	Lord's	1899
		104	115m		-/14	England	Manchester	1902
		185*	230m		-/25?	England	Sydney	1903-04

		113	189m		-/12	England	Adelaide	1903-04
		166	241m		-/18	England	Sydney	1907-08
		159	178m		1/15	South Africa	Melbourne	1910-11
		214*	242m		-/26	South Africa	Adelaide	1910-11
		113	226m	206	-/12	England	Sydney	1911-12
Turner,A	(1)	136	279m	222	-/15	West Indies	Adelaide	1975-76
Walters,KD	(15)	155 §	322m		2/11	England	Brisbane[2]	1965-66
		115	263m		-/5	England	Melbourne	1965-66
		118	214m	185	-/12	West Indies	Sydney	1968-69
		110	194m		-/13	West Indies	Adelaide	1968-68
		242)	480m	412	-/24	West Indies	Sydney	1968-69
		103)	196m	181	-/7			
		102	208m		2/14	India	Madras[1]	1969-70
		112	328m		-/9	England	Brisbane[2]	1970-71
		102*	200m		-/15	West Indies	Bridgetown	1972-73
		112	148m		1/19	West Indies	Port-of-Spain	1972-73
		104*	165m	138	-/15	New Zealand	Auckland	1973-74
		103	140m	119	1/11	England	Perth	1974-75
		107	247m		-/9	Pakistan	Adelaide	1976-77
		250	394m	342	2/30	New Zealand	Christchurch	1976-77
		107	276m	206	-/6	New Zealand	Melbourne	1980-81
Waugh,ME	(20)	138 §	237m	186	-/18	England	Adelaide	1990-91
		139*	307m	188	3/11	West Indies	St John's	1990-91
		112	327m	234	-/9	West Indies	Melbourne	1992-93
		137	239m	219	-/18	England	Birmingham	1993
		111	187m	139	-/15	New Zealand	Hobart	1993-94
		113*	283m	222	-/13	South Africa	Durban[2]	1993-94
		140	323m	215	1/14	England	Brisbane[2]	1994-95
		126	276m	192	-/12	West Indies	Kingston	1994-95
		116	262m	106	1/8	Pakistan	Sydney	1995-96
		111	261m	223	1/7	Sri Lanka	Perth	1995-96
		116	323m	229	1/17	South Africa	Port Elizabeth	1996-97
		100	211m	186	1/12	South Africa	Sydney	1997-98
		115*	404m	305	-/16	South Africa	Adelaide	1997-98
		153*	334m	266	4/13	India	Bangalore	1997-98
		121	293m	205	-/10	England	Sydney	1998-99
		117	334m	232	1/9	Pakistan	Karachi[1]	1998-99
		100	200m	148	-/17	Pakistan	Brisbane[2]	1999-2000
		119	271m	175	-/12	West Indies	Perth	2000-01
		108	209m	170	-/14	England	Lord's	2001
		120	352m	176	2/16	England	The Oval	2001
Waugh,SR	(32)	177*	308m	242	-/24	England	Leeds	1989
		152*	329m	249	-/17	England	Lord's	1989
		134*	234m	234	-/14	Sri Lanka	Hobart	1989-90
		100	269m	207	-/5	West Indies	Sydney	1992-93
		157*	405m	305	-/19	England	Leeds	1993
		147*	380m	281	-/15	New Zealand	Brisbane[2]	1993-94
		164 §	380m	276	-/19	South Africa	Adelaide	1993-94
		200	555m	425	1/17	West Indies	Kingston	1994-95
		112*	366m	275	-/7	Pakistan	Brisbane[2]	1995-96
		131*	329m	252	-/12	Sri Lanka	Melbourne	1995-96
		170	421m	316	-/13	Sri Lanka	Adelaide	1995-96
		160	501m	366	-/22	South Africa	Johannesburg[3]	1996-97
		108)	241m	173	-/13)	England	Manchester	1997
		116)	383m	270	-/10)			
		112	330m	232	-/13	England	Brisbane[2]	1998-99
		122*	315m	198	-/13	England	Melbourne	1998-99

		157	391m	326	1/16	Pakistan	Rawalpindi[2]	1998-99
		100	251m	165	1/11	West Indies	Kingston	1998-99
		199	507m	377	1/20	West Indies	Bridgetown	1998-99
		151* §	430m	351	-/18	Zimbabwe	Harare	1999-2000
		150	402m	323	-/17	India	Adelaide	1999-2000
		151*	415m	310	-/23	New Zealand	Wellington	1999-2000
		121*	362m	237	-/13	West Indies	Melbourne	2000-01
		103	300m	238	1/9	West Indies	Sydney	2000-01
		110	309m	201	1/11	India	Kolkata	2000-01
		105	245m	181	-/13	England	Birmingham	2001
		157*	312m	256	1/21	England	The Oval	2001
		103*	292m	191	2/13	Pakistan	Sharjah	2002-03
		102	182m	135	-/18	England	Sydney	2002-03
		115	314m	233	-/8	West Indies	Bridgetown	2002-03
		100*	200	133	1/10	Bangladesh	Darwin	2003-04
		156*	411m	291	-/17	Bangladesh	Cairns	2003-04
Wellham,DM	(1)	103 §	266m	222	-/12	England	The Oval	1981
Wessels,KC	(4)	162 §	464m	343	-/17	England	Brisbane[2]	1982-83
		141 §	252m	188	-/21	Sri Lanka	Kandy	1982-83
		179	330m	233	1/24	Pakistan	Adelaide	1983-84
		173	482m	351	-/14	West Indies	Sydney	1984-85
Wood,GM	(9)	126	337m		1/8	West Indies	Georgetown	1977-78
		100	392m	283	-/6	England	Melbourne	1978-79
		112	363m	295	-/10	England	Lord's	1980
		111 §	318m	229	-/12	New Zealand	Brisbane[2]	1980-81
		125	286m	217	1/10	India	Adelaide	1980-81
		100	375m	305	-/3	Pakistan	Melbourne	1981-82
		100	261m	249	-/10	New Zealand	Auckland	1981-82
		172	601m	449	-/21	England	Nottingham	1985
		111	391m	287	-/14	West Indies	Perth	1988-89
Woodfull,WM	(7)	141	295m		-/12	England	Leeds	1926
		117	259m		-/6	England	Manchester	1926
		111	258m	286	-/6	England	Sydney	1928-29
		107	271m	309	-/7	England	Melbourne	1928-29
		102	325m	381	-/3	England	Melbourne	1928-29
		155	325m	391	-/9	England	Lord's	1930
		161	300m		-/5	South Africa	Melbourne	1931-32
Yallop,GN	(8)	121 §	228m		-/13	India	Adelaide	1977-78
		102 §	347m	307	-/8	England	Brisbane[2]	1978-79
		121	266m	212	-/13	England	Sydney	1978-79
		167	520m	392	-/14	India	Calcutta	1979-80
		172	504m		-/19	Pakistan	Faisalabad	1979-80
		114	177m	125	-/17	England	Manchester	1981
		141	402m	274	-/13	Pakistan	Perth	1983-84
		268	716m	517	-/29	Pakistan	Melbourne	1983-84

ENGLAND (708)			Time	Balls	6/4	Opponents		
Abel,R	(2)	120	n240h		-/11	South Africa	Cape Town	1888-89
		132*	325m		-/11	Australia	Sydney	1891-92
Allen,GOB	(1)	122 §	170m		1/14	New Zealand	Lord's	1931
Ames,LEG	(8)	105	220m		-/17	West Indies	Port-of-Spain	1929-30
		149	160m		-/17	West Indies	Kingston	1929-30
		137 §	205m		2/18	New Zealand	Lord's	1931
		103	144m		-/11	New Zealand	Christchurch	1932-33
		120	262m	333	-/14	Australia	Lord's	1934
		126	251m		-/16	West Indies	Kingston	1934-35

		148*	210m		1/14	South Africa	The Oval	1935
		115	145m	168	-/13	South Africa	Cape Town	1938-39
Amiss,DL	(11)	112	304m		-/15	Pakistan	Lahore[2]	1972-73
		158	326m		-/27	Pakistan	Hyderabad	1972-73
		138* §	365m		-/12	New Zealand	Nottingham	1973
		174	396m	429	-/19	West Indies	Port-of-Spain	1973-74
		262*	570m	563	1/40	West Indies	Kingston	1973-74
		118	340m	246	-/15	West Indies	Georgetown	1973-74
		188	>360h		-/29	India	Lord's	1974
		183	421m	370	-/19	Pakistan	The Oval	1974
		164*	406m	351	-/25	New Zealand	Christchurch	1974-75
		203	443m	320	-/28	West Indies	The Oval	1976
		179	496m	393	1/22	India	Delhi	1976-77
Atherton,MA	(16)	151 §	497m	382	-/16	New Zealand	Nottingham	1990
		131	338m	276	-/12	India	Manchester	1990
		105	451m	349	-/8	Australia	Sydney	1990-91
		144	412m	296	-/17	West Indies	Georgetown	1993-94
		135	539m	383	-/13	West Indies	St John's	1993-94
		101	325m	264	-/13	New Zealand	Nottingham	1994
		111	408m	307	-/14	New Zealand	Manchester	1994
		113	336m	247	-/17	West Indies	Nottingham	1995
		185*	645m	492	-/29	South Africa	Johannesburg[3]	1995-96
		160	467m	376	-/20	India	Nottingham	1996
		118	398m	311	-/11	New Zealand	Christchurch	1996-97
		103	365m	279	-/12	South Africa	Birmingham	1998
		108	380m	274	-/15	South Africa	Port Elizabeth	1999-2000
		136	471m	330	1/19	Zimbabwe	Nottingham	2000
		108	444m	331	-/13	West Indies	The Oval	2000
		125	579m	430	-/9	Pakistan	Karachi[1]	2000-01
Athey,CWJ	(1)	123	315m	203	-/14	Pakistan	Lord's	1987
Bailey,TE	(1)	134*	390m		-/13	New Zealand	Christchurch	1950-51
Bakewell,AH	(1)	107 §	230m		-/10	West Indies	The Oval	1933
Barber,RW	(1)	185	296m	272	-/19	Australia	Sydney	1965-66
Barnes,W	(1)	134	285h		-/7	Australia	Adelaide	1884-85
Barnett,CJ	(2)	129	341m		1/13	Australia	Adelaide	1936-37
		126	172m	183	-/18	Australia	Nottingham	1938
Barrington,KF	(20)	128 §	330h		-/20	West Indies	Bridgetown	1959-60
		121	350m		-/10	West Indies	Port-of-Spain	1959-60
		139 §	430m		-/19	Pakistan	Lahore[2]	1961-62
		151*	420m		-/15	India	Bombay[2]	1961-62
		172	406m		-/26	India	Kanpur	1961-62
		113*	360h		-/13	India	Delhi	1961-62
		132*	227m		2/16	Australia	Adelaide	1962-63
		101	320m	344	-/4	Australia	Sydney	1962-63
		126 §	254m		1/15	New Zealand	Auckland	1962-63
		256	685m	621	-/26	Australia	Manchester	1964
		148*	432m		-/9	South Africa	Durban[2]	1964-65
		121	329m		1/16	South Africa	Johannesburg[3]	1964-65
		137	437m		1/11	New Zealand	Birmingham	1965
		163	339m	291	-/26	New Zealand	Leeds	1965
		102	329m		-/4	Australia	Adelaide	1965-66
		115	178m		2/8	Australia	Melbourne	1965-66
		148	310m		-/17	Pakistan	Lord's	1967
		109*	410m		-/5	Pakistan	Nottingham	1967
		142	347m		-/14	Pakistan	The Oval	1967
		143	390m		2/14	West Indies	Port-of-Spain	1967-68

Bell,IR	(5)	162*	233m	168	1/25	Bangladesh	Chester-le-Street	2005
		115	372m	272	-/7	Pakistan	Faisalabad	2005-06
		100*	254m	168	-/9	Pakistan	Lord's	2006
		106*	198m	135	1/13	Pakistan	Manchester	2006
		119	267m	206	-/12	Pakistan	Leeds	2006
Botham,IT	(14)	103	313m		1/12	New Zealand	Christchurch	1977-78
		100 §	190m		-/11	Pakistan	Birmingham	1978
		108	a180h			Pakistan	Lord's	1978
		137	201m	152	5/16	India	Leeds	1979
		119*	224m	212	-/15	Australia	Melbourne	1979-80
		114	206m	144	-/17	India	Bombay[3]	1979-80
		149*	219m	148	1/27	Australia	Leeds	1981
		118	123m	102	6/13	Australia	Manchester	1981
		142	347m		2/12	India	Kanpur	1981-82
		128	199m	169	2/19	India	Manchester	1982
		208	276m	226	4/19	India	The Oval	1982
		103	156m	103	3/14	New Zealand	Nottingham	1983
		138	236m	167	2/22	New Zealand	Wellington	1983-84
		138	249m	174	4/13	Australia	Brisbane[2]	1986-87
Bowley,EH	(1)	109	128m		1/11	New Zealand	Auckland	1929-30
Boycott,G	(22)	113	297m	314	-/10	Australia	The Oval	1964
		117	423m	396	-/12	South Africa	Port Elizabeth	1964-65
		246* §	573m	555	1/29	India	Leeds	1967
		116	293m	254	-/20	West Indies	Georgetown	1967-68
		128	335m		-/18	West Indies	Manchester	1969
		106	269m	273	-/16	West Indies	Lord's	1969
		142*	412m		-/12	Australia	Sydney	1970-71
		119*	250m		-/12	Australia	Adelaide	1970-71
		121*	309m		-/12	Pakistan	Lord's	1971
		112	265m	206	1/14	Pakistan	Leeds	1971
		115	221m		-/20	New Zealand	Leeds	1973
		112	415m	385	-/12	West Indies	Port-of-Spain	1973-74
		107	419m	314	-/11	Australia	Nottingham	1977
		191	620m	469	-/23	Australia	Leeds	1977
		(His 100th first-class century)						
		100*	325m		-/8	Pakistan	Hyderabad	1977-78
		131	417m		-/10	New Zealand	Nottingham	1978
		155	458m	341	-/12	India	Birmingham	1979
		125	418m	293	-/6	India	The Oval	1979
		128*	316m	252	-/12	Australia	Lord's	1980
		104*	345m		-/8	West Indies	St John's	1980-81
		137	441m	321	-/7	Australia	The Oval	1981
		105	441m	278	-/7	India	Delhi	1981-82
Braund,LC	(3)	103*	222m		1∆/12	Australia	Adelaide	1901-02
		102	171m		-/15	Australia	Sydney	1903-04
		104 §	240h		-/12	South Africa	Lord's	1907
Briggs,J	(1)	121	150h		-/15	Australia	Melbourne	1884-85
Broad,BC	(6)	162	435m	314	-/25	Australia	Perth	1986-87
		116	307m	263	1/12	Australia	Adelaide	1986-87
		112	329m	225	-/9	Australia	Melbourne	1986-87
		116	421m	339	-/13	Pakistan	Faisalabad	1987-88
		139	434m	361	-/13	Australia	Sydney	1987-88
		114 §	341m	244	-/11	New Zealand	Christchurch	1987-88
Brown,JT	(1)	140	148m		-/16	Australia	Melbourne	1894-95
Butcher,MA	(8)	116	322m	252	-/18	South Africa	Leeds	1998
		116	278m	236	-/16	Australia	Brisbane[2]	1998-99
		173*	315m	227	1/23	Australia	Leeds	2001

		105	399m	295	-/10	Sri Lanka	Lord's	2002
		123	313m	226	-/18	Sri Lanka	Manchester	2002
		124	337m	276	-/19	Australia	Sydney	2002-03
		137	380m	256	1/21	Zimbabwe	Lord's	2003
		106	235m	182	-/21	South Africa	Nottingham	2003
Chapman,APF	(1)	121	152m	166	4/12	Australia	Lord's	1930
Collingwood,PD	(2)	134* §	355m	252	4/13	India	Nagpur	2005-06
		186	440m	327	-/23	Pakistan	Lord's	2006
Compton,DCS	(17)	102 §	138m	172	-/15	Australia	Nottingham	1938
		120 §	140m		-/16	West Indies	Lord's	1939
		147)	286m	350	-/14	Australia	Adelaide	1946-47
		103*)	284m	353	-/10			
		163 §	270m		-/19	South Africa	Nottingham	1947
		208	355m		-/20	South Africa	Lord's	1947
		115	190m		-/17	South Africa	Manchester	1947
		113	110m		-/15	South Africa	The Oval	1947
		184	410m	482	-/19	Australia	Nottingham	1948
		145*	327m	322	-/16	Australia	Manchester	1948
		114	156m	201	-/14	South Africa	Johannesburg[2]	1948-49
		114	240h		-/13	New Zealand	Leeds	1949
		116	220m		-/11	New Zealand	Lord's	1949
		112	320m		-/11	South Africa	Nottingham	1951
		133	349m		-/17	West Indies	Port-of-Spain	1953-54
		278	290m		1/34	Pakistan	Nottingham	1954
		158	339m		-/22	South Africa	Manchester	1955
Cook,AN	(3)	104* §	364m	243	-/12	India	Nagpur	2005-06
		105 §	327m	279	-/10	Pakistan	Lord's	2006
		127	341m	260	-/18	Pakistan	Manchester	2006
Cowdrey,MC	(22)	102	239m		-/15	Australia	Melbourne	1954-55
		101	369m		1/9	South Africa	Cape Town	1956-57
		154 §	500m		-/16	West Indies	Birmingham	1957
		152	321m		-/14	West Indies	Lord's	1957
		100*	365m	302	-/7	Australia	Sydney	1958-59
		160	278m	279	4/14	India	Leeds	1959
		114	406m		-/11	West Indies	Kingston	1959-60
		119	270h		-/15	West Indies	Port-of-Spain	1959-60
		155	260m		-/22	South Africa	The Oval	1960
		159 §	263m		-/21	Pakistan	Birmingham	1962
		182	323m		1/23	Pakistan	The Oval	1962
		113	270m		-/7	Australia	Melbourne	1962-63
		128*	235m		-/10	New Zealand	Wellington	1962-63
		107	380m		-/17	India	Calcutta	1963-64
		151	374m		1/23	India	Delhi	1963-64
		119	298m		-/13	New Zealand	Lord's	1965
		105	188m	170	-/11	South Africa	Nottingham	1965
		104	197m			Australia	Melbourne	1965-66
		101	345m		-/12	West Indies	Kingston	1967-68
		148	271m		-/21	West Indies	Port-of-Spain	1967-68
		104	244m		-/15	Australia	Birmingham	1968
		(In his 100th Test match)						
		100	227m		-/12	Pakistan	Lahore[2]	1968-69
Crawley,JP	(4)	106	257m	217	-/12	Pakistan	The Oval	1996
		112 §	358m	198	1/9	Zimbabwe	Bulawayo[2]	1996-97
		156* §	320m	249	1/19	Sri Lanka	The Oval	1998
		100* §	190m	132	-/8	India	Lord's	2002
Denness,MH	(4)	118	244m	228	-/12	India	Lord's	1974
		100	214m	193	-/10	India	Birmingham	1974

		188	492m	448	-/17	Australia	Melbourne	1974-75
		181	414m	392	-/25	New Zealand	Auckland	1974-75
Denton,D	(1)	104	100m		-/18	South Africa	Johannesburg[1]	1909-10
Dexter,ER	(9)	141	257m		-/24	New Zealand	Christchurch	1958-59
		136* §	285h		1/19	West Indies	Bridgetown	1959-60
		110	255h			West Indies	Georgetown	1959-60
		180	344m		-/31	Australia	Birmingham	1961
		126*	256m		-/15	India	Kanpur	1961-62
		205	495m		-/22	Pakistan	Karachi[1]	1961-62
		172	228m		5/18	Pakistan	The Oval	1962
		174	481m	382	-/22	Australia	Manchester	1964
		172	339m		-/27	South Africa	Johannesburg[3]	1964-65
D'Oliveira,BL	(5)	109 §	185m		-/13	India	Leeds	1967
		158	315m		-/21	Australia	The Oval	1968
		114*	285m		-/9	Pakistan	Dacca	1968-69
		117	346m		-/11	Australia	Melbourne	1970-71
		100	216m		2/13	New Zealand	Christchurch	1970-71
Douglas,JWHT	(1)	119 §	225m		-/14	South Africa	Durban[1]	1913-14
Duleepsinhji,KS	(3)	117	131m		1/10	New Zealand	Auckland	1929-30
		173 §	292m	321	-/21	Australia	Lord's	1930
		109	135h		-/13	New Zealand	The Oval	1931
Edrich,JH	(12)	120 §	318m	287	2/9	Australia	Lord's	1964
		310* §	532m	450	5/52	New Zealand	Leeds	1965
		109	310m		-/11	Australia	Melbourne	1965-66
		103	253m		-/12	Australia	Sydney	1965-66
		146	469m		1/10	West Indies	Bridgetown	1967-68
		164	462m		-/20	Australia	The Oval	1968
		115	296m	306	-/20	New Zealand	Lord's	1969
		155	347m		-/19	New Zealand	Nottingham	1969
		115*	346m		-/16	Australia	Perth	1970-71
		130	354m		-/14	Australia	Adelaide	1970-71
		100*	198m		1/9	India	Manchester	1974
		175	542m	420	-/21	Australia	Lord's	1975
Edrich,WJ	(6)	219	436m		-/25	South Africa	Durban[2]	1938-39
		119	314m	379	-/7	Australia	Sydney	1946-47
		189	362m		1/24	South Africa	Lord's	1947
		191	320m		3/22	South Africa	Manchester	1947
		111	314m	312	1/13	Australia	Leeds	1948
		100	185m		-/14	New Zealand	The Oval	1949
Evans,TG	(2)	104	140m		-/17	West Indies	Manchester	1950
		104	130m		-/16	India	Lord's	1952
Fane,FL	(1)	143	n240h		-/17	South Africa	Johannesburg[1]	1905-06
Fletcher,KWR	(7)	113	295m	259	-/13	India	Bombay[2]	1972-73
		178	379m		2/21	New Zealand	Lord's	1973
		129*	365m	357	-/19	West Indies	Bridgetown	1973-74
		123*	334m		-/8	India	Manchester	1974
		122	513m	377	-/10	Pakistan	The Oval	1974
		146	446m	424	-/11	Australia	Melbourne	1974-75
		216	443m	413	-/30	New Zealand	Auckland	1974-75
Flintoff,A	(5)	137 §	215m	163	3/23	New Zealand	Christchurch	2001-02
		142	205m	146	5/18	South Africa	Lord's	2003
		102*	327m	224	1/13	West Indies	St John's	2003-04
		167	274m	191	7/17	West Indies	Birmingham	2004
		102	201m	132	1/14	Australia	Nottingham	2005
Foster,RE	(1)	287 §	419m		-/37	Australia	Sydney	1903-04
Fowler,G	(3)	105 §	324m	303	-/8	New Zealand	The Oval	1983
		106	366m	259	-/13	West Indies	Lord's	1984

		201	565m	411	3/21	India	Madras[1]	1984-85
Fry,CB	(2)	144	213m		-/23	Australia	The Oval	1905
		129	285h		-/7	South Africa	The Oval	1907
Gatting,MW	(10)	136	310m	255	-/21	India	Bombay[3]	1984-85
		207	504m	308	3/20	India	Madras[1]	1984-85
		160	356m	266	-/21	Australia	Manchester	1985
		100*	216m	127	-/13	Australia	Birmingham	1985
		183*	383m	294	2/20	India	Birmingham	1986
		121	259m	198	-/13	New Zealand	The Oval	1986
		100	180m	141	-/15	Australia	Adelaide	1986-87
		124	401m	281	-/16	Pakistan	Birmingham	1987
		150*	346m	302	-/21	Pakistan	The Oval	1987
		117	410m	286	-/14	Australia	Adelaide	1994-95
Gibb,PA	(2)	106 §	192m	192	-/7	South Africa	Johannesburg[1]	1938-39
		120	451m		-/2	South Africa	Durban[2]	1938-39
Gooch,GA	(20)	123	211m	162	1/17	West Indies	Lord's	1980
		116	310m		-/13	West Indies	Bridgetown	1980-81
		153	315m		2/21	West Indies	Kingston	1980-81
		127	227m		-/20	India	Madras[1]	1981-82
		196	423m	310	-/27	Australia	The Oval	1985
		114	355m	280	1/12	India	Lord's	1986
		183	441m	368	-/22	New Zealand	Lord's	1986
		146	410m	303	-/15	West Indies	Nottingham	1988
		154	393m	281	1/19	New Zealand	Birmingham	1990
		333)	627m	485	3/43	India	Lord's	1990
		123)	147m	113	4/13			
		116	237m	163	-/16	India	Manchester	1990
		117	214m	188	-/12	Australia	Adelaide	1990-91
		154*	452m	331	-/18	West Indies	Leeds	1991
		174	329m	252	-/19	Sri Lanka	Lord's	1991
		114	294m	220	2/15	New Zealand	Auckland	1991-92
		135	415m	301	1/19	Pakistan	Leeds	1992
		133	309m	247	2/21	Australia	Manchester	1993
		120	324m	265	1/18	Australia	Nottingham	1993
		210	418m	317	-/29	New Zealand	Nottingham	1994
Gower,DI	(18)	111 §	251m	253	-/14	New Zealand	The Oval	1978
		102	254m	221	-/9	Australia	Perth	1978-79
		200* §	365m	279	1/24	India	Birmingham	1979
		154*	461m		1/16	West Indies	Kingston	1980-81
		114	370m	259	-/16	Australia	Adelaide	1982-83
		112*	281m	196	-/14	New Zealand	Leeds	1983
		108	228m	198	-/16	New Zealand	Lord's	1983
		152	426m	318	-/16	Pakistan	Faisalabad	1983-84
		173*	423m	284	-/16	Pakistan	Lahore[2]	1983-84
		166	379m	283	-/17	Australia	Nottingham	1985
		215	449m	314	1/25	Australia	Birmingham	1985
		157	337m	215	-/20	Australia	The Oval	1985
		131	281m	202	-/14	New Zealand	The Oval	1986
		136	277m	175	-/19	Australia	Perth	1986-87
		106	273m	198	-/16	Australia	Lord's	1989
		157*	365m	271	-/21	India	The Oval	1990
		100	254m	170	-/8	Australia	Melbourne	1990-91
		123	312m	236	-/15	Australia	Sydney	1990-91
Grace,WG	(2)	152 §	235m		-/12	Australia	The Oval	1880
		170	270m		-/22	Australia	The Oval	1886
Graveney,TW	(11)	175 §	503m		-/17	India	Bombay[2]	1951-52
		111	166m	168	-/14	Australia	Sydney	1954-55

		258	471m		-/30	West Indies	Nottingham	1957
		164	324m		-/17	West Indies	The Oval	1957
		153	247m		-/22	Pakistan	Lord's	1962
		114	200m	214	-/15	Pakistan	Nottingham	1962
		109	230m		1/11	West Indies	Nottingham	1966
		165	361m		-/19	West Indies	The Oval	1966
		151	300h		2/12	India	Lord's	1967
		118	250m		-/20	West Indies	Port-of-Spain	1967-68
		105	275m		-/9	Pakistan	Karachi[1]	1968-69
Greig,AW	(8)	148	360m	291	-/24	India	Bombay[2]	1972-73
		139 §	197m		-/16	New Zealand	Nottingham	1973
		148	404m	320	2/15	West Indies	Bridgetown	1973-74
		121	311m	254	1/14	West Indies	Georgetown	1973-74
		106	188m	180	1/8	India	Lord's	1974
		110	296m	229	-/17	Australia	Brisbane[2]	1974-75
		116	340m	264	-/15	West Indies	Leeds	1976
		103	426m	343	1/7	India	Calcutta	1976-77
Griffith,SC	(1)	140 §	354m		-/15	West Indies	Port-of-Spain	1947-48
Gunn,G	(2)	119 §	150m		-/20	Australia	Sydney	1907-08
		122*	287m		1!/7	Australia	Sydney	1907-08
Gunn,W	(1)	102*	250m		-/8	Australia	Manchester	1893
Hammond,WR	(22)	251	461m	605	-/30	Australia	Sydney	1928-29
		200	398m	472	-/17	Australia	Melbourne	1928-29
		119*)	263m	374	-/19	Australia	Adelaide	1928-29
		177)	440m	603	-/17			
		138*	200m		-/13	South Africa	Birmingham	1929
		101*	>120h		1/5	South Africa	The Oval	1929
		113	325m	356	-/14	Australia	Leeds	1930
		136*	220m		-/6	South Africa	Durban[2]	1930-31
		100*	100m		-/13	New Zealand	The Oval	1931
		112	192m	242	-/16	Australia	Sydney	1932-33
		101	208m	205	-/12	Australia	Sydney	1932-33
		227	396m		-/22	New Zealand	Christchurch	1932-33
		336*	325m	398	10/34	New Zealand	Auckland	1932-33
		167	190m		-/21	India	Manchester	1936
		217	290m		-/30	India	The Oval	1936
		231*	458m		-/27	Australia	Sydney	1936-37
		140	219m		1/14	New Zealand	Lord's	1937
		240	369m	385	-/32	Australia	Lord's	1938
		181	337m	371	-/16	South Africa	Cape Town	1938-39
		120	178m	177	-/16	South Africa	Durban[2]	1938-39
		140	349m		-/7	South Africa	Durban[2]	1938-39
		138	180h		-/21	West Indies	The Oval	1939
Hampshire,JH	(1)	107 §	288m	258	-/15	West Indies	Lord's	1969
Hardstaff,J,jr	(4)	114 §	250m		-/9	New Zealand	Lord's	1937
		103	n180h		-/16	New Zealand	The Oval	1937
		169*	326m	395	-/20	Australia	The Oval	1938
		205*	315m		-/16	India	Lord's	1946
Hayes,FC	(1)	106* §	240m		-/12	West Indies	The Oval	1973
Hayward,TW	(3)	122	>180h		1!/15	South Africa	Johannesburg[1]	1895-96
		130	255h		-/18	Australia	Manchester	1899
		137	270h		-/20	Australia	The Oval	1899
Hearne,JW	(1)	114	225m	243	-/11	Australia	Melbourne	1911-12
Hendren,EH	(7)	132	140m		-/20	South Africa	Leeds	1924
		142	190m		2/14	South Africa	The Oval	1924
		127*	208m		-/18	Australia	Lord's	1926

		169	308m	314	-/16	Australia	Brisbane[1]	1928-29
		205*	398m		-/29	West Indies	Port-of-Spain	1929-30
		123			-/21	West Indies	Georgetown	1929-30
		132	243m	245	-/22	Australia	Manchester	1934
Hick,GA	(6)	178	390m	319	1/20	India	Bombay[3]	1992-93
		110	272m	182	3/6	South Africa	Leeds	1994
		118*	302m	213	-/17	West Indies	Nottingham	1995
		141	393m	252	-/25	South Africa	Centurion	1995-96
		107	347m	238	-/18	Sri Lanka	The Oval	1998
		101 §	270m	197	-/13	Zimbabwe	Lord's	2000
Hill,AJL	(1)	124				South Africa	Cape Town	1895-96
Hobbs,JB	(15)	187	225m		-/23	South Africa	Cape Town	1909-10
		126*	227m	206	-/8	Australia	Melbourne	1911-12
		187	334m	351	-/16	Australia	Adelaide	1911-12
		178	268m		-/22	Australia	Melbourne	1911-12
		107	167m	203	-/15	Australia	Lord's	1912
		122	210m		-/10	Australia	Melbourne	1920-21
		123	151m		-/13	Australia	Adelaide	1920-21
		211	280m		-/16	South Africa	Lord's	1924
		115	219m		-/7	Australia	Sydney	1924-25
		154	288m		-/11	Australia	Melbourne	1924-25
		119	294m		-/7	Australia	Adelaide	1924-25
		119	247m		-/10	Australia	Lord's	1926
		100	227m		-/10	Australia	The Oval	1926
		159	240h		-/20	West Indies	The Oval	1928
		142	278m	301	-/11	Australia	Melbourne	1928-29
Hussain,N	(14)	128 §	327m	227	1/18	India	Birmingham	1996
		107#	239m	180	-/12	India	Nottingham	1996
		113 §	357m	276	-/14	Zimbabwe	Bulawayo[2]	1996-97
		207	437m	336	-/38	Australia	Birmingham	1997
		105	250m	181	-/15	Australia	Leeds	1997
		106	378m	318	-/14	West Indies	St John's	1997-98
		105	391m	294	-/17	South Africa	Lord's	1998
		146*	635m	463	-/17	South Africa	Durban[2]	1999-2000
		109	298m	255	3/12	Sri Lanka	Galle	2000-01
		106	323m	244	-/14	New Zealand	Christchurch	2001-02
		155	459m	331	-/25	India	Lord's	2002
		110	271m	194	1/18	India	Leeds	2002
		116	354m	251	-/18	South Africa	Nottingham	2003
		103*	295m	204	-/15	New Zealand	Lord's	2004
Hutchings,KL	(1)	126	163m		1!/21	Australia	Melbourne	1907-08
Hutton,L	(19)	100	202m		-/8	New Zealand	Manchester	1937
		100 §	199m	227	-/14	Australia	Nottingham	1938
		364	797m	844	-/35	Australia	The Oval	1938
		196 §	310m		-/21	West Indies	Lord's	1939
		165*	310m		-/17	West Indies	The Oval	1939
		122#	300m	356	-/5	Australia	Sydney	1946-47
		100	277m		-/8	South Africa	Leeds	1947
		158	290m	362	-/16	South Africa	Johannesburg[2]	1948-49
		123	249m		-/13	South Africa	Johannesburg[2]	1948-49
		101	>240h		-/14	New Zealand	Leeds	1949
		206	300h		-/25	New Zealand	The Oval	1949
		202*	470m		-/22	West Indies	The Oval	1950
		156*	370m		-/11	Australia	Adelaide	1950-51
		100	300h			South Africa	Leeds	1951
		150	317m		-/20	India	Lord's	1952

		104	315m		-/10	India	Manchester	1952
		145	325m	308	-/16	Australia	Lord's	1953
		169	457m		1/24	West Indies	Georgetown	1953-54
		205	534m		1/23	West Indies	Kingston	1953-54
Illingworth,R	(2)	113	195h		-/12	West Indies	Lord's	1969
		107	270m		1/8	India	Manchester	1971
Insole,DJ	(1)	110*	373m		-/7	South Africa	Durban[2]	1956-57
Jackson,Hon.FS	(5)	103	135h		-/13	Australia	The Oval	1893
		118	173m		-/18	Australia	The Oval	1899
		128	255m		-/16	Australia	Manchester	1902
		144*	268m		-/18	Australia	Leeds	1905
		113	223m		-/12	Australia	Manchester	1905
Jardine,DR	(1)	127	300h		-/5	West Indies	Manchester	1933
Jessop,GL	(1)	104	77m		-/17	Australia	The Oval	1902
Jones,GO	(1)	100	192m	146	1/15	New Zealand	Leeds	2004
Key,RWT	(1)	221 §	426m	288	-/31	West Indies	Lord's	2004
Knight,B R	(2)	125 §	218m		-/14	New Zealand	Auckland	1962-63
		127	224m		-/16	India	Kanpur	1963-64
Knight,NV	(1)	113	258m	176	-/16	Pakistan	Leeds	1996
Knott,APE	(5)	101	181m		1/11	New Zealand	Auckland	1970-71
		116	188m	173	-/22	Pakistan	Birmingham	1971
		106*	227m	205	-/9	Australia	Adelaide	1974-75
		116	305m	212	-/14	West Indies	Leeds	1976
		135	292m	214	-/18	Australia	Nottingham	1977
Lamb,AJ	(14)	107	260m	202	1/8	India	The Oval	1982
		102* §	297m	293	-/10	New Zealand	The Oval	1983
		137*	262m	219	-/22	New Zealand	Nottingham	1983
		110	360m	259	-/13	West Indies	Lord's	1984
		100	228m	186	-/15	West Indies	Leeds	1984
		100*	251m	185	-/15	West Indies	Manchester	1984
		107 §	267m	195	1/10	Sri Lanka	Lord's	1984
		113	338m	212	-/15	West Indies	Lord's	1988
		125	281m	205	-/24	Australia	Leeds	1989
		132	364m	209	-/16	West Indies	Kingston	1989-90
		119	338m	225	-/14	West Indies	Bridgetown	1989-90
		139	276m	187	-/22	India	Lord's	1990
		109	205m	231	2/8	India	Manchester	1990
		142	303m	141	-/15	New Zealand	Wellington	1991-92
Legge,GB	(1)	196	281m		-/23	New Zealand	Auckland	1929-30
Lewis,AR	(1)	125	267m	228	1/16	India	Kanpur	1972-73
Lewis,CC	(1)	117	170m	140	2/15	India	Madras[1]	1992-93
Leyland,M	(9)	137 §	301m	330	-/18	Australia	Melbourne	1928-29
		102			-/10	South Africa	Lord's	1929
		109	211m	258	1/14	Australia	Lord's	1934
		153	314m	314	-/19	Australia	Manchester	1934
		110	165m	174	1/15	Australia	The Oval	1934
		161	235m		1/17	South Africa	The Oval	1935
		126	251m		-/11	Australia	Brisbane[2]	1936-37
		111*	194m		-/11	Australia	Melbourne	1936-37
		187	381m	431	-/17	Australia	The Oval	1938
Lloyd,D	(1)	214*	448m	396	-/17	India	Birmingham	1974
Luckhurst,BW	(4)	131	340m		-/13	Australia	Perth	1970-71
		109	328m		-/11	Australia	Melbourne	1970-71
		108* §	327m	279	-/14	Pakistan	Birmingham	1971
		101	231m	170	1/10	India	Manchester	1971
MacLaren,AC	(5)	120	220m		-/12	Australia	Melbourne	1894-95

		109	189m		-/15	Australia	Sydney	1897-98
		124	317m		-/10	Australia	Adelaide	1897-98
		116	206m		-/20	Australia	Sydney	1901-02
		140	217m		-/22	Australia	Nottingham	1905
Makepeace,JWH	(1)	117	260m		-/4	Australia	Melbourne	1920-21
Mann,FG	(1)	136*	237m		1/12	South Africa	Port Elizabeth	1948-49
May,PBH	(13)	138 §	380m		-/19	South Africa	Leeds	1951
		135	249m		-/24	West Indies	Port-of-Spain	1953-54
		104	298m	281	-/10	Australia	Sydney	1954-55
		112	270m		-/18	South Africa	Lord's	1955
		117	270h		-/16	South Africa	Manchester	1955
		101	317m		-/12	Australia	Leeds	1956
		285*	595m		2/25	West Indies	Birmingham	1957
		104	183m		-/14	West Indies	Nottingham	1957
		113*	174m		2/12	New Zealand	Leeds	1958
		101	156m		4/7	New Zealand	Manchester	1958
		113	315m	298	-/11	Australia	Melbourne	1958-59
		124*	251m		-/14	New Zealand	Auckland	1958-59
		106	218m		-/18	India	Nottingham	1959
Mead,CP	(4)	102	>210h		-/12	South Africa	Johannesburg[1]	1913-14
		117	225h		-/8	South Africa	Port Elizabeth	1913-14
		182*	309m		-/21	Australia	The Oval	1921
		181	454m		-/13	South Africa	Durban[2]	1922-23
Milburn,C	(2)	126*	179m		3/17	West Indies	Lord's	1966
		139	301m		1/17	Pakistan	Karachi[1]	1968-69
Milton,CA	(1)	104* §	297m		-/12	New Zealand	Leeds	1958
Murray,JT	(1)	112 §	267m		-/13	West Indies	The Oval	1966
Parfitt,PH	(7)	111	312m		-/11	Pakistan	Karachi[1]	1961-62
		101*	197m		2/9	Pakistan	Birmingham	1962
		119	265m		-/18	Pakistan	Leeds	1962
		101*	225m	187	-/9	Pakistan	Nottingham	1962
		131* §	289m		-/14	New Zealand	Auckland	1962-63
		121	328m		-/18	India	Kanpur	1963-64
		122*	333m	289	-/18	South Africa	Johannesburg[3]	1964-65
Parks,JM	(2)	101* §	≥210m			West Indies	Port-of-Spain	1959-60
		108*	247m		-/10	South Africa	Durban[2]	1964-65
Pataudi,Nawab of,sr	(1)	102 §	317m	380	-/6	Australia	Sydney	1932-33
Paynter,E	(4)	216*	319m	331	1/26	Australia	Nottingham	1938
		117 §)	176m	179	1/8	South Africa	Johannesburg[1]	1938-39
		100 §)	192m	162	-/10			
		243	334m	419	-/24	South Africa	Durban[2]	1938-39
Pietersen,KP	(5)	158	286m	158	7/15	Australia	The Oval	2005
		100	202m	137	3/6	Pakistan	Faisalabad	2005-06
		158	301m	205	2/19	Sri Lanka	Lord's	2006
		142	225m	157	3/20	Sri Lanka	Birmingham	2006
		135	272m	169	2/20	Pakistan	Leeds	2006
Place,W	(1)	107	367m		-/6	West Indies	Kingston	1947-48
Pullar,G	(4)	131	320m		-/14	India	Manchester	1959
		175	360m	354	1/15	South Africa	The Oval	1960
		119	313m		-/14	India	Kanpur	1961-62
		165	414m		-/16	Pakistan	Dacca	1961-62
Radley,CT	(2)	158	648m	500	-/15	New Zealand	Auckland	1977-78
		106 §	310m		-/11	Pakistan	Birmingham	1978
Ramprakash,MR	(2)	154	529m	388	-/20	West Indies	Bridgetown	1997-98
		133	365m	232	-/18	Australia	The Oval	2001
Randall,DW	(7)	174 §	448m	353	-/21	Australia	Melbourne	1976-77

		150	582m	498	-/13	Australia	Sydney	1978-79
		126	353m	290	1/11	India	Lord's	1982
		105	249m	156	-/11	Pakistan	Birmingham	1982
		115	266m	215	-/13	Australia	Perth	1982-83
		164	365m	269	2/20	New Zealand	Wellington	1983-84
		104	347m	338	-/12	New Zealand	Auckland	1983-84
Ranjitsinhji,KS	(2)	154* §	185m		-/23	Australia	Manchester	1896
		175	223m		-/24	Australia	Sydney	1897-98
Read,WW	(1)	117	137m	155	-/20	Australia	The Oval	1884
Rhodes,W	(2)	179	397m		-/14	Australia	Melbourne	1911-12
		152	310m		-/21	South Africa	Johannesburg[1]	1913-14
Richards,CJ	(1)	133	240m	207	-/16	Australia	Perth	1986-87
Richardson,PE	(5)	104	222m		-/11	Australia	Manchester	1956
		117 §	528m		-/6	South Africa	Johannesburg[3]	1956-57
		126	278m		-/10	West Indies	Nottingham	1957
		107	295m		-/10	West Indies	The Oval	1957
		100 §	286m		-/7	New Zealand	Birmingham	1958
Robertson,JDB	(2)	133	345m		-/14	West Indies	Port-of-Spain	1947-48
		121 §	225h		1/11	New Zealand	Lord's	1949
Robins,RWV	(1)	108	130m		-/12	South Africa	Manchester	1935
Robinson,RT	(4)	160	508m	391	-/17	India	Delhi	1984-85
		175 §	408m	271	-/27	Australia	Leeds	1985
		148	392m	293	-/18	Australia	Birmingham	1985
		166 §	528m	366	-/16	Pakistan	Manchester	1987
Russell,CAG	(5)	135*	250m		1/10	Australia	Adelaide	1920-21
		101	244m		-/9	Australia	Manchester	1921
		102*	163m		-/11	Australia	The Oval	1921
		140)	320m		-/11	South Africa	Durban[2]	1922-23
		111)	265m		-/10			
Russell,RC	(2)	128*	350m	294	-/14	Australia	Manchester	1989
		124	383m	261	-/13	India	Lord's	1996
Sandham,A	(2)	152 §	360m		-/16	West Indies	Bridgetown	1929-30
		325	600m		-/28	West Indies	Kingston	1929-30
Sharp,J	(1)	105	176m	174	-/11	Australia	The Oval	1909
Sharpe,PJ	(1)	111	269m		-/14	New Zealand	Nottingham	1969
Sheppard,Rev.DS	(3)	119	350m		-/9	India	The Oval	1952
		113	296m		1/15	Australia	Manchester	1956
		113	301m		-/5	Australia	Melbourne	1962-63
Shrewsbury,A	(3)	105*	320m		-/10	Australia	Melbourne	1884-85
		164	411m		-/16	Australia	Lord's	1886
		106	250m		-/9	Australia	Lord's	1893
Simpson,RT	(4)	103 §	a145m		3/11	New Zealand	Manchester	1949
		156*	338m		-/12	Australia	Melbourne	1950-51
		137	250m		-/21	South Africa	Nottingham	1951
		101	203m		-/9	Pakistan	Nottingham	1954
Smith,MJK	(3)	100 §	214m		-/12	India	Manchester	1959
		108	a300h		2/?	West Indies	Port-of-Spain	1959-60
		121	320m		1/12	South Africa	Cape Town	1964-65
Smith,RA	(9)	143	355m	285	-/15	Australia	Manchester	1989
		101	206m	150	-/16	Australia	Nottingham	1989
		100* §	196m	155	-/14	India	Lord's	1990
		121*	243m	197	-/11	India	Manchester	1990
		148*	413m	271	-/20	West Indies	Lord's	1991
		109	353m	256	-/13	West Indies	The Oval	1991
		127 §	326m	231	-/18	Pakistan	Birmingham	1992
		128	448m	338	-/20	Sri Lanka	Colombo (SSC)	1992-93

		175	418m	315	3/25	West Indies	St John's	1993-94
Spooner,RH	(1)	119 §	<180h		1/13	South Africa	Lord's	1912
Steel,AG	(2)	135*	238m		-/16	Australia	Sydney	1882-83
		148	230m		-/13	Australia	Lord's	1884
Steele,DS	(1)	106 §	368m	296	-/9	West Indies	Nottingham	1976
Stewart,AJ	(15)	113* §	308m	240	-/14	Sri Lanka	Lord's	1991
		148	355m	265	-/17	New Zealand	Christchurch	1991-92
		107	320m	243	-/13	New Zealand	Wellington	1991-92
		190 §	351m	261	-/31	Pakistan	Birmingham	1992
		118)	347m	221	-/18	West Indies	Bridgetown	1993-94
		143)	475m	319	-/20			
		119	289m	229	-/20	New Zealand	Lord's	1994
		170	438m	315	-/24	Pakistan	Leeds	1996
		101*	408m	267	-/8	Zimbabwe	Harare	1996-97
		173	364m	277	1/23	New Zealand	Auckland	1996-97
		164	422m	317	-/24	South Africa	Manchester	1998
		107	212m	160	-/16	Australia	Melbourne	1998-99
		124*	382m	283	-/21	Zimbabwe	Lord's	2000
		105	186m	153	-/13	West Indies	Manchester	2000
		(In his 100th Test match)						
		123	273m	190	-/17	Sri Lanka	Manchester	2002
Stoddart,AE	(2)	134	230m		-/15	Australia	Adelaide	1891-92
		173	320m		1∆/14	Australia	Melbourne	1894-95
Strauss,AJ	(10)	112 §	305m	215	-/13	New Zealand	Lord's	2004
		137 §	298m	202	-/20	West Indies	Lord's	2004
		126 §	301m	228	-/17	South Africa	Port Elizabeth	2004-05
		136	383m	285	-/16	South Africa	Durban[2]	2004-05
		147	353m	250	1/23	South Africa	Johannesburg[3]	2004-05
		106	246m	158	2/9	Australia	Manchester	2005
		129	351m	210	-/17	Australia	The Oval	2005
		128	331m	240	1/17	India	Mumbai[3]	2005-06
		128	300m	214	/-13	Pakistan	Lord's	2006
		116	250m	171	-/16	Pakistan	Leeds	2006
Subba Row,R	(3)	100 §	270m			West Indies	Georgetown	1959-60
		112 §	244m		-/13	Australia	Birmingham	1961
		137	400m		1/15	Australia	The Oval	1961
Sutcliffe,H	(16)	122	200m		-/11	South Africa	Lord's	1924
		115 §	247m		-/11	Australia	Sydney	1924-25
		176)	431m		-/17	Australia	Melbourne	1924-25
		127)	379m		-/12			
		143	295m		-/14	Australia	Melbourne	1924-25
		161	439m		-/16	Australia	The Oval	1926
		102				South Africa	Johannesburg[1]	1927-28
		135	385m	462	-/9	Australia	Melbourne	1928-29
		114	225m		-/7	South Africa	Birmingham	1929
		100	176m		-/10	South Africa	Lord's	1929
		104)	210m		-/9	South Africa	The Oval	1929
		109*)	200m		-/11			
		161	404m	387	-/10	Australia	The Oval	1930
		117 §	220m		-/10	New Zealand	The Oval	1931
		109*	195m		1/9	New Zealand	Manchester	1931
		194	436m	496	-/13	Australia	Sydney	1932-33
Tate,MW	(1)	100*	<120h		-/12	South Africa	Lord's	1929
Tavaré,CJ	(2)	149	455m	303	-/18	India	Delhi	1981-82
		109 §	312m	255	-/11	New Zealand	The Oval	1983
Thorpe,GP	(16)	114* §	334m	280	-/11	Australia	Nottingham	1993
		123	301m	218	-/19	Australia	Perth	1994-95

		119 §	338m	245	-/17	New Zealand	Auckland	1996-97
		108	330m	249	-/12	New Zealand	Wellington	1996-97
		138	290m	245	-/19	Australia	Birmingham	1997
		103	392m	268	-/8	West Indies	Bridgetown	1997-98
		118	432m	301	-/2	Pakistan	Lahore[2]	2000-01
		113*	330m	267	-/11	Sri Lanka	Colombo (SSC)	2000-01
		138	329m	261	1/17	Pakistan	Manchester	2001
		200*	330m	231	4/28	New Zealand	Christchurch	2001-02
		123	316m	229	-/12	Sri Lanka	Birmingham	2002
		124	316m	244	-/16	South Africa	The Oval	2003
		119*	312m	217	-/13	West Indies	Bridgetown	2003-04
		104*	236m	171	-/13	New Zealand	Nottingham	2004
		114	392m	239	-/9	West Indies	Manchester	2004
		118*	313m	209	-/15	South Africa	Durban[2]	2004-05
Trescothick,ME	(14)	122 §	394m	348	-/12	Sri Lanka	Kandy	2000-01
		117	365m	272	1/15	Pakistan	Manchester	2001
		161	296m	232	-/23	Sri Lanka	Birmingham	2002
		219	570m	374	2/16	South Africa	The Oval	2003
		113 §	249m	194	3/16	Bangladesh	Dhaka	2003-04
		132	232m	165	-/13	New Zealand	Leeds	2004
		105)	254m	182	-/19	West Indies	Birmingham	2004
		107)	196m	158	1/15			
		132	344m	261	3/20	South Africa	Durban[2]	2004-05
		180	367m	248	4/24	South Africa	Johannesburg[3]	2004-05
		194	367m	259	-/23	Bangladesh	Lord's	2005
		151	192m	148	2/21	Bangladesh	Chester-le-Street	2005
		193	467m	305	2/20	Pakistan	Multan[2]	2005-06
		106	251m	180	1/16	Sri Lanka	Lord's	2006
Tyldesley,GE	(3)	122	253m		-/16	South Africa	Johannesburg[1]	1927-28
		100	165m		-/5	South Africa	Durban[2]	1927-28
		122 §	210h		1/13	West Indies	Lord's	1928
Tyldesley,JT	(4)	112				South Africa	Cape Town	1898-99
		138	262m		-/20	Australia	Birmingham	1902
		100	168m		-/12	Australia	Leeds	1905
		112*	212m		-/15	Australia	The Oval	1905
Ulyett,G	(1)	149	240m		-/13	Australia	Melbourne	1881-82
Valentine,BH	(2)	136 §	177m		1/13	India	Bombay[1]	1933-34
		112	160m	147	1/12	South Africa	Cape Town	1938-39
Vaughan,MP	(15)	120	341m	223	1/16	Pakistan	Manchester	2001
		115	276m	219	-/17	Sri Lanka	Lord's	2002
		100	217m	141	-/11	India	Lord's	2002
		197	354m	258	-/23	India	Nottingham	2002
		195	379m	279	-/29	India	The Oval	2002
		177	371m	306	3/22	Australia	Adelaide	2002-03
		145	277m	218	3/19	Australia	Melbourne	2002-03
		183	399m	278	1/27	Australia	Sydney	2002-03
		156	415m	286	1/24	South Africa	Birmingham	2003
		105	448m	333	-/11	Sri Lanka	Kandy	2003-04
		140	346m	267	-/20	West Indies	St John's	2003-04
		103)	228m	154	-/12	West Indies	Lord's	2004
		101*)	168m	145	-/11			
		120	203m	174	-/15	Bangladesh	Lord's	2005
		166	281m	215	1/20	Australia	Manchester	2005
Walters,CF	(1)	102	151m		-/14	India	Madras[1]	1933-34
Ward,Albert	(1)	117	224m		-/11	Australia	Sydney	1894-95
Warner,PF	(1)	132* §			-/19	South Africa	Johannesburg[1]	1898-99

Washbrook,C	(6)	112	247m	299	1/8	Australia	Melbourne	1946-47
		143	317m	312	-/22	Australia	Leeds	1948
		195	297m	308	-/18	South Africa	Johannesburg[2]	1948-49
		103*	180h		-/12	New Zealand	Leeds	1949
		114 §	320m		1/14	West Indies	Lord's	1950
		102	320m		-/9	West Indies	Nottingham	1950
Watkins,AJ	(2)	111	220m		-/15	South Africa	Johannesburg[2]	1948-49
		137 §	540h		-/15	India	Delhi	1951-52
Watson,W	(2)	109 §	346m	356	-/16	Australia	Lord's	1953
		116 §	259m		-/16	West Indies	Kingston	1953-54
White,C	(1)	121	343m	265	2/12	India	Ahmedabad	2001-02
Willey,P	(2)	100*	236m	203	-/16	West Indies	The Oval	1980
		102*	223m	203	1/15	West Indies	St John's	1980-81
Wood,H	(1)	134*				South Africa	Cape Town	1891-92
Woolley,FE	(5)	133*	215m		-/12	Australia	Sydney	1911-12
		115*	206m		1/11	South Africa	Johannesburg[1]	1922-23
		134*	145m		-/20	South Africa	Lord's	1924
		123	146m		1/15	Australia	Sydney	1924-25
		154	165m		-/20	South Africa	Manchester	1929
Woolmer,RA	(3)	149	499m	390	-/20	Australia	The Oval	1975
		120	306m	247	-/13	Australia	Lord's	1977
		137	386m	338	-/22	Australia	Manchester	1977
Worthington,TS	(1)	128	>210h		-/19	India	The Oval	1936
Wyatt,RES	(2)	113	245m		-/14	South Africa	Manchester	1929
		149	305m		-/17	South Africa	Nottingham	1935

SOUTH AFRICA (239)			Time	Balls	6/4	Opponents		
Alma,HM	(1)	149	408m	317	-/20	New Zealand	Cape Town	2005-06
Balaskas,XC	(1)	122*	198m		-/15	New Zealand	Wellington	1931-32
Barlow,EJ	(6)	114 §	354m		-/13	Australia	Brisbane[2]	1963-64
		109	273m		-/11	Australia	Melbourne	1963-64
		201	392m		-/27	Australia	Adelaide	1963-64
		138	344m		-/16	England	Cape Town	1964-65
		127	362m		1/11	Australia	Cape Town	1969-70
		110	323m	247	1/13	Australia	Johannesburg[3]	1969-70
Bland,KC	(3)	126	324m	333	1/13	Australia	Sydney	1963-64
		144*	248m		2/17	England	Johannesburg[3]	1964-65
		127	≤270h		-/16	England	The Oval	1965
Boucher,MV	(4)	100	209m	183	-/16	West Indies	Centurion	1998-99
		125	322m	236	-/18	Zimbabwe	Harare	1999-2000
		108	290m	220	1/14	England	Durban[2]	1999-2000
		122*	250m	173	-/21	West Indies	Cape Town	2003-04
Catterall,RH	(3)	120	195m		2/15	England	Birmingham	1924
		120	200m		-/16	England	Lord's	1924
		119	135m		2/14	England	Durban[2]	1927-28
Christy,JAJ	(1)	103 §	126m		-/10	New Zealand	Christchurch	1931-32
Cronje,WJ	(6)	135	527m	411	-/12	India	Port Elizabeth	1992-93
		122	412m	297	-/11	Sri Lanka	Colombo (SSC)	1993-94
		122	250m	122	1/16	Australia	Johannesburg[3]	1993-94
		112	288m	235	1/10	New Zealand	Cape Town	1994-95
		101	227m	155	3/7	New Zealand	Auckland	1994-95
		126	288m	212	-/16	England	Nottingham	1998
Cullinan,DJ	(14)	102	358m	232	-/17	Sri Lanka	Colombo (PSS)	1993-94
		153*	354m	261	1/15	India	Calcutta	1996-97
		122*	262m	194	1/15	India	Johannesburg[3]	1996-97
		113	222m	160	1/13	Sri Lanka	Cape Town	1997-98

		103	307m	185	-/13	Sri Lanka	Centurion	1997-98
		168	425m	307	-/20	West Indies	Cape Town	1998-99
		275*	658m	490	2/27	New Zealand	Auckland	1998-99
		152	327m	272	1/22	New Zealand	Wellington	1998-99
		108	251m	170	-/17	England	Johannesburg[3]	1999-2000
		120	354m	255	1/10	England	Cape Town	1999-2000
		114*	273m	224	1/12	Sri Lanka	Galle	2000-01
		112	289m	232	3/12	Sri Lanka	Cape Town	2000-01
		103	216m	155	-/14	West Indies	Port-of-Spain	2000-01
		134	367m	262	-/14	West Indies	Bridgetown	2000-01
Dalton,EL	(2)	117	140m		-/18	England	The Oval	1935
		102	209m	237	-/9	England	Johannesburg[1]	1938-39
de Villiers,AB	(3)	136*	276m	169	1/11	England	Centurion	2004-05
		178		352	1/15	West Indies	Bridgetown	2004-05
		114	251m	173	1/13	West Indies	St John's	2004-05
Dippenaar,HH	(3)	100	238m	192	-/21	New Zealand	Johannesburg[3]	2000-01
		178*	514m	369	2/25	Bangladesh	Chittagong[1]	2002-03
		110	372m	245	-/11	England	Port Elizabeth	2004-05
Endean,WR	(3)	162*	452m		-/9	Australia	Melbourne	1952-53
		116	275m		-/9	New Zealand	Auckland	1952-53
		116*	≥240h		-/16	England	Leeds	1955
Faulkner,GA	(4)	123	170m		-/17	England	Johannesburg[1]	1909-10
		204	313m		-/26	Australia	Melbourne	1910-11
		115	239m		-/10	Australia	Adelaide	1910-11
		122*	257m	270	-/13	Australia	Manchester	1912
Frank,CN	(1)	152	512m		-/17	Australia	Johannesburg[1]	1921-22
Gibbs,HH	(14)	211*	659m	468	3/23	New Zealand	Christchurch	1998-99
		120	316m	250	-/16	New Zealand	Wellington	1998-99
		147 §	213m	164	2/28	Zimbabwe	Harare	2001-02
		107	204m	145	2/16	India	Bloemfontein	2001-02
		196	442m	354	1/25	India	Port Elizabeth	2001-02
		104	298m	197	-/15	Australia	Durban[2]	2001-02
		114	215m	190	2/17	Bangladesh	Potchefstrrom	2002-03
		228	383m	240	6/29	Pakistan	Cape Town	2002-03
		179	305m	236	1/29	England	Birmingham	2003
		183	324m	258	1/35	England	The Oval	2003
		142	264m	175	-/23	West Indies	Durban[2]	2003-04
		142	305m	223	4/15	West Indies	Cape Town	2003-04
		192	474m	335	3/24	West Indies	Centurion	2003-04
		161	484m	307	-/25	England	Johannesburg[3]	2004-05
Goddard,TL	(1)	112	251m		3/10	England	Johannesburg[3]	1964-65
Hall,AJ	(1)	164 §	569m	454	-/17	India	Kanpur	2004-05
Hathorn,CMH	(1)	102	135h		-/15	England	Johannesburg[1]	1905-06
Hudson,AC	(4)	163 §	521m	384	-/24	West Indies	Bridgetown	1991-92
		102	249m	175	-/13	Australia	Cape Town	1993-94
		135 §	311m	236	2/18	Zimbabwe	Harare	1994-95
		146	302m	244	-/24	India	Calcutta	1996-97
Irvine,BL	(1)	102	178m	146	2/9	Australia	Port Elizabeth	1969-70
Kallis,JH	(24)	101	357m	279	-/6	Australia	Melbourne	1997-98
		132	357m	266	-/16	England	Manchester	1998
		110	429m	327	-/9	West Indies	Cape Town	1998-99
		148*	450m	340	1/17	New Zealand	Christchurch	1998-99
		115	339m	268	3/13	Zimbabwe	Harare	1999-2000
		105	315m	229	2/10	England	Cape Town	1999-2000
		160	345m	289	-/26	New Zealand	Bloemfontein	2000-01
		157*	381m	272	5/14	Zimbabwe	Harare	2001-02

		189*	581m	443	3/19	Zimbabwe	Bulawayo[2]	2001-02
		139*	266m	228	1/18	Bangladesh	Potchefstrrom	2002-03
		105	319m	236	1/11	Pakistan	Durban[2]	2002-03
		158	411m	297	1/17	West Indies	Johannesburg[3]	2003-04
		177	479m	344	-/20	West Indies	Durban[2]	2003-04
		130*	262m	191	5/7	West Indies	Cape Town	2003-04
		130*	247m	199	1/14	West Indies	Centurion	2003-04
		150*	404m	312	-/19	New Zealand	Hamilton	2003-04
		121	399m	259	-/12	India	Kolkata	2004-05
		162	364m	264	1/21	England	Durban[2]	2004-05
		149	493m	334	-/11	England	Cape Town	2004-05
		136*	277m	217	1/16	England	Centurion	2004-05
		109*	411m	346	-/15	West Indies	Georgetown	2004-05
		147	394m	287	1/14	West Indies	St John's	2004-05
		111	361m	275	-/17	Australia	Sydney	2005-06
		114	344m	223	-/17	Australia	Durban[2]	2005-06
Kirsten,G	(21)	110	353m	241	-/16	England	Johannesburg[3]	1995-96
		102)	241m	171	-/15	India	Calcutta	1996-97
		133)	315m	197	-/18			
		103	290m	204	-/15	India	Cape Town	1996-97
		100*	299m	208	-/15	Pakistan	Faisalabad	1997-98
		108*	235m	159	1/17	Australia	Adelaide	1997-98
		210	652m	525	1/24	England	Manchester	1998
		134	448m	305	-/15	West Indies	Centurion	1998-99
		128	361m	282	-/15	New Zealand	Auckland	1998-99
		275	878m	642	-/26	England	Durban[2]	1999-2000
		180	574m	461	-/20	Sri Lanka	Durban[2]	2000-01
		150	447m	308	1/13	West Indies	Georgetown	2000-01
		220	442m	286	1/33	Zimbabwe	Harare	2001-02
		153	437m	359	-/20	Australia	Sydney	2001-02
		150 §	326m	223	-/14	Bangladesh	East London	2002-03
		160	372m	227	1/17	Bangladesh	Potchefstrrom	2002-03
		108	284m	244	-/15	England	Lord's	2003
		130	458m	323	-/17	England	Leeds	2003
		118	316m	232	1/11	Pakistan	Faisalabad	2003-04
		137	275m	218	-/20	West Indies	Durban[2]	2003-04
		137	308m	213	1/18	New Zealand	Hamilton	2003-04
Kirsten,PN	(1)	104	295m	226	-/13	England	Leeds	1994
Klusener,L	(4)	102*	143m	100	-/13	India	Cape Town	1996-97
		174	333m	221	2/25	England	Port Elizabeth	1999-2000
		118*	244m	220	2/13	Sri Lanka	Kandy	2000-01
		108	195m	124	1/18	India	Bloemfontein	2001-02
Lindsay,DT	(3)	182	274m		5/25	Australia	Johannesburg[3]	1966-67
		137	253m		-/14	Australia	Durban[2]	1966-67
		131	160m		4/14	Australia	Johannesburg[3]	1966-67
McGlew,DJ	(7)	255* §	534m		-/19	New Zealand	Wellington	1952-53
		104*	280m		-/19	England	Manchester	1955
		133	398m		-/13	England	Leeds	1955
		108	315m		1/12	Australia	Johannesburg[3]	1957-58
		105	572m		-/4	Australia	Durban[2]	1957-58
		127*	312m		-/10	New Zealand	Durban[2]	1961-62
		120	302m		1/10	New Zealand	Johannesburg[3]	1961-62
McKenzie,ND	(2)	120	277m	207	-/20	New Zealand	Port Elizabeth	2000-01
		103	266m	191	1/11	Sri Lanka	Centurion	2000-01
McLean,RA	(5)	101	144m		-/11	New Zealand	Durban[2]	1953-54
		142	205m		1/21	England	Lord's	1955

		100	260m		-/14	England	Durban[2]	1956-57
		109	157m	153	-/14	England	Manchester	1960
		113	174m		1/16	New Zealand	Cape Town	1961-62
McMillan,BM	(3)	113 §	226m	180	-/15	Pakistan	Johannesburg[3]	1994-95
		100*	299m	168	3/9	England	Johannesburg[3]	1995-96
		103*	348m	235	-/9	India	Cape Town	1996-97
Melville,A	(4)	103	210m		-/10	England	Durban[2]	1938-39
		189)	360h		1/16	England	Nottingham	1947
		104*)	138m		-/15			
		117	253m		-/13	England	Lord's	1947
Mitchell,B	(8)	123	340m		-/9	England	Cape Town	1930-31
		113 §	181m		-/6	New Zealand	Christchurch	1931-32
		164*	333m		-/17	England	Lord's	1935
		128	280m		-/11	England	The Oval	1935
		109	190m	234	-/14	England	Durban[2]	1938-39
		120)	391m		-/14	England	The Oval	1947
		189*)	410m					
		120	344m		-/11	England	Cape Town	1948-49
Murray,ARA	(1)	109 §	219m			New Zealand	Wellington	1952-53
Nourse,AD	(9)	231	298m	346	-/36	Australia	Johannesburg[1]	1935-36
		120	268m	295	1/12	England	Cape Town	1938-39
		103	364m	345	-/6	England	Durban[2]	1938-39
		149	240m		1/15	England	Nottingham	1947
		115	145m		2/13	England	Manchester	1947
		112	209m		-/11	England	Cape Town	1948-49
		129*	319m		-/11	England	Johannesburg[2]	1948-49
		114	274m	279	-/9	Australia	Cape Town	1949-50
		208	555m		-/25	England	Nottingham	1951
Nourse,AW	(1)	111	228m		-/13	Australia	Johannesburg[1]	1921-22
Owen-Smith,HG	(1)	129	160m		2/15	England	Leeds	1929
Pithey,AJ	(1)	154	440m		1/13	England	Cape Town	1964-65
Pollock,RG	(7)	122	221m	234	1/19	Australia	Sydney	1963-64
		175	283m		3/18	Australia	Adelaide	1963-64
		137	272m	236	-/18	England	Port Elizabeth	1964-65
		125	140m	145	-/21	England	Nottingham	1965
		209	361m		-/30	Australia	Cape Town	1966-67
		105	179m		1/13	Australia	Port Elizabeth	1966-67
		274	417m	401	-/43	Australia	Durban[2]	1969-70
Pollock,SM	(2)	111	123m	111	3/16	Sri Lanka	Centurion	2000-01
		106*	241m	190	-/13	West Indies	Bridgetown	2000-01
Prince,AG	(4)	139*	351m	218	2/18	Zimbabwe	Centurion	2004-05
		131	321m	254	1/13	West Indies	St John's	2004-05
		119	395m	271	-/13	Australia	Sydney	2005-06
		108*	400m	286	-/9	New Zealand	Cape Town	2005-06
Rhodes,JN	(3)	101* §	255m	202	1/14	Sri Lanka	Moratuwa	1993-94
		117	298m	200	1/14	England	Lord's	1998
		103*	104m	95	6/8	West Indies	Centurion	1998-99
Richards,BA	(2)	140	181m	164	1/20	Australia	Durban[2]	1969-70
		126	236m	212	3/16	Australia	Port Elizabeth	1969-70
Richardson,DJ	(1)	109	302m	206	-/7	New Zealand	Cape Town	1994-95
Rowan,EAB	(3)	156*	368m		-/18	England	Johannesburg[2]	1948-49
		143	388m	369	-/14	Australia	Durban[2]	1949-50
		236	550m		-/28	England	Leeds	1951
Rudolph,JA	(5)	222* §	521m	383	2/29	Bangladesh	Chittagong[1]	2002-03
		101	275m	215	-/13	West Indies	Cape Town	2003-04
		154*	439m	312	1/27	New Zealand	Auckland	2003-04

		102	413m	297	-/12	Sri Lanka	Galle	2004-05
		102*	431m	283	-/13	Australia	Perth	2005-06
Sherwell,PW	(1)	115	105m		-/18	England	Lord's	1907
Siedle,IJ	(1)	141	297m		-/13	England	Cape Town	1930-31
Sinclair,JH	(3)	106	142m		1!/9	England	Cape Town	1898-99
		101	125m		2!/14	Australia	Johannesburg[1]	1902-03
		104	83m		6!/18	Australia	Cape Town	1902-03
Smith,GC	(11)	200 §	338m	287	-/25	Bangladesh	East London	2002-03
		151	338m	216	-/18	Pakistan	Cape Town	2002-03
		277 §	541m	373	-/35	England	Birmingham	2003
		259	574m	370	-/34	England	Lord's	2003
		132	266m	184	-/22	West Indies	Johannesburg[3]	2003-04
		139	300m	180	2/21	West Indies	Centurion	2003-04
		125*	295m	203	-/17	New Zealand	Wellington	2003-04
		121 §	167m	107	2/17	Zimbabwe	Cape Town	2004-05
		148	469m	313	-/17	West Indies	Port-of-Spain	2004-05
		104	276m	203	1/13	West Indies	Bridgetown	2004-05
		126	256m	173	-/19	West Indies	St John's	2004-05
Snooke,SJ	(1)	103	215m			Australia	Adelaide	1910-11
Symcox,PL	(1)	108	226m	157	-/17	Pakistan	Johannesburg[3]	1997-98
Taylor,HW	(7)	109	198m		1/11	England	Durban[1]	1913-14
		176	308m		-/25	England	Johannesburg[1]	1922-23
		101	225h		1/11	England	Johannesburg[1]	1922-23
		102	270m		1/6	England	Durban[2]	1922-23
		101	145m		-/9	England	Johannesburg[1]	1927-28
		121	220m		-/12	England	The Oval	1929
		117	167m		-/15	England	Cape Town	1930-31
Van der Bijl,PGV	(1)	125	438m	458	1/11	England	Durban[2]	1938-39
Viljoen,KG	(2)	111	210m		1/9	Australia	Melbourne	1931-32
		124	280m		-/10	England	Manchester	1935
Wade,WW	(1)	125	290m		-/12	England	Port Elizabeth	1948-49
Waite,JHB	(4)	113	340m		-/12	England	Manchester	1955
		115	305m		-/11	Australia	Johannesburg[3]	1957-58
		134	513m		-/6	Australia	Durban[2]	1957-58
		101	206m		-/13	New Zealand	Johannesburg[3]	1961-62
Wessels,KC	(2)	118 §	372m	264	-/18	India	Durban[2]	1992-93
		105 §	298m	217	-/15	England	Lord's	1994
White,GC	(2)	147	>240h		2!/19	England	Johannesburg[1]	1905-06
		118	240h		1/10	England	Durban[1]	1909-10
Winslow,PL	(1)	108	190m		3/13	England	Manchester	1955
Zulch,JW	(2)	105	184m		-/9	Australia	Adelaide	1910-11
		150	298m		-/15	Australia	Sydney	1910-11
WEST INDIES (404)			Time	Balls	6/4	Opponents		
Adams,JC	(6)	137	414m	262	-/21	England	Georgetown	1993-94
		125*	406m	312	-/14	India	Nagpur	1994-95
		174*	451m	371	-/19	India	Mohali	1994-95
		151	308m	226	-/24	New Zealand	Wellington	1994-95
		208*	433m	333	1/31	New Zealand	St John's	1995-96
		101*	505m	373	-/6	Zimbabwe	Kingston	1999-2000
Alexander,FCM	(1)	108	212m	186	1/9	Australia	Sydney	1960-61
Arthurton,KLT	(2)	157* §	447m	343	1/16	Australia	Brisbane[2]	1992-93
		126	323m	232	2/11	England	Kingston	1993-94
Atkinson,DS	(1)	219	411m		1/29	Australia	Bridgetown	1954-55
Bacchus,SFAF	(1)	250	512m	375	-/33	India	Kanpur	1978-79
Baichan,L	(1)	105* §	373m		-/5	Pakistan	Lahore[2]	1974-75

Barrow,I	(1)	105	235m		-/9	England	Manchester	1933
Best,CA	(1)	164	423m	245	-/19	England	Bridgetown	1989-90
Bravo,DJJ	(2)	107	272m	235	-/13	South Africa	St John's	2004-05
		113 §	290m	202	-/15	Australia	Hobart	2005-06
Butcher,BF	(7)	103	≥180h		-/15	India	Calcutta	1958-59
		142	335m		-/10	India	Madras[2]	1958-59
		133	244m	261	2/17	England	Lord's	1963
		117	210m		1/10	Australia	Port-of-Spain	1964-65
		209*	461m		-/22	England	Nottingham	1966
		101	249m	134	-/14	Australia	Sydney	1968-69
		118	191m		-/18	Australia	Adelaide	1968-69
Campbell,SL	(4)	208	675m	496	-/29	New Zealand	Bridgetown	1995-96
		113	407m	327	-/9	Australia	Brisbane[2]	1996-97
		105	366m	271	-/16	Australia	Bridgetown	1998-99
		170	344m	262	2/23	New Zealand	Hamilton	1999-2000
Carew,GM	(1)	107	162m		-/16	England	Port-of-Spain	1947-48
Carew,MC	(1)	109 §	318m		-/12	New Zealand	Auckland	1968-69
Chanderpaul,S	(14)	137*	442m	272	-/13	India	Bridgetown	1996-97
		118	385m	263	1/15	England	Georgetown	1997-98
		140	367m	290	-/23	India	Georgetown	2001-02
		101*	365m	231	-/13	India	Bridgetown	2001-02
		136*	675m	510	-/17	India	St John's	2001-02
		140	368m	258	1/17	India	Kolkata	2002-03
		100	108m	72	2/15	Australia	Georgetown	2002-03
		104	229m	154	1/17	Australia	St John's	2002-03
		109	239m	171	1/20	South Africa	Durban[2]	2003-04
		101*	271m	190	-/11	Bangladesh	Kingston	2003-04
		128*	383m	270	-/15	England	Lord's	2004
		203*	541m	370	-/23	South Africa	Georgetown	2004-05
		127	403m	287	-/13	South Africa	St John's	2004-05
		153*		254	2/10	Pakistan	Bridgetown	2004-05
Christiani,RJ	(1)	107 §	194m		-/9	India	Delhi	1948-49
Davis,CA	(4)	103	372m		-/6	England	Lord's	1969
		125*	n300h		-/15	India	Georgetown	1970-71
		105	330h			India	Port-of-Spain	1970-71
		183	602m		-/21	New Zealand	Bridgetown	1971-72
Depeiza,CC	(1)	122	330m		-/16	Australia	Bridgetown	1954-55
Dujon,PJL	(5)	110	239m		-/14	India	St John's	1982-83
		130	262m	187	2/15	Australia	Port-of-Spain	1983-84
		101	247m	228	-/12	England	Manchester	1984
		139	240m	158	-/21	Australia	Perth	1984-85
		106*	316m	175	-/13	Pakistan	Port-of-Spain	1987-88
Foster,MLC	(1)	125 §	232m		-/16	Australia	Kingston	1972-73
Fredericks,RC	(8)	163	408m		-/20	New Zealand	Kingston	1971-72
		150	510m		-/17	England	Birmingham	1973
		100	212m		-/13	India	Calcutta	1974-75
		104	215m		-/17	India	Bombay[3]	1974-75
		169	212m	145	1/27	Australia	Perth	1975-76
		138	282m	253	1/14	England	Lord's	1976
		109	156m	124	-/18	England	Leeds	1976
		120	380m		-/12	Pakistan	Port-of-Spain	1976-77
Ganga,D	(3)	113	311m	225	1/19	Australia	Georgetown	2002-03
		117	326m	238	1/17	Australia	Port-of-Spain	2002-03
		135		294	-/15	India	Bassaterre	2005-06
Ganteaume,AG	(1)	112 §	300m		-/13	England	Port-of-Spain	1947-48
Gayle,CH	(7)	175	394m	255	-/34	Zimbabwe	Bulawayo[2]	2001-02

		204	482m	332	2/29	New Zealand	St George's	2001-02
		116	167m	120	1/20	South Africa	Cape Town	2003-04
		107	226m	159	-/17	South Africa	Centurion	2003-04
		141	394m	293	-/18	Bangladesh	Gros Islet	2003-04
		105	133m	87	1/16	England	The Oval	2004
		317	630m	483	3/37	South Africa	St John's	2004-05
Gomes,HA	(9)	101 §	205m		-/11	Australia	Georgetown	1977-78
		115	343m	269	-/11	Australia	Kingston	1977-78
		126*	344m	252	-/11	Australia	Sydney	1981-82
		124*	402m	273	-/9	Australia	Adelaide	1981-82
		123	446m	333	-/12	India	Port-of-Spain	1982-83
		143	380m	279	-/16	England	Birmingham	1984
		104*	314m	197	-/14	England	Leeds	1984
		127	472m	297	-/9	Australia	Perth	1984-85
		120*	304m	217	-/10	Australia	Adelaide	1984-85
Gomez,GE	(1)	101 §	255m		-/7	India	Delhi	1948-49
Greenidge,CG	(19)	107 §	260m	208	2/14	India	Bangalore	1974-75
		134)	250m	198	-/18	England	Manchester	1976
		101)	245m	155	-/13			
		115	214m	147	2/14	England	Leeds	1976
		100	≥210h		3/15	Pakistan	Kingston	1976-77
		154*	248m		1/14	India	St John's	1982-83
		194	552m	368	-/23	India	Kanpur	1983-84
		120*	270m	189	3/10	Australia	Georgetown	1983-84
		127	286m	193	-/17	Australia	Kingston	1983-84
		214*	300m	241	-/29	England	Lord's	1984
		223	598m	425	-/30	England	Manchester	1984
		100	316m	235	-/12	New Zealand	Port-of-Spain	1984-85
		213	534m	381	7/20	New Zealand	Auckland	1986-87
		141	362m	265	4/14	India	Calcutta	1987-88
		103	246m	192	-/14	England	Lord's	1988
		104	294m	249	-/8	Australia	Adelaide	1988-89
		117	236m	182	1/11	India	Bridgetown	1988-89
		149	380m	207	3/18	England	St John's	1989-90
		(In his 100th Test match)						
		226	677m	480	3/11	Australia	Bridgetown	1990-91
Griffith,AFG	(1)	114 §	463m	346	1/10	New Zealand	Hamilton	1999-2000
Haynes,DL	(18)	105 §	435m	323	-/16	New Zealand	Dunedin	1979-80
		122	263m	199	3/17	New Zealand	Christchurch	1979-80
		184	490m	395	1/27	England	Lord's	1980
		136	372m		1/10	India	St John's	1982-83
		103*	270m	184	-/9	Australia	Georgetown	1983-84
		145	383m	222	1/19	Australia	Bridgetown	1983-84
		125	436m	269	-/17	England	The Oval	1984
		131	472m	283	-/14	England	St John's	1985-86
		121	311m	269	-/20	New Zealand	Wellington	1986-87
		100	243m	176	-/12	Australia	Perth	1988-89
		143	316m	272	-/16	Australia	Sydney	1988-89
		112*	177m	128	3/11	India	Bridgetown	1988-89
		109	303m	176	-/10	England	Bridgetown	1989-90
		167	533m	317	1/24	England	St John's	1989-90
		117	351m	204	-/8	Pakistan	Karachi[1]	1990-91
		111	318m	223	-/17	Australia	Georgetown	1990-91
		143*	406m	289	-/20	Pakistan	Port-of-Spain	1992-93
		125	351m	206	1/14	Pakistan	Bridgetown	1992-93
Headley,GA	(10)	176 §	390h		-/16	England	Bridgetown	1929-30

		114)	200m		-/10	England	Georgetown	1929-30
		112)	257m		1/12			
		223	390h		-/28	England	Kingston	1929-30
		102*	247m		-/10	Australia	Brisbane[1]	1930-31
		105	146m		-/13	Australia	Sydney	1930-31
		169*	375h		-/18	England	Manchester	1933
		270*	493m		-/30	England	Kingston	1934-35
		106)	250m		-/13	England	Lord's	1939
		107)	230m		-/8			
Hinds,WW	(5)	165	361m	236	-/24	Pakistan	Bridgetown	1999-2000
		113	296m	200	2/14	India	Kingston	2001-02
		113	215m	143	4/8	Sri Lanka	Gros Islet	2002-03
		100	251m	200	-/16	India	Kolkata	2002-03
		213	455m	297	2/34	South Africa	Georgetown	2004-05
Holford,DAJ	(1)	105*	320m		-/6	England	Lord's	1966
Holt,JK	(2)	166	284m		1/26	England	Bridgetown	1953-54
		123	255m		-/17	India	Delhi	1958-59
Hooper,CL	(13)	100*	277m	171	3/7	India	Calcutta	1987-88
		134	315m	226	2/11	Pakistan	Lahore[2]	1990-91
		111	282m	202	1/14	England	Lord's	1991
		178*	297m	248	4/19	Pakistan	St John's	1992-93
		127	285m	180	2/14	England	The Oval	1995
		102	306m	228	1/10	Australia	Brisbane[2]	1996-97
		129	275m	212	-/17	India	Kingston	1996-97
		106	135m	90	4/14	Pakistan	Karachi[1]	1997-98
		108*	216m	150	-/17	England	St John's	1997-98
		149 §	277m	211	1/18	Zimbabwe	Bulawayo[2]	2001-02
		233	630m	402	3/29	India	Georgetown	2001-02
		115	345m	235	-/18	India	Bridgetown	2001-02
		136	401m	278	3/13	India	St John's	2001-02
Hunte,CC	(8)	142 §	300h		-/17	Pakistan	Bridgetown	1957-58
		260	506m		1/28	Pakistan	Kingston	1957-58
		114	253m		-/9	Pakistan	Georgetown	1957-58
		110	270m		-/9	Australia	Melbourne	1960-61
		182	500m		-/27	England	Manchester	1963
		108*	300h			England	The Oval	1963
		135	300h		-/19	England	Manchester	1966
		101	285m		-/16	India	Bombay[2]	1966-67
Jacobs,RD	(3)	113*	257m	214	4/11	South Africa	Bridgetown	2000-01
		118	240m	204	5/11	India	St John's	2001-02
		107*	309m	207	3/8	England	St John's	2003-04
Julien,BD	(2)	121	171m		2/18	England	Lord's	1973
		101	192m		-/12	Pakistan	Karachi[1]	1974-75
Kallicharran,AI	(12)	100* §	258m		1/7	New Zealand	Georgetown	1971-72
		101	179m		1/13	New Zealand	Port-of-Spain	1971-72
		158	369m	334	-/18	England	Port-of-Spain	1973-74
		119	251m	191	-/18	England	Bridgetown	1973-74
		124 §	281m	226	2/15	India	Bangalore	1974-75
		115			1/18	Pakistan	Karachi[1]	1974-75
		101	267m	207	-/13	Australia	Brisbane[2]	1975-76
		103*	257m		-/8	India	Port-of-Spain	1975-76
		127	256m		-/17	Australia	Port-of-Spain	1977-78
		126	263m	260	1/18	Australia	Kingston	1977-78
		187	396m		-/26	India	Bombay[3]	1978-79
		106	221m	176	-/14	Australia	Adelaide	1979-80
Kanhai,RB	(15)	256	400m		-/42	India	Calcutta	1958-59

		217	420h		-/32	Pakistan	Lahore[1]	1958-59
		110	378m		1/19	England	Port-of-Spain	1959-60
		117)	149m		2/14	Australia	Adelaide	1960-61
		115)	222m		-/12			
		138	298m		-/19	India	Kingston	1961-62
		139			2/11	India	Port-of-Spain	1961-62
		129	372m		-/17	Australia	Bridgetown	1964-65
		121	182m		2/12	Australia	Port-of-Spain	1964-65
		104	215m		-/14	England	The Oval	1966
		153	300m		1/19	England	Port-of-Spain	1967-68
		150	412m	301	-/21	England	Georgetown	1967-68
		158*	390h		-/17	India	Kingston	1970-71
		105	305m		-/11	Australia	Bridgetown	1972-73
		157	340m		-/21	England	Lord's	1973
King,CL	(1)	100*	129m	109	4/10	New Zealand	Christchurch	1979-80
Lambert,CB	(1)	104	364m	232	1/10	England	St John's	1997-98
Lara,BC	(32)	277	474m	372	-/38	Australia	Sydney	1992-93
		167	256m	210	2/25	England	Georgetown	1993-94
		375	766m	538	-/45	England	St John's	1993-94
		147	247m	181	-/23	New Zealand	Wellington	1994-95
		145	281m	216	-/16	England	Manchester	1995
		152	253m	182	-/28	England	Nottingham	1995
		179	267m	206	1/26	England	The Oval	1995
		132	223m	185	1/22	Australia	Perth	1996-97
		103	215m	175	1/11	India	St John's	1996-97
		115	266m	207	1/11	Sri Lanka	Arnos Vale	1996-97
		213	468m	344	3/28	Australia	Kingston	1998-99
		153*	352m	256	1/19	Australia	Bridgetown	1998-99
		100	101m	84	3/15	Australia	St John's	1998-99
		112	199m	158	1/13	England	Manchester	2000
		182	351m	234	1/30	Australia	Adelaide	2000-01
		178	361m	293	-/19	Sri Lanka	Galle	2001-02
		221)	447m	354	2/23	Sri Lanka	Colombo (SSC)	2001-02
		130)	257m	215	1/14			
		110	183m	157	-/20	Australia	Georgetown	2002-03
		122	298m	208	1/13	Australia	Port-of-Spain	2002-03
		209	452m	360	1/24	Sri Lanka	Gros Islet	2002-03
		191	271m	203	4/23	Zimbabwe	Bulawayo[2]	2003-04
		202	439m	274	2/32	South Africa	Johannesburg[3]	2003-04
		115	326m	238	1/16	South Africa	Cape Town	2003-04
		400*	778m	582	4/43	England	St John's	2003-04
		120	169m	147	-/12	Bangladesh	Kingston	2003-04
		196	430m	285	-/25	South Africa	Port-of-Spain	2004-05
		176		224	1/21	South Africa	Bridgetown	2004-05
		130	166m	120	4/16	Pakistan	Bridgetown	2004-05
		153	298m	233	2/20	Pakistan	Kingston	2004-05
		226	405m	298	-/22	Australia	Adelaide	2005-06
		120		307	-/10	India	Gros Islet	2005-06
Lloyd,CH	(19)	118 §	273m		1/17	England	Port-of-Spain	1967-68
		113*	178m		2/14	England	Bridgetown	1967-68
		129 §	208m		1/18	Australia	Brisbane[2]	1968-69
		178	358m		1/24	Australia	Georgetown	1972-73
		132	a240h		2/15	England	The Oval	1973
		163	205m	149	2/22	India	Bangalore	1974-75
		242*	429m		4/19	India	Bombay[3]	1974-75
		149	218m	186	1/22	Australia	Perth	1975-76

		102	206m	121	-/14	Australia	Melbourne	1975-76
		102	175m		2/12	India	Bridgetown	1975-76
		157	290m		3/21	Pakistan	Bridgetown	1976-77
		121	187m	156	-/17	Australia	Adelaide	1979-80
		101	205m	159	-/11	England	Manchester	1980
		100	238m		-/17	England	Bridgetown	1980-81
		143	310mm		2/13	India	Port-of-Spain	1982-83
		106	218m		1/11	India	St John's	1982-83
		103	320m		1/6	India	Delhi	1983-84
		161*	496m		-/12	India	Calcutta	1983-84
		114	208m	154	3/14	Australia	Brisbane[2]	1984-85
Logie,AL	(2)	130	273m		2/12	India	Bridgetown	1982-83
		101	188m	136	-/15	India	Calcutta	1987-88
McMorris,EDAS	(1)	125 §	342m		-/11	India	Kingston	1961-62
Martin,FR	(1)	123*	347m		-/11	Australia	Sydney	1930-31
Murray,JR	(1)	101*	114m	88	2/11	New Zealand	Wellington	1994-95
Nurse,SM	(6)	201	382m		-/30	Australia	Bridgetown	1964-65
		137	345m		2/14	England	Leeds	1966
		136	331m		-/12	England	Port-of-Spain	1967-68
		137	200m		1/18	Australia	Sydney	1968-69
		168 §	215m		2/22	New Zealand	Auckland	1968-69
		258	476m		1/35	New Zealand	Christchurch	1968-69
Pairaudeau,BH	(1)	115 §	272m		-/16	India	Port-of-Spain	1952-53
Rae,AF	(4)	104	255m		-/11	India	Bombay[2]	1948-49
		109	230m		3/5	India	Madras[1]	1948-49
		106	280m		-/15	England	Lord's	1950
		109	300h			England	The Oval	1950
Richards,IVA	(24)	192*	319m	297	6/20	India	Delhi	1974-75
		101	182m	136	-/17	Australia	Adelaide	1975-76
		142	242m		1/10	India	Bridgetown	1975-76
		130	290m	203	-/21	India	Port-of-Spain	1975-76
		177	343m	296	2/23	India	Port-of-Spain	1975-76
		232 §	438m	313	4/31	England	Nottingham	1976
		135	288m	261	-/18	England	Manchester	1976
		291	472m	386	-/38	England	The Oval	1976
		140	329m	259	-/20	Australia	Brisbane[2]	1979-80
		145	196m	159	1/25	England	Lord's	1980
		120	417m	263	-/15	Pakistan	Multan[1]	1980-81
		182*	383m		2/23	England	Bridgetown	1980-81
		114	305m		1/21	England	St John's	1980-81
		109	258m		2/9	India	Georgetown	1982-83
		120	267m		1/13	India	Bombay[3]	1983-84
		178	377m	229	-/30	Australia	St John's	1983-84
		117	204m	154	1/17	England	Birmingham	1984
		208	376m	245	3/22	Australia	Melbourne	1984-85
		105	192m	147	3/13	New Zealand	Bridgetown	1984-85
		110*	87m	58	7/7	England	St John's	1985-86
		109*	179m	114	-/13	India	Delhi	1987-88
		123	302m	169	-/13	Pakistan	Port-of-Spain	1987-88
		146	195m	150	3/21	Australia	Perth	1988-89
		110	304m	178	1/13	India	Kingston	1988-89
Richardson,RB	(16)	131*	481m	313	-/17	Australia	Bridgetown	1983-84
		154	468m	326	1/21	Australia	St John's	1983-84
		138	331m	232	-/24	Australia	Brisbane[2]	1984-85
		185	455m	346	-/26	New Zealand	Georgetown	1984-85
		102	176m	140	1/19	England	Port-of-Spain	1985-86

		160	348m	278	-/18	England	Bridgetown	1985-86
		122	286m	194	-/12	Australia	Melbourne	1988-89
		106	194m	160	-/16	Australia	Adelaide	1988-89
		194	459m	367	-/20	India	Georgetown	1988-89
		156	482m	314	-/20	India	Kingston	1988-89
		104*	315m	240	-/15	Australia	Kingston	1990-91
		182	344m	259	2/26	Australia	Georgetown	1990-91
		104	273m	229	-/13	England	Birmingham	1991
		121	458m	312	1/11	England	The Oval	1991
		109	330m	253	-/11	Australia	Sydney	1992-93
		100	344m	223	1/12	Australia	Kingston	1994-95
Roach,CA	(2)	122	165m		-/20	England	Bridgetown	1929-30
		209	303m		3/22	England	Georgetown	1929-30
Rowe,LG	(7)	214 §)	427m		1/19	New Zealand	Kingston	1971-72
		100*)	153m		-/13			
		120	303m	258	1/17	England	Kingston	1973-74
		302	612m	430	1/36	England	Bridgetown	1973-74
		123	437m	340	1/10	England	Port-of-Spain	1973-74
		107	267m	235	-/14	Australia	Brisbane[2]	1975-76
		100	186m	165	1/10	New Zealand	Christchurch	1979-80
Samuels,MN	(1)	104 §	253m	182	-/18	India	Kolkata	2002-03
Samuels,RG	(1)	125	329m	219	3/15	New Zealand	St John's	1995-96
Sarwan,RR	(8)	119 §	307m	228	-/19	Bangladesh	Dhaka	2002-03
		105	208m	139	1/17	Australia	St John's	2002-03
		114	312m	225	-/18	South Africa	Durban[2]	2003-04
		119	350m	273	-/15	South Africa	Centurion	2003-04
		261*	573m	402	3/32	Bangladesh	Kingston	2003-04
		139	301m	226	-/25	England	Birmingham	2004
		107*	348m	221	-/11	South Africa	Port-of-Spain	2004-05
		127	388m	279	2/14	South Africa	St John's	2004-05
		116		174	1/17	India	Bassaterre	2005-06
Shillingford,IT	(1)	120	345m		1/15	Pakistan	Georgetown	1976-77
Simmons,PV	(1)	110	253m	178	2/8	Australia	Melbourne	1992-93
Smith,DR	(1)	105* §	135m	105	2/15	South Africa	Cape Town	2003-04
Smith,DS	(1)	108 §	275m	188	-/18	England	Kingston	2003-04
Smith,OG	(4)	104 §	218m		-/14	Australia	Kingston	1954-55
		161 §	412m		1/18	England	Birmingham	1957
		168	416m		3/10	England	Nottingham	1957
		100	<180h		2/10	India	Delhi	1958-59
Sobers,GS	(26)	365*	614m		-/38	Pakistan	Kingston	1957-58
		125)	260m		-/15	Pakistan	Georgetown	1957-58
		109*)			-/9			
		142* §	365m		1/8	India	Bombay[2]	1958-59
		198	340m		-/28	India	Kanpur	1958-59
		106*	a195h		-/11	India	Calcutta	1958-59
		226	647m		-/24	England	Bridgetown	1959-60
		147	371m		-/17	England	Kingston	1959-60
		145	420h		1/18	England	Georgetown	1959-60
		132	174m		-/21	Australia	Brisbane[2]	1960-61
		168	270m	224	1/25	Australia	Sydney	1960-61
		153	280m		4/11	India	Kingston	1961-62
		104			2/13	India	Kingston	1961-62
		102	251m		-/14	England	Leeds	1963
		161	248m		1/26	England	Manchester	1966
		163*	330m		-/13	England	Lord's	1966
		174	243m		-/24	England	Leeds	1966

		113*	357m		1/14	England	Kingston	1967-68
		152	440m	362	-/18	England	Georgetown	1967-68
		110	134m		2/15	Australia	Adelaide	1968-69
		113	144m	126	-/20	Australia	Sydney	1968-69
		108*	150m		2/14	India	Georgetown	1970-71
		178	329m		1/19	India	Bridgetown	1970-71
		132				India	Port-of-Spain	1970-71
		142	363m		-/18	New Zealand	Bridgetown	1971-72
		150*	288m	227	-/19	England	Lord's	1973
Solomon,JS	(1)	100*	281m		-/9	India	Delhi	1958-59
Stollmeyer,JB	(4)	160	308m		-/12	India	Madras[1]	1948-49
		104	242m		-/6	Australia	Sydney	1951-52
		152	326m		-/14	New Zealand	Auckland	1951-52
		104*	163m			India	Port-of-Spain	1952-53
Walcott,CL	(15)	152 §	259m		-/12	India	Delhi	1948-49
		108	164m		2/11	India	Calcutta	1948-49
		168*	285m		-/24	England	Lord's	1950
		115	168m		-/13	New Zealand	Auckland	1951-52
		125	255m		1/15	India	Georgetown	1952-53
		118	241m		-/11	India	Kingston	1952-53
		220	428m		1/28	England	Bridgetown	1953-54
		124	211m		1/18	England	Port-of-Spain	1953-54
		116	262m		-/20	England	Kingston	1953-54
		108	208m		-/14	Australia	Kingston	1954-55
		126)	267m		-/14	Australia	Port-of-Spain	1954-55
		110)	147m		-/17			
		155)	294m		-/23	Australia	Kingston	1954-55
		110)	196m		-/14			
		145	273m		-/19	Pakistan	Georgetown	1957-58
Weekes,ED	(15)	141	232m		-/15	England	Kingston	1947-48
		128 §	194m		-/16	India	Delhi	1948-49
		194	368m		-/18	India	Bombay[2]	1948-49
		162)	199m		-/24	India	Calcutta	1948-49
		101)	187m		-/5			
		129	220m		-/17	England	Nottingham	1950
		207	431m		-/20	India	Port-of-Spain	1952-53
		161	338m		-/22	India	Port-of-Spain	1952-53
		109	173m		-/13	India	Kingston	1952-53
		206	354m		-/25	England	Port-of-Spain	1953-54
		139	210m		1/24	Australia	Port-of-Spain	1954-55
		123	148m		-/17	New Zealand	Dunedin	1955-56
		103	142m		-/16	New Zealand	Christchurch	1955-56
		156	211m		-/19	New Zealand	Wellington	1955-56
		197 §	330m		-/18	Pakistan	Bridgetown	1957-58
Weekes,KH	(1)	137	135m		1/18	England	The Oval	1939
Williams,AB	(2)	100 §	169m	118	-/19	Australia	Georgetown	1977-78
		111	214m		-/11	India	Calcutta	1978-79
Williams,SC	(1)	128	452m	299	1/11	India	Port-of-Spain	1996-97
Worrell,FMM	(9)	131*	215m		-/14	England	Georgetown	1947-48
		261	335m		2/35	England	Nottingham	1950
		138	305m		-/17	England	The Oval	1950
		108	247m		-/7	Australia	Melbourne	1951-52
		100	151m		-/13	New Zealand	Auckland	1951-52
		237	569m		-/35	India	Kingston	1952-53
		167	438m		-/23	England	Port-of-Spain	1953-54
		191*	575m		-/26	England	Nottingham	1957
		197*	682m		2/17	England	Bridgetown	1959-60

NEW ZEALAND (200)			Time	Balls	6/4	Opponents		
Astle,NJ	(11)	125 §	214m	154	2/22	West Indies	Bridgetown	1995-96
		103	217m	165	1/12	West Indies	St John's	1995-96
		102* §	278m	214	-/13	England	Auckland	1996-97
		114	258m	192	-/16	Zimbabwe	Auckland	1997-98
		101	220m	175	3/7	England	Manchester	1999
		141	549m	408	2/16	Zimbabwe	Wellington	2001-02
		156*	408m	275	1/22	Australia	Perth	2001-02
		222	231m	168	11/29	England	Christchurch	2001-02
		103	284m	207	-/14	India	Ahmedabad	2003-04
		114	279m	203	-/17	Sri Lanka	Napier	2004-05
		128		217	-/21	Zimbabwe	Bulawayo[2]	2005-06
Barton,PT	(1)	109	276m		-/20	South Africa	Port Elizabeth	1961-62
Bell,MD	(1)	105	270m	163	-/17	Pakistan	Hamilton	2000-01
Bracewell,JG	(1)	110	270m	200	-/10	England	Nottingham	1986
Burgess,MG	(5)	119*	255m		-/12	Pakistan	Dacca	1969-70
		104	237m	176	1/12	England	Auckland	1970-71
		101	185m		1/15	West Indies	Kingston	1971-72
		105	228m		-/12	England	Lord's	1973
		111	254m		-/9	Pakistan	Lahore[2]	1976-77
Cairns,CL	(5)	120	122m	96	9/10	Zimbabwe	Auckland	1995-96
		126	202m	260	3/16	India	Hamilton	1998-99
		109	204m	138	2/14	Australia	Wellington	1999-2000
		124	251m	174	2/13	Zimbabwe	Harare	2001-02
		158	213m	171	7/18	South Africa	Auckland	2003-04
Coney,JV	(3)	174*	488m	374	1/26	England	Wellington	1983-84
		111*	385m	243	-/12	Pakistan	Dunedin	1984-85
		101*	282m	192	-/14	Australia	Wellington	1985-86
Congdon,BE	(7)	104	320m		-/7	England	Christchurch	1965-66
		166*	527m		1/14	West Indies	Port-of-Spain	1971-72
		126	258m		-/11	West Indies	Bridgetown	1971-72
		176	409m		-/19	England	Nottingham	1973
		175	515m		-/12	England	Lord's	1973
		132	390m	360	-/14	Australia	Wellington	1973-74
		107*	297m	251	-/11	Australia	Christchurch	1976-77
Crowe,JJ	(3)	128	384m	285	-/20	England	Auckland	1983-84
		112	286m	207	1/10	West Indies	Kingston	1984-85
		120*	609m	397	-/13	Sri Lanka	Colombo (CCC)	1986-87
Crowe,MD	(17)	100	276m	247	-/19	England	Wellington	1983-84
		188	571m	462	1/26	West Indies	Georgetown	1984-85
		188	472m	328	-/26	Australia	Brisbane[2]	1985-86
		137	283m	226	-/21	Australia	Christchurch	1985-86
		106	339m	247	-/11	England	Lord's	1986
		119	381m	308	-/15	West Indies	Wellington	1986-87
		104	382m	264	1/8	West Indies	Auckland	1986-87
		137	234m	184	1/17	Australia	Adelaide	1987-88
		143	402m	333	-/14	England	Wellington	1987-88
		174	592m	410	-/16	Pakistan	Wellington	1988-89
		113	227m	174	-/17	India	Auckland	1989-90
		108*	552m	306	1/14	Pakistan	Lahore[2]	1990-91
		299	610m	523	3/29	Sri Lanka	Wellington	1990-91
		140	182m	163	3/17	Zimbabwe	Harare	1992-93
		107	159m	121	4/10	Sri Lanka	Colombo (SSC)	1992-93
		142	366m	255	3/20	England	Lord's	1994
		115	333m	237	-/15	England	Manchester	1994
Dempster,CS	(2)	136	274m		-/8	England	Wellington	1929-30

		120	235m		-/10	England	Lord's	1931
Donnelly,MP	(1)	206	355m		-/26	England	Lord's	1949
Dowling,GT	(3)	129	378m		-/17	India	Bombay[2]	1964-65
		143	343m		2/16	India	Dunedin	1967-68
		239	556m	519	5/28	India	Christchurch	1967-68
Edgar,BA	(3)	129 §	414m		-/14	Pakistan	Christchurch	1978-79
		127	432m	317	-/7	West Indies	Auckland	1979-80
		161	516m	418	-/22	Australia	Auckland	1981-82
Fleming,SP	(9)	127	367m	253	1/18	England	Auckland	1996-97
		174*	475m	333	1/16	Sri Lanka	Colombo (RPS)	1997-98
		105	316m	223	-/15	Australia	Perth	2001-02
		130	275m	230	-/20	West Indies	Bridgetown	2001-02
		274*	653m	476	1/28	Sri Lanka	Colombo (PSS)	2002-03
		192	479m	332	-/31	Pakistan	Hamilton	2003-04
		117	281m	198	2/16	England	Nottingham	2004
		202	445m	318	1/21	Bangladesh	Chittagong[1]	2004-05
		262	576m	423	2/31	South Africa	Cape Town	2005-06
Franklin,J.EC		122*	359m	268	1/14	South Africa	Cape Town	2005-06
Franklin,TJ	(1)	101	432m	310	-/8	England	Lord's	1990
Greatbatch,MJ	(3)	107* §	407m	325	-/12	England	Auckland	1987-88
		146* §	656m	485	-/17	Australia	Perth	1989-90
		133	427m	317	-/16	Pakistan	Hamilton	1992-93
Guy,JW	(1)	102 §	473m		-/13	India	Hyderabad	1955-56
Hadlee,RJ	(2)	103	114m	92	2/11	West Indies	Christchurch	1979-80
		151*	407m	243	2/14	Sri Lanka	Colombo (CCC)	1986-87
Hadlee,WA	(1)	116	147m		-/11	England	Christchurch	1946-47
Harris,PGZ	(1)	101	266m		2/10	South Africa	Cape Town	1961-62
Hastings,BF	(4)	117*	278m		2/12	West Indies	Christchurch	1968-69
		105	273m		-/15	West Indies	Bridgetown	1971-72
		110	275m		-/10	Pakistan	Auckland	1972-73
		101	281m	274	-/8	Australia	Wellington	1973-74
Horne,MJ	(4)	133 §	326m	259	2/9	Australia	Hobart	1997-98
		157	396m	260	4/19	Zimbabwe	Auckland	1997-98
		100	367m	224	-/13	England	Lord's	1999
		110	339m	277	-/13	Zimbabwe	Bulawayo[2]	2001-02
Howarth,GP	(6)	122)	515m		-/12	England	Auckland	1977-78
		102)	320m		-/13			
		123	340m		-/14	England	Lord's	1978
		114	286m		1/11	Pakistan	Napier	1978-79
		147	358m	261	-/13	West Indies	Christchurch	1979-80
		137 §	353m		-/15	India	Wellington	1980-81
Jarvis,TW	(1)	182	540m	555	-/19	West Indies	Georgetown	1971-72
Jones,AH	(7)	150	444m	383	-/11	Australia	Adelaide	1987-88
		170	634m	448	2/15	India	Auckland	1989-90
		186	562m	454	-/15	Sri Lanka	Wellington	1990-91
		122)	288m	217	-/8	Sri Lanka	Hamilton	1990-91
		100*)	255m	175	-/8			
		143	462m	398	-/15	England	Wellington	1991-92
		143	351m	283	-/11	Australia	Perth	1993-94
Latham,RT	(1)	119 §	282m	214	1/14	Zimbabwe	Bulawayo[1]	1992-93
Lees,WK	(1)	152	338m		2/21	Pakistan	Karachi[1]	1976-77
McCullum,BB	(2)	143 §	339m	243	2/10	Bangladesh	Dhaka	2004-05
		111 §	148m	112	1/15	Zimbabwe	Harare	2005-06
McGregor,SN	(1)	111	340m		-/12	Pakistan	Lahore[1]	1955-56
McMillan,CD	(6)	139 §	263	209	-/18	Zimbabwe	Wellington	1997-98
		142 §	283m	179	6/13	Sri Lanka	Colombo (RPS)	1997-98

		107*	295m	210	3/9	England	Manchester	1999
		142	311m	209	2/18	Zimbabwe	Wellington	2001-02
		106 §	180m	140	-/18	Bangladesh	Hamilton	2001-02
		100*	194m	130	1/7	India	Mohali	2003-04
Marshall,HJH	(2)	146 §	338m	256	1/23	Australia	Christchurch	2004-05
		160 §	323m	249	2/22	Sri Lanka	Napier	2004-05
Mills,JE	(1)	117 §	258m		-/13	England	Wellington	1929-30
Morrison,JFM	(1)	117	261m	246	-/11	Australia	Sydney	1973-74
Oram,JDP	(3)	119*	301m	216	-/19	South Africa	Hamilton	2003-04
		126*	258m	178	3/12	Australia	Brisbane[2]	2004-05
		133	285m	169	2/18	South Africa	Centurion	2005-06
Page,ML	(1)	104	215m		-/15	England	Lord's	1931
Parker,JM	(3)	108	258m	233	-/10	Australia	Sydney	1973-74
		121	408m	297	-/18	England	Auckland	1974-75
		104	289m		-/11	India	Bombay[3]	1976-77
Parore,AC	(2)	100* §	298m	249	-/9	West Indies	Christchurch	1994-95
		110	308m	243	1/14	Australia	Perth	2001-02
Pollard,V	(2)	116	437m		-/10	England	Nottingham	1973
		105*	235m		-/14	England	Lord's	1973
Rabone,GO	(1)	107	n360h		-/9	South Africa	Durban[2]	1953-54
Redmond,RE	(1)	107 §	145m		-/20	Pakistan	Auckland	1972-73
Reid,JF	(6)	123*	446m		-/11	India	Christchurch	1980-81
		180	685m	445	-/16	Sri Lanka	Colombo (CCC)	1983-84
		106	291m	325	-/8	Pakistan	Hyderabad	1984-85
		148	572m	427	-/15	Pakistan	Wellington	1984-85
		158*	486m	318	-/17	Pakistan	Auckland	1984-85
		108 §	365m	256	-/16	Australia	Brisbane[2]	1985-86
Reid,JR	(6)	135	196m		2/18	South Africa	Cape Town	1953-54
		119*	210h		1/10	India	Delhi	1955-56
		120	273m		-/15	India	Calcutta	1955-56
		142	259m		2/21	South Africa	Johannesburg[3]	1961-62
		100	252m		-/13	England	Christchurch	1962-63
		128	268m		3/15	Pakistan	Karachi[1]	1964-65
Richardson,MH	(4)	106	422m	280	1/14	Pakistan	Hamilton	2000-01
		143 §	356m	191	-/14	Bangladesh	Hamilton	2001-02
		145	550m	410	-/19	India	Mohali	2003-04
		101	435m	309	-/10	England	Lord's	2004
Rutherford,KR	(3)	107*	263m	181	-/12	England	Wellington	1987-88
		105	277m	227	2/13	Sri Lanka	Moratuwa	1992-93
		102	260m	215	1/9	Australia	Christchurch	1992-93
Sinclair,BW	(3)	138	346m		-/22	South Africa	Auckland	1963-64
		130	373m		-/12	Pakistan	Lahore[2]	1964-65
		114	229m		-/11	England	Auckland	1965-66
Sinclair,MS	(3)	214 §	532m	447	-/22	West Indies	Wellington	1999-2000
		150	399m	321	1/23	South Africa	Port Elizabeth	2001-02
		204*	520m	348	2/27	Pakistan	Christchurch	2000-01
Smith,IDS	(2)	113*	239m	182	2/9	England	Auckland	1983-84
		173	237m	136	3/23	India	Auckland	1989-90
Spearman,CM	(1)	112	334m	219	1/9	Zimbabwe	Auckland	1995-96
Styris,SB	(5)	107 §	232m	178	1/8	West Indies	St George's	2001-02
		119	297m	231	2/10	India	Mohali	2003-04
		170	313m	220	2/12	South Africa	Auckland	2003-04
		108	258m	174	-/16	England	Nottingham	2004
		103*	192m	121	2/15	West Indies	Auckland	2005-06
Sutcliffe,B	(5)	101	170m		-/12	England	Manchester	1949
		116	267m		-/12	England	Christchurch	1950-51

		137* §	300h		-/15	India	Hyderabad	1955-56
		230*	>480h		-/30	India	Delhi	1955-56
		151*	357m		-/24	India	Calcutta	1964-65
Taylor,BR	(2)	105 §	158m		3/14	India	Calcutta	1964-65
		124 §	111m	102	5/14	West Indies	Auckland	1968-69
Thomson,SA	(1)	120*	233m	167	2/12	Pakistan	Christchurch	1993-94
Turner,GM	(7)	110 §	445m		-/7	Pakistan	Dacca	1969-70
		223*	572m		-/26	West Indies	Kingston	1971-72
		259	704m	759	-/22	West Indies	Georgetown	1971-72
		101)	282m	260	-/9	Australia	Christchurch	1973-74
		110*)	370m	355	-/11			
		117	411m		-/9	India	Christchurch	1975-76
		113	246m	236	-/14	India	Kanpur	1976-77
Vettori,DL	(2)	137*	223m	170	1/23	Pakistan	Hamilton	2003-04
		127	139m	98b	2/20	Zimbabwe	Harare	2005-06
Vincent,L	(3)	104 §	273m	207	1/15	Australia	Perth	2001-02
		106	321m	227	2/14	India	Mohali	2003-04
		224	529m	348	4/25	Sri Lanka	Wellington	2004-05
Vivian,HG	(1)	100 §	139m		-/14	South Africa	Wellington	1931-32
Wright,JG	(12)	110	460m	434	1/10	India	Auckland	1980-81
		141	352m	262	-/26	Australia	Christchurch	1981-82
		130	387m	297	-/24	England	Auckland	1983-84
		107	235m	200	1/17	Pakistan	Karachi[1]	1984-85
		119	427m	344	-/8	England	The Oval	1986
		138	575m	466	-/14	West Indies	Wellington	1986-87
		103	352m	276	-/16	England	Auckland	1987-88
		185	553m	443	-/23	India	Christchurch	1989-90
		113*	278m	208	1/12	India	Napier	1989-90
		117*	248m	197	1/17	Australia	Wellington	1989-90
		101	185m	140	-/14	Sri Lanka	Hamilton	1990-91
		116	406m	334	-/15	England	Wellington	1991-92
Young,BA	(2)	120	416m	314	-/7	Pakistan	Christchurch	1993-94
		267*	605m	421	-/37	Sri Lanka	Dunedin	1996-97
INDIA (339)			Time	Balls	6/4	Opponents		
Adhikari,HR	(1)	114* §	245m		-/10	West Indies	Delhi	1948-49
Agarkar,AB	(1)	109* §	238m	190	-/16	England	Lord's	2002
Amarnath,M	(11)	100	264m		-/4	Australia	Perth	1977-78
		101*	288m	223	-/5	West Indies	Kanpur	1978-79
		109*	391m	284	-/15	Pakistan	Lahore[2]	1982-83
		120	282m	200	1/15	Pakistan	Lahore[2]	1982-83
		103*	236m	188	-/12	Pakistan	Karachi[1]	1982-83
		117	375m		-/14	West Indies	Port-of-Spain	1982-83
		116	282m		-/10	West Indies	St John's	1982-83
		101*	408m		-/8	Pakistan	Lahore[2]	1984-85
		116*	395m	201	-/9	Sri Lanka	Kandy	1985-86
		138	382m	312	-/10	Australia	Sydney	1985-86
		131	454m	301	-/14	Sri Lanka	Nagpur	1986-87
Amarnath,NB	(1)	118 §	203m		-/21	England	Bombay[1]	1933-34
Amarnath,S	(1)	124 §	259m		1/16	New Zealand	Auckland	1975-76
Amre,PK	(1)	103 §	374m	298	-/11	South Africa	Durban[2]	1992-93
Apte,ML	(1)	163*	584m			West Indies	Port-of-Spain	1952-53
Azharuddin,M	(22)	110 §	442m	324	-/10	England	Calcutta	1984-85
		105	279m	218	-/18	England	Madras[1]	1984-85
		122	374m	270	-/16	England	Kanpur	1984-85
		199	500m		1/16	Sri Lanka	Kanpur	1986-87

		141	400m		-/11	Pakistan	Calcutta	1986-87
		110	308m	211	-/14	Pakistan	Jaipur	1986-87
		109	249m	175	-/10	Pakistan	Faisalabad	1989-90
		192	421m	259	-/26	New Zealand	Auckland	1989-90
		121	174m	112	-/22	England	Lord's	1990
		179	279m	243	1/21	England	Manchester	1990
		106	185m	162	-/17	Australia	Adelaide	1991-92
		182	326m	197	1/26	England	Calcutta	1992-93
		108	290m	217	1/11	Sri Lanka	Bangalore	1993-94
		152	361m	260	1/16	Sri Lanka	Ahmedabad	1993-94
		109	126m	78	1/18	South Africa	Calcutta	1996-97
		163*	312m	222	1/25	South Africa	Kanpur	1996-97
		115	175m	109	1/19	South Africa	Cape Town	1996-97
		126	289m	199	-/11	Sri Lanka	Colombo (RPS)	1997-98
		108*	227m	174	-/14	Sri Lanka	Colombo (SSC)	1997-98
		163*	311m	246	3/18	Australia	Calcutta	1997-98
		103*	230m	156	-/14	New Zealand	Wellington	1998-99
		102	224m	170	2/13	South Africa	Bangalore	1999-200
Baig,AA	(1)	112 §	261m		-/12	England	Manchester	1959
Bangar,SB	(1)	100* §	183m	154	2/12	Zimbabwe	Nagpur	2001-02
Borde,CG	(5)	109	255m		-/16	West Indies	Delhi	1958-59
		177*	533		-/13	Pakistan	Madras[2]	1960-61
		109	152m		-/17	New Zealand	Bombay[2]	1964-65
		121			-/15	West Indies	Bombay[2]	1966-67
		125	340m		-/14	West Indies	Madras[1]	1966-67
Contractor,NJ	(1)	108	397m		-/10	Australia	Bombay[2]	1959-60
Das,SS	(2)	110	256m	175	-/19	Zimbabwe	Nagpur	2000-01
		105	293m	203	-/19	Zimbabwe	Nagpur	2001-02
Dasgupta,D	(1)	100 §	338m	254	-/15	England	Mohali	2001-02
Dhoni,MS	(1)	148	229m	153	4/19	Pakistan	Faisalabad	2005-06
Dravid,RS	(23)	148	540m	362	-/21	South Africa	Johannesburg[3]	1996-97
		118 §	422m	300	-/17	Zimbabwe	Harare	1998-99
		190)	493m	354	-/31	New Zealand	Hamilton	1998-99
		103*)	163m	136	-/16			
		107	314m	218	-/12	Sri Lanka	Colombo (SSC)	1998-99
		144	418m	327	-/18	New Zealand	Mohali	1999-2000
		200*	551m	350	-/27	Zimbabwe	Delhi	2000-01
		162	408m	301	1/20	Zimbabwe	Nagpur	2000-01
		180	444m	353	-/21	Australia	Kolkata	2000-01
		144*	436m	345	-/23	West Indies	Georgetown	2001-02
		115	338m	244	-/16	England	Nottingham	2002
		148	429m	307	-/23	England	Leeds	2002
		217*	629m	468	-/28	England	The Oval	2002
		100*	345m	242	-/12	West Indies	Mumbai[3]	2002-03
		222	578m	387	1/28	New Zealand	Ahmedabad	2003-04
		233	594m	446	1/23	Australia	Adelaide	2003-04
		270	740m	495	1/34	Pakistan	Rawalpindi[2]	2003-04
		160	387m	304	-/12	Bangladesh	Chittagong[1]	2004-05
		110)	290m	222	1/15	Pakistan	Kolkata	2004-05
		135)	374m	283	-/15			
		128*	331m	233	-/19	Pakistan	Lahore[2]	2005-06
		103	342m	220	-/16	Pakistan	Faisalabad	2005-06
		146		234	-/16	West Indies	Gros Islet	2005-06
Durani,SA	(1)	104	194m		-/14	West Indies	Port-of-Spain	1961-62
Engineer,FM	(2)	109	159m		-/18	West Indies	Madras[1]	1966-67
		121	283m	182	-/14	England	Bombay[2]	1972-73

Gaekwad,AD	(2)	102	357m		-/10	West Indies	Kanpur	1978-79
		201	671m	436	-/17	Pakistan	Jullundur	1983-84
Gambhir,G	(1)	139	286m	196	-/19	Bangladesh	Chittagong[1]	2004-05
Ganguly,SC	(12)	131 §	434m	301	-/20	England	Lord's	1996
		136	361m	268	2/17	England	Nottingham	1996
		147	426m	390	2/19	Sri Lanka	Colombo (SSC)	1997-98
		109	324m	240	2/10	Sri Lanka	Mohali	1997-98
		173	516m	361	2/25	Sri Lanka	Mumbai[3]	1997-98
		101*	138m	111	2/16	New Zealand	Hamilton	1998-99
		125	323m	252	-/20	New Zealand	Ahmedabad	1999-2000
		136	456m	284	1/21	Zimbabwe	Delhi	2001-02
		128	261m	167	3/14	England	Leeds	2002
		100*	269m	211	3/8	New Zealand	Ahmedabad	2003-04
		144	291m	196	-/18	Australia	Brisbane[2]	2003-04
		101		262	-/10	Zimbabwe	Bulawayo[2]	2005-06
Gavaskar,SM	(34)	116	265m		-/11	West Indies	Georgetown	1970-71
		117*	340m		-/10	West Indies	Bridgetown	1970-71
		124)	392m		-/11	West Indies	Port-of-Spain	1970-71
		220)	505m		-/22			
		101	290m		-/8	England	Manchester	1974
		116 §	368m		1/15	New Zealand	Auckland	1975-76
		156	488m	352	-/13	West Indies	Port-of-Spain	1975-76
		102	245m		-/13	West Indies	Port-of-Spain	1975-76
		119	265m		-/20	New Zealand	Bombay[3]	1976-77
		108	341m	220	-/13	England	Bombay[3]	1976-77
		113 §	320m	264	-/12	Australia	Brisbane[2]	1977-78
		127	270m		-/20	Australia	Perth	1977-78
		118	354m		-12	Australia	Melbourne	1977-78
		111)	357m		-/15	Pakistan	Karachi[1]	1978-79
		137)	315m	240	-/20			
		205	398m		2/29	West Indies	Bombay[3]	1978-79
		107)	315h		-/18	West Indies	Calcutta	1978-79
		182*)	399m	264	-/19			
		120	344m	218	-/18	West Indies	Delhi	1978-79
		221	489m	443	-/21	England	The Oval	1979
		115	329m	238	1/17	Australia	Delhi	1979-80
		123	303m	239	-/17	Australia	Bombay[3]	1979-80
		166	593m	393	1/15	Pakistan	Madras[1]	1979-80
		172	708m	476	-/21	England	Bangalore	1981-82
		155 §	399m	293	1/24	Sri Lanka	Madras[1]	1982-83
		127*	433m	262	-/19	Pakistan	Faisalabad	1982-83
		147*	330m		1/17	West Indies	Georgetown	1982-83
		103*	236m	190	-/10	Pakistan	Bangalore	1983-84
		121	224m	128	2/15	West Indies	Delhi	1983-84
		236*	644m	425	-/23	West Indies	Madras[1]	1983-84
		166*	551m	416	-/16	Australia	Adelaide	1985-86
		172	413m	400	-/19	Australia	Sydney	1985-86
		103	302m	203	-/11	Australia	Bombay[3]	1986-87
		176	506m	302	-/22	Sri Lanka	Kanpur	1986-87
Hanumant Singh	(1)	105 §	149m		-/16	England	Delhi	1963-64
Hazare,VS	(7)	116)	275m		-/14	Australia	Adelaide	1947-48
		145)	313m		-/17			
		134*	371m		-/18	West Indies	Bombay[2]	1948-49
		122	241m		-/14	West Indies	Bombay[2]	1948-49
		164*	515m		-/15	England	Delhi	1951-52
		155	321m		-/19	England	Bombay[2]	1951-52

		146*	285m		-/18	Pakistan	Bombay^2	1952-53
Jaisimha,ML	(3)	127	249m		2/14	England	Delhi	1961-62
		129	299m		1/18	England	Calcutta	1963-64
		101	291m		-/9	Australia	Brisbane^2	1967-68
Kambli,VG	(4)	224	608m	411	-/23	England	Bombay^3	1992-93
		227 §	413m	301	-/28	Zimbabwe	Delhi	1992-93
		125	358m	220	1/16	Sri Lanka	Colombo (SSC)	1993-94
		120	315m	240	2/15	Sri Lanka	Colombo (PSS)	1993-94
Kapil Dev	(8)	126*	224m	124	1/11	West Indies	Delhi	1978-79
		116	173m	98	2/16	England	Kanpur	1981-82
		100*	142m	95	3/13	West Indies	Port-of-Spain	1982-83
		119	214m	138	-/21	Australia	Madras^1	1986-87
		163	240m	165	1/19	Sri Lanka	Kanpur	1986-87
		109	164m	124	-/18	West Indies	Madras^1	1987-88
		110	197m	142	-/19	England	The Oval	1990
		129	256m	180	1/14	South Africa	Port Elizabeth	1992-93
Kirmani,SMH	(2)	101*	306m	206	-/16	Australia	Bombay^3	1979-80
		102	319m	230	-/10	England	Bombay^3	1984-85
Kripal Singh,AG	(1)	100* §	246m		-/12	New Zealand	Hyderabad	1955-56
Kunderan,BK	(2)	192	410m		-/31	England	Madras^2	1963-64
		100	241m		-/15	England	Delhi	1963-64
Laxman,VVS	(10)	167	255m	198	-/27	Australia	Sydney	1999-2000
		281	631m	452	-/44	Australia	Kolkata	2000-01
		130	369m	244	-/14	West Indies	St John's	2001-02
		154*	530m	396	-/17	West Indies	Kolkata	2002-03
		104*	428m	262	-/11	New Zealand	Mohali	2003-04
		148	356m	282	-/18	Australia	Adelaide	2003-04
		178	403m	298	-/30	Australia	Sydney	2003-04
		140		221	-/21	Zimbabwe	Bulawayo^2	2005-06
		104	398m	237	-/14	Sri Lanka	Ahmedabad	2005-06
		100		231	-/15	West Indies	Bassaterre	2005-06
Manjrekar,SV	(4)	108	343m	221	-/15	West Indies	Bridgetown	1988-89
		113* §	351m	243	-/13	Pakistan	Karachi^1	1989-90
		218	511m	401	-/28	Pakistan	Lahore^2	1989-90
		100* §	529m	422	-/7	Zimbabwe	Harare	1992-93
Manjrekar,VL	(7)	133	266m		-/19	England	Leeds	1952
		118	249m		-/15	West Indies	Kingston	1952-53
		118 §	235m		-/20	New Zealand	Hyderabad	1955-56
		177	555h		-/20	New Zealand	Delhi	1955-56
		189*	444m		-/28	England	Delhi	1961-62
		108	294m		-/14	England	Madras^2	1963-64
		102*	200m		-/14	New Zealand	Madras^2	1964-65
Mankad,MH	(5)	116	180h		1/13	Australia	Melbourne	1947-48
		111	300m		-/6	Australia	Melbourne	1947-48
		184	270m		1/19	England	Lord's	1952
		223	472m		-/22	New Zealand	Bombay^2	1955-56
		231	525m		-/21	New Zealand	Madras^2	1955-56
Merchant,VM	(3)	114	255m		-/13	England	Manchester	1936
		128	315h		-/15	England	The Oval	1946
		154	440m		-/20	England	Delhi	1951-52
Modi,RS	(1)	112	284m		-/12	West Indies	Bombay^2	1948-49
Mohammad Kaif (1)		148*		243	-/12	West Indies	Gros Islet	2005-06
Mongia,NR	(1)	152 §	497m	365	1/18	Australia	Delhi	1996-97
Mushtaq Ali	(2)	112	160m		-/17	England	Manchester	1936
		106 §	203m		-/9	West Indies	Calcutta	1948-49
Nadkarni,RG	(1)	122*	418m		-/15	England	Kanpur	1963-64

Pataudi,Nawab of,jr	(6)	103	168m		2/16	England	Madras^2	1961-62
		203*	430m		2/23	England	Delhi	1963-64
		128* §	343m	311	-/17	Australia	Madras^2	1964-65
		153	285m		-/29	New Zealand	Calcutta	1964-65
		113	233m		2/16	New Zealand	Delhi	1964-65
		148	350m		1/15	England	Leeds	1967
Patel,BP	(1)	115*	420m		-/10	West Indies	Port-of-Spain	1975-76
Patil,SM	(4)	174	301m	240	1/22	Australia	Adelaide	1980-81
		129*	212m	196	2/18	England	Manchester	1982
		114* §	216m		1/13	Sri Lanka	Madras^1	1982-83
		127	330h	231	-/18	Pakistan	Faisalabad	1984-85
Phadkar,DG	(2)	123	254m		-/15	Australia	Adelaide	1947-48
		115	389m		1/10	England	Calcutta	1951-52
Prabhakar,M	(1)	120	405m	274	-/16	West Indies	Mohali	1994-95
Ramchand,GS	(2)	106*	220m		-/14	New Zealand	Calcutta	1955-56
		109	248m		-/19	Australia	Bombay^2	1956-57
Ramesh,S	(2)	143 §	317m	214	1/18	Sri Lanka	Colombo (SSC)	1998-99
		110	228m	169	-/13	New Zealand	Ahmedabad	1999-2000
Ratra,A	(1)	115*	369m	284	-/12	West Indies	St John's	2001-02
Roy,Pankaj	(5)	140	329m		-/20	England	Bombay^2	1951-52
		111	232m		-/15	England	Madras^1	1951-52
		150	376m		-/20	West Indies	Kingston	1952-53
		100	308m		-/15	New Zealand	Calcutta	1955-56
		173	472m		-/12	New Zealand	Madras^2	1955-56
Sardesai,DN	(5)	200*	550m		-/25	New Zealand	Bombay^2	1964-65
		106	140m		-/18	New Zealand	Delhi	1964-65
		212	487m		1/17	West Indies	Kingston	1970-71
		112	278m		-/11	West Indies	Port-of-Spain	1970-71
		150	288m		-/20	West Indies	Bridgetown	1970-71
Sehwag,VK	(12)	105 §	272m	173	-/19	South Africa	Bloemfontein	2001-02
		106	257m	183	-/18	England	Nottingham	2002
		147 §	301m	206	3/24	West Indies	Mumbai^3	2002-03
		130	315m	225	2/16	New Zealand	Mohali	2003-04
		195	312m	233	5/16	Australia	Melbourne	2003-04
		309 §	531m	375	6/39	Pakistan	Multan^2	2003-04
		155	356m	221	-/21	Australia	Chennai^1	2004-05
		164	328m	228	2/24	South Africa	Kanpur	2004-05
		173	352m	244	2/19	Pakistan	Mohali	2004-05
		201	325m	262	2/28	Pakistan	Bangalore	2004-05
		254	328m	247	1/47	Pakistan	Lahore^2	2005-06
		180		190	2/20	West Indies	Gros Islet	2005-06
Shastri,RJ	(11)	128	488m	327	-/15	Pakistan	Karachi^1	1982-83
		102	370m		-/5	West Indies	St John's	1982-83
		139	405m	270	2/16	Pakistan	Faisalabad	1984-85
		142	389m	322	1/17	England	Bombay^3	1984-85
		111	455m	357	-/13	England	Calcutta	1984-85
		121*	388m	287	6/9	Australia	Bombay^3	1986-87
		125	>450h		1/8	Pakistan	Jaipur	1986-87
		107	441m	282	-/12	West Indies	Bridgetown	1988-89
		100	245m	185	1/12	England	Lord's	1990
		187	559m	435	-/23	England	The Oval	1990
		206	572m	472	2/17	Australia	Sydney	1991-92
Shodhan,RH	(1)	110 §	215m		-/15	Pakistan	Calcutta	1952-53
Sidhu,NS	(9)	116 §	295m	195	4/12	New Zealand	Bangalore	1988-89
		116	358m	237	-/13	West Indies	Kingston	1988-89
		106	403m	273	-/9	England	Madras^1	1992-93

		104	384m	273	-/7	Sri Lanka	Colombo (SSC)	1993-94
		124	280m	223	8/9	Sri Lanka	Lucknow[2]	1993-94
		107	296m	240	-/17	West Indies	Nagpur	1994-95
		201	673m	491	1/19	West Indies	Port-of-Spain	1996-97
		111	260m	200	2/13	Sri Lanka	Colombo (RPS)	1997-98
		131	476m	372	2/14	Sri Lanka	Mohali	1997-98
Solkar,ED	(1)	102	363m		-/8	West Indies	Bombay[3]	1974-75
Srikkanth,K	(2)	116	190m	119	1/19	Australia	Sydney	1985-86
		123	227m	149	2/18	Pakistan	Madras[1]	1986-87
Tendulkar,SR	(35)	119*	225m	189	-/17	England	Manchester	1990
		148*	298m	215	-/14	Australia	Sydney	1991-92
		114	228m	161	-/16	Australia	Perth	1991-92
		111	370m	270	-/19	South Africa	Johannesburg[3]	1992-93
		165	361m	296	1/24	England	Madras[1]	1992-93
		104*	217m	163	1/11	Sri Lanka	Colombo (SSC)	1993-94
		142	260m	224	-/22	Sri Lanka	Lucknow[2]	1993-94
		179	412m	319	1/24	West Indies	Nagpur	1994-95
		122	262m	176	1/19	England	Birmingham	1996
		177	462m	360	-/26	England	Nottingham	1996
		169	333m	253	-/26	South Africa	Cape Town	1996-97
		143	294m	247	-/20	Sri Lanka	Colombo (RPS)	1997-98
		139	403m	266	-/16	Sri Lanka	Colombo (SSC)	1997-98
		148	320m	244	3/21	Sri Lanka	Mumbai[3]	1997-98
		155*	286m	191	4/14	Australia	Chennai[1]	1997-98
		177	298m	207	3/29	Australia	Bangalore	1997-98
		113	200m	151	-/13	New Zealand	Wellington	1998-99
		136	430m	273	-/18	Pakistan	Chennai[1]	1998-99
		124*	308m	234	1/10	Sri Lanka	Colombo (SSC)	1998-99
		126*	397m	248	-/14	New Zealand	Mohali	1999-2000
		217	494m	343	-/29	New Zealand	Ahmedabad	1999-2000
		116	283m	119	1/9	Australia	Melbourne	1999-2000
		122	283m	233	-/19	Zimbabwe	Delhi	2000-01
		201*	392m	284	-/27	Zimbabwe	Nagpur	2000-01
		126	346m	230	2/15	Australia	Chennai[1]	2000-01
		155	233m	184	1/23	South Africa	Bloemfontein	2001-02
		102	254m	197	1/12	England	Ahmedabad	2001-02
		176	444m	316	-/22	Zimbabwe	Nagpur	2001-02
		117	356m	260	-/14	West Indies	Port-of-Spain	2001-02
		193	434m	330	3/19	England	Leeds	2002
		176	419m	298	-/26	West Indies	Kolkata	2002-03
		241*	613m	436	-/33	Australia	Sydney	2003-04
		194*	493m	348	-/21	Pakistan	Multan[2]	2003-04
		248*	552m	379	-/35	Bangladesh	Dhaka	2004-05
		109	310m	196	1/14	Sri Lanka	Delhi	2005-06
Umrigar,PR	(12)	130*	262m		-/11	England	Madras[1]	1951-52
		102	168m		1/15	Pakistan	Bombay[2]	1952-53
		130	327m		2/12	West Indies	Port-of-Spain	1952-53
		117	232m		-/16	West Indies	Kingston	1952-53
		108	280m		-/13	Pakistan	Peshawar[1]	1954-55
		223 §	503m		-/26	New Zealand	Hyderabad	1955-56
		118	260m		-/13	England	Manchester	1959
		115	339m		-/11	Pakistan	Kanpur	1960-61
		117			-/14	Pakistan	Madras[2]	1960-61
		112				Pakistan	Delhi	1960-61
		147*	400m		-/16	England	Kanpur	1961-62
		172*	248m			West Indies	Port-of-Spain	1961-62

Vengsarkar,DB	(17)	157*	379m	299	1/18	West Indies	Calcutta	1978-79
		109	336m	223	-/11	West Indies	Delhi	1978-79
		103	353m	295	-/13	England	Lord's	1979
		112	366m	283	2/12	Australia	Bangalore	1979-80
		146*	522m	370	1/11	Pakistan	Delhi	1979-80
		157	334m	264	-/21	England	Lord's	1982
		159	370m	238	1/20	West Indies	Delhi	1983-84
		100	108m	142	-/13	West Indies	Bombay[3]	1983-84
		137	360m	255	1/17	England	Kanpur	1984-85
		126*	327m	213	-/16	England	Lord's	1986
		102*	282m	216	-/10	England	Leeds	1986
		164*	432m	303	1/21	Australia	Bombay[3]	1986-87
		153	335m		-/13	Sri Lanka	Nagpur	1986-87
		166	429m	266	-/14	Sri Lanka	Cuttack	1986-87
		109	400m	295	-/10	Pakistan	Ahmedabad	1986-87
		102	405m	257	-/8	West Indies	Delhi	1987-88
		102#	346m	266	-/11	West Indies	Calcutta	1987-88
Viswanath,GR	(14)	137 §	354m		-/25	Australia	Kanpur	1969-70
		113	267m	214	1/18	England	Bombay[2]	1972-73
		139	376m	263	-/23	West Indies	Calcutta	1974-75
		112	220m		-/15	West Indies	Port-of-Spain	1975-76
		103*	147m		-/8	New Zealand	Kanpur	1976-77
		145 §	360m		-/16	Pakistan	Faisalabad	1978-79
		124	346m		-/17	West Indies	Madras[1]	1978-79
		179	419m	261	-/21	West Indies	Kanpur	1978-79
		113	351m	337	-/14	England	Lord's	1979
		161*	405m	297	1/11	Australia	Bangalore	1979-80
		131	277m	207	-/18	Australia	Delhi	1979-80
		114	274m	222	-/11	Australia	Melbourne	1980-81
		107	268m	200	-/14	England	Delhi	1981-82
		222	638m	373	-/31	England	Madras[1]	1981-82
Wadekar,AL	(1)	143	371m		-/12	New Zealand	Wellington	1967-68
Wasim Jaffer	(2)	100	306m	198	-/12	England	Nagpur	2005-06
		212	503m	399	1/24	West Indies	St John's	2005-06
Yashpal Sharma	(2)	100*	280m	239	3/10	Australia	Delhi	1979-80
		140	492m	301	2/18	England	Madras[1]	1981-82
Yuvraj Singh	(2)	112	197m	129	2/15	Pakistan	Lahore[2]	2003-04
		122		144	1/19	Pakistan	Karachi[1]	2005-06

PAKISTAN (293)			Time	Balls	6/4	Opponents		
Aamer Malik	(2)	117	409m	300	-/15	India	Faisalabad	1989-90
		113	344m	276	-/11	India	Lahore[2]	1989-90
Aamer Sohail	(5)	205	343m	284	-/32	England	Manchester	1992
		105	280m	200	-/17	Australia	Lahore[2]	1994-95
		160	441m	297	1/17	West Indies	Rawalpindi[2]	1997-98
		160	354m	255	-/21	West Indies	Karachi[1]	1997-98
		133	345m	272	1/18	Australia	Karachi[1]	1998-99
Abdur Razzaq	(3)	100*	330m	225	-/12	England	Faisalabad	2000-01
		110* §	121m	100	3/16	Bangladesh	Multan[2]	2001-02
		134	340m	235	4/17	Bangladesh	Dhaka	2001-02
Ali Naqvi	(1)	115 §	356m	270	-/14	South Africa	Rawalpindi[2]	1997-98
Alimuddin	(2)	103*	325m		-/15	India	Karachi[1]	1954-55
		109	232m		-/17	England	Karachi[1]	1961-62
Asif Iqbal	(11)	146	190m	244	2/21	England	The Oval	1967
		104*	192m	170	-/16	England	Birmingham	1971
		175	274m		1/18	New Zealand	Dunedin	1972-73

		102	195m		-/16	England	Lahore[2]	1972-73
		166	334m		-/15	New Zealand	Lahore[2]	1976-77
		152*	268m		-/14	Australia	Adelaide	1976-77
		120	245m		-/15	Australia	Sydney	1976-77
		135	245m		1/20	West Indies	Kingston	1976-77
		104 §	178m		-/15	India	Faisalabad	1978-79
		104	237m		-/10	New Zealand	Napier	1978-79
		134*	306m		1/18	Australia	Perth	1978-79
Azhar Mahmood	(3)	128* §	351m	267	1/11	South Africa	Rawalpindi[2]	1997-98
		132	198m	163	-/24	South Africa	Durban[2]	1997-98
		136	304m	215	2/16	South Africa	Johannesburg[3]	1997-98
Basit Ali	(1)	103	197m	139	3/9	New Zealand	Christchurch	1993-94
Faisal Iqbal	(1)	139 §		220	1/16	India	Karachi[1]	2005-06
Hanif Mohammad	(12)	142	518m		1/17	India	Bahawalpur	1954-55
		103	270h		-/8	New Zealand	Dacca	1955-56
		337 §	973m		-/24	West Indies	Bridgetown	1957-58
		103	390h		-/7	West Indies	Karachi[1]	1958-59
		101*	365m		-/10	Australia	Karachi[1]	1959-60
		160	380m		-/17	India	Bombay[2]	1960-61
		111)	497m		-/14	England	Dacca	1961-62
		104)	396m		-/8			
		104	193m		-/8	Australia	Melbourne	1964-65
		100*	203m		-/18	New Zealand	Christchurch	1964-65
		203*	445m		-/33	New Zealand	Lahore[2]	1964-65
		187*	540h		-/21	England	Lord's	1967
Haroon Rashid	(3)	122 §	298m		1/18	England	Lahore[2]	1977-78
		108	214m		6/10	England	Hyderabad	1977-78
		153 §	323m	242	3/16	Sri Lanka	Karachi[1]	1981-82
Ijaz Ahmed	(12)	122	297m	221	2/17	Australia	Faisalabad	1988-89
		121	450m	331	-/11	Australia	Melbourne	1989-90
		137	442m	332	2/17	Australia	Sydney	1995-96
		103	312m	213	2/13	New Zealand	Christchurch	1995-96
		141	279m	201	2/20	England	Leeds	1996
		125	269m	201	1/19	New Zealand	Rawalpindi[2]	1996-97
		113 §	324m	245	-/11	Sri Lanka	Colombo (RPS)	1996-97
		151	485m	337	1/15	West Indies	Karachi[1]	1997-98
		155	386m	282	-/24	Australia	Peshawar[2]	1998-99
		120*	325m	251	-/16	Australia	Karachi[1]	1998-99
		211	519m	372	1/23	Sri Lanka	Dhaka	1998-99
		115	230m	160	-/16	Australia	Perth	1999-2000
Ijaz Faqih	(1)	105 §	330m	241	4/7	India	Ahmedabad	1986-87
Imran Farhat	(2)	128	343m	226	-/18	South Africa	Faisalabad	2003-04
		101	266m	204	-/14	India	Lahore[2]	2003-04
Imran Khan	(6)	123	302m	199	-/13	West Indies	Lahore[2]	1980-81
		117	192m	121	5/10	India	Faisalabad	1982-83
		135*	>300h	230	5/14	India	Madras[1]	1986-87
		118	256m	201	1/11	England	The Oval	1987
		109*	201m	145	1/17	India	Karachi[1]	1989-90
		136	485m	361	-/10	Australia	Adelaide	1989-90
Imran Nazir	(2)	131 §	261m	180	-/20	West Indies	Bridgetown	1999-2000
		127 §	291m	203	3/18	New Zealand	Lahore[2]	2001-02
Imtiaz Ahmed	(3)	209	380m		-/28	New Zealand	Lahore[1]	1955-56
		122	250m		-/14	West Indies	Kingston	1957-58
		135	320m		-/11	India	Madras[2]	1960-61
Intikhab Alam	(1)	138	270m		4/15	England	Hyderabad	1972-73
Inzamamul Haq	(25)	123	314m	225	1/11	West Indies	St John's	1992-93

		135*	251m	195	1/19	New Zealand	Wellington	1993-94
		100*	197m	125	-/13	Sri Lanka	Kandy	1994-95
		101	205m	168	2/12	Zimbabwe	Harare	1994-95
		148	299m	218	1/19	England	Lord's	1996
		177	443m	320	2/19	West Indies	Rawalpindi[2]	1997-98
		200*	535m	397	2/23	Sri Lanka	Dhaka	1998-99
		118	276m	191	-/12	Australia	Hobart	1999-2000
		138	336m	243	1/17	Sri Lanka	Karachi[1]	1999-2000
		135	406m	254	-/20	West Indies	Georgetown	1999-2000
		112	215m	163	-/18	Sri Lanka	Galle	1999-2000
		142	361m	257	-/22	England	Karachi[1]	2000-01
		130	318m	241	1/22	New Zealand	Christchurch	2000-01
		114	215m	153	1/18	England	Manchester	2001
		105* §	205m	163	1/15	Bangladesh	Multan[2]	2001-02
		329	579m	436	9/38	New Zealand	Lahore[2]	2001-02
		112	142m	107	1/20	Zimbabwe	Harare	2002-03
		138*	316m	232	1/20	Bangladesh	Multan[2]	2003-04
		118	323m	243	-/14	India	Lahore[2]	2003-04
		117	332m	244	1/10	Sri Lanka	Karachi[1]	2004-05
		184	361m	264	-/25	India	Bangalore	2004-05
		(In his 100th Test match)						
		117*	244m	194	-/14	West Indies	Kingston	2004-05
		109)	326m	200	-/13	England	Faisalabad	2005-06
		100*)	243m	134	1/9			
		119	251m	193	1/12	India	Faisalabad	2005-06
Javed Burki	(3)	138 §	375h		1/17	England	Lahore[2]	1961-62
		140	356m		-/18	England	Dacca	1961-62
		101	225m		-/15	England	Lord's	1962
Javed Miandad	(23)	163 §	259m		-/22	New Zealand	Lahore[2]	1976-77
		206	410m		2/29	New Zealand	Karachi[1]	1976-77
		154* §	430m		3/13	India	Faisalabad	1978-79
		100	311m		1/8	India	Karachi[1]	1978-79
		160*	420m		1/17	New Zealand	Christchurch	1978-79
		129*	388m	284	-/15	Australia	Perth	1978-79
		106*	217m		1/11	Australia	Faisalabad	1979-80
		138	416m	264	2/13	Australia	Lahore[2]	1982-83
		126	276m	200	3/10	India	Faisalabad	1982-83
		280*	606m	460	1/19	India	Hyderabad	1982-83
		131	361m	271	-/13	Australia	Adelaide	1983-84
		104)	269m	217	-/12	New Zealand	Hyderabad	1984-85
		103*)	245m	198	1/13			
		203*	465m		1/22	Sri Lanka	Faisalabad	1985-86
		260	617m	521	1/28	England	The Oval	1987
		114	405m	235	-/12	West Indies	Georgetown	1987-88
		102	436m	265	-/18	West Indies	Port-of-Spain	1987-88
		211	636m	441	1/29	Australia	Karachi[1]	1988-89
		107	254m	186	-/17	Australia	Faisalabad	1988-89
		118	360m	277	-/8	New Zealand	Wellington	1988-89
		271	558m	465	5/28	New Zealand	Auckland	1988-89
		145	369m	291	-/10	India	Lahore[2]	1989-90
		(In his 100th Test match)						
		153*	415m	337	-/19	England	Birmingham	1992
Kamran Akmal	(4)	109	238m	154	-/16	India	Mohali	2004-05
		154	326m	242	-/14	England	Lahore[2]	2005-06
		102*	108m	81	2/11	India	Lahore[2]	2005-06
		113	203m	148	-/18	India	Karachi[1]	2005-06

Khalid Ibadulla	(1)	166 §	330m	319	-/20	Australia	Karachi[1]	1964-65
Majid Khan	(8)	158	303m		-/18	Australia	Melbourne	1972-73
		110	269m		-/15	New Zealand	Auckland	1972-73
		100	247m		-/9	West Indies	Karachi[1]	1974-75
		112	128m		2/18	New Zealand	Karachi[1]	1976-77
		167	360h		-/25	West Indies	Georgetown	1976-77
		119*	411m		-/13	New Zealand	Napier	1978-79
		108	219m		-/16	Australia	Melbourne	1978-79
		110*	282m		-/14	Australia	Lahore[2]	1979-80
Mansoor Akhtar	(1)	111	289m	191	-/18	Australia	Faisalabad	1982-83
Mohammad Hafeez	(1)	102*	210m	144	1/11	Bangladesh	Peshawar[2]	2003-04
Mohammad Ilyas	(1)	126	205m		1/15	New Zealand	Karachi[1]	1964-65
Mohammad Wasim	(2)	109* §	217m	165	-/17	New Zealand	Lahore[2]	1996-97
		192 §	555m	408	-/23	Zimbabwe	Harare	1997-98
Mohsin Khan	(7)	129	296m	173	-/17	Sri Lanka	Lahore[2]	1981-82
		200	496m	386	-/23	England	Lord's	1982
		135	349m	218	-/17	Australia	Lahore[2]	1982-83
		101* §	168m	161	1/10	India	Lahore[2]	1982-83
		149	393m	296	-/16	Australia	Adelaide	1983-84
		152	354m	239	1/19	Australia	Melbourne	1983-84
		104	258m	136	-/3	England	Lahore[2]	1983-84
Moin Khan	(4)	115* §	233m	185	1/13	Australia	Lahore[2]	1994-95
		117*	283m	208	2/13	Sri Lanka	Sialkot	1994-95
		105	282m	191	1/10	England	Leeds	1996
		137	222m	174	2/20	New Zealand	Hamilton	2003-04
Mudassar Nazar	(10)	114 §	591m		-/12	England	Lahore[2]	1977-78
		126	447m	337	-/13	India	Bangalore	1979-80
		119	294m	199	-/10	India	Karachi[1]	1982-83
		231	627m	444	1/21	India	Hyderabad	1982-83
		152*	495m	296	-/15	India	Lahore[2]	1982-83
		152	458m	308	-/14	India	Karachi[1]	1982-83
		199	552m	408	-/24	India	Faisalabad	1984-85
		106	255m	187	-/11	New Zealand	Hyderabad	1984-85
		124	416m	362	-/16	England	Birmingham	1987
		120	323m	257	-/18	England	Lahore[2]	1987-88
Mushtaq Mohammad	(10)	101	210m		-/19	India	Delhi	1960-61
		100*	324m		-/9	England	Nottingham	1962
		100	351m	283	-/13	England	Birmingham	1971
		121	292m	271	-/14	Australia	Sydney	1972-73
		201	383m		-/20	New Zealand	Dunedin	1972-73
		157	469m		-/17	England	Hyderabad	1972-73
		123	466m		-/12	West Indies	Lahore[2]	1974-75
		101			-/9	New Zealand	Hyderabad	1976-77
		107	298m		-/11	New Zealand	Karachi[1]	1976-77
		121	371m		-/14	West Indies	Port-of-Spain	1976-77
Nasim-ul-Ghani	(1)	101	180m		1/16	England	Lord's	1962
Nazir Mohammad	(1)	124*	517m			India	Lucknow[1]	1952-53
Qasim Omar	(3)	113	283m	224	-/12	Australia	Adelaide	1983-84
		210	685m	442	-/27	India	Faisalabad	1984-85
		206 §				Sri Lanka	Faisalabad	1985-86
Rameez Raja	(2)	122	388m	242	-/17	Sri Lanka	Colombo (PSS)	1985-86
		114	302m	279	1/12	India	Jaipur	1986-87
Rashid Latif	(1)	150	326m	234	1/17	West Indies	Sharjah	2001-02
Sadiq Mohammad	(5)	137	313m		-/15	Australia	Melbourne	1972-73
		166	362m		-/19	New Zealand	Wellington	1972-73
		119	375m		-/12	England	Lahore[2]	1972-73

		103*			-/14	New Zealand	Hyderabad	1976-77
		105	296m		-/10	Australia	Melbourne	1976-77
Saeed Ahmed	(5)	150	349m		-/16	West Indies	Georgetown	1957-58
		166	461m		-/19	Australia	Lahore[2]	1959-60
		121 §	345m		-/11	India	Bombay[2]	1960-61
		103	245m		-/10	India	Madras[2]	1960-61
		172	341m		1/17	New Zealand	Karachi[1]	1964-65
Saeed Anwar	(11)	169	307m	248	-/26	New Zealand	Wellington	1993-94
		136 §	319m	218	-/12	Sri Lanka	Colombo (PSS)	1994-95
		176	378m	264	-/26	England	The Oval	1996
		149	305m	214	-/20	New Zealand	Rawalpindi[2]	1996-97
		118	312m	209	-/18	South Africa	Durban[2]	1997-98
		145	383m	278	-/12	Australia	Rawalpindi[2]	1998-99
		126	289m	226	3/18	Australia	Peshawar[2]	1998-99
		188*	452m	259	1/23	India	Calcutta	1998-99
		119	254m	174	-/20	Australia	Brisbane[2]	1999-2000
		123	339m	237	2/12	Sri Lanka	Galle	1999-2000
		101 §	131m	104	1/17	Bangladesh	Multan[2]	2001-02
Saleem Malik	(15)	100* §	272m	191	-/10	Sri Lanka	Karachi[1]	1981-82
		107	251m	168	-/14	India	Faisalabad	1982-83
		116	393m	270	-/17	England	Faisalabad	1983-84
		102*	205m	157	-/15	India	Faisalabad	1984-85
		119*	267m	169	1/21	New Zealand	Karachi[1]	1984-85
		102	267m	237	-/6	England	The Oval	1987
		102*	216m	144	-/13	India	Karachi[1]	1989-90
		102	268m	208	-/7	West Indies	Karachi[1]	1990-91
		101	287m	201	-/10	Sri Lanka	Sialkot	1991-92
		165	370m	297	1/19	England	Birmingham	1992
		140	285m	200	-/20	New Zealand	Wellington	1993-94
		237	443m	328	-/34	Australia	Rawalpindi[2]	1994-95
		143	313m	242	-/19	Australia	Lahore[2]	1994-95
		100*	289m	223	-/10	England	The Oval	1996
		155	338m	240	-/26	Sri Lanka	Colombo (SSC)	1996-97
Salman Butt	(2)	108	276m	185	-/16	Australia	Sydney	2004-05
		122 §	403m	256	-/12	England	Multan[2]	2005-06
Saqlain Mushtaq	(1)	101*	430m	291	1/11	New Zealand	Christchurch	2000-01
Shahid Afridi	(5)	141 §	305m	191	3/21	India	Chennai[1]	1998-99
		107 §	208m	149	3/16	West Indies	Sharjah	2001-02
		122		95	6/9	West Indies	Bridgetown	2004-05
		103	111m	80	7/7	India	Lahore[2]	2005-06
		156	208m	128	6/20	India	Faisalabad	2005-06
Shoaib Malik	(1)	14*		369	2/21	Sri Lanka	Colombo (SSC)	2005-06
Shoaib Mohammad	(7)	101	240h		-/10	India	Madras[1]	1986-87
		163	720m	516	1/17	New Zealand	Wellington	1988-89
		112	350m	254	-/17	New Zealand	Auckland	1988-89
		203*	486m	335	-/19	India	Lahore[2]	1989-90
		203*	656m	411	-/23	New Zealand	Karachi[1]	1990-91
		105	351m	223	1/15	New Zealand	Lahore[2]	1990-91
		142	527m	368	-/20	New Zealand	Faisalabad	1990-91
Taslim Arif	(1)	210*	435m		-/20	Australia	Faisalabad	1979-80
Taufeeq Umar	(4)	104 §	231m	164	-/15	Bangladesh	Multan[2]	2001-02
		111 §	360m	229	-/13	Zimbabwe	Harare	2002-03
		135	334m	254	1/20	South Africa	Cape Town	2002-03
		111	322m	247	-/16	South Africa	Lahore[2]	2003-04
Wajatullah Wasti	(2)	133 §)	335m	238	2/18	Sri Lanka	Lahore[2]	1998-99
		121*)	425m	303	1/12			

Waqar Hassan	(1)	189	430m		-/30	New Zealand	Lahore[1]	1955-56
Wasim Akram	(3)	123	244m	195	1/18	Australia	Adelaide	1989-90
		257*	489m	370	12/22	Zimbabwe	Sheikhapura	1996-97
		100	160m	89	6/8	Sri Lanka	Galle	1999-2000
Wasim Raja	(4)	107*	340m		1/10	West Indies	Karachi[1]	1974-75
		117*	260m		1/12	West Indies	Bridgetown	1976-77
		125	258m	207	2/17	India	Jullundur	1983-84
		112	300m	210	2/14	England	Faisalabad	1983-84
Wazir Mohammad	(2)	106	a180h		-/17	West Indies	Kingston	1957-58
		189	403m		-/22	West Indies	Port-of-Spain	1957-58
Yasir Hameed	(2)	170)	312m	253	-/25	Bangladesh	Karachi[1]	2003-04
		105)	229m	161	-/15			
Younis Khan	(12)	107 §	320m	250	-/11	Sri Lanka	Rawalpindi[2]	1999-2000
		116	363m	281	1/9	Sri Lanka	Galle	1999-2000
		149* §	253m	182	4/14	New Zealand	Auckland	2000-01
		119	270m	217	-/20	Bangladesh	Chittagong[1]	2001-02
		153	412m	291	1/15	West Indies	Sharjah	2001-02
		124	318m	215	1/12	Sri Lanka	Karachi[1]	2004-05
		147	370m	258	-/19	India	Kolkata	2004-05
		267	690m	504	1/32	India	Bangalore	2004-05
		106	260m	190	-/14	West Indies	Kingston	2004-05
		199	476m	336	-/26	India	Lahore[2]	2005-06
		194	454m	299	1/22	India	Faisalabad	2005-06
		173	405m	285	-/22	England	Leeds	2006
Yousuf Youhana	(19)	120*	306m	206	1/15	Zimbabwe	Lahore[2]	1998-99
		115	358m	245	-/14	West Indies	Bridgetown	1999-2000
		103*	335m	231	1/8	West Indies	St John's	1999-2000
		124	374m	308	1/8	England	Lahore[2]	2000-01
		117 §	313m	242	1/14	England	Karachi[1]	2000-01
		203	528m	429	3/27	New Zealand	Christchurch	2000-01
		102* §	230m	153	-/14	Bangladesh	Multan[2]	2001-02
		204*	325m	243	2/34	Bangladesh	Chittagong[1]	2001-02
		146	363m	276	1/18	West Indies	Sharjah	2001-02
		159	365m	282	-/21	Zimbabwe	Bulawayo[2]	2002-03
		112	219m	164	2/16	India	Multan[2]	2003-04
		111	195m	134	4/11	Australia	Melbourne	2004-05
		104	228m	179	-/13	India	Kolkata	2004-05
		223	602m	373	2/26	England	Lahore[2]	2005-06
		173	270m	199	2/22	India	Lahore[2]	2005-06
		126	232m	179	4/11	India	Faisalabad	2005-06
		202	468m	330	1/26	England	Lord's	2006
		192	343m	261	2/25	England	Leeds	2006
		128	349m	236	-/18	England	The Oval	2006
Zaheer Abbas	(12)	274 §	550m		-/38	England	Birmingham	1971
		240	550m	410	-/22	England	The Oval	1974
		101	224m		1/13	Australia	Adelaide	1976-77
		176 §	315m		2/24	India	Faisalabad	1978-79
		235*	391m		2/29	India	Lahore[2]	1978-79
		135	388m	282	1/15	New Zealand	Auckland	1978-79
		134 §	269m	148	2/12	Sri Lanka	Lahore[2]	1981-82
		126	279m	205	3/12	Australia	Faisalabad	1982-83
		215	334m	254	2/23	India	Lahore[2]	1982-83
		(His 100th first-class century)						
		186	328m	246	-/23	India	Karachi[1]	1982-83
		168	264m	176	1/23	India	Faisalabad	1982-83
		168*	500m	341	1/6	India	Lahore[2]	1984-85

SRI LANKA (135)			Time	Balls	6/4	Opponents		
Arnold,RP	(3)	123	310m	208	-/20	Pakistan	Lahore[2]	1998-99
		104*	377m	243	-/14	Zimbabwe	Harare	1999-2000
		109	364m	236	-/13	England	Manchester	2002
Atapattu,MS	(16)	108	341m	244	-/14	India	Mohali	1997-98
		223 §	569m	448	1/29	Zimbabwe	Kandy	1997-98
		216*	627m	437	-/24	Zimbabwe	Bulawayo[2]	1999-2000
		207*	659m	457	1/19	Pakistan	Kandy	1999-2000
		120	372m	291	-/15	South Africa	Kandy	2000-01
		201*	684m	536	-/14	England	Galle	2000-01
		108	309m	228	-/11	India	Colombo (SSC)	2001-02
		201 §	320m	259	-/27	Bangladesh	Colombo (SSC)	2001-02
		100*	193m	126	-/11	Zimbabwe	Galle	2001-02
		185	492m	351	-/24	England	Lord's	2002
		118	404m	275	-/15	West Indies	Gros Islet	2002-03
		118	283m	219	-/19	Australia	Colombo (SSC)	2003-04
		170	333m	253	-/21	Zimbabwe	Harare	2003-04
		249	516m	324	1/36	Zimbabwe	Bulawayo[2]	2003-04
		133	333m	268	-/19	Australia	Cairns	2004-05
		127	304m	244	-/22	New Zealand	Napier	2004-05
de Silva,PA	(20)	122 §	510m		3/17	Pakistan	Faisalabad	1985-86
		105	265m		-/16	Pakistan	Karachi[1]	1985-86
		167	491m	361	1/17	Australia	Brisbane[2]	1989-90
		267 §	509m	380	-/40	New Zealand	Wellington	1990-91
		123	261m	193	5/6	New Zealand	Auckland	1990-91
		148	388m	297	1/17	India	Colombo (PSS)	1993-94
		127	211m	156	1/19	Pakistan	Colombo (PSS)	1994-95
		105	402m	316	-/11	Pakistan	Faisalabad	1994-95
		168	508m	383	1/14	Pakistan	Colombo (RPS)	1996-97
		138*)	273m	208	-/19	Pakistan	Colombo (SSC)	1996-97
		103*)	169m	99	1/11			
		126	293m	211	-/16	India	Colombo (RPS)	1997-98
		146)	365m	228	-/20	India	Colombo (SSC)	1997-98
		120)	267m	198	-/13			
		110*	378m	263	1/15	India	Mohali	1997-98
		143*	460m	310	2/16	Zimbabwe	Colombo (SSC)	1997-98
		152	461m	292	-/17	England	The Oval	1998
		112	377m	276	-/12	Pakistan	Rawalpindi[2]	1999-2000
		106	336m	243	1/10	England	Galle	2000-01
		206 §	318m	234	1/28	Bangladesh	Colombo (PSS)	2002-03
Dias,RL	(3)	109	260m	179	1/14	Pakistan	Lahore[2]	1981-82
		108 §	272m	215	-/18	New Zealand	Colombo (SSC)	1983-84
		106	312m	216	-/17	India	Kandy	1985-86
Dilshan,TM	(4)	163*	478m	343	-/18	Zimbabwe	Harare	1999-2000
		100	162m	129	1/13	England	Kandy	2003-04
		104	244m	188	1/12	Australia	Galle	2003-04
		168	215m	179	1/19	Bangladesh	Colombo (PSS)	2005-06
Gurusinha,AP	(7)	116*	495m	307	-/14	Pakistan	Colombo (PSS)	1985-86
		119)	362m	261	1/17	New Zealand	Hamilton	1990-91
		102)	331m	239	1/9			
		137	525m	399	-/18	Australia	Colombo (SSC)	1992-93
		128 §	607m	461	1/14	Zimbabwe	Harare	1994-95
		127	516m	429	1/11	New Zealand	Dunedin	1994-95
		143	353m	274	1/15	Australia	Melbourne	1995-96
Jayasuriya,ST	(14)	112	272m	188	2/14	Australia	Adelaide	1995-96
		113	290m	212	1/9	Pakistan	Colombo (SSC)	1996-97

		340	799m	578	2/36	India	Colombo (RPS)	1997-98
		199	419m	226	-/16	India	Colombo (SSC)	1997-98
		213	346m	278	1/33	England	The Oval	1998
		188	467m	358	2/17	Pakistan	Kandy	1999-2000
		148	190m	156	1/24	South Africa	Galle	2000-01
		111	191m	138	1/16	India	Galle	2000-01
		145	214m	164	6/13	Bangladesh	Colombo (PSS)	2002-03
		139	292m	212	-/17	Zimbabwe	Kandy	2001-02
		131	204m	145	2/17	Australia	Kandy	2003-04
		157	228m	147	3/19	Zimbabwe	Harare	2003-04
		253	490m	348	4/33	Pakistan	Faisalabad	2004-05
		107	115m	129	1/14	Pakistan	Karachi[1]	2004-05
Jayawardene,DPMD	(16)	167	338m	278	-/18	New Zealand	Galle	1997-98
		242	677m	465	2/30	India	Colombo (SSC)	1998-99
		167 §	216m	183	1/14	South Africa	Galle	2000-01
		101*	339m	289	2/22	South Africa	Colombo (SSC)	2000-01
		101	180m	165	1/12	England	Kandy	2000-01
		104	217m	149	-/17	India	Kandy	2001-02
		139	341m	216	1/14	India	Colombo (SSC)	2001-02
		150 §	180m	115	1/26	Bangladesh	Colombo (SSC)	2001-02
		107	222m	168	-/17	England	Lord's	2002
		134	351m	246	1/14	England	Colombo (SSC)	2003-04
		100*	174m	152	1/7	Zimbabwe	Bulawayo[2]	2003-04
		237	563m	415	3/25	South Africa	Galle	2004-05
		141	338m	243	1/19	New Zealand	Napier	2004-05
		119	366m	220	-/12	England	Lord's	2006
		374	752m	572	1/43	South Africa	Colombo (SSC)	2006-07
		123	359m	248	3/11	South Africa	Colombo (PSS)	2006-07
Kaluwitharana,RS	(3)	132* §	203m	158	-/26	Australia	Colombo (SSC)	1992-93
		103 §	134m	104	2/13	New Zealand	Dunedin	1996-97
		100	178m	144	-/16	Pakistan	Lahore[2]	1998-99
Kuruppu,DSBP	(1)	201* §	778m	562	-/24	New Zealand	Colombo (CCC)	1986-87
Madugalle,RS	(1)	103	403m	280	-/10	India	Colombo (SSC)	1985-86
Mahanama,RS	(4)	153	361m	297	-/18	New Zealand	Moratuwa	1992-93
		109	217m	154	-/14	New Zealand	Colombo (SSC)	1992-93
		151	520m	362	-/19	India	Colombo (PSS)	1993-94
		225	753m	561	-/27	India	Colombo (RPS)	1997-98
Mendis,LRD	(4)	105 §)	179m	123	1/17	India	Madras[1]	1982-83
		105)	236m		-/12			
		111	197m	143	3/11	England	Lord's	1984
		124	318m	228	2/12	India	Kandy	1985-86
Ranatunga,A	(4)	111	400m	290	1/4	India	Colombo (SSC)	1985-86
		135*	341m	208	4/14	Pakistan	Colombo (PSS)	1985-86
		127	266m	192	3/15	Australia	Colombo (SSC)	1992-93
		131 §	204m	140	1/18	South Africa	Moratuwa	1992-93
Ranatunga,S	(2)	118 §	467m	342	-/17	Zimbabwe	Harare	1994-95
		100*	421m	352	-/15	Zimbabwe	Bulawayo[2]	1994-95
Samaraweera,TT	(5)	103* §	196m	176	-/10	India	Colombo (SSC)	2001-02
		123* §	270m	166	-/12	Zimbabwe	Colombo (SSC)	2001-02
		142	491m	408	-/13	England	Colombo (SSC)	2003-04
		100	330m	232	-/10	Pakistan	Faisalabad	2004-05
		138	292m	217	-/20	Bangladesh	Colombo (PSS)	2005-06
Sangakkara,KC	(10)	105* §	329m	226	-/13	India	Galle	2001-02
		140 §	529m	373	-/16	West Indies	Galle	2001-02
		128* §	289m	186	-/22	Zimbabwe	Colombo (SSC)	2001-02
		230 §	480m	327	3/32	Pakistan	Lahore[2]	2001-02

		270	468m	365	2/36	Zimbabwe	Bulawayo²	2003-04
		232	529m	357	1/31	South Africa	Colombo (SSC)	2004-05
		138	348m	251	1/20	Pakistan	Karachi¹	2004-05
		157*	411m	284	-/24	West Indies	Kandy	2005-06
		185	448m	326	-/22	Pakistan	Colombo (SSC)	2005-06
		287	675m	457	-/35	South Africa	Colombo (SSC)	2006-07
Silva,SAR	(2)	102* §	316m	255	-/12	England	Lord's	1984
		111	492m	347	-/11	India	Colombo (PSS)	1985-86
Tharanga,WU	(1)	165	442m	302	2/19	Bangladesh	Bogra	2005-06
Tillakaratne,HP	(11)	116	451m	287	-/14	Zimbabwe	Harare	1994-95
		108	332m	258	-/14	New Zealand	Dunedin	1994-95
		115	226m	176	-/20	Pakistan	Faisalabad	1994-95
		119	267m	206	-/12	Australia	Perth	1995-96
		126*	409m	326	-/13	Zimbabwe	Colombo (SSC)	1996-97
		103	349m	228	-/10	Pakistan	Colombo (RPS)	1996-97
		136*	312m	213	-/16	India	Colombo (SSC)	2001-02
		105*	385m	247	-/3	West Indies	Galle	2001-02
		204*	538m	343	-/23	West Indies	Colombo (SSC)	2001-02
		104*	331m	231	-/17	South Africa	Centurion	2002-03
		144*	456m	314	-/24	New Zealand	Colombo (PSS)	2002-03
van Dort,MG	(2)	140	255m	185	1/16	Bangladesh	Colombo (SSC)	2002-03
		105	396m	303	-/9	England	Birmingham	2006
Wettimuny,S	(2)	157	372m	330	-/21	Pakistan	Faisalabad	1981-82
		190	636m	471	-/21	England	Lord's	1984

ZIMBABWE (42)			Time	Balls	6/4	Opponents		
Arnott,KJ	(1)	101* §	248m	200	-/12	New Zealand	Bulawayo¹	1992-93
Campbell,ADR	(2)	102	253m	186	-/15	India	Nagpur	2000-01
		103	294m	229	-/10	West Indies	Bulawayo²	2001-02
Carlisle,SV	(2)	118	398m	213	2/15	Australia	Sydney	2003-04
		103*	225m	173	-/9	Bangladesh	Bulawayo²	2003-04
Flower,A	(12)	115	289m	236	-/15	India	Delhi	1992-93
		156	336m	245	1/18	Pakistan	Harare	1994-95
		112 §	364m	331	-/12	England	Bulawayo²	1996-97
		105*	337m	238	-/10	Sri Lanka	Colombo (SSC)	1997-98
		100*	292m	217	-/6	Pakistan	Bulawayo²	1997-98
		129	422m	304	-/8	Sri Lanka	Harare	1999-2000
		113* §	431m	290	-/12	West Indies	Port-of-Spain	1999-2000
		183*	466m	351	2/24	India	Delhi	2000-01
		232*	542m	448	2/30	India	Nagpur	2000-01
		142)	289m	200	1/21	South Africa	Harare	2001-02
		199*)	590m	470	1/24			
		114*	216m	150	-/13	Bangladesh	Chittagong¹	2001-02
Flower,GW	(6)	201*	654m	523	1/10	Pakistan	Harare	1994-95
		110	392m	287	1/14	Pakistan	Sheikhapura	1996-97
		104)	345m	288	-/10	New Zealand	Harare	1997-98
		151)	335m	240	3/12			
		156*	512m	329	2/13	Pakistan	Bulawayo²	1997-98
		106*	273m	196	4/12	India	Nagpur	2000-01
Goodwin,MW	(3)	166* §	316m	204	-/17	Pakistan	Bulawayo²	1997-98
		113	324m	240	-/10	West Indies	Kingston	1999-2000
		148*	335m	251	-/20	England	Nottingham	2000
Gripper,TR	(1)	112	352m	263	-/15	Bangladesh	Chittagong¹	2001-02
Houghton,DL	(4)	121 §	414m	322	-/15	India	Harare	1992-93
		266	675m	541	3/30	Sri Lanka	Bulawayo²	1994-95
		142	394m	268	2/17	Sri Lanka	Harare	1994-95

		104#	306m	204	-/12	New Zealand	Auckland	1995-96
Johnson,NC	(1)	107 §	164m	117	-/16	Pakistan	Peshawar[2]	1998-99
Masakadza,H	(1)	119 §	388m	316	-/12	West Indies	Harare	2001-02
Strang,PA	(1)	106*	325m	207	-/10	Pakistan	Sheikhapura	1996-97
Streak,HH	(1)	127*	358m	264	1/12	West Indies	Harare	2003-04
Taibu,T	(1)	153	340m	292	2/19	Bangladesh	Dhaka	2004-05
Vermeulen,MA	(1)	118	433m	304	1/14	West Indies	Bulawayo[2]	2003-04
Whittall,GJ	(4)	113*	243m	192	-/9	Pakistan	Harare	1994-95
		203*	453m	359	2/22	New Zealand	Bulawayo[2]	1997-98
		188*	472m	429	2/27	New Zealand	Harare	2000-01
		119 §	258m	194	-/16	Bangladesh	Bulawayo[2]	2000-01
Wishart,CB	(1)	114	173m	145	2/11	Bangladesh	Chittagong[1]	2001-02

BANGLADESH (12)			Time	Balls	6/4	Opponents		
Aminul Islam	(1)	145 §	535m	380	-/17	India	Dhaka	2000-01
Habibul Bashar	(3)	108	283m	209	-/15	Zimbabwe	Chittagong[1]	2001-02
		108	278m	218	-/11	Pakistan	Peshawar[2]	2003-04
		113	197m	131	-/15	West Indies	Gros Islet	2003-04
Javed Omar	(1)	119	492m	357	-/17	Pakistan	Karachi[1]	2003-04
Khaled Mashud	(1)	103*	334m	281	-/13	West Indies	Gros Islet	2003-04
Mohammad Ashraful	(3)	114 §	248m	211	-/16	Sri Lanka	Colombo (SSC)	2001-02
		158*	275m	194	3/24	India	Chittagong[1]	2004-05
		136	250m	184	3/15	Sri Lanka	Chittagong[2]	2005-06
Mohammad Rafique	(1)	111	230m	152	1/11	West Indies	Gros Islet	2003-04
Nafis Iqbal	(1)	121	468m	355	-/18	Zimbabwe	Dhaka	2004-05
Shahriar Nafees	(1)	138	274m	189	-/19	Australia	Fatullah	2005-06

NINETY-NINES IN TEST MATCHES

Seventy-six Test innings of ninety-nine have been made by sixty-eight batsmen (M.J.K.Smith, G.Boycott, R.B.Richardson, J.G.Wright, M.A.Atherton, Saleem Malik, G.S.Blewett and S.C.Ganguly doing so twice in their careers). G.Boycott, S.R.Waugh, A.J.Tudor, S.M.Pollock and A.J.Hall are the only players to register a not out 99. In the Third Test between England and Pakistan at Karachi[1] in 1972-73 three batsmen, Majid Khan, Mushtaq Mohammad and D.L.Amiss were dismissed for 99. (§ on debut).

AUSTRALIA	How out	Opponent		
C.Hill	c A.O.Jones b S.F.Barnes	England	Melbourne	1901-02
C.G.Macartney	cw E.J.Smith b F.R.Foster	England	Lord's	1912
A.G.Chipperfield §	cw L.E.G.Ames b K.Farnes	England	Nottingham	1934
W.A.Brown	run out	India	Melbourne	1947-48
K.R.Miller	b D.V.P.Wright	England	Adelaide	1950-51
A.R.Morris	run out	South Africa	Melbourne	1952-53
C.C.McDonald	cw J.H.B.Waite b E.R.H.Fuller	South Africa	Cape Town	1957-58
R.M.Cowper	c F.J.Titmus b I.J.Jones	England	Melbourne	1965-66
I.M.Chappell	c A.L.Wadekar b B.S.Bedi	India	Calcutta	1969-70
R.Edwards	lbw b R.A.Woolmer	England	Lord's	1975
K.J.Hughes	c J.M.Brearley b D.L.Underwood	England	Perth	1979-80
D.M.Jones	lbw b D.K.Morrison	New Zealand	Perth	1989-90
M.E.Waugh	b P.C.R.Tufnell	England	Lord's	1993
M.J.Slater	cw T.E.Blain b D.N.Patel	New Zealand	Perth	1993-94
S.R.Waugh*	not out	England	Perth	1994-95
G.S.Blewett	b C.E.Cuffy	West Indies	Adelaide	1996-97
G.S.Blewett	b S.B.Doull	New Zealand	Hobart	1997-98
S.K.Warne	c M.H.Richardson b D.L.Vettori	New Zealand	Perth	2001-02
M.L.Hayden	c V.K.Sehwag b Harbhajan Singh	India	Brisbane[2]	2003-04
S.M.Katich	lbw b M.Kartik	India	Nagpur	2004-05
J.L.Langer	cw D.C.Ramdin b F.H.Edwards	West Indies	Adelaide	2005-06

ENGLAND	How out	Opponent		
H.Sutcliffe	b G.F.Bissett	South Africa	Cape Town	1927-28
E.Paynter	lbw b W.J.O'Reilly	Australia	Lord's	1938
N.W.D.Yardley	c L.Tuckett b O.C.Dawson	South Africa	Nottingham	1947
M.J.K.Smith	cw J.H.B.Waite b G.Griffin	South Africa	Lord's	1960
M.J.K.Smith	run out	Pakistan	Lahore[2]	1961-62
E.R.Dexter	b G.D.McKenzie	Australia	Brisbane[2]	1962-63
D.L.Amiss	c Sarfraz Nawaz b Intikhab Alam	Pakistan	Karachi[1]	1972-73
G.Boycott	cw D.L.Murray b B.D.Julien	West Indies	Port-of-Spain	1973-74
G.Boycott*	not out	Australia	Perth	1979-80
G.A.Gooch	run out	Australia	Melbourne	1979-80
M.D.Moxon	c J.J.Crowe b E.J.Chatfield	New Zealand	Auckland	1987-88
M.A.Atherton	run out	Australia	Lord's	1993
M.A.Atherton	c and b B.M.McMillan	South Africa	Leeds	1994
A.J.Tudor*	not out	New Zealand	Birmingham	1999
M.E.Trescothick	cw D.Dasgupta b A.Kumble	India	Ahmedabad	2001-02

SOUTH AFRICA	How out	Opponent		
G.A.Faulkner	c F.E.Wooley b G.J.Thompson	England	Cape Town	1909-10
B.Mitchell	cw S.C.Griffith b A.V.Bedser	England	Port Elizabeth	1948-49
T.L.Goddard	c M.C.Cowdrey b J.B.Statham	England	The Oval	1960
J.H.Kallis	run out	Australia	Melbourne	2001-02
N.D.McKenzie	run out	Australia	Cape Town	2001-02
S.M.Pollock*	not out	Sri Lanka	Centurion	2002-03
A.J.Hall*	not out	England	Leeds	2003

WEST INDIES	How out	Opponent		
R.J.Christiani §	lbw b K.Cranston	England	Bridgetown	1947-48
A.F.Rae	b T.B.Burtt	New Zealand	Auckland	1951-52
R.B.Kanhai	run out	India	Madras[2]	1958-59
M.L.C.Foster	b S.Abid Ali	India	Port-of-Spain	1970-71
R.B.Richardson	b Kapil Dev	India	Port-of-Spain	1988-89
R.B.Richardson	lbw b M.E.Waugh	Australia	Bridgetown	1990-91

NEW ZEALAND	How out	Opponent		
J.E.F.Beck	run out	South Africa	Cape Town	1953-54
R.J.Hadlee	cw R.W.Taylor b R.G.D.Willis	England	Christchurch	1983-84
J.G.Wright	cw G.C.Dyer b C.J.McDermott	Australia	Melbourne	1987-88
D.N.Patel	run out	England	Christchurch	1991-92
J.G.Wright	st R.C.Russell b P.C.R.Tufnell	England	Christchurch	1991-92
M.H.Richardson	lbw b M.L.Nkala	Zimbabwe	Harare	1999-2000
S.P.Fleming	c G.Kirsten b A.A.Donald	South Africa	Bloemfontein	2000-01
B.B.McCullum	lbw b S.L.Malinga	Sri Lanka	Napier	2004-05

INDIA	How out	Opponent		
Pankaj Roy	c R.Benaud b L.F.Kline	Australia	Delhi	1959-60
M.L.Jaisimha	run out	Pakistan	Kanpur	1960-61
A.L.Wadekar	c A.P.Sheahan b R.B.Simpson	Australia	Melbourne	1967-68
R.F.Surti	c M.G.Burgess b G.A.Bartlett	New Zealand	Auckland	1967-68
N.S.Sidhu	lbw b M.Muralidaran	Sri Lanka	Bangalore	1993-94
S.C.Ganguly	c H.P.Tillakaratne b K.R.Pushpakumara	Sri Lanka	Nagpur	1997-98
S.C.Ganguly	b S.J.Harmison	England	Nottingham	2002

PAKISTAN	How out	Opponent		
Maqsood Ahmed	st N.S.Tamhane b S.P.Gupte	India	Lahore[1]	1954-55
Majid Khan	c D.L.Amiss b P.I.Pocock	England	Karachi[1]	1972-73

Mushtaq Mohammad	run out	England	Karachi[1]	1972-73
Javed Miandad	c sub (K.Srikkanth) b S.Madan Lal	India	Bangalore	1983-84
Saleem Malik	c D.I.Gower b P.H.Edmonds	England	Leeds	1987
Saleem Malik	c C.E.Eksteen b A.A.Donald	South Africa	Johannesburg[3]	1994-95
Aamer Sohail	b G.D.McGrath	Australia	Brisbane[2]	1995-96
Inzamamul Haq	lbw b W.P.U.J.C.Vaas	Sri Lanka	Lahore[2]	2001-02
Asim Kamal §	b A.Nel	South Africa	Lahore[2]	2003-04

SRI LANKA	How out	Opponent		
R.P.Arnold	c Yousuf Yohana b Arshad Khan	Pakistan	Peshawar[2]	1999-2000
D.P.M.D.Jayawardene	run out	West Indies	Galle	2001-02

ZIMBABWE	How out	Opponent		
A.D.R.Campbell	cw H.P.Tillakaratne b K.R.Pushpakumara	Sri Lanka	Harare	1994-95

THE NERVOUS NINETIES *(§ first Test, † last Test, ¶ only Test)*

AUSTRALIA		Opponents		
A.C.Bannerman	94	England	Sydney	1882-83
A.C.Bannerman	91	England	Sydney	1891-92
G.H.S.Trott	92	England	The Oval	1893
G.H.S.Trott	95	England	Melbourne	1894-95
C.Hill	96	England	Sydney	1897-98
C.Hill	99	England	Melbourne	1901-02
C.Hill	98 + 97	England	Adelaide	1901-02
C.Hill	91	South Africa	Cape Town	1902-03
V.S.Ransford	95	South Africa	Melbourne	1910-11
W.Bardsley	94	South Africa	Sydney	1910-11
R.B.Minnett §	90	England	Sydney	1911-12
W.W.Armstrong	90	England	Melbourne	1911-12
C.Hill	98	England	Adelaide	1911-12
C.G.Macartney	99	England	Lord's	1912
J.M.Gregory	93	England	Sydney	1920-21
T.J.E.Andrews	92	England	Leeds	1921
T.J.E.Andrews	94	England	The Oval	1921
A.J.Richardson §	98	England	Sydney	1924-25
J.M.Taylor	90	England	Melbourne	1924-25
S.J.McCabe	90	West Indies	Adelaide	1930-31
W.H.Ponsford	92*	West Indies	Adelaide	1930-31
A.G.Chipperfield §	99	England	Nottingham	1934
S.J.McCabe	93	England	Sydney	1936-37
C.L.McCool	95	England	Brisbane[2]	1946-47
D.Tallon	92	England	Melbourne	1946-47
W.A.Brown	99	India	Melbourne	1947-48
S.J.E.Loxton	93	England	Leeds	1948
K.R.Miller	99	England	Adelaide	1950-51
A.L.Hassett	92	England	Melbourne	1950-51
A.R.Morris	99	South Africa	Melbourne	1952-53
R.N.Harvey	92*	England	Sydney	1954-55
R.G.Archer	98	West Indies	Bridgetown	1954-55
R.Benaud	97	England	Lord's	1956
C.C.McDonald	99	South Africa	Cape Town	1957-58
R.N.Harvey	96	Pakistan	Dacca	1959-60
R.B.Simpson	92	West Indies	Brisbane[2]	1960-61
C.C.McDonald	91	West Indies	Melbourne	1960-61
R.B.Simpson	92	West Indies	Melbourne	1960-61

W.M.Lawry	98	England	Brisbane[2]	1962-63
R.B.Simpson	91	England	Sydney	1962-63
I.R.Redpath §	97	South Africa	Melbourne	1963-64
B.K.Shepherd	96	South Africa	Melbourne	1963-64
R.Benaud	90	South Africa	Sydney	1963-64
P.J.P.Burge	91	South Africa	Adelaide	1963-64
B.C.Booth	98	England	Manchester	1964
W.M.Lawry	94	England	The Oval	1964
R.M.Cowper	99	England	Melbourne	1965-66
W.M.Lawry	98	South Africa	Johannesburg[3]	1966-67
R.B.Simpson	94	South Africa	Durban[2]	1966-67
R.M.Cowper	92	India	Adelaide	1967-68
K.D.Walters	93	India	Brisbane[2]	1967-68
K.D.Walters	94*	India	Sydney	1967-68
I.R.Redpath	92	England	Leeds	1968
I.M.Chappell	96	West Indies	Adelaide	1968-69
I.M.Chappell	99	India	Calcutta	1969-70
R.W.Marsh	92*	England	Melbourne	1970-71
R.W.Marsh	91	England	Manchester	1972
R.W.Marsh	97	West Indies	Kingston	1972-73
I.M.Chappell	97	West Indies	Port-of-Spain	1972-73
K.D.Walters	94	New Zealand	Adelaide	1973-74
I.R.Redpath	93	New Zealand	Wellington	1973-74
I.M.Chappell	90	England	Brisbane[2]	1974-75
R.Edwards	99	England	Lord's	1975
R.B.McCosker	95*	England	Leeds	1975
G.J.Gilmour	95	West Indies	Adelaide	1975-76
G.M.Wood	90	West Indies	Kingston	1977-78
P.M.Toohey	97	West Indies	Kingston	1977-78
W.M.Darling	91	England	Sydney	1978-79
K.J.Hughes	92	India	Calcutta	1979-80
B.M.Laird §	93	West Indies	Brisbane[2]	1979-80
K.J.Hughes	99	England	Perth	1979-80
G.S.Chappell	98*	England	Sydney	1979-80
J.M.Wiener †	93	Pakistan	Lahore[2]	1979-80
R.W.Marsh	91	New Zealand	Perth	1980-81
G.N.Yallop	98	Sri Lanka	Kandy	1982-83
K.J.Hughes	94	Pakistan	Melbourne	1983-84
A.R.Border	98*	West Indies	Port-of-Spain	1983-84
A.R.Border	98	West Indies	St John's	1983-84
K.C.Wessels	98	West Indies	Adelaide	1984-85
K.C.Wessels	90	West Indies	Melbourne	1984-85
W.B.Phillips	91	England	Leeds	1985
G.M.Ritchie	94	England	Lord's	1985
G.R.Marsh	92	India	Sydney	1985-86
G.M.Ritchie	92	New Zealand	Wellington	1985-86
D.M.Jones	93	England	Adelaide	1986-87
P.R.Sleep	90	New Zealand	Melbourne	1987-88
S.R.Waugh	90	West Indies	Brisbane[2]	1988-89
S.R.Waugh	91	West Indies	Perth	1988-89
D.C.Boon	94	England	Lord's	1989
S.R.Waugh	92	England	Manchester	1989
D.M.Jones	99	New Zealand	Perth	1989-90
D.C.Boon	94*	England	Melbourne	1990-91
D.C.Boon	97	England	Sydney	1990-91
G.R.Marsh	94	West Indies	Georgetown	1990-91

M.A.Taylor	94	India	Brisbane[2]	1991-92
A.R.Border	91*	India	Adelaide	1991-92
G.R.J.Matthews	96	Sri Lanka	Moratuwa	1992-93
D.C.Boon	93	England	Manchester	1993
M.E.Waugh	99	England	Lord's	1993
M.J.Slater	99	New Zealand	Perth	1993-94
M.J.Slater	92	South Africa	Sydney	1993-94
D.C.Boon	96	South Africa	Cape Town	1993-94
M.J.Slater	95	South Africa	Durban[2]	1993-94
S.R.Waugh	98	Pakistan	Rawalpindi[2]	1994-95
M.G.Bevan	91	Pakistan	Lahore[2]	1994-95
S.R.Waugh	94*	England	Melbourne	1994-95
M.A.Taylor	90	England	Adelaide	1994-95
S.R.Waugh	99*	England	Perth	1994-95
M.A.Taylor	96	Sri Lanka	Perth	1995-96
R.T.Ponting §	96	Sri Lanka	Perth	1995-96
G.S.Blewett	99	West Indies	Adelaide	1996-97
G.S.Blewett	91	New Zealand	Brisbane[2]	1997-98
S.R.Waugh	96	New Zealand	Perth	1997-98
G.S.Blewett	99	New Zealand	Hobart	1997-98
S.R.Waugh	96	South Africa	Melbourne	1997-98
I.A.Healy	90	India	Chennai[1]	1997-98
M.J.Slater	91	India	Bangalore	1997-98
D.S.Lehmann	98	Pakistan	Rawalpindi[2]	1998-99
M.A.Taylor	92	Pakistan	Peshawar[2]	1998-99
M.J.Slater	96	Pakistan	Karachi[1]	1998-99
S.R.Waugh	96	England	Sydney	1998-99
R.T.Ponting	96	Sri Lanka	Kandy	1999-2000
M.J.Slater	96	Sri Lanka	Galle	1999-2000
M.E.Waugh	90	Zimbabwe	Harare	1999-2000
M.J.Slater	97	Pakistan	Hobart	1999-2000
M.J.Slater	91	India	Melbourne	1999-2000
M.J.Slater	96	India	Sydney	1999-2000
R.T.Ponting	92	West Indies	Adelaide	2000-01
M.L.Hayden	97	India	Kolkata	2000-01
A.C.Gilchrist	90	England	Lord's	2001
M.L.Hayden	91	New Zealand	Hobart	2000-01
S.K.Warne	99	New Zealand	Perth	2001-02
S.R.Waugh	90	South Africa	Melbourne	2001-02
M.L.Hayden	96	South Africa	Cape Town	2001-02
A.C.Gilchrist	91	South Africa	Durban[2]	2001-02
D.R.Martyn	95	England	Adelaide	2002-03
D.S.Lehmann	96	West Indies	Bridgetown	2002-03
M.L.Hayden	99	India	Brisbane[2]	2003-04
R.T.Ponting	92	Sri Lanka	Colombo (SSC)	2003-04
D.R.Martyn	97	Sri Lanka	Cairns	2004-05
M.J.Clarke	91	India	Nagpur	2004-05
S.M.Katich	99	India	Nagpur	2004-05
D.R.Martyn	97	India	Nagpur	2004-05
J.L.Langer	97	Pakistan	Perth	2004-05
R.T.Ponting	98	Pakistan	Perth	2004-05
M.J.Clarke	91	England	Lord's	2005
S.K.Warne	90	England	Manchester	2005
J.L.Langer	99	West Indies	Adelaide	2005-06
M.L.Hayden	90	South Africa	Sydney	2005-06
M.L.Hayden	90	South Africa	Cape Town	2005-06

ENGLAND		Opponents		
W.H.Scotton	90	Australia	The Oval	1884
W.W.Read	94	Australia	The Oval	1886
F.S.Jackson §	91	Australia	Lord's	1893
A.Ward †	93	Australia	Melbourne	1894-95
R.Abel	94	Australia	Lord's	1896
K.S.Ranjitsinhji	93*	Australia	Nottingham	1899
T.W.Hayward	90	Australia	Adelaide	1901-02
A.C.MacLaren	92	Australia	Sydney	1901-02
T.W.Hayward	91	Australia	Sydney	1903-04
J.T.Tyldesley	97	Australia	Melbourne	1903-04
G.L.Jessop	93	South Africa	Lord's	1907
J.B.Hobbs	93*	South Africa	Johannesburg[1]	1909-10
W.Rhodes	92	Australia	Manchester	1912
J.B.Hobbs	92	South Africa	Johannesburg[1]	1913-14
J.B.Hobbs	97	South Africa	Durban[2]	1913-14
F.E.Woolley	95 + 93	Australia	Lord's	1921
C.A.G.Russell	96	South Africa	Johannesburg[1]	1922-23
E.H.Hendren	92	Australia	Adelaide	1924-25
H.Sutcliffe	94	Australia	Leeds	1926
H.Sutcliffe	99	South Africa	Cape Town	1927-28
R.E.S.Wyatt	91	South Africa	Cape Town	1927-28
W.R.Hammond	90	South Africa	Durban[2]	1927-28
D.R.Jardine	98	Australia	Adelaide	1928-29
E.H.Hendren	95	Australia	Melbourne	1928-29
F.E.Woolley	95*	South Africa	Leeds	1929
E.H.Hendren	93	South Africa	Cape Town	1930-31
M.Leyland	91	South Africa	Johannesburg[1]	1930-31
H.Larwood †	98	Australia	Sydney	1932-33
J.Hardstaff, jr	94	India	Manchester	1936
E.Paynter	99	Australia	Lord's	1938
P.A.Gibb §	93	South Africa	Johannesburg[1]	1938-39
B.H.Valentine	97	South Africa	Johannesburg[1]	1938-39
L.Hutton	92	South Africa	Johannesburg[1]	1938-39
J.Hardstaff, jr	94	West Indies	The Oval	1939
L.Hutton	94	Australia	Adelaide	1946-47
N.W.D.Yardley	99	South Africa	Nottingham	1947
J.Hardstaff, jr	98	West Indies	Bridgetown	1947-48
C.Washbrook	97	South Africa	Johannesburg[2]	1948-49
T.E.Bailey	93	New Zealand	Lord's	1949
R.T.Simpson	94	West Indies	Nottingham	1950
L.Hutton	98*	South Africa	Manchester	1951
T.E.Bailey	95	South Africa	Leeds	1951
R.T.Spooner	92	India	Calcutta	1951-52
D.C.S.Compton	93	West Indies	Bridgetown	1953-54
T.W.Graveney	92	West Indies	Port-of-Spain	1953-54
D.C.S.Compton	93	Pakistan	Manchester	1954
P.B.H.May	91	Australia	Melbourne	1954-55
P.B.H.May	97	South Africa	Leeds	1955
C.Washbrook	98	Australia	Leeds	1956
D.C.S.Compton	94	Australia	The Oval	1956
P.B.H.May	92	Australia	Sydney	1958-59
R.Subba Row	94	India	The Oval	1959
M.J.K.Smith	98	India	The Oval	1959
M.C.Cowdrey	97	West Indies	Kingston	1959-60
M.J.K.Smith	96	West Indies	Port-of-Spain	1959-60

R.Subba Row	90	South Africa	Lord's	1960
M.J.K.Smith	99	South Africa	Lord's	1960
M.C.Cowdrey	93	Australia	Leeds	1961
P.B.H.May	95	Australia	Manchester	1961
M.J.K.Smith	99	Pakistan	Lahore[2]	1961-62
T.W.Graveney	97	Pakistan	Birmingham	1962
E.R.Dexter	99	Australia	Brisbane[2]	1962-63
E.R.Dexter	93	Australia	Melbourne	1962-63
K.F.Barrington	94	Australia	Sydney	1962-63
M.C.Cowdrey	93*	Australia	The Oval	1964
R.W.Barber	97	South Africa	Johannesburg[3]	1964-65
K.F.Barrington	93	South Africa	Johannesburg[3]	1964-65
K.F.Barrington	91	South Africa	Lord's	1965
C.Milburn §	94	West Indies	Manchester	1966
T.W.Graveney	96	West Indies	Lord's	1966
J.M.Parks	91	West Indies	Lord's	1966
M.C.Cowdrey	96	West Indies	Nottingham	1966
K.F.Barrington	93	India	Leeds	1967
K.F.Barrington	97	India	Lord's	1967
J.H.Edrich	96	West Indies	Kingston	1967-68
G.Boycott	90	West Indies	Bridgetown	1967-68
T.W.Graveney	96	Australia	Birmingham	1968
A.P.E.Knott	96*	Pakistan	Karachi[1]	1968-69
A.P.E.Knott	96	New Zealand	Auckland	1970-71
A.P.E.Knott	90	India	The Oval	1971
B.W.Luckhurst	96	Australia	Nottingham	1972
A.P.E.Knott	92	Australia	The Oval	1972
B.Wood §	90	Australia	The Oval	1972
K.W.R.Fletcher	97*	India	Madras[1]	1972-73
D.L.Amiss	99	Pakistan	Karachi[1]	1972-73
G.Boycott	92	New Zealand	Lord's	1973
G.Boycott	97	West Indies	The Oval	1973
G.Boycott	93	West Indies	Port-of-Spain	1973-74
G.Boycott	99	West Indies	Port-of-Spain	1973-74
J.H.Edrich	96	India	Lord's	1974
D.L.Amiss	90	Australia	Melbourne	1974-75
A.W.Greig	96	Australia	Lord's	1975
D.S.Steele	92	Australia	Leeds	1975
J.H.Edrich	96	Australia	The Oval	1975
J.M.Brearley	91	India	Bombay[3]	1976-77
A.W.Greig	91	Australia	Lord's	1977
G.Miller	98*	Pakistan	Lahore[2]	1977-78
G.A.Gooch	91*	New Zealand	The Oval	1978
R.W.Taylor	97	Australia	Adelaide	1978-79
G.Boycott	99*	Australia	Perth	1979-80
D.I.Gower	98*	Australia	Sydney	1979-80
G.A.Gooch	99	Australia	Melbourne	1979-80
G.Miller	98	India	Manchester	1982
D.W.Randall	95	India	The Oval	1982
E.E.Hemmings	95	Australia	Sydney	1982-83
C.L.Smith	91	New Zealand	Auckland	1983-84
R.T.Robinson	96	India	Kanpur	1984-85
D.I.Gower	90	West Indies	St John's	1985-86
C.W.J.Athey	96	Australia	Perth	1986-87
M.W.Gatting	96	Australia	Sydney	1986-87
D.J.Capel	98	Pakistan	Karachi[1]	1987-88

G.A.Gooch	93	Pakistan	Karachi[1]	1987-88
M.D.Moxon	99	New Zealand	Auckland	1987-88
R.C.Russell §	94	Sri Lanka	Lord's	1988
R.A.Smith	96	Australia	Lord's	1989
A.J.Stewart	91	Australia	Sydney	1990-91
A.J.Lamb	91	Australia	Perth	1990-91
R.A.Smith	96	New Zealand	Christchurch	1991-92
A.J.Lamb	93	New Zealand	Christchurch	1991-92
M.A.Atherton	99	Australia	Lord's	1993
G.A.Hick	96	West Indies	Kingston	1993-94
M.A.Atherton	99	South Africa	Leeds	1994
G.A.Hick	98*	Australia	Sydney	1994-95
R.A.Smith	95	West Indies	Lord's	1995
G.P.Thorpe	94	West Indies	Manchester	1995
G.A.Hick	96	West Indies	The Oval	1995
R.C.Russell	91	West Indies	The Oval	1995
M.A.Atherton	95	West Indies	The Oval	1995
N.V.Knight	96	Zimbabwe	Bulawayo[2]	1996-97
M.A.Atherton	94*	New Zealand	Christchurch	1996-97
M.A.Atherton	98*	South Africa	Nottingham	1998
N.Hussain	94	South Africa	Leeds	1998
A.J.Tudor	99*	New Zealand	Birmingham	1999
A.J.Stewart	95	South Africa	Durban[2]	1999-2000
C.White	93	Pakistan	Lahore[2]	2000-01
M.E.Trescothick	99	India	Ahmedabad	2001-02
M.A.Butcher	92	India	Ahmedabad	2001-02
M.A.Butcher	94	Sri Lanka	Birmingham	2002
C.White	94*	India	Nottingham	2002
A.Flintoff	95	South Africa	The Oval	2003
N. Hussain	95	Bangladesh	Chittagong[1]	2003-04
G.P.Thorpe	90	West Indies	Port-of-Spain	2003-04
A.Flintoff	94	New Zealand	Leeds	2004
A.J.Strauss	90	West Indies	Manchester	2004
R.W.T.Key	93*	West Indies	Manchester	2004
A.J.Strauss	94*	South Africa	Port Elizabeth	2004-05
M.E.Trescothick	90	Australia	Birmingham	2005
P.D.Collingwood	96	Pakistan	Lahore[2]	2005-06
I.R.Bell	92	Pakistan	Lahore[2]	2005-06
K.P.Pietersen	96	Pakistan	The Oval	2006

SOUTH AFRICA		Opponents		
L.J.Tancred	97	Australia	Johannesburg[1]	1902-03
C.B.Llewellyn	90	Australia	Johannesburg[1]	1902-03
A.W.Nourse	93*	England	Johannesburg[1]	1905-06
G.A.Faulkner	99	England	Cape Town	1909-10
A.W.Nourse	92*	Australia	Melbourne	1910-11
G.A.Faulkner	92	Australia	Sydney	1910-11
H.W.Taylor	93	Australia	Lord's	1912
H.W.Taylor	93	England	Durban[1]	1913-14
H.W.Taylor	91	England	Durban[2]	1922-23
R.H.Catterall	95	England	The Oval	1924
R.H.Catterall	98	England	Birmingham	1929
H.G.Deane	93	England	The Oval	1929
B.Mitchell	95	Australia	Adelaide	1931-32
H.B.Cameron	90	England	Lord's	1935
A.D.Nourse	91	Australia	Durban[2]	1935-36

P.G.V.van der Bijl †	97	England	Durban[2]	1938-39
K.G.Viljoen	93	England	Manchester	1947
A.D.Nourse	97	England	The Oval	1947
B.Mitchell †	99	England	Port Elizabeth	1948-49
P.N.F.Mansell §	90	England	Leeds	1951
K.J.Funston	92	Australia	Adelaide	1952-53
J.C.Watkins	92	Australia	Melbourne	1952-53
W.R.Endean	93	New Zealand	Johannesburg[2]	1953-54
R.A.McLean	93	England	Johannesburg[3]	1956-57
T.L.Goddard	90	Australia	Johannesburg[3]	1957-58
S.O'Linn	98	England	Nottingham	1960
T.L.Goddard	99	England	The Oval	1960
T.L.Goddard	93	Australia	Sydney	1963-64
E.J.Barlow	92	New Zealand	Wellington	1963-64
E.J.Barlow	96	England	Johannesburg[3]	1964-65
A.J.Pithey	95	England	Johannesburg[3]	1964-65
R.G.Pollock	90	Australia	Johannesburg[3]	1966-67
J.N.Rhodes	91	India	Johannesburg[3]	1992-93
B.M.McMillan	98	India	Johannesburg[3]	1992-93
K.C.Wessels	95*	India	Port Elizabeth	1992-93
A.C.Hudson	90	Sri Lanka	Moratuwa	1993-94
K.C.Wessels	92	Sri Lanka	Colombo (SSC)	1993-94
A.C.Hudson	90	Australia	Adelaide	1993-94
B.M.McMillan	93	England	The Oval	1994
D.J.Cullinan	94	England	The Oval	1994
D.J.Richardson	93	New Zealand	Johannesburg[3]	1994-95
D.J.Cullinan	96	New Zealand	Auckland	1994-95
B.M.McMillan	98*	Zimbabwe	Harare	1995-96
D.J.Cullinan	91	England	Port Elizabeth	1995-96
A.M.Bacher	96	Australia	Centurion	1996-97
G.Kirsten	98	Pakistan	Rawalpindi[2]	1997-98
A.M.Bacher	96	Pakistan	Sheikhapura	1997-98
S.M.Pollock	92	Sri Lanka	Cape Town	1997-98
J.N.Rhodes	95	England	Birmingham	1998
J.H.Kallis	95	India	Bangalore	1999-2000
L.Klusener	97	India	Bangalore	1999-2000
L.Klusener	95*	Sri Lanka	Colombo (SSC)	2000-01
M.V.Boucher	92	Sri Lanka	Cape Town	2000-01
L.Klusener	97	Sri Lanka	Cape Town	2000-01
J.H.Kallis	99	Australia	Melbourne	2001-02
N.D.McKenzie	99	Australia	Cape Town	2001-02
H.H.Gibbs	92	Sri Lanka	Centurion	2002-03
S.M.Pollock	99*	Sri Lanka	Centurion	2002-03
H.H.Dippenaar	92	England	Lord's	2003
N.D.McKenzie	90	England	Nottingham	2003
A.J.Hall	99*	England	Leeds	2003
G.Kirsten	90	England	The Oval	2003
H.H.Gibbs	98	Pakistan	Faisalabad	2003-04
J.H.Kallis	92	New Zealand	Hamilton	2003-04
J.A.Rudolph	93*	New Zealand	Wellington	2003-04
J.A.Rudolph	93	England	Port Elizabeth	2004-05
H.H.Gibbs	98	England	Johannesburg[3]	2004-05
A.B.de Villiers	92	England	Centurion	2004-05
A.B.de Villiers	98	Zimbabwe	Cape Town	2004-05
H.H.Gibbs	94	Australia	Melbourne	2005-06
A.G.Prince	93	Australia	Johannesburg[3]	2005-06

A.G.Prince	93	New Zealand	Centurion	2005-06
J.A.Rudolph	90	Sri Lanka	Colombo(SSC)	2006-07
A.B.de Villiers	95	Sri Lanka	Colombo(PSS)	2006-07
H.H.Gibbs	92	Sri Lanka	Colombo(PSS)	2006-07

WEST INDIES		Opponents		
R.K.Nunes †	92	England	Kingston	1929-30
J.E.D.Sealy	92	England	Port-of-Spain	1934-35
L.N.Constantine	90	England	Port-of-Spain	1934-35
G.A.Headley	93	England	Port-of-Spain	1934-35
J.E.D.Sealy	91	England	Kingston	1934-35
V.H.Stollmeyer ¶	96	England	The Oval	1939
R.J.Christiani §	99	England	Bridgetown	1947-48
F.M.M.Worrell §	97	England	Port-of-Spain	1947-48
E.D.Weekes	90	India	Madras[1]	1948-49
A.F.Rae	97	India	Bombay[2]	1948-49
A.F.Rae	99	New Zealand	Auckland	1951-52
C.L.Walcott	98	India	Bridgetown	1952-53
J.K.Holt §	94	England	Kingston	1953-54
E.D.Weekes	90*	England	Kingston	1953-54
E.D.Weekes	94	England	Georgetown	1953-54
C.L.Walcott	90	England	Birmingham	1957
E.D.Weekes	90	England	Lord's	1957
R.B.Kanhai	96	Pakistan	Port-of-Spain	1957-58
R.B.Kanhai	99	India	Madras[2]	1958-59
C.C.Hunte	92	India	Delhi	1958-59
G.S.Sobers	92	England	Port-of-Spain	1959-60
J.S.Solomon	96	India	Bridgetown	1961-62
F.M.M.Worrell	98*	India	Kingston	1961-62
R.B.Kanhai	90	England	Manchester	1963
R.B.Kanhai	92	England	Leeds	1963
S.M.Nurse	93	England	Nottingham	1966
G.S.Sobers	94	England	Nottingham	1966
R.B.Kanhai	90	India	Calcutta	1966-67
G.S.Sobers	95	India	Madras[1]	1966-67
G.S.Sobers	95*	England	Georgetown	1967-68
R.B.Kanhai	94	Australia	Brisbane[2]	1968-69
M.C.Carew	90	Australia	Adelaide	1968-69
S.M.Nurse	95	New Zealand	Auckland	1968-69
M.C.Carew	91	New Zealand	Christchurch	1968-69
B.F.Butcher †	91	England	Leeds	1969
G.S.Sobers	93	India	Kingston	1970-71
M.L.C.Foster	99	India	Port-of-Spain	1970-71
C.A.Davis	90	New Zealand	Port-of-Spain	1971-72
R.C.Fredericks	98	Australia	Bridgetown	1972-73
D.L.Murray	90	Australia	Bridgetown	1972-73
A.I.Kallicharran	91	Australia	Port-of-Spain	1972-73
C.H.Lloyd	94	England	Birmingham	1973
R.C.Fredericks	94	England	Kingston	1973-74
A.I.Kallicharran	93	England	Kingston	1973-74
R.C.Fredericks	98	England	Georgetown	1973-74
C.G.Greenidge §	93	India	Bangalore	1974-75
A.I.Kallicharran	98	India	Bombay[3]	1974-75
D.L.Murray	91	India	Bombay[3]	1974-75
A.I.Kallicharran	92*	Pakistan	Lahore[2]	1974-75
K.D.Boyce	95*	Australia	Adelaide	1975-76

I.V.A.Richards	98	Australia	Melbourne	1975-76
C.H.Lloyd	91*	Australia	Melbourne	1975-76
A.I.Kallicharran	93	India	Bridgetown	1975-76
A.I.Kallicharran	97	England	Nottingham	1976
I.V.A.Richards	92	Pakistan	Bridgetown	1976-77
C.G.Greenidge	91 + 96	Pakistan	Georgetown	1976-77
A.I.Kallicharran	92	Australia	Port-of-Spain	1977-78
S.F.A.F.Bacchus	98	India	Bangalore	1978-79
A.I.Kallicharran	98	India	Madras[1]	1978-79
H.A.Gomes	91	India	Madras[1]	1978-79
I.V.A.Richards	96	Australia	Melbourne	1979-80
C.G.Greenidge	91 + 97	New Zealand	Christchurch	1979-80
D.L.Haynes	96	England	Port-of-Spain	1980-81
C.H.Lloyd	95	England	Kingston	1980-81
H.A.Gomes	90*	England	Kingston	1980-81
D.L.Haynes	92	India	Bridgetown	1982-83
M.D.Marshall	92	India	Kanpur	1983-84
P.J.L.Dujon	98	India	Ahmedabad	1983-84
A.L.Logie	97	Australia	Port-of-Spain	1983-84
H.A.Gomes	92*	England	Lord's	1984
C.G.Greenidge	95	Australia	Adelaide	1984-85
D.L.Haynes	90	New Zealand	Georgetown	1984-85
A.L.Logie	93	Australia	Perth	1988-89
R.B.Richardson	93	India	Bridgetown	1988-89
R.B.Richardson	99	India	Port-of-Spain	1988-89
A.L.Logie	98	England	Port-of-Spain	1989-90
R.B.Richardson	99	Australia	Bridgetown	1990-91
B.C.Lara	96	Pakistan	Port-of-Spain	1992-93
J.C.Adams	95*	England	Kingston	1993-94
B.C.Lara	91	India	Mohali	1994-95
S.L.Campbell	93	England	Lord's	1995
R.B.Richardson †	93	England	The Oval	1995
R.I.C.Holder	91*	India	Port-of-Spain	1996-97
S.Chanderpaul	95	Pakistan	Rawalpindi[2]	1997-98
C.L.Hooper	94*	England	Port-of-Spain	1997-98
B.C.Lara	93	England	Georgetown	1997-98
P.A.Wallace	92	England	St John's	1997-98
A.L.Logie	95*	England	Lord's	1988
J.C.Adams	94	Australia	Kingston	1998-99
J.C.Adams	98	England	Birmingham	2000
R.D.Jacobs	96*	Australia	Perth	2000-01
R.R.Sarwan	91	South Africa	Georgetown	2000-01
R.D.Jacobs	93*	South Africa	Port-of-Spain	2000-01
B.C.Lara	91	South Africa	St John's	2000-01
M.N.Samuels	91	Bangladesh	Dhaka	2002-03
R.D.Jacobs	91*	Bangladesh	Dhaka	2002-03
B.C.Lara	91	Australia	Port-of-Spain	2002-03
R.R.Sarwan	90	England	St John's	2003-04
S.Chanderpaul	97*	England	Lord's	2004
B.C.Lara	95	England	Birmingham	2004
S.Chanderpaul	92	Pakistan	Bridgetown	2004-05
D.Ganga	95	New Zealand	Auckland	2005-06
S.Chanderpaul	97*	India	Bassaterre	2005-06

NEW ZEALAND

R.C.Blunt	96	England	Lord's	1931
W.A.Hadlee	93	England	Manchester	1937

F.B.Smith	96	England	Leeds	1949
J.R.Reid	93	England	The Oval	1949
J.E.F.Beck	99	South Africa	Cape Town	1953-54
N.S.Harford §	93	Pakistan	Lahore[1]	1955-56
J.W.Guy	91	India	Calcutta	1955-56
J.R.Reid	92	South Africa	Cape Town	1961-62
J.R.Reid	97	Pakistan	Wellington	1964-65
R.W.Morgan	97	Pakistan	Christchurch	1964-65
B.A.G.Murray	90	Pakistan	Lahore[2]	1969-70
G.M.Turner	95	West Indies	Port-of-Spain	1971-72
G.M.Turner	98	England	Christchurch	1974-75
M.G.Burgess	95	India	Wellington	1975-76
R.W.Anderson §	92	Pakistan	Lahore[2]	1976-77
G.P.Howarth	94	England	The Oval	1978
J.G.Wright	93	England	Leeds	1983
R.J.Hadlee	92*	England	Nottingham	1983
R.J.Hadlee	99	England	Christchurch	1983-84
J.V.Coney	92	Sri Lanka	Colombo (CCC)	1983-84
J.F.Reid	97	Pakistan	Karachi[1]	1984-85
J.V.Coney	98	Australia	Christchurch	1985-86
J.V.Coney	93	Australia	Auckland	1985-86
J.G.Wright	99	Australia	Melbourne	1987-88
M.J.Greatbatch	90*	India	Hyderabad	1988-89
J.G.Wright	98	England	Lord's	1990
D.N.Patel	99	England	Christchurch	1991-92
J.G.Wright	99	England	Christchurch	1991-92
M.D.Crowe	98	Australia	Wellington	1992-93
S.P.Fleming §	92	India	Hamilton	1993-94
B.A.Young	94	England	Lord's	1994
R.G.Twose	94	Zimbabwe	Auckland	1995-96
S.P.Fleming	92*	Pakistan	Lahore[2]	1996-97
C.L.Cairns	93	Pakistan	Lahore[2]	1996-97
N.J.Astle	96	Zimbabwe	Bulawayo[2]	1997-98
D.L.Vettori	90	Zimbabwe	Bulawayo[2]	1997-98
S.P.Fleming	91	Australia	Brisbane[2]	1997-98
C.D.McMillan	92	India	Hamilton	1998-99
M.J.Horne	93	South Africa	Auckland	1998-99
N.J.Astle	93	West Indies	Wellington	1999-2000
M.H.Richardson	99	Zimbabwe	Harare	2000-01
S.P.Fleming	99	South Africa	Bloemfontein	2000-01
C.D.McMillan	98	Pakistan	Hamilton	2000-01
M.H.Richardson	95	West Indies	St George's	2000-01
J.D.P.Oram	97	Pakistan	Wellington	2003-04
J.D.P.Oram	90	South Africa	Auckland	2003-04
M.H.Richardson	93	England	Lord's	2004
B.B.McCullum	96	England	Lord's	2004
S.P.Fleming	97	England	Leeds	2004
B.B.McCullum	99	Sri Lanka	Napier	2004-05
L.Vincent †	92	Zimbabwe	Bulawayo[2]	2005-06
S.P.Fleming	97	West Indies	Wellington	2005-06
INDIA		Opponents		
M.H.Mankad	96	West Indies	Port-of-Spain	1952-53
V.L.Manjrekar	90	New Zealand	Calcutta	1955-56
Pankaj Roy	90	West Indies	Bombay[2]	1958-59
N.J.Contractor	92	West Indies	Delhi	1958-59
C.G.Borde	96	West Indies	Delhi	1958-59

Pankaj Roy	99	Australia	Delhi	1959-60
M.L.Jaisimha	99	Pakistan	Kanpur	1960-61
N.J.Contractor	92	Pakistan	Delhi	1960-61
V.L.Manjrekar	96	England	Kanpur	1961-62
C.G.Borde	93	West Indies	Kingston	1961-62
S.A.Durani	90	England	Bombay[2]	1963-64
Hanumant Singh	94	Australia	Madras[2]	1964-65
F.M.Engineer	90	New Zealand	Madras[2]	1964-65
A.L.Wadekar	91	England	Leeds	1967
A.L.Wadekar	99	Australia	Melbourne	1967-68
R.F.Surti	99	New Zealand	Auckland	1967-68
Nawab of Pataudi, jr	95	Australia	Bombay[2]	1969-70
A.V.Mankad	97	Australia	Delhi	1969-70
A.L.Wadekar	91*	Australia	Delhi	1969-70
A.L.Wadekar	90	England	Kanpur	1972-73
G.R.Viswanath	97*	West Indies	Madras[1]	1974-75
G.R.Viswanath	95	West Indies	Bombay[3]	1974-75
M.Amarnath	90	Australia	Perth	1977-78
S.M.Gavaskar	97	Pakistan	Lahore[2]	1978-79
C.P.S.Chauhan	93	Pakistan	Lahore[2]	1978-79
G.R.Viswanath	96	Australia	Calcutta	1979-80
C.P.S.Chauhan	97	Australia	Adelaide	1980-81
R.J.Shastri	93	England	Delhi	1981-82
Kapil Dev	97	England	The Oval	1982
D.B.Vengsarkar	90	Sri Lanka	Madras[1]	1982-83
M.Amarnath	91	West Indies	Bridgetown	1982-83
D.B.Vengsarkar	94	West Indies	St John's	1982-83
Kapil Dev	98	West Indies	St John's	1982-83
S.M.Gavaskar	90	West Indies	Ahmedabad	1983-84
M.Amarnath	95	England	Madras[1]	1984-85
D.B.Vengsarkar	98*	Sri Lanka	Colombo (SSC)	1985-86
S.M.Gavaskar	90	Australia	Madras[1]	1986-87
S.M.Gavaskar	91	Pakistan	Madras[1]	1986-87
D.B.Vengsarkar	96	Pakistan	Madras[1]	1986-87
S.M.Gavaskar †	96	Pakistan	Bangalore	1986-87
J.Arun Lal	93	West Indies	Calcutta	1987-88
K.Srikkanth	94	New Zealand	Bombay[3]	1988-89
N.S.Sidhu	97	Pakistan	Sialkot	1989-90
W.V.Raman	96	New Zealand	Christchurch	1989-90
M.Prabhakar	95	New Zealand	Napier	1989-90
S.V.Manjrekar	93	England	Manchester	1990
M.Prabhakar	95	Sri Lanka	Colombo (SSC)	1993-94
N.S.Sidhu	99	Sri Lanka	Bangalore	1993-94
S.R.Tendulkar	96	Sri Lanka	Bangalore	1993-94
N.S.Sidhu	98	New Zealand	Hamilton	1993-94
M.Azharuddin	97	West Indies	Nagpur	1994-95
R.S.Dravid §	95	England	Lord's	1996
S.R.Tendulkar	92	West Indies	Bridgetown	1996-97
A.D.Jadeja	96	West Indies	St John's	1996-97
R.S.Dravid	92	West Indies	Georgetown	1996-97
R.S.Dravid	92	Sri Lanka	Nagpur	1997-98
S.C.Ganguly	99	Sri Lanka	Nagpur	1997-98
R.S.Dravid	93	Sri Lanka	Mumbai[3]	1997-98
V.V.S.Laxman	95	Australia	Calcutta	1997-98
N.S.Sidhu	97	Australia	Calcutta	1997-98
S.Ramesh	96	Pakistan	Delhi	1998-99
S.R.Tendulkar	97	South Africa	Mumbai[2]	1999-2000

S.B.Joshi	92	Bangaldesh	Dhaka	2000-01
S.C.Ganguly	98*	Sri Lanka	Kandy	2001-02
S.R.Tendulkar	90	England	Bangalore	2001-02
R.S.Dravid	91	West Indies	St John's	2001-02
S.R.Tendulkar	92	England	Nottingham	2002
S.C.Ganguly	99	England	Nottingham	2002
R.S.Dravid	92	Australia	Melbourne	2003-04
R.S.Dravid	91*	Australia	Sydney	2003-04
V.K.Sehwag	90	Pakistan	Lahore[2]	2003-04
G.Gambhir	96	South Africa	Kanpur	2004-05
S.R.Tendulkar	94	Pakistan	Mohali	2004-05
K.D.Karthik	93	Pakistan	Kolkata	2004-05
G.Gambhir	97	Zimbabwe	Harare	2005-06
R.S.Dravid	98	Zimbabwe	Harare	2005-06
I.K.Pathan	93	Sri Lanka	Delhi	2005-06
V.V.S.Laxman	90	Pakistan	Faisalabad	2005-06
I.K.Pathan	90	Pakistan	Faisalabad	2005-06
Mohammad Kaif †	91	England	Nagpur	2005-06
R.S.Dravid	95	England	Mohali	2005-06
PAKISTAN		Opponents		
Hanif Mohammad	96	India	Bombay[2]	1952-53
Waqar Hassan	97	India	Calcutta	1952-53
Maqsood Ahmed	99	India	Lahore[1]	1954-55
A.H.Kardar	93	India	Karachi[1]	1954-55
Imtiaz Ahmed	91	West Indies	Bridgetown	1957-58
Wazir Mohammad	97*	West Indies	Georgetown	1957-58
Saeed Ahmed	97	West Indies	Port-of-Spain	1957-58
Saeed Ahmed	91	Australia	Karachi[1]	1959-60
Imtiaz Ahmed †	98	England	The Oval	1962
Abdul Kadir §	95	Australia	Karachi[1]	1964-65
Hanif Mohammad	93	Australia	Melbourne	1964-65
Shafqat Rana	95	New Zealand	Lahore[2]	1969-70
Asif Iqbal	92	New Zealand	Dacca	1969-70
Sadiq Mohammad	91	England	Leeds	1971
Majid Khan	99	England	Karachi[1]	1972-73
Mushtaq Mohammad	99	England	Karachi[1]	1972-73
Majid Khan	98	England	The Oval	1974
Sadiq Mohammad	98*	Pakistan	Karachi[1]	1974-75
Majid Khan	98	New Zealand	Hyderabad	1976-77
Zaheer Abbas	90	Australia	Melbourne	1976-77
Majid Khan	92	West Indies	Port-of-Spain	1976-77
Sadiq Mohammad	97	England	Leeds	1978
Zaheer Abbas	96	India	Faisalabad	1978-79
Wasim Raja	97	India	Delhi	1979-80
Wasim Raja	94*	India	Kanpur	1979-80
Taslim Arif §	90	India	Calcutta	1979-80
Mudassar Nazar	95	Australia	Melbourne	1981-82
Zaheer Abbas	90	Australia	Melbourne	1981-82
Javed Miandad	92	Sri Lanka	Karachi[1]	1982-83
Zaheer Abbas	91	Australia	Faisalabad	1982-83
Mohsin Khan	94	India	Lahore[2]	1982-83
Mohsin Khan	91	India	Karachi[1]	1982-83
Javed Miandad	99	India	Bangalore	1983-84
Sarfraz Nawaz †	90	England	Lahore[2]	1983-84
Qasim Omar	96	New Zealand	Dunedin	1984-85
Javed Miandad	94	India	Madras[1]	1986-87

Saleem Malik	99	England	Leeds	1987
Saleem Yousuf	91	England	Birmingham	1987
Aamer Malik	98*	England	Karachi[1]	1987-88
Shoaib Mohammad	94	Australia	Karachi[1]	1988-89
Shoaib Mohammad	95	India	Karachi[1]	1989-90
Rameez Raja	98	Sri Lanka	Sialkot	1991-92
Imran Khan	93*	Sri Lanka	Sialkot	1991-92
Javed Miandad	92	New Zealand	Hamilton	1992-93
Basit Ali	92*	West Indies	Bridgetown	1992-93
Saeed Anwar	94	Sri Lanka	Colombo (PSS)	1993-94
Saleem Malik	99	South Africa	Johannesburg[3]	1994-95
Inzamamul Haq	95	South Africa	Johannesburg[3]	1994-95
Inzamamul Haq	95	Sri Lanka	Peshawar[2]	1994-95
Aamer Sohail	99	Australia	Brisbane[2]	1995-96
Moin Khan	98	Sri Lanka	Colombo (SSC)	1996-97
Inzamamul Haq	96	South Africa	Faisalabad	1997-98
Inzamamul Haq	92*	West Indies	Peshawar[2]	1997-98
Moin Khan	97	Zimbabwe	Bulawayo[2]	1997-98
Inzamamul Haq	97	Australia	Peshawar[2]	1998-99
Yousuf Youhana	95	Australia	Brisbane[2]	1999-2000
Mohammad Wasim	91	Australia	Hobart	1999-2000
Younis Khan	91	New Zealand	Auckland	2001-02
Rashid Latif	94	Bangladesh	Dhaka	2001-02
Inzamamul Haq	99	Sri Lanka	Lahore[2]	2001-02
Asim Kamal §	99	South Africa	Lahore[2]	2003-04
Asim Kamal	91	India	Mohali	2004-05
Yasir Hameed	91	India	Multan[2]	2004-05
Shahid Afridi	92	England	Faisalabad	2005-06
Inzamamul Haq	99	England	Lahore[2]	2005-06
Yousuf Youhana	97	India	Karachi[1]	2005-06
Abdur Razzaq	90	India	Karachi[1]	2005-06
Mohammad Hafeez	95	England	The Oval	2006
Imran Farhat	91	England	The Oval	2006

SRI LANKA		Opponents		
R.L.Dias	98	Pakistan	Faisalabad	1981-82
R.S.Madugalle	91*	Pakistan	Faisalabad	1981-82
R.L.Dias	97	India	Madras[1]	1982-83
A.Ranatunga	90	Australia	Kandy	1982-83
S.Wettimuny	91	Australia	Kandy	1982-83
L.R.D.Mendis	94	England	Lord's	1984
R.L.Dias	95	India	Colombo (PSS)	1985-86
J.R.Ratnayeke	93	India	Kanpur	1986-87
P.A.de Silva	96	New Zealand	Auckland	1990-91
H.P.Tillakaratne	93	New Zealand	Colombo (SSC)	1992-93
H.P.Tillakaratne	93*	England	Colombo (SSC)	1992-93
P.A.de Silva	93	India	Colombo (SSC)	1993-94
H.P.Tillakaratne	92	South Africa	Moratuwa	1993-94
C.I.Dunusinghe §	91	New Zealand	Napier	1994-95
A.Ranatunga	90	New Zealand	Dunedin	1994-95
S.T.Jayasuriya	90	West Indies	Arnos Vale	1996-97
M.S.Atapattu	98	India	Mumbai[3]	1997-98
D.P.M.D.Jayawardene	91	Zimbabwe	Harare	1999-2000
R.P.Arnold	99	Pakistan	Peshawar[2]	1999-2000
D.P.M.D.Jayawardene	98	South Africa	Durban[2]	2000-01
K.Sangakkara	98	South Africa	Centurion	2000-01
K.Sangakkara	95	England	Kandy	2000-01

D.P.M.D.Jayawardene	99	West Indies	Galle	2001-02
S.T.Jayasuriya	92	Zimbabwe	Colombo,SSC	2001-02
H.P.Tillakaratne	96	Zimbabwe	Colombo,SSC	2001-02
U.D.U.Chandana	92	Zimbabwe	Galle	2001-02
H.P.Tillakaratne	93	New Zealand	Kandy	2002-03
Abdur Razzaq	90	India	Karachi[1]	2005-06
Mohammad Hafeez	95	England	The Oval	2006
Imran Farhat	91	England	The Oval	2006
ZIMBABWE		Opponents		
G.W.Flower	96	India	Delhi	1992-93
A.D.R.Campbell	99	Sri Lanka	Harare	1994-95
M.W.Goodwin	91	Australia	Harare	1999-2000
G.J.Rennie	93	New Zealand	Wellington	2000-01
C.B.Wishart	93	West Indies	Harare	2001-02
A.M.Blignaut	92	West Indies	Harare	2001-02
C.B.Wishart	94	Bangladesh	Dhaka	2001-02
A.Flower	92	India	Delhi	2001-02
D.D.Ebrahim	94	India	Delhi	2001-02
C.B.Wishart †	96	West Indies	Bulawayo[2]	2001-02
A.M.Blignaut	91	West Indies	Harare	2003-04
T.Taibu	92	Bangladesh	Chittagong[1]	2004-05
BANGLADESH		Opponents		
Habibul Bashar	97	Pakistan	Peshawar[2]	2003-04
Mohammad Ashraful	98	Zimbabwe	Harare	2003-04
Habibul Bashar	94	Zimbabwe	Chittagong[1]	2004-05

There have been 726 scores in the nineties recorded in Test cricket (151 for Australia; 151 for England; 75 for South Africa; 105 for West Indies; 52 for New Zealand; 81 for India; 69 for Pakistan; 27 for Sri Lanka; 12 for Zimbabwe and 3 for Bangladesh). The following players scored these nineties:

10 S.R.Waugh(A)
9 R.S.Dravid(I), M.J.Slater(A)
8 A.I.Kallicharran(W)
7 Inzamamul Haq(P)
6 G.Boycott(E), S.P.Fleming(N), C.G.Greenidge(W), M.L.Hayden(A), C.Hill(A), R.B.Kanhai(W), B.C.Lara(W), S.R.Tendulkar(I)
5 M.A.Atherton(E), K.F.Barrington(E), D.C.Boon(A), S.M.Gavaskar(I), H.H.Gibbs(SA), R.T.Ponting(A), G.S.Sobers(W), H.P.Tillakaratne(SL)
4 S.Chanderpaul(W), I.M.Chappell(A), M.C.Cowdrey(E), A.B.de Villiers(SA), T.W.Graveney(E), Javed Miandad(P), A.P.E.Knott(E), A.L.Logie(W), Majid Khan(P), R.W.Marsh(A), P.B.H.May(E), R.B.Richardson(W), N.S.Sidhu(I), R.B.Simpson(A), M.J.K.Smith(E), M.A.Taylor(A), D.B.Vengsarkar(I), A.L.Wadekar(I), E.D.Weekes(W), K.C.Wessels(A2/SA2), J.G.Wright(N), Zaheer Abbas(P)
2 D.L.Amiss(E), T.J.E.Andrews(A), Asim Kamal(P), N.J.Astle(N), A.M.Bacher(SA), T.E.Bailey(E), A.C.Bannerman(A), E.J.Barlow(SA), R.Benaud(A), A.M.Blignaut(Z), C.G.Borde(I), M.A.Butcher(E), M.C.Carew(W), R.H.Catterall(SA), C.P.S.Chauhan(I), M.J.Clarke(A), N.J.Contractor(I), R.M.Cowper(A), P.A.de Silva(SL), E.R.Dexter(E), G.A.Faulkner(SA), A.Flintoff(E), G.Gambhir(I), D.I.Gower(E), A.W.Greig(E), Habibul Bashar (B), R.J.Hadlee(N), Hanif Mohammad(P), R.N.Harvey(A), T.W.Hayward(E), A.C.Hudson(SA), N.Hussain(E), Imtiaz Ahmed(P), S.T.Jayasuriya(SL), D.M.Jones(A), Kapil Dev(I), G.Kirsten(SA), A.J.Lamb(E), J.L.Langer(A), V.V.S.Laxman(I), D.S.Lehmann(A), S.J.McCabe(A), B.B.McCullum(N), C.C.McDonald(A), N.D.McKenzie(SA), C.D.McMillan(N), V.L.Manjrekar(I), G.R.Marsh(A), G.Miller(E), B.Mitchell(SA), Mohsin Khan(P), Moin Khan(P), D.L.Murray(W), A.D.Nourse(SA), A.W.Nourse(SA), S.M.Nurse(W), J.D.P.Oram(N), I.K.Pathan(I), S.M.Pollock(SA), M.Prabhakar(I), A.G.Prince(SA), A.F.Rae(W), A.Ranatunga(SL), J.N.Rhodes(SA), G.M.Ritchie(A), Pankaj Roy(I), R.C.Russell(E), Saeed Ahmed(P), Saleem Malik(P), K.C.Sangakkara(SL), R.R.Sarwan(W), J.E.D.Sealy(W), Shoaib Mohammad(P), A.J.Stewart(E), A.J.Strauss(E), R.Subba Row(E), H.Sutcliffe(E), G.P.Thorpe(E), M.E.Trescothick(E), G.H.S.Trott(A), G.M.Turner(N),

C.L.Walcott(W), S.K.Warne(A), C.Washbrook(E), Wasim Raja(P), M.E.Waugh(A), C.White(E), F.M.M.Worrell(W), Yousuf Youhana(P)

1 Aamer Malik(P), Aamer Sohail(P), Abdur Razzaq(P), Abdul Kadir(P), R.Abel(E), R.W.Anderson(N), R.G.Archer(A), W.W.Armstrong(A), R.P.Arnold(SL), Arun Lal(I), Asif Iqbal(P), M.S.Atapattu(SL), C.W.J.Athey(E), M.Azharuddin(I), S.F.A.F.Bacchus(W), R.W.Barber(E), W.Bardsley(A), Basit Ali(P), J.E.F.Beck(N), I.R.Bell(E), M.G.Bevan(A), R.C.Blunt(N), B.C.Booth(A), M.V.Boucher(SA), K.D.Boyce(W), J.M.Brearley(E), W.A.Brown(A), P.J.P.Burge(A), M.G.Burgess(N), B.F.Butcher(W), C.L.Cairns(N), H.B.Cameron(SA), A.D.R.Campbell(Z), S.L.Campbell(W), D.J.Capel(E), U.D.U.Chandana(SL), G.S.Chappell(A), A.G.Chipperfield(A), R.J.Christiani(W), P.D.Collingwood(E), L.N.Constantine(W), M.D.Crowe(N), W.M.Darling(A), C.A.Davis(W), H.G.Deane(SA), H.H.Dippenaar(SA), P.J.L.Dujon(W), C.I.Dunusinghe(SL), S.A.Durani(I), D.D.Ebrahim(Z), R.Edwards(A), W.R.Endean(SA), F.M.Engineer(I), K.W.R.Fletcher(E), A.Flower(Z), G.W.Flower(Z), M.L.C.Foster(W), K.J.Funston(SA), D.Ganga(W), M.W.Gatting(E), P.A.Gibb(E), G.J.Gilmour(A), M.W.Goodwin(Z), M.J.Greatbatch(N), J.M.Gregory(A), J.W.Guy(N), W.A.Hadlee(N), A.J.Hall(SA), W.R.Hammond(E), Hanumant Singh(I), N.S.Harford(N), A.L.Hassett(A), G.A.Headley(W), I.A.Healy(A), E.E.Hemmings(E), R.I.C.Holder(W), J.K.Holt(W), C.L.Hooper(W), M.J.Horne(N), G.P.Howarth(N), C.C.Hunte(W), Imran Farhat(P), Imran Khan(P), F.S.Jackson(E), A.D.Jadeja(I), M.L.Jaisimha(I), D.R.Jardine(E), G.L.Jessop(E), S.B.Joshi(I), A.H.Kardar(P), K.D.Karthik(I), S.M.Katich(A), R.W.T.Key(E), N.V.Knight(E), B.M.Laird(A), H.Larwood(E), M.Leyland(E), C.B.Llewellyn(SA), S.J.E.Loxton(A), B.W.Luckhurst(E), C.G.Macartney(A), C.L.McCool(A), R.B.McCosker(A), A.C.MacLaren(E), R.A.McLean(SA), R.S.Madugalle(SL), S.V.Manjrekar(I), A.V.Mankad(I), M.H.Mankad(I), P.N.F.Mansell(SA), Maqsood Ahmed(P), M.D.Marshall(W), G.R.J.Matthews(A), L.R.D.Mendis(SL), C.Milburn(E), K.R.Miller(A), R.B.Minnett(A), Mohammad Ashraful(B), Mohammad Hafeez(P), Mohammad Kaif(I), Mohammad Wasim(P), R.W.Morgan(N), A.R.Morris(A), M.D.Moxon(E), Mudassar Nazar(P), B.A.G.Murray(N), Mushtaq Mohammad(P), Nawab of Pataudi jr(I), R.K.Nunes(W), S.O'Linn(SA), J.M.Parks(E), D.N.Patel(N), E.Paynter(E), W.B.Phillips(A), K.P.Pietersen(E), A.J.Pithey(SA), R.G.Pollock(SA), W.H.Ponsford(A), Qasim Omar(P), W.V.Raman(I), Rameez Raja(P), S.Ramesh(I), D.W.Randall(E), K.S.Ranjitsinhji(E), V.S.Ransford(A), J.R.Ratnayeke(SL), W.W.Read(E), J.F.Reid(N), G.J.Rennie(Z), W.Rhodes(E), A.J.Richardson(A), D.J.Richardson(SA), R.T.Robinson(E), C.A.G.Russell(E), Saeed Anwar(P), Saleem Yousuf(P), M.N.Samuels(W), Sarfraz Nawaz(P), W.H.Scotton(E), Shafqat Rana(P), V.K.Sehwag(I), Shahid Afridi(P), R.J.Shastri(I), B.K.Shepherd(A), R.T.Simpson(E), P.R.Sleep(A), C.L.Smith(E), F.B.Smith(N), J.S.Solomon(W), R.T.Spooner(E), K.Srikkanth(I), D.S.Steele(E), V.H.Stollmeyer(W), R.F.Surti(I), D.Tallon(A), L.J.Tancred(SA), Taslim Arif(P), J.M.Taylor(A), R.W.Taylor(E), P.M.Toohey(A), A.J.Tudor(E), R.G.Twose(N), J.T.Tyldesley(E), B.H.Valentine(E), P.G.V.van der Bijl(SA), D.L.Vettori(N), K.G.Viljoen(SA), L.Vincent(N), P.A.Wallace(W), Waqar Hassan(P), A.Ward(E), J.C.Watkins(SA), Wazir Mohammad(P), S.Wettimuny(SL), J.M.Wiener(A), B.Wood(E), R.E.S.Wyatt(E), G.M.Wood(A), G.N.Yallop(A), N.W.D.Yardley(E), Yasir Hameed(P), B.A.Young(N), Younis Khan(P)

MOST FIFTIES *(All scores of 50 and over)*

Player	Country	50s	Inns	A	E	SA	W	N	I	P	SL	Z	B
A.R.Border	Australia	**90**	265	-	29	1	17	11	13	14	5	-	-
S.R.Waugh	Australia	**82**	260	-	24	9	16	9	7	6	6	3	2
S.M.Gavaskar	India	**79**	214	12	20	-	20	5	-	17	5	-	-
B.C.Lara	West Indies	**79**	225	20	18	13	-	6	8	4	7	1	2
S.R.Tendulkar	India	**76**	211	14	14	6	10	8	-	7	10	6	1
I.V.A.Richards	West Indies	**69**	182	19	23	-	-	3	15	9	-	-	-
R.S.Dravid	India	**69**	174	10	9	6	13	6	-	7	8	8	1
Inzamamul Haq	Pakistan	**69**	185	7	15	5	8	7	5	-	12	6	2
M.E.Waugh	Australia	**67**	209	-	17	8	17	7	5	9	4	1	-
Javed Miandad	Pakistan	**66**	189	13	11	-	6	13	19	-	3	1	-
G.A.Gooch	England	**66**	215	20	-	0	18	7	13	6	2	-	-
J.H.Kallis	South Africa	**64**	170	8	11	-	16	8	5	3	5	6	2
R.T.Ponting	Australia	**64**	173	-	9	13	10	6	8	7	6	2	2
G.Boycott	England	**64**	193	21	-	3	20	8	6	6	-	-	-
M.A.Atherton	England	**62**	212	16	-	11	10	10	6	7	0	2	-
M.C.Cowdrey	England	**60**	188	16	-	10	16	10	5	3	-	-	-

A.J.Stewart	England	**60**	235	14	-	9	9	9	5	6	4	4	-
M.A.Taylor	Australia	**59**	186	-	21	5	6	7	5	12	3	-	-
C.H.Lloyd	West Indies	**58**	175	18	18	-	-	0	19	3	-	-	-
D.L.Haynes	West Indies	**57**	202	19	18	1	-	8	6	5	0	-	-
D.I.Gower	England	**57**	204	21	-	-	7	8	8	11	2	-	-
G.S.Sobers	West Indies	**56**	160	10	23	-	-	1	15	7	-	-	-
K.F.Barrington	England	**55**	131	18	-	8	7	4	12	6	-	-	-
G.S.Chappell	Australia	**55**	151	-	21	-	12	6	3	12	0	-	-
G.Kirsten	South Africa	**55**	176	7	12	-	5	7	6	8	6	2	2
G.P.Thorpe	England	**55**	179	11	-	7	14	5	2	7	5	1	3
C.G.Greenidge	West Indies	**53**	185	12	15	-	-	7	13	6	-	-	-
D.C.Boon	Australia	**53**	190	-	15	3	11	11	8	2	3	-	-
L.Hutton	England	**52**	138	19	-	11	11	7	4	0	-	-	-
S.Chanderpaul	West Indies	**52**	168	6	11	7	-	5	15	5	1	1	1
D.B.Vengsarkar	India	**52**	185	9	11	-	13	3	-	10	6	-	-
J.L.Langer	Australia	**51**	171	-	7	4	10	9	7	10	2	0	1
M.L.Hayden	Australia	**50**	148	-	5	11	7	6	9	3	4	2	2
S.P.Fleming	New Zealand	**50**	171	7	6	5	6	-	3	6	9	5	2
G.R.Viswanath	India	**49**	155	13	16	-	11	5	-	4	0	-	-
K.D.Walters	Australia	**48**	123	-	17	3	11	7	8	2	-	-	-
N.Hussain	England	**47**	171	13	-	8	5	6	6	3	3	1	2
W.R.Hammond	England	**46**	140	16	-	20	2	5	3	-	-	-	-
D.C.S.Compton	England	**45**	131	14	-	18	4	4	2	3	-	-	-
D.P.M.D.Jayawardene	Sri Lanka	**45**	136	1	10	7	2	5	8	6	-	4	2
R.N.Harvey	Australia	**45**	137	-	18	13	6	-	6	2	-	-	-
Yousuf Youhana	Pakistan	**44**	117	3	8	1	5	4	10	-	2	7	4
Saleem Malik	Pakistan	**44**	154	7	13	1	4	7	5	-	6	1	-
S.T.Jayasuriya	Sri Lanka	**44**	178	4	3	6	5	4	5	10	-	4	3
J.B.Hobbs	England	**43**	102	27	-	14	2	-	-	-	-	-	-
R.B.Kanhai	West Indies	**43**	137	15	14	-	-	-	11	3	-	-	-
M.E.Trescothick	England	**43**	143	7	-	6	5	4	4	5	7	1	4
R.B.Richardson	West Indies	**43**	146	16	10	0	-	3	7	6	1	-	-
M.Azharuddin	India	**43**	147	5	9	6	3	5	-	6	9	0	-
D.G.Bradman	Australia	**42**	80	-	31	4	2	-	5	-	-	-	-
A.Ranatunga	Sri Lanka	**42**	155	4	5	5	1	7	6	10	-	4	-
P.A.de Silva	Sri Lanka	**42**	159	7	4	3	2	6	8	9	-	2	1
W.M.Lawry	Australia	**40**	123	-	20	5	7	-	8	0	-	-	-
I.M.Chappell	Australia	**40**	136	-	20	0	12	3	3	2	-	-	-
C.L.Hooper	West Indies	**40**	173	7	8	5	-	0	8	7	4	1	-
Most for the other countries:													
A.Flower	Zimbabwe	**39**	112	0	1	4	2	6	10	7	7	-	2
Habibul Bashar	Bangladesh	**27**	83	2	2	2	2	1	1	7	3	7	-

MOST CONSECUTIVE FIFTIES

SEVEN									
E.D.Weekes	West Indies	141	128	194	162	101	90	56	1947-48 to 1948-49
A.Flower	Zimbabwe	65	183*	70	55	232*	79	73	2000-01
Inzamamul Haq	Pakistan	50	117*	53	72	109	100*	97	2004-05 to 2005-06
SIX									
J.Ryder	Australia	78*	58	56	142	201*	88		1921-22 to 1924-25
E.H.Hendren	England	77	205*	56	123	61	55		1929-30
G.A.Headley	West Indies	93	53	270*	106	107	51		1934-35 to 1939
A.Melville	South Africa	67	78	103	189	104*	117		1938-39 to 1947
G.S.Sobers	West Indies	52	52	80	365*	125	109*		1957-58
E.R.Dexter	England	85	172	70	99	93	52		1962 to 1962-63
K.F.Barrington	England	63	132*	101	94	126	76		1962-63
K.D.Walters	Australia	76	118	110	50	242	103		1968-69

G.S.Chappell	Australia	68	54*	52	70	121	67	1975-76 to 1976-77
G.R.Viswanath	India	59	54	79	89	73	145	1977-78 to 1978-79
Zaheer Abbas	Pakistan	91	126	52	215	186	168	1982-83
A.R.Border	Australia	80	65*	76	51*	50	56	1989 to 1989-90
M.A.Taylor	Australia	108	52	101	77	59	101*	1989-90
R.S.Dravid	India	92	93	85	52	56	86	1997-98
J.H.Kallis	South Africa	177	73	130*	130*	92	150*	2003-04

G.Boycott (England) scored nine fifties in ten innings in 1970-71 and 1971: 70, 50, 77, 142,12, 76*, 58, 119*, 121*, 112. A.Flower's 2000-01 sequence also ran to nine fifties in ten innings: 65; 183*; 70; 55; 232*; 79; 73; 23; 51; 83. M.A.Noble (Australia) is the only player to score two separate not out fifties on the same day: 60* and 59* v England at Manchester in 1899 on the second day.*

MOST RUNS FROM STROKES WORTH FOUR OR MORE IN AN INNINGS

runs	6s	5s	4s							
238	5	-	52	J.H.Edrich	310*	England	v	New Zealand	Leeds	1965
223	11	1	38	M.L.Hayden	380	Australia	v	Zimbabwe	Perth	2003-04
206	9	-	38	Inzamamul Haq	329	Pakistan	v	New Zealand	Lahore[2]	2001-02
201	4	1	43	B.C.Lara	400*	West Indies	v	England	St John's	2003-04
196	10	-	34	W.R.Hammond	336*	England	v	New Zealand	Auckland	1932-33
194	1	-	47	V.K.Sehwag	254	India	v	Pakistan	Lahore[2]	2005-06
192	6	-	39	V.K.Sehwag	309	India	v	Pakistan	Multan[2]	2003-04
190	3	-	43	G.A.Gooch	333	England	v	India	The Oval	1990
184	-	-	46	D.G.Bradman	334	Australia	v	England	Leeds	1930
180	2	-	43	D.G.Bradman	304	Australia	v	England	Leeds	1934
180	-	-	45	B.C.Lara	375	West Indies	v	England	St John's	1993-94
178	11	-	28	N.J.Astle	222	New Zealand	v	England	Christchurch	2001-02
178	1	-	43	D.P.M.D.Jayawardene	374	Sri Lanka	v	South Africa	Colombo (SSC)	2006-07
177	-	1	43	R.G.Pollock	274	South Africa	v	Australia	Durban[2]	1969-70
176	-	-	44	V.V.S.Laxman	281	India	v	Australia	Kolkata	2000-01
168	-	-	42	R.B.Kanhai	256	West Indies	v	India	Calcutta	1958-59
166	1	-	40	D.L.Amiss	262*	England	v	West Indies	Kingston	1973-74
166	3	-	37	C.H.Gayle	317	West Indies	v	South Africa	St John's	2004-05
160	-	-	40	P.A.de Silva	267	Sri Lanka	v	New Zealand	Wellington	1990-91
160	12	-	22	Wasim Akram	257*	Pakistan	v	Sri Lanka	Sheikhupura	1996-97
158	3	-	35	D.L.Houghton	266	Zimbabwe	v	Sri Lanka	Bulawayo[2]	1994-95
157	-	1	38	G.S.Sobers	365*	West Indies	v	Pakistan	Kingston	1957-58
156	2	-	36	S.T.Jayasuriya	340	Sri Lanka	v	India	Colombo (RPS)	1997-98
156	2	-	36	K.C.Sangakkara	270	Sri Lanka	v	Zimbabwe	Bulawayo[2]	2003-04
156	4	-	33	S.T.Jayasuriya	253	Sri Lanka	v	Pakistan	Faisalabad	2004-05
152	2	-	35	F.M.M.Worrell	261	West Indies	v	England	Nottingham	1957
152	-	-	38	Zaheer Abbas	274	Pakistan	v	England	Birmingham	1971
152	-	-	38	I.V.A.Richards	291	West Indies	v	England	The Oval	1976
152	-	-	38	B.C.Lara	277	West Indies	v	Australia	Sydney	1992-93
152	-	-	38	N.Hussain	207	England	v	Australia	Birmingham	1997
152	6	-	29	H.H.Gibbs	228	South Africa	v	Pakistan	Cape Town	2002-03
150	1	-	36	L.G.Rowe	302	West Indies	v	England	Bridgetown	1973-74
150	3	-	33	K.C.Sangakkara	230	Sri Lanka	v	Pakistan	Lahore[2]	2001-02
150	1	-	36	M.S.Atapattu	249	Sri Lanka	v	Zimbabwe	Bulawayo[2]	2003-04

CENTURY BEFORE LUNCH

FIRST DAY	Lunch score					
V.T.Trumper (104)	103*	Australia	v	England	Manchester	1902
C.G.Macartney (151)	112*	Australia	v	England	Leeds	1926
D.G.Bradman (334)	105*	Australia	v	England	Leeds	1930
Majid Khan (112)	108*	Pakistan	v	New Zealand	Karachi[1]	1976-77

OTHER DAYS	Overnight score	Lunch score						Day
K.S.Ranjitsinhji (154*)	41*	154*	England	v	Australia	Manchester	1896	3
C.Hill (142)	22*	138*	Australia	v	South Africa	Johannesburg[1]	1902-03	3
W.Bardsley (164)	32*	150*	Australia	v	South Africa	Lord's	1912	2
C.P.Mead (182*	19*	128*	England	v	Australia	The Oval	1921	2
J.B.Hobbs (211)	12*	114*	England	v	South Africa	Lord's	1924	2
H.G.Owen-Smith (129)	27*	129	South Africa	v	England	Leeds	1929	3
W.R.Hammond (336*)	41*	152*	England	v	New Zealand	Auckland	1932-33	2
L.E.G.Ames (148*)	25*	148*	England	v	South Africa	The Oval	1935	3
S.J.McCabe (189*)	59*	159*	Australia	v	South Africa	Johannesburg[1]	1935-36	4
G.S.Chappell (176)	76*	176	Australia	v	New Zealand	Christchurch	1981-82	2
M.A.Taylor (334*)	112*	225*	Australia	v	Pakistan	Peshawar[2]	1998-99	2
Inzamamul Haq (112)	-	103*	Pakistan	v	Zimbabwe	Harare	2002-03	3
B.C.Lara (191)	77*	191*	West Indies	v	Zimbabwe	Bulawayo[2]	2003-04	2
I.R.Bell (162*)	57*	162*	England	v	Bangladesh	Chester-le-Street	2005	2

ONE HUNDRED RUNS BETWEEN LUNCH AND TEA

112	J.M.Gregory (119)	Australia	v	South Africa	Johannesburg[1]	1921-22
115	D.G.Bradman (334)	Australia	v	England	Leeds	1930
150	W.R.Hammond (336*)	England	v	New Zealand	Christchurch	1932-33
107	D.G.Bradman (244)	Australia	v	England	The Oval	1934
127	S.J.McCabe (232)	Australia	v	England	Nottingham	1938
114	F.M.M.Worrell (261)	West Indies	v	England	Nottingham	1950
173	D.C.S.Compton (278)	England	v	Pakistan	Nottingham	1954
121	R.Benaud (121)	Australia	v	West Indies	Kingston	1954-55
103	G.S.Sobers (174)	West Indies	v	England	Leeds	1966
100	K.R.Stackpole (138)	Australia	v	South Africa	Cape Town	1966-67
100	K.D.Walters (112)	Australia	v	West Indies	Port-of-Spain	1972-73
106	D.W.Hookes (143*)	Australia	v	Sri Lanka	Kandy	1982-83
103	M.Azharuddin (179)	India	v	England	Manchester	1990
105	P.A.de Silva (206)	Sri Lanka	v	Bangladesh	Colombo (PSS)	2002-03
105†	M.L.Hayden (380)	Australia	v	Zimbabwe	Perth	2003-04
100†	A.C.Gilchrist (113*)	Australia	v	Zimbabwe	Perth	2003-04
101	L.Vincent (224)	New Zealand	v	Sri Lanka	Wellington	2004-05
109	V.K.Sehwag (254)	India	v	Pakistan	Lahore[2]	2005-06
103	T.M.Dilshan (168)	Sri Lanka	v	Bangladesh	Colombo,PSS	2005-06

† Hayden and Gilchrist both scored 100 runs in the same session.

ONE HUNDRED RUNS BETWEEN TEA AND STUMPS

113	G.J.Bonnor (128)	Australia	v	England	Sydney	1884-85
112	V.T.Trumper (185*)	Australia	v	England	Sydney	1903-04
133	V.T.Trumper (159)	Australia	v	South Africa	Melbourne	1910-11
102	C.A.G.Russell (102*)	England	v	Australia	The Oval	1921
101	D.G.Bradman (254)	Australia	v	England	Lord's	1930
102	D.G.Bradman (304)	Australia	v	England	Leeds	1934
104	A.Melville (104*)	South Africa	v	England	Nottingham	1947
107	D.G.Bradman (201)	Australia	v	India	Adelaide	1947-48
105	D.T.Lindsay (131)	South Africa	v	Australia	Johannesburg[3]	1966-67
103	K.D.Walters (103)	Australia	v	England	Perth	1974-75
106	I.T.Botham (149*)	England	v	Australia	Leeds	1981
140	I.D.S.Smith (173)	New Zealand	v	India	Auckland	1989-90
106	R.B.Richardson (182)	West Indies	v	Australia	Georgetown	1990-91
110	M.E.Waugh (139*)	Australia	v	West Indies	St John's	1990-91
121	V.V.S.Laxman (167)	India	v	Australia	Sydney	1999-2000
139	N.J.Astle (222)	New Zealand	v	England	Christchurch	2001-02

101	D.S.Lehmann (177)	Australia	v	Bangladesh	Cairns	2003-04
107	M.L.Hayden (380)	Australia	v	Zimbabwe	Perth	2003-04
112	C.H.Gayle (116)	West Indies	v	South Africa	Cape Town	2003-04
105	D.R.Smith (105*)	West Indies	v	South Africa	Cape Town	2003-04
105	C.L.Cairns (158)	New Zealand	v	South Africa	Auckland	2003-04
127	D.L.Vettori (127)	New Zealand	v	Zimbabwe	Harare	2005-06

FASTEST FIFTIES

Min						
22	V.T.Trumper (63)	Australia	v	South Africa	Johannesburg[1]	1902-03
28	J.T Brown (140)	England	v	Australia	Melbourne	1894-95
29	S.A.Durani (61*)	India	v	England	Kanpur	1963-64
30	E.A.V.Williams (72)	West Indies	v	England	Bridgetown	1947-48
30	B.R.Taylor (124)	New Zealand	v	West Indies	Auckland	1968-69
31	W.J.OReilly (56*)	Australia	v	South Africa	Johannesburg[1]	1935-36
32	W.J.Cronje (82)	South Africa	v	Sri Lanka	Centurion	1997-98
33	C.A.Roach (56)	West Indies	v	England	The Oval	1933
34	C.R.Browne (70*)	West Indies	v	England	Georgetown	1929-30
35	J.H.Sinclair (104)	South Africa	v	Australia	Cape Town	1902-03
35	C.G.Macartney (56)	Australia	v	South Africa	Sydney	1910-11
35	J.W.Hitch (51*)	England	v	Australia	The Oval	1921
36	Tapash Baisya (66)	Bangladesh	v	New Zealand	Chittagong[1]	2004-05
36	J.H.Kallis (54)	South Africa	v	Zimbabwe	Cape Town	2004-05
37	A.Flintoff (58)	England	v	West Indies	Lord's	2004
38	R.Benaud (121)	Australia	v	West Indies	Kingston	1954-55
40	J.Darling (160)	Australia	v	England	Sydney	1897-98
40	S.J.McCabe (189*)	Australia	v	South Africa	Johannesburg[1]	1935-36
41	J.M.Gregory (119)	Australia	v	South Africa	Johannesburg[1]	1921-22
41	C.H.Gayle (66)	West Indies	v	England	Lord's	2004
41	Mohammad Rafique	Bangladesh	v	Australia	Chittagong[2]	2005-06
42	T.G.Evans (73)	England	v	India	Nottingham	1959
42	A.Flintoff (75*)	England	v	New Zealand	Wellington	2001-02
43	G.L.Jessop (104)	England	v	Australia	The Oval	1902
43	S.M.Pollock (111)	South Africa	v	Sri Lanka	Centurion	2000-01
43	J.L.Langer (123)	Australia	v	New Zealand	Hobart	2001-02
44	Harbhajan Singh (54)	India	v	England	Nottingham	2002
44	M.E.Trescothick (70)	England	v	Sri Lanka	Colombo (SSC)	2003-04
44	N.B.Mahwire (50*)	Zimbabwe	v	New Zealand	Bulawayo[2]	2005-06
45	J.J.Lyons (55)	Australia	v	England	Lord's	1890
45	G.L.Jessop (93)	England	v	South Africa	Lord's	1907
45	P.W.Sherwell (115)	South Africa	v	England	Lord's	1907
45	F.B.Smith (54*)	New Zealand	v	England	Leeds	1949
45	R.R.Lindwall (50)	Australia	v	England	Lord's	1953
45	L.K.Germon (55)	New Zealand	v	Pakistan	Lahore[2]	1996-97
45	P.L.Symcox (54)	South Africa	v	Australia	Adelaide	1997-98
45	A.Symonds (72)	Australia	v	South Africa	Melbourne	2005-06

FASTEST FIFTIES (by balls)

Balls						
24	J.H.Kallis (54)	South Africa	v	Zimbabwe	Cape Town	2004-05
26	I.T.Botham (66)	England	v	India	Delhi	1981-82
26	Shahid Afridi (58)	Pakistan	v	India	Bangalore	2004-05
27	Yousuf Youhana (50)	Pakistan	v	South Africa	Cape Town	2002-03
30	Kapil Dev (73)	India	v	Pakistan	Karachi[1]	1982-83
31	W.J.Cronje (82)	South Africa	v	Sri Lanka	Centurion	1997-98
32	I.V.A.Richards (61)	West Indies	v	India	Kingston	1982-83

32	I.T.Botham (59)	England	v	New Zealand	The Oval	1986
33	R.C.Fredericks (169)	West Indies	v	Australia	Perth	1975-76
33	Kapil Dev (59)	India	v	Pakistan	Karachi	1978-79
33	Kapil Dev (65)	India	v	England	Manchester	1982
33	Mudassar Nazar (57)	Pakistan	v	Sri Lanka	Karachi[1]	1985-86
33	A.J.Lamb (60)	England	v	New Zealand	Auckland	1991-92
33	A.Flintoff (75*)	England	v	New Zealand	Wellington	2001-02
33	Harbhajan Singh (54)	India	v	England	Nottingham	2002
33	A.M.Blignaut (50)	Zimbabwe	v	Pakistan	Harare	2002-03
33	V.K.Sehwag (180)	India	v	West Indies	Gros Islet	2005-06
34	I.D.S.Smith (61)	New Zealand	v	Pakistan	Faisalabad	1990-91
34	C.H.Gayle (317)	West Indies	v	South Africa	St John's	2004-05
34	N.B.Mahwire (50*)	Zimbabwe	v	New Zealand	Bulawayo[2]	2005-06
34	M.S.Dhoni (148)	India	v	Pakistan	Faisalabad	2005-06
35	I.V.A.Richards (110*)	West Indies	v	England	St John's	1985-86
35	R.B.Richardson (106)	West Indies	v	Australia	Adelaide	1988-89
35	M.Azahruddin (109)	India	v	South Africa	Calcutta	1996-97
35	S.M.Pollock (111)	South Africa	v	Sri Lanka	Centurion	2000-01
35	S.T.Jayasuriya (89)	Sri Lanka	v	Bangladesh	Colombo (SSC)	2001-02
35	Tapash Baisya (66)	Bangladesh	v	New Zealand	Chittagong[1]	2004-05
36	B.R.Taylor (124)	New Zealand	v	West Indies	Auckland	1968-69
36	C.H.Gayle (105)	West Indies	v	England	The Oval	2004
37	S.M.Gavaskar (121)	India	v	West Indies	Delhi	1983-84
37	Wasim Akram (52)	Pakistan	v	Australia	Perth	1999-2000
37	S.Chanderpaul (100)	West Indies	v	Australia	Georgetown	2002-03
37	C.H.Gayle (116)	West Indies	v	South Africa	Cape Town	2003-04
37	C.L.Cairns (82)	New Zealand	v	England	Lord's	2004
37	S.K.Warne (50*)	Australia	v	New Zealand	Wellington	2004-05
37	Habibul Bashar (63)	Bangladesh	v	England	Chester-le-Street	2005
38	S.Chanderpaul (71)	West Indies	v	Australia	Sydney	1996-97
38	C.D.McMillan (88)	New Zealand	v	Zimbabwe	Auckland	1997-98
38	B.C.Lara (68)	West Indies	v	South Africa	Centurion	1998-99
38	A.F.G.Griffith (54*)	West Indies	v	Zimbabwe	Kingston	1999-2000
38	Habibul Bashar (61)	Bangladesh	v	New Zealand	Hamilton	2001-02
38	N.J.Astle (65)	New Zealand	v	England	Auckland	2001-02
38	A.Flintoff (58)	England	v	West Indies	Lord's	2004
38	Shahid Afridi (122)	Pakistan	v	West Indies	Bridgetown	2004-05
39	M.J.Greatbatch (87)	New Zealand	v	Zimbabwe	Bulawayo[1]	1992-93
39	A.D.R.Campbell (63)	Zimbabwe	v	Pakistan	Rawalpindi[2]	1993-94
39	G.P.Wickramasinghe (51)	Sri Lanka	v	South Africa	Cape Town	1997-98
39	M.E.Trescothick (70)	England	v	Sri Lanka	Colombo (SSC)	2003-04
39	A.M.Blignaut (61)	Zimbabwe	v	South Africa	Cape Town	2004-05
40	I.T.Botham (81)	England	v	West Indies	Lord's	1984
40	B.C.Lara (53)	West Indies	v	England	Leeds	1995
40	G.P.Thorpe (82*)	England	v	Australia	Nottingham	1997
40	S.T.Jayasuriya (50)	Sri Lanka	v	India	Mumbai[3]	1997-98
40	P.L.Symcox (54)	South Africa	v	Australia	Adelaide	1997-98
40	B.B.McCullum (111)	New Zealand	v	Zimbabwe	Harare	2005-06
40	A.Symonds (72)	Australia	v	South Africa	Melbourne	2005-06
41	R.J.Hadlee (51)	New Zealand	v	Australia	Brisbane[2]	1985-86
41	L.Klusener (108)	South Africa	v	India	Bloemfontein	2001-02
41	C.L.Cairns (158)	New Zealand	v	South Africa	Auckland	2003-04
41	Mohammad Rafique	Bangladesh	v	Australia	Chittagong[2]	2005-06
42	D.I.Gower (73)	England	v	Pakistan	Manchester	1992
42	J.L.Langer (122*)	Australia	v	New Zealand	Hamilton	1999-2000
42	C.D.McMillan (70)	New Zealand	v	Bangladesh	Wellington	2001-02
42	Shahid Afridi (60)	Pakistan	v	India	Karachi[1]	2005-06

43	J.M.Gregory (119)	Australia	v	South Africa	Johannesburg[1]	1921-22
43	A.Ranatunga (131)	Sri Lanka	v	South Africa	Moratuwa	1993-94
43	D.R.Martyn (64*)	Australia	v	England	The Oval	2001
43	B.C.Lara (152)	West Indies	v	England	Nottingham	1995
43	M.V.Boucher (68)	South Africa	v	England	Lord's	2003
43	K.C.Sangakkara (64)	Sri Lanka	v	South Africa	Colombo (SSC)	2004-05
44	A.Flower (51)	Zimbabwe	v	India	Bulawayo[2]	2000-01
44	D.P.M.D.Jayawardene (150)	Sri Lanka	v	Bangladesh	Colombo (SSC)	2001-02
44	R.R.Sarwan (66)	West Indies	v	Sri Lanka	Colombo (SSC)	2001-02
44	K.C.Sangakkara (56)	Sri Lanka	v	Zimbabwe	Galle	2001-02
44	S.R.Tendulkar (92)	India	v	England	Nottingham	2002
44	S.T.Jayasuriya (85)	Sri Lanka	v	England	Colombo (SSC)	2003-04
44	C.H.Gayle (66)	West Indies	v	England	Lord's	2004
45	W.J.OReilly (56*)	Australia	v	South Africa	Johannesburg[1]	1935-36
45	C.L.Hooper (73*)	West Indies	v	England	Leeds	1995
45	P.A.Patel (62)	India	v	Australia	Sydney	2003-04
45	Yuvraj Singh (122)	India	v	Pakistan	Karachi[1]	2005-06
46	R.S.Kaluwitharana (103)	Sri Lanka	v	New Zealand	Dunedin	1996-97
46	L.Klusener (58)	South Africa	v	Pakistan	Sheikhupura	1997-98
46	R.S.Kaluwitharana (51)	Sri Lanka	v	Zimbabwe	Kandy	1997-98
46	A.C.Gilchrist (86)	Australia	v	Pakistan	Brisbane[2]	1999-2000
46	Habibul Bashar (51)	Bangladesh	v	Pakistan	Chittagong[1]	2001-02
46	D.L.Vettori (127)	New Zealand	v	Zimbabwe	Harare	2005-06
46	Shahid Afridi (92)	Pakistan	v	England	Faisalabad	2005-06
46	A.Symonds (55)	Australia	v	South Africa	Cape Town	2005-06
47	P.V.Simmons (87)	West Indies	v	Pakistan	Bridgetown	1992-93
47	C.L.Cairns (120)	New Zealand	v	Zimbabwe	Auckland	1995-96
47	S.T.Jayasuriya (72)	Sri Lanka	v	Pakistan	Colombo (SSC)	1996-97
47	P.A.de Silva (78)	Sri Lanka	v	West Indies	Arnos Vale	1996-97
47	S.T.Jayasuriya (59)	Sri Lanka	v	New Zealand	Colombo (RPS)	1997-98
47	D.L.Vettori (51)	New Zealand	v	England	The Oval	1999
47	A.C.Gilchrist (54)	Australia	v	England	Nottingham	2001
47	A.C.Gilchrist (113*)	Australia	v	Zimbabwe	Perth	2003-04
47	M.S.Dhoni (69)	India	v	West Indies	St John's	2005-06
48	B.C.Lara (88)	West Indies	v	Australia	St John's	1994-95
48	A.J.Stewart (73)	England	v	Zimbabwe	Bulwayo[2]	1996-97
48	I.A.Healy (63)	Australia	v	England	Nottingham	1997
48	C.L.Hooper (106)	West Indies	v	Pakistan	Karachi[1]	1997-98
48	M.J.Slater (77)	Australia	v	England	Birmingham	2001
48	M.Muralidaran (67)	Sri Lanka	v	India	Kandy	2001-02
48	T.J.Friend (60*)	Zimbabwe	v	India	Nagpur	2001-02
48	S.K.Warne (77)	Australia	v	England	Brisbane[2]	2002-03
48	M.L.Hayden (101*)	Australia	v	Zimbabwe	Sydney	2003-04
48	A.M.Blignaut (52)	Zimbabwe	v	South Africa	Centurion	2004-05
48	A.Flintoff (68)	England	v	Australia	Birmingham	2005
48	V.K.Sehwag (254)	India	v	Pakistan	Lahore[2]	2005-06
49	R.T.Ponting (67)	Australia	v	India	Melbourne	1999-2000
49	M.E.Trescothick (55)	England	v	Australia	The Oval	2001
49	J.L.Langer (123)	Australia	v	New Zealand	Hobart	2001-02
49	A.Flintoff (137)	England	v	New Zealand	Christchurch	2001-02
49	Abdur Razzaq (110*)	Pakistan	v	Bangladesh	Multan[2]	2001-02
49	S.R.Waugh (77)	Australia	v	England	Melbourne	2002-03
49	Habibul Bashar (71)	Bangladesh	v	Pakistan	Karachi[1]	2003-04
49	V.K.Sehwag (173)	India	v	Pakistan	Mohali	2004-05
49	Aftab Ahmed (82*)	Bangladesh	v	England	Chester-le-Street	2005
49	W.P.U.J.C.Vaas (65)	Sri Lanka	v	Bangladesh	Colombo (PSS)	2005-06

49	M.S.Dhoni (51*)	India	v	Sri Lanka	Delhi	2005-06
49	D.Mohammed (52)	West Indies	v	India	St John's	2005-06
50	R.S.Mahanama (109)	Sri Lanka	v	New Zealand	Colombo (SSC)	1992-93
50	M.E.Waugh (70)	Australia	v	England	Nottingham	1993
50	M.E.Waugh (126)	Australia	v	West Indies	Kingston	1994-95
50	C.L.Hooper (108*)	West Indies	v	England	St John's	1997-98
50	S.R.Tendulkar (53)	India	v	Sri Lanka	Colombo (SSC)	1998-99
50	C.L.Cairns (72)	New Zealand	v	West Indies	Hamilton	1999-2000
50	H.H.Gibbs (147)	South Africa	v	Zimbabwe	Harare	2001-02
50	G.C.Smith (85*)	South Africa	v	England	Birmingham	2003
50	S.T.Jayasuriya (107)	Sri Lanka	v	Pakistan	Karachi[1]	2004-05
50	Shahid Afridi (59)	Pakistan	v	India	Kolkata	2004-05
50	Kamran Akmal (102*)	Pakistan	v	India	Lahore[2]	2005-06
50	S.P.Fleming (97)	New Zealand	v	West Indies	Wellington	2005-06

FASTEST CENTURIES

Min						
70	J.M.Gregory (119)	Australia	v	South Africa	Johannesburg[1]	1921-22
75	G.L.Jessop (104)	England	v	Australia	The Oval	1902
78	R.Benaud (121)	Australia	v	West Indies	Kingston	1954-55
80	J.H.Sinclair (104)	South Africa	v	Australia	Cape Town	1902-03
81	I.V.A.Richards (110*)	West Indies	v	England	St John's	1985-86
86	B.R.Taylor (124)	New Zealand	v	West Indies	Auckland	1968-69
91	J.Darling (160)	Australia	v	England	Sydney	1897-98
91	S.J.McCabe (189*)	Australia	v	South Africa	Johannesburg[1]	1935-36
94	V.T.Trumper (185*)	Australia	v	England	Sydney	1903-04
95	J.T.Brown (140)	England	v	Australia	Melbourne	1894-95
95	P.W.Sherwell (115)	South Africa	v	England	Lord's	1907
98	D.Denton (104)	England	v	South Africa	Johannesburg[1]	1909-10
98	C.Hill (191)	Australia	v	South Africa	Sydney	1910-11
98	D.G.Bradman (167)	Australia	v	South Africa	Melbourne	1931-32
98	B.C.Lara (100)	West Indies	v	Australia	St John's	1998-99
98	S.M.Pollock (111)	South Africa	v	Sri Lanka	Centurion	2000-01
99	C.G.Macartney (116)	Australia	v	South Africa	Durban[1]	1921-22
99	D.G.Bradman (334)	Australia	v	England	Leeds	1948
99	C.H.Gayle (116)	West Indies	v	South Africa	Cape Town	2003-04
100	G.J.Bonnor (128)	Australia	v	England	Sydney	1884-85
100	C.Hill (100)	Australia	v	South Africa	Mebourne	1910-11
100	L.E.G.Ames (149)	England	v	West Indies	Kingston	1929-30
100	W.R.Hammond (100*)	England	v	New Zealand	The Oval	1931
100	W.R.Hammond (167)	England	v	India	Manchester	1936

FASTEST CENTURIES (by balls)

Balls						
56	I.V.A.Richards (110*)	West Indies	v	England	St John's	1985-86
67	J.M.Gregory (119)	Australia	v	South Africa	Johannesburg[1]	1921-22
69	S.Chanderpaul (100)	West Indies	v	Australia	Georgetown	2002-03
71	R.C.Fredericks (169)	West Indies	v	Australia	Perth	1975-76
74	Majid Khan (112)	Pakistan	v	New Zealand	Karachi[1]	1976-77
74	Kapil Dev (163)	India	v	Sri Lanka	Kanpur	1986-87
74	M.Azahruddin (109)	India	v	South Africa	Calcutta	1996-97
76	G.L.Jessop (104)	England	v	Australia	The Oval	1902
78	Shahid Afridi (122)	Pakistan	v	West Indies	Bridgetown	2004-05
78	Shahid Afridi (103)	Pakistan	v	India	Lahore[2]	2005-06
78	V.K.Sehwag (180)	India	v	West Indies	Gros Islet	2005-06
79	C.H.Gayle (116)	West Indies	v	South Africa	Cape Town	2003-04

80	C.L.Hooper (106)	West Indies	v	Pakistan	Karachi[1]	1997-98
80	C.H.Gayle (105)	West Indies	v	England	The Oval	2004
81	D.P.M.D.Jayawardene (150)	Sri Lanka	v	Bangladesh	Colombo (SSC)	2001-02
81	Kamran Akmal (102*)	Pakistan	v	India	Lahore[2]	2005-06
82	B.C.Lara (100)	West Indies	v	Australia	St John's	1998-99
82	D.L.Vettori (127)	New Zealand	v	Zimbabwe	Harare	2005-06
83	B.R.Taylor (124)	New Zealand	v	West Indies	Auckland	1968-69
84	A.C.Gilchrist (122)	Australia	v	India	Mumbai[3]	2000-01
84	A.C.Gilchrist (113*)	Australia	v	Zimbabwe	Perth	2003-04
84	M.L.Hayden (101*)	Australia	v	Zimbabwe	Sydney	2003-04
85	C.H.Lloyd (163)	West Indies	v	India	Bangalore	1974-75
86	I.T.Botham (118)	England	v	Australia	Manchester	1981
86	Kapil Dev (116)	India	v	England	Kanpur	1981-82
86	C.L.Cairns (120)	New Zealand	v	Zimbabwe	Auckland	1995-96
86	Wasim Akram (100)	Pakistan	v	Sri Lanka	Galle	1999-2000
86	A.C.Gilchrist (113*)	Australia	v	New Zealand	Wellington	2004-05
87	I.T.Botham (147*)	England	v	Australia	Leeds	1981
87	M.Azharuddin (121)	India	v	England	Lord's	1990
88	R.R.Lindwall (100)	Australia	v	England	Melbourne	1946-47
88	R.J.Hadlee (103)	New Zealand	v	West Indies	Christchurch	1979-80
90	S.T.Jayasuriya (157)	Sri Lanka	v	Zimbabwe	Harare	2003-04
91	A.C.Gilchrist (138*)	Australia	v	South Africa	Cape Town	2001-02
92	Abdur Razzaq (110*)	Pakistan	v	Bangladesh	Multan[2]	2001-02
93	D.R.Smith (105*)	West Indies	v	South Africa	Cape Town	2003-04
93	M.S.Dhoni (148)	India	v	Pakistan	Faisalabad	2005-06
94	Zaheer Abbas (168)	Pakistan	v	India	Faisalabad	1982-83
94	S.M.Gavaskar (121)	India	v	West Indies	Delhi	1983-84
94	A.C.Gilchrist (133)	Australia	v	England	Sydney	2002-03
94	A.C.Gilchrist (113*)	Australia	v	Zimbabwe	Perth	2003-04
94	B.B.McCullum (111)	New Zealand	v	Zimbabwe	Harare	2005-06
95	D.T.Lindsay (131)	South Africa	v	Australia	Johannesburg[3]	1966-67
95	Kapil Dev (100*)	India	v	West Indies	Port-of-Spain	1982-83
95	I.D.S.Smith (173)	New Zealand	v	India	Auckland	1989-90
95	G.A.Gooch (123)	England	v	India	Lord's	1990
95	J.N.Rhodes (103*)	South Africa	v	West Indies	Centurion	1998-99
95	S.M.Pollock (111)	South Africa	v	Sri Lanka	Centurion	2000-01
96	M.Azahruddin (115)	India	v	South Africa	Cape Town	1996-97
96	C.H.Gayle (317)	West Indies	v	South Africa	St John's	2004-05
96	Shahid Afridi (156)	Pakistan	v	India	Faisalabad	2005-06
97	K.Srikkanth (116)	India	v	Australia	Sydney	1985-86
98	G.S.Sobers (113)	West Indies	v	Australia	Sydney	1968-69
98	R.S.Kaluwitharana (103)	Sri Lanka	v	New Zealand	Dunedin	1996-97
99	I.T.Botham (103)	England	v	New Zealand	Nottingham	1983
99	P.A.de Silva (103*)	Sri Lanka	v	Pakistan	Colombo (SSC)	1996-97
100	L.Klusener (102*)	South Africa	v	India	Cape Town	1996-97
100	B.C.Lara (112)	West Indies	v	England	Manchester	2000
101	Kapil Dev (126*)	India	v	West Indies	Delhi	1978-79
102	I.V.A.Richards (109*)	West Indies	v	India	Delhi	1987-88
102	J.L.Langer (122*)	Australia	v	New Zealand	Hamilton	1999-2000
102	Saeed Anwar (101)	Pakistan	v	Bangladesh	Multan[2]	2001-02
102	Inzamamul Haq (112)	Pakistan	v	Zimbabwe	Harare	2002-03
103	S.T.Jayasuriya (148)	Sri Lanka	v	South Africa	Galle	2000-01
103	A.C.Gilchrist (104)	Australia	v	India	Bangalore	2004-05
104	I.T.Botham (108)	England	v	Pakistan	Lord's	1978
104	A.C.Gilchrist (101*)	Australia	v	West Indies	Port-of-Spain	2002-03
104	A.C.Gilchrist (121)	Australia	v	New Zealand	Christchurch	2004-05

104	R.T.Ponting (105)	Australia	v	New Zealand	Auckland	2004-05
104	T.M.Dilshan (168	Sri Lanka	v	Bangladesh	Colombo (PSS)	2005-06
105	I.V.A.Richards (145)	West Indies	v	England	Lord's	1980
105	Kapil Dev (109)	India	v	West Indies	Madras[1]	1987-88
105	S.T.Jayasuriya (111)	Sri Lanka	v	India	Galle	2001-02
105	Yousuf Youhana (223)	Pakistan	v	England	Lahore[2]	2005-06
106	S.C.Ganguly (101*)	India	v	New Zealand	Hamilton	1998-99
107	C.H.Lloyd (242*)	West Indies	v	India	Bombay[3]	1974-75
107	S.R.Tendulkar (177)	India	v	Australia	Bangalore	1997-98
107	N.C.Johnson (107)	Zimbabwe	v	Pakistan	Peshawar[2]	1998-98
107	S.T.Jayasuriya (131)	Sri Lanka	v	Australia	Kandy	2003-04
107	V.K.Sehwag (309)	India	v	Pakistan	Multan[2]	2003-04
107	G.C.Smith (121)	South Africa	v	Zimbabwe	Cape Town	2004-05
108	M.D.Crowe (107)	New Zealand	v	Sri Lanka	Colombo (SSC)	1992-93
109	D.C.S.Compton (113)	England	v	South Africa	The Oval	1947
109	C.L.King (100*)	West Indies	v	New Zealand	Christchurch	1979-80
109	Kapil Dev (119)	India	v	Australia	Madras[1]	1986-87
109	A.C.Gilchrist (113)	Australia	v	Pakistan	Sydney	2004-05
110	R.E.Redmond (107)	New Zealand	v	Pakistan	Auckland	1972-73
110	R.C.Fredericks (109)	West Indies	v	England	Leeds	1976
110	L.R.D.Mendis (105)	Sri Lanka	v	India	Madras[2]	1982-83
110	S.R.Waugh (134*)	Australia	v	Sri Lanka	Hobart	1989-90
110	A.C.Gilchrist (149*)	Australia	v	Pakistan	Hobart	1999-2000
110	Yuvraj Singh (112)	India	v	Pakistan	Lahore[2]	2003-04
110	S.T.Jayasuriya (107)	Sri Lanka	v	Pakistan	Karachi[1]	2004-05
112	A.Flintoff (142)	England	v	South Africa	Lord's	2003
112	C.L.Cairns (158)	New Zealand	v	South Africa	Auckland	2003-04
113	R.T.Ponting (144)	Australia	v	England	Leeds	2001
113	R.T.Ponting (169)	Australia	v	Zimbabwe	Sydney	2003-04
114	A.Rantunga (131)	Sri Lanka	v	South Africa	Moratuwa	1993-94
114	V.V.S.Laxman (167)	India	v	Australia	Sydney	1999-2000
114	A.Flintoff (137)	England	v	New Zealand	Christchurch	2001-02
114	N.J.Astle (222)	New Zealand	v	England	Christchurch	2001-02

FASTEST DOUBLE CENTURIES

Min						
214	D.G.Bradman (334)	Australia	v	England	Leeds	1930
217	N.J.Astle (222)	New Zealand	v	England	Christchurch	2001-02
223	S.J.McCabe (232)	Australia	v	England	Nottingham	1938
226	V.T.Trumper (214*)	Australia	v	South Africa	Adelaide	1910-11
234	D.G.Bradman (254)	Australia	v	England	Lord's	1930
240	W.R.Hammond (336*)	England	v	New Zealand	Auckland	1932-33
241	E.S.Gregory (201)	Australia	v	England	Sydney	1894-95
245	D.C S.Compton (278)	England	v	Pakistan	Nottingham	1954
251	D.G Bradman (223)	Australia	v	West Indies	Brisbane[1]	1930-31
253	D.G.Bradman (226)	Australia	v	South Africa	Brisbane[2]	1931-32

FASTEST DOUBLE CENTURIES (by balls)

Balls						
153	N.J.Astle (222)	New Zealand	v	England	Christchurch	2001-02
182	V.K.Sehwag (254)	Pakistan	v	India	Lahore[2]	2005-06
211	H.H.Gibbs (228)	South Africa	v	Pakistan	Cape Town	2002-03
212	A.C.Gilchrist (204*)	Australia	v	South Africa	Johannesburg[3]	2001-02
222	I.T.Botham (208)	England	v	India	The Oval	1982

222	V.K.Sehwag (309)	India	v	Pakistan	Multan[2]	2003-04
229	P.A.de Silva (206)	Sri Lanka	v	Bangladesh	Colombo (PSS)	2002-03
231	G.P.Thorpe (200*)	England	v	New Zealand	Christchurch	2001-02
232	C.G.Greenidge (214*)	West Indies	v	England	Lord's	1984
240	C.H.Lloyd (242*)	West Indies	v	India	Bombay[3]	1974-75
241	Zaheer Abbas (215)	Pakistan	v	India	Lahore[2]	1982-83
242	D.G.Bradman (244)	Australia	v	England	The Oval	1934
242	I.V.A.Richards (208)	West Indies	v	Australia	Melbourne	1984-85
243	Yousuf Youhana (204*)	Pakistan	v	Bangladesh	Chittagong[1]	2001-02

FASTEST TRIPLE CENTURIES

Min						
288	W.R.Hammond (336*)	England	v	New Zealand	Auckland	1932-33
336	D.G.Bradman (334)	Australia	v	England	Leeds	1930

W.R.Hammond's third hundred was scored in 48 minutes. D.G.Bradman scored his three hundreds in 99, 115 and 122 minutes respectively and reached 309 at the end of the first day.*

MOST RUNS IN A DAY

								Day
309	(0-309*)	D.G.Bradman (334)	Australia	v	England	Leeds	1930	1
295	(41*-336*)	W.R.Hammond (336*)	England	v	New Zealand	Auckland	1932-33	2
273	(5*-278)	D.C.S.Compton (278)	England	v	Pakistan	Nottingham	1954	2
271	(0-271*)	D.G.Bradman (304)	Australia	v	England	Leeds	1934	2
244	(0-244)	D.G.Bradman (244)	Australia	v	England	The Oval	1934	1
239	(0-239*)	F.M.M.Worrell (261)	West Indies	v	England	Nottingham	1950	2
228	(0-228*)	V.K.Sehwag (309)	India	v	Pakistan	Multan[2]	2003-04	1
228	(0-228)	H.R.Gibbs (228)	South Africa	v	Pakistan	Cape Town	2002-03	1
227	(86*-313*)	B.C.Lara (400*)	West Indies	v	England	St John's	2003-04	2
223	(0-223*)	W.R.Hammond (227)	England	v	New Zealand	Christchurch	1932-33	1
223	(0-223*)	D.G.Bradman (223)	Australia	v	West Indies	Brisbane[1]	1930-31	1
222	(112*-334*)	M.A.Taylor (334*)	Australia	v	Pakistan	Peshawar[2]	1998-99	2
222	(0-222)	N.J.Astle (222)	New Zealand	v	England	Christchurch	2001-02	5
217	(0-217)	W.R.Hammond (217)	England	v	India	The Oval	1936	1
214	(73*-287)	R.E.Foster (287)	England	v	Australia	Sydney	1903-04	3
214	(0-214*)	C.G.Greenidge (214*)	West Indies	v	England	Lord's	1984	4
213	(19*-232)	S.J.McCabe (232)	Australia	v	England	Nottingham	1938	3
210	(0-210*)	W.R.Hammond (240)	England	v	Australia	Lord's	1938	1
209	(0-209)	C.A.Roach (209)	West Indies	v	England	Georgetown	1929-30	1
208	(20*-228*)	G.S.Sobers (365*)	West Indies	v	Pakistan	Kingston	1957-58	3
208	(0-208*)	V.T.Trumper (214*)	Australia	v	South Africa	Adelaide	1910-11	3
206	(0-206)	P.A.de Silva (206)	Sri Lanka	v	Bangladesh	Colombo (PSS)	2002-03	2
206	(0-206)	L.Hutton (206)	England	v	New Zealand	The Oval	1949	2
205	(7*-212*)	B.C.Lara (213)	West Indies	v	Australia	Kingston	1998-99	2
205	(0-205*)	W.H.Ponsford (266)	Australia	v	England	The Oval	1934	1
205	(0-205)	Aamer Sohail (205)	Pakistan	v	England	Manchester	1992	1
203	(0-203*)	R B Kanhai (256)	West Indies	v	India	Calcutta	1958-59	1
203	(0-203)	H.L.Collins (203)	Australia	v	South Africa	Johannesburg[1]	1921-22	1
203	(0*-203*)	P.A.de Silva (267)	Sri Lanka	v	New Zealand	Wellington	1990-91	2
202	(0-202*)	G.Kirsten (220)	South Africa	v	Zimbabwe	Harare	2000-01	1
202	(0-202*)	B.C.Lara (226)	West Indies	v	Australia	Adelaide	2005-06	1
201	(0-201)	D.G.Bradman (201)	Australia	v	India	Adelaide	1947-48	1
200	(0-200*)	I.V.A.Richards (291)	West Indies	v	England	The Oval	1976	1
200	(0-200*)	G.P.Thorpe (200*)	England	v	New Zealand	Christchurch	2001-02	4
200	(0-200*)	D.G.Bradman (226)	Australia	v	South Africa	Brisbane[2]	1931-32	1
200	(0-200)	G.C.Smith (200)	South Africa	v	Bangladesh	East London	2002-03	1

FEWEST RUNS IN A DAY

								Day
52	(52*)	Mudassar Nazar(114)	Pakistan	v	England	Lahore[2]	1977-78	1
54	(0*-54*)	M.L.Jaisimha (99)	India	v	Pakistan	Kanpur	1960-61	3
56	(1*-57*)	D.J.McGlew (70)	South Africa	v	Australia	Johannesburg[3]	1957-58	4
59	(0*-59*)	M.L.Jaisimha (74)	India	v	Australia	Calcutta	1959-60	4

SLOWEST FIFTIES

Min						
357	T.E.Bailey (68)	England	v	Australia	Brisbane[2]	1958-59
350	C.J.Tavaré (82)	England	v	Pakistan	Lord's	1982
333	B.A.Young (51)	New Zealand	v	South Africa	Durban[2]	1994-95
326	S.M.Gavaskar (51)	India	v	Sri Lanka	Colombo (SSC)	1985-86
318	Rameez Raja (62)	Pakistan	v	West Indies	Karachi[1]	1986-87
316	C.P.S.Chauhan (61)	India	v	Pakistan	Kanpur	1979-80
315	Shoaib Mohammad (53*)	Pakistan	v	Zimbabwe	Lahore[2]	1993-94
313	D.J.McGlew (70)	South Africa	v	Australia	Johannesburg[3]	1957-58
312	J.J.Crowe (120*)	New Zealand	v	Sri Lanka	Colombo (CCC)	1986-87
310	B.A.Edgar (55)	New Zealand	v	Australia	Wellington	1981-82
310	A.R.Border (75)	Australia	v	West Indies	Sydney	1988-89
306	C.J.Tavaré (78)	England	v	Australia	Manchester	1981
304	P.L.Taylor (54*)	Australia	v	Pakistan	Karachi[1]	1988-89
302	D.N.Sardesai (60)	India	v	West Indies	Bridgetown	1961-62
300	G.S.Camacho (57)	West Indies	v	England	Bridgetown	1967-68
297	R.G.Hart (57*)	New Zealand	v	West Indies	Bridgetown	2001-02
296	C.Z.Harris (56)	New Zealand	v	Sri Lanka	Moratuwa	1992-93
296	B.A.Young (56)	New Zealand	v	England	Wellington	1996-97
294	C.L.Smith (91)	England	v	New Zealand	Auckland	1983-84
290	G.Boycott (63)	England	v	Pakistan	Lahore[2]	1977-78
290	K.R.Rutherford (50*)	New Zealand	v	Australia	Auckland	1985-86
290	E.J.Gray (50)	New Zealand	v	England	Nottingham	1986
290	H.D.P.K.Dharmasena (54)	Sri Lanka	v	Zimbabwe	Bulawayo[2]	1994-95
289	C.J.Tavaré (56)	England	v	India	Bombay[3]	1981-82
289	B.A.Edgar (74)	New Zealand	v	Australia	Perth	1985-86
288	R.J.Shastri (109)	India	v	West Indies	Bridgetown	1988-89
285	P.R.Umrigar (78)	India	v	Australia	Bombay[2]	1956-57
285	G.A.Gooch (84)	England	v	West Indies	The Oval	1988
284	K.S.More (55)	India	v	South Africa	Durban[2]	1992-93
284	J.G.Wright (72)	New Zealand	v	Australia	Wellington	1992-93
283	N.Hussain (146*)	England	v	South Africa	Durban[2]	1999-2000
282	E.D.A.S.McMorris (73)	West Indies	v	England	Kingston	1959-60
280	P.E.Richardson (117)	England	v	South Africa	Johannesburg[3]	1956-57
279	Asif Mujtaba (54*)	Pakistan	v	Zimbabwe	Rawalpindi[2]	1993-94
278	G.Boycott (77)	England	v	Australia	Perth	1978-79
277	P.A.de Silva (110*)	Sri Lanka	v	India	Mohali	1997-98
275	W.M.Lawry (57)	Australia	v	England	Melbourne	1962-63
275	S.Ranatunga (118)	Sri Lanka	v	Zimbabwe	Harare	1994-95
275	Abdur Razzaq (71)	Pakistan	v	India	Mohali	2004-05
274	M.N.Samuels (51)	West Indies	v	South Africa	Georgetown	2000-01
273	C.Z.Harris (68*)	New Zealand	v	South Africa	Auckland	1998-99
272	A.P.Gurusinha (128)	Sri Lanka	v	Zimbabwe	Harare	1994-95
271	B.A.Young (51)	New Zealand	v	South Africa	Cape Town	1994-95
270	Mudassar Nazar (111)	Pakistan	v	England	Lahore[2]	1977-78
270	M.D.Crowe (108*)	New Zealand	v	Pakistan	Lahore[2]	1990-91
270	Saqlain Mushtaq (78)	Pakistan	v	Zimbabwe	Sheikhupura	1996-97

SLOWEST CENTURIES

Min						
557	Mudassar Nazar (111)	Pakistan	v	England	Lahore[2]	1977-78
545	D.J.McGlew (105)	South Africa	v	Australia	Durban[2]	1957-58
535	A.P.Gurusinha (128)	Sri Lanka	v	Zimbabwe	Harare	1994-95
516	J.J.Crowe (120*)	New Zealand	v	Sri Lanka	Colombo (CCC)	1986-87
500	S.V.Manjrekar (104)	India	v	Zimbabwe	Harare	1992-93
499	J.C.Adams (101*)	West Indies	v	Zimbabwe	Kingston	1999-2000
488	P.E.Richardson (117)	England	v	South Africa	Johannesburg[3]	1956-57
487	C.T.Radley (158)	England	v	New Zealand	Auckland	1977-78
468	Hanif Mohammad (142)	Pakistan	v	India	Bahawalpur	1954-55
467	N.Hussain (146*)	England	v	South Africa	Durban[2]	1999-2000
462	M.J.Greatbatch (146*)	New Zealand	v	Australia	Perth	1989-90
461	M.D.Crowe (108*)	New Zealand	v	Pakistan	Lahore[2]	1990-91
460	Hanif Mohammad (111)	Pakistan	v	England	Dacca	1961-62
458	K.W.R.Fletcher (122)	England	v	Pakistan	The Oval	1974
458	N.J.Astle (141)	New Zealand	v	Zimbabwe	Wellington	2000-01
457	S.A.R.Silva (111)	Sri Lanka	v	India	Colombo (SSC)	1985-86
457	S.Chanderpaul (136*)	West Indies	v	India	St John's	2001-02
455	G.P.Howarth (122)	New Zealand	v	England	Auckland	1977-78
440	A.J.Watkins (137*)	England	v	India	Delhi	1951-52
438	G.Boycott (105)	England	v	India	Delhi	1981-82
437	D.B.Vengsarkar (146*)	India	v	Pakistan	Delhi	1979-80
437	A.P.Gurusinha (116*)	Sri Lanka	v	Pakistan	Colombo (PSS)	1985-86
436	A.J.Hall (163)	South Africa	v	India	Kanpur	2004-05
435	J.W.Guy (102)	New Zealand	v	India	Hyderabad	1955-56
434	M.C.Cowdrey (154)	England	v	West Indies	Birmingham	1957
434	T.J.Franklin (101)	New Zealand	v	England	Lord's	1990
430	S.Ranatunga (118)	Sri Lanka	v	Zimbabwe	Harare	1994-95
428	S.M.Gavaskar (172)	India	v	England	Bangalore	1981-82
427	R.J.Shastri (109)	India	v	West Indies	Bridgetown	1988-89
426	Saqlain Mushtaq (101*)	Pakistan	v	New Zealand	Christchurch	2000-01
425	H.A.Gomes (127)	West Indies	v	Australia	Perth	1984-85
424	R.J.Shastri (125)	India	v	Pakistan	Jaipur	1986-87
424	M.A.Atherton (105)	England	v	Australia	Sydney	1990-91
422	R.J.Shastri (111)	India	v	England	Calcutta	1984-85
421	S.Ranatunga (100*)	Sri Lanka	v	Zimbabwe	Bulawayo[2]	1994-95
420	M.D.Crowe (188)	New Zealand	v	West Indies	Georgetown	1984-85
416	W.J.Cronje (135)	South Africa	v	India	Port Elizabeth	1992-93
416	A.J.Stewart (143)	England	v	West Indies	Bridgetown	1993-94
416	N.S.Sidhu (131)	India	v	Sri Lanka	Mohali	1996-97
416	V.V.S.Laxman (154*)	India	v	West Indies	Kolkata	2002-03
414	J.H.B.Waite (134)	South Africa	v	Australia	Durban[2]	1957-58
414	A.W.Greig (103)	England	v	India	Calcutta	1976-77
414	J.G.Wright (110)	New Zealand	v	India	Auckland	1980-81
413	J.A.Rudolph (102*)	South Africa	v	Australia	Perth	2005-06
412	J.G.Wright (138)	New Zealand	v	West Indies	Wellington	1986-87
411	D.W.Randall (150)	England	v	Australia	Sydney	1978-79
410	M.A.Atherton (151)	England	v	New Zealand	Nottingham	1990
409	M.L.Apte (163*)	India	v	West Indies	Port-of-Spain	1952-53
409	M.P.Vaughan (105)	England	v	Sri Lanka	Kandy	2003-04
408	M.Amarnath (101)	India	v	Pakistan	Lahore[2]	1984-85
406	J.A.Rudolph (102)	South Africa	v	Sri Lanka	Galle	2004-05
405	M.H.Richardson (106)	New Zealand	v	Pakistan	Hamilton	2000-01
404	Nafis Iqbal (121)	Bangladesh	v	Zimbabwe	Dhaka	2004-05
404	J.F.Reid (148)	New Zealand	v	Pakistan	Wellington	1984-85

403	T.T.Samaraweera (142)	Sri Lanka	v	England	Colombo (SSC)	2003-04
402	M.H.Richardson (101)	New Zealand	v	England	Lord's	2004
399	V.V.S.Laxman (104*)	India	v	New Zealand	Mohali	2003-04
396	R.A.Woolmer (149)	England	v	Australia	The Oval	1975
395	A.P.Gurusinha (127)	Sri Lanka	v	New Zealand	Dunedin	1994-95
392	J.F.Reid (180)	New Zealand	v	Sri Lanka	Colombo (CCC)	1983-84
392	M.J.Greatbatch (107*)	New Zealand	v	England	Auckland	1987-88
390	R.A.Smith (128)	England	v	Sri Lanka	Colombo (SSC)	1992-93
390	K.F.Barrington (109*)	England	v	Pakistan	Nottingham	1967
390	M.A.Butcher (105)	England	v	Sri Lanka	Lord's	2002
390	J.N.Gillespie (201*)	Australia	v	Bangladesh	Chittagong[2]	2005-0-
388	H.A.Gomes (127*)	West Indies	v	Australia	Adelaide	1981-82
388	J.L.Langer (127)	Australia	v	Pakistan	Hobart	1999-2000
387	M.A.Atherton (111)	England	v	New Zealand	Manchester	1994
386	C.A.Davis (183)	West Indies	v	New Zealand	Bridgetown	1971-72
385	D.M.Jones (210)	Australia	v	India	Madras[1]	1986-87
385	Imran Khan (136)	Pakistan	v	Australia	Adelaide	1989-90
385	R.S.Dravid (148)	India	v	South Africa	Johannesburg[3]	1996-97
384	M.A.Taylor (100)	Australia	v	India	Adelaide	1991-92
383	H.H.Gibbs (211*)	South Africa	v	New Zealand	Christchurch	1998-99
383	M.S.Atapattu (201*)	Sri Lanka	v	England	Galle	2000-01
382	D.L.Haynes (105)	West Indies	v	New Zealand	Dunedin	1979-80
382	A.Flower (113*)	Zimbabwe	v	West Indies	Port-of-Spain	1999-2000
381	G.Kirsten (275)	South Africa	v	England	Durban[2]	1999-2000
380	M.G.Vandort (105)	Sri Lanka	v	England	Birmingham	2006
379	G.Boycott (107)	England	v	Australia	Nottingham	1977
379	M.R.Ramprakash (154)	England	v	West Indies	Bridgetown	1997-98
378	G.P.Thorpe (103)	England	v	West Indies	Bridgetown	1997-98
378	D.R.Martyn (161)	Australia	v	Sri Lanka	Kandy	2003-04
377	M.R.Ramprakash (154)	England	v	West Indies	Bridgetown	1997-98
376	B.A.Edgar (127)	New Zealand	v	West Indies	Auckland	1979-80
375	G.P.Thorpe (103)	England	v	West Indies	Bridgetown	1997-98
374	Javed Omar (119)	Bangladesh	v	Pakistan	Peshawar[2]	2003-04
372	M.A.Vermeulen (118)	Zimbabwe	v	West Indies	Bulawayo[2]	2004-05
371	J.H.Kallis (109*)	South Africa	v	West Indies	Georgetown	2004-05
370	H.P.Tillakaratne (116)	Sri Lanka	v	Zimbabwe	Harare	1994-95
370	H.P.Tillakaratne (105*)	Sri Lanka	v	West Indies	Galle	2001-02

SLOWEST DOUBLE CENTURIES

Min						
776	D.S.B.P.Kuruppu (201*)	Sri Lanka	v	New Zealand	Colombo (CCC)	1986-87
741	G.Kirsten (275)	South Africa	v	England	Durban[2]	1999-2000
677	M.S.Atapattu (201*)	Sri Lanka	v	England	Galle	2000-01
671	N.S.Sidhu (201)	India	v	West Indies	Port-of-Spain	1996-97
666	G.W.Flower (201*)	Zimbabwe	v	Pakistan	Harare	1994-95
656	Shoaib Mohammad (203*)	Pakistan	v	New Zealand	Karachi[1]	1990-91
652	A.D.Gaekwad (201)	India	v	Pakistan	Jullundur	1983-84
652	R.S.Mahanama (225)	Sri Lanka	v	India	Colombo (RPS)	1997-98
651	S.L.Campbell (208)	West Indies	v	New Zealand	Bridgetown	1995-96
645	R.S.Dravid (270)	India	v	Pakistan	Rawalpindi[2]	2003-04
644	H.H.Gibbs (211*)	South Africa	v	New Zealand	Christchurch	1998-99
635	G.Kirsten (210)	South Africa	v	England	Manchester	1998
608	R.B.Simpson (311)	Australia	v	England	Manchester	1964
596	A.R.Border (205)	Australia	v	New Zealand	Adelaide	1987-88
595	G.S.Sobers (226)	West Indies	v	England	Bridgetown	1959-60
591	Javed Miandad (211)	Pakistan	v	Australia	Karachi[1]	1988-89

584	Hanif Mohammad (337)	Pakistan	v	West Indies	Bridgetown	1957-58
579	R.S.Dravid (217)	India	v	England	The Oval	2002
574	J.N.Gillespie (201*)	Australia	v	Bangladesh	Chittagong[2]	2005-06
570	S.G.Barnes (234)	Australia	v	England	Sydney	1946-47
570	M.S.Atapattu (216*)	Sri Lanka	v	Zimbabwe	Bulawayo[2]	1999-2000
568	G.R.Viswanath (222)	India	v	England	Madras[1]	1981-82
567	Yousuf Youhana (223)	Pakistan	v	England	Lahore[2]	2005-06
566	A.R.Border (200*)	Australia	v	England	Leeds	1993
562	C.G.Greenidge (226)	West Indies	v	Australia	Bridgetown	1990-91
556	R.J.Shastri (206)	India	v	Australia	Sydney	1991-92
555	G.N.Yallop (268)	Australia	v	Pakistan	Melbourne	1983-84
553	Younis Khan (267)	Pakistan	v	India	Bangalore	2004-05
550	S.R.Waugh (200)	Australia	v	West Indies	Kingston	1994-95
550	M.S.Atapattu (223)	Sri Lanka	v	Zimbabwe	Kandy	1997-98
545	R.S.Dravid (222)	India	v	New Zealand	Ahmedabad	2003-04
537	M.E.Trescothick (219)	England	v	South Africa	The Oval	2003
535	R.M.Cowper (307)	Australia	v	England	Melbourne	1965-66
534	Inzamamul Haq (200*)	Pakistan	v	Sri Lanka	Dhaka	1998-99
532	S.R.Tendulkar (241*)	India	v	Australia	Sydney	2003-04
531	W.M.Lawry (210)	Australia	v	West Indies	Bridgetown	1964-65
531	H.P.Tillakaratne (204*)	Sri Lanka	v	West Indies	Colombo (SSC)	2001-02
524	D.L.Houghton (266)	Zimbabwe	v	Sri Lanka	Bulawayo[2]	1994-95
521	Yousuf Youhana (103)	Pakistan	v	New Zealand	Christchurch	2000-01
521	R.S.Dravid (233)	India	v	Australia	Adelaide	2003-04
518	K.F.Barrington (256)	England	v	Australia	Manchester	1964
518	L.Vincent (224)	New Zealand	v	Sri Lanka	Wellington	2004-05
515	D.M.Jones (216)	Australia	v	West Indies	Adelaide	1988-89
514	M.S.Sinclair (204*)	New Zealand	v	Pakistan	Christchurch	2000-01
513	V.G.Kambli (224)	India	v	England	Bombay[3]	1992-93
512	M.A.Taylor (219)	Australia	v	England	Nottingham	1989
512	D.P.M.D.Jayawardene(237)	Sri Lanka	v	South Africa	Galle	2004-05
511	B.A.Young (267*)	New Zealand	v	Sri Lanka	Dunedin	1996-97
509	S.Chanderpaul (203*)	West Indies	v	South Africa	Georgetown	2004-05

SLOWEST TRIPLE CENTURIES

Min						
858	Hanif Mohammad (337)	Pakistan	v	West Indies	Bridgetown	1957-58
753	R.B.Simpson (311)	Australia	v	England	Manchester	1964
723	S.T.Jayasuriya (340)	Sri Lanka	v	India	Colombo (RPS)	1997-98
693	R.M.Cowper (307)	Australia	v	England	Melbourne	1965-66
681	M.A.Taylor (334*)	Australia	v	Pakistan	Peshawar[2]	1998-99
662	L.Hutton (364)	England	v	Australia	The Oval	1938
610	B.C.Lara (375)	West Indies	v	England	St John's	1993-94
605	L.G.Rowe (302)	West Indies	v	England	Bridgetown	1973-74

LONGEST INDIVIDUAL INNINGS

Min						
970	Hanif Mohammad (337)	Pakistan	v	West Indies	Bridgetown	1957-57
878	G.Kirsten (275)	South Africa	v	England	Durban[2]	1999-2000
799	S.T.Jayasuriya (340)	Sri Lanka	v	India	Colombo (RPS)	1997-98
797	L.Hutton (364)	England	v	Australia	The Oval	1938
778	D.S.B.P.Kuruppu (201*)	Sri Lanka	v	New Zealand	Colombo (CCC)	1986-87
778	B.C.Lara (400*)	West Indies	v	England	St John's	2003-04
768	B.C.Lara (375)	West Indies	v	England	St John's	1993-94
762	R.B.Simpson (311)	Australia	v	England	Manchester	1964
753	R.S.Mahanama (225)	Sri Lanka	v	India	Colombo (RPS)	1997-98

752	D.P.M.D.Jayawardene (374)	Sri Lanka	v	South Africa	Colombo (SSC)	2006-07
740	R.S.Dravid (270)	India	v	Pakistan	Rawalpindi^{2}	2003-04
727	R.M.Cowper (307)	Australia	v	England	Melbourne	1965-66
720	Shoaib Mohammad (163)	Pakistan	v	New Zealand	Wellington	1988-89
720	M.A.Taylor (334*)	Australia	v	England	Peshawar^{2}	1998-99
716	G.N.Yallop (268)	Australia	v	Pakistan	Melbourne	1983-84
708	S.M.Gavaskar (172)	India	v	England	Bangalore	1981-82
704	G.M.Turner (259)	New Zealand	v	West Indies	Georgetown	1971-72
690	Younis Khan (267)	Pakistan	v	India	Bangalore	2004-05
685	K.F.Barrington (256)	England	v	Australia	Manchester	1964
685	J.F.Reid (180)	New Zealand	v	Sri Lanka	Colombo (CCC)	1983-84
685	Qasim Omar (210)	Pakistan	v	India	Faisalabad	1984-85
684	M.S.Atapattu (201*)	Sri Lanka	v	England	Galle	2000-01
682	F.M.M.Worrell (197*)	West Indies	v	England	Bridgetown	1959-60
680	Imtiaz Ahmed (209)	Pakistan	v	New Zealand	Lahore^{1}	1955-56
677	C.G.Greenidge (226)	West Indies	v	Australia	Bridgetown	1990-91
677	D.P.M.D.Jayawardene (242)	Sri Lanka	v	India	Colombo (SSC)	1998-99
675	D.L.Houghton (266)	Zimbabwe	v	Sri Lanka	Bulawayo^{2}	1994-95
675	S.L.Campbell (208)	West Indies	v	New Zealand	Bridgetown	1995-96
675	S.Chanderpaul (136*)	West Indies	v	India	St John's	2001-02
673	N.S.Sidhu (201)	India	v	West Indies	Port-of-Spain	1996-97
671	A.D.Gaekwad (201)	India	v	Pakistan	Jullundur	1983-84
675	K.C.Sangakkara (287)	Sri Lanka	v	South Africa	Colombo (SSC)	2006-07
659	H.H.Gibbs (211*)	South Africa	v	New Zealand	Christchurch	1998-99
659	M.S.Atapattu (207*)	Sri Lanka	v	Pakistan	Kandy	2000-01
658	D.J.Cullinan (275*)	South Africa	v	New Zealand	Auckland	1998-99
656	M.J.Greatbatch (146*)	New Zealand	v	Australia	Perth	1989-90
656	Shoaib Mohammad (203*)	Pakistan	v	New Zealand	Karachi^{1}	1990-91
654	G.W.Flower (201*)	Zimbabwe	v	Pakistan	Harare	1994-95
653	S.P.Fleming (274*)	New Zealand	v	Sri Lanka	Colombo (PSS)	2002-03
652	G.Kirsten (210)	South Africa	v	England	Manchester	1998
648	C.T.Radley (158)	England	v	New Zealand	Auckland	1977-78
647	G.S.Sobers (226)	West Indies	v	England	Bridgetown	1959-60
645	M.A.Atherton (185*)	England	v	South Africa	Johannesburg^{3}	1995-96
644	S.M.Gavaskar (236*)	India	v	West Indies	Madras^{1}	1983-84
642	S.G.Barnes (234)	Australia	v	England	Sydney	1946-47
638	G.R.Viswanath (222)	India	v	England	Madras^{1}	1981-82
636	S.Wettimuny (190)	Sri Lanka	v	England	Lord's	1984
636	Javed Miandad (211)	Pakistan	v	Australia	Karachi^{1}	1988-89
634	A.H.Jones (170*)	New Zealand	v	India	Auckland	1989-90
635	N.Hussain (146*)	England	v	South Africa	Durban^{2}	1999-2000
631	V.V.S.Laxman (281)	India	v	Australia	Kolkata	2000-01
630	C.L.Hooper (233)	West Indies	v	India	Georgetown	2001-02
630	C.H.Gayle (317)	West Indies	v	South Africa	St John's	2004-05
629	R.S.Dravid (217)	India	v	England	The Oval	2002
627	Mudassar Nazar (231)	Pakistan	v	India	Hyderabad	1982-83
627	G.A.Gooch (333)	England	v	India	Lord's	1990
627	M.S.Atapattu (216*)	Sri Lanka	v	Zimbabwe	Bulawayo^{2}	1999-2000
622	M.L.Hayden (380)	Australia	v	Zimbabwe	Perth	2003-04
620	G.Boycott (191)	England	v	Australia	Leeds	1977
617	Javed Miandad (260)	Pakistan	v	England	The Oval	1987
614	G.S.Sobers (365*)	West Indies	v	Pakistan	Kingston	1957-58
613	S.R.Tendulkar (241*)	India	v	Australia	Sydney	2003-04
612	L.G.Rowe (302)	West Indies	v	England	Bridgetown	1973-74
610	M.D.Crowe (699)	New Zealand	v	Sri Lanka	Wellington	1990-91
609	J.J.Crowe (120*)	New Zealand	v	Sri Lanka	Colombo (CCC)	1986-87

608	V.G.Kambli (224)	India	v	England	Bombay[3]	1992-93
607	A.P.Gurusinha (128)	Sri Lanka	v	Zimbabwe	Harare	1994-95
606	Javed Miandad (280*)	Pakistan	v	India	Hyderabad	1982-83
605	B.A.Young (267*)	New Zealand	v	Sri Lanka	Dunedin	1996-97
602	C.A.Davis (183)	West Indies	v	New Zealand	Bridgetown	1971-72
602	Yousuf Youhana (223)	Pakistan	v	England	Lahore[2]	2005-06
601	G.M.Wood (172)	Australia	v	England	Nottingham	1985
600	A.Sandham (325)	England	v	West Indies	Kingston	1929-30

AN HOUR BEFORE SCORING FIRST RUN

Min						
101	G.I.Allott (0)	New Zealand	v	South Africa	Auckland	1998-99
97	T.G.Evans (10*)	England	v	Australia	Adelaide	1946-47
84	R.K.Chauhan (9)	India	v	Sri Lanka	Ahmedabad	1993-94
82	P.I.Pocock (13)	England	v	West Indies	Georgetown	1967-68
74	J.T.Murray (3*)	England	v	Australia	Sydney	1962-63
72	C.G.Rackemann (9)	Australia	v	England	Sydney	1990-91
72	H.H.Streak (19*)	Zimbabwe	v	Pakistan	Karachi[2]	1993-94
72	P.M.Such (0)	England	v	New Zealand	Manchester	1999
70	W.L.Murdoch (17)	Australia	v	England	Sydney	1882-83
69	R.M.Hogg (7*)	Australia	v	West Indies	Adelaide	1984-85
67	C.J.Tavaré (82)	England	v	Pakistan	Lord's	1982
66	J.G.Wright (38)	New Zealand	v	Australia	Wellington	1981-82
65	Shujauddin (45)	Pakistan	v	Australia	Lahore[2]	1959-60
64	C.E.Eksteen (21)	South Africa	v	New Zealand	Auckland	1994-95
63	C.J.Tavaré (9)	England	v	Australia	Perth	1982-83
63	P.C.R.Tufnell (2*)	England	v	India	Bombay[3]	1992-93
62	M.A.Taylor (49)	Australia	v	England	Sydney	1994-95

AN HOUR WITHOUT ADDING TO SCORE

Min						
94	M.C.Snedden (23)	New Zealand	v	Australia	Wellington	1989-90
91	J.J.Crowe (21)	New Zealand	v	West Indies	Bridgetown	1984-85
90	B.Mitchell (58)	South Africa	v	Australia	Brisbane[2]	1931-32
90	C.J.Tavaré (89)	England	v	Australia	Perth	1982-83
89	R.J.Shastri (23)	India	v	South Africa	Johannesburg[3]	1992-93
87	I.K.Pathan (55)	India	v	Australia	Bangalore	2004-05
86	R.J.Shastri (14)	India	v	South Africa	Durban[2]	1992-93
82	M.D.Bell (25)	New Zealand	v	India	Hamilton	1998-99
79	T.E.Bailey (8)	England	v	South Africa	Leeds	1955
77	D.B.Close (20)	England	v	West Indies	Manchester	1976
75	A.Ranatunga (37)	Sri Lanka	v	New Zealand	Colombo (CCC)	1983-84
73	N.Hussain (146*)	England	v	South Africa	Durban[2]	1999-2000
72	N.C.Johnson (52*)	Zimbabwe	v	Sri Lanka	Bulawayo[2]	1999-2000
71	R.C.Russell (29*)	England	v	South Africa	Johannesburg[3]	1995-96
70	D.L.Haynes (9)	West Indies	v	New Zealand	Auckland	1979-80
69	G.A.Gooch (84)	England	v	West Indies	The Oval	1988
67	W.H.Scotton (34)	England	v	Australia	The Oval	1886
67	S.R.Tendulkar (126*)	India	v	New Zealand	Mohali	1999-2000
66	S.M.Gavaskar (52)	India	v	Sri Lanka	Colombo (PSS)	1985-86
65	Nawab of Pataudi, jr (5)	India	v	England	Bombay[2]	1972-73
65	R.G.Twose (36)	New Zealand	v	India	Cuttack	1995-96
64	Anil Dalpat (15)	Pakistan	v	New Zealand	Wellington	1984-85
64	M.A.Taylor (11)	Australia	v	England	Sydney	1990-91
64	S.Chanderpaul (80)	West Indies	v	England	The Oval	1995
63	D.R.Jardine (24)	England	v	Australia	Brisbane[2]	1932-33

63	W.R.Endean (18)	South Africa	v	England	Johannesburg[3]	1956-57
63	W.R.Playle (18)	New Zealand	v	England	Leeds	1958
63	J.M.Brearley (48)	England	v	Australia	Birmingham	1981
63	S.R.Waugh (47*)	Australia	v	England	Nottingham	1993
63	A.J.Stewart (81)	England	v	South Africa	Port Elizabeth	1995-96
62	K.F.Barrington (137)	England	v	New Zealand	Birmingham	1965
62	R.J.Shastri (5)	India	v	South Africa	Port Elizabeth	1992-93
62	M.P.Vaughan (156)	England	v	South Africa	Birmingham	2003
61	J.F.Reid (148)	New Zealand	v	Pakistan	Wellington	1984-85
61	M.D.Marshall (6*)	West Indies	v	England	Birmingham	1991
61	H.J.H.Marshall (40*)	New Zealand	v	South Africa	Johannesburg[3]	2000-01
60	B.Mitchell (73)	South Africa	v	England	Johannesburg[1]	1938-39
60	T.E.Bailey (80)	England	v	South Africa	Durban[2]	1956-57
60	H.A.Gomes (5)	West Indies	v	England	Port-of-Spain	1980-81
60	C.J.Tavaré (82)	England	v	Pakistan	Lord's	1982
60	A.R.Border (9)	Australia	v	Pakistan	Faisalabad	1982-83
60	S.M.Gavaskar (51)	India	v	Sri Lanka	Colombo (SSC)	1985-86
60	J.J.Crowe (120*)	New Zealand	v	Sri Lanka	Colombo (CCC)	1986-87
60	G.A.Hick (59)	England	v	West Indies	Bridgetown	1993-94
60	Rajin Saleh (60)	Bangladesh	v	Pakistan	Karachi[1]	2003-04
60	M.P.Vaughan (48)	England	v	Bangladesh	Dhaka	2003-04

BATSMEN DISMISSED FOR A 'PAIR'

FOUR TIMES

B.S.Chandrasekhar (India): v NZ 1975-76; v E 1976-77; v A 1977-78 (twice).
C.A.Walsh (West Indies): v P 1997-98; v N 1999-2000; v A 2000-01; v SA 2000-01.
M.Dillon (West Indies): v A 1998-99; v A 2000-01; v P 2001-02; N 2001-02.
M.S.Atapattu (Sri Lanka): v I 1990-91; v I 1993-94; v E 2000-01; v P 2004-05.
C.S.Martin v P 2000-01; v P 2001-02; v A 2004-05 v W 2005-06.

THREE TIMES

R.Peel (England):v A 1894-95 (twice), 1896.
R.W.Blair (New Zealand): v WI 1955-56; v E 1962-63; v SA 1963-64.
D.L.Underwood (England):v WI 1966; v A 1974-75; v WI 1976.
B.S.Bedi (India):v E 1974; v WI 1974-75; v E 1976-77.
A.G.Hurst (Australia):v E 1978-79 (twice); v P 1978-79.
C.E.L.Ambrose (West Indies):v E 1988; v P 1990-91; v E 1991.
D.K.Morrison (New Zealand): v A 1987-88; v SL 1990-91; v A 1993-94.
D.E.Malcolm (England): v NZ 1990; v P 1992; v A 1997.
G.D.McGrath (Australia): v P 1995-96; v E 1998-99 (twice).
A.B.Agarkar (India): v A 1999-2000 (twice); v A 2000-01.
Manjural Islam (Bangladesh): v Z 2000-01; v N 2001-02; v SL 2002-03.
A.Nehra (India): v Z 2000-01; v W 2001-02; v A 2003-04.
Zaheer Khan v SA 2001-02; v N 2002-03; v A 2004-05.

TWICE

AUSTRALIA: K.D.Mackay v E 1956; v I 1959-60. G.D.McKenzie v SA 1963-64; v E 1968. J.W.Gleeson v SA 1969-70; v E 1970-71. W.M.Clark v WI 1977-78 (twice). R.M.Hogg v I 1979-80; v WI 1984-85. R.G.Holland v E 1985; v NZ 1985-86. M.E.Waugh v SL 1992-93 (twice). S.K.Warne v I 2000-01; v P 2002-03.
ENGLAND: A.V.Bedser v A 1948; v WI 1950. D.L.Amiss v A 1968, 1974-75. P.I.Pocock v WI 1984 (twice). N.A.Foster v WI 1985-86; v P 1987-88. D.Gough v A 1997; 2001. A.R.Caddick v A 1997; v W 1997-98. A.Flintoff v SA 1998; v I 2002. M.A.Atherton v A 1998-99; v SA 1999-2000 M.J.Hoggard v A 2002-03; v A 2005.
SOUTH AFRICA: L.J.Tancred v E 1907, 1912. Q.McMillan v A 1931-32 (twice). R.J.Crisp v A 1935-36 (twice). M.Ntini v SL 2004-05; v A 2005-06. A.Nel v P 2003-04, v SL 2006-07.
WEST INDIES: C.A.Roach v E 1929-30, 1933. A.L.Valentine v E 1950, 1953-54. A.I.Kallicharran v E 1973-74; v NZ 1979-80. D.Williams v A 1992-93; v E 1997-98. P.T.Collins v A 1998-99; v SL 2001-02. R.R.Sarwan v A 2000-01; v E

2003-04. C.H.Gayle v SL 2001-02; v I 2005-06. D.Ramnarine v SL 2001-02; v P 2001-02. R.D.Jacobs v I 2002-03; v E 2004.
NEW ZEALAND: S.B.Doull v W 1994-95; v E 1996-97. P.J.Wiseman v I 1998-99; v I 1999-2000.
INDIA: M.Amarnath v WI 1983-84 (twice). Maninder Singh v P 1982-83; v WI 1987-88. J.Srinath v SA 1999-2000; v W 2001-02.
PAKISTAN: Aaqib Javed v A 1989-90; v E 1992. Waqar Younis v NZ 1990-91; A 2002-03. Mushtaq Ahmed v A 1994-95; v Z 1998-99. Shabbir Ahmed v WI 2004-05; v E 2005-06.
SRI LANKA: G.P.Wickramasinghe v P 1999-2000 (twice). M.Muralidaran v W 2000-01; v A 2003-04. R.P.Arnold v E 2000-01; v SA 2002-03.
ZIMBABWE: G.W.Flower v P 1993-94; v I 2000-01. H.K.Olonga v E 1996-97; v SL 2001-02. A.G.Huckle v SL 1997-98; v P 1997-98. M.Mbangwa v N 1997-98; v W 1999-2000.
BANGLADESH: Mohammad Sharif v Z 2000-01; v P 2001-02. Mohammad Ashraful v A 2003-04; v N 2004-05.

ONCE
AUSTRALIA: P.S.McDonnell v E 1882-83. T.W.Garrett v E 1882-83. E.Evans v E 1886. P.G.McShane v E 1887-88. A.C.Bannerman v E 1888. M.A.Noble v E 1899. E.S.Gregory v E 1899. C.E.McLeod v E 1901-02. J.Darling v E 1902. J.J.Kelly v E 1902. H.Trumble v E 1903-04. V.T.Trumper v E 1907-08. J.V.Saunders v E 1907-08. C.V.Grimmett v E 1930. W.A.S.Oldfield v SA 1931-32. J.H.W.Fingleton v E 1932-33. V.Y.Richardson v E 1932-33. C.L.Badcock v E 1938. I.W.G.Johnson v E 1946-47. J.Moroney v E 1950-51. J.B.Iverson v E 1950-51. L.V.Maddocks v E 1956. R.N.Harvey v E 1956. A.T.W.Grout v WI 1960-61. R.Benaud v E 1961. A.N.Connolly v WI 1968-69. R.Edwards v E 1972. K.R.Stackpole v NZ 1973-74. G.Dymock v E 1974-75. R.W.Marsh v E 1977. J.R.Thomson v E 1977. C.S.Serjeant v I 1977-78. A.L.Mann v I 1977-78. D.W.Hookes v P 1979-80. G.M.Wood v NZ 1980-81. M.R.Whitney v E 1981. B.Yardley v P 1982-83. R.J.Bright v P 1982-83. C.G.Rackemann v WI 1984-85. K.J.Hughes v WI 1984-85. M.G.Hughes v E 1986-87. D.M.Jones v P 1988-89. B.A.Reid v WI 1990-91. I.A.Healy v WI 1992-93. A.R.Border v WI 1992-93. J.L.Langer v NZ 1992-93. M.A.Taylor v P 1994-95. P.E.McIntyre v A 1994-95. B.P.Julian v W 1994-95. C.J.McDermott v P 1995-96. C.R.Miller v P 1998-99. S.C.G.MacGill v W 1998-99. R.T.Ponting v P 1999-2000. A.C.Gilchrist v I 2000-01.
ENGLAND: G.F.Grace v A 1880. W.Attewell v A 1891-92. G.A.Lohmann v SA 1895-96. E.G.Arnold v A 1903-04. A.E.Knight v A 1903-04. E.G.Hayes v SA 1905-06. M.C.Bird v SA 1909-10. H.Strudwick v A 1921. P.Holmes v SA 1927-28. C.I.J.Smith v WI 1934-35. J.T.Ikin v A 1946-47. J.J.Warr v A 1950-51. F.Ridgway v I 1951-52. R.T.Spooner v SA 1955. J.H.Wardle v A 1956. F.S.Trueman v A 1958-59. T.E.Bailey v A 1958-59. G.Pullar v P 1961-62. M.J.K.Smith v I 1961-62. J.T.Murray v P 1967. B.W.Luckhurst v P 1971. A.P.E.Knott v NZ 1973. G.G.Arnold v A 1974-75. G.A.Gooch v A 1975. A.Ward v WI 1976. J.C.Balderstone v WI 1976. M.Hendrick v NZ 1977-78. R.A.Woolmer v A 1981. I.T.Botham v A 1981. E.E.Hemmings v A 1982-83. N.G.Cowans v I 1984-85. D.J.Capel v P 1987-88. W.Larkins v WI 1989-90. R.J.Bailey v WI 1989-90. C.C.Lewis v A 1993. P.C.R.Tufnell v A 1994-95. J.P.Crawley v A 1994-95. P.A.J.DeFreitas v A 1994-95. M.R.Ramprakash v W 1995. R.K.Illingworth v W 1995. M.A.Butcher v W 1997-98. G.P.Thorpe v SA 1998. A.D.Mullally v A 1998-99. P.M.Such v A 1998-99. G.M.Hamilton v SA 1999-2000. G.A.Hick v W 2000. E.S.H.Giddins v W 2000. N.Hussain v W 2000. A.J.Stewart v A 2002-03. I.R.Bell v A 2005.
SOUTH AFRICA: C.S.Wimble v E 1891-92. J.T.Willoughby v E 1895-96. J.J.Kotze v A 1902-03. P.S.Twentyman-Jones v A 1902-03. A.E.E.Vogler v A 1910-11. T.A.Ward v A 1912. C.B.Llewellyn v E 1912. P.T.Lewis v E 1913-14. J.L.Cox v E 1913-14. C.D.Dixon v E 1913-14. G.A.L.Hearne v E 1922-23. A.E.Hall v E 1922-23. F.Nicholson v A 1935-36. X.C.Balaskas v A 1935-36. C.N.McCarthy v E 1948-49. D.J.McGlew v E 1955. W.R.Endean v E 1955. P.S.Heine v E 1956-57. C.Wesley v E 1960. M.A.Seymour v A 1969-70. A.A.Donald v WI 1991-92. C.R.Matthews v E 1994. D.J.Richardson v P 1994-95. G.Kirsten v W 2000-01. J.M.Kemp v W 2000-01.
WEST INDIES: C.R.Browne v E 1929-30. H.C.Griffith v E 1933. E.E.Achong v E 1934-35. J.Trim v A 1951-52. A.P.Binns v A 1954-55. O.G.Smith v A 1954-55. S.Ramadhin v E 1957. E.D.Weekes v E 1957. F.C.M.Alexander v E 1957. L.R.Gibbs v P 1958-59. F.M.M.Worrell v A 1960-61. J.S.Solomon v I 1961-62. J.L.Hendriks v E 1966. W.W.Hall v E 1967-68. D.L.Murray v I 1974-75. C.G.Greenidge v A 1975-76. J.Garner v P 1976-77. D.A.Murray v P 1980-81. A.L.Logie v I 1983-84. M.A.Holding v A 1984-85. P.J.L.Dujon v P 1986-87. A.H.Gray v P 1986-87. K.L.T.Arthurton v A 1992-93. J.R.Murray v P 1992-93. C.O.Browne v SL 1996-97. R.N.Lewis v SA 1998-99. A.F.G.Griffith v Z 1999-2000. M.I.Black v A 2000-01. N.A.M.McLean 2000-01. J.C.Adams v A 2000-01. C.E.Cuffy v P 2001-02. J.J.C.Lawson v A 2002-03. D.S.Smith v A 2002-03. F.H.Edwards v Z 2003-04. D.B.Powell v SL 2005-06.
NEW ZEALAND: K.C.James v E 1929-30. F.T.Badcock v E 1929-30. J.Cowie v E 1937. C.G.Rowe v A 1945-46. L.A.Butterfield v A 1945-46. L.S.M.Miller v SA 1953-54. M.B.Poore v E 1954-55. I.A.Colquhoun v E 1954-55. J.A.Hayes v E 1954-55. A.R.MacGibbon v I 1955-56. H.B.Cave v WI 1955-56. N.S.Harford v E 1958. R.C.Motz v SA 1961-62. M.J.F.Shrimpton v SA 1963-64. A.E.Dick v P 1964-65. G.A.Bartlett v E 1965-66. T.W.Jarvis v P 1972-73. W.K.Lees v E 1977-78. B.P.Bracewell v E 1978. B.L.Cairns v A 1980-81. B.A.Edgar v A 1980-81. G.B.Troup v I 1980-81. J.V.Coney

v A 1981-82. I.D.S.Smith v A 1981-82. J.G.Bracewell v P 1984-85. K.R.Rutherford v WI 1984-85. J.G.Wright v E 1986. C.M.Kuggeleijn v I 1988-89. M.C.Snedden v I 1988-89. B.R.Hartland v E 1991-92. M.L.Su'a v P 1992-93. D.J.Nash v SL 1994-95. C.Z.Harris N v W 1995-96. D.N.Patel v E 1996-97. S.P.Fleming v A 1997-98. D.L.Vettori v SL 1997-98. R.G.Twose v E 1999. S.B.OConnor v A 1999-2000. J.E.C.Franklin v P 2000-01.

INDIA: V.S.Hazare v E 1951-52. G.S.Ramchand v E 1952. Pankaj Roy v E 1952. P.G.Joshi v WI 1952-53. C.V.Gadkari v WI 1952-53. N.S.Tamhane v WI 1958-59. Surendranath v E 1959. R.B.Desai v A 1959-60. D.N.Sardesai v WI 1961-62. M.L.Jaisimha v NZ 1969-70. E.A.S.Prasanna v WI 1974-75. F.M.Engineer v WI 1974-75. D.B.Vengsarkar v WI 1978-79. Yashpal Sharma v A 1979-80. R.M.H.Binny v P 1979-80. D.R.Doshi v P 1982-83. S.Venkataraghavan v WI 1982-83. R.G.Patel v NZ 1988-89. B.K.Venkatesh Prasad v W 1996-97. Harvinder Singh v A 1997-98. Harbhajan Singh v W 2001-02. V.V.S.Laxman v N 2002-03. L.Balaji v P 2003-04.

PAKISTAN: M.E.Z.Ghazali v E 1954. Nasim-ul-Ghani v WI 1957-58. Wazir Mohammad v WI 1957-58. Imtiaz Ahmed v E 1961-62. Javed Burki v NZ 1964-65. Salim Altaf v A 1976-77. Iqbal Qasim v E 1978. Majid Khan v A 1978-79. Wasim Bari v A 1978-79. Sikander Bakht v A 1978-79. Mudassar Nazar v E 1982. Wasim Akram v SL 1985-86. Saeed Anwar v WI 1990-91. Aamer Sohail v NZ 1992-93. Manzoor Elahi v Z 1994-95. Rashid Latif v SA 1997-98. Saleem Malik v A 1998-99. Azhar Mahmood v I 1998-99. Saleem Elahi v E 2001. Taufeeq Umar v A 2002-03. Mohammad Zahid v SA 2002-03. Shoaib Akhtar v A 2004-05.Danish Kaneria v I 2004-05.

SRI LANKA: B.R.Jurangpathy v I 1986-87. R.G.de Alwis v I 1986-87. R.J.Ratnayake v I 1990-91. G.F.Labrooy v I 1990-91. A.Ranatunga v P 1991-92. S.D.Anurasiri v P 1991-92. C.I.Dunusinghe v N 1994-95. H.M.K.R.B.Herath v P 1999-2000. D.N.T.Zoysa v E 2000-01. W.P.U.J.C.Vaas v W 2001-02. K.H.R.K.Fernando v SA 2002-03. S.L.Malinga v A 2004-05. W.U.Tharanga v E 2006.

ZIMBABWE: D.H.Brain v I 1992-93. S.G.Peall v P 1993-94. H.H.Streak v N 1997-98. G.J.Rennie v N 1997-98. D.P.Viljoen v P 1997-98. B.A.Murphy v W 1999-2000. M.L.Nkala v N 2000-01. M.A.Vermeulen v E 2003. C.B.Mpofu v N 2005-06.

BANGLADESH: Aminul Islam v SL 2002-03. Alamgir Kabir v SL 2002-03. Talha Jubair v SL 2002-03. Alok Kapali v A 2003-04. Khaled Mashud v P 2003-04. Habibul Bashar v Z 2003-04. Tareq Aziz v N 2004-05. Rajin Saleh v I 2004-05. Manjural Islam[2] v I 2004-05. Moshrafe Bin Mortaza v E 2005. Enamul Haque[2] v A 2005-06.

THREE PAIRS IN A MATCH BY THE SAME TEAM

M.B.Poore, I.A.Colquhoun, J A.Hayes	New Zealand	v	England	Auckland	1954-55
D L.Amiss, D L.Underwood, G G.Arnold	England	v	Australia	Adelaide	1974-75
Majid Khan, Wasim Bari, Sikander Bakht	Pakistan	v	Australia	Perth	1978-79
M.S.Ataputta, R.J.Ratnayake, G.F.Labrooy	Sri Lanka	v	India	Chandigarh	1990-91

BATSMEN DISMISSED FOR A 'KING PAIR'

W.Attewell	England	v	Australia	Sydney	1891-92
A.E.E.Vogler	South Africa	v	Australia	Sydney	1910-11
T.A.Ward	South Africa	v	Australia	Manchester	1912
R.J.Crisp	South Africa	v	Australia	Durban[2]	1935-36
I.A.Colquhoun	New Zealand	v	England	Auckland	1954-55
C.Wesley	South Africa	v	England	Nottingham	1960
G.B.Troup	New Zealand	v	India	Wellington	1980-81
D.J.Richardson	South Africa	v	Pakistan	Johannesburg[3]	1994-95
A.G.Huckle	Zimbabwe	v	Pakistan	Harare	1997-98
A.B.Agarkar	India	v	Australia	Melbourne	1999-2000
A.C.Gilchrist	Australia	v	India	Kolkata	2000-01

BATSMEN DISMISSED FOR A PAIR BY THE SAME FIELDING COMBINATION

R.Peel	st Jarvis b Turner	England	v	Australia	Sydney	1894-95
J.Darling	c Braund b Barnes	Australia	v	England	Sheffield	1902
P.T.Lewis	c Woolley b Barnes	South Africa	v	England	Durban[1]	1913-14
P.G.Joshi	c Worrell b Valentine	India	v	West Indies	Bridgetown	1952-53
K.D.Mackay	c Oakman b Laker	Australia	v	England	Manchester	1956
Maninder Singh	c Richardson b Walsh	India	v	West Indies	Bombay[3]	1987-88

G.M.Hamilton	c Pollock b Donald	England	v	South Africa	Johannesburg[3]	1999-2000
C.B.Mpofu	st McCullum b Vettori	Zimbabwe	v	New Zealand	Harare	2005-06

BATSMEN DISMISSED FOR A PAIR ON THE SAME DAY

R.Peel	England	v	Australia	Sydney	1894-95
C.E.McLeod	Australia	v	England	Stdney	1901-02
P.S.Twentyman-Jones	South Africa	v	Australia	Cape Town	1902-03
A.E.E.Vogler	South Africa	v	Australia	Sydney	1910-11
T.A.Ward	South Africa	v	Australia	Manchester	1912
A.V.Bedser	England	v	West Indies	The Oval	1950
Pankaj Roy	India	v	England	Manchester	1952
M.E.Z.Ghazali	Pakistan	v	England	Manchester	1954
R.N.Harvey	Australia	v	England	Manchester	1956
F.M.M.Worrell	West Indies	v	Australia	Melbourne	1960-61
H.K.Olonga	Zimbabwe	v	Sri Lanka	Galle	2001-02
C.S.Martin	New Zealand	v	Pakistan	Lahore[2]	2001-02
M.A.Vermeulen	Zimbabwe	v	England	Chester-le-Street	2003
Manjural Islam[2]	Bangladesh	v	India	Chittagong[1]	2004-05
C.B.Mpofu	Zimbabwe	v	New Zealand	Harare	2005-06

FASTEST PAIRS

Timed from the start of first innings to dismissal in the second innings

120 mins	M.E.Z.Ghazali	Pakistan	v	England	Manchester	1954
124 mins	R.N.Harvey	Australia	v	England	Manchester	1956
152 mins	M.A.Vermeulen	Zimbabwe	v	England	Chester-le-Street	2003
164 mins	Pankaj Roy	India	v	England	Manchester	1952
184 mins	Manjural Islam[2]	Bangladesh	v	India	Chittagong[1]	2004-05

MOST 'DUCKS'

Player	Country	0s	Tests	A	E	SA	W	N	I	P	SL	Z	B
C.A.Walsh	West Indies	**43**	132	13	8	4	-	3	3	8	3	1	-
S.K.Warne	Australia	**34**	139	-	10	4	5	0	6	4	5	0	-
G.D.McGrath	Australia	**33**	117	-	9	5	6	3	3	5	1	0	0
M.Muralidaran	Sri Lanka	**27**	107	4	1	8	3	3	1	4	-	2	1
M.Dillon	West Indies	**26**	38	6	-	5	-	2	6	4	2	-	-
C.E.L.Ambrose	West Indies	**26**	98	8	11	2	-	0	0	5	0	0	-
D.K.Morrison	New Zealand	**24**	48	7	4	1	1	-	2	6	3	-	-
B.S.Chandrasekhar	India	**23**	58	6	8	-	4	3	-	2	-	-	-
M.S.Atapattu	Sri Lanka	**22**	88	2	2	4	1	3	4	4	-	2	0
S.R.Waugh	Australia	**22**	168	-	6	2	3	3	3	5	0	0	0
Waqar Younis	Pakistan	**21**	87	4	2	3	1	3	1	-	3	4	0
B.S.Bedi	India	**20**	67	1	11	-	7	1	-	0	-	-	-
M.A.Atherton	England	**20**	115	7	-	5	5	1	1	1	0	0	-
A.R.Caddick	England	**19**	62	7	-	3	5	1	0	1	2	0	-
Wasim Bari	Pakistan	**19**	81	11	4	-	2	0	2	-	-	-	-
D.L.Underwood	England	**19**	86	8	-	-	7	0	2	1	1	-	-
M.E.Waugh	Australia	**19**	128	-	0	1	4	1	4	4	5	0	-
I.A.Healy	Australia	**18**	119	-	3	1	10	2	0	1	1	0	-
C.S.Martin	New Zealand	**17**	31	4	1	4	3	-	-	5	-	0	0
G.P.Wickramasinghe	Sri Lanka	**17**	40	1	1	0	1	3	2	9	-	0	-
J.A.Snow	England	**17**	49	6	-	1	7	1	1	1	-	-	-
J.Garner	West Indies	**17**	58	4	5	-	-	4	0	4	-	-	-
A.A.Donald	South Africa	**17**	72	4	5	-	5	0	1	2	0	0	-
T.G.Evans	England	**17**	91	5	-	6	1	3	1	1	-	-	-
Wasim Akram	Pakistan	**17**	104	1	1	0	7	1	2	-	3	2	0
D.E.Malcolm	England	**16**	40	6	-	0	3	2	2	3	0	-	-

Danish Kaneria	Pakistan	**16**	40	2	2	2	4	1	4	-	0	-	1
K.R.Rutherford	New Zealand	**16**	56	3	3	2	3	-	1	2	2	-	-
J.E.Emburey	England	**16**	64	5	-	-	6	-	2	1	2	-	-
G.W.Flower	Zimbabwe	**16**	67	0	2	3	2	0	3	3	3	-	0
M.W.Gatting	England	**16**	79	6	-	-	2	2	3	3	0	-	-
D.C.Boon	Australia	**16**	107	-	5	0	3	3	0	2	3	-	-
B.C.Lara	West Indies	**16**	127	5	4	1	-	1	3	1	1	-	-
Kapil Dev	India	**16**	131	3	4	0	4	2	-	2	1	0	-
P.C.R.Tufnell	England	**15**	42	8	-	1	4	0	0	1	1	0	-
Zaheer Khan	India	**15**	42	4	0	2	1	3	-	1	2	2	0
E.A.S.Prasanna	India	**15**	49	7	4	-	2	2	-	0	-	-	-
M.J.Hoggard	England	**15**	58	4	-	2	1	1	4	2	0	0	0
G.D.McKenzie	Australia	**15**	60	-	7	3	1	-	4	0	-	-	-
M.A.Holding	West Indies	**15**	60	5	4	-	-	2	4	-	-	-	-
H.H.Streak	Zimbabwe	**15**	65	1	1	1	1	4	2	4	1	-	0
M.Ntini	South Africa	**15**	69	4	2	-	3	1	1	1	3	-	0
L.R.Gibbs	West Indies	**15**	79	5	5	-	-	0	2	3	-	-	-
M.D.Marshall	West Indies	**15**	81	3	6	-	-	1	2	3	-	-	-
D.B.Vengsarkar	India	**15**	116	1	3	-	5	3	-	2	1	-	-
H.K.Olonga	Zimbabwe	**14**	30	0	3	1	1	2	2	0	5	-	0
P.T.Collins	West Indies	**14**	32	3	2	1	-	0	4	1	3	0	0
D.R.Doshi	India	**14**	33	4	4	-	-	1	-	5	0	-	-
R.M.Hogg	Australia	**14**	38	-	7	-	2	1	3	1	0	-	-
Pankaj Roy	India	**14**	43	8	1	-	2	1	-	2	-	-	-
S.Ramadhin	West Indies	**14**	43	7	6	-	-	1	0	0	-	-	-
S.J.Harmison	England	**14**	44	4	-	4	1	1	1	-	-	1	1
D.W.Randall	England	**14**	47	6	-	-	1	2	3	2	-	-	-
J.R.Thomson	Australia	**14**	51	-	5	-	6	0	2	1	-	-	-
Mushtaq Ahmed	Pakistan	**14**	52	7	2	0	1	1	0	-	1	2	-
D.Gough	England	**14**	58	9	-	1	1	1	-	1	1	0	-
A.Flintoff	England	**14**	61	1	-	4	0	2	4	0	2	0	-
D.L.Vettori	New Zealand	**14**	70	2	2	1	0	-	2	1	4	1	1
M.V.Boucher	South Africa	**14**	95	3	3	-	3	3	0	1	1	0	0
N.Hussain	England	**14**	95	3	-	2	5	0	0	0	1	2	1
I.T.Botham	England	**14**	102	10	-	-	1	1	1	1	0	-	-
S.P.Fleming	New Zealand	**14**	102	6	1	1	0	-	1	3	2	0	0
S.T.Jayasuriya	Sri Lanka	**14**	105	2	1	5	2	1	1	0	-	2	0
A.J.Stewart	England	**14**	133	6	-	2	2	1	2	0	1	0	-
T.M.Alderman	Australia	**13**	41	-	4	-	6	0	-	2	1	-	-
J.G.Bracewell	New Zealand	**13**	41	3	3	-	0	-	2	4	1	-	-
Saqlain Mushtaq	Pakistan	**13**	49	3	0	3	1	2	3	-	0	1	0
C.G.Borde	India	**13**	55	4	4	-	4	0	-	1	-	-	-
S.Venkataraghavan	India	**13**	57	5	2	-	5	1	-	0	-	-	-
F.E.Woolley	England	**13**	64	7	-	6	-	0	0	-	-	-	-
J.Srinath	India	**13**	67	1	1	4	2	2	-	1	0	2	0
J.B.Statham	England	**13**	70	5	-	5	2	0	0	1	-	-	-
J.N.Gillespie	Australia	**13**	71	-	5	2	0	1	2	2	1	0	0
C.J.McDermott	Australia	**13**	71	-	4	0	3	0	3	3	0	-	-
G.Kirsten	South Africa	**13**	101	3	2	-	5	0	1	1	1	0	0
C.L.Hooper	West Indies	**13**	102	5	3	0	-	0	0	5	0	0	-
A.Kumble	India	**13**	110	1	3	1	2	1	-	2	1	2	-
Inzamamul Haq	Pakistan	**13**	112	3	3	1	0	2	1	-	2	0	1
G.A.Gooch	England	**13**	118	5	-	0	3	4	1	0	0	-	-
A.D.Mullally	England	**12**	19	6	-	1	-	2	0	2	0	1	-
R.W.Blair	New Zealand	**12**	19	-	6	4	2	-	-	-	-	-	-
R.C.Motz	New Zealand	**12**	32	-	2	6	0	-	1	3	-	-	-

A.L.Valentine	West Indies	**12**	36	5	4	-	-	1	2	0	-	-	-
M.R.Ramprakash	England	**12**	52	0	-	2	5	2	0	2	1	0	-
E.S.Gregory	Australia	**12**	58	-	11	1	-	-	-	-	-	-	-
C.H.Gayle	West Indies	**12**	61	1	1	1	-	0	3	0	4	2	0
R.D.Jacobs	West Indies	**12**	65	1	2	3	-	0	3	2	0	1	0
M.Amarnath	India	**12**	69	3	3	-	5	0	-	1	0	-	-
M.E.Trescothick	England	**12**	76	2	-	3	1	2	0	2	2	0	0
A.C.Gilchrist	Australia	**12**	84	-	1	2	0	1	4	0	4	0	0
R.J.Hadlee	New Zealand	**12**	86	3	5	-	1	-	3	2	0	-	-
G.S.Chappell	Australia	**12**	87	-	4	-	3	3	1	1	0	-	-
R.G.D.Willis	England	**12**	90	5	-	-	3	1	2	0	1	-	-
G.S.Sobers	West Indies	**12**	93	6	1	-	-	2	2	1	-	-	-
A.Ranatunga	Sri Lanka	**12**	93	1	1	1	-	1	2	6	-	-	-
R.W.Marsh	Australia	**12**	96	-	6	-	1	1	1	3	-	-	-
G.P.Thorpe	England	**12**	100	2	-	4	4	0	0	1	0	0	1
Saleem Malik	Pakistan	**12**	103	4	1	0	1	4	2	-	0	0	-
S.M.Gavaskar	India	**12**	125	3	2	-	5	-	-	1	1	-	-
S.R.Tendulkar	India	**12**	132	4	0	1	3	1	-	2	0	1	0
J.W.Gleeson	Australia	**11**	29	-	5	3	2	-	1	-	-	-	-
Maninder Singh	India	**11**	35	1	0	-	4	-	-	5	1	-	-
S.C.G.MacGill	Australia	**11**	39	-	3	0	5	-	2	0	1	0	0
R.A.McLean	South Africa	**11**	40	3	5	-	-	3	-	-	-	-	-
Khaled Mashud	Bangladesh	**11**	41	1	1	0	2	0	1	4	1	1	-
E.J.Chatfield	New Zealand	**11**	43	0	5	-	1	-	3	2	0	-	-
M.J.K.Smith	England	**11**	50	2	-	2	2	2	3	0	-	-	-
A.V.Bedser	England	**11**	51	5	-	2	3	1	0	0	-	-	-
F.M.M.Worrell	West Indies	**11**	51	8	2	-	-	-	1	-	-	-	-
A.T.W.Grout	Australia	**11**	51	-	4	2	3	-	1	1	-	-	-
D.M.Jones	Australia	**11**	52	-	3	-	1	2	2	3	0	-	-
V.L.Manjrekar	India	**11**	55	4	-	-	5	1	-	1	-	-	-
Harbhajan Singh	India	**11**	57	3	1	1	3	1	-	2	0	0	-
G.A.Hick	England	**11**	65	2	-	0	5	0	1	1	2	0	-
F.S.Trueman	England	**11**	67	6	-	2	1	1	1	0	-	-	-
W.J.Cronje	South Africa	**11**	68	3	5	-	1	0	2	0	0	0	-
I.M.Chappell	Australia	**11**	75	-	5	4	0	0	2	0	-	-	-
N.J.Astle	New Zealand	**11**	79	1	1	0	1	-	2	2	2	2	0
M.L.Hayden	Australia	**11**	83	-	2	6	2	1	0	0	0	0	0
C.G.Greenidge	West Indies	**11**	108	5	3	-	-	0	3	0	-	-	-
A.R.Border	Australia	**11**	156	-	3	0	4	2	2	0	0	-	-
A.G.Hurst	Australia	**10**	12	-	6	-	-	-	2	2	-	-	-
Manjural Islam[1]	Bangladesh	**10**	17	-	-	1	1	2	-	1	3	2	-
A.Nehra	India	**10**	17	3	2	0	3	0	-	0	0	2	0
F.H.Edwards	West Indies	**10**	24	2	4	1	-	1	-	0	0	2	0
P.I.Pocock	England	**10**	25	0	-	-	7	-	3	0	0	-	-
A.N.Connolly	Australia	**10**	29	-	4	1	2	-	3	-	-	-	-
S.L.Boock	New Zealand	**10**	30	0	2	-	3	-	-	5	0	-	1
S.B.Doull	New Zealand	**10**	32	1	2	3	2	-	1	1	0	0	-
J.Briggs	England	**10**	33	9	-	1	-	-	-	-	-	-	-
B.K.Venkatesh Prasad	India	**10**	33	1	0	2	3	2	-	1	1	-	-
Fazal Mahmood	Pakistan	**10**	34	0	3	-	5	0	2	-	-	-	-
A.F.A.Lilley	England	**10**	35	9	-	1	-	-	-	-	-	-	-
D.N.Patel	New Zealand	**10**	37	2	3	0	1	-	-	4	0	0	-
A.A.Mallett	Australia	**10**	38	-	4	-	3	1	1	1	-	-	-
G.R.Dilley	England	**10**	41	2	-	-	5	1	1	1	-	-	-
Shoaib Akhtar	Pakistan	**10**	42	4	1	1	0	1	2	-	1	0	0
I.R.Bishop	West Indies	**10**	43	5	1	-	-	0	1	2	1	-	-

David Gower, a fine batsman and former English captain, made 114 against Australia in Adelaide in December 1982.

Frank Tyson bowled a devastating spell against Australia at the MCG in January 1955, taking 7 for 27 and spearheading England to victory.

Umpire Darrell Hair lifts off the bails after Pakistan refuses to take to the field following ball tampering allegations. The match was subsequently awarded to England, culminating in a controversial end to the fourth and final Test match between England and Pakistan in London in 2006.

South Africa's Graeme Pollock made 122 against Australia at the SCG in 1964. The wicketkeeper is the legendary Wally Grout.

P.A.J.DeFreitas	England	**10**	44	4	-	0	4	1	0	1	0	-	-
I.W.G.Johnson	Australia	**10**	45	-	6	1	1	0	1	1	-	-	-
C.M.Old	England	**10**	46	4	-	-	3	0	0	3	-	-	-
Intikhab Alam	Pakistan	**10**	47	1	4	-	1	3	1	-	-	-	-
D.L.Amiss	England	**10**	50	7	-	-	0	0	2	1	-	-	-
Iqbal Qasim	Pakistan	**10**	50	0	5	-	2	0	3	-	0	-	-
M.G.Hughes	Australia	**10**	53	-	3	1	5	0	1	0	0	-	-
R.W.Taylor	England	**10**	58	3	-	-	-	3	2	2	0	-	-
A.D.R.Campbell	Zimbabwe	**10**	60	0	1	2	1	2	2	1	1	-	0
A.I.Kallicharran	West Indies	**10**	66	1	4	-	-	3	2	0	-	-	-
D.J.Cullinan	South Africa	**10**	70	3	1	-	1	0	1	2	1	1	-
K.J.Hughes	Australia	**10**	70	-	3	-	4	1	1	1	-	-	-
D.K.Lillee	Australia	**10**	70	-	3	-	4	0	0	3	0	-	-
A.R.Butcher	England	**10**	71	3	-	1	3	2	0	-	0	0	1
D.C.S.Compton	England	**10**	78	7	-	1	0	0	1	1	-	-	-
Zaheer Abbas	Pakistan	**10**	78	3	2	-	2	2	1	-	-	-	-
G.R.Viswanath	India	**10**	91	1	3	-	1	2	-	3	0	-	-
S.Chanderpaul	West Indies	**10**	98	1	4	1	-	1	0	3	-	0	0
G.Boycott	England	**10**	108	3	-	1	4	2	0	0	-	-	-
D.L.Haynes	West Indies	**10**	116	1	2	0	-	3	1	3	0	-	-
I.V.A.Richards	West Indies	**10**	121	5	2	-	-	0	1	2	-	-	-

MOST CONSECUTIVE DUCKS

FIVE

R.G.Holland	(including two pairs	Australia	v	England	1985
	in consecutive Tests)	Australia	v	New Zealand	1985-86
A.B.Agarkar	(including two pairs in consecutive Tests)	India	v	Australia	1999-2000†
Mohammad Asif		Pakistan	v	India	2005-06
		Pakistan	v	Sri Lanka	2005-06
		Pakistan	v	England	2006

FOUR

R.Peel	(2 pairs in consecutive Tests)	England	v	Australia	1894-95
R.J.Crisp	(2 pairs in consecutive Tests)	South Africa	v	Australia	1935-36†
Pankaj Roy	(including one pair)	India	v	England	1952
L.S.M.Miller	(including one pair)	New Zealand	v	South Africa	1953-54
R.B.Desai		India	v	England	1959
	(including one pair)	India	v	Australia	1959-60
W.M.Clark	(2 pairs in consecutive Tests)	Australia	v	West Indies	1977-78
P.I.Pocock	(2 pairs in consecutive Tests)	England	v	West Indies	1984
N.A.Foster	(including one pair)	England	v	Australia	1985
		England	v	West Indies	1985-86
R.G.de Alwis	(including one pair)	Sri Lanka	v	India	1986-87
		Sri Lanka	v	Australia	1987-88
M.E.Waugh	(2 pairs in consecutive Tests)	Australia	v	Sri Lanka	1992-93
M.L.Su'a	(including one pair)	New Zealand	v	Sri Lanka	1992-93
		New Zealand	v	Pakistan	1992-93
		New Zealand	v	Australia	1992-93
D.K.Morrison	(including one pair)	New Zealand	v	Australia	1993-94
M.Mbangwa	(including one pair)	Zimbabwe	v	New Zealand	1997-98
		Zimbabwe	v	Pakistan	1997-98
A.D.Mullally	(including one pair)	England	v	Australia	1998-99
G.D.McGrath	(including two pairs)	Australia	v	England	1998-99†
M.Dillon	(including two pairs)	West Indies	v	Australia	1998-99
		West Indies	v	Australia	2000-01

P.T.Collins	(including two pairs)	West Indies	v	Australia	1998-99
		West Indies	v	Sri Lanka	2001-02
C.S.Martin		New Zealand	v	South Africa	2000-01
	(including one pair)	New Zealand	v	Pakistan	2000-01
M.Dillon	(including one pair)	West Indies	v	Pakistan	2001-02
		West Indies	v	New Zealand	2001-02
A.Nel		South Africa	v	Australia	2001-02
D.Ramnarine	(2 'pairs' in consecutive Tests)	West Indies	v	Sri Lanka	2001-02
		West Indies	v	Pakistan	2001-02
	(including one pair)	South Africa	v	Pakistan	2003-04
		South Africa	v	West Indies	2003-04
Shabbir Ahmed	(including one pair)	Pakistan	v	West Indies	2004-05
	(including one pair)	Pakistan	v	England	2005-06

† Agarkar's sequence was 1st ball; 1st ball + 1st ball; 1st ball + 2nd ball. Crisp was dismissed four times in five balls (in his last four Test innings); McGrath was dismissed 2nd ball in each innings.

MOST DUCKS IN A SERIES

					Innings	
SIX	A.G.Hurst	Australia	v	England	12	1978-79
FIVE	Pankaj Roy	India	v	England	7	1952
	N.A.T.Adcock	South Africa	v	Australia	8	1957-58
	R.C.Motz	New Zealand	v	South Africa	9	1961-62
	W.M.Clark	Australia	v	West Indies	7	1977-78
	M.Amarnath	India	v	West Indies	6	1983-84
	A.D.Mullally	England	v	Australia	7	1998-99
	G.D.McGrath	Australia	v	England	7	1998-99
	A.B.Agarkar	India	v	Australia	6	1999-2000
	G.P.Wickramasinghe	Sri Lanka	v	Pakistan	6	1999-2000

MOST INNINGS IN CAREER WITHOUT A DUCK

47	G.O.Jones	England	2003-04	to	2006#
44	J.W.Burke	Australia	1950-51	to	1958-59
40	R.A.Duff	Australia	1901-02	to	1907-08
40	A.B.de Villiers	South Africa	2004-05	to	2006-07#
38	B.P.Patel	India	1974	to	1977-78
37	R.J.Christiani	West Indies	1947-48	to	1953-54
36	D.L.Houghton	Zimbabwe	1992-93	to	1997-98
35	Waqar Hassan	Pakistan	1952-53	to	1959-60
34	B.D.Julien	West Indies	1973	to	1976-77
33	Yasir Hameed	Pakistan	2003-04	to	2004-05#
32	J.W.Zulch	South Africa	1909-10	to	1921-22
32	M.J.Clarke	Australia	2004-05	to	2005-06#
31	H.L.Collins	Australia	1920-21	to	1926
28	P.D.Collingwood	England	2003-04	to	2006#
27	W.W.Read	England	1882-83	to	1893
26	W.Bates	England	1881-82	to	1886-87

 # current player.

MOST INNINGS BEFORE FIRST DUCK

75	P.A.de Silva	Sri Lanka	1984	to	1994-95
58	C.H.Lloyd	West Indies	1966-67	to	1973-74
51	A.K.Davidson	Australia	1953	to	1961
46	B.F.Butcher	West Indies	1958-59	to	1966-67
44	M.J.Slater	Australia	1993	to	1994-95
44	R.T.Ponting	Australia	1995-96	to	1999-2000
41	R.N.Harvey	Australia	1947-48	to	1953
41	G.S.Sobers	West Indies	1953-54	to	1958-59

41	K.D.Ghavri	India	1974-75	to	1979-80
40	W.H.Ponsford	Australia	1924-25	to	1932-33
40	Sadiq Mohammad	Pakistan	1969-70	to	1976-77
40	A.J.Stewart	England	1989-90	to	1992-93
38	M.A.Taylor	Australia	1988-89	to	1990-91
37	A.P.Sheahan	Australia	1967-68	to	1969-70
37	J.C.Adams	West Indies	1991-92	to	1995-96
37	R.S.Dravid	India	1996	to	1998-99
36	J.M.Parks	England	1954	to	1964-65
36	R.G.Nadkarni	India	1955-56	to	1961-62
36	R.W.Barber	England	1960	to	1965-66
36	Imran Farhat	Pakistan	2000-01	to	2006
35	G.A.Faulkner	South Africa	1905-06	to	1912
35	S.M.Katich	Australia	2001	to	2005-06

MOST CONSECUTIVE INNINGS WITHOUT A DUCK

119	D.I.Gower	England	1982	to	1990-91
96	R.B.Richardson	West Indies	1984-85	to	1991
89	A.R.Border	Australia	1982-83	to	1988-89
86	A.J.Stewart	England	1993-94	to	1998-99
78	K.F.Barrington	England	1962	to	1967-68
75	P.A.de Silva	Sri Lanka	1984	to	1994-95
74	C.H.Lloyd	West Indies	1976	to	1984
72	H.W.Taylor	South Africa	1912	to	1931-32
72	G.M.Turner §	New Zealand	1968-69	to	1982-83
72	R.S.Dravid	India	1999-2000	to	2003-04
68	K.D.Walters	Australia	1969-70	to	1976-77
67	W.R.Hammond	England	1929	to	1936
67	G.Boycott	England	1969	to	1978-79
67	M.L.Hayden	Australia	2002-03	to	2005
66	H.A.Gomes	West Indies	1977-78	to	1984-85
63	M.E.Waugh	Australia	1992-93	to	1996-97
63	G.A.Hick	England	1992-93	to	1998
62	A.P.E.Knott	England	1974	to	1981
62	G.R.Marsh	Australia	1986-87	to	1990-91
60	G.A.Gooch	England	1990	to	1994
60	C.L.Hooper	West Indies	1997-98	to	2002-03
60	J.L.Langer	Australia	1998-99	to	2001-02

§ Turner was dismissed for a duck in his first innings & did not make another one in his career.

FEWEST DUCKS IN A CAREER

Ducks	Innings					
0	47	G.O.Jones	England	2003-04	to	2006#
0	44	J.W.Burke	Australia	1950-51	to	1958-59
0	40	R.A.Duff	Australia	1901-02	to	1907-08
0	40	A.B.de Villiers	South Africa	2004-05	to	2006-07#
0	38	B.P.Patel	India	1974	to	1977-78
0	37	R.J.Christiani	West Indies	1947-48	to	1953-54
0	36	D.L.Houghton	Zimbabwe	1992-93	to	1997-98
0	35	Waqar Hassan	Pakistan	1952-53	to	1959-60
0	34	B.D.Julien	West Indies	1973	to	1976-77
1	74	C.L.Walcott	West Indies	1947-48	to	1959-60
1	73	G.M.Turner	New Zealand	1968-69	to	1982-83
1	69	A.L.Hassett	Australia	1938	to	1953
1	65	M.H.Richardson	New Zealand	2000-01	to	2004-05

1	61	A.K.Davidson	Australia	1953	to	1962-63
1	56	P.E.Richardson	England	1956	to	1963
1	55	C.G.Macartney	Australia	1907-08	to	1926
1	53	G.M.Ritchie	Australia	1982-83	to	1986-87
1	48	W.H.Ponsford	Australia	1924-25	to	1934
1	48	E.D.Solkar	India	1969-70	to	1976-77
1	48	W.B.Phillips	Australia	1983-84	to	1985-86
1	46	S.J.Snooke	South Africa	1905-06	to	1922-23
1	46	J.E.Cheetham	South Africa	1948-49	to	1955
1	45	R.W.Barber	England	1960	to	1968
1	42	C.Kelleway	Australia	1910-11	to	1928-29
1	41	R.G.Pollock	South Africa	1963-64	to	1969-70
1	40	A.Shrewsbury	England	1881-82	to	1893
2	84	H.Sutcliffe	England	1924	to	1935
2	83	C.C.McDonald	Australia	1951-52	to	1961
2	78	Saeed Ahmed	Pakistan	1957-58	to	1972-73
2	76	H.W.Taylor	South Africa	1912	to	1931-32
2	74	A.H.Jones	New Zealand	1986-87	to	1994-95
2	66	C.Washbrook	England	1937	to	1956
2	57	K.D.Ghavri	India	1974-75	to	1980-81
2	56	J.B.Stollmeyer	West Indies	1939	to	1954-55
2	53	G.R.J.Matthews	Australia	1983-84	to	1992-93
2	52	N.J.Contractor	India	1955-56	to	1961-62
2	50	P.Willey	England	1976	to	1986
3	93	G.R.Marsh	Australia	1985-86	to	1991-92
3	85	J.V.Coney	New Zealand	1973-74	to	1986-87
3	83	A.W.Nourse	South Africa	1902-03	to	1924
3	80	B.Mitchell	South Africa	1930-31	to	1948-49
3	79	Mohsin Khan	Pakistan	1977-78	to	1986-87
3	78	B.F.Butcher	West Indies	1958-59	to	1969
3	70	G.N.Yallop	Australia	1975-76	to	1984-85
3	70	A.P.Gurusinha	Sri Lanka	1985-86	to	1996-97
4	175	C.H.Lloyd	West Indies	1966-67	to	1984-85
4	140	W.R.Hammond	England	1927-28	to	1946-47
4	125	K.D.Walters	Australia	1965-66	to	1980-81
4	103	K.C.Sangakkara	Sri Lanka	2000-01	20	2006-07#
4	102	J.B.Hobbs	England	1907-08	to	1930
4	100	Mushtaq Mohammad	Pakistan	1958-59	to	1978-79
5	186	M.A.Taylor	Australia	1988-89	to	1998-99
5	174	R.S.Dravid	India	1996	to	2005-06#
5	147	M.Azharuddin	India	1984-85	to	1999-2000
5	138	L.Hutton	England	1937	to	1954-55
5	131	K.F.Barrington	England	1955	to	1968
6	189	Javed Miandad	Pakistan	1976-77	to	1993-94
7	204	D.I.Gower	England	1978	to	1992

Partnerships

HIGHEST PARTNERSHIP FOR EACH WICKET

1st	413	M.H.Mankad (231), Pankaj Roy (173)	IND	v	NZ	Madras[2]	1955-56
2nd	576	S.T.Jayasuriya (340), R.S.Mahanama (225)	SL	v	IND	Colombo (RPS)	1997-98
3rd	624	K.C.Sangakarra (287), D.P.M.D.Jayawardene (375)	SL	v	SA	Colombo(SSC)	2006-07
4th	411	P.B.H.May (285*), M.C.Cowdrey (154)	ENG	v	WI	Birmingham	1957
5th	405	S.G.Barnes (234), D.G.Bradman (234)	AUS	v	ENG	Sydney	1946-47
6th	346	J.H.W.Fingleton (136), D.G.Bradman (270)	AUS	v	ENG	Melbourne	1936-37
7th	347	D.S.Atkinson (219), C.C.Depeiza (122)	WI	v	AUS	Bridgetown	1954-55
8th	313	Wasim Akram (257*), Saqlain Mushtaq (78)	PAK	v	ZIM	Sheikhupura	1996-97
9th	195	M.V.Boucher (78), P.L.Symcox (108)	SA	v	PAK	Johannesburg[3]	1997-98
10th	151	B.F.Hastings (110), R.O.Collinge (68*)	NZ	v	PAK	Auckland	1972-73
	151	Azhar Mahmood (128*), Mushtaq Ahmed (59)	PAK	v	SA	Rawalpindi[2]	1997-98

PARTNERSHIPS OF 300 AND OVER

Runs	Wkt				
624	3rd	K.C.Sangakarra (287), D.P.M.D.Jayawardene (375)	SL v SA	Colombo(SSC)	2006-07
576	2nd	S.T.Jayasuriya (340), R.S.Mahanama (225)	SL v IND	Colombo (RPS)	1997-98
467	3rd	A.H.Jones (186), M.D.Crowe (299)	NZ v SL	Wellington	1990-91
363	3rd	Younis Khan (173), Yousuf Youhana (192)	PAK v ENG	Leeds	2006
451	2nd	W.H.Ponsford (266), D.G.Bradman (244)	AUS v ENG	The Oval	1934
451	3rd	Mudassar Nazar (231), Javed Miandad (280*)	PAK v IND	Hyderabad	1982-83
438	2nd	M.S.Atapattu (249), K.C.Sangakkara (270)	SL v ZIM	Bulawayo[2]	2003-04
446	2nd	C.C.Hunte (260), G.S.Sobers (365*)	WI v PAK	Kingston	1957-58
429*	3rd	J.A.Rudolph (222*), H.H.Dippenaar (178*)	SA v BAN	Chittagong[1]	2002-03
413	1st	M.H.Mankad (231), Pankaj Roy (173)	IND v NZ	Madras[2]	1955-56
411	4th	P.B.H.May (285*), M.C.Cowdrey (154)	ENG v WI	Birmingham	1957
410	1st	V.K.Sehwag (254), R.S.Dravid (128*)	IND v PAK	Lahore[2]	2005-06
405	5th	S.G.Barnes (234), D.G.Bradman (234)	AUS v ENG	Sydney	1946-47
399	4th	G.S.Sobers (226), F.M.M.Worrell (197*)	WI v E	Bridgetown	1959-60
397	3rd	Qasim Omar (206), Javed Miandad (203*)	PAK v SL	Faisalabad	1985-86
388	4th	W.H.Ponsford (181), D.G.Bradman (304)	AUS v ENG	Leeds	1934
387	1st	G.M.Turner (259), T.W.Jarvis (182)	NZ v WI	Georgetown	1971-72
385	5th	S.R.Waugh (160), G.S.Blewett (214*)	AUS v SA	Johannesburg[3]	1996-97
382	2nd	L.Hutton (364), M.Leyland (187)	ENG v AUS	The Oval	1938
382	1st	W.M.Lawry (210), R.B.Simpson (201)	AUS v WI	Bridgetown	1964-65
376	5th	V.V.S.Laxman (281), R.S.Dravid (180)	IND v AUS	Kolkata	2000-01
370	3rd	W.J.Edrich (189), D.C.S.Compton (208)	ENG v SA	Lord's	1947
369	2nd	J.H.Edrich (310*), K.F.Barrington (163)	ENG v NZ	Leeds	1965
368	1st	G.C.Smith (151), H.H.Gibbs (228)	SA v PAK	Cape Town	2002-03
359	1st	L.Hutton (158), C.Washbrook (195)	ENG v SA	Johannesburg[2]	1948-49
353	4th	S.R.Tendulkar (241*), V.V.S.Laxman (178)	IND v AUS	Sydney	2003-04
352*§	3rd	Ijaz Ahmed (211), Inzamamul Haq (200*)	PAK v SL	Dhaka	1998-99
351	2nd	G.A.Gooch (196), D.I.Gower (157)	ENG v AUS	The Oval	1985
350	4th	Mushtaq Mohammad (201), Asif Iqbal (175)	PAK v NZ	Dunedin	1972-73
347	7th	D.S.Atkinson (219), C.C.Depeiza (122)	WI v AUS	Bridgetown	1954-55
346	6th	J.H.W.Fingleton (136), D.G.Bradman (270)	AUS v ENG	Melbourne	1936-37
344*	2nd	S.M.Gavaskar (182*), D.B.Vengsarkar (157*)	IND v WI	Calcutta	1978-79
341	3rd	E.J.Barlow (201), R.G.Pollock (175)	SA v AUS	Adelaide	1963-64
338	3rd	E.D.Weekes (206), F.M.M.Worrell (167)	WI v ENG	Port-of-Spain	1953-54
338	1st	G.C.Smith (277), H.H.Gibbs (179)	SA v ENG	Birmingham	2003
336	4th	W.M.Lawry (151), K.D.Walters (242)	AUS v WI	Sydney	1968-69
336	3rd	V.K.Sehwag (309), S.R.Tendulkar (194*)	IND v PAK	Multan[2]	2003-04
335	1st	M.S.Atapattu (207*), S.T.Jayasuriya (188)	SL v PAK	Kandy	1999-2000

332*	5th	A.R.Border (200*), S.R.Waugh (157*)	AUS v ENG	Leeds	1993
331	2nd	R.T.Robinson (148), D.I.Gower (215)	ENG v AUS	Birmingham	1985
331	2nd	C.H.Gayle (317), R.R.Sarwan (127)	WI v SA	St John's	2004-05
329	1st	G.R.Marsh (138), M.A.Taylor (219)	AUS v ENG	Nottingham	1989
327	5th	J.L.Langer (144), R.T.Ponting (197)	AUS v PAK	Perth	1999-2000
324	3rd	Younis Khan (267), Inzamamul Haq (184)	PAK v IND	Bangalore	2004-05
323	1st	J.B.Hobbs (178), W.Rhodes (179)	ENG v AUS	Melbourne	1911-12
323	3rd	Aamer Sohail (160), Inzamamul Haq (177)	PAK v WI	Rawalpindi[2]	1997-98
322	4th	Javed Miandad (153*), Saleem Malik (165)	PAK v ENG	Birmingham	1992
322	5th	B.C.Lara (213), J.C.Adams (94)	WI v AUS	Kingston	1998-99
320	4th	J.N.Gillespie (201*), M.E.K.Hussey (182)	AUS v BAN	Chittagong[2]	2005-06
319	3rd	A.Melville (189), A.D.Nourse (149)	SA v ENG	Nottingham	1947
319	3rd	Younis Khan (199), Yousuf Youhana (173)	PAK v IND	Lahore[2]	2005-06
317	6th	D.R.Martyn (133), A.C.Gilchrist (204*)	AUS v SA	Johannesburg[3]	2001-02
316†	3rd	G.R.Viswanath (222), Yashpal Sharma (140)	IND v ENG	Madras[1]	1981-82
315*	2nd	H.H.Gibbs (211*), J.H.Kallis (148*)	SA v NZ	Christchurch	1998-99
315	3rd	R.T.Ponting (206), D.S.Lehmann (160)	AUS v WI	Port-of-Spain	2002-03
313	8th	Wasim Akram (257*), Saqlain Mushtaq (78)	PAK v ZIM	Sheikhupura	1996-97
308	7th	Waqar Hassan (189), Imtiaz Ahmed (209)	PAK v NZ	Lahore[1]	1955-56
308	3rd	R.B.Richardson (154), I.V.A.Richards (178)	WI v AUS	St Johns	1983-84
308	3rd	G.A.Gooch (333), A.J.Lamb (139)	ENG v IND	Lord's	1990
303	3rd	I.V.A.Richards (232), A.I.Kallicharran (97)	WI v ENG	Nottingham	1976
303	3rd	M.A.Atherton (135), R.A.Smith (175)	ENG v WI	St John's	1993-94
303	5th	R.S.Dravid (233), V.V.S.Laxman (148)	IND v AUS	Adelaide	2003-04
301	2nd	A.R.Morris (182), D.G.Bradman (173*)	AUS v ENG	Leeds	1948
301	1st	G.C.Smith (139), H.H.Gibbs (192)	SA v WI	Centurion	2003-04

§ 366 runs were added for this wicket in two separate partnerships, Inzamamul Haq retiring hurt and being succeeded by Yousuf Youhana after 352 runs had been scored. † 415 runs were scored for this wicket in two separate partnerships, D.B.Vengsarkar retiring hurt and being succeeded by Yashpal Sharma after 99 runs had been added.

MOST CENTURY PARTNERSHIPS IN AN INNINGS

FOUR		Opponents		
England	382 (2nd), 135 (3rd), 215 (6th), 106 (7th)	Australia	The Oval	1938
West Indies	267 (4th), 101 (6th), 118 (7th), 106 (9th)	India	Delhi	1948-49
Pakistan	152 (1st), 112 (2nd), 154 (3rd), 121 (4th)	West Indies	Bridgetown	1957-58
India	144 (3rd), 172 (4th), 109 (5th), 102 (6th)	West Indies	Kanpur	1978-79

SUMMARY OF CENTURY PARTNERSHIPS

Country	1st	2nd	3rd	4th	5th	6th	7th	8th	9th	10th	Total
Australia	96	143	133	130	102	62	30	16	8	4	724
England	162	156	141	137	85	80	38	14	8	4	825
South Africa	55	43	57	45	22	25	19	16	3	1	286
West Indies	59	70	84	87	64	59	18	2	4	1	448
New Zealand	34	36	39	37	36	21	18	12	2	4	239
India	56	71	78	64	55	32	21	13	7	2	399
Pakistan	39	45	65	57	33	34	14	5	7	3	302
Sri Lanka	15	15	41	26	31	19	6	5	2	0	160
Zimbabwe	10	9	5	13	6	9	7	4	0	0	63
Bangladesh	1	10	1	5	2	0	0	0	0	0	19
Total	527	598	644	601	436	341	171	87	41	19	3465

BATSMEN SHARING IN MOST CENTURY PARTNERSHIPS

Player	Country	Total	1st	2nd	3rd	4th	5th	6th	7th	8th	9th	10th
S.R.Waugh	Australia	**64**	0	1	1	20	23	12	4	1	2	0
A.R.Border	Australia	**63**	0	2	15	20	16	8	1	1	0	0
R.S.Dravid	India	**63**	1	22	20	7	9	2	0	2	0	0
B.C.Lara	West Indies	**60**	0	6	25	20	5	3	1	0	0	0
S.R.Tendulkar	India	**59**	0	0	26	13	13	4	2	0	0	1
S.M.Gavaskar	India	**58**	22	18	8	6	2	1	0	0	1	0
R.T.Ponting	Australia	**57**	0	27	8	4	15	2	1	1	0	0
Javed Miandad	Pakistan	**50**	0	2	22	15	8	3	0	0	0	0
J.L.Langer	Australia	**48**	14	18	5	5	3	3	0	0	0	0
G.Boycott	England	**47**	20	8	9	8	0	2	0	0	0	0
M.E.Waugh	Australia	**47**	0	0	25	12	7	2	1	0	0	0
C.G.Greenidge	West Indies	**46**	22	9	5	4	2	3	1	0	0	0
M.A.Atherton	England	**45**	23	11	5	4	0	2	0	0	0	0
G.Kirsten	South Africa	**45**	13	14	8	5	2	1	0	2	0	0
G.S.Chappell	Australia	**44**	0	2	15	13	11	2	1	0	0	0
I.V.A.Richards	West Indies	**44**	0	11	12	12	5	2	1	1	0	0
D.C.Boon	Australia	**43**	6	13	16	5	1	1	0	1	0	0
M.L.Hayden	Australia	**43**	18	14	6	2	1	2	0	0	0	0
G.S.Sobers	West Indies	**43**	0	3	4	12	12	10	2	0	0	0
M.C.Cowdrey	England	**42**	5	9	6	13	4	3	1	0	1	0
Inzamamul Haq	Pakistan	**42**	0	1	15	15	5	4	2	0	0	0
G.A.Gooch	England	**41**	18	11	7	2	2	1	0	0	0	0
L.Hutton	England	**41**	17	13	7	1	0	2	1	0	0	0
C.H.Lloyd	West Indies	**41**	0	0	6	14	9	10	1	0	1	0
S.Chanderpaul	West Indies	**40**	0	2	3	9	16	10	0	0	0	0
D.L.Haynes	West Indies	**40**	18	15	5	1	0	1	0	0	0	0
M.A.Taylor	Australia	**40**	17	13	5	3	1	1	0	0	0	0
D.I.Gower	England	**39**	0	7	10	11	5	3	2	1	0	0
J.H.Kallis	South Africa	**38**	0	7	17	8	3	1	0	2	0	0
A.J.Stewart	England	**37**	7	7	3	9	8	1	0	1	0	1
N.Hussain	England	**36**	0	8	13	10	4	0	1	0	0	0
D.P.M.D.Jayawardene	Sri Lanka	**36**	0	0	18	8	8	0	0	2	0	0
M.E.Trescothick	England	**36**	19	10	4	2	1	0	0	0	0	0
K.F.Barrington	England	**35**	0	6	10	14	4	1	0	0	0	0
D.G.Bradman	Australia	**35**	0	14	11	3	6	1	0	0	0	0
P.A.de Silva	Sri Lanka	**35**	0	0	16	10	5	3	1	0	0	0
G.P.Thorpe	England	**35**	0	0	7	13	6	6	3	0	0	0
R.B.Kanhai	West Indies	**34**	2	9	11	7	3	2	0	0	0	0
W.R.Hammond	England	**33**	1	6	12	11	2	1	0	0	0	0
H.Sutcliffe	England	**33**	21	10	1	0	0	1	0	0	0	0
Yousuf Youhana	Pakistan	**32**	0	0	7	17	2	4	1	0	1	0
M.Azharuddin	India	**32**	0	1	3	14	7	4	2	1	0	0
J.H.Edrich	England	**32**	9	11	6	5	1	0	0	0	0	0
R.N.Harvey	Australia	**32**	0	6	13	9	3	1	0	0	0	0
J.B.Hobbs	England	**32**	24	6	1	0	0	0	1	0	0	0
S.C.Ganguly	India	**31**	0	1	4	12	11	1	1	1	0	0
M.S.Atapattu	Sri Lanka	**30**	9	7	10	2	1	1	0	0	0	0
I.M.Chappell	Australia	**30**	0	18	8	1	1	2	0	0	0	0
D.C.S.Compton	England	**30**	0	0	14	7	7	1	0	1	0	0
A.Ranatunga	Sri Lanka	**30**	0	0	1	11	12	6	0	0	0	0
D.B.Vengsarkar	India	**30**	0	9	9	9	1	2	0	0	0	0
Yousuf Youhana	Pakistan	**32**	0	0	7	17	2	4	1	0	1	0

The most for the other countries are:

S.P.Fleming	New Zealand	**29**	1	3	9	7	2	5	0	2	0	0
A.Flower	Zimbabwe	**18**	0	0	0	11	3	3	1	0	0	0
Habibul Bashar	Bangladesh	**13**	0	9	0	4	0	0	0	0	0	0

HIGHEST WICKET PARTNERSHIPS FOR EACH COUNTRY

AUSTRALIA

1st	382	W.M.Lawry (210), R.B.Simpson (201)	v	West Indies	Bridgetown	1964-65
2nd	451	W.H.Ponsford (266), D.G.Bradman (244)	v	England	The Oval	1934
3rd	315	R.T.Ponting (206), D.S.Lehmann (160)	v	West Indies	Port-of-Spain	2002-03
4th	388	W.H.Ponsford (181), D.G.Bradman (304)	v	England	Leeds	1934
5th	405	S.G.Barnes (234), D.G.Bradman (234)	v	England	Sydney	1946-47
6th	346	J.H.W.Fingleton (136), D.G.Bradman (270)	v	England	Melbourne	1936-37
7th	217	K.D.Walters (250), G.J.Gilmour (101)	v	New Zealand	Christchurch	1976-77
8th	243	R.J.Hartigan (116), C.Hill (160)	v	England	Adelaide	1907-08
9th	154	S.E.Gregory (201), J.M.Blackham (74)	v	England	Sydney	1894-95
10th	127	J.M.Taylor (108), A.A.Mailey (46*)	v	England	Sydney	1924-25

ENGLAND

1st	359	L.Hutton (158), C.Washbrook (195)	v	South Africa	Johannesburg[2]	1948-49
2nd	382	L.Hutton (364), M.Leyland (187)	v	Australia	The Oval	1938
3rd	370	W.J.Edrich (189), D.C.S.Compton (208)	v	South Africa	Lord's	1947
4th	411	P.B.H.May (285*), M.C.Cowdrey (154)	v	West Indies	Birmingham	1957
5th	254	K.W.R.Fletcher (113), A.W.Greig (148)	v	India	Bombay[2]	1972-73
6th	281	G.P.Thorpe (200*), A.Flintoff (137)	v	New Zealand	Christchurch	2001-02
7th	197	M.K.J.Smith (96), J.M.Parks (101*)	v	West Indies	Port-of-Spain	1959-60
8th	246	L.E.G.Ames (137), G.O.B.Allen (122)	v	New Zealand	Lord's	1931
9th	163*	M.C.Cowdrey (128*), A.C.Smith (69*)	v	New Zealand	Wellington	1962-62
10th	130	R.E.Foster (287), W.Rhodes (40*)	v	Australia	Sydney	1903-04

SOUTH AFRICA

1st	368	G.C.Smith (151), H.H.Gibbs (228)	v	Pakistan	Cape Town	2002-03
2nd	315*	H.H.Gibbs (211*), J.H.Kallis (148*)	v	New Zealand	Christchurch	1998-99
3rd	429*	J.A.Rudolph (222*), H.H.Dippenaar (178*)	v	Bangladesh	Chittagong[1]	2002-03
4th	249	J.H.Kallis (177), G.Kirsten (137)	v	West Indies	Durban[2]	2003-04
5th	267	J.H.Kallis (147), A.G.Prince (131)	v	West Indies	St John's	2004-05
6th	200	R.G.Pollock (274), H.R.Lance (61)	v	Australia	Durban[2]	1969-70
7th	246	D.J.McGlew (255*), A.R.A.Murray (109)	v	New Zealand	Wellington	1952-53
8th	150	N.D.McKenzie (103), S.M.Pollock (111)	v	Sri Lanka	Centurion	2000-01
	150	G.Kirsten (130), M.Zondeki (59)	v	England	Leeds	2003
9th	195	M.V.Boucher (78), P.L.Symcox (108)	v	Pakistan	Johannesburg[3]	1997-98
10th	103	H.G.Owen-Smith (129), A.J.Bell (26*)	v	England	Leeds	1929

WEST INDIES

1st	298	C.G.Greenidge (149), D.L.Haynes (167)	v	England	St John's	1989-90
2nd	446	C.C.Hunte (260), G.S.Sobers (365*)	v	Pakistan	Kingston	1957-58
3rd	338	E.D.Weekes (206), F.M.M.Worrell (167)	v	England	Port-of-Spain	1953-54
4th	399	G.S.Sobers (226), F.M.M.Worrell (197*)	v	England	Bridgetown	1959-60
5th	322	B.C.Lara (213), J.C.Adams (94)	v	Australia	Kingston	1998-99
6th	282*	B.C.Lara (400*), R.D.Jacobs (107*)	v	England	St John's	2003-04
7th	347	D.S.Atkinson (219), C.C.Depeiza (122)	v	Australia	Bridgetown	1954-55
8th	148	J.C.Adams (101*), F.A.Rose (69)	v	Zimbabwe	Kingston	1999-00
9th	161	C.H.Lloyd (161*), A.M.E.Roberts (68)	v	India	Calcutta	1983-84
10th	106	C.L.Hooper (178*), C.A.Walsh (30)	v	Pakistan	St John's	1992-93

NEW ZEALAND

1st	387	G.M.Turner (259), T.W.Jarvis (182)	v	West Indies	Georgetown	1971-72
2nd	241	J.G.Wright (116), A.H.Jones (143)	v	England	Wellington	1991-92
3rd	467	A.H.Jones (186), M.D.Crowe (299)	v	Sri Lanka	Wellington	1990-91
4th	243	M.J.Horne (157), N.J.Astle (114)	v	Zimbabwe	Auckland	1997-98
5th	222	N.J.Astle (141), C.D.McMillan (142)	v	Zimbabwe	Wellington	2000-01
6th	246*	J.J.Crowe (120*), R.J.Hadlee (151*)	v	Sri Lanka	Colombo (CCC)	1986-87
7th	225	C.L.Cairns (158), J.D.P.Oram (90)	v	South Africa	Auckland	2003-04
8th	256	S.P.Fleming (262), J.E.C.Franklin (122*)	v	South Africa	Cape Town	2005-06
9th	136	I.D.S.Smith (173), M.C.Snedden (22)	v	India	Auckland	1989-90
10th	151	B.F.Hastings (110), R.O.Collinge (68*)	v	Pakistan	Auckland	1972-73

INDIA

1st	413	M.H.Mankad (231), Pankaj Roy (173)	v	New Zealand	Madras[2]	1955-56
2nd	344*	S.M.Gavaskar (182*), D.B.Vengsarkar (157*)	v	West Indies	Calcutta	1978-79
3rd	336	V.K.Sehwag (309), S.R.Tendulkar (194*)	v	Pakistan	Multan[2]	2003-04
4th	353	S.R.Tendulkar (241*), V.V.S.Laxman (178)	v	Australia	Sydney	2003-04
5th	376	V.V.S.Laxman (281), R.S.Dravid (180)	v	Australia	Calcutta	2000-01
6th	298*	D.B.Vengsarkar (164*), R.J.Shastri (121*)	v	Australia	Bombay[3]	1986-87
7th	235	R.J.Shastri (142), S.M.H.Kirmani (102)	v	England	Bombay[2]	1984-85
8th	161	M.Azharuddin (109), A.Kumble (88)	v	South Africa	Calcutta	1996-97
9th	149	P.G.Joshi (52*), R.B.Desai (85)	v	Pakistan	Bombay[2]	1960-61
10th	133	S.R.Tendulkar (248*), Zaheer Khan (75)	v	Bangladesh	Dhaka	2004-05

PAKISTAN

1st	298	Aamer Sohail (160), Ijaz Ahmed (151)	v	West Indies	Karachi[1]	1997-98
2nd	291	Zaheer Abbas (274), Mushtaq Mohammad (100)	v	England	Birmingham	1971
3rd	451	Mudassar Nazar (231), Javed Miandad (280*)	v	India	Hyderabad	1982-83
4th	350	Mushtaq Mohammad (201), Asif Iqbal (175)	v	New Zealand	Dunedin	1972-73
5th	281	Javed Miandad (163), Asif Iqbal (166)	v	New Zealand	Lahore[2]	1976-77
6th	269	Yousuf Youhana (223), Kamran Akmal (223)	v	England	Lahore[2]	2005-06
7th	308	Waqar Hassan (189), Imtiaz Ahmed (209)	v	New Zealand	Lahore[1]	1955-56
8th	313	Wasim Akram (257*), Saqlain Mushtaq (78)	v	Zimbabwe	Sheikhupura	1996-97
9th	190	Asif Iqbal (146), Intikhab Alam (51)	v	England	The Oval	1967
10th	151	Azhar Mahmood (128*), Mushtaq Ahmed (59)	v	South Africa	Rawalpindi[2]	1997-98

SRI LANKA

1st	335	M.S.Atapattu (207), S.T.Jayasuriya (188)	v	Pakistan	Kandy	1999-00
2nd	576	S.T.Jayasuriya (340), R.S.Mahanama (225)	v	India	Colombo (RPS)	1997-98
3rd	624	K.C.Sangakarra (287), D.P.M.D.Jayawardene (375)	v	South Africa	Colombo(SSC)	2006-07
4rd	262	T.T.Samaraweera (142), D.P.M.D.Jayawardene (134)	v	England	Colombo (SSC)	2003-04
5th	240*	A.P.Gurusinha (116*), A.Ranatunga (135*)	v	Pakistan	Colombo (PSS)	1985-86
6th	280	T.T.Samaraweera (138), T.M.Dilshan (168)	v	Bangladesh	Colombo (PSS)	2005-06
7th	189*	P.A.de Silva (143*), A.Ranatunga (87*)	v	Zimbabwe	Colombo (SSC)	1997-98
8th	194*	H.P.Tillakaratne (136*), T.T.Samaraweera (103*)	v	India	Colombo (SSC)	2001-02
9th	170	D.P.M.D.Jayawardene (237), W.P.U.J.C.Vaas (69)	v	South Africa	Galle	2004-05
10th	105	W.P.U.J.C.Vaas (50*), K.M.D.Kulasekara (64)	v	England	Lord's	2006

ZIMBABWE

1st	164	D.D.Ebrahim (75), A.D.R.Campbell (106)	v	West Indies	Bulawayo[2]	2000-01
2nd	135	M.H.Dekker (68*), A.D.R.Campbell (75)	v	Pakistan	Rawalpindi[2]	1993-94
3rd	194	A.D.R.Campbel (99), C.L.Houghton (142)	v	Sri Lanka	Harare	1994-95
4th	269	G.W.Flower (201*), A.Flower (156)	v	Pakistan	Harare	1994-95
5th	277*	M.W.Goodwin (166*), A.Flower (100*)	v	Pakistan	Bulawayo[2]	1997-98
6th	165	D.L.Houghton (121), A.Flower (59)	v	India	Harare	1992-93
7th	154	H.H.Streak (83*), A.M.Blignaut (92)	v	West Indies	Harare	2000-01

8th	168	H.H.Streak (127*), A.M.Blignaut (91)	v	West Indies	Harare	2003-04
9th	87	P.A.Strang (106*), B.C.Strang (42)	v	Pakistan	Sheikhupura	1996-97
10th	97*	A.Flower (183*), H.K.Olonga (11*)	v	India	Delhi	2000-01

BANGLADESH

1st	133	Javed Omer (43), Nafis Iqbal (121)	v	Zimbabwe	Dhaka	2004-05
2nd	187	Shahriar Nafees (138), Habibul Bashar (76)	v	Australia	Fatullah	2005-06
3rd	84	Javed Omer (62), Aminul Islam (84)	v	Zimbabwe	Bulawayo[2]	2000-01
4th	120	Habibul Bashar (77), Manjural Islam[2] (35)	v	West Indies	Kingston	2003-04
5th	126	Aminul Islam (56), Mohammad Ashraful (114)	v	Sri Lanka	Colombo (SSC)	2001-02
6th	97	Mohammad Ashraful (98), Mushfiqur Rahman (44)	v	Zimbabwe	Harare	2003-04
7th	93	Aminul Islam (145), Khaled Mashud (32)	v	India	Dhaka	2000-01
8th	87	Mohammad Ashraful (81), Mohammad Rafique (111)	v	West Indies	Gros Islet	2003-04
9th	74	Khaled Mashud (103*), Tapash Baisya (26)	v	West Indies	Gros Islet	2003-04
10th	69	Mohammad Rafique (65), Shahadat Hossain (3*)	v	Australia	Chittagong[2]	2005-06

Bowling

TWO HUNDRED TEST WICKETS

Opponents

Player (Country)	Tests	Wkts	Avge	A	E	SA	WI	NZ	I	P	SL	Z	B
S.K.Warne (A)	139	**679**	25.37	-	172	130	65	103	43	90	59	6	11
M.Muralidaran (SL)	106	**652**	21.89	50	93	104	70	52	66	78	-	87	50
G.D.McGrath (A)	118	**539**	21.59	-	136	57	107	57	51	80	37	6	5
A.Kumble (I)	110	**533**	28.82	88	78	66	74	50	-	62	66	38	10
C.A.Walsh (W)	132	**519**	24.44	135	145	51	-	43	65	63	8	9	-
Kapil Dev (I)	131	**434**	29.64	79	85	8	89	25	-	99	45	4	-
R.J.Hadlee (N)	86	**431**	22.29	130	97	-	51	-	65	51	37	-	-
Wasim Akram (P)	104	**414**	23.62	50	57	13	79	60	45	-	63	47	0
C.E.L.Ambrose (W)	98	**405**	20.99	128	164	21	-	13	15	42	14	8	-
S.M.Pollock (SA)	102	**395**	23.42	40	91	-	65	43	39	37	48	23	9
I.T.Botham (E)	102	**383**	28.40	148	-	-	61	64	59	40	11	-	-
M.D.Marshall (W)	81	**376**	20.94	87	127	-	-	36	76	50	-	-	-
Waqar Younis (P)	87	**373**	23.56	30	50	24	55	70	8	-	56	62	18
Imran Khan (P)	88	**362**	22.81	64	47	-	80	31	94	-	46	-	-
D.K.Lillee (A)	70	**355**	23.92	-	167	-	55	38	21	71	3	-	-
A.A.Donald (SA)	72	**330**	22.25	53	86	-	43	21	57	27	29	14	-
R.G.D.Willis (E)	90	**325**	25.20	128	-	-	38	60	62	34	3	-	-
L.R.Gibbs (W)	79	**309**	29.09	103	100	-	-	11	63	32	-	-	-
F.S.Trueman (E)	67	**307**	21.57	79	-	27	86	40	53	22	-	-	-
W.P.U.J.C.Vaas (SL)	94	**307**	29.51	37	38	27	43	36	25	46	-	48	7
D.L.Underwood (E)	86	**297**	25.83	105	-	-	38	48	62	36	8	-	-
C.J.McDermott (A)	71	**291**	28.63	-	84	21	59	48	34	18	27	-	-
M.Ntini (SA)	69	**274**	28.28	39	54	-	53	40	11	17	35	6	19
B.S.Bedi (I)	67	**266**	28.71	56	85	-	62	57	-	6	-	-	-
J.Garner (W)	58	**259**	20.97	89	92	-	-	36	7	35	-	-	-
J.N.Gillespie (A)	71	**259**	26.13	-	65	24	50	26	43	10	12	10	19
J.B.Statham (E)	70	**252**	24.84	69	-	69	42	20	25	27	-	-	-
M.A.Holding (W)	60	**249**	23.68	76	96	-	-	16	61	-	-	-	-
R.Benaud (A)	63	**248**	27.03	-	83	52	42	-	52	19	-	-	-
G.D.McKenzie (A)	60	**246**	29.78	-	96	41	47	-	47	15	-	-	-
B.S.Chandrasekhar (I)	58	**242**	29.74	38	95	-	65	36	-	8	-	-	-
Harbhajan Singh (I)	57	**238**	29.81	56	33	16	45	17	-	15	21	31	4
A.V.Bedser (E)	51	**236**	24.89	104	-	54	11	13	44	10	-	-	-
J.Srinath (I)	67	**236**	30.49	30	17	64	25	33	-	17	17	30	3
Abdul Qadir (P)	67	**236**	32.80	45	82	-	42	26	27	-	14	-	-
G.S.Sobers (W)	93	**235**	34.03	51	102	-	-	19	59	4	-	-	-
A.R.Caddick (E)	62	**234**	29.91	64	-	16	53	47	7	23	16	8	-
D.Gough (E)	58	**229**	28.39	74	-	43	31	25	-	24	16	16	-
R.R.Lindwall (A)	61	**228**	23.03	-	114	31	41	2	36	4	-	-	-
M.J.Hoggard (E)	58	**222**	29.79	22	-	26	29	26	36	27	30	3	23
C.L.Cairns (N)	62	**218**	29.40	39	47	9	17	-	19	16	19	39	13
D.L.Vettori (N)	70	**218**	34.61	51	26	15	23	-	19	4	31	23	26
C.V.Grimmett (A)	37	**216**	24.21	-	106	77	33	-	-	-	-	-	-
H.H.Streak (Z)	65	**216**	28.17	7	24	3	21	32	24	44	39	-	20
M.G.Hughes (A)	53	**212**	28.38	-	75	4	53	25	23	16	16	-	-
B.Lee (A)	53	**209**	31.29	-	42	49	46	32	21	5	-	6	8
Saqlain Mushtaq (P)	49	**208**	29.83	30	24	18	22	18	25	-	34	28	9
A.M.E.Roberts (W)	47	**202**	25.61	51	50	-	-	3	67	31	-	-	-
J.A.Snow (E)	49	**202**	26.66	83	-	4	72	20	16	7	-	-	-
J.R.Thomson (A)	51	**200**	28.00	-	100	-	62	6	22	10	-	-	-

LEADING WICKET TAKERS FOR EACH COUNTRY

AUSTRALIA	Tests	Balls	Runs	Wkts	Avge	5wi	10w	Best
S.K.Warne	139	39070	17226	679	25.37	36	10	8/71
G.D.McGrath	118	27885	11642	539	21.59	28	3	8/24
D.K.Lillee	70	18467	8493	355	23.92	23	7	7/83
C.J.McDermott	71	16586	8332	291	28.63	14	2	8/97
J.N.Gillespie	71	14234	6770	259	26.13	8	0	7/37
R.Benaud	63	19108	6704	248	27.03	16	1	7/72
G.D.McKenzie	60	17681	7328	246	29.78	16	3	8/71
R.R.Lindwall	61	13650	5251	228	23.03	12	0	7/38
C.V.Grimmett	37	14513	5231	216	24.21	21	7	7/40
M.G.Hughes	53	12285	6017	212	28.38	7	1	8/87
B.Lee	53	10990	6541	209	31.29	7	0	5/30
J.R.Thomson	51	10535	5601	200	28.00	8	0	6/46
S.C.G.MacGill	39	10066	5305	189	28.06	11	2	8/108
A.K.Davidson	44	11587	3819	186	20.53	14	2	7/93
G.F.Lawson	46	11118	5501	180	30.56	11	2	8/112
K.R.Miller	55	10461	3906	170	22.97	7	1	7/60
T.M.Alderman	41	10181	4616	170	27.15	14	1	6/47
W.A.Johnston	40	11048	3826	160	23.91	7	0	6/44
W.J.O'Reilly	27	10024	3254	144	22.59	11	3	7/54
H.Trumble	32	8099	3072	141	21.78	9	3	8/65
M.H.N.Walker	34	10094	3792	138	27.47	6	0	8/143
A.A.Mallett	38	9990	3940	132	29.84	6	1	8/59
B.Yardley	33	8909	3986	126	31.63	6	1	7/98
R.M.Hogg	38	7633	3503	123	28.47	6	2	6/74
M.A.Noble	42	7159	3025	121	25.00	9	2	7/17
B.A.Reid	27	6244	2784	113	24.63	5	2	7/51
M.S.Kasprowicz	38	7158	3716	113	32.88	4	0	7/36
I.W.G.Johnson	45	8780	3182	109	29.19	3	0	7/44
P.R.Reiffel	35	6403	2804	104	26.96	5	0	6/71
G.Giffen	31	6391	2791	103	27.09	7	1	7/117
A.N.Connolly	29	7818	2981	102	29.22	4	0	6/47
C.T.B.Turner	17	5179	1670	101	16.53	11	2	7/43

ENGLAND	Tests	Balls	Runs	Wkts	Avge	5wi	10w	Best
I.T.Botham	102	21815	10878	383	28.40	27	4	8/34
R.G.D.Willis	90	17357	8190	325	25.20	16	0	8/43
F.S.Trueman	67	15178	6625	307	21.57	17	3	8/31
D.L.Underwood	86	21862	7674	297	25.83	17	6	8/51
J.B.Statham	70	16056	6261	252	24.84	9	1	7/39
A.V.Bedser	51	15918	5876	236	24.89	15	5	7/44
A.R.Caddick	62	13558	6999	234	29.91	13	1	7/46
D.Gough	58	11819	6503	229	28.39	9	0	6/42
M.J.Hoggard	58	12168	6607	222	29.76	6	1	7/61
J.A.Snow	49	12021	5387	202	26.66	8	1	7/40
J.C.Laker	46	12027	4101	193	21.24	9	3	10/53
S.F.Barnes	27	7873	3106	189	16.43	24	7	9/103
A.Flintoff	61	11536	5720	179	31.95	2	0	5/58
S.J.Harmison	44	9683	5053	175	28.87	8	1	7/12
G.A.R.Lock	49	13147	4451	174	25.58	9	3	7/35
M.W.Tate	39	12523	4055	155	26.16	7	1	6/42
F.J.Titmus	53	15118	4931	153	32.22	7	0	7/79
A.R.C.Fraser	39	9295	4104	150	27.36	10	1	8/53
J.E.Emburey	65	15571	5728	147	38.96	6	0	7/78
H.Verity	40	11173	3510	144	24.37	5	2	8/43

C.M.Old	46	8858	4020	143	28.11	4	0	7/50
A.W.Greig	58	9802	4541	141	32.20	6	2	8/86
P.A.J.DeFreitas	44	9838	4700	140	33.57	4	0	7/70
A.F.Giles	52	11688	5544	140	39.60	5	0	5/57
G.R.Dilley	41	8192	4107	138	29.76	6	0	6/38
T.E.Bailey	61	9712	3856	132	29.21	5	1	7/34
D.G.Cork	37	7678	3906	131	29.81	5	0	7/43
D.E.Malcolm	40	8468	4748	128	37.09	5	2	9/57
W.Rhodes	58	8231	3425	127	26.96	6	1	8/68
P.H.Edmonds	51	12028	4273	125	34.18	2	0	7/66
D.A.Allen	39	11297	3779	122	30.97	4	0	5/30
R.Illingworth	61	11934	3807	122	31.20	3	0	6/29
P.C.R.Tufnell	42	11288	4560	121	37.68	5	2	7/47
J.Briggs	33	5332	2094	118	17.74	9	4	8/11
G.G.Arnold	34	7650	3254	115	28.29	6	0	6/45
G.A.Lohmann	18	3821	1205	112	10.75	9	5	9/28
D.V.P.Wright	34	8135	4224	108	39.11	6	1	7/105
J.H.Wardle	28	6597	2080	102	20.39	5	1	7/36
R.Peel	20	5216	1715	101	16.98	5	1	7/31
C.Blythe	19	4546	1863	100	18.63	9	4	8/59

SOUTH AFRICA	Tests	Balls	Runs	Wkts	Avge	5wi	10w	Best
S.M.Pollock	102	25172	9253	395	23.42	16	1	7/87
M.Ntini	69	14598	7751	274	28.28	14	4	7/37
A.A.Donald	72	15519	7344	330	22.25	20	3	8/71
J.H.Kallis	101	13529	6304	199	31.67	4	0	6/54
H.J.Tayfield	37	13568	4405	170	25.91	14	2	9/113
P.R.Adams	45	8850	4405	134	32.87	4	1	7/128
N.Boje	43	8620	4265	100	42.65	3	0	5/62
T.L.Goddard	41	11736	3226	123	26.22	5	0	6/53
P.M.Pollock	28	6522	2806	116	24.18	9	1	6/38
N.A.T.Adcock	26	6391	2195	104	21.10	5	0	6/43

WEST INDIES	Tests	Balls	Runs	Wkts	Avge	5wi	10w	Best
C.A.Walsh	132	30019	12688	519	24.44	22	3	7/37
C.E.L.Ambrose	98	22103	8501	405	20.99	22	3	8/45
M.D.Marshall	81	17585	7876	376	20.94	22	4	7/22
L.R.Gibbs	79	27115	8989	309	29.09	18	2	8/38
J.Garner	58	13175	5433	259	20.97	7	0	6/56
M.A.Holding	60	12680	5898	249	23.68	13	2	8/92
G.S.Sobers	93	21599	7999	235	34.03	6	0	6/73
A.M.E.Roberts	47	11136	5174	202	25.61	11	2	7/54
W.W.Hall	48	10421	5066	192	26.38	9	1	7/69
I.R.Bishop	43	8407	3910	161	24.28	6	0	6/40
S.Ramadhin	43	13939	4579	158	28.98	10	1	7/49
A.L.Valentine	36	12953	4215	139	30.32	8	2	8/104
M.Dillon	38	8710	4406	131	33.63	2	0	5/71
C.E.H.Croft	27	6165	2913	125	23.30	3	0	8/29
V.A.Holder	40	9095	3627	109	33.27	3	0	6/28
P.T.Collins	32	6964	3671	106	34.63	3	0	6/53

NEW ZEALAND	Tests	Balls	Runs	Wkts	Avge	5wi	10w	Best
R.J.Hadlee	86	21918	9611	431	22.29	36	9	9/52
C.L.Cairns	62	11698	6410	218	29.40	13	1	7/27
D.L.Vettori	70	17072	7547	218	34.61	12	2	7/87
D.K.Morrison	48	10064	5549	160	34.68	10	0	7/89
B.L.Cairns	43	10628	4279	130	32.91	6	1	7/74
E.J.Chatfield	43	10360	3958	123	32.17	3	1	6/73

	Tests	Balls	Runs	Wkts	Avge	5wi	10w	Best
R.O.Collinge	35	7689	3393	116	29.25	3	0	6/63
B.R.Taylor	30	6334	2953	111	26.60	4	0	7/74
J.G.Bracewell	41	8403	3653	102	35.81	4	1	6/32
R.C.Motz	32	7034	3148	100	31.48	5	0	6/63
INDIA	Tests	Balls	Runs	Wkts	Avge	5wi	10w	Best
A.Kumble	110	34445	15363	533	28.82	33	8	10/74
Kapil Dev	131	28741	12867	434	29.64	23	2	9/83
B.S.Bedi	67	21367	7637	266	28.71	14	1	7/98
B.S.Chandrasekhar	58	15963	7199	242	29.74	16	2	8/79
J.Srinath	67	15104	7196	236	30.49	10	1	8/86
Harbhajan Singh	57	15062	7097	238	29.81	19	4	8/84
E.A.S.Prasanna	49	14353	5742	189	30.38	10	2	8/76
M.H.Mankad	44	14686	5236	162	32.32	8	2	8/52
S.Venkataraghavan	57	14877	5634	156	36.11	3	1	8/72
R.J.Shastri	80	15751	6187	151	40.97	2	0	5/75
S.P.Gupte	36	11284	4403	149	29.55	12	1	9/102
Zaheer Khan	42	7967	4399	121	36.35	3	0	5/29
D.R.Doshi	33	9322	3502	114	30.71	6	0	6/102
K.D.Ghavri	39	7042	3656	109	33.54	4	0	5/33
N.S.Yadav	35	8349	3580	102	35.09	3	0	5/76
PAKISTAN	Tests	Balls	Runs	Wkts	Avge	5wi	10w	Best
Wasim Akram	104	22627	9779	414	23.62	25	5	7/119
Waqar Younis	87	16224	8788	373	23.56	22	5	7/76
Imran Khan	88	19458	8258	362	22.81	23	6	8/58
Abdul Qadir	67	17126	7742	236	32.80	15	5	9/56
Saqlain Mushtaq	49	14070	6206	208	29.83	13	3	8/164
Mushtaq Ahmed	52	12532	6100	185	32.97	10	3	7/56
Sarfraz Nawaz	55	13931	5798	177	32.75	4	1	9/86
Iqbal Qasim	50	13019	4807	171	28.11	8	2	7/49
Danish Kaneria	40	11035	5566	169	32.93	11	2	7/77
Shoaib Akhtar	42	7490	4239	165	25.69	12	2	6/11
Fazal Mahmood	34	9834	3434	139	24.70	13	4	7/42
Intikhab Alam	47	10474	4494	125	35.92	5	2	7/52
SRI LANKA	Tests	Balls	Runs	Wkts	Avge	5wi	10w	Best
M.Muralidaran	107	35816	14275	652	21.89	56	18	9/51
W.P.U.J.C.Vaas	94	20414	9062	307	29.51	11	2	7/71
S.T.Jayasuriya	105	7966	3271	96	34.07	2	0	5/34
G.P.Wickramasinghe	40	7260	3559	85	41.87	3	0	6/60
R.J.Ratnayake	23	4961	2563	73	35.11	5	0	6/66
H.D.P.K.Dharmasena	31	6939	2920	69	42.31	3	0	6/72
D.N.T.Zoysa	30	4422	2157	64	33.70	1	0	5/20
C.R.D.Fernando	24	3496	2201	69	31.89	3	0	5/42
S.L.Malinga	19	3165	2034	62	32.80	1	0	5/80
A.L.F.de Mel	17	3518	2180	59	36.94	3	0	6/109
K.R.Pushpakumara	23	3792	2242	58	38.65	4	0	7/116
J.R.Ratnayeke	22	3833	1972	56	35.21	4	0	8/83
ZIMBABWE	Tests	Balls	Runs	Wkts	Avge	5wi	10w	Best
H.H.Streak	65	13535	6085	216	28.17	7	0	6/73
P.A.Strang	24	5714	2522	70	36.02	4	1	4/109
R.W.Price	18	5135	2475	69	35.87	5	1	6/73
H.K.Olonga	30	4502	2620	68	38.52	2	0	5/70
B.C.Strang	26	5432	2203	56	39.33	1	0	5/101
A.M.Blignaut	19	3185	1964	54	36.37	3	0	5/73
G.J.Whittall	46	4686	2088	51	40.94	0	0	4/18

BANGLADESH	Tests	Balls	Runs	Wkts	Avge	5wi	10w	Best
Mohammad Rafique	26	7233	3184	87	36.59	7	0	6/77
Mashrafe Bin Mortaza	20	3560	1874	50	37.48	0	0	4/60
Tapash Baisya	21	2476	2137	36	59.36	0	0	4/72
Enamul Haque[2]	10	2385	1198	32	37.43	3	1	7/95
Manjural Islam[1]	17	2970	1605	28	57.32	1	0	6/81

MOST ECONOMICAL CAREER BOWLING *(Qualification: 25 wickets)*

Player	Country	Runs/100 balls	Tests	Balls	Runs	Wkts	Avge
W.Attewell	England	**21.96**	10	2850	626	28	22.35
T.L.Goddard	South Africa	**27.49**	41	11736	3226	123	26.22
R.G.Nadkarni	India	**27.92**	41	9165	2559	88	29.07
H.Ironmonger	Australia	**28.33**	14	4695	1330	74	17.97
J.C.Watkins	South Africa	**29.09**	15	2805	816	29	28.13
K.D.Mackay	Australia	**29.71**	37	5792	1721	50	34.42
G.E.Gomez	West Indies	**30.37**	29	5236	1590	58	27.41
P.R.Umrigar	India	**31.17**	59	4725	1473	35	42.08
R.G.Barlow	England	**31.23**	17	2456	767	34	22.55
H.Verity	England	**31.42**	40	11173	3510	144	24.37
E.R.H.Toshack	Australia	**31.50**	12	3140	989	47	21.04
J.H.Wardle	England	**31.53**	28	6597	2080	102	20.39
G.A.Lohmann	England	**31.54**	18	3821	1205	112	10.75
D.S.Atkinson	West Indies	**31.67**	22	5201	1647	47	35.04
R.Illingworth	England	**31.85**	61	11934	3801	122	31.20

LEAST ECONOMICAL CAREER BOWLING *(Qualification: 100 wickets)*

Player	Country	Runs/100 balls	Tests	Balls	Runs	Wkts	Avge
B.Lee	Australia	**59.52**	53	10990	6541	209	31.29
Shoaib Akhtar	Pakistan	**56.60**	42	7490	4239	165	25.69
D.E.Malcolm	England	**55.99**	40	8480	4748	128	37.09
Zaheer Khan	India	**55.22**	42	7967	4399	121	36.35
D.K.Morrison	New Zealand	**55.14**	48	10064	5549	160	34.68
D.Gough	England	**55.01**	58	11821	6503	229	28.40
C.L.Cairns	New Zealand	**54.79**	62	11698	6410	218	29.40
M.J.Hoggard	England	**54.30**	58	12168	6607	222	29.76
Waqar Younis	Pakistan	**54.17**	87	16224	8788	373	23.56
P.T.Collins	West Indies	**53.23**	31	6718	3576	104	34.38
J.R.Thomson	Australia	**53.18**	51	10535	5601	200	28.00
M.Ntini	South Africa	**53.10**	69	14598	7751	274	28.28
S.C.G.MacGill	Australia	**52.70**	39	10066	5305	189	28.06
K.D.Ghavri	India	**51.96**	39	7036	3656	109	33.54
D.V.P.Wright	England	**51.92**	34	8135	4224	108	39.11
M.S.Kasprowicz	Australia	**51.91**	38	7158	3716	113	32.88
A.R.Caddick	England	**51.62**	62	13558	6999	234	29.91
S.J.Harmison	England	**52.18**	44	9683	5053	175	28.87
D.G.Cork	England	**50.73**	34	6472	3283	105	31.26
M.Dillon	West Indies	**50.58**	38	8710	4406	131	33.63
Danish Kaneria	Pakistan	**50.44**	40	11035	5566	169	32.93
C.J.McDermott	Australia	**50.24**	71	16586	8332	291	28.63
G.R.Dilley	England	**50.13**	41	8192	4107	138	29.76

BEST STRIKE RATES *(Qualification: 25 wickets)*

Player	Country	Balls/wkt	Tests	Balls	Runs	Wkts	Avge
G.A.Lohmann	England	**34.11**	18	3821	1205	112	10.75
A.E.Trott	Australia/England	**36.46**	5	948	390	26	15.00
M.J.Proctor	South Africa	**36.92**	7	1514	616	41	15.02
J.J.Ferris	Australia/England	**37.73**	9	2302	775	61	12.70
Mohammad Asif	Pakistan	**38.63**	6	1159	635	30	21.16
S.E.Bond	New Zealand	**38.72**	14	2478	1378	64	21.53
B.J.T.Bosanquet	England	**38.80**	7	970	604	25	24.16
G.F.Bissett	South Africa	**39.56**	4	989	469	25	18.76
S.F.Barnes	England	**41.65**	27	7873	3106	189	16.43
A.E.E.Vogler	South Africa	**43.18**	15	2764	1455	64	22.73
E.A.Martindale	West Indies	**43.37**	10	1809	1045	43	24.30
Waqar Younis	Pakistan	**43.49**	87	16224	8788	373	23.56

WORST STRIKE RATES *(Qualification: 50 wickets)*

Player	Country	Balls/wkt	Tests	Balls	Runs	Wkts	Avge
C.L.Hooper	West Indies	**120.95**	120	13788	5635	114	49.43
K.D.Mackay	Australia	**115.84**	37	5792	1721	50	34.42
N.J.Astle	New Zealand	**110.47**	79	5634	2099	51	41.15
C.G.Borde	India	**109.52**	55	5695	2417	52	46.48
J.E.Emburey	England	**104.70**	64	15391	5646	147	38.41
R.J.Bright	Australia	**104.55**	25	5541	2180	53	41.13
R.J.Shastri	India	**104.31**	80	15751	6185	151	40.96
R.G.Nadkarni	India	**104.15**	41	9165	2559	88	29.08
F.M.M.Worrell	West Indies	**103.49**	51	7141	2672	69	38.72
G.R.J.Matthews	Australia	**102.80**	33	6271	2942	61	48.23
H.J.Howarth	New Zealand	**102.71**	30	8833	3178	86	36.95
K.J.O'Keeffe	Australia	**101.58**	24	5384	2018	53	38.08
H.D.P.K.Dharmasena	Sri Lanka	**100.56**	31	6939	2920	69	42.31
N.B.F.Mann	South Africa	**99.93**	19	5796	1920	58	33.10
P.I.Pocock	England	**99.25**	25	6650	2976	67	44.42
F.J.Titmus	England	**98.81**	53	15118	4931	153	32.23
R.Illingworth	England	**97.82**	61	11934	3801	122	31.20
B.C.Strang	Zimbabwe	**97.00**	26	5432	2203	56	39.34
R.B.Simpson	Australia	**96.92**	62	6881	3001	71	42.27
D.G.Phadkar	India	**96.68**	31	5994	2285	62	36.85
P.H.Edmonds	England	**96.22**	51	12028	4273	125	34.18
A.M.B.Rowan	South Africa	**96.17**	15	5193	2084	54	38.59
W.R.Hammond	England	**96.01**	85	7969	3138	83	37.81

BEST BOWLING AVERAGES *(Qualification: 25 wickets)*

Player	Country	Tests	Balls	Runs	Wkts	Avge	5wi	10w
G.A.Lohmann	England	18	3821	1205	112	**10.75**	9	5
J.J.Ferris	Australia/England	9	2302	775	61	**12.70**	6	1
A.E.Trott	Australia/England	5	948	390	26	**15.00**	2	0
M.J.Proctor	South Africa	7	1514	616	41	**15.02**	1	0
W.Barnes	England	21	2289	793	51	**15.54**	3	0
W.Bates	England	15	2364	821	50	**16.42**	4	1
S.F.Barnes	England	27	7873	3106	189	**16.43**	24	7
C.T.B.Turner	Australia	17	5179	1670	101	**16.53**	11	2
R.Peel	England	20	5216	1715	101	**16.98**	5	1
J.Briggs	England	33	5332	2094	118	**17.74**	9	4
R.Appleyard	England	9	1596	534	31	**17.87**	1	0
W.S.Lees	England	5	1256	467	26	**17.96**	2	0
H.Ironmonger	Australia	14	4695	1330	74	**17.97**	4	2

G.B.Lawrence	South Africa	5	1334	512	28	**18.28**	2	0
F.R.Spofforth	Australia	18	4185	1731	94	**18.41**	7	4
F.H.Tyson	England	17	3452	1413	76	**18.56**	4	1
C.Blythe	England	19	4446	1863	100	**18.63**	9	4
G.F.Bissett	South Africa	4	989	469	25	**18.76**	2	0
A.S.Kennedy	England	5	1683	599	31	**19.32**	2	0

WORST BOWLING AVERAGES *(Qualification: 50 wickets)*

Player	Country	Tests	Balls	Runs	Wkts	Avge	5wi	10w
C.L.Hooper	West Indies	102	13788	5625	114	**49.43**	4	0
Mohammad Sami	Pakistan	28	5982	3531	73	**48.37**	2	0
G.R.J.Matthews	Australia	33	6271	2942	61	**48.23**	2	1
P.J.Wiseman	New Zealand	25	5660	2903	61	**47.59**	2	0
A.B.Agarkar	India	26	4857	2745	58	**47.32**	1	0
C.G.Borde	India	55	5695	2417	52	**46.48**	1	0
P.I.Pocock	England	25	6650	2976	67	**44.42**	3	0
F.H.Edwards	West Indies	24	4045	2675	62	**43.14**	4	0
N.Boje	South Africa	43	8620	4265	100	**42.65**	3	0
H.D.P.K.Dharmasena	Sri Lanka	31	6939	2920	69	**42.31**	3	0
R.B.Simpson	Australia	62	6881	3001	71	**42.27**	2	0
D.N.Patel	New Zealand	37	6594	3154	75	**42.05**	3	0
G.P.Wickramasinghe	Sri Lanka	40	7260	3559	85	**41.87**	3	0
M.E.Waugh	Australia	128	4853	2429	59	**41.17**	1	0
N.J.Astle	New Zealand	79	5634	2099	51	**41.15**	0	0
R.J.Bright	Australia	25	5541	2180	53	**41.13**	4	1
R.J.Shastri	India	80	15751	6185	151	**40.96**	2	0
G.J.Whittall	Zimbabwe	46	4686	2088	51	**40.94**	0	0
S.Madan Lal	India	39	5997	2846	71	**40.08**	4	0

MOST FIVE WICKETS IN AN INNINGS

Player	Country	5wkts	Tests	A	E	SA	W	N	I	P	SL	Z	B
M.Muralidaran	Sri Lanka	**56**	107	5	6	11	8	4	4	5	-	6	7
R.J.Hadlee	New Zealand	**36**	86	14	8	-	4	-	4	4	2	-	-
S.K.Warne	Australia	**36**	139	-	10	7	3	3	1	6	4	0	1
A.Kumble	India	**33**	110	9	4	3	4	3	-	4	4	2	0
I.T.Botham	England	**27**	102	9	-	-	3	6	6	2	1	-	-
G.D.McGrath	Australia	**28**	118	-	9	2	8	2	2	3	2	0	0
Wasim Akram	Pakistan	**25**	104	4	2	0	4	6	2	-	3	4	0
S.F.Barnes	England	**24**	27	12	-	12	-	-	-	-	-	-	-
D.K.Lillee	Australia	**23**	70	-	11	-	3	4	0	5	0	-	-
Imran Khan	Pakistan	**23**	88	3	4	-	6	1	6	-	3	-	-
Kapil Dev	India	**23**	131	7	4	0	4	0	-	7	1	0	-
M.D.Marshall	West Indies	**22**	81	7	6	-	-	1	6	2	-	-	-
Waqar Younis	Pakistan	**22**	87	0	3	1	3	5	0	-	4	5	1
C.E.L.Ambrose	West Indies	**22**	98	8	8	2	-	1	1	1	1	0	-
C.A.Walsh	West Indies	**22**	132	4	5	2	-	3	4	4	0	0	-
C.V.Grimmett	Australia	**21**	37	-	11	8	2	-	-	-	-	-	-
A.A.Donald	South Africa	**20**	72	2	9	-	2	0	3	1	2	1	-
Harbhajan Singh	India	**19**	57	7	3	1	5	0	-	1	1	1	0
L.R.Gibbs	West Indies	**18**	79	6	7	-	-	0	4	1	-	-	-
F.S.Trueman	England	**17**	67	5	-	1	6	2	2	1	-	-	-
D.L.Underwood	England	**17**	86	4	-	-	1	6	1	4	1	-	-
B.S.Chandrasekhar	India	**16**	58	3	8	-	4	1	-	0	-	-	-
G.D.McKenzie	Australia	**16**	60	-	6	3	2	-	4	1	-	-	-
R.Benaud	Australia	**16**	63	-	4	5	1	-	5	1	-	-	-
R.G.D.Willis	England	**16**	90	7	-	-	2	3	3	1	0	-	-

S.M.Pollock	South Africa	**16**	102	1	3	-	4	1	2	3	1	1	0
A.V.Bedser	England	**15**	51	7	-	3	1	0	4	0	-	-	-
Abdul Qadir	Pakistan	**15**	67	3	8	-	1	2	0	-	1	-	-
H.J.Tayfield	South Africa	**14**	37	4	7	-	-	3	-	-	-	-	-
T.M.Alderman	Australia	**14**	41	-	11	-	1	0	-	2	0	-	-
A.K.Davidson	Australia	**14**	44	-	5	2	5	-	2	0	-	-	-
B.S.Bedi	India	**14**	67	5	4	-	1	4	-	0	-	-	-
M.Ntini	South Africa	**14**	69	2	2	-	5	4	0	0	0	0	1
C.J.McDermott	Australia	**14**	71	-	8	0	1	1	3	1	0	-	-
Fazal Mahmood	Pakistan	**13**	34	4	2	-	3	0	4	-	-	-	-
A.R.C.Fraser	England	**13**	46	3	-	3	5	0	2	-	-	-	-
Saqlain Mushtaq	Pakistan	**13**	49	1	1	1	2	0	4	-	1	2	1
M.A.Holding	West Indies	**13**	60	5	6	-	-	0	2	-	-	-	-
A.R.Caddick	England	**13**	62	4	-	1	5	3	0	0	0	0	-
C.L.Cairns	New Zealand	**13**	62	1	4	-	2	-	0	1	2	2	1
S.P.Gupte	India	**12**	36	0	1	-	4	4	-	3	-	-	-
Shoaib Akhtar	Pakistan	**12**	42	3	1	1	1	3	0	-	2	0	1
R.R.Lindwall	Australia	**12**	61	-	6	2	2	0	2	0	-	-	-
D.L.Vettori	New Zealand	**12**	70	6	0	0	0	-	1	0	2	0	3
T.Richardson	England	**11**	14	14	-	-	-	-	-	-	-	-	-
C.T.B.Turner	Australia	**11**	17	-	17	-	-	-	-	-	-	-	-
W.J.O'Reilly	Australia	**11**	27	-	8	2	-	1	-	-	-	-	-
S.C.G.MacGill	Australia	**11**	39	-	3	0	2	-	0	2	0	0	4
Danish Kaneria	Pakistan	**11**	40	2	0	1	1	1	2	-	1	-	3
G.F.Lawson	Australia	**11**	46	-	7	-	2	0	-	2	0	-	-
A.M.E.Roberts	West Indies	**11**	47	2	4	-	-	0	4	1	-	-	-
W.P.U.J.C.Vaas	Sri Lanka	**11**	94	1	1	1	3	4	0	1	-	0	0
S.Ramadhin	West Indies	**10**	43	1	5	-	-	3	1	0	-	-	-
D.K.Morrison	New Zealand	**10**	48	2	1	0	2	-	3	1	1	-	-
E.A.S.Prasanna	India	**10**	49	5	0	-	1	4	-	0	-	-	-
Mushtaq Ahmed	Pakistan	**10**	52	2	2	1	2	3	0	-	0	0	-
J.Srinath	India	**10**	67	0	0	4	0	2	-	2	1	1	0

The most for Zimbabwe is 7 by H.H.Streak in 65 Tests; and for Bangladesh 7 in 26 Tests by Mohammad Rafique.

MOST WICKETS IN A CAREER WITHOUT TAKING FIVE WICKETS IN AN INNINGS

Player	Country	Tests	Balls	Mdns	Runs	Wkts	Avge	Best
M.Hendrick	ENG	30	6208	249	2248	87	25.83	4/28
B.M.McMillan	SAF	38	6048	255	2537	75	33.82	4/65
D.R.Hadlee	NZ	26	4883	114	2389	71	33.64	4/30
B.R.Knight	ENG	29	5377	204	2223	70	31.75	4/38
E.R.Dexter	ENG	62	5317	186	2306	66	34.93	4/10
W.K.M.Benjamin	WI	21	3694	136	1648	61	27.01	4/46
Wasim Raja	PAK	57	4082	134	1826	51	35.80	4/50
G.J.Whittall	ZIM	46	4686	208	2088	51	40.94	4/18
N.J.Astle	NZ	79	5634	315	2099	51	41.15	3/27
Mashrafe Bin Mortaze	BAN	20	3560	134	1874	50	37.48	4/60
J.C.Alabaster	NZ	21	3992	178	2863	49	38.02	4/46
R.K.Chauhan	IND	21	4749	238	1857	47	39.51	4/48
B.L.D'Oliveira	ENG	44	5706	318	1859	47	39.55	3/46
Saleem Altaf	PAK	21	4001	122	1710	46	37.17	4/11
W.W.Davis	WI	15	2773	53	1472	45	32.71	4/19
W.M.Clark	AUS	10	2793	63	1264	44	28.72	4/46
A.Nehra	IND	17	3447	122	1866	44	42.40	4/72
N.A.M.McLean	WI	19	3299	85	1873	44	42.56	3/53
W.J.Cronje	SA	68	3800	243	1288	43	29.95	3/14
C.E.Cuffy	WI	15	3366	145	1455	43	33.83	4/82

R.W.Blair	NZ	19	3525	114	1515	43	35.23	4/85
R.W.Barber	ENG	28	3426	101	1806	42	43.00	4/132
A.W.Nourse	SA	45	3234	120	1553	41	37.87	4/25
S.D.Anurasiri	SL	18	3973	150	1548	41	37.75	4/71
W.J.Edrich	ENG	39	3234	81	1693	41	41.29	4/68
V.Pollard	NZ	32	4421	207	1853	40	46.32	3/3

THIRTY-FIVE WICKETS IN A TEST SERIES

Player (Country)	Opp	Season	Tests	Balls	Mdns	Runs	Wkts	Avge	5wi	10w	Best
S.F.Barnes (E)	SA	1913-14	4	1356	56	536	49	10.93	7	3	9/103
J.C.Laker (E)	Aus	1956	5	1703	127	442	46	9.60	4	2	10/53
C.V.Grimmett (A)	SA	1935-36	5	2077	140	642	44	14.59	5	3	7/40
T.M.Alderman (A)	Eng	1981	6	1950	76	893	42	21.26	4	0	6/135
R.M.Hogg (A)	Eng	1978-79	6	1740	60	527	41	12.85	5	2	6/74
T.M.Alderman (A)	Eng	1989	6	1622	68	712	41	17.36	6	1	6/128
Imran Khan (P)	Ind	1982-83	6	1339	69	558	40	13.95	4	2	8/60
S.K.Warne (A)	Eng	2005	5	1517	37	797	40	19.92	3	2	6/46
A.V.Bedser (E)	Aus	1953	5	1591	58	682	39	17.48	5	1	7/44
D.K.Lillee (A)	Eng	1981	6	1870	81	870	39	22.30	2	1	7/89
M.W.Tate (E)	Aus	1924-25	5	2528	62	881	38	23.18	5	1	6/99
W.J.Whitty (A)	SA	1910-11	5	1395	55	632	37	17.08	2	0	6/17
H.J.Tayfield (SA)	Eng	1956-57	5	2280	105	636	37	17.18	4	1	9/113
G.D.McGrath (A)	Eng	1997	6	1499	67	701	36	19.47	2	0	8/38
A.E.E.Vogler (SA)	Eng	1909-10	5	1349	33	783	36	21.75	4	1	7/94
A.A.Mailey (A)	Eng	1920-21	5	1465	27	946	36	26.27	4	2	9/121
G.A.Lohmann (E)	SA	1895-96	3	520	38	203	35	5.80	4	2	9/28
M.D.Marshall (W)	Eng	1988	5	1219	49	443	35	12.66	3	1	7/22
B.S.Chandrasekhar (I)	Eng	1972-73	5	1747	83	662	35	18.91	4	0	8/79

MOST WICKETS IN A TEST SERIES FOR EACH COUNTRY

(§ in first series. # in last series. † in only series.)

AUSTRALIA	Opp	Season	Tests	Balls	Mdns	Runs	Wkts	Avge	5wi	10w	Best
C.V.Grimmett #	SA	1935-36	5	2077	140	642	44	14.59	5	3	7/40
T.M.Alderman §	ENG	1981	6	1950	76	893	42	21.26	4	0	6/135
R.M.Hogg §	ENG	1978-79	6	1740	60	527	41	12.85	5	2	6/74
T.M.Alderman	ENG	1989	6	1622	68	712	41	17.36	6	1	6/128
S.K.Warne	ENG	2005	5	1517	37	797	40	19.92	3	2	6/46
D.K.Lillee	ENG	1981	6	1870	81	870	39	22.30	2	1	7/89
W.J.Whitty	SA	1910-11	5	1395	55	632	37	17.08	2	0	6/17
G.D.McGrath	ENG	1997	6	1499	67	701	36	19.47	2	0	8/38
A.A.Mailey §	ENG	1920-21	5	1465	27	946	36	26.27	4	2	9/121
G.F.Lawson	ENG	1982-83	5	1384	51	687	34	20.20	4	1	6/47
G.Giffen	ENG	1894-95	5	2060	111	820	34	24.11	3	0	6/155
S.K.Warne	ENG	1993	6	2639	178	877	34	25.79	1	0	5/82
C.V.Grimmett	SA	1931-32	5	1836	108	557	33	16.87	3	1	7/83
J.R.Thomson	ENG	1974-75	5	1401	34	592	33	17.93	2	0	6/46
C.V.Grimmett	WI	1930-31	5	1433	60	593	33	17.96	2	1	7/87
A.K.Davidson	WI	1960-61	4	1391	25	612	33	18.54	5	1	6/53
G.D.McGrath	ENG	2001	5	1166	56	542	32	16.93	4	0	7/76
M.A.Noble	ENG	1901-02	5	1380	68	608	32	19.00	4	1	7/17
C.J.McDermott	ENG	1994-95	5	1397	56	675	32	21.09	4	0	6/38
H.V.Hordern #	ENG	1911-12	5	1665	43	780	32	24.37	4	2	7/90
H.Ironmonger	SA	1931-32	4	1331	112	296	31	9.54	3	1	6/18
D.K.Lillee	ENG	1972	5	1499	83	548	31	17.67	3	1	6/66
S.K.Warne	ENG	2001	5	1172	41	580	31	18.71	3	1	7/165

R.Benaud	ENG	1958-59	5	1866	65	584	31	18.83	2	0	5/83
C.J.McDermott	IND	1991-92	5	1586	75	670	31	21.61	3	1	5/54
J.V.Saunders #	ENG	1907-08	5	1603	52	716	31	23.09	3	0	5/28
M.G.Hughes	ENG	1993	6	1778	79	845	31	27.25	1	0	5/92
G.D.McGrath	WI	1998-99	4	1198	59	508	30	16.93	4	1	5/28
R.Benaud	SA	1957-58	5	1937	56	658	30	21.93	4	0	5/49
G.D.McKenzie	WI	1968-69	5	1649	27	758	30	25.26	1	1	8/71
C.J.McDermott	ENG	1985	6	1406	21	901	30	30.03	2	0	8/141
A.K.Davidson	IND	1959-60	5	1469	85	431	29	14.86	2	1	7/93
R.Benaud	IND	1959-60	5	1934	146	568	29	19.58	2	0	5/43
G.D.McKenzie	ENG	1964	5	1536	61	654	29	22.55	2	0	7/153
G.F.Lawson	ENG	1989	6	1663	68	791	29	27.27	1	0	6/72
J.R.Thomson	WI	1975-76	6	1205	15	831	29	28.65	2	0	6/50
C.V.Grimmett	ENG	1930	5	2098	78	925	29	31.89	4	1	6/167
A.A.Mallett	IND	1969-70	5	1792	129	535	28	19.10	3	1	6/64
S.K.Warne	ENG	2005	4	1061	29	551	28	19.67	1	1	6/46
H.Trumble	ENG	1901-02	5	1604	93	561	28	20.03	2	0	6/74
W.J.O'Reilly	ENG	1934	5	2002	128	698	28	24.92	2	1	7/54
W.M.Clark §	IND	1977-78	5	1585	27	701	28	25.03	0	0	4/46
S.K.Warne	PAK	2002-03	3	744	29	342	27	12.66	2	1	7/94
B.A.Reid	ENG	1990-91	4	1039	47	432	27	16.00	2	1	7/51
W.J.O'Reilly	SA	1935-36	5	1502	112	460	27	17.03	2	0	5/20
S.C.G.MacGill	ENG	1998-99	4	1112	33	478	27	17.70	2	1	7/50
R.R.Lindwall	ENG	1948	5	1337	57	530	27	19.62	2	0	6/20
S.K.Warne	ENG	1994-95	5	1537	84	549	27	20.33	2	1	8/71
W.A.Johnston	ENG	1948	5	1856	91	630	27	23.33	1	0	5/36
E.A.McDonald	ENG	1921	5	1235	32	668	27	24.74	2	0	5/32
D.K.Lillee	WI	1975-76	5	1035	7	712	27	26.37	1	0	5/63
W.J.O'Reilly	ENG	1932-33	5	2302	144	724	27	26.81	2	1	5/63
H.Trumble	ENG	1902	3	1036	55	371	26	14.26	2	2	8/65
G.D.McGrath	WI	1996-97	5	1205	61	453	26	17.42	1	0	5/50
R.R.Lindwall	ENG	1953	5	1444	62	490	26	18.84	3	0	5/54
S.K.Warne	SL	2003-04	3	1008	37	521	26	20.03	4	2	5/65
M.H.N.Walker	WI	1972-73	5	1627	83	539	26	20.73	3	0	6/114
E.Jones	ENG	1899	5	1276	73	657	26	25.26	2	1	7/88
J.W.Gleeson	WI	1968-69	5	2006	57	844	26	32.46	2	0	5/61
A.K.Davidson	SA	1957-58	5	1613	47	425	25	17.00	2	0	6/34
W.J.O'Reilly	ENG	1936-37	5	1982	89	555	25	22.20	2	0	5/51
A.G.Hurst	ENG	1978-79	6	1634	44	577	25	23.08	1	0	5/28
D.K.Lillee	ENG	1974-75	6	1462	36	596	25	23.84	0	0	4/49
C.V.Grimmett	ENG	1934	5	2379	148	668	25	26.72	2	0	7/83

ENGLAND	Opp	Season	Tests	Balls	Mdns	Runs	Wkts	Avge	5wi	10w	Best
S.F.Barnes #	SA	1913-14	4	1356	56	536	49	10.93	7	3	9/103
J.C.Laker	AUST	1956	5	1703	127	442	46	9.60	4	2	10/53
A.V.Bedser	AUST	1953	5	1591	58	682	39	17.48	5	1	7/44
M.W.Tate	AUST	1924-25	5	2528	62	881	38	23.18	5	1	6/99
G.A.Lohmann	SA	1895-96	3	520	38	203	35	5.80	4	2	9/28
G.A.R.Lock	NZ	1958	5	1056	93	254	34	7.47	3	1	7/35
S.F.Barnes	SA	1912	3	768	38	282	34	8.29	5	3	8/29
F.S.Trueman	WI	1963	5	1420	53	594	34	17.47	4	2	7/44
I.T.Botham	AUST	1981	6	1635	81	700	34	20.58	3	1	6/95
S.F.Barnes	AUST	1911-12	5	1782	64	778	34	22.88	3	0	5/44
H.Larwood #	AUST	1932-33	5	1322	42	644	33	19.51	2	1	5/28
F.R.Foster §	AUST	1911-12	5	1660	58	692	32	21.62	3	0	6/91
T.Richardson	AUST	1894-95	5	1747	63	849	32	26.53	4	0	6/104
W.Rhodes	AUST	1903-04	5	1032	36	488	31	15.74	3	1	8/68

A.S.Kennedy †	SA	1922-23	5	1683	91	599	31	19.32	2	0	5/76
J.A.Snow	AUST	1970-71	6	1805	47	708	31	22.83	2	0	7/40
I.T.Botham	AUST	1985	6	1510	36	855	31	27.58	1	0	5/109
A.V.Bedser	AUST	1950-51	5	1560	34	482	30	16.06	2	1	5/46
A.V.Bedser	SA	1951	5	1655	84	517	30	17.23	3	1	7/58
J.N.Crawford #	AUST	1907-08	5	1426	36	742	30	24.73	3	0	5/48
F.S.Trueman §	IND	1952	4	718	25	386	29	13.31	2	0	8/31
D.L.Underwood	IND	1976-77	5	1517	95	509	29	17.55	1	0	5/84
R.G.D.Willis	AUST	1981	6	1516	56	666	29	22.96	1	0	8/43
F.H.Tyson	AUST	1954-55	5	1208	16	583	28	20.82	2	1	7/27
M.W.Tate §	SA	1924	5	1304	68	424	27	15.70	1	0	6/42
J.B.Statham	SA	1960	5	1218	54	491	27	18.18	2	1	6/63
A.R.C.Fraser	WI	1997-98	6	1124	50	492	27	18.22	2	1	8/53
J.A.Snow	WI	1967-68	4	990	29	504	27	18.66	3	1	7/49
R.G.D.Willis	AUST	1977	5	1000	36	534	27	19.77	3	0	7/78
R.Peel	AUST	1894-95	5	1831	77	721	27	26.70	1	0	6/67
F.J.Titmus	IND	1963-64	5	2393	156	747	27	27.66	2	0	6/73
C.Blythe	SA	1907	3	603	26	270	26	10.38	3	1	8/59
J.H.Wardle	SA	1956-57	4	1118	37	359	26	13.80	3	1	7/36
J.K.Lever §	IND	1976-77	5	898	29	380	26	14.61	2	1	7/46
W.S.Lees †	SA	1905-06	5	1256	69	467	26	17.96	2	0	6/78
W.Voce	AUST	1936-37	5	1297	20	560	26	21.53	1	1	6/41
D.G.Cork §	WI	1995	5	1106	30	661	26	25.42	1	0	7/43
M.J.Hoggard #	SA	2004-05	5	1203	37	663	26	25.50	2	1	7/61
F.S.Trueman	SA	1960	5	1083	31	508	25	20.32	1	0	5/27
D.Gough	WI	2000	5	1043	33	530	25	21.20	1	0	5/109
A.Fielder #	AUST	1907-08	4	1299	31	627	25	25.08	1	0	6/82
J.C.White	AUST	1928-29	5	2440	134	760	25	30.40	3	1	8/126

SOUTH AFRICA	Opp	Season	Tests	Balls	Mdns	Runs	Wkts	Avge	5wi	10w	Best
H.J.Tayfield	ENG	1956-57	5	2280	105	636	37	17.18	4	1	9/113
A.E.E.Vogler	ENG	1909-10	5	1349	33	783	36	21.75	4	1	7/94
A.A.Donald	ENG	1998	5	1460	69	653	33	19.78	4	0	6/88
H.J.Tayfield	AUST	1952-53	5	2228	58	843	30	28.10	2	1	7/81
S.M.Pollock	WI	1998-99	5	1184	44	483	29	16.65	3	0	5/43
M.Ntini	WI	2003-04	4	1121	45	620	29	21.37	3	0	5/49
G.A.Faulkner	ENG	1909-10	5	1255	45	635	29	21.89	2	0	6/87
G.B.Lawrence †	NZ	1961-62	5	1334	62	512	28	18.28	2	0	8/53
A.E.Hall §	ENG	1922-23	4	1505	82	501	27	18.55	2	1	7/63
M.J.Procter #	AUST	1969-70	4	858	50	353	26	13.57	1	0	6/73
T.L.Goddard	AUST	1966-67	5	1533	101	422	26	16.23	1	0	6/53
H.J.Tayfield	ENG	1955	5	1881	124	568	26	21.84	3	0	5/60
N.A.T.Adcock	ENG	1960	5	1578	69	587	26	22.57	2	0	6/65
C.B.Llewellyn	AUST	1902-03	3	796	23	448	25	17.92	4	1	6/92
G.F.Bissett †	ENG	1927-28	4	989	28	469	25	18.76	2	0	7/29
T.L.Goddard §	ENG	1955	5	1894	148	528	25	21.12	2	0	5/31
J.M.Blanckenberg	ENG	1922-23	5	1510	60	613	25	24.52	2	0	6/76
M.Ntini	ENG	2004-05	5	1329	49	627	25	25.08	0	0	4/50
R.O.Schwarz	AUST	1910-11	5	1006	19	651	25	26.04	2	0	6/47
P.M.Pollock	AUST	1963-64	5	1275	11	710	25	28.40	2	0	6/95
J.T.Partridge §	AUST	1963-64	5	1980	33	833	25	33.32	2	0	7/91

WEST INDIES	Opp	Season	Tests	Balls	Mdns	Runs	Wkts	Avge	5wi	10w	Best
M.D.Marshall	ENG	1988	5	1219	49	443	35	12.66	3	1	7/22
C.A.Walsh	ENG	2000	5	1322	92	436	34	12.82	2	1	6/74
C.E.L.Ambrose	AUST	1992-93	5	1563	77	542	33	16.42	3	1	7/25
M.D.Marshall	IND	1983-84	6	1326	59	621	33	18.81	2	0	6/37

A.L.Valentine §	ENG	1950	4	2535	197	674	33	20.42	2	2	8/104
C.E.H.Croft §	PAK	1976-77	5	1307	45	676	33	20.48	1	0	8/29
C.C.Griffith	ENG	1963	5	1343	54	519	32	16.21	3	0	6/36
A.M.E.Roberts	IND	1974-75	5	1251	51	585	32	18.28	3	1	7/64
J.Garner	AUST	1983-84	5	1253	55	523	31	16.87	3	0	6/60
C.E.L.Ambrose	WI	1997-98	6	1235	61	428	30	14.25	2	0	5/25
W.W.Hall	IND	1958-59	5	1330	65	530	30	17.66	2	1	6/50
M.A.Holding	IND	1983-84	6	1342	43	663	30	22.10	1	0	5/102
J.Garner	ENG	1984	5	1307	60	540	29	18.62	1	0	5/55
M.A.Holding	ENG	1976	4	957	54	356	28	12.71	3	1	8/92
A.M.E.Roberts	ENG	1976	5	1330	69	537	28	19.17	3	1	6/37
M.D.Marshall	AUST	1984-85	5	1277	47	554	28	19.78	4	1	5/38
C.E.L.Ambrose	ENG	1991	5	1494	63	560	28	20.00	2	0	6/52
A.L.Valentine	IND	1952-53	5	2580	178	828	28	29.57	2	0	5/64
W.W.Hall	IND	1961-62	5	1006	37	475	27	15.74	2	0	6/49
J.Garner	ENG	1985-86	5	937	30	436	27	16.14	0	0	4/43
M.D.Marshall	ENG	1985-86	5	1017	36	482	27	17.85	0	0	4/38
M.D.Marshall	NZ	1984-85	4	1021	30	486	27	18.00	1	1	7/80
I.R.Bishop	ENG	1995	6	1455	49	649	27	24.03	1	0	5/32
J.Garner	ENG	1980	5	1276	73	371	26	14.26	0	0	4/30
R.Gilchrist #	IND	1958-59	4	1189	73	419	26	16.11	1	0	6/55
C.A.Walsh	IND	1987-88	4	823	24	437	26	16.80	2	0	5/54
C.E.L.Ambrose	ENG	1993-94	5	1346	62	519	26	19.96	2	1	6/24
C.A.Walsh	AUST	1998-99	4	1249	38	543	26	20.88	1	0	5/39
L.R.Gibbs	ENG	1963	5	1497	74	554	26	21.30	2	1	5/98
C.E.L.Ambrose	AUST	1988-89	5	1227	38	558	26	21.46	1	0	5/72
S.Ramadhin §	ENG	1950	4	2267	170	604	26	23.23	3	1	6/86
L.R.Gibbs	AUST	1972-73	5	1950	108	696	26	26.76	1	0	5/102
C.A.Walsh	ENG	1995	6	1740	57	786	26	30.23	1	0	5/45
C.A.Walsh	SA	2000-01	5	1582	87	492	25	19.68	1	0	6/61
J.Garner §	PAK	1976-77	5	1317	41	688	25	27.52	0	0	4/48

NEW ZEALAND	Opp	Season	Tests	Balls	Mdns	Runs	Wkts	Avge	5wi	10w	Best
R.J.Hadlee	AUST	1985-86	3	1017	42	401	33	12.15	5	2	9/52
B.R.Taylor	WI	1971-72	4	1034	39	478	27	17.70	2	0	7/74
R.J.Hadlee	SL	1983-84	3	707	48	230	23	10.00	2	1	5/29
A.R.McGibbon	SA	1953-54	5	1369	36	454	22	20.63	0	0	4/62
J.C.Alabaster	SA	1961-62	5	1347	60	617	22	28.04	0	0	4/59
R.J.Hadlee	ENG	1983	4	1392	65	559	21	26.61	2	0	6/53
D.L.Vettori	BAN	2004-05	2	670	49	224	20	11.20	3	1	6/28
A.R.McGibbon #	ENG	1958	5	1054	50	389	20	19.45	1	0	5/64
F.J.Cameron §	SA	1961-62	5	1208	54	493	20	24.65	2	0	5/48

INDIA	Opp	Season	Tests	Balls	Mdns	Runs	Wkts	Avge	5wi	10w	Best
B.S.Chandrasekhar	ENG	1972-73	5	1747	83	662	35	18.91	4	0	8/79
M.H.Mankad	ENG	1951-52	5	2224	151	571	34	16.79	1	1	8/55
S.P.Gupte	NZ	1955-56	5	2140	152	669	34	19.67	4	0	7/128
Harbhajan Singh	AUST	2000-01	3	1071	44	545	32	17.03	4	2	8/84
Kapil Dev	PAK	1979-80	6	1271	53	566	32	17.68	3	1	7/56
B.S.Bedi	AUST	1977-78	5	1759	39	740	31	23.87	3	1	5/55
Kapil Dev	WI	1983-84	6	1223	39	537	29	18.51	2	1	9/83
Kapil Dev	AUST	1979-80	6	1339	53	625	28	22.32	2	0	5/74
B.S.Chandrasekhar	AUST	1977-78	5	1579	24	704	28	25.14	3	1	6/52
D.R.Doshi §	AUST	1979-80	6	1838	87	630	27	23.33	2	0	6/103
K.D.Ghavri	WI	1978-79	6	1230	42	634	27	23.48	1	0	5/51
A.Kumble	AUST	2004-05	4	1185	29	685	27	25.37	3	1	7/48
S.P.Gupte	WI	1952-53	5	1977	87	789	27	29.22	3	0	7/162

	Opp	Season	Tests	Balls	Mdns	Runs	Wkts	Avge	5wi	10w	Best
E.A.S.Prasanna	AUST	1969-70	5	1770	107	672	26	25.84	3	1	6/74
M.H.Mankad	PAK	1952-53	4	1592	100	514	25	20.56	3	1	8/52
B.S.Bedi	ENG	1976-77	5	1788	106	574	25	22.96	2	0	6/71
B.S.Bedi	ENG	1972-73	5	2237	134	632	25	25.28	1	0	5/63
Kapil Dev	AUST	1991-92	5	1704	76	645	25	25.80	2	0	5/97
E.A.S.Prasanna	AUST	1967-68	4	1581	34	686	25	27.44	2	0	6/104

PAKISTAN	Opp	Season	Tests	Balls	Mdns	Runs	Wkts	Avge	5wi	10w	Best
Imran Khan	IND	1982-83	6	1339	69	558	40	13.95	4	2	8/60
Abdul Qadir	ENG	1987-88	3	1408	69	437	30	14.56	3	2	9/56
Waqar Younis	NZ	1990-91	3	869	50	315	29	10.86	3	2	7/76
Waqar Younis	ZIM	1993-94	3	784	31	373	27	13.81	4	1	7/91
Wasim Akram	NZ	1993-94	3	958	41	431	25	17.24	2	0	7/119
Imran Khan	WI	1976-77	5	1417	54	790	25	31.60	1	0	6/90
Saqlain Mushtaq	IND	1998-99	3	1127	46	503	24	20.95	4	2	5/93
Sikander Bakht	IND	1979-80	5	1269	47	641	24	26.70	3	1	8/69
Imran Khan	WI	1987-88	3	779	16	416	23	18.08	2	1	7/80
Khan Mohammad	IND	1954-55	4	1013	54	350	22	15.90	2	0	5/73
Pervez Sajjad	NZ	1969-70	3	1146	71	342	22	15.54	2	0	7/74
Waqar Younis	ENG	1992	5	996	29	557	22	25.31	3	0	5/52
Abdul Qadir	AUS	1982-83	3	1275	48	562	22	25.54	2	1	7/142

SRI LANKA	Opp	Season	Tests	Balls	Mdns	Runs	Wkts	Avge	5wi	10w	Best
M.Muralidaran	ZIM	2001-02	3	1219	84	294	30	9.80	2	1	9/51
M.Muralidaran	AUS	2003-04	3	1255	37	649	28	23.17	4	1	6/59
M.Muralidaran	ENG	2003-04	3	1390	109	320	26	12.30	1	1	7/46
W.P.U.J.C.Vaas	WI	2001-02	3	842	32	401	26	15.42	2	1	7/71
M.Muralidaran	SA	2000-01	3	1366	52	480	26	18.46	3	1	7/84
M.Muralidaran	PAK	1999-2000	3	1279	50	516	26	19.84	1	1	6/71
M.Muralidaran	ENG	2006	3	878	35	405	24	16.87	2	2	8/70
M.Muralidaran	WI	2001-02	3	1306	53	536	24	22.33	3	2	6/81
M.Muralidaran	IND	2001-02	3	1065	51	444	23	19.30	2	1	8/87
M.Muralidaran	SA	2006-07	2	978	31	397	22	18.04	3	2	7/97
R.J.Ratnayake	IND	1985-86	3	997	35	459	20	22.95	2	0	6/85

ZIMBABWE	Opp	Season	Tests	Balls	Mdns	Runs	Wkts	Avge	5wi	10w	Best
H.H.Streak	PAK	1994-95	3	708	31	298	22	13.54	2	0	6/90
R.W.Price	WI	2003-04	2	836	32	396	19	20.84	2	1	6/73
A.G.Huckle	NZ	1997-98	2	706	23	373	16	23.31	2	1	6/111

BANGLADESH	Opp	Season	Tests	Balls	Mdns	Runs	Wkts	Avge	5wi	10w	Best
Enamul Haque[2] #	ZIM	2004-05	2	722	31	300	18	16.66	3	1	7/95
Mohammad Rafique	PAK	2003-04	3	976	43	405	17	23.82	2	0	5/36
Khaled Mahmud	PAK	2003-04	3	594	26	257	11	23.36	0	0	4/37
Mohammad Rafique	AUS	2005-06	2	713	26	305	11	27.72	1	0	5/62

MOST WICKETS IN A TEST SERIES FOR A LOSING SIDE *(§ in first series. # in last series.)*

Player (Country)	Opp	Season	Tests	Balls	Mdns	Runs	Wkts	Avge	5wi	10w	Best
T.M.Alderman (A) §	ENG	1981	6	1950	76	893	42	21.26	4	0	6/135
R.M.Hogg (A) §	ENG	1978-79	6	1740	60	527	41	12.85	5	2	6/74
S.K.Warne (A)	ENG	2005	5	1517	37	797	40	19.92	3	2	6/46
D.K.Lillee (A)	ENG	1981	6	1870	81	870	39	22.30	2	1	7/89
M.W.Tate (E)	AUS	1924-25	5	2528	62	881	38	23.18	5	1	6/99
C.A.Walsh (W)	ENG	2000	5	1322	92	436	34	12.82	2	1	6/74
F.S.Trueman (E)	WI	1963	5	1420	53	594	34	17.47	4	2	7/44
G.Giffen (A)	ENG	1894-95	5	2060	111	820	34	24.11	3	0	6/155
A.A.Donald (SA)	ENG	1998	5	1460	69	653	33	19.78	4	0	6/88

H.V.Hordern (A) #	ENG	1911-12	5	1665	43	780	32	24.37	4	2	7/90
B.S.Bedi (I)	AUS	1977-78	5	1759	39	740	31	23.87	3	1	5/55
A.V.Bedser (E)	AUS	1950-51	5	1560	34	482	30	16.06	2	1	5/46
J.N.Crawford (E) #	AUS	1907-08	5	1426	36	742	30	24.73	3	0	5/48
C.J.McDermott (A)	ENG	1985	6	1406	21	901	30	30.03	2	0	8/141
Kapil Dev (I)	WI	1983-84	6	1223	39	537	29	18.51	2	1	9/83
M.Muralidaran (SL)	AUS	2003-04	3	1255	37	649	28	23.17	4	1	6/59
B.S.Chandrasekhar (I)	AUS	1977-78	5	1579	24	704	28	25.14	3	1	6/52
A.R.C.Fraser (E)	WI	1997-98	6	1124	50	492	27	18.22	2	1	8/53
A.E.Hall (SA) §	ENG	1922-23	4	1505	82	501	27	18.55	2	1	7/63
K.D.Ghavri (I)	WI	1978-79	6	1230	42	634	27	23.48	1	0	5/51
A.Kumble (I)	AUS	2004-05	4	1185	29	685	27	25.37	3	1	7/48
W.J.O'Reilly (A)	ENG	1932-33	5	2302	144	724	27	26.81	2	1	5/63
S.P.Gupte (I)	WI	1952-53	5	1977	87	789	27	29.22	3	0	7/162
M.Muralidaran (SL)	SA	2000-01	3	1366	52	480	26	18.46	3	1	7/84
R.R.Lindwall (A)	ENG	1953	5	1444	62	490	26	18.84	3	0	5/54
M.Muralidaran (SL)	PAK	1999-2000	3	1279	50	516	26	19.84	1	1	6/71
C.A.Walsh (W)	AUS	1998-99	4	1249	38	543	26	20.88	1	0	5/39
W.Voce (E)	AUS	1936-37	5	1297	20	560	26	21.53	1	1	6/41
H.J.Tayfield (SA)	ENG	1955	5	1881	124	568	26	21.84	3	0	5/60
N.A.T.Adcock (SA)	ENG	1960	5	1578	69	587	26	22.57	2	0	6/65
E.A.S.Prasanna (I)	AUS	1969-70	5	1770	107	672	26	25.84	3	1	6/74
L.R.Gibbs (W)	AUS	1972-73	5	1950	108	696	26	26.76	1	0	5/102
C.B.Llewellyn (SA)	AUS	1902-03	3	796	23	448	25	17.92	4	1	6/92
C.A.Walsh (W)	SA	2000-01	5	1582	87	492	25	19.68	1	0	6/61
T.L.Goddard (SA) §	ENG	1955	5	1894	148	528	25	21.12	2	0	5/31
B.S.Bedi (I)	ENG	1976-77	5	1788	106	574	25	22.96	2	0	6/71
A.G.Hurst (A)	ENG	1978-79	6	1634	44	577	25	23.08	1	0	5/28
A.Fielder (E) #	AUS	1907-08	4	1299	31	627	25	25.08	1	0	6/82
M.Ntini (SA)	ENG	2004-05	5	1329	49	627	25	25.08	0	0	4/50
Kapil Dev (I)	AUS	1991-92	5	1704	76	645	25	25.80	2	0	5/97
R.O.Schwarz (SA)	AUS	1910-11	5	1006	19	651	25	26.04	2	0	6/47
E.A.S.Prasanna (I)	AUS	1967-68	4	1581	34	686	25	27.44	2	0	6/104
Imran Khan (P)	WI	1976-77	5	1417	54	790	25	31.60	1	0	6/90

MOST WICKETS IN A TEST MATCH

19/90(9/37 + 10/53)	J.C.Laker	England	v	Australia	Manchester	1956
17/159(8/56 + 9/103)	S.F.Barnes	England	v	South Africa	Johannesburg[1]	1913-14
16/136(8/61 + 8/75)	N.D.Hirwani §	India	v	West Indies	Madras[1]	1987-88
16/137(8/84 + 8/53)	R.A.L.Massie §	Australia	v	England	Lord's	1972
16/220(7/155 + 9/65)	M.Muralidaran	Sri Lanka	v	England	The Oval	1998
15/28(7/17 + 8/11)	J.Briggs	England	v	South Africa	Cape Town	1888-89
15/45(7/38 + 8/7)	G.A Lohmann	England	v	South Africa	Port Elizabeth	1895-96
15/99(8/59 + 7/40)	C.Blythe	England	v	South Africa	Leeds	1907
15/104(7/61 + 8/43)	H.Verity	England	v	Australia	Lord's	1934
15/123(9/52 + 6/71)	R.J.Hadlee	New Zealand	v	Australia	Brisbane[2]	1985-86
15/124(7/56 + 8/68)	W.Rhodes	England	v	Australia	Melbourne	1903-04
15/217(7/133 + 8/84)	Harbhajan Singh	India	v	Australia	Chennai[1]	2000-01
14/90(7/46 + 7/44)	F.R.Spofforth	Australia	v	England	The Oval	1882
14/99(7/55 + 7/44)	A.V.Bedser	England	v	Australia	Nottingham	1953
14/102(7/28 + 7/74)	W.Bates	England	v	Australia	Melbourne	1882-83
14/116(8/58 + 6/58)	Imran Khan	Pakistan	v	Sri Lanka	Lahore[2]	1981-82
14/124(9/69+ 5/55)	J.M.Patel	India	v	Australia	Kanpur	1959-60
14/144(7/56 + 7/88)	S.F.Barnes #	England	v	South Africa	Durban[1]	1913-14
14/149(8/92 + 6/57)	M.A.Holding	West Indies	v	England	The Oval	1976
14/149(4/75 + 10/74)	A.Kumble	India	v	Pakistan	Delhi	1998-99

14/191(7/120 + 7/71)	W.P.U.J.C.Vaas	Sri Lanka	v	West Indies	Colombo (SSC)	2001-02
14/199(7/116 + 7/83)	C.V.Grimmett	Australia	v	South Africa	Adelaide	1931-32

TEN WICKETS IN A MATCH *(§ In first Test. # In last Test. † In only Test)*

AUSTRALIA (86)		Opponents		
16/137(8/84 + 8/53)	R.A.L.Massie §	England	Lord's	1972
14/90(7/46 + 7/44)	F.R.Spofforth	England	The Oval	1882
14/199(7/116 + 7/83)	C.V.Grimmett	South Africa	Adelaide	1931-32
13/77(7/17 + 6/60)	M.A.Noble	England	Melbourne	1901-02
13/110(6/48 + 7/62)	F.R.Spofforth	England	Melbourne	1878-79
13/148(6/97 + 7/51)	B.A.Reid	England	Melbourne	1990-91
13/173(7/100 + 6/73)	C.V.Grimmett #	South Africa	Durban[2]	1935-36
13/217(5/130 + 8/87)	M.G.Hughes	West Indies	Perth	1988-89
13/236(4/115 + 9/121)	A.A.Mailey	England	Melbourne	1920-21
12/87(5/44 + 7/43)	C.T.B.Turner	England	Sydney	1887-88
12/89(6/59 + 6/30)	H.Trumble	England	The Oval	1896
12/107(5/57 + 7/50)	S.C.G.MacGill	England	Sydney	1998-99
12/124(5/31 + 7/93)	A.K.Davidson	India	Kanpur	1959-60
12/126(6/66 + 6/60)	B.A.Reid	India	Melbourne	1991-92
12/128(7/56 + 5/72)	S.K.Warne	South Africa	Sydney	1993-94
12/166(5/99 + 7/67)	G.Dymock	India	Kanpur	1979-80
12/173(8/65 + 4/108)	H.Trumble	England	The Oval	1902
12/175(5/85 + 7/90)	H.V.Hordern	England	Sydney	1911-12
12/246(6/122 + 6/124)	S.K.Warne	England	The Oval	2005
11/24(5/6 + 6/18)	H.Ironmonger	South Africa	Melbourne	1931-32
11/31(5/2 + 6/29)	E.R.H.Toshack	India	Brisbane[2]	1947-48
11/77(7/23 + 4/54)	S.K.Warne	Pakistan	Brisbane[2]	1995-96
11/79(7/23 + 4/56)	H.Ironmonger	West Indies	Melbourne	1930-31
11/82(5/45 + 6/37)	C.V.Grimmett §	England	Sydney	1924-25
11/85(7/58 + 4/27)	C.G.Macartney	England	Leeds	1909
11/95(4/68 + 7/27)	M.R.Whitney	India	Perth	1991-92
11/96(7/46 + 4/50)	A.R.Border	West Indies	Sydney	1988-89
11/103(5/51 + 6/52)	M.A.Noble	England	Sheffield	1902
11/105(6/52 + 5/53)	R.Benaud	India	Calcutta	1956-57
11/109(5/75 + 6/34)	S.K.Warne	South Africa	Sydney	1997-98
11/110(3/39 + 8/71)	S.K.Warne	England	Brisbane[2]	1994-95
11/117(4/73 + 7/44)	F.R.Spofforth	England	Sydney	1882-83
11/118(5/32 + 6/86)	C.G.Rackemann	Pakistan	Perth	1983-84
11/123(5/51 + 6/72)	D.K.Lillee	New Zealand	Auckland	1976-77
11/129(4/75 + 7/54)	W.J.O'Reilly	England	Nottingham	1934
11/134(6/47 + 5/87)	G.F.Lawson	England	Brisbane[2]	1982-83
11/138(6/60 + 5/78)	D.K.Lillee	England	Melbourne	1979-80
11/157(8/97 + 3/60)	C.J.McDermott	England	Perth	1990-91
11/159(7/89 + 4/70)	D.K.Lillee	England	The Oval	1981
11/165(7/68 + 4/97)	G.E.Palmer	England	Sydney	1881-82
11/165(6/26 + 5/139)	D.K.Lillee	England	Melbourne	1976-77
11/181(8/112 + 3/69)	G.F.Lawson	West Indies	Adelaide	1984-85
11/183(7/87 + 4/96)	C.V.Grimmett	West Indies	Adelaide	1930-31
11/188(7/94 + 4/94)	S.K.Warne	Pakistan	Colombo (PSS)	2002-03
11/222(5/135 + 6/87)	A.K.Davidson	West Indies	Brisbane[2]	1960-61
11/229(7/165 + 4/64)	S.K.Warne	England	Brisbane[2]	2002-03
10/27(6/17 + 4/10)	G.D.McGrath	West Indies	Brisbane[2]	2000-01
10/63(5/27 + 5/36)	C.T.B.Turner	England	Lord's	1888
10/66(5/30 + 5/36)	R.M.Hogg	England	Melbourne	1978-79
10/78(5/50 + 5/28)	G.D.McGrath	West Indies	Port-of-Spain	1998-99
10/88(5/32 + 5/56)	C.V.Grimmett	South Africa	Cape Town	1935-36

10/91(6/58 + 4/33)	G.D.McKenzie	India	Madras[2]	1964-65
10/103(5/48 + 5/55)	G.D.McGrath	India	Sydney	1999-2000
10/110(3/70 + 7/40)	C.V.Grimmett	South Africa	Johannesburg[1]	1935-36
10/111(7/87 + 3/24)	R.J.Bright	Pakistan	Karachi[1]	1979-80
10/113(4/31 + 6/82)	M.G.Bevan	West Indies	Adelaide	1996-97
10/113(5/81 + 5/32)	C.R.Miller	West Indies	Adelaide	2000-01
10/115(6/72 + 4/43)	N.J.N.Hawke	West Indies	Georgetown	1964-65
10/122(5/66 + 5/56)	W.J.O'Reilly	England	Leeds	1938
10/122(5/65 + 5/57)	R.M.Hogg	England	Perth	1978-79
10/126(7/65 + 3/61)	G.E.Palmer	England	Melbourne	1882-83
10/127(7/83 + 3/44)	D.K.Lillee	West Indies	Melbourne	1981-82
10/128(4/75 + 6/53)	H.Trumble	England	Manchester	1902
10/129(5/63 + 5/66)	W.J.O'Reilly	England	Melbourne	1932-33
10/133(5/77 + 5/56)	S.C.G.MacGill	Bangladesh	Cairns	2003-04
10/135(6/82 + 4/53)	D.K.Lillee	Pakistan	Melbourne	1976-77
10/144(4/54 + 6/90)	F R.Spofforth	England	Sydney	1884-85
10/144(5/91 + 5/53)	A.A.Mallett	India	Madras[1]	1969-70
10/144(6/54 + 4/90)	R.G.Holland	West Indies	Sydney	1984-85
10/151(7/66 + 3/85)	G.D.McKenzie	India	Melbourne	1967-68
10/151(5/107 + 5/44)	T.M.Alderman	England	Leeds	1989
10/152(5/72 + 5/80)	K.R.Miller	England	Lord's	1956
10/155(5/65 + 5/90)	S.K.Warne	Sri Lanka	Kandy	2003-04
10/159(8/71 + 2/88)	G.D.McKenzie	West Indies	Melbourne	1968-69
10/159(5/116 + 5/43)	S.K.Warne	Sri Lanka	Galle	2003-04
10/160(4/88 + 6/72)	G.Giffen	England	Sydney	1891-92
10/161(5/95 + 5/66)	H.V.Hordern #	England	Sydney	1911-12
10/162(4/116 + 6/46)	S.K.Warne	England	Birmingham	2005
10/164(7/88 + 3/76)	E.Jones	England	Lord's	1899
10/168(5/76 + 5/92)	C.J.McDermott	India	Adelaide	1991-92
10/174(6/106 + 4/68)	R.G.Holland	New Zealand	Sydney	1985-86
10/181(5/58 + 5/123)	D.K.Lillee	England	The Oval	1972
10/185(3/87 + 7/98)	B.Yardley	West Indies	Sydney	1981-82
10/201(5/107 + 5/94)	C.V.Grimmett	England	Nottingham	1930
10/239(4/129 + 6/110)	L.O.Fleetwood-Smith	England	Adelaide	1936-37
10/249(5/103 + 5/146)	G.R.J.Matthews	India	Madras[1]	1986-87
10/302(5/160 + 5/142)	A.A.Mailey	England	Adelaide	1920-21
ENGLAND (94)		Opponents		
19/90(9/37 + 10/53)	J.C.Laker	Australia	Manchester	1956
17/159(8/56 + 9/103)	S.F.Barnes	South Africa	Johannesburg[1]	1913-14
15/28(7/17 + 8/11)	J.Briggs	South Africa	Cape Town	1888-89
15/45(7/38 + 8/7)	G.A Lohmann	South Africa	Port Elizabeth	1895-96
15/99(8/59 + 7/40)	C.Blythe	South Africa	Leeds	1907
15/104(7/61 + 8/43)	H.Verity	Australia	Lord's	1934
15/124(7/56 + 8/68)	W.Rhodes	Australia	Melbourne	1903-04
14/99(7/55 + 7/44)	A.V.Bedser	Australia	Nottingham	1953
14/102(7/28 + 7/74)	W.Bates	Australia	Melbourne	1882-83
14/144(7/56 + 7/88)	S.F.Barnes #	South Africa	Durban[1]	1913-14
13/57(5/28 + 8/29)	S.F.Barnes	South Africa	The Oval	1912
13/71(5/20 + 8/51)	D.L.Underwood	Pakistan	Lord's	1974
13/91(6/54 + 7/37)	J.J.Ferris ¶	South Africa	Cape Town	1891-92
13/106(6/58 + 7/48)	I.T.Botham	India	Bombay[3]	1979-80
13/156(8/86 + 5/70)	A.W.Greig	West Indies	Port-of-Spain	1973-74
13/163(6/42 + 7/121)	S.F.Barnes	Australia	Melbourne	1901-02
13/244(7/168 + 6/76)	T.Richardson	Australia	Manchester	1896
13/256(5/130 + 8/126)	J.C.White	Australia	Adelaide	1928-29
12/71(9/28 + 3/43)	G.A.Lohmann	South Africa	Johannesburg[1]	1895-96

12/89(5/53 + 7/36)	J.H.Wardle	South Africa	Cape Town	1956-57
12/97(6/12 + 6/85)	D.L.Underwood	New Zealand	Christchurch	1970-71
12/101(7/52 + 5/49)	R.Tattersall	South Africa	Lord's	1951
12/101(6/41 + 6/60)	D.L.Underwood	New Zealand	The Oval	1969
12/102(6/50 + 6/52)	F.Martin §	Australia	The Oval	1890
12/104(7/36 + 5/68)	G.A.Lohmann	Australia	The Oval	1886
12/112(7/58 + 5/54)	A.V.Bedser	South Africa	Manchester	1951
12/119(5/75 + 7/44)	F.S.Trueman	West Indies	Birmingham	1963
12/130(7/70 + 5/60)	G.Geary	South Africa	Johannesburg[1]	1927-28
12/136(6/49 + 6/87)	J.Briggs	Australia	Adelaide	1891-92
12/171(7/71 + 5/100)	A.P.Freeman	South Africa	Manchester	1929
12/205(5/144 + 7/61)	M.J.Hoggard	South Africa	Johannesburg[3]	2004-05
11/48(5/28 + 6/20)	G.A.R.Lock	West Indies	The Oval	1957
11/65(4/14 + 7/51)	G.A.R.Lock	New Zealand	Leeds	1958
11/68(7/31 + 4/37)	R.Peel	Australia	Manchester	1888
11/70(4/38 + 7/32)	D.L.Underwood	New Zealand	Lord's	1969
11/74(5/29 + 6/45)	J.Briggs	Australia	Lord's	1886
11/76(6/48 + 5/28)	W.H.Lockwood	Australia	Manchester	1902
11/76(6/19 + 5/57)	S.J.Harmison	Pakistan	Manchester	2006
11/83(6/65 + 5/18)	N.G.B.Cook	Pakistan	Karachi[1]	1983-84
11/84(5/31 + 6/53)	G.A.R.Lock	New Zealand	Christchurch	1958-59
11/88(5/58 + 6/30)	F.S.Trueman	Australia	Leeds	1961
11/90(6/7 + 5/83)	A.E.R.Gilligan	South Africa	Birmingham	1924
11/93(4/41 + 7/52)	A.V.Bedser	India	Manchester	1946
11/93(7/66 + 4/27)	P.C.R.Tufnell	Australia	The Oval	1997
11/96(5/37 + 6/59)	C.S.Marriott †	West Indies	The Oval	1933
11/97(6/63 + 5/34)	J.B.Statham	South Africa	Lord's	1960
11/98(7/44 + 4/54)	T.E.Bailey	West Indies	Lord's	1957
11/102(6/44 + 5/58)	C.Blythe	Australia	Birmingham	1909
11/110(8/53 + 3/57)	S.F.Barnes	South Africa	Lord's	1912
11/110(5/25 + 6/85)	A.R.C.Fraser	West Indies	Port-of-Spain	1997-98
11/113(5/58 + 6/55)	J.C.Laker	Australia	Leeds	1956
11/118(6/68 + 5/50)	C.Blythe	South Africa	Cape Town	1905-06
11/140(6/101 + 5/39)	I.T.Botham	New Zealand	Lord's	1978
11/145(7/49 + 4/96)	A.V.Bedser §	India	Lord's	1946
11/147(4/100 + 7/47)	P.C.R.Tufnell	New Zealand	Christchurch	1991-92
11/149(4/79 + 7/70)	W.Voce	West Indies	Port-of-Spain	1929-30
11/152(6/100 + 5/52)	F.S.Trueman	West Indies	Lord's	1963
11/153(7/49 + 4/104)	H.Verity	India	Madras[1]	1933-34
11/163(6/104 + 5/59)	N.A.Foster	India	Madras[1]	1984-85
11/173(6/39 + 5/134)	T.Richardson	Australia	Lord's	1896
11/176(6/78 + 5/98)	I.T.Botham	Australia	Perth	1979-80
11/215(7/113 + 4/102)	D.L.Underwood	Australia	Adelaide	1974-75
11/228(6/130 + 5/98)	M.W.Tate	Australia	Sydney	1924-25
10/49(5/29 + 5/20)	F.E.Woolley	Australia	The Oval	1912
10/57(6/41 + 4/16)	W.Voce	Australia	Brisbane[2]	1936-37
10/60(6/41 + 4/19)	J.T.Hearne	Australia	The Oval	1896
10/70(7/46 + 3/24)	J.K.Lever §	India	Delhi	1976-77
10/78(5/35 + 5/43)	G.O.B.Allen	India	Lord's	1936
10/82(4/37 + 6/45)	D.L.Underwood	Australia	Leeds	1972
10/87(8/35 + 2/52)	G.A.Lohmann	Australia	Sydney	1886-87
10/93(5/54 + 5/39)	A.P.Freeman	West Indies	Manchester	1928
10/104(7/46 + 3/58)	C.Blythe #	South Africa	Cape Town	1909-10
10/104(6/77 + 4/27)	R.M.Ellison	Australia	Birmingham	1985
10/105(5/46 + 5/59)	A.V.Bedser	Australia	Melbourne	1950-51
10/105(5/57 + 5/48)	S.F.Barnes	South Africa	Durban[1]	1913-14

10/115(6/52 + 4/63)	S.F.Barnes	South Africa	Leeds	1912
10/119(4/64 + 6/55)	J.C.Laker	South Africa	The Oval	1951
10/122(5/60 + 5/62)	A.R.C.Fraser	South Africa	Nottingham	1998
10/124(5/96 + 5/28)	H.Larwood	Australia	Sydney	1932-33
10/130(4/45 + 6/85)	F.H.Tyson	Australia	Sydney	1954-55
10/137(4/60 + 6/77)	D.E.Malcolm	West Indies	Port-of-Spain	1989-90
10/138(1/81 + 9/57)	D.E.Malcolm	South Africa	The Oval	1994
10/142(4/82 + 6/60)	G.A Lohmann	Australia	Sydney	1891-92
10/142(8/58 + 2/84)	J.A.Snow	West Indies	Georgetown	1967-68
10/148(5/34 + 5/114)	J.Briggs	Australia	The Oval	1893
10/149(5/98 + 5/51)	A.W.Greig	New Zealand	Auckland	1977
10/156(5/49 + 5/107)	T.Richardson §	Australia	Manchester	1893
10/175(5/95 + 5/80)	D.V.P.Wright	South Africa	Lord's	1947
10/179(5/102 + 5/77)	K.Farnes §	Australia	Nottingham	1934
10/195(5/105 + 5/90)	G.T.S.Stevens	West Indies	Bridgetown	1929-30
10/204(8/94 + 2/110)	T.Richardson #	Australia	Sydney	1897-98
10/207(7/115 + 3/92)	A.P.Freeman	South Africa	Leeds	1929
10/215(3/121 + 7/94)	A.R.Caddick #	Australia	Sydney	2002-03
10/253(6/125 + 4/128)	I.T.Botham	Australia	The Oval	1981

¶ *Ferris's only Test for England.*

SOUTH AFRICA (21)		Opponents		
13/132(6/95 + 7/37)	M.Ntini	West Indies	Port-of-Spain	2004-05
13/165(6/84 + 7/81)	H.J.Tayfield	Australia	Melbourne	1952-53
13/192(4/79 + 9/113)	H.J.Tayfield	England	Johannesburg[3]	1956-57
12/127(4/57 + 8/70)	S.J.Snooke	England	Johannesburg[1]	1905-06
12/139(5/55 + 7/84)	A.A.Donald	India	Port Elizabeth	1992-93
12/181(5/87 + 7/94)	A.E.E.Vogler	England	Johannesburg[1]	1909-10
11/112(4/49 + 7/63)	A.E.Hall §	England	Cape Town	1922-23
11/113(3/42 + 8/71)	A.A.Donald	Zimbabwe	Harare	1995-96
11/127(6/53 + 5/74)	A.A.Donald	England	Johannesburg[3]	1999-2000
11/150(5/63 + 6/87)	E.P.Nupen	England	Johannesburg[1]	1930-31
11/196(6/128 + 5/68)	S.F.Burke §	New Zealand	Cape Town	1961-62
10/87(5/53 + 5/34)	P.M.Pollock	England	Nottingham	1965
10/88(4/56 + 6/32)	A.Nel	West Indies	Bridgetown	2004-05
10/106(5/37 + 5/69)	P.R.Adams	Bangladesh	Chittagong[1]	2002-03
10/108(6/81 + 4/27)	P.S.de Villiers	Pakistan	Johannesburg[3]	1994-95
10/116(5/43 + 5/73)	C.B.Llewellyn	Australia	Johannesburg[1]	1902-03
10/123(4/80 + 6/43)	P.S.de Villiers	Australia	Sydney	1993-94
10/145(5/94 + 5/51)	M.Ntini	England	Lord's	2003
10/147(4/91 + 6/56)	S.M.Pollock	India	Bloemfontein	2001-02
10/220(5/75 + 5/145)	M.Ntini	England	Lord's	2003
10/178(6/100 + 4/78)	M.Ntini	Australia	Johannesburg[3]	2005-06

WEST INDIES (26)		Opponents		
14/149(8/92 + 6/57)	M.A.Holding	England	The Oval	1976
13/55(7/37 + 6/18)	C.A.Walsh	New Zealand	Wellington	1994-95
12/121(7/64 + 5/57)	A.M.E.Roberts	India	Madras[1]	1974-75
11/84(5/60 + 6/24)	C.E.L.Ambrose	England	Port-of-Spain	1993-94
11/89(5/34 + 6/55)	M.D.Marshall	India	Port-of-Spain	1988-89
11/107(5/45 + 6/62)	M.A.Holding	Australia	Melbourne	1981-82
11/120(4/40 + 7/80)	M.D.Marshall	New Zealand	Bridgetown	1984-85
11/126(6/50 + 5/76)	W.W.Hall	India	Kanpur	1958-59
11/134(7/78 + 4/56)	C.D.Collymore	Pakistan	Kingston	2004-05
11/147(5/70 + 6/77)	K.D.Boyce	England	The Oval	1973
11/152(5/66 + 6/86)	S.Ramadhin	England	Lord's	1950
11/157(5/59 + 6/98)	L.R.Gibbs	England	Manchester	1963

11/204(8/104 + 3/100)	A.L.Valentine §	England	Manchester	1950
11/229(5/137 + 6/92)	W.Ferguson	England	Port-of-Spain	1947-48
10/92(6/32 + 4/60)	M.D.Marshall	England	Lord's	1988
10/96(5/41 + 5/55)	H.H.H.Johnson §	England	Kingston	1947-48
10/101(6/62 + 4/39)	C A Walsh	India	Kingston	1988-89
10/106(5/37 + 5/69)	L R Gibbs	England	Manchester	1966
10/107(5/69 + 5/38)	M.D.Marshall	Australia	Adelaide	1984-85
10/113(7/55 + 3/58)	G.E.Gomez	Australia	Sydney	1951-52
10/117(4/43 + 6/74)	C.A.Walsh	England	Lord's	2000
10/120(6/74 + 4/46)	C.E.L.Ambrose	Australia	Adelaide	1992-93
10/123(5/60 + 5/63)	A.M.E.Roberts	England	Lord's	1976
10/127(2/82 + 8/45)	C.E.L.Ambrose	England	Bridgetown	1989-90
10/160(4/121 + 6/39)	A.L.Valentine	England	The Oval	1950
10/174(5/105 + 5/69)	K.C.G.Benjamin	England	Nottingham	1995

NEW ZEALAND (21)		Opponents		
15/123(9/52 + 6/71)	R.J.Hadlee	Australia	Brisbane[2]	1985-86
12/149(5/62 + 7/87)	D.L.Vettori	Australia	Auckland	1999-2000
12/170(6/70 + 6/100)	D.L.Vettori	Bangladesh	Chittagong[1]	2004-05
11/58(4/35 + 7/23)	R.J.Hadlee	India	Wellington	1975-76
11/102(5/34 + 6/68)	R.J.Hadlee	West Indies	Dunedin	1979-80
11/152(7/52 + 4/100)	C.Pringle	Pakistan	Faisalabad	1990-91
11/155(5/65 + 6/90)	R.J.Hadlee	Australia	Perth	1985-86
11/169(6/76 + 5/93)	D.J.Nash	England	Lord's	1994
11/180(6/76 + 5/104)	C.S.Martin	Pakistan	Auckland	2003-04
10/88(6/49 + 4/39)	R.J.Hadlee	India	Bombay[3]	1988-89
10/99(6/51 + 4/48)	S.E.Bond	Zimbabwe	Bulawayo[2]	2005-06
10/100(3/73 + 7/27)	R.J.Hadlee	England	Wellington	1977-78
10/100(7/74 + 6/26)	C.L.Cairns	West Indies	Hamilton	1999-2000
10/102(5/73 + 5/29)	R.J.Hadlee	Sri Lanka	Colombo (CCC)	1983-84
10/106(4/74 + 6/32)	J.G.Bracewell	Australia	Auckland	1985-86
10/124(4/51 + 6/73)	E.J.Chatfield	West Indies	Port-of-Spain	1984-85
10/140(6/80 + 4/60)	J.Cowie	England	Manchester	1937
10/140(4/73 + 6/67)	R.J.Hadlee	England	Nottingham	1986
10/144(7/74 + 3/70)	B.L.Cairns	England	Leeds	1983
10/166(4/71 + 6/95)	G.B.Troup	West Indies	Auckland	1979-80
10/176(5/109 + 5/67)	R.J.Hadlee	Australia	Melbourne	1987-88

INDIA (37)		Opponents		
16/136(8/61 + 8/75)	N.D.Hirwani §	West Indies	Madras[1]	1987-88
15/217(7/133 + 8/84)	Harbhajan Singh	Australia	Chennai[1]	2000-01
14/124(9/69+ 5/55)	J.M.Patel	Australia	Kanpur	1959-60
14/149(4/75 + 10/74)	A.Kumble	Pakistan	Delhi	1998-99
13/131(8/52 + 5/79)	M.H.Mankad	Pakistan	Delhi	1952-53
13/132(5/46 + 8/86)	J.Srinath	Pakistan	Calcutta	1998-99
13/181(7/48 + 6/133)	A.Kumble	Australia	Chennai[1]	2004-05
13/196(7/123 + 6/73)	Harbhajan Singh	Australia	Kolkata	2000-01
12/104(6/52 + 6/52)	B.S.Chandrasekhar	Australia	Melbourne	1977-78
12/108(8/55 + 4/53)	M.H.Mankad	England	Madras[1]	1951-52
12/126(7/59 + 5/67)	I.K.Pathan	Zimbabwe	Harare	2005-06
12/152(8/72 + 4/80)	S.Venkataraghavan	New Zealand	Delhi	1964-65
12/181(6/64 + 6/117)	L.Shivaramakrishnan	England	Bombay[3]	1984-85
12/279(8/141 + 4/138)	A.Kumble	Australia	Sydney	2003-04
11/96(5/45 + 6/51)	I.K.Pathan	Bangladesh	Dhaka	2004-05
11/122(5/31 + 6/91)	R.G.Nadkarni	Australia	Madras[2]	1964-65
11/125(5/38 + 6/87)	S.L.Venkatapathy Raju	Sri Lanka	Ahmedabad	1993-94
11/128(4/69 + 7/59)	A.Kumble	Sri Lanka	Lucknow[2]	1993-94

11/140(3/64 + 8/76)	E.A.S.Prasanna	New Zealand	Auckland	1975-76
11/146(4/90 + 7/56)	Kapil Dev	Pakistan	Madras[1]	1979-80
11/224(5/146 + 6/78)	Harbhajan Singh	Australia	Bangalore	2004-05
11/235(7/157 + 4/78)	B.S.Chandrasekhar	West Indies	Bombay[2]	1966-67
10/107(3/56 + 7/51)	Maninder Singh	Sri Lanka	Nagpur	1986-87
10/126(7/27 + 6/91)	Maninder Singh	Pakistan	Bangalore	1986-87
10/130(7/49 + 6/87)	Ghulam Ahmed	Australia	Calcutta	1956-57
10/134(4/67 + 6/67)	A.Kumble	New Zealand	Kanpur	1999-2000
10/141(7/62 + 3/79)	Harbhajan Singh	Pakistan	Bangalore	2004-05
10/135(1/52 + 9/83)	Kapil Dev	West Indies	Ahmedabad	1983-84
10/153(5/60 + 5/93)	B.K.Venkatesh Prasad	South Africa	Durban[2]	1996-97
10/157(6/72 + 4/85)	A.Kumble	Sri Lanka	Delhi	2005-06
10/163(3/98 + 7/63)	A.Kumble	Pakistan	Kolkata	2004-05
10/174(4/100 + 6/74)	E.A.S.Prasanna	Australia	Madras[1]	1969-70
10/177(6/105 + 4/72)	S.A.Durani	England	Madras[2]	1961-62
10/188(4/130 + 6/58)	C.Sharma	England	Birmingham	1986
10/194(5/89 + 5/105)	B.S.Bedi	Australia	Perth	1977-78
10/223(9/102 + 1/121)	S.P.Gupte	West Indies	Kanpur	1958-59
10/233(7/115 + 3/118)	A.Kumble	England	Ahmedabad	2001-02

PAKISTAN (44)		Opponents		
14/116(8/58 + 6/58)	Imran Khan	Sri Lanka	Lahore[2]	1981-82
13/101(9/56 + 4/45)	Abdul Qadir	England	Lahore[2]	1987-88
13/114(6/34 + 7/80)	Fazal Mahmood	Australia	Karachi[1]	1956-57
13/135(7/91 + 6/44)	Waqar Younis	Zimbabwe	Karachi[2]	1993-94
12/94(6/42 + 6/52)	Fazal Mahmood	India	Lucknow[1]	1952-53
12/94(5/52 + 7/42)	Danish Kaneria	Bangladesh	Multan[2]	2001-02
12/99(6/53 + 6/46)	Fazal Mahmood	England	The Oval	1954
12/100(6/34 + 6/66)	Fazal Mahmood	West Indies	Dacca	1958-59
12/130(7/76 + 5/54)	Waqar Younis	New Zealand	Faisalabad	1990-91
12/165(6/102 + 6/63)	Imran Khan	Australia	Sydney	1976-77
11/71(6/44 + 5/27)	Mohammad Asif	Sri Lanka	Kandy	2005-06
11/78(5/48 + 6/30)	Shoaib Akhtar	New Zealand	Wellington	2003-04
11/79(3/19 + 8/60)	Zulfiqar Ahmed	New Zealand	Karachi[1]	1955-56
11/79(5/37 + 6/42)	Imran Khan	India	Karachi[1]	1982-83
11/110(6/61 + 5/49)	Wasim Akram	West Indies	St John's	1999-2000
11/118(4/69 + 7/49)	Iqbal Qasim	Australia	Karachi[1]	1979-80
11/119(6/34 + 5/85)	Waqar Younis	Sri Lanka	Kandy	1994-95
11/121(7/80 + 4/41)	Imran Khan	West Indies	Georgetown	1987-88
11/125(2/39 + 9/86)	Sarfraz Nawaz	Australia	Melbourne	1978-79
11/130(4/64 + 7/66)	Intikhab Alam	New Zealand	Dunedin	1972-73
11/130(7/52 + 4/78)	Mohammad Zahid §	New Zealand	Rawalpindi[2]	1996-97
11/160(6/62 + 5/98)	Wasim Akram	Australia	Melbourne	1989-90
11/179(4/60 + 7/119)	Wasim Akram	New Zealand	Wellington	1993-94
11/180(6/98 + 5/82)	Imran Khan	India	Faisalabad	1982-83
11/190(8/69 + 3/121)	Sikander Bakht	India	Delhi	1979-80
11/218(4/76 + 7/142)	Abdul Qadir	Australia	Faisalabad	1982-83
10/77(3/37 + 7/40)	Imran Khan	England	Leeds	1987
10/79(6/49 + 4/30)	Shoaib Akhtar	Bangladesh	Peshawar[2]	2003-04
10/106(5/35 + 5/71)	Wasim Akram	Zimbabwe	Faisalabad	1996-97
10/106(3/20 + 7/86)	Waqar Younis	New Zealand	Lahore[1]	1990-91
10/106(6/48 + 4/58)	Mushtaq Ahmed	West Indies	Peshawar[2]	1997-98
10/128(5/56 + 5/72)	Wasim Akram	New Zealand	Dunedin	1984-85
10/133(6/78 + 4/55)	Waqar Younis	South Africa	Port Elizabeth	1997-98
10/143(4/59 + 6/84)	Mushtaq Ahmed	New Zealand	Lahore[2]	1996-97
10/155(7/66 + 3/89)	Saqlain Mushtaq	Zimbabwe	Bulawayo[2]	2002-03
10/171(3/115 + 7/56)	Mushtaq Ahmed	New Zealand	Christchurch	1995-96

10/175(4/135 + 6/40)	Iqbal Qasim	India	Bombay[3]	1979-80
10/182(5/91 + 5/91)	Intikhab Alam	New Zealand	Dacca	1969-70
10/186(5/88 + 5/98)	Abdul Qadir	England	Karachi[1]	1987-88
10/187(5/94 + 8/93)	Saqlain Mushtaq	India	Chennai[1]	1998-99
10/190(3/72 + 7/118)	Danish Kaneria	Sri Lanka	Karachi[1]	2004-05
10/194(5/84 + 5/110)	Abdul Qadir	England	Lahore[2]	1983-84
10/211(7/96 + 3/115)	Abdul Qadir	England	The Oval	1987
10/216(5/94 + 5/122)	Saqlain Mushtaq	India	Delhi	1998-99

SRI LANKA (21)		Opponents		
16/220(7/155 + 9/65)	M.Muralidaran	England	The Oval	1998
14/191(7/120 + 7/71)	W.P.U.J.C.Vaas	West Indies	Colombo (SSC)	2001-02
12/225(5/128 + 7/97)	M.Muralidaran	South Africa	Colombo(PSS)	2006-07
13/115(9/51 + 4/64)	M.Muralidaran	Zimbabwe	Kandy	2001-02
13/171(6/87 + 7/84)	M.Muralidaran	South Africa	Galle	2000-01
12/117(5/23 + 7/94)	M.Muralidaran	Zimbabwe	Kandy	1997-98
11/93(7/46 + 4/47)	M.Muralidaran	England	Galle	2003-04
11/132(3/62 + 8/70)	M.Muralidaran	England	Nottingham	2006
11/161(5/122 + 6/39)	M.Muralidaran	South Africa	Durban[2]	2000-01
11/170(6/126 + 5/44)	M.Muralidaran	West Indies	Galle	2001-02
11/196(8/87 + 3/109)	M.Muralidaran	India	Colombo (SSC)	2001-02
11/212(6/59 + 5/153)	M.Muralidaran	Australia	Galle	2003-04
10/83(2/37 + 8/46)	M.Muralidaran	West Indies	Kandy	2005-06
10/90(5/47 + 5/43)	W.P.U.J.C.Vaas	New Zealand	Napier	1994-95
10/98(5/39 + 5/59)	M.Muralidaran	Bangladesh	Colombo (PSS)	2002-03
10/111(5/13 + 5/98)	M.Muralidaran	Bangladesh	Colombo (SSC)	2001-02
10/115(6/86 + 4/29)	M.Muralidaran	England	Birmingham	2006
10/135(4/54 + 6/81)	M.Muralidaran	West Indies	Kandy	2001-02
10/148(4/77 + 6/71)	M.Muralidaran	Pakistan	Peshawar[2]	1999-2000
10/172(4/41 + 6/131)	M.Muralidaran	South Africa	Colombo(SSC)	2006-07
10/210(5/109 + 5/101)	U.D.U.Chandana	Australia	Cairns	2004-05

ZIMBABWE (3)		Opponents		
11/257(6/111 + 5/146)	A.G.Huckle	New Zealand	Bulawayo[2]	1997-98
10/158(8/109 + 2/49)	P.A.Strang	New Zealand	Bulawayo[2]	2000-01
10/161(6/73 + 4/88)	R.W.Price	West Indies	Harare	2003-04

BANGLADESH (1)		Opponents		
12/200(7/95 + 5/105)	Enamul Haque[2]	Zimbabwe	Dhaka	2004-05

DISTRIBUTION OF TEN WICKETS IN A MATCH

Taken Against	A	E	SA	WI	NZ	I	P	SL	Z	B	Total Against
					Taken For						
Australia	0	38	4	4	5	11	6	2	0	0	70
England	43	0	8	15	5	5	6	4	0	0	86
South Africa	7	26	0	0	0	1	1	4	0	0	39
West Indies	15	12	2	0	4	4	4	4	1	0	45
New Zealand	2	8	2	2	0	3	11	1	2	0	31
India	12	7	2	4	2	0	7	1	0	0	35
Pakistan	5	3	1	1	2	6	0	1	0	0	19
Sri Lanka	2	0	0	0	1	5	4	0	0	0	12
Zimbabwe	0	0	1	0	1	1	3	2	0	1	9
Bangladesh	1	0	1	0	1	1	2	2	0	0	8
Total For	87	94	21	26	21	37	44	21	3	1	355

MOST 'FIVE FORS' IN CONSECUTIVE INNINGS

6	C.T.B.Turner (Australia)	5/44)	v	England	Sydney	1887-88
		7/43)				
		5/27)	v	England	Lord's	1888
		5/36)				
		6/112	v	England	The Oval	1888
		5/86	v	England	Manchester	1888
5	T.Richardson (England)	6/104	v	Australia	Melbourne	1894-95
		6/39)	v	Australia	Lord's	1896
		5/134)				
		7/168)	v	Australia	Manchester	1896
		6/76)				
5	A.V.Bedser (England)	5/27	v	India	Manchester	1952
		5/41	v	India	The Oval	1952
		7/55)	v	Australia	Nottingham	1953
		7/44)				
		5/105	v	Australia	Lord's	1953
4	J.Briggs (England)	6/49)	v	Australia	Adelaide	1891-92
		6/87)				
		5/34)	v	Australia	The Oval	1893
		5/114)				
4	S.F.Barnes (England)	5/57)	v	South Africa	Durban[1]	1913-14
		5/48)				
		8/56)	v	South Africa	Johannesburg[1]	1913-14
		9/103)				
4	J.C.Laker (England)	5/58)	v	Australia	Leeds	1956
		6/55)				
		9/37)	v	Australia	Manchester	1956
		10/53)				
4	F.S.Trueman (England)	6/100)	v	West Indies	Lord's	1963
		5/52)				
		5/75)	v	West Indies	Birmingham	1963
		7/44)				
4	D.K.Lillee (Australia)	5/51)	v	New Zealand	Auckland	1976-77
		6/72)				
		6/26)	v	England	Melbourne	1976-77
		5/139)				
4	R.M.Hogg (Australia)	5/65)	v	England	Perth	1978-79
		5/57)				
		5/30)	v	England	Melbourne	1978-79
		5/36)				
4	Imran Khan (Pakistan)	8/60	v	India	Karachi[1]	1982-83
		6/98)	v	India	Faisalabad	1982-83
		5/82)				
		6/35	v	India	Hyderabad,Pak	1982-83
4	M.D.Marshall (West Indies)	5/82	v	Australia	Brisbane[2]	1984-85
		5/69)	v	Australia	Adelaide	1984-85
		5/38)				
		5/86	v	Australia	Melbourne	1984-85
4	Waqar Younis (Pakistan)	7/86	v	New Zealand	Lahore[2]	1990-91
		7/76)	v	New Zealand	Faisalabad	1990-91
		5/54)				
		5/76	v	West Indies	Karachi[1]	1990-91
4	Saqlain Mushtaq (Pakistan)	5/94)	v	India	Chennai[1]	1998-99
		5/93)				

		5/94)	v	India	Delhi	1998-99
		5/122)				
4	Harbhajan Singh (India)	7/123)	v	Australia	Kolkata	2000-01
		6/73)				
		7/133)	v	Australia	Chennai[1]	2000-01
		8/84)				
4	M.Muralidaran (Sri Lanka)	5/13)	v	Bangladesh	Colombo (SSC)	2001-02
		5/98)				
		6/126)	v	West Indies	Galle	2001-02
		5/44)				
4	S.K.Warne (Australia)	5/116)	v	Sri Lanka	Galle	2003-04
		5/43)				
		5/65)	v	Sri Lanka	Kandy	2003-04
		5/90)				

TEN WICKETS IN LAST TEST

13/91(6/54 + 7/37)	J.J.Ferris ¶	England	v	South Africa	Cape Town	1891-92
10/204(8/94 + 2/110)	T.Richardson	England	v	Australia	Sydney	1897-98
10/104(7/46 + 3/58)	C.Blythe	England	v	South Africa	Cape Town	1909-10
10/161(5/95 + 5/66)	H.V.Hordern	Australia	v	England	Sydney	1911-12
14/144(7/56 + 7/88)	S.F.Barnes	England	v	South Africa	Durban[1]	1913-14
11/96(5/37 + 6/59)	C.S.Marriott #	England	v	West Indies	The Oval	1933
13/173(7/100 + 6/73)	C.V.Grimmett §	Australia	v	South Africa	Durban[2]	1935-36
10/215(3/121 + 7/94)	A.R.Caddick	England	v	Australia	Sydney	2002-03
12/225(5/128 + 7/97)	M.Muralidaran †	Sri Lanka	v	South Africa	Colombo(PSS)	2006-07

¶ His only Test for England. # His only Test. § Grimmett took 10/88 v South Africa (Cape Town); 10/110 v South Africa (Johannesburg[1]); & 13/173 v South Africa (Durban[2]) in his last 3 Tests. † current player.

NINE WICKETS OR MORE IN AN INNINGS

O	M	R	W						
51.2	23	53	10	J.C.Laker	England	v	Australia	Manchester	1956
26.3	9	74	10	A.Kumble	India	v	Pakistan	Delhi	1998-99
14.2	6	28	9	G.A.Lohmann	England	v	South Africa	Johannesburg[1]	1895-96
16.4	4	37	9	J.C.Laker	England	v	Australia	Manchester	1956
40	19	51	9	M.Muralidaran	Sri Lanka	v	Zimbabwe	Kandy	2001-02
23.4	4	52	9	R.J.Hadlee	New Zealand	v	Australia	Brisbane[2]	1985-86
37	13	56	9	Abdul Qadir	Pakistan	v	England	Lahore[2]	1987-88
16.3	2	57	9	D.E.Malcolm	England	v	South Africa	The Oval	1994
54.2	27	65	9	M.Muralidaran	Sri Lanka	v	England	The Oval	1998
35.5	16	69	9	J.M.Patel	India	v	Australia	Kanpur	1959-60
30.3	6	83	9	Kapil Dev	India	v	West Indies	Ahmedabad	1983-84
35.4	7	86	9	Sarfraz Nawaz	Pakistan	v	Australia	Melbourne	1978-79
49.4	16	95	9	J.M.Noreiga	West Indies	v	India	Port-of-Spain	1970-71
34.3	11	102	9	S.P.Gupte	India	v	West Indies	Kanpur	1958-59
38.4	7	103	9	S.F.Barnes	England	v	South Africa	Johannesburg[1]	1913-14
37	11	113	9	H.J.Tayfield	South Africa	v	England	Johannesburg[3]	1956-57
47	8	121	9	A.A.Mailey	Australia	v	England	Melbourne	1920-21

EIGHT WICKETS IN AN INNINGS *(§ In first Test. # In last Test)*

8/7	G.A.Lohmann	England	v	South Africa	Port Elizabeth	1895-96
8/11	J.Briggs	England	v	South Africa	Cape Town	1888-89
8/24	G.D.McGrath	Australia	v	Pakistan	Perth	2004-05
8/29	S.F.Barnes	England	v	South Africa	The Oval	1912
8/29	C.E.H.Croft	West Indies	v	Pakistan	Port-of-Spain	1976-77
8/31	F.Laver	Australia	v	England	Manchester	1909

8/31	F.S.Trueman	England	v	India	Manchester	1952
8/34	I.T.Botham	England	v	Pakistan	Lord's	1978
8/35	G.A.Lohmann	England	v	Australia	Sydney	1886-87
8/38	L.R.Gibbs	West Indies	v	India	Bridgetown	1961-62
8/38	G.D.McGrath	Australia	v	England	Lord's	1997
8/43	A.E.Trott §	Australia	v	England	Adelaide	1894-95
8/43	H.Verity	England	v	Australia	Lord's	1934
8/43	R.G.D.Willis	England	v	Australia	Leeds	1981
8/45	C.E.L.Ambrose	West Indies	v	England	Bridgetown	1989-90
8/46	M.Muralidaran	Sri Lanka	v	West Indies	Kandy	2005-06
8/51	D.L.Underwood	England	v	Pakistan	Lord's	1974
8/52	M.H.Mankad	India	v	Pakistan	Delhi	1952-53
8/53	G.B.Lawrence	South Africa	v	New Zealand	Johannesburg[3]	1961-62
8/53	R.A.L.Massie §	Australia	v	England	Lord's	1972
8/53	A.R.C.Fraser	England	v	West Indies	Port-of-Spain	1997-98
8/55	M.H.Mankad	India	v	England	Madras[1]	1951-52
8/56	S.F.Barnes	England	v	South Africa	Johannesburg[1]	1913-14
8/58	G.A.Lohmann	England	v	Australia	Sydney	1891-92
8/58	Imran Khan	Pakistan	v	Sri Lanka	Lahore[2]	1981-82
8/59	C.Blythe	England	v	South Africa	Leeds	1907
8/59	A.A.Mallett	Australia	v	Pakistan	Adelaide	1972-73
8/60	Imran Khan	Pakistan	v	India	Karachi[1]	1982-83
8/61	N.D.Hirwani §	India	v	West Indies	Madras[1]	1987-88
8/64	L.Klusener	South Africa	v	India	Calcutta	1996-97
8/65	H.Trumble	Australia	v	England	The Oval	1902
8/68	W.Rhodes	England	v	Australia	Melbourne	1903-04
8/69	H.J.Tayfield	South Africa	v	England	Durban[2]	1956-57
8/69	Sikander Bakht	Pakistan	v	India	Delhi	1979-80
8/70	S.J.Snooke	South Africa	v	England	Johannesburg[1]	1905-06
8/70	M.Muralidaran	Sri Lanka	v	England	Nottingham	2006
8/71	G.D.McKenzie	Australia	v	West Indies	Melbourne	1968-69
8/71	S.K.Warne	Australia	v	England	Brisbane[2]	1994-95
8/71	A.A.Donald	South Africa	v	Zimbabwe	Harare	1995-96
8/72	S.Venkataraghavan	India	v	New Zealand	Delhi	1964-65
8/75	N.D.Hirwani §	India	v	West Indies	Madras[1]	1987-88
8/75	A.R.C.Fraser	England	v	West Indies	Bridgetown	1993-94
8/76	E.A.S.Prasanna	India	v	New Zealand	Auckland	1975-76
8/79	B.S.Chandrasekhar	India	v	England	Delhi	1972-73
8/81	L.C.Braund	England	v	Australia	Melbourne	1903-04
8/83	J.R.Ratnayeke	Sri Lanka	v	Pakistan	Sialkot	1985-86
8/84	R.A.L.Massie §	Australia	v	England	Lord's	1972
8/84	Harbhajan Singh	India	v	Australia	Chennai[1]	2000-01
8/85	Kapil Dev	India	v	Pakistan	Lahore[2]	1982-83
8/86	A.W.Greig	England	v	West Indies	Port-of-Spain	1973-74
8/86	J.Srinath	India	v	Pakistan	Calcutta	1998-99
8/87	M.G.Hughes	Australia	v	West Indies	Perth	1988-89
8/87	M.Muralidaran	Sri Lanka	v	India	Colombo (SSC)	2001-02
8/92	M.A.Holding	West Indies	v	England	The Oval	1976
8/94	T.Richardson #	England	v	Australia	Sydney	1897-98
8/97	C.J.McDermott	Australia	v	England	Perth	1990-91
8/103	I.T.Botham	England	v	West Indies	Lord's	1984
8/104	A.L.Valentine §	West Indies	v	England	Manchester	1950
8/106	Kapil Dev	India	v	Australia	Adelaide	1985-86
8/107	B.J.T.Bosanquet	England	v	Australia	Nottingham	1905
8/107	N.A.Foster	England	v	Pakistan	Leeds	1987
8/108	S.C.G.MacGill	Australia	v	Bangladesh	Fatullah	2005-06

8/109	P.A.Strang	Zimbabwe	v	New Zealand	Bulawayo[2]	2000-01
8/112	G.F.Lawson	Australia	v	West Indies	Adelaide	1984-85
8/126	J.C.White	England	v	Australia	Adelaide	1928-29
8/141	C.J.McDermott	Australia	v	England	Manchester	1985
8/141	A.Kumble	India	v	Australia	Sydney	2003-04
8/143	M.H.N.Walker	Australia	v	England	Melbourne	1974-75
8/164	Saqlain Mushtaq	Pakistan	v	England	Lahore[2]	2000-01
Best for Bangladesh						
7/95	Enamul Haque[2]	Bangladesh	v	Zimbabwe	Dhaka	2004-05

MOST WICKETS IN A TEST FOR A LOSING SIDE

13/132	J.Srinath	India	v	Pakistan	Calcutta	1998-99
13/163	S.F.Barnes	England	v	Australia	Melbourne	1901-02
13/217	M.G.Hughes	Australia	v	West Indies	Perth	1988-89
13/244	T.Richardson	England	v	Australia	Manchester	1896
12/87	C.T.B.Turner	Australia	v	England	Sydney	1887-88
12/89	H.Trumble	Australia	v	England	The Oval	1896
12/121	A.M.E.Roberts	West Indies	v	India	Madras[1]	1974-75
12/124	A.K.Davidson	Australia	v	India	Kanpur	1959-60
12/128	S.K.Warne	Australia	v	South Africa	Sydney	1993-94
12/149	D.L.Vettori	New Zealand	v	Australia	Auckland	1999-00
12/166	G.Dymock	Australia	v	India	Kanpur	1979-80
12/173	H.Trumble	Australia	v	England	The Oval	1902
12/246	S.K.Warne	Australia	v	England	The Oval	2005

MOST WICKETS IN AN INNINGS FOR A LOSING SIDE

9/83	Kapil Dev	India	v	West Indies	Ahmedabad	1983-84
9/95	J.M.Noreiga	West Indies	v	India	Port of Spain	1970-71
9/102	S.P.Gupte	India	v	West Indies	Kanpur	1958-59
8/53	A.R.C.Fraser	England	v	West Indies	Port of Spain	1997-98
8/58	G.A.Lohmann	England	v	Australia	Sydney	1891-92
8/65	H.Trumble	Australia	v	England	The Oval	1902
8/79	B.S.Chandrasekhar	India	v	England	Delhi	1972-73
8/81	L.C.Braund	England	v	Australia	Melbourne	1903-04
8/83	J.R.Ratnayeke	Sri Lanka	v	Pakistan	Sialkot	1985-86
8/86	J.Srinath	India	v	Pakistan	Calcutta	1998-99
8/87	M.G.Hughes	Australia	v	West Indies	Perth	1988-89
8/94	T.Richardson	England	v	Australia	Sydney	1897-98
8/103	I.T.Botham	England	v	West Indies	Lord's	1984
8/104	A.L.Valentine	West Indies	v	England	Manchester	1950
8/107	N.A.Foster	England	v	Pakistan	Leeds	1987
8/109	P.A.Strang	Zimbabwe	v	New Zealand	Bulawayo[2]	2000-01
8/112	G.F.Lawson	Australia	v	West Indies	Adelaide	1984-85
8/143	M.H.N.Walker	Australia	v	England	Melbourne	1974-75

OLDEST PLAYERS TO TAKE 10 OR MORE WICKETS IN A MATCH

Years	Days	Player	Date of Birth				
49	314	H.Ironmonger	7.04.1882	11/24	Australia v South Africa	Melbourne	1931-32
48	313	H.Ironmonger	7.04.1882	11/79	Australia v West Indies	Melbourne	1930-31
44	69	C.V.Grimmett	25.12.1891	13/173	Australia v South Africa	Durban[2]	1935-36
44	54	C.V.Grimmett	25.12.1891	10/110	Australia v South Africa	Johannesburg[1]	1935-36
44	10	C.V.Grimmett	25.12.1891	10/88	Australia v South Africa	Cape Town	1935-36
41	73	A.P.Freeman	17.05.1888	10/207	England v South Africa	Leeds	1929
41	59	A.P.Freeman	17.05.1888	12/171	England v South Africa	Manchester	1929
41	39	C.V.Grimmett	25.12.1891	14/199	Australia v South Africa	Adelaide	1931-32
40	305	S.F.Barnes	19.04.1873	14/144	England v South Africa	Durban[1]	1913-14

40	255	S.F.Barnes	19.04.1873	17/159	England v South Africa	Johannesburg[1]	1913-14
40	242	S.F.Barnes	19.04.1873	10/105	England v South Africa	Durban[1]	1913-14
40	68	A.P.Freeman	17.05.1888	10/93	England v West Indies	Manchester	1928
39	116	S.F.Barnes	19.04.1873	13/57	England v South Africa	The Oval	1912
39	82	S.F.Barnes	19.04.1873	10/115	England v South Africa	Leeds	1912
39	54	S.F.Barnes	19.04.1873	11/110	England v South Africa	Lord's	1912
39	37	R.G.Holland	19.10.1946	10/174	Australia v New Zealand	Sydney	1985-86
38	355	C.V.Grimmett	25.12.1891	11/183	Australia v West Indies	Adelaide	1930-31
38	173	C.V.Grimmett	25.12.1891	10/201	Australia v England	Nottingham	1930
38	75	R.G.Holland	19.10.1946	10/144	Australia v West Indies	Sydney	1984-85
37	353	J.C.White	19.02.1891	13/256	England v Australia	Adelaide	1928-29
37	335	C.S.Marriott	14.09.1895	11/96	England v West Indies	The Oval	1933
37	263	H.H.H.Johnson	13.07.1910	10/96	West Indies v England	Kingston	1947-48
37	149	R.J.Hadlee	3.07.1951	10/88	New Zealand v India	Bombay[3]	1988-89
36	315	C.R.Miller	6.02.1964	10/113	Australia v West Indies	Adelaide	2000-01
36	211	K.R.Miller	28.11.1919	10/152	Australia v England	Lord's	1956
36	180	R.J.Hadlee	3.07.1951	10/176	New Zealand v Australia	Melbourne	1987-88
36	0	S.K.Warne	13.09.1969	12/246	Australia v England	The Oval	2005
35	328	S.K.Warne	13.09.1969	10/162	Australia v England	Birmingham	2005
35	250	E.A.S.Prasanna	22.05.1940	11/140	India v New Zealand	Auckland	1975-76
35	133	Imran Khan	25.11.1952	11/121	Pakistan v West Indies	Georgetown	1987-88
35	93	H.Trumble	12.05.1867	12/173	Australia v England	The Oval	1902
35	75	H.Trumble	12.05.1867	10/128	Australia v England	Manchester	1902
35	40	R.J.Hadlee	3.07.1951	10/140	New Zealand v England	Nottingham	1986
35	27	J.M.Patel	26.11.1924	14/124	India v Australia	Kanpur	1959-60
Oldest for the other countries:							
34	39	A.A.Donald	20.10.1966	11/127	South Africa v England	Johannesburg[3]	1999-2000
34	120	M.Muralidaran	17.04.1972	12/225	Sri Lanka v South Africa	Colombo (PSS)	2006-07
30	50	P.A.Strang	28.07.1970	10/158	Zimbabwe v New Zealand	Bulawayo[2]	2000-01

OLDEST PLAYERS TO TAKE FIVE OR MORE WICKETS IN AN INNINGS

Years	Days	Player	Date of Birth				
49	314	H.Ironmonger	7.04.1882	6/18	Australia v South Africa	Melbourne	1931-32
49	311	H.Ironmonger	7.04.1882	5/6	Australia v South Africa	Melbourne	1931-32
49	240	H.Ironmonger	7.04.1882	5/42	Australia v South Africa	Brisbane[2]	1931-32
48	312	H.Ironmonger	7.04.1882	7/23	Australia v West Indies	Melbourne	1930-31
46	272	D.D.Blackie	5.04.1882	6/94	Australia v England	Melbourne	1928-29
45	157	A.J.Traicos	17.05.1947	5/85	Zimbabwe v India	Harare	1992-93
44	69	C.V.Grimmett	25.12.1891	6/73	Australia v South Africa	Durban[2]	1935-36
44	65	C.V.Grimmett	25.12.1891	7/100	Australia v South Africa	Durban[2]	1935-36
44	54	C.V.Grimmett	25.12.1891	7/40	Australia v South Africa	Johannesburg[1]	1935-36
44	10	C.V.Grimmett	25.12.1891	5/56	Australia v South Africa	Cape Town	1935-36
44	9	C.V.Grimmett	25.12.1891	5/32	Australia v South Africa	Cape Town	1935-36
42	242	F.E.Woolley	27.05.1887	7/76	England v New Zealand	Wellington	1929-30
42	241	C.V.Grimmett	25.12.1891	5/64	Australia v England	The Oval	1934
42	168	C.V.Grimmett	25.12.1891	5/81	Australia v England	Nottingham	1934
41	137	E.E.Hemmings	20.02.1949	6/58	England v New Zealand	Birmingham	1990
41	73	A.P.Freeman	17.05.1888	5/100	England v South Africa	Manchester	1929
41	72	A.P.Freeman	17.05.1888	7/71	England v South Africa	Manchester	1929
41	61	L.R.Gibbs	29.09.1934	5/102	West Indies v Australia	Brisbane[2]	1975-76
41	56	A.P.Freeman	17.05.1888	7/115	England v South Africa	Leeds	1929
40	305	S.F.Barnes	19.04.1873	7/88	England v South Africa	Durban[1]	1913-14
40	301	S.F.Barnes	19.04.1873	7/56	England v South Africa	Durban[1]	1913-14
40	261	S.F.Barnes	19.04.1873	5/102	England v South Africa	Johannesburg[1]	1913-14
40	255	S.F.Barnes	19.04.1873	9/103	England v South Africa	Johannesburg[1]	1913-14
40	251	S.F.Barnes	19.04.1873	8/56	England v South Africa	Johannesburg[1]	1913-14

40	242	S.F.Barnes	19.04.1873	5/48	England v South Africa	Durban[1]	1913-14
40	238	S.F.Barnes	19.04.1873	5/57	England v South Africa	Durban[1]	1913-14
40	223	A.A.Mailey	3.01.1886	6/138	Australia v England	The Oval	1926
40	203	C.P.Carter	23.04.1881	6/91	South Africa v Australia	Johannesburg[1]	1921-22
40	121	L.R.Gibbs	29.09.1934	7/98	West Indies v India	Bombay[3]	1974-75
40	99	W.J.O'Reilly	20.12.1905	5/14	Australia v New Zealand	Wellington	1945-46
40	86	G.W.A.Chubb	12.04.1911	6/51	South Africa v England	Manchester	1951
40	77	L.R.Gibbs	29.09.1934	6/76	West Indies v India	Delhi	1974-75
40	72	F.R.Brown	16.12.1910	5/49	England v Australia	Melbourne	1950-51
40	70	G.W.A.Chubb	12.04.1911	5/77	South Africa v England	Lord's	1951
40	68	A.P.Freeman	17.05.1888	5/39	England v West Indies	Manchester	1928
40	65	A.P.Freeman	17.05.1888	5/54	England v West Indies	Manchester	1928
40	39	C.V.Grimmett	25.12.1891	7/83	Australia v South Africa	Adelaide	1931-32
40	35	C.V.Grimmett	25.12.1891	7/116	Australia v South Africa	Adelaide	1931-32
40	12	C.V.Grimmett	25.12.1891	6/92	Australia v South Africa	Melbourne	1931-32
39	281	D.S.de Silva	11.06.1942	5/59	Sri Lanka v Pakistan	Faisalabad	1981-82
39	231	F.J.Laver	7.12.1869	8/31	Australia v England	Manchester	1909
39	182	R.Peel	12.02.1857	6/23	England v Australia	The Oval	1896
39	130	L.R.Gibbs	29.09.1934	6/108	West Indies v England	Port-of-Spain	1973-74
39	124	S.F.Barnes	19.04.1873	5/30	England v Australia	The Oval	1912
39	116	S.F.Barnes	19.04.1873	8/29	England v South Africa	The Oval	1912
39	115	S.F.Barnes	19.04.1873	5/28	England v South Africa	The Oval	1912
39	80	S.F.Barnes	19.04.1873	6/52	England v South Africa	Leeds	1912
39	76	R.Illingworth	8.06.1932	5/70	England v India	The Oval	1971
39	54	S.F.Barnes	19.04.1873	6/85	England v South Africa	Lord's	1912
39	52	S.F.Barnes	19.04.1873	5/25	England v South Africa	Lord's	1912
39	34	R.G.Holland	19.10.1946	6/106	Australia v New Zealand	Sydney	1985-86
39	26	C.V.Grimmett	25.12.1891	5/49	Australia v West Indies	Brisbane[1]	1930-31
39	6	R.J.Hadlee	3.07.1951	5/53	New Zealand v England	Birmingham	1990
39	5	A.A.Mailey	3.01.1886	5/92	Australia v England	Melbourne	1924-25

YOUNGEST PLAYERS TO TAKE 10 OR MORE WICKETS IN A MATCH

Years	Days	Player	Date of Birth				
18	43	Enamul Haque[2]	5.12.1986	11/199	Bangladesh v Zimbabwe	Dhaka	2004-05
18	256	Wasim Akram	3.06.1966	10/128	Pakistan v New Zealand	Dunedin	1984-85
18	334	S.Venkataraghavan	21.04.1946	12/152	India v New Zealand	Delhi	1964-65
18	338	L.Shivaramakrishnan	31.12.1965	12/181	India v England	Bombay[3]	1984-85
18	341	Waqar Younis	16.11.1971	10/106	Pakistan v New Zealand	Lahore[1]	1990-91
18	349	Waqar Younis	16.11.1971	12/130	Pakistan v New Zealand	Faisalabad	1990-91
19	89	N.D.Hirwani	18.10.1968	16/136	India v West Indies	Madras[1]	1987-88
20	42	A.L.Valentine	28.04.1930	11/204	West Indies v England	Manchester	1950
20	46	I.K.Pathan	27.10.1984	11/96	India v Bangladesh	Dhaka	2004-05
20	47	W.P.U.J.C.Vaas	27.01.1974	10/90	Sri Lanka v New Zealand	Napier	1994-95
20	110	A.L.Valentine	28.04.1930	10/160	West Indies v England	The Oval	1950
20	121	Mohammad Zahid	2.08.1976	11/130	Pakistan v New Zealand	Rawalpindi[2]	1996-97
20	182	W.Voce	8.08.1909	11/149	England v West Indies	Port-of-Spain	1929-30
20	186	C.Sharma	3.01.1966	10/188	India v England	Birmingham	1986
20	255	Harbhajan Singh	3.07.1980	13/196	India v Australia	Kolkata	2000-01
20	258	Danish Kaneria	16.12.1980	12/94	Pakistan v Bangladesh	Multan[2]	2001-02
20	261	Harbhajan Singh	3.07.1980	15/217	India v Australia	Chennai[1]	2000-01
Youngest for the other countries:							
21	76	D.L.Vettori	27.01.1979	12/149	New Zealand v Australia	Auckland	1999-2000
23	274	G.E.Palmer	22.05.1859	11/165	Australia v England	Sydney	1881-82
24	40	P.M.Pollock	30.06.1941	10/87	South Africa v England	Nottingham	1965
26	8	A.G.Huckle	21.09.1971	11/257	Zimbabwe v New Zealand	Bulawayo[2]	1997-98

YOUNGEST PLAYERS TO TAKE FIVE OR MORE WICKETS IN AN INNINGS

Years	Days	Player	Date of Birth				
16	307	Nasim-ul-Ghani	14.05.1941	5/116	Pakistan v West Indies	Georgetown	1957-58
16	321	Nasim-ul-Ghani	14.05.1941	6/67	Pakistan v West Indies	Port-of-Spain	1957-58
18	36	Enamul Haque[2]	5.12.1986	6/45	Bangladesh v Zimbabwe	Chittagong[1]	2004-05
18	41	Enamul Haque[2]	5.12.1986	7/95	Bangladesh v Zimbabwe	Dhaka	2004-05
18	43	Enamul Haque[2]	5.12.1986	5/105	Bangladesh v Zimbabwe	Dhaka	2004-05
18	49	D.L.Vettori	27.01.1979	5/84	New Zealand v Sri Lanka	Hamilton	1996-97
18	236	#Shahid Afridi	#1.03.1980	5/52	Pakistan v Australia	Karachi[1]	1998-99
18	253	Wasim Akram	3.06.1966	5/56	Pakistan v New Zealand	Dunedin	1984-85
18	256	Wasim Akram	3.06.1966	5/72	Pakistan v New Zealand	Dunedin	1984-85
18	294	R.J.Shastri	27.05.1962	5/125	India v New Zealand	Auckland	1980-81
18	301	E.Chigumbura	14.03.1986	5/54	Zimbabwe v Bangladesh	Chittagong[1]	2004-05
18	319	Shahid Nazir	4.12.1977	5/53	Pakistan v Zimbabwe	Sheikhupura	1996-97
18	332	S.Venkataraghavan	21.04.1946	8/72	India v New Zealand	Delhi	1964-65
18	334	L.Shivaramakrishnan	31.12.1965	6/64	India v England	Bombay[3]	1984-85
18	338	L.Shivaramakrishnan	31.12.1965	6/117	India v England	Bombay[3]	1984-85
18	341	Waqar Younis	16.11.1971	7/86	Pakistan v New Zealand	Lahore[2]	1990-91
18	346	Waqar Younis	16.11.1971	7/76	Pakistan v New Zealand	Faisalabad	1990-91
18	349	Waqar Younis	16.11.1971	5/54	Pakistan v New Zealand	Faisalabad	1990-91
18	351	L.Shivaramakrishnan	31.12.1965	6/99	India v England	Delhi	1984-85
18	364	Waqar Younis	16.11.1971	5/76	Pakistan v West Indies	Karachi[1]	1990-91
19	8	Waqar Younis	16.11.1971	5/46	Pakistan v West Indies	Faisalabad	1990-91
19	88	N.D.Hirwani	18.10.1968	8/61	India v West Indies	Madras[1]	1987-88
19	89	N.D.Hirwani	18.10.1968	8/75	India v West Indies	Madras[1]	1987-88
19	95	A.Cotter	3.12.1884	6/40	Australia v England	Melbourne	1903-04
19	101	K.R.Pushpakumara	21.07.1975	7/116	Sri Lanka v Zimbabwe	Harare	1994-95
19	136	D.L.Vettori	27.01.1979	5/84	New Zealand v Sri Lanka	Hamilton	1996-97
19	247	C.Sharma	3.01.1966	5/118	India v Sri Lanka	Colombo (PSS)	1985-86
19	253	J.J.Ferris	21.05.1867	5/76	Australia v England	Sydney	1886-87
19	214	Shahadat Hossain	7.8.1986	5/86	Bangladesh v Sri Lanka	Bogra	2005-06
19	253	M.G.Melle	3.06.1930	5/113	South Africa v Australia	Johannesburg[2]	1949-50
19	271	C.N.McCarthy	24.03.1929	6/43	South Africa v England	Durban[2]	1948-49
19	272	H.H.Streak	16.03.1974	5/56	Zimbabwe v Pakistan	Rawalpindi[2]	1993-94
19	281	J.J.Ferris	21.05.1867	5/71	Australia v England	Sydney	1886-87
19	324	P.R.Adams	20.01.1977	6/55	South Africa v India	Kanpur	1996-97
19	327	C.N.McCarthy	24.03.1929	5/114	South Africa v England	Johannesburg[2]	1948-49
19	356	Umar Gul	14.04.1984	5/31	Pakistan v India	Lahore[2]	2003-04
19	364	R.B.Desai	20.06.1939	5/89	India v England	Lord's	1959
20	2	G.D.McKenzie	24.06.1941	5/37	Australia v England	Lord's	1961
20	14	Mohammad Sami	24.02.1981	5/36	Pakistan v New Zealand	Auckland	2000-01
20	27	Waqar Younis	16.11.1971	5/84	Pakistan v Sri Lanka	Sialkot	1991-92
20	30	N.D.Hirwani	18.10.1968	6/59	India v New Zealand	Bangalore	1988-89
20	41	A.L.Valentine	28.04.1930	8/104	West Indies v England	Manchester	1950
20	44	W.P.U.J.C.Vaas	27.01.1974	5/47	Sri Lanka v New Zealand	Napier	1994-95
20	44	I.K.Pathan	27.10.1984	5/45	India v Bangladesh	Dhaka	2004-05
20	46	I.K.Pathan	27.10.1984	6/51	India v Bangladesh	Dhaka	2004-05
20	47	W.P.U.J.C.Vaas	27.01.1974	5/43	Sri Lanka v New Zealand	Napier	1994-95
20	51	Waqar Younis	16.11.1971	5/65	Pakistan v Sri Lanka	Faisalabad	1991-92
20	52	W.P.U.J.C.Vaas	27.01.1974	6/87	Sri Lanka v New Zealand	Dunedin	1994-95
20	52	I.K.Pathan	27.10.1984	5/32	India v Bangladesh	Chittagong[1]	2004-05
20	75	C.J.McDermott	14.04.1965	6/70	Australia v England	Lord's	1985
20	106	Azeem Hafeez	29.07.1963	5/100	Pakistan v Australia	Perth	1983-84
20	110	A.L.Valentine	28.04.1930	6/39	West Indies v England	The Oval	1950
20	110	V.Razdan	25.08.1969	5/79	India v Pakistan	Sialkot	1989-90
20	111	C.J.McDermott	14.04.1965	8/141	Australia v England	Manchester	1985

20	112	Saqlain Mushtaq	29.12.1976	5/89	Pakistan v Sri Lanka	Colombo (RPS)	1996-97
20	121	Mohammad Zahid	2.08.1976	7/66	Pakistan v New Zealand	Rawalpindi[2]	1996-97
20	134	Azeem Hafeez	29.07.1963	5/167	Pakistan v Australia	Adelaide	1983-84
20	143	G.P.Wickramasinghe	14.08.1971	5/73	Sri Lanka v Pakistan	Faisalabad	1991-92
20	154	C.Sharma	3.01.1966	5/64	India v England	Lord's	1986
20	165	P.M.Pollock	30.06.1941	6/38	South Africa v New Zealand	Durban[2]	1961-62
20	182	W.Voce	8.08.1909	7/70	England v West Indies	Port-of-Spain	1929-30
20	185	C.Sharma	3.01.1966	6/58	India v England	Birmingham	1986
20	188	Kapil Dev	6.01.1959	5/146	India v England	Birmingham	1979
20	204	Arif Butt	17.05.1944	6/89	Pakistan v Australia	Melbourne	1964-65
20	215	Waqar Younis	16.11.1971	5/91	Pakistan v England	Lord's	1992
20	251	Harbhajan Singh	3.07.1980	7/123	India v Australia	Kolkata	2000-01
20	252	Waqar Younis	16.11.1971	5/113	Pakistan v England	Leeds	1992
20	255	A.Cotter	3.12.1884	7/148	Australia v England	The Oval	1905
20	255	Harbhajan Singh	3.07.1980	6/73	India v Australia	Kolkata	2000-01
20	256	Danish Kaneria	16.12.1980	6/42	Pakistan v Bangladesh	Multan[2]	2001-02
20	258	Danish Kaneria	16.12.1980	6/52	Pakistan v Bangladesh	Multan[2]	2001-02
20	259	Harbhajan Singh	3.07.1980	7/133	India v Australia	Chennai[1]	2000-01
20	262	Harbhajan Singh	3.07.1980	8/84	India v Australia	Chennai[1]	2000-01
20	264	C.L.Cairns	13.06.1970	5/75	New Zealand v Sri Lanka	Auckland	1990-91
20	267	Waqar Younis	16.11.1971	5/52	Pakistan v England	The Oval	1992
20	283	Kapil Dev	6.01.1959	5/82	India v Australia	Delhi	1979-80
20	284	Saqlain Mushtaq	29.12.1976	5/129	Pakistan v South Africa	Faisalabad	1997-98
20	294	Kapil Dev	6.01.1959	5/74	India v Australia	Calcutta	1979-80
20	298	R.L.Johnson	30.07.1982	5/73	England v Zimbabwe	Lord's	2003
20	305	T.J.Friend	7.01.1981	5/31	Zimbabwe v Bangladesh	Dhaka	2001-02
20	313	D.J.J.Bravo	7.10.1983	6/55	West Indies v England	Manchester	2004
20	323	H.H.Streak	16.03.1974	6/90	Zimbabwe v Pakistan	Harare	1994-95
20	329	H.H.Streak	16.03.1974	5/70	Zimbabwe v Pakistan	Bulawayo[2]	1994-95
20	331	J.J.C.Lawson	13.01.1982	6/3	West Indies v Bangladesh	Dhaka	2002-03
20	333	Kapil Dev	6.01.1959	5/58	India v Pakistan	Delhi	1979-80
20	355	Kapil Dev	6.01.1959	6/63	India v Pakistan	Kanpur	1979-80
20	356	H.J.Tayfield	30.01.1929	7/23	South Africa v Australia	Durban[2]	1949-50
20	361	E.P.Nupen	1.01.1902	5/53	South Africa v England	Johannesburg[1]	1922-23
20	363	J.M.Blanckenberg	31.12.1892	5/83	South Africa v England	Johannesburg[1]	1913-14

#Medical tests organised by the Pakistan Cricket Board in 1996, showed that Shahid Afridi was born in circa 1977 and was at least 19 years of age at that time.

DISTRIBUTION OF FIVE WICKETS IN AN INNINGS

Taken					Taken For						Total
Against	A	E	SA	WI	NZ	I	P	SL	Z	B	Against
Australia	0	231	39	59	33	53	30	11	2	1	459
England	272	0	90	86	33	56	33	8	2	0	580
South Africa	64	99	0	6	10	11	5	14	2	1	212
West Indies	78	85	15	0	21	38	29	13	3	0	282
New Zealand	21	59	25	19	0	29	43	15	3	1	215
India	40	49	8	47	22	0	36	13	5	1	221
Pakistan	38	36	8	20	17	37	0	16	7	2	181
Sri Lanka	13	8	8	6	13	15	23	0	1	2	89
Zimbabwe	1	3	3	2	8	7	13	11	0	5	53
Bangladesh	5	4	5	3	5	4	7	8	4	0	45
Total For	532	574	201	248	162	250	219	109	29	13	2337

FIVE WICKETS IN AN INNINGS

(§ In first Test appearance against that country; † on Test debut; # Ferris & Trott had previously played for Australia and Traicos for South Africa.)

AUSTRALIA *(532)*			Opponents		
Alderman,TM	(14)	†§ 5/62	England	Nottingham	1981
		6/135	England	Leeds	1981
		5/42	England	Birmingham	1981
		5/109	England	Manchester	1981
		6/128	West Indies	Perth	1984-85
		5/107)	England	Leeds	1989
		5/44)			
		6/128	England	Lord's	1989
		5/66	England	Manchester	1989
		5/69	England	Nottingham	1989
		5/66	England	The Oval	1989
		5/105	Pakistan	Melbourne	1989-90
		5/65	Pakistan	Sydney	1989-90
		6/47	England	Brisbane[2]	1990-91
Archer,RG	(1)	5/53	England	The Oval	1956
Armstrong,WW	(3)	5/122	England	Leeds	1905
		5/27	England	Birmingham	1909
		6/34	England	Lord's	1909
Benaud,R	(16)	§ 7/72	India	Madras[2]	1956-57
		6/52)	India	Calcutta	1956-57
		5/53)			
		5/49	South Africa	Cape Town	1957-58
		5/114	South Africa	Durban[2]	1957-58
		5/84	South Africa	Johannesburg[3]	1957-58
		5/82	South Africa	Port Elizabeth	1957-58
		5/83	England	Sydney	1958-59
		5/91	England	Adelaide	1958-59
		5/93	Pakistan	Karachi[1]	1959-60
		5/76	India	Delhi	1959-60
		5/43	India	Madras[2]	1959-60
		5/96	West Indies	Adelaide	1960-61
		6/70	England	Manchester	1961
		6/115	England	Brisbane[2]	1962-63
		5/68	South Africa	Brisbane[2]	1963-64
Bevan,MG	(1)	6/82	West Indies	Adelaide	1996-97
Bichel,AJ	(1)	5/60	West Indies	Melbourne	2000-01
Blackie,DD	(1)	6/94	England	Melbourne	1928-29
Border,AR	(2)	7/46	West Indies	Sydney	1988-89
		5/68	West Indies	Georgetown	1990-91
Boyle,HF	(1)	6/42	England	Manchester	1884
Bright,RJ	(4)	§ 7/87	Pakistan	Karachi[1]	1979-80
		5/172	Pakistan	Lahore[2]	1979-80
		5/68	England	Birmingham	1981
		5/94	India	Madras[1]	1986-87
Callaway,ST	(1)	5/37	England	Adelaide	1894-95
Chappell,GS	(1)	5/61	Pakistan	Sydney	1972-73
Clark,SR	(1)	§ 5/55	South Africa	Cape Town	2005-06
Clarke,MJ	(1)	6/9	India	Mumbai[3]	2004-05
Connolly,AN	(4)	5/72	England	Leeds	1968
		5/122	West Indies	Adelaide	1968-69
		5/47	South Africa	Cape Town	1969-70
		6/47	South Africa	Port Elizabeth	1969-70

Cook,SH	(1)	†§ 5/39	New Zealand	Perth	1997-98
Cooper,WH	(1)	†§ 6/120	England	Melbourne	1881-82
Cotter,A	(7)	6/40	England	Melbourne	1903-04
		7/148	England	The Oval	1905
		6/101	England	Sydney	1907-08
		5/142	England	Melbourne	1907-08
		5/38	England	Leeds	1909
		6/95	England	The Oval	1909
		§ 6/69	South Africa	Sydney	1910-11
Davidson,AK	(14)	§ 6/34	South Africa	Johannesburg[3]	1957-58
		5/38	South Africa	Port Elizabeth	1957-58
		6/64	England	Melbourne	1958-59
		5/31)	India	Kanpur	1959-60
		7/93)			
		§ 5/135)	West Indies	Brisbane[2]	1960-61
		§ 6/87)			
		6/83	West Indies	Melbourne	1960-61
		5/80	West Indies	Sydney	1960-61
		5/84	West Indies	Melbourne	1960-61
		5/42	England	Lord's	1961
		5/63	England	Leeds	1961
		6/75	England	Melbourne	1962-63
		5/25	England	Sydney	1962-63
Dodemaide,AIC	(1)	†§ 6/58	New Zealand	Melbourne	1987-88
Dymock,G	(5)	†§ 5/58	New Zealand	Adelaide	1973-74
		5/99)	India	Kanpur	1979-80
		7/67)			
		6/34	England	Perth	1979-80
		5/104	West Indies	Adelaide	1979-80
Ferris,JJ	(4)	†§ 5/76	England	Sydney	1886-87
		5/71	England	Sydney	1886-87
		5/26	England	Lord's	1888
		5/49	England	The Oval	1890
Fleetwood-Smith,LO	(2)	§ 5/124	England	Melbourne	1936-37
		6/110	England	Adelaide	1936-37
Fleming,DW	(3)	5/46	England	Perth	1998-99
		5/59	Pakistan	Brisbane[2]	1999-2000
		§ 5/30	India	Adelaide	1999-2000
Garrett,TW	(2)	6/78	England	Sydney	1881-82
		5/80	England	Melbourne	1881-82
Giffen,G	(7)	7/117	England	Sydney	1884-85
		6/72	England	Sydney	1891-92
		5/43	England	Lord's	1893
		7/128	England	The Oval	1893
		6/155	England	Melbourne	1894-95
		5/76	England	Adelaide	1894-95
		5/26	England	Sydney	1894-95
Gillespie,JN	(8)	5/54	South Africa	Port Elizabeth	1996-97
		7/37	England	Leeds	1997
		5/88	England	Perth	1998-99
		5/89	West Indies	Adelaide	2000-01
		6/40	West Indies	Melbourne	2000-01
		5/53	England	Lord's	2001
		5/39	West Indies	Georgetown	2002-03
		5/56	India	Nagpur	2004-05
Gilmour,GJ	(3)	5/64	New Zealand	Auckland	1973-74

		§ 6/85	England	Leeds	1975
		5/34	West Indies	Melbourne	1975-76
Gleeson,JW	(3)	§ 5/122	West Indies	Brisbane[2]	1968-69
		5/61	West Indies	Melbourne	1968-69
		5/125	South Africa	Johannesburg[3]	1969-70
Gregory,JM	(4)	7/69	England	Melbourne	1920-21
		6/58	England	Nottingham	1921
		§ 6/77	South Africa	Durban[1]	1921-22
		5/111	England	Sydney	1924-25
Grimmett,CV	(21)	†§ 5/45)	England	Sydney	1924-25
		6/37)			
		5/88	England	Leeds	1926
		6/131	England	Brisbane[1]	1928-29
		5/102	England	Adelaide	1928-29
		5/107)	England	Nottingham	1930
		5/94)			
		6/167	England	Lord's	1930
		5/135	England	Leeds	1930
		§ 7/87	West Indies	Adelaide	1930-31
		5/49	West Indies	Brisbane[1]	1930-31
		6/92	South Africa	Melbourne	1931-32
		7/116)	South Africa	Adelaide	1931-32
		7/83)			
		5/81	England	Nottingham	1934
		5/64	England	The Oval	1934
		5/32)	South Africa	Cape Town	1935-36
		5/56)			
		7/40	South Africa	Johannesburg[1]	1935-36
		7/100)	South Africa	Durban[2]	1935-36
		6/73)			
Hawke,NJN	(6)	6/139	South Africa	Adelaide	1963-64
		5/75	England	Leeds	1964
		6/47	England	The Oval	1964
		6/72	West Indies	Georgetown	1964-65
		7/105	England	Sydney	1965-66
		5/54	England	Adelaide	1965-66
Hazlitt,GR	(1)	7/25	England	The Oval	1912
Higgs,JD	(2)	5/148	England	Sydney	1979-80
		§ 7/143	India	Madras[1]	1979-80
Hogan,TG	(1)	†§ 5/66	Sri Lanka	Kandy	1982-83
Hogg,RM	(6)	†§ 6/74	England	Brisbane[2]	1978-79
		5/65)	England	Perth	1978-79
		5/57)			
		5/30)	England	Melbourne	1978-79
		5/36)			
		6/77	West Indies	Bridgetown	1983-84
Holland,RG	(3)	6/54	West Indies	Sydney	1984-85
		§ 5/68	England	Lord's	1985
		6/106	New Zealand	Sydney	1985-86
Horan,TP	(1)	6/40	England	Sydney	1884-85
Hordern,HV	(5)	†§ 5/66	South Africa	Melbourne	1910-11
		§ 5/85)	England	Sydney	1911-12
		7/90)			
		5/95)	England	Sydney	1911-12
		5/66)			
Hornibrook,PM	(1)	7/92	England	The Oval	1930

Howell,WP	(1)	5/81	South Africa	Cape Town	1902-03
Hughes,MG	(7)	§ 5/67	Sri Lanka	Perth	1987-88
		§ 5/130)	West Indies	Perth	1988-89
		8/87)			
		5/88	Sri Lanka	Hobart	1989-90
		5/111	Pakistan	Adelaide	1989-90
		5/64	West Indies	Adelaide	1992-93
		5/92	England	Nottingham	1993
Hurst,AG	(2)	5/28	England	Sydney	1978-79
		5/94	Pakistan	Perth	1978-79
Ironmonger,H	(4)	7/23	West Indies	Melbourne	1930-31
		§ 5/42	South Africa	Brisbane[2]	1931-32
		5/6)	South Africa	Melbourne	1931-32
		6/18)			
Iverson,JB	(1)	6/27	England	Sydney	1950-51
Jenner,TJ	(1)	5/90	West Indies	Port-of-Spain	1972-73
Johnson,IWG	(3)	§ 6/42	England	Sydney	1946-47
		5/34	South Africa	Durban[2]	1949-50
		7/44	West Indies	Georgetown	1954-55
Johnston,WA	(7)	§ 5/36	England	Nottingham	1948
		§ 6/44	South Africa	Johannesburg[2]	1949-50
		5/35	England	Brisbane[2]	1950-51
		6/62	West Indies	Adelaide	1951-52
		5/110	South Africa	Adelaide	1952-53
		6/152	South Africa	Melbourne	1952-53
		5/85	England	Melbourne	1954-55
Jones,E	(3)	6/82	England	Sydney	1897-98
		5/88	England	Nottingham	1899
		7/88	England	Lord's	1899
Kasprowicz,MS	(4)	7/36	England	The Oval	1997
		5/28	India	Bangalore	1997-98
		7/39	Sri Lanka	Darwin	2004-05
		5/30	Pakistan	Perth	2004-05
Katich,SM	(1)	§ 6/65	Zimbabwe	Sydney	2003-04
Kelleway,C	(1)	5/33	South Africa	Manchester	1912
Kendall,TK	(1)	†§ 7/55	England	Melbourne	1876-77
Kline,LF	(1)	§ 7/75	Pakistan	Lahore[2]	1959-60
Laughlin,TJ	(1)	5/101	West Indies	Kingston	1977-78
Laver,FJ	(2)	7/64	England	Nottingham	1905
		8/31	England	Manchester	1909
Lawson,GF	(11)	7/81	England	Lord's	1981
		5/108	England	Perth	1982-83
		6/47)	England	Brisbane[2]	1982-83
		5/87)			
		5/66	England	Adelaide	1982-83
		5/49	Pakistan	Brisbane[2]	1983-84
		5/59	Pakistan	Sydney	1983-84
		5/116	West Indies	Brisbane[2]	1984-85
		8/112	West Indies	Adelaide	1984-85
		5/103	England	Nottingham	1985
		6/72	England	Manchester	1989
Lee,B	(7)	†§ 5/47	India	Melbourne	1999-2000
		5/77	New Zealand	Hamilton	1999-2000
		5/61	West Indies	Perth	2000-01
		5/67	New Zealand	Brisbane[2]	2001-02
		5/30	West Indies	Brisbane[2]	2005-06

		5/93	South Africa	Perth	2005-06
		5/69	South Africa	Durban[2]	2005-06
Lillee,DK	(23)	†§ 5/84	England	Adelaide	1970-71
		6/66	England	Manchester	1972
		5/58)	England	The Oval	1972
		5/123)			
		5/15	England	Birmingham	1975
		5/63	West Indies	Melbourne	1975-76
		5/163	Pakistan	Adelaide	1976-77
		6/82	Pakistan	Melbourne	1976-77
		5/51)	New Zealand	Auckland	1976-77
		6/72)			
		6/26)	England	Melbourne	1976-77
		5/139)			
		5/78	West Indies	Adelaide	1979-80
		6/60)	England	Melbourne	1979-80
		5/78)			
		6/53	New Zealand	Brisbane[2]	1980-81
		5/65	New Zealand	Perth	1980-81
		5/46	England	Nottingham	1981
		7/89	England	The Oval	1981
		5/18	Pakistan	Perth	1981-82
		5/81	Pakistan	Brisbane[2]	1981-82
		7/83	West Indies	Melbourne	1981-82
		6/171	Pakistan	Adelaide	1983-84
Lindwall,RR	(12)	7/63	England	Sydney	1946-47
		7/38	India	Adelaide	1947-48
		5/70	England	Lord's	1948
		6/20	England	The Oval	1948
		5/32	South Africa	Cape Town	1949-50
		5/52	West Indies	Sydney	1951-52
		5/60	South Africa	Brisbane[2]	1952-53
		5/57	England	Nottingham	1953
		5/66	England	Lord's	1953
		5/54	England	Leeds	1953
		6/95	West Indies	Georgetown	1954-55
		7/43	India	Madras[2]	1956-57
Lyons,JJ	(1)	5/30	England	Lord's	1890
Macartney,CG	(2)	7/58	England	Leeds	1909
		5/44	South Africa	Cape Town	1921-22
McCool,CL	(3)	5/109	England	Sydney	1946-47
		5/44	England	Sydney	1946-47
		5/41	South Africa	Cape Town	1949-50
McDermott,CJ	(14)	6/70	England	Lord's	1985
		8/141	England	Manchester	1985
		5/97	New Zealand	Melbourne	1987-88
		5/97	England	Adelaide	1990-91
		8/97	England	Perth	1990-91
		5/80	West Indies	Kingston	1990-91
		5/54	India	Brisbane[2]	1991-92
		5/76)	India	Adelaide	1991-92
		5/62)			
		6/53	England	Brisbane[2]	1994-95
		5/42	England	Melbourne	1994-95
		5/101	England	Sydney	1994-95
		6/38	England	Perth	1994-95

		5/49	Pakistan	Sydney	1995-96
McDonald,EA	(2)	5/32	England	Nottingham	1921
		5/143	England	The Oval	1921
MacGill,SCG	(11)	§ 5/66	Pakistan	Rawalpindi[2]	1998-99
		5/57)	England	Sydney	1998-99
		7/50)			
		7/104	West Indies	Sydney	2000-01
		5/152	England	Melbourne	2002-03
		5/75	West Indies	Bridgetown	2002-03
		§ 5/65	Bangladesh	Darwin	2003-04
		5/77)	Bangladesh	Cairns	2003-04
		5/56)			
		5/87	Pakistan	Sydney	2004-05
		8/108	Bangladesh	Fatullah	2005-06
McGrath,GD	(28)	§ 5/68	West Indies	Bridgetown	1994-95
		6/47	West Indies	Port-of-Spain	1994-95
		5/61	Pakistan	Hobart	1995-96
		5/40	Sri Lanka	Melbourne	1995-96
		5/50	West Indies	Melbourne	1996-97
		6/86	South Africa	Centurion	1996-97
		8/38	England	Lord's	1997
		7/76	England	The Oval	1997
		5/32	New Zealand	Brisbane[2]	1997-98
		5/66	Pakistan	Karachi[1]	1998-99
		6/85	England	Brisbane[2]	1998-99
		5/50)	West Indies	Port of Spain	1998-99
		5/28)			
		5/93	West Indies	Kingston	1998-99
		5/92	West Indies	Bridgetown	1998-99
		5/48)	India	Sydney	1999-2000
		5/55)			
		6/17	West Indies	Brisbane[2]	2000-01
		5/54	England	Lord's	2001
		5/49	England	Nottingham	2001
		7/76	England	Leeds	2001
		5/43	England	The Oval	2001
		5/21	South Africa	Johannesburg[3]	2001-02
		5/37	Sri Lanka	Darwin	2004-05
		8/24	Pakistan	Perth	2004-05
		6/115	New Zealand	Christchurch	2004-05
		5/53	England	Lord's	2005
		5/115	England	Manchester	2005
Mackay,KD	(2)	§ 6/42	Pakistan	Dacca	1959-60
		5/121	England	The Oval	1961
McKenzie,GD	(16)	†§ 5/37	England	Lord's	1961
		5/89	England	Adelaide	1962-63
		5/53	England	Nottingham	1964
		7/153	England	Manchester	1964
		§ 6/58	India	Madras[2]	1964-65
		§ 6/69	Pakistan	Karachi[1]	1964-65
		5/33	West Indies	Port-of-Spain	1964-65
		5/134	England	Melbourne	1965-66
		6/48	England	Adelaide	1965-66
		5/46	South Africa	Johannesburg[3]	1966-67
		5/65	South Africa	Cape Town	1966-67
		5/65	South Africa	Port Elizabeth	1966-67

		7/66	India	Melbourne	1967-68
		8/71	West Indies	Melbourne	1968-69
		5/69	India	Bombay[2]	1969-70
		6/67	India	Calcutta	1969-70
McLeod,CE	(2)	5/65	England	Adelaide	1897-98
		5/125	England	Manchester	1905
McLeod,RW	(1)	†§ 5/55	England	Melbourne	1891-92
Mailey,AA	(6)	5/160)	England	Adelaide	1920-21
		5/142)			
		9/121	England	Melbourne	1920-21
		5/119	England	Sydney	1920-21
		5/92	England	Melbourne	1924-25
		6/138	England	The Oval	1926
Mallett,AA	(6)	6/64	India	Delhi	1969-70
		5/91)	India	Madras[1]	1969-70
		5/53)			
		§ 5/126	South Africa	Cape Town	1969-70
		5/114	England	Leeds	1972
		§ 8/59	Pakistan	Adelaide	1972-73
Malone,MF	(1)	†§ 5/63	England	The Oval	1977
Massie,RAL	(2)	†§ 8/84)	England	Lord's	1972
		8/53)			
Matthews,GRJ	(2)	5/103)	India	Madras[1]	1986-87
		5/146)			
May,TBA	(3)	5/9	West Indies	Adelaide	1992-93
		5/89	England	Birmingham	1993
		5/65	New Zealand	Hobart	1993-94
Meckiff,I	(2)	†§ 5/125	South Africa	Johannesburg[3]	1957-58
		6/38	England	Melbourne	1958-59
Midwinter,WE	(1)	†§ 5/78	England	Melbourne	1876-77
Miller,CR	(3)	§ 5/55	New Zealand	Auckland	1999-2000
		5/81)	West Indies	Adelaide	2000-01
		5/32)			
Miller,KR	(7)	§ 7/60	England	Brisbane[2]	1946-47
		§ 5/40	South Africa	Johannesburg[2]	1949-50
		5/60	West Indies	Melbourne	1951-52
		5/26	West Indies	Sydney	1951-52
		6/107	West Indies	Kingston	1954-55
		5/72)	England	Lord's	1956
		5/80)			
Noble,MA	(9)	†§ 6/49	England	Melbourne	1897-98
		5/84	England	Melbourne	1897-98
		7/17)	England	Melbourne	1901-02
		6/60)			
		5/54	England	Sydney	1901-02
		6/98	England	Melbourne	1901-02
		5/51)	England	Sheffield	1902
		6/52)			
		7/11	England	Sydney	1903-04
O'Connor,JDA	(1)	†§ 5/40	England	Adelaide	1907-08
O'Keeffe,KJ	(1)	5/101	New Zealand	Christchurch	1976-77
O'Reilly,WJ	(11)	5/63)	England	Melbourne	1932-33
		5/66)			
		7/54	England	Nottingham	1934
		7/189	England	Manchester	1934
		5/20	South Africa	Johannesburg[1]	1935-36

Player	No.	Figures	Opponent	Venue	Season
		5/49	South Africa	Durban[2]	1935-36
		5/102	England	Brisbane[2]	1936-37
		5/51	England	Melbourne	1936-37
		5/66)	England	Leeds	1938
		5/56)			
		§ 5/14	New Zealand	Wellington	1945-46
Palmer,GE	(6)	7/68	England	Sydney	1881-82
		5/46	England	Sydney	1881-82
		7/65	England	Melbourne	1882-83
		5/103	England	Melbourne	1882-83
		6/111	England	Lord's	1884
		5/81	England	Adelaide	1884-85
Pascoe,LS	(1)	5/59	England	Lord's	1980
Philpott,PI	(1)	§ 5/90	England	Brisbane[2]	1965-66
Rackemann,CG	(3)	§ 5/32)	Pakistan	Perth	1983-84
		§ 6/86)			
		§ 5/161	West Indies	St John's	1983-84
Reid,BA	(5)	6/97)	England	Melbourne	1990-91
		7/51)			
		6/66)	India	Melbourne	1991-92
		6/60)			
		5/112	West Indies	Brisbane[2]	1992-93
Reiffel,PR	(5)	§ 5/65	England	Leeds	1993
		6/71	England	Birmingham	1993
		5/39	Sri Lanka	Adelaide	1995-96
		5/73	West Indies	Perth	1996-97
		5/49	England	Leeds	1997
Renneberg,DA	(2)	5/97	South Africa	Johannesburg[3]	1966-67
		§ 5/39	India	Adelaide	1967-68
Ring,DT	(2)	§ 6/80	West Indies	Brisbane[2]	1951-52
		§ 6/72	South Africa	Brisbane[2]	1952-53
Saunders,JV	(6)	†§ 5/43	England	Sydney	1901-02
		5/50	England	Sheffield	1902
		§ 7/34	South Africa	Johannesburg[1]	1902-03
		5/65	England	Adelaide	1907-08
		5/28	England	Melbourne	1907-08
		5/82	England	Sydney	1907-08
Sievers,MW	(1)	5/21	England	Melbourne	1936-37
Simpson,RB	(2)	5/57	England	Sydney	1962-63
		5/59	India	Sydney	1967-68
Sleep,PR	(1)	5/72	England	Sydney	1986-87
Spofforth,FR	(7)	6/48)	England	Melbourne	1878-79
		7/62)			
		7/46)	England	The Oval	1882
		7/44)			
		7/44	England	Sydney	1882-83
		6/90	England	Sydney	1884-85
		5/30	England	Sydney	1884-85
Taylor,PL	(1)	†§ 6/78	England	Sydney	1986-87
Thomson,JR	(8)	§ 6/46	England	Brisbane[2]	1974-75
		5/93	England	Perth	1974-75
		5/38	England	Birmingham	1975
		5/62	West Indies	Melbourne	1975-76
		6/50	West Indies	Sydney	1975-76
		6/77	West Indies	Bridgetown	1977-78
		5/73	England	Brisbane[2]	1982-83

		5/50	England	Sydney	1982-83
Toshack,ERH	(4)	§ 6/82	England	Brisbane[2]	1946-47
		§ 5/2)	India	Brisbane[2]	1947-48
		§ 6/29)			
		5/40	England	Lord's	1948
Trott,AE	(1)	†§ 8/43	England	Adelaide	1894-95
Trumble,H	(9)	6/59)	England	The Oval	1896
		6/30)			
		5/60	England	Leeds	1899
		6/74	England	Adelaide	1901-02
		5/62	England	Melbourne	1901-02
		6/53	England	Manchester	1902
		8/65	England	The Oval	1902
		5/34	England	Melbourne	1903-04
		7/28	England	Melbourne	1903-04
Turner,CTB	(11)	†§ 6/15	England	Sydney	1886-87
		5/41	England	Sydney	1886-87
		5/44)	England	Sydney	1887-88
		7/43)			
		5/27)	England	Lord's	1888
		5/36)			
		6/112	England	The Oval	1888
		5/86	England	Manchester	1888
		5/51	England	Melbourne	1891-92
		6/67	England	Lord's	1893
		5/32	England	Melbourne	1894-95
Walker,MHN	(6)	6/15	Pakistan	Sydney	1972-73
		§ 6/114	West Indies	Kingston	1972-73
		5/97	West Indies	Bridgetown	1972-73
		5/75	West Indies	Port-of-Spain	1972-73
		8/143	England	Melbourne	1974-75
		5/48	England	Birmingham	1975
Wall,TW	(3)	†§ 5/66	England	Melbourne	1928-29
		§ 5/14	South Africa	Brisbane[2]	1931-32
		5/72	England	Adelaide	1932-33
Walters,KD	(1)	5/66	West Indies	Georgetown	1972-73
Ward,FA	(1)	†§ 6/102	England	Brisbane[2]	1936-37
Warne,SK	(36)	§ 7/52	West Indies	Melbourne	1992-93
		5/82	England	Birmingham	1993
		6/31	New Zealand	Hobart	1993-94
		7/56)	South Africa	Sydney	1993-94
		5/72)			
		§ 5/89	Pakistan	Karachi[1]	1994-95
		6/136	Pakistan	Lahore[2]	1994-95
		8/71	England	Brisbane[2]	1994-95
		6/64	England	Melbourne	1994-95
		7/23	Pakistan	Brisbane[2]	1995-96
		6/48	England	Manchester	1997
		5/88	New Zealand	Hobart	1997-98
		5/75)	South Africa	Sydney	1997-98
		6/34)			
		5/52	Sri Lanka	Kandy	1999-2000
		5/110	Pakistan	Hobart	1999-2000
		5/71	England	Birmingham	2001
		6/33	England	Nottingham	2001
		7/165	England	The Oval	2001

		5/113	South Africa	Adelaide	2001-02
		6/161	South Africa	Cape Town	2001-02
		7/97	Pakistan	Colombo (PSS)	2002-03
		5/74	Pakistan	Sharjah	2002-03
		5/116)	Sri Lanka	Galle	2003-04
		5/43)			
		5/90)	Sri Lanka	Kandy	2003-04
		5/65)			
		6/125	India	Chennai[1]	2004-05
		5/39	New Zealand	Christchurch	2004-05
		6/46	England	Birmingham	2005
		6/122)	England	The Oval	2005
		6/124)			
		5/48	West Indies	Brisbane[2]	2005-06
		6/80	West Indies	Adelaide	2005-06
		6/86	South Africa	Durban[2]	2005-06
		5/113	Bangladesh	Chittagong[2]	2005-06
Waugh,ME	(1)	5/40	England	Adelaide	1994-95
Waugh,SR	(3)	5/69	England	Perth	1986-87
		5/92	West Indies	Melbourne	1988-89
		5/28	South Africa	Cape Town	1993-94
Whitney,MR	(2)	§ 7/89	West Indies	Adelaide	1988-89
		7/27	India	Perth	1991-92
Whitty,WJ	(3)	6/17	South Africa	Melbourne	1910-11
		6/104	South Africa	Adelaide	1910-11
		5/55	South Africa	Manchester	1912
Yardley,B	(6)	6/84	Pakistan	Perth	1981-82
		7/187	Pakistan	Melbourne	1981-82
		7/98	West Indies	Sydney	1981-82
		5/132	West Indies	Adelaide	1981-82
		5/107	England	Perth	1982-83
		§ 5/88	Sri Lanka	Kandy	1982-83

ENGLAND *(574)*			Opponents		
Allen,DA	(4)	5/67	India	Calcutta	1961-62
		5/30	Pakistan	Dacca	1961-62
		5/41	South Africa	Durban[2]	1964-65
		5/123	New Zealand	Auckland	1965-66
Allen,GOB	(5)	5/14	New Zealand	The Oval	1931
		§ 5/35)	India	Lord's	1936
		§ 5/43)			
		7/80	India	The Oval	1936
		5/36	Australia	Brisbane[2]	1936-37
Allom,MJC	(1)	†§ 5/38	New Zealand	Christchurch	1929-30
Allott,PJW	(1)	§ 6/61	West Indies	Leeds	1984
Anderson,JM	(2)	†§ 5/73	Zimbabwe	Lord's	2003
		5/105	South Africa	Nottingham	2003
Appleyard,R	(1)	†§ 5/51	Pakistan	Nottingham	1954
Arnold,EG	(1)	§ 5/37	South Africa	Lord's	1907
Arnold,GG	(6)	5/58	Pakistan	The Oval	1967
		§ 6/45	India	Delhi	1972-73
		5/131	New Zealand	Nottingham	1973
		5/27	New Zealand	Leeds	1973
		§ 5/113	West Indies	The Oval	1973
		5/86	Australia	Sydney	1974-75
Bailey,TE	(5)	†§ 6/118	New Zealand	Leeds	1949

		6/84	New Zealand	Manchester	1949
		7/34	West Indies	Kingston	1953-54
		5/20	South Africa	Johannesburg[3]	1956-57
		7/44	West Indies	Lord's	1957
Barlow,RG	(3)	5/19	Australia	The Oval	1882
		7/40	Australia	Sydney	1882-83
		7/44	Australia	Manchester	1886
Barnes,SF	(24)	†§ 5/65	Australia	Sydney	1901-02
		6/42)	Australia	Melbourne	1901-02
		7/121)			
		6/49	Australia	Sheffield	1902
		5/72	Australia	Melbourne	1907-08
		7/60	Australia	Sydney	1907-08
		6/63	Australia	Leeds	1909
		5/56	Australia	Manchester	1909
		5/44	Australia	Melbourne	1911-12
		5/105	Australia	Adelaide	1911-12
		5/74	Australia	Melbourne	1911-12
		§ 5/25)	South Africa	Lord's	1912
		§ 6/85)			
		6/52	South Africa	Leeds	1912
		5/28)	South Africa	The Oval	1912
		8/29)			
		5/30	Australia	The Oval	1912
		5/57)	South Africa	Durban[1]	1913-14
		5/48)			
		8/56)	South Africa	Johannesburg[1]	1913-14
		9/103)			
		5/102	South Africa	Johannesburg[1]	1913-14
		7/56)	South Africa	Durban[1]	1913-14
		7/88)			
Barnes,W	(3)	6/31	Australia	Melbourne	1884-85
		6/28	Australia	Sydney	1886-87
		5/32	Australia	The Oval	1888
Bates,W	(4)	7/28)	Australia	Melbourne	1882-83
		7/74)			
		5/31	Australia	Adelaide	1884-85
		5/24	Australia	Sydney	1884-85
Bedser,AV	(15)	†§ 7/49	India	Lord's	1946
		7/52	India	Manchester	1946
		5/127	West Indies	Nottingham	1950
		5/46)	Australia	Melbourne	1950-51
		5/59)			
		6/37	South Africa	Nottingham	1951
		7/58)	South Africa	Manchester	1951
		5/54)			
		5/27	India	Manchester	1952
		5/41	India	The Oval	1952
		7/55)	Australia	Nottingham	1953
		7/44)			
		5/105	Australia	Lord's	1953
		5/115	Australia	Manchester	1953
		6/95	Australia	Leeds	1953
Berry,R	(1)	†§ 5/63	West Indies	Manchester	1950
Birkenshaw,J	(1)	§ 5/57	Pakistan	Karachi[1]	1972-73
Blythe,C	(9)	6/68)	South Africa	Cape Town	1905-06

		5/50)			
		8/59)	South Africa	Leeds	1907
		7/40)			
		5/61	South Africa	The Oval	1907
		6/44)	Australia	Birmingham	1909
		5/58)			
		5/63	Australia	Manchester	1909
		7/46	South Africa	Cape Town	1909-10
Bosanquet,BJT	(2)	6/51	Australia	Sydney	1903-04
		8/107	Australia	Nottingham	1905
Botham,IT	(27)	†§ 5/74	Australia	Nottingham	1977
		5/21	Australia	Leeds	1977
		5/73	New Zealand	Christchurch	1977-78
		5/109	New Zealand	Auckland	1977-78
		8/34	Pakistan	Lord's	1978
		6/34	New Zealand	Nottingham	1978
		6/101)	New Zealand	Lord's	1978
		5/39)			
		§ 5/70	India	Birmingham	1979
		5/35	India	Lord's	1979
		6/78)	Australia	Perth	1979-80
		5/98)			
		6/58)	India	Bombay[3]	1979-80
		7/48)			
		6/95	Australia	Leeds	1981
		5/11	Australia	Birmingham	1981
		6/125	Australia	The Oval	1981
		5/61	India	Bombay[3]	1981-82
		5/46	India	Lord's	1982
		5/74	Pakistan	Leeds	1982
		5/59	New Zealand	Wellington	1983-84
		8/103	West Indies	Lord's	1984
		5/72	West Indies	The Oval	1984
		6/90	Sri Lanka	Lord's	1984
		5/109	Australia	Lord's	1985
		5/71	West Indies	Port-of-Spain	1985-86
		5/41	Australia	Melbourne	1986-87
Bowes,WE	(6)	§ 6/34	New Zealand	Auckland	1932-33
		6/142	Australia	Leeds	1934
		5/55	Australia	The Oval	1934
		5/100	South Africa	Manchester	1935
		5/49	Australia	The Oval	1938
		6/33	West Indies	Manchester	1939
Bradley,WM	(1)	†§ 5/67	Australia	Manchester	1899
Braund,LC	(3)	†§ 5/61	Australia	Sydney	1901-02
		5/95	Australia	Melbourne	1901-02
		8/81	Australia	Melbourne	1903-04
Brearley,W	(1)	5/110	Australia	The Oval	1905
Briggs,J	(9)	5/29)	Australia	Lord's	1886
		6/45)			
		5/25	Australia	The Oval	1888
		7/17)	South Africa	Cape Town	1888-89
		8/11)			
		6/49)	Australia	Adelaide	1891-92
		6/87)			
		5/34)	Australia	The Oval	1893

		5/114)			
Brown,DJ	(2)	5/63	Australia	Sydney	1965-66
		5/42	Australia	Lord's	1968
Brown,FR	(1)	5/49	Australia	Melbourne	1950-51
Buckenham,CP	(1)	5/115	South Africa	Johannesburg[1]	1909-10
Caddick,AR	(13)	6/65	West Indies	Port-of-Spain	1993-94
		5/63	West Indies	Bridgetown	1993-94
		5/50	Australia	Birmingham	1997
		5/42	Australia	The Oval	1997
		5/67	West Indies	Port-of-Spain	1997-98
		5/32	New Zealand	Birmingham	1999
		7/46	South Africa	Durban[2]	1999-2000
		5/16	West Indies	Lord's	2000
		5/14	West Indies	Leeds	2000
		5/101	Australia	Lord's	2001
		6/122	New Zealand	Christchurch	2001-02
		6/63	New Zealand	Wellington	2001-02
		7/94	Australia	Sydney	2002-03
Carr,DW	(1)	†§ 5/146	Australia	The Oval	1909
Cartwright,TW	(1)	6/94	South Africa	Nottingham	1965
Clark,EW	(1)	5/98	Australia	The Oval	1934
Coldwell,LJ	(1)	†§ 6/85	Pakistan	Lord's	1962
Compton,DCS	(1)	5/70	South Africa	Cape Town	1948-49
Cook,NGB	(4)	†§ 5/35	New Zealand	Lord's	1983
		5/63	New Zealand	Nottingham	1983
		§ 6/65)	Pakistan	Karachi[1]	1983-84
		§ 5/18)			
Copson,WH	(1)	†§ 5/85	West Indies	Lord's	1939
Cork,DG	(5)	†§ 7/43	West Indies	Lord's	1995
		§ 5/84	South Africa	Johannesburg[3]	1995-96
		5/113	Pakistan	Leeds	1996
		5/93	South Africa	Birmingham	1998
		6/119	South Africa	Lord's	1998
Cowans,NG	(2)	6/77	Australia	Melbourne	1982-83
		5/42	Pakistan	Lahore[2]	1983-84
Crawford,JN	(3)	5/79	Australia	Melbourne	1907-08
		5/48	Australia	Melbourne	1907-08
		5/141	Australia	Sydney	1907-08
Croft,RDB	(1)	5/95	New Zealand	Christchurch	1996-97
DeFreitas,PAJ	(4)	5/86	Pakistan	Karachi[1]	1987-88
		5/53	New Zealand	Nottingham	1990
		§ 7/70	Sri Lanka	Lord's	1991
		5/71	New Zealand	Nottingham	1994
Dilley,GR	(6)	5/68	Australia	Brisbane[2]	1986-87
		5/92	Pakistan	Birmingham	1987
		6/154	Pakistan	The Oval	1987
		6/38	New Zealand	Christchurch	1987-88
		5/60	New Zealand	Auckland	1987-88
		5/55	West Indies	Lord's	1988
Douglas,JWHT	(1)	5/46	Australia	Melbourne	1911-12
Edmonds,PH	(2)	†§ 5/28	Australia	Leeds	1975
		7/66	Pakistan	Karachi[1]	1977-78
Ellison,RM	(3)	§ 6/77	Australia	Birmingham	1985
		5/46	Australia	The Oval	1985
		5/78	West Indies	Kingston	1985-86
Emburey,JE	(6)	5/124	West Indies	Port-of-Spain	1980-81

Player	No.	Figures	Opponent	Venue	Season
		§ 6/33	Sri Lanka	Colombo (PSS)	1981-82
		5/82	Australia	Leeds	1985
		5/78	West Indies	Port-of-Spain	1985-86
		5/80	Australia	Brisbane[2]	1986-87
		7/78	Australia	Sydney	1986-87
Emmett,T	(1)	7/68	Australia	Melbourne	1876-77
Farnes,K	(3)	†§ 5/102)	Australia	Nottingham	1934
		†§ 5/77)			
		6/96	Australia	Melbourne	1936-37
Fender,PGH	(2)	5/122	Australia	Melbourne	1920-21
		5/90	Australia	Sydney	1920-21
Ferris,JJ #	(2)	†§ 6/54)	South Africa	Cape Town	1891-92
		†§ 7/37)			
Fielder,A	(1)	6/82	Australia	Sydney	1907-08
Flintoff,A	(2)	5/58	West Indies	Bridgetown	2003-04
		5/78	Australia	The Oval	2005
Flowers,W	(1)	5/46	Australia	Sydney	1884-85
Foster,FR	(4)	†§ 5/92	Australia	Sydney	1911-12
		6/91	Australia	Melbourne	1911-12
		5/36	Australia	Adelaide	1911-12
		§ 5/16	South Africa	Lord's	1912
Foster,NA	(5)	5/67	Pakistan	Lahore[2]	1983-84
		§ 6/104)	India	Madras[1]	1984-85
		§ 5/59)			
		8/107	Pakistan	Leeds	1987
		5/64	West Indies	The Oval	1988
Fraser,ARC	(13)	§ 5/28	West Indies	Kingston	1989-90
		§ 5/104	India	Lord's	1990
		5/124	India	Manchester	1990
		6/82	Australia	Melbourne	1990-91
		5/87	Australia	The Oval	1993
		8/75	West Indies	Bridgetown	1993-94
		5/73	Australia	Sydney	1994-95
		5/66	West Indies	Lord's	1995
		8/53	West Indies	Port-of-Spain	1997-98
		5/40	West Indies	Port-of-Spain	1997-98
		5/60)	South Africa	Nottingham	1998
		5/62)			
		5/42	South Africa	Leeds	1998
Freeman,AP	(5)	5/54)	West Indies	Manchester	1928
		5/39)			
		7/115	South Africa	Leeds	1929
		7/71)	South Africa	Manchester	1929
		5/100)			
Geary,G	(4)	7/70)	South Africa	Johannesburg[1]	1927-28
		5/60)			
		5/35	Australia	Sydney	1928-29
		5/105	Australia	Melbourne	1928-29
Giddins,ESH	(1)	§ 5/15	Zimbabwe	Lord's	2000
Gifford,N	(1)	5/55	Pakistan	Karachi[1]	1972-73
Giles,AF	(5)	5/75	Pakistan	Faisalabad	2000-01
		§ 5/67	India	Ahmedabad	2001-02
		5/116	Sri Lanka	Kandy	2003-04
		5/81	West Indies	Lord's	2004
		5/57	West Indies	Birmingham	2004
Gilligan,AER	(2)	6/7)	South Africa	Birmingham	1924
		5/83)			

Goddard,TWJ	(1)	§ 6/29	New Zealand	Manchester	1937
Gough,D	(9)	6/49	Australia	Sydney	1994-95
		5/40	New Zealand	Wellington	1996-97
		5/149	Australia	Leeds	1997
		6/42	South Africa	Leeds	1998
		5/96	Australia	Melbourne	1998-99
		5/70	South Africa	Johannesburg[3]	1999-2000
		5/109	West Indies	Birmingham	2000
		5/61	Pakistan	Lord's	2001
		5/103	Australia	Leeds	2001
Greenhough,T	(1)	5/35	India	Lord's	1959
Greig,AW	(6)	5/24	India	Calcutta	1972-73
		6/164	West Indies	Bridgetown	1973-74
		8/86)	West Indies	Port-of-Spain	1973-74
		5/70)			
		5/98)	New Zealand	Auckland	1974-75
		5/51)			
Gunn,J	(1)	5/76	Australia	Adelaide	1901-02
Haigh,S	(1)	6/11	South Africa	Cape Town	1898-99
Hammond,WR	(2)	†§ 5/36	South Africa	Johannesburg[1]	1927-28
		5/57	Australia	Adelaide	1936-37
Harmison,SJ	(8)	§ 5/35	Bangladesh	Dhaka	2003-04
		§ 7/12	West Indies	Kingston	2003-04
		6/61	West Indies	Port-of-Spain	2003-04
		6/46	West Indies	The Oval	2004
		5/38	Bangladesh	Chester-le-Street	2005
		5/43	Australia	Lord's	2005
		6/19)	Pakistan	Manchester	2006
		5/57)			
Headley,DW	(1)	6/66	Australia	Melbourne	1998-99
Hearne,JT	(4)	§ 5/76	Australia	Lord's	1896
		6/41	Australia	The Oval	1896
		5/42	Australia	Sydney	1897-98
		6/98	Australia	Melbourne	1897-98
Hearne,JW	(1)	5/49	South Africa	Johannesburg[1]	1913-14
Hemmings,EE	(1)	6/58	New Zealand	Birmingham	1990
Heseltine,C	(1)	†§ 5/38	South Africa	Johannesburg[1]	1895-96
Higgs,K	(2)	6/91	West Indies	Lord's	1966
		5/58	Pakistan	The Oval	1967
Hilton,MJ	(1)	§ 5/61	India	Kanpur	1951-52
Hirst,GH	(3)	5/77	Australia	The Oval	1902
		5/48	Australia	Melbourne	1903-04
		5/58	Australia	Birmingham	1909
Hoggard,MJ	(6)	§ 7/63	New Zealand	Christchurch	2001-02
		5/92	Sri Lanka	Birmingham	2002
		5/144)	South Africa	Johannesburg[3]	2004-05
		7/61)			
		5/73	Bangladesh	Chester-le-Street	2005
		6/57	India	Nagpur	2005-06
Hollies,WE	(5)	7/50	West Indies	Georgetown	1934-35
		§ 5/123	South Africa	Nottingham	1947
		§ 5/131	Australia	The Oval	1948
		5/133	New Zealand	Lord's	1949
		5/63	West Indies	Manchester	1950
Howorth,R	(1)	§ 6/124	West Indies	Bridgetown	1947-48
Illingworth,R	(3)	6/29	India	Lord's	1967

		6/87	Australia	Leeds	1968
		5/70	India	The Oval	1971
Jackson,Hon.FS	(1)	5/52	Australia	Nottingham	1905
Jenkins,RO	(1)	§ 5/116	West Indies	Lord's	1950
Johnson,RL	(2)	†§ 6/33	Zimbabwe	Chester-le-Street	2003
		§ 5/49	Bangladesh	Chittagong[1]	2003-04
Jones,IJ	(1)	6/118	Australia	Adelaide	1965-66
Jones,SP	(3)	5/57	West Indies	Port-of-Spain	2003-04
		6/53	Australia	Manchester	2005
		5/44	Australia	Nottingham	2005
Kennedy,AS	(2)	5/88	South Africa	Durban[2]	1922-23
		5/76	South Africa	Durban[2]	1922-23
Kirtley,RJ	(1)	†§ 6/34	South Africa	Nottingham	2003
Laker,JC	(9)	†§ 7/103	West Indies	Bridgetown	1947-48
		6/55	South Africa	The Oval	1951
		5/56	South Africa	The Oval	1955
		5/58)	Australia	Leeds	1956
		6/55)			
		9/37)	Australia	Manchester	1956
		10/53)			
		5/17	New Zealand	Leeds	1958
		5/107	Australia	Sydney	1958-59
Langridge,J	(2)	†§ 7/56	West Indies	Manchester	1933
		5/63	India	Madras[1]	1933-34
Larter,JDF	(2)	†§ 5/57	Pakistan	The Oval	1962
		5/68	South Africa	Nottingham	1965
Larwood,H	(4)	6/32	Australia	Brisbane[1]	1928-29
		§ 5/57	South Africa	Birmingham	1929
		5/96)	Australia	Sydney	1932-33
		5/28)			
Lawrence,DV	(1)	5/106	West Indies	The Oval	1991
Lees,WS	(2)	†§ 5/34	South Africa	Johannesburg[1]	1905-06
		6/78	South Africa	Johannesburg[1]	1905-06
Lever,JK	(3)	†§ 7/46	India	Delhi	1976-77
		5/59	India	Madras[1]	1976-77
		5/100	India	Bangalore	1981-82
Lever,P	(2)	§ 5/70	India	Manchester	1971
		6/38	Australia	Melbourne	1974-75
Lewis,CC	(3)	§ 6/111	West Indies	Birmingham	1991
		5/31	New Zealand	Auckland	1991-92
		5/72	India	Birmingham	1996
Loader,PJ	(1)	§ 6/36	West Indies	Leeds	1957
Lock,GAR	(9)	5/45	Australia	The Oval	1953
		5/28)	West Indies	The Oval	1957
		6/20)			
		5/17	New Zealand	Lord's	1958
		7/51	New Zealand	Leeds	1958
		7/35	New Zealand	Manchester	1958
		5/31)	New Zealand	Christchurch	1958-59
		6/53)			
		6/65	India	Madras[2]	1961-62
Lockwood,WH	(5)	†§ 6/101	Australia	Lord's	1893
		7/71	Australia	The Oval	1899
		6/48)	Australia	Manchester	1902
		5/28)			
		5/45	Australia	The Oval	1902

Lohmann,GA	(9)	7/36)	Australia	The Oval	1886
		5/68)			
		8/35	Australia	Sydney	1886-87
		5/17	Australia	Sydney	1887-88
		8/58	Australia	Sydney	1891-92
		§ 7/38)	South Africa	Port Elizabeth	1895-96
		§ 8/7)			
		9/28	South Africa	Johannesburg[1]	1895-96
		7/42	South Africa	Cape Town	1895-96
Macaulay,GG	(1)	†§ 5/64	South Africa	Cape Town	1922-23
Malcolm,DE	(5)	6/77	West Indies	Port-of-Spain	1989-90
		5/94	New Zealand	Lord's	1990
		5/46	New Zealand	Birmingham	1990
		5/94	Pakistan	The Oval	1992
		§ 9/57	South Africa	The Oval	1994
Mallender,NA	(1)	†§ 5/50	Pakistan	Leeds	1992
Marriott,CS	(2)	†§ 5/37)	West Indies	The Oval	1933
		†§ 6/59)			
Martin,F	(2)	†§ 6/50)	Australia	The Oval	1890
		†§ 6/52)			
Miller,G	(1)	5/44	Australia	Sydney	1978-79
Morley,F	(1)	†§ 5/56	Australia	The Oval	1880
Mullally,AD	(1)	§ 5/105	Australia	Brisbane	1998-99
Nichols,MS	(2)	§ 5/55	India	Bombay[1]	1933-34
		§ 6/35	South Africa	Nottingham	1935
Old,CM	(4)	§ 5/113	New Zealand	Lord's	1973
		5/21	India	Lord's	1974
		6/54	New Zealand	Wellington	1977-78
		7/50	Pakistan	Birmingham	1978
Paine,GAE	(1)	5/168	West Indies	Kingston	1934-35
Panesar,MS	(1)	5/78	Sri Lanka	Nottingham	2006
Parkin,CH	(2)	5/60	Australia	Adelaide	1920-21
		5/38	Australia	Manchester	1921
Peate,E	(2)	5/43	Australia	Sydney	1881-82
		6/85	Australia	Lord's	1884
Peebles,IAR	(3)	6/204	Australia	The Oval	1930
		6/63	South Africa	Johannesburg[1]	1930-31
		§ 5/77	New Zealand	Lord's	1931
Peel,R	(5)	†§ 5/51	Australia	Adelaide	1884-85
		5/18	Australia	Sydney	1887-88
		7/31	Australia	Manchester	1888
		6/67	Australia	Sydney	1894-95
		6/23	Australia	The Oval	1896
Perks,RTD	(2)	†§ 5/100	South Africa	Durban[2]	1938-39
		§ 5/156	West Indies	The Oval	1939
Pocock,PI	(3)	§ 6/79	Australia	Manchester	1968
		5/169	Pakistan	Hyderabad	1972-73
		5/110	West Indies	Port-of-Spain	1973-74
Pollard,R	(1)	†§ 5/24	India	Manchester	1946
Price,JSE	(1)	5/73	India	Calcutta	1963-64
Pringle,DR	(3)	§ 5/108	West Indies	Birmingham	1984
		5/95	West Indies	Leeds	1988
		5/100	West Indies	Lord's	1991
Relf,AE	(1)	5/85	Australia	Lord's	1909
Rhodes,W	(6)	7/17	Australia	Birmingham	1902
		5/63	Australia	Sheffield	1902

		5/94	Australia	Sydney	1903-04
		7/56)	Australia	Melbourne	1903-04
		8/68)			
		5/83	Australia	Manchester	1909
Richardson,T	(11)	†§ 5/49)	Australia	Manchester	1893
		†§ 5/107)			
		5/181	Australia	Sydney	1894-95
		5/57	Australia	Melbourne	1894-95
		5/75	Australia	Adelaide	1894-95
		6/104	Australia	Melbourne	1894-95
		6/39)	Australia	Lord's	1896
		5/134)			
		7/168)	Australia	Manchester	1896
		6/76)			
		8/94	Australia	Sydney	1897-98
Robins,RWV	(1)	§ 6/32	West Indies	Lord's	1933
Sharpe,JW	(1)	6/84	Australia	Melbourne	1891-92
Shaw,A	(1)	†§ 5/38	Australia	Melbourne	1876-77
Shuttleworth,K	(1)	†§ 5/47	Australia	Brisbane[2]	1970-71
Silverwood,CEW	(1)	5/91	South Africa	Cape Town	1999-2000
Simpson-Hayward,GHT	(2)	†§ 6/43	South Africa	Johannesburg[1]	1909-10
		5/69	South Africa	Johannesburg[1]	1909-10
Sims,JM	(1)	§ 5/73	India	The Oval	1936
Small,GC	(2)	§ 5/48	Australia	Melbourne	1986-87
		5/75	Australia	Sydney	1986-87
Smith,CA	(1)	†§ 5/19	South Africa	Port Elizabeth	1888-89
Smith,CIJ	(1)	†§ 5/16	West Indies	Bridgetown	1934-35
Snow,JA	(8)	7/49	West Indies	Kingston	1967-68
		5/86	West Indies	Bridgetown	1967-68
		6/60	West Indies	Georgetown	1967-68
		5/114	West Indies	Lord's	1969
		6/114	Australia	Brisbane[2]	1970-71
		7/40	Australia	Sydney	1970-71
		5/57	Australia	Lord's	1972
		5/92	Australia	Nottingham	1972
Statham,JB	(9)	5/60	Australia	Melbourne	1954-55
		7/39	South Africa	Lord's	1955
		5/118	West Indies	Nottingham	1957
		7/57	Australia	Melbourne	1958-59
		5/31	India	Nottingham	1959
		6/63)	South Africa	Lord's	1960
		5/34)			
		5/53	Australia	Manchester	1961
		5/40	South Africa	The Oval	1965
Stevens,GTS	(2)	§ 5/105)	West Indies	Bridgetown	1929-30
		§ 5/90)			
Such,PM	(2)	†§ 6/67	Australia	Manchester	1993
		5/81	Australia	Sydney	1998-99
Tate,MW	(7)	6/42	South Africa	Leeds	1924
		§ 6/130)	Australia	Sydney	1924-25
		§ 5/98)			
		6/99	Australia	Melbourne	1924-25
		5/75	Australia	Melbourne	1924-25
		5/115	Australia	Sydney	1924-25
		5/124	Australia	Leeds	1930
Tattersall,R	(4)	6/44	New Zealand	Wellington	1950-51

		7/52)	South Africa	Lord's	1951
		5/49)			
		6/48	India	Kanpur	1951-52
Titmus,FJ	(7)	7/79	Australia	Sydney	1962-63
		5/103	Australia	Sydney	1962-63
		§ 5/116	India	Madras[2]	1963-64
		6/73	India	Kanpur	1963-64
		5/66	South Africa	Durban[2]	1964-65
		5/19	New Zealand	Leeds	1965
		5/83	West Indies	Manchester	1966
Trott,AE #	(1)	†§ 5/51	South Africa	Johannesburg[1]	1898-99
Trueman,FS	(17)	8/31	India	Manchester	1952
		5/48	India	The Oval	1952
		5/90	Australia	Lord's	1956
		5/63	West Indies	Nottingham	1957
		§ 5/31	New Zealand	Birmingham	1958
		5/35	West Indies	Port-of-Spain	1959-60
		5/27	South Africa	Nottingham	1960
		5/58)	Australia	Leeds	1961
		6/30)			
		6/31	Pakistan	Lord's	1962
		5/62	Australia	Melbourne	1962-63
		7/75	New Zealand	Christchurch	1962-63
		6/100)	West Indies	Lord's	1963
		5/52)			
		5/75)	West Indies	Birmingham	1963
		7/44)			
		5/48	Australia	Lord's	1964
Tudor,AJ	(1)	5/44	Australia	Nottingham	2001
Tufnell,PCR	(5)	5/61	Australia	Sydney	1990-91
		§ 6/25	West Indies	The Oval	1991
		§ 5/94	Sri Lanka	Lord's	1991
		§ 7/47	New Zealand	Christchurch	1991-92
		7/66	Australia	The Oval	1997
Tyson,FH	(4)	6/85	Australia	Sydney	1954-55
		7/27	Australia	Melbourne	1954-55
		§ 6/28	South Africa	Nottingham	1955
		6/40	South Africa	Port Elizabeth	1956-57
Ulyett,G	(1)	7/36	Australia	Lord's	1884
Underwood,DL	(17)	§ 5/52	Pakistan	Nottingham	1967
		7/50	Australia	The Oval	1968
		5/94	Pakistan	Dacca	1968-69
		§ 7/32	New Zealand	Lord's	1969
		6/41)	New Zealand	The Oval	1969
		6/60)			
		6/12)	New Zealand	Christchurch	1970-71
		6/85)			
		5/108	New Zealand	Auckland	1970-71
		6/45	Australia	Leeds	1972
		5/20)	Pakistan	Lord's	1974
		8/51)			
		7/113	Australia	Adelaide	1974-75
		5/39	West Indies	Lord's	1976
		5/84	India	Bombay[3]	1976-77
		6/66	Australia	Manchester	1977
		§ 5/28	Sri Lanka	Colombo (PSS)	1981-82

Verity,H	(5)	5/33	Australia	Sydney	1932-33
		7/49	India	Madras[1]	1933-34
		7/61)	Australia	Lord's	1934
		8/43)			
		5/70	South Africa	Cape Town	1938-39
Voce,W	(3)	7/70	West Indies	Port-of-Spain	1929-30
		5/58	South Africa	Durban[2]	1930-31
		6/41	Australia	Brisbane[2]	1936-37
Wardle,JH	(5)	7/56	Pakistan	The Oval	1954
		5/79	Australia	Sydney	1954-55
		5/53)	South Africa	Cape Town	1956-57
		7/36)			
		5/61	South Africa	Durban[2]	1956-57
Warren,AR	(1)	†§ 5/57	Australia	Leeds	1905
White,C	(3)	5/57	West Indies	Leeds	2000
		5/32	West Indies	The Oval	2000
		5/127	Australia	Perth	2002-03
White,JC	(3)	5/107	Australia	Melbourne	1928-29
		5/130)	Australia	Adelaide	1928-29
		8/126)			
Willis,RGD	(16)	5/61	Australia	Melbourne	1974-75
		5/42	West Indies	Leeds	1976
		5/27	India	Calcutta	1976-77
		6/53	India	Bangalore	1976-77
		7/78	Australia	Lord's	1977
		5/88	Australia	Nottingham	1977
		5/102	Australia	The Oval	1977
		5/32	New Zealand	Wellington	1977-78
		5/47	Pakistan	Lord's	1978
		5/42	New Zealand	The Oval	1978
		5/44	Australia	Perth	1978-79
		5/65	West Indies	Nottingham	1980
		8/43	Australia	Leeds	1981
		6/101	India	Lord's	1982
		5/66	Australia	Brisbane[2]	1982-83
		5/35	New Zealand	Lord's	1983
Woolley,FE	(4)	5/41	South Africa	The Oval	1912
		5/29)	Australia	The Oval	1912
		5/20)			
		7/76	New Zealand	Wellington	1929-30
Wright,DVP	(6)	5/167	Australia	Brisbane[2]	1946-47
		7/105	Australia	Sydney	1946-47
		5/95)	South Africa	Lord's	1947
		5/80)			
		5/141	West Indies	The Oval	1950
		5/48	New Zealand	Wellington	1950-51

SOUTH AFRICA *(201)*			Opponents		
Adams,PR	(4)	6/55	India	Kanpur	1996-97
		§ 5/37)	Bangladesh	Chittagong[1]	2002-03
		§ 3/69)			
		7/128	Pakistan	Lahore[2]	2003-04
Adcock,NAT	(5)	5/43	New Zealand	Johannesburg[2]	1953-54
		5/45	New Zealand	Johannesburg[2]	1953-54
		6/43	Australia	Durban[2]	1957-58

		5/62	England	Birmingham	1960
		6/65	England	The Oval	1960
Ashley,WH	(1)	†§ 7/95	England	Cape Town	1888-89
Balaskas,XC	(1)	5/49	England	Lord's	1935
Barlow,EJ	(1)	5/85	Australia	Cape Town	1966-67
Bell,AJ	(4)	†§ 6/99	England	Lord's	1929
		5/140	Australia	Sydney	1931-32
		5/69	Australia	Melbourne	1931-32
		5/142	Australia	Adelaide	1931-32
Bissett,GF	(2)	†§ 5/37	England	Cape Town	1927-28
		7/29	England	Durban[2]	1927-28
Blanckenberg,JM	(4)	5/83	England	Johannesburg[1]	1913-14
		§ 5/78	Australia	Durban[1]	1921-22
		6/76	England	Johannesburg[1]	1922-23
		5/61	England	Cape Town	1922-23
Boje,N	(3)	5/83	India	Bangalore	1999-2000
		5/62	Sri Lanka	Colombo (SSC)	2000-01
		5/88	Sri Lanka	Galle	2004-05
Bromfield,HD	(1)	§ 5/88	England	Cape Town	1964-65
Burke,SF	(2)	†§ 6/128)	New Zealand	Cape Town	1961-62
		†§ 5/68)			
Carter,CP	(2)	6/50	England	Durban[1]	1913-14
		6/91	Australia	Johannesburg[1]	1921-22
Chubb,GWA	(2)	5/77	England	Lord's	1951
		6/51	England	Manchester	1951
Crisp,RJ	(1)	5/99	England	Manchester	1935
de Villiers,PS	(5)	6/43	Australia	Sydney	1993-94
		5/64	New Zealand	Dunedin[2]	1994-95
		5/61	New Zealand	Cape Town	1994-95
		§ 6/81	Pakistan	Johannesburg[3]	1994-95
		5/23	Pakistan	Durban[2]	1997-98
Donald,AA	(20)	5/55)	India	Port Elizabeth	1992-93
		7/84)			
		§ 5/69	Sri Lanka	Moratuwa	1993-94
		§ 5/74	England	Lord's	1994
		§ 8/71	Zimbabwe	Harare	1995-96
		5/46	England	Cape Town	1995-96
		5/40	India	Durban[2]	1996-97
		5/36	Australia	Centurion	1996-97
		5/79	Pakistan	Durban[2]	1997-98
		6/59	Australia	Melbourne	1997-98
		5/54	Sri Lanka	Centurion	1997-98
		5/32	England	Lord's	1998
		6/88	England	Manchester	1998
		5/109	England	Nottingham	1998
		5/71	England	Leeds	1998
		5/49	West Indies	Port Elizabeth	1998-99
		5/49	West Indies	Centurion	1998-99
		6/53	England	Johannesburg[3]	1999-2000
		5/74	England	Johannesburg[3]	1999-2000
		5/47	England	Cape Town	1999-2000
Faulkner,GA	(4)	6/17	England	Leeds	1907
		5/120	England	Durban[1]	1909-10
		6/87	England	Durban[1]	1909-10
		7/84	England	The Oval	1912
Fuller,ERH	(1)	5/66	Australia	Melbourne	1952-53

Goddard,TL	(5)	5/69	England	Leeds	1955
		5/31	England	The Oval	1955
		5/80	England	Nottingham	1960
		5/60	Australia	Adelaide	1963-64
		6/53	Australia	Johannesburg[3]	1966-67
Gordon,N	(2)	†§ 5/103	England	Johannesburg[1]	1938-39
		5/157	England	Cape Town	1938-39
Hall,AE	(3)	†§ 7/63	England	Cape Town	1922-23
		6/82	England	Johannesburg[1]	1922-23
		6/100	England	Johannesburg[1]	1927-28
Hayward,M	(1)	§ 5/56	Pakistan	Durban[2]	2002-03
Heine,PS	(4)	†§ 5/60	England	Lord's	1955
		5/86	England	Manchester	1955
		§ 6/58	Australia	Johannesburg[3]	1957-58
		6/96	Australia	Johannesburg[3]	1957-58
Ironside,DEJ	(1)	†§ 5/51	New Zealand	Johannesburg[2]	1953-54
Kallis,JH	(4)	5/90	West Indies	Cape Town	1998-99
		6/67	West Indies	Bridgetown	2000-01
		5/21	Bangladesh	Potchefstroom	2002-03
		6/54	England	Leeds	2003
Klusener,L	(1)	†§ 8/64	India	Calcutta	1996-97
Langeveldt,CK	(1)	†§ 5/46	England	Cape Town	2004-05
Langton,ABC	(1)	5/58	England	Johannesburg[1]	1938-39
Lawrence,GB	(2)	8/53	New Zealand	Johannesburg[3]	1961-62
		5/52	New Zealand	Johannesburg[3]	1961-62
Llewellyn,CB	(4)	§ 6/92	Australia	Johannesburg[1]	1902-03
		5/43)	Australia	Johannesburg[1]	1902-03
		5/73)			
		6/97	Australia	Cape Town	1902-03
McCarthy,CN	(2)	†§ 6/43	England	Durban[2]	1948-49
		5/114	England	Johannesburg[2]	1948-49
McMillan,Q	(2)	§ 5/66	New Zealand	Christchurch	1931-32
		5/125	New Zealand	Wellington	1931-32
Mann,NBF	(1)	6/59	England	Durban[2]	1948-49
Matthews,CR	(2)	5/80	Australia	Cape Town	1993-94
		§ 5/42	New Zealand	Johannesburg[3]	1994-95
Melle,MG	(2)	†§ 5/113	Australia	Johannesburg[2]	1949-50
		6/71	Australia	Brisbane[2]	1952-53
Middleton,J	(2)	†§ 5/64	England	Port Elizabeth	1895-96
		5/51	England	Johannesburg[1]	1898-99
Mitchell,B	(1)	5/87	Australia	Durban[2]	1935-36
Nel,A	(3)	5/87	West Indies	Cape Town	2003-04
		6/81	England	Centurion	2004-05
		6/32	West Indies	Bridgetown	2004-05
Ntini,M	(14)	§ 6/66	New Zealand	Bloemfontein	2000-01
		§ 5/19	Bangladesh	East London	2002-03
		5/75)	England	Lord's	2003
		5/145)			
		5/94	West Indies	Johannesburg[3]	2003-04
		5/66	West Indies	Durban[2]	2003-04
		5/49	West Indies	Centurion	2003-04
		6/95)	West Indies	Port-of-Spain	2004-05
		7/37)			
		5/64	Australia	Perth	2005-06
		5/64	Australia	Johannesburg[3]	2005-06
		5/94)	New Zealand	Centurion	2005-06

		5/51)			
		5/35	New Zealand	Johannesburg[3]	2005-06
Nupen,EP	(5)	§ 5/53	England	Johannesburg[1]	1922-23
		5/83	England	Durban[2]	1927-28
		5/63)	England	Johannesburg[1]	1930-31
		6/87)			
		6/46	England	Johannesburg[1]	1930-31
Parker,GM	(1)	†§ 6/152	England	Birmingham	1924
Partridge,JT	(3)	5/123	Australia	Sydney	1963-64
		7/91	Australia	Sydney	1963-64
		6/86	New Zealand	Auckland	1963-64
Pegler,SJ	(2)	6/105	Australia	Manchester	1912
		7/65	England	Lord's	1912
Pithey,DB	(1)	6/58	New Zealand	Dunedin	1963-64
Pollock,PM	(9)	†§ 6/38	New Zealand	Durban[2]	1961-62
		§ 6/95	Australia	Brisbane[2]	1963-64
		5/83	Australia	Sydney	1963-64
		6/47	New Zealand	Wellington	1963-64
		5/129	England	Johannesburg[3]	1964-65
		5/53)	England	Nottingham	1965
		5/34)			
		5/43	England	The Oval	1965
		5/39	Australia	Johannesburg[3]	1969-70
Pollock,SM	(16)	5/32	England	Cape Town	1995-96
		5/37	Pakistan	Faisalabad	1997-98
		7/87	Australia	Adelaide	1997-98
		6/50	Pakistan	Durban[2]	1997-98
		5/53	England	Leeds	1998
		§ 5/54	West Indies	Johannesburg[3]	1998-99
		5/43	West Indies	Port Elizabeth	1998-99
		5/83	West Indies	Durban	1998-99
		5/33	New Zealand	Wellington	1998-99
		§ 5/39	Zimbabwe	Bloemfontein	1999-2000
		6/30	Sri Lanka	Cape Town	2000-01
		5/28	West Indies	Kingston	2000-01
		6/56	India	Bloemfontein	2001-02
		5/40	India	Port Elizabeth	2001-02
		6/39	England	Nottingham	2003
		6/78	Pakistan	Faisalalabad	2003-04
Procter,MJ	(1)	6/73	Australia	Port Elizabeth	1969-70
Promnitz,HLE	(1)	†§ 5/58	England	Johannesburg[1]	1927-28
Quinn,NA	(1)	6/92	England	Leeds	1929
Rose-Innes,A	(1)	†§ 5/43	England	Port Elizabeth	1888-89
Rowan,AMB	(4)	5/80	England	Cape Town	1948-49
		5/167	England	Port Elizabeth	1948-49
		5/68	England	Nottingham	1951
		5/174	England	Leeds	1951
Rowe,GA	(1)	†§ 5/115	England	Johannesburg[1]	1895-96
Schultz,BN	(2)	5/48	Sri Lanka	Colombo (SSC)	1993-94
		5/63	Sri Lanka	Colombo (PSS)	1993-94
Schwarz,RO	(2)	§ 5/102	Australia	Sydney	1910-11
		6/47	Australia	Sydney	1910-11
Sinclair,JH	(1)	6/26	England	Cape Town	1898-99
Snooke,SJ	(1)	8/70	England	Johannesburg[1]	1905-06
Steyn,DW	(2)	5/47	New Zealand	Centurion	2005-06
		5/82	Sri Lanka	Colombo (PSS)	2006-07

Tayfield,HJ	(14)	7/23	Australia	Durban[2]	1949-50
		6/84)	Australia	Melbourne	1952-53
		7/81)			
		5/62	New Zealand	Auckland	1952-53
		6/62	New Zealand	Durban[2]	1953-54
		6/13	New Zealand	Johannesburg[2]	1953-54
		5/80	England	Lord's	1955
		5/94	England	Leeds	1955
		5/60	England	The Oval	1955
		5/130	England	Cape Town	1956-57
		8/69	England	Durban[2]	1956-57
		9/113	England	Johannesburg[3]	1956-57
		6/78	England	Port Elizabeth	1956-57
		5/120	Australia	Cape Town	1957-58
Terbrugge,DJ	(1)	§ 5/46	Bangladesh	East London	2002-03
Tuckett,L	(2)	†§ 5/68	England	Nottingham	1947
		5/115	England	Lord's	1947
Vincent,CL	(3)	6/131	England	Durban[2]	1927-28
		5/105	England	The Oval	1929
		6/51	England	Durban[2]	1930-31
Vogler,AEE	(5)	7/128	England	Lord's	1907
		5/87)	England	Johannesburg[1]	1909-10
		7/94)			
		5/83	England	Johannesburg[1]	1909-10
		5/72	England	Cape Town	1909-10
Zondeki,M	(1)	6/39 §	Zimbabwe	Centurion	2004-05
WEST INDIES *(248)*			Opponents		
Adams,JC	(1)	5/17	New Zealand	Bridgetown	1995-96
Ambrose,CEL	(22)	5/72	Australia	Perth	1988-89
		8/45	England	Bridgetown	1989-90
		5/35	Pakistan	Lahore[2]	1990-91
		6/52	England	Leeds	1991
		5/74	England	Nottingham	1991
		§ 6/34	South Africa	Bridgetown	1991-92
		5/66	Australia	Brisbane[2]	1992-93
		6/74	Australia	Adelaide	1992-93
		7/25	Australia	Perth	1992-93
		5/60)	England	Port-of-Spain	1993-94
		6/24)			
		5/45	Australia	Port-of-Spain	1994-95
		5/96	England	The Oval	1995
		5/68	New Zealand	St John's	1995-96
		5/55	Australia	Melbourne	1996-97
		5/43	Australia	Perth	1996-97
		5/87	India	Port-of-Spain	1996-97
		5/37	Sri Lanka	St John's	1996-97
		5/52	England	Port-of-Spain	1997-98
		5/25	England	Port-of-Spain	1997-98
		6/51	South Africa	Port Elizabeth	1998-99
		5/94	Australia	St John's	1998-99
Atkinson,DS	(3)	5/56	Australia	Bridgetown	1954-55
		5/66	New Zealand	Wellington	1955-56
		7/53	New Zealand	Auckland	1955-56
Atkinson,ES	(1)	5/42	Pakistan	Kingston	1957-58
Benjamin,KCG	(4)	§ 6/66	England	Kingston	1993-94

		5/65	India	Mohali	1994-95
		5/109)	England	Nottingham	1995
		5/69)			
Bishop,IR	(6)	6/87	India	Bridgetown	1988-89
		5/84	England	St John's	1989-90
		5/41	Pakistan	Lahore[2]	1990-91
		6/40	Australia	Perth	1992-93
		5/43	Pakistan	Port-of-Spain	1992-93
		5/32	England	Leeds	1995
Boyce,KD	(2)	§ 5/70)	England	The Oval	1973
		§ 6/77)			
Bravo,DDJ	(2)	6/55	England	Manchester	2004
		6/84	Australia	Adelaide	2005-06
Butcher,BF	(1)	§ 5/34	England	Port-of-Spain	1967-68
Clarke,ST	(1)	5/126	India	Bangalore	1978-79
Collins,PT	(3)	§ 6/76	New Zealand	Bridgetown	2001-02
		§ 5/26	Bangladesh	Dhaka	2002-03
		6/53	Bangladesh	Kingston	2003-04
Collymore,CD	(3)	§ 6/66	Sri Lanka	Gros Islet	2002-03
		7/57	Sri Lanka	Kingston	2002-03
		7/78	Pakistan	Kingston	2004-05
Constantine,LN	(2)	5/87	England	Georgetown	1929-30
		5/73	England	The Oval	1939
Croft,CEH	(3)	8/29	Pakistan	Port-of-Spain	1976-77
		5/40	England	Port-of-Spain	1980-81
		6/74	England	St John's	1980-81
Daniel,WW	(1)	5/39	India	Ahmedabad	1983-84
Dewdney,DT	(1)	5/21	New Zealand	Auckland	1955-56
Dillon,M	(2)	§ 5/111	Pakistan	Karachi[1]	1997-98
		5/71	India	Kingston	2001-02
Drakes,VC	(1)	§ 5/93	Australia	Georgetown	2002-03
Edwards,FH	(4)	§ 5/36	Sri Lanka	Kingston	2002-03
		§ 5/133	Zimbabwe	Harare	2003-04
		§ 5/38	Pakistan	Bridgetown	2004-05
		5/65	New Zealand	Wellington	2005-06
Edwards,RM	(1)	5/84	New Zealand	Wellington	1968-69
Ferguson,W	(3)	5/137)	England	Port-of-Spain	1947-48
		6/92)			
		5/116	England	Georgetown	1947-48
Garner,J	(7)	6/56	New Zealand	Auckland	1979-80
		5/56	Australia	Adelaide	1981-82
		6/75	Australia	Georgetown	1983-84
		6/60	Australia	Port-of-Spain	1983-84
		5/63	Australia	St John's	1983-84
		5/55	England	Birmingham	1984
		5/51	New Zealand	Wellington	1986-87
Gayle,CH	(2)	5/34	England	Birmingham	2004
		5/91	Pakistan	Bridgetown	2004-05
Gibbs,LR	(18)	5/80	Pakistan	Georgetown	1957-58
		§ 5/66	Australia	Sydney	1960-61
		5/97	Australia	Adelaide	1960-61
		8/38	India	Bridgetown	1961-62
		§ 5/59)	England	Manchester	1963
		§ 6/98)			
		6/29	Australia	Georgetown	1964-65
		5/37)	England	Manchester	1966

		5/69)			
		6/39	England	Leeds	1966
		5/51	India	Calcutta	1966-67
		6/60	England	Georgetown	1967-68
		5/88	Australia	Brisbane[2]	1968-69
		5/102	Australia	Port-of-Spain	1972-73
		6/108	England	Port-of-Spain	1973-74
		6/76	India	Delhi	1974-75
		7/98	India	Bombay[3]	1974-75
		5/102	Australia	Brisbane[2]	1975-76
Gilchrist,R	(1)	6/55	India	Calcutta	1958-59
Goddard,JDC	(1)	5/31	England	Georgetown	1947-48
Gomez,GE	(1)	7/55	Australia	Sydney	1951-52
Griffith,CC	(5)	5/91	England	Lord's	1963
		6/36	England	Leeds	1963
		6/71	England	The Oval	1963
		6/46	Australia	Port-of-Spain	1964-65
		5/69	England	Port-of-Spain	1967-68
Griffith,HC	(2)	6/103	England	The Oval	1928
		5/63	England	Port-of-Spain	1929-30
Hall,WW	(9)	6/50)	India	Kanpur	1958-59
		5/76)			
		5/87	Pakistan	Lahore[1]	1958-59
		7/69	England	Kingston	1959-60
		6/90	England	Georgetown	1959-60
		§ 5/63	Australia	Brisbane[2]	1960-61
		6/49	India	Kingston	1961-62
		5/20	India	Port-of-Spain	1961-62
		5/60	Australia	Kingston	1964-65
Harper,RA	(1)	6/57	England	Manchester	1984
Holder,VA	(3)	6/39	India	Bombay[3]	1974-75
		5/108	Australia	Adelaide	1975-76
		6/28	Australia	Port-of-Spain	1977-78
Holding,MA	(13)	6/65	India	Port-of-Spain	1975-76
		5/17	England	Manchester	1976
		8/92)	England	The Oval	1976
		6/57)			
		6/67	England	Lord's	1980
		5/56	England	Kingston	1980-81
		5/45)	Australia	Melbourne	1981-82
		6/62)			
		5/64	Australia	Sydney	1981-82
		5/72	Australia	Adelaide	1981-82
		5/102	India	Bombay[3]	1983-84
		5/43	England	The Oval	1984
		6/21	Australia	Perth	1984-85
Holford,DAJ	(1)	5/23	India	Bridgetown	1975-76
Hooper,CL	(4)	5/40	Pakistan	Bridgetown	1992-93
		5/116	India	Nagpur	1994-95
		5/26	Sri Lanka	Arnos Vale	1996-97
		5/80	England	Bridgetown	1997-98
Inshan Ali	(1)	5/59	New Zealand	Port-of-Spain	1971-72
Johnson,HHH	(2)	†§ 5/41)	England	Kingston	1947-48
		†§ 5/55)			
Jones,PE	(1)	5/85	India	Bombay[2]	1948-49
Julien,BD	(1)	5/57	England	Bridgetown	1973-74

Kentish,ESM	(1)	5/49	England	Kingston	1953-54
King,FM	(1)	5/74	India	Port-of-Spain	1952-53
King,LA	(1)	†§ 5/46	India	Kingston	1961-62
King,RD	(1)	5/51	Zimbabwe	Kingston	1999-2000
Lawson,JJC	(2)	§ 6/3	Bangladesh	Dhaka	2002-03
		7/78	Australia	St John's	2002-03
Marshall,MD	(22)	5/37	India	Port-of-Spain	1982-83
		6/37	India	Calcutta	1983-84
		5/72	India	Madras[1]	1983-84
		5/42	Australia	Bridgetown	1983-84
		5/51	Australia	Kingston	1983-84
		6/85	England	Lord's	1984
		7/53	England	Leeds	1984
		5/35	England	The Oval	1984
		5/82	Australia	Brisbane[2]	1984-85
		5/69)	Australia	Adelaide	1984-85
		5/38)			
		5/86	Australia	Melbourne	1984-85
		7/80	New Zealand	Bridgetown	1984-85
		5/33	Pakistan	Lahore[2]	1986-87
		5/65	Pakistan	Bridgetown	1987-88
		6/69	England	Nottingham	1988
		6/32	England	Lord's	1988
		7/22	England	Manchester	1988
		5/29	Australia	Sydney	1988-89
		5/60	India	Bridgetown	1988-89
		5/34)	India	Port-of-Spain	1988-89
		6/55)			
Martindale,EA	(3)	5/73	England	Manchester	1933
		5/93	England	The Oval	1933
		5/22	England	Bridgetown	1934-35
Noreiga,JM	(2)	9/95	India	Port-of-Spain	1970-71
		5/129	India	Port-of-Spain	1970-71
Parry,DR	(1)	5/15	Australia	Port-of-Spain	1977-78
Patterson,BP	(5)	§ 5/24	India	Delhi	1987-88
		5/68	India	Bombay[3]	1987-88
		5/39	Australia	Melbourne	1988-89
		5/83	Australia	Kingston	1990-91
		5/81	England	Birmingham	1991
Perry,NO	(1)	†§ 5/70	Australia	Kingston	1998-99
Powell,DB	(1)	5/25	Sri Lanka	Kandy	2005-06
Ramadhin,S	(10)	5/66)	England	Lord's	1950
		6/86)			
		5/135	England	Nottingham	1950
		§ 5/90	Australia	Brisbane[2]	1951-52
		§ 5/86	New Zealand	Christchurch	1951-52
		5/26	India	Bridgetown	1952-53
		6/113	England	Georgetown	1953-54
		6/23	New Zealand	Dunedin	1955-56
		5/46	New Zealand	Christchurch	1955-56
		7/49	England	Birmingham	1957
Ramnarine,D	(1)	5/78	South Africa	Bridgetown	2000-01
Roberts,AME	(11)	5/50	India	Calcutta	1974-75
		7/64)	India	Madras[1]	1974-75
		5/57)			
		§ 5/66	Pakistan	Lahore[2]	1974-75

		7/54	Australia	Perth	1975-76
		5/60)	England	Lord's	1976
		5/63)			
		6/37	England	Manchester	1976
		5/56	Australia	Port-of-Spain	1977-78
		5/72	England	Nottingham	1980
		5/39	India	Kingston	1982-83
Rose,FA	(2)†§	6/100	India	Kingston	1996-97
	§	7/84	South Africa	Durban	1998-99
Scott,OC	(1)	5/266	England	Kingston	1929-30
Shepherd,JN	(1)†§	5/104	England	Manchester	1969
Smith,OG	(1)	5/90	India	Delhi	1958-59
Sobers,GS	(6)	5/120	Australia	Melbourne	1960-61
		5/63	India	Kingston	1961-62
		5/60	England	Birmingham	1963
		5/41	England	Leeds	1966
		6/73	Australia	Brisbane[2]	1968-69
		5/42	England	Leeds	1969
Taylor,J	(1)†§	5/109	Pakistan	Port-of-Spain	1957-58
Trim,J	(1) §	5/34	Australia	Melbourne	1951-52
Valentine,AL	(8)†§	8/104	England	Manchester	1950
		6/39	England	The Oval	1950
	§	5/99	Australia	Brisbane[2]	1951-52
		6/102	Australia	Adelaide	1951-52
		5/88	Australia	Melbourne	1951-52
		5/127	India	Georgetown	1952-53
		5/64	India	Kingston	1952-53
		5/32	New Zealand	Christchurch	1955-56
Walsh,CA	(22)	5/73	New Zealand	Auckland	1986-87
	§	5/54	India	Delhi	1987-88
		5/54	India	Bombay[3]	1987-88
		6/62	India	Kingston	1988-89
		5/68	England	Kingston	1989-90
		5/94	England	Bridgetown	1993-94
		6/79	India	Bombay[3]	1994-95
		7/37)	New Zealand	Wellington	1994-95
		6/18)			
		6/54	Australia	St John's	1994-95
		5/45	England	Birmingham	1995
		5/98	Australia	Sydney	1996-97
		5/74	Australia	Perth	1996-97
		5/79	Pakistan	Peshawar[2]	1997-98
		5/143	Pakistan	Rawalpindi[2]	1997-98
		6/80	South Africa	Centurion	1998-99
		5/39	Australia	Bridgetown	1998-99
		5/22	Pakistan	Bridgetown	1999-2000
		5/83	Pakistan	St John's	1999-2000
		5/36	England	Birmingham	2000
		6/74	England	Lord's	2000
		6/61	South Africa	Port-of-Spain	2000-01
Worrell,FMM	(2)	6/38	Australia	Adelaide	1951-52
		7/70	England	Leeds	1957
NEW ZEALAND *(162)*			Opponents		
Bartlett,GA	(1) §	6/38	India	Christchurch	1967-68
Bond,SE	(4) §	5/78	West Indies	Bridgetown	2001-02

		5/104	West Indies	St George's	2001-02
		6/41	Zimbabwe	Bulawayo[2]	2005-06
		5/69	West Indies	Auckland	2005-06
Boock,SL	(4)	5/67	England	Auckland	1977-78
		§ 5/28	Sri Lanka	Kandy	1983-84
		7/87	Pakistan	Hyderabad	1984-85
		5/117	Pakistan	Wellington	1984-85
Bracewell,JG	(4)	§ 5/75	India	Auckland	1980-81
		6/32	Australia	Auckland	1985-86
		6/51	India	Bombay[3]	1988-89
		6/85	Australia	Wellington	1989-90
Burtt,TB	(3)	5/97	England	Leeds	1949
		6/162	England	Manchester	1949
		§ 5/69	West Indies	Christchurch	1951-52
Butler,IG	(1)	6/46	Pakistan	Wellington	2003-04
Cairns,BL	(6)	5/55	India	Madras[1]	1976-77
		6/85	West Indies	Christchurch	1979-80
		5/87	Australia	Brisbane[2]	1980-81
		5/33	India	Wellington	1980-81
		7/74	England	Leeds	1983
		7/143	England	Wellington	1983-84
Cairns,CL	(13)	§ 5/75	Sri Lanka	Auckland	1990-91
		6/52	England	Auckland	1991-92
		5/137	Pakistan	Rawalpindi[2]	1996-97
		5/50	Zimbabwe	Harare	1997-98
		5/62	Sri Lanka	Colombo (SSC)	1997-98
		6/77	England	Lord's	1999
		5/31	England	The Oval	1999
		§ 7/27	West Indies	Hamilton	1999-2000
		5/44	West Indies	Wellington	1999-2000
		5/31	Zimbabwe	Bulawayo[2]	2000-01
		5/146	Australia	Brisbane[2]	2001-02
		§ 7/53	Bangladesh	Hamilton	2001-02
		5/79	England	Nottingham	2004
Cameron,FJ	(3)	5/83	South Africa	Johannesburg[3]	1961-62
		5/48	South Africa	Cape Town	1961-62
		5/34	Pakistan	Auckland	1964-65
Chatfield,EJ	(3)	5/95	England	Leeds	1983
		5/63	Sri Lanka	Colombo (CCC)	1983-84
		§ 6/73	West Indies	Port-of-Spain	1984-85
Collinge,RO	(3)	5/74	England	Leeds	1973
		5/82	Australia	Auckland	1973-74
		6/63	India	Christchurch	1975-76
Congdon,BE	(1)	5/65	India	Auckland	1975-76
Cowie,J	(4)	6/67	England	Manchester	1937
		§ 6/40	Australia	Wellington	1945-46
		6/83	England	Christchurch	1946-47
		5/127	England	Leeds	1949
Cresswell,GF	(1)	†§ 6/168	England	The Oval	1949
Cunis,RS	(1)	6/76	England	Auckland	1970-71
Davis,HT	(1)	5/63	Sri Lanka	Hamilton	1996-97
Doull,SB	(6)	§ 5/66	Pakistan	Auckland	1993-94
		5/73	South Africa	Dunedin[2]	1994-95
		5/46	Pakistan	Lahore[2]	1996-97
		5/75	England	Wellington	1996-97
		§ 5/58	Sri Lanka	Dunedin	1996-97

		§ 7/65	India	Wellington	1998-99
Franklin,JEC	(3)	§ 5/28	Bangladesh	Dhaka	2004-05
		6/119	Australia	Auckland	2004-05
		5/53	West Indies	Wellington	2005-06
Hadlee,RJ	(36)	7/23	India	Wellington	1975-76
		5/121	Pakistan	Lahore[2]	1976-77
		6/26	England	Wellington	1977-78
		5/84	England	Lord's	1978
		5/62	Pakistan	Christchurch	1978-79
		5/104	Pakistan	Auckland	1978-79
		§ 5/34)	West Indies	Dunedin	1979-80
		§ 6/68)			
		5/87	Australia	Perth	1980-81
		6/57	Australia	Melbourne	1980-81
		5/47	India	Christchurch	1980-81
		5/63	Australia	Auckland	1981-82
		6/100	Australia	Christchurch	1981-82
		6/53	England	The Oval	1983
		5/93	England	Lord's	1983
		5/28	England	Christchurch	1983-84
		5/73)	Sri Lanka	Colombo (CCC)	1983-84
		5/29)			
		6/51	Pakistan	Dunedin	1984-85
		9/52)	Australia	Brisbane[2]	1985-86
		6/71)			
		5/65	Australia	Sydney	1985-86
		5/65)	Australia	Perth	1985-86
		6/90)			
		7/116	Australia	Christchurch	1985-86
		6/80	England	Lord's	1986
		6/80	England	Nottingham	1986
		6/105	West Indies	Auckland	1986-87
		6/50	West Indies	Christchurch	1986-87
		5/68	Australia	Adelaide	1987-88
		5/109)	Australia	Melbourne	1987-88
		5/67)			
		5/65	India	Bangalore	1988-89
		6/49	India	Bombay[3]	1988-89
		5/39	Australia	Wellington	1989-90
		5/53	England	Birmingham	1990
Hart,MN	(1)	§ 5/77	South Africa	Johannesburg[3]	1994-95
Howarth,HJ	(2)	5/34	India	Nagpur	1969-70
		§ 5/80	Pakistan	Karachi[1]	1969-70
MacGibbon,AR	(1)	5/64	England	Birmingham	1958
Martin,CS	(7)	§ 5/71	Zimbabwe	Wellington	2000-01
		6/76)	South Africa	Auckland	2003-04
		5/104)			
		5/55	South Africa	Wellington	2003-04
		5/142	Australia	Brisbane[2]	2004-05
		6/54	Sri Lanka	Wellington	2004-05
		5/37	South Africa	Johannesburg[3]	2005-06
Moir,AM	(2)†§	6/155	England	Christchurch	1950-51
		5/62	England	Auckland	1954-55
Morrison,DK	(10)	§ 5/69	England	Christchurch	1987-88
		5/75	India	Christchurch	1989-90
		5/98	India	Napier	1989-90

		5/145	India	Auckland	1989-90
		§ 5/153	Sri Lanka	Wellington	1990-91
		5/51	Pakistan	Hamilton	1992-93
		7/89	Australia	Wellington	1992-93
		6/37	Australia	Christchurch	1992-93
		§ 6/69	West Indies	Christchurch	1994-95
		5/61	West Indies	St John's	1995-96
Motz,RC	(5)	5/108	England	Birmingham	1965
		5/86	India	Dunedin	1967-68
		6/63	India	Christchurch	1967-68
		6/69	West Indies	Wellington	1968-69
		5/113	West Indies	Christchurch	1968-69
Nash,DJ	(3)	6/76)	England	Lord's	1994
		5/93)			
		6/27	India	Mohali	1999-2000
O'Connor,SB	(1)	5/51	Australia	Hamilton	1999-2000
O'Sullivan,DR	(1)	5/148	Australia	Adelaide	1973-74
Patel,DN	(3)	§ 6/113	Zimbabwe	Bulawayo[1]	1992-93
		6/50	Zimbabwe	Harare	1992-93
		5/93	Australia	Canterbury	1992-93
Pringle,C	(1)	7/52	Pakistan	Faisalabad	1990-91
Rabone,GO	(1)	6/68	South Africa	Cape Town	1953-54
Reid,JR	(1)	6/60	South Africa	Dunedin	1963-64
Snedden,MC	(1)	§ 5/68	West Indies	Christchurch	1986-87
Su'a,ML	(2)	5/85	Zimbabwe	Harare	1992-93
		§ 5/73	Pakistan	Hamilton	1992-93
Taylor,BR	(4)	†§ 5/86	India	Calcutta	1964-65
		5/26	India	Bombay[2]	1964-65
		7/74	West Indies	Bridgetown	1971-72
		5/41	West Indies	Port-of-Spain	1971-72
Troup,GB	(1)	6/95	West Indies	Auckland	1979-80
Tuffey,DR	(2)	§ 6/54	England	Auckland	2001-02
		5/87	Pakistan	Hamilton	2003-04
Vettori,DL	(12)	5/84	Sri Lanka	Hamilton	1996-97
		6/64	Sri Lanka	Colombo (SSC)	1997-98
		6/127	India	Kanpur	1999-2000
		5/62)	Australia	Auckland	1999-2000
		7/87)	Australia	Auckland	1999-2000
		5/138	Australia	Hobart	2001-02
		6/87	Australia	Perth	2001-02
		6/28	Bangladesh	Dhaka	2004-05
		6/70)	Bangladesh	Chittagong[1]	2004-05
		6/100)			
		5/152	Australia	Adelaide	2004-05
		5/106	Australia	Christchurch	2004-05
Watson,W	(1)	6/78	Pakistan	Lahore[2]	1990-91
Wiseman,PJ	(2)	†§ 5/82	Sri Lanka	Colombo (RPS)	1997-98
		§ 5/90	Zimbabwe	Bulawayo[2]	2000-01
INDIA *(250)*			Opponents		
Abid Ali,S	(1)	†§ 6/55	Australia	Adelaide	1967-68
Agarkar,AB	(1)	6/41	Australia	Adelaide	2003-04
Amar Singh,L	(2)	7/86	England	Madras[1]	1933-34
		6/35	England	Lord's	1936
Amarnath,NB	(2)	5/118	England	Lord's	1946
		5/96	England	Manchester	1946

Arshad Ayub	(3)	5/50	New Zealand	Bombay[3]	1988-89
		5/104	West Indies	Georgetown	1988-89
		5/117	West Indies	Port-of-Spain	1988-89
Balaji,L	(1)	5/76	Pakistan	Mohali	2004-05
Bedi,BS	(14)	6/127	New Zealand	Christchurch	1967-68
		6/42	New Zealand	Bombay[2]	1969-70
		5/37	Australia	Delhi	1969-70
		7/98	Australia	Calcutta	1969-70
		5/63	England	Calcutta	1972-73
		6/226	England	Lord's	1974
		5/82	West Indies	Port-of-Spain	1975-76
		5/27	New Zealand	Bombay[3]	1976-77
		5/48	New Zealand	Madras[1]	1976-77
		5/110	England	Calcutta	1976-77
		6/71	England	Bangalore	1976-77
		5/55	Australia	Brisbane[2]	1977-78
		5/89)	Australia	Perth	1977-78
		5/105)			
Binny,RMH	(2)	5/40	England	Lord's	1986
		6/56	Pakistan	Calcutta	1986-87
Borde,CG	(1)	5/88	England	Madras[2]	1963-64
Chandrasekhar,BS	(16)	§ 7/157	West Indies	Bombay[2]	1966-67
		5/127	England	Lord's	1967
		6/38	England	The Oval	1971
		8/79	England	Delhi	1972-73
		5/65	England	Calcutta	1972-73
		6/90	England	Madras[1]	1972-73
		5/135	England	Bombay[2]	1972-73
		6/94	New Zealand	Auckland	1975-76
		6/120	West Indies	Port-of-Spain	1975-76
		5/153	West Indies	Kingston	1975-76
		5/50	England	Madras[1]	1976-77
		6/76	England	Bangalore	1976-77
		6/52)	Australia	Melbourne	1977-78
		6/52)			
		5/136	Australia	Adelaide	1977-78
		5/115	West Indies	Bombay[3]	1978-79
Desai,RB	(2)	5/89	England	Lord's	1959
		6/56	New Zealand	Bombay[2]	1964-65
Doshi,DR	(6)	†§ 6/103	Australia	Madras[1]	1979-80
		5/43	Australia	Bombay[3]	1979-80
		§ 5/39	England	Bombay[3]	1981-82
		6/102	England	Manchester	1982
		§ 5/85	Sri Lanka	Madras[1]	1982-83
		5/90	Pakistan	Lahore[2]	1982-83
Durani,SA	(3)	5/47	England	Calcutta	1961-62
		6/105	England	Madras[2]	1961-62
		6/73	Australia	Calcutta	1964-65
Ghavri,KD	(4)	5/33	England	Bombay[3]	1976-77
		5/51	West Indies	Bangalore	1978-79
		5/52	England	Bombay[3]	1979-80
		5/107	Australia	Sydney	1980-81
Ghulam Ahmed	(4)	§ 5/70	England	Kanpur	1951-52
		5/100	England	Leeds	1952
		5/109	Pakistan	Dacca	1954-55
		7/49	Australia	Calcutta	1956-57

Gupte,SP	(12)	§ 7/162	West Indies	Port-of-Spain	1952-53
		5/107	West Indies	Port-of-Spain	1952-53
		5/180	West Indies	Kingston	1952-53
		5/18	Pakistan	Dacca	1954-55
		5/133	Pakistan	Lahore[1]	1954-55
		5/63	Pakistan	Peshawar[1]	1954-55
		§ 7/128	New Zealand	Hyderabad	1955-56
		5/45	New Zealand	Bombay[2]	1955-56
		6/90	New Zealand	Calcutta	1955-56
		5/72	New Zealand	Madras[2]	1955-56
		9/102	West Indies	Kanpur	1958-59
		5/90	England	Kanpur	1961-62
Harbhajan Singh	(18)	7/123)	Australia	Kolkata	2000-01
		6/73)			
		7/133)	Australia	Chennai[1]	2000-01
		8/84)			
		§ 5/51	England	Mohali	2001-02
		5/71	England	Ahmedabad	2001-02
		6/62	Zimbabwe	Delhi	2001-02
		5/138	West Indies	Kingston	2001-02
		5/115	England	The Oval	2002
		7/48	West Indies	Mumbai[3]	2002-03
		5/115	West Indies	Kolkata	2002-03
		5/146)	Australia	Bangalore	2004-05
		6/78)			
		5/29	Australia	Mumbai[3]	2004-05
		7/87	South Africa	Kolkata	2004-05
		6/152	Pakistan	Bangalore	2004-03
		7/62	Sri Lanka	Ahmedabad	2005-06
		5/147	West Indies	Bassaterre	2005-06
Hirwani,ND	(4)	†§ 8/61)	West Indies	Madras[1]	1987-88
		†§ 8/75)			
		§ 6/59	New Zealand	Bangalore	1988-89
		6/59	New Zealand	Cuttack	1994-95
Joshi,SB	(1)	§ 5/142	Bangladesh	Dhaka	2000-01
Kapil Dev	(23)	§ 5/146	England	Birmingham	1979
		5/82	Australia	Delhi	1979-80
		5/74	Australia	Calcutta	1979-80
		5/58	Pakistan	Delhi	1979-80
		6/63	Pakistan	Kanpur	1979-80
		7/56	Pakistan	Madras[1]	1979-80
		5/97	Australia	Sydney	1980-81
		5/28	Australia	Melbourne	1980-81
		5/70	England	Bombay[3]	1981-82
		6/91	England	Calcutta	1981-82
		5/125	England	Lord's	1982
		§ 5/110	Sri Lanka	Madras[1]	1982-83
		5/102	Pakistan	Karachi[1]	1982-83
		7/220	Pakistan	Faisalabad	1982-83
		8/85	Pakistan	Lahore[2]	1982-83
		5/68	Pakistan	Bangalore	1983-84
		6/77	West Indies	Delhi	1983-84
		9/83	West Indies	Ahmedabad	1983-84
		8/106	Australia	Adelaide	1985-86
		5/58	West Indies	Port-of-Spain	1988-89
		6/84	West Indies	Kingston	1988-89

		5/97	Australia	Melbourne	1991-92
		5/130	Australia	Adelaide	1991-92
Kumar,VV	(1)	†§ 5/64	Pakistan	Delhi	1960-61
Kumble,AR	(32)	6/53	South Africa	Johannesburg[3]	1992-93
		6/64	England	Madras[1]	1992-93
		§ 5/70	Zimbabwe	Delhi	1992-93
		§ 5/87	Sri Lanka	Colombo (SSC)	1993-94
		7/59	Sri Lanka	Lucknow[2]	1993-94
		5/81	New Zealand	Bangalore	1994-95
		§ 5/67	Australia	Delhi	1996-97
		5/120	West Indies	Kingston	1996-97
		5/104	West Indies	Port-of-Spain	1996-97
		5/62	Australia	Calcuttta	1997-98
		6/98	Australia	Bangalore	1997-98
		§ 6/70	Pakistan	Chennai[1]	1998-99
		10/74	Pakistan	Delhi	1998-99
		6/67	New Zealand	Kanpur	1999-2000
		5/82	New Zealand	Ahmedabad	1999-2000
		6/143	South Africa	Bangalore	1999-2000
		8/81	England	Mohali	2001-02
		7/115	England	Ahmedabad	2001-02
		5/63	Zimbabwe	Nagpur	2001-02
		5/30	West Indies	Chennai[1]	2002-03
		5/154	Australia	Adelaide	2003-04
		6/176	Australia	Melbourne	2003-04
		8/141	Australia	Sydney	2003-04
		6/72	Pakistan	Multan[2]	2003-04
		7/48)	Australia	Chennai[1]	2004-05
		6/133)			
		5/90	Australia	Mumbai[3]	2004-05
		6/131	South Africa	Kanpur	2004-05
		7/63	Pakistan	Kolkata	2004-05
		6/72	Sri Lanka	Delhi	2005-06
		5/89	Sri Lanka	Ahmedabad	2005-06
		5/76	England	Mohali	2005-06
Kuruvilla,A	(1)	5/68	West Indies	Bridgetown	1996-97
Madan Lal,S	(4)	5/134	New Zealand	Christchurch	1975-76
		§ 5/72	Australia	Brisbane[2]	1977-78
		5/23	England	Bombay[3]	1981-82
		5/85	England	Delhi	1981-82
Maninder Singh	(3)	7/51	Sri Lanka	Nagpur	1986-87
		5/135	Pakistan	Madras[1]	1986-87
		7/27	Pakistan	Bangalore	1986-87
Mankad,MH	(8)	5/101	England	Manchester	1946
		8/55	England	Madras[1]	1951-52
		5/196	England	Lord's	1952
		§ 8/52)	Pakistan	Delhi	1952-53
		§ 5/79)			
		5/72	Pakistan	Bombay[2]	1952-53
		5/228	West Indies	Kingston	1952-53
		5/64	Pakistan	Peshawar[1]	1954-55
Nadkarni,RG	(4)	6/105	Australia	Bombay[2]	1959-60
		5/31)	Australia	Madras[2]	1964-65
		6/91)			
		6/43	New Zealand	Wellington	1967-68
Nissar, Mahomed	(3)	†§ 5/93	England	Lord's	1932

		5/90	England	Bombay[1]	1933-34
		5/120	England	The Oval	1936
Patel,JM	(2)	9/69)	Australia	Kanpur	1959-60
		5/55)			
Phadkar,DG	(3)	7/159	West Indies	Madras[1]	1948-49
		5/72	Pakistan	Calcutta	1952-53
		5/64	West Indies	Bridgetown	1952-53
Pathan,IK	(7)	5/45)	Bangladesh	Dhaka	2004-05
		6/51)			
		5/32	Bangladesh	Chittagong[1]	2004-05
		5/58	Zimbabwe	Bulawayo[2]	2005-06
		7/59)	Zimbabwe	Harare	2005-06
		5/67)			
		5/61	Pakistan	Karachi[1]	2005-06
Prabhakar,M	(3)	§ 5/104	Pakistan	Karachi[1]	1989-90
		6/132	Pakistan	Faisalabad	1989-90
		5/101	Australia	Perth	1991-92
Prasanna,EAS	(10)	6/141	Australia	Melbourne	1967-68
		6/104	Australia	Brisbane[2]	1967-68
		§ 6/94	New Zealand	Dunedin	1967-68
		5/32	New Zealand	Wellington	1967-68
		5/51	New Zealand	Nagpur	1969-70
		5/121	Australia	Bombay[2]	1969-70
		5/42	Australia	Delhi	1969-70
		6/74	Australia	Madras[1]	1969-70
		5/70	West Indies	Madras[1]	1974-75
		8/76	New Zealand	Auckland	1975-76
Ramchand,GS	(1)	6/49	Pakistan	Karachi[1]	1954-55
Rangachari,CR	(1)	§ 5/107	West Indies	Delhi	1948-49
Razdan,V	(1)	5/79	Pakistan	Sialkot	1989-90
Sharma,C	(4)	5/118	Sri Lanka	Colombo (PSS)	1985-86
		5/64	England	Lord's	1986
		6/58	England	Birmingham	1986
		§ 5/55	West Indies	Delhi	1987-88
Shastri,RJ	(2)	5/125	New Zealand	Auckland	1980-81
		5/75	Pakistan	Nagpur	1983-84
Shinde,SG	(1)	6/91	England	Delhi	1951-52
Shivaramakrishnan,L	(3)	§ 6/64)	England	Bombay[3]	1984-85
		§ 6/117)			
		6/99	England	Delhi	1984-85
Srinath,J	(10)	6/21	South Africa	Ahmedabad	1996-97
		5/104	South Africa	Johannesburg[3]	1996-97
		5/95	New Zealand	Hamilton	1998-99
		5/46)	Pakistan	Calcutta	1998-99
		8/86)			
		6/45	New Zealand	Mohali	1999-2000
		5/60	Zimbabwe	Delhi	2000-01
		5/114	Sri Lanka	Galle	2001-02
		5/140	South Africa	Bloemfontein	2001-02
		6/76	South Africa	Port Elizabeth	2001-02
Surendranath,R	(2)	5/115	England	Manchester	1959
		5/89	England	The Oval	1959
Surti,RF	(1)	§ 5/74	Australia	Adelaide	1967-68
Umrigar,PR	(2)	6/78	Pakistan	Bahawalpur	1954-55
		5/107	West Indies	Port-of-Spain	1961-62
Venkatapathy Raju,SL	(5)	§ 6/12	Sri Lanka	Chandigarh	1990-91

		5/38)	Sri Lanka	Ahmedabad	1993-94
		6/87)			
		§ 5/60	West Indies	Bombay[3]	1994-95
		5/127	West Indies	Nagpur	1994-95
Venkatesh Prasad,BK	(7)	5/76	England	Lord's	1996
		6/104	South Africa	Calcutta	1996-97
		5/60)	South Africa	Durban[2]	1996-97
		5/93)			
		5/82	West Indies	Bridgetown	1996-97
		§ 6/33	Pakistan	Chennai[1]	1998-99
		5/72	Sri Lanka	Kandy	2001-02
Venkataraghavan,S	(3)	8/72	New Zealand	Delhi	1964-65
		6/74	New Zealand	Hyderabad	1969-70
		5/95	West Indies	Port-of-Spain	1970-71
Yadav,NS	(3)	§ 5/131	West Indies	Bombay[3]	1983-84
		5/99	Australia	Sydney	1985-86
		§ 5/76	Sri Lanka	Nagpur	1986-87
Zaheer Khan	(3)	§ 5/53	New Zealand	Wellington	2002-03
		5/29	New Zealand	Hamilton	2002-03
		5/95	Australia	Brisbane[2]	2003-04

PAKISTAN *(219)*			Opponents		
Aamer Nazir	(1)	5/46	Zimbabwe	Harare	1994-95
Aaqib Javed	(1)	5/84	Sri Lanka	Faisalabad	1995-96
Abdul Qadir	(15)	6/44	England	Hyderabad	1977-78
		§ 5/76	Australia	Karachi[1]	1982-83
		7/142	Australia	Lahore[2]	1982-83
		5/166	Australia	Melbourne	1983-84
		5/74	England	Karachi[1]	1983-84
		5/84)	England	Lahore[2]	1983-84
		5/110)			
		5/108	New Zealand	Hyderabad	1984-85
		5/44	Sri Lanka	Karachi[1]	1985-86
		6/16	West Indies	Faisalabad	1986-87
		7/96	England	The Oval	1987
		9/56	England	Lahore[2]	1987-88
		5/88)	England	Karachi[1]	1987-88
		5/98)			
		6/160	New Zealand	Auckland	1988-89
Abdur Razzaq	(1)	5/35	Sri Lanka	Karachi[1]	2004-05
Arif Butt	(1)	†§ 6/89	Australia	Melbourne	1964-65
Arshad Khan	(1)	§ 5/38	Sri Lanka	Dhaka	1998-99
Asif Iqbal	(2)	§ 5/48	New Zealand	Wellington	1964-65
		5/52	New Zealand	Auckland	1964-65
Asif Masood	(1)	5/111	England	Birmingham	1971
Azeem Hafeez	(4)	§ 5/100	Australia	Perth	1983-84
		5/167	Australia	Adelaide	1983-84
		6/46	India	Lahore[2]	1984-85
		5/127	New Zealand	Wellington	1984-85
Danish Kaneria	(11)	§ 6/42)	Bangladesh	Multan[2]	2001-02
		§ 6/52)			
		7/77	Bangladesh	Dhaka	2001-02
		§ 5/110	New Zealand	Lahore[2]	2001-02
		§ 5/46	South Africa	Lahore[2]	2003-04
		7/118	Sri Lanka	Karachi[1]	2004-05
		5/125	Australia	Melbourne	2004-05

		7/188	Australia	Sydney	2004-05
		6/150	Pakistan	Mohali	2004-05
		5/127	Pakistan	Bangalore	2004-05
		5/46	West Indies	Kingston	2004-05
D'Souza,A	(1)	5/112	England	Karachi[1]	1961-62
Ehteshamuddin	(1)	5/47	India	Kanpur	1979-80
Fazal Mahmood	(13)	5/52)	India	Lucknow[1]	1952-53
		7/42)			
		6/53)	England	The Oval	1954
		6/46)			
		5/48	India	Karachi[1]	1954-55
		§ 6/34)	Australia	Karachi[1]	1956-57
		§ 7/80)			
		6/83	West Indies	Port-of-Spain	1957-58
		6/34)	West Indies	Dacca	1958-59
		6/66)			
		5/71	Australia	Dacca	1959-60
		5/74	Australia	Karachi[1]	1959-60
		5/26	India	Calcutta	1960-61
Haseeb Ahsan	(2)	5/121	India	Kanpur	1960-61
		6/202	India	Madras[2]	1960-61
Imran Khan	(23)	5/122	Australia	Melbourne	1976-77
		6/102)	Australia	Sydney	1976-77
		6/63)			
		6/90	West Indies	Kingston	1976-77
		5/106	New Zealand	Napier	1978-79
		5/114	India	Madras[1]	1979-80
		5/63	India	Calcutta	1979-80
		5/62	West Indies	Multan	1980-81
		§ 8/58)	Sri Lanka	Lahore[2]	1981-82
		§ 6/58)			
		7/52	England	Birmingham	1982
		5/49	England	Leeds	1982
		8/60	India	Karachi[1]	1982-83
		6/98)	India	Faisalabad	1982-83
		5/82)			
		6/35	India	Hyderabad	1982-83
		5/40	Sri Lanka	Sialkot	1985-86
		5/59	West Indies	Lahore[2]	1986-87
		6/46	West Indies	Karachi[1]	1986-87
		7/40	England	Leeds	1987
		6/129	England	Birmingham	1987
		7/80	West Indies	Georgetown	1987-88
		5/115	West Indies	Port-of-Spain	1987-88
Intikhab Alam	(5)	5/91)	New Zealand	Dacca	1969-70
		5/91)			
		7/52	New Zealand	Dunedin	1972-73
		6/127	New Zealand	Auckland	1972-73
		5/116	England	The Oval	1974
Iqbal Qasim	(8)	6/40	India	Bombay[3]	1979-80
		7/49	Australia	Karachi[1]	1979-80
		6/89	West Indies	Faisalabad	1980-81
		6/141	Sri Lanka	Faisalabad	1981-82
		5/78	New Zealand	Hyderabad	1984-85
		5/48	India	Bangalore	1986-87
		5/83	England	Faisalabad	1987-88

		5/35	Australia	Karachi[1]	1988-89
Khan Mohammad	(4)	§ 5/61	England	Lord's	1954
		5/74	India	Bahawalpur	1954-55
		5/73	India	Karachi[1]	1954-55
		6/21	New Zealand	Dacca	1955-56
Mahmood Hussain	(2)	6/67	India	Dacca	1954-55
		5/129	India	Bombay[2]	1960-61
Mohammad Akram	(1)	5/138	Australia	Perth	1999-2000
Mohammad Asif	(2)	6/44)	Sri Lanka	Kandy	2005-06
		5/27)			
Mohammad Nazir	(3)	†§ 7/99	New Zealand	Karachi[1]	1969-70
		5/44	West Indies	Faisalabad	1980-81
		5/72	India	Nagpur	1983-84
Mohammad Sami	(2)	†§ 5/36	New Zealand	Auckland	2000-01
		5/44	New Zealand	Hamilton	2003-04
Mohammad Zahid	(1)	†§ 7/66	New Zealand	Rawalpindi[2]	1996-97
Mudassar Nazar	(1)	6/32	England	Lord's	1982
Munir Malik	(1)	§ 5/128	England	Leeds	1962
Mushtaq Ahmed	(10)	5/115	Australia	Hobart	1995-96
		5/95	Australia	Sydney	1995-96
		§ 7/56	New Zealand	Christchurch	1995-96
		5/57	England	Lord's	1996-97
		6/78	England	The Oval	1996-97
		6/84	New Zealand	Lahore[2]	1996-97
		6/87	New Zealand	Rawalpindi[2]	1996-97
		5/35)	West Indies	Peshawar[2]	1997-98
		5/71)			
		6/78	South Africa	Durban[2]	1997-98
Mushtaq Mohammad	(3)	5/49	New Zealand	Dunedin	1972-73
		5/28	West Indies	Port-of-Spain	1976-77
		5/59	New Zealand	Christchurch	1978-79
Nasim-ul-Ghani	(2)	5/116	West Indies	Georgetown	1957-58
		6/67	West Indies	Port-of-Spain	1957-58
Pervez Sajjad	(3)	5/42	New Zealand	Auckland	1964-65
		5/33	New Zealand	Karachi[1]	1969-70
		7/74	New Zealand	Lahore[2]	1969-70
Saleem Jaffer	(1)	§ 5/40	New Zealand	Wellington	1988-89
Saqlain Mushtaq	(13)	5/89	Sri Lanka	Colombo (RPS)	1996-97
		§ 5/129	South Africa	Rawalpindi[2]	1997-98
		§ 5/54	West Indies	Karachi[1]	1997-98
		5/32	Zimbabwe	Lahore	1998-99
		§ 5/94)	India	Chennai[1]	1998-99
		§ 5/93)			
		5/94)	India	Delhi	1998-99
		5/122)			
		6/46	Australia	Hobart	1999-2000
		5/121	West Indies	Bridgetown	1999-2000
		§ 8/164	England	Lahore[2]	2000-01
		5/35	Bangladesh	Chittagong[1]	2001-02
		7/66	Zimbabwe	Bulawayo[2]	2002-03
Sarfraz Nawaz	(4)	§ 6/89	West Indies	Lahore[2]	1974-75
		5/39	England	Leeds	1978
		5/70	India	Karachi[1]	1978-79
		9/86	Australia	Melbourne	1978-79
Shabbir Ahmed	(2)	†§ 5/48	Bangladesh	Karachi[1]	2003-04
		§ 5/117	New Zealand	Hamilton	2003-04

Shahid Afridi	(1)	†§ 5/52	Australia	Karachi[1]	1998-99
Shahid Nazir	(1)	†§ 5/53	Zimbabwe	Sheikhupura	1996-97
Shoaib Akhtar	(12)	5/43	South Africa	Durban[2]	1997-98
		5/75	Sri Lanka	Peshawar[2]	1999-2000
		5/24	West Indies	Sharjah	2001-02
		§ 6/11	New Zealand	Lahore[2]	2001-02
		5/21	Australia	Colombo (PSS)	2002-03
		6/49	Bangladesh	Peshawar[2]	2003-04
		5/48)	New Zealand	Wellington	2003-04
		6/30)			
		5/60	Sri Lanka	Faisalabad	2004-05
		5/99	Australia	Perth	2004-05
		5/109	Australia	Melbourne	2004-05
		5/71	England	Lahore[2]	2005-06
Sikander Bakht	(3)	8/69	India	Delhi	1979-80
		5/55	India	Bombay[3]	1979-80
		5/56	India	Kanpur	1979-80
Tahir Naqqash	(2)	§ 5/40	England	Birmingham	1982
		5/76	India	Bangalore	1983-84
Tauseef Ahmed	(3)	5/54	Sri Lanka	Karachi[1]	1985-86
		6/45	Sri Lanka	Kandy	1985-86
		5/54	India	Bangalore	1986-87
Umar Gul	(2)	5/31	India	Lahore2	2003-04
		5/123	England	Leeds	2006
Waqar Younis	(22)	7/86	New Zealand	Lahore[2]	1990-91
		7/76)	New Zealand	Faisalabad	1990-91
		5/54)			
		§ 5/76	West Indies	Karachi[1]	1990-91
		5/46	West Indies	Faisalabad	1990-91
		§ 5/84	Sri Lanka	Sialkot	1991-92
		5/65	Sri Lanka	Faisalabad	1991-92
		5/91	England	Lord's	1992
		5/113	England	Leeds	1992
		5/52	England	The Oval	1992
		5/22	New Zealand	Hamilton	1992-93
		5/104	West indies	Bridgetown	1992-93
		§ 7/91)	Zimbabwe	Karachi[2]	1993-94
		§ 6/44)			
		5/88	Zimbabwe	Rawalpindi[2]	1993-94
		5/100	Zimbabwe	Lahore[2]	1993-94
		6/78	New Zealand	Christchurch	1993-94
		6/34)	Sri Lanka	Kandy	1994-95
		5/85)			
		6/78	South Africa	Port Elizabeth	1997-98
		5/106	Zimbabwe	Bulawayo[2]	1997-98
		6/55	Bangladesh	Dhaka	2001-02
Wasim Akram	(25)	5/56)	New Zealand	Dunedin	1984-85
		5/72)			
		§ 6/91	West Indies	Faisalabad	1986-87
		5/96	India	Calcutta	1986-87
		5/101	India	Sialkot	1989-90
		§ 6/62)	Australia	Melbourne	1989-90
		§ 5/98)			
		5/100	Australia	Adelaide	1989-90
		5/28	West Indies	Lahore[2]	1990-91
		5/128	England	Manchester	1992

		6/67	England	The Oval	1992
		5/45	New Zealand	Hamilton	1992-93
		§ 5/65	Zimbabwe	Rawalpindi[2]	1993-94
		6/43	New Zealand	Auckland	1993-94
		7/119	New Zealand	Wellington	1993-94
		5/43	Sri Lanka	Colombo (PSS)	1994-95
		5/64	Australia	Karachi[1]	1994-95
		5/43	Zimbabwe	Bulawayo[2]	1994-95
		5/55	Sri Lanka	Peshawar[2]	1995-96
		5/53	New Zealand	Christchurch	1995-96
		6/48	Zimbabwe	Faisalabad	1996-97
		5/52	Zimbabwe	Peshawar[2]	1998-99
		6/61)	West Indies	St Johns	1999-2000
		5/49)			
		5/45	Sri Lanka	Colombo (SSC)	2000-01
Zulfiqar Ahmed	(2)	§ 5/37)	New Zealand	Karachi[1]	1955-56
		§ 6/42)			
SRI LANKA *(109)*			Opponents		
Ahangama,FS	(1)	5/52	India	Kandy	1985-86
Bandaratilake,MRCN	(1)	5/36	New Zealand	Galle	1997-98
Chandana,UDU	(3)	†§ 6/179	Pakistan	Dhaka	1998-99
		5/109)	Australia	Cairns	2004-05
		5/101)			
de Mel,ALF	(3)	§ 5/68	India	Madras[1]	1982-83
		5/64	India	Colombo (SSC)	1985-86
		6/109	Pakistan	Karachi[1]	1985-86
de Silva,DS	(1)	5/59	Pakistan	Faisalabad	1981-82
de Silva,KSC	(1)	§ 5/85	Pakistan	Colombo (SSC)	1996-97
Dharmasena,HDPK	(3)	§ 6/99	Pakistan	Colombo (PSS)	1994-95
		5/57	India	Mumbai[3]	1997-98
		6/72	New Zealand	Galle	1997-98
Fernando,CRD	(3)	§ 5/98	South Africa	Durban[2]	2000-01
		§ 5/42	India	Galle	2001-02
		5/60	Bangladesh	Colombo (PSS)	2005-06
Jayasuriya,ST	(2)	5/43	Zimbabwe	Galle	2001-02
		5/34	South Africa	Colombo (SSC)	2004-05
John,VB	(2)	5/60	New Zealand	Wellington	1982-83
		5/86	New Zealand	Kandy	1983-84
Kuruppuarachchi,AK	(1)	†§ 5/44	Pakistan	Colombo (CCC)	1985-86
Labrooy,GF	(1)	5/133	Australia	Brisbane[2]	1989-90
Malinga,SL	(1)	§ 5/80	New Zealand	Napier	2004-05
Muralidaran,M	(56)	§ 5/104	South Africa	Moratuwa	1993-94
		5/101	South Africa	Colombo (SSC)	1993-94
		5/162	India	Lucknow[2]	1993-94
		5/64	New Zealand	Napier	1994-95
		5/68	Pakistan	Faisalabad	1995-96
		5/33	Zimbabwe	Faisalabad	1996-97
		6/98	Pakistan	Colombo (RPS)	1996-97
		5/34	West Indies	St John's	1996-97
		5/113	West Indies	Arnos Vale	1996-97
		5/23)	Zimbabwe	Kandy	1997-98
		7/94)			
		5/63	South Africa	Centurion	1997-98
		5/90	New Zealand	Colombo (RPS)	1997-98
		5/30	New Zealand	Colombo (SSC)	1997-98

		7/155)	England	The Oval	1998
		9/65)	England	The Oval	1998
		5/71	Australia	Galle	1999-2000
		6/71	Pakistan	Peshawar[2]	1999-2000
		5/115	Pakistan	Colombo (SSC)	2000-01
		6/87)	South Africa	Galle	2000-01
		7/84)			
		5/68	South Africa	Colombo (SSC)	2000-01
		5/122)	South Africa	Durban[2]	2000-01
		6/39)			
		5/49	India	Galle	2001-02
		8/87	India	Colombo,SSC	2001-02
		§ 5/13)	Bangladesh	Colombo,SSC	2001-02
		§ 5/98)			
		6/126)	West Indies	Galle	2001-02
		5/44)			
		6/80	West Indies	Kandy	2001-02
		9/51	Zimbabwe	Kandy	2001-02
		5/67	Zimbabwe	Galle	2001-02
		5/143	England	Birmingham	2002
		5/39)	Bangladesh	Colombo (PSS)	2002-03
		5/59)			
		5/49	New Zealand	Kandy	2002-03
		5/138	West Indies	Gros Islet	2002-03
		7/46	England	Galle	2003-04
		6/59)	Australia	Galle	2003-04
		5/153)			
		5/173	Australia	Kandy	2003-04
		5/123	Australia	Colombo (SSC)	2003-04
		6/45	Zimbabwe	Harare	2003-04
		6/36	West Indies	Colombo (SSC)	2005-06
		8/46	West Indies	Kandy	2005-06
		6/18	Bangladesh	Colombo (RPS)	2005-06
		7/100	India	Delhi	2005-06
		6/54	Bangladesh	Chittagong[2]	2005-06
		5/79	Bangladesh	Bogra	2005-06
		5/39	Pakistan	Kandy	2005-06
		6/86	England	Birmingham	2006
		8/70	England	Nottingham	2006
		6/131	South Africa	Colombo (SSC)	2006-07
		5/128)	South Africa	Colombo(PSS)	2006-07
		7/97)			
Nissanka,RAP	(1)	5/64	West Indies	Kingston	2002-03
Pushpakumara,KR	(4)	7/116	Zimbabwe	Harare	1994-95
		5/41	West Indies	Arnos Vale	1996-97
		5/122	India	Nagpur	1997-98
		5/56	Zimbabwe	Harare	1999-2000
Ramanayake,CPH	(1)	5/82	Australia	Moratuwa	1992-93
Ratnayake,RJ	(5)	§ 6/85	India	Colombo (SSC)	1985-86
		5/49	India	Colombo (PSS)	1985-86
		6/66	Australia	Hobart	1989-90
		5/77	New Zealand	Hamilton	1990-91
		§ 5/69	England	Lord's	1991
Ratnayeke,JR	(4)	5/42	New Zealand	Colombo (SSC)	1983-84
		8/83	Pakistan	Sialkot	1985-86

		5/37	Pakistan	Colombo (CCC)	1985-86
		5/85	India	Cuttack	1986-87
Vaas,WPUJC	(11)	§ 5/47)	New Zealand	Napier	1994-95
		§ 5/43)			
		6/87	New Zealand	Dunedin	1994-95
		5/99	Pakistan	Peshawar[2]	1995-96
		6/73	England	Colombo,SSC	2000-01
		7/120)	West Indies	Colombo,SSC	2001-02
		7/71)			
		5/31	Australia	Darwin	2004-05
		6/29	South Africa	Colombo (SSC)	2004-05
		6/108	New Zealand	Wellington	2004-05
		6/22	West Indies	Kandy	2005-06
Wickramasinghe,GP	(3)	5/73	Pakistan	Faisalabad	1991-92
		6/103	Pakistan	Lahore[2]	1999-2000
		6/60	Zimbabwe	Bulawayo[2]	1999-2000
Zoysa,DNT	(1)	5/20	Zimbabwe	Harare	2003-04
ZIMBABWE *(29)*			Opponents		
Blignaut,AM	(3)	†§ 5/73	Bangladesh	Bulawayo[2]	2000-01
		5/74	India	Harare	2000-01
		5/79	Pakistan	Harare	2002-03
Brain,DH	(1)	5/42	Pakistan	Lahore[2]	1993-94
Chigumbura,E	(1)	†§ 5/54	Bangladesh	Chittagong[1]	2004-05
Friend,TJ	(1)	§ 5/31	Bangladesh	Dhaka	2001-02
Hondo,DT	(1)	6/59	Bangladesh	Dhaka	2004-05
Huckle,AG	(2)	6/111)	New Zealand	Bulawayo[2]	1997-98
		5/146)			
Olonga,HK	(2)	§ 5/70	India	Harare	1998-99
		5/93	Pakistan	Harare	2002-03
Price,RW	(5)	5/181	South Africa	Bulawayo[2]	2001-02
		§ 5/182	India	Nagpur	2001-02
		6/121	Australia	Sydney	2003-04
		6/73	West Indies	Harare	2003-04
		5/199	West Indies	Bulawayo[2]	2003-04
Strang,BC	(1)	§ 5/101	South Africa	Harare	1995-96
Strang,PA	(4)	5/106	Sri Lanka	Colombo (SSC)	1996-97
		5/212	Pakistan	Sheikhupura	1996-97
		§ 5/123	England	Bulawayo[2]	1996-97
		8/109	New Zealand	Bulawayo[2]	2000-01
Streak,HH	(7)	5/56	Pakistan	Rawalpindi[2]	1993-94
		6/90	Pakistan	Harare	1994-95
		5/70	Pakistan	Bulawayo[2]	1994-95
		5/93	Australia	Harare	1999-2000
		5/23	West Indies	Port-of-Spain	1999-2000
		6/87	England	Lord's	2000
		6/73	India	Harare	2005-06
Traicos,AJ #	(1)	†§ 5/85	India	Harare	1992-93
BANGLADESH *(13)*			Opponents		
Enamul Haque[2]	(3)	§ 6/45	Zimbabwe	Chittagong[1]	2004-05
		7/95)	Zimbabwe	Dhaka	2004-05
		5/105)			
Manjural Islam	(1)	†§ 6/81	Zimbabwe	Bulawayo[2]	2000-01
Mohammad Rafique	(7)	6/77	South Africa	Dhaka	2002-03
		5/118	Pakistan	Peshawar[2]	2003-04

		5/36	Pakistan	Multan[2]	2003-04
		§ 6/122	New Zealand	Dhaka	2004-05
		5/65	Zimbabwe	Chittagong[1]	2004-05
		5/114	Sri Lanka	Colombo,RPS	2005-06
		5/62	Australia	Fatullah	2005-06
Naimur Rahman	(1)†§	6/132	India	Dhaka	2000-01
Shahadat Hossain	(1)	5/86	Sri Lanka	Bogra	2005-06

HAT-TRICKS IN TEST MATCHES

F.R.Spofforth | Australia | v England | Melbourne | 1878-1879
V.P.F.A.Royle (bowled), F.A.Mackinnon (bowled), T.Emmett (caught)

W.Bates | England | v Australia | Melbourne | 1882-83
P.S.McDonnell (bowled), G.Giffen (caught & bowled), G.J.Bonnor (caught)

J.Briggs | England | v Australia | Sydney | 1891-92
W.F.Giffen (bowled), S.T.Callaway (caught), J.M.Blackham (lbw)

G.A.Lohmann | England | v South Africa | Port Elizabeth | 1895-96
F.J.Cook (bowled), J.Middleton (bowled), J.T.Willoughby (caught)

J.T.Hearne | England | v Australia | Leeds | 1899
C.Hill (bowled), S.E.Gregory (caught), M.A.Noble (caught)

H.Trumble | Australia | v England | Melbourne | 1901-02
A.O.Jones (caught), J.R.Gunn (caught), S.F.Barnes (caught & bowled)

§ H.Trumble | Australia | v England | Melbourne | 1903-04
W.Rhodes (caught), A.E.Knight (caught wicket-keeper), A.F.A.Lilley (lbw)

¶ T.J.Matthews (2) | Australia | v South Africa | Manchester | 1912
1st innings: R.Beaumont (bowled), S.J.Pegler (lbw), T.A.Ward (lbw)
2nd innings: H.W.Taylor (bowled), R.O.Schwartz (caught & bowled), T.A.Ward (caught & bowled)

† M.J.C.Allom | England | v New Zealand | Christchurch | 1929-30
T.C.Lowry (lbw), K.C.James (caught wicket-keeper), F.T.Badcock (bowled)

T.W.J.Goddard | England | v South Africa | Johannesburg[1] | 1938-39
A.D.Nourse (caught & bowled), N.Gordon (stumped), W.W.Wade (bowled)

P.J.Loader | England | v West Indies | Leeds | 1957
J.D.C.Goddard (bowled), S.Ramadhin (caught), R.Gilchrist (bowled)

L.F.Kline | Australia | v South Africa | Cape Town | 1957-58
E.R.H.Fuller (caught), H.J.Tayfield (lbw), N.A.T.Adcock (caught)

W.W.Hall | West Indies | v Pakistan | Lahore[1] | 1958-59
Mushtaq Mohammad (lbw), Fazal Mahmood (caught), Nasim-ul-Ghani (bowled)

§ G.M.Griffin | South Africa | v England | Lord's | 1960
M.J.K.Smith (caught wicket-keeper), P.M.Walker (bowled), F.S.Trueman (bowled)

L.R.Gibbs | West Indies | v Australia | Adelaide | 1960-61
K.D.Mackay (lbw), A.T.W.Grout (caught), F.M.Misson (bowled)

† P.J.Petherick | New Zealand | v Pakistan | Lahore[2] | 1976-77
Javed Miandad (caught), Wasim Raja (caught & bowled), Intikhab Alam (caught)

C.A.Walsh | West Indies | v Australia | Brisbane[2] | 1988-89
A.I.C.Dodemaide (caught), M.R.J.Veletta (caught), G.M.Wood (lbw)

M.G.Hughes | Australia | v West Indies | Perth | 1988-89
C.E.L.Ambrose (caught wicket-keeper), B.P.Patterson (caught), C.G.Greenidge (lbw)

† D.W.Fleming | Australia | v Pakistan | Rawalpindi[2] | 1994-95
Aamer Malik (caught), Inzamamul Haq (lbw), Saleem Malik (caught wicket-keeper)

S.K.Warne | Australia | v England | Melbourne | 1994-95
P.A.J.DeFreitas (lbw), D.Gough (caught wicket-keeper), D.E.Malcolm (caught)

D.G.Cork | England | v West Indies | Old Trafford | 1995
R.B.Richardson (bowled), J.R.Murray (lbw), C.L.Hooper (lbw)

D.Gough | England | v Australia | Sydney | 1998-99
I.A.Healy (caught wicket-keeper), S.C.G.MacGill (bowled), C.R.Miller (bowled)

Wasim Akram | Pakistan | v Sri Lanka | Lahore[2] | 1998-99

R.S.Kaluwitharana (bowled), M.R.C.N.Bandaratilleke (bowled), G.P.Wickramasinghe (bowled)

Wasim Akram	Pakistan	v	Sri Lanka	Dhaka	1998-99
	D.A.Gunawardene (caught), W.P.U.J.C.Vaas (bowled), D.P.M.D.Jayawardene (caught)				
D.N.T.Zoysa	Sri Lanka	v	Zimbabwe	Harare	1999-2000
	T.R.Gripper (lbw), M.W.Goodwin (caught wicket-keeper), N.C.Johnson (lbw)				
Abdur Razzaq	Pakistan	v	Sri Lanka	Galle	1999-2000
	R.S.Kaluwitharana (caught wicket-keeper), H.M.R.K.B.Herath (lbw), K.R.Pushpakumara (lbw)				
G.D.McGrath	Australia	v	West Indies	Perth	2000-01
	S.L.Campbell (caught), B.C.Lara (caught), J.C.Adams (caught)				
Harbhajan Singh	India	v	Australia	Kolkata	2000-01
	R.T.Ponting (lbw), A.C.Gilchrist (lbw), S.K.Warne (caught)				
Mohammad Sami	Pakistan	v	Sri Lanka	Lahore[2]	2001-02
	T.C.B.Fernando (lbw), D.N.T.Zoysa (lbw), M.Muralidaran (bowled)				
# J.J.C.Lawson	West Indies	v	Australia	Bridgetown	2002-03
	B.Lee (bowled), S.C.G.MacGill (bowled), J.L.Langer (lbw)				
Alok Kapali	Bangladesh	v	Pakistan	Peshawar[2]	2003
	Shabbir Ahmed (caught), Danish Kaneria (lbw), Umar Gul (lbw)				
A.M.Blignaut	Zimbabwe	v	Bangladesh	Harare	2003-04
	Hannan Sarkar (lbw), Mohammad Ashraful (caught), Mushfiqur Rahman (caught wicket-keeper)				
M.J.Hoggard	England	v	West Indies	Bridgetown	2003-04
	R.R.Sarwan (caught), S.Chanderpaul (lbw), R.O.Hinds (caught)				
J.E.C.Franklin	New Zealand	v	Bangladesh	Dhaka	2004-05
	Manjural Islam[2] (caught wicket-keeper), Mohammad Rafique (caught), Tapash Baisya (bowled)				
I.K.Pathan	India	v	Pakistan	Karachi[1]	2005-06
	Salman Butt (caught), Younis Khan (lbw), Yousuf Youhana (bowled)				

§ Trumble & Griffin did the hat-trick in their last Tests. ¶ Matthews did the hat-trick in each innings on the second afternoon of the match. † Allom, Petherick & Fleming did the hat-trick on debut. # Walsh, Hughes and Lawson did the hat-trick over two innings (Hughes's hat-trick was spread over 3 overs - last ball of an over, first ball of next over - last over of 1st innings - and first ball of 2nd innings. Zoysa's hat-trick was from his first three balls in the match. Pathan's hat-trick was from the 4th, 5th & 6th balls of the first over of the match.

FOUR WICKETS IN FIVE BALLS

M.J.C.Allom	England	v	New Zealand	Christchurch	1929-30
In his first Test - in his eighth over (W0WWW).					
C.M.Old	England	v	Pakistan	Birmingham	1978
In the same over (WW0WW) his third ball was a no ball.					
Wasim Akram	Pakistan	v	West Indies	Lahore[2]	1990-91
In the same over (WW1WW) - a catch was dropped from the third ball.					

THREE WICKETS IN FOUR BALLS

F.R.Spofforth	Australia	v	England	The Oval	1882
F.R.Spofforth	Australia	v	England	Sydney	1884-85
J.Briggs	England	v	South Africa	Cape Town	1888-89
W.P.Howell	Australia	v	South Africa	Cape Town	1902-03
M.J.C.Allom	England	v	New Zealand	Christchurch	1929-30
E.P.Nupen	South Africa	v	England	Johannesburg[1]	1930-31
W J.O'Reilly	Australia	v	England	Manchester	1934
W.Voce	England	v	Australia	Sydney	1936-37
R.R.Lindwall	Australia	v	England	Adelaide	1946-47
K.Cranston	England	v	South Africa	Leeds	1947
C.N.McCarthy	South Africa	v	England	Durban[2]	1948-49
R.Appleyard	England	v	New Zealand	Auckland	1954-55
R.Benaud	Australia	v	West Indies	Georgetown	1954-55
Fazal Mahmood	Pakistan	v	Australia	Karachi[1]	1956-57

J.W.Martin	Australia	v	West Indies	Melbourne	1960-61
L.R.Gibbs	West Indies	v	Australia	Sydney	1960-61
K.D.Mackay	Australia	v	England	Birmingham	1961
W.W.Hall	West Indies	v	India	Port-of-Spain	1961-62
D.Shackleton	England	v	West Indies	Lord's	1963
G.D.McKenzie	Australia	v	West Indies	Port-of-Spain	1964-65
F.J.Titmus	England	v	New Zealand	Leeds	1965
P.Lever	England	v	Pakistan	Leeds	1971
D.K.Lillee	Australia	v	England	Manchester	1972
D.K.Lillee	Australia	v	England	The Oval	1972
C.M.Old	England	v	Pakistan	Birmingham	1978
S.T.Clarke	West Indies	v	Pakistan	Karachi[1]	1980-81
R.J.Hadlee	New Zealand	v	Australia	Melbourne	1980-81
R.J.Shastri	India	v	New Zealand	Wellington	1980-81
I.T.Botham	England	v	Australia	Leeds	1985
Kapil Dev	India	v	Australia	Adelaide	1985-86
C.G.Rackemann	Australia	v	Pakistan	Adelaide	1989-90
D.E.Malcolm	England	v	West Indies	Port-of-Spain	1989-90
Wasim Akram	Pakistan	v	West Indies	Lahore[2]	1990-91
A.R.Border	Australia	v	West Indies	Georgetown	1990-91
Wasim Akram	Pakistan	v	England	Lord's	1992
S.K.Warne	Australia	v	England	Brisbane[2]	1994-95
P.A.Strang	Zimbabwe	v	Sri Lanka	Colombo (RPS)	1996-97
S.M.Pollock	South Africa	v	Pakistan	Faisalabad	1997-98
†J.N.Gillespie	Australia	v	England	Perth	1998-99
Waqar Younis	Pakistan	v	Zimbabwe	Peshawar[2]	1998-99
M.S.Kasprowicz	Australia	v	Pakistan	Perth	1999-2000
A.R.Caddick	England	v	West Indies	Leeds	2000
D.Gough	England	v	Pakistan	Lord's	2001
G.D.McGrath	Australia	v	South Africa	Johannesburg[3]	2001-02
Shoaib Akhtar	Pakistan	v	Australia	Colombo (PSS)	2002-03
J.H.Kallis	South Africa	v	Bangladesh	Potchefstroom	2002-03
J.J.C.Lawson	West indies	v	Bangladesh	Dhaka	2002-03
A.Flintoff	England	v	Australia	Birmingham	2005
J.E.C.Franklin	New Zealand	v	Zimbabwe	Harare	2005-06
J.H.Kallis	South Africa	v	Australia	Melbourne	2005-06
A.Kumble	India	v	England	Mohali	2005-06

K.Cranston, F.J.Titmus, C.M.Old and Wasim Akram each took four wickets in an over. † Gillespie took four wickets in 6 balls (W0WW1W) thus he achieved three wickets in 4 balls twice.

BOWLERS UNCHANGED IN A COMPLETED INNINGS

AUSTRALIA		Opponents		
G.E.Palmer (7/68)	E.Evans (3/64)	England (133)	Sydney	1881-82
F.R.Spofforth (5/30)	G.E.Palmer (4/32)	England (77)	Sydney	1884-85
C.T.B.Turner (6/15)	J.J.Ferris (4/27)	England (45)	Sydney	1886-87
C.T.B.Turner (5/36)	J.J.Ferris (5/26)	England (62)	Lord's	1888
G.Giffen (5/26)	C.T.B.Turner (4/33)	England (72)	Sydney	1894-95
H.Trumble (3/38)	M.A.Noble (7/17)	England (61)	Melbourne	1901-02
M.A.Noble (5/54)	J.V.Saunders (5/43)	England (99)	Sydney	1901-02
G.D.McGrath (5/28)	J.N.Gillespie (4/18)	West Indies (51)	Port-of-Spain	1998-99

ENGLAND		Opponents		
F.Morley (2/34)	R.G.Barlow (7/40)	Australia (83)	Sydney	1882-83
G.A.Lohmann (7/36)	J.Briggs(3/28)	Australia (68)	The Oval	1886
G.A.Lohmann (5/17)	R.Peel (5/18)	Australia (42)	Sydney	1887-88
J.Briggs (8/11)	A.J.Fothergill (1/30)	South Africa (43)	Cape Town	1888-89

J.J.Ferris (7/37)	F.Martin (2/39)	South Africa (83)	Cape Town	1891-92
J.Briggs (6/49)	G.A.Lohmann (3/46)	Australia (100)	Adelaide	1891-92
T.Richardson (6/39)	G.A.Lohmann (3/13)	Australia (53)	Lord's	1896
S.Haigh (6/11)	A.E.Trott (4/19)	South Africa (35)	Cape Town	1898-99
S.F.Barnes (6/42)	C.Blythe (4/64)	Australia (112)	Melbourne	1901-02
G.H.Hirst (4/28)	C.Blythe (6/44)	Australia (74)	Birmingham	1909
F.R.Foster (5/16)	S.F.Barnes (5/25)	South Africa (58)	Lord's	1912
A.E.R.Gilligan (6/7)	M.W.Tate (4/12)	South Africa (30)	Birmingham	1924
G.O.B.Allen (5/36)	W.Voce (4/16)	Australia (58)	Brisbane[2]	1936-37
PAKISTAN		Opponents		
Fazal Mahmood (6/34)	Khan Mohammad (4/43)	Australia (80)	Karachi[1]	1956-57
Wasim Akram (4/32)	Waqar Younis (6/34)	Sri Lanka (71)	Kandy	1994-95
WEST INDIES		Opponents		
C.E.L.Ambrose (6/24)	C.A.Walsh (3/16)	England (46)	Port-of-Spain	1993-94

BOWLER DISMISSING ALL ELEVEN BATSMEN IN A MATCH

J.C.Laker	19/90	England	v	Australia	Manchester	1956
S.Venkataraghavan	12/152	India	v	New Zealand	Delhi	1964-65
G.Dymock	12/166	Australia	v	India	Kanpur	1979-80
Abdul Qadir	13/101	Pakistan	v	England	Lahore[2]	1987-88
Waqar Younis	12/130	Pakistan	v	New Zealand	Faisalabad	1990-91
M.Muralidaran	13/171	Sri Lanka	v	South Africa	Galle	2000-01

MOST LBWs IN AN INNINGS BY ONE BOWLER

FIVE					
T.M.Alderman	Australia	v	Pakistan	Melbourne	1989-90
C.E.L.Ambrose	West Indies	v	England	Bridgetown	1989-90
Mohammad Zahid	Pakistan	v	New Zealand	Rawalpindi[2]	1996-97
R.L.Johnson	England	v	Zimbabwe	Chester-le-Street	2003
FOUR					
P.S.Heine	South Africa	v	England	Leeds	1955
G.A.R.Lock	England	v	New Zealand	Leeds	1958
Abdul Qadir	Pakistan	v	England	Karachi[1]	1977-78
Kapil Dev	India	v	Australia	Kanpur	1979-80
R.J.Hadlee	New Zealand	v	West Indies	Dunedin	1979-80
L.S.Pascoe	Australia	v	England	Lord's	1980
R.M.Ellison	England	v	West Indies	Kingston	1985-86
Abdul Qadir	Pakistan	v	England	Faisalabad	1987-88
N.D.Hirwani	India	v	New Zealand	Bangalore	1988-89
T.M.Alderman	Australia	v	England	Leeds	1989
T.M.Alderman	Australia	v	England	Lord's	1989
G.P.Wickramasinghe	Sri Lanka	v	Pakistan	Faisalabad	1991-92
Waqar Younis	Pakistan	v	Zimbabwe	Karachi[2]	1993-94
Shahid Nazir	Pakistan	v	Zimbabwe	Sheikhupura	1996-97
Wasim Akram	Pakistan	v	West Indies	Peshawar[2]	1997-98
D.Gough	England	v	South Africa	Leeds	1998
A.Kumble	India	v	New Zealand	Kanpur	1999-2000
W.P.U.J.C.Vaas	Sri Lanka	v	West Indies (in each innings)	Colombo (SSC)	2001-02
I.K.Pathan	India	v	Bangladesh	Dhaka	2004-05
W.P.U.J.C.Vaas	Sri Lanka	v	West Indies	Colombo (SSC)	2005-06
A. Kumble	India	v	West Indies	Kingston	2005-06

MOST LBWs IN A MATCH BY ONE BOWLER

EIGHT					
Mohammad Zahid	Pakistan	v	New Zealand	Rawalpindi[2]	1996-97
W.P.U.J.C.Vaas	Sri Lanka	v	West Indies	Colombo (SSC)	2001-02
SEVEN					
R.J.Hadlee	New Zealand	v	West Indies	Dunedin	1979-80
Abdul Qadir	Pakistan	v	England	Faisalabad	1987-88
Waqar Younis	Pakistan	v	Zimbabwe	Karachi[2]	1993-94
I.K.Pathan	India	v	Bangladesh	Dhaka	2004-05
SIX					
Imran Khan	Pakistan	v	India	Faisalabad	1982-83
T.M.Alderman	Australia	v	Pakistan	Melbourne	1989-90
C.E.L.Ambrose	West Indies	v	England	Bridgetown	1989-90
Waqar Younis	Pakistan	v	West Indies	St John's	1992-93
G.D.McGrath	Australia	v	West Indies	Port-of-Spain	1998-99
G.D.McGrath	Australia	v	West Indies	Bridgetown	1998-99
W.P.U.J.C.Vaas	Sri Lanka	v	West Indies	Colombo (SSC)	2005-06
FIVE					
Fazal Mahmood	Pakistan	v	India	Lucknow[1]	1952-53
Kapil Dev	India	v	Australia	Kanpur	1979-80
N.D.Hirwani	India	v	New Zealand	Bangalore	1988-89
T.M.Alderman	Australia	v	England	Leeds	1989
T.M.Alderman	Australia	v	England	Lord's	1989
Wasim Akram	Pakistan	v	West Indies	Lahore[2]	1990-91
G.P.Wickramasinghe	Sri Lanka	v	Pakistan	Faisalabad	1991-92
C.C.Lewis	England	v	New Zealand	Auckland	1991-92
Mushtaq Ahmed	Pakistan	v	New Zealand	Lahore[2]	1996-97
H.H.Streak	Zimbabwe	v	West Indies	Port-of-Spain	1999-2000
R.L.Johnson	England	v	Zimbabwe	Chester-le-Street	2003
C.L.Cairns	New Zealand	v	England	Nottingham	2004

FOUR OR MORE BOWLERS CONCEDING 100 RUNS IN AN INNINGS

SIX BOWLERS

Sri Lanka (3d-713) v Zimbabwe Bulayawo[2] 2003-04

(D.T.Hondo 0/116; T.Panyangara 1/120; T.Mupariwa 0/136; M.L.Nkala 1/111; E.Chigumbura 1/108; S.Matsikenyeri 0/112)

FIVE BOWLERS

Australia (8d-758) v West Indies Kingston 1954-55

(D.T.Dewdney 1/115; F.M.King 2/126; D.S.Atkinson 1/132; O.G.Smith 2/145; F.M.M.Worrell 1/116 - nb G.S.Sobers 1/99 in the same innings)

West Indies (8d-652) v England Lord's 1973

(G.G.Arnold 0/111; R.G.D.Willis 4/118; A.W.Greig 3/180; D.L.Underwood 0/105; R.Illingworth 1/114)

Australia (6d-607) v New Zealand Brisbane[2] 1993-94

(D.K.Morrison 0/104; C.L.Cairns 1/128; S.B.Doull 2/105; R.P.de Groen 1/120; D.N.Patel 1/125)

Australia (6d-735) v Zimbabwe Perth 2003-04

(H.H.Streak 0/131; A.M.Blignaut 0/115; S.M.Ervine 4/146; R.W.Price 0/187; T.R.Gripper 2/142)

FOUR BOWLERS

England (849) v West Indies Kingston 1929-30

(H.C.Griffith 2/555; G.Gladstone 1/139; O.C.Scott 5/266; F.R.Martin 1/128)

Australia (6d-729) v England Lord's 1930

(G.O.B.Allen 0/115; M.W.Tate 1/148; J.C.White 1/172; R.W.V.Robins 1/172)

Australia (554) v South Africa Melbourne 1931-32

(A.J.Bell 1/101; N.A.Quinn 1/113; C.L.Vincent 4/154; Q.McMillan 4/150)

England (524) v Australia Sydney 1932-33
(T.W.Wall 3/104; L.E.Nagel 2/110; W.J.O'Reilly 3/117; C.V.Grimmett 1/118)

Australia (701) v England The Oval 1934
(W.E.Bowes 4/164; G.O.B.Allen 4/170; E.W.Clark 2/110; H.Verity 0/123)

England (8d-658) v Australia Nottingham 1938
(E.L.McCormick 1/108; W.J.O'Reilly 3/164; L.O.Fleetwood-Smith 4/153; F.A.Ward 0/142)

England (5-654) v South Africa Durban[2] 1938-39
(A.B.C.Langton 1/132; N.Gordon 1/174; B.Mitchell 1/133; E.L.Dalton 2/100)

Australia (674) v India Adelaide 1947-48
(C.R.Rangachari 4/141; M.H.Mankad 2/170; C.T.Sarwate 0/121; V.S.Hazare 0/110)

Australia (7d-549) v South Africa Port Elizabeth 1949-50
(C.N.McCarthy 0/121; M.G.Melle 2/132; H.J.Tayfield 2/103; N.B.F.Mann 2/154)

Australia (530) v South Africa Adelaide 1952-53
(M.G.Melle 1/105; E.R.H.Fuller 2/119; H.J.Tayfield 4/142; P.N.F.Mansell 2/113)

West Indies (8d-681) v England Port-of-Spain 1953-54
(F.S.Trueman 1/131; T.E.Bailey 0/104; J.C.Laker 2/154; G.A.R.Lock 2/178)

England (6d-558) v Pakistan Nottingham 1954
(Fazal Mahmood 0/148; Khan Mohammad 3/155; A.H.Kardar 1/110; Khalid Wazir 2/116)

Australia (8d-601) v England Brisbane[2] 1954-55
(A.V.Bedser 1/131; J.B.Statham 2/123; F.H.Tyson 1/160; T.E.Bailey 3/140)

England (5d-544) v Pakistan Birmingham 1962
(Mahmood Hussain 2/130; A.D'Souza 1/161; Intikhab Alam 2/117; Nasim-ul-Ghani 0/109)

South Africa (595) v Australia Adelaide 1963-64
(R.A.Gaunt 2/115; G.D.McKenzie 1/135; N.J.N.Hawke 3/139; R.Benaud 0/101)

Australia (8d-656) v England Manchester 1964
(J.S.E.Price 3/183; T.W.Cartwright 2/118; F.J.Titmus 0/100; J.B.Mortimore 0/122)

Australia (6d-650) v West Indies Bridgetown 1964-65
(W.W.Hall 2/117; C.C.Griffith 0/131; G.S.Sobers 1/143; L.R.Gibbs 2/168)

Australia (516) v England Adelaide 1965-66
(I.J.Jones 6/118; D.J.Brown 1/109; F.J.Titmus 3/116; D.A.Allen 0/103)

Australia (547) v West Indies Sydney 1968-69
(W.W.Hall 3/113; R.M.Edwards 2/139; G.S.Sobers 0/109; L.R.Gibbs 2/124)

New Zealand (9d-551) v England Lord's 1973
(J.A.Snow 3/109; G.G.Arnold 1/108; C.M.Old 5/113; N.Gifford 0/107)

Australia (6d-511) v New Zealand Wellington 1973-74
(M.G.Webb 2/114; R.O.Collinge 1/103; D.R.Hadlee 2/107; H.J.Howarth 0/113)

Pakistan (7d-600) v England The Oval 1974
(G.G.Arnold 1/106; R.G.D.Willis 2/102; C.M.Old 0/143; D.L.Underwood 2/106)

West Indies (585) v Australia Perth 1975-76
(D.K.Lillee 2/123; J.R.Thomson 3/128; G.J.Gilmour 2/103; A.A.Mallett 0/103)

Pakistan (9d-565) v New Zealand Karachi[1] 1976-77
(R.O.Collinge 2/141; R.J.Hadlee 4/138; B.L.Cairns 1/142; D.R.O'Sullivan 2/131)

India (7d-644) v West Indies Kanpur 1978-79
(M.D.Marshall 1/123; V.A.Holder 0/118; R.R.Jumadeen 3/137; D.R.Parry 2/127)

England (5d-633) v India Birmingham 1979
(Kapil Dev 5/146; K.D.Ghavri 0/129; B.S.Chandrasekhar 0/113; S.Venkataraghavan 0/107)

Australia (528) v India Adelaide 1980-81
(Kapil Dev 2/112; K.D.Ghavri 0/106; D.R.Doshi 3/146; N.S.Yadav 4/143)

Pakistan (7d-500) v Sri Lanka Lahore[2] 1981-82
(A.L.F.de Mel 3/120; J.R.Ratnayeke 3/121; D.S.de Silva 1/129; R.G.C.E.Wijesuriya 0/105)

Pakistan (652) v India Faisalabad 1982-83
(Kapil Dev 7/220; S.Madan Lal 2/109; D.R.Doshi 0/130; Maninder Singh 1/103)

Pakistan (3d-581) v India Hyderabad 1982-83
(Kapil Dev 0/111; B.S.Sandhu 2/107; Maninder Singh 0/135; D.R.Doshi 1/143)

Pakistan (624) v Australia Adelaide 1983-84
(G.F.Lawson 2/127; R.M.Hogg 1/123; D.K.Lillee 6/171; T.G.Hogan 1/107)

West Indies (606) v England Birmingham 1984
(R.G.D.Willis 2/108; I.T.Botham 1/127; D.R.Pringle 5/108; N.G.B.Cook 1/127)

India (8d-553) v England Kanpur 1984-85
(N.G.Cowans 2/115; N.A.Foster 3/123; P.H.Edmonds 1/112; C.S.Cowdrey 1/103)

New Zealand (7d-533) v Australia Brisbane[2] 1985-86
(C.J.McDermott 1/119; D.R.Gilbert 2/102; G.R.J.Matthews 3/110; R.G.Holland 0/106)

England (8d-592) v Australia Perth 1986-87
(G.F.Lawson 0/126; C.D.Matthews 3/112; B.A.Reid 4/115; G.R.J.Matthews 1/124)

Australia (5d-514) v England Adelaide 1986-87
(G.R.Dilley 1/111; P.A.J.DeFreitas 1/128; J.E.Emburey 1/117; P.H.Edmonds 2/134)

India (7d-676) v Sri Lanka Kanpur 1986-87
(A.L.F.de Mel 1/119; G.F.Labrooy 1/164; J.R.Ratnayeke 4/132; E.A.R.de Silva 0/133)

Australia (7d-601) v England Leeds 1989
(P.A.J.DeFreitas 2/140; N.A.Foster 3/109; P.J.Newport 2/153; D.R.Pringle 0/123)

Pakistan (5-699) v India Lahore[2] 1989-90
(M.Prabhakar 1/107; Maninder Singh 2/191; Arshad Ayub 0/182; R.J.Shastri 105)

England (4d-653) v India Lord's 1990
(Kapil Dev 1/120; M.Prabhakar 1/187; S.K.Sharma 1/122; N.D.Hirwani 1/102)

India (454) v England Lord's 1990
D.E.Malcolm 1/106; A.R.C.Fraser 5/104; C.C.Lewis 1/108; E.E.Hemmings 2/109)

India (9d-606) v England The Oval 1990
(D.E.Malcolm 2/110; A.R.C.Fraser 2/112; N.F.Williams 2/148; E.E.Hemmings 2/117)

England (9d-580) v New Zealand Christchurch 1991-92
(D.K.Morrison 2/133; C.L.Cairns 1/118; C.Pringle 3/127; D.N.Patel 2/132)

Australia (4d-653) v England Leeds 1993
(M.J.McCague 0/110; M.C.Ilott 3/161; A.R.Caddick 0/138; M.P.Bicknell 1/155)

Pakistan (5d-548) v New Zealand Wellington 1993-94
(D.K.Morrison 2/139; R.P.de Groen 0/104; S.B.Doull 0/112; M.N.Hart 1/102)

West Indies (5d-593) v England St John's 1993-94
(A.R.C.Fraser 2/121; A.R.Caddick 3/158; P.C.R.Tufnell 0/110; C.C.Lewis 0/140)

West Indies (8d-592) v England The Oval 1995
(D.E.Malcolm 3/160; A.R.C.Fraser 1/155; M.Watkinson 0/113; D.G.Cork 3/145)

Australia (8d-628) v South Africa Johannesburg[3] 1996-97
(A.A.Donald 2/136; S.M.Pollock 2/105; L.Klusener 1/122; P.R.Adams 1/163)

New Zealand (7d-586) v Sri Lanka Dunedin 1996-97
(W.P.U.J.C.Vaas 4/144; D.N.T.Zoysa 1/112; G.P.Wickramasinghe 1/117; M.Muralidaran 0/136)

South Africa (5d-552) v England Manchester 1998
(D.Gough 3/116; D.G.Cork 0/109; R.D.B.Croft 0/103; A.F.Giles 1/106)

New Zealand (9d-496) v England Manchester 1999
(A.R.Caddick 2/112; D.W.Headley 1/115; P.C.R.Tufnell 2/111; P.M.Such 4/114)

India (7d-657) v Australia Kolkata 2000-01
(G.D.McGrath 3/103; J.N.Gillespie 2/115; S.K.Warne 1/152; M.S.Kasprowicz 0/139)

Australia (576) v England Birmingham 2001
(D.Gough 3/152; A.R.Caddick 1/163; C.White 1/101; A.F.Giles 1/108)

West Indies (6d-559) v Zimbabwe Bulawayo[2] 2001-02
(H.H.Streak 2/110; A.M.Blignaut 0/116; B.C.Strang 2/111; R.W.Price 2/157)

Australia (4d-641) v England The Oval 2001
(D.Gough 1/113; A.R.Caddick 0/146; J.Ormond 1/115; P.C.R.Tufnell 1/174)

Sri Lanka (9d-627) v West Indies Colombo (SSC) 2001-02
(M.Dillon 2/131; P.T.Collins 3/156; M.I.Black 1/123; C.L.Hooper 2/112)

Australia (554) v South Africa Sydney 2001-02
(A.A.Donald 1/119; S.M.Pollock 3/109; J.H.Kallis 1/129; C.W.Henderson 0/112)

Australia (7d-652) v South Africa Johannesburg[3] 2001-02
(M.Ntini 1/124; J.H.Kallis 2/116; A.Nel 2/121; N.Boje 1/153)

India (8d-628) v England Leeds 2002
(M.J.Hoggard 1/102; A.R.Caddick 3/150; A.J.Tudor 2/146; A.F.Giles 1/134)

Australia (492) v England Brisbane[2] 2002-03
(A.R.Caddick 3/108; M.J.Hoggard 0/122; C.White 2/105; A.F.Giles 4/101)

West Indies (536) v Bangladesh Dhaka 2002-03
(Tapash Baisya 2/117; Talha Jubair 3/135; Naimur Rahman 1/118; Enamul Haque 1/101)

Australia (6d-551) v England Melbourne 2002-03
(A.R.Caddick 1/126; S.J.Harmison 0/108; C.White 3/133; R.K.J.Dawson 2/121)

South Africa (7d-620) v Pakistan Cape Town 2002-03
(Waqar Younis 1/121; Mohammad Sami 1/124; Mohammad Zahid 2/108; Saqlain Mushtaq 3/237)

Australia (4d-576) v West Indies Port-of-Spain 2002-03
(M.Dillon 2/124; P.T.Collins 0/123; V.C.Drakes 1/112; M.N.Samuels 1/111)

South Africa (6d-682) v England Lord's 2003
(D.Gough 0/127; S.J.Harmison 1/103; A.Flintoff 1/115; A.F.Giles 1/142)

England (9d-604) v South Africa The Oval 2003
(S.M.Pollock 3/111; M.Ntini 1/129; A.J.Hall 2/111; J.H.Kallis 2/117)

Australia (556) v India Adelaide 2003-04
(A.B.Agarkar 2/119; I.K.Pathan 1/136; A.Nehra 2/115; A.Kumble 5/154)

New Zealand (563) v Pakistan Hamilton 2003-04
(Mohammad Sami 0/126; Shabbir Ahmed 2/117; Umar Gul 2/118; Danish Kaneria 2/112)

South Africa (9d-658) v West Indies Durban[2] 2003-04
(M.Dillon 1/111; F.H.Edwards 1/115; A.Sanford 3/170; V.C.Drakes 2/113)

New Zealand (595) v South Africa Auckland 2003-04
(S.M.Pollock 4/113; M.Ntini 3/110; J.H.Kallis 1/108; N.Boje 1/108)

India (5d-675) v Pakistan Multan[2] 2003-04
(Shoaib Akhtar 0/119; Mohammad Sami 2/110; Shabbir Ahmed 0/122; Saqlain Mushtaq 1/204)

Australia (8d-575) v New Zealand Adelaide 2004-05
(C.S.Martin 0/118; J.E.C.Franklin 0/102; D.L.Vettori 5/152; P.J.Wiseman 3/140)

India (526) v Bangladesh Dhaka 2004-05
(Tapash Baisya 2/113; Mashrafe Bin Mortaza 2/125; Mushfiqur Rahman 2/104; Mohammad Rafique 2/113)

India (516) v Pakistan Mohali 2004-05
(Mohammad Sami 2/120; Naved-ul-Hasan 1/133; Abdur Razzaq 1/107; Danish Kaneria 6/150)

Pakistan (570) v India Bangalore 2004-05
(I.K.Pathan 0/105; L.Balaji 2/114; A.Kumble 0/159; Harbhajan Singh 6/152)

West Indies (747) v South Africa St John's 2004-05
(S.M.Pollock 0/111; M.Ntini 1/106; M.Zondeki 3/120; G.C.Smith 2/145)

England (3d-528) v Bangladesh Lord's 2005
(Mashrafe Bin Mortaza 2/107; Shahadat Hossain 0/101; Anwar Hossain[2] 0/110; Mohammad Rafique 1/150)

New Zealand (9d-452) v Zimbabwe Harare 2005-06
(H.H.Streak 2/102; N.B.Mahwire 3/115; C.B.Mpofu 2/100; A.G.Cremer 1/113)

Pakistan (8d-636) v England Lahore[2] 2005-06
(M.J.Hoggard 2/106; A.Flintoff 1/111; S.J.Harmison 1/154; L.E.Plunkett 1/125)

Pakistan (7d-679) v India Lahore[2] 2005-06
(I.K.Pathan 1/133; A.B.Agarkar 2/122; Harbhajan Singh 0/176; A.Kumble 2/178)

Pakistan (558) v India Faisalabad 2005-06
(I.K.Pathan 0/106; Zaheer Khan 3/135; Harbhajan Singh 0/101; A.Kumble 3/150)

India (603) v Pakistan Faisalabad 2005-06
(Shoaib Akhtar 1/100; Mohammad Asif 1/103; Abdul Razzaq 2/126; Danish Kaneria 3/165)

Pakistan (7d-599) v India Karachi[1] 2005-06
(I.K.Pathan 1/106; Zaheer Khan 1/103; R.P.Singh 1/115; A.Kumble 3/151)

England (515) v Pakistan Leeds 2006
(Mohammad Sami 2/135; Umar Gul 5/123; Shahid Nazir 1/101; Dabish Kaneria 2/111)

Pakistan (504) v England The Oval 2006
(M.J.Hoggard 3/124; S.J.Harmison 4/125; S.I.Mahmood 2/101; M.S.Panesar 1/103)

Wicket-keeping

MOST DISMISSALS IN TEST CAREER

Player	Country	Tests	Dis	C	S	A	E	SA	W	N	I	P	SL	Z	B
						Opponents									
I.A.Healy	A	119	**395**	366	29	-	135	33	78	42	26	45	34	2	-
M.V.Boucher	SA	95	**362**	348	14	43	71	-	57	38	21	30	57	25	20
R.W.Marsh	A	96	**355**	343	12	-	148	-	65	58	16	68	-	-	-
A.C.Gilchrist	A	84	**348**	315	33	-	70	44	52	41	50	38	27	11	15
A.J.Stewart	E	133	**277**	263¡	14	84	-	55	37	31	12	23	24	11	-
P.J.L.Dujon	W	81	**272**	267¶	5	86	84	-	-	20	60	22	-	-	-
A.P.E.Knott	E	95	**269**	250	19	105	-	-	43	26	54	41	-	-	-
Wasim Bari	P	81	**228**	201	27	66	54	-	21	32	55	-	-	-	-
T.G.Evans	E	91	**219**	173	46	76	-	59	37	28	12	7	-	-	-
R.D.Jacobs	W	65	**219**	207	12	44	39	51	-	8	18	13	12	16	17
A.C.Parore	N	78	**204**	197#	7	25	46	20	15	-	18	18	26	31	5
S.M.H.Kirmani	I	88	**198**	160	38	41	42	-	36	28	-	50	1	-	-
D.L.Murray	W	62	**189**	181	8	42	94	-	-	7	27	21	-	-	-
A.T.W.Grout	A	51	**187**	163	24	-	76	33	41	-	20	17	-	-	-
I.D.S.Smith	N	63	**176**	168	8	39	42	-	16	-	29	23	27	-	-
R.W.Taylor	E	57	**174**	167	7	57	-	-	-	45	40	29	3	-	-
R.C.Russell	E	54	**165**	153	12	28	-	27	52	16	20	16	6	-	-
K.C.Sangakkara	SL	62	**162**	142¢	20	18	40	22	15	3	14	13	-	10	26
A.Flower	Z	63	**160**	151†	9	3	9	8	8	31	19	38	33	-	11
D.J.Richardson	SA	42	**152**	150	2	40	15	-	6	23	32	13	17	6	-
Moin Khan	P	69	**148**	128!	20	22	17	16	25	16	7	-	40	5	-
J.H.B.Waite	SA	50	**141**	124	17	28	56	-	-	57	-	-	-	-	-
Rashid Latif	P	37	**130**	119	11	17	15	4	6	27	-	-	12	23	26
K.S.More	I	49	**130**	110	20	13	37	11	21	13	-	21	11	3	-
W.A.S.Oldfield	A	54	**130**	78	52	-	90	27	13	-	-	-	-	-	-
G.O.Jones	E	31	**124**	119	5	16	-	16	15	14	10	23	17	-	13
R.S.Kaluwitharana	SL	49	**119**	93	26	21	4	21	9	15	9	19	-	18	-
J.M.Parks	E	46	**114**	103§	11	21	-	30	31	22	9	1	-	-	-
N.R.Mongia	I	44	**107**	99	8	17	8	20	19	12	0	11	18	2	-
Saleem Yousuf	P	32	**104**	91	13	15	15	-	22	22	11	-	19	-	-
J.R.Murray	W	31	**102**	99•	3	36	30	1	-	7	17	9	2	-	-
Kamran Akmal	P	27	**106**	90	16	7	27	5	16	-	31	-	11	9	-

Best for Bangladesh is:

Player	Country	Tests	Dis	C	S	A	E	SA	W	N	I	P	SL	Z	B
Khaled Mashud	B	41	**83**	75	8	3	11	3	12	7	6	9	13	19	-

¶ Including 2 catches in 2 Tests when not keeping wicket. ¡ including 31 catches in 46 Tests when not keeping wickets. # includes 3 catches in 11 Tests when not keeping wicket. † includes 9 catches in 8 Tests when not keeping wicket. ! includes 1 catches in 3 Tests when not keeping wicket. § Including 2 catches in 3 Tests when not keeping wicket. • includes 1 catch in 2 Tests when not keeping wickets. ¢ includes 20 catches in 16 matches when not keeping wickets.

MOST DISMISSALS IN A SERIES *(§ In first series. # In last series)*

AUSTRALIA

Total	C	S	Tests	Player	Opponents	Season
28	28	0	5	R.W.Marsh	England	1982-83
27	25	2	6	I.A.Healy	England	1997
26	26	0	6	R.W.Marsh	West Indies	1975-76
26	21	5	6	I.A.Healy	England	1993
26	24	2	5	A.C.Gilchrist	England	2001

Total	C	S	Tests	Player	Opponents	Season
25	23	2	5	I.A.Healy	England	1994-95
25	23	2	5	A.C.Gilchrist	England	2002-03
24	24	0	5	I.A.Healy	England	1990-91
23	20	3	5	A.T.W.Grout	West Indies	1960-61
23	21	2	5	R.W.Marsh	England	1972
23	23	0	6	R.W.Marsh	England	1981
23	19	4	5	I.A.Healy	West Indies	1992-93
22 §	22	0	5	S.J.Rixon	India	1977-78
21 #	13	8	5	R.A.Saggers	South Africa	1949-50
21 §	16	5	5	G.R.A.Langley	West Indies	1951-52
21	20	1	5	A.T.W.Grout	England	1961
21 #	21	0	5	R.W.Marsh	Pakistan	1983-84
21	19	2	5	A.C.Gilchrist	West Indies	2000-01
20	16	4	5	D.Tallon	England	1946-47
20	16	4	4	G.R.A.Langley	West Indies	1954-55
20	17	3	5	A.T.W.Grout	England	1958-59
20 §	19	1	5	H.B.Taber	South Africa	1966-67

ENGLAND

Total	C	S	Tests	Player	Opponents	Season
27	25	2	5	R.C.Russell	South Africa	1995-96
24	21	3	6	A.P.E.Knott	Australia	1970-71
23	22	1	6	A.P.E.Knott	Australia	1974-75
23	23	0	6	A.J.Stewart	Australia	1997
23	23	0	5	A.J.Stewart	South Africa	1998
21	21	0	5	H.Strudwick	South Africa	1913-14
21	20	1	5	S.J.Rhodes	Australia	1994-95
20	20	0	5	T.G.Evans	South Africa	1956-57
20	18	2	6	R.W.Taylor	Australia	1978-79
20	19	1	6	P.R.Downton	Australia	1985

SOUTH AFRICA

Total	C	S	Tests	Player	Opponents	Season
26	23	3	5	J.H.B.Waite	New Zealand	1961-62
26	25	1	5	M.V.Boucher	England	1998
24	24	0	5	D.T.Lindsay	Australia	1966-67
23	16	7	5	J.H.B.Waite	New Zealand	1953-54
19	19	0	5	M.V.Boucher	England	1999-2000

WEST INDIES

Total	C	S	Tests	Player	Opponents	Season
24 §	22	2	5	D.L.Murray	England	1963
23	22	1	5	F.C.M.Alexander	England	1959-60
23	23	0	5	P.J.L.Dujon	Australia	1990-91
21	20	1	5	R.D.Jacobs	England	2000
21	20	1	5	R.D.Jacobs	Australia	2000-01
21	21	0	5	R.D.Jacobs	Australia	2000-01
20	19	1	5	P.J.L.Dujon	South Africa	1983-84
20	20	0	5	P.J.L.Dujon	England	1988

NEW ZEALAND

Total	C	S	Tests	Player	Opponents	Season
23 §	21	2	5	A.E.Dick	South Africa	1961-62
16	16	0	3	I.D.S.Smith	Sri Lanka	1990-91
16	16	0	3	A.C.Parore	Pakistan	2000-01
14	14	0	5	E.C.Petrie	England	1958
14	14	0	4	A.C.Parore	England	1999

INDIA

Total	C	S	Tests	Player	Opponents	Season
19 §	12	7	5	N.S.Tamhane	Pakistan	1954-55
19	17	2	6	S.M.H.Kirmani	Pakistan	1979-80
16	16	0	3	K.S.More	England	1986
14	11	3	6	S.M.H.Kirmani	Australia	1979-80
14	13	1	6	S.M.H.Kirmani	Pakistan	1982-83
14	14	0	3	N.R.Mongia	South Africa	1996-97

PAKISTAN

Total	C	S	Tests	Player	Opponents	Season
18	17	1	3	Rashid Latif	Bangladesh	2003-04
17	15	2	6	Wasim Bari	India	1982-83
16	14	2	5	Wasim Bari	West Indies	1987-77
16	14	2	6	Wasim Bari	India	1979-80
16	14	2	4	Kamran Akmal	England	2006
16	15	1	2	Kamran Akmal	West Indies	2004-05
15	15	0	5	Wasim Bari	Australia	1983-84
15	15	0	5	Saleem Yousuf	England	1987
15	15	0	3	Saleem Yousuf	New Zealand	1990-91

SRI LANKA

Total	C	S	Tests	Player	Opponents	Season
22	21	1	3	S.A.R.Silva	India	1985-86
15	15	0	3	H.P.Tillakaratne	New Zealand	1990-91
13	12	1	3	K.C.Sangakkara	England	2000-01
13	9	4	3	K.C.Sangakkara	England	2003-04
11	7	4	3	K.C.Sangakkara	Australia	2003-04

ZIMBABWE

Total	C	S	Tests	Player	Opponents	Season
13	13	0	2	W.R.James	Sri Lanka	1994-95
13	13	0	3	A.Flower	Pakistan	1994-95
10	10	0	3	A.Flower	Sri Lanka	1999-2000

BANGLADESH

Total	C	S	Tests	Player	Opponents	Season
8	7	1	2	Khaled Mashud	England	2003-04
8	6	2	2	Khaled Mashud	Zimbabwe	2003-04
7	6	1	2	Khaled Mashud	West Indies	2002-03
7	6	1	2	Khaled Mashud	Zimbabwe	2004-05

MOST DISMISSALS IN A MATCH *(§ In first Test)*

AUSTRALIA

Dismissals	Player	Opponents	Venue	Season
10 (10c)	A.C.Gilchrist	New Zealand	Hamilton	1999-2000
9 (8c, 1s)	G.R.A.Langley	England	Lord's	1956
9 (9c)	R.W.Marsh	England	Brisbane[2]	1982-83
9 (9c)	I.A.Healy	England	Brisbane[2]	1994-95
8 (8c)	J.J.Kelly	England	Sydney	1901-02
8 (8c)	G.R.A.Langley	West Indies	Kingston	1954-55
8 (6c, 2s)	A.T.W.Grout	Pakistan	Lahore[2]	1959-60
8 (8c)	A.T.W.Grout	England	Lord's	1961
8 (7c, 1s) §	H.B.Taber	South Africa	Johannesburg[3]	1966-67
8 (8c)	R.W.Marsh	West Indies	Melbourne	1975-76
8 (8c)	R.W.Marsh	New Zealand	Christchurch	1976-77
8 (7c, 1s)	R.W.Marsh	India	Sydney	1980-81
8 (8c)	R.W.Marsh	England	Adelaide	1982-83

8 (8c)	I.A.Healy	West Indies	Adelaide	1992-93
8 (8c)	I.A.Healy	England	Melbourne	1994-95
8 (8c)	I.A.Healy	Sri Lanka	Adelaide	1995-96
8 (7c, 1s)	A.C.Gilchrist	West Indies	Brisbane[2]	2000-01
8 (8c)	A.C.Gilchrist	Sri Lanka	Darwin	2004-05
ENGLAND				
11 (11c)	R.C.Russell	South Africa	Johannesburg[3]	1995-96
10 (10c)	R.W.Taylor	India	Bombay[3]	1979-80
9 (7c, 2s)	R.C.Russell	South Africa	Port Elizabeth	1995-96
9 (9c)	G.O.Jones	Bangladesh	Chester-le-Street	2005
8 (6c, 2s)	L.E.G.Ames	West Indies	The Oval	1933
8 (8c)	J.M.Parks	New Zealand	Christchurch	1965-66
8 (8c)	A.J.Stewart	Australia	Manchester	1997
8 (8c)	A.J.Stewart	South Africa	Nottingham	1998
8 (8c) §	C.M.W.Read	New Zealand	Birmingham	1999
8 (8c)	A.J.Stewart	South Africa	Durban[2]	1999-2000
SOUTH AFRICA				
9 (9c)	D.J.Richardson	India	Port Elizabeth	1992-93
9 (8c, s1)	M.V.Boucher	Pakistan	Port Elizabeth	1997-98
8 (8c)	D.T.Lindsay	Australia	Johannesburg[3]	1966-67
8 (8c)	D.J.Richardson	Sri Lanka	Colombo (SSC)	1993-94
8 (8c)	M.V.Boucher	Sri Lanka	Durban[2]	2000-01
8 (8c)	M.V.Boucher	Sri Lanka	Centurion	2002-03
8 (8c)	M.V.Boucher	Zimbabwe	Centurion	2004-05
WEST INDIES				
9 (9c)	D.A.Murray	Australia	Melbourne	1981-82
9 (9c)	C.O.Browne	England	Lord's	1995
9 (8c, 1s)	R.D.Jacobs	Australia	Sydney	2000-01
8 (8c)	J.R.Murray	Australia	Perth	1992-93
NEW ZEALAND				
8 (8c)	W.K.Lees	Sri Lanka	Wellington	1982-83
8 (8c)	I.D.S.Smith	Sri Lanka	Hamilton	1990-91
7 (6c, 1s) §	A.E.Dick	South Africa	Durban[2]	1961-62
7 (7c)	R.I.Harford	India	Wellington	1967-68
7 (7c)	I.D.S.Smith	India	Wellington	1980-81
7 (7c)	I.D.S.Smith	England	Leeds	1983
7 (7c)	A.C.Parore	Pakistan	Auckland	2000-01
7 (7c)	A.C.Parore	Pakistan	Hamilton	2000-01
INDIA				
8 (8c)	N.R.Mongia	South Africa	Durban[2]	1996-97
8 (8c)	N.R.Mongia	Pakistan	Calcutta	1998-99
7 (1c, 6s)	K.S.More	West Indies	Chennai[1]	1987-88
7 (5c, 2s)	K.S.More	England	Bombay[3]	1992-93
PAKISTAN				
9 (9c)	Rashid Latif	New Zealand	Auckland	1993-94
9 (9c)	Kamran Akmal	West Indies	Kingston	2004-05
8 (8c)	Wasim Bari	England	Leeds	1971
8 (7c, 1s)	Rashid Latif	Australia	Sydney	1995-96
SRI LANKA				
9 (9c)	S.A.R.Silva	India	Colombo (SSC)	1985-86
9 (8c, 1s)	S.A.R.Silva	India	Colombo (PSS)	1985-86

7 (7c) §	H.P.Tillakaratne	New Zealand	Hamilton	1990-91
7 (7c)	C.I.Dunusinghe	New Zealand	Napier	1994-95

ZIMBABWE

7 (7c)	W.R.James	Sri Lanka	Bulawayo[2]	1994-95
7 (5c, 2s)	T.Taibu	Bangladesh	Harare	2003-04

BANGLADESH

7 (5c, 2s)	Khaled Mashud	Zimbabwe	Harare	2003-04

MOST DISMISSALS IN AN INNINGS *(§ In first Test. # in last Test)*

AUSTRALIA

6 (6c) §	A.T.W.Grout	South Africa	Johannesburg[3]	1957-58
6 (6c)	R.W.Marsh	England	Brisbane[2]	1982-83
6 (6c)	I.A.Healy	England	Birmingham	1997
5 (1c, 4s)	W.A.S.Oldfield	England	Melbourne	1924-25
5 (2c, 3s)	G.R.A.Langley	West Indies	Georgetown	1954-55
5 (5c)	G.R.A.Langley	West Indies	Kingston	1954-55
5 (5c)	G.R.A.Langley	England	Lord's	1956
5 (4c, 1s)	A.T.W.Grout	South Africa	Durban[2]	1957-58
5 (5c)	A.T.W.Grout	Pakistan	Lahore[2]	1959-60
5 (4c, 1s)	A.T.W.Grout	West Indies	Brisbane[2]	1960-61
5 (5c)	A.T.W.Grout	England	Lord's	1961
5 (5c)	A.T.W.Grout	England	Sydney	1965-66
5 (5c) §	H.B.Taber	South Africa	Johannesburg[3]	1966-67
5 (5c)	H.B.Taber	West Indies	Sydney	1968-69
5 (5c) #	H.B.Taber	South Africa	Port Elizabeth	1969-70
5 (5c)	R.W.Marsh	England	Manchester	1972
5 (5c)	R.W.Marsh	England	Nottingham	1972
5 (5c)	R.W.Marsh	New Zealand	Sydney	1973-74
5 (5c)	R.W.Marsh	New Zealand	Christchurch	1973-74
5 (5c)	R.W.Marsh	West Indies	Melbourne	1975-76
5 (5c)	R.W.Marsh	New Zealand	Christchurch	1976-77
5 (5c) §	J.A.Maclean	England	Brisbane[2]	1978-79
5 (5c)	K.J.Wright	Pakistan	Melbourne	1978-79
5 (5c)	R.W.Marsh	West Indies	Brisbane[2]	1979-80
5 (5c)	R.W.Marsh	India	Sydney	1980-81
5 (5c)	R.W.Marsh	Pakistan	Perth	1981-82
5 (5c)	R.W.Marsh	Pakistan	Perth	1983-84
5 (5c) #	R.W.Marsh	Pakistan	Sydney	1983-84
5 (5c)	W.B.Phillips	West Indies	Kingston	1983-84
5 (5c)	I.A.Healy	Pakistan	Adelaide	1989-90
5 (5c)	I.A.Healy	England	Melbourne	1990-91
5 (5c)	I.A.Healy	England	Adelaide	1990-91
5 (5c)	I.A.Healy	New Zealand	Brisbane[2]	1993-94
5 (5c)	I.A.Healy	Pakistan	Rawalpindi[2]	1994-95
5 (4c, 1s) §	P.A.Emery	Pakistan	Lahore[2]	1994-95
5 (5c)	I.A.Healy	England	Brisbane[2]	1994-95
5 (5c)	I.A.Healy	England	Melbourne	1994-95
5 (5c)	I.A.Healy	Sri Lanka	Adelaide	1995-96
5 (5c)	I.A.Healy	South Africa	Johannesburg[3]	1996-97
5 (5c)	I.A.Healy	England	Perth	1998-99
5 (5c)	A.C.Gilchrist	New Zealand (1st innings)	Hamilton	1999-2000
5 (5c)	A.C.Gilchrist	New Zealand (2nd innings)	Hamilton	1999-2000
5 (4c, 1s)	A.C.Gilchrist	West Indies	Brisbane[2]	2000-01
5 (5c)	A.C.Gilchrist	England	Leeds	2001

5 (4c, 1s)	A.C.Gilchrist	England	Sydney	2002-03
5 (5c)	A.C.Gilchrist	Sri Lanka	Darwin	2004-05
5 (4c, 1s)	A.C.Gilchrist	England	Nottingham	2002-03

ENGLAND

7 (7c)	R.W.Taylor	India	Bombay[3]	1979-80
6 (6c)	J.T.Murray	India	Lord's	1967
6 (6c)	R.C.Russell	Australia	Melbourne	1990-91
6 (6c)	R.C.Russell	South Africa (1st Innings)	Johannesburg[3]	1995-96
6 (6c)	A.J.Stewart	Australia	Manchester	1997
6 (5c, 1s)	C.M.W.Read	New Zealand	Birmingham	1999
6 (6c)	G.O.Jones	Bangladesh	Chester-le-Street	2005
5 (5c)	J.G.Binks	India	Calcutta	1963-64
5 (3c, 2s)	J.M.Parks	Australia	Sydney	1965-66
5 (5c)	J.M.Parks	New Zealand	Christchurch	1965-66
5 (4c, 1s)	A.P.E.Knott	India	Manchester	1974
5 (5c)	R.W.Taylor	New Zealand	Nottingham	1978
5 (5c)	R.W.Taylor	Australia	Brisbane[2]	1978-79
5 (5c)	C.J.Richards	Australia	Melbourne	1986-87
5 (5c)	R.C.Russell	West Indies	Bridgetown	1989-90
5 (5c)	R.C.Russell	South Africa (2nd Innings)	Johannesburg[3]	1995-96
5 (4c, 1s)	R.C.Russell	South Africa	Port Elizabeth	1995-96
5 (5c)	A.J.Stewart	South Africa	Lord's	1998
5 (5c)	A.J.Stewart	South Africa	Nottingham	1998
5 (5c)	A.J.Stewart	Australia	Lord's	2001
5 (5c)	J.S.Foster	New Zealand	Christchurch	2001-02
5 (5c)	C.M.W.Read	Bangladesh	Chittagong	2003-04
5 (5c)	G.O.Jones	India	Mumbai[3]	2005-06
5 (5c)	G.O.Jones	Sri Lanka	Lord's	2006
5 (4c, 1s)	G.O.Jones	Pakistan	Manchester	2006

SOUTH AFRICA

6 (6c)	D.T.Lindsay	Australia	Johannesburg[3]	1966-67
6 (6c)	M.V.Boucher	Pakistan	Port Elizabeth	1997-98
6 (6c)	M.V.Boucher	Sri Lanka	Cape Town	1997-98
6 (6c)	M.V.Boucher	Zimbabwe	Centurion	2004-05
5 (5c)	D.J.Richardson	India	Port Elizabeth	1992-93
5 (5c)	M.V.Boucher	England	Lord's	1998
5 (5c)	M.V.Boucher	England	Johannesburg[3]	1999-2000
5 (5c)	M.V.Boucher	India	Bombay[3]	1999-2000
5 (5c)	M.V.Boucher	West Indies	Kingston	2000-01
5 (5c)	M.V.Boucher	Sri Lanka	Centurion	2002-03
5 (5c)	M.V.Boucher	Australia	Johannesburg[3]	1999-2000

WEST INDIES

7 (7c)	R.D.Jacobs	Australia	Sydney	2000-01
5 (5c)	F.C.M.Alexander	England	Bridgetown	1959-60
5 (5c)	D.L.Murray	England	Leeds	1976
5 (5c)	D.L.Murray	Pakistan	Georgetown	1976-77
5 (5c)	D.A.Murray	India	Delhi	1978-79
5 (5c)	D.A.Murray	Australia	Melbourne	1981-82
5 (5c)	P.J.L.Dujon	India	Kingston	1982-83
5 (5c)	P.J.L.Dujon	England	Bridgetown	1985-86
5 (5c)	P.J.L.Dujon	Australia	St John's	1990-91
5 (5c)	D.Williams	Australia	Brisbane[2]	1992-93
5 (5c)	J.R.Murray	Australia	Perth	1992-93
5 (5c)	C.O.Browne	England	Nottingham	1995

5 (5c)	C.O.Browne	New Zealand	St John's	1995-96
5 (4c, 1s)	R.D.Jacobs	India	Bombay[3]	2002-03
NEW ZEALAND				
7 (7c)	I.D.S.Smith	Sri Lanka	Hamilton	1990-91
5 (5c)	R.I.Harford	India	Wellington	1967-68
5 (5c)	K.J.Wadsworth	Pakistan	Auckland	1972-73
5 (5c)	W.K.Lees	Sri Lanka	Wellington	1982-83
5 (4c, 1s)	I.D.S.Smith	England	Auckland	1983-84
5 (5c)	I.D.S.Smith	Sri Lanka	Auckland	1990-91
5 (5c)	A.C.Parore	England	Auckland	1991-92
5 (4c, 1s)	A.C.Parore	Sri Lanka	Colombo (SSC)	1992-93
5 (5c)	A.C.Parore	Zimbabwe	Harare	2000-01
5 (5c)	A.C.Parore	Pakistan	Auckland	2000-01
INDIA				
6 (5c, 1s)	S.M.H.Kirmani	New Zealand	Christchurch	1975-76
5 (3c, 2s)	B.K.Kunderan	England	Bombay[1]	1961-62
5 (5c)	S.M.H.Kirmani	Pakistan	Faisalabad	1982-83
5 (0c, 5s)	K.S.More	West Indies	Chennai[1]	1987-88
5 (5c)	N.R.Mongia	South Africa	Durban[2]	1996-97
5 (5c)	N.R.Mongia	Pakistan	Calcutta	1998-99
PAKISTAN				
7 (7c)	Wasim Bari	New Zealand	Auckland	1978-79
6 (6c)	Rashid Latif	Zimbabwe	Bulawayo[2]	1997-98
5 (4c, 1s)	Imtiaz Ahmed	Australia	Lahore[2]	1959-60
5 (5c)	Wasim Bari	England	Leeds	1971
5 (5c)	Saleem Yousuf	Sri Lanka	Karachi[1]	1985-86
5 (5c)	Saleem Yousuf	New Zealand	Faisalabad	1990-91
5 (4c, 1s)	Moin Khan	West Indies	Bridgetown	1992-93
5 (5c)	Rashid Latif	Zimbabwe	Lahore[2]	1993-94
5 (5c)	Rashid Latif	New Zealand	Auckland	1993-94
5 (4c, s1)	Rashid Latif	Australia	Sydney	1995-96
5 (5c)	Rashid Latif	New Zealand	Christchurch	1995-96
5 (4c, 1s)	Kamran Akmal	West Indies	Bridgetown	2004-05
5 (5c)	Kamran Akmal	West Indies	Kingston	2004-05
SRI LANKA				
6 (6c)	S.A.R.Silva	India	Colombo (SSC)	1985-86
5 (5c)	S.A.R.Silva	India	Colombo (PSS)	1985-86
5 (5c)	H.P.Tillakaratne	New Zealand	Hamilton	1990-91
5 (5c)	P.B.Dasanayake	Zimbabwe	Harare	1994-95
5 (5c)	R.S.Kaluwitharana	South Africa	Centurion	2000-01
5 (5c)	K.C.Sangakkara	England	Lord's	2002
5 (5c)	K.C.Sangakkara	Bangladesh	Colombo (PSS)	2005-06
ZIMBABWE				
5 (5c)	W.R.James	Sri Lanka	Bulawayo[2]	1994-95
5 (5c)	A.Flower	England	Nottingham	2000
4 (4c)	A.Flower	New Zealand	Harare	1992-93
4 (4c)	A.Flower	Pakistan	Karachi[2]	1993-94
4 (4c)	W.R.James	Sri Lanka	Harare	1994-95
4 (4c)	A.Flower	Pakistan	Harare	1994-95
4 (4c)	A.Flower	Sri Lanka	Bulawayo[2]	1999-2000
4 (4c)	A.Flower	Sri Lanka	Harare	1999-2000
4 (4c)	A.Flower	West Indies	Kingston	1999-2000
4 (4c)	A.Flower	England	Nottingham	2000

4 (4c)	A.Flower	India		Harare	2001
4 (4c)	T.Taibu	Bangladesh		Harare	2003-04

BANGLADESH

4 (4c)	Khaled Mashud	Sri Lanka		Colombo (SSC)	2002-03
4 (4c)	Khaled Mashud	West Indies		Chittagong	2002-03
4 (2c, 2s)	Khaled Mashud	Zimbabwe		Harare	2003-04
4 (3c, 1s)	Khaled Mashud	India		Chittagong	2004-05
4 (4c)	Khaled Mashud	Sri Lanka		Colombo (RPS)	2005-06

MOST STUMPINGS IN A SERIES

9	A.F.A.Lilley	England	v	Australia	in Australia	1903-04
9	P.W.Sherwell	South Africa	v	Australia	in Australia	1910-11
8	W.A.S.Oldfield	Australia	v	England	in Australia	1924-25
8	R.A.Saggers	Australia	v	South Africa	in South Africa	1949-50

MOST STUMPINGS IN A MATCH

6	K.S.More	India	v	West Indies	Chennai[1]	1987-88
5	P.Sen	India	v	England	Madras[1]	1951-52
4	J.M.Blackham	Australia	v	England	Lord's	1888
4	A.H.Jarvis	Australia	v	England	Sydney	1894-95
4	W.A.S.Oldfield	Australia	v	England	Melbourne	1924-25
4	W.A.S.Oldfield	Australia	v	England	Sydney	1924-25
4	W.A.S.Oldfield	Australia	v	West Indies	Adelaide	1930-31
4	R.A.Saggers	Australia	v	South Africa	Port Elizabeth	1949-50
4	G.R.A.Langley	Australia	v	West Indies	Brisbane[2]	1951-52
4	Rajindernath	India	v	Pakistan	Bombay[2]	1952-53
4	Wasim Bari	Pakistan	v	Australia	Melbourne	1976-77

MOST STUMPINGS IN AN INNINGS

5	K.S.More	India	v	West Indies	Chennai[1]	1987-88
4	W.A.S.Oldfield	Australia	v	England	Melbourne	1924-25
4	P.Sen	India	v	England	Madras[1]	1951-52
3	A.H.Jarvis	Australia	v	England	Sydney	1894-95
3	J.J.Kelly	Australia	v	South Africa	Cape Town	1902-03
3	A.F.A.Lilley	England	v	Australia	Sydney	1903-04
3	P.W.Sherwell	South Africa	v	Australia	Sydney	1910-11
3	H.Carter	Australia	v	England	Melbourne	1920-21
3	T.A.Ward	South Africa	v	Australia	Johannesburg[1]	1921-22
3	W.A.S.Oldfield	Australia	v	West Indies	Adelaide	1930-31
3	W.A.S.Oldfield	Australia	v	England	Brisbane[2]	1936-37
3	D.Tallon	Australia	v	England	Sydney	1946-47
3	R.A.Saggers	Australia	v	South Africa	Cape Town	1949-60
3	G.R.A.Langley	Australia	v	West Indies	Brisbane[2]	1951-52
3	G.R.A.Langley	Australia	v	West Indies	Georgetown	1954-55
3	A.P.E.Knott	England	v	Australia	Leeds	1968
3	P.B.Dassanayake	Sri Lanka	v	South Africa	Colombo (SSC)	1993-94
3	R.S.Kaluwitharana	Sri Lanka	v	Australia	Cairns	2004-05
3	Kamran Akmal	Pakistan	v	Australia	Sydney	2004-05

COMPLETED INNINGS WITHOUT EXTRAS

Total	Wicket-keeper					
328	N.S.Tamhane	India	v	Pakistan	Lahore[1]	1954-55
252	W.Farrimond	England	v	South Africa	Durban[2]	1930-31
247	J.M.Parks	England	v	South Africa	Nottingham	1960
236	G.MacGregor	England	v	Australia	Melbourne	1891-92
200	R.W.Marsh	Australia	v	Pakistan	Melbourne	1972-73
174	J.J.Kelly	Australia	v	England	Melbourne	1897-98
134	M.V.Boucher	South Africa	v	Pakistan	Port Elizabeth	1997-98
128	R.W.Marsh	Australia	v	West Indies	Sydney	1975-76
126	J.Hunter	England	v	Australia	Melbourne	1884-85
111	A.F.A.Lilley	England	v	Australia	Melbourne	1903-04
104	R.D.Jacobs	West Indies	v	Zimbabwe	Bulawayo[2]	2003-04
96	R.W.Taylor	England	v	India	Lord's	1979
94	T.G.Evans	England	v	New Zealand	Birmingham	1958
92	G.MacGregor	England	v	Australia	The Oval	1890
84	T.G.Evans	England	v	Australia	Manchester	1956
77	S.C.Guillen	New Zealand	v	West Indies	Auckland	1955-56
74	T.G.Evans	England	v	New Zealand	Lord's	1958
62	J.M.Blackham	Australia	v	England	Lord's	1888
42	A.P.E.Knott	England	v	India	Lord's	1974
30	H.R.Butt	England	v	South Africa	Port Elizabeth	1895-96
26	T.G.Evans	England	v	New Zealand	Auckland	1954-55

MOST BYES CONCEDED IN AN INNINGS

37	F.E.Woolley	England	v	Australia (327)	The Oval	1934
(At the age of 47, standing-in for the injured L.E.G.Ames).						
33	J.T.Murray	England	v	India (390)	Bombay[2]	1961-62
33	J.M.Parks	England	v	West Indies (9d-391)	Kingston	1967-68
31	W.L.Cornford	England	v	New Zealand (387)	Auckland	1929-30
31	A.T.W.Grout	Australia	v	Pakistan (366)	Lahore[2]	1959-60
30	M.Bissett	South Africa	v	England (417)	Cape Town	1909-10
30	W.Carkeek	Australia	v	South Africa (329)	Nottingham	1912
30	E.A.C.Hunte	West Indies	v	England (327)	Georgetown	1929-30
30	T.G.Evans	England	v	New Zealand (189)	Wellington	1950-51

NO BYES CONCEDED IN TOTAL OF 500 RUNS

3d-713	T.Taibu	Zimbabwe	v	Sri Lanka	Bulawayo[2]	2003-04
4-671	H.P.Tillakaratne	Sri Lanka	v	New Zealand	Wellington	1990-91
5d-660	A.C.Parore	New Zealand	v	West Indies	Wellington	1994-95
8d-659	T.G.Evans	England	v	Australia	Sydney	1946-47
9d-658	R.D.Jacobs	West Indies	v	South Africa	Durban[2]	2003-04
652	S.M.H.Kirmani	India	v	Pakistan	Faisalabad	1982-83
4d-632	A.J.Stewart	England	v	Australia	Lord's	1993
619	J.L.Hendriks	West Indies	v	Australia	Sydney	1968-69
5d-616	I.D.S.Smith	New Zealand	v	Pakistan	Auckland	1988-89
6d-610	S.S.Dighe	India	v	Sri Lanka	Colombo (SSC)	2001-02
6d-609	A.Flower	Zimbabwe	v	India	Nagpur	2000-01
7d-601	R C Russell	England	v	Australia	Leeds	1989
3d-600	A.Flower	Zimbabwe	v	South Africa	Harare	2001-02
4d-599	Moin Khan	Pakistan	v	Australia	Peshawar[2]	1998-99
595	M.V.Boucher	South Africa	v	New Zealand	Auckland	2003-04
5d-593	R.C.Russell	England	v	West Indies	St John's	1993-94
7d-586	R.S.Kaluwitharana	Sri Lanka	v	New Zealand	Dunedin	1996-97

8d-567	A.C.Parore	New Zealand	v	England	Nottingham	1994
9d-566	R.D.Jacobs	West Indies	v	England	Birmingham	2004
6d-560	R.J.Blakey	England	v	India	Madras[1]	1992-93
9d-559	W.W.Wade	South Africa	v	England	Cape Town	1938-39
4d-556	Khaled Mashud	Bangladesh	v	Australia	Cairns	2003-04
556	P.A.Patel	India	v	Australia	Adelaide	2003-04
5d-555	Khaled Mashud	Bangladesh	v	Sri Lanka	Colombo (SSC)	2001-02
6d-551	J.S.Foster	England	v	Australia	Melbourne	2002-03
9d-551	A.P.E.Knott	England	v	New Zealand	Lord's	1973
551	J.J.Kelly	Australia	v	England	Sydney	1897-98
7d-548	L.K.Germon	New Zealand	v	West Indies	St John's	1995-96
545	K.C.Sangakkara	Sri Lanka	v	England	Birmingham	2002
5d-544	Imtiaz Ahmed	Pakistan	v	England	Birmingham	1962
3d-543	T.M.Findlay	West Indies	v	New Zealand	Georgetown	1971-72
9d-541	Khaled Mashud	Bangladesh	v	Sri Lanka	Colombo (PSS)	2002-03
9d-536	I.A.Healy	Australia	v	West Indies	Bridgetown	1990-91
536	Khaled Mashud	Bangladesh	v	West Indies	Dhaka	2002-03
9d-532	A.P.E.Knott	England	v	Australia	The Oval	1975
531	D.T.Lindsay	South Africa	v	England	Johannesburg[3]	1964-65
528	S.M.H.Kirmani	India	v	Australia	Adelaide	1980-81
528	R.C.Russell	England	v	Australia	Lord's	1989
7d-526	A.P.E.Knott	England	v	West Indies	Port-of-Spain	1967-68
521	W.A.S.Oldfield	Australia	v	England	Brisbane[1]	1928-29
520	J.H.B.Waite	South Africa	v	Australia	Melbourne	1952-53
517	I.A.Healy	Australia	v	South Africa	Adelaide	1997-98
515	P.J.L.Dujon	West Indies	v	Australia	Adelaide	1988-89
4d-514	R.G.de Alwis	Sri Lanka	v	Australia	Kandy	1982-83
5d-514	C.J.Richards	England	v	Australia	Adelaide	1986-87
9d-513	R.D.Jacobs	West Indies	v	India	St John's	2001-02
513	Moin Khan	Pakistan	v	Australia	Rawalpindi[2]	1998-99
6d-512	B.N.French	England	v	New Zealand	Wellington	1987-88
510	J.L.Hendriks	West Indies	v	Australia	Melbourne	1968-69
509	W.B.Phillips	Australia	v	West Indies	Bridgetown	1983-84
6d-507	K.J.Wadsworth	New Zealand	v	Pakistan	Dunedin	1972-73
7d-504	K.C.Sangakkara	Sri Lanka	v	South Africa	Cape Town	2000-01
8d-503	S.M.H.Kirmani	India	v	Pakistan	Faisalabad	1978-79
6d-500	R.S.Kaluwitharana	Sri Lanka	v	Australia	Melbourne	1995-96
7d-500	R.C.Russell	England	v	West Indies	St John's	1997-98

Fielding

MOST CATCHES IN TESTS

Player	Country	Tests	C	A	E	SA	WI	NZ	I	P	SL	Z	B
				Opponents									
M.E.Waugh	A	128	**181**	-	43	19	45	10	29	23	7	5	-
B.C.Lara	W	127	**161**	34	45	19	-	13	22	8	14	3	3
M.A.Taylor	A	104	**157**	-	46	17	28	25	10	20	11	-	-
A.R.Border	A	156	**156**	-	57	5	19	31	14	22	8	-	-
S.P.Fleming	N	102	**152**	17	28	11	18	-	20	14	16	22	6
R.S.Dravid	I	103	**145**	32	21	13	20	12	-	15	8	18	6
H.P.Tillakaratne	SL	83	**122**†	11	16	9	4	37	16	13	-	14	2
G.S.Chappell	A	87	**122**	-	61	-	16	18	5	22	0	-	-
I.V.A.Richards	W	121	**122**	24	29	-	-	7	39	23	-	-	-
I.T.Botham	E	102	**120**	57	-	-	19	14	14	14	2	-	-
M.C.Cowdrey	E	114	**120**	40	-	22	21	15	11	11	-	-	-
S.K.Warne	A	139	**120**	-	25	19	19	18	10	13	15	0	1
R.T.Ponting	A	104	**119**	-	21	24	14	11	19	11	10	4	4
C.L.Hooper	W	102	**115**	38	24	14	-	1	18	14	4	2	0
S.R.Waugh	A	168	**112**	-	29	9	19	18	12	14	7	4	0
D.P.M.D.Jayawardene	SL	83	**111**	10	24	9	12	9	8	20	-	17	2
R.B.Simpson	A	62	**110**	-	30	27	29	-	21	3	-	-	-
W.R.Hammond	E	85	**110**	43	-	30	22	9	6	-	-	-	-
G.S.Sobers	W	93	**109**	27	40	-	-	11	27	4	-	-	-
M.L.Hayden	A	83	**108**	-	22	21	23	4	15	3	9	4	7
S.M.Gavaskar	I	125	**108**	19	35	-	17	11	-	19	7	-	-
I.M.Chappell	A	75	**105**	-	31	11	24	16	17	6	-	-	-
M.Azharuddin	I	99	**105**	14	9	13	20	4	0	14	27	4	-
G.P.Thorpe	E	100	**105**	19	-	8	27	16	8	13	9	1	4
G.A.Gooch	E	118	**103**	29	-	1	28	13	21	7	4	-	-

† includes 32 catches in 11 Tests as a wicket-keeper (also made two stumpings).

The most successful catchers for the other countries are:

Player	Country	Tests	C	A	E	SA	WI	NZ	I	P	SL	Z	B
J.H.Kallis	SA	101	**94**	10	19	-	21	10	15	7	14	4	4
Javed Miandad	P	124	**93**	12	20	-	12	20	18	-	11	-	-
A.D.R.Campbell	Z	60	**60**	1	10	3	3	10	4	18	6	-	5
Habibul Bashar	B	42	**19**	0	0	0	4	1	2	1	3	8	-

MOST CATCHES IN A SERIES *(§ In first Test series)*

AUSTRALIA

C	Tests	Player	Against	Season
15 §	5	J.M.Gregory	England	1920-21
14	6	G.S.Chappell	England	1974-75
13 §	5	R.B.Simpson	South Africa	1957-58
13	5	R.B.Simpson	West Indies	1960-61
12	5	D.F.Whatmore	India	1979-80
12	6	A.R.Border	England	1981
11	5	R.B.Simpson	West Indies	1964-65
11	5	I.M.Chappell	England	1974-75
11	6	I.R.Redpath	England	1974-75
11	6	A.R.Border	England	1985
11	6	M.A.Taylor	England	1993
11	5	M.E.Waugh	West Indies	2000-01
11	3	R.T.Ponting	South Africa	2001-02

ENGLAND

12 §	5	L.C.Braund	Australia	1901-02
12	5	W.R.Hammond	Australia	1934
12	3	J.T.Ikin	South Africa	1951
12	6	A.W.Greig	Australia	1974-75
12	6	I.T.Botham	Australia	1981
11	3	A.W.Greig	Pakistan	1974
11	6	I.T.Botham	Australia	1978-79
11	4	G.A.Hick	Australia	1998-99
11	5	M.E.Trescothick	South Africa	2004-05

SOUTH AFRICA

12	5	A.E.E.Vogler	England	1909-10
12	5	B.Mitchell	England	1930-31
12	5	T.L.Goddard	England	1956-57
11	5	A.W.Nourse	England	1922-23
10	5	W.R.Endean	England	1956-57
10	5	W.J.Cronje	West Indies	1998-99
10	5	D.J.Cullinan	West Indies	2000-01

WEST INDIES

13	6	B.C.Lara	England	1997-98
13	4	B.C.Lara	India	2005-06
12	5	G.S.Sobers	Australia	1960-61
11	4	E.D.Weekes	England	1950
11	5	G.S.Sobers	India	1961-62
10	5	G.S.Sobers	England	1966
10	4	R.C.Fredericks	England	1973-74
10	4	I.V.A.Richards	India	1988-89
10	4	D.R.E.Joseph	Australia	1998-99
10	5	B.C.Lara	England	2000

NEW ZEALAND

10	2	S.P.Fleming	Zimbabwe	1997-98
10	4	S.P.Fleming	England	1999
9	3	B.A.Young	Pakistan	1993-94
9	3	S.P.Fleming	Australia	1997-98
9	3	S.P.Fleming	West Indies	2005-06

INDIA

13	4	R.S.Dravid	Australia	2004-05
12	5	E.D.Solkar	England	1972-73
10	4	A.L.Wadekar	New Zealand	1967-68
10	4	E.D.Solkar	Australia	1969-70
10	3	M.Azharuddin	Sri Lanka	1993-94
10	4	R.S.Dravid	England	2002

PAKISTAN

9	5	W.Mathias	West Indies	1957-58
9	2	Taufeeq Umar	South Africa	2003-04
8	3	Majid Khan	New Zealand	1972-73
8	6	Javed Miandad	India	1979-80
8	3	Yousuf Youhana	England	2000-01

SRI LANKA

9	3	D.P.M.D.Jayawardene	Pakistan	1999-2000
8	2	H.P.Tillakaratne	New Zealand	1992-93
8	2	R.S.Mahanama	Zimbabwe	1996-97

8	2	R.S.Mahanama	New Zealand	1996-97
8	3	S.T.Jayasuriya	New Zealand	1997-98
8	2	D.P.M.D.Jayawardene	Zimbabwe	2003-04

ZIMBABWE

7	3	M.H.Dekker	Sri Lanka	1994-95
7	2	A.D.R.Campbell	England	1996-97

BANGLADESH

4	2	Aminul Islam	Pakistan	2001-02
4	3	Rajin Saleh	Pakistan	2003-04

MOST CATCHES IN A MATCH *(§ In first Test. # In last Test)*

AUSTRALIA

7	G.S.Chappell	v	England	Perth	1974-75
7	M.L.Hayden	v	Sri Lanka	Galle	2003-04
6	J.M.Gregory	v	England	Sydney	1920-21
6 #	V.Y.Richardson	v	South Africa	Durban[2]	1935-36
6 #	R.N.Harvey	v	England	Sydney	1962-63
6	I.M.Chappell	v	New Zealand	Adelaide	1973-74
6	D.F.Whatmore	v	India	Kanpur	1979-80
6	M.E.Waugh	v	India	Chennai[1]	2000-01

ENGLAND

6	A.Shrewsbury	v	Australia	Sydney	1887-88
6	F.E.Woolley	v	Australia	Sydney	1911-12
6	M.C.Cowdrey	v	West Indies	Lord's	1963
6	A.W.Greig	v	Pakistan	Leeds	1974
6	A.J.Lamb	v	New Zealand	Lord's	1983
6	G.A.Hick	v	Pakistan	Leeds	1992

SOUTH AFRICA

6	A.E.E.Vogler	v	England	Durban[1]	1909-10
6	B.Mitchell	v	Australia	Melbourne	1931-32
5	G.A.Faulkner	v	England	Cape Town	1909-10
5	B.Mitchell	v	England	Johannesburg[1]	1930-31
5	W.R.Endean	v	New Zealand	Johannesburg[2]	1953-54
5	P.R.Adams	v	England	Lord's	2003

WEST INDIES

6	G.S.Sobers	v	England	Lord's	1973
6	J.C.Adams	v	England	Bridgetown	1993-94

NEW ZEALAND

7	S.P.Fleming	v	Zimbabwe	Harare	1997-98
6	B.A.Young	v	Pakistan	Auckland	1993-94
6	S.P.Fleming	v	Australia	Brisbane[2]	1997-98
6	S.P.Fleming	v	West Indies	Wellington	2005-06
5	S.P.Fleming	v	India	Wellington	1998-99
5	C.Z.Harris	v	Zimbabwe	Bulawayo[2]	1997-98
5	M.S.Sinclair	v	Bangladesh	Chittagong	2004-05

INDIA

7 §	Yajurvindra Singh	v	England	Bangalore	1976-77
6	E.D.Solkar	v	West Indies	Port-of-Spain	1970-71
6	V.K.Sehwag	v	England	Leeds	2002

PAKISTAN

6	Taufeeq Umar	v	South Africa	Faisalabad	2003-04

5	Majid Khan	v	Australia	Karachi[1]	1979-80
5	Inzamamul Haq	v	Zimbabwe	Rawalpindi[2]	1993-94
5	Wajahatullah Wasti	v	Sri Lanka	Dhaka	1998-99
5	Shadab Kabir	v	Bangladesh	Chittagong	2001-02

SRI LANKA

7	H.P.Tillakaratne	v	New Zealand	Colombo (SSC)	1992-93
6	D.P.M.D.Jayawardene	v	Pakistan	Peshawar[2]	1999-2000
6	D.P.M.D.Jayawardene	v	Zimbabwe	Harare	2003-04
5	Y.Goonasekera	v	New Zealand	Wellington	1982-83
5	R.S.Mahanama	v	Zimbabwe	Colombo(RPS)	1996-97
5	S.T.Jayasuriya	v	New Zealand	Galle	1997-98
5	H.P.Tillakaratne	v	New Zealand	Galle	1997-98
5	H.P.Tillakaratne	v	Zimbabwe	Colombo(SSC)	2001-02

ZIMBABWE

4	M.H.Dekker	v	Sri Lanka	Harare	1994-95
4	A.D.R.Campbell	v	England	Harare	1996-97
4	G.W.Flower	v	England	Nottingham	2000
4	A.D.R.Campbell	v	Bangladesh	Harare	2000-01
4	A.D.R.Campbell	v	Pakistan	Harare	2002-03

BANGLADESH

4	Rajin Saleh	v	Pakistan	Karachi[1]	2003-04
3	Al Sahariar	v	India	Dhaka	2000-01
3	Aminul Islam	v	Pakistan	Chittagong	2001-02
3	Hannan Sarkar	v	Zimbabwe	Harare	2003-04

MOST CATCHES IN AN INNINGS *(§ In first Test. # In last Test)*

AUSTRALIA

5	V.Y.Richardson #	v	South Africa	Durban[2]	1935-36
4	S.J.E.Loxton	v	England	Brisbane[2]	1950-51
4	G.B.Hole	v	South Africa	Sydney	1952-53
4	R.G.Archer	v	West Indies	Georgetown	1954-55
4	A.K.Davidson	v	India	Delhi	1959-60
4	R.B.Simpson	v	West Indies	Sydney	1960-61
4	R.N.Harvey #	v	England	Sydney	1962-63
4	R.B.Simpson	v	West Indies	Bridgetown	1964-65
4	I.M.Chappell	v	New Zealand	Adelaide	1973-74
4	G.S.Chappell	v	England	Perth	1974-75
4	A.Turner	v	Pakistan	Sydney	1976-77
4	D.F.Whatmore	v	India	Kanpur	1979-80
4	A.R.Border	v	Pakistan	Karachi[1]	1979-80
4	D.C.Boon	v	Pakistan	Karachi[1]	1988-89
4	M.A.Taylor	v	West Indies	Bridgetown	1994-95
4	M.J.Slater	v	England	Melbourne	1998-99
4	M.E.Waugh	v	India	Melbourne	1999-2000
4	M.E.Waugh	v	India	Chennai[1]	2000-01
4	M.L.Hayden	v	India	Brisbane[2]	2003-04
4	M.L.Hayden	v	Sri Lanka	Galle	2003-04

ENGLAND

4	L.C.Braund	v	Australia	Sheffield	1902
4	W.Rhodes	v	Australia	Manchester	1905
4	L.C.Braund	v	Australia	Sydney	1907-08
4	F.E.Woolley	v	Australia	Sydney	1911-12

4	A.P.F.Chapman	v	West Indies	The Oval	1928
4	H.Larwood	v	Australia	Brisbane[1]	1928-29
4	J.E.McConnon	v	Pakistan	Manchester	1954
4	P.B.H.May	v	Australia	Adelaide	1954-55
4	P.H.Parfitt	v	Australia	Nottingham	1972
4	A.W.Greig	v	Pakistan	Leeds	1974
4	P.H.Edmonds	v	New Zealand	Christchurch	1977-78
4	A.J.Lamb	v	New Zealand	Lord's	1983
4	G.A.Hick	v	Pakistan	Leeds	1992
4	G.A.Hick	v	India	Calcutta	1992-93
4	G.A.Hick	v	New Zealand	Nottingham	1994
4	N.V.Knight	v	New Zealand	Christchurch	1996-97
4	G.P.Thorpe	v	Pakistan	Faisalabad	2000-01
4	M.E.Trescothick	v	Sri Lanka	Lord's	2002
4	M.E.Trescothick	v	Zimbabwe	Lord's	2003
SOUTH AFRICA					
4	A.E.E.Vogler	v	England	Durban[1]	1909-10
4	A.W.Nourse	v	England	Durban[2]	1922-23
4	B.Mitchell	v	Australia	Melbourne	1931-32
4	T.L.Goddard	v	Australia	Sydney	1963-64
4	A.J.Traicos §	v	Australia	Durban[2]	1969-70
4	A.C.Hudson	v	India	Cape Town	1992-93
4	H.H.Gibbs	v	West Indies	Durban[2]	1998-99
4	G.Kirsten	v	England	Cape Town	1999-2000
WEST INDIES					
4	E.D.Weekes	v	India	Kingston	1952-53
4	G.S.Sobers	v	England	Port-of-Spain	1959-60
4	G.S.Sobers	v	England	Nottingham	1966
4	R.C.Fredericks	v	Australia	Port-of-Spain	1972-73
4	G.S.Sobers	v	England	Lord's	1973
4	I.V.A.Richards	v	India	Kingston	1988-89
4	A.L.Logie	v	Pakistan	Lahore[2]	1990-91
4	J.C.Adams	v	England	Bridgetown	1993-94
4	B.C.Lara	v	Australia	Kingston	1994-95
4	C.L.Hooper	v	South Africa	Port Elizabeth	1998-99
4	B.C.Lara	v	India	Kingston	2005-2006
NEW ZEALAND					
5	S.P.Fleming	v	Zimbabwe	Harare	1997-98
4	J.J.Crowe	v	West Indies	Bridgetown	1984-85
4	M.D.Crowe	v	West Indies	Kingston	1984-85
4	S.P.Fleming	v	Australia	Brisbane[2]	1997-98
4	S.P.Fleming	v	Zimbabwe	Harare	2005-06
4	S.P.Fleming	v	West Indies	Wellington	2005-06
INDIA					
5	Yajurvindra Singh §	v	England	Bangalore	1976-77
5	M Azharuddin	v	Pakistan	Karachi[1]	1989-90
5	K.Srikkanth	v	Australia	Perth	1991-92
4	A.L.Wadekar	v	England	Birmingham	1967
4	A.L.Wadekar	v	New Zealand	Christchurch	1967-68
4	E.D.Solkar	v	West Indies	Port-of-Spain	1970-71
4	S.Venkataraghavan	v	New Zealand	Madras[1]	1976-77
4	D.B.Vengsarkar	v	England	Bombay[3]	1984-85
4	V.V.S.Laxman	v	England	Mohali	2001-02
4	Mohammad Kaif	v	Australia	Mumbai[3]	2004-05

PAKISTAN

4	W.Mathias	v	West Indies	Bridgetown	1957-58
4	Hanif Mohammad	v	England	Dacca	1968-69
4	Aamer Malik §	v	England	Faisalabad	1987-88
4	Inzamamul Haq	v	Zimbabwe	Rawalpindi[2]	1993-94
4	Saleem Elahi	v	Sri Lanka	Colombo (SSC)	1996-97
4	Taufeeq Umar	v	South Africa	Faisalabad	2003-04

SRI LANKA

4	Y.Goonasekera	v	New Zealand	Wellington	1982-83
4	H.P.Tillakaratne	v	New Zealand	Colombo (SSC)	1992-93
4	R.S.Mahanama	v	New Zealand	Dunedin	1996-97
4	R.S.Mahanama	v	Zimbabwe	Colombo (PIS)	1996-97
4	P.A.de Silva	v	India	Mumbai[3]	1997-98
4	R.P.Arnold	v	Pakistan	Rawalpindi[2]	1999-2000
4	H.P.Tillakaratne	v	England	Birmingham	2002
4	K.C.Sangakkara	v	Bangladesh	Colombo (PSS)	2002-03
4	D.P.M.D.Jayawardene	v	Zimbabwe	Harare	2003-04
4	D.P.M.D.Jayawardene	v	West Indies	Kandy	2005-06

ZIMBABWE

4	M.H.Dekker	v	Sri Lanka	Harare	1994-95

BANGLADESH

3	Al Sahariar	v	India	Dhaka	2000-01
3	Aminul Islam	v	Pakistan	Chittagong	2001-02
3	Rajin Saleh	v	Pakistan	Karachi[1]	2003-04

MOST SUBSTITUTE CATCHES BY ONE FIELDER IN AN INNINGS

FOUR					
Younis Khan	Pakistan	v	Bangladesh	Multan[2]	2001-02
THREE					
H.Strudwick	England	v	Australia	Melbourne	1903-04
Haroon Rashid	Pakistan	v	England	Leeds	1982
Gursharan Singh	India	v	West Indies	Ahmedabad	1983-84
Mashrafe Bin Mortaze	Bangladesh	v	Oakistan	Multan[2]	2003-04

MOST SUBSTITUTE CATCHES BY ONE FIELDER IN A MATCH

FOUR					
Gursharan Singh	India	v	West Indies	Ahmedabad	1983-84
Younis Khan	Pakistan	v	Bangladesh	Multan[2]	2001-02
THREE					
H.Strudwick	England	v	Australia	Melbourne	1903-04
J.E.D.Sealy	West Indies	v	England	Port-of-Spain	1929-30
W.V.Rodriguez	West Indies	v	India	Port-of-Spain	1961-62
Yajurvindra Singh	India	v	West Indies	Chennai[1]	1978-79
Haroon Rashid	Pakistan	v	England	Leeds	1982
M.J.Greatbatch	New Zealand	v	England	Christchurch	1987-88
W.V.Raman	India	v	England	Chennai[1]	1992-93
V.K.Sehwag	India	v	Zimbabwe	Nagpur	2001-02
Mashrafe Bin Mortaze	Bangladesh	v	Pakistan	Multan[2]	2003-04
D.R.Smith	West indies	v	Australia	Hobart	2005-06

All Round

1000 RUNS AND 100 WICKETS

	Tests	Runs	Wkts	Tests for Double
AUSTRALIA				
R.Benaud	63	2201	248	32
A.K.Davidson	44	1328	186	34
G.Giffen	31	1238	103	30
J.N.Gillespie	71	1218	259	70
M.G.Hughes	53	1032	212	52
I.W.G.Johnson	45	1000	109	45
B.Lee	53	1029	209	52
R.R.Lindwall	61	1502	228	38
K.R.Miller	55	2958	170	33
M.A.Noble	42	1997	121	27
S.K.Warne	139	2946	679	58
ENGLAND				
T.E.Bailey	61	2290	132	47
I.T.Botham	102	5200	383	21
J.E.Emburey	64	1721	147	46
A.Flintoff	61	3077	179	43
A.F.Giles	52	1347	140	43
A.W.Greig	58	3599	141	37
R.Illingworth	61	1836	122	47
W.Rhodes	58	2325	127	44
M.W.Tate	39	1198	155	33
F.J.Titmus	53	1449	153	40
SOUTH AFRICA				
T.L.Goddard	41	2516	123	36
J.H.Kallis	101	7950	199	53
S.M.Pollock	102	3515	395	26
WEST INDIES				
C.E.L.Ambrose	98	1439	405	69
C.L.Hooper	102	5762	114	90
M.D.Marshall	81	1810	376	49
G.S.Sobers	93	8032	235	48
NEW ZEALAND				
J.G.Bracewell	41	1001	102	41
C.L.Cairns	62	3320	218	33
R.J.Hadlee	86	3124	431	28
D.L.Vettori	70	2128	218	47
INDIA				
Kapil Dev	131	5248	434	25
A.Kumble	110	2025	533	56
M.H.Mankad	44	2109	162	23
R.J.Shastri	80	3830	151	44
J.Srinath	67	1009	236	67
PAKISTAN				
Abdul Qadir	67	1029	236	62
Imran Khan	88	3807	362	30
Intikhab Alam	47	1493	125	41
Sarfraz Nawaz	55	1045	177	55

Waqar Younis	87	1010	373	86
Wasim Akram	104	2898	414	45
SRI LANKA				
M.Muralidaran	107	1093	652	95
W.P.U.J.C.Vaas	94	2503	307	40
ZIMBABWE				
H.H.Streak	65	1990	216	47

1000 RUNS, 50 WICKETS AND 50 CATCHES

AUSTRALIA	Tests	Runs	Wkts	Catches
R.Benaud	63	2201	248	65
R.B.Simpson	62	4869	71	110
S.K.Warne	139	2946	679	120
M.E.Waugh	128	8029	59	181
S.R.Waugh	168	10927	91	112
ENGLAND				
I.T.Botham	102	5200	383	120
A.W.Greig	58	3599	141	87
W.R.Hammond	85	7249	83	110
W.Rhodes	58	2325	127	60
F.E.Woolley	64	3283	83	64
SOUTH AFRICA				
J.H.Kallis	101	7950	199	93
S.M.Pollock	102	3515	395	66
WEST INDIES				
C.L.Hooper	102	5762	114	115
G.S.Sobers	93	8032	235	109
INDIA				
Kapil Dev	131	5248	434	64
A.Kumble	110	2025	533	50
SRI LANKA				
S.T.Jayasuriya	105	6745	96	78
M.Muralidaran	107	1093	652	57

1000 RUNS AND 100 WICKET-KEEPING DISMISSALS

AUSTRALIA	Tests	Runs	Dismissals	Tests for Double
A.C.Gilchrist	84	5029	348	22
I.A.Healy	119	4356	395	36
R.W.Marsh	96	3633	355	25
W.A.S.Oldfield	54	1427	130	41
ENGLAND				
T.G.Evans	91	2439	219	42
G.O.Jones	31	1109	127	27
A.P.E.Knott	95	4389	269	30
J.M.Parks	46	1962	114	41
R.C.Russell	54	1897	165	37
A.J.Stewart	133	8463	277	65
R.W.Taylor	57	1156	174	47

SOUTH AFRICA				
M.V.Boucher	94	3565	360	30
D.J.Richardson	42	1359	152	28
J.H.B.Waite	50	2405	141	36
WEST INDIES				
P.J.L.Dujon	81	3322	272	30
R.D.Jacobs	65	2531	219	28
D.L.Murray	62	1993	189	33
NEW ZEALAND				
A.C.Parore	78	2865	204	49
I.D.S.Smith	63	1815	177	42
INDIA				
S.M.H.Kirmani	88	2759	198	42
N.R.Mongia	44	1442	107	41
K.S.More	49	1285	130	39
PAKISTAN				
Moin Khan	69	2741	148	49
Rashid Latif	37	1381	130	28
Saleem Yousuf	32	1055	104	32
Wasim Bari	81	1366	228	53
Kamran Akmal	27	1253	106	26
SRI LANKA				
R.S.Kaluwitharana	49	1933	119	42
K.C.Sangakkara	62	4796	162	34
ZIMBABWE				
A.Flower	63	4794	160	39

250 RUNS AND 20 WICKETS IN A SERIES

Player	Tests	Runs	Wkts				
G.Giffen	5	475	34	Australia	v	England	1894-95
L.C.Braund §	5	256	21	England	v	Australia	1901-02
G.A.Faulkner	5	545	29	South Africa	v	England	1909-10
G.J.Thompson	5	267	23	England	v	South Africa	1909-10
J.M.Gregory §	5	442	23	Australia	v	England	1920-21
K.R.Miller	5	362	20	Australia	v	West Indies	1951-52
K.R.Miller	5	439	20	Australia	v	West Indies	1954-55
R.Benaud	5	329	30	Australia	v	South Africa	1957-58
G.S.Sobers	5	424	23	West Indies	v	India	1961-62
G.S.Sobers	5	322	20	West Indies	v	England	1963
G.S.Sobers	5	722	20	West Indies	v	England	1966
T.L.Goddard	5	294	26	South Africa	v	Australia	1966-67
A.W.Greig	5	430	24	England	v	West Indies	1973-74
I.T.Botham	6	291	23	England	v	Australia	1978-79
Kapil Dev	6	278	32	India	v	Pakistan	1979-80
I T.Botham	6	399	34	England	v	Australia	1981
Kapil Dev	6	318	22	India	v	England	1981-82
R.J.Hadlee	4	301	21	New Zealand	v	England	1983
I.T.Botham	6	250	31	England	v	Australia	1985
J.H.Kallis	5	267	20	South Africa	v	West Indies	2000-01

S.M.Pollock	5	302	20	South Africa	v	West Indies	2000-01
Flintoff,A	5	402	24	England	v	Australia	2005

§ in first Test series.

250 RUNS, 20 WICKETS AND 10 CATCHES IN A SERIES

Player	Tests	Runs	Wkts	C	Series			
L.C.Braund §	5	256	21	12	England	v	Australia	1901-02
J.M.Gregory §	5	442	23	15	Australia	v	England	1920-21
G.S.Sobers	5	424	23	11	West Indies	v	India	1961-62
G.S.Sobers	5	722	20	10	West Indies	v	England	1966
I.T.Botham	6	291	23	11	England	v	Australia	1978-79
I T.Botham	6	399	34	12	England	v	Australia	1981

250 RUNS AND 20 WICKET-KEEPING DISMISSALS IN A SERIES

	Tests	Runs	Dismissals				
J H.B Waite	5	263	26	South Africa	v	New Zealand	1961-62
D T.Lindsay	5	606	24	South Africa	v	Australia	1966-67
A P.E.Knott	6	364	23	England	v	Australia	1974-75
P.J.L.Dujon	5	305	20	West Indies	v	England	1988
I.A.Healy	6	296	26	Australia	v	England	1993
A.J.Stewart	6	268	23	England	v	Australia	1997
A.J.Stewart	5	465	23	England	v	South Africa	1998
R.D.Jacobs	5	317	20	West Indies	v	South Africa	1998-99
A.C.Gilchrist	5	333	21	Australia	v	West Indies	2000-01
R.D.Jacobs	5	288	21	West Indies	v	Australia	2000-01
R.D.Jacobs	5	317	20	West Indies	v	South Africa	2000-01
A.C.Gilchrist	5	340	26	Australia	v	England	2001
A.C.Gilchrist	5	333	25	Australia	v	England	2002-03

500 RUNS IN A SERIES BY A WICKET-KEEPER

	Tests	Runs	Avge				
B.K.Kunderan	5	525	52.50	India	v	England	1963-64
D.T.Lindsay	5	606	86.57	South Africa	v	Australia	1966-67
A.Flower	2	540	270.00	Zimbabwe	v	India	2000-01

MATCH DOUBLE - 100 RUNS AND 10 WICKETS

A.K.Davidson	44	5/135)	Australia	v	West Indies	Brisbane[2]	1960-61
	80	6/87)					
I.T.Botham	114	6/58)	England	v	India	Bombay[3]	1979-80
		7/48)					
Imran Khan	117	6/98)	Pakistan	v	India	Faisalabad	1982-83
		5/82)					

A CENTURY AND 5 WICKETS IN AN INNINGS OF THE SAME MATCH

AUSTRALIA	Opponents				
C.Kelleway	114	5/33	South Africa	Manchester	1912
J.M.Gregory	100	7/69	England	Melbourne	1920-21
K.R.Miller	109	6/107	West Indies	Kingston	1954-55
R.Benaud	100	5/84	South Africa	Johannesburg[3]	1957-58

ENGLAND

A.W.Greig	148	6/164	West Indies	Bridgetown	1973-74
I.T.Botham	103	5/73	New Zealand	Christchurch	1977-78
I.T.Botham	108	8/34	Pakistan	Lord's	1978
I.T.Botham	114	6/58 + 7/48	India	Bombay[3]	1979-80
I.T.Botham	149*	6/95	Australia	Leeds	1981
I.T.Botham	138	5/59	New Zealand	Wellington	1983-84

SOUTH AFRICA

J.H.Sinclair	106	6/26	England	Cape Town	1898-99
G.A.Faulkner	123	5/120	England	Johannesburg[1]	1909-10
J.H.Kallis	110	5/90	West Indies	Cape Town	1998-99
J.H.Kallis	139*	5/21	Bangladesh	Potchefstroom	2002-03

WEST INDIES

D.S.Atkinson	219	5/56	Australia	Bridgetown	1954-55
O.G.Smith	100	5/90	India	Delhi	1958-59
G.S.Sobers	104	5/63	India	Kingston	1961-62
G.S.Sobers	174	5/41	England	Leeds	1966

NEW ZEALAND

B.R.Taylor §	105	5/86	India	Calcutta	1964-65

§ in first Test.

INDIA

M.H.Mankad	184	5/196	England	Lord's	1952
P.R.Umrigar	172*	5/107	West Indies	Port-of-Spain	1961-62

PAKISTAN

Mushtaq Mohammad	201	5/49	New Zealand	Dunedin	1972-73
Mushtaq Mohammad	121	5/28	West Indies	Port-of-Spain	1976-77
Imran Khan	117	6/88 + 5/82	India	Faisalabad	1982-83
Wasim Akram	123	5/100	Australia	Adelaide	1989-90

ZIMBABWE

P.A.Strang	106*	5/212	Pakistan	Sheikhupura	1996-97

A 50 AND 10 WICKETS IN THE SAME MATCH

AUSTRALIA			Opponents		
H.Trumble	64* + 7*	8/65 + 4/108	England	The Oval	1902
A.K.Davidson	44 + 80	5/132 + 6/87	West Indies	Brisbane[2]	1960-61
A.R.Border	75 + 16*	7/46 + 4/50	West Indies	Sydney	1988-89
M.G.Bevan	85*	4/31 + 6/82	West Indies	Adelaide	1996-97

ENGLAND			Opponents		
W.Bates	55	7/28 + 7/74	Australia	Melbourne	1882-83
F.E.Woolley	62 + 4	5/29 + 5/20	Australia	The Oval	1912
A.W.Greig	51	5/98 + 5/51	New Zealand	Auckland	1974-75
J.K.Lever §	53	7/46 + 3/24	India	Delhi	1976-77
I.T.Botham	114	6/58 + 7/48	India	Bombay[3]	1979-80

§ in first Test.

SOUTH AFRICA			Opponents		
P.S.de Villiers	66*	6/81 + 4/27	Pakistan	Johannesburg[3]	1994-95

WEST INDIES			Opponents		
K.D.Boyce	72 + 9	5/70 + 6/77	England	The Oval	1973
M.D.Marshall	63	4/40 + 7/80	New Zealand	Bridgetown	1984-85

NEW ZEALAND

	Opponents				
R.J.Hadlee	51 + 17	5/34 + 6/68	West Indies	Dunedin	1979-80
R.J.Hadlee	54	9/52 + 6/71	Australia	Brisbane[2]	1985-86
R.J.Hadlee	68	6/80 + 4/60	England	Nottingham	1986
D.J.Nash	56	6/76 + 5/93	England	Lord's	1994
C.L.Cairns	72	3/73 + 7/27	West Indies	Hamilton	2004-05

INDIA	Opponents				
Kapil Dev	84	4/90 + 7/56	Pakistan	Chennai[1]	1979-80

PAKISTAN	Opponents				
Imran Khan	117	6/98 + 5/82	India	Faisalabad	1982-83
Abdul Qadir	61	5/88 + 5/98	England	Karachi[1]	1987-88

A CENTURY AND 5 DISMISSALS IN AN INNINGS BY A WICKET-KEEPER

D.T.Lindsay	182	6c	South Africa	v	Australia	Johannesburg[3]	1966-67
I.D.S.Smith	113*	4c, 1s	New Zealand	v	England	Auckland	1983-84
S.A.R.Silva	111	5c	Sri Lanka	v	India	Colombo (PSS)	1985-86
A.C.Gilchrist	113	4c, 1s	Australia	v	England	Sydney	2002-03

A 50 AND 10 DISMISSALS IN THE SAME MATCH

AUSTRALIA			Opponents		
A.C.Gilchrist	75	5c + 5c	New Zealand	Hamilton	1999-2000

The Captains

RESULT SUMMARY	Tests as				Opponents							Results			Toss
AUSTRALIA (42)	Captain	E	SA	W	N	I	P	SL	Z	B	W	L	D	Tie	Won
D.W.Gregory	**3**	3	-	-	-	-	-	-	-	-	2	1	0	0	2
W.L.Murdoch	**16**	16	-	-	-	-	-	-	-	-	5	7	4	0	7
T.P.Horan	**2**	2	-	-	-	-	-	-	-	-	0	2	0	0	1
H.H.Massie	**1**	1	-	-	-	-	-	-	-	-	1	0	0	0	1
J.M.Blackham	**8**	8	-	-	-	-	-	-	-	-	3	3	2	0	4
H.J.H.Scott	**3**	3	-	-	-	-	-	-	-	-	0	3	0	0	1
P.S.McDonnell	**6**	6	-	-	-	-	-	-	-	-	1	5	0	0	4
G.Giffen	**4**	4	-	-	-	-	-	-	-	-	2	2	0	0	3
G.H.S.Trott	**8**	8	-	-	-	-	-	-	-	-	5	3	0	0	5
J.Darling	**21**	18	3	-	-	-	-	-	-	-	7	4	10	0	7
H.Trumble	**2**	2	-	-	-	-	-	-	-	-	2	0	0	0	1
M.A.Noble	**15**	15	-	-	-	-	-	-	-	-	8	5	2	0	11
C.Hill	**10**	5	5	-	-	-	-	-	-	-	5	5	0	0	5
E.S.Gregory	**6**	3	3	-	-	-	-	-	-	-	2	1	3	0	1
W.W.Armstrong	**10**	10	-	-	-	-	-	-	-	-	8	0	2	0	4
H.L.Collins	**11**	8	3	-	-	-	-	-	-	-	5	2	4	0	7
W.Bardsley	**2**	2	-	-	-	-	-	-	-	-	0	0	2	0	1
J.Ryder	**5**	5	-	-	-	-	-	-	-	-	1	4	0	0	2
W.M.Woodfull	**25**	15	5	5	-	-	-	-	-	-	14	7	4	0	12
V.Y.Richardson	**5**	-	5	-	-	-	-	-	-	-	4	0	1	0	1
D.G.Bradman	**24**	19	-	-	-	5	-	-	-	-	15	3	6	0	10
W.A.Brown	**1**	-	-	-	1	-	-	-	-	-	1	0	0	0	0
A.L.Hassett	**24**	10	10	4	-	-	-	-	-	-	14	4	6	0	18
A.R.Morris	**2**	1	-	1	-	-	-	-	-	-	0	2	0	0	2
I.W.G.Johnson	**17**	9	-	5	-	2	1	-	-	-	7	5	5	0	6
R.R.Lindwall	**1**	-	-	-	-	1	-	-	-	-	0	0	1	0	0
I.D.Craig	**5**	-	5	-	-	-	-	-	-	-	3	0	2	0	3
R.Benaud	**28**	14	1	5	-	5	3	-	-	-	12	4	11	1	11
R.N.Harvey	**1**	1	-	-	-	-	-	-	-	-	1	0	0	0	0
R.B.Simpson	**39**	8	9	10	-	10	2	-	-	-	12	12	15	0	19
B.C.Booth	**2**	2	-	-	-	-	-	-	-	-	0	1	1	0	1
W.M.Lawry	**25**	9	4	5	-	7	-	-	-	-	9	8	8	0	8
B.N.Jarman	**1**	1	-	-	-	-	-	-	-	-	0	0	1	0	1
I.M.Chappell	**30**	16	-	5	6	-	3	-	-	-	15	5	10	0	17
G.S.Chappell	**48**	15	-	12	8	3	9	1	-	-	21	13	14	0	29
G.N.Yallop	**7**	6	-	-	-	-	1	-	-	-	1	6	0	0	6
K.J.Hughes	**28**	6	-	7	-	6	9	-	-	-	4	13	11	0	13
A.R.Border	**93**	29	6	18	17	11	6	6	-	-	32	22	38	1	46
M.A.Taylor	**50**	16	6	9	3	4	9	3	-	-	26	13	11	0	26
S.R.Waugh	**57**	9	6	12	6	10	6	3	3	2	41	9	7	0	31
A.C.Gilchrist	**6**	1	-	1	-	3	-	1	-	-	4	1	1	0	4
R.T.Ponting	**29**	5	6	3	5	1	3	4	-	2	21	3	5	0	10
	681	311	77	102	46	68	52	18	3	4	314	178	187	2	341

	Tests as				Opponents							Results			Toss
ENGLAND (77)	Captain	A	SA	W	N	I	P	SL	Z	B	W	L	D	Tie	Won
James Lillywhite	**2**	2	-	-	-	-	-	-	-	-	1	1	0	0	0
Lord Harris	**4**	4	-	-	-	-	-	-	-	-	2	1	1	0	2
A.Shaw	**4**	4	-	-	-	-	-	-	-	-	0	2	2	0	4
A.N.Hornby	**2**	2	-	-	-	-	-	-	-	-	0	1	1	0	1
Hon.I.F.W.Bligh	**4**	4	-	-	-	-	-	-	-	-	2	2	0	0	3

A.Shrewsbury	**7**	7	-	-	-	-	-	-	-	-	5	2	0	0	3
A.G.Steel	**4**	4	-	-	-	-	-	-	-	-	3	1	0	0	2
W.W.Read	**2**	1	1	-	-	-	-	-	-	-	2	0	0	0	0
W.G.Grace	**13**	13	-	-	-	-	-	-	-	-	8	3	2	0	4
C.A.Smith	**1**	-	1	-	-	-	-	-	-	-	1	-	0	0	0
M.P.Bowden	**1**	-	1	-	-	-	-	-	-	-	1	0	0	0	1
A.E.Stoddart	**8**	8	-	-	-	-	-	-	-	-	3	4	1	0	2
T.C.O'Brien	**1**	-	1	-	-	-	-	-	-	-	1	0	0	0	0
Lord Hawke	**4**	-	4	-	-	-	-	-	-	-	4	0	0	0	4
A.C.MacLaren	**22**	22	-	-	-	-	-	-	-	-	4	11	7	0	11
P.F.Warner	**10**	5	5	-	-	-	-	-	-	-	4	6	0	0	5
Hon F.S.Jackson	**5**	5	-	-	-	-	-	-	-	-	2	0	3	0	5
R.E.Foster	**3**	-	3	-	-	-	-	-	-	-	1	0	2	0	3
F.L.Fane	**5**	3	2	-	-	-	-	-	-	-	2	3	0	0	3
A.O.Jones	**2**	2	-	-	-	-	-	-	-	-	0	2	0	0	1
H.D.G.Leveson Gower	**3**	-	3	-	-	-	-	-	-	-	1	2	0	0	0
J.W.H.T.Douglas	**18**	12	6	-	-	-	-	-	-	-	8	8	2	0	7
C.B.Fry	**6**	3	3	-	-	-	-	-	-	-	4	0	2	0	4
Hon.L.H.Tennyson	**3**	3	-	-	-	-	-	-	-	-	0	1	2	0	2
F.T.Mann	**5**	-	5	-	-	-	-	-	-	-	2	1	2	0	3
A.E.R.Gilligan	**9**	5	4	-	-	-	-	-	-	-	4	4	1	0	2
A.W.Carr	**6**	4	2	-	-	-	-	-	-	-	1	0	5	0	3
A.P.F.Chapman	**17**	9	5	3	-	-	-	-	-	-	9	2	6	0	9
R.T.Stanyforth	**4**	-	4	-	-	-	-	-	-	-	2	1	1	0	0
G.T.S.Stevens	**1**	-	1	-	-	-	-	-	-	-	0	1	0	0	0
J.C.White	**4**	1	3	-	-	-	-	-	-	-	1	1	2	0	3
A.H.H.Gilligan	**4**	-	-	-	4	-	-	-	-	-	1	0	3	0	1
Hon.F.S.G.Calthorpe	**4**	-	-	4	-	-	-	-	-	-	1	1	2	0	2
R.E.S.Wyatt	**16**	5	5	5	1	-	-	-	-	-	3	5	8	0	12
D.R.Jardine	**15**	5	-	2	4	4	-	-	-	-	9	1	5	0	7
C.F.Walters	**1**	1	-	-	-	-	-	-	-	-	0	1	0	0	0
G.O.B.Allen	**11**	5	-	3	-	3	-	-	-	-	4	5	2	0	6
R.W.V.Robins	**3**	-	-	-	3	-	-	-	-	-	1	0	2	0	2
W.R.Hammond	**20**	8	5	3	1	3	-	-	-	-	4	3	13	0	12
N.W.D.Yardley	**14**	6	5	3	-	-	-	-	-	-	4	7	3	0	9
K.Cranston	**1**	-	-	-	1	-	-	-	-	-	0	0	1	0	0
F.G.Mann	**7**	-	5	-	2	-	-	-	-	-	2	0	5	0	5
F.R.Brown	**15**	5	5	1	4	-	-	-	-	-	5	6	4	0	3
N.D.Howard	**4**	-	-	-	-	4	-	-	-	-	1	0	3	0	2
D.B.Carr	**1**	-	-	-	-	1	-	-	-	-	0	1	0	0	1
L.Hutton	**23**	10	-	5	2	4	2	-	-	-	11	4	8	0	7
D.S.Sheppard	**2**	-	-	-	-	-	2	-	-	-	1	0	1	0	1
P.B.H.May	**41**	13	10	8	7	3	-	-	-	-	20	10	11	0	26
M.C.Cowdrey	**27**	6	5	10	-	2	4	-	-	-	8	4	15	0	17
E.R.Dexter	**30**	10	-	5	3	5	7	-	-	-	9	7	14	0	13
M.J.K.Smith	**25**	5	8	1	6	5	-	-	-	-	5	3	17	0	10
D.B.Close	**7**	-	-	1	-	3	3	-	-	-	6	0	1	0	4
T.W.Graveney	**1**	1	-	-	-	-	-	-	-	-	0	0	1	0	0
R.Illingworth	**31**	11	-	6	8	3	3	-	-	-	12	5	14	0	15
A.R.Lewis	**8**	-	-	-	-	5	3	-	-	-	1	2	5	0	3
M.H.Denness	**19**	6	-	5	2	3	3	-	-	-	6	5	8	0	9
J.H.Edrich	**1**	1	-	-	-	-	-	-	-	-	0	1	0	0	0
A.W.Greig	**14**	4	-	5	-	5	-	-	-	-	3	5	6	0	6
J.M.Brearley	**31**	18	-	-	3	5	5	-	-	-	18	4	9	0	13
G.Boycott	**4**	-	-	-	3	-	1	-	-	-	1	1	2	0	3
I.T.Botham	**12**	3	-	9	-	-	-	-	-	-	0	4	8	0	6

K.W.R.Fletcher	**7**	-	-	-	-	6	-	1	-	-	1	1	5	0	5
R.G.D.Willis	**18**	5	-	-	7	3	3	-	-	-	7	5	6	0	8
D.I.Gower	**32**	12	-	10	-	6	3	1	-	-	5	18	9	0	14
M.W.Gatting	**23**	6	-	1	6	2	8	-	-	-	2	5	16	0	14
J.E.Emburey	**2**	-	-	2	-	-	-	-	-	-	0	2	0	0	1
C.S.Cowdrey	**1**	-	-	1	-	-	-	-	-	-	0	1	0	0	0
G.A.Gooch	**34**	8	-	8	6	5	5	2	-	-	10	12	12	0	16
A.J.Lamb	**3**	1	-	2	-	-	-	-	-	-	0	3	0	0	2
A.J.Stewart	**15**	5	5	1	-	1	1	2	-	-	4	8	3	0	5
M.A.Atherton	**54**	15	8	17	6	3	3	-	2	-	13	21	20	0	23
N.Hussain	**45**	8	6	4	6	7	4	6	4	-	17	15	13	0	19
M.A.Butcher	**1**	-	-	-	1	-	-	-	-	-	0	0	1	0	1
M.P.Vaughan	**33**	5	9	8	2	-	2	3	-	4	19	6	8	0	14
M.E.Trescothick	**2**	-	-	-	1	-	1	-	-	-	1	1	0	0	0
A.Flintoff	**6**	-	-	-	-	3	-	3	-	-	2	2	2	0	3
A.J.Strauss	**4**	-	-	-	-	-	4	-	-	-	3	0	1	0	2
	852	311	130	134	88	94	67	18	6	4	298	245	309	0	409

SOUTH AFRICA (32)	Tests as Captain	Opponents									Results				Toss Won
		A	E	W	N	I	P	SL	Z	B	W	L	D	Tie	
O.R.Dunell	**1**	-	1	-	-	-	-	-	-	-	0	1	0	0	1
W.H.Milton	**2**	-	2	-	-	-	-	-	-	-	0	2	0	0	1
E.A.Halliwell	**3**	1	2	-	-	-	-	-	-	-	0	3	0	0	1
A.R.Richards	**1**	-	1	-	-	-	-	-	-	-	0	1	0	0	0
M.Bisset	**2**	-	2	-	-	-	-	-	-	-	0	2	0	0	0
H.M.Taberer	**1**	1	-	-	-	-	-	-	-	-	0	0	1	0	1
J.H.Anderson	**1**	1	-	-	-	-	-	-	-	-	0	1	0	0	0
P.W.Sherwell	**13**	5	8	-	-	-	-	-	-	-	5	6	2	0	5
S.J.Snooke	**5**	-	5	-	-	-	-	-	-	-	3	2	0	0	3
F.Mitchell	**3**	2	1	-	-	-	-	-	-	-	0	3	0	0	2
L.J.Tancred	**3**	1	2	-	-	-	-	-	-	-	0	2	1	0	2
H.W.Taylor	**18**	3	15	-	-	-	-	-	-	-	1	10	7	0	11
H.G.Deane	**12**	-	12	-	-	-	-	-	-	-	2	4	6	0	9
E.P.Nupen	**1**	-	1	-	-	-	-	-	-	-	1	0	0	0	0
H.B.Cameron	**9**	5	2	-	2	-	-	-	-	-	2	5	2	0	3
H.F.Wade	**10**	5	5	-	-	-	-	-	-	-	1	4	5	0	5
A.Melville	**10**	-	10	-	-	-	-	-	-	-	0	4	6	0	4
A.D.Nourse	**15**	5	10	-	-	-	-	-	-	-	1	9	5	0	7
J.E.Cheetham	**15**	5	3	-	7	-	-	-	-	-	7	5	3	0	6
D.J.McGlew	**14**	1	8	-	5	-	-	-	-	-	4	6	4	0	4
C.B.van Ryneveld	**8**	4	4	-	-	-	-	-	-	-	2	4	2	0	3
T.L.Goddard	**13**	5	5	-	3	-	-	-	-	-	1	2	10	0	4
P.L.van der Merwe	**8**	5	3	-	-	-	-	-	-	-	4	1	3	0	4
A.Bacher	**4**	4	-	-	-	-	-	-	-	-	4	0	0	0	4
K.C.Wessels	**16**	5	3	1	-	4	-	3	-	-	5	3	8	0	11
W.J.Cronje	**53**	7	15	5	7	8	6	2	3	-	27	11	15	0	22
G.Kirsten	**1**	-	-	-	-	-	1	-	-	-	0	0	1	0	0
S.M.Pollock	**26**	3	-	5	3	2	2	8	2	1	14	5	7	0	9
M.V.Boucher	**4**	3	-	-	-	-	-	-	-	1	2	2	0	0	2
G.C.Smith	**39**	5	10	8	6	2	2	2	2	2	15	12	12	0	23
J.H.Kallis	**1**	1	-	-	-	-	-	-	-	-	0	1	0	0	1
A.G.Prince	**2**	-	-	-	-	-	-	2	-	-	0	2	0	0	1
	314	77	130	19	33	16	11	17	7	4	101	113	100	0	149

WEST INDIES (28)	Tests as Captain	Opponents									Results				Toss Won
		A	E	SA	N	I	P	SL	Z	B	W	L	D	Tie	
R.K.Nunes	**4**	-	4	-	-	-	-	-	-	-	0	3	1	0	2
E.L.G.Hoad	**1**	-	1	-	-	-	-	-	-	-	0	0	1	0	1
N.Betancourt	**1**	-	1	-	-	-	-	-	-	-	0	1	0	0	0
M.P.Fernandes	**1**	-	1	-	-	-	-	-	-	-	1	0	0	0	1
G.C.Grant	**12**	5	7	-	-	-	-	-	-	-	3	7	2	0	5
R.C.Grant	**3**	-	3	-	-	-	-	-	-	-	0	1	2	0	2
G.A.Headley	**1**	-	1	-	-	-	-	-	-	-	0	0	1	0	1
G.E.Gomez	**1**	-	1	-	-	-	-	-	-	-	0	0	1	0	0
J.D.C.Goddard	**22**	4	11	-	2	5	-	-	-	-	8	7	7	0	12
J.B.Stollmeyer	**13**	3	5	-	-	5	-	-	-	-	3	4	6	0	7
D.S.Atkinson	**7**	3	-	-	4	-	-	-	-	-	3	3	1	0	3
F.C.M.Alexander	**18**	-	5	-	-	5	8	-	-	-	7	4	7	0	9
F.M.M.Worrell	**15**	5	5	-	-	5	-	-	-	-	9	3	2	1	9
G.S.Sobers	**39**	10	13	-	8	8	-	-	-	-	9	10	20	0	27
R.B.Kanhai	**13**	5	8	-	-	-	-	-	-	-	3	3	7	0	6
C.H.Lloyd	**74**	22	18	-	3	20	1	-	-	-	36	12	26	0	35
A.I.Kallicharran	**9**	3	-	-	-	6	-	-	-	-	1	2	6	0	4
D.L.Murray	**1**	1	-	-	-	-	-	-	-	-	0	0	1	0	1
I.V.A.Richards	**50**	11	19	-	7	8	5	-	-	-	27	8	15	0	23
C.G.Greenidge	**1**	-	-	-	-	-	1	-	-	-	0	1	0	0	1
D.L.Haynes	**4**	-	1	-	-	-	3	-	-	-	1	1	2	0	2
R.B.Richardson	**24**	9	10	1	-	-	3	1	-	-	11	6	7	0	12
C.A.Walsh	**22**	5	1	-	4	7	3	2	-	-	6	7	9	0	13
B.C.Lara	**44**	9	14	8	2	5	-	2	2	2	10	24	10	0	20
J.C.Adams	**15**	5	5	-	-	-	3	-	2	-	4	8	3	0	9
C.L.Hooper	**22**	-	-	5	2	8	2	3	2	-	4	11	7	0	15
R.D.Jacobs	**2**	-	-	-	-	-	-	-	-	2	2	0	0	0	1
S.Chanderpaul	**14**	3	-	4	3	-	2	2	-	-	1	10	3	0	11
	433	102	134	19	35	82	41	10	6	4	149	136	147	1	231

NEW ZEALAND (25)	Tests as Captain	Opponents									Results				Toss Won
		A	E	SA	W	I	P	SL	Z	B	W	L	D	Tie	
T.C.Lowry	**7**	-	7	-	-	-	-	-	-	-	0	2	5	0	5
M.L.Page	**7**	-	5	2	-	-	-	-	-	-	0	3	4	0	4
W.A.Hadlee	**8**	1	7	-	-	-	-	-	-	-	0	2	6	0	4
B.Sutcliffe	**4**	-	-	2	2	-	-	-	-	-	0	3	1	0	4
W.M.Wallace	**2**	-	-	2	-	-	-	-	-	-	0	1	1	0	0
G.O.Rabone	**5**	-	2	3	-	-	-	-	-	-	0	4	1	0	2
H.B.Cave	**9**	-	-	-	1	5	3	-	-	-	0	5	4	0	5
J.R.Reid	**34**	-	13	8	3	4	6	-	-	-	3	18	13	0	17
M.E.Chapple	**1**	-	1	-	-	-	-	-	-	-	0	0	1	0	0
B.W.Sinclair	**3**	-	2	-	-	1	-	-	-	-	0	1	2	0	3
G.T.Dowling	**19**	-	5	-	5	6	3	-	-	-	4	7	8	0	10
B.E.Congdon	**17**	6	5	-	3	-	3	-	-	-	1	7	9	0	4
G.M.Turner	**10**	2	-	-	-	6	2	-	-	-	1	6	3	0	2
J.M.Parker	**1**	-	-	-	-	-	1	-	-	-	0	0	1	0	0
M.G.Burgess	**10**	1	6	-	-	-	3	-	-	-	1	6	3	0	4
G.P.Howarth	**30**	5	7	-	7	3	3	5	-	-	11	7	12	0	17
J.V.Coney	**15**	6	3	-	3	-	3	-	-	-	5	4	6	0	8
J.J.Crowe	**6**	3	2	-	-	-	-	1	-	-	0	1	5	0	3
J.G.Wright	**14**	2	4	-	-	6	2	-	-	-	3	3	8	0	8
M.D.Crowe	**16**	4	3	-	-	-	3	4	2	-	2	7	7	0	8
I.D.S.Smith	**1**	-	-	-	-	-	-	1	-	-	0	0	1	0	1

K.R.Rutherford	**18**	2	3	4	2	1	4	2	-	-	2	11	5	0	12
L.K.Germon	**12**	-	2	-	2	3	3	-	2	-	1	5	6	0	6
S.P.Fleming	**78**	14	11	9	7	9	6	9	9	4	27	26	25	0	37
D.J.Nash	**3**	-	-	3	-	-	-	-	-	-	0	1	2	0	3
	330	46	88	33	35	44	45	22	13	4	61	130	139	0	165

INDIA (29)	Tests as Captain	Opponents A	E	SA	W	N	P	SL	Z	B	Results W	L	D	Tie	Toss Won
C.K.Nayudu	**4**	-	4	-	-	-	-	-	-	-	0	3	1	0	1
Maharajkumar of Vizianagram	**3**	-	3	-	-	-	-	-	-	-	0	2	1	0	1
Nawab of Pataudi, sr	**3**	-	3	-	-	-	-	-	-	-	0	1	2	0	3
N.B.Amarnath	**15**	5	-	-	5	-	5	-	-	-	2	6	7	0	4
V.S.Hazare	**14**	-	9	-	5	-	-	-	-	-	1	5	8	0	8
M.H.Mankad	**6**	-	-	-	1	-	5	-	-	-	0	1	5	0	1
Ghulam Ahmed	**3**	-	-	-	2	1	-	-	-	-	0	2	1	0	1
P.R.Umrigar	**8**	3	-	-	1	4	-	-	-	-	2	2	4	0	6
H.R.Adhikari	**1**	-	-	-	1	-	-	-	-	-	0	0	1	0	1
D.K.Gaekwad	**4**	-	4	-	-	-	-	-	-	-	0	4	0	0	2
Pankaj Roy	**1**	-	1	-	-	-	-	-	-	-	0	1	0	0	1
G.S.Ramchand	**5**	5	-	-	-	-	-	-	-	-	1	2	2	0	4
N.J.Contractor	**12**	-	5	-	2	-	5	-	-	-	2	2	8	0	7
Nawab of Pataudi, jr	**40**	11	8	-	10	11	-	-	-	-	9	19	12	0	20
C.G.Borde	**1**	1	-	-	-	-	-	-	-	-	0	1	0	0	0
A.L.Wadekar	**16**	-	11	-	5	-	-	-	-	-	4	4	8	0	7
S.Venkataraghavan	**5**	-	4	-	1	-	-	-	-	-	0	2	3	0	2
S.M.Gavaskar	**47**	9	14	-	6	4	13	1	-	-	9	8	30	0	22
B.S.Bedi	**22**	5	5	-	4	5	3	-	-	-	6	11	5	0	13
G.R.Viswanath	**2**	-	1	-	-	-	1	-	-	-	0	1	1	0	2
Kapil Dev	**34**	6	3	-	11	-	8	6	-	-	4	7	22	1	15
D.B.Vengsarkar	**10**	-	-	-	7	3	-	-	-	-	2	5	3	0	5
R.J.Shastri	**1**	-	-	-	1	-	-	-	-	-	1	0	0	0	1
K.Srikkanth	**4**	-	-	-	-	-	4	-	-	-	0	0	4	0	2
M.Azharuddin	**47**	8	9	4	3	9	3	8	3	-	14	14	19	0	29
S.R.Tendulkar	**25**	4	-	8	5	3	-	5	-	-	4	9	12	0	15
S.C.Ganguly	**49**	9	7	4	8	3	4	3	8	3	21	13	15	0	21
R.S.Dravid	**17**	2	3	-	4	1	5	2	-	-	5	4	8	0	10
V.K.Sehwag	**1**	-	-	-	-	-	-	1	-	-	1	0	0	0	1
	400	68	94	16	82	44	56	26	11	3	88	129	182	1	205

PAKISTAN (25)	Tests as Captain	Opponents A	E	SA	W	N	I	SL	Z	B	Results W	L	D	Tie	Toss Won
A.H.Kardar	**23**	1	4	-	5	3	10	-	-	-	6	6	11	0	10
Fazal Mahmood	**10**	2	-	-	3	-	5	-	-	-	2	2	6	0	6
Imtiaz Ahmed	**4**	1	3	-	-	-	-	-	-	-	0	2	2	0	4
Javed Burki	**5**	-	5	-	-	-	-	-	-	-	0	4	1	0	3
Hanif Mohammad	**11**	2	3	-	-	6	-	-	-	-	2	2	7	0	6
Saeed Ahmed	**3**	-	3	-	-	-	-	-	-	-	0	0	3	0	1
Intikhab Alam	**17**	3	6	-	2	6	-	-	-	-	1	5	11	0	12
Majid Khan	**3**	-	3	-	-	-	-	-	-	-	0	0	3	0	1
Mushtaq Mohammad	**19**	5	-	-	5	6	3	-	-	-	8	4	7	0	10
Wasim Bari	**6**	-	6	-	-	-	-	-	-	-	0	2	4	0	4
Asif Iqbal	**6**	-	-	-	-	-	6	-	-	-	0	2	4	0	3
Javed Miandad	**34**	9	8	-	4	7	-	6	-	-	14	6	14	0	12
Imran Khan	**48**	8	8	-	9	2	15	6	-	-	14	8	26	0	25

Zaheer Abbas	**14**	3	3	-	-	3	5	-	-	-	3	1	10	0	6
Wasim Akram	**25**	6	3	-	6	1	3	2	4	-	12	8	5	0	8
Waqar Younis	**17**	3	2	2	2	1	-	1	3	3	10	7	0	0	8
Saleem Malik	**12**	3	-	1	-	3	-	2	3	-	7	3	2	0	6
Rameez Raja	**5**	-	-	-	-	-	-	5	-	-	1	2	2	0	2
Saeed Anwar	**7**	-	-	3	-	2	-	2	-	-	1	4	2	0	3
Aamer Sohail	**6**	3	-	2	-	-	-	-	1	-	1	2	3	0	2
Rashid Latif	**6**	-	-	1	-	-	-	-	2	3	4	1	1	0	2
Moin Khan	**13**	-	3	-	3	2	-	4	1	-	4	2	7	0	5
Inzamamul Haq	**25**	1	7	1	1	3	8	4	-	-	8	9	8	0	13
Yousuf Youhana	**3**	2	-	1	-	-	-	-	-	-	1	2	0	0	2
Younis Khan	**2**	-	-	-	1	-	1	-	-	-	1	1	0	0	0
	324	52	67	11	41	45	56	32	14	6	100	85	139	0	153

	Tests as				Opponents							Results			Toss
SRI LANKA (10)	Captain	A	E	SA	W	N	I	P	Z	B	W	L	D	Tie	Won
B.Warnapura	**4**	-	1	-	-	-	1	2	-	-	0	3	1	0	2
L.R.D.Mendis	**19**	1	1	-	-	4	6	7	-	-	2	8	9	0	10
D.S.De Silva	**2**	-	-	-	-	2	-	-	-	-	0	2	0	0	1
R.S.Madugalle	**2**	1	1	-	-	-	-	-	-	-	0	2	0	0	0
A.Ranatunga	**56**	7	2	5	3	12	13	7	7	-	12	19	25	0	29
P.A.de Silva	**6**	1	1	-	-	-	-	4	-	-	0	4	2	0	3
H.P.Tillakaratne	**11**	3	3	-	2	2	-	1	-	-	1	4	6	0	3
S.T.Jayasuriya	**38**	3	6	7	3	-	3	7	6	3	18	12	8	0	26
M.S.Atapattu	**18**	2	-	3	2	2	3	2	2	2	8	6	4	0	8
D.P.M.D.Jayawardene	**9**	-	3	2	-	-	-	2	-	2	5	2	2	0	2
	165	18	18	17	10	22	26	32	15	7	46	62	57	0	84

	Tests as				Opponents							Results			Toss
ZIMBABWE (7)	Captain	A	E	SA	W	N	I	P	SL	B	W	L	D	Tie	Won
D.L.Houghton	**4**	-	-	-	-	2	2	-	-	-	0	2	2	0	1
A.Flower	**20**	-	2	2	2	2	-	6	6	-	1	10	9	0	10
A.D.R.Campbell	**21**	1	2	1	-	4	1	8	4	-	2	12	7	0	15
H.H.Streak	**21**	2	2	2	4	3	4	-	-	4	4	11	6	0	13
B.A.Murphy	**1**	-	-	-	-	-	-	-	-	1	0	0	1	0	1
S.V.Carlisle	**6**	-	-	-	-	-	2	-	3	1	1	5	0	0	4
T.Taibu	**10**	-	-	2	-	2	2	-	2	2	0	9	1	0	5
	83	3	6	7	6	13	11	14	15	8	8	49	26	0	49

	Tests as				Opponents							Results			Toss
BANGLADESH (4)	Captain	A	E	SA	W	N	I	P	SL	Z	W	L	D	Tie	Won
Naimur Rahman	**7**	-	-	-	-	-	1	1	1	4	0	6	1	0	3
Khaled Mashud	**12**	-	-	2	2	4	-	2	2	-	0	12	0	0	7
Khaled Mahmud	**9**	2	2	2	-	-	-	3	-	-	0	9	0	0	5
Habibul Bashar	**16**	2	2	-	2	-	2	-	4	4	1	12	3	0	7
	44	4	4	4	4	4	3	6	7	8	1	39	4	0	22

MOST CONSECUTIVE MATCHES AS CAPTAIN

			From	To
Australia	93	A.R.Border	1984-85	1993-94
England	52	M.A.Atherton	1993	1997-98
South Africa	36	G.C.Smith	2002-03	# 2005-06
West Indies	39	G.S.Sobers	1964-65	1971-72
New Zealand	61	S.P.Fleming	1999	# 2005-06
India	37	M.Azharuddin	1989-90	1996
Pakistan	23	A.H.Kardar	1952-53	1957-58
Sri Lanka	38	S.T.Jayasuriya	1999-2000	2002-03
Zimbabwe	19	A.D.R.Campbell	1996-97	1999-2000
Bangladesh	10	Khaled Mashud	2001-02	2002-03

In addition to those listed above, the following had unbroken captaincy runs of 20 or more matches.

50	M.A.Taylor (A)
35	P.B.H.May (E)
34	J.R.Reid (N)
33	S.C.Ganguly (I)
30	I.M.Chappell (A), S.R.Waugh (A)
29	C.H.Lloyd (W)
28	A.Ranatunga (SL)
26	W.J.Cronje(SA) - twice
25	W.M.Woodfull (A), R.Illingworth (E), D.I.Gower (E)
23	C.H.Lloyd (W), M.W.Gatting (E), N.Hussain (E), R.T.Ponting (A)
22	B.S.Bedi (I), S.M.Gavaskar (I), A.Ranatunga (SL), C.L.Hooper (W)
21	Nawab of Pataudi, jr (I), S.M.Pollock (SA)
20	M.J.K.Smith (E), W.M.Lawry (A), J.M.Brearley (E), Kapil Dev (I)

 # denotes current unbroken run.

WINNING ALL FIVE TOSSES IN A SERIES

Captains				Venue	
Hon F.S.Jackson	England	v	Australia	England	1905
M.A.Noble	Australia	v	England	England	1909
H.G.Deane	South Africa	v	England	South Africa	1927-28
J.D.C.Goddard	West Indies	v	India	India	1948-49
A.L.Hassett	Australia	v	England	England	1953
P.B.H.May (3))	England	v	West Indies	West Indies	1959-60
M.C.Cowdrey (2))					
M.C.Cowdrey	England	v	South Africa	England	1960
Nawab of Pataudi, jr	India	v	England	India	1963-64
G.S.Sobers	West Indies	v	England	England	1966
G.S.Sobers	West Indies	v	New Zealand	West Indies	1971-72
C.H.Lloyd	West Indies	v	India	West Indies	1982-83
M.A.Taylor	Australia	v	England	Australia	1998-99

The following Australian captains won five tosses during 6 match series in Australia: I.M.Chappell v England 1974-75; G.S.Chappell v West Indies 1975-76; G.N.Yallop v England 1978-79. K.W.R.Fletcher (England) won five successive tosses during the 6 match series in India in 1981-82. M.A.Taylor (Australia) won five successive tosses during the 6 match series in England in 1997. M.C.Cowdrey won the toss for England in nine consecutive Tests from 1959-60 to 1961. R.B.Richardson (West Indies) won the toss in all 4 Tests in the series against Australia in the West Indies in 1994-95 and 8 consecutive tosses from 1993-94 to 1995. M.A.Taylor (2 v P 1998-99; 5 v E 1998-99) and S.R.Waugh (4 v W 1998-99; 1 v SL 1999-2000) won the toss in 12 consecutive Tests for Australia.

CAPTAINS WHO SENT THE OPPOSITION IN

(§ In first match as captain. # In last Test as captain. ¶ In only Test as captain.)

AUSTRALIA	Opponents	Result		
P.S.McDonnell §	England	Lost by 13 runs	Sydney	1886-87
P.S.McDonnell	England	Lost by 126 runs	Sydney	1887-88
G.Giffen §	England	Lost by 94 runs	Melbourne	1894-95
M.A.Noble	England	Won by 9 wickets	Lord's	1909
A.L.Hassett	West Indies	Won by 7 wickets	Sydney	1951-52
A.L.Hassett	England	Drawn	Leeds	1953
A.R.Morris #	England	Lost by 38 runs	Sydney	1954-55
I.W.G.Johnson	England	Drawn	Sydney	1954-55
R.Benaud	England	Won by 9 wickets	Melbourne	1958-59
R.Benaud	Pakistan	Won by 8 wickets	Dacca	1959-60
R.Benaud	West Indies	Won by 2 wickets	Melbourne	1960-61
R.B.Simpson §	South Africa	Won by 8 wickets	Melbourne	1963-64
R.B.Simpson	Pakistan	Drawn	Melbourne	1964-65
R.B.Simpson	West Indies	Drawn	Port-of-Spain	1964-65
R.B.Simpson	South Africa	Lost by 8 wickets	Durban[2]	1966-67
W.M.Lawry	West Indies	Won by innings + 30 runs	Melbourne	1968-69
W.M.Lawry	India	Won by 10 wickets	Calcutta	1969-70
W.M.Lawry	England	Drawn	Perth	1970-71
I.M.Chappell §	England	Lost by 62 runs	Sydney	1970-71
I.M.Chappell	New Zealand	Drawn	Sydney	1973-74
I.M.Chappell	England	Won by 9 wickets	Perth	1974-75
I.M.Chappell	England	Drawn	Melbourne	1974-75
G.S.Chappell	West Indies	Won by 8 wickets	Melbourne	1975-76
G.S.Chappell	West Indies	Won by 7 wickets	Sydney	1975-76
G.S.Chappell	New Zealand	Won by 10 wickets	Auckland	1976-77
G.S.Chappell	England	Drawn	The Oval	1977
R.B.Simpson	West Indies	Lost by 198 runs	Port-of-Spain	1977-78
G.N.Yallop	England	Lost by 166 runs	Perth	1978-79
G.N.Yallop	England	Lost by 205 runs	Adelaide	1978-79
G.N.Yallop #	Pakistan	Lost by 71 runs	Melbourne	1978-79
K.J.Hughes §	Pakistan	Won by 7 wickets	Perth	1978-79
G.S.Chappell	England	Won by 6 wickets	Sydney	1979-80
G.S.Chappell	West Indies	Lost by 408 runs	Adelaide	1979-80
G.S.Chappell	New Zealand	Won by 10 wickets	Brisbane[2]	1980-81
G.S.Chappell	New Zealand	Won by 8 wickets	Perth	1980-81
G.S.Chappell	India	Lost by 59 runs	Melbourne	1980-81
K.J.Hughes	England	Won by 4 wickets	Nottingham	1981
K.J.Hughes	England	Drawn	Lord's	1981
G.S.Chappell	Pakistan	Won by 10 wickets	Brisbane[2]	1981-82
G.S.Chappell	New Zealand	Drawn	Wellington	1981-82
G.S.Chappell	England	Drawn	Perth	1982-83
G.S.Chappell	England	Won by 7 wickets	Brisbane[2]	1982-83
G.S.Chappell	England	Lost by 3 runs	Melbourne	1982-83
K.J.Hughes	Pakistan	Won by 10 wickets	Sydney	1983-84
K.J.Hughes	West Indies	Lost by innings + 112 runs	Perth	1984-85
A.R.Border	West Indies	Drawn	Melbourne	1984-85
A.R.Border	England	Won by 4 wickets	Lord's	1985
A.R.Border	New Zealand	Won by 4 wickets	Sydney	1985-86
A.R.Border	England	Lost by 7 wickets	Brisbane[2]	1986-87
A.R.Border	New Zealand	Won by 9 wickets	Brisbane[2]	1987-88
A.R.Border	New Zealand	Drawn	Melbourne	1987-88
A.R.Border	West Indies	Lost by 169 runs	Perth	1988-89

A.R.Border	West Indies	Lost by 285 runs	Melbourne	1988-89
A.R.Border	Pakistan	Drawn	Sydney	1989-90
A.R.Border	England	Won by 10 wickets	Brisbane[2]	1990-91
A.R.Border	West Indies	Lost by 343 runs	Bridgetown	1990-91
A.R.Border	India	Won by 10 wickets	Brisbane[2]	1991-92
A.R.Border	New Zealand	Drawn	Wellington	1992-93
M.A.Taylor	South Africa	Won by 2 wickets	Port Elizabeth	1996-97
M.A.Taylor	England	Drawn	Lord's	1997
M.A.Taylor	England	Won by innings + 61 runs	Leeds	1997
M.A.Taylor	England	Won by 7 wickets	Perth	1998-99
M.A.Taylor	England	Lost by 12 runs	Melbourne	1998-99
S.R.Waugh	Pakistan	Won by 10 wickets	Brisbane[2]	1999-2000
S.R.Waugh	Pakistan	Won by 4 wickets	Hobart	1999-2000
S.R.Waugh	New Zealand	Won by 6 wickets	Hamilton	1999-2000
S.R.Waugh	West Indies	Won by innings + 126 runs	Brisbane[2]	2000-01
S.R.Waugh	West Indies	Won by innings + 27 runs	Perth	2000-01
S.R.Waugh	India	Won by 10 wickets	Mumbai[3]	2000-01
S.R.Waugh	England	Won by innings + 118 runs	Birmingham	2001
S.R.Waugh	England	Won by 8 wickets	Lord's	2001
S.R.Waugh	South Africa	Won by 9 wickets	Melbourne	2001-02
S.R.Waugh	Bangladesh	Won by an innings and 132 runs	Darwin	2003-04
S.R.Waugh	Bangladesh	Won by an innings and 98 runs	Cairns	2003-04
R.T.Ponting	New Zealand	Won by 9 wickets	Christchurch	2004-05
R.T.Ponting	England	Lost by 2 runs	Birmingham	2005
ENGLAND	Opponents	Result		
A.E.Stoddart	Australia	Lost by innings + 147 runs	Sydney	1894-95
Lord Hawke	South Africa	Won by innings + 33 runs	Cape Town	1895-96
A.C.MacLaren	Australia	Lost by 229 runs	Melbourne	1901-02
A.O.Jones #	Australia	Lost by 49 runs	Sydney	1907-08
J.W.H.T.Douglas	Australia	Won by innings + 225 runs	Melbourne	1911-12
A.W.Carr	Australia	Drawn	Leeds	1926
A.P.F.Chapman	South Africa	Lost by 28 runs	Johannesburg[1]	1930-31
A.P.F.Chapman #	South Africa	Drawn	Durban[2]	1930-31
R.E.S.Wyatt	West Indies	Won by 4 wickets	Bridgetown	1934-35
R.E.S.Wyatt	West Indies	Lost by 217 runs	Port-of-Spain	1934-35
R.E.S.Wyatt #	South Africa	Drawn	The Oval	1935
G.O.B.Allen §	India	Won by 9 wickets	Lord's	1936
W.R.Hammond #	New Zealand	Drawn	Christchurch	1946-47
F.R.Brown §	New Zealand	Drawn	Manchester	1949
L.Hutton	Pakistan	Drawn	Lord's	1954
L.Hutton	Australia	Lost by innings + 154 runs	Brisbane[2]	1954-55
L.Hutton #	New Zealand	Won by 8 wickets	Dunedin	1954-55
P.B.H.May	Australia	Lost by 10 wickets	Adelaide	1958-59
E.R.Dexter	New Zealand	Won by innings + 47 runs	Wellington	1962-63
E.R.Dexter	Australia	Drawn	Lord's	1964
M.J.K.Smith	South Africa	Drawn	Johannesburg[3]	1964-65
M.J.K.Smith	South Africa	Drawn	The Oval	1965
D.B.Close #	Pakistan	Won by 8 wickets	The Oval	1967
R.Illingworth	Australia	Drawn	Nottingham	1972
M.H.Denness	Australia	Lost by 163 runs	Adelaide	1974-75
M.H.Denness	New Zealand	Drawn	Christchurch	1974-75
M.H.Denness #	Australia	Lost by innings + 85 runs	Birmingham	1975
A.W.Greig #	Australia	Lost by 45 runs	Melbourne	1976-77
G.Boycott	New Zealand	Lost by 72 runs	Wellington	1977-78
J.M.Brearley	Australia	Lost by 138 runs	Perth	1979-80
I.T.Botham	West Indies	Lost by innings + 79 runs	Port-of-Spain	1980-81

I.T.Botham	West Indies	Lost by 298 runs	Bridgetown	1980-81
J.M.Brearley #	Australia	Drawn	The Oval	1981
K.W.R.Fletcher	India	Drawn	Madras[1]	1981-82
R.G.D.Willis	Australia	Lost by 8 wickets	Adelaide	1982-83
D.I.Gower	Sri Lanka	Drawn	Lord's	1984
D.I.Gower	Australia	Drawn	Manchester	1985
D.I.Gower	Australia	Won by innings + 118 runs	Birmingham	1985
D.I.Gower	West Indies	Lost by innings + 30 runs	Bridgetown	1985-86
D.I.Gower	West Indies	Lost by 240 runs	St John's	1985-86
M.W.Gatting	New Zealand	Drawn	The Oval	1986
M.W.Gatting	Australia	Won by innings + 14 runs	Melbourne	1986-87
M.W.Gatting	Pakistan	Drawn	Birmingham	1987
M.W.Gatting	New Zealand	Drawn	Auckland	1987-88
G.A.Gooch	Sri Lanka	Won by 7 wickets	Lord's	1988
D.I.Gower	Australia	Lost by 210 runs	Leeds	1989
G.A.Gooch	West Indies	Drawn	Port-of-Spain	1989-90
A.J.Lamb §	West Indies	Lost by 164 runs	Bridgetown	1989-90
G.A.Gooch	Pakistan	Drawn	Birmingham	1992
G.A.Gooch	Australia	Lost by 179 runs	Manchester	1993
M.A.Atherton	Australia	Lost by 295 runs	Melbourne	1994-95
M.A.Atherton	South Africa	Drawn	Johannesburg[3]	1995-96
M.A.Atherton	Pakistan	Drawn	Leeds	1996
M.A.Atherton	New Zealand	Won by 4 wickets	Christchurch	1996-97
M.A.Atherton	New Zealand	Drawn	Auckland	1996-97
M.A.Atherton	West Indies	Won by 3 wickets	Port-of-Spain	1997-98
A.J.Stewart	South Africa	Lost by 10 wickets	Lord's	1998
A.J.Stewart	South Africa	Won by 8 wickets	Nottingham	1998
N.Hussain	New Zealand	Lost by 83 runs	The Oval	1999
N.Hussain	South Africa	Drawn	Port Elizabeth	1999-2000
N.Hussain	South Africa	Won by 2 wickets	Centurion	1999-2000
N.Hussain	Zimbabwe	Won by innings + 209 runs	Lord's	2000
N.Hussain	West Indies	Won by 2 wickets	Lord's	2000
N.Hussain	Sri Lanka	Won by innings + 111 runs	Birmingham	2002
N.Hussain	Australia	Lost 384 runs	Brisbane[2]	2002-03
M.P.Vaughan	West Indies	Won by 8 wickets	Bridgetown	2003-04
M.P.Vaughan	New Zealand	Won by 9 wickets	Leeds	2004
M.P.Vaughan	South Africa	Drawn	Centurion	2004-05
M.P.Vaughan	Bangladesh	Won by innings + 261 runs	Lord's	2005
M.P.Vaughan	Bangladesh	Won by innings + 27 runs	Chester-le-Street	2005

SOUTH AFRICA	Opponents	Result		
E.A.Halliwell §	England	Lost by 288 runs	Port Elizabeth	1895-96
P.W.Sherwell	Australia	Lost by 530 runs	Melbourne	1910-11
P.W.Sherwell #	Australia	Lost by 7 wickets	Sydney	1910-11
H.W.Taylor	England	Lost by innings + 18 runs	Birmingham	1924
H.G.Deane	England	Lost by 87 runs	Cape Town	1927-28
H.G.Deane	England	Won by 4 wickets	Johannesburg[1]	1927-28
H.G.Deane	England	Won by 8 wickets	Durban[2]	1927-28
H.G Deane	England	Drawn	The Oval	1929
T.L.Goddard	Australia	Drawn	Sydney	1963-64
P.L.van der Merwe #	Australia	Won by 7 wickets	Port Elizabeth	1966-67
K.C.Wessels §	West Indies	Lost by 52 runs	Bridgetown	1991-92
K.C.Wessels	India	Won by 9 wickets	Port Elizabeth	1992-93
K.C.Wessels	Australia	Drawn	Durban[2]	1993-94
W.J.Cronje	England	Drawn	Centurion	1995-96
W.J.Cronje	Australia	Won by 8 wickets	Centurion	1996-97
W.J.Cronje	Pakistan	Lost by 29 runs	Durban[2]	1997-98

W.J.Cronje	England	Drawn	Birmingham	1998
W.J.Cronje	West Indies	Won by 9 wickets	Durban[2]	1998-99
W.J.Cronje	Zimbabwe	Won by innings + 13 runs	Bloemfontein	1999-2000
W.J.Cronje	Zimbabwe	Won by innings + 219 runs	Harare	1999-2000
W.J.Cronje	England	Won by innings + 21 runs	Johannesburg[3]	1999-2000
S.M.Pollock	New Zealand	Won by 7 wickets	Port Elizabeth	2000-01
S.M.Pollock	New Zealand	Drawn	Johannesburg[3]	2000-01
S.M.Pollock	India	Won by 9 wickets	Bloemfontein	2001-02
M.V.Boucher	Australia	Won by 5 wickets	Durban[2]	2001-02
S.M.Pollock	Sri Lanka	Won by 3 wickets	Centurion	2002-03
G.C.Smith	England	Won by innings + 92 runs	Lord's	2003
G.C.Smith	West Indies	Won by innings + 65 runs	Durban[2]	2003-04
G.C.Smith	New Zealand	Won by 6 wickets	Wellington	2003-04
G.C.Smith	England	Drawn	Durban[2]	2004-05
G.C.Smith	Zimbabwe	Won by an innings + 62 runs	Centurion	2004-05
G.C.Smith	New Zealand	Drawn	Cape Town	2005-06
G.C.Smith	New Zealand	Won by 4 wickets	Johannesburg[3]	2005-06

WEST INDIES	Opponents	Result		
R.S.Grant	England	Drawn	Manchester	1939
F.C.M.Alexander	Pakistan	Lost by 41 runs	Dacca	1958-59
F.M.M.Worrell	India	Won by innings + 30 runs	Bridgetown	1961-62
G.S.Sobers	Australia	Lost by 382 runs	Sydney	1968-69
G.S.Sobers	New Zealand	Won by 5 wickets	Auckland	1968-69
G.S.Sobers	India	Drawn	Kingston	1970-71
G.S.Sobers	New Zealand	Drawn	Port-of-Spain	1971-72
R.B.Kanhai	England	Won by 7 wickets	Port-of-Spain	1973-74
R.B.Kanhai	England	Drawn	Bridgetown	1973-74
C.H.Lloyd	Pakistan	Drawn	Lahore[2]	1974-75
C.H.Lloyd	India	Won by 10 wickets	Kingston	1975-76
C.H.Lloyd	Pakistan	Drawn	Georgetown	1976-77
C.H.Lloyd	Pakistan	Lost by 266 runs	Port-of-Spain	1976-77
C.H.Lloyd	Australia	Won by innings + 106 runs	Port-of-Spain	1977-78
C.H.Lloyd	Australia	Won by 9 wickets	Bridgetown	1977-78
A.I.Kallicharran	India	Drawn	Bombay[3]	1978-79
D.L.Murray ¶	Australia	Drawn	Brisbane[2]	1979-80
C.H.Lloyd	England	Drawn	Manchester	1980
I.V.A.Richards §	England	Drawn	Kingston	1980
C.H.Lloyd	Australia	Won by 5 wickets	Adelaide	1981-82
C.H.Lloyd	India	Won by 4 wickets	Kingston	1982-83
C.H.Lloyd	India	Drawn	Port-of-Spain	1982-83
C.H.Lloyd	India	Won by 10 wickets	Bridgetown	1982-83
C.H.Lloyd	India	Drawn	St John's	1982-83
I.V.A.Richards	Australia	Drawn	Port-of-Spain	1983-84
C.H.Lloyd	Australia	Won by 10 wickets	Bridgetown	1983-84
C.H.Lloyd	Australia	Won by 10 wickets	Kingston	1983-84
C.H.Lloyd	England	Won by 9 wickets	Lord's	1984
C.H.Lloyd	Australia	Won by 8 wickets	Brisbane[2]	1984-85
I.V.A.Richards	New Zealand	Won by 10 wickets	Bridgetown	1984-85
I.V.A.Richards	England	Won by 7 wickets	Port-of-Spain	1985-86
I.V.A.Richards	England	Won by 10 wickets	Port-of-Spain	1985-86
I.V.A.Richards	New Zealand	Drawn	Wellington	1986-87
I.V.A.Richards	India	Drawn	Bombay[3]	1987-88
I.V.A.Richards	Pakistan	Won by 2 wickets	Bridgetown	1987-88
I.V.A.Richards	England	Won by 10 wickets	Leeds	1988
I.V.A.Richards	India	Won by 8 wickets	Bridgetown	1988-89
I.V.A.Richards	India	Won by 7 wickets	Kingston	1988-89

I.V.A.Richards	Australia	Drawn	Port-of-Spain	1990-91
I.V.A.Richards	England	Lost by 115 runs	Leeds	1991
I.V.A.Richards	England	Won by 7 wickets	Birmingham	1991
R.B.Richardson	England	Won by innings + 44 runs	Georgetown	1993-94
R.B.Richardson	England	Lost by 208 runs	Bridgetown	1993-94
C.A.Walsh	New Zealand	Drawn	Christchurch	1994-95
R.B.Richardson	Australia	Drawn	St John's	1994-95
R.B.Richardson	Australia	Won by 9 wickets	Port-of-Spain	1994-95
R.B.Richardson	England	Won by 9 wickets	Leeds	1995
C.A.Walsh	New Zealand	Won by 10 wickets	Bridgetown	1995-96
C.A.Walsh	Australia	Lost by 123 runs	Brisbane^2	1996-97
C.A.Walsh	Sri Lanka	Won by 6 wickets	St John's	1996-97
B.C.Lara	England	Drawn	Bridgetown	1997-98
B.C.Lara	England	Won by innings + 52 runs	St John's	1997-98
B.C.Lara	South Africa	Lost by 178 runs	Port Elizabeth	1998-99
B.C.Lara	South Africa	Lost by 351 runs	Centurion	1998-99
B.C.Lara	New Zealand	Lost by innings + 105 runs	Wellington	1999-2000
J.C.Adams	Pakistan	Drawn	Georgetown	1999-2000
J.C.Adams	Pakistan	Won by 1 wkt	St John's	1999-2000
J.C.Adams	England	Won by innings + 93 runs	Birmingham	2000
J.C.Adams	England	Lost by 158 runs	The Oval	2000
J.C.Adams	Australia	Lost by 352 runs	Melbourne	2000-01
C.L.Hooper	South Africa	Drawn	Bridgetown	2000-01
C.L.Hooper	South Africa	Lost by 82 runs	St John's	2000-01
C.L.Hooper	Zimbabwe	Drawn	Harare	2001-02
C.L.Hooper	Pakistan	Lost by 244 runs	Sharjah	2001-02
C.L.Hooper	India	Drawn	Georgetown	2001-02
C.L.Hooper	India	Lost by 7 runs	Port-of-Spain	2001-02
C.L.Hooper	India	Won by 10 wickets	Bridgetown	2001-02
C.L.Hooper	India	Drawn	St John's	2001-02
C.L.Hooper	New Zealand	Lost by 204 runs	Bridgetown	2001-02
C.L.Hooper	New Zealand	Drawn	St George's	2001-02
R.D.Jacobs §	Bangladesh	Won by innings + 310 runs	Dhaka	2002-03
B.C.Lara	Australia	Lost by 9 wickets	Bridgetown	2002-03
B.C.Lara	South Africa	Lost 10 wickets	Centurion	2003-04
B.C.Lara	Sri Lanka	Won by 7 wickets	Kingston	2003-04
B.C.Lara	England	Lost 210 runs	Lord's	2004
S.Chanderpaul	Sri Lanka	Lost 240 runs	Kandy	2005-06
S.Chanderpaul	Australia	Lost 379 runs	Brisbane^2	2005-06
S.Chanderpaul	New Zealand	Lost 27 runs	Auckland	2005-06

NEW ZEALAND	Opponents	Result		
T.C.Lowry	England	Drawn	Auckland	1929-30
T.C.Lowry #	England	Drawn	Manchester	1931
B.Sutcliffe	West Indies	Drawn	Auckland	1951-52
B.Sutcliffe	South Africa	Lost by 9 wickets	Johannesburg^2	1953-54
J.R.Reid	South Africa	Drawn	Auckland	1963-64
J.R.Reid	Pakistan	Drawn	Lahore^2	1964-65
G.T.Dowling	India	Lost by 272 runs	Auckland	1967-68
G.T.Dowling	West Indies	Won by 6 wickets	Wellington	1968-69
G.T.Dowling	England	Drawn	Auckland	1970-71
B.E.Congdon	England	Drawn	Lord's	1973
B.E.Congdon	Australia	Won by 5 wickets	Christchurch	1973-74
B.E.Congdon	Australia	Lost by 297 runs	Auckland	1973-74
G.M.Turner	Australia	Drawn	Christchurch	1976-77
M.G.Burgess	Pakistan	Lost by 128 runs	Christchurch	1978-79
G.P.Howarth	West Indies	Drawn	Christchurch	1979-80

G.P.Howarth	West Indies	Drawn	Auckland	1979-80
G.P.Howarth	Australia	Drawn	Melbourne	1980-81
G.P.Howarth	Australia	Won by 5 wickets	Auckland	1981-82
G.P.Howarth	Australia	Lost by 8 wickets	Christchurch	1981-82
G.P.Howarth	Sri Lanka	Won by 6 wickets	Wellington	1982-83
G.P.Howarth	England	Won by 5 wickets	Leeds	1983
G.P Howarth	England	Lost by 127 runs	Lord's	1983
G.P.Howarth	Sri Lanka	Drawn	Colombo (SSC)	1983-84
G.P.Howarth	Pakistan	Won by innings + 99 runs	Auckland	1984-85
G.P.Howarth	Pakistan	Won by 2 wickets	Dunedin	1984-85
G.P.Howarth #	West Indies	Lost by 10 wickets	Kingston	1984-85
J.V.Coney	Australia	Won by innings + 41 runs	Brisbane[2]	1985-86
J.V.Coney	Australia	Won by 6 wickets	Perth	1985-86
J.V.Coney	Australia	Drawn	Wellington	1985-86
J.V.Coney	Australia	Drawn	Christchurch	1985-86
J.V.Coney	England	Won by 8 wickets	Nottingham	1986
J.V.Coney #	West Indies	Won by 5 wickets	Christchurch	1986-87
J.J.Crowe §	Sri Lanka	Drawn	Colombo (CCC)	1986-87
J.J.Crowe	England	Drawn	Christchurch	1987-88
J.G.Wright	Australia	Drawn	Perth	1989-90
J.G.Wright	England	Drawn	Lord's	1990
J.G.Wright #	England	Lost by 114 runs	Birmingham	1990
M.D.Crowe	Pakistan	Lost by 65 runs	Faisalabad	1990-91
I.D.S.Smith ¶	Sri Lanka	Drawn	Auckland	1990-91
M.D.Crowe	England	Lost by innings + 4 runs	Christchurch	1991-92
M.D.Crowe	England	Lost by 168 runs	Auckland	1991-92
K.R.Rutherford §	Pakistan	Lost by 33 runs	Hamilton	1992-93
M.D.Crowe	Australia	Lost by innings + 60 runs	Christchurch	1992-93
M.D.Crowe	Australia	Drawn	Perth	1993-94
K.R.Rutherford	Pakistan	Won 5 wickets	Christchurch	1993-94
K.R.Rutherford	Sri Lanka	Lost by 241 runs	Napier	1994-95
K.R.Rutherford	Sri Lanka	Drawn	Dunedin	1994-95
L.K.Germon	Pakistan	Lost by 161 runs	Christchurch	1995-96
L.K.Germon	West indies	Drawn	St John's	1995-96
S.P.Fleming	Zimbabwe	Drawn	Harare	1997-98
S.P.Fleming	Australia	Lost by 186 runs	Brisbane[2]	1997-98
D.J.Nash	South Africa	Drawn	Auckland	1998-99
S.P.Fleming	India	Drawn	Mohali	1999-2000
S.P.Fleming	Pakistan	Lost by 299 runs	Auckland	2000-01
S.P.Fleming	Pakistan	Won by innings + 185 runs	Hamilton	2000-01
S.P.Fleming	Australia	Drawn	Brisbane[2]	2001-02
S.P.Fleming	Australia	Drawn	Hobart	2001-02
S.P.Fleming	Bangladesh	Won by innings + 74 runs	Wellington	2001-02
S.P.Fleming	England	Lost by 98 runs	Christchurch	2001-02
S.P.Fleming	England	Drawn	Wellington	2001-02
S.P.Fleming	India	Won by 10 wickets	Wellington	2002-03
S.P.Fleming	India	Won by 4 wickets	Hamilton	2002-03
S.P.Fleming	South Africa	Won by 9 wickets	Auckland	2003-04
S.P.Fleming	Australia	Drawn	Wellington	2004-05
S.P.Fleming	Sri Lanka	Won by innings + 38 runs	Wellington	2004-05
S.P.Fleming	West Indies	Drawn	Napier	2005-06

INDIA	Opponents	Result		
Nawab of Pataudi, sr	England	Drawn	Manchester	1946
N.B.Amarnath	Pakistan	Drawn	Calcutta	1952-53
P.R.Umrigar	Australia	Lost by 94 runs	Calcutta	1956-57
Nawab of Pataudi, jr	England	Drawn	Kanpur	1963-64

Nawab of Pataudi, jr	Australia	Drawn	Calcutta	1964-65
Nawab of Pataudi, jr	Australia	Lost by 39 runs	Brisbane[2]	1967-68
Nawab of Pataudi, jr	Australia	Lost by 144 runs	Sydney	1967-68
Nawab of Pataudi, jr	New Zealand	Lost by 6 wickets	Christchurch	1967-68
A.L.Wadekar	West Indies	Drawn	Bridgetown	1970-71
Nawab of Pataudi, jr	West Indies	Lost by 267 runs	Bangalore	1974-75
B.S.Bedi	West Indies	Drawn	Port-of-Spain	1975-76
S.M.Gavaskar	Australia	Drawn	Adelaide	1980-81
S.M.Gavaskar	New Zealand	Lost by 62 runs	Wellington	1980-81
S.M.Gavaskar	Pakistan	Drawn	Lahore[2] (1st)	1982-83
S.M.Gavaskar	Pakistan	Drawn	Lahore[2] (5th)	1982-83
Kapil Dev	Pakistan	Drawn	Jullundur	1983-84
Kapil Dev	West Indies	Lost by 138 runs	Ahmedabad	1983-84
Kapil Dev	Australia	Drawn	Melbourne	1985-86
Kapil Dev	England	Won by 5 wickets	Lord's	1986
D.B.Vengsarkar	West Indies	Drawn	Georgetown	1988-89
D.B.Vengsarkar	West Indies	Lost by 217 runs	Port-of-Spain	1988-89
K.Srikkanth §	Pakistan	Drawn	Karachi[1]	1989-90
M.Azharuddin	New Zealand	Drawn	Auckland	1990-91
M.Azharuddin	England	Lost by 247 runs	Lord's	1990
M.Azharuddin	Australia	Drawn	Sydney	1991-92
M.Azharuddin	Australia	Lost by 38 runs	Adelaide	1991-92
M.Azharuddin	South Africa	Drawn	Durban[2]	1992-93
M.Azharuddin	Sri Lanka	Drawn	Kandy	1993-94
M.Azharuddin	England	Drawn	Lord's	1996
S.R.Tendulkar	India	Lost by 328 runs	Durban[2]	1996-97
S.R.Tendulkar	West Indies	Lost by 38 runs	Bridgetown	1996-97
S.R.Tendulkar	Sri Lanka	Drawn	Colombo (SSC)	1997-98
S.R.Tendulkar	Sri Lanka	Drawn	Mohali	1997-98
M.Azharuddin	Zimbabwe	Lost by 61 runs	Harare	1998-99
M.Azharuddin	New Zealand	Drawn	Hamilton	1998-99
S.R.Tendulkar	Australia	Lost by 180 runs	Melbourne	1999-2000
S.R.Tendulkar	Australia	Lost by innings + 141 runs	Sydney	1999-2000
S.C.Ganguly	Sri Lanka	Won by 7 wickets	Kandy	2001-02
S.C.Ganguly	South Africa	Drawn	Port Elizabeth	2001-02
S.C.Ganguly	England	Won by 10 wickets	Mohali	2001-02
S.C.Ganguly	West Indies	Lost by 155 runs	Kingston	2001-02
S.C.Ganguly	Australia	Drawn	Brisbane[2]	2003-04
S.C.Ganguly	Pakistan	Won by Innings + 131 runs	Rawalpindi[2]	2003-04
S.C.Ganguly	Bangladesh	Won by innings + 140 runs	Dhaka	2004-05
S.C.Ganguly	Pakistan	Drawn	Mohali	2004-05
S.C.Ganguly	Zimbabwe	Won by 10 wickets	Harare	2005-06
R.S.Dravid	Pakistan	Lost by 341 runs	Karachi[1]	2005-06
R.S.Dravid	England	Lost by 212 runs	Mumbai[3]	2005-06

PAKISTAN	Opponents	Result		
Fazal Mahmood §	West Indies	Won by 10 wickets	Karachi[1]	1958-59
Javed Burki	England	Lost by innings + 117 runs	Leeds	1962
Javed Burki	England	Drawn	Nottingham	1962
Hanif Mohammad	New Zealand	Drawn	Wellington	1964-65
Hanif Mohammad	New Zealand	Won by innings + 64 runs	Rawalpindi[1]	1964-65
Intikhab Alam	Australia	Lost by 52 runs	Sydney	1972-73
Mushtaq Mohammad	India	Won by 8 wickets	Lahore[2]	1978-79
Mushtaq Mohammad	New Zealand	Drawn	Auckland	1978-79
Javed Miandad	Australia	Lost by 286 runs	Perth	1981-82
Javed Miandad	Sri Lanka	Won by innings + 102 runs	Lahore[2]	1981-82
Imran Khan	Australia	Won by 9 wickets	Lahore[2]	1982-83

Imran Khan	India	Won by innings + 86 runs	Karachi[1]	1982-83
Imran Khan	India	Won by 10 wickets	Faisalabad	1982-83
Zaheer Abbas	Australia	Lost by innings + 9 runs	Perth	1983-84
Zaheer Abbas	England	Drawn	Lahore[2]	1983-84
Javed Miandad	Sri Lanka	Won by 8 wickets	Sialkot	1985-86
Imran Khan	India	Drawn	Calcutta	1986-87
Imran Khan	England	Drawn	Manchester	1987
Imran Khan	West Indies	Drawn	Port-of-Spain	1987-88
Imran Khan	New Zealand	Drawn	Wellington	1988-89
Imran Khan	India	Drawn	Faisalabad	1989-90
Imran Khan	India	Drawn	Lahore[2]	1989-90
Imran Khan	India	Drawn	Sialkot	1989-90
Imran Khan	Australia	Lost by 92 runs	Melbourne	1989-90
Javed Miandad	New Zealand	Won by innings + 43 runs	Karachi[1]	1990-91
Imran Khan	Sri Lanka	Won by 3 wickets	Faisalabad	1991-92
Wasim Akram	West Indies	Lost by 10 wickets	Bridgetown	1992-93
Saleem Malik §	New Zealand	Won 5 wickets	Auckland	1993-94
Saleem Malik	Sri Lanka	Won by innings + 52 runs	Kandy	1994-95
Saleem Malik	Australia	Drawn	Rawalpindi[2]	1994-95
Rameez Raja	Sri Lanka	Lost by 42 runs	Faisalabad	1995-96
Wasim Akram	New Zealand	Won by innings + 13 runs	Rawalpindi[2]	1996-97
Wasim Akram	West Indies	Won by innings + 29 runs	Rawalpindi[2]	1997-98
Aamer Sohail	South Africa	Drawn	Johannesburg[3]	1997-98
Rashid Latif	South Africa	Lost by 259 runs	Port Elizabeth	1997-98
Moin Khan	Zimbabwe	Drawn	Lahore[2]	1998-99
Saeed Anwar	Sri Lanka	Lost by 57 runs	Peshawar[2]	1999-2000
Moin Khan	New Zealand	Drawn	Christchurch	2000-01
Waqar Younis	England	Lost by innings + 9 runs	Lord's	2001
Waqar Younis	Bangladesh	Won by innings + 178 runs	Dhaka	2001-02
Waqar Younis	South Africa	Lost by 10 wickets	Durban[2]	2002-03
Rashid Latif	Bangladesh	Won by 7 wickets	Karachi[1]	2003-04
Inzamamul Haq	New Zealand	Drawn	Hamilton	2003-04
Inzamamul Haq	Sri Lanka	Won by 6 wickets	Karachi[1]	2004-05
Inzamamul Haq	Australia	Lost by 491 runs	Perth	2004-05
Inzamamul Haq	Sri Lanka	Drawn	Colombo (SSC)	2005-06
Inzamamul Haq	Sri Lanka	Won by 8 wickets	Kandy	2005-06
Inzamamul Haq	England	Match awarded to England	The Oval	2006

SRI LANKA	Opponents	Result		
D.S.de Silva §	New Zealand	Lost by innings + 25 runs	Christchurch	1982-83
L.R.D.Mendis	Pakistan	Won by 8 wickets	Colombo (CCC)	1985-86
A.Ranatunga §	Australia	Drawn	Brisbane[2]	1989-90
A.Ranatunga	Australia	Lost by 173 runs	Hobart	1989-90
A.Ranatunga	New Zealand	Drawn	Wellington	1990-91
A.Ranatunga	New Zealand	Drawn	Hamilton	1990-91
P.A.de Silva	Pakistan	Drawn	Gujranwala	1991-92
A.Ranatunga	Australia	Lost by 16 runs	Colombo (SSC)	1992-93
A.Ranatunga	Australia	Drawn	Colombo (RPS)	1992-93
A.Ranatunga	New Zealand	Drawn	Moratuwa	1992-93
A.Ranatunga	Australia	Lost by 10 wickets	Melbourne	1995-96
A.Ranatunga	Zimbabwe	Won by 10 wickets	Colombo (SSC)	1996-97
A.Ranatunga	New Zealand	Lost by innings + 36 runs	Dunedin	1996-97
A.Ranatunga	West Indies	Drawn	Arnos Vale	1996-97
A.Ranatunga	India	Drawn	Mumbai[3]	1997-98
A.Ranatunga	England	Won by 10 wickets	The Oval	1998
A.Ranatunga	India	Drawn	Colombo (SSC)	1998-99
S.T.Jayasuriya	Zimbabwe	Drawn	Bulawayo[2]	1999-2000

S.T.Jayasuriya	Zimbabwe	Won by 6 wickets	Harare	1999-2000
S.T.Jayasuriya	Zimbabwe	Drawn	Harare	1999-2000
S.T.Jayasuriya	Pakistan	Won by 2 wickets	Rawalpindi[2]	1999-2000
S.T.Jayasuriya	Pakistan	Lost by 222 runs	Karachi[1]	1999-2000
S.T.Jayasuriya	South Africa	Lost by 7 runs	Kandy	2000-01
S.T.Jayasuriya	South Africa	Drawn	Colombo (SSC)	2000-01
S.T.Jayasuriya	South Africa	Lost by innings + 7 runs	Centurion	2000-01
S.T.Jayasuriya	India	Won by 10 wickets	Galle	2001-02
S.T.Jayasuriya	Pakistan	Won by 8 wickets	Lahore[2]	2001-02
S.T.Jayasuriya	Bangladesh	Won by innings + 196 runs	Colombo (PSS)	2002-03
M.S.Atapattu	Zimbabwe	Won by innings + 240 runs	Harare	2003-04
M.S.Atapattu	Zimbabwe	Won by innings + 254 runs	Bulawayo[2]	2003-04
M.S.Atapattu	Australia	Lost by innings + 149 runs	Darwin	2004-05
M.S.Atapattu	Australia	Drawn	Cairns	2004-05
M.S.Atapattu	Bangladesh	Won by innings + 96 runs	Colombo (RPS)	2005-06

ZIMBABWE	Opponents	Result		
A.Flower	Pakistan	Lost by 52 runs	Rawalpindi[2]	1993-94
A.Flower	Pakistan	Drawn	Lahore[2]	1993-94
A.Flower	New Zealand	Drawn	Hamilton	1995-96
A.D.R.Campbell	England	Drawn	Harare	1996-97
A.D.R.Campbell	Pakistan	Won by 7 wickets	Peshawar[2]	1998-99
A.Flower	West Indies	Lost by 35 runs	Port-of-Spain	1999-2000
A.Flower	England	Drawn	Nottingham	2000
H.H.Streak	Bangladesh	Won by innings + 32 runs	Bulawayo[2]	2000-01
H.H.Streak	Bangladesh	Won by 8 wickets	Harare	2000-01
B.A.Murphy §	Bangladesh	Drawn	Dhaka	2001-02
S.V.Carlisle	Sri Lanka	Lost by innings + 166 runs	Colombo (SSC)	2001-02
A.D.R.Campbell	Pakistan	Lost by 119 runs	Harare	2002-03
H.H.Streak	England	Lost by innings + 92 runs	Lord's	2003
H.H.Streak	Australia	Lost by innings + 175 runs	Perth	2003-04
H.H.Streak	Bangladesh	Drawn	Bulawayo[2]	2003-04
T.Taibu	New Zealand	Lost by innings + 294 runs	Harare	2005-06

BANGLADESH	Opponents	Result		
Naimur Rahman	Zimbabwe	Lost by 8 wickets	Chaittagong	2001-02
Khaled Mashud	New Zealand	Lost by innings + 52 runs	Hamilton	2001-02
Khaled Mashud	Sri Lanka	Lost by 288 runs	Colombo (SSC)	2002-03
Khaled Mashud	South Africa	Lost by innings + 107 runs	East London	2002-03
Khaled Mahmud	England	Lost by 329 runs	Chittagong[1]	2003-04

CAPTAINS WHO SENT THE OPPOSITION IN — SUMMARY

Country	Captains	Instances	W	L	D
Australia	17	76	40	20	16
England	32	70	21	24	25
South Africa	11	33	18	7	8
West Indies	16	78	32	21	25
New Zealand	17	66	18	18	30
India	14	47	6	17	24
Pakistan	17	47	18	13	16
Sri Lanka	6	33	11	9	13
Zimbabwe	6	16	3	7	6
Bangladesh	3	5	0	5	0
Totals	139	471	167	141	163

CENTURY ON DEBUT AS CAPTAIN

0	143	G.H.S.Trott	Australia	v	England	Lord's	1896
109	50*	A.C.MacLaren	England	v	Australia	Sydney	1897-98
133	22	M.A.Noble	Australia	v	England	Sydney	1903-04
191		C.Hill	Australia	v	South Africa	Sydney	1910-11
109	8	H.W.Taylor	South Africa	v	England	Durban[1]	1913-14
12	158	W.W.Armstrong	Australia	v	England	Sydney	1920-21
112		A.L.Hassett	Australia	v	South Africa	Johannesburg[2]	1949-50
164*		V.J.Hazare	India	v	England	Delhi	1951-52
10	104	J.B.Stollmeyer	West Indies	v	Australia	Sydney	1951-52
107	68	G.O.Rabone	New Zealand	v	South Africa	Durban[2]	1953-54
104*	48	D.J.McGlew	South Africa	v	England	Manchester	1955
239	5	G.T.Dowling	New Zealand	v	India	Christchurch	1967-68
126		B.E.Congdon	New Zealand	v	West Indies	Bridgetown	1971-72
30	163	C.H.Lloyd	West Indies	v	India	Bangalore	1974-75
123	109*	G.S.Chappell	Australia	v	West Indies	Brisbane[2]	1975-76
116	35*	S.M.Gavaskar	India	v	New Zealand	Auckland	1975-76
7	102	G.N.Yallop	Australia	v	England	Brisbane[2]	1978-79
120*		J.J.Crowe	New Zealand	v	Sri Lanka	Colombo (CCC)	1986-87
10	102	D.B.Vengsarkar	India	v	West Indies	Delhi	1987-88
119	10	A.J.Lamb	England	v	West Indies	Bridgetown	1989-90
121		D.L.Houghton	Zimbabwe	v	India	Harare	1992-93
203*		S.Chanderpaul	West Indies	v	South Africa	Georgetown	2004-05
30	128	A.J.Strauss	England	v	Pakistan	Lord's	2006

HIGHEST INDIVIDUAL INNINGS BY CAPTAINS

400*	B.C.Lara	West Indies	v	England	St John's	2003-04
374	D.P.M.D.Jayawardene	Sri Lanka	v	South Africa	Colombo (SSC)	2006-07
334*	M.A.Taylor	Australia	v	Pakistan	Peshawar[2]	1998-99
333	G.A.Gooch	England	v	India	Lord's	1990
311	R.B.Simpson	Australia	v	England	Manchester	1964
299	M.D.Crowe	New Zealand	v	Sri Lanka	Wellington	1990-91
285*	P.B.H.May	England	v	West Indies	Birmingham	1957
277	G.C.Smith	South Africa	v	England	Birmingham	2003
274*	S.P.Fleming	New Zealand	v	Sri Lanka	Colombo (PSS)	2002-03
270	D.G.Bradman	Australia	v	England	Melbourne	1936-37
262	S.P.Fleming	New Zealand	v	South Africa	Cape Town	2005-06
259	G.C.Smith	South Africa	v	England	Lord's	2003
257*	Wasim Akram	Pakistan	v	Zimbabwe	Sheikhupura	1996-97
249	M.S.Atapattu	Sri Lanka	v	Zumbabwe	Bulawayo[2]	2003-04
242*	C.H.Lloyd	West Indies	v	India	Bombay[3]	1974-75
240	W.R.Hammond	England	v	Australia	Lord's	1938
239	G.T.Dowling	New Zealand	v	India	Christchurch	1967-68
237	Saleem Malik	Pakistan	v	Australia	Rawalpindi[2]	1994-95
235	G.S.Chappell	Australia	v	Pakistan	Faisalabad	1979-80
234	D.G.Bradman	Australia	v	England	Sydney	1946-47
225	R.B.Simpson	Australia	v	England	Adelaide	1965-66
219	D.S.Atkinson	West Indies	v	Australia	Bridgetown	1954-55
217	S.R.Tendulkar	India	v	New Zealand	Ahmedabad	1999-2000
215	D.I.Gower	England	v	Australia	Birmingham	1985
213	B.C.Lara	West Indies	v	Australia	Kingston	1998-99
212	D.G.Bradman	Australia	v	England	Adelaide	1936-37
211	W.L.Murdoch	Australia	v	England	The Oval	1884
211	Javed Miandad	Pakistan	v	Australia	Karachi[1]	1988-89
209	B.C.Lara	West Indies	v	Sri Lanka	Gros Islet	2002-03

208	A.D.Nourse	South Africa	v	England	Nottingham	1951
207	R.T.Ponting	Australia	v	Pakistan	Sydney	2004-05
205	L.Hutton	England	v	West Indies	Kingston	1953-54
205	E.R.Dexter	England	v	Pakistan	Karachi[1]	1961-62
205	W.M.Lawry	Australia	v	West Indies	Melbourne	1968-69
205	S.M.Gavaskar	India	v	West Indies	Bombay[3]	1978-79
205	A.R.Border	Australia	v	New Zealand	Adelaide	1987-88
204	G.S.Chappell	Australia	v	India	Sydney	1980-81
203*	Nawab of Pataudi jr	India	v	England	Delhi	1963-64
203*	Hanif Mohammad	Pakistan	v	New Zealand	Lahore[2]	1964-65
203*	Javed Miandad	Pakistan	v	Sri Lanka	Faisalabad	1985-86
203*	S.Chanderpaul	West Indies	v	South Africa	Georgetown	2004-05
203	H.L.Collins	Australia	v	South Africa	Johannesburg[1]	1921-22
202	B.C.Lara	West Indies	v	South Africa	Johannesburg[3]	2003-04
202	S.P.Fleming	New Zealand	v	Bangladesh	Chittagong[1]	2004-05
201*	J.Ryder	Australia	v	England	Adelaide	1924-25
201	D.G.Bradman	Australia	v	India	Adelaide	1947-48
201	R.B.Simpson	Australia	v	West Indies	Bridgetown	1964-65
201	G.S.Chappell	Australia	v	Pakistan	Brisbane[2]	1981-82
200*	A.R.Border	Australia	v	England	Leeds	1993

CENTURIES BY RIVAL CAPTAINS IN THE SAME TEST

H.W.Taylor	South Africa	109	J.W.H.T.Douglas	England	119	Durban[2]	1913-14
A.P.F.Chapman	England	121	W.M.Woodfull	Australia	155	Lord's	1930
W.R.Hammond	England	240	D.G.Bradman	Australia	102*	Lord's	1938
A.Melville	South Africa	103	W.R.Hammond	England	140	Durban[2]	1938-39
L.Hutton	England	145	A.L.Hassett	Australia	104	Lord's	1953
P.B.H.May	England	117	D.J.McGlew	South Africa	104*	Manchester	1955
D.J.McGlew	South Africa	120	J.R.Reid	New Zealand	142	Johannesburg[1]	1961-62
E.R.Dexter	England	174	R.B.Simpson	Australia	311	Manchester	1964
G.S.Sobers	West Indies	113*	M.C.Cowdrey	England	101	Kingston	1967-68
W.M.Lawry	Australia	151	G.S.Sobers	West Indies	113	Sydney	1968-69
G.S.Sobers	West Indies	142	B.E.Congdon	New Zealand	126	Bridgetown	1971-72
R.B.Kanhai	West Indies	105	I.M.Chappell	Australia	106*	Bridgetown	1972-73
B.E.Congdon	New Zealand	132	I.M.Chappell	Australia	145 + 121	Wellington	1973-74
S.M.Gavaskar	India	205	A.I.Kallicharran	West Indies	187	Bombay[3]	1978-79
Javed Miandad	Pakistan	106*	G.S.Chappell	Australia	235	Faisalabad	1979-80
Imran Khan	Pakistan	117	S.M.Gavaskar	India	127*	Faisalabad	1982-83
C.H.Lloyd	West Indies	143	Kapil Dev	India	100*	Port-of-Spain	1982-83
Kapil Dev	India	119	A.R.Border	Australia	106	Madras[1]	1986-87
M.W.Gatting	England	150*	Imran Khan	Pakistan	118	The Oval	1987
D.B.Vengsarkar	India	102	I.V.A.Richards	West Indies	146	Delhi	1987-88
Javed Miandad	Pakistan	107	A.R.Border	Australia	113*	Faisalabad	1988-89
G.A.Gooch	England	333 + 123	M.Azharuddin	India	121	Lord's	1990
G.A.Gooch	England	116	M.Azharuddin	India	179	Manchester	1990
B.C.Lara	West Indies	213	S.R.Waugh	Australia	100	Kingston	1998-99
B.C.Lara	West Indies	153*	S.R.Waugh	Australia	199	Bridgetown	1998-99
N.Hussain	England	110	S.C.Ganguly	India	128	Leeds	2002
H.P.Tillakaratne	Sri Lanka	144	S.P.Fleming	New Zealand	274*	Colombo (PSS)	2002-03
G.C.Smith	South Africa	132	B.C.Lara	West Indies	202	Johannesburg[3]	2003-04
B.C.Lara	West Indies	400*	M.P.Vaughan	England	140	St John's	2003-04
S.Chanderpaul	West Indies	127	G.C.Smith	South Africa	126	St John's	2004-05
M.P.Vaughan	England	166	R.T.Ponting	Australia	156	Manchester	2005
Inzamamul Haq	Pakistan	119	R.S.Dravid	India	103	Faisalabad	2005-06
B.C.Lara	West Indies	120	R.S.Dravid	India	146	Gros Islet	2005-06

CENTURY IN EACH INNINGS BY A CAPTAIN

189	104*	A.Melville	South Africa	v	England	Nottingham	1947
132	127*	D.G.Bradman	Australia	v	India	Melbourne	1947-48
153	115	R.B.Simpson	Australia	v	Pakistan	Karachi[1]	1964-65
145	121	I.M.Chappell	Australia	v	New Zealand	Wellington	1973-74
123	109*	G.S.Chappell	Australia	v	West Indies	Brisbane[2]	1975-76
107	182*	S.M.Gavaskar	India	v	West Indies	Calcutta	1978-79
140	114*	A.R.Border	Australia	v	New Zealand	Christchurch	1985-86
333	123	G.A.Gooch	England	v	India	Lord's	1990
103	101*	M.P.Vaughan	England	v	West Indies	Lord's	2004
149	104*	R.T.Ponting	Australia	v	West Indies	Brisbane[2]	2005-06
109	100*	Inzamamul Haq	Pakistan	v	England	Faisalabad	2005-06
120	143*	R.T.Ponting	Australia	v	South Africa	Sydney	2005-06
103	116	R.T.Ponting	Australia	v	South Africa	Durban[2]	2005-06

CENTURY AND A NINETY IN SAME MATCH BY A CAPTAIN

104	93	Hanif Mohammad	Pakistan	v	Australia	Melbourne	1964-65
152	95*	G.S.Sobers	West Indies	v	England	Georgetown	1967-68
119	94	L.R.D.Mendis	Sri Lanka	v	England	Lord's	1984
94*	118	M.A.Atherton	England	v	New Zealand	Christchurch	1996-97
334*	94	M.A.Taylor	Australia	v	Pakistan	Peshawar[2]	1998-99
91	122	B.C.Lara	West Indies	v	Australia	Port-of-Spain	2002-03
92	153*	S.Chanderpaul	West Indies	v	Pakistan	Bridgetown	2004-05

TEN WICKETS IN A MATCH BY A CAPTAIN

13/55	C.A.Walsh	West Indies	v	New Zealand	Wellington	1994-95
13/135	Waqar Younis	Pakistan	v	Zimbabwe	Karachi[2]	1993-94
12/100	Fazal Mahmood	Pakistan	v	West Indies	Dacca	1958-59
11/79	Imran Khan	Pakistan	v	India	Karachi[1]	1982-83
11/90	A.E.R.Gilligan	England	v	South Africa	Birmingham	1924
11/96	A.R.Border	Australia	v	West Indies	Sydney	1988-89
11/121	Imran Khan	Pakistan	v	West Indies	Georgetown	1987-88
11/130	Intikhab Alam	Pakistan	v	New Zealand	Dunedin	1972-73
11/150	E.P.Nupen	South Africa	v	England	Johannesburg[1]	1930-31
11/180	Imran Khan	Pakistan	v	India	Faisalabad	1982-83
10/77	Imran Khan	Pakistan	v	England	Leeds	1987
10/78	G.O.B.Allen	England	v	India	Lord's	1936
10/106	Wasim Akram	Pakistan	v	Zimbabwe	Faisalabad	1996-97
10/135	Kapil Dev	India	v	West Indies	Ahmedabad	1983-84
10/182	Intikhab Alam	Pakistan	v	New Zealand	Dacca	1969-70
10/194	B.S.Bedi	India	v	Australia	Perth	1977-78

SIX WICKETS IN AN INNINGS BY A CAPTAIN

9/83	Kapil Dev	India	v	West Indies	Ahmedabad	1983-84
8/60	Imran Khan	Pakistan	v	India	Karachi[1]	1982-83
8/106	Kapil Dev	India	v	Australia	Adelaide	1985-86
7/37	C.A.Walsh	West Indies	v	New Zealand	Wellington	1994-95
7/40	Imran Khan	Pakistan	v	England	Leeds	1987
7/44	I.W.G.Johnson	Australia	v	West Indies	Georgetown	1954-55
7/46	A.R.Border	Australia	v	West Indies	Sydney	1988-89
7/52	Intikhab Alam	Pakistan	v	New Zealand	Dunedin	1972-73
7/52	Imran Khan	Pakistan	v	England	Birmingham	1982

7/53	D.S.Atkinson	West Indies	v	New Zealand	Auckland	1955-56
7/80	G.O.B.Allen	England	v	India	The Oval	1936
7/80	Imran Khan	Pakistan	v	West Indies	Georgetown	1987-88
7/91	Waqar Younis	Pakistan	v	Zimbabwe	Karachi[2]	1993-94
7/100	M.A.Noble	Australia	v	England	Sydney	1903-04
6/7	A.E.R.Gilligan	England	v	South Africa	Birmingham	1924
6/18	C.A.Walsh	West Indies	v	New Zealand	Wellington	1994-95
6/30	S.M.Pollock	South Africa	v	Sri Lanka	Cape Town	2000-01
6/34	Fazal Mahmood	Pakistan	v	West Indies	Dacca	1958-59
6/35	Imran Khan	Pakistan	v	India	Hyderabad,Pak	1982-83
6/44	Waqar Younis	Pakistan	v	Zimbabwe	Karachi[2]	1993-94
6/46	Imran Khan	Pakistan	v	West Indies	Karachi[1]	1986-87
6/48	Wasim Akram	Pakistan	v	Zimbabwe	Faisalabad	1996-97
6/55	Waqar Younis	Pakistan	v	Bangladesh	Dhaka	2001-02
6/56	S.M.Pollock	South Africa	v	India	Bloemfontein	2001-02
6/60	J.R.Reid	New Zealand	v	South Africa	Dunedin	1963-64
6/66	Fazal Mahmood	Pakistan	v	West Indies	Dacca	1958-59
6/68	G.O.Rabone	New Zealand	v	South Africa	Cape Town	1953-54
6/70	R.Benaud	Australia	v	England	Manchester	1961
6/71	B.S.Bedi	India	v	England	Bangalore	1976-77
6/73	G.S.Sobers	West Indies	v	Australia	Brisbane[2]	1968-69
6/77	Kapil Dev	India	v	West Indies	Delhi	1983-84
6/79	C.A.Walsh	West Indies	v	India	Bombay[3]	1994-95
6/87	E.P.Nupen	South Africa	v	England	Johannesburg[1]	1930-31
6/98	Imran Khan	Pakistan	v	India	Faisalabad	1982-83
6/101	R.G.D.Willis	England	v	India	Lord's	1982
6/115	R.Benaud	Australia	v	England	Brisbane[2]	1962-63
6/127	Intikhab Alam	Pakistan	v	New Zealand	Auckland	1972-73
6/129	Imran Khan	Pakistan	v	England	Birmingham	1987
6/132	Naimur Rahman	Bangladesh	v	India	Dhaka	2000-01
6/155	G.Giffen	Australia	v	England	Melbourne	1894-95

A CENTURY AND FIVE WICKETS IN AN INNINGS BY A CAPTAIN

219	5/56	D.S.Atkinson	West Indies	v	Australia	Bridgetown	1954-55
174	5/41	G.S.Sobers	West Indies	v	England	Leeds	1966
121	5/28	Mushtaq Mohammad	Pakistan	v	West Indies	Port-of-Spain	1976-77
117	6/98) 5/82)	Imran Khan	Pakistan	v	India	Faisalabad	1982-83

A HUNDRED RUNS AND EIGHT WICKETS IN A MATCH BY A CAPTAIN

121	56	5/28	3/69	Mushtaq Mohammad	Pakistan	v	West Indies	Port-of-Spain	1976-77
174		5/41	3/39	G.S.Sobers	West Indies	v	England	Leeds	1966
117		6/98	5/82	Imran Khan	Pakistan	v	India	Faisalabad	1982-83
67*	46	5/49	3/66	Imran Khan	Pakistan	v	England	Leeds	1982
35	68	3/71	5/36	G.O.B.Allen	England	v	Australia	Brisbane[2]	1936-37

YOUNGEST CAPTAINS

Years	Days						
20	358	T.Taibu	Zimbabwe	v	Sri Lanka	Harare	2003-04
21	77	Nawab of Pataudi, jr	India	v	West Indies	Bridgetown	1961-62
22	15	Waqar Younis	Pakistan	v	Zimbabwe	Karachi[2]	1993-94
22	82	G.C.Smith	South Africa	v	Bangladesh	Chittagong[1]	2002-03
22	194	I.D.Craig	Australia	v	South Africa	Johannesburg[3]	1957-58

22	260	Javed Miandad	Pakistan	v	Australia	Karachi[1]	1979-80
22	306	M.Bisset	South Africa	v	England	Johannesburg[1]	1898-99
23	144	M.P.Bowden	England	v	South Africa	Cape Town	1888-89
23	169	S.R.Tendulkar	India	v	Australia	Delhi	1996-97
23	217	G.C.Grant	West Indies	v	Australia	Adelaide	1930-31
23	292	Hon I.F.W.Bligh	England	v	Australia	Melbourne	1882-83
23	319	S.P.Fleming	New Zealand	v	England	Christchurch	1996-97
23	353	A.D.R.Campbell	Zimbabwe	v	Sri Lanka	Colombo (RPS)	1996-97
24	23	Javed Burki	Pakistan	v	England	Birmingham	1962
24	48	Kapil Dev	India	v	West Indies	Kingston	1982-83
24	125	W.J.Cronje	South Africa	v	Australia	Adelaide	1993-94
24	194	I.T.Botham	England	v	West Indies	Nottingham	1980
24	222	H.W.Taylor	South Africa	v	England	Durban[1]	1913-14
24	342	B.A.Murphy	Zimbabwe	v	Bangladesh	Dhaka	2001-02
25	40	D.B.Carr	England	v	India	Madras[1]	1951-52
25	57	K.J.Hughes	Australia	v	Pakistan	Perth	1978-79
25	81	M.V.Boucher	South Africa	v	Australia	Johannesburg[3]	2001-02
25	117	D.S.Sheppard	England	v	Pakistan	Nottingham	1954
25	133	D.I.Gower	England	v	Pakistan	Lord's	1982
25	135	M.A.Atherton	England	v	Australia	Birmingham	1993
25	138	P.W.Sherwell	South Africa	v	England	Johannesburg[1]	1905-06
25	160	P.B.H.May	England	v	South Africa	Nottingham	1955
25	217	A.Flower	Zimbabwe	v	Pakistan	Karachi[2]	1993-94
25	223	H.B.Cameron	South Africa	v	England	Johannesburg[1]	1930-31
25	229	R.J.Shastri	India	v	West Indies	Madras[1]	1987-88
25	234	C.A.Smith	England	v	South Africa	Port Elizabeth	1888-89
25	252	J.M.Parker	New Zealand	v	Pakistan	Karachi[1]	1976-77
25	309	P.A.de Silva	Sri Lanka	v	England	Lord's	1991
25	313	Khaled Mashud	Bangladesh	v	New Zealand	Auckland	2001-02
25	324	W.L.Murdoch	Australia	v	England	The Oval	1880
25	345	A.P.F.Chapman	England	v	Australia	The Oval	1926

OLDEST CAPTAINS

Years	Days						
50	320	W.G.Grace	England	v	Australia	Nottingham	1899
45	245	G.O.B.Allen	England	v	West Indies	Kingston	1947-48
43	276	W.R.Hammond	England	v	New Zealand	Christchurch	1946-47
43	232	W.Bardsley	Australia	v	England	Manchester	1926
42	247	N.Betancourt	West Indies	v	England	Port-of-Spain	1929-30
42	130	E.S.Gregory	Australia	v	England	The Oval	1912
42	89	R.B.Simpson	Australia	v	West Indies	Kingston	1977-78
42	86	W.W.Armstrong	Australia	v	England	The Oval	1921
41	330	J.W.H.T.Douglas	England	v	South Africa	Manchester	1924
41	289	M.H.Mankad	India	v	West Indies	Madras[1]	1958-59
41	178	V.Y.Richardson	Australia	v	South Africa	Durban[2]	1935-36
41	95	N.B.Amarnath	India	v	Pakistan	Calcutta	1952-53
41	80	R.Illingworth	England	v	West Indies	Lord's	1973
41	44	T.W.Graveney	England	v	Australia	Leeds	1968
40	279	A.D.Nourse	South Africa	v	England	The Oval	1951
40	277	D.S.de Silva	Sri Lanka	v	New Zealand	Wellington	1982-83
40	245	F.R.Brown	England	v	South Africa	The Oval	1951
40	223	J.M.Blackham	Australia	v	England	Sydney	1894-95
40	125	C.H.Lloyd	West Indies	v	Australia	Sydney	1984-85
40	109	C.B.Fry	England	v	Australia	The Oval	1912
40	3	G.A.Gooch	England	v	Australia	Leeds	1993

General

MOST TEST MATCH APPEARANCES FOR EACH COUNTRY

For	Total		A	E	SA	WI	NZ	I	P	SL	Z	B
			Opponents									
Australia	**168**	S.R.Waugh	-	46	16	32	23	18	20	8	3	2
England	**133**	A.J.Stewart	33	-	23	24	16	9	13	9	6	-
South Africa	**102**	S.M.Pollock	13	23	-	15	11	9	10	13	5	3
West Indies	**132**	C.A.Walsh	38	36	10	-	10	15	18	3	2	-
New Zealand	**102**	S.P.Fleming	14	16	13	11	-	13	9	11	11	4
India	**132**	S.R.Tendulkar	21	17	16	16	16	-	16	16	9	3
Pakistan	**124**	Javed Miandad	24	22	-	17	18	28	-	12	3	-
Sri Lanka	**107**	M.Muralidaran	10	13	15	10	10	15	14	-	14	6
Zimbabwe	**67**	G.W.Flower	1	6	5	4	10	8	14	13	-	6
Bangladesh	**42**	Habibul Bashar	4	4	4	4	2	3	6	7	8	-

MOST CONSECUTIVE APPEARANCES

		From		To	
153	A.R.Border (Australia)	Melbourne	1978-79	Durban[2]	1993-94
107	M.E.Waugh (Australia)	Manchester	1993	Sharjah	2002-03
106	S.M.Gavaskar (India)	Bombay[3]	1974-75	Madras[1]	1986-87
93 †	R.S.Dravid (India)	Lord's	1996	Delhi	# 2005-06
87	G.R.Viswanath (India)	Georgetown	1970-71	Karachi[1]	1982-83
85 †	G.S.Sobers (West Indies)	Port-of-Spain	1954-55	Port-of-Spain	1971-72
84 †	S.R.Tendulkar (India)	Karachi[1]	1989-90	Harare	2000-01
84 §	A.C.Gilchrist (Australia)	Brisbane[2]	1999-2000	Chittagong[2]	# 2005-06
76	M.L.Hayden (Australia)	Hamilton	1999-2000	Chittagong[2]	# 2005-06
75	M.V.Boucher (South Africa)	Johannesburg[3]	1997-98	Colombo (SSC)	2004-05
72	D.L.Haynes (West Indies)	Brisbane[2]	1979-80	Lord's	1988
71 †	I.M.Chappell (Australia)	Adelaide	1965-66	Melbourne	1975-76
69	M.Azharuddin (India)	Kingston	1988-89	Colombo (SSC)	1998-99
66	Kapil Dev (India)	Faisalabad	1978-79	Delhi	1984-85
65	A.P.E.Knott (England)	Auckland	1970-71	The Oval	1977
65	I.T.Botham (England)	Wellington	1977-78	Karachi[1]	1983-84
65	Kapil Dev (India)	Madras[1]	1984-85	Hamilton	1993-94
64 †	I.A.Healy (Australia)	Karachi[1]	1988-89	Rawalpindi[2]	1994-95
64	B.C.Lara (West Indies)	Bridgetown	1991-92	Wellington	1999-2000
63	M.A.Atherton (England)	Bombay[3]	1992-93	Leeds	1998
63	S.P.Fleming (New Zealand)	Edgbaston	1999	Johannesburg[3]	# 2005-06
62	A.J.Stewart (England)	Lord's	1996	The Oval	2001
61 †	R.B.Kanhai (West Indies)	Birmingham	1957	Sydney	1968-69
61	I.V.A.Richards (West Indies)	Nottingham	1980	Madras[1]	1987-88
60	D.C.Boon (Australia)	Wellington	1989-90	Adelaide	1995-96
60	A.Kumble (India)	Harare	1992-93	Bangalore	1999-2000
60	J.H.Kallis (South Africa)	Melbourne	1997-98	Cape Town	2002-03
58 §	J R.Reid (New Zealand)	Manchester	1949	Leeds	1965
58 §	A.W.Greig (England)	Manchester	1972	The Oval	1977
56	S.M.H.Kirmani (India)	Madras[1]	1979-80	Kanpur	1984-85
56 †	A.D.R.Campbell (Zimbabwe)	Harare	1992-93	Bulawayo[2]	2001-02
56	S.C.Ganguly (India)	Colombo (RPS)	1997-98	Ahmedabad	2003-04
55	I.A.Healy (Australia)	Brisbane[2]	1994-95	Harare	1999-2000
54	G.D.McGrath (Australia)	Brisbane[2]	1998-99	Melbourne	2002-03
53	Javed Miandad (Pakistan)	Lahore[2]	1977-78	Sydney	1983-84

53	K.J.Hughes (Australia)	Brisbane[2]	1978-79	Sydney	1982-83
53	C.A.Walsh (West Indies)	St John's	1989-90	Port-of-Spain	1996-97
53 †	G.Kirsten (South Africa)	Melbourne	1993-94	Wellington	1998-99
53	M.S.Atapattu (Sri Lanka)	Kingstown	1996-97	Colombo (PSS)	2002-03
52	F.E.Woolley (England)	The Oval	1909	The Oval	1926
52	P.B.H.May (England)	The Oval	1953	Leeds	1959
52 †	R.W.Marsh (Australia)	Brisbane[2]	1970-71	The Oval	1977
52	M.A.Taylor (Australia)	Cape Town	1993-94	Sydney	1998-99
52 †	A.Flower (Zimbabwe)	Harare	1992-93	Harare	2000-01
52	J.L.Langer (Australia)	The Oval	2001	The Oval	2005
51 †	G.S.Chappell (Australia)	Perth	1970-71	The Oval	1977
51	D.I.Gower (England)	Bombay[3]	1981-82	Lord's	1986
51	A.C.Parore (New Zealand)	Lahore[2]	1996-97	Auckland	2001-02
50	R.J.Shastri (India)	Jullundur	1983-84	Sialkot	1989-90

The most for Bangladesh is 30 by Habibul Bashar.

§ Entire Test career. # To date. † from debut (note: Kapil Dev played 66 consecutive Tests from his debut, before being dropped for one Test for disciplinary reasons. He then played a further 65 consecutive Tests before retiring).

LONGEST CAREERS *(From debut to final day of last match)*

Years	Days		Team (s)	From		To	
30	315	W.Rhodes	England	Nottingham	1899	Kingston	1929-30
26	355	D.B.Close	England	Manchester	1949	Manchester	1976
25	13	F.E.Woolley	England	The Oval	1909	The Oval	1934
24	10	G.A.Headley	West Indies	Bridgetown	1929-30	Kingston	1953-54
23	41	A.J.Traicos	South Africa/Zimbabwe	Durban[2]	1969-70	Delhi	1992-93
22	233	J.B.Hobbs	England	Melbourne	1907-08	The Oval	1930
22	120	G.Gunn	England	Sydney	1907-08	Kingston	1929-30
22	18	E.S.Gregory	Australia	Lord's	1890	The Oval	1912
21	336	F.R.Brown	England	The Oval	1931	Lord's	1953
21	313	A.W.Nourse	South Africa	Johannesburg[1]	1902-03	The Oval	1924
20	218	Imran Khan	Pakistan	Birmingham	1971	Faisalabad	1991-92
20	132	R.B.Simpson	Australia	Johannesburg[1]	1957-58	Kingston	1977-78
20	79	M.C.Cowdrey	England	Brisbane[2]	1954-55	Melbourne	1974-75
20	6	G.S.Sobers	West Indies	Kingston	1953-54	Port-of-Spain	1973-74
20	3	Mushtaq Mohammed	Pakistan	Lahore[1]	1958-59	Perth	1978-79
Longest for the other countries:							
19	0	N.B.Amarnath	India	Bombay[1]	1933-34	Calcutta	1952-53
18	72	B.Sutcliffe	New Zealand	Christchurch	1946-47	Birmingham	1965
18	174	A.Ranatunga	Sri Lanka	Colombo (PSS)	1981-82	Colombo (SSC)	2000-01
11	134	G.W.Flower	Zimbabwe	Harare	1992-93	Bulawayo[2]	2003-04
5	161	Habibul Bashar	Bangladesh	Dhaka	2000-01	Chittagong[2]	2005-06
		Khaled Mashud	Bangladesh	Dhaka	2000-01	Chittagong[2]	2005-06
		Mohammad Rafique	Bangladesh	Dhaka	2000-01	Chittagong[2]	2005-06

LONGEST INTERVALS BETWEEN APPEARANCES

Years	Days		Team (s)	From		To	
22	222	A.J.Traicos	Sth Africa/Zimb	Port Elizabeth	1969-70	Harare	1992-93
17	316	G.Gunn	England	Sydney	1911-12	Bridgetown	1929-30
17	111	Younis Ahmed	Pakistan	Lahore[2]	1969-70	Jaipur	1986-87
14	92	J.M.M.Commaille	South Africa	Cape Town	1909-10	Birmingham	1924
14	28	D.C.Cleverley	New Zealand	Christchurch	1931-32	Wellington	1945-46
13	53	F.Mitchell	England/South Africa	Cape Town	1898-99	Manchester	1912
13	32	G.M.Carew	West Indies	Bridgetown	1934-35	Port-of-Spain	1947-48
12	160	N.B.Amarnath	India	Madras[1]	1933-34	Lord's	1946

12	81	W.E.Hollies	England	Kingston	1934-35	Nottingham	1947
12	10	Nawab of Pataudi, sr	England/India	Nottingham	1934	Lord's	1946
11	361	F.R.Brown	England	Manchester	1937	The Oval	1949
11	345	H.L.Jackson	England	Manchester	1949	Leeds	1961
11	320	G.A.Faulkner	South Africa	The Oval	1912	Lord's	1924
11	306	S.J.Pegler	South Africa	The Oval	1912	Birmingham	1924
11	298	M.P.Donnelly	New Zealand	The Oval	1937	The Oval	1949
11	225	D.Shackleton	England	Delhi	1951-52	Lord's	1963
10	158	S.J.Snooke	South Africa	The Oval	1912	Durban[2]	1922-23
10	48	J.Langridge	England	Lord's	1936	The Oval	1946
10	12	M.P.Bicknell	England	Birmingham	1993	Leeds	2003
Longest for Australia:							
9	305	R.B.Simpson	Australia	Sydney	1967-68	Brisbane[2]	1977-78

The most matches between appearances is 115 by M.P.Bicknell (as above).

PLAYERS WHO REPRESENTED TWO COUNTRIES

Player	Country (Tests)	Seasons	Country (Tests)	Seasons	Total Tests
Amir Elahi	India (1)	1947-48	Pakistan (5)	1952-53	6
J.J.Ferris	Australia (8)	1886-87 to 1890	England (1)	1891-92	9
S.C.Guillen	West Indies (5)	1951-52	New Zealand (3)	1955-56	8
Gul Mahomed	India (8)	1946 to 1952-53	Pakistan (1)	1956-57	9
F.Hearne	England (2)	1888-89	South Africa (4)	1891-92 to 1895-96	6
A.H.Kardar	India (3)	1946 §	Pakistan (23)	1952-53 to 1957-58	26
W.E.Midwinter	Australia (8)	1876-77 to 1886-87	England (4)	1881-82	12
F.Mitchell	England (2)	1898-99	South Africa (3)	1912	5
W.L.Murdoch	Australia (18)	1876-77 to 1890	England (1)	1891-92	19
Nawab of Pataudi, sr	England (3)	1932-33 to 1934	India (3)	1946	6
A.J.Traicos	South Africa (3)	1969-70	Zimbabwe (4)	1992-93	7
A.E.Trott	Australia (3)	1894-95	England (2)	1898-99	5
K.C.Wessels	Australia (24)	1982-83 to 1985-86	South Africa (16)	1991-92 to 1994	40
S.M.J.Woods	Australia (3)	1888	England (3)	1895-96	6

§ As "Abdul Hafeez".

YOUNGEST TEST PLAYERS

YearsDays *(see footnote about Hasan Raza & Shahid Afridi)*

Years	Days						
15	124	Mushtaq Mohammad	Pakistan	v	West Indies	Lahore[1]	1958-59
15	128	Mohammad Sharif	Bangladesh	v	Zimbabwe	Bulawayo[2]	2001-02
16	189	Aaqib Javed	Pakistan	v	New Zealand	Wellington	1988-89
16	205	S.R.Tendulkar	India	v	Pakistan	Karachi[1]	1989-90
16	221	Aftab Baloch	Pakistan	v	New Zealand	Dacca	1969-70
16	223	Talha Jubair	Bangladesh	v	Sri Lanka	Colombo (PSS)	2002-03
16	248	Nasim-ul-Ghani	Pakistan	v	West Indies	Bridgetown	1957-58
16	267	Mushfiqur Rahim	Bangladesh	v	England	Lord's	2005
16	320	Enamul Haque[2]	Bangladesh	v	England	Dhaka	2003-04
16	352	Khalid Hassan	Pakistan	v	England	Nottingham	1954
16	362	Mohammad Ashraful	Bangladesh	v	Sri Lanka	Colombo (PSS)	2001-02
17	5	Zahid Fazal	Pakistan	v	West Indies	Karachi[1]	1990-91
17	68	Ataur Rehmann	Pakistan	v	England	Birmingham	1992
17	78	Imran Nazir	Pakistan	v	Sri Lanka	Lahore[2]	1998-99
17	118	L.Shivaramakrishnan	India	v	West Indies	St John's	1982-83
17	122	J.E.D.Sealy	West Indies	v	England	Bridgetown	1929-30
17	129	Fazl-e-Akbar	Pakistan	v	South Africa	Durban[2]	1997-98
17	152	P.A.Patel	India	v	England	Nottingham	2002
17	189	C.D.U.S.Weerasinghe	Sri Lanka	v	India	Colombo (PSS)	1985-86

17	193	Maninder Singh	India	v	Pakistan	Karachi[1]	1932-83
17	239	I.D.Craig	Australia	v	South Africa	Melbourne	1952-53
17	245	G.S.Sobers	West Indies	v	England	Kingston	1953-54
17	265	V.L.Mehra	India	v	New Zealand	Bombay[2]	1955-56
17	265	Harbhajan Singh	India	v	Australia	Bangalore	1997-98
17	300	Hanif Mohammad	Pakistan	v	India	Delhi	1952-53
17	324	Yasir Ali	Pakistan	v	Bangladesh	Multan[2]	2003-04
17	341	Intikhab Alam	Pakistan	v	Australia	Karachi[1]	1959-60
17	352	H.Masakadza	Zimbabwe	v	West Indies	Harare	2001-02
17	364	Waqar Younis	Pakistan	v	India	Karachi[1]	1989-90
18	10	D.L.Vettori	New Zealand	v	England	Wellington	1996-97
18	13	A.G.Milkha Singh	India	v	Australia	Madras[2]	1959-60
18	26	Majid Khan	Pakistan	v	Australia	Karachi[1]	1964-65
18	31	M.R.Bynoe	West Indies	v	Pakistan	Lahore[1]	1958-59
18	34	Mashrafe Bin Mortaza	Bangladesh	v	Zimbabwe	Dhaka	2001-02
18	41	Salahuddin	Pakistan	v	New Zealand	Rawalpindi[1]	1964-65
18	41	P.Utseya	Zimbabwe	v	Sri Lanka	Harare	2003-04
18	44	Khalid Wazir	Pakistan	v	England	Lord's	1954
18	53	E.Chigumbura	Zimbabwe	v	Sri Lanka	Harare	2003-04
18	60	B.R.M.Taylor	Zimbabwe	v	Sri Lanka	Harare	2003-04
18	66	T.Taibu	Zimbabwe	v	West Indies	Bulawayo[2]	2001-02
18	74	J.B.Stollmeyer	West Indies	v	England	Lord's	1939
18	78	A.Ranatunga	Sri Lanka	v	England	Colombo (PSS)	1981-82
18	81	B.R.Jurangpathy	Sri Lanka	v	India	Kandy	1985-86
18	83	Nazmul Hossain	Bangladesh	v	India	Chittagong[1]	2004-05
18	109	A.G.Cremer	Zimbabwe	v	Bangladesh	Chittagong[1]	2004-05
18	119	Ranjan Das	Bangladesh	v	India	Dhaka	2000-01
18	130	Irfan Fazil	Pakistan	v	Sri Lanka	Karachi[1]	1999-2000
18	136	Ijaz Ahmed	Pakistan	v	India	Madras[1]	1986-87
18	138	T.Panyangara	Zimbabwe	v	Sri Lanka	Harare	2003-04
18	147	C.M.Bandara	Sri Lanka	v	New Zealand	Colombo (RPS)	1997-98
18	149	D.B.Close	England	v	New Zealand	Manchester	1949
18	173	A.T.Roberts	West Indies	v	New Zealand	Auckland	1955-56
18	186	Haseeb Ahsan	Pakistan	v	West Indies	Bridgetown	1957-58
18	190	Imran Khan	Pakistan	v	England	Birmingham	1971
18	194	Qaisar Abbas	Pakistan	v	England	Lahore[2]	2000-01
18	197	D.L.Freeman	New Zealand	v	England	Christchurch	1932-33
18	208	Alok Kapali	Bangladesh	v	Sri Lanka	Colombo (SSC)	2002-03
18	212	H.K.Olonga	Zimbabwe	v	Pakistan	Harare	1994-95
18	230	Tushar Imran	Bangladesh	v	Sri Lanka	Colombo (SSC)	2002-03
18	232	T.W.Garrett	Australia	v	England	Melbourne	1876-77
18	236	Wasim Akram	Pakistan	v	New Zealand	Auckland	1984-85
18	242	A.P.H.Scott	West Indies	v	India	Kingston	1952-53
18	249	B.S.Chandrasekhar	India	v	England	Bombay[2]	1963-64
18	255	Saqlain Mushtaq	Pakistan	v	Sri Lanka	Peshawar[2]	1995-96
18	256	Shadab Kabir	Pakistan	v	England	Lord's	1996
18	260	Mohammad Ilyas	Pakistan	v	Australia	Melbourne	1964-65
18	267	H.G.Vivian	New Zealand	v	England	The Oval	1931
18	270	R.J.Shastri	India	v	New Zealand	Wellington	1980-81
18	288	C.Sharma	India	v	Pakistan	Lahore[2]	1984-85
18	292	Imran Farhat	Pakistan	v	New Zealand	Auckland	2000-01
18	293	Shahadat Hossain	Bangladesh	v	England	Lord's	2005
18	295	R.O.Collinge	New Zealand	v	Pakistan	Wellington	1964-65
18	298	D.N.T.Zoysa	Sri Lanka	v	New Zealand	Dunedin	1996-97
18	311	P.A.de Silva	Sri Lanka	v	England	Lord's	1984
18	312	S.Venkataraghavan	India	v	New Zealand	Madras[2]	1964-65

18	316	B.P.Bracewell	New Zealand	v	England	The Oval	1978
18	318	Shahid Nazir	Pakistan	v	Zimbabwe	Sheikhupura	1996-97
18	323	Saleem Malik	Pakistan	v	Sri Lanka	Karachi[1]	1981-82
18	332	Salman Butt	Pakistan	v	Bangladesh	Multan[2]	2003-04
18	340	P.R.Adams	South Africa	v	England	Port Elizabeth	1995-96
18	351	Aftab Ahmed	Bangladesh	v	New Zealand	Chittagong[1]	2004-05
18	353	Saleem Elahi	Pakistan	v	Australia	Brisbane[2]	1995-96
18	363	Anwar Hossain	Bangladesh	v	West Indies	Dhaka	2002-03
18	363	J.E.Taylor	West Indies	v	Sri Lanka	Gros Islet	2003-04

Hasan Raza (Pakistan), allegedly born 11 March 1982, made his debut in 1996-97 v Zimbabwe at Faisalabad on 24 October 1996 which would make him 14 years 227 days old on his debut. However, medical tests organized by the PCB prior to his debut showed that he was born circa 1981 and was at least 15 years of age. Similarly Shahid Afridi (Pakistan) allegedly born 1 March 1980, made his debut in 1998-99 v Australia at Karachi[1] on 22 October 1998 which would make him 18 years 235 days old on debut. The 1996-97 PCB tests showed he was born circa 1977 and that he was at least 21 at that time.

OLDEST PLAYERS ON TEST DEBUT

Years	Days						
49	119	J.Southerton	England	v	Australia	Melbourne	1876-77
47	284	Miran Bux	Pakistan	v	India	Lahore[1]	1954-55
46	253	D.D.Blackie	Australia	v	England	Sydney	1928-29
46	237	H.Ironmonger	Australia	v	England	Brisbane[2]	1928-29
45	154	A.J.Traicos #	Zimbabwe	v	India	Harare	1992-93
42	242	N.Betancourt	West Indies	v	England	Port-of-Spain	1929-30
41	337	E.R.Wilson	England	v	Australia	Sydney	1920-21
41	27	R.J.D.Jamshedji	India	v	England	Bombay[1]	1933-34
40	345	C.A.Wiles	West Indies	v	England	Manchester	1933
40	295	O.Henry	South Africa	v	India	Durban[2]	1992-93
40	216	S.Kinneir	England	v	Australia	Sydney	1911-12
40	110	H.W.Lee	England	v	South Africa	Johannesburg[1]	1930-31
40	56	G.W.A.Chubb	South Africa	v	England	Nottingham	1951
40	37	C.Ramaswami	India	v	England	Manchester	1936

 # Traicos had previously played three Tests for South Africa in 1969-70.

The oldest player to make his debut for New Zealand was H.M.McGirr who was 38 years 101 days old when he appeared against England at Auckland in 1929-30; for Sri Lanka D.S.de Silva who was 39 years 251 days old when he made his debut in his country's inaugural Test against England at Colombo (PSS) in 1981-82; for Zimbabwe A.C.Waller who was 37 years 84 days old when he appeared against England at Bulawayo[2] in 1996-97; and for Bangladesh Enamul Haque who was 35 years 58 days when he debuted against Zimbabwe at Harare in 2001-02.

OLDEST TEST PLAYERS *(Age on final day of their last Test match)*

Years	Days						
52	165	W.Rhodes	England	v	West Indies	Kingston	1929-30
50	327	H.Ironmonger	Australia	v	England	Sydney	1932-33
50	320	W.G.Grace	England	v	Australia	Nottingham	1899
50	303	G.Gunn	England	v	West Indies	Kingston	1929-30
49	139	J.Southerton	England	v	Australia	Melbourne	1876-77
47	302	Miran Bux	Pakistan	v	India	Peshawar[1]	1954-55
47	249	J.B.Hobbs	England	v	Australia	The Oval	1930
47	87	F.E.Woolley	England	v	Australia	The Oval	1934
46	309	D.D.Blackie	Australia	v	England	Adelaide	1928-29
46	206	A.W.Nourse	South Africa	v	England	The Oval	1924
46	202	H.Strudwick	England	v	Australia	The Oval	1926
46	41	E.H.Hendren	England	v	West Indies	Kingston	1934-35
45	305	A.J.Traicos	Zimbabwe	v	India	Delhi	1992-93

45	245	G.O.B.Allen	England	v	West Indies	Kingston	1947-48
45	215	P.Holmes	England	v	India	Lord's	1932
45	140	D.B.Close	England	v	West Indies	Manchester	1976
44	341	E.G.Wynyard	England	v	South Africa	Johannesburg[1]	1905-06
44	317	J.M.M.Commaille	South Africa	v	England	Cape Town	1927-28
44	238	R.Abel	England	v	Australia	Manchester	1902
44	236	G.A.Headley	West Indies	v	England	Kingston	1953-54
44	105	Amir Elahi	Pakistan	v	India	Calcutta	1952-53
44	69	C.V.Grimmett	Australia	v	South Africa	Durban[2]	1935-36

ON THE FIELD THROUGHOUT A MATCH

						Days
Nazar Mohammad	Pakistan	v	India	Lucknow[1]	1952-53	4
D.J.McGlew	South Africa	v	New Zealand	Wellington	1952-53	4
C.A.Milton	England	v	New Zealand	Leeds	1958	5#†
J.H.Edrich	England	v	New Zealand	Leeds	1965	5
D.Lloyd	England	v	India	Birmingham	1974	3
G.Boycott	England	v	Australia	Leeds	1977	4
Taslim Arif	Pakistan	v	Australia	Faisalabad	1979-80	5∫
S.M.Gavaskar	India	v	West Indies	Georgetown	1982-83	5#
D.S.B.P.Kuruppu	Sri Lanka	v	New Zealand	Colombo (CCC)	1986-87	5†
M.A.Taylor	Australia	v	Pakistan	Sydney	1989-90	6§
M.A.Taylor	Australia	v	South Africa	Melbourne	1993-94	5∫
G.W.Flower	Zimbabwe	v	Pakistan	Harare	1994-95	4
B.A.Young	New Zealand	v	Sri Lanka	Dunedin	1996-97	5
R.S.Dravid	India	v	Pakistan	Lahore[2]	2005-06	5
W.U.Tharanga	Sri Lanka	v	Bangladesh	Bogra	2005-06	4

† In first Test. # Rain prevented play on two days. ∫ Rain prevented play on one day. § Rain prevented play on three days.

Umpires

MOST TEST MATCHES

Tests		Home Country	From	To
113 †	S.A.Bucknor	West Indies	1988-89	2006
92	D.R.Shepherd	England	1985	2004-05
76 †	R.E.Koertzen	South Africa	1992-93	2006
76 †	D.B.Hair	Australia	1991-92	2006
73	S.Venkataraghavan	India	1992-93	2003-04
66	H.D.Bird	England	1973	1996
59 †	D.J.Harper	Australia	1998-99	2005-06
48	F.Chester	England	1924	1955
44	D.L.Orchard	South Africa	1995-96	2003-04
42	C.S.Elliott	England	1957	1974
39	R.S.Dunne	New Zealand	1988-89	2001-02
38	R.B.Tiffin	Zimbabwe	1995-96	2003-04
37 †	S.J.A.Taufel	Australia	2000-01	2006
37 †	B.F.Bowden	New Zealand	1999-2000	2006-07
36	D.J.Constant	England	1971	1988
36	S.G.Randell	Australia	1984-85	1997-98
34	Khizer Hayat	Pakistan	1979-80	1996-97
34 †	Aleem Dar	Pakistan	2003-04	2006-07
33	J.S.Buller	England	1956	1969
33	A.R.Crafter	Australia	1978-79	1991-92
32	R.W.Crockett	Australia	1901-02	1924-25
32 †	E.A.R.de Silva	Sri Lanka	2000-01	2005-06
31	D.Sang Hue	West Indies	1961-62	1980-81
29	J.Phillips	England	1893	1905-06
29	F.S.Lee	England	1949	1962
29	C.J.Egar	Australia	1960-61	1968-69
29	L.H.Barker	West Indies	1983-84	1996-97
28	Mahboob Shah	Pakistan	1974-75	1996-97
28	D.M.Archer	West Indies	1980-81	1991-92
28	I.D.Robinson	Zimbabwe	1992-93	2001-02
27	R.C.Bailhache	Australia	1974-75	1988-89
26	B.J.Meyer	England	1978	1993
26	V.K.Ramaswamy	India	1984-85	1999-2000
26	B.L.Aldridge	New Zealand	1985-86	1995-96
26	C.J.Mitchley	South Africa	1992-93	1999-2000
25	L.P.Rowan	Australia	1962-63	1970-71
25	R.Gosein	West Indies	1964-65	1977-78
25	K.T.Francis	Sri Lanka	1981-82	1999-2000
25	P.Willey	England	1995-96	2003-04

† current Test umpire.

C.J.Egar & L.P.Rowan stood together in 19 Tests, four more than the partnership of R.Gosein & D.Sang Hue.

Individual Career Records

These career records for all players appearing in official Test matches are complete to 22 August 2006.
(* not out; # retired hurt)

AUSTRALIA (397 Players)						BATTING AND FIELDING							BOWLING					
Player	M	I	NO	Runs	HS	Avge	100	50	0	C/S	Balls	Mdns	Runs	Wkts	Avge	5wi	10w	Best
a'Beckett,EL	4	7	0	143	41	20.42	0	0	0	4	1062	47	317	3	105.66	0	0	1/41
Alderman,TM	41	53	22	203	26*	6.54	0	0	13	27	10181	432	4616	170	27.15	14	1	6/47
Alexander,G	2	4	0	52	33	13.00	0	0	0	2	168	13	93	2	46.50	0	0	2/69
Alexander,HH	1	2	1	17	17*	17.00	0	0	1	0	276	3	154	1	154.00	0	0	1/129
Allan,FE	1	1	0	5	5	5.00	0	0	0	0	180	15	80	4	20.00	0	0	2/30
Allan,PJ	1					0	0	0	0	192	6	83	2		41.5 0	0	0	2/58
Allen,RC	1	2	0	44	30	22.00	0	0	0	2								
Andrews,TJE	16	23	1	592	94	26.90	0	4	0	12	156	5	116	1	116.00	0	0	1/23
Angel,J	4	7	1	35	11	5.83	0	0	2	1	748	24	463	10	46.30	0	0	3/54
Archer,KA	5	9	0	234	48	26.00	0	0	1	0								
Archer,RG	19	30	1	713	128	24.58	1	2	4	20	3576	160	1318	48	27.45	1	0	5/53
Armstrong,WW	50	84	10	2863	159*	38.68	6	8	6	44	8022	407	2923	87	33.59	3	0	6/35
Badcock,CL	7	12	1	160	118	14.54	1	0	4	3								
Bannerman,AC	28	50	2	1108	94	23.08	0	8	3	21	292	17	163	4	40.75	0	0	3/111
Bannerman,C	3	6	2	239	165#	59.75	1	0	0	0								
Bardsley,W	41	66	5	2469	193*	40.47	6	14	6	12								
Barnes,SG	13	19	2	1072	234	63.05	3	5	1	14	594	11	218	4	54.50	0	0	2/25
Barnett,BA	4	8	1	195	57	27.85	0	1	0	3/2								
Barrett,JE	2	4	1	80	67*	26.66	0	1	1	1								
Beard,GR	3	5	0	114	49	22.80	0	0	0	0	259	17	109	1	109.00	0	0	1/26
Benaud,J	3	5	0	223	142	44.60	1	0	0	0	24	1	12	2	6.00	0	0	2/12
Benaud,R	63	97	7	2201	122	24.45	3	9	8	65	19108	805	6704	248	27.03	16	1	7/72
Bennett,MJ	3	5	2	71	23	23.66	0	0	0	5	665	24	325	6	54.16	0	0	3/79
Bevan,MG	18	30	3	785	91	29.07	0	6	4	8	1285	30	703	29	24.24	1	1	6/82
Bichel,AJ	19	22	1	355	71	16.90	0	1	3	16	3337	111	1870	58	32.24	1	0	5/60
Blackham,JM	35	62	11	800	74	15.68	0	4	6	37/24								
Blackie,DD	3	6	3	24	11*	8.00	0	0	2	2	1260	51	444	14	31.71	1	0	6/94
Blewett,GS	46	79	4	2552	214	34.02	4	15	6	45	1436	60	720	14	51.42	0	0	2/9
Bonnor,GJ	17	30	0	512	128	17.06	1	2	5	16	164	16	84	2	42.00	0	0	1/5
Boon,DC	107	190	20	7422	200	43.65	21	32	16	99	36	3	14	0	-	0	0	0/0
Booth,BC	29	48	6	1773	169	42.21	5	10	5	17	436	27	146	3	48.66	0	0	2/33
Border,AR	156	265	44	11174	205	50.56	27	63	11	156	4009	197	1525	39	39.10	2	1	7/46
Boyle,HF	12	16	4	153	36*	12.75	0	0	2	10	1743	175	641	32	20.03	1	0	6/42
Bracken,NW	5	6	2	70	37	17.50	0	0	0	2	1110	53	505	12	42.08	0	0	4/48
Bradman,DG	52	80	10	6996	334	99.94	29	13	7	32	160	3	72	2	36.00	0	0	1/8
Bright,RJ	25	39	8	445	33	14.35	0	0	6	13	5541	298	2180	53	41.13	4	1	7/87
Bromley,EH	2	4	0	38	26	9.50	0	0	0	2	60	4	19	0	-	0	0	0/0
Brown,WA	22	35	1	1592	206*	46.82	4	9	1	14	988	72	440	12	36.66	0	0	3/88
Bruce,W	14	26	2	702	80	29.25	0	5	1	12								
Burge,PJP	42	68	8	2290	181	38.16	4	12	5	23								
Burke,JW	24	44	7	1280	189	34.59	3	5	0	18	814	41	230	8	28.75	0	0	4/37
Burn,EJK	2	4	0	41	19	10.25	0	0	1	0								
Burton,FJ	2	4	2	4	2*	2.00	0	0	0	1/1								
Callaway,ST	3	6	1	87	41	17.40	0	0	1	0	471	33	142	6	23.66	1	0	5/37
Callen,IW	1	2	2	26	22*	-	0	0	0	1	440	5	191	6	31.83	0	0	3/83
Campbell,GD	4	4	0	10	6	2.50	0	0	2	1	951	29	503	13	38.69	0	0	3/79
Carkeek,W	6	5	2	16	6*	5.33	0	0	0	6/0								
Carlson,PH	2	4	0	23	21	5.75	0	0	2	2	368	10	99	2	49.50	0	0	2/41

AUSTRALIA (cont.)	**BATTING AND FIELDING**										**BOWLING**							
Player	M	I	NO	Runs	HS	Avge	100	50	0	C/S	Balls	Mdns	Runs	Wkts	Avge	5wi	10w	Best
Carter,H	28	47	9	873	72	22.97	0	4	4	44/21								
Chappell,GS	87	151	19	7110	247*	53.86	24	31	12	122	5327	208	1913	47	40.70	1	0	5/61
Chappell,IM	75	136	10	5345	196	42.42	14	26	11	105	2873	87	1316	20	65.80	0	0	2/21
Chappell,TM	3	6	1	79	27	15.80	0	0	0	2								
Charlton,PC	2	4	0	29	11	7.25	0	0	0	0	45	1	24	3	8.00	0	0	3/18
Chipperfield,AG	14	20	3	552	109	32.47	1	2	1	15	924	28	437	5	87.40	0	0	3/91
Clark,SR	4	5	2	31	13*	10.33	0	0	1	2	882	38	394	21	18.76	1	0	5/55
Clark,WM	10	19	2	98	33	5.76	0	0	8	6	2793	63	1265	44	28.75	0	0	4/46
Clarke,MJ	21	32	3	1079	151	37.20	2	4	0	17	158	3	75	8	9.37	1	0	6/9
Colley,DJ	3	4	0	84	54	21.00	0	1	0	1	729	20	312	6	52.00	0	0	3/83
Collins,HL	19	31	1	1352	203	45.06	4	6	0	13	654	31	252	4	63.00	0	0	2/47
Coningham,A	1	2	0	13	10	6.50	0	0	0	0	186	9	76	2	38.00	0	0	2/17
Connolly,AN	29	45	20	260	37	10.40	0	0	10	17	7818	289	2981	102	29.22	4	0	6/47
Cook,SH	2	2	2	3	3*	-	0	0	0	0	224	10	142	7	20.28	1	0	5/39
Cooper,BB	1	2	0	18	15	9.00	0	0	0	2								
Cooper,WH	2	3	1	13	7	6.50	0	0	0	1	446	31	226	9	25.11	1	0	6/120
Corling,GE	5	4	1	5	3	1.66	0	0	2	0	1159	50	447	12	37.25	0	0	4/60
Cosier,GJ	18	32	1	897	168	28.93	2	3	3	14	899	30	341	5	68.19	0	0	2/26
Cottam,JT	1	2	0	4	3	2.00	0	0	0	1								
Cotter,A	21	37	2	457	45	13.05	0	0	6	8	4633	86	2549	89	28.64	7	0	7/148
Coulthard,G	1	1	1	6	6*	-	0	0	0	0								
Cowper,RM	27	46	2	2061	307	46.84	5	10	3	21	3005	138	1139	36	31.63	0	0	4/48
Craig,ID	11	18	0	358	53	19.88	0	2	3	2								
Crawford,WPA	4	5	2	53	34	17.66	0	0	1	1	437	27	107	7	15.28	0	0	3/28
Cullen,DJ	1						0	0	0	0	84	0	54	1	54.00	0	0	1/25
Dale,AC	2	3	0	6	5	2.00	0	0	1	0	348	19	187	6	31.16	0	0	3/71
Darling,J	34	60	2	1657	178	28.56	3	8	8	27								
Darling,LS	12	18	1	474	85	27.88	0	3	2	8	162	7	65	0	-	0	0	0/3
Darling,WM	14	27	1	697	91	26.80	0	6	1	5								
Davidson,AK	44	61	7	1328	80	24.59	0	5	1	42	11587	431	3819	186	20.53	14	2	7/93
Davis,IC	15	27	1	692	105	26.61	1	4	3	9								
Davis,SP	1	1	0	0	0	0.00	0	0	1	0	150	4	70	0	-	0	0	0/70
de Courcy,JH	3	6	1	81	41	16.20	0	0	0	3								
Dell,AR	2	2	2	6	3*	-	0	0	0	0	559	18	160	6	26.66	0	0	3/65
Dodemaide,AIC	10	15	6	202	50	22.44	0	1	0	6	2184	92	953	34	28.02	1	0	6/58
Donnan,H	5	10	1	75	15	8.33	0	0	1	1	54	2	22	0	-	0	0	0/22
Dooland,B	3	5	1	76	29	19.00	0	0	0	3	880	9	419	9	46.55	0	0	4/69
Duff,RA	22	40	3	1317	146	35.59	2	6	0	14	180	8	85	4	21.25	0	0	2/43
Duncan,JRF	1	1	0	3	3	3.00	0	0	0	0	112	4	30	0	-	0	0	0/30
Dyer,GC	6	6	0	131	60	21.83	0	1	1	22/2								
Dymock,G	21	32	7	236	31*	9.43	0	0	7	1	5545	179	2116	78	27.12	5	1	7/67
Dyson,J	30	58	7	1359	127*	26.64	2	5	4	10								
Eady,CJ	2	4	1	20	10*	6.66	0	0	0	2	223	14	112	7	16.00	0	0	3/30
Eastwood,KH	1	2	0	5	5	2.50	0	0	1	0	40	0	21	1	21.00	0	0	1/21
Ebeling,HI	1	2	0	43	41	21.50	0	0	0	0	186	9	89	3	29.66	0	0	3/74
Edwards,JD	3	6	1	48	26	9.60	0	0	3	1								
Edwards,R	20	32	3	1171	170*	40.37	2	9	4	7	12	0	20	0	-	0	0	0/20
Edwards,WJ	3	6	0	68	30	11.33	0	0	2	0								
Elliott,MTG	21	36	1	1172	199	33.48	3	4	5	14	12	1	4	0	-	0	0	0/0
Emery,PA	1	1	1	8	8*	-	0	0	0	5/1								
Emery,SH	4	2	0	6	5	3.00	0	0	0	2	462	13	249	5	49.80	0	0	2/46
Evans,E	6	10	2	82	33	10.25	0	0	3	5	1237	166	332	7	47.42	0	0	3/64
Fairfax,AG	10	12	4	410	65	51.25	0	4	0	15	1520	54	645	21	30.71	0	0	4/31

AUSTRALIA (cont.)	**BATTING AND FIELDING**										**BOWLING**							
Player	M	I	NO	Runs	HS	Avge	100	50	0	C/S	Balls	Mdns	Runs	Wkts	Avge	5wi	10w	Best
Favell,LE	19	31	3	757	101	27.03	1	5	2	9								
Ferris,JJ	8	16	4	98	20*	8.16	0	0	1	4	2030	224	684	48	14.25	4	0	5/26
Fingleton,JHW	18	29	1	1189	136	42.46	5	3	3	13								
Fleetwood-Smith,LO	10	11	5	54	16*	9.00	0	0	2	0	3093	78	1570	42	37.38	2	1	6/110
Fleming,DW	20	19	3	305	71*	19.06	0	2	7	9	4129	153	1942	75	25.89	3	0	5/30
Francis,BC	3	5	0	52	27	10.40	0	0	1	1								
Freeman,EW	11	18	0	345	76	19.16	0	2	0	5	2183	58	1128	34	33.17	0	0	4/52
Freer,FAW	1	1	1	28	28*	-	0	0	0	0	160	3	74	3	24.66	0	0	2/49
Gannon,JB	3	5	4	3	3*	3.00	0	0	1	3	726	13	361	11	32.81	0	0	4/77
Garrett,TW	19	33	6	339	51*	12.55	0	1	5	7	2728	296	970	36	26.94	2	0	6/78
Gaunt,RA	3	4	2	6	3	3.00	0	0	0	1	716	14	310	7	44.28	0	0	3/53
Gehrs,DRA	6	11	0	221	67	20.09	0	2	1	6	6	0	4	0	-	0	0	0/4
Giffen,G	31	53	0	1238	161	23.35	1	6	5	24	6391	434	2791	103	27.09	7	1	7/117
Giffen,WF	3	6	0	11	3	1.8	3	0	0	1	1							
Gilbert,DR	9	12	4	57	15	7.12	0	0	1	0	1647	49	843	16	52.68	0	0	3/48
Gilchrist,AC	84	119	18	5029	204*	49.79	16	21	12	315/33								
Gillespie,JN	71	93	28	1218	201*	18.73	1	2	13	27	14234	630	6770	259	26.13	8	0	7/37
Gilmour,GJ	15	22	1	483	101	23.00	1	3	3	8	2661	51	1406	54	26.03	3	0	6/85
Gleeson,JW	29	46	8	395	45	10.39	0	0	11	17	8857	378	3367	93	36.20	3	0	5/61
Graham,H	6	10	0	301	107	30.10	2	0	2	3								
Gregory,DW	3	5	2	60	43	20.00	0	0	0	0	20	1	9	0	-	0	0	0/9
Gregory,EJ	1	2	0	11	11	5.50	0	0	1	1								
Gregory,ES	58	100	7	2282	201	24.53	4	8	12	25	30	0	33	0	-	0	0	0/4
Gregory,JM	24	34	3	1146	119	36.96	2	7	3	37	5582	138	2648	85	31.15	4	0	7/69
Gregory,RG	2	3	0	153	80	51.00	0	2	0	1	24	0	14	0	-	0	0	0/14
Grimmett,CV	37	50	10	557	50	13.92	0	1	7	17	14513	736	5231	216	24.21	21	7	7/40
Groube,TU	1	2	0	11	11	5.50	0	0	1	0								
Grout,ATW	51	67	8	890	74	15.08	0	3	11	163/24								
Guest,CEJ	1	1	0	11	11	11.00	0	0	0	0	144	0	59	0	-	0	0	0/8
Hamence,RA	3	4	1	81	30*	27.00	0	0	0	1								
Hammond,JR	5	5	2	28	19	9.33	0	0	1	2	1031	47	488	15	32.53	0	0	4/38
Harry,J	1	2	0	8	6	4.00	0	0	0	1								
Hartigan,MJ	2	4	0	170	116	42.50	1	0	0	1	12	0	7	0	-	0	0	0/7
Hartkopf,AEV	1	2	0	80	80	40.00	0	1	1	0	240	2	134	1	134.00	0	0	1/120
Harvey,MR	1	2	0	43	31	21.50	0	0	0	0								
Harvey,RN	79	137	10	6149	205	48.41	21	24	7	64	414	23	120	3	40.00	0	0	1/8
Hassett,AL	43	69	3	3073	198*	46.56	10	11	1	30	111	2	78	0	-	0	0	0/1
Hawke,NJN	27	37	15	365	45*	16.59	0	0	6	9	6974	238	2677	91	29.41	6	1	7/105
Hauritz,NM	1	2	0	15	15	7.50	0	0	1	1	162	4	103	5	20.60	0	0	3/16
Hayden,ML	83	148	12	7138	380	52.48	25	25	11	108	54	0	40	0	-	0	0	0/7
Hazlitt,GR	9	12	4	89	34*	11.12	0	0	2	4	1563	74	623	23	27.08	1	0	7/25
Healy,IA	119	182	23	4356	161*	27.39	4	22	18	366/29								
Hendry,HSTL	11	18	2	335	112	20.93	1	0	1	10	1706	73	640	16	40.00	0	0	3/36
Hibbert,PA	1	2	0	15	13	7.50	0	0	0	1								
Higgs,JD	22	36	16	111	16	5.55	0	0	5	3	4752	176	2057	66	31.16	2	0	7/143
Hilditch,AMJ	18	34	0	1073	119	31.55	2	6	3	13								
Hill,C	49	89	2	3412	191	39.21	7	19	9	33								
Hill,JC	3	6	3	21	8*	7.00	0	0	1	2	606	29	273	8	34.12	0	0	3/35
Hoare,DE	1	2	0	35	35	17.50	0	0	1	2	232	0	156	2	78.00	0	0	2/68
Hodge,BJ	5	9	2	409	203*	58.42	1	1	0	9	12	0	8	0	-	0	0	0/8
Hodges,JR	2	4	1	10	8	3.33	0	0	1	0	136	9	84	6	14.00	0	0	2/7
Hogan,TG	7	12	1	205	42*	18.63	0	0	1	2	1436	54	706	15	47.06	1	0	5/66

AUSTRALIA (cont.)	**BATTING AND FIELDING**										**BOWLING**							
Player	M	I	NO	Runs	HS	Avge	100	50	0	C/S	Balls	Mdns	Runs	Wkts	Avge	5wi	10w	Best
Hogg,GB	4	5	1	38	17*	9.50	0	0	0	0	774	25	452	9	50.22	0	0	2/40
Hogg,RM	38	58	13	439	52	9.75	0	1	14	7	7633	230	3503	123	28.47	6	2	6/74
Hohns,TV	7	7	1	136	40	22.66	0	0	1	3	1528	84	580	17	34.11	0	0	3/59
Hole,GB	18	33	2	789	66	25.45	0	6	2	21	398	14	126	3	42.00	0	0	1/9
Holland,RG	11	15	4	35	10	3.18	0	0	7	5	2889	124	1352	34	39.76	3	2	6/54
Hookes,DW	23	41	3	1306	143*	34.36	1	8	4	12	96	4	41	1	41.00	0	0	1/4
Hopkins,AJY	20	33	2	509	43	16.41	0	0	4	11	1327	49	696	26	26.76	0	0	4/81
Horan,TP	15	27	2	471	124	18.84	1	1	3	6	373	45	143	11	13.00	1	0	6/40
Hordern,HV	7	13	2	254	50	23.09	0	1	1	6	2148	49	1075	46	23.36	5	2	7/90
Hornibrook,PM	6	7	1	60	26	10.00	0	0	1	7	1579	63	664	17	39.05	1	0	7/92
Howell,WP	18	27	6	158	35	7.52	0	0	8	12	3892	245	1407	49	28.71	1	0	5/81
Hughes,KJ	70	124	6	4415	213	37.41	9	22	10	50	85	4	28	0	-	0	0	0/0
Hughes,MG	53	70	8	1032	72*	16.64	0	2	10	23	12285	499	6017	212	28.38	7	1	8/87
Hunt,WA	1	1	0	0	0	0.00	0	0	1	1	96	2	39	0	-	0	0	0/14
Hurst,AG	12	20	3	102	26	6.00	0	0	10	3	3054	74	1200	43	27.90	2	0	5/28
Hurwood,A	2	2	0	5	5	2.50	0	0	1	2	517	28	170	11	15.45	0	0	4/22
Hussey,MEK	11	19	4	1139	182	75.93	4	4	0	3	24	0	18	0	-	0	0	0/2
Inverarity,RJ	6	11	1	174	56	17.40	0	1	1	4	372	26	93	4	23.25	0	0	3/26
Iredale,FA	14	23	1	807	140	36.68	2	4	2	16	12	1	3	0	-	0	0	0/3
Ironmonger,H	14	21	5	42	12	2.62	0	0	6	3	4695	328	1330	74	17.97	4	2	7/23
Iverson,JB	5	7	3	3	1*	0.75	0	0	2	2	1108	29	320	21	15.23	1	0	6/27
Jackson,A	8	11	1	474	164	47.40	1	2	1	7								
Jaques,PA	2	3	0	96	66	32.00	0	1	0	1								
Jarman,BN	19	30	3	400	78	14.81	0	2	5	50/4								
Jarvis,AH	11	21	3	303	82	16.83	0	1	1	9/9								
Jenner,TJ	9	14	5	208	74	23.11	0	1	1	5	1881	62	749	24	31.20	1	0	5/90
Jennings,CB	6	8	2	107	32	17.83	0	0	2	5								
Johnson,IWG	45	66	12	1000	77	18.51	0	6	10	30	8780	330	3182	109	29.19	3	0	7/44
Johnson,LJ	1	1	1	25	25*	-	0	0	0	2	282	10	74	6	12.33	0	0	3/8
Johnston,WA	40	49	25	273	29	11.37	0	0	7	16	11048	372	3826	160	23.91	7	0	6/44
Jones,DM	52	89	11	3631	216	46.55	11	14	11	34	198	15	64	1	64.00	0	0	1/5
Jones,E	19	26	1	126	20	5.04	0	0	5	21	3754	161	1857	64	29.01	3	1	7/88
Jones,SP	12	24	4	428	87	21.40	0	1	3	12	262	26	112	6	18.66	0	0	4/47
Joslin,LR	1	2	0	9	7	4.50	0	0	0	0								
Julian,BP	7	9	1	128	56*	16.00	0	1	3	4	1098	43	599	15	39.93	0	0	4/36
Kasprowicz,MS	38	54	12	445	25	10.59	0	0	7	16	7158	246	3716	113	32.88	4	0	7/36
Katich,SM	22	36	3	1258	125	38.12	2	8	1	14	659	10	406	12	33.83	1	0	6/65
Kelleway,C	26	42	4	1422	147	37.42	3	6	1	24	4363	146	1683	52	32.36	1	0	5/33
Kelly,JJ	36	56	17	664	46*	17.02	0	0	7	43/20								
Kelly,TJD	2	3	0	64	35	21.33	0	0	0	1								
Kendall,TK	2	4	1	39	17*	13.00	0	0	0	2	563	56	215	14	15.35	1	0	7/55
Kent,MF	3	6	0	171	54	28.50	0	2	0	6								
Kerr,RB	2	4	0	31	17	7.75	0	0	1	1								
Kippax,AF	22	34	1	1192	146	36.12	2	8	1	13	72	5	19	0	-	0	0	0/2
Kline,LF	13	16	9	58	15*	8.28	0	0	3	9	2373	113	776	34	22.82	1	0	7/75
Laird,BM	21	40	2	1341	92	35.28	0	11	2	16	18	1	12	0	-	0	0	0/3
Langer,JL	99	171	10	7371	250	45.78	22	29	9	67	6	0	3	0	-	0	0	0/3
Langley,GRA	26	37	12	374	53	14.96	0	1	3	83/15								
Laughlin,TJ	3	5	0	87	35	17.40	0	0	0	3	516	16	262	6	43.66	1	0	5/101
Laver,FJ	15	23	6	196	45	11.52	0	0	4	8	2361	121	964	37	26.05	2	0	8/31
Law,SG	1	1	1	54	54*	-	0	1	0	1	18	1	9	0	-	0	0	0/9
Lawry,WM	67	123	12	5234	210	47.15	13	27	6	30	14	1	6	0	-	0	0	0/0
Lawson,GF	46	68	12	894	74	15.96	0	4	6	10	11118	386	5501	180	30.56	11	2	8/112

AUSTRALIA (cont.)			**BATTING AND FIELDING**								**BOWLING**							
Player	M	I	NO	Runs	HS	Avge	100	50	0	C/S	Balls	Mdns	Runs	Wkts	Avge	5wi	10w	Best
Lee,B	53	58	11	1029	64	21.89	0	3	9	14	10990	375	6541	209	31.29	7	0	5/30
Lee,PK	2	3	0	57	42	19.00	0	0	1	1	436	19	212	5	42.40	0	0	4/111
Lehmann,DS	27	42	2	1798	177	44.95	5	10	2	11	974	36	412	15	27.46	0	0	3/42
Lillee,DK	70	90	24	905	73*	13.71	0	1	10	23	18467	652	8493	355	23.92	23	7	7/83
Lindwall,RR	61	84	13	1502	118	21.15	2	5	9	26	13650	419	5251	228	23.03	12	0	7/38
Love,HSB	1	2	0	8	5	4.00	0	0	0	3/0								
Love,ML	5	8	3	243	100*	48.60	1	1	2	7								
Loxton,SJE	12	15	0	554	101	36.93	1	3	1	7	906	20	349	8	43.62	0	0	3/55
Lyons,JJ	14	27	0	731	134	27.07	1	3	1	3	316	17	149	6	24.83	1	0	5/30
McAlister,PA	8	16	1	252	41	16.79	0	0	0	10								
McCabe,SJ	39	62	5	2748	232	48.21	6	13	4	41	3746	127	1543	36	42.86	0	0	4/13
Macartney,CG	35	55	4	2131	170	41.78	7	9	1	17	3561	177	1240	45	27.55	2	1	7/58
McCool,CL	14	17	4	459	104*	35.30	1	1	0	14	2504	44	958	36	26.61	3	0	5/41
McCormick,EL	12	14	5	54	17*	6.00	0	0	3	8	2107	50	1079	36	29.97	0	0	4/101
McCosker,RB	25	46	5	1622	127	39.56	4	9	5	21								
McDermott,CJ	71	90	13	940	42*	12.20	0	0	13	19	16586	579	8332	291	28.63	14	2	8/97
McDonald,CC	47	83	4	3107	170	39.32	5	17	2	14	8	0	3	0	-	0	0	0/3
McDonald,EA	11	12	5	116	36	16.57	0	0	1	3	2885	90	1431	43	33.27	2	0	5/32
McDonnell,PS	19	34	1	955	147	28.93	3	2	6	6	52	1	53	0	-	0	0	0/11
MacGill,SCG	39	43	9	347	43	10.20	0	1	11	16	10066	339	5305	189	28.06	11	2	8/108
McGrath,GD	118	131	49	629	61	7.67	0	1	33	37	27885	1400	11642	539	21.59	28	3	8/24
McIlwraith,J	1	2	0	9	7	4.50	0	0	0	1								
McIntyre,PE	2	4	1	22	16	7.33	0	0	2	0	393	10	194	5	38.80	0	0	3/103
Mackay,KD	37	52	7	1507	89	33.48	0	13	6	16	5792	267	1721	50	34.41	2	0	6/42
McKenzie,GD	60	89	12	945	76	12.27	0	2	15	34	17681	547	7328	246	29.78	16	3	8/71
McKibbin,TR	5	8	2	88	28*	14.66	0	0	2	4	1032	41	496	17	29.17	0	0	3/35
McLaren,JW	1	2	2	0	0*	-	0	0	0	0	144	3	70	1	70.00	0	0	1/23
Maclean,JA	4	8	1	79	33*	11.28	0	0	2	18/0								
McLeod,CE	17	29	5	573	112	23.87	1	4	5	9	3374	171	1325	33	40.15	2	0	5/65
McLeod,RW	6	11	0	146	31	13.27	0	0	0	3	1089	67	382	12	31.83	1	0	5/53
McShane,PG	3	6	1	26	12*	5.20	0	0	3	2	108	9	48	1	48.00	0	0	1/39
Maddocks,LV	7	12	2	177	69	17.70	0	1	3	18/1								
Maguire,JN	3	5	1	28	15*	7.00	0	0	2	2	616	21	323	10	32.30	0	0	4/57
Mailey,AA	21	29	9	222	46*	11.10	0	0	3	14	6119	115	3358	99	33.91	6	2	9/121
Mallett,AA	38	50	13	430	43*	11.62	0	0	10	30	9990	419	3940	132	29.84	6	1	8/59
Malone,MF	1	1	0	46	46	46.00	0	0	0	0	342	24	77	6	12.83	1	0	5/63
Mann,AL	4	8	0	189	105	23.62	1	0	2	2	552	4	316	4	79.00	0	0	3/12
Marr,AP	1	2	0	5	5	2.50	0	0	1	0	48	6	14	0	-	0	0	0/3
Marsh,GR	50	93	7	2854	138	33.18	4	15	3	38								
Marsh,RW	96	150	13	3633	132	26.51	3	16	12	343/12	72	1	54	0	-	0	0	0/11
Martin,JW	8	13	1	214	55	17.83	0	1	3	5	1846	57	832	17	48.94	0	0	3/56
Martyn,DR	65	106	14	4361	165	47.40	13	23	7	33	468	16	168	2	84.00	0	0	1/0
Massie,HH	9	16	0	249	55	15.56	0	1	2	5								
Massie,RAL	6	8	1	78	42	11.14	0	0	3	1	1739	74	647	31	20.87	2	1	8/53
Matthews,CD	3	5	0	54	32	10.80	0	0	1	1	570	18	313	6	52.16	0	0	3/95
Matthews,GRJ	33	53	8	1849	130	41.08	4	12	2	17	6271	257	2942	61	48.22	2	1	5/103
Matthews,TJ	8	10	1	153	53	17.00	0	1	1	7	1081	46	419	16	26.18	0	0	4/29
May,TBA	24	28	12	225	42*	14.06	0	0	3	6	6577	321	2606	75	34.74	3	0	5/9
Mayne,LC	6	11	3	76	13	9.50	0	0	0	3	1251	37	628	19	33.05	0	0	4/43
Mayne,RE	4	4	1	64	25*	21.33	0	0	1	2	6	0	1	0	-	0	0	0/1
Meckiff,I	18	20	7	154	45*	11.84	0	0	2	9	3734	120	1423	45	31.62	2	0	6/38
Meuleman,KD	1	1	0	0	0	0.00	0	0	1	1								
Midwinter,WE	8	14	1	174	37	13.38	0	0	1	5	949		333	14	23.78	1	0	5/78

AUSTRALIA (cont.)	**BATTING AND FIELDING**										**BOWLING**							
Player	M	I	NO	Runs	HS	Avge	100	50	0	C/S	Balls	Mdns	Runs	Wkts	Avge	5wi	10w	Best
Miller,CR	18	24	3	174	43	8.28	0	0	7	6	4091	163	1805	69	26.15	3	1	5/32
Miller,KR	55	87	7	2958	147	36.97	7	13	5	38	10461	337	3906	170	22.97	7	1	7/60
Minnett,RB	9	15	0	391	90	26.06	0	3	3	0	589	26	290	11	26.36	0	0	4/34
Misson,FM	5	5	3	38	25*	19.00	0	0	1	6	1197	30	616	16	38.50	0	0	4/58
Moody,TM	8	14	0	456	106	32.57	2	3	1	9	432	19	147	2	73.50	0	0	1/17
Moroney,J	7	12	1	383	118	34.81	2	1	3	0								
Morris,AR	46	79	3	3533	206	46.48	12	12	4	15	111	1	50	2	25.00	0	0	1/5
Morris,S	1	2	1	14	10*	14.00	0	0	0	0	136	14	73	2	36.50	0	0	2/73
Moses,H	6	10	0	198	33	19.79	0	0	0	1								
Moss,JK	1	2	1	60	38*	60.00	0	0	0	0								
Moule,WH	1	2	0	40	34	20.00	0	0	0	1	51	4	23	3	7.66	0	0	3/23
Muller,SA	2	2	2	6	6*	-	0	0	0	2	348	8	258	7	36.85	0	0	3/68
Murdoch,WL	18	33	5	896	211	32.00	2	1	3	14/0								
Musgrove,HA	1	2	0	13	9	6.50	0	0	0	0								
Nagel,LE	1	2	1	21	21*	21.00	0	0	1	0	262	9	110	2	55.00	0	0	2/110
Nash,LJ	2	2	0	30	17	15.00	0	0	0	6	311	12	126	10	12.60	0	0	4/18
Nicholson,MJ	1	2	0	14	9	7.00	0	0	0	0	150	4	115	4	28.75	0	0	3/56
Nitschke,HC	2	2	0	53	47	26.50	0	0	0	3								
Noble,MA	42	73	7	1997	133	30.25	1	16	4	26	7159	361	3025	121	25.00	9	2	7/17
Noblet,G	3	4	1	22	13*	7.33	0	0	1	1	774	25	183	7	26.14	0	0	3/21
Nothling,OE	1	2	0	52	44	26.00	0	0	0	0	276	15	72	0	-	0	0	0/12
O'Brien,LPJ	5	8	0	211	61	26.37	0	2	1	3								
O'Connor,JDA	4	8	1	86	20	12.28	0	0	0	3	692	24	340	13	26.15	1	0	5/40
O'Donnell,SP	6	10	3	206	48	29.42	0	0	1	4	940	37	504	6	84.00	0	0	3/37
Ogilvie,AD	5	10	0	178	47	17.79	0	0	3	5								
O'Keeffe,KJ	24	34	9	644	85	25.76	0	1	3	15	5384	189	2018	53	38.07	1	0	5/101
Oldfield,WAS	54	80	17	1427	65*	22.65	0	4	9	78/52								
O'Neill,NC	42	69	8	2779	181	45.55	6	15	6	21	1392	48	667	17	39.23	0	0	4/41
O'Reilly,WJ	27	39	7	410	56*	12.81	0	1	6	7	10024	585	3254	144	22.59	11	3	7/54
Oxenham,RK	7	10	0	151	48	15.10	0	0	2	4	1802	112	522	14	37.28	0	0	4/39
Palmer,GE	17	25	4	296	48	14.09	0	0	3	13	4517	452	1678	78	21.51	6	2	7/65
Park,RL	1	1	0	0	0	0.00	0	0	1	0	6	0	9	0	-	0	0	0/9
Pascoe,LS	14	19	9	106	30*	10.60	0	0	3	2	3403	112	1668	64	26.06	1	0	5/59
Pellew,CE	10	14	1	484	116	37.23	2	1	0	4	78	3	34	0	-	0	0	0/3
Phillips,WB	27	48	2	1485	159	32.28	2	7	1	52/0								
Phillips,WN	1	2	0	22	14	11.00	0	0	0	0								
Philpott,PI	8	10	1	93	22	10.33	0	0	0	5	2262	67	1000	26	38.46	1	0	5/90
Ponsford,WH	29	48	4	2122	266	48.22	7	6	1	21								
Ponting,RT	104	173	24	8692	257	58.33	31	33	8	119	527	23	231	5	46.20	0	0	1/0
Pope,RJ	1	2	0	3	3	1.50	0	0	1	0								
Rackemann,CG	12	14	4	53	15*	5.30	0	0	5	2	2719	132	1137	39	29.15	3	1	6/86
Ransford,VS	20	38	6	1211	143*	37.84	1	7	2	10	43	3	28	1	28.00	0	0	1/9
Redpath,IR	66	120	11	4737	171	43.45	8	31	9	83	64	2	41	0	-	0	0	0/0
Reedman,JC	1	2	0	21	17	10.50	0	0	0	1	57	2	24	1	24.00	0	0	1/12
Reid,BA	27	34	14	93	13	4.65	0	0	6	5	6244	244	2784	113	24.63	5	2	7/51
Reiffel,PR	35	50	14	955	79*	26.52	0	6	5	15	6403	279	2804	104	26.96	5	0	6/71
Renneberg,DA	8	13	7	22	9	3.66	0	0	3	2	1598	42	830	23	36.08	2	0	5/39
Richardson,AJ	9	13	0	403	100	31.00	1	2	1	1	1812	91	521	12	43.41	0	0	2/20
Richardson,VY	19	30	0	706	138	23.53	1	1	5	24								
Rigg,KE	8	12	0	401	127	33.41	1	1	0	5								
Ring,DT	13	21	2	426	67	22.42	0	4	2	5	3024	69	1305	35	37.28	2	0	6/72
Ritchie,GM	30	53	5	1690	146	35.20	3	7	1	14	6	0	10	0	-	0	0	0/10
Rixon,SJ	13	24	3	394	54	18.76	0	2	4	42/5								

AUSTRALIA (cont.)	BATTING AND FIELDING										BOWLING							
Player	M	I	NO	Runs	HS	Avge	100	50	0	C/S	Balls	Mdns	Runs	Wkts	Avge	5wi	10w	Best
Robertson,GR	4	7	0	140	57	20.00	0	1	2	1	898	19	515	13	39.61	0	0	4/72
Robertson,WR	1	2	0	2	2	1.00	0	0	1	0	44	3	24	0	-	0	0	0/24
Robinson,RD	3	6	0	100	34	16.66	0	0	0	4								
Robinson,RH	1	2	0	5	3	2.50	0	0	0	1								
Rorke,GF	4	4	2	9	7	4.50	0	0	1	1	703	26	203	10	20.29	0	0	3/23
Rutherford,JW	1	1	0	30	30	30.00	0	0	0	0	36	2	15	1	15.00	0	0	1/11
Ryder,J	20	32	5	1394	201*	51.62	3	9	1	17	1897	71	743	17	43.70	0	0	2/20
Saggers,RA	6	5	2	30	14	10.00	0	0	0	16/8								
Saunders,JV	14	23	6	39	11*	2.29	0	0	8	5	3565	116	1796	79	22.73	6	0	7/34
Scott,HJH	8	14	1	359	102	27.61	1	1	0	8	28	1	26	0	-	0	0	0/9
Sellers,RHD	1	1	0	0	0	0.00	0	0	1	1	30	1	17	0	-	0	0	0/17
Serjeant,CS	12	23	1	522	124	23.72	1	2	4	13								
Sheahan,AP	31	53	6	1594	127	33.91	2	7	3	17								
Shepherd,BK	9	14	2	502	96	41.83	0	5	1	2	26	1	9	0	-	0	0	0/3
Sievers,MW	3	6	1	67	25*	13.40	0	0	0	4	602	25	161	9	17.88	1	0	5/21
Simpson,RB	62	111	7	4869	311	46.81	10	27	8	110	6881	253	3001	71	42.26	2	0	5/57
Sincock,DJ	3	4	1	80	29	26.66	0	0	0	2	724	7	410	8	51.25	0	0	3/67
Slater,KN	1	1	1	1	1*	-	0	0	0	0	256	9	101	2	50.50	0	0	2/40
Slater,MJ	74	131	7	5312	219	42.83	14	21	9	33	25	1	10	1	10.00	0	0	1/4
Sleep,PR	14	21	1	483	90	24.15	0	3	4	4	2982	132	1397	31	45.06	1	0	5/72
Slight,J	1	2	0	11	11	5.50	0	0	1	0								
Smith,DBM	2	3	1	30	24*	15.00	0	0	1	0								
Smith,SB	3	5	0	41	12	8.20	0	0	0	1								
Spofforth,FR	18	29	6	217	50	9.43	0	1	6	11	4185	416	1731	94	18.41	7	4	7/44
Stackpole,KR	43	80	5	2807	207	37.42	7	14	5	47	2321	86	1001	15	66.73	0	0	2/33
Stevens,GB	4	7	0	112	28	16.00	0	0	0	2								
Symonds,A	10	15	0	286	72	19.06	0	2	2	10	894	33	409	9	45.44	0	0	3/50
Taber,HB	16	27	5	353	48	16.04	0	0	3	56/4								
Tait,SW	2	3	2	8	4	8.00	0	0	0	0	288	5	210	5	42.00	0	0	3/97
Tallon,D	21	26	3	394	92	17.13	0	2	3	50/8								
Taylor,JM	20	28	0	997	108	35.60	1	8	1	11	114	5	45	1	45.00	0	0	1/25
Taylor,MA	104	186	13	7525	334*	43.49	19	40	5	157	42	3	26	1	26.00	0	0	1/11
Taylor,PL	13	19	3	431	87	26.93	0	2	1	10	2227	101	1068	27	39.55	1	0	6/78
Thomas,G	8	12	1	325	61	29.54	0	3	0	3								
Thoms,GR	1	2	0	44	28	22.00	0	0	0	0								
Thomson,AL	4	5	4	22	12*	22.00	0	0	1	0	1519	33	654	12	54.50	0	0	3/79
Thomson,JR	51	73	20	679	49	12.81	0	0	14	20	10535	301	5601	200	28.00	8	0	6/46
Thomson,NFD	2	4	0	67	41	16.75	0	0	0	3	112	16	31	1	31.00	0	0	1/14
Thurlow,HM	1	1	0	0	0	0.00	0	0	1	0	234	7	86	0	-	0	0	0/33
Toohey,PM	15	29	1	893	122	31.89	1	7	3	9	2	0	4	0	-	0	0	0/4
Toshack,ERH	12	11	6	73	20*	14.60	0	0	1	4	3140	155	989	47	21.04	4	1	6/29
Travers,JPF	1	2	0	10	9	5.00	0	0	0	1	48	2	14	1	14.00	0	0	1/14
Tribe,GE	3	3	1	35	25*	17.50	0	0	0	0	760	9	330	2	165.00	0	0	2/48
Trott,AE	3	5	3	205	85*	102.50	0	2	1	4	474	17	192	9	21.33	1	0	8/43
Trott,GHS	24	42	0	921	143	21.92	1	4	7	21	1891	47	1019	29	35.13	0	0	4/71
Trumble,H	32	57	14	851	70	19.79	0	4	7	45	8099	452	3072	141	21.78	9	3	8/65
Trumble,JW	7	13	1	243	59	20.25	0	1	1	3	600	59	222	10	22.20	0	0	3/29
Trumper,VT	48	89	8	3163	214*	39.04	8	13	7	31	546	20	317	8	39.62	0	0	3/60
Turner,A	14	27	1	768	136	29.53	1	3	2	15								
Turner,CTB	17	32	4	323	29	11.53	0	0	6	8	5179	457	1670	101	16.53	11	2	7/43
Veivers,TR	21	30	4	813	88	31.26	0	7	3	7	4191	195	1375	33	41.66	0	0	4/68
Veletta,MRJ	8	11	0	207	39	18.81	0	0	0	12								
Waite,MG	2	3	0	11	8	3.66	0	0	1	1	552	23	190	1	190.00	0	0	1/150

AUSTRALIA (cont.)				**BATTING AND FIELDING**							**BOWLING**							
Player	M	I	NO	Runs	HS	Avge	100	50	0	C/S	Balls	Mdns	Runs	Wkts	Avge	5wi	10w	Best
Walker,MHN	34	43	13	586	78*	19.53	0	1	5	12	10094	380	3792	138	27.47	6	0	8/143
Wall,TW	18	24	5	121	20	6.36	0	0	5	11	4812	154	2010	56	35.89	3	0	5/14
Walters,FH	1	2	0	12	7	6.00	0	0	0	2								
Walters,KD	74	125	14	5357	250	48.26	15	33	4	43	3295	79	1425	49	29.08	1	0	5/66
Ward,FA	4	8	2	36	18	6.00	0	0	2	1	1268	30	574	11	52.18	1	0	6/102
Warne,SK	139	192	16	2946	99	16.73	0	11	34	120	39070	1711	17226	679	25.37	36	10	8/71
Watkins,JR	1	2	1	39	36	39.00	0	0	0	1	48	1	21	0	-	0	0	0/21
Watson,GD	5	9	0	97	50	10.77	0	1	3	1	552	23	254	6	42.33	0	0	2/67
Watson,SR	2	2	0	47	31	23.50	0	0	0	0	150	5	85	2	42.50	0	0	1/25
Watson,WJ	4	7	1	106	30	17.66	0	0	1	2	6	0	5	0	-	0	0	0/5
Waugh,ME	128	209	17	8029	153*	41.81	20	47	19	181	4853	171	2429	59	41.16	1	0	5/40
Waugh,SR	168	260	46	10927	200	51.06	32	50	22	112	7805	332	3445	92	37.44	3	0	5/28
Wellham,DM	6	11	0	257	103	23.36	1	0	0	5								
Wessels,KC	24	42	1	1761	179	42.95	4	9	3	18	90	3	42	0	-	0	0	0/2
Whatmore,DF	7	13	0	293	77	22.53	0	2	1	13	30	2	11	0	-	0	0	0/11
Whitney,MR	12	19	8	68	13	6.18	0	0	4	2	2672	90	1325	39	33.97	2	1	7/27
Whitty,WJ	14	19	7	161	39*	13.41	0	0	3	4	3357	163	1373	65	21.12	3	0	6/17
Wiener,JM	6	11	0	281	93	25.54	0	2	0	4	78	4	41	0	-	0	0	0/19
Williams,BA	4	6	3	23	10*	7.66	0	0	1	4	852	43	406	9	45.11	0	0	4/53
Wilson,JW	1						0	0	0	0	216	17	64	1	64.00	0	0	1/25
Wilson,P	1	2	2	0	0*	-	0	0	0	0	72	2	50	0	-	0	0	0/50
Wood,GM	59	112	6	3374	172	31.83	9	13	9	41								
Woodcock,AJ	1	1	0	27	27	27.00	0	0	0	1								
Woodfull,WM	35	54	4	2300	161	46.00	7	13	6	7								
Woods,SMJ	3	6	0	32	18	5.33	0	0	2	1	217	18	121	5	24.20	0	0	2/35
Woolley,RD	2	2	0	21	13	10.50	0	0	0	7/0								
Worrall,J	11	22	3	478	76	25.15	0	5	2	13	255	29	127	1	127.00	0	0	1/97
Wright,KJ	10	18	5	219	55*	16.84	0	1	2	31/4								
Yallop,GN	39	70	3	2756	268	41.13	8	9	3	23	192	5	116	1	116.00	0	0	1/21
Yardley,B	33	54	4	978	74	19.56	0	4	8	31	8909	379	3986	126	31.63	6	1	7/98
Young,S	1	2	1	4	4*	4.00	0	0	1	0	48	3	13	0	-	0	0	0/5
Zoehrer,TJ	10	14	2	246	52*	20.50	0	1	0	18/1								

ENGLAND (633 players)				**BATTING AND FIELDING**							**BOWLING**							
Player	M	I	NO	Runs	HS	Avge	100	50	0	C/S	Balls	Mdns	Runs	Wkts	Avge	5wi	10w	Best
Abel,R	13	22	2	744	132*	37.20	2	2	1	13								
Absolom,CA	1	2	0	58	52	29.00	0	1	0	0								
Adams,CJ	5	8	0	104	31	13.00	0	0	0	6	120	5	59	1	59.00	0	0	1/42
Afzaal,U	3	6	1	83	54	16.60	0	1	0	0	54	0	49	1	49.00	0	0	1/49
Agnew,JP	3	4	3	10	5	10.00	0	0	0	0	552	12	373	4	93.25	0	0	2/51
Allen,DA	39	51	15	918	88	25.50	0	5	4	10	11297	685	3779	122	30.97	4	0	5/30
Allen,GOB	25	33	2	750	122	24.19	1	3	1	20	4386	116	2379	81	29.37	5	1	7/80
Allom,MJC	5	3	2	14	8*	14.00	0	0	0	0	817	28	265	14	18.92	1	0	5/38
Allott,PJW	13	18	3	213	52*	14.20	0	1	2	4	2225	76	1084	26	41.69	1	0	6/61
Ames,LEG	47	72	12	2434	149	40.56	8	7	5	74/23								
Amiss,DL	50	88	10	3612	262*	46.30	11	11	10	24								
Anderson,JM	13	17	12	89	21*	17.80	0	0	0	4	2221	80	1353	41	33.00	2	0	5/73
Andrew,KV	2	4	1	29	15	9.66	0	0	0	1/0								
Appleyard,R	9	9	6	51	19*	17.00	0	0	0	4	1596	70	554	31	17.87	1	0	5/51
Archer,AG	1	2	1	31	24*	31.00	0	0	0	0								

ENGLAND (cont.)			**BATTING AND FIELDING**								**BOWLING**							
Player	M	I	NO	Runs	HS	Avge	100	50	0	C/S	Balls	Mdns	Runs	Wkts	Avge	5wi	10w	Best
Armitage,T	2	3	0	33	21	11.00	0	0	0	0	12	0	15	0	-	0	0	0/15
Arnold,EG	10	15	3	160	40	13.33	0	0	5	8	1677	64	788	31	25.41	1	0	5/37
Arnold,GG	34	46	11	421	59	12.02	0	1	5	9	7650	284	3254	115	28.29	6	0	6/45
Arnold,J	1	2	0	34	34	17.00	0	0	1	0								
Astill,WE	9	15	0	190	40	12.66	0	0	2	7	2182	98	856	25	34.24	0	0	4/58
Atherton,MA	115	212	7	7728	185*	37.69	16	46	20	83	408	12	302	2	151.00	0	0	1/20
Athey,CWJ	23	41	1	919	123	22.97	1	4	2	13								
Attewell,W	10	15	6	150	43*	16.66	0	0	4	9	2850	326	626	28	22.35	0	0	4/42
Bailey,RJ	4	8	0	119	43	14.87	0	0	2	0								
Bailey,TE	61	91	14	2290	134*	29.74	1	10	7	32	9712	379	3856	132	29.21	5	1	7/34
Bairstow,DL	4	7	1	125	59	20.83	0	1	1	12/1								
Bakewell,AH	6	9	0	409	107	45.44	1	3	0	3	18	0	8	0	-	0	0	0/8
Balderstone,JC	2	4	0	39	35	9.75	0	0	2	1	96	0	80	1	80.00	0	0	1/80
Barber,RW	28	45	3	1495	185	35.59	1	9	1	21	3426	101	1806	42	43.00	0	0	4/132
Barber,W	2	4	0	83	44	20.75	0	0	0	1	2	0	0	1	0.00	0	0	1/0
Barlow,GD	3	5	1	17	7*	4.25	0	0	1	0								
Barlow,RG	17	30	4	591	62	22.73	0	2	3	14	2456	325	767	34	22.55	3	0	7/40
Barnes,SF	27	39	9	242	38*	8.06	0	0	8	12	7873	356	3106	189	16.43	24	7	9/103
Barnes,W	21	33	2	725	134	23.38	1	5	3	19	2289	271	793	51	15.54	3	0	6/28
Barnett,CJ	20	35	4	1098	129	35.41	2	5	1	14	256	11	93	0	-	0	0	0/1
Barnett,KJ	4	7	0	207	80	29.57	0	2	1	1	36	0	32	0	-	0	0	0/32
Barratt,F	5	4	1	28	17	9.33	0	0	0	2	750	33	235	5	47.00	0	0	1/8
Barrington,KF	82	131	15	6806	256	58.67	20	35	5	58	2715	102	1300	29	44.82	0	0	3/4
Barton,VA	1	1	0	23	23	23.00	0	0	0	0								
Bates,W	15	26	2	656	64	27.33	0	5	0	9	2364	282	821	50	16.42	4	1	7/28
Batty,GJ	7	8	1	144	38	20.57	0	0	1	3	1394	34	733	11	66.63	0	0	3/55
Bean,G	3	5	0	92	50	18.40	0	1	0	4								
Bedser,AV	51	71	15	714	79	12.75	0	1	11	26	15918	574	5876	236	24.89	15	5	7/44
Bell,IR	18	32	5	1287	162*	47.66	5	7	3	18	102	3	64	1	64.00	0	0	1/33
Benjamin,JE	1	1	0	0	0	0.00	0	0	1	0	168	3	80	4	20.00	0	0	4/42
Benson,MR	1	2	0	51	30	25.50	0	0	0	0								
Berry,R	2	4	2	6	4*	3.00	0	0	1	2	653	47	228	9	25.33	1	0	5/63
Bicknell,MP	4	7	0	45	15	6.42	0	0	3	2	1080	39	543	14	38.78	0	0	4/84
Binks,JG	2	4	0	91	55	22.75	0	1	0	8/0								
Bird,MC	10	16	1	280	61	18.66	0	2	2	5	264	12	120	8	15.00	0	0	3/11
Birkenshaw,J	5	7	0	148	64	21.14	0	1	1	3	1017	33	469	13	36.07	1	0	5/57
Blackwell,ID	1	1	0	4	4	4.00	0	0	0	0	114	2	71	0	-	0	0	0/28
Blakey,RJ	2	4	0	7	6	1.75	0	0	2	2/0								
Bligh,Hon.IFW	4	7	1	62	19	10.33	0	0	2	7								
Blythe,C	19	31	12	183	27	9.63	0	0	4	6	4546	231	1863	100	18.62	9	4	8/59
Board,JH	6	12	2	108	29	10.80	0	0	3	8/3								
Bolus,JB	7	12	0	496	88	41.33	0	4	0	2	18	0	16	0	-	0	0	0/16
Booth,MW	2	2	0	46	32	23.00	0	0	0	0	312	8	130	7	18.57	0	0	4/49
Bosanquet,BJT	7	14	3	147	27	13.36	0	0	0	9	970	10	604	25	24.16	2	0	8/107
Botham,IT	102	161	6	5200	208	33.54	14	22	14	120	21815	788	10878	383	28.40	27	4	8/34
Bowden,MP	2	2	0	25	25	12.50	0	0	1	1								
Bowes,WE	15	11	5	28	10*	4.66	0	0	2	2	3655	131	1519	68	22.33	6	0	6/33
Bowley,EH	5	7	0	252	109	36.00	1	0	0	2	252	7	116	0	-	0	0	0/7
Boycott,G	108	193	23	8114	246*	47.72	22	42	10	33	944	45	382	7	54.57	0	0	3/47
Bradley,WM	2	2	1	23	23*	23.00	0	0	1	0	625	49	233	6	38.83	1	0	5/67
Braund,LC	23	41	3	987	104	25.97	3	2	7	39	3805	144	1810	47	38.51	3	0	8/81
Brearley,JM	39	66	3	1442	91	22.88	0	9	6	52								
Brearley,W	4	5	2	21	11*	7.00	0	0	2	0	705	25	359	17	21.11	1	0	5/110

ENGLAND (cont.)	**BATTING AND FIELDING**										**BOWLING**							
Player	M	I	NO	Runs	HS	Avge	100	50	0	C/S	Balls	Mdns	Runs	Wkts	Avge	5wi	10w	Best
Brennan,DV	2	2	0	16	16	8.00	0	0	1	0/1								
Briggs,J	33	50	5	815	121	18.11	1	2	10	12	5332	386	2095	118	17.75	9	4	8/11
Broad,BC	25	44	2	1661	162	39.54	6	6	3	10	6	0	4	0	-	0	0	0/4
Brockwell,W	7	12	0	202	49	16.83	0	0	1	6	582	31	309	5	61.80	0	0	3/33
Bromley-Davenport,HR	4	6	0	128	84	21.33	0	1	1	1	155	6	98	4	24.50	0	0	2/46
Brookes,D	1	2	0	17	10	8.50	0	0	0	1								
Brown,A	2	1	1	3	3*	-	0	0	0	1	323	9	150	3	50.00	0	0	3/27
Brown,DJ	26	34	5	342	44*	11.79	0	0	6	7	5098	182	2237	79	28.31	2	0	5/42
Brown,FR	22	30	1	734	79	25.31	0	5	1	22	3260	117	1398	45	31.06	1	0	5/49
Brown,G	7	12	2	299	84	29.90	0	2	2	9/3								
Brown,JT	8	16	3	470	140	36.15	1	1	2	7	35	0	22	0	-	0	0	0/22
Brown,SJE	1	2	1	11	10*	11.00	0	0	0	1	198	4	138	2	69.00	0	0	1/60
Buckenham,CP	4	7	0	43	17	6.14	0	0	1	2	1182	25	593	21	28.23	1	0	5/115
Butcher,AR	1	2	0	34	20	17.00	0	0	0	0	12	0	9	0	-	0	0	0/9
Butcher,MA	71	131	7	4288	173*	34.58	8	23	10	61	901	27	541	15	36.06	0	0	4/42
Butcher,RO	3	5	0	71	32	14.20	0	0	1	3								
Butler,HJ	2	2	1	15	15*	15.00	0	0	1	1	552	30	215	12	17.91	0	0	4/34
Butt,HR	3	4	1	22	13	7.33	0	0	1	1/1								
Caddick,AR	62	95	12	861	49*	10.37	0	0	19	21	13558	501	6999	234	29.91	13	1	7/46
Calthorpe,Hon.FSG	4	7	0	129	49	18.42	0	0	1	3	204	8	91	1	91.00	0	0	1/38
Capel,DJ	15	25	1	374	98	15.58	0	2	4	6	2000	52	1064	21	50.66	0	0	3/88
Carr,AW	11	13	1	237	63	19.75	0	1	0	3								
Carr,DB	2	4	0	135	76	33.75	0	1	0	0	210	6	140	2	70.00	0	0	2/84
Carr,DW	1	1	0	0	0	0.00	0	0	1	0	414	3	282	7	40.28	1	0	5/146
Cartwright,TW	5	7	2	26	9	5.20	0	0	2	2	1611	97	544	15	36.26	1	0	6/94
Chapman,APF	26	36	4	925	121	28.90	1	5	2	32	40	1	20	0	-	0	0	0/10
Charlwood,HRJ	2	4	0	63	36	15.75	0	0	1	0								
Chatterton,W	1	1	0	48	48	48.00	0	0	0	0								
Childs,JH	2	4	4	2	2*	-	0	0	0	1	516	29	183	3	61.00	0	0	1/13
Christopherson,S	1	1	0	17	17	17.00	0	0	0	0	136	13	69	1	69.00	0	0	1/52
Clark,EW	8	9	5	36	10	9.00	0	0	1	0	1931	71	899	32	28.09	1	0	5/98
Clarke,R	2	3	0	96	55	32.00	0	1	0	1	174	11	60	4	15.00	0	0	2/7
Clay,JC	1	0	0	0	0		0	0	0	1	192	7	75	0	-	0	0	0/30
Close,DB	22	37	2	887	70	25.34	0	4	3	24	1212	56	532	18	29.55	0	0	4/35
Coldwell,LJ	7	7	5	9	6*	4.50	0	0	1	1	1668	60	610	22	27.72	1	0	6/85
Collingwood,PD	15	28	3	1027	186	41.08	2	3	0	20	432	11	245	1	245.00	0	0	1/33
Compton,DCS	78	131	15	5807	278	50.06	17	28	10	49	2710	71	1410	25	56.40	1	0	5/70
Cook,AN	9	16	2	761	127	54.35	3	3	0	7								
Cook,C	1	2	0	4	4	2.00	0	0	1	0	180	4	127	0	-	0	0	0/40
Cook,G	7	13	0	203	66	15.61	0	2	1	9	42	3	27	0	-	0	0	0/4
Cook,NGB	15	25	4	179	31	8.52	0	0	2	5	4174	220	1689	52	32.48	4	1	6/65
Cope,GA	3	3	0	40	22	13.33	0	0	1	1	864	29	277	8	34.62	0	0	3/102
Copson,WH	3	1	0	6	6	6.00	0	0	0	1	762	31	297	15	19.79	1	0	5/85
Cork,DG	37	56	8	864	59	18.00	0	3	5	18	7678	264	3906	131	29.81	5	0	7/43
Cornford,WL	4	4	0	36	18	9.00	0	0	0	5/3								
Cottam,RMH	4	5	1	27	13	6.75	0	0	0	2	903	41	327	14	23.35	0	0	4/50
Coventry,Hon.CJ	2	2	1	13	12	13.00	0	0	0	0								
Cowans,NG	19	29	7	175	36	7.95	0	0	5	9	3452	113	2003	51	39.27	2	0	6/77
Cowdrey,CS	6	8	1	101	38	14.42	0	0	1	5	399	2	309	4	77.25	0	0	2/65
Cowdrey,MC	114	188	15	7624	182	44.06	22	38	9	120	119	0	104	0	-	0	0	0/1
Coxon,A	1	2	0	19	19	9.50	0	0	1	0	378	13	172	3	57.33	0	0	2/90
Cranston,J	1	2	0	31	16	15.50	0	0	0	1								

ENGLAND (cont.)	**BATTING AND FIELDING**										**BOWLING**							
Player	M	I	NO	Runs	HS	Avge	100	50	0	C/S	Balls	Mdns	Runs	Wkts	Avge	5wi	10w	Best
Cranston,K	8	14	0	209	45	14.92	0	0	2	3	1010	37	461	18	25.61	0	0	4/12
Crapp,JF	7	13	2	319	56	29.00	0	3	1	7								
Crawford,JN	12	23	2	469	74	22.33	0	2	1	13	2203	61	1150	39	29.48	3	0	5/48
Crawley,JP	37	61	9	1800	156*	34.61	4	9	4	29								
Croft,RDB	21	34	8	421	37*	16.19	0	0	2	10	4619	195	1825	49	37.24	1	0	5/95
Curtis,TS	5	9	0	140	41	15.55	0	0	1	3	18	0	7	0	-	0	0	0/7
Cuttell,WR	2	4	0	65	21	16.25	0	0	0	2	285	32	73	6	12.16	0	0	3/17
Dawson,EW	5	9	0	175	55	19.44	0	1	0	0								
Dawson,RKJ	7	13	3	114	19*	11.40	0	0	0	3	1116	20	677	11	61.54	0	0	4/134
Dean,H	3	4	2	10	8	5.00	0	0	10	2	447	23	153	11	13.90	0	0	4/19
DeFreitas,PAJ	44	68	5	934	88	14.82	0	4	1	14	9838	367	4700	140	33.57	4	0	7/70
Denness,MH	28	45	3	1667	188	39.69	4	7	2	28								
Denton,D	11	22	1	424	104	20.19	1	1	4	8								
Dewes,JG	5	10	0	121	67	12.10	0	1	1	0								
Dexter,ER	62	102	8	4502	205	47.89	9	27	6	29	5317	186	2306	66	34.93	0	0	4/10
Dilley,GR	41	58	19	521	56	13.35	0	2	10	10	8192	279	4107	138	29.76	6	0	6/38
Dipper,AE	1	2	0	51	40	25.50	0	0	0	0								
Doggart,GHG	2	4	0	76	29	19.00	0	0	1	3								
d'Oliveira,BL	44	70	8	2484	158	40.06	5	15	4	29	5706	318	1859	47	39.55	0	0	3/46
Dollery,HE	4	7	0	72	37	10.28	0	0	2	1								
Dolphin,A	1	2	0	1	1	0.50	0	0	1	1/0								
Douglas,JWHT	23	35	2	962	119	29.15	1	6	3	9	2812	66	1486	45	33.02	1	0	5/46
Downton,PR	30	48	8	785	74	19.62	0	4	4	70/5								
Druce,NF	5	9	0	252	64	28.00	0	1	0	5								
Ducat,A	1	2	0	5	3	2.50	0	0	0	1								
Duckworth,G	24	28	12	234	39*	14.62	0	0	2	45/15								
Duleepsinhji,KS	12	19	2	995	173	58.52	3	5	0	10	6	0	7	0	-	0	0	0/7
Durston,FJ	1	2	1	8	6*	8.00	0	0	0	0	202	2	136	5	27.20	0	0	4/102
Ealham,MA	8	13	3	210	53*	21.00	0	2	0	4	1060	43	488	17	28.70	0	0	4/21
Edmonds,PH	51	65	15	875	64	17.50	0	2	5	42	12028	613	4273	125	34.18	2	0	7/66
Edrich,JH	77	127	9	5138	310*	43.54	12	24	6	43	30	1	23	0	-	0	0	0/6
Edrich,WJ	39	63	2	2440	219	40.00	6	13	3	39	3234	81	1693	41	41.29	0	0	4/68
Elliott,H	4	5	1	61	37*	15.25	0	0	0	8/3								
Ellison,RM	11	16	1	202	41	13.46	0	0	1	2	2264	90	1048	35	29.94	3	1	6/77
Emburey,JE	64	96	20	1713	75	22.53	0	10	16	34	15391	741	5646	147	38.40	6	0	7/78
Emmett,GM	1	2	0	10	10	5.00	0	0	1	0								
Emmett,T	7	13	1	160	48	13.33	0	0	1	9	728	92	284	9	31.55	1	0	7/68
Evans,AJ	1	2	0	18	14	9.00	0	0	0	0								
Evans,TG	91	133	14	2439	104	20.49	2	8	17	173/46								
Fagg,AE	5	8	0	150	39	18.75	0	0	0	5								
Fairbrother,NH	10	15	1	219	83	15.64	0	1	1	4	12	0	9	0	-	0	0	0/9
Fane,FL	14	27	1	682	143	26.23	1	3	3	6								
Farnes,K	15	17	5	58	20	4.83	0	0	4	1	3932	103	1719	60	28.65	3	1	6/96
Farrimond,W	4	7	0	116	35	16.57	0	0	0	5/2								
Fender,PGH	13	21	1	380	60	19.00	0	2	3	14	2178	66	1185	29	40.86	2	0	5/90
Ferris,JJ	1	1	0	16	16	16.00	0	0	0	0	272	27	91	13	7.00	2	1	7/37
Fielder,A	6	12	5	78	20	11.14	0	0	0	4	1491	42	711	26	27.34	1	0	6/82
Fishlock,LB	4	5	1	47	19*	11.75	0	0	1	1								
Flavell,JA	4	6	2	31	14	7.75	0	0	0	0	792	25	367	7	52.42	0	0	2/65
Fletcher,KWR	59	96	14	3272	216	39.90	7	19	6	54	285	6	193	2	96.50	0	0	1/6
Flintoff,A	61	98	11	3077	167	35.36	5	22	14	44	11536	404	5720	179	31.95	2	0	5/58
Flowers,W	8	14	0	254	56	18.14	0	1	0	2	858	92	296	14	21.14	1	0	5/46
Ford,FGJ	5	9	0	168	48	18.66	0	0	1	5	204	6	129	1	129.00	0	0	1/47

ENGLAND (cont.)				**BATTING AND FIELDING**							**BOWLING**							
Player	M	I	NO	Runs	HS	Avge	100	50	0	C/S	Balls	Mdns	Runs	Wkts	Avge	5wi	10w	Best
Foster,FR	11	15	1	330	71	23.57	0	3	1	11	2447	108	926	45	20.57	4	0	6/91
Foster,JS	7	12	3	226	48	25.11	0	0	1	17/1								
Foster,NA	29	45	7	446	39	11.73	0	0	9	7	6261	239	2891	88	32.85	5	1	8/107
Foster,RE	8	14	1	602	287	46.30	1	1	1	13								
Fothergill,AJ	2	2	0	33	32	16.50	0	0	0	0	321	42	90	8	11.25	0	0	4/19
Fowler,G	21	37	0	1307	201	35.32	3	8	3	10	18	1	11	0	-	0	0	0/0
Fraser,ARC	46	67	15	388	32	7.46	0	0	9	9	10876	439	4836	177	27.32	13	2	8/53
Freeman,AP	12	16	5	154	50*	14.00	0	1	2	4	3732	142	1707	66	25.86	5	3	7/71
French,BN	16	21	4	308	59	18.11	0	1	2	38/1								
Fry,CB	26	41	3	1223	144	32.18	2	7	3	17	10	1	3	0	-	0	0	0/3
Gallian,JER	3	6	0	74	28	12.33	0	0	2	1	84	1	62	0	-	0	0	0/6
Gatting,MW	79	138	14	4409	207	35.55	10	21	16	59	752	29	317	4	79.25	0	0	1/14
Gay,LH	1	2	0	37	33	18.50	0	0	0	3/1								
Geary,G	14	20	4	249	66	15.56	0	2	3	13	3810	181	1353	46	29.41	4	1	7/70
Gibb,PA	8	13	0	581	120	44.69	2	3	1	3/1								
Giddins,ESH	4	7	3	10	7	2.50	0	0	3	0	444	21	240	12	20.00	1	0	5/15
Gifford,N	15	20	9	179	25*	16.27	0	0	1	8	3084	174	1026	33	31.09	1	0	5/55
Giles,AF	52	77	12	1347	59	20.72	0	4	8	32	11688	388	5544	140	39.60	5	0	5/57
Gilligan,AER	11	16	3	209	39*	16.07	0	0	2	3	2404	73	1046	36	29.05	2	1	6/7
Gilligan,AHH	4	4	0	71	32	17.75	0	0	0	0								
Gimblett,H	3	5	1	129	67*	32.25	0	1	0	1								
Gladwin,C	8	11	5	170	51*	28.33	0	1	0	2	2129	89	571	15	38.06	0	0	3/21
Goddard,TWJ	8	5	3	13	8	6.50	0	0	1	3	1563	62	588	22	26.72	1	0	6/29
Gooch,GA	118	215	6	8900	333	42.58	20	46	13	103	2655	122	1069	23	46.47	0	0	3/39
Gough,D	58	86	18	855	65	12.57	0	2	14	13	11819	370	6503	229	28.39	9	0	6/42
Gover,AR	4	1	1	2	2*	-	0	0	0	1	816	26	359	8	44.87	0	0	3/85
Gower,DI	117	204	18	8231	215	44.25	18	39	7	74	36	0	20	1	20.00	0	0	1/1
Grace,EM	1	2	0	36	36	18.00	0	0	1	1								
Grace,GF	1	2	0	0	0	0.00	0	0	2	2								
Grace,WG	22	36	2	1098	170	32.29	2	5	2	39	666	65	236	9	26.22	0	0	2/12
Graveney,TW	79	123	13	4882	258	44.38	11	20	8	80	260	6	167	1	167.00	0	0	1/34
Greenhough,T	4	4	1	4	2	1.33	0	0	1	1	1129	66	357	16	22.31	1	0	5/35
Greenwood,A	2	4	0	77	49	19.25	0	0	0	2								
Greig,AW	58	93	4	3599	148	40.43	8	20	5	87	9802	338	4541	141	32.20	6	2	8/86
Greig,IA	2	4	0	26	14	6.50	0	0	0	0	188	6	114	4	28.50	0	0	4/53
Grieve,BAF	2	3	2	40	14*	40.00	0	0	0	0								
Griffith,SC	3	5	0	157	140	31.40	1	0	1	5/0								
Gunn,G	15	29	1	1120	122*	40.00	2	7	3	15	12	0	8	0	-	0	0	0/8
Gunn,JR	6	10	2	85	24	10.62	0	0	1	3	999	54	387	18	21.50	1	0	5/76
Gunn,W	11	20	2	392	102*	21.77	1	1	1	5								
Habib,A	2	3	0	26	19	8.66	0	0	0	0								
Haig,NE	5	9	0	126	47	14.00	0	0	2	4	1026	54	448	13	34.46	0	0	3/73
Haigh,S	11	18	3	113	25	7.53	0	0	4	8	1294	61	622	24	25.91	1	0	6/11
Hallows,C	2	2	1	42	26	42.00	0	0	0	0								
Hamilton,GM	1	2	0	0	0	0.00	0	0	2	0	90	1	63	0	-	0	0	0/63
Hammond,WR	85	140	16	7249	336*	58.45	22	24	4	110	7969	300	3138	83	37.80	2	0	5/36
Hampshire,JH	8	16	1	403	107	26.86	1	2	2	9								
Hardinge,HTW	1	2	0	30	25	15.00	0	0	0	0								
Hardstaff,J jr	23	38	3	1636	205*	46.74	4	10	4	9								
Hardstaff,J sr	5	10	0	311	72	31.10	0	3	0	1								
Harmison,SJ	44	58	16	504	42	12.00	0	0	14	5	9683	326	5053	175	28.87	8	1	7/12
Harris,Lord	4	6	1	145	52	29.00	0	1	0	2	32	1	29	0	-	0	0	0/14
Hartley,JC	2	4	0	15	9	3.75	0	0	2	2	192	2	115	1	115.00	0	0	1/62

ENGLAND (cont.)			**BATTING AND FIELDING**								**BOWLING**							
Player	M	I	NO	Runs	HS	Avge	100	50	0	C/S	Balls	Mdns	Runs	Wkts	Avge	5wi	10w	Best
Hawke,Lord	5	8	1	55	30	7.85	0	0	2	3								
Hayes,EG	5	9	1	86	35	10.75	0	0	2	2	90	1	52	1	52.00	0	0	1/28
Hayes,FC	9	17	1	244	106*	15.25	1	0	6	7								
Hayward,TW	35	60	2	1999	137	34.46	3	12	7	19	893	42	514	14	36.71	0	0	4/22
Headley,DW	15	26	4	186	31	8.45	0	0	3	7	3026	82	1671	60	27.85	1	0	6/60
Hearne,A	1	1	0	9	9	9.00	0	0	0	1								
Hearne,F	2	2	0	47	27	23.50	0	0	0	1								
Hearne,GG	1	1	0	0	0	0.00	0	0	1	0								
Hearne,JT	12	18	4	126	40	9.00	0	0	3	4	2976	211	1082	49	22.08	4	1	6/41
Hearne,JW	24	36	5	806	114	26.00	1	2	3	13	2926	56	1462	30	48.73	1	0	5/49
Hegg,WK	2	4	0	30	15	7.50	0	0	0	8/0								
Hemmings,EE	16	21	4	383	95	22.52	0	2	5	5	4437	207	1825	43	42.44	1	0	6/58
Hendren,EH	51	83	9	3525	205*	47.63	7	21	4	33	47	0	31	1	31.00	0	0	1/27
Hendrick,M	30	35	15	128	15	6.40	0	0	8	25	6208	249	2248	87	25.83	0	0	4/28
Heseltine,C	2	2	0	18	18	9.00	0	0	1	3	157	3	84	5	16.79	1	0	5/38
Hick,GA	65	114	6	3383	178	31.32	6	18	11	90	3057	128	1306	23	56.78	0	0	4/126
Higgs,K	15	19	3	185	63	11.56	0	1	2	4	4112	194	1473	71	20.74	2	0	6/91
Hill,A	2	4	2	101	49	50.50	0	0	1	1	340	37	130	7	18.57	0	0	4/27
Hill,AJL	3	4	0	251	124	62.75	1	1	0	1	40	4	8	4	2.00	0	0	4/8
Hilton,MJ	4	6	1	37	15	7.40	0	0	2	1	1244	65	477	14	34.07	1	0	5/61
Hirst,GH	24	38	3	790	85	22.57	0	5	5	18	4010	146	1770	59	30.00	3	0	5/48
Hitch,JW	7	10	3	103	51*	14.71	0	1	1	4	462	5	325	7	46.42	0	0	2/31
Hobbs,JB	61	102	7	5410	211	56.94	15	28	4	17	376	15	165	1	165.00	0	0	1/19
Hobbs,RNS	7	8	3	34	15*	6.80	0	0	1	8	1291	67	481	12	40.08	0	0	3/25
Hoggard,MJ	58	79	26	426	38	8.03	0	0	15	23	12168	435	6607	222	29.76	6	1	7/61
Hollies,WE	13	15	8	37	18*	5.28	0	0	4	2	3554	176	1332	44	30.27	5	0	7/50
Hollioake,AJ	4	6	0	65	45	10.83	0	0	1	4	144	2	67	2	33.50	0	0	2/31
Hollioake,BC	2	4	0	44	28	11.00	0	0	1	2	252	4	199	4	49.75	0	0	2/105
Holmes,ERT	5	9	2	114	85*	16.28	0	1	2	4	108	4	76	2	38.00	0	0	1/10
Holmes,P	7	14	1	357	88	27.46	0	4	3	3								
Hone,L	1	2	0	13	7	6.50	0	0	0	2/0								
Hopwood,JL	2	3	1	12	8	6.00	0	0	0	0	462	32	155	0	-	0	0	0/16
Hornby,AN	3	6	0	21	9	3.50	0	0	1	0	28	7	0	1	0.00	0	0	1/0
Horton,MJ	2	2	0	60	58	30.00	0	1	0	2	238	18	59	2	29.50	0	0	2/24
Howard,ND	4	6	1	86	23	17.20	0	0	0	4								
Howell,H	5	8	6	15	5	7.50	0	0	0	0	918	23	559	7	79.85	0	0	4/115
Howorth,R	5	10	2	145	45*	18.12	0	0	0	2	1536	61	635	19	33.42	1	0	6/124
Humphries,J	3	6	1	44	16	8.80	0	0	0	7/0								
Hunter,J	5	7	2	93	39*	18.60	0	0	0	8/3								
Hussain,N	95	171	16	5764	207	37.18	14	33	14	67	30	0	15	0	-	0	0	0/15
Hutchings,KL	7	12	0	341	126	28.41	1	1	1	9	90	1	81	1	81.00	0	0	1/5
Hutton,L	79	138	15	6971	364	56.67	19	33	5	57	260	4	232	3	77.33	0	0	1/2
Hutton,RA	5	8	2	219	81	36.50	0	2	1	9	738	27	257	9	28.55	0	0	3/72
Iddon,J	5	7	1	170	73	28.33	0	2	3	0	66	3	27	0	-	0	0	0/3
Igglesden,AP	3	5	3	6	3*	3.00	0	0	2	1	555	11	329	6	54.83	0	0	2/91
Ikin,JT	18	31	2	606	60	20.89	0	3	4	31	572	12	354	3	118.00	0	0	1/38
Illingworth,R	61	90	11	1836	113	23.24	2	5	7	45	11934	715	3807	122	31.20	3	0	6/29
Illingworth,RK	9	14	7	128	28	18.28	0	0	3	5	1485	77	615	19	32.36	0	0	4/96
Ilott,MC	5	6	2	28	15	7.00	0	0	0	0	1042	38	542	12	45.16	0	0	3/48
Insole,DJ	9	17	2	408	110*	27.20	1	1	2	8								
Irani,RC	3	5	0	86	41	17.20	0	0	0	2	192	10	112	3	37.33	0	0	1/22
Jackman,RD	4	6	0	42	17	7.00	0	0	2	0	1070	45	445	14	31.78	0	0	4/110
Jackson,HL	2	2	1	15	8	15.00	0	0	3	1	498	30	155	7	22.14	0	0	2/26

ENGLAND (cont.)	BATTING AND FIELDING										BOWLING							
Player	M	I	NO	Runs	HS	Avge	100	50	0	C/S	Balls	Mdns	Runs	Wkts	Avge	5wi	10w	Best
Jackson,Hon.FS	20	33	4	1415	144*	48.79	5	6	0	10	1587	77	799	24	33.29	1	0	5/52
James,SP	2	4	0	71	36	17.75	0	0	1	0								
Jameson,JA	4	8	0	214	82	26.75	0	1	0	0	42	2	17	1	17.00	0	0	1/17
Jardine,DR	22	33	6	1296	127	48.00	1	10	2	26	6	0	10	0	-	0	0	0/10
Jarvis,PW	9	15	2	132	29*	10.15	0	0	1	2	1912	61	965	21	45.95	0	0	4/107
Jenkins,RO	9	12	1	198	39	18.00	0	0	0	4	2118	51	1098	32	34.31	1	0	5/116
Jessop,GL	18	26	0	569	104	21.88	1	3	3	11	732	28	354	10	35.40	0	0	4/68
Johnson,RL	3	4	0	59	26	14.75	0	0	0	0	547	25	275	16	17.18	2	0	6/33
Jones,AO	12	21	0	291	34	13.85	0	0	2	15	228	14	133	3	44.33	0	0	3/73
Jones,GO	31	47	4	1109	100	25.79	1	6	0	119/5								
Jones,IJ	15	17	9	38	16	4.75	0	0	2	4	3546	98	1769	44	40.20	1	0	6/118
Jones,SP	18	18	5	205	44	15.76	0	0	3	4	2821	78	1666	59	28.23	3	0	6/53
Jupp,H	2	4	0	68	63	17.00	0	1	1	2								
Jupp,VWC	8	13	1	208	38	17.33	0	0	0	5	1301	55	616	28	22.00	0	0	4/37
Kabir Ali	1	2	0	10	9	5.00	0	0	0	0	216	5	136	5	27.20	0	0	3/80
Keeton,WW	2	4	0	57	25	14.25	0	0	1	0								
Kennedy,AS	5	8	2	93	41*	15.50	0	0	1	5	1683	91	599	31	19.32	2	0	5/76
Kenyon,D	8	15	0	192	87	12.80	0	1	1	5								
Key,RWT	15	26	1	775	221	31.00	1	3	2	11								
Killick,ET	2	4	0	81	31	20.25	0	0	0	2								
Kilner,R	9	8	1	233	74	33.28	0	2	0	6	2368	82	734	24	30.58	0	0	4/51
King,JH	1	2	0	64	60	32.00	0	1	0	0	162	5	99	1	99.00	0	0	1/99
Kinneir,SP	1	2	0	52	30	26.00	0	0	0	0								
Kirtley,RJ	4	7	1	32	12	5.33	0	0	0	3	1079	50	561	19	29.52	1	0	6/34
Knight,AE	3	6	1	81	70*	16.20	0	1	3	1								
Knight,BR	29	38	7	812	127	26.19	2	0	2	14	5377	204	2223	70	31.75	0	0	4/38
Knight,DJ	2	4	0	54	38	13.50	0	0	0	1								
Knight,NV	17	30	0	719	113	23.96	1	4	1	26								
Knott,APE	95	149	15	4389	135	32.75	5	30	8	250/19								
Knox,NA	2	4	1	24	8*	8.00	0	0	0	0	126	2	105	3	35.00	0	0	2/39
Laker,JC	46	63	15	676	63	14.08	0	2	6	12	12027	674	4101	193	21.24	9	3	10/53
Lamb,AJ	79	139	10	4656	142	36.09	14	18	9	75	30	2	23	1	23.00	0	0	1/6
Langridge,J	8	9	0	242	70	26.88	0	1	0	6	1074	51	413	19	21.73	2	0	7/56
Larkins,W	13	25	1	493	64	20.54	0	3	6	8								
Larter,JDF	10	7	2	16	10	3.20	0	0	2	5	2172	87	941	37	25.43	2	0	5/57
Larwood,H	21	28	3	485	98	19.40	0	2	4	15	4969	167	2212	78	28.35	4	1	6/32
Lathwell,MN	2	4	0	78	33	19.50	0	0	1	0								
Lawrence,DV	5	6	0	60	34	10.00	0	0	0	0	1089	34	676	18	37.55	1	0	5/106
Leadbeater,E	2	2	0	40	38	20.00	0	0	0	3	289	8	218	2	109.00	0	0	1/38
Lee,HW	1	2	0	19	18	9.50	0	0	0	0								
Lees,WS	5	9	3	66	25*	11.00	0	0	0	2	1256	69	467	26	17.96	2	0	6/78
Legge,GB	5	7	1	299	196	49.83	1	0	2	1	30	0	34	0	-	0	0	0/34
Leslie,CFH	4	7	0	106	54	15.14	0	1	1	1	96	10	44	4	11.00	0	0	3/31
Lever,JK	21	31	5	306	53	11.76	0	1	2	11	4433	140	1951	73	26.72	3	1	7/46
Lever,P	17	18	2	350	88*	21.87	0	2	1	11	3571	92	1509	41	36.80	2	0	6/38
Leveson Gower,HDG	3	6	2	95	31	23.75	0	0	0	1								
Levett,WHV	1	2	1	7	5	7.00	0	0	0	3/0								
Lewis,AR	9	16	2	457	125	32.64	1	3	2	0								
Lewis,CC	32	51	3	1105	117	23.02	1	4	6	25	6852	220	3490	93	37.52	3	0	6/111
Lewis,J	1	2	0	27	20	13.50	0	0	0	0	246	9	122	3	40.66	0	0	3/68
Leyland,M	41	65	5	2764	187	46.06	9	10	6	13	1103	35	585	6	97.50	0	0	3/91
Lilley,AFA	35	52	8	903	84	20.52	0	4	10	70/22	25	1	23	1	23.00	0	0	1/23

ENGLAND (cont.)	**BATTING AND FIELDING**										**BOWLING**							
Player	M	I	NO	Runs	HS	Avge	100	50	0	C/S	Balls	Mdns	Runs	Wkts	Avge	5wi	10w	Best
Lillywhite, James jr	2	3	1	16	10	8.00	0	0	0	1	340	37	126	8	15.75	0	0	4/70
Lloyd,D	9	15	2	552	214*	42.46	1	0	0	11	24	0	17	0	-	0	0	0/4
Lloyd,TA	1	1	1	10	10*	-	0	0	0	0								
Loader,PJ	13	19	6	76	17	5.84	0	0	3	2	2662	115	878	39	22.51	1	0	6/36
Lock,GAR	49	63	9	742	89	13.74	0	3	8	59	13147	819	4451	174	25.58	9	3	7/35
Lockwood,WH	12	16	3	231	52*	17.76	0	1	3	4	1973	100	883	43	20.53	5	1	7/71
Lohmann,GA	18	26	2	213	62*	8.87	0	1	7	28	3830	364	1205	112	10.75	9	5	9/28
Lowson,FA	7	13	0	245	68	18.84	0	2	2	5								
Lucas,AP	5	9	1	157	55	19.62	0	1	0	1	120	13	54	0	-	0	0	0/23
Luckhurst,BW	21	41	5	1298	131	36.05	4	5	4	14	57	2	32	1	32.00	0	0	1/9
Lyttelton,Hon.A	4	7	1	94	31	15.66	0	0	0	2	48	5	19	4	4.75	0	0	4/19
Macaulay,GG	8	10	4	112	76	18.66	0	1	1	5	1701	79	662	24	27.58	1	0	5/64
MacBryan,JCW	1	0	0	0	0		0	0	0	0								
McCague,MJ	3	5	0	21	11	4.19	0	0	2	1	593	17	390	6	65.00	0	0	4/121
McConnon,JE	2	3	1	18	11	9.00	0	0	0	4	216	12	74	4	18.50	0	0	3/19
McGahey,CP	2	4	0	38	18	9.50	0	0	1	1								
McGrath,A	4	5	0	201	81	40.20	0	2	0	3	102	0	56	4	14.00	0	0	3/16
MacGregor,G	8	11	3	96	31	12.00	0	0	1	14/3								
McIntyre,AJW	3	6	0	19	7	3.16	0	0	1	8/0								
MacKinnon,FA	1	2	0	5	5	2.50	0	0	1	0								
MacLaren,AC	35	61	4	1931	140	33.87	5	8	4	29								
McMaster,JEP	1	1	0	0	0	0.00	0	0	1	0								
Maddy,DL	3	4	0	46	24	11.50	0	0	0	4	84	1	40	0	-	0	0	0/40
Mahmood,SI	5	5	1	51	34	12.75	0	0	0	0	822	21	498	15	33.20	0	0	4/22
Makepeace,JWH	4	8	0	279	117	34.87	1	2	0	0								
Malcolm,DE	40	58	19	236	29	6.05	0	0	16	7	8480	253	4748	128	37.09	5	2	9/57
Mallender,NA	2	3	0	8	4	2.66	0	0	0	0	449	20	215	10	21.50	1	0	5/50
Mann,FG	7	12	2	376	136*	37.59	1	0	0	3								
Mann,FT	5	9	1	281	84	35.12	0	2	0	4								
Marks,VJ	6	10	1	249	83	27.66	0	3	0	0	1082	54	484	11	44.00	0	0	3/78
Marriott,CS	1	1	0	0	0	0.00	0	0	1	1	247	8	96	11	8.72	2	1	6/59
Martin,F	2	2	0	14	13	7.00	0	0	0	2	410	30	141	14	10.07	2	1	6/50
Martin,JW	1	2	0	26	26	13.00	0	0	1	0	270	6	129	1	129.00	0	0	1/111
Martin,PJ	8	13	0	115	29	8.84	0	0	2	6	1452	73	580	17	34.11	0	0	4/60
Mason,JR	5	10	0	129	32	12.90	0	0	1	3	324	13	149	2	74.50	0	0	1/8
Matthews,ADG	1	1	1	2	2*	-	0	0	0	1	180	8	65	2	32.50	0	0	1/13
May,PBH	66	106	9	4537	285*	46.77	13	22	8	42								
Maynard,MP	4	8	0	87	35	10.87	0	0	2	3								
Mead,CP	17	26	2	1185	182*	49.37	4	3	3	4								
Mead,W	1	2	0	7	7	3.50	0	0	1	1	265	24	91	1	91.00	0	0	1/91
Midwinter,WE	4	7	0	95	36	13.57	0	0	0	5	776	79	272	10	27.20	0	0	4/81
Milburn,C	9	16	2	654	139	46.71	2	2	1	7								
Miller,AM	1	2	2	24	20*	-	0	0	0	0								
Miller,G	34	51	4	1213	98*	25.80	0	7	5	17	5149	219	1859	60	30.98	1	0	5/44
Milligan,FW	2	4	0	58	38	14.50	0	0	0	1	45	2	29	0	-	0	0	0/0
Millman,G	6	7	2	60	32*	12.00	0	0	2	13/2								
Milton,CA	6	9	1	204	104*	25.50	1	0	0	5	24	2	12	0	-	0	0	0/12
Mitchell,A	6	10	0	298	72	29.80	0	2	1	9	6	0	4	0	-	0	0	0/4
Mitchell,F	2	4	0	88	41	22.00	0	0	0	2								
Mitchell,TB	5	6	2	20	9	5.00	0	0	1	1	894	21	498	8	62.25	0	0	2/49
Mitchell-Innes,NS	1	1	0	5	5	5.00	0	0	0	0								
Mold,AW	3	3	1	0	0*	0.00	0	0	2	1	491	32	234	7	33.42	0	0	3/44
Moon,LJ	4	8	0	182	36	22.75	0	0	1	4/0								

ENGLAND (cont.)			**BATTING AND FIELDING**								**BOWLING**							
Player	M	I	NO	Runs	HS	Avge	100	50	0	C/S	Balls	Mdns	Runs	Wkts	Avge	5wi	10w	Best
Morley,F	4	6	2	6	2*	1.50	0	0	2	4	972	124	296	16	18.50	1	0	5/56
Morris,H	3	6	0	115	44	19.16	0	0	0	3								
Morris,JE	3	5	2	71	32	23.66	0	0	0	3								
Mortimore,JB	9	12	2	243	73*	24.30	0	1	1	3	2162	133	733	13	56.38	0	0	3/36
Moss,AE	9	7	1	61	26	10.16	0	0	1	1	1657	79	626	21	29.80	0	0	4/35
Moxon,MD	10	17	1	455	99	28.43	0	3	2	10	48	2	30	0	-	0	0	0/3
Mullally,AD	19	27	4	127	24	5.52	0	0	12	6	4525	213	1812	58	31.24	1	0	5/105
Munton,TA	2	2	1	25	25*	25.00	0	0	1	0	405	15	200	4	50.00	0	0	2/22
Murdoch,WL	1	1	0	12	12	12.00	0	0	0	0/1								
Murray,JT	21	28	5	506	112	22.00	1	2	3	52/3								
Newham,W	1	2	0	26	17	13.00	0	0	0	0								
Newport,PJ	3	5	1	110	40*	27.50	0	0	1	1	669	18	417	10	41.70	0	0	4/87
Nichols,MS	14	19	7	355	78*	29.58	0	2	0	11	2565	97	1152	41	28.09	2	0	6/35
Oakman,ASM	2	2	0	14	10	7.00	0	0	0	7	48	3	21	0	-	0	0	0/21
O'Brien,TC	5	8	0	59	20	7.37	0	0	3	4								
O'Connor,J	4	7	0	153	51	21.85	0	1	1	2	162	6	72	1	72.00	0	0	1/31
Old,CM	46	66	9	845	65	14.82	0	2	10	22	8858	311	4020	143	28.11	4	0	7/50
Oldfield,N	1	2	0	99	80	49.50	0	1	0	0								
Ormond,J	2	4	1	38	18	12.66	0	0	1	0	372	12	185	2	92.50	0	0	1/70
Padgett,DEV	2	4	0	51	31	12.75	0	0	0	0	12	0	8	0	-	0	0	0/8
Paine,GAE	4	7	1	97	49	16.16	0	0	1	5	1044	39	467	17	27.47	1	0	5/168
Palairet,LCH	2	4	0	49	20	12.25	0	0	0	2								
Palmer,CH	1	2	0	22	22	11.00	0	0	1	0	30	1	15	0	-	0	0	0/15
Palmer,KE	1	1	0	10	10	10.00	0	0	0	0	378	7	189	1	189.00	0	0	1/113
Panesar,MS	10	13	8	51	26	10.20	0	0	3	2	2408	104	1037	32	32.40	2	0	5/72
Parfitt,PH	37	52	6	1882	131*	40.91	7	6	5	42	1326	68	574	12	47.83	0	0	2/5
Parker,CWL	1	1	1	3	3*	-	0	0	0	0	168	16	32	2	16.00	0	0	2/32
Parker,PWG	1	2	0	13	13	6.50	0	0	1	0								
Parkhouse,WGA	7	13	0	373	78	28.69	0	2	1	3								
Parkin,CH	10	16	3	160	36	12.30	0	0	1	3	2095	55	1128	32	35.25	2	0	5/38
Parks,JH	1	2	0	29	22	14.50	0	0	0	0	126	9	36	3	12.00	0	0	2/26
Parks,JM	46	68	7	1962	108*	32.16	2	9	3	103/11	54	1	51	1	51.00	0	0	1/43
Pataudi, Nawab of, sr	3	5	0	144	102	28.80	1	0	0	0								
Patel,MM	2	2	0	45	27	22.50	0	0	0	2	276	8	180	1	180.00	0	0	1/101
Paynter,E	20	31	5	1540	243	59.23	4	7	3	7								
Peate,E	9	14	8	70	13	11.66	0	0	1	2	2096	250	683	31	22.03	2	0	6/85
Peebles,IAR	13	17	8	98	26	10.88	0	0	3	5	2882	78	1391	45	30.91	3	0	6/63
Peel,R	20	33	4	427	83	14.72	0	3	8	17	5216	444	1715	101	16.98	5	1	7/31
Penn,F	1	2	1	50	27*	50.00	0	0	0	0	12	1	2	0	-	0	0	0/2
Perks,RTD	2	2	2	3	2*	-	0	0	0	1	829	17	355	11	32.27	2	0	5/100
Philipson,H	5	8	1	63	30	9.00	0	0	0	8/3								
Pietersen,KP	18	34	1	1597	158	48.39	5	6	2	11	84	1	76	1	76.00	0	0	1/11
Pigott,ACS	1	2	1	12	8*	12.00	0	0	0	0	102	7	75	2	37.50	0	0	2/75
Pilling,R	8	13	1	91	23	7.58	0	0	1	10/4								
Place,W	3	6	1	144	107	28.80	1	0	0	0								
Plunkett,LE	6	9	1	69	28	8.62	0	0	4	2	1004	26	601	16	37.56	0	0	3/17
Pocock,PI	25	37	4	206	33	6.24	0	0	10	15	6650	281	2976	67	44.41	3	0	6/79
Pollard,R	4	3	2	13	10*	13.00	0	0	0	3	1102	63	378	15	25.20	1	0	5/24
Poole,CJ	3	5	1	161	69*	40.25	0	2	0	1	30	1	9	0	-	0	0	0/9
Pope,GH	1	1	1	8	8*	-	0	0	0	0	218	12	85	1	85.00	0	0	1/49
Pougher,AD	1	1	0	17	17	17.00	0	0	0	2	105	8	26	3	8.66	0	0	3/26
Price,JSE	15	15	6	66	32	7.33	0	0	5	7	2724	90	1401	40	35.02	1	0	5/73

ENGLAND (cont.)			**BATTING AND FIELDING**								**BOWLING**							
Player	M	I	NO	Runs	HS	Avge	100	50	0	C/S	Balls	Mdns	Runs	Wkts	Avge	5wi	10w	Best
Price,WFF	1	2	0	6	6	3.00	0	0	1	2/0								
Prideaux,RM	3	6	1	102	64	20.40	0	1	0	0	12	2	0	0	-	0	0	0/0
Pringle,DR	30	50	4	695	63	15.10	0	1	6	10	5287	192	2518	70	35.97	3	0	5/95
Pullar,G	28	49	4	1974	175	43.86	4	12	3	2	66	3	37	1	37.00	0	0	1/1
Quaife,WG	7	13	1	228	68	19.00	0	1	1	4	15	1	6	0	-	0	0	0/6
Radford,NV	3	4	1	21	12*	7.00	0	0	1	0	678	15	351	4	87.75	0	0	2/131
Radley,CT	8	10	0	481	158	48.10	2	2	1	4								
Ramprakash,MR	52	92	6	2350	154	27.32	2	12	12	39	895	16	477	4	119.25	0	0	1/2
Randall,DW	47	79	5	2470	174	33.37	7	12	14	31	16	0	3	0	-	0	0	0/1
Ranjitsinhji,KS	15	26	4	989	175	44.95	2	6	2	13	97	6	39	1	39.00	0	0	1/23
Read,CMW	13	19	3	325	55	20.31	0	1	5	37/5								
Read,HD	1	0	0	0	0		0	0	0	0	270	14	200	6	33.33	0	0	4/136
Read,JM	17	29	2	461	57	17.07	0	2	3	8								
Read,WW	18	27	1	720	117	27.69	1	5	0	16	60	2	63	0	-	0	0	0/27
Reeve,DA	3	5	0	124	59	24.80	0	1	1	1	149	8	60	2	30.00	0	0	1/4
Relf,AE	13	21	3	416	63	23.11	0	1	1	14	1764	91	624	25	24.96	1	0	5/85
Rhodes,HJ	2	1	1	0	0*	-	0	0	0	0	449	10	244	9	27.11	0	0	4/50
Rhodes,SJ	11	17	5	294	65*	24.50	0	1	1	46/3								
Rhodes,W	58	98	21	2325	179	30.19	2	11	6	60	8225	365	3425	127	26.96	6	1	8/68
Richards,CJ	8	13	0	285	133	21.92	1	0	2	20/1								
Richardson,DW	1	1	0	33	33	33.00	0	0	0	1								
Richardson,PE	34	56	1	2061	126	37.47	5	9	1	6	120	9	48	3	16.00	0	0	2/10
Richardson,T	14	24	8	177	25*	11.06	0	0	3	5	4498	191	2220	88	25.22	11	4	8/94
Richmond,TL	1	2	0	6	4	3.00	0	0	0	0	114	3	86	2	43.00	0	0	2/69
Ridgway,F	5	6	0	49	24	8.16	0	0	2	3	793	23	379	7	54.14	0	0	4/83
Robertson,JDB	11	21	2	881	133	46.36	2	6	0	6	138	4	58	2	29.00	0	0	2/17
Robins,RWV	19	27	4	612	108	26.60	1	4	4	12	3318	77	1758	64	27.46	1	0	6/32
Robinson,RT	29	49	5	1601	175	36.38	4	6	5	8	6	1	0	0	-	0	0	0/0
Roope,GRJ	21	32	4	860	77	30.71	0	7	3	35	172	5	76	0	-	0	0	0/2
Root,CF	3	0	0	0	0		0	0	0	1	642	47	194	8	24.25	0	0	4/84
Rose,BC	9	16	2	358	70	25.57	0	2	0	4								
Royle,VPFA	1	2	0	21	18	10.50	0	0	0	2	16	1	6	0	-	0	0	0/6
Rumsey,FE	5	5	3	30	21*	15.00	0	0	0	0	1145	53	461	17	27.11	0	0	4/25
Russell,CAG	10	18	2	910	140	56.87	5	2	2	8								
Russell,RC	54	86	16	1897	128*	27.10	2	6	8	153/12								
Russell,WE	10	18	1	362	70	21.29	0	2	2	4	144	9	44	0	-	0	0	0/19
Saggers,MJ	3	3	0	1	1	0.33	0	0	2	1	493	20	247	7	35.28	0	0	2/29
Salisbury,IDK	15	25	3	368	50	16.72	0	1	4	5	2492	50	1539	20	76.94	0	0	4/163
Sandham,A	14	23	0	879	325	38.21	2	3	3	4								
Schofield,CP	2	3	0	67	57	22.33	0	1	1	0	108	2	73	0	-	0	0	0/73
Schultz,SS	1	2	1	20	20	20.00	0	0	0	0	34	3	26	1	26.00	0	0	1/16
Scotton,WH	15	25	2	510	90	22.17	0	3	2	4	20	1	20	0	-	0	0	0/20
Selby,J	6	12	1	256	70	23.27	0	2	0	1/0								
Selvey,MWW	3	5	3	15	5*	7.50	0	0	1	1	492	9	343	6	57.16	0	0	4/41
Shackleton,D	7	13	7	113	42	18.83	0	0	0	1	2078	96	768	18	42.66	0	0	4/72
Shah,OA	1	2	0	126	88	63.00	0	1	0	1								
Sharp,J	3	6	2	188	105	47.00	1	1	0	1	183	3	111	3	37.00	0	0	3/67
Sharpe,JW	3	6	4	44	26	22.00	0	0	0	2	975	61	305	11	27.72	1	0	6/84
Sharpe,PJ	12	21	4	786	111	46.23	1	4	1	17								
Shaw,A	7	12	1	111	40	10.09	0	0	1	4	1096	155	285	12	23.75	1	0	5/38
Sheppard,DS	22	33	2	1172	119	37.80	3	6	2	12								
Sherwin,M	3	6	4	30	21*	15.00	0	0	1	5/2								
Shrewsbury,A	23	40	4	1277	164	35.47	3	4	1	29	12	2	2	0	-	0	0	0/2

ENGLAND (cont.)				**BATTING AND FIELDING**							**BOWLING**							
Player	M	I	NO	Runs	HS	Avge	100	50	0	C/S	Balls	Mdns	Runs	Wkts	Avge	5wi	10w	Best
Shuter,J	1	1	0	28	28	28.00	0	0	0	0								
Shuttleworth,K	5	6	0	46	21	7.66	0	0	1	1	1071	20	427	12	35.58	1	0	5/47
Sidebottom,A	1	1	0	2	2	2.00	0	0	0	0	112	3	65	1	65.00	0	0	1/65
Sidebottom,RJ	1	1	0	4	4	4.00	0	0	0	0	120	2	64	0	-	0	0	0/26
Silverwood,CEW	6	7	3	29	10	7.25	0	0	2	2	828	27	444	11	40.36	1	0	5/91
Simpson,RT	27	45	3	1401	156*	33.35	4	6	6	5	45	2	22	2	11.00	0	0	2/4
Simpson-Hayward,GHT	5	8	1	105	29*	15.00	0	0	1	1	898	18	420	23	18.26	2	0	6/43
Sims,JM	4	4	0	16	12	4.00	0	0	1	6	887	21	480	11	43.63	1	0	5/73
Sinfield,RA	1	1	0	6	6	6.00	0	0	0	0	378	16	123	2	61.50	0	0	1/51
Slack,WN	3	6	0	81	52	13.50	0	1	2	3								
Smailes,TF	1	1	0	25	25	25.00	0	0	0	0	120	3	62	3	20.66	0	0	3/44
Small,GC	17	24	7	263	59	15.47	0	1	4	9	3927	154	1871	55	34.01	2	0	5/48
Smith,AC	6	7	3	118	69*	29.50	0	1	0	20/0								
Smith,AM	1	2	1	4	4*	4.00	0	0	1	0	138	2	89	0	-	0	0	0/89
Smith,CA	1	1	0	3	3	3.00	0	0	0	0	154	16	61	7	8.71	1	0	5/19
Smith,CIJ	5	10	0	102	27	10.20	0	0	2	1	930	40	393	15	26.20	1	0	5/16
Smith,CL	8	14	1	392	91	30.15	0	2	1	5	102	4	39	3	13.00	0	0	2/31
Smith,D	2	4	0	128	57	32.00	0	1	1	1								
Smith,DM	2	4	0	80	47	20.00	0	0	1	0								
Smith,DR	5	5	1	38	34	9.50	0	0	2	2	972	47	359	6	59.83	0	0	2/60
Smith,DV	3	4	1	25	16*	8.33	0	0	1	0	270	13	97	1	97.00	0	0	1/12
Smith,EJ	11	14	1	113	22	8.69	0	0	2	17/3								
Smith,ET	3	5	0	87	64	17.40	0	1	2	5								
Smith,H	1	1	0	7	7	7.00	0	0	0	1/0								
Smith,MJK	50	78	6	2278	121	31.63	3	11	11	53	214	4	128	1	128.00	0	0	1/10
Smith,RA	62	112	15	4236	175	43.67	9	28	8	39	24	2	6	0	-	0	0	0/6
Smith,TPB	4	5	0	33	24	6.60	0	0	0	1	538	5	319	3	106.33	0	0	2/172
Smithson,GA	2	3	0	70	35	23.33	0	0	1	0								
Snow,JA	49	71	14	772	73	13.54	0	2	17	16	12021	415	5387	202	26.66	8	1	7/40
Southerton,J	2	3	1	7	6	3.50	0	0	1	2	263	30	107	7	15.28	0	0	4/46
Spooner,RH	10	15	0	481	119	32.06	1	4	2	4								
Spooner,RT	7	14	1	354	92	27.23	0	3	3	10/2								
Stanyforth,RT	4	6	1	13	6*	2.60	0	0	1	7/2								
Staples,SJ	3	5	0	65	39	13.00	0	0	0	0	1149	50	435	15	29.00	0	0	3/50
Statham,JB	70	87	28	675	38	11.44	0	0	13	28	16056	595	6261	252	24.84	9	1	7/39
Steel,AG	13	20	3	600	148	35.29	2	0	1	5	1360	108	605	29	20.86	0	0	3/27
Steele,DS	8	16	0	673	106	42.06	1	5	1	7	88	5	39	2	19.50	0	0	1/1
Stephenson,JP	1	2	0	36	25	18.00	0	0	0	0								
Stevens,GTS	10	17	0	263	69	15.47	0	1	2	9	1186	24	648	20	32.40	2	1	5/90
Stevenson,GB	2	2	1	28	27*	28.00	0	0	0	0	312	7	183	5	36.59	0	0	3/111
Stewart,AJ	133	235	21	8463	190	39.54	15	45	14	263/14	20	0	13	0	-	0	0	0/5
Stewart,MJ	8	12	1	385	87	35.00	0	2	1	6								
Stoddart,AE	16	30	2	996	173	35.57	2	3	3	6	162	7	94	2	47.00	0	0	1/10
Storer,W	6	11	0	215	51	19.54	0	1	0	11/0	168	5	108	2	54.00	0	0	1/24
Strauss,AJ	31	58	2	2597	147	46.37	10	7	4	39								
Street,GB	1	2	1	11	7*	11.00	0	0	0	0/1								
Strudwick,H	28	42	13	230	24	7.93	0	0	5	61/12								
Studd,CT	5	9	1	160	48	20.00	0	0	2	5	384	60	98	3	32.66	0	0	2/35
Studd,GB	4	7	0	31	9	4.42	0	0	1	8								
Subba Row,R	13	22	1	984	137	46.85	3	4	0	5	6	0	2	0	-	0	0	0/2
Such,PM	11	16	5	67	14*	6.09	0	0	3	4	3124	135	1242	37	33.56	2	0	6/67
Sugg,FH	2	2	0	55	31	27.50	0	0	0	0								

ENGLAND (cont.)			BATTING AND FIELDING								BOWLING							
Player	M	I	NO	Runs	HS	Avge	100	50	0	C/S	Balls	Mdns	Runs	Wkts	Avge	5wi	10w	Best
Sutcliffe,H	54	84	9	4555	194	60.73	16	23	2	23								
Swetman,R	11	17	2	254	65	16.93	0	1	2	24/2								
Tate,FW	1	2	1	9	5*	9.00	0	0	0	2	96	4	51	2	25.50	0	0	2/7
Tate,MW	39	52	5	1198	100*	25.48	1	5	5	11	12523	581	4055	155	26.16	7	1	6/42
Tattersall,R	16	17	7	50	10*	5.00	0	0	1	8	4228	212	1513	58	26.08	4	1	7/52
Tavaré,CJ	31	56	2	1755	149	32.50	2	12	5	20	30	3	11	0	-	0	0	0/0
Taylor,JP	2	4	2	34	17*	17.00	0	0	1	0	288	9	156	3	52.00	0	0	1/18
Taylor,K	3	5	0	57	24	11.40	0	0	0	1	12	0	6	0	-	0	0	0/6
Taylor,LB	2	1	1	1	1*	-	0	0	0	1	381	11	178	4	44.50	0	0	2/34
Taylor,RW	57	83	12	1156	97	16.28	0	3	10	167/7	12	0	6	0	-	0	0	0/6
Tennyson,LH	9	12	1	345	74*	31.36	0	4	1	6	6	0	1	0	-	0	0	0/1
Terry,VP	2	3	0	16	8	5.33	0	0	0	2								
Thomas,JG	5	10	4	83	31*	13.83	0	0	3	0	774	18	504	10	50.40	0	0	4/70
Thompson,GJ	6	10	1	273	63	30.33	0	2	0	5	1367	66	638	23	27.73	0	0	4/50
Thomson,NI	5	4	1	69	39	23.00	0	0	1	3	1488	68	568	9	63.11	0	0	2/55
Thorpe,GP	100	179	28	6744	200*	44.66	16	39	12	105	138	7	37	0	-	0	0	0/0
Titmus,FJ	53	76	11	1449	84*	22.29	0	10	4	35	15118	777	4931	153	32.22	7	0	7/79
Tolchard,RW	4	7	2	129	67	25.80	0	1	1	5								
Townsend,CL	2	3	0	51	38	17.00	0	0	0	0	140	5	75	3	25.00	0	0	3/50
Townsend,DCH	3	6	0	77	36	12.83	0	0	0	1	6	0	9	0	-	0	0	0/9
Townsend,LF	4	6	0	97	40	16.16	0	0	0	2	399	22	205	6	34.16	0	0	2/22
Tremlett,MF	3	5	2	20	18*	6.66	0	0	2	0	492	13	226	4	56.50	0	0	2/98
Trescothick,ME	76	143	10	5825	219	43.79	14	29	12	95	294	6	151	1	151.00	0	0	1/34
Trott,AE	2	4	0	23	16	5.75	0	0	1	0	474	37	198	17	11.65	1	0	5/49
Trueman,FS	67	85	14	981	39*	13.81	0	0	11	64	15178	522	6625	307	21.57	17	3	8/31
Tudor,AJ	10	16	4	229	99*	19.08	0	1	2	3	1512	51	963	28	34.39	1	0	5/44
Tufnell,NC	1	1	0	14	14	14.00	0	0	0	0/1								
Tufnell,PCR	42	59	29	153	22*	5.10	0	0	15	12	11288	505	4560	121	37.68	5	2	7/47
Turnbull,MJL	9	13	2	224	61	20.36	0	1	1	1								
Tyldesley,GE	14	20	2	990	122	55.00	3	6	2	2	3	0	2	0	-	0	0	0/2
Tyldesley,JT	31	55	1	1661	138	30.75	4	9	4	16								
Tyldesley,RK	7	7	1	47	29	7.83	0	0	1	1	1615	76	619	19	32.57	0	0	3/50
Tylecote,EFS	6	9	1	152	66	19.00	0	1	4	5/5								
Tyler,EJ	1	1	0	0	0	0.00	0	0	1	0	145	6	65	4	16.25	0	0	3/49
Tyson,FH	17	24	3	230	37*	10.95	0	0	3	4	3452	97	1411	76	18.56	4	1	7/27
Udal,SD	4	7	1	109	33*	18.16	0	0	1	1	596	13	344	8	43.00	0	0	4/14
Ulyett,G	25	39	0	949	149	24.33	1	7	6	19	2627	299	1020	50	20.40	1	0	7/36
Underwood,DL	86	116	35	937	45*	11.56	0	0	19	44	21862	1239	7674	297	25.83	17	6	8/51
Valentine,BH	7	9	2	454	136	64.85	2	1	0	2								
Vaughan,MP	64	115	9	4587	197	43.27	15	14	7	37	936	21	527	6	87.83	0	0	2/71
Verity,H	40	44	12	669	66*	20.90	0	3	4	30	11173	604	3510	144	24.37	5	2	8/43
Vernon,GF	1	2	1	14	11*	14.00	0	0	0	0								
Vine,J	2	3	2	46	36	46.00	0	0	0	0								
Voce,W	27	38	15	308	66	13.39	0	1	6	15	6360	211	2733	98	27.88	3	2	7/70
Waddington,A	2	4	0	16	7	4.00	0	0	1	1	276	7	119	1	119.00	0	0	1/35
Wainwright,E	5	9	0	132	49	14.66	0	0	0	2	127	6	73	0	-	0	0	0/11
Walker,PM	3	4	0	128	52	32.00	0	1	0	5	78	3	34	0	-	0	0	0/8
Walters,CF	11	18	3	784	102	52.26	1	7	0	6								
Ward,Alan	5	6	1	40	21	8.00	0	0	4	3	761	20	453	14	32.35	0	0	4/61
Ward,Albert	7	13	0	487	117	37.46	1	3	1	1								
Ward,IJ	5	9	1	129	39	16.12	0	0	1	1								
Wardle,JH	28	41	8	653	66	19.78	0	2	5	12	6597	403	2080	102	20.39	5	1	7/36
Warner,PF	15	28	2	622	132*	23.92	1	3	4	3								

ENGLAND (cont.)				BATTING AND FIELDING							BOWLING							
Player	M	I	NO	Runs	HS	Avge	100	50	0	C/S	Balls	Mdns	Runs	Wkts	Avge	5wi	10w	Best
Warr,JJ	2	4	0	4	4	1.00	0	0	3	0	584	6	281	1	281.00	0	0	1/76
Warren,A	1	1	0	7	7	7.00	0	0	0	1	236	9	113	6	18.83	1	0	5/57
Washbrook,C	37	66	6	2569	195	42.81	6	12	2	12	36	0	33	1	33.00	0	0	1/25
Watkin,SL	3	5	0	25	13	5.00	0	0	1	1	534	17	305	11	27.72	0	0	4/65
Watkins,AJ	15	24	4	810	137*	40.50	2	4	2	17	1364	45	554	11	50.36	0	0	3/20
Watkinson,M	4	6	1	167	82*	33.40	0	1	1	1	672	24	348	10	34.80	0	0	3/64
Watson,W	23	37	3	879	116	25.85	2	3	3	8								
Webbe,AJ	1	2	0	4	4	2.00	0	0	1	2								
Wellard,AW	2	4	0	47	38	11.75	0	0	1	2	456	9	237	7	33.85	0	0	4/81
Wells,AP	1	2	1	3	3*	3.00	0	0	1	0								
Wharton,A	1	2	0	20	13	10.00	0	0	0	0								
Whitaker,JJ	1	1	0	11	11	11.00	0	0	0	1								
White,C	30	50	7	1052	121	24.46	1	5	8	14	3959	119	2220	59	37.62	3	0	5/32
White,DW	2	2	0	0	0	0.00	0	0	2	0	220	5	119	4	29.75	0	0	3/65
White,JC	15	22	9	239	29	18.38	0	0	1	6	4801	253	1581	49	32.26	3	1	8/126
Whysall,WW	4	7	0	209	76	29.85	0	2	0	7	16	0	9	0	-	0	0	0/9
Wilkinson,LL	3	2	1	3	2	3.00	0	0	0	0	573	9	271	7	38.71	0	0	2/12
Willey,P	26	50	6	1184	102*	26.90	2	5	2	3	1091	49	456	7	65.14	0	0	2/73
Williams,NF	1	1	0	38	38	38.00	0	0	0	0	246	5	148	2	74.00	0	0	2/148
Willis,RGD	90	128	55	840	28*	11.50	0	0	2	39	17357	554	8190	325	25.20	16	0	8/43
Wilson,CEM	2	4	1	42	18	14.00	0	0	0	0								
Wilson,D	6	7	1	75	42	12.50	0	0	0	1	1472	93	466	11	42.36	0	0	2/17
Wilson,ER	1	2	0	10	5	5.00	0	0	0	0	123	5	36	3	12.00	0	0	2/28
Wood,A	4	5	1	80	53	20.00	0	1	1	10/1								
Wood,B	12	21	0	454	90	21.61	0	2	1	6	98	4	50	0	-	0	0	0/2
Wood,GEC	3	2	0	7	6	3.50	0	0	0	5/1								
Young,RA	2	4	0	27	13	6.75	0	0	1	6/0								
Wood,H	4	4	1	204	134*	68.00	1	1	0	2/1								
Wood,R	1	2	0	6	6	3.00	0	0	1	0								
Woods,SMJ	3	4	0	122	53	30.50	0	1	0	4	195	8	129	5	25.80	0	0	3/28
Woolley,FE	64	98	7	3283	154	36.07	5	23	3	64	6495	251	2815	83	33.91	4	1	7/76
Woolmer,RA	19	34	2	1059	149	33.09	3	2	4	10	546	16	299	4	74.75	0	0	1/8
Worthington,TS	9	11	0	321	128	29.18	1	1	4	8	633	18	316	8	39.50	0	0	2/19
Wright,CW	3	4	0	125	71	31.25	0	1	0	0								
Wright,DVP	34	39	13	289	45	11.11	0	0	7	10	8135	177	4224	108	39.11	6	1	7/105
Wyatt,RES	40	64	6	1839	149	31.70	2	12	6	16	1395	67	642	18	35.66	0	0	3/4
Wynyard,EG	3	6	0	72	30	12.00	0	0	2	0	24	0	17	0	-	0	0	0/2
Yardley,NWD	20	34	2	812	99	25.37	0	4	2	14	1662	41	707	21	33.66	0	0	3/67
Young,HI	2	2	0	43	43	21.50	0	0	1	1	556	38	262	12	21.83	0	0	4/30
Young,JA	8	10	5	28	10*	5.60	0	0	3	5	2368	119	757	17	44.52	0	0	3/65

SOUTH AFRICA (299 players)				BATTING AND FIELDING							BOWLING							
Player	M	I	NO	Runs	HS	Avge	100	50	0	C/S	Balls	Mdns	Runs	Wkts	Avge	5wi	10w	Best
Ackerman,HD	4	8	0	161	57	20.12	0	1	0	1								
Adams,PR	45	55	15	360	35	9.00	0	0	8	29	8850	338	4405	134	32.87	4	1	7/128
Adcock,NAT	26	39	12	146	24	5.40	0	0	9	4	6391	218	2195	104	21.10	5	0	6/43
Amla,HM	7	13	0	364	149	28.00	1	1	1	6	6	0	4	0	-	0	0	0/4
Anderson,JH	1	2	0	43	32	21.50	0	0	0	1								
Ashley,WH	1	2	0	1	1	0.50	0	0	1	0	173	18	95	7	13.57	1	0	7/95
Bacher,A	12	22	1	679	73	32.33	0	6	1	10								
Bacher,AM	19	33	1	833	96	26.03	0	5	3	11	6	0	4	0	-	0	0	0/4

SOUTH AFRICA (cont.)					**BATTING AND FIELDING**						**BOWLING**							
Player	M	I	NO	Runs	HS	Avge	100	50	0	C/S	Balls	Mdns	Runs	Wkts	Avge	5wi	10w	Best
Balaskas,XC	9	13	1	174	122*	14.50	1	0	5	5	1572	28	806	22	36.63	1	0	5/49
Barlow,EJ	30	57	2	2516	201	45.74	6	15	3	35	3021	115	1362	40	34.05	1	0	5/85
Baumgartner,HV	1	2	0	19	16	9.50	0	0	0	1	166	3	99	2	49.50	0	0	2/99
Beaumont,R	5	9	0	70	31	7.77	0	0	2	2	6	1	0	0	-	0	0	0/0
Begbie,DW	5	7	0	138	48	19.71	0	0	0	2	160	0	130	1	130.00	0	0	1/38
Bell,AJ	16	23	12	69	26*	6.27	0	0	6	6	3342	89	1567	48	32.64	4	0	6/99
Bisset,M	3	6	2	103	35	25.75	0	0	0	2/1								
Bissett,GF	4	4	2	38	23	19.00	0	0	0	0	989	28	469	25	18.76	2	0	7/29
Blanckenberg,JM	18	30	7	455	59	19.78	0	2	2	9	3888	132	1817	60	30.28	4	0	6/76
Bland,KC	21	39	5	1669	144*	49.08	3	9	2	10	394	18	125	2	62.50	0	0	2/16
Bock,EG	1	2	2	11	9*	-	0	0	0	0	138	2	91	0	-	0	0	0/42
Boje,N	43	62	10	1306	85	25.11	0	4	5	18	8620	291	4265	100	42.65	3	0	5/62
Bond,GE	1	1	0	0	0	0.00	0	0	1	0	16	0	16	0	-	0	0	0/16
Bosch,T	1	2	2	5	5*	-	0	0	0	0	237	9	104	3	34.66	0	0	2/61
Botha,J	1	1	1	20	20*	-	0	0	0	0	117	2	103	2	51.50	0	0	1/26
Botten,JT	3	6	0	65	33	10.83	0	0	2	1	828	37	337	8	42.12	0	0	2/56
Boucher,MV	95	134	17	3565	125	30.47	4	23	14	348/14	8	0	6	1	6.00	0	0	1/6
Brann,WH	3	5	0	71	50	14.20	0	1	1	2								
Briscoe,AW	2	3	0	33	16	11.00	0	0	0	1								
Bromfield,HD	9	12	7	59	21	11.80	0	0	3	13	1810	101	599	17	35.23	1	0	5/88
Brown,LS	2	3	0	17	8	5.66	0	0	0	0	318	7	189	3	63.00	0	0	1/30
Burger,CGD	2	4	1	62	37*	20.66	0	0	0	1								
Burke,SF	2	4	1	42	20	14.00	0	0	1	0	660	37	257	11	23.36	2	1	6/128
Buys,ID	1	2	1	4	4*	4.00	0	0	1	0	144	4	52	0	-	0	0	0/20
Cameron,HB	26	45	4	1239	90	30.21	0	10	3	39/12								
Campbell,T	5	9	3	90	48	15.00	0	0	1	7/1								
Carlstein,PR	8	14	1	190	42	14.61	0	0	1	3								
Carter,CP	10	15	5	181	45	18.10	0	0	3	2	1475	47	694	28	24.78	2	0	6/50
Catterall,RH	24	43	2	1555	120	37.92	3	11	3	12	342	7	162	7	23.14	0	0	3/15
Chapman,HW	2	4	1	39	17	13.00	0	0	0	1	126	1	104	1	104.00	0	0	1/51
Cheetham,JE	24	43	6	883	89	23.86	0	5	1	13	6	0	2	0	-	0	0	0/2
Chevalier,GA	1	2	1	0	0*	0.00	0	0	1	1	253	11	100	5	20.00	0	0	3/68
Christy,JAJ	10	18	0	618	103	34.33	1	5	1	3	138	4	92	2	46.00	0	0	1/15
Chubb,GWA	5	9	3	63	15*	10.50	0	0	0	0	1425	63	577	21	27.47	2	0	6/51
Cochran,JAK	1	1	0	4	4	4.00	0	0	0	0	138	5	47	0	-	0	0	0/47
Coen,SK	2	4	2	101	41*	50.50	0	0	0	1	12	0	7	0	-	0	0	0/7
Commaille,JMM	12	22	1	355	47	16.90	0	0	1	1								
Commins,JB	3	6	1	125	45	25.00	0	0	1	2								
Conyngham,DP	1	2	2	6	3*	-	0	0	0	1	366	22	103	2	51.50	0	0	1/40
Cook,FJ	1	2	0	7	7	3.50	0	0	1	0								
Cook,SJ	3	6	0	107	43	17.83	0	0	1	0								
Cooper,AHC	1	2	0	6	6	3.00	0	0	1	1								
Cox,JL	3	6	1	17	12*	3.40	0	0	3	1	576	24	245	4	61.25	0	0	2/74
Cripps,G	1	2	0	21	18	10.50	0	0	0	0	15	0	23	0	-	0	0	0/23
Crisp,RJ	9	13	1	123	35	10.25	0	0	5	3	1428	30	747	20	37.34	1	0	5/99
Cronje,WJ	68	111	9	3714	135	36.41	6	23	11	33	3800	243	1288	43	29.95	0	0	3/14
Cullinan,DJ	70	115	12	4554	275*	44.21	14	20	10	67	120	3	71	2	35.50	0	0	1/10
Curnow,SH	7	14	0	168	47	12.00	0	0	0	5								
Dalton,EL	15	24	2	698	117	31.72	2	3	1	5	864	7	490	12	40.83	0	0	4/59
Davies,EQ	5	8	3	9	3	1.80	0	0	2	0	768	7	481	7	68.71	0	0	4/75
Dawson,AC	2	1	0	10	10	10.00	0	0	0	0	252	14	117	5	23.40	0	0	2/20
Dawson,OC	9	15	1	293	55	20.92	0	1	1	10	1294	41	578	10	57.80	0	0	2/57
Deane,HG	17	27	2	628	93	25.12	0	3	1	8								

SOUTH AFRICA (cont.)				**BATTING AND FIELDING**									**BOWLING**					
Player	M	I	NO	Runs	HS	Avge	100	50	0	C/S	Balls	Mdns	Runs	Wkts	Avge	5wi	10w	Best
de Bruyn,Z	3	5	1	155	83	38.75	0	1	0	0	216	7	92	3	30.66	0	0	2/32
de Villiers,AB	22	40	1	1607	178	41.20	3	10	0	29/1	198	6	99	2	49.50	0	0	2/49
de Villiers,PS	18	26	7	359	67*	18.89	0	2	3	11	4805	221	2063	85	24.27	5	2	6/23
Dippenaar,HH	37	60	5	1715	177*	31.18	3	7	7	27	12	1	1	0	-	0	0	0/1
Dixon,CD	1	2	0	0	0	0.00	0	0	2	1	240	6	118	3	39.33	0	0	2/62
Donald,AA	72	94	33	652	37	10.68	0	0	17	18	15519	661	7344	330	22.25	20	3	8/71
Dower,RR	1	2	0	9	9	4.50	0	0	1	2								
Draper,RG	2	3	0	25	15	8.33	0	0	0	0								
Duckworth,CAR	2	4	0	28	13	7.00	0	0	0	3								
Dumbrill,R	5	10	0	153	36	15.30	0	0	0	3	816	40	336	9	37.33	0	0	4/30
Duminy,JP	3	6	0	30	12	5.00	0	0	1	2	60	0	39	1	39.00	0	0	1/17
Dunell,OR	2	4	1	42	26*	14.00	0	0	1	1								
du Preez,JH	2	2	0	0	0	0.00	0	0	2	2	144	12	51	3	17.00	0	0	2/22
du Toit,JF	1	2	2	2	2*	-	0	0	0	1	85	5	47	1	47.00	0	0	1/47
Dyer,DV	3	6	0	96	62	16.00	0	1	0	0								
Eksteen,CE	7	11	2	91	22	10.11	0	0	1	5	1536	97	494	8	61.75	0	0	3/12
Elgie,MK	3	6	0	75	56	12.50	0	1	2	4	66	2	46	0	-	0	0	0/18
Elworthy,S	4	5	1	72	48	18.00	0	0	0	1	867	35	444	13	34.15	0	0	4/66
Endean,WR	28	52	4	1630	162*	33.95	3	8	3	41/0								
Farrer,WS	6	10	2	221	40	27.62	0	0	0	2								
Faulkner,GA	25	47	4	1754	204	40.79	4	8	2	20	4227	124	2180	82	26.58	4	0	7/84
Fellows-Smith,JP	4	8	2	166	35	27.66	0	0	0	2	114	1	61	0	-	0	0	0/13
Fichardt,CG	2	4	0	15	10	3.75	0	0	1	2								
Finlason,CE	1	2	0	6	6	3.00	0	0	1	0	12	0	7	0	-	0	0	0/7
Floquet,CE	1	2	1	12	11*	12.00	0	0	0	0	48	2	24	0	-	0	0	0/24
Francis,HH	2	4	0	39	29	9.75	0	0	0	1								
Francois,CM	5	9	1	252	72	31.50	0	1	0	5	684	36	225	6	37.50	0	0	3/23
Frank,CN	3	6	0	236	152	39.33	1	0	0	0								
Frank,WHB	1	2	0	7	5	3.50	0	0	0	0	58	3	52	1	52.00	0	0	1/52
Fuller,ERH	7	9	1	64	17	8.00	0	0	2	3	1898	61	668	22	30.36	1	0	5/66
Fullerton,GM	7	13	0	325	88	25.00	0	3	1	10/2								
Funston,KJ	18	33	1	824	92	25.75	0	5	2	7								
Gamsy,D	2	3	1	39	30*	19.50	0	0	0	5/0								
Gibbs,HH	79	135	6	5728	228	44.40	14	22	7	72	6	0	4	0	-	0	0	0/4
Gleeson,RA	1	2	1	4	3	4.00	0	0	0	2								
Glover,GK	1	2	1	21	18*	21.00	0	0	0	0	65	4	28	1	28.00	0	0	1/28
Goddard,TL	41	78	5	2516	112	34.46	1	18	4	48	11736	706	3226	123	26.22	5	0	6/53
Gordon,N	5	6	2	8	7*	2.00	0	0	3	1	1966	28	807	20	40.34	2	0	5/103
Graham,R	2	4	0	6	4	1.50	0	0	2	2	240	13	127	3	42.33	0	0	2/22
Grieveson,RE	2	2	0	114	75	57.00	0	1	0	7/3								
Griffin,GM	2	4	0	25	14	6.25	0	0	1	0	432	14	192	8	24.00	0	0	4/87
Hall,AE	7	8	2	11	5	1.83	0	0	4	4	2361	107	886	40	22.15	3	1	7/63
Hall,AJ	19	30	4	735	163	28.26	1	3	6	15	2838	91	1511	39	38.74	0	0	3/1
Hall,GG	1	1	0	0	0	0.00	0	0	1	0	186	7	94	1	94.00	0	0	1/94
Halliwell,EA	8	15	0	188	57	12.53	0	1	3	9/2								
Halse,CG	3	3	3	30	19*	-	0	0	0	1	587	7	260	6	43.33	0	0	3/50
Hands,PAM	7	12	0	300	83	25.00	0	2	2	3	37	0	18	0	-	0	0	0/1
Hands,RHM	1	2	0	7	7	3.50	0	0	1	0								
Hanley,MA	1	1	0	0	0	0.00	0	0	1	0	232	7	88	1	88.00	0	0	1/57
Harris,TA	3	5	1	100	60	25.00	0	1	0	1								
Hartigan,GPD	5	10	0	114	51	11.40	0	1	3	0	252	7	141	1	141.00	0	0	1/72
Harvey,RL	2	4	0	51	28	12.75	0	0	0	0								
Hathorn,CMH	12	20	1	325	102	17.10	1	0	1	5								

SOUTH AFRICA (cont.)					**BATTING AND FIELDING**						**BOWLING**							
Player	M	I	NO	Runs	HS	Avge	100	50	0	C/S	Balls	Mdns	Runs	Wkts	Avge	5wi	10w	Best
Hayward,M	16	17	8	66	14	7.33	0	0	3	4	2821	90	1609	54	29.79	1	0	5/56
Hearne,F	4	8	0	121	30	15.13	0	0	2	2	62	0	40	2	20.00	0	0	2/40
Hearne,GAL	3	5	0	59	28	11.80	0	0	2	3								
Heine,PS	14	24	3	209	31	9.95	0	0	3	8	3890	106	1455	58	25.08	4	0	6/58
Henderson,CW	7	7	0	65	30	9.28	0	0	1	2	1962	79	928	22	42.18	0	0	4/116
Henry,O	3	3	0	53	34	17.66	0	0	0	2	427	15	189	3	63.00	0	0	2/56
Hime,CFW	1	2	0	8	8	4.00	0	0	1	0	55	4	31	1	31.00	0	0	1/20
Hudson,AC	35	63	3	2007	163	33.45	4	13	7	36								
Hutchinson,P	2	4	0	14	11	3.50	0	0	2	3								
Ironside,DEJ	3	4	2	37	13	18.50	0	0	0	1	986	41	275	15	18.33	1	0	5/51
Irvine,BL	4	7	0	353	102	50.42	1	2	0	2								
Jack,SD	2	2	0	7	7	3.50	0	0	1	1	462	24	196	8	24.50	0	0	4/69
Johnson,CL	1	2	0	10	7	5.00	0	0	0	1	140	12	57	0	-	0	0	0/57
Kallis,JH	101	170	27	7950	189*	55.59	24	40	6	94	13529	609	6304	199	31.67	4	0	6/54
Keith,HJ	8	16	1	318	73	21.20	0	2	3	9	108	2	63	0	-	0	0	0/19
Kemp,JM	4	6	0	80	55	13.33	0	1	2	3	479	20	222	9	24.66	0	0	3/33
Kempis,GA	1	2	1	0	0*	0.00	0	0	1	0	168	17	76	4	19.00	0	0	3/53
Kirsten,G	101	176	15	7289	275	45.27	21	34	13	83	349	19	142	2	71.00	0	0	1/0
Kirsten,PN	12	22	2	626	104	31.30	1	4	2	8	54	1	30	0	-	0	0	0/5
Klusener,L	49	69	11	1906	174	32.86	4	8	4	34	6887	318	3033	80	37.91	1	0	8/64
Kotze,JJ	3	5	0	2	2	0.40	0	0	4	3	413	8	243	6	40.50	0	0	3/64
Kuiper,AP	1	2	0	34	34	17.00	0	0	1	1								
Kuys,F	1	2	0	26	26	13.00	0	0	1	0	60	4	31	2	15.50	0	0	2/31
Lance,HR	13	22	1	591	70	28.14	0	5	1	7	948	38	479	12	39.91	0	0	3/30
Langeveldt,CK	6	4	2	14	8	7.00	0	0	1	2	999	27	593	16	37.06	1	0	5/46
Langton,ACB	15	23	4	298	73*	15.68	0	2	5	8	4199	104	1827	40	45.67	1	0	5/58
Lawrence,GB	5	8	0	141	43	17.62	0	0	2	2	1334	62	512	28	18.28	2	0	8/53
le Roux,FL	1	2	0	1	1	0.50	0	0	1	0	54	3	24	0	-	0	0	0/5
Lewis,PT	1	2	0	0	0	0.00	0	0	2	0								
Liebenberg,GFJ	5	8	0	104	45	13.00	0	0	2	1								
Lindsay,DT	19	31	1	1130	182	37.66	3	5	2	57/2								
Lindsay,JD	3	5	2	21	9*	7.00	0	0	2	4/1								
Lindsay,NV	1	2	0	35	29	17.50	0	0	0	1								
Ling,WVS	6	10	0	168	38	16.79	0	0	3	1	18	0	20	0	-	0	0	0/20
Llewellyn,CB	15	28	1	544	90	20.14	0	4	6	7	2292	55	1421	48	29.60	4	1	6/92
Lundie,EB	1	2	1	1	1	1.00	0	0	0	0	286	9	107	4	26.75	0	0	4/101
Macaulay,MJ	1	2	0	33	21	16.50	0	0	0	0	276	17	73	2	36.50	0	0	1/10
McCarthy,CN	15	24	15	28	5	3.11	0	0	6	6	3499	64	1510	36	41.94	2	0	6/43
McGlew,DJ	34	64	6	2440	255*	42.06	7	10	4	18	32	0	23	0	-	0	0	0/7
McKenzie,ND	41	65	4	2028	120	33.24	2	13	6	37	72	0	63	0	-	0	0	0/1
McKinnon,AH	8	13	7	107	27	17.83	0	0	0	1	2546	153	925	26	35.57	0	0	4/128
McLean,RA	40	73	3	2120	142	30.28	5	10	11	23	4	0	1	0	-	0	0	0/1
McMillan,BM	38	62	12	1968	113	39.36	3	13	3	49	6048	255	2537	75	33.82	0	0	4/65
McMillan,Q	13	21	4	306	50*	18.00	0	1	4	8	2021	38	1243	36	34.52	2	0	5/66
Mann,NBF	19	31	1	400	52	13.33	0	1	4	3	5796	260	1920	58	33.10	1	0	6/59
Mansell,PNF	13	22	2	355	90	17.75	0	2	3	15	1506	31	736	11	66.90	0	0	3/58
Markham,LA	1	1	0	20	20	20.00	0	0	0	0	104	1	72	1	72.00	0	0	1/34
Marx,WFE	3	6	0	125	36	20.83	0	0	1	0	228	1	144	4	36.00	0	0	3/85
Matthews,CR	18	25	6	348	62*	18.31	0	1	4	4	3980	231	1502	52	28.88	2	0	5/42
Meintjes,DJ	2	3	0	43	21	14.33	0	0	0	3	246	7	115	6	19.16	0	0	3/38
Melle,MG	7	12	4	68	17	8.50	0	0	1	4	1667	20	851	26	32.73	2	0	6/71
Melville,A	11	19	2	894	189	52.58	4	3	2	8								
Middleton,J	6	12	5	52	22	7.42	0	0	2	1	1064	61	442	24	18.41	2	0	5/51

SOUTH AFRICA (cont.)	BATTING AND FIELDING										BOWLING							
Player	M	I	NO	Runs	HS	Avge	100	50	0	C/S	Balls	Mdns	Runs	Wkts	Avge	5wi	10w	Best
Mills,CH	1	2	0	25	21	12.50	0	0	0	2	140	7	83	2	41.50	0	0	2/83
Milton,WH	3	6	0	68	21	11.33	0	0	0	1	79	5	48	2	24.00	0	0	1/5
Mitchell,B	42	80	9	3471	189*	48.88	8	21	3	56	2519	26	1380	27	51.11	1	0	5/87
Mitchell,F	3	6	0	28	12	4.67	0	0	1	0								
Morkel,DPB	16	28	1	663	88	24.55	0	4	3	13	1704	55	821	18	45.61	0	0	4/93
Murray,ARA	10	14	1	289	109	22.23	1	1	1	3	2374	111	710	18	39.44	0	0	4/169
Nel,A	23	25	6	135	18*	7.10	0	0	8	9	4959	187	2503	84	29.79	3	1	6/32
Nel,JD	6	11	0	150	38	13.63	0	0	1	1								
Newberry,C	4	8	0	62	16	7.75	0	0	1	3	558	15	268	11	24.36	0	0	4/72
Newson,ES	3	5	1	30	16	7.50	0	0	0	3	874	15	265	4	66.25	0	0	2/58
Ngam,M	3	1	1	0	0*	-	0	0	0	1	392	15	189	11	17.18	0	0	3/26
Nicholson,F	4	8	1	76	29	10.85	0	0	4	3/0								
Nicolson,JFW	3	5	0	179	78	35.80	0	1	0	0	24	0	17	0	-	0	0	0/5
Norton,NO	1	2	0	9	7	4.50	0	0	0	0	90	4	47	4	11.75	0	0	4/47
Nourse,AD	34	62	7	2960	231	53.81	9	14	3	12	20	1	9	0	-	0	0	0/0
Nourse,AW	45	83	8	2234	111	29.78	1	15	3	43	3234	120	1553	41	37.87	0	0	4/25
Ntini,M	69	78	23	574	32*	10.43	0	0	15	18	14598	539	7751	274	28.28	14	4	7/37
Nupen,EP	17	31	7	348	69	14.50	0	2	5	9	4159	133	1788	50	35.75	5	1	6/46
Ochse,AE	2	4	0	16	8	4.00	0	0	0	0								
Ochse,AL	3	4	1	11	4*	3.66	0	0	0	1	649	10	362	10	36.20	0	0	4/79
O'Linn,S	7	12	1	297	98	27.00	0	2	0	4								
Ontong,JL	2	4	1	57	32	19.00	0	0	1	1	185	2	133	1	133.00	0	0	1/79
Owen-Smith,HGO	5	8	2	252	129	42.00	1	1	0	4	156	0	113	0	-	0	0	0/3
Palm,AW	1	2	0	15	13	7.50	0	0	0	1								
Parker,GM	2	4	2	3	2*	1.50	0	0	2	0	366	2	273	8	34.12	1	0	6/152
Parkin,DC	1	2	0	6	6	3.00	0	0	1	1	130	4	82	3	27.33	0	0	3/82
Partridge,JT	11	12	5	73	13*	10.42	0	0	0	6	3684	136	1373	44	31.20	3	0	7/91
Pearse,COC	3	6	0	55	31	9.16	0	0	2	1	144	0	106	3	35.33	0	0	3/56
Pegler,SJ	16	28	5	356	35*	15.47	0	0	6	5	2989	84	1572	47	33.44	2	0	7/65
Peterson,RJ	5	6	1	159	78	31.80	0	1	0	4	785	37	403	8	50.37	0	0	3/46
Pithey,AJ	17	27	1	819	154	31.50	1	4	2	3	12	0	5	0	-	0	0	0/5
Pithey,DB	8	12	1	138	55	12.54	0	1	1	6	1424	67	577	12	48.08	1	0	6/58
Plimsoll,JB	1	2	1	16	8*	16.00	0	0	0	0	237	9	143	3	47.66	0	0	3/128
Pollock,PM	28	41	13	607	75*	21.67	0	2	3	9	6522	270	2806	116	24.18	9	1	6/38
Pollock,RG	23	41	4	2256	274	60.97	7	11	1	17	414	17	204	4	51.00	0	0	2/50
Pollock,SM	102	147	37	3515	111	31.95	2	15	9	66	25172	1158	9253	395	23.42	16	1	7/87
Poore,RM	3	6	0	76	20	12.66	0	0	0	3	9	0	4	1	4.00	0	0	1/4
Pothecary,JE	3	4	0	26	12	6.50	0	0	0	2	828	32	354	9	39.33	0	0	4/58
Powell,AW	1	2	0	16	11	8.00	0	0	0	2	20	1	10	1	10.00	0	0	1/10
Pretorius,D	4	4	1	22	9	7.33	0	0	1	0	570	18	430	6	71.66	0	0	4/115
Prince,AG	23	36	3	1258	139*	38.12	4	3	2	9	78	1	31	1	31.00	0	0	1/2
Prince,CFH	1	2	0	6	5	3.00	0	0	0	0								
Pringle,MW	4	6	2	67	33	16.75	0	0	0	0	652	21	270	5	54.00	0	0	2/62
Procter,MJ	7	10	1	226	48	25.11	0	0	1	4	1514	80	616	41	15.02	1	0	6/73
Promnitz,HLE	2	4	0	14	5	3.50	0	0	0	2	528	30	161	8	20.12	1	0	5/58
Quinn,NA	12	18	3	90	28	6.00	0	0	1	1	2922	103	1145	35	32.71	1	0	6/92
Reid,N	1	2	0	17	11	8.50	0	0	0	0	126	3	63	2	31.50	0	0	2/63
Rhodes,JN	52	80	9	2532	117	35.66	3	17	4	34	12	1	5	0	-	0	0	0/0
Richards,AR	1	2	0	6	6	3.00	0	0	1	0								
Richards,BA	4	7	0	508	140	72.57	2	2	0	3	72	3	26	1	26.00	0	0	1/12
Richards,WHM	1	2	0	4	4	2.00	0	0	1	0								
Richardson,DJ	42	64	8	1359	109	24.26	1	8	7	150/2								
Robertson,JB	3	6	1	51	17	10.20	0	0	0	2	738	26	321	6	53.50	0	0	3/143

SOUTH AFRICA (cont.)				**BATTING AND FIELDING**									**BOWLING**					
Player	M	I	NO	Runs	HS	Avge	100	50	0	C/S	Balls	Mdns	Runs	Wkts	Avge	5wi	10w	Best
Rose-Innes,A	2	4	0	14	13	3.50	0	0	2	2	128	8	89	5	17.79	1	0	5/43
Routledge,TW	4	8	0	72	24	9.00	0	0	1	2								
Rowan,AMB	15	23	6	290	41	17.05	0	0	3	7	5193	136	2084	54	38.59	4	0	5/68
Rowan,EAB	26	50	5	1965	236	43.66	3	12	4	14	19	1	7	0	-	0	0	0/0
Rowe,GA	5	9	3	26	13*	4.33	0	0	3	4	998	50	456	15	30.40	1	0	5/115
Rudolph,JA	35	63	7	2028	222*	36.21	5	8	8	22	664	13	432	4	108.00	0	0	1/1
Rushmere,MW	1	2	0	6	3	3.00	0	0	0	0								
Samuelson,SV	1	2	0	22	15	11.00	0	0	0	1	108	2	64	0	-	0	0	0/64
Schultz,BN	9	8	2	9	6	1.50	0	0	3	2	1733	82	749	37	20.24	2	0	5/48
Schwarz,RO	20	35	8	374	61	13.85	0	1	6	18	2639	66	1417	55	25.76	2	0	6/47
Seccull,AW	1	2	1	23	17*	23.00	0	0	0	1	60	2	37	2	18.50	0	0	2/37
Seymour,MA	7	10	3	84	36	12.00	0	0	3	2	1458	36	588	9	65.33	0	0	3/80
Shalders,WA	12	23	1	355	42	16.13	0	0	4	3	48	3	6	1	6.00	0	0	1/6
Shepstone,GH	2	4	0	38	21	9.50	0	0	1	2	115	9	47	0	-	0	0	0/8
Sherwell,PW	13	22	4	427	115	23.72	1	1	1	20/16								
Siedle,IJ	18	34	0	977	141	28.73	1	5	3	7	19	1	7	1	7.00	0	0	1/7
Sinclair,JH	25	47	1	1069	106	23.23	3	3	7	9	3598	110	1996	63	31.68	1	0	6/26
Smith,CJE	3	6	1	106	45	21.20	0	0	0	2								
Smith,FW	3	6	1	45	12	9.00	0	0	1	2/0								
Smith,GC	47	82	5	3879	277	50.37	11	14	5	56	1247	27	724	8	90.50	0	0	2/145
Smith,VI	9	16	6	39	11*	3.90	0	0	4	3	1655	55	769	12	64.08	0	0	4/143
Snell,RP	5	8	1	95	48	13.57	0	0	1	1	1025	42	538	19	28.31	0	0	4/74
Snooke,SD	1	1	0	0	0	0.00	0	0	1	2								
Snooke,SJ	26	46	1	1008	103	22.40	1	5	1	24	1620	62	702	35	20.05	1	1	8/70
Solomon,WRT	1	2	0	4	2	2.00	0	0	0	1								
Stewart,RB	1	2	0	13	9	6.50	0	0	0	2								
Steyn,DW	8	13	4	70	13	7.77	0	0	2	2	680	37	1124	32	35.12	1	0	5/47
Steyn,PJR	3	6	0	127	46	21.16	0	0	0	0								
Stricker,LA	13	24	0	342	48	14.25	0	0	5	3	174	3	105	1	105.00	0	0	1/36
Strydom,PC	2	3	0	35	30	11.66	0	0	0	1	36	0	27	0	-	0	0	0/27
Susskind,MJ	5	8	0	268	65	33.50	0	4	0	1								
Symcox,PL	20	27	1	741	108	28.50	1	4	1	5	3561	135	1603	37	43.32	0	0	4/69
Taberer,HM	1	1	0	2	2	2.00	0	0	0	0	60	2	48	1	48.00	0	0	1/25
Tancred,AB	2	4	1	87	29	29.00	0	0	0	2								
Tancred,LJ	14	26	1	530	97	21.20	0	2	5	3								
Tancred,VM	1	2	0	25	18	12.50	0	0	0	0								
Tapscott,GL	1	2	0	5	4	2.50	0	0	0	1								
Tapscott,LE	2	3	1	58	50*	29.00	0	1	0	0	12	1	2	0	-	0	0	0/2
Tayfield,HJ	37	60	9	862	75	16.90	0	2	5	26	13568	602	4405	170	25.91	14	2	9/113
Taylor,AI	1	2	0	18	12	9.00	0	0	0	0								
Taylor,D	2	4	0	85	36	21.25	0	0	0	0								
Taylor,HW	42	76	4	2936	176	40.77	7	17	2	19	342	18	156	5	31.20	0	0	3/15
Terbrugge,DJ	7	8	5	16	4*	5.33	0	0	2	4	1012	44	517	20	25.85	1	0	5/46
Theunissen,NHCD	1	2	1	2	2*	2.00	0	0	1	0	80	5	51	0	-	0	0	0/51
Thornton,G	1	1	1	1	1*	-	0	0	0	1	24	0	20	1	20.00	0	0	1/20
Tomlinson,DS	1	1	0	9	9	9.00	0	0	0	0	60	0	38	0	-	0	0	0/38
Traicos,AJ	3	4	2	8	5*	4.00	0	0	1	4	470	24	207	4	51.75	0	0	2/70
Trimborn,PHJ	4	4	2	13	11*	6.50	0	0	1	7	747	31	257	11	23.36	0	0	3/12
Tsolekile,TL	3	5	0	47	22	9.40	0	0	1	6/0								
Tuckett,L	9	14	3	131	40*	11.90	0	0	3	9	2104	47	980	19	51.57	2	0	5/68
Tuckett,LR	1	2	1	0	0*	0.00	0	0	1	2	120	4	69	0	-	0	0	0/24

Twentyman-Jones,PS

SOUTH AFRICA (cont.) — **BATTING AND FIELDING** — **BOWLING**

Player	M	I	NO	Runs	HS	Avge	100	50	0	C/S	Balls	Mdns	Runs	Wkts	Avge	5wi	10w	Best
	1	2	0	0	0	0.00	0	0	2	0								
van der Bijl,PGV	5	9	0	460	125	51.11	1	2	0	1								
van der Merwe,EA	2	4	1	27	19	9.00	0	0	1	3/0								
van der Merwe,PL	15	23	2	533	76	25.38	0	3	3	11	79	7	22	1	22.00	0	0	1/6
van Jaarsveld,M	9	15	2	397	73	30.53	0	3	0	11	42	0	28	0	-	0	0	0/28
van Ryneveld,CB	19	33	6	724	83	26.81	0	3	0	14	1554	27	671	17	39.47	0	0	4/67
Varnals,GD	3	6	0	97	23	16.16	0	0	0	0	12	1	2	0	-	0	0	0/2
Viljoen,KG	27	50	2	1365	124	28.43	2	9	5	5	48	1	23	0	-	0	0	0/10
Vincent,CL	25	38	12	526	60	20.23	0	2	4	27	5851	194	2631	84	31.32	3	0	6/51
Vintcent,CH	3	6	0	26	9	4.33	0	0	1	1	369	23	193	4	48.25	0	0	3/88
Vogler,AEE	15	26	6	340	65	17.00	0	2	4	20	2764	96	1455	64	22.73	5	1	7/94
Wade,HF	10	18	2	327	40*	20.43	0	0	4	4								
Wade,WW	11	19	1	511	125	28.38	1	3	3	15/2								
Waite,JHB	50	86	7	2405	134	30.44	4	16	9	124/17								
Walter,KA	2	3	0	11	10	3.66	0	0	1	3	495	20	197	6	32.83	0	0	4/63
Ward,TA	23	42	9	459	64	13.90	0	2	5	19/13								
Watkins,JC	15	27	1	612	92	23.53	0	3	2	12	2805	134	816	29	28.13	0	0	4/22
Wesley,C	3	5	0	49	35	9.80	0	0	2	1								
Wessels,KC	16	29	2	1027	118	38.04	2	6	2	12								
Westcott,RJ	5	9	0	166	62	18.44	0	1	2	0	32	0	22	0	-	0	0	0/22
White,GC	17	31	2	872	147	30.06	2	4	3	10	498	14	301	9	33.44	0	0	4/47
Willoughby,CM	2						0	0	0	0	300	18	125	1	125.00	0	0	1/47
Willoughby,JT	2	4	0	8	5	2.00	0	0	2	0	275	12	159	6	26.50	0	0	2/37
Wimble,CS	1	2	0	0	0	0.00	0	0	2	0								
Winslow,PL	5	9	0	186	108	20.66	1	0	1	1								
Wynne,OE	6	12	0	219	50	18.25	0	1	0	3								
Zondeki,M	5	4	0	82	59	20.50	0	1	0	1	692	21	438	16	27.37	1	0	6/39
Zulch,JW	16	32	2	985	150	32.83	2	4	0	4	24	0	28	0	-	0	0	0/2

WEST INDIES (265 players) — **BATTING AND FIELDING** — **BOWLING**

Player	M	I	NO	Runs	HS	Avge	100	50	0	C/S	Balls	Mdns	Runs	Wkts	Avge	5wi	10w	Best
Achong,EE	6	11	1	81	22	8.10	0	0	2	6	918	34	378	8	47.25	0	0	2/64
Adams,JC	54	90	17	3012	208*	41.26	6	14	7	48	2853	99	1336	27	49.48	1	0	5/17
Alexander,FCM	25	38	6	961	108	30.03	1	7	5	85/5								
Allan,DW	5	7	1	75	40*	12.50	0	0	0	15/3								
Allen,IBA	2	2	2	5	4*	-	0	0	0	1	282	4	180	5	36.00	0	0	2/69
Ambrose,CEL	98	145	29	1439	53	12.41	0	1	26	18	22103	1000	8501	405	20.99	22	3	8/45
Arthurton,KLT	33	50	5	1382	157*	30.71	2	8	8	22	473	14	183	1	183.00	0	0	1/17
Asgarali,NS	2	4	0	62	29	15.50	0	0	1	0								
Atkinson,DS	22	35	6	922	219	31.79	1	5	4	11	5201	311	1647	47	35.04	3	0	7/53
Atkinson,ES	8	9	1	126	37	15.75	0	0	3	2	1634	77	589	25	23.56	1	0	5/42
Austin,RA	2	2	0	22	20	11.00	0	0	0	2	6	0	5	0	-	0	0	0/5
Bacchus,SFAF	19	30	0	782	250	26.07	1	3	7	17	6	0	3	0	-	0	0	0/3
Baichan,L	3	6	2	184	105*	46.00	1	0	0	2								
Banks,OAC	10	16	4	321	50*	26.75	0	1	1	6	2401	62	1367	28	48.82	0	0	4/87
Baptiste,EAE	10	11	1	233	87*	23.30	0	1	1	2	1362	60	563	16	35.19	0	0	3/31
Barrett,AG	6	7	1	40	19	6.67	0	0	1	0	1612	83	603	13	46.38	0	0	3/43
Barrow,IM	11	19	2	276	105	16.24	1	0	3	17/5								
Bartlett,EL	5	8	1	131	84	18.71	0	1	1	2								
Baugh,CS	5	10	0	196	68	19.60	0	1	0	4/1								
Benjamin,KCG	26	36	8	222	43*	7.93	0	0	8	2	5132	158	2785	92	30.27	4	1	6/66

WEST INDIES (cont.)				**BATTING AND FIELDING**							**BOWLING**							
Player	M	I	NO	Runs	HS	Avge	100	50	0	C/S	Balls	Mdns	Runs	Wkts	Avge	5wi	10w	Best
Benjamin,WKM	21	26	1	470	85	18.80	0	2	4	12	3694	136	1648	61	27.02	0	0	4/46
Bernard,DE	1	2	0	11	7	5.50	0	0	0	0	66	1	61	0	-	0	0	0/61
Best,CA	8	13	1	342	164	28.50	1	1	1	8	30	0	21	0	-	0	0	0/2
Best,TL	12	19	2	174	27	10.23	0	0	3	1	1851	38	1171	26	45.03	0	0	4/46
Betancourt,N	1	2	0	52	39	26.00	0	0	0	0								
Binns,AP	5	8	1	64	27	9.14	0	0	3	14/3								
Birkett,LS	4	8	0	136	64	17.00	0	1	1	4	126	1	71	1	71.00	0	0	1/16
Bishop,IR	43	63	11	632	48	12.15	0	0	10	8	8413	288	3909	161	24.28	6	0	6/40
Black,MI	6	11	3	21	6	2.63	0	0	4	0	954	27	597	12	49.75	0	0	4/83
Boyce,KD	21	30	3	657	95*	24.33	0	4	4	5	3501	99	1801	60	30.02	2	1	6/77
Bradshaw,IDR	5	8	1	96	33	13.71	0	0	1	3	1021	33	540	9	60.00	0	0	3/73
Bravo,DJJ	16	30	1	956	113	32.96	2	5	2	13	2403	76	1295	36	35.97	2	0	6/55
Breese,GR	1	2	0	5	5	2.50	0	0	1	1	188	3	135	2	67.50	0	0	2/108
Browne,CO	20	30	6	387	68	16.12	0	1	7	79/2								
Browne,CR	4	8	1	176	70*	25.14	0	1	2	1	840	38	288	6	48.00	0	0	2/72
Butcher,BF	44	78	6	3104	209*	43.11	7	16	3	15	256	15	90	5	18.00	1	0	5/34
Butler,LS	1	1	0	16	16	16.00	0	0	0	0	240	7	151	2	75.50	0	0	2/151
Butts,CG	7	8	1	108	38	15.43	0	0	1	2	1554	70	595	10	59.50	0	0	4/73
Bynoe,MR	4	6	0	111	48	18.50	0	0	0	4	30	4	5	1	5.00	0	0	1/5
Camacho,GS	11	22	0	640	87	29.09	0	4	1	4	18	1	12	0	-	0	0	0/12
Cameron,FJ	5	7	1	151	75*	25.17	0	1	1	0	786	34	278	3	92.67	0	0	2/74
Cameron,JH	2	3	0	6	5	2.00	0	0	1	0	232	6	88	3	29.33	0	0	3/66
Campbell,SL	52	93	4	2882	208	32.38	4	18	7	46								
Carew,GM	4	7	1	170	107	28.33	1	0	1	1	18	2	2	0	-	0	0	0/2
Carew,MC	19	36	3	1127	109	34.15	1	5	1	13	1174	46	437	8	54.63	0	0	1/11
Challenor,G	3	6	0	101	46	16.83	0	0	2	0								
Chanderpaul,S	98	168	22	6531	203*	44.73	14	38	10	41	1590	51	786	8	98.25	0	0	1/2
Chang,HS	1	2	0	8	6	4.00	0	0	0	0								
Christiani,CM	4	7	2	98	32*	19.60	0	0	1	6/1								
Christiani,RJ	22	37	3	896	107	26.35	1	4	0	19/2	234	1	108	3	36.00	0	0	3/52
Clarke,CB	3	4	1	3	2	1.00	0	0	1	0	456	2	261	6	43.50	0	0	3/59
Clarke,ST	11	16	5	172	35*	15.64	0	0	2	2	2477	81	1169	42	27.83	1	0	5/126
Collins,PT	32	47	7	235	24	5.87	0	0	14	7	6964	221	3671	106	34.63	3	0	6/53
Collymore,CD	23	40	21	147	16	7.73	0	0	9	5	4735	184	2219	75	29.58	4	1	7/57
Constantine,L	18	33	0	635	90	19.24	0	4	4	28	3583	125	1746	58	30.10	2	0	5/75
Croft,CEH	27	37	22	158	33	10.53	0	0	6	8	6165	211	2913	125	23.30	3	0	8/29
Cuffy,CE	15	23	9	58	15	4.14	0	0	6	5	3366	143	1455	43	33.84	0	0	4/82
Cummins,AC	5	6	1	98	50	19.60	0	1	1	1	618	11	342	8	42.75	0	0	4/54
da Costa,OC	5	9	1	153	39	19.13	0	0	1	5	372	13	175	3	58.33	0	0	1/14
Daniel,WW	10	11	4	46	11	6.57	0	0	2	4	1754	60	910	36	25.28	1	0	5/39
Davis,BA	4	8	0	245	68	30.63	0	3	0	1								
Davis,CA	15	29	5	1301	183	54.21	4	4	1	4	894	32	330	2	165.00	0	0	1/27
Davis,WW	15	17	4	202	77	15.54	0	1	2	10	2773	53	1472	45	32.71	0	0	4/19
de Caires,FI	3	6	0	232	80	38.67	0	2	1	1	12	0	9	0	-	0	0	0/9
Deonarine,N	4	6	1	107	40	21.40	0	0	0	2	341	17	151	2	75.50	0	0	1/5
Depeiza,CC	5	8	2	187	122	31.17	1	0	1	7/4	30	0	15	0	-	0	0	0/3
Dewdney,DT	9	12	5	17	5*	2.43	0	0	3	0	1641	65	807	21	38.43	1	0	5/21
Dhanraj,R	4	4	0	17	9	4.25	0	0	0	1	1087	32	595	8	74.38	0	0	2/49
Dillon,M	38	68	3	546	43	8.40	0	0	26	16	8710	267	4406	131	33.63	2	0	5/71
Dowe,UG	4	3	2	8	5*	8.00	0	0	0	3	1014	30	534	12	44.50	0	0	4/69
Drakes,VC	12	20	2	386	67	21.44	0	1	2	2	2611	65	1359	33	41.18	1	0	5/93
Dujon,PJL	81	115	11	3322	139	31.94	5	16	8	267/5								
Edwards,FH	24	39	11	119	20	4.25	0	0	10	4	4045	75	2675	62	43.14	4	0	5/36

WEST INDIES (cont.)					**BATTING AND FIELDING**								**BOWLING**					
Player	M	I	NO	Runs	HS	Avge	100	50	0	C/S	Balls	Mdns	Runs	Wkts	Avge	5wi	10w	Best
Edwards,RM	5	8	1	65	22	9.29	0	0	2	0	1311	25	626	18	34.78	1	0	5/84
Ferguson,W	8	10	3	200	75	28.57	0	2	1	11	2568	83	1165	34	34.26	3	1	6/92
Fernandes,MP	2	4	0	49	22	12.25	0	0	1	0								
Findlay,TM	10	16	3	212	44*	16.31	0	0	1	19/2								
Foster,MLC	14	24	5	580	125	30.53	1	1	0	3	1776	106	600	9	66.67	0	0	2/41
Francis,GN	10	18	4	81	19*	5.79	0	0	4	7	1619	54	763	23	33.17	0	0	4/40
Frederick,MC	1	2	0	30	30	15.00	0	0	1	0								
Fredericks,RC	59	109	7	4334	169	42.49	8	26	7	62	1187	41	548	7	78.29	0	0	1/12
Fuller,RL	1	1	0	1	1	1.00	0	0	0	0	48	2	12	0	-	0	0	0/2
Furlonge,HA	3	5	0	99	64	19.80	0	1	1	0								
Ganga,D	38	67	1	1765	135	26.74	3	7	7	25	162	2	86	0	-	0	0	0/0
Ganteaume,AG	1	1	0	112	112	112.00	1	0	0	0								
Garner,J	58	68	14	672	60	12.44	0	1	17	42	13175	576	5433	259	20.98	7	0	6/56
Garrick,LV	1	2	0	27	27	13.50	0	0	1	2								
Gaskin,BBM	2	3	0	17	10	5.67	0	0	1	1	474	24	158	2	79.00	0	0	1/15
Gayle,CH	61	108	3	4089	317	38.94	7	25	12	65	4274	151	1825	49	37.24	2	0	5/34
Gibbs,GL	1	2	0	12	12	6.00	0	0	1	1	24	1	7	0	-	0	0	0/2
Gibbs,LR	79	109	39	488	25	6.97	0	0	15	52	27115	1313	8989	309	29.09	18	2	8/38
Gibson,OD	2	4	0	93	37	23.25	0	0	0	0	472	9	275	3	91.67	0	0	2/81
Gilchrist,R	13	14	3	60	12	5.45	0	0	4	4	3227	124	1521	57	26.68	1	0	6/55
Gladstone,G	1	1	1	12	12*	-	0	0	0	0	300	5	189	1	189.00	0	0	1/139
Goddard,JDC	27	39	11	859	83*	30.68	0	4	5	22	2931	148	1050	33	31.82	1	0	5/31
Gomes,HA	60	91	11	3171	143	39.64	9	13	5	18	2401	79	930	15	62.00	0	0	2/20
Gomez,GE	29	46	5	1243	101	30.32	1	8	5	18	5236	289	1590	58	27.41	1	1	7/55
Grant,GC	12	22	6	413	71*	25.81	0	3	1	10	24	0	18	0	-	0	0	0/1
Grant,RS	7	11	1	220	77	22.00	0	1	3	13	986	32	353	11	32.09	0	0	3/68
Gray,AH	5	8	2	48	12*	8.00	0	0	2	6	888	37	377	22	17.14	0	0	4/39
Greenidge,AE	6	10	0	222	69	22.20	0	2	2	5								
Greenidge,CG	108	185	16	7558	226	44.72	19	34	11	96	26	3	4	0	-	0	0	0/0
Greenidge,GA	5	9	2	209	50	29.86	0	1	1	3	156	4	75	0	-	0	0	0/2
Grell,MG	1	2	0	34	21	17.00	0	0	0	1	30	1	17	0	-	0	0	0/7
Griffith,AFG	14	27	1	638	114	24.54	1	4	4	5								
Griffith,CC	28	42	10	530	54	16.56	0	1	5	16	5631	177	2683	94	28.54	5	0	6/36
Griffith,HC	13	23	5	91	18	5.06	0	0	6	4	2663	89	1243	44	28.25	2	0	6/103
Guillen,SC	5	6	2	104	54	26.00	0	1	1	9/2								
Hall,WW	48	66	14	818	50*	15.73	0	2	7	11	10421	312	5066	192	26.39	9	1	7/69
Harper,RA	25	32	3	535	74	18.45	0	3	5	36	3615	183	1291	46	28.07	1	0	6/57
Haynes,DL	116	202	25	7487	184	42.30	18	39	10	65	18	0	8	1	8.00	0	0	1/2
Headley,GA	22	40	4	2190	270*	60.83	10	5	2	14	398	7	230	0	-	0	0	0/0
Headley,RGA	2	4	0	62	42	15.50	0	0	0	2								
Hendriks,JL	20	32	8	447	64	18.63	0	2	4	42/5								
Hinds,RO	9	16	1	363	84	24.20	0	2	1	4	998	42	390	5	78.00	0	0	2/83
Hinds,WW	45	80	2	2608	213	33.43	5	14	6	33	1123	41	591	16	36.93	0	0	3/79
Hoad,ELG	4	8	0	98	36	12.25	0	0	1	1								
Holder,RIC	11	17	2	380	91	25.33	0	2	1	9								
Holder,VA	40	59	11	682	42	14.21	0	0	7	16	9095	367	3627	109	33.28	3	0	6/28
Holding,MA	60	76	10	910	73	13.79	0	6	15	22	12680	459	5898	249	23.69	13	2	8/92
Holford,DAJ	24	39	5	768	105*	22.59	1	3	3	18	4816	164	2009	51	39.39	1	0	5/23
Holt,JK	17	31	2	1066	166	36.76	2	5	2	8	30	2	20	1	20.00	0	0	1/20
Hooper,CL	102	173	15	5762	233	36.47	13	27	13	115	13788	531	5635	114	49.43	4	0	5/26
Howard,AB	1	0	0	0	0	-	0	0	0	0	372	16	140	2	70.00	0	0	2/140
Hunte,CC	44	78	6	3245	260	45.07	8	13	5	16	270	11	110	2	55.00	0	0	1/17
Hunte,EAC	3	6	1	166	58	33.20	0	2	0	5/0								

WEST INDIES (cont.)	**BATTING AND FIELDING**										**BOWLING**							
Player	M	I	NO	Runs	HS	Avge	100	50	0	C/S	Balls	Mdns	Runs	Wkts	Avge	5wi	10w	Best
Hylton,LG	6	8	2	70	19	11.67	0	0	0	1	965	31	418	16	26.13	0	0	4/27
Imtiaz Ali	1	1	1	1	1*	-	0	0	0	0	204	10	89	2	44.50	0	0	2/37
Inshan Ali	12	18	2	172	25	10.75	0	0	3	7	3718	137	1621	34	47.68	1	0	5/59
Jacobs,RD	65	112	20	2577	118	28.01	3	14	12	207/12								
Johnson,HHH	3	4	0	38	22	9.50	0	0	1	0	789	37	238	13	18.31	2	1	5/41
Johnson,TF	1	1	1	9	9*	-	0	0	0	1	240	3	129	3	43.00	0	0	2/53
Jones,CEL	4	7	0	63	19	9.00	0	0	0	3	102	11	11	0	-	0	0	0/2
Jones,PE	9	11	2	47	10*	5.22	0	0	1	4	1842	64	751	25	30.04	1	0	5/85
Joseph,DRE	4	7	0	141	50	20.14	0	1	0	10								
Joseph,SC	4	8	0	133	45	16.62	0	0	1	3	12	0	8	0	-	0	0	0/8
Julien,BD	24	34	6	866	121	30.93	2	3	0	14	4542	192	1868	50	37.36	1	0	5/57
Jumadeen,RR	12	14	10	84	56	21.00	0	1	2	4	3140	140	1141	29	39.34	0	0	4/72
Kallicharran,AI	66	109	10	4399	187	44.43	12	21	10	51	406	14	158	4	39.50	0	0	2/16
Kanhai,RB	79	137	6	6227	256	47.53	15	28	7	50/0	183	8	85	0	-	0	0	0/1
Kentish,ESM	2	2	1	1	1*	1.00	0	0	1	1	540	31	178	8	22.25	1	0	5/49
King,CL	9	16	3	418	100*	32.15	1	2	3	5	582	24	282	3	94.00	0	0	1/30
King,FM	14	17	3	116	21	8.29	0	0	4	5	2869	140	1159	29	39.97	1	0	5/74
King,LA	2	4	0	41	20	10.25	0	0	1	2	476	19	154	9	17.11	1	0	5/46
King,RD	19	27	8	66	12*	3.47	0	0	7	2	3442	119	1733	53	32.69	1	0	5/51
Lambert,CB	5	9	0	284	104	31.56	1	1	1	8	10	0	5	1	5.00	0	0	1/4
Lara,BC	127	225	6	11464	400*	52.34	32	47	16	161	60	1	28	0	-	0	0	0/0
Lashley,PD	4	7	0	159	49	22.71	0	0	1	4	18	2	1	1	1.00	0	0	1/1
Lawson,JJC	13	21	6	52	14	3.46	0	0	6	3	2364	55	1512	51	29.64	2	0	7/78
Legall,RA	4	5	0	50	23	10.00	0	0	0	8/1								
Lewis,DM	3	5	2	259	88	86.33	0	3	0	8								
Lewis,RN	4	8	0	88	40	11.00	0	0	3	0	759	24	388	1	388.00	0	0	1/67
Lloyd,CH	110	175	14	7515	242*	46.68	19	39	4	90	1716	75	622	10	62.20	0	0	2/13
Logie,AL	52	78	9	2470	130	35.80	2	16	8	57	7	1	4	0	-	0	0	0/0
McGarrell,NC	4	6	2	61	33	15.25	0	0	1	2	1212	65	453	17	26.65	0	0	4/23
McLean,NAM	19	32	2	368	46	12.27	0	0	6	5	3299	85	1873	44	42.57	0	0	3/53
McMorris,EDAS	13	21	0	564	125	26.86	1	3	1	5								
McWatt,CA	6	9	2	202	54	28.86	0	2	0	9/1	24	2	16	1	16.00	0	0	1/16
Madray,IS	2	3	0	3	2	1.00	0	0	1	2	210	6	108	0	-	0	0	0/12
Marshall,MD	81	107	11	1810	92	18.85	0	10	15	25	17584	613	7876	376	20.95	22	4	7/22
Marshall,NE	1	2	0	8	8	4.00	0	0	1	0	279	22	62	2	31.00	0	0	1/22
Marshall,RE	4	7	0	143	30	20.43	0	0	1	1	52	2	15	0	-	0	0	0/3
Marshall,XM	2	4	0	17	10	4.25	0	0	0	1								
Martin,FR	9	18	1	486	123*	28.59	1	0	1	2	1346	27	619	8	77.38	0	0	3/91
Martindale,EA	10	14	3	58	22	5.27	0	0	3	5	1605	40	804	37	21.73	3	0	5/22
Mattis,EH	4	5	0	145	71	29.00	0	1	1	3	36	1	14	0	-	0	0	0/4
Mendonça,IL	2	2	0	81	78	40.50	0	1	0	8/2								
Merry,CA	2	4	0	34	13	8.50	0	0	0	1								
Miller,R	1	1	0	23	23	23.00	0	0	0	0	96	8	28	0	-	0	0	0/28
Mohammed,D	3	5	1	139	52	34.75	0	1	0	0	647	11	430	7	61.42	0	0	3/112
Morton,RS	4	7	1	193	70*	32.16	0	2	1	6	36	0	22	0	-	0	0	0/7
Moseley,EA	2	4	0	35	26	8.75	0	0	1	1	522	13	261	6	43.50	0	0	2/70
Mudie,GH	1	1	0	5	5	5.00	0	0	0	0	174	12	40	3	13.33	0	0	2/23
Murray,DA	19	31	3	601	84	21.46	0	3	3	57/5								
Murray,DL	62	96	9	1993	91	22.91	0	11	7	181/8								
Murray,JR	33	45	4	918	101*	22.39	1	3	9	99/3								
Nagamootoo,MV	5	8	1	185	68	26.43	0	1	0	2	1494	70	637	12	53.08	0	0	3/119
Nanan,R	1	2	0	16	8	8.00	0	0	0	2	216	7	91	4	22.75	0	0	2/37
Neblett,JM	1	2	1	16	11*	16.00	0	0	0	0	216	11	75	1	75.00	0	0	1/44

WEST INDIES (cont.)	**BATTING AND FIELDING**										**BOWLING**							
Player	M	I	NO	Runs	HS	Avge	100	50	0	C/S	Balls	Mdns	Runs	Wkts	Avge	5wi	10w	Best
Noreiga,JM	4	5	2	11	9	3.67	0	0	1	2	1322	47	493	17	29.00	2	0	9/95
Nunes,RK	4	8	0	245	92	30.63	0	2	1	2/0								
Nurse,SM	29	54	1	2523	258	47.60	6	10	3	21	42	4	7	0	-	0	0	0/0
Padmore,AL	2	2	1	8	8*	8.00	0	0	1	0	474	23	135	1	135.00	0	0	1/36
Pagon,DJ	2	3	0	37	35	12.33	0	0	1	0								
Pairaudeau,BH	13	21	0	454	115	21.62	1	3	3	6	6	0	3	0	-	0	0	0/3
Parry,DR	12	20	3	381	65	22.41	0	3	3	4	1909	65	936	23	40.70	1	0	5/15
Passailaigue,CC	1	2	1	46	44	46.00	0	0	0	3	12	0	15	0	-	0	0	0/15
Patterson,BP	28	38	16	145	21*	6.59	0	0	8	5	4829	109	2874	93	30.90	5	0	5/24
Payne,TRO	1	1	0	5	5	5.00	0	0	0	5/0								
Perry,NO	4	7	1	74	26	12.33	0	0	2	1	804	24	446	10	44.60	1	0	5/70
Phillip,N	9	15	5	297	47	29.70	0	0	1	5	1820	46	1042	28	37.21	0	0	4/48
Pierre,LR	1	0	0	0	0	-	0	0	0	0	42	0	28	0	-	0	0	0/9
Powell,DB	17	26	0	157	16	6.03	0	0	7	1	3143	99	1755	43	40.81	0	0	4/83
Powell,RL	2	3	0	53	30	17.66	0	0	1	1	78	2	49	0	-	0	0	0/13
Rae,AF	15	24	2	1016	109	46.18	4	4	1	10								
Ragoonath,S	2	4	1	13	9	4.33	0	0	1	0								
Ramadhin,S	43	58	14	361	44	8.20	0	0	14	9	13939	813	4579	158	28.98	10	1	7/49
Ramdass,R	1	2	0	26	23	13.00	0	0	0	2								
Ramdin,DC	12	22	4	478	71	26.55	0	3	0	29/0								
Ramnarine,D	12	21	4	106	35*	6.24	0	0	8	8	3495	169	1383	45	30.73	1	0	5/78
Reifer,FL	4	8	0	63	29	7.88	0	0	3	4								
Richards,IVA	121	182	12	8540	291	50.24	24	45	10	122	5170	203	1964	32	61.38	0	0	2/17
Richardson,RB	86	146	12	5949	194	44.40	16	27	8	90	66	4	18	0	-	0	0	0/0
Rickards,KR	2	3	0	104	67	34.67	0	1	0	0								
Roach,CA	16	32	1	952	209	30.71	2	6	6	5	222	5	103	2	51.50	0	0	1/18
Roberts,AME	47	62	11	762	68	14.94	0	3	6	9	11135	382	5174	202	25.61	11	2	7/54
Roberts,AT	1	2	0	28	28	14.00	0	0	1	0								
Roberts,LA	1	1	0	0	0	0.00	0	0	1	0								
Rodriguez,WV	5	7	0	96	50	13.71	0	1	1	3	573	10	374	7	53.43	0	0	3/51
Rose,FA	19	28	2	344	69	13.23	0	1	2	4	3124	102	1637	53	30.89	2	0	7/84
Rowe,LG	30	49	2	2047	302	43.55	7	7	2	17	86	3	44	0	-	0	0	0/1
St Hill,EL	2	4	0	18	12	4.50	0	0	1	0	558	29	221	3	73.67	0	0	2/110
St Hill,WH	3	6	0	117	38	19.50	0	0	0	1	12	0	9	0	-	0	0	0/9
Samuels,MN	23	41	4	1044	104	28.21	1	7	4	9	1308	32	703	5	140.60	0	0	2/49
Samuels,RG	6	12	2	372	125	37.20	1	1	0	8								
Sandford,A	11	17	2	72	18*	4.80	0	0	2	4	2217	69	1316	30	43.86	0	0	4/132
Sarwan,RR	63	114	7	4207	261*	39.31	9	26	9	44	1747	33	970	21	46.19	0	0	4/37
Scarlett,RO	3	4	1	54	29*	18.00	0	0	0	2	804	53	209	2	104.50	0	0	1/46
Scott,APH	1	1	0	5	5	5.00	0	0	0	0	264	9	140	0	-	0	0	0/52
Scott,OC	8	13	3	171	35	17.10	0	0	1	0	1405	18	925	22	42.05	1	0	5/266
Sealey,BJ	1	2	0	41	29	20.50	0	0	0	0	30	1	10	1	10.00	0	0	1/10
Sealy,JED	11	19	2	478	92	28.12	0	3	2	6/1	156	4	94	3	31.33	0	0	2/7
Shepherd,JN	5	8	0	77	32	9.63	0	0	2	4	1445	70	479	19	25.21	1	0	5/104
Shillingford,GC	7	8	1	57	25	8.14	0	0	1	2	1181	38	537	15	35.80	0	0	3/63
Shillingford,IT	4	7	0	218	120	31.14	1	0	0	1								
Shivnarine,S	8	14	1	379	63	29.15	0	4	2	6	336	10	167	1	167.00	0	0	1/13
Simmons,PV	26	47	2	1002	110	22.27	1	4	4	26	624	27	257	4	64.25	0	0	2/34
Singh,CK	2	3	0	11	11	3.67	0	0	2	2	506	35	166	5	33.20	0	0	2/28
Small,JA	3	6	0	79	52	13.17	0	1	2	3	366	11	184	3	61.33	0	0	2/67
Small,MA	2	1	1	3	3*	-	0	0	0	0	270	7	153	4	38.25	0	0	3/40
Smith,CW	5	10	1	222	55	24.67	0	1	0	4/1								
Smith,DR	10	14	1	320	105*	24.61	1	0	4	9	651	20	344	7	49.14	0	0	3/71

WEST INDIES (cont.)				**BATTING AND FIELDING**									**BOWLING**					
Player	M	I	NO	Runs	HS	Avge	100	50	0	C/S	Balls	Mdns	Runs	Wkts	Avge	5wi	10w	Best
Smith,DS	16	30	1	735	108	25.34	1	3	4	13								
Smith,OG	26	42	0	1331	168	31.69	4	6	8	9	4431	229	1625	48	33.85	1	0	5/90
Sobers,GS	93	160	21	8032	365*	57.78	26	30	12	109	21599	974	7999	235	34.04	6	0	6/73
Solomon,JS	27	46	7	1326	100*	34.00	1	9	7	13	702	39	268	4	67.00	0	0	1/20
Stayers,SC	4	4	1	58	35*	19.33	0	0	0	0	636	20	364	9	40.44	0	0	3/65
Stollmeyer,JB	32	56	5	2159	160	42.33	4	12	2	20	990	30	507	13	39.00	0	0	3/32
Stollmeyer,VH	1	1	0	96	96	96.00	0	1	0	0								
Stuart,CEL	6	9	2	24	12*	3.43	0	0	2	2	1116	37	628	20	31.40	0	0	3/33
Taylor,JE	7	11	3	90	23	11.25	0	0	0	0	1006	28	612	18	34.00	1	0	5/50
Taylor,JO	3	5	3	4	4*	2.00	0	0	2	0	672	33	273	10	27.30	1	0	5/109
Thompson,PIC	2	3	1	17	10*	8.50	0	0	0	0	228	1	215	5	43.00	0	0	2/58
Trim,J	4	5	1	21	12	5.25	0	0	2	2	794	28	291	18	16.17	1	0	5/34
Valentine,AL	36	51	21	141	14	4.70	0	0	12	13	12953	789	4215	139	30.32	8	2	8/104
Valentine,VA	2	4	1	35	19*	11.67	0	0	1	0	288	14	104	1	104.00	0	0	1/55
Walcott,CL	44	74	7	3798	220	56.69	15	14	1	53/11	1194	72	408	11	37.09	0	0	3/50
Walcott,LA	1	2	1	40	24	40.00	0	0	0	0	48	1	32	1	32.00	0	0	1/17
Wallace,PA	7	13	0	279	92	21.46	0	2	1	9								
Walsh,CA	132	185	61	936	30*	7.55	0	0	43	29	30019	1145	12688	519	24.45	22	3	7/37
Washington,DM	1	1	1	7	7*	-	0	0	0	3	174	4	93	0	-	0	0	0/20
Watson,CD	7	6	1	12	5	2.40	0	0	2	1	1458	47	724	19	38.11	0	0	4/62
Weekes,ED	48	81	5	4455	207	58.62	15	19	6	49	122	3	77	1	77.00	0	0	1/8
Weekes,KH	2	3	0	173	137	57.67	1	0	0	0								
White,AW	2	4	1	71	57*	23.67	0	1	0	1	491	27	152	3	50.67	0	0	2/34
Wight,CV	2	4	1	67	23	22.33	0	0	0	0	30	1	6	0	-	0	0	0/6
Wight,GL	1	1	0	21	21	21.00	0	0	0	0								
Wiles,CA	1	2	0	2	2	1.00	0	0	1	0								
Willett,ET	5	8	3	74	26	14.80	0	0	2	0	1326	78	482	11	43.82	0	0	3/33
Williams,AB	7	12	0	469	111	39.08	2	1	1	5								
Williams,D	11	19	1	242	65	13.44	0	1	7	40/2								
Williams,EAV	4	6	0	113	72	18.83	0	1	1	2	796	46	241	9	26.78	0	0	3/51
Williams,SC	31	52	3	1183	128	24.14	1	3	6	27	18	0	19	0	-	0	0	0/19
Wishart,KL	1	2	0	52	52	26.00	0	1	1	0								
Worrell,FMM	51	87	9	3860	261	49.49	9	22	11	43	7141	274	2672	69	38.72	2	0	7/70

NEW ZEALAND (232 players)				**BATTING AND FIELDING**									**BOWLING**					
Player	M	I	NO	Runs	HS	Avge	100	50	0	C/S	Balls	Mdns	Runs	Wkts	Avge	5wi	10w	Best
Adams,AR	1	2	0	18	11	9.00	0	0	0	1	190	5	105	6	17.50	0	0	3/44
Alabaster,JC	21	34	6	272	34	9.71	0	0	2	7	3992	178	1863	49	38.02	0	0	4/46
Allcott,CFW	6	7	2	113	33	22.60	0	0	0	3	1206	41	541	6	90.16	0	0	2/102
Allott,GI	10	15	7	27	8*	3.37	0	0	4	2	2023	62	1111	19	58.47	0	0	4/74
Anderson,RW	9	18	0	423	92	23.50	0	3	1	1								
Anderson,WM	1	2	0	5	4	2.50	0	0	0	1								
Andrews,B	2	3	2	22	17	22.00	0	0	0	1	256	3	154	2	77.00	0	0	2/40
Astle,NJ	79	133	10	4650	222	37.80	11	24	11	68	5634	315	2099	51	41.15	0	0	3/27
Badcock,FT	7	9	2	137	64	19.57	0	2	3	1	1608	66	610	16	38.12	0	0	4/80
Barber,RT	1	2	0	17	12	8.50	0	0	0	1								
Bartlett,GA	10	18	1	263	40	15.47	0	0	4	8	1768	64	792	24	33.00	1	0	6/38
Barton,PT	7	14	0	285	109	20.35	1	1	1	4								
Beard,DD	4	7	2	101	31	20.20	0	0	0	2	806	37	302	9	33.55	0	0	3/22
Beck,JEF	8	15	0	394	99	26.26	0	3	1	0								
Bell,MD	13	23	1	484	105	22.00	1	2	4	10								

NEW ZEALAND (cont.)				**BATTING AND FIELDING**							**BOWLING**							
Player	M	I	NO	Runs	HS	Avge	100	50	0	C/S	Balls	Mdns	Runs	Wkts	Avge	5wi	10w	Best
Bell,W	2	3	3	21	21*	-	0	0	0	1	491	13	235	2	117.50	0	0	1/54
Bilby,GP	2	4	0	55	28	13.75	0	0	0	3								
Blain,TE	11	20	3	456	78	26.82	0	2	2	19/2								
Blair,RW	19	34	6	189	64*	6.75	0	1	12	5	3525	114	1515	43	35.23	0	0	4/85
Blunt,RC	9	13	1	330	96	27.50	0	1	1	5	936	34	472	12	39.33	0	0	3/17
Bolton,BA	2	3	0	59	33	19.66	0	0	1	1								
Bond,SE	14	14	7	123	41*	17.57	0	0	1	5	2478	91	1378	64	21.53	4	1	6/51
Boock,SL	30	41	8	207	37	6.27	0	0	10	14	6598	327	2564	74	34.64	4	0	7/87
Bracewell,BP	6	12	2	24	8	2.40	0	0	5	1	1036	29	585	14	41.78	0	0	3/110
Bracewell,JG	41	60	11	1001	110	20.42	1	4	13	31	8403	360	3653	102	35.81	4	1	6/32
Bradburn,GE	7	10	2	105	30*	13.12	0	0	1	6	867	28	460	6	76.66	0	0	3/134
Bradburn,WP	2	4	0	62	32	15.50	0	0	0	2								
Brown,VR	2	3	1	51	36*	25.50	0	0	1	3	342	13	176	1	176.00	0	0	1/17
Burgess,MG	50	92	6	2684	119*	31.20	5	14	5	34	498	27	212	6	35.33	0	0	3/23
Burke,C	1	2	0	4	3	2.00	0	0	0	0	66	2	30	2	15.00	0	0	2/30
Burtt,TB	10	15	3	252	42	21.00	0	0	1	2	2593	119	1170	33	35.45	3	0	6/162
Butler,IG	8	10	2	76	26	9.50	0	0	2	4	1368	37	884	24	36.83	1	0	6/46
Butterfield,LA	1	2	0	0	0	0.00	0	0	2	0	78	6	24	0	-	0	0	0/24
Cairns,BL	43	65	8	928	64	16.28	0	2	7	30	10628	447	4280	130	32.92	6	1	7/74
Cairns,CL	62	104	5	3320	158	33.53	5	22	7	14	11698	413	6410	218	29.40	13	1	7/27
Cameron,FJ	19	30	20	116	27*	11.60	0	0	4	2	4570	220	1849	62	29.82	3	0	5/34
Cave,HB	19	31	5	229	22*	8.80	0	0	5	8	4074	242	1467	34	43.14	0	0	4/21
Chapple,ME	14	27	1	497	76	19.11	0	3	2	10	248	17	84	1	84.00	0	0	1/24
Chatfield,EJ	43	54	33	180	21*	8.57	0	0	11	7	10360	489	3958	123	32.17	3	1	6/73
Cleverley,DC	2	4	3	19	10*	19.00	0	0	0	0	222	3	130	0	-	0	0	0/51
Collinge,RO	35	50	13	533	68*	14.40	0	2	9	10	7689	228	3393	116	29.25	3	0	6/63
Colquhoun,IA	2	4	2	1	1*	0.50	0	0	2	4/0								
Coney,JV	52	85	14	2668	174*	37.57	3	16	3	64	2835	135	966	27	35.77	0	0	3/28
Congdon,BE	61	114	7	3448	176	32.22	7	19	9	44	5620	197	2154	59	36.50	1	0	5/65
Cowie,J	9	13	4	90	45	10.00	0	0	3	3	2028	65	969	45	21.53	4	1	6/40
Cresswell,GF	3	5	3	14	12*	7.00	0	0	1	0	650	30	292	13	22.46	1	0	6/168
Cromb,IB	5	8	2	123	51*	20.50	0	1	1	1	960	36	442	8	55.25	0	0	3/113
Crowe,JJ	39	65	4	1601	128	26.24	3	6	6	41	18	1	9	0	-	0	0	0/0
Crowe,MD	77	131	11	5444	299	45.36	17	18	9	71	1377	52	676	14	48.28	0	0	2/25
Cumming,CD	5	9	1	208	74	26.00	0	1	1	2								
Cunis,RS	20	31	8	295	51	12.82	0	1	6	1	4250	140	1887	51	37.00	1	0	6/76
d'Arcy,JW	5	10	0	136	33	13.60	0	0	0	0								
Davis,HT	5	7	4	20	8*	6.66	0	0	0	4	1010	26	499	17	29.35	1	0	5/63
de Groen,RP	5	10	4	45	26	7.50	0	0	1	0	1060	44	505	11	45.90	0	0	3/40
Dempster,CS	10	15	4	723	136	65.72	2	5	0	2	5	0	10	0	-	0	0	0/10
Dempster,EW	5	8	2	106	47	17.66	0	0	2	1	544	17	219	2	109.50	0	0	1/24
Dick,AE	17	30	4	370	50*	14.23	0	1	4	47/4								
Dickinson,GR	3	5	0	31	11	6.20	0	0	0	3	451	13	245	8	30.62	0	0	3/66
Donnelly,MP	7	12	1	582	206	52.90	1	4	2	7	30	0	20	0	-	0	0	0/20
Doull,SB	32	50	11	570	46	14.61	0	0	10	16	6053	251	2872	98	29.30	6	0	7/65
Dowling,GT	39	77	3	2306	239	31.16	3	11	6	23	36	2	19	1	19.00	0	0	1/19
Drum,CJ	5	5	2	10	4	3.33	0	0	1	4	806	27	482	16	30.12	0	0	3/36
Dunning,JA	4	6	1	38	19	7.60	0	0	2	2	830	20	493	5	98.60	0	0	2/35
Edgar,BA	39	68	4	1958	161	30.59	3	12	7	14/0	18	1	3	0	-	0	0	0/3
Edwards,GN	8	15	0	377	55	25.13	0	3	2	7/0								
Emery,RWG	2	4	0	46	28	11.50	0	0	0	0	46	0	52	2	26.00	0	0	2/52
Fisher,FE	1	2	0	23	14	11.50	0	0	0	0	204	6	78	1	78.00	0	0	1/78
Fleming,SP	102	173	10	6545	274*	40.15	9	41	14	152								

NEW ZEALAND (cont.)				**BATTING AND FIELDING**										**BOWLING**				
Player	M	I	NO	Runs	HS	Avge	100	50	0	C/S	Balls	Mdns	Runs	Wkts	Avge	5wi	10w	Best
Foley,H	1	2	0	4	2	2.00	0	0	0	0								
Franklin,JEC	19	25	5	460	122*	23.00	1	1	3	7	3205	99	1969	70	28.12	3	0	6/119
Freeman,DL	2	2	0	2	1	1.00	0	0	0	0	240	3	169	1	169.00	0	0	1/91
Fulton,PG	5	7	0	185	75	26.42	0	1	0	3								
Gallichan,N	1	2	0	32	30	16.00	0	0	0	0	264	11	113	3	37.66	0	0	3/99
Gedye,SG	4	8	0	193	55	24.12	0	2	0	0								
Germon,LK	12	21	3	382	55	21.22	0	1	3	27/2								
Gillespie,SR	1	1	0	28	28	28.00	0	0	0	0	162	2	79	1	79.00	0	0	1/79
Gray,EJ	10	16	0	248	50	15.50	0	1	0	6	2076	87	886	17	52.11	0	0	3/73
Greatbatch,MJ	41	71	5	2021	146*	30.62	3	10	9	27	6	1	0	0	-	0	0	0/0
Guillen,SC	3	6	0	98	41	16.33	0	0	2	4/1								
Guy,JW	12	23	2	440	102	20.95	1	3	3	2								
Hadlee,DR	26	42	5	530	56	14.32	0	1	9	8	4883	114	2389	71	33.64	0	0	4/30
Hadlee,RJ	86	134	19	3124	151*	27.16	2	15	12	39	21918	809	9611	431	22.29	36	9	9/52
Hadlee,WA	11	19	1	543	116	30.16	1	2	1	6								
Harford,NS	8	15	0	229	93	15.26	0	2	4	0								
Harford,RI	3	5	2	7	6	2.33	0	0	1	11/0								
Harris,CZ	23	42	4	777	71	20.44	0	5	9	14	2560	106	1170	16	73.12	0	0	2/16
Harris,PGZ	9	18	1	378	101	22.23	1	1	3	6	42	2	14	0	-	0	0	0/14
Harris,RM	2	3	0	31	13	10.33	0	0	0	0								
Hart,MN	14	24	4	353	45	17.65	0	0	3	9	3086	127	1438	29	49.58	1	0	5/77
Hart,RG	11	19	3	260	57*	16.25	0	1	4	29/1								
Hartland,BR	9	18	0	303	52	16.83	0	1	3	5								
Haslam,MJ	4	2	1	4	3	4.00	0	0	0	2	493	19	245	2	122.50	0	0	1/33
Hastings,BF	31	56	6	1510	117*	30.20	4	7	6	23	22	0	9	0	-	0	0	0/3
Hayes,JA	15	22	7	73	19	4.86	0	0	4	3	2675	86	1217	30	40.56	0	0	4/36
Henderson,M	1	2	1	8	6	8.00	0	0	0	1	90	3	64	2	32.00	0	0	2/38
Horne,MJ	35	65	2	1788	157	28.38	4	5	4	17	66	7	26	0	-	0	0	0/4
Horne,PA	4	7	0	71	27	10.14	0	0	2	3								
Hough,KW	2	3	2	62	31*	62.00	0	0	0	1	462	23	175	6	29.16	0	0	3/79
How,JM	4	6	1	61	37	12.20	0	0	2	6								
Howarth,GP	47	83	5	2531	147	32.44	6	11	7	29	614	20	271	3	90.33	0	0	1/13
Howarth,HJ	30	42	18	291	61	12.12	0	1	7	33	8833	393	3178	86	36.95	2	0	5/34
James,KC	11	13	2	52	14	4.72	0	0	4	11/5								
Jarvis,TW	13	22	1	625	182	29.76	1	2	6	3	12	1	3	0	-	0	0	0/0
Jones,AH	39	74	8	2922	186	44.27	7	11	2	25	328	8	194	1	194.00	0	0	1/40
Jones,RA	1	2	0	23	16	11.50	0	0	0	0								
Kennedy,RJ	4	5	1	28	22	7.00	0	0	2	2	636	17	380	6	63.33	0	0	3/28
Kerr,JL	7	12	1	212	59	19.27	0	1	2	4								
Kuggeleijn,CM	2	4	0	7	7	1.75	0	0	3	1	97	2	67	1	67.00	0	0	1/50
Larsen,GR	8	13	4	127	26*	14.11	0	0	2	5	1967	109	689	24	28.70	0	0	3/57
Latham,RT	4	7	0	219	119	31.28	1	0	1	5	18	2	6	0	-	0	0	0/6
Lees,WK	21	37	4	778	152	23.57	1	1	4	52/7	5	0	4	0	-	0	0	0/4
Leggat,IB	1	1	0	0	0	0.00	0	0	1	2	24	0	6	0	-	0	0	0/6
Leggat,JG	9	18	2	351	61	21.93	0	2	1	0								
Lissette,AF	2	4	2	2	1*	1.00	0	0	2	1	288	16	124	3	41.33	0	0	2/73
Loveridge,GR	1	1	1	4	4*	-	0	0	0	0								
Lowry,TC	7	8	0	223	80	27.87	0	2	2	8	12	1	5	0	-	0	0	0/0
McCullum,BB	23	35	2	1083	143	32.81	2	6	3	56/5								
McEwan,PE	4	7	1	96	40*	16.00	0	0	1	5	36	1	13	0	-	0	0	0/6
MacGibbon,AR	26	46	5	814	66	19.85	0	3	7	13	5659	228	2160	70	30.85	1	0	5/64
McGirr,HM	2	1	0	51	51	51.00	0	1	0	0	180	5	115	1	115.00	0	0	1/65
McGregor,SN	25	47	2	892	111	19.82	1	3	5	9								

NEW ZEALAND (cont.)				BATTING AND FIELDING							BOWLING							
Player	M	I	NO	Runs	HS	Avge	100	50	0	C/S	Balls	Mdns	Runs	Wkts	Avge	5wi	10w	Best
McLeod,EG	1	2	1	18	16	18.00	0	0	0	0	12	0	5	0	-	0	0	0/5
McMahon,TG	5	7	4	7	4*	2.33	0	0	2	7/1								
McMillan,CD	55	91	10	3116	142	38.46	6	19	7	22	1802	101	1257	28	44.89	0	0	3/48
McRae,DAN	1	2	0	8	8	4.00	0	0	1	0	84	3	44	0	-	0	0	0/44
Marshall,HJH	13	19	2	652	160	38.35	2	2	1	1	6	0	4	0	-	0	0	0/4
Marshall,JAH	5	7	0	166	52	23.71	0	1	0	3								
Martin,CS	31	41	18	48	7	2.08	0	0	17	9	5806	213	3413	99	34.47	7	1	6/54
Mason,MJ	1	2	0	3	3	1.50	0	0	1	0	132	5	105	0	-	0	0	0/32
Matheson,AM	2	1	0	7	7	7.00	0	0	0	2	282	9	136	2	68.00	0	0	2/7
Meale,T	2	4	0	21	10	5.25	0	0	0	0								
Merritt,WE	6	8	1	73	19	10.42	0	0	1	2	936	10	617	12	51.41	0	0	4/104
Meuli,EM	1	2	0	38	23	19.00	0	0	0	0								
Milburn,BD	3	3	2	8	4*	8.00	0	0	1	6/2								
Miller,LSM	13	25	0	346	47	13.84	0	0	5	1	2	0	1	0	-	0	0	0/1
Mills,JE	7	10	1	241	117	26.77	1	0	2	1								
Mills,KD	7	12	3	120	31	13.33	0	0	2	2	1041	50	534	17	31.41	0	0	4/43
Moir,AM	17	30	8	327	41*	14.86	0	0	5	2	2650	82	1418	28	50.64	2	0	6/155
Moloney,DAR	3	6	0	156	64	26.00	0	1	1	3	12	1	9	0	-	0	0	0/9
Mooney,FLH	14	22	2	343	46	17.15	0	0	1	22/8	8	1	0	0	-	0	0	0/0
Morgan,RW	20	34	1	734	97	22.24	0	5	5	12	1114	38	609	5	121.80	0	0	1/16
Morrison,BD	1	2	0	10	10	5.00	0	0	1	1	186	5	129	2	64.50	0	0	2/129
Morrison,DK	48	71	26	379	42	8.42	0	0	24	14	10064	313	5549	160	34.68	10	0	7/89
Morrison,JFM	17	29	0	656	117	22.62	1	3	4	9	264	17	71	2	35.50	0	0	2/52
Motz,RC	32	56	3	612	60	11.54	0	3	12	9	7034	279	3148	100	31.48	5	0	6/63
Murray,BAG	13	26	1	598	90	23.92	0	5	1	21	6	1	0	1	0.00	0	0	1/0
Murray,DJ	8	16	1	303	52	20.20	0	1	3	6								
Nash,DJ	32	45	14	729	89*	23.51	0	4	5	13	6196	312	2649	93	28.48	3	1	6/27
Newman,J	3	4	0	33	19	8.25	0	0	0	0	425	11	254	2	127.00	0	0	2/76
O'Brien,IE	2	3	0	10	5	3.33	0	0	1	1	258	7	197	2	98.50	0	0	1/73
O'Connor,SB	19	27	9	103	20	5.72	0	0	4	6	3667	149	1724	53	32.52	1	0	5/51
Oram,JDP	20	35	7	1203	133	42.96	3	4	2	12	3256	144	1392	38	36.63	0	0	4/41
O'Sullivan,DR	11	21	4	158	23*	9.29	0	0	2	2	2744	75	1224	18	68.00	1	0	5/148
Overton,GWF	3	6	1	8	3*	1.60	0	0	2	1	729	23	258	9	28.66	0	0	3/65
Owens,MB	8	12	6	16	8*	2.66	0	0	5	3	1074	42	585	17	34.41	0	0	4/99
Page,ML	14	20	0	492	104	24.60	1	2	1	6	379	11	231	5	46.20	0	0	2/21
Papps,MHW	6	12	1	229	86	20.81	0	2	4	7								
Parker,JM	36	63	2	1498	121	24.55	3	5	4	30	40	2	24	1	24.00	0	0	1/24
Parker,NM	3	6	0	89	40	14.83	0	0	0	2								
Parore,AC	78	128	19	2865	110	26.28	2	14	6	197/7								
Patel,DN	37	66	8	1200	99	20.68	0	5	10	15	6594	253	3154	75	42.05	3	0	6/50
Patel,JS	1	1	1	27	27*	-	0	0	0	1	252	8	117	3	39.00	0	0	3/117
Petherick,PJ	6	11	4	34	13	4.85	0	0	1	4	1305	37	681	16	42.56	0	0	3/90
Petrie,EC	14	25	5	258	55	12.90	0	1	2	25/0								
Playle,WR	8	15	0	151	65	10.06	0	1	3	4								
Pocock,BA	15	29	0	665	85	22.93	0	6	4	5	24	0	20	0	-	0	0	0/10
Pollard,V	32	59	7	1266	116	24.34	2	7	4	19	4421	207	1853	40	46.32	0	0	3/3
Poore,MB	14	24	1	355	45	15.43	0	0	6	1	788	24	367	9	40.77	0	0	2/28
Priest,MW	3	4	0	56	26	14.00	0	0	0	0	377	15	158	3	52.66	0	0	2/42
Pringle,C	14	21	4	175	30	10.29	0	0	7	3	2985	113	1389	30	46.30	1	1	7/52
Puna,N	3	5	3	31	18*	15.50	0	0	0	1	480	20	240	4	60.00	0	0	2/40
Rabone,GO	12	20	2	562	107	31.22	1	2	0	5	1385	48	635	16	39.68	1	0	6/68
Redmond,RE	1	2	0	163	107	81.50	1	1	0	0								
Reid,JF	19	31	3	1296	180	46.28	6	2	4	9	18	1	7	0	-	0	0	0/0

NEW ZEALAND (cont.)					**BATTING AND FIELDING**						**BOWLING**							
Player	M	I	NO	Runs	HS	Avge	100	50	0	C/S	Balls	Mdns	Runs	Wkts	Avge	5wi	10w	Best
Reid,JR	58	108	5	3428	142	33.28	6	22	5	43/1	7725	444	2835	85	33.35	1	0	6/60
Richardson,MH	38	65	3	2776	145	44.77	4	19	1	26	66	0	21	1	21.00	0	0	1/16
Roberts,ADG	7	12	1	254	84*	23.09	0	1	2	4	440	15	182	4	45.50	0	0	1/12
Roberts,AW	5	10	1	248	66*	27.55	0	3	0	4	459	19	209	7	29.85	0	0	4/101
Robertson,GK	1	1	0	12	12	12.00	0	0	0	0	144	6	91	1	91.00	0	0	1/91
Rowe,CG	1	2	0	0	0	0.00	0	0	2	1								
Rutherford,KR	56	99	8	2465	107*	27.08	3	18	16	32	256	3	161	1	161.00	0	0	1/38
Scott,RH	1	1	0	18	18	18.00	0	0	0	0	138	3	74	1	74.00	0	0	1/74
Scott,VJ	10	17	1	458	84	28.62	0	3	1	7	18	0	14	0	-	0	0	0/5
Sewell,DG	1	1	1	1	1*	-	0	0	0	0	138	3	90	0	-	0	0	0/9
Shrimpton,MJF	10	19	0	265	46	13.94	0	0	6	2	257	1	158	5	31.60	0	0	3/35
Sinclair,BW	21	40	1	1148	138	29.43	3	3	5	8	60	3	32	2	16.00	0	0	2/32
Sinclair,IM	2	4	1	25	18*	8.33	0	0	2	1	233	9	120	1	120.00	0	0	1/79
Sinclair,MS	25	42	5	1365	214	36.89	3	4	4	22	24	0	13	0	-	0	0	0/13
Smith,FB	4	6	1	237	96	47.40	0	2	0	1								
Smith,HD	1	1	0	4	4	4.00	0	0	0	0	120	0	113	1	113.00	0	0	1/113
Smith,IDS	63	88	17	1815	173	25.56	2	6	7	168/8	18	1	5	0	-	0	0	0/5
Snedden,CA	1					-	0	0	0	0	96	5	46	0	-	0	0	0/46
Snedden,MC	25	30	8	327	33*	14.86	0	0	6	7	4775	194	2199	58	37.91	1	0	5/68
Sparling,JT	11	20	2	229	50	12.72	0	1	2	3	708	33	327	5	65.40	0	0	1/9
Spearman,CM	19	37	2	922	112	26.34	1	3	3	21								
Stead,GR	5	8	0	278	78	34.75	0	2	0	2	6	0	1	0	-	0	0	0/1
Stirling,DA	6	9	2	108	26	15.42	0	0	0	1	902	24	601	13	46.23	0	0	4/88
Styris,SB	27	44	4	1527	170	38.17	5	6	5	23	1900	74	973	20	48.65	0	0	3/28
Su'a,ML	13	18	5	165	44	12.69	0	0	5	8	2843	92	1377	36	38.25	2	0	5/73
Sutcliffe,B	42	76	8	2727	230*	40.10	5	15	5	20	538	10	344	4	86.00	0	0	2/38
Taylor,BR	30	50	6	898	124	20.40	2	2	8	10	6334	206	2953	111	26.60	4	0	7/74
Taylor,DD	3	5	0	159	77	31.80	0	1	0	2								
Thomson,K	2	4	1	94	69	31.33	0	1	1	0	21	1	9	1	9.00	0	0	1/9
Thomson,SA	19	35	4	958	120*	30.90	1	5	3	7	1990	74	953	19	50.15	0	0	3/63
Tindill,EWT	5	9	1	73	37*	9.12	0	0	1	6/1								
Troup,GB	15	18	6	55	13*	4.58	0	0	7	2	3183	105	1454	39	37.28	1	1	6/95
Truscott,PB	1	2	0	29	26	14.50	0	0	0	1								
Tuffey,DR	22	30	7	263	39	11.43	0	0	5	12	4110	181	2057	66	31.16	2	0	6/54
Turner,GM	41	73	6	2991	259	44.64	7	14	1	42	12	1	5	0	-	0	0	0/5
Twose,RG	16	27	2	628	94	25.12	0	6	5	5	211	2	130	3	43.33	0	0	2/36
Vance,RH	4	7	0	207	68	29.57	0	1	0	0								
Vaughan,JTC	6	12	1	201	44	18.27	0	0	0	4	1040	41	450	11	40.90	0	0	4/27
Vettori,DL	70	100	15	2128	137*	25.03	2	11	14	35	17072	714	7547	218	34.61	12	2	7/87
Vincent,L	22	38	1	1295	224	35.00	3	9	4	20	6	0	2	0	-	0	0	0/2
Vivian,GE	5	6	0	110	43	18.33	0	0	1	3	198	7	107	1	107.00	0	0	1/14
Vivian,HG	7	10	0	421	100	42.10	1	5	0	4	1311	44	633	17	37.23	0	0	4/58
Wadsworth,KJ	33	51	4	1010	80	21.48	0	5	5	92/4								
Walker,BGK	5	8	2	118	27*	19.66	0	0	1	0	669	17	399	5	79.80	0	0	2/92
Wallace,WM	13	21	0	439	66	20.90	0	5	0	5	6	0	5	0	-	0	0	0/5
Walmsley,KP	3	5	0	13	5	2.60	0	0	2	0	774	26	391	9	43.44	0	0	3/70
Ward,JT	8	12	6	75	35*	12.50	0	0	2	16/1								
Watson,W	15	18	6	60	11	5.00	0	0	3	4	3486	182	1387	40	34.67	1	0	6/78
Watt,L	1	2	0	2	2	1.00	0	0	1	0								
Webb,MG	3	2	0	12	12	6.00	0	0	1	0	732	6	471	4	117.75	0	0	2/114
Webb,PN	2	3	0	11	5	3.66	0	0	0	2								
Weir,GL	11	16	2	416	74*	29.71	0	3	1	3	342	7	209	7	29.85	0	0	3/38
White,DJ	2	4	0	31	18	7.75	0	0	0	0	3	0	5	0	-	0	0	0/5

NEW ZEALAND (cont.)					**BATTING AND FIELDING**						**BOWLING**							
Player	M	I	NO	Runs	HS	Avge	100	50	0	C/S	Balls	Mdns	Runs	Wkts	Avge	5wi	10w	Best
Whitelaw,PE	2	4	2	64	30	32.00	0	0	0	0								
Wiseman,PJ	25	34	7	366	36	13.55	0	0	5	11	5660	208	2903	61	47.59	2	0	5/82
Wright,JG	82	148	7	5334	185	37.82	12	23	7	38	30	1	5	0	-	0	0	0/1
Young,BA	35	68	4	2034	267*	31.78	2	12	5	54								
Yuile,BW	17	33	6	481	64	17.81	0	1	3	12	2897	168	1213	34	35.67	0	0	4/43

INDIA (256 players)					**BATTING AND FIELDING**						**BOWLING**							
Player	M	I	NO	Runs	HS	Avge	100	50	0	C/S	Balls	Mdns	Runs	Wkts	Avge	5wi	10w	Best
Abid Ali,S	29	53	3	1018	81	20.36	0	6	3	32	4164	119	1980	47	42.12	1	0	6/55
Adhikari,HR	21	36	8	872	114*	31.14	1	4	5	8	170	2	82	3	27.33	0	0	3/68
Agarkar,AB	26	39	5	868	109*	25.52	1	0	9	6	4857	168	2745	58	47.32	1	0	6/41
Amar Singh,L	7	14	1	292	51	22.46	0	1	1	3	2182	95	858	28	30.64	2	0	7/86
Amarnath,M	69	113	10	4378	138	42.50	11	24	5	47	3676	101	1782	32	55.68	0	0	4/63
Amarnath,NB	24	40	4	878	118	24.38	1	4	12	13	4241	195	1481	45	32.91	2	0	5/96
Amarnath,S	10	18	0	550	124	30.55	1	3	1	4	11	0	5	1	5.00	0	0	1/5
Amir Elahi	1	2	0	17	13	8.50	0	0	0	0								
Amre,PK	11	13	3	425	103	42.50	1	3	0	9								
Ankola,SA	1	1	0	6	6	6.00	0	0	0	0	180	7	128	2	64.00	0	0	1/35
Apte,AL	1	2	0	15	8	7.50	0	0	0	0								
Apte,ML	7	13	2	542	163*	49.27	1	3	1	2	6	0	3	0	-	0	0	0/3
Arshad Ayub	13	19	4	257	57	17.13	0	1	1	2	3663	150	1438	41	35.07	3	0	5/50
Arun Lal,J	16	29	1	729	93	26.03	0	6	1	13	16	1	7	0	-	0	0	0/0
Arun,B	2	2	1	4	2*	4.00	0	0	0	2	252	12	116	4	29.00	0	0	3/76
Azad,KBJ	7	12	0	135	24	11.25	0	0	2	3	750	28	373	3	124.33	0	0	2/84
Azharuddin,M	99	147	9	6215	199	45.03	22	21	5	105	13	0	16	0	-	0	0	0/4
Badani,HK	4	7	1	94	38	15.66	0	0	0	6	48	2	17	0	-	0	0	0/17
Bahutule,SV	2	4	1	39	21*	13.00	0	0	2	1	366	8	203	3	67.66	0	0	1/32
Baig,AA	10	18	0	428	112	23.77	1	2	1	6	18	0	15	0	-	0	0	0/2
Balaji,L	8	9	0	51	31	5.66	0	0	4	1	1756	64	1004	27	37.18	1	0	5/76
Banerjee,SN	1	2	0	13	8	6.50	0	0	0	0	273	8	127	5	25.40	0	0	4/54
Banerjee,SS	1	1	0	0	0	0.00	0	0	1	3	306	3	181	5	36.20	0	0	4/120
Banerjee,ST	1	1	0	3	3	3.00	0	0	0	0	108	4	47	3	15.66	0	0	3/47
Bangar,SB	12	18	2	470	100*	29.37	1	3	2	4	762	35	343	7	49.00	0	0	2/23
Baqa Jilani,M	1	2	1	16	12	16.00	0	0	0	0	90	4	55	0	-	0	0	0/55
Bedi,BS	67	101	28	656	50*	8.98	0	1	20	26	21364	1096	7637	266	28.71	14	1	7/98
Bhandari,P	3	4	0	77	39	19.25	0	0	0	1	78	2	39	0	-	0	0	0/12
Bhat,AR	2	3	1	6	6	3.00	0	0	1	0	438	22	151	4	37.75	0	0	2/65
Binny,RMH	27	41	5	830	83*	23.05	0	5	7	11	2870	76	1534	47	32.63	2	0	6/56
Borde,CG	55	97	11	3061	177*	35.59	5	18	13	37	5695	236	2417	52	46.48	1	0	5/88
Chandrasekhar,BS	58	80	39	167	22	4.07	0	0	23	25	15963	584	7199	242	29.74	16	2	8/79
Chauhan,CPS	40	68	2	2084	97	31.57	0	16	6	38	174	2	106	2	53.00	0	0	1/4
Chauhan,RK	21	17	3	98	23	7.00	0	0	1	12	4749	238	1857	47	39.51	0	0	4/48
Chopra,AS	10	19	0	437	60	23.00	0	2	1	15								
Chopra,N	1	2	0	7	4	3.50	0	0	0	0	144	3	78	0	-	0	0	0/78
Chowdhury,NR	2	2	1	3	3*	3.00	0	0	1	0	516	21	205	1	205.00	0	0	1/130
Colah,SHM	2	4	0	69	31	17.25	0	0	0	2								
Contractor,NJ	31	52	1	1611	108	31.58	1	11	2	18	186	7	80	1	80.00	0	0	1/9
Dahiya,V	2	1	1	2	2*	-	0	0	0	6/0								
Dani,HT	1					-	0	0	0	1	60	5	19	1	19.00	0	0	1/9

INDIA (cont.)				**BATTING AND FIELDING**									**BOWLING**					
Player	M	I	NO	Runs	HS	Avge	100	50	0	C/S	Balls	Mdns	Runs	Wkts	Avge	5wi	10w	Best
Das,SS	23	40	2	1326	110	34.89	2	9	3	34	66	2	35	0	-	0	0	0/7
Dasgupta,D	8	13	1	344	100	28.66	1	2	2	13/0								
Desai,RB	28	44	13	418	85	13.48	0	1	8	9	5597	178	2761	74	37.31	2	0	6/56
Dhoni,MS	14	20	1	604	148	31.78	1	3	0	38/9	6	0	13	0	-	0	0	0/13
Dighe,SS	6	10	1	141	47	15.66	0	0	1	12/2								
Dilawar Hussain	3	6	0	254	59	42.33	0	3	0	6/1								
Divecha,RV	5	5	0	60	26	12.00	0	0	0	5	1044	44	361	11	32.81	0	0	3/102
Doshi,DR	33	38	10	129	20	4.60	0	0	14	10	9322	456	3502	114	30.71	6	0	6/102
Dravid,RS	103	174	22	9026	270	59.38	23	46	5	145	120	4	39	1	39.00	0	0	1/18
Durani,SA	29	50	2	1202	104	25.04	1	7	4	14	6446	317	2657	75	35.42	3	1	6/73
Engineer,FM	46	87	3	2611	121	31.08	2	16	7	66/16								
Gadkari,CV	6	10	4	129	50*	21.50	0	1	2	6	102	4	45	0	-	0	0	0/8
Gaekwad,AD	40	70	4	1985	201	30.07	2	10	4	15	334	8	187	2	93.50	0	0	1/4
Gaekwad,DK	11	20	1	350	52	18.42	0	1	3	5	12	0	12	0	-	0	0	0/4
Gaekwad,HG	1	2	0	22	14	11.00	0	0	0	0	222	21	47	0	-	0	0	0/47
Gambhir,G	13	21	2	684	139	36.00	1	3	1	12								
Gandhi,DJ	4	7	1	204	88	34.00	0	2	2	3								
Gandotra,A	2	4	0	54	18	13.50	0	0	0	1	6	0	5	0	-	0	0	0/5
Ganesh,D	4	7	3	25	8	6.25	0	0	0	0	461	15	287	5	57.40	0	0	2/28
Ganguly,SC	88	140	12	5215	173	40.74	12	25	8	58	2516	86	1419	26	54.57	0	0	3/28
Gavaskar,SM	125	214	16	10122	236*	51.12	34	45	12	108	380	15	206	1	206.00	0	0	1/34
Ghavri,KD	39	57	14	913	86	21.23	0	2	2	16	7036	233	3656	109	33.54	4	0	5/33
Ghorpade,JM	8	15	0	229	41	15.26	0	0	3	4	150	1	131	0	-	0	0	0/17
Ghulam Ahmed	22	31	9	192	50	8.72	0	1	9	11	5650	254	2052	68	30.17	4	1	7/49
Gopalan,MJ	1	2	1	18	11*	18.00	0	0	0	3	114	7	39	1	39.00	0	0	1/39
Gopinath,CD	8	12	1	242	50*	22.00	0	1	4	2	48	2	11	1	11.00	0	0	1/11
Guard,GM	2	2	0	11	7	5.50	0	0	0	2	396	16	182	3	60.66	0	0	2/69
Guha,S	4	7	2	17	6	3.40	0	0	1	2	674	23	311	3	103.66	0	0	2/55
Gul Mahomed	8	15	0	166	34	11.07	0	0	2	3	77	4	24	2	12.00	0	0	2/21
Gupte,BP	3	3	2	28	17*	28.00	0	0	0	0	678	28	349	3	116.33	0	0	1/54
Gupte,SP	36	42	13	183	21	6.31	0	0	6	14	11284	608	4403	149	29.55	12	1	9/102
Gursharan Singh	1	1	0	18	18	18.00	0	0	0	2								
Hanumant Singh	14	24	2	686	105	31.18	1	5	3	11	66	0	51	0	-	0	0	0/5
Harbhajan Singh	57	79	18	986	66	16.16	0	2	11	28	15062	509	7097	238	29.81	19	4	8/84
Hardikar,MS	2	4	1	56	32*	18.66	0	0	1	3	108	7	55	1	55.00	0	0	1/9
Harvinder Singh	3	4	1	6	6	2.00	0	0	2	0	273	6	185	4	46.25	0	0	2/62
Hazare,VS	30	52	6	2192	164*	47.65	7	9	4	11	2840	99	1220	20	61.00	0	0	4/29
Hindlekar,DD	4	7	2	71	26	14.20	0	0	0	3/0								
Hirwani,ND	17	22	12	54	17	5.40	0	0	5	5	4298	155	1987	66	30.10	4	1	8/61
Ibrahim,KC	4	8	0	169	85	21.12	0	1	1	0								
Indrajitsinhji,KS	4	7	1	51	23	8.50	0	0	1	6/3								
Irani,JK	2	3	2	3	2*	3.00	0	0	1	2/1								
Jadeja,AD	15	24	2	576	96	26.18	0	4	1	5								
Jahangir Khan,M	4	7	0	39	13	5.57	0	0	1	4	606	28	255	4	63.75	0	0	4/60
Jai,LP	1	2	0	19	19	9.50	0	0	1	0								
Jaisimha,ML	39	71	4	2056	129	30.68	3	12	9	17	2097	109	829	9	92.11	0	0	2/54
Jamshedji,RJD	1	2	2	5	4*	-	0	0	0	2	210	4	137	3	45.66	0	0	3/137
Jayantilal,HK	1	1	0	5	5	5.00	0	0	0	0								
Johnson,DJ	2	3	1	8	5	4.00	0	0	0	0	240	6	143	3	47.66	0	0	2/52
Joshi,PG	12	20	1	207	52*	10.89	0	1	3	18/9								
Joshi,SB	15	19	2	352	92	20.70	0	1	2	7	3451	146	1470	41	35.85	1	0	5/142
Kambli,VG	17	21	1	1084	227	54.20	4	3	3	7								
Kanitkar,HH	2	4	0	74	45	18.50	0	0	0	0	6	0	2	0	-	0	0	0/2

INDIA (cont.)					BATTING AND FIELDING						BOWLING							
Player	M	I	NO	Runs	HS	Avge	100	50	0	C/S	Balls	Mdns	Runs	Wkts	Avge	5wi	10w	Best
Kanitkar,HS	2	4	0	111	65	27.75	0	1	0	0								
Kapil Dev	131	184	15	5248	163	31.05	8	27	16	64	27740	1060	12867	434	29.64	23	2	9/83
Kapoor,AR	4	6	1	97	42	19.40	0	0	0	1	642	26	255	6	42.50	0	0	2/19
Kardar,AH	3	5	0	80	43	16.00	0	0	1	1								
Karim,SS	1	1	0	15	15	15.00	0	0	0	1/0								
Karthik,KD	10	13	0	245	93	18.84	0	1	0	29/4								
Kartik,M	8	10	1	88	43	9.77	0	0	2	2	1932	74	820	24	34.16	0	0	4/44
Kenny,RB	5	10	1	245	62	27.22	0	3	2	1								
Kirmani,SMH	88	124	22	2759	102	27.04	2	12	7	160/38	19	0	13	1	13.00	0	0	1/9
Kishenchand,G	5	10	0	89	44	8.89	0	0	5	1								
Kripal Singh,AG	14	20	5	422	100*	28.13	1	2	4	4	1518	76	584	10	58.40	0	0	3/43
Krishnamurthy,P	5	6	0	33	20	5.50	0	0	2	7/1								
Kulkarni,NM	3	2	1	5	4	5.00	0	0	0	1	738	28	332	2	166.00	0	0	1/70
Kulkarni,RR	3	2	0	2	2	1.00	0	0	1	1	366	5	227	5	45.40	0	0	3/85
Kulkarni,UN	4	8	5	13	7	4.33	0	0	1	0	448	5	238	5	47.60	0	0	2/37
Kumar,VV	2	2	0	6	6	3.00	0	0	1	2	605	46	202	7	28.85	1	0	5/64
Kumble,A	110	140	27	2025	88	17.92	0	4	13	50	34445	1412	15364	533	28.82	33	8	10/74
Kunderan,BK	18	34	4	981	192	32.70	2	3	1	23/7	24	0	13	0	-	0	0	0/13
Kuruvilla,A	10	11	1	66	35*	6.60	0	0	5	0	1765	59	892	25	35.68	1	0	5/68
Lall Singh	1	2	0	44	29	22.00	0	0	0	1								
Lamba,R	4	5	0	102	53	20.40	0	1	1	5								
Laxman,VVS	77	124	14	4704	281	42.76	10	25	8	81	252	10	100	1	100.00	0	0	1/32
Madan Lal	39	62	16	1042	74	22.65	0	5	7	15	5997	188	2846	71	40.08	4	0	5/23
Mahomed Nissar	6	11	3	55	14	6.87	0	0	2	2	1211	34	707	25	28.28	3	0	5/90
Maka,ES	2	1	1	2	2*	-	0	0	0	2/1								
Malhotra,AO	7	10	1	226	72*	25.11	0	1	2	2	18	1	3	0	-	0	0	0/0
Maninder Singh	35	38	12	99	15	3.80	0	0	11	9	8218	359	3288	88	37.36	3	2	7/27
Manjrekar,SV	37	61	6	2043	218	37.14	4	9	3	25/1	17	0	15	0	-	0	0	0/4
Manjrekar,VL	55	92	10	3208	189*	39.12	7	15	11	19/2	204	17	44	1	44.00	0	0	1/16
Mankad,AV	22	42	3	991	97	25.41	0	6	3	12	41	1	43	0	-	0	0	0/0
Mankad,MH	44	72	5	2109	231	31.47	5	6	7	33	14686	777	5236	162	32.32	8	2	8/52
Mantri,MK	4	8	1	67	39	9.57	0	0	2	8/1								
Meherhomji,KR	1	1	1	0	0*	-	0	0	0	1/0								
Mehra,VL	8	14	1	329	62	25.30	0	2	1	1	36	1	6	0	-	0	0	0/1
Merchant,VM	10	18	0	859	154	47.72	3	3	2	7	54	0	40	0	-	0	0	0/17
Mhambrey,PL	2	3	1	58	28	29.00	0	0	0	1	258	6	148	2	74.00	0	0	1/43
Milkha Singh,AG	4	6	0	92	35	15.33	0	0	0	2	6	0	2	0	-	0	0	0/2
Modi,RS	10	17	1	736	112	46.00	1	6	0	3	30	1	14	0	-	0	0	0/14
Mohammad Kaif	13	22	2	624	148*	31.20	1	3	1	15	18	0	4	0	-	0	0	0/4
Mohanty,DS	2	1	1	0	0*	-	0	0	0	0	430	10	239	4	59.75	0	0	4/78
Mongia,NR	44	68	8	1442	152	24.03	1	6	6	99/8								
More,KS	49	64	14	1285	73	25.70	0	7	7	110/20	12	0	12	0	-	0	0	0/12
Muddiah,VM	2	3	1	11	11	5.50	0	0	1	0	318	17	134	3	44.66	0	0	2/40
Mushtaq Ali,S	11	20	1	612	112	32.21	2	3	1	7	378	9	202	3	67.33	0	0	1/45
Nadkarni,RG	41	67	12	1414	122*	25.70	1	7	6	22	9165	665	2559	88	29.07	4	1	6/43
Naik,SS	3	6	0	141	77	23.50	0	1	1	0								
Naoomal Jaoomal	3	5	1	108	43	27.00	0	0	0	0	108	0	68	2	34.00	0	0	1/4
Narasimha Rao,MV	4	6	1	46	20*	9.20	0	0	0	8	463	11	227	3	75.66	0	0	2/46
Navle,JG	2	4	0	42	13	10.50	0	0	0	1/0								
Nayak,SV	2	3	1	19	11	9.50	0	0	0	1	231	6	132	1	132.00	0	0	1/16
Nayudu,CK	7	14	0	350	81	25.00	0	2	0	4	858	24	386	9	42.88	0	0	3/40
Nayudu,CS	11	19	3	147	36	9.18	0	0	3	3	522	6	359	2	179.50	0	0	1/19

INDIA (cont.)					**BATTING AND FIELDING**							**BOWLING**						
Player	M	I	NO	Runs	HS	Avge	100	50	0	C/S	Balls	Mdns	Runs	Wkts	Avge	5wi	10w	Best
Nazir Ali,S	2	4	0	30	13	7.50	0	0	0	0	138	1	83	4	20.75	0	0	4/83
Nehra,A	17	25	11	77	19	5.50	0	0	10	5	3447	122	1866	44	42.40	0	0	4/72
Nyalchand,S	1	2	1	7	6*	7.00	0	0	0	0	384	33	97	3	32.33	0	0	3/97
Pai,AM	1	2	0	10	9	5.00	0	0	0	0	114	5	31	2	15.50	0	0	2/29
Palia,PE	2	4	1	29	16	9.66	0	0	0	0	42	3	13	0	-	0	0	0/2
Pandit,CS	5	8	1	171	39	24.42	0	0	0	14/2								
Parkar,GAHM	1	2	0	7	6	3.50	0	0	0	1								
Parkar,RD	2	4	0	80	35	20.00	0	0	0	0								
Parsana,DD	2	2	0	1	1	0.50	0	0	1	0	120	6	50	1	50.00	0	0	1/32
Patankar,CT	1	2	1	14	13	14.00	0	0	0	3/1								
Pataudi, Nawab of, jr	46	83	3	2793	203*	34.91	6	16	7	27	132	6	88	1	88.00	0	0	1/10
Pataudi, Nawab of, sr	3	5	0	55	22	11.00	0	0	0	0								
Patel,BP	21	38	5	972	115*	29.45	1	5	0	17								
Patel,JM	7	10	1	25	12	2.77	0	0	5	2	1725	94	637	29	21.96	2	1	9/69
Patel,MM	6	7	2	32	13	6.40	0	0	2	3	1374	49	680	24	28.33	0	0	4/25
Patel,PA	19	28	7	669	69	31.85	0	4	4	39/7								
Patel,RGM	1	2	0	0	0	0.00	0	0	2	1	84	0	51	0	-	0	0	0/14
Pathan,IK	25	32	2	835	93	27.83	0	6	4	8	5078	185	2802	91	30.79	7	2	7/59
Patiala,Yuvraj of	1	2	0	84	60	42.00	0	1	0	2								
Patil,SM	29	47	4	1588	174	36.93	4	7	4	12	645	29	240	9	26.66	0	0	2/28
Patil,SR	1	1	1	14	14*	-	0	0	0	1	138	7	51	2	25.50	0	0	1/15
Phadkar,DG	31	45	7	1229	123	32.34	2	8	3	21	5994	277	2285	62	36.85	3	0	7/159
Piyush Chawla	1	1	0	1	1	1.00	0	0	0	0	85	3	53	1	53.00	0	0	1/8
Prabhakar,M	39	58	9	1600	120	32.65	1	9	3	20	7475	274	3581	96	37.30	3	0	6/132
Prasad,MSK	6	10	1	106	19	11.77	0	0	0	15/0								
Prasanna,EAS	49	84	20	735	37	11.48	0	0	15	18	14353	602	5742	189	30.38	10	2	8/76
Punjabi,PH	5	10	0	164	33	16.40	0	0	0	5								
Rai Singh,K	1	2	0	26	24	13.00	0	0	0	0								
Rajinder Pal	1	2	1	6	3*	6.00	0	0	0	0	78	4	22	0	-	0	0	0/3
Rajindernath	1					-	0	0	0	0/4								
Rajput,LS	2	4	0	105	61	26.25	0	1	1	1								
Raman,WV	11	19	1	448	96	24.88	0	4	4	6	348	20	129	2	64.50	0	0	1/7
Ramaswami,C	2	4	1	170	60	56.66	0	1	0	0								
Ramchand,GS	33	53	5	1180	109	24.58	2	5	6	20	4976	256	1899	41	46.31	1	0	6/49
Ramesh,S	19	37	1	1367	143	37.97	2	8	3	18	54	0	43	0	-	0	0	0/5
Ramji,L	1	2	0	1	1	0.50	0	0	1	1	138	5	64	0	-	0	0	0/64
Rangachari,CR	4	6	3	8	8*	2.66	0	0	3	0	846	11	493	9	54.77	1	0	5/107
Rangnekar,KM	3	6	0	33	18	5.50	0	0	2	1								
Ranjane,VB	7	9	3	40	16	6.66	0	0	1	1	1265	33	649	19	34.15	0	0	4/72
Rathour,V	6	10	0	131	44	13.10	0	0	0	12								
Ratra,A	6	10	1	163	115*	18.11	1	0	1	11/2	6	0	1	0	-	0	0	0/1
Razdan,V	2	2	1	6	6*	6.00	0	0	1	0	240	6	141	5	28.20	1	0	5/79
Reddy,B	4	5	1	38	21	9.50	0	0	2	9/2								
Rege,MR	1	2	0	15	15	7.50	0	0	1	1								
Roy,AK	4	7	0	91	48	13.00	0	0	2	0								
Roy,Pankaj	43	79	4	2442	173	32.56	5	9	14	16	104	4	66	1	66.00	0	0	1/6
Roy,Praanab	2	3	1	71	60*	35.50	0	1	0	1								
Sandhu,BS	8	11	4	214	71	30.57	0	2	1	1	1020	32	557	10	55.70	0	0	3/87
Sanghvi,RL	1	2	0	2	2	1.00	0	0	1	0	74	3	78	2	39.00	0	0	2/67
Sarandeep Singh	3	2	1	43	39*	43.00	0	0	0	1	678	27	340	10	34.00	0	0	4/136
Sardesai,DN	30	55	4	2001	212	39.23	5	9	4	4	59	2	45	0	-	0	0	0/3

INDIA (cont.)	**BATTING AND FIELDING**										**BOWLING**							
Player	M	I	NO	Runs	HS	Avge	100	50	0	C/S	Balls	Mdns	Runs	Wkts	Avge	5wi	10w	Best
Sarwate,CT	9	17	1	208	37	13.00	0	0	4	0	658	5	374	3	124.66	0	0	1/16
Saxena,RC	1	2	0	25	16	12.50	0	0	0	0	12	0	11	0	-	0	0	0/11
Sehwag,VK	48	79	3	4013	309	52.80	12	12	8	37	1192	33	628	12	52.33	0	0	3/33
Sekhar,TAP	2	1	1	0	0*	-	0	0	0	0	204	3	129	0	-	0	0	0/43
Sen,PK	14	18	4	165	25	11.78	0	0	1	20/11								
Sengupta,AK	1	2	0	9	8	4.50	0	0	0	0								
Sharma,AK	1	2	0	53	30	26.50	0	0	0	1	24	0	9	0	-	0	0	0/9
Sharma,C	23	27	9	396	54	22.00	0	1	2	7	3470	61	2163	61	35.45	4	1	6/58
Sharma,G	5	4	1	11	10*	3.66	0	0	2	2	1307	57	418	10	41.80	0	0	4/88
Sharma,PH	5	10	0	187	54	18.70	0	1	0	1	24	0	8	0	-	0	0	0/2
Sharma,SK	2	3	1	56	38	28.00	0	0	1	1	414	9	247	6	41.16	0	0	3/37
Shastri,RJ	80	121	14	3830	206	35.79	11	12	9	36	15751	657	6185	151	40.96	2	0	5/75
Shinde,SG	7	11	5	85	14	14.16	0	0	0	0	1515	59	717	12	59.75	1	0	6/91
Shivaramakrishnan,L	9	9	1	130	25	16.25	0	0	1	9	2367	74	1145	26	44.03	3	1	6/64
Shodhan,RH	3	4	1	181	110	60.33	1	0	0	1	60	3	26	0	-	0	0	0/1
Shukla,RC	1					-	0	0	0	0	294	9	152	2	76.00	0	0	2/82
Siddiqui,IR	1	2	1	29	24	29.00	0	0	0	1	114	5	48	1	48.00	0	0	1/32
Sidhu,NS	51	78	2	3202	201	42.13	9	15	9	9	6	0	9	0	-	0	0	0/9
Singh,R	1	1	0	0	0	0.00	0	0	1	1	240	8	176	3	58.66	0	0	2/74
Singh,RP	2	3	2	6	6	6.00	0	0	0	0	522	8	345	9	38.33	0	0	4/89
Singh,RR	1	2	0	27	15	13.50	0	0	0	5	60	4	32	0	-	0	0	0/16
Singh,VR	2	1	0	2	2	2.00	0	0	0	0	282	7	158	2	79.00	0	0	2/61
Sohoni,SW	4	7	2	83	29*	16.60	0	0	0	2	532	20	202	2	101.00	0	0	1/16
Solkar,ED	27	48	6	1068	102	25.42	1	6	1	53	2265	82	1070	18	59.44	0	0	3/28
Sood,MM	1	2	0	3	3	1.50	0	0	1	0								
Sreesanth,S	5	7	3	75	29*	18.75	0	0	2	1	1019	41	566	19	29.78	0	0	4/70
Srikkanth,K	43	72	3	2062	123	29.88	2	12	7	40	216	3	114	0	-	0	0	0/1
Srinath,J	67	92	21	1009	76	14.21	0	4	13	22	15104	599	7196	236	30.49	10	1	8/86
Srinivasan,TE	1	2	0	48	29	24.00	0	0	0	0								
Subramanya,V	9	15	1	263	75	18.78	0	2	1	9	444	17	201	3	67.00	0	0	2/32
Sunderam,GR	2	1	1	3	3*	-	0	0	0	0	396	12	166	3	55.33	0	0	2/46
Surendranath	11	20	7	136	27	10.46	0	0	4	4	2602	144	1053	26	40.50	2	0	5/75
Surti,RF	26	48	4	1263	99	28.70	0	9	5	26	3870	115	1962	42	46.71	1	0	5/74
Swamy,VN	1					-	0	0	0	0	108	5	45	0	-	0	0	0/15
Tamhane,NS	21	27	5	225	54*	10.22	0	1	8	35/16								
Tarapore,KK	1	1	0	2	2	2.00	0	0	0	0	114	2	72	0	-	0	0	0/72
Tendulkar,SR	132	211	22	10469	248*	55.39	35	41	12	83	3330	75	1884	37	50.91	0	0	3/10
Umrigar,PR	59	94	8	3631	223	42.22	12	14	5	33	4725	262	1473	35	42.08	2	0	6/74
Vengsarkar,DB	116	185	22	6868	166	42.13	17	35	15	78	47	1	36	0	-	0	0	0/3
Venkatapathy Raju,SL	28	34	10	240	31	10.00	0	0	3	6	7602	362	2857	93	30.72	5	1	6/12
Venkataraghavan,S	57	76	12	748	64	11.68	0	2	13	44	14877	696	5634	156	36.11	3	1	8/72
Venkataramana,M	1	2	2	0	0*	-	0	0	0	1	70	1	58	1	58.00	0	0	1/10
Venkatesh Prasad,BK	33	47	20	203	30*	7.51	0	0	10	6	7041	275	3360	96	35.00	7	1	6/33
Vijay Bharadwaj,R	3	3	0	28	22	9.33	0	0	1	3	247	8	107	1	107.00	0	0	1/26
Viswanath,GR	91	155	10	6080	222	41.93	14	35	10	63	70	1	46	1	46.00	0	0	1/11
Viswanath,S	3	5	0	31	20	6.20	0	0	2	11/0								
Vizanagram,Maharajkumar of	3	6	2	33	19*	8.25	0	0	0	1								
Wadekar,AL	37	71	3	2113	143	31.07	1	14	7	46	61	1	55	0	-	0	0	0/0

INDIA (cont.)				BATTING AND FIELDING									BOWLING					
Player	M	I	NO	Runs	HS	Avge	100	50	0	C/S	Balls	Mdns	Runs	Wkts	Avge	5wi	10w	Best
Wasim Jaffer	14	26	0	883	212	33.96	2	6	2	15	66	3	18	2	9.00	0	0	2/18
Wassan,AS	4	5	1	94	53	23.50	0	1	1	1	712	16	504	10	50.40	0	0	4/108
Wazir Ali,S	7	14	0	237	42	16.92	0	0	1	1	30	1	25	0	-	0	0	0/0
Yadav,NS	35	40	12	403	43	14.39	0	0	4	10	8360	339	3580	102	35.09	3	0	5/76
Yadav,V	1	1	0	30	30	30.00	0	0	0	1/2								
Yajurvindra Singh	4	7	1	109	43*	18.16	0	0	4	11	120	3	50	0	-	0	0	0/2
Yashpal Sharma	37	59	11	1606	140	33.45	2	9	0	16	30	2	17	1	17.00	0	0	1/6
Yograj Singh	1	2	0	10	6	5.00	0	0	0	0	90	3	63	1	63.00	0	0	1/63
Yohannan,T	3	4	4	13	8*	-	0	0	0	1	486	17	256	5	51.20	0	0	2/56
Yuvraj Singh	19	29	5	830	122	34.58	2	3	3	21	144	1	90	1	90.00	0	0	1/25
Zaheer Khan	42	54	15	507	75	13.00	0	1	15	10	7967	267	4399	121	36.35	3	0	5/29

PAKISTAN (186 players)				BATTING AND FIELDING									BOWLING					
Player	M	I	NO	Runs	HS	Avge	100	50	0	C/S	Balls	Mdns	Runs	Wkts	Avge	5wi	10w	Best
Aamer Malik	14	19	3	565	117	35.31	2	3	3	15/1	156	5	89	1	89.00	0	0	1/0
Aamer Nazir	6	11	6	31	11	6.20	0	0	2	2	1057	24	597	20	29.85	1	0	5/46
Aamer Sohail	47	83	3	2823	205	35.28	5	13	6	36	2383	80	1049	25	41.96	0	0	4/54
Aaqib Javed	22	27	7	101	28*	5.05	0	0	8	2	3918	136	1874	54	34.70	1	0	5/84
Abdul Kadir	4	8	0	272	95	34.00	0	2	2	0/1								
Abdul Qadir	67	77	11	1029	61	15.59	0	3	7	15	17126	608	7742	236	32.80	15	5	9/56
Abdur Razzaq	43	72	8	1828	134	28.56	3	6	4	12	6650	202	3520	95	37.05	1	0	5/35
Afaq Hussain	2	4	4	66	35*	-	0	0	0	2	240	7	106	1	106.00	0	0	1/40
Aftab Baloch	2	3	1	97	60*	48.50	0	1	0	0	44	0	17	0	-	0	0	0/2
Aftab Gul	6	8	0	182	33	22.75	0	0	0	3	6	0	4	0	-	0	0	0/4
Agha Saadat Ali	1	1	1	8	8*	-	0	0	0	3								
Agha Zahid	1	2	0	15	14	7.50	0	0	0	0								
Akram Raza	9	12	2	153	32	15.30	0	0	3	8	1526	61	732	13	56.30	0	0	3/46
Ali Naqvi	5	9	1	242	115	30.25	1	0	0	1	12	0	11	0	-	0	0	0/11
Ali Rizvi	1					-	0	0	0	0	111	1	72	2	36.00	0	0	2/72
Alimuddin	25	45	2	1091	109	25.37	2	7	6	8	84	0	75	1	75.00	0	0	1/17
Amir Elahi	5	7	1	65	47	10.83	0	0	1	0	400	5	248	7	35.42	0	0	4/134
Anil Dalpat	9	12	1	167	52	15.18	0	1	0	22/3								
Anwar Hussain	4	6	0	42	17	7.00	0	0	0	0	36	1	29	1	29.00	0	0	1/25
Anwar Khan	1	2	1	15	12	15.00	0	0	0	0	32	0	12	0	-	0	0	0/12
Arif Butt	3	5	0	59	20	11.80	0	0	1	0	666	26	288	14	20.57	1	0	6/89
Arshad Khan	9	8	2	31	9*	5.16	0	0	1	0	2538	119	960	32	30.00	1	0	5/38
Ashfaq Ahmed	1	2	1	1	1*	1.00	0	0	1	0	138	9	53	2	26.50	0	0	2/31
Ashraf Ali	8	8	3	229	65	45.80	0	2	0	17/5								
Asif Iqbal	58	99	7	3575	175	38.85	11	12	9	36	3864	181	1502	53	28.33	2	0	5/48
Asif Masood	16	19	10	93	30*	10.33	0	0	5	5	3038	78	1568	38	41.26	1	0	5/111
Asif Mujtaba	25	41	3	928	65*	24.42	0	8	5	19	666	26	303	4	75.75	0	0	1/0
Asim Kamal	12	20	1	717	99	37.73	0	8	2	10								
Ata-ur-Rehman	13	15	6	76	19	8.44	0	0	3	2	1973	62	1071	31	34.54	0	0	4/50
Atif Rauf	1	2	0	25	16	12.50	0	0	0	0								
Atiq-uz-Zaman	1	2	0	26	25	13.00	0	0	0	5/0								
Azam Khan	1	1	0	14	14	14.00	0	0	0	0								
Azeem Hafeez	18	21	5	134	24	8.37	0	0	2	1	4351	172	2204	63	34.98	4	0	6/46
Azhar Khan	1	1	0	14	14	14.00	0	0	0	0	18	1	2	1	2.00	0	0	1/1
Azhar Mahmood	21	34	4	900	136	30.00	3	1	5	14	3015	111	1402	39	35.94	0	0	4/50
Azmat Rana	1	1	0	49	49	49.00	0	0	0	0								
Basit Ali	19	33	1	858	103	26.81	1	5	5	6	6	0	6	0	-	0	0	0/6

PAKISTAN (cont.)				BATTING AND FIELDING							BOWLING							
Player	M	I	NO	Runs	HS	Avge	100	50	0	C/S	Balls	Mdns	Runs	Wkts	Avge	5wi	10w	Best
Bazid Khan	1	2	0	32	23	16.00	0	0	0	2								
Danish Kaneria	40	54	27	175	29	6.48	0	0	16	11	11035	339	5566	169	32.93	11	2	7/77
d'Souza,A	6	10	8	76	23*	38.00	0	0	0	3	1587	56	745	17	43.82	1	0	5/112
Ehteshamuddin	5	3	1	2	2	1.00	0	0	1	2	940	40	375	16	23.43	1	0	5/47
Faisal Iqbal	17	30	2	763	139	27.25	1	5	3	11	6	0	7	0	-	0	0	0/7
Farhan Adil	1	2	0	33	25	16.50	0	0	0	0								
Farooq Hameed	1	2	0	3	3	1.50	0	0	1	0	184	1	107	1	107.00	0	0	1/82
Farrukh Zaman	1					-	0	0	0	0	80	2	15	0	-	0	0	0/7
Fazal Mahmood	34	50	6	620	60	14.09	0	1	10	11	9834	560	3434	139	24.70	13	4	7/42
Fazl-e-Akbar	5	8	4	52	25	13.00	0	0	2	2	882	24	511	11	46.45	0	0	3/85
Ghazali,MEZ	2	4	0	32	18	8.00	0	0	2	0	48	1	18	0	-	0	0	0/18
Ghulam Abbas	1	2	0	12	12	6.00	0	0	1	0								
Gul Mohammad	1	2	1	39	27*	39.00	0	0	0	0								
Hanif Mohammad	55	97	8	3915	337	43.98	12	15	5	40/0	206	9	95	1	95.00	0	0	1/1
Haroon Rashid	23	36	1	1217	153	34.77	3	5	2	16	8	0	3	0	-	0	0	0/3
Hasan Raza	7	10	1	235	68	26.11	0	2	1	5	6	0	1	0	-	0	0	0/1
Haseeb Ahsan	12	16	7	61	14	6.77	0	0	3	1	2835	100	1330	27	49.25	2	0	6/202
Humayun Farhat	1	2	0	54	28	27.00	0	0	0	0/0								
Iftikhar Anjum	1	1	1	9	9*	-	0	0	0	0	84	1	62	0	-	0	0	0/8
Ijaz Ahmed[1]	60	92	4	3315	211	37.67	12	12	7	45	180	1	77	2	38.50	0	0	1/9
Ijaz Ahmed[2]	2	3	0	29	16	9.66	0	0	0	3	24	0	6	0	-	0	0	0/1
Ijaz Butt	8	16	2	279	58	19.92	0	1	1	5/0								
Ijaz Faqih	5	8	1	183	105	26.14	1	0	2	0	534	9	299	4	74.75	0	0	1/38
Imran Farhat	21	39	0	1287	128	33.00	2	8	1	26	247	3	192	3	64.00	0	0	2/69
Imran Khan	88	126	25	3807	136	37.69	6	18	8	28	19458	727	8258	362	22.81	23	6	8/58
Imran Nazir	8	13	0	427	131	32.84	2	1	2	4								
Imtiaz Ahmed	41	72	1	2079	209	29.28	3	11	9	77/16	6	1	0	0	-	0	0	0/0
Intikhab Alam	47	77	10	1493	138	22.28	1	8	10	20	10474	383	4494	125	35.95	5	2	7/52
Inzamamul Haq	112	185	20	8497	329	51.49	25	44	13	79	9	0	8	0	-	0	0	0/8
Iqbal Qasim	50	57	15	549	56	13.07	0	1	10	42	13019	649	4807	171	28.11	8	2	7/49
Irfan Fazil	1	2	1	4	3	4.00	0	0	0	2	48	0	65	2	32.50	0	0	1/30
Israr Ali	4	8	1	33	10	4.71	0	0	1	1	318	12	165	6	27.50	0	0	2/29
Jalaluddin	6	3	2	3	2	3.00	0	0	0	0	1197	51	537	11	48.81	0	0	3/77
Javed Akhtar	1	2	1	4	2*	4.00	0	0	0	0	96	5	52	0	-	0	0	0/52
Javed Burki	25	48	4	1341	140	30.47	3	4	3	7	42	2	23	0	-	0	0	0/2
Javed Miandad	124	189	21	8832	280*	52.57	23	43	6	93/1	1470	32	682	17	40.11	0	0	3/74
Kabir Khan	4	5	2	24	10	8.00	0	0	1	1	655	15	370	9	41.11	0	0	3/26
Kamran Akmal	27	45	2	1253	154	29.14	4	3	7	90/16								
Kardar,AH	23	37	3	847	93	24.91	0	5	1	15	2712	139	954	21	45.42	0	0	3/35
Khalid Hasan	1	2	1	17	10	17.00	0	0	0	0	126	1	116	2	58.00	0	0	2/116
Khalid Ibadulla	4	8	0	253	166	31.62	1	0	0	3	336	21	99	1	99.00	0	0	1/42
Khalid Wazir	2	3	1	14	9*	7.00	0	0	0	0								
Khan Mohammad	13	17	7	100	26*	10.00	0	0	3	4	3157	153	1292	54	23.92	4	0	6/21
Liaqat Ali	5	7	3	28	12	7.00	0	0	1	1	808	23	359	6	59.83	0	0	3/80
Mahmood Hussain	27	39	6	336	35	10.18	0	0	8	5	5910	225	2628	68	38.64	2	0	6/67
Majid Khan	63	106	5	3931	167	38.92	8	19	9	70	3584	124	1456	27	53.92	0	0	4/45
Mansoor Akhtar	19	29	3	655	111	25.19	1	3	4	9								
Manzoor Elahi	6	10	2	123	52	15.37	0	1	3	7	444	23	194	7	27.71	0	0	2/38
Maqsood Ahmed	16	27	1	507	99	19.50	0	2	2	13	462	21	191	3	63.66	0	0	2/12
Masood Anwar	1	2	0	39	37	19.50	0	0	0	0	161	4	102	3	34.00	0	0	2/59
Mathias,W	21	36	3	783	77	23.72	0	3	3	22	24	0	20	0	-	0	0	0/20
Miran Bux	2	3	2	1	1*	1.00	0	0	1	0	348	22	115	2	57.50	0	0	2/82
Misbah-ul-Haq	5	9	0	120	28	13.33	0	0	0	1								

PAKISTAN (cont.)				**BATTING AND FIELDING**									**BOWLING**					
Player	M	I	NO	Runs	HS	Avge	100	50	0	C/S	Balls	Mdns	Runs	Wkts	Avge	5wi	10w	Best
Mohammad Akram	9	15	6	24	10*	2.66	0	0	5	4	1477	37	859	17	50.52	1	0	5/138
Mohammad Asif	6	8	3	18	12*	3.60	0	0	5	2	1159	40	635	30	21.16	2	1	6/44
Mohammad Aslam	1	2	0	34	18	17.00	0	0	0	0								
Mohammad Farooq	7	9	4	85	47	17.00	0	0	1	1	1422	50	682	21	32.47	0	0	4/70
Mohammad Hafeez	4	7	1	309	102*	51.50	1	2	0	2	228	16	74	1	74.00	0	0	1/14
Mohammad Hussain	2	3	0	18	17	6.00	0	0	1	1	180	7	87	3	29.00	0	0	2/66
Mohammad Ilyas	10	19	0	441	126	23.21	1	2	1	6	84	1	63	0	-	0	0	0/1
Mohammad Khalil	2	4	1	9	5	3.00	0	0	1	0	290	3	200	0	-	0	0	0/38
Mohammad Munaf	4	7	2	63	19	12.60	0	0	0	0	769	31	341	11	31.00	0	0	4/42
Mohammad Nazir	14	18	10	144	29*	18.00	0	0	3	4	3262	162	1124	34	33.05	3	0	7/99
Mohammad Ramzan	1	2	0	36	29	18.00	0	0	0	1								
Mohammad Sami	28	43	11	337	49	10.53	0	0	7	6	5982	163	3531	73	48.37	2	0	5/36
Mohammad Wasim	18	28	2	783	192	30.11	2	2	3	22/2								
Mohammad Zahid	5	6	1	7	6*	1.40	0	0	4	0	792	17	502	15	33.46	1	1	7/66
Mohsin Kamal	9	11	7	37	13*	9.25	0	0	1	4	1348	28	822	24	34.25	0	0	4/116
Mohsin Khan	48	79	6	2709	200	37.10	7	9	3	34	86	4	30	0	-	0	0	0/0
Moin Khan	69	104	8	2741	137	28.55	4	15	5	128/20								
Mudassar Nazar	76	116	8	4114	231	38.09	10	17	7	48	5967	217	2532	66	38.36	1	0	6/32
Mufassir-ul-Haq	1	1	1	8	8*	-	0	0	0	1	222	12	84	3	28.00	0	0	2/50
Munir Malik	3	4	1	7	4	2.33	0	0	1	1	684	21	358	9	39.77	1	0	5/128
Mushtaq Ahmed	52	72	15	655	59	11.49	0	2	14	23	12532	405	6100	185	32.97	10	3	7/56
Mushtaq Mohammad	57	100	7	3643	201	39.17	10	19	4	42	5260	177	2309	79	29.22	3	0	5/28
Nadeem Abbasi	3	2	0	46	36	23.00	0	0	0	6/0								
Nadeem Ghauri	1	1	0	0	0	0.00	0	0	1	0	48	1	20	0	-	0	0	0/20
Nadeem Khan	2	3	1	34	25	17.00	0	0	0	0	432	10	230	2	115.00	0	0	2/147
Nasim-ul-Ghani	29	50	5	747	101	16.60	1	2	8	11	4406	204	1959	52	37.67	2	0	6/67
Naushad Ali	6	11	0	156	39	14.18	0	0	0	9/0								
Naved Anjum	2	3	0	44	22	14.66	0	0	0	0	342	14	162	4	40.50	0	0	2/57
Naved Ashraf	2	3	0	64	32	21.33	0	0	0	0								
Naved Latif	1	2	0	20	20	10.00	0	0	1	0								
Naved-ul-Hasan	8	13	3	176	42*	17.60	0	0	2	3	1421	31	931	16	58.18	0	0	3/30
Nazar Mohammad	5	8	1	277	124*	39.57	1	1	1	7	12	1	4	0	-	0	0	0/4
Niaz Ahmed	2	3	3	17	16*	-	0	0	0	1	294	14	94	3	31.33	0	0	2/72
Pervez Sajjad	19	20	11	123	24	13.66	0	0	2	9	4145	217	1410	59	23.89	3	0	7/74
Qaiser Abbas	1	1	0	2	2	2.00	0	0	0	0	96	3	35	0	-	0	0	0/35
Qasim Umar	26	43	2	1502	210	36.63	3	5	2	15	6	1	0	0	-	0	0	0/0
Rameez Raja	57	94	5	2833	122	31.83	2	22	7	34								
Rashid Khan	4	6	3	155	59	51.66	0	1	1	2	738	32	360	8	45.00	0	0	3/129
Rashid Latif	37	57	9	1381	150	28.77	1	7	4	119/11	12	0	10	0	-	0	0	0/10
Rehman,SF	1	2	0	10	8	5.00	0	0	20	1	204	3	99	1	99.00	0	0	1/43
Riaz Afridi	1	1	0	9	9	9.00	0	0	0	0	186	10	87	2	43.50	0	0	2/42
Rizwan-uz-Zaman	11	19	1	345	60	19.16	0	3	2	4	132	7	46	4	11.50	0	0	3/26
Sadiq Mohammad	41	74	2	2579	166	35.81	5	10	6	28	200	5	98	0	-	0	0	0/0
Saeed Ahmed	41	78	4	2991	172	40.41	5	16	2	13	1980	89	802	22	36.45	0	0	4/64
Saeed Anwar	55	91	2	4052	188*	45.52	11	25	8	18	48	3	23	0	-	0	0	0/0
Salahuddin	5	8	2	117	34*	19.50	0	0	0	3	546	27	187	7	26.71	0	0	2/36
Saleem Altaf	21	31	12	276	53*	14.52	0	1	6	3	4001	122	1710	46	37.17	0	0	4/11

PAKISTAN (cont.)				**BATTING AND FIELDING**									**BOWLING**					
Player	M	I	NO	Runs	HS	Avge	100	50	0	C/S	Balls	Mdns	Runs	Wkts	Avge	5wi	10w	Best
Saleem Elahi	13	24	1	436	72	18.95	0	1	4	10/1								
Saleem Jaffar	14	14	6	42	10*	5.25	0	0	12	2	2531	93	1139	36	31.63	1	0	5/40
Saleem Malik	103	154	22	5768	237	43.69	15	29	2	65	734	20	414	5	82.80	0	0	1/3
Saleem Yousuf	32	44	5	1055	91*	27.05	0	5	4	91/13								
Salman Butt	14	26	0	777	122	29.88	2	4	4	7	24	0	18	0	-	0	0	0/18
Saqlain Mushtaq	49	78	14	927	101*	14.48	1	2	13	15	14070	538	6206	208	29.83	13	3	8/164
Sarfraz Nawaz	55	72	13	1045	90	17.71	0	4	6	26	13951	486	5798	177	32.75	4	1	9/86
Shabbir Ahmed	10	15	5	88	24*	8.80	0	0	4	3	2576	97	1175	51	23.03	2	0	5/48
Shadab Kabir	5	7	0	148	55	21.14	0	1	0	11	6	0	9	0	-	0	0	0/9
Shafiq Ahmed	6	10	1	99	27*	11.00	0	0	3	0	8	0	1	0	-	0	0	0/1
Shafqat Rana	5	7	0	221	95	31.57	0	2	1	5	36	1	9	1	9.00	0	0	1/2
Shahid Afridi	26	46	1	1683	156	37.40	5	8	6	10	3122	69	1640	47	34.89	1	0	5/52
Shahid Israr	1	1	1	7	7*	-	0	0	0	2/0								
Shahid Mahboob	1					-	0	0	0	0	294	12	131	2	65.50	0	0	2/131
Shahid Mahmood	1	2	0	25	16	12.50	0	0	0	0	36	1	23	0	-	0	0	0/23
Shahid Nazir	10	12	3	102	18	11.33	0	0	1	4	1406	45	769	23	33.43	1	0	5/53
Shahid Saeed	1	1	0	12	12	12.00	0	0	0	0	90	0	43	0	-	0	0	0/7
Shakeel Ahmed[1]	3	5	0	74	33	14.80	0	0	1	4/0								
Shakeel Ahmed[2]	1	1	0	1	1	1.00	0	0	0	1	325	12	139	4	34.75	0	0	4/91
Sharpe,DA	3	6	0	134	56	22.33	0	1	0	2								
Shoaib Akhtar	42	62	11	534	47	10.47	0	0	10	11	7490	218	4239	165	25.69	12	2	6/11
Shoaib Malik	15	24	4	798	148*	39.90	1	4	2	5	1303	32	748	13	57.53	0	0	4/42
Shoaib Mohammad	45	68	7	2705	203*	44.34	7	13	6	22	396	16	170	5	34.00	0	0	2/8
Shujauddin	19	32	6	395	47	15.19	0	0	3	8	2313	121	801	20	40.05	0	0	3/18
Sikander Bakht	26	35	12	146	22*	6.34	0	0	4	7	4870	147	2412	67	36.00	3	1	8/69
Tahir Naqqash	15	19	5	300	57	21.42	0	1	1	3	2800	108	1398	34	41.11	2	0	5/40
Talat Ali	10	18	2	370	61	23.12	0	2	2	4	20	1	7	0	-	0	0	0/1
Taslim Arif	6	10	2	501	210*	62.62	1	2	1	6/3	30	0	28	1	28.00	0	0	1/28
Taufeeq Umar	25	46	2	1729	135	39.29	4	9	3	33	78	2	44	0	-	0	0	0/0
Tauseef Ahmed	34	38	20	318	35*	17.66	0	0	6	9	7778	359	2950	93	31.72	3	0	6/45
Umar Gul	11	14	1	67	14	5.15	0	0	4	4	2390	58	1440	45	32.00	2	0	5/31
Wajahatullah Wasti	6	10	1	329	133	36.55	2	0	0	7	18	2	8	0	-	0	0	0/0
Waqar Hasan	21	35	1	1071	189	31.50	1	6	0	10	6	0	10	0	-	0	0	0/10
Waqar Younis	87	120	21	1010	45	10.20	0	0	21	18	16224	516	8788	373	23.56	22	5	7/76
Wasim Akram	104	147	19	2898	257*	22.64	3	7	17	43	22627	871	9779	414	23.62	25	5	7/119
Wasim Bari	81	112	26	1366	85	15.88	0	6	19	201/27	8	0	2	0	-	0	0	0/2
Wasim Raja	57	92	14	2821	125	36.16	4	18	8	20	4082	134	1826	51	35.80	0	0	4/50
Wazir Mohammad	20	33	4	801	189	27.62	2	3	8	5	24	0	15	0	-	0	0	0/2
Yasir Ali	1	2	2	1	1*	-	0	0	0	0	120	5	55	2	27.50	0	0	1/12
Yasir Hameed	17	33	3	1168	170	38.93	2	7	0	13	6	0	5	0	-	0	0	0/5
Younis Ahmed	4	7	1	177	62	29.50	0	1	1	0	6	0	6	0	-	0	0	0/6
Younis Khan	47	83	4	3884	267	49.16	12	15	9	49	264	7	169	2	84.50	0	0	1/24
Yousuf Youhana	70	117	9	5737	223	53.12	19	25	8	58	6	0	3	0	-	0	0	0/3
Zaheer Abbas	78	124	11	5062	274	44.79	12	20	10	34	370	9	132	3	44.00	0	0	2/21
Zahid Fazal	9	16	0	288	78	18.00	0	1	0	5								
Zahoor Elahi	2	3	0	30	22	10.00	0	0	0	1								
Zakir Khan	2	2	2	9	9*	-	0	0	0	1	444	13	259	5	51.80	0	0	3/80
Zulfiqar Ahmed	9	10	4	200	63*	33.33	0	1	1	5	1285	78	366	20	18.29	2	1	6/42
Zulqarnain	3	4	0	24	13	6.00	0	0	0	8/2								

SRI LANKA (104 players)				BATTING AND FIELDING								BOWLING						
Player	M	I	NO	Runs	HS	Avge	100	50	0	C/S	Balls	Mdns	Runs	Wkts	Avge	5wi	10w	Best
Ahangama,FS	3	3	1	11	11	5.50	0	0	1	1	801	32	348	18	19.33	1	0	5/52
Amalean,KN	2	3	2	9	7*	9.00	0	0	0	1	244	2	156	7	22.28	0	0	4/97
Amerasinghe,AMJG	2	4	1	54	34	18.00	0	0	0	3	300	9	150	3	50.00	0	0	2/73
Anurasiri,SD	18	22	5	91	24	5.35	0	0	3	4	3973	152	1548	41	37.75	0	0	4/71
Arnold,RP	44	69	4	1821	123	28.01	3	10	7	51	1334	45	598	11	54.36	0	0	3/76
Atapattu,MS	88	152	15	5330	249	38.90	16	15	22	57	48	0	24	1	24.00	0	0	1/9
Bandara,CM	8	11	3	124	43	15.50	0	0	2	4	1152	29	633	16	39.56	0	0	3/84
Bandaratilleke,MRCN	7	9	1	93	25	11.62	0	0	1	0	1722	83	698	23	30.34	1	0	5/36
Chandana,UDU	16	24	1	616	92	26.78	0	2	0	7	2685	64	1535	37	41.48	3	1	6/179
Dassanayake,PB	11	17	2	196	36	13.06	0	0	3	19/5								
de Alwis,RG	11	19	0	152	28	8.00	0	0	5	21/2								
de Mel,ALF	17	28	5	326	34	14.17	0	0	5	9	3518	92	2180	59	36.94	3	0	6/109
de Saram,SI	4	5	0	117	39	23.40	0	0	0	1								
de Silva,AM	3	3	0	10	9	3.33	0	0	1	4/1								
de Silva,DS	12	22	3	406	61	21.36	0	2	3	5	3031	108	1347	37	36.40	1	0	5/59
de Silva,EAR	10	16	4	185	50	15.41	0	1	3	4	2328	87	1032	8	129.00	0	0	2/67
de Silva,GRA	4	7	2	41	14	8.20	0	0	2	0	962	41	385	7	55.00	0	0	2/38
de Silva,KSC	8	12	5	65	27	9.28	0	0	2	5	1585	42	889	16	55.56	1	0	5/85
de Silva,PA	93	159	11	6361	267	42.97	20	22	7	43	2595	77	1208	29	41.65	0	0	3/30
de Silva,SKL	3	4	2	36	20*	18.00	0	0	1	1/0								
de Silva,WRS	2	2	1	10	5*	10.00	0	0	0	0	288	11	146	7	20.85	0	0	4/35
Dharmasena,HDPK	31	51	7	868	62*	19.72	0	3	4	14	6939	264	2920	69	42.31	3	0	6/72
Dias,RL	20	36	1	1285	109	36.71	3	8	2	6	24	0	17	0	-	0	0	0/17
Dilshan,TM	39	63	7	2056	168	36.71	4	9	6	44	528	20	271	6	45.16	0	0	2/4
Dunusinghe,CI	5	10	0	160	91	16.00	0	1	3	13/2								
Fernando,CRD	24	51	10	124	16	5.90	0	0	5	8	3496	95	2201	69	31.89	3	0	5/42
Fernando,ERNS	5	10	0	112	46	11.20	0	0	3	0								
Fernando,KADM	2	3	1	56	51*	28.00	0	1	0	0	126	2	107	1	107.00	0	0	1/29
Fernando,KHRK	2	4	0	38	24	9.50	0	0	2	1	234	7	108	4	27.00	0	0	3/63
Fernando,TCB	9	8	3	132	45	26.40	0	0	1	4	1270	31	792	18	44.00	0	0	4/27
Gallage,IS	1	1	0	3	3	3.00	0	0	0	0	150	5	77	0	-	0	0	0/24
Goonasekera,Y	2	4	0	48	23	12.00	0	0	0	6								
Goonatilleke,HM	5	10	2	177	56	22.12	0	1	1	10/3								
Gunawardene,DA	6	11	0	181	43	16.45	0	0	1	2								
Guneratne,RPW	1	2	2	0	0*	-	0	0	0	0	102	1	84	0	-	0	0	0/84
Gurusinha,AP	41	70	7	2452	143	38.92	7	8	3	33/0	1408	47	681	20	34.05	0	0	2/7
Hathurusingha,UC	26	44	1	1274	83	29.62	0	8	2	7	1962	99	789	17	46.41	0	0	4/66
Herath,HMKRB	12	16	2	123	33*	8.78	0	0	4	2	2395	80	1204	35	34.40	0	0	4/38
Hettiarachchi,D	1	2	1	0	0*	0.00	0	0	1	0	162	7	41	2	20.50	0	0	2/36
Jayasekera,RSA	1	2	0	2	2	1.00	0	0	1	0								
Jayasuriya,ST	105	178	14	6745	340	41.12	14	30	14	78	7966	312	3271	96	34.07	2	0	5/34
Jayawardene,DMPD	83	136	10	6253	374	49.62	16	29	7	111	458	16	228	4	57.00	0	0	2/32
Jayawardene,HAPW	7	5	0	81	42	16.20	0	0	1	15/3								
Jeganathan,S	2	4	0	19	8	4.75	0	0	1	0	30	2	12	0	-	0	0	0/12
John,VB	6	10	5	53	27*	10.60	0	0	4	2	1281	53	614	28	21.92	2	0	5/60
Jurangpathy,BR	2	4	0	1	1	0.25	0	0	3	2	150	3	93	1	93.00	0	0	1/69
Kalavitigoda,S	1	2	0	8	7	4.00	0	0	0	2								

SRI LANKA (cont.)				**BATTING AND FIELDING**							**BOWLING**							
Player	M	I	NO	Runs	HS	Avge	100	50	0	C/S	Balls	Mdns	Runs	Wkts	Avge	5wi	10w	Best
Kalpage,RS	11	18	2	294	63	18.37	0	2	0	10	1576	49	774	12	64.50	0	0	2/27
Kaluperuma,LWS	2	4	1	12	11*	4.00	0	0	2	2	162	4	93	0	-	0	0	0/24
Kaluperuma,SMS	4	8	0	88	23	11.00	0	0	1	6	240	8	124	2	62.00	0	0	2/17
Kaluwitharana,RS	49	78	4	1933	132	26.12	3	9	6	93/26								
Kapugedera,CK	4	7	1	151	63	25.16	0	2	1	2								
Kulasekara,KMDN	4	7	0	115	64	16.42	0	1	2	0	612	20	302	4	75.50	0	0	2/45
Kuruppu,DSBP	4	7	1	320	201*	53.33	1	0	0	1/0								
Kuruppuarachchi,AK	2	2	2	0	0*	-	0	0	0	0	272	6	149	8	18.62	1	0	5/44
Labrooy,GF	9	14	3	158	70*	14.36	0	1	3	3	2158	58	1194	27	44.22	1	0	5/133
Lakshitha,MKGCP	2	3	0	42	40	14.00	0	0	1	1	288	10	158	5	31.60	0	0	2/33
Liyanage,DK	9	9	0	69	23	7.66	0	0	1	0	1355	47	666	17	39.17	0	0	4/56
Lokuarachchi,KS	4	5	1	94	28*	23.50	0	0	0	1	594	20	295	5	59.00	0	0	2/47
Madugalle,RS	21	39	4	1029	103	29.40	1	7	4	9	84	2	38	0	-	0	0	0/0
Madurasinghe,MAWR	3	6	1	24	11	4.80	0	0	1	0	396	12	172	3	57.33	0	0	3/60
Mahanama,RS	52	89	1	2576	225	29.27	4	11	7	56	36	0	30	0	-	0	0	0/3
Maharoof,MF	15	23	4	449	72	23.63	0	3	0	5	1944	72	1095	20	54.75	0	0	4/52
Malinga,SL	19	24	10	125	26	8.92	0	0	6	9	3165	72	2034	62	32.80	1	0	5/80
Mendis,LRD	24	43	1	1329	124	31.64	4	8	2	9								
Mirando,MTT	1	2	0	24	13	12.00	0	0	0	0	90	1	59	0	-	0	0	0/23
Mubarak,J	8	14	1	236	48	18.15	0	0	2	10	78	2	42	0	-	0	0	0/1
Muralidaran,M	107	138	49	1093	67	12.28	0	1	27	57	35816	1556	14275	652	21.89	56	18	9/51
Nawaz,MN	1	2	1	99	78*	99.00	0	1	0	0								
Nissanka,RAP	4	5	2	18	12*	6.00	0	0	2	0	587	21	366	10	36.60	1	0	5/64
Perera,ASA	3	4	1	77	43*	25.66	0	0	0	1	408	12	180	1	180.00	0	0	1/104
Perera,PDRL	8	9	6	33	11*	11.00	0	0	1	2	1130	31	661	17	38.88	0	0	3/40
Pushpakumara,KR	23	31	12	166	44	8.73	0	0	5	10	3792	98	2242	58	38.65	4	0	7/116
Ramanayake,CPH	18	24	9	143	34*	9.53	0	0	7	6	3654	109	1880	44	42.72	1	0	5/82
Ramyakumara,WMG	2	3	0	38	14	12.66	0	0	0	0	114	4	66	2	33.00	0	0	2/49
Ranasinghe,AN	2	4	0	88	77	22.00	0	1	1	0	114	1	69	1	69.00	0	0	1/23
Ranatunga,A	93	155	12	5105	135*	35.69	4	38	12	47	2373	114	1040	16	65.00	0	0	2/17
Ranatunga,D	2	3	0	87	45	29.00	0	0	0	0								
Ranatunga,S	9	17	1	531	118	33.18	2	2	1	2								
Ratnayake,RJ	23	36	6	433	56	14.43	0	2	5	9	4961	136	2563	73	35.10	5	0	6/66
Ratnayeke,JR	22	38	6	807	93	25.21	0	5	5	1	3833	118	1972	56	35.21	4	0	8/83
Samarasekera,MAR	4	7	0	118	57	16.85	0	1	1	3	192	5	104	3	34.66	0	0	2/38
Samaraweera,DP	7	14	0	211	42	15.07	0	0	1	5								
Samaraweera,TT	39	58	8	2089	142	41.78	5	13	4	30	1285	36	671	14	47.92	0	0	4/49
Sangakkara,KC	62	103	5	4796	287	48.93	10	22	4	142/20	6	0	4	0	-	0	0	0/4
Senanayake,CP	3	5	0	97	64	19.40	0	1	1	2								
Silva,KJ	7	4	1	6	6*	2.00	0	0	3	1	1533	72	647	20	32.34	0	0	4/16
Silva,SAR	9	16	2	353	111	25.21	2	0	1	33/1								
Tharanga,WU	10	19	1	591	165	32.83	1	3	4	10								
Tillakaratne,HP	83	131	25	4545	204*	42.87	11	20	9	122/2	76	3	25	0	-	0	0	0/0
Upashantha,KEA	2	3	0	10	6	3.33	0	0	0	0	306	5	200	4	50.00	0	0	2/41
Vaas,WPUJC	94	136	26	2503	74*	22.75	0	11	9	28	20414	777	9062	307	29.51	11	2	7/71
Vandort,MG	6	11	2	461	140	51.22	2	2	2	2								
Warnapura,B	4	8	0	96	38	12.00	0	0	1	2	90	4	46	0	-	0	0	0/1

SRI LANKA (cont.)	BATTING AND FIELDING										BOWLING							
Player	M	I	NO	Runs	HS	Avge	100	50	0	C/S	Balls	Mdns	Runs	Wkts	Avge	5wi	10w	Best
Warnaweera,KPJ	10	12	3	39	20	4.33	0	0	3	0	2333	90	1021	32	31.90	0	0	4/25
Weerasinghe,CDUS	1	1	0	3	3	3.00	0	0	0	0	114	8	36	0	-	0	0	0/8
Wettimuny,MD	2	4	0	28	17	7.00	0	0	1	2								
Wettimuny,S	23	43	1	1221	190	29.07	2	6	5	10	24	0	37	0	-	0	0	0/16
Wickramasinghe,GP	40	64	5	555	51	9.40	0	1	17	18	7260	248	3559	85	41.87	3	0	6/60
Wickremasinghe,AGD	3	3	1	17	13*	8.50	0	0	0	9/1								
Wijegunawardene,KIW	2	4	1	14	6*	4.66	0	0	0	0	364	16	147	7	21.00	0	0	4/51
Wijesuriya,RGCE	4	7	2	22	8	4.40	0	0	2	1	586	23	294	1	294.00	0	0	1/68
Wijetunge,PK	1	2	0	10	10	5.00	0	0	1	0	312	5	118	2	59.00	0	0	1/58
Zoysa,DNT	30	40	6	288	28*	8.47	0	0	9	4	4422	160	2157	64	33.70	1	0	5/20

ZIMBABWE (74 players)	BATTING AND FIELDING										BOWLING							
Player	M	I	NO	Runs	HS	Avge	100	50	0	C/S	Balls	Mdns	Runs	Wkts	Avge	5wi	10w	Best
Arnott,KJ	4	8	1	302	101*	43.14	1	1	1	4								
Blignaut,AM	19	36	3	884	92	26.78	0	6	6	13	3185	103	1964	54	36.37	3	0	5/73
Brain,DH	9	13	2	115	28	10.45	0	0	4	1	1810	54	915	30	30.50	1	0	5/42
Brandes,EA	10	15	3	121	39	10.08	0	0	2	4	1996	69	951	26	36.57	0	0	3/45
Brent,GB	4	6	0	35	25	5.83	0	0	3	1	818	39	314	7	44.85	0	0	3/21
Briant,GA	1	2	0	17	16	8.50	0	0	0	0								
Bruk-Jackson,GK	2	4	0	39	31	9.75	0	0	1	0								
Burmester,MG	3	4	2	54	30*	27.00	0	0	1	1	436	22	227	3	75.66	0	0	3/78
Butchart,IP	1	2	0	23	15	11.50	0	0	0	1	18	0	11	0	-	0	0	0/11
Campbell,ADR	60	109	4	2858	103	27.21	2	18	10	60	66	2	28	0	-	0	0	0/1
Carlisle,SV	37	66	6	1615	118	26.91	2	8	7	34								
Chigumbura,E	6	12	0	187	71	15.58	0	1	5	2	829	22	498	9	55.33	1	0	5/54
Coventry,CK	2	4	0	88	37	22.00	0	0	0	3								
Cremer,AG	6	12	1	29	12	2.63	0	0	4	3	870	16	595	13	45.76	0	0	3/86
Crocker,GJ	3	4	1	69	33	23.00	0	0	0	0	456	20	217	3	72.33	0	0	2/65
Dabengwa,KM	3	6	0	90	35	15.00	0	0	1	1	438	10	249	5	49.80	0	0	3/127
Dekker,MH	14	22	1	333	68*	15.85	0	2	4	12	60	4	15	0	-	0	0	0/5
Duffin,T	2	4	0	80	56	20.00	0	1	0	1								
Ebrahim,DD	29	55	1	1225	94	22.68	0	10	8	17								
Ervine,SM	5	8	0	261	86	32.62	0	3	1	7	570	18	388	9	43.11	0	0	4/146
Evans,CN	3	6	0	52	22	8.66	0	0	0	1	54	0	35	0	-	0	0	0/8
Ewing,GM	3	6	0	108	71	18.00	0	1	2	1	426	11	260	2	130.00	0	0	1/27
Ferreira,NR	1	2	0	21	16	10.50	0	0	0	0								
Flower,A	63	112	19	4794	232*	51.54	12	27	5	151/9	3	0	4	0	-	0	0	0/0
Flower,GW	67	123	6	3457	201*	29.54	6	15	16	43	3378	122	1537	25	61.48	0	0	4/41
Friend,TJ	13	19	4	447	81	29.80	0	3	4	2	2000	63	1090	25	43.60	1	0	5/31
Goodwin,MW	19	37	4	1414	166*	42.84	3	8	4	10	119	3	69	0	-	0	0	0/3
Gripper,TR	20	38	1	809	112	21.86	1	5	5	14	793	21	509	6	84.83	0	0	2/91
Hondo,DT	9	15	7	83	19	10.37	0	0	1	5	1486	50	774	21	36.85	1	0	6/59
Houghton,DL	22	36	2	1464	266	43.05	4	4	0	17	5	0	0	0	-	0	0	0/0
Huckle,AG	8	14	3	74	28*	6.72	0	0	7	3	1568	48	872	25	34.88	2	1	6/109
James,WR	4	4	0	61	33	15.25	0	0	0	16/0								
Jarvis,MP	5	3	1	4	2*	2.00	0	0	1	2	1273	88	393	11	35.72	0	0	3/30

ZIMBABWE (cont.)				BATTING AND FIELDING										BOWLING				
Player	M	I	NO	Runs	HS	Avge	100	50	0	C/S	Balls	Mdns	Runs	Wkts	Avge	5wi	10w	Best
Johnson,NC	13	23	1	532	107	24.18	1	4	3	12	1186	50	594	15	39.59	0	0	4/77
Lock,ACI	1	2	1	8	8*	8.00	0	0	1	0	180	5	105	5	21.00	0	0	3/68
Madondo,TN	3	4	1	90	74*	30.00	0	1	1	1								
Mahwire,NB	10	17	6	147	50*	13.36	0	1	2	1	1287	35	915	18	50.83	0	0	4/92
Maregwede,A	2	4	0	74	50	18.50	0	0	1	1								
Marillier,DA	5	7	1	185	73	30.83	0	2	0	2	616	21	322	11	29.27	0	0	4/57
Masakadza,H	15	30	1	785	119	27.06	1	3	5	8	126	4	39	2	19.50	0	0	1/9
Matambanadzo,EZ	3	5	1	17	7	4.25	0	0	1	0	384	10	250	4	62.50	0	0	2/62
Matsikenyeri,S	8	16	1	351	57	23.40	0	2	0	7	483	6	345	2	172.50	0	0	1/58
Mbangwa,M	15	25	8	34	8	2.00	0	0	9	2	2596	149	1006	32	31.43	0	0	3/23
Mpofu,CB	6	12	6	17	7	2.83	0	0	3	0	830	22	556	8	69.50	0	0	4/109
Mupariwa,T	1	2	0	15	14	15.00	0	0	0	0	204	1	136	0	-	0	0	0/136
Murphy,BA	11	15	3	123	30	10.25	0	0	3	11	2153	67	1113	18	61.83	0	0	3/32
Mutendera,DT	1	2	0	10	10	5.00	0	0	1	0	84	4	29	0	-	0	0	0/29
Mwayenga,W	1	2	1	15	14*	15.00	0	0	0	0	126	6	79	1	79.00	0	0	1/79
Nkala,ML	10	15	2	187	47	14.38	0	0	4	4	1452	53	727	11	66.09	0	0	3/82
Olonga,HK	30	45	11	184	24	5.41	0	0	14	10	4502	129	2620	68	38.52	2	0	5/70
Panyangara,T	3	6	2	128	40*	32.00	0	0	0	0	535	21	286	8	35.75	0	0	3/28
Peall,SG	4	6	2	60	30	15.00	0	0	3	1	888	45	303	4	75.75	0	0	2/89
Price,RW	18	30	7	236	36	9.83	0	0	4	3	5135	198	2475	69	35.87	5	1	6/73
Pycroft,AJ	3	5	0	152	60	30.40	0	1	0	2								
Ranchod,U	1	2	0	8	7	4.00	0	0	5	0	72	0	45	1	45.00	0	0	1/45
Rennie,GJ	23	46	1	1023	93	22.73	0	7	1	13	126	0	84	1	84.00	0	0	1/40
Rennie,JA	4	6	1	62	22	12.40	0	0	0	1	724	37	293	3	97.66	0	0	2/22
Rogers,BG	4	8	0	90	36	11.25	0	0	2	1	18	0	17	0	-	0	0	0/17
Shah,AH	3	5	0	122	62	24.40	0	1	2	0	186	9	125	1	125.00	0	0	1/46
Sibanda,V	3	6	0	48	18	8.00	0	0	2	4								
Strang,BC	26	45	9	465	53	12.91	0	1	8	11	5433	306	2203	56	39.33	1	0	5/101
Strang,PA	24	41	10	839	106*	27.06	1	2	3	15	5720	211	2522	70	36.02	4	1	8/109
Streak,HH	65	107	18	1990	127*	22.36	1	11	15	17	13535	592	6085	216	28.17	7	0	6/73
Taibu,T	24	46	3	1273	153	29.60	1	9	5	48/0	48	1	27	1	27.00	0	0	1/27
Taylor,BRM	10	20	0	422	78	21.10	0	3	1	7	42	0	38	0	-	0	0	0/6
Traicos,AJ	7	10	4	19	5*	3.16	0	0	1	8	1611	58	769	18	42.72	1	0	5/86
Utseya,P	1	2	0	45	45	22.50	0	0	1	2	72	2	55	0	-	0	0	0/55
Vermeulen,MA	8	16	0	414	118	25.87	1	2	3	6	6	0	5	0	-	0	0	0/5
Viljoen,DP	2	4	0	57	38	14.25	0	0	2	1	105	2	65	1	65.00	0	0	1/14
Waller,AC	2	3	0	69	50	23.00	0	1	0	1								
Watambwa,BT	6	8	5	11	4*	3.66	0	0	2	0	931	36	490	14	35.00	0	0	4/64
Whittall,AR	10	18	3	114	17	7.60	0	0	1	8	1562	48	736	7	105.14	0	0	3/73
Whittall,GJ	46	82	7	2207	203*	29.42	4	10	6	19	4686	208	2088	51	40.94	0	0	4/18
Wishart,CB	27	50	1	1098	114	22.40	1	5	6	16								

BANGLADESH (45 players)	**BATTING AND FIELDING**										**BOWLING**							
Player	M	I	NO	Runs	HS	Avge	100	50	0	C/S	Balls	Mdns	Runs	Wkts	Avge	5wi	10w	Best
Abdur Razzak	1	2	0	15	15	7.50	0	0	1	0	180	5	99	0	-	0	0	0/99
Aftab Ahmed	10	20	1	395	82*	20.78	0	1	2	4	210	4	176	3	58.66	0	0	1/33
Akram Khan	8	16	0	259	44	16.18	0	0	0	3								
Al Sahariar	15	30	0	683	70	22.76	0	4	2	10								
Alamgir Kabir	3	5	1	8	4	2.00	0	0	2	0	261	6	221	0	-	0	0	0/39
Alok Kapali	17	34	1	584	85	17.69	0	2	6	5	1103	15	709	6	118.16	0	0	3/3
Aminul Islam	13	26	1	530	145	21.20	1	2	3	5	198	1	149	1	149.00	0	0	1/66
Anwar Hossain[1]	1	2	0	14	12	7.00	0	0	0	0								
Anwar Hossain[2]	3	6	3	22	13	7.33	0	0	1	0	348	5	307	0	-	0	0	0/95
Ehsanul Haque	1	2	0	7	5	3.50	0	0	0	0	18	0	19	0	-	0	0	0/19
Enamul Haque[1]	10	19	4	180	24*	12.00	0	0	3	1	2230	86	1027	18	57.05	0	0	4/136
Enamul Haque[2]	10	18	11	28	9	4.00	0	0	3	2	2385	80	1198	32	37.43	3	1	7/95
Fahim Muntasir	3	6	0	52	33	8.66	0	0	1	1	576	15	342	5	68.40	0	0	3/131
Faisal Hossain	1	2	0	7	5	3.50	0	0	0	0								
Habibul Bashar	42	83	1	2838	113	34.61	3	24	6	19	234	1	195	0	-	0	0	0/1
Hannan Sarkar	17	33	0	662	76	20.06	0	5	5	7								
Hasibul Hossain	5	10	1	97	31	10.77	0	0	2	1	780	23	571	6	95.16	0	0	2/125
Javed Omar	35	70	1	1525	119	22.10	1	6	3	8	6	0	12	0	-	0	0	0/12
Khaled Mahmud	12	23	1	266	45	12.09	0	0	4	2	1620	65	832	13	64.00	0	0	4/37
Khaled Mashud	41	79	9	1361	103*	19.44	1	3	11	75/8								
Manjural Islam[1]	17	33	11	81	21	3.68	0	0	10	4	2970	103	1605	28	57.32	1	0	6/81
Manjural Islam[2]	6	11	1	257	69	25.70	0	1	2	3	749	19	401	5	80.20	0	0	3/84
Mashrafe Bin Mortaza	20	38	4	283	48	8.32	0	0	6	5	3560	134	1874	50	37.48	0	0	4/60
Mehrab Hossain	9	18	0	241	71	13.38	0	1	1	5/0	12	0	5	0	-	0	0	0/5
Mohammad Ashraful	33	65	3	1511	158*	29.05	3	6	9	10	834	8	626	9	69.55	0	0	2/42
Mohammad Rafique	26	47	5	982	111	23.38	1	4	5	6	7233	272	3184	87	36.59	7	0	6/77
Mohammad Salim	2	4	1	49	26	16.33	0	0	1	3/1								
Mohammad Sharif	8	16	2	86	24*	6.14	0	0	7	5	1353	41	911	14	65.07	0	0	4/98
Mushfiqur Rahim	2	4	0	24	19	12.00	0	0	1	1								
Mushfiqur Rahman	10	19	2	232	46*	13.64	0	0	5	6	1365	45	823	13	63.30	0	0	4/65
Nafees Iqbal	11	22	0	518	121	23.54	1	2	2	2								
Naimur Rahman	8	15	1	210	48	15.00	0	0	1	4	1321	45	718	12	59.83	1	0	6/132
Nazmul Hossain	1	2	1	8	8*	8.00	0	0	1	0	155	4	114	2	57.00	0	0	2/114
Rafiqul Islam	1	2	0	7	6	3.50	0	0	0	0								
Rajin Saleh	17	33	1	930	89	29.06	0	6	4	11	402	4	244	2	122.00	0	0	1/9
Ranjan Das	1	2	0	2	2	1.00	0	0	1	1	132	3	72	1	72.00	0	0	1/64
Sanwar Hossain	9	18	0	345	49	19.16	0	0	1	1	444	5	310	5	62.00	0	0	2/128
Shahadat Hossain	7	14	3	55	13	5.00	0	0	2	3	1071	21	793	16	49.56	1	0	5/86
Shahriar Hossain	3	5	0	99	48	19.80	0	0	0	0/1								
Shahriar Nafees	6	12	0	402	138	33.50	1	2	1	6								
Syed Rasel	4	8	2	30	19	5.00	0	0	1	0	551	17	360	9	40.00	0	0	4/129
Talha Jubair	7	14	6	52	31	6.50	0	0	6	1	1090	21	771	14	55.07	0	0	3/135
Tapash Baisya	21	40	6	384	66	11.29	0	2	9	6	2476	93	2137	36	59.36	0	0	4/72
Tareq Aziz	3	6	4	22	10*	11.00	0	0	2	1	360	7	261	1	261.00	0	0	1/76
Tushar Imran	4	8	0	55	28	6.87	0	0	3	1								

COMPLETE TEST RECORD FOR PLAYERS REPRESENTING TWO COUNTRIES

	BATTING AND FIELDING										BOWLING							
Player	M	I	NO	Runs	HS	Avge	100	50	0	C/S	Balls	Mdns	Runs	Wkts	Avge	5wi	10w	Best
Amir Elahi (I/P)	6	9	1	82	47	10.25	0	0	1	0	400	5	248	7	35.42	0	0	4/134
Ferris,JJ (A/E)	9	17	4	114	20*	8.76	0	0	1	4	2302	251	775	61	12.70	6	1	7/37
Guillen,SC (W/N)	8	12	2	202	54	20.20	0	1	3	13/3								
Gul Mahomed (I/P)	9	17	1	205	34	12.81	0	0	2	3	77	4	24	2	12.00	0	0	2/21
Hearne,F (E/SA)	6	10	0	168	30	16.80	0	0	2	3	62	0	40	2	20.00	0	0	2/40
Kardar,AH (I/P)	26	42	3	927	93	23.76	0	5	2	16	2712	139	954	21	45.42	0	0	3/35
Midwinter,WE (A/E)	12	21	1	269	37	13.45	0	0	1	10	1725	183	605	24	25.20	1	0	5/78
Mitchell,F (E/SA)	5	10	0	116	41	11.60	0	0	0	2								
Murdoch,WL (A/E)	19	34	5	908	211	31.31	2	1	3	13/2								
Pataudi, Nawab of, sr (E/I)	6	10	0	199	102	19.90	1	0	0	0								
Traicos,AJ (SA/Z)	7	10	4	19	5*	3.16	0	0	2	8	1611	58	769	18	42.72	0	0	3/186
Trott,AE (A/E)	5	9	3	228	85*	38.00	0	2	2	4	948	54	390	26	15.00	2	0	8/43
Wessels,KC (A/SA)	40	71	3	2788	179	41.00	6	15	5	30	90	3	42	0	-	0	0	0/2
Woods,SMJ (A/E)	6	10	0	154	53	15.40	0	1	2	5	412	26	250	10	25.00	0	0	3/28